WORLD CIVILIZATIONS

Comprehensive Volume

WORLD CIVILIZATIONS

Comprehensive Volume

PHILIP J. ADLER
EAST CAROLINA UNIVERSITY

WEST PUBLISHING COMPANY
Minneapolis/St. Paul   New York   Los Angeles   San Francisco

PRODUCTION CREDITS

Photo Research Kathy Ringrose
Design and layout Diane Beasley
Cartography Maryland Cartographics, Inc.
Map Proofreading William J. McMullen
Proofreading Lynn Reichel
Composition Carlisle Communications
Index Terry Casey
Cover Image Transparency of BENIN, Seventeenth Century (plaque with two figures holding containers), photograph number 64.798. Courtesy of Museum Für Völkerkunde, Austria.

British Library Cataloguing-in-Publication Data. A catalogue record for this book is available from the British Library.

Library of Congress Cataloging-in-Publication Data

Adler, Philip J.
    World Civilizations / Philip J. Adler
        p.   cm.
    Includes bibliographical references (p.) and Index.
    ISBN 0-314-06799-X (hard : alk. paper). — ISBN 0-314-06800-7 (v.   1 : soft : alk. paper). — ISBN 0-314-06801-5 (v. 2 : soft : alk.   paper)
    1. Civilization—History.   I. Title
CB69.A35 1996   95-34878
909—dc20   CIP

WEST'S COMMITMENT TO THE ENVIRONMENT

In 1906, West Publishing Company began recycling materials left over from the production of books. This began a tradition of efficient and responsible use of resources. Today, 100% of our legal bound volumes are printed on acid-free, recycled paper consisting of 50% new paper pulp and 50% paper that has undergone a de-inking process. We also use vegetable-based inks to print all of our books. West recycles nearly 27,700,000 pounds of scrap paper annually—the equivalent of 229,300 trees. Since the 1960s, West has devised ways to capture and recycle waste inks, solvents, oils, and vapors created in the printing process. We also recycle plastics of all kinds, wood, glass, corrugated cardboard, and batteries, and have eliminated the use of polystyrene book packaging. We at West are proud of the longevity and the scope of our commitment to the environment.

West pocket parts and advance sheets are printed on recyclable paper and can be collected and recycled with newspapers. Staples do not have to be removed. Bound volumes can be recycled after removing the cover.

Production, Prepress, Printing and Binding by West Publishing Company.

Printed with **Printwise**
Environmentally Advanced Water Washable Ink

An
Dora, die glaubte

CONTENTS IN BRIEF

CONTENTS

PART 2

CLASSICAL MEDITERRANEAN CIVILIZATIONS 500 B.C.E. – 500 C.E. 91

PART 3

EQUILIBRIUM AMONG POLYCENTRIC CIVILIZATIONS 500–1500 C.E.   179

PART 4

DISEQUILIBRIUM: THE WESTERN EXPANSION 1500–1800 C.E.   337

PART 5

INDUSTRY AND WESTERN HEGEMONY 1880–1920   445

PART 6

EQUILIBRIUM REESTABLISHED: THE TWENTIETH-CENTURY WORLD   610

MAPS

PREFACE

More than most of us are aware, our end-of-the-twentieth-century lives are intertwined not only with one another, but with the past. "We live in a global village" and "those who do not know their history are condemned to repeat it" are familiar clichés. But clichés become clichés because they possess demonstrable truth. A recognition of our cultural interdependency and of the debts that the present owes the past is one of the requisites of an educated individual. By common consent, the study of history is a chief avenue toward that status. That is why surveys of history, national and international, are among the most common and most popular of the social science requirements in most American colleges.

The history of world civilizations can neither be summed up easily, nor exhausted in its detail. *World Civilizations* attempts to walk a middle line; its narrative embraces every major civilized epoch in every part of the globe, but the treatment of topics is selective and follows definite patterns.

This book is a brief survey of the history of civilized life since its inceptions in the Middle East some five thousand years ago. It is meant to be used in conjunction with a lecture course at the introductory level. A majority of the students in such a course will probably be encountering many of the topics for the first time, and this book reflects that fact. The needs and interests of the freshman and sophomore students in two- and four-year colleges and universities have been kept constantly in mind by the author, whose familiarity with those needs has been sharpened by thirty years of classroom experience.

While it deals with the history of civilization throughout the globe, this book does not attempt to be comprehensive in detail, nor evenly balanced among the multiple fields of history. It deliberately tilts toward social and cultural topics and toward the long-term processes that affect the lives of the millions, rather than the acts of "the captains and the kings." The evolution of law and the formative powers of religion upon early government, as examples, receive considerably more attention than wars and diplomatic arrangements. The rise of an industrial working class in European cities garners more space than the trade policies of the European governments. Such selectivity is forced upon any author of any text, but the firm intent to keep this a *concise* survey necessitated a particularly close review of the material. It is hoped that the result will prove both thought provoking and highly readable.

✤ ORGANIZATION

The organization of *World Civilizations* is largely dictated by its nature: as a history, the basic order is *chronological.* There are six parts, dealing with six chronological eras from Ancient Civilizations (3000–500 B.C.E. to Recent Times (post-1920 C.E.). The parts have several binding threads of development in common, but the main point of reference is the relative degree of contact with other civilizations. This ranges from near-perfect isolation, as, for example, in ancient China, to close and continual interaction, as in the late twentieth-century world.

The second organizing principle is the *prioritization of certain topics and processes.* Sociocultural and economic affairs are generally emphasized, and the longer term is kept in perspective while some short-term phenomena are deliberately minimized. In terms of the space allotted, the more recent epochs of history are emphasized, in line with the recognition of growing global interdependence and cultural contact.

Although this text was from its inception meant as a world history and contains proportionately more material on non-Western peoples and cultures than any other currently in print, the Western nations also receive considerable attention. (In this respect, Western means not only European but also North American since the eighteenth century.) The treatment adopted in this book should allow any student to find an adequate explanation of the rise of the West to temporary dominion in modern times and the reasons for the reestablishment of worldwide cultural equilibrium in the latter half of the twentieth century.

✤ PEDAGOGY

An important feature of *World Civilizations* is its division into a number of short chapters. Each of the sixty-two chapters is meant to constitute a unit suitable in scope for a single lecture, short enough to allow easy digestion, and with strong logical coherence. Each chapter offers the following features:

- A chapter outline.
- A brief chapter chronology.
- A chapter summary.
- A "Test Your Knowledge" section at the end of the chapter.
- Terms and individuals for identification (in boldface type).
- Key terms and concepts (in italic type).
- An excerpt from primary documents.
- A biography of a contemporary figure.
- A brief bibliography of recent and older works at the end of the chapter.
- Color illustrations and abundant maps.

Other features include the following:

- An end-of-book glossary gives explanations of unfamiliar terms.
- Each of the six parts begins with a short essay that describes the chapter contents and major trends covered in that part.
- A "Link" feature at the beginning of each part provides a comparative capsule overview of the characteristics and achievements of the epoch as experienced by the different peoples and regions.

✤ SUPPLEMENTS

The following supplements are available for the instructor:

- **Instructor's Manual with Test Bank,** by Raymond Hylton of Virginia Union University, includes chapter outlines, lecture topics, definitions of terms to know, and chapter summaries. The Test Bank includes more than 3,000 multiple-choice, true/false, long and short essay, matching, and fill-in-the-blank questions.
- **Westest 3.1 Computerized Testing**. Call-in testing is available.
- **Lecture Notes,** by Marsha Beal of Vincennes University, provide lectures to accompany the text.
- **Map Transparency Acetates** include approximately 50 full-color maps from the text.

- **West's History Videodisc II:** *The Sights and Sounds of History* includes short, focused video clips, photos, artwork, animations, music, and dramatic readings that "bring to life" historical topics and events that are most difficult for students to appreciate from a core textbook alone.

The following supplements are available for the student:

- **Study Guide,** by Raymond Hylton of Virginia Union University, includes chapter outlines, sample test questions, and identification terms.
- **Map Exercise Workbook,** by Arthur Durand of Metropolitan State College, features approximately 30 map exercise sets that help students feel comfortable with and learn from maps that they encounter in the core textbook.
- **Primary Source Supplement,** by Robert Welborn of Clayton State College, is a collection of primary source documents with accompanying exercises. It teaches students to think critically by using primary sources in studying history.

✤ ACKNOWLEDGMENTS

The author is happy to acknowledge the sustained aid given him by many individuals during the long incubation period of this text. Colleagues in the History Department at East Carolina University, at the annual meetings of the test planners and graders of the Advanced Placement in European History, and in several professional organizations, notably the American Association for the Advancement of Slavic Studies, are particularly to be thanked. I would also like to thank Enrique Ramirez of Tyler Junior College and Raymond Hylton of Virginia Union University for their input on the Biography and Primary Source Document segments of this text.

In addition, the following reviewers' comments were essential to the gradual transformation of a manuscript into a book; I am indebted to all of them and to the students in HIST 1030-1031 who suffered through the early versions of the work.

Marsha Beal
Vincennes University

Laura Blunk
Cuyahoga Community College

William Brazill
Wayne State University

Orazio A. Ciccarelli
University of Southern Mississippi

Robert Clouse
Indiana State University

Sara Crook
Peru State University

Sonny Davis
Texas A & M University at Kingsville

Arthur Durand
Metropolitan Community College

Frank N. Egerton
University of Wisconsin—Parkside

Ken Fenster
DeKalb College

Tom Fiddick
University of Evansville

David Fischer
Midlands Technical College

Jerry Gershenhorn
North Carolina Central University

Erwin Grieshaber
Mankato State University

Eric Haines
Bellevue Community College

Mary Headberg
Saginaw Valley State University

Charles Holt
Morehead State University

Raymond Hylton
Virginia Union University

Fay Jensen
DeKalb College—North Campus

Aman Kabourou
Dutchess Community College

Lois Lucas
West Virginia State College

Ed Massey
Bee County College

Bob McGregor
University of Illinois—Springfield

John Mears
Southern Methodist University

Will Morris
Midland College

Gene Mueller
Henderson State University

Tim Myers
Butler County Community College

William Paquette
Tidewater Community College

Nancy Rachels
Hillsborough Community College

Enrique Ramirez
Tyler Junior College

Robin Rudoff
East Texas State University

Shapur Shahbazi
Eastern Oregon State University

John Simpson
Pierce College

John S. H. Smith
Northern Nevada Community College

Maureen Sowa
Bristol Community College

Susan Tindall
Georgia State University

Bill Warren
Valley City State University

Robert Welborn
Clayton State College

David Wilcox
Houston Community College

Steve Wiley
Anoka-Ramsey Community College

John Yarnevich
Trukee Meadows Community College—Old Towne Mall Campus

Finally, Joan Gill and Becky Stovall, my acquisition and developmental editors at West Publishing Company, are responsible for many of this book's best points; without their help and guidance, the project certainly would not have been completed. I also want to thank Christine Hurney, my production editor, for many a long day's careful work.

Note: Throughout the work the pinyin orthography has been adopted for Chinese names. The older Wade-Giles system has been included in parentheses as the first mention and retained in a few cases where common usage demands it (Chiang Kai-shek, for example).

About the Author

PHILIP J. ADLER has taught college courses in world history to undergraduates for almost thirty years prior to his recent retirement. Dr. Adler took his Ph.D at the University of Vienna following military service overseas in the 1950s. His dissertation was in the activity of the South Slav emigres during World War I, and his academic specialty was the modern history of eastern Europe and the Austro-Hungarian empire. His research has been supported by Fulbright and National Endowment for the Humanities grants. Adler has published widely in the historical journals of this country and German-speaking Europe. He is currently professor emeritus at East Carolina University where he spend most of his teaching career.

INTRODUCTION TO THE STUDENT

❧ WHY IS HISTORY WORTH STUDYING?

A few years ago a book about women in the past appeared with an eye-catching title: *Herstory.* Suddenly, the real meaning of a commonly used word became a lot clearer. History is indeed a *story,* not specifically about women or men, but about all those who have left some imprint on the age in which they lived.

History can be defined most simply as the story of human actions in past times. Those actions tend to fall into broad patterns, regardless of whether they occurred yesterday or five thousand years ago. Physical needs, such as the need for food, water, and breathable air, dictate some actions. Others stem from emotional and intellectual needs, such as religious belief or the search for immortality. Human action also results from desires rather than absolute needs. Some desires are so common that they recur in every generation; some examples might be literary ambition, or scientific curiosity, or the quest for political power over others.

History is the record of how people tried to meet those needs or fulfill those desires, successfully in some cases, unsuccessfully in others. Many generations of our ancestors have found familiarity with that record to be useful in guiding their own actions. The study of past human acts also encourages us to see our own present possibilities, both individual and collective. Perhaps that is history's greatest value and has been the source of its continuous fascination for men and women who have sought the good life.

Many people are naturally attracted toward the study of history, but others find it difficult or (even worse) "irrelevant." Some students—perhaps yourself!—dread history courses, saying that they can see no point in learning about the past. My life, they say, is here and now; leave the past to the past. What can be said in response to justify the study of history?

Insofar as people are ignorant of their past, they are also ignorant of much of their present, for the one grows directly out of the other. If we ignore or forget the experience of those who lived before us, we are like an amnesia victim, constantly puzzled by what should be familiar, surprised by what should be predictable. Not only do we not know what we should know, but we cannot perceive our true possibilities, because we have nothing to measure them against. The nonhistorical mind does not know what it is missing—and contrary to the old saying, that can definitely hurt you!

A word of caution here: this is not a question of "history repeats itself." This often-quoted cliché is clearly nonsense if taken literally. History does *not* repeat itself exactly, and the difference in details is always important. But history does exhibit general patterns, dictated by common human needs and desires. Some knowledge of and respect for those patterns has been a vital part of the mental equipment of all human societies.

But there is another, more personal reason to learn about the past. Adult persons who know none of their history are really in the position of a young child. They are *objects,* not subjects. Like the child, they are acted upon by forces, limited by restrictions, or compelled by a logic that they not only can do little about, but may not even perceive. They are manipulated by others' ideas, wishes, and ambitions. They never attain control of their lives, or, at least, not until the young child grows up. The sad thing is that the unhistorical adult *has* grown up, physically, but less so mentally.

The historically unconscious are confined within a figurative wooden packing crate, into which they were put by the accident of birth into a given society, at a given time, in a given place. The boards forming the box enclose these people, blocking their view in all directions. One board of the box might be the religion—or lack of it— into which they were born; another, the economic position of their family; another, their physical appearance, race, or ethnic group. Other boards could be whether they were born in a city slum or a small village, or whether they had a chance at formal education in school (about three-fourths of the world's children never go beyond the third year of school). These and many other facts are the boards of the boxes into which we are all born.

If we are to fully realize our potential as human beings, some (at least some!) of the boards must be removed so we can see out, gain other vistas and visions, and have a chance to measure and compare our experiences with others outside. Here "outside" refers to the cross section of the collective experience of other human beings, either now in the present, or what is more manageable for study, in the knowable past.

Thus, the real justification for studying history is that it lets us see out, beyond our individual birth-box, into the rich variety of others' lives and thoughts. History is a factual introduction into humans' past achievements; its breadth and complexity vary, depending on the type. But whatever the type of history we study, by letting us see and giving us perspective that enables us to contrast and compare our lives with those of others, history liberates us from the invisible boards that confine us all within our birth-box.

For many people, the study of history has been a form of liberation. Through history, they have become aware of the ways other people have dealt with the same concerns and questions that puzzle them. They have been able to gain a perspective on their own life, both as an individual and as a member of the greater society in which they work and act. Perhaps, they have successfully adapted some of the solutions that history has revealed to them and experienced the pleasure of applying a historical lesson to their own advantage. For all these reasons, the study of the historical past is indeed worth the effort. *Not* to have some familiarity with the past is to abdicate some part of our human potential.

✤ ABOUT THIS BOOK

Organization

The textbook you are holding is a beginning survey of world history. It is meant to be studied as part of a lecture course at the freshman/sophomore level, a course in which a majority of the students will probably be encountering world history for the first time in any depth.

Some students may at first be confused by dates followed by "B.C.E.," meaning "before the common era," and "C.E." meaning "common era." These terms are used to reflect a global perspective and they correspond to the Western equivalent B.C. (before Christ) and A.D. (*anno Domini*). Also, a caution about the word *century* is in order: the term "17th Century" C.E. refers to the years 1601 to 1699 in the Common Era. "The 1700's" refers to the years 1700–1799. With a little practice these terms become second nature and will increase your fluency in history.

Although this text includes a large number of topics, it is not meant to be comprehensive. Your instructor's lectures will almost certainly bring up many points that are not discussed in the book; that is proper and should be expected. To do well in your tests, you must pay close attention to the material covered in the lectures, which may not be in this book.

Three principles have guided the organization of this book. First, the basic order is dictated by *chronology,* for this is a history text and history can be defined as action-in-time. After an introductory chapter on prehistory, we look first at Mesopotamia and Egypt, then at India and China. In these four river valley environments, humans were first successful in adapting nature to their needs on a large scale, a process which we call civilization. Between about 2500 B.C.E. and about 1000 C.E., the river valley civilizations matured and developed a "classic" culture in most phases of life: a fashion of thinking and acting that would be a model for emulation so long as that civilization was vital and capable of defending itself.

By 500 B.C.E. the Near Eastern civilizations centered in Egypt and Mesopotamia were in decline and had been replaced by Mediterranean-based ones, which drew on the older civilizations to some extent but also added some novel and distinct features of their own. First, the Greeks, then, the Romans succeeded in bringing much of the known world under their influence, culminating in the great Roman Empire reaching from Spain to the Persians. For the West, the greatest single addition to civilized life in this era was the combination of Jewish theology and Greco-Roman philosophy and science. During the same epoch (500 B.C.E.–500 C.E.), the civilizations of East and South Asia were also experiencing growth and change of huge dimensions. India's Hindu religion and philosophy were being challenged by Buddhism, while China recovered from political dismemberment and became the permanent chief factor in East Asian affairs. Japan emerged slowly from a prehistoric stage under Chinese tutelage, while the southeastern part of the Asian continent attained a high civilization created in part by Indian traders and Buddhist missionaries.

From 500 to about 1500 C.E., the various civilized regions (including sub-Saharan Africa and the Americas) were either still isolated from one another or maintained a power equilibrium. After 500, Mediterranean civilization underwent much more radical changes than occurred elsewhere on the globe, and by about 1000, an amalgam of Greco-Roman, Germanic, and Jewish-Christian beliefs called Europe, or Western Christianity, had emerged. By 1500, this civilization began to rise to a position of worldwide domination, marked by the voyages of discovery and ensuing colonization. In the next three centuries, the Europeans and their colonial outposts slowly wove a web of worldwide commercial and technological interests anchored on military force. Our book's treatment of the entire post-1500 age will give much attention to the West, but also to the impacts of Western culture and ideas upon non-Western peoples. In particular, it will look at the Black African civilization encountered by the early European traders and what became of it and at the Native American civilizations of Latin America and their fate under Spanish conquest and rule.

From 1800 through World War I, Europe led the world in practically every field of material human life, including military affairs, science, commerce, and living standards. This was the golden age of Europe's imperial control of the rest of the world. The Americas, much of Asia, Oceania, and coastal Africa all were the tails of the European dog; all became formal or informal colonies at one time, and some remained under direct European control until the mid-twentieth century.

After World War I, the pendulum of power swung steadily away from Europe and toward what had been the periphery: first, North America; then, Russia, Japan, and the non-Western peoples. As we approach the end of the present century, the world has not only shrunk, but has again been anchored on multiple power bases, both Western and non-Western. A degree of equilibrium is rapidly being restored, this time built on a foundation of Western technology that has been adopted throughout the globe.

Our periodization scheme, then, will be a sixfold one:

- Ancient Civilizations, 3500 B.C.E.–500 B.C.E.
- Classical Mediterranean Civilizations, 500 B.C.E.–500 C.E.
- Equilibrium among Polycentric Civilizations, 500–1500 C.E.
- Disequilibrium: The Western Expansion, 1500–1800 C.E.
- Industry and Western Hegemony, 1800–1920.
- Equilibrium Reasserted: The Twentieth-Century World.

Each period will be introduced by a brief summary and by an outline comparing the various contemporary civilizations. These six outlines are termed *Links* and will afford a nutshell overview of the topics covered in the following part of the book.

Text Emphases and Coverage

As a second principle of organization, this book reflects the author's particular concerns, so the material treated is selective.

There is a definite tilt toward social and economic topics in the broadest sense, although these are usually introduced by a treatment of political events. Wars and military matters are treated only as they seem relevant to other topics. Only the most prominent and most recognizably important governmental, military, or diplomatic facts and figures are mentioned in the text. The author believes that students who are interested in such factual details will hear them in lectures or can easily find them in the library or an encyclopedia. Others, who are less interested in such details, will appreciate the relative focus on broad topics and long-term trends.

The third organizing principle of the book is its approach to Western and non-Western history. A prominent place is given throughout to the history of the Western world. Why this emphasis in a world that has grown much smaller and more intricately connected over the last generation?

At least three reasons come to mind: (1) Western culture and ideas have dominated most of the world for the past five hundred years, and much of this text deals with that period; (2) the rest of the planet has been westernized in important ways during the twentieth century, either voluntarily or involuntarily; and most importantly (3) the majority of the people reading this book are themselves members and products of Western civilization. If one agrees with the philosopher Socrates that to "know thyself" is the source of all knowledge, then a beginning has to be made by exploring one's own roots—roots growing from a Western soil.

About one-third of the text chapters deal with the period since the end of the eighteenth century, and about one-fifth with history since World War I. This emphasis on the most recent past fits with the interests of most students; but should you be particularly attracted to any or all of the earlier periods, be assured that an immense amount of interesting writing on almost all of the world's peoples in any epoch is available. The end-of-chapter bibliographies will provide a good starting point for further inquiry.

Many instructors will wish to supplement the text by assigning outside readings and/or by material in their lectures. The bibliographies are helpful sources for much of the information omitted from the text and for much else besides; your college library will have many of the titles listed. They have been chosen because they are up-to-date, readily available, and highly readable.

As a good student, your best resource, always, is your own sense of curiosity. Keep it active as you go through these pages; remember, this and every textbook are the *beginning,* not the ending of your search for useful knowledge. Good luck!

PART 1

ANCIENT CIVILIZATIONS
3500–500 B.C.E.

The first eight chapters of this book examine the growth of civilized life in four quite different areas of the globe before 500 B.C.E. In the first chapter, which deals with the enormous stretch of time between the advent of *Homo sapiens* throughout much of the earth and about 5000 B.C.E., we look at the general conditions of life and at the achievements of human beings before history. These "breakthroughs" are truly impressive, and it is a mark of their fundamental importance that we so rarely think about them: we cannot envision an existence in which they were unknown. Metalworking, writing, art, settled habitation, and religious belief are just a few of the triumphs of prehistoric humans' imagination and skill.

Most important of all, the commitment to growing, rather than chasing or gathering, food gradually took root among widely scattered groups in the late Neolithic Age (c. 8000–5000). This Agricultural Revolution is one of the two epoch-making changes in human life to date, the other being the Industrial Revolution commencing in the late eighteenth century. Agriculture generated the material basis of civilization as that word is generally understood. Urban living, statutory law, government by officials, writing beyond mere record keeping, military forces, and socioeconomic classes are all indirect products of the adoption of food growing as the primary source of sustenance for a given people or tribe.

Chapters 2 through 7 examine the establishment and development of urban life in the river valleys of western Asia, northeast Africa, India, and China. First in chronology was probably Mesopotamia, but it was quickly rivaled by the civilization of the Nile valley of Egypt. Both of these began to take definite form about 3500 B.C.E. and reached their apex between c. 1500 and 1200. Somewhat later, the plains of the Indus River in India's far west produced a highly organized and urban society that prospered until about the middle of the second millennium B.C.E., when it went into decline and was forgotten for many centuries. Simultaneous with the decline of the Indus valley civilization, the north-central region of China gave birth to a civilized state ruled by the Shang dynasts. Like the others, this society was founded on a mastery of irrigated farming. Unlike the Mesopotamians and the Indus peoples, both the Egyptians and the Chinese maintained the major elements of their early civilizations down to modern days.

Part 1 also provides brief accounts of a few of the other major contributors to world civilization before 500 B.C.E. Thus, Chapter 4 puts the warlike Assyrians and the first of the several Persian empires into perspective, and Chapter 5 examines the small but crucially important nation of the Jews and their religious convictions. Finally, Chapter 8 offers a comparative glance at the daily lives and social attitudes of the ancient civilizations, as we can know about them from both archaeology and history. In this chapter, as indeed throughout the book, special attention is devoted to the nonelite working people and to the relations between the sexes.

	Law and Government	Economy
MESOPOTAMIANS, EGYPTIANS, HEBREWS	*Mesopotamia:* Early law based on different treatment for differing classes. Property better protected than people, but some care for all persons' interests. Government originally theocratic but becomes monarchic after c. 2000 B.C.E. when contesting city-states are conquered by external invader and put under centralized rule. *Egypt:* Law is the divine justice of the pharaoh, administered by his officials. Government displays great stability under god-king until as late as 1000 B.C.E., when foreign invasions multiply after failed attempt at empire. *Israel:* Law is based on the Covenant with Yahweh which provides a divinely approved, ethical foundation for ancient custom. The twelve tribes of Israel dream of a messiah who will lead them to an earthly kingdom but are repeatedly disappointed after Solomon's reign, and fall under alien rule.	Mesopotamia is very active in commerce originating in large towns and cities which are themselves dependent on intensive irrigation farming. Trade with the Indus valley, the Black Sea region, Egypt and Persia, is attested to by archaeology. Skilled craftsmen as well as priests and governors supply the export trade. Egypt is the most fertile part of the world and can export grain as well as copper to its neighbors, while remaining almost self-sufficient for millennia. Unlike Mesopotamia, no large urban areas and relatively little contact with others through most of this epoch. The Hebrews sporadically play an intermediary role in the trade between the Nile and the eastern Mediterranean civilizations, but their economy is basically agrarian and pastoral throughout this period.
INDIANS	Law remains customary and unwritten in a wholly oral culture even long after the Aryan invasion introduces the Sanskrit language. The priestly caste of brahmins retain their law-making position as the Aryan-Indian amalgam produces Vedic Hindu belief. Important concepts and laws are memorized by succeeding generations, dominated by caste self-interest. Government is presumed to be theocratic in the Indus valley civilization; no evidence is available even as late as the end of the epoch. Coming of Aryans brings the rule of warrior-kings who attempt to remain separate from their subjects but gradually are absorbed into the Indian mass. Aryans slowly spread east into the Ganges plain and fragment into many petty principalities which rule north India.	Indian and other South Asian cultures are overwhelmingly agrarian into modern times. Large towns exist from earliest times (Harappa, Mohenjo-daro), but the large majority of people live in villages, with little contact outside their own region. Trade with Mesopotamia and later with Persia is active; at the end of the period, colonization and trade with Southeast Asians (Malay peninsula, Thailand) are beginning.
CHINESE	China develops writing early and keeps extensive records from c. 1000 B.C.E. Chinese law, which is customary in this period, looks to the protection of property and maintenance of the clan/family as determining factors for justice. Government is monarchic and warrior oriented, with Shang conquerors as models for the succeeding Zhou. Zhou dynasts lose grip on outlying "warlords" by the end of the period, and the Era of Warring States opens.	As in South Asia, most Chinese live in villages, raising grain and engaging in pastoral agriculture. A few large towns exist, but as yet play only a minor role in the economy. Trade with others is negligible in this era, China is still isolated from the rest of the world. Rice culture has not yet begun, as the south remains unconquered. Contact with India, Vietnam, and Japan is not yet undertaken.

3500–500 B.C.E. ANCIENT CIVILIZATIONS

Peoples: Mesopotamians, Egyptians, Hebrews, Indians, Chinese

Religion and Philosophy	Arts and Culture	Science and Technology
Religious belief dictates the type of government in the earliest period, but gradually separates the king from the priest. Mesopotamia adopts a pessimistic view of the human-god relationship and the afterlife. Egypt had an uniquely optimistic relationship with its gods, lasting until invasions force a reconciliation after 1000. Jews pioneer monotheist theocracy and elevate Yahweh into a supreme and universal ruler of all, with a special relationship with his chosen people based on love and immortal rewards for the faithful.	Mesopotamians produce first monumental architecture, first urban society, first sophisticated writing system, and much else. Arts flourish under priestly and royal patronage, but relatively little has survived time and wars. Egypt's pyramids are the most impressive ancient construction of all; massive sculpture, interior fresco painting, and ceramics are other Egyptian strengths in art. At the end of the period, Hebrews produce the Bible as literature and history of the race.	Mesopotamians play a huge role in early science: chronology, calendar, math, physics, and astronomy are all highly developed by 2500. Technology (mudbrick construction, city sanitation, hydraulics for city and farming, etc.) also has a major place in the daily life of the city-states. Egypt also develops considerable science, but is not so consistently innovative. Medicine and pharmacy are strengths as are skill in construction and stonework. A solar calendar is developed. Jews lag in both science and technology, remaining dependent on others throughout this period.
Religion of India is a mixture of Indus civilization belief and Aryan "sky gods." The Vedas brought by the Aryans become sacred scripture for emerging Vedic Hinduism by 1000. Brahmin priestly castes are co-rulers with the warriors who conquer North India and impose Aryan rule. South India is not conquered, but is strongly influenced by Vedic beliefs. At the end of the period, Buddhism begins to gain ground rapidly among all Indians, and has an enormous impact on philosophy as well as theology.	South Asian art largely reflects the religious mythology, as it does elsewhere until modern times. Much has been lost to the climate. Some sculpture and minor arts survive from ruins of Indus valley towns. Stone temples and carvings survive in limited numbers; the extensive sacred literature is entirely oral into the first centuries C.E., when the Vedas, Upanishads, and other Hindu and Buddhist epics that date in oral form from 1700–500 B.C.E. are first written.	Indians master metalworking (weapons, utensils) early, progressing rapidly through bronze to iron age by 1000 B.C.E. Mathematics are especially important, navigation arts are well developed, and engineering skills enable them to erect massive temples and fortresses. Lack of written data hinders detailed knowledge of Indian science in this era.
Chinese religion is conditioned by ancestral continuity; honor of lineage is all-important, with gods playing relatively minor roles. There is no state theology, but the emperor supposedly enjoys the "mandate of heaven" to rule and serves as high priest. At the end of the period, the Confucian ethical and philosophical system, which will be a substitute for supernatural religion for educated classes, is beginning. The peasant majority goes on with superstition-ridden Dao.	Chinese arts in several formats take on lasting features during Zhou dynasty: bronzes, landscape painting, nature poetry, ceramics, silk, and pagoda architecture. Language arts are highly developed, despite difficulties of ideographic language. Reverence for education and for the aged are already apparent. Supreme importance of the family continually emphasized in this patriarchal society.	Metal technology well advanced in China: Bronze Age commences by 3000 B.C.E. and iron introduced, probably from India, by 600s. Shang bronzes finest ever cast, while Zhou dynasty sees major improvements in agricultural productivity and weaponry. Copper coins circulate; laqueurware and silkprocessing are major home industries.

CHAPTER 1

PREHISTORY

c. 50,000 B.C.E.	*Homo sapiens* appear
c. 10,000 B.C.E.	Beginnings of agriculture, private property, specialization of labor
c. 7000 B.C.E.	Bronze Age begins
c. 3500 B.C.E.	Irrigation civilizations in Mesopotamia, Egypt
c. 1500 B.C.E.	Iron Age

History, in the strict sense, means a systematic written record of the human past. But most people don't use history in the strict sense. They define the word "history" as whatever has happened in the past to humans, and that, of course, is a much bigger proposition. Humans have inhabited the earth for a very long time. Present-day human beings evolved over millions of years, and the majority of that period is still a totally closed book to modern science. Indeed, you can think of human evolution as a vast black space penetrated by only an occasional pinpoint of light, representing our current knowledge.

Every few years, new evidence is discovered that extends the age of the genus *Homo* further back in time. A humanlike creature, or **hominid,** walked about in East Africa well over 3 million years ago by latest reckoning. (The oldest hominid generally accepted as such is "Lucy," a female whose fossilized bones were discovered in Ethiopia two decades ago.) *Homo sapiens,* "thinking man," is much younger, however. This modern variety of humans—the originator of all people now living—is apparently no more than about 50,000 years old. Where they first appeared and why they were so successful in extending their habitation over the entire globe in a relatively short time (perhaps 20,000 years) remain mysteries that the anthropologists and their scientific cousins, the archaeologists, would love to solve.

❖ DEFINITION OF TERMS

Certain words and phrases will be constantly recurring in this book and in the lectures that accompany it. Accordingly, we should establish some definitions at the outset:

History The systematic written record of what people have done in the past. In this context, the past can mean 10,000 years ago or yesterday. History depends on memory; it is remembered activities. What has happened but been forgotten—which is, of course, the vast majority of what has happened—is technically not history.

Prehistory Whatever happened to people in the period prior to writing.

Culture The human-created part of the environment, the "way of life" of a distinct group of humans interacting with one another. In prehistory, culture is often associated with particular tools.

Civilization A complex, developed culture usually associated with specific achievements such as agriculture, urban life, specialized labor, and a system of writing.

Archaeology The study of prehistoric and/or historical cultures through examination of their artifacts (anything made by humans). The name means "the study of origins," and like almost every other scientific name in the English language, it is derived from Greek.

Anthropology Another Greek name, referring to the science that studies humans as a species rather than studying a special aspect of their activity.

Archaeologists are crucial to the study of prehistoric humans. In that transitional period when writing is just beginning to develop, the **paleontologists** and the **paleographers** (students of anything old and of old writing, respectively) are essential to the historian, also.

❧ THE PALEOLITHIC AGE

The very lengthy period extending from about the appearance of the first hominids to about 7000 B.C.E. is known as the Paleolithic Age, so called because tools were made of stone and were still quite crude (*paleo* = old; *lithos* = stone). By the end of the Paleolithic, humans inhabited all the continents except Antarctica. Paleolithic peoples were hunters and foragers, but life was not easy and famine was always near at hand.

Paleolithic hunting and gathering was done in groups, and success depended more on organization and cooperation than on individual bravery or strength. The family was the basic social unit, but it was normally an extended family that included uncles, aunts, in-laws, and other relatives rather than the nuclear family (mother, father, children) that is common today. A unit larger than the nuclear family was necessary for protection. But the total number able to live and hunt together was probably quite small—no more than forty or so. More than that would have been very difficult to maintain when the hunting was poor or the wild fruits and seeds were not plentiful.

Although conflicts frequently arose over hunting grounds, water, theft, or other problems, the Paleolithic era probably saw less warfare than any time in later history. So much open space capable of sustaining life was available that the weaker units probably just moved on when they were confronted with force or threats.

Human Development during the Paleolithic

During the Paleolithic, both the appearance of humans and their vital capacity to reason and plan changed considerably. Due to the extensive work of anthropologists since World War II, we know that several different hominids evolved during this time. Evidence uncovered in East Africa and Europe indicates that some subspecies came to an evolutionary dead end, however. A good example is the famous **Neanderthal Man** who flourished in western Germany about 30,000 years ago and then disappeared at about the same time that *Homo sapiens* appeared in Europe.

Climatic changes probably affected and perhaps even caused these evolutionary developments. We know that the end of the last of several Ice Ages coincided with the appearance of *Homo sapiens* throughout the Northern Hemisphere. It is entirely possible that the pre–*Homo sapiens* inhabitants of Europe, such as Neanderthal Man, failed to adapt to the changed climate, in the same way that some zoologists believe that the dinosaurs failed to adapt much earlier.

During the Paleolithic, humans became more upright, and their skull changed shape to encompass a gradually enlarging brain. Their bodies grew less hairy and their arms shorter. Hip structure changed to allow a more erect gait. Eyesight grew sharper and the sense of smell less so. All these changes and many others were adaptations that reflected both humans' changed physical environment and their increasing mastery and manipulation of that environment.

The *changed physical environment* was reflected in the substitution of semipermanent shelter for the nomadism of an earlier day. By the late Paleolithic, groups were living in caves, lean-tos and other shelters for long periods of time, perhaps several months. Where earlier a group rarely remained more than a few weeks at a given locale, now they could stay in one place several months to await the ripening of certain fruit or the migration of the animals. Even more important, humans' ability to master their physical environment was constantly increasing as they learned to make clothing for cold seasons, to kindle fire where and when it was needed, and to devise new tools for new tasks. The earliest human artwork came in the late Paleolithic, and the caves of southern France and Spain where they were found (Lascaux) are world famous for their lifelike portraits of deer and other animals. In such ways, humans began to bend the physical world to their will. As they developed an ability to plan and to remember what had been successful in the past so they could repeat it, humans in the late Paleolithic were making rapid strides toward civilization. They would reach that state in the next age—the Neolithic.

The Leakey Family

Louis, Mary, and Richard Leakey form a remarkable, two-generation family of distinguished African anthropologists. Their work has transformed the knowledge of ancient hominids held by the contemporary scientific world.

Louis Leakey (1903–1972) was born to British missionaries in Kenya. He grew up in intimate association with the native Kikuyu people, even undergoing the complicated and painful rites of initiation into manhood among them. He became interested in African anthropology very early and, after getting a degree at Cambridge in 1926, devoted the rest of his life to the subject. He made some initial excavations in the Olduvai river gorge in Kenya in 1931–1932, where later he and his wife would make their most exciting discoveries. Returning there throughout the 1930s and 1940s, Leakey supervised excavations that revolutionized existing beliefs about the age and development of humanlike creatures.

Many of his views remain controversial, but they have formed the point of departure for most anthropology in Africa for a generation. The outstanding trio of female primate researchers Jane Goodall, Dian Fossey, and Caroline Tutin were all Louis Leakey's students in Africa.

Mary Douglas Leakey (1913–) married Louis in 1936, after completing her own university work and beginning an anthropology career in Britain. She took up African fieldwork with the same intensity as her husband. In 1960, their discovery of *australopithecine* (southern hominid) fossils in Olduvai and in the neighboring site at Laetoli ignited ongoing arguments about the origins of *homo habilis* ("tool-using man"). In 1976, Mary Leakey discovered a complete run of bipedal footprints dating back at least two and one-half million years in the fossilized earth at Laetoli, moving the age of erect-walking hominids back very considerably from what had been previously thought.

Richard Leakey (1944–) has continued his parents' work with somewhat different emphasis in contemporary Kenya. A trained anthropologist, he has written two very popular books on Africa (*People of the Lake* and *Origins*) that summarize his parents' scientific contributions as well as his own research in the field. More recently, he has served as a government official for the republic of Kenya and is an internationally known environmentalist active in the protection and expansion of the magnificent Kenyan wilderness reserves. Kenya's problems associated with the pressure exerted by a rapidly growing population (4 percent per year, among the world's highest rates) and limited agricultural possibilities have been steadily mounting, and Richard Leakey has been a leader in seeking solutions that conform to both environmental demands and the urgent political realities of a developing country.

■ Richard Leakey holds two of the Australopithecine skulls discovered in east Africa.

⚜ THE NEOLITHIC AGE: AGRICULTURE

Although the Paleolithic saw notable developments, it was in the New Stone (Neolithic) Age that humans made the breakthrough to advanced culture and eventually civilization. As we saw, Paleolithic groups were essentially nomadic. They depended on either hunting and gathering or on raising animals for food. Both the hunter-gatherers and the herders followed a pastoral life; the former moved with the seasons and the migration of the animals they hunted, and the latter had to move with their animals when the grazing was exhausted. Both had no reason to attempt to settle down and every reason not to. In the following age, this situation changed. The gradual adoption of agriculture demanded a *sedentary,* or settled, life.

The beginnings of farming used to be called the "**Agricultural Revolution.**" Now, we know that if this was a revolution, it was a very slow one. Most peoples took about five to ten generations (200–400 years) to complete it. Gradually, hunting-herding as the primary way to gain food gave way to sowing and harvesting. Usually, agriculture went hand in hand with hunting for a long, long time. Some members of the group would hunt while others engaged in raising some form of grain from wild grasses, the usual form of agriculture. When agriculture became the primary way of getting something to eat, the Agricultural Revolution was complete for that group.

Slow though the transition may have been, "revolution" is not altogether an inappropriate word because the adop-

■ Several Neolithic hunters had to collaborate to bring down the large game animals that iron weaponry allowed them to kill and butcher.

■ **A Neolithic Village.** This diorama recreates daily tasks in Neolithic society. In the background hunters drive wild horses off a rocky cliff while others slaughter them below. Tool-shapers assist in erecting village housing. Women dry meat and prepare fur clothing. Children assist where they can.

tion of the agricultural lifestyle did lead to revolutionary changes in the long run. First, it meant that people settled down permanently. To be near the cultivated area, people settled in villages and then in towns, where they lived and worked in many new, specialized occupations that were unknown to pre-agricultural society. These settlements could not depend on the luck of hunting or fishing or on sporadic harvests of wild seeds and berries to supply their daily needs. Only regularized farming could support the specialists who populated the towns, and only intensive agriculture could produce the dependable surplus of food that was necessary to allow the population to grow. Of course, occasional years of famine still occurred. But the lean years were far less frequent than when people depended on hunting-gathering for sustenance. Thus, one major result of agriculture was a steadily *expanding population* that lived in *permanent settlements.*

Secondly, agriculture was the force behind creating the concept of "mine versus thine," that is, *privately owned property* in land. Until farming became common, there was no concept of private property; land, water, game, and fish "belonged" to all who needed them. But once a group had labored hard to establish a productive farm, they wanted permanent possession. After all, they had to clear the land, supply water at the right time, and organize labor for the harvest. Who would do that if they had no assurance that next year and the next the land would still be in their possession?

Thirdly, agriculture necessitated the development of *systematized regulation* to enforce the rights of one party over those of another when disputes arose over property. Codes of law, enforced by organized authority, or government officials, were very important results of agriculture's introduction.

A fourth change was the increasing *specialization of labor*. It made no sense for a Neolithic farmer to try to be a soldier or a carpenter, as well as a food grower. Efforts were more productive for the entire community if people specialized; the same applied to the carpenter and the soldier, who were not expected to farm.

Agriculture also led to an *enlarged public role for women* in Neolithic society, apparently a direct result of the fact that the very first farmers were probably women. The association of women with fertility, personified in a whole series of Earth-Mother goddesses in various cultures, was also important in this development. As the persons who brought forth life, women were seen as the key to assuring that the Earth-Mother would respond to the villagers' prayers for food from her womb. In many areas where agriculture became important, *female-centered religious cults* and female priestesses replaced male gods and priests.

These alterations in lifestyle came about gradually, of course, as a group learned to depend on crop growing for its main food supply. When that change took place varied sharply from one continent or region to the next. In a few places, it has still not occurred. A few nomadic tribes or hunter-gatherer groups can still be found, although they are fast disappearing under the intrusions of modern communications and technology.

Where were the first agricultural societies? For many years, researchers believed agriculture must have emerged first in the Near or Middle East and spread gradually from there into Asia and Africa. According to this "**diffusion theory**" of cultural accomplishment, knowledge of new techniques spreads through human contacts, as water might spread on blotting paper. But now it is known that as early as 7000 B.C.E. agriculture had developed in at least four separate areas independent of outside influences: the Near East, Central America, North China, and West Africa. Slightly later, the first domesticated animals were being raised as a part of village life. The raising of pigs, sheep, cattle, and goats for food and fiber goes back at least as far as 4000 B.C.E. (The horse comes considerably later, as we shall see.) Map 1.1 shows where some common plant and animal species were first cultivated or domesticated.

Irrigation Civilizations

Several of the earliest civilizations developed in the plains bordering on major rivers or in the valleys the rivers created. Not coincidentally, four of the most important civilizations, which we will examine in the next chapters, emerged in this way. The development of high civilization was dependent on intensive, productive agriculture, and the development of agriculture was in turn dependent on the excellent soil and regular supply of water provided by

■ The faint outlines of ancient irrigation canals and ditches are still visible from the air two thousand years after their abandonment.

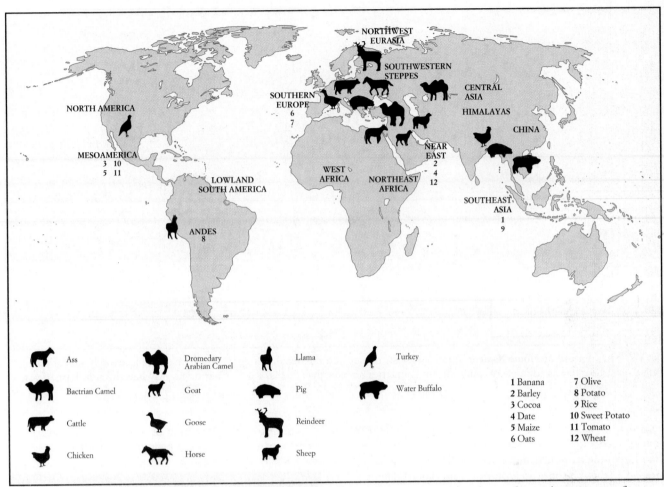

NORTHWEST
EURASIA

SOUTHWESTERN
STEPPES

CENTRAL
ASIA

SOUTHERN
EUROPE
6
7

HIMALAYAS

NORTH AMERICA

CHINA

MESOAMERICA
3 10
5 11

NEAR
EAST
2
4
12

WEST
AFRICA

NORTHEAST
AFRICA

LOWLAND
SOUTH AMERICA

SOUTHEAST
ASIA
1
9

ANDES
8

	Ass		Dromedary Arabian Camel		Llama		Turkey
	Bactrian Camel		Goat		Pig		Water Buffalo
	Cattle		Goose		Reindeer		
	Chicken		Horse		Sheep		

1 Banana	7 Olive
2 Barley	8 Potato
3 Cocoa	9 Rice
4 Date	10 Sweet Potato
5 Maize	11 Tomato
6 Oats	12 Wheat

⊙ **MAP 1.1 Origin of Crops and Domestic Animals.** This shows the areas where particular plant and animal species were first cultivated or domesticated. In the case of some species (e.g., the pig), there seems to have been independent development in different areas. In most cases, however, the contact between neighboring cultures facilitated the rapid spread of plant and animal cultivation around the globe.

the river. In ancient *Mesopotamia,* the dual drainage of the Tigris and Euphrates Rivers made the first urban civilization possible. In *Egypt,* the Nile, the world's longest river at more than 4,000 miles, was the life-giving source of everything the people needed and cherished. In *India,* the beginnings of civilization are traced to the extensive fields on both sides of the Indus River, which flows more than 2,000 miles from the slopes of the Himalayas to the ocean. Finally, in *China,* the valley of the Yellow River, which is about 2,700 miles long, was the cradle of the oldest continuous civilization in world history.

The rivers were not just the source of good crops and essential water. They also provided a sure and generally easy form of transport and communication, allowing inter-village trade and encouraging central authorities to extend their powers over a much greater area than would have been possible if they had only overland contacts.

But the rivers had very different natures. The Tigris and the Yellow were as destructive in their unpredictable flooding as the Nile and the Indus were peaceful and friendly. The Yellow River was so ruinous at times that its ancient name was the "sorrow of China." But without its dependable source of water, early farming in North China would have been impossible.

Climate, too, made a difference among the early civilizations. Egypt and most of the Indus valley have temperate climates that change little over the course of the year and are suitable for crops all year long. It is not at all

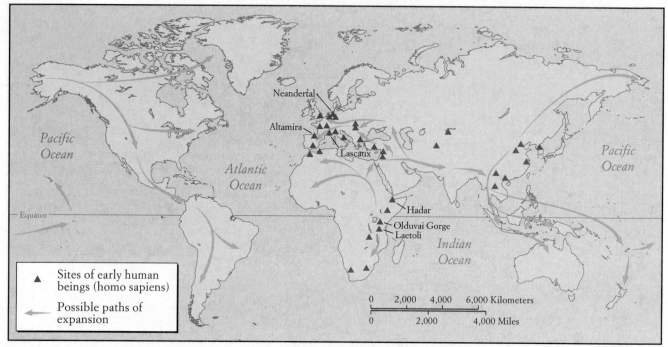

⊙ **MAP 1.2 Spread of *Homo Sapiens.*** Anthropologists disagree on the detail, but agree that human beings entirely similar to ourselves probably existed in every continent but Antarctica no later than 20,000 B.C.E. Their origin may have been in East Africa.

unusual for an Egyptian family farm to grow three crops annually. North China and Mesopotamia, on the other hand, experience much more severe changes of weather, not only from season to season but from day to day.

In the Near East, the climate has changed significantly over the past two millennia. What was once a relatively moderate place, with adequate rain for growing grain crops, has gradually become an arid desert, with very intense heat much of the year. Present-day Iraq, which occupies the old Mesopotamia, is a very difficult place to farm even with modern irrigation techniques. This change is a big part of the reason why Mesopotamia, after thousands of years of leadership, sank slowly into stagnation in later days.

⚜ METAL AND ITS USES

The first metal used by humans seems to have been soft copper. When combined with lead and tin ores, copper becomes the more useful *bronze.* Bronze has some advantages over copper: it is harder (and therefore more suitable for weaponry), and more resistant to weathering. But it has several disadvantages when compared to other metals: it is relatively difficult to make; its weight is

■ The discovery of how to smelt and temper iron tools and weapons was a major turning point in the civilized development of every people.

excessive for many uses; and it cannot keep a fine edge for tools and cutting weapons. Above all, bronze was difficult to obtain in the ancient world and very expensive.

The period when bronze art objects and bronze weapons predominated in a given part of the world is called its Bronze Age. In western Asia where civilizations first appeared, the Bronze Age extended from about 7000 B.C.E. to about 1500 B.C.E., when a major innovation in human technology made its first appearance: the smelting of *iron*.

Iron is the key metal of history. Wherever it has come into common use, certain advances have occurred. Iron plowshares open areas to cultivation that previously could not be tilled. Iron weapons and body armor give warfare a new look. Iron tools enable new technical progress and expanded production. Iron utensils are cheaper than other metals, last longer, resist fiery heat, and do not easily shatter or lose their edge.

Iron ore is one of the more common metallic ores, and it is often found on or very near the earth's surface (unlike copper and lead). It is easily segregated from the surrounding soils or rock. The crucial breakthrough was learning how to temper the ore, that is, how to purify it so that the iron could be formed and used without shattering. The Indo-European people known as Hittites, who lived in modern-day Turkey, were apparently the first to smelt iron. By 1200 B.C.E., the knowledge of iron was spreading rapidly among Middle Eastern and Egyptian peoples.

Summary

The prehistory of the human race is immeasurably longer than the short period (5,000 years or so) of which we have historical knowledge. During the last 50,000 years of the prehistorical period, men and women became physically and mentally indistinguishable from ourselves and spread across the earth. Developing agriculture to supplement hunting and gathering, humans slowly attained that advanced state we call civilization in the later part of the Neolithic Age, around 3000 B.C.E. Urban life was now possible, a system of record keeping evolved, and advanced weapons and tools of metal were invented.

In the next chapters of this book, we will examine the four earliest centers of advanced civilization, one by one, and look at the reasons why each of them became such a center. We will see that both the similarities and the contrasts among these civilizations were remarkable and gave each of them a particular atmosphere that would last for thousands of years, and in some cases until the present day.

Identification Terms

Agricultural Revolution	culture	hominid	paleographers
civilization	diffusion theory	Neanderthal Man	paleontologists

Test Your Knowledge

1. Which of the following statements most aptly describes Paleolithic society?
   a. The hunt was the only way to obtain food regularly.
   b. There was constant fighting among families and clans.
   c. The individual was more important than the group.
   d. Cooperation was necessary for survival.
2. The Agricultural Revolution occurred first during the
   a. Neolithic.
   b. Bronze Age.
   c. Paleolithic.
   d. Mesozoic.
3. Among the major changes that occur as a result of the adoption of agriculture by any group is:
   a. the abandonment of traditional village life.
   b. a decrease in trading.
   c. an increase in population.
   d. a reduction in animal raising.
4. Which of the following was *not* a characteristic of most early civilizations?
   a. A dependable source of water for agriculture.
   b. A religion based on female fertility rites.
   c. Attempts at total self-sufficiency in consumption.
   d. Water-based communication and transport.
5. Which of these was of decisive importance to Neolithic agriculture?
   a. The development of chemical fertilizers.
   b. The mastery of irrigation techniques.
   c. The development of insecticides.
   d. The creation of a law code.
6. The increase in the number of humans during the Neolithic Age was primarily caused by
   a. the disappearance of epidemic disease.
   b. a surplus of food.
   c. decreased intergroup violence.
   d. a greater respect for the aged.

Bibliography

Childe, V. G. *What Happened in History,* 1985. An anthropologist looks at humans' early presence.

Cole, S. *The Neolithic Revolution,* 1970. Covers the Near East and parts of Europe.

Fiedel, S. *Prehistory of the Americas,* 1988. Reflects the most recent material.

Hallo, W., and W. K. Simpson. *The Ancient Near East,* 1971. A readable survey that examines both Mesopotamia and Egypt. Discusses mainly political affairs.

Jones, W. D. *Venus and Sothis: How the Ancient Near East Was Rediscovered,* 1982. Very interesting account of early archaeology.

Leakey, R. E., and R. Lewin. *Origins: What New Discoveries Reveal,* 1977. Well illustrated and controversial.

———. *The Making of Mankind,* 1981. Perhaps the best account of early hominids, heavily illustrated and clearly written. The author takes sharp issue with the conclusions of his father Louis Leakey on this topic.

Quennell, M. C., and H. B. Quennell. *Everyday Life in the New Stone, Bronze, and Early Iron Ages,* 1955. One of the very best of the *Everyday Life* series.

Starr, C. G. *Early Man,* 1968. A brief, well-illustrated survey that discusses early Near Eastern civilizations as well as prehistory.

MESOPOTAMIA

c. 5000 B.C.E.	Sumerians arrive in Mesopotamia
c. 3500 B.C.E.	Cuneiform writing
c. 3000 B.C.E.	Sumerian city-states
c. 2200 B.C.E.	Sargon of Akkad
1700s B.C.E.	Hammurabi/oldest surviving law code
c. 1500 B.C.E.	Hittites conquer Mesopotamia

The land the ancient Greeks called Mesopotamia ("land between the rivers") is now the eastern half of Iraq. The rivers are the Euphrates and the Tigris. They originate in present-day Turkey and parallel one another for about 400 miles before joining together to flow into the head of the Persian Gulf (see Map 2.1).

In the lower courses of the rivers, in the third millennium B.C.E., originated the first extensive urban civilization of the world. This civilization was supported by extensive irrigation farming, pioneered by a people called **Sumerians,** who came into lower Mesopotamia from somewhere to the east around 5000 B.C.E. Gradually, the Sumerians created a series of small competing kingdoms, each of which was centered on a good-sized town. Here they developed a series of ideas and techniques that would provide the foundation of a distinct and highly influential civilization.

✤ SUMERIAN CIVILIZATION

The Sumerians were the first people to do an enormous number of highly significant things. They built the first large cities, as distinct from towns (the largest apparently containing upward of 100,000 people); they developed the first sophisticated system of writing; they built the first monumental buildings, using as the basic principle of support the post-and-lintel system, which is still the normal way of piercing walls for light and air. They were probably the inventors of the wheel, and they were the first to design and build a gravity-flow irrigation system. They had the first school system known to history, and they were the first to use sunbaked brick. They were possibly the first to use the plow, and among the first to make bronze metal.

What we know of them is extremely impressive, but nonetheless we know a good deal not only because they left extensive records of their own, but also because they had enormous influence on their neighbors and their successors in Mesopotamia.

The Sumerians were not the only settlers of the broad plain on either side of the two rivers; in fact, they were not the first people in those regions. Most of their neighboring tribes were members of the **Semitic** language family; that is, they spoke a language that was related to many others, which, collectively, are called the Semitic family by modern linguists. (Note: A language group or family is related by its grammar and sometimes by its vocabulary and alphabet. The Semitic family is one of the major language

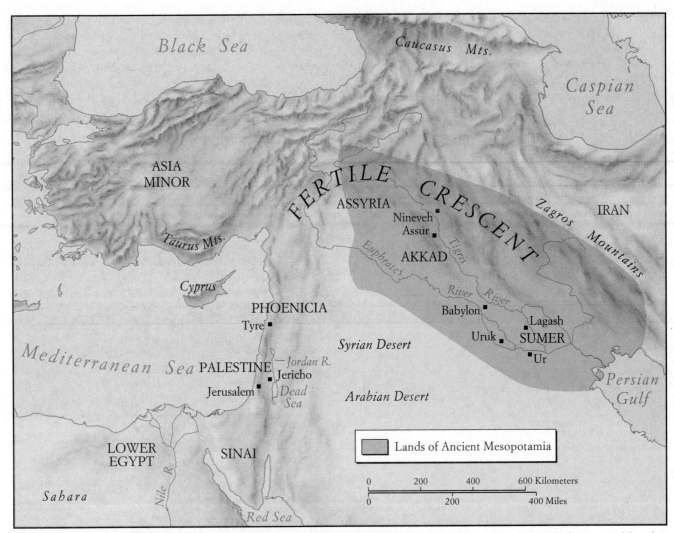

⊙ **MAP 2.1   The Ancient Near East.** The Mesopotamian city-states were concentrated on the rich agricultural plain created by silt from the Tigris and Euphrates Rivers as they flowed toward the head of the Persian Gulf.

families in the world and includes both Hebrew and Arabic as well as many others.)

By somewhere around 3000 B.C.E., the Sumerians had extended their domain upriver into the Semite-inhabited places. Either by coercion or peaceably, they began to civilize these *barbarians* (a Greek word meaning people who speak a different language and are supposedly inferior). Large towns grew up, with neighborhoods of craftsmen, merchants, and laborers. Trade grew rapidly, not only between food-growing villages and the towns, but among the towns scattered for hundreds of miles along the banks of the rivers. Trade wars and disputes over water—essential for irrigation—assured that no centralized governing power was possible. Whenever a city

managed to seize control of substantial supplies of water and trade, the others upstream or downstream would band together against it, or its subjects would rebel. Conflicts seem to have been the order of the day, with city-state vying against city-state in a constant struggle for mastery over the precious irrigated lands. The early history of Mesopotamia under the Sumerians is a tale of great technological and cultural advances, marred by strife, disunion, and unceasing warfare.

Not until about 2200 B.C.E. was the land between the rivers brought under one effective rule, and that was imposed by a Semitic invader known as **Sargon** the Great, who conquered the entire plain. Sargon established his capital in the new town of Akkad, near modern-day

Baghdad, capital of Iraq. Although the Akkadian empire lasted less than a century, its influence was great, for it spread Sumerian culture and methods far and wide in the Near and Middle East, through that wide belt of land reaching from Mesopotamia to Egypt that is called the **Fertile Crescent** (see Map 2.1).

Although the Sumerian city-states never united until they were overwhelmed by outsiders, their cultural and religious achievements and beliefs would be picked up by their conquerors and essentially retained by all their successors in Mesopotamia. Perhaps the most important of all the Sumerian accomplishments was the gradual invention of a system of *writing*.

The Evolution of Writing

Some type of marks on some type of medium (clay, paper, wood, stone) had been in use long, long before 3500 B.C.E.

What the Sumerians of that epoch did, to justify the claim of having invented writing, was to move beyond pictorial writing, or symbols derived from pictures, into a further phase of conveying meaning through abstract marks.

All writing derives from a picture originally. This is called pictography, and it has been used from one end of the earth to the other. Pictography had several obvious disadvantages, though. For one thing, it could not convey the meaning of abstractions (things that have no material, tangible existence). Nor could it communicate the tense of a verb, nor the degree of an adjective or adverb, nor many other things that language has to handle well.

The way that the Sumerians (and later peoples) got around these difficulties was to gradually expand their pictorial writing to a much more sophisticated level, so that it included special signs for abstractions, tenses, and so on—signs that had nothing to do with tangible objects. These are called conventional signs and may be invented

■ After earlier experimentation with pictographic writing, the Sumerians devised a script called cuneiform (wedge-shaped). Since this system of signs transcribed sounds rather than pictures or ideas, it was adaptable to other languages as well; thus, cuneiform writing was later used by the Babylonians and Assyrians.

Original pictograph	Pictograph in position of later cuneiform	Early Babylonian	Assyrian	Original or derived meaning
				Bird
				Fish
				Donkey
				Ox
				Sun Day
				Grain
				Orchard
				To plow To till
				Boomerang To throw To throw down
				To stand To go

■ This example of cuneiform writing describes an old Babylonian sacred marriage rite.

fying and standardizing their pictures, so that they could be written more rapidly and recognized more easily by strangers.

A big breakthrough came sometime in the third millennium, when a series of clever scribes began to use written signs to indicate the sounds of the spoken language. This was the beginning of the *phonetic written language,* where the signs had a direct connection with the oral language. Although the Sumerians did not progress as far as an alphabet, they started down the path that would culminate in one about 2,500 years later.

The basic format of the written language after about 3500 B.C.E. was a script written in wedge-shaped characters, the **cuneiform,** on clay tablets about the size of your hand. Tens of thousands of these tablets covered by cuneiform writings have been dug up in modern times. Most of them pertain to contracts between private parties or between a private party and the officials. But other tablets contain prayers of all sorts, proclamations by officials, law codes and judgments, and some letters and poetry. Sumerian cuneiform remained the basic script of most Near and Middle Eastern languages until about 1000 B.C.E., when its use began to fade out.

Mathematics and Chronology

After the invention of writing, perhaps the most dramatic advance made by these early inhabitants of Mesopotamia was in mathematics and chronology. Sumerian math was based on units of 60, and this, of course, is the reason why we still measure time in intervals of 60 seconds and 60 minutes. Much of our basic geometry and trigonometry also stems from the Sumerians. Their calendar was based on the movement of the moon and was thus a lunar

for any meaning desired by their users. For example, if both of us agree that the signs "cc~" stand for "the boy in the blue suit," then that is what they mean when we see them on a piece of paper, or a rock surface, or wherever. If we further agree that by adding the vertical stroke "!" we make a verb into a future tense, then it's future tense so far as we're concerned. Very slowly, the Sumerians expanded their pictographs in this way, while simultaneously simpli-

■ These carved Sumerian seals were equivalent to signatures, identifying the authors of the documents they marked. Some have been found as far away as India.

The *Epic of Gilgamesh*

Stories of the Great Deluge occur in many ancient cultural traditions. In each case, the story tells of a disastrous flood that engulfed the entire earth and nearly annihilated humanity. The most familiar flood story in the Western world is found in the Book of Genesis in the Old Testament.

In the Middle Eastern tradition, the narrative of the Deluge is first found in the *Epic of Gilgamesh*. In this version, the main focus of the story is on the inevitability of death and the defeat of the hero as he attempts to achieve immortality. The Mesopotamian counterpart of the biblical Noah is Utnapishtim. Here his description of the flood is contrasted with the version recounted in Genesis:

GILGAMESH

... The gods of the abyss rose up; Nergal pulled out the dams of the netherworld, Ninurta the war-lord threw down the dikes ... a stupor of despair went up to heaven when the god of storms turned daylight into darkness, when he smashed the earth like a teacup. One whole day the tempest raged, gathering fury as it went, and it poured over the people like the tide of battle; a man could not see his brother nor could the people be seen from heaven. Even the gods were terrified at the flood, they fled to the highest heaven ... they crouched against the walls, cowering ... the gods of heaven and hell wept ... for six days and six nights the winds blew, tempest and flood raged together like warring hosts ... I looked at the face of the earth, and all was silence, all mankind was turned into clay ... I bowed low, and I wept ...

GENESIS

All the fountains of the great deep burst forth and the floodgates of the heavens were opened. And rain fell on the earth for forty days and forty nights .... The waters increased and bore up the ark, and it rose above the earth. The waters rose higher and higher, and increased greatly on the earth ... the waters rose higher and higher, so that all the highest mountains everywhere under the heavens were covered. All flesh that moved on the earth died: birds, cattle, wild animals, all creatures that crawl upon the earth, and all men. Only Noah and those with him in the ark were saved.

Gilgamesh is a grim tale that speaks of death and the afterlife in pessimistic and fearful tones. Indicative is this description by Gilgamesh's companion Enkidu of a vivid dream he had had, foreshadowing his approaching death:

I stood alone before an awful Being; his face was somber like the blackbird of the storm. He fell upon me with the talons of an eagle, and he held me fast, pinioned by his claws until I smothered; then he transformed me so that my arms became wings covered with feathers ... and he led me away, to the house from which those who enter never return ... whose people sit in darkness, dust their food and clay their meat. They are clothed like birds with wings for coverings, they see no light, they sit in darkness ....

The epic ends with the failure of Gilgamesh's quest for the secret of immortal life. The somber funeral chant seem to underline the poets sense of resignation and futility:

The king has laid himself down, and will not rise again
The Lord of Kullab [i.e., Gilgamesh] will not rise again,
He overcame evil, but he will not rise again,
Though he was strong of arm, he will not rise again,
Possessing wisdom and a comely face, he will not rise again ....

SOURCE: *Reprinted with permission. Penguin Classics, 1960, Second revised edition, 1972. Copyright © N. K. Sanders, 1960, 1964, 1972.*

calendar, as were the calendars of most other ancient peoples. The year was based on the passage of seasons and the position of the stars; it was subdivided into lunar months, corresponding to the period between one full moon and the next. In calculating the year's length, the Sumerians arrived at a figure very close to our own, though they were not quite as close as the Egyptians were. All in all, Sumerian math including its further development by the Babylonians and Persians has held up very well and has been influential in all later Western theory of science, including that of the Greeks.

Religion and the Afterlife

Our knowledge of the Sumerians' religion is sketchy and unsure. Apparently, they believed in a host of gods (**polytheism,** or "many gods") of various ranks. There were many male and female deities, each with specific competencies in human affairs.

The gods were much like superhumans, with all the faults and weaknesses of men and women. Some of them lived forever; others died just as humans did. Some were immensely powerful, others rather insignificant. Each major city developed its own set of powerful gods and attempted to please its chief gods by building enormous temples, called ziggurats. The best-known ziggurat was erected by the powerful city of **Babylon** long after the Sumerian epoch. It was the Tower of Babel of biblical fame.

The gods were frequently cruel toward their human creatures and were highly unpredictable. There is no trace of a loving relationship between deity and men; nor is there any trace of ethics in Mesopotamian religion. The demands of the gods had no intrinsic connection with doing good or avoiding evil on earth. The gods often punished humans, but not for what we would call sin. When comprehensible at all, the reasons for the punishment were petty and unworthy, but generally, they were simply unknowable. The punishments often took the form of natural catastrophes, such as droughts or floods. To avert punishment, the gods had to be appeased with frequent, costly rituals and ceremonies, which were the responsibility of a hereditary priesthood. The priests used their power as interpreters of the will of the gods to create large and wealthy temple communities, supported by the offerings of the citizens. In some Sumerian cities, the priests seem to have been the true rulers for a time. This practice ended with the conquest by Sargon the Great, who made the royal throne the undisputed center of authority.

■ Now in a German museum, this magnificent portal known as the Ishtar Gate was erected in the walls of one of the Mesopotamian cities. It shows the advanced artistic achievement of the age.

The religion was certainly not an optimistic one, and it seems to have had no clear ideas on the nature of the afterlife or who, if anyone, could enjoy immortality. The best approach seemed to be to honor and obey the gods as well as you could, to appease them by making offerings through their very powerful priests, and to hope for the best in the afterlife, if there was one. The concept of a heaven or a hell seems to have been very vague.

Much of what is known about Mesopotamian religious belief derives from their literature, in which several major myths of Western civilization, including the Flood and the Garden of Eden, find their first expressions. Particularly important is the creation myth embraced in the long poem called the *Epic of Gilgamesh.* Gilgamesh is a man, a king of one of the city-states, who desires the secret of immortal life, but the gods, jealous of his power, defeat him. *Gilgamesh* is the first epic poem in world literature (see the Document in this chapter).

Law and Government

One of the earliest known complete code of laws originated in post-Sumerian Mesopotamia, in the 1700s B.C.E. during the reign of the emperor Hammurabi (see the Biography in this chapter). His code certainly had predecessors that have been lost, because its legal concepts and

Hammurabi

The Babylonian emperor Hammurabi, who ruled Mesopotamia from c. 1792 to c. 1750 B.C.E., is best known for the code of laws that bears his name, one of the earliest law codes yet discovered. Hammurabi's empire stretched from the desolate mountains of Zagros in western Iran, to the edge of the Arabian desert; it was centered on the great city of Babylon in central Mesopotamia. Though nature has not been generous with this region, he was successful in bringing prosperity and peace to the majority of his subjects.

Like all Middle Eastern kingdoms, Hammurabi's empire was originally created by conquest. He formed coalitions with his Semite neighbors and won the loyalty of the smaller Amorite city-states that surrounded his own. Babylon emerged as a center of both manufacturing and trade, and its influence reached from the head of the Persian Gulf to the eastern shore of the Mediterranean.

Hammurabi was a tireless builder, spending much time repairing older temples and constructing new ones dedicated to Babylon's many gods. Among his more important economic undertakings was the construction of several new canals to move the waters of the Tigris farther into the desert and allow new agricultural colonies to flourish. He established a courier service and built roads so the messengers could travel quickly. His government combined a central court with subordinate local lords, a system that would later be used effectively by the Persian Empire.

But the emperor's main concern was to maintain order through good law. To that effect, he gave his subjects a complex law code. Its 282 decrees, collectively termed the Code of Hammurabi, were inscribed on stone stelae or columns and erected in many public places. One was discovered in Persian Susa and is now in the Louvre in Paris.

The code dealt primarily with civil affairs such as marriage and inheritance, family relations, property rights, and business practices. Criminal offenses were punished with varying degrees of severity, depending on the social status of the offender and the victim. Trial by ordeal, retribution by retaliatory action, and capital punishment were common practices. Children were often made to suffer for the sins of the fathers. But judges made a clear distinction between intentional and unintentional injuries, and monetary fines were normally used as punishment where no malicious intent was manifested. The "eye for an eye" morality often associated with Hammurabi's code was relatively restricted in application.

The code made theft a serious crime and devoted great attention to crimes against property in general. Marriage and inheritance, business contracts, and commercial transactions of all kinds were strictly regulated and enforced. Workers had to do an adequate job or be punished for negligence. Official fee tables were ordained for medical care, and woe to the doctor who was found guilty of malpractice! Although the code did not concern itself with religious belief or practice, it did accord considerable powers to the administering judges, who were often priests. In general, it established strict standards of justice and public morality.

Hammurabi stands forth after four thousand years as a ruler of exceptional ability. His subjects enjoyed a period of prosperity, in part because of the personal interest he took in all branches of government. In the prologue to the code, he stated: "When Marduk sent me to rule the people . . . I established law and justice in the land, and promoted the welfare of the people." It is a proud boast, and one that apparently has been validated by history. Long after the emperor's death, his law was still the basis of a great civilization.

vocabulary are much too sophisticated for it to have been a first effort.

The code is based on two distinctive principles: punishment depended on the social rank of the violator, and offenders were subjected to the same damages or injury that they caused to others. These ideas would be incorporated into many later codes over the next two thousand years. A commoner would get a different, more severe punishment than a noble or official would receive for the same offense. And a slave (of whom there were many) would be treated more harshly still. If in the same social class as the victim, the offender would have to give "an eye for an eye, a tooth for a tooth." The victim had the right to demand personal compensation from the person who had caused him grief—a legal concept that is gradually being reintroduced into American criminal law. Another basic principle of Mesopotamian law was that the government should act as an impartial referee among its subject citizens, seeing to it that the wronged party got satisfaction from the evildoer.

People were not equal before the law: husbands had a great deal of power over wives, fathers over children, rich over poor, free citizens over slaves. Nevertheless, there was a definite attempt to protect the defenseless, and to see that all received justice.

Much of Hammurabi's code dealt with social and family problems, such as the support of widows and orphans, illegitimacy, adultery, and rape. Clearly, the position of women was inferior to men, but they did have certain legal rights and were not just the property of their male relatives. A wife could divorce her husband, and if the husband was found to be at fault, she was entitled to the property she had brought into the marriage. A woman could also enter into contracts and have custody over minor children under certain conditions—two rights that many later civilizations denied them.

Government in Mesopotamia can be divided into two types: the **theocracy** of the early city-states of the Sumerians, and the kingdom-empires of their successors, starting with Sargon the Great of Akkad. The cities were ruled by a king, assisted by noble officials and priests. In Sumerian times, the kings were no more than figureheads for the priests, but later they exercised decisive power.

Social Structure

There were three social classes in Mesopotamia: (1) A small group of nobles and priests were great landlords and had a monopoly on the higher offices of the city. (2) The freemen were the most numerous class; they did the bulk of the city's work and trading and owned and worked most of the outlying farmlands. (3) The slaves, who at times were very numerous, often possessed considerable skills and were given some responsible positions. Freemen had some political rights; slaves had none.

As we will repeatedly see, slaves were common in most ancient societies, and enslavement was by no means the morally contemptible and personally humiliating condition it would frequently become later. Slavery had nothing much to do with race or ethnicity and everything to do with bad luck, such as being on the losing side of a war or falling into debt. Most slaves in Mesopotamia—and elsewhere—had run up debts that they could not otherwise repay. It was not at all uncommon to become someone's slave for a few years and then resume your freedom when you had paid off what you owed. Hereditary slavery was rare. Many owners routinely freed their slaves in their wills as a mark of piety and benevolence.

Maltreatment of slaves did occur, but mostly to fieldworkers, miners, or criminals who had been enslaved as punishment and had had no personal contacts with their owner. On the other side, in all ancient societies many slaves engaged in business, many had advanced skills in the crafts, and some managed to accumulate enough money working on their own accounts that they could buy their freedom. The conditions of slavery in the ancient world varied so enormously that we cannot generalize about them with any accuracy except to say that slaves were politically and legally inferior to free citizens.

⚜ SUCCESSORS TO SUMERIA

After the conquest by Sargon of Akkad, Mesopotamia was subjected to a long series of foreign invasions and conquests by nomadic peoples eager to enjoy the fruits of civilized life. These barbaric nomads generally adopted the beliefs and values of those they had conquered. After the Akkadians, the most important of them were, in sequence:

1. The Amorites, or Old Babylonians, a Semitic people who conquered the plains under their great emperor Hammurabi in the 1700s B.C.E.
2. The Hittites, an Indo-European group of tribes who came out of southern Russia into modern-day Turkey and constructed an empire there that reached far into the east and south. The Hittites were a remarkable people who took over the river plain around 1500. They were skilled administrators and established the first example of a multinational state, which worked fairly well.

■ The so-called Marsh Arabs of the Tigris-Euphrates delta have changed little in two thousand years. They still derive a simple living from reed-gathering and fishing activities which also occupied their ancestors.

3. After the Hittites fell to unknown invaders around 1200, the Assyrians gradually established themselves, operating from their northern Mesopotamian center at Nineveh. The Imperial Assyrian period from around 800–600 B.C.E. will be dealt with in Chapter 4.

4. Finally, after a very brief period under the New Babylonians (or Chaldees as the Old Testament calls them), the plains fell to the mighty Persian Empire in the 500s B.C.E. and stayed under Persian (Iranian) rule for most of the next thousand years (see Chapter 4).

✤ THE DECLINE OF MESOPOTAMIA IN WORLD HISTORY

The valley of the Tigris and Euphrates Rivers ceased to be of central importance in the ancient world after the Persian conquest. The Persians did not choose to make their capital there, nor did they adopt the ideas and the cultural models of their new province, as all previous conquerors had. The Persians were already far advanced beyond barbarism when they conquered Mesopotamia and perhaps were not so easily impressed.

More importantly, the cities' food supply was declining as the irrigated farms of the lower plains no longer produced abundant harvests. Thanks to several thousand years of salt deposits from the evaporated waters of the canals and ditches, the fields, unrenewed by fertilizers and exposed to a gradually harshening climate of sandstorms and great heat, were simply not capable of producing as much as the population needed. Various problems contributed to the decline of Mesopotamia, but it is certain that it proceeded in part from one of the first known examples of long-term environmental degradation. The once thriving city-states and rich fields were gradually abandoned, and the center of power and culture moved elsewhere.

Mesopotamia slowly receded into the background of civilized activities from the Persian conquest until the ninth century C.E., when for a time it became the political and spiritual center of the far-flung world of Islam. But it was not until the mid-twentieth century, with the rise of Muslim fundamentalism and the coming of the Oil Age, that the area again became a vital world center.

Summary

The Sumerians were the first civilized inhabitants of the dual-river plain and left their several successors-in-power a variety of techniques and attitudes that they adopted and adapted. Of all the Sumerian achievements, none are more important than the invention of writing and the mastery of town building and urban living skills. Their religious beliefs seem harsh and pessimistic now, but apparently reflected their perceptions of the world around them.

During the many centuries from 3500 to the Persian conquest, the Mesopotamian valley was the most important single contributor to the spread of civilization in southern Asia and the eastern Mediterranean. Its science and laws, its arts and architecture were strongly reflected in both the classical Greek tradition and the ideas and beliefs of the Hebrews—two very notable ancestors of the Western world.

Test Your Knowledge

1. The founders of ancient Mesopotamian civilization were the
   a. Sumerians.
   b. Amorites.
   c. Semites.
   d. Babylonians.
2. The Tigris and Euphrates were important to Mesopotamians primarily because
   a. they kept out potential raiders.
   b. they made irrigation possible.
   c. they drained off the water from the frequent storms.
   d. they brought the people together.
3. The Mesopotamian ziggurat was a
   a. military fort.
   b. temple of worship.
   c. household shrine.
   d. royal palace.
4. Pictographs are a form of writing that
   a. uses pictures and words.
   b. uses agreed-on signs to make pictures.
   c. puts abstract ideas into pictorial form.
   d. uses pictures of material objects to form meanings.
5. Mesopotamians considered their gods to be
   a. about equal in power.
   b. the creators of people and the universe.
   c. responsive to human needs and wants.
   d. disembodied spirits.
6. The *Epic of Gilgamesh* deals with the
   a. struggle between good and evil.
   b. details of death and the afterlife.
   c. proof of the existence of gods.
   d. conflict between men and women.
7. The law code of King Hammurabi
   a. ensured equal treatment for all offenders.
   b. was the first law code ever written.
   c. used fines and financial punishments exclusively.
   d. ordered punishments in accord with the social rank of the offender.

Identification Terms

Babylon	Fertile Crescent	Sargon	Sumerians
cuneiform	polytheism	Semitic	Hittites

Bibliography

Crawford, H. *Sumer and the Sumerians,* 1991. More recent than Kramer, but not as witty.

Frankfort, H. *The Birth of Civilization in the Near East,* 1951. A classic work; demands some thought, but well worth it. Compares Mesopotamia and Egypt in several ways. See also the next entry.

Frankfort, H., et al. *Before Philosophy: The Intellectual Adventure of Ancient Man,* 1946.

Kramer, S. *History Begins at Sumer,* 1981. A classic rendition of why the Sumerians are important.

Mallowan, M. E. *Early Mesopotamia and Iran,* 1966. Strong on the technical achievements.

Saggs, H. F. *Civilization before Greece and Rome,* 1989. Very up-to-date on the findings of the last twenty years.

EGYPT

c. 3100–2200 B.C.E.	Old Kingdom
c. 2600–2100 B.C.E.	Pyramids built
c. 2200–2100 B.C.E.	First Intermediate Period
c. 2100–1650 B.C.E.	Middle Kingdom
c. 1650–1570 B.C.E.	Second Intermediate Period
1500s	Hyksos invasion
c. 1550–700 B.C.E.	New Kingdom
c. 1550–1250 B.C.E.	Empire
1300s	Akhnaton
	Tutankhamen
525 B.C.E.	PERSIAN CONQUEST

It would be hard to find two other ancient civilizations that present as sharp a contrast in some respects as Mesopotamia on one end of the Fertile Crescent and Egypt on the other. Although they were only some 800 miles apart over countryside that is relatively easy to cross and were both based on intensive irrigated farming, the two civilizations evolved very different patterns of beliefs and values. Unlike Mesopotamia, Egypt was an island in time and space that enjoyed a thousand years or more of civilized living with little disturbance from the outside world.

⚜ THE NATURAL ENVIRONMENT

Like Mesopotamia, Egypt was dependent on the waters of a great river system. Egypt is, and has always been, the valley of the Nile—a green strip averaging about 30 miles wide, with fierce desert hills on either side. The 1,000 mile river itself originates far to the south in the lakes of central Africa and flows north until it empties into the Mediterranean Sea at Alexandria.

Unlike the Tigris and Euphrates, the Nile is a benevolent river, and without it life in Egypt would have been unthinkable. In contrast to the frequent destructive flooding of the Tigris, the Nile annually would swell gently until it overflowed its low banks and spread out over the valley floor, carrying with it a load of extremely fertile silt. Two or three weeks later, the flood would subside, and the river would recede, depositing the silt to renew the valley with a fresh layer of good topsoil. The receding waters were trapped in a series of small reservoirs connected to an intricate system of ditches that would later convey the water into the surrounding fields for irrigation.

The entire year is one long growing season in Egypt. The climate is moderate and constant, with no storms and no frosts ever. The sun shines in modern Egypt an average of 361 days per year, and there is no reason to think that it was any different four thousand years ago. Rain is almost unknown, and the temperature is in the 70s year-round. These advantages make Egypt an ideal area for intensive agriculture, and it has supported three crops a year for a very long time. In Mesopotamia, by contrast, farmers have always had to cope with excessive heat, drought, sandstorms, occasional floods, and insect invasions.

Egypt's Protective Isolation

But not only in agriculture was Egypt blessed by its environment. The country was also protected against invasion by the deserts on the east and west of the valley and by the cataracts (falls) of the northerly flowing Nile, which prevented easy passage into Egypt from the south, where enemies (Nubians, Ethiopians) dwelled. On the north, the sea gave the Nile delta some protection from unwanted intruders, while still allowing the Egyptians to develop maritime operations. Unlike Mesopotamia, which had no real natural boundaries and was repeatedly invaded from all sides, Egypt was secure in its geographic isolation. Only on the northeast where the narrow Sinai peninsula links Egypt to Asia (see Map 3.1) was a land-based invasion possible, and most of Egypt's eventual conquerors arrived from this direction.

Egypt's natural walls kept it safe from external danger for a very long time, however. For about 2,500 years, Egyptian civilization developed in almost unbroken safety. But this isolation also had its drawbacks. When serious external challenges finally did come, the Egyptian governing class and general society were not prepared to resist effectively and could not adequately respond to the new situation.

Egypt's Uniqueness

No other ancient civilization was so "different" as Egypt. The country possessed everything needed for a decent life: excellent agriculture, natural barriers against invasion, great natural resources, and a skilled and numerous population. Together, they gave Egypt advantages that could only be envied.

In fact, over time the Egyptian educated class, especially the officials and priests, developed a sort of superiority complex toward foreigners that is rivaled in history only by that of the Chinese. The Egyptians were convinced that the gods smiled upon them and their land, that they already possessed the best of all worlds in Egypt, and that they could learn nothing of significant value from others. When the king dealt with foreign traders, he could

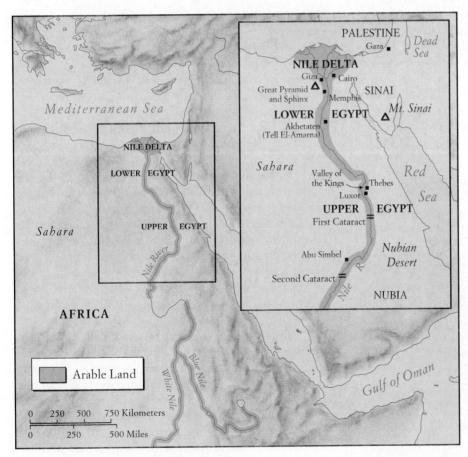

⊙ MAP 3.1 Ancient Egypt and the Nile. The first tourist to leave an account of Egypt was the Greek Herodotus in the fifth century B.C.E. He called Egypt "the gift of the Nile," a phrase that still describes the relation of the river and the people. The arable portion of the Nile valley extended about 800 miles upriver in ancient times.

successfully pretend to his own people that the foreigners had come to "give tribute," while the king showed his own generosity by showering "gifts" in return.

So secure were the Egyptians for so long that their security eventually turned into a weakness. Their conviction of superiority became a kind of mental cage, hemming in their imaginations and preventing the Egyptians from responding to change, even as change became increasingly necessary. In short, they lost their abilities to adapt effectively. But this weakness took a very long time to show itself—about two thousand years!

✤ THE PHARAOH: EGYPT'S GOD-KING

As is true of almost all early peoples, the Egyptians' religious beliefs reflected their environment to some extent, and the fully developed religion had enormous impact on the nature of their government.

In contrast to Mesopotamia, Egypt was quickly and easily unified; around 3100 B.C.E all the middle and lower reaches of the Nile valley came under one ruler. From the Mediterranean Sea southward to the Nubian desert, the country and the numerous already-civilized villagers came under the control of a **pharaoh** (meaning "from the great house"). The first pharaoh was called Menes, but he appears to have been merely a legend—or if he existed in fact, we know nothing of him but his name.

The period from 3100 to about 2500 B.C.E was Egypt's foundation period and the time of its greatest triumphs and cultural achievements. During these centuries, the land was ruled by an unbroken line of god-kings who

■ Still the world's largest edifice, the Great Pyramid was built to house the remains of the pharaoh Khufu (Cheops) in the Old Kingdom. It contains more than two million blocks of limestone weighing an average two and one half tons each; all had to be transported from far up the Nile.

apparently faced no serious threats either inside or outside their domain.

It is important to recognize that the pharaoh was not *like* a god; instead, he *was* a god, a god who chose to live on earth for a time. From the moment that his days-long coronation ceremony was completed, he was no longer a mortal man. He had become immortal, a reincarnation of the great divinity **Horus.** The pharaoh's will was law, and his wisdom was all-knowing. What he desired was by definition correct and just. What he did was the will of the almighty gods, speaking through him as one of them. His regulations must be carried out without question; otherwise, the gods might cease to smile on Egypt. His wife and family, especially his son who would succeed him, shared to some degree in this celestial glory, but only the reigning pharaoh was divine. Such powers in the monarch are quite rare in history, and Egypt's god-king was truly extraordinary in his powers and in the prestige he enjoyed among his people.

Government under the Pharaoh

The pharaoh governed through a bureaucracy, mainly composed of noble landowners who were responsible to him but were granted great local powers. When a weak pharaoh came to the throne, the power of the central authority could and occasionally did break down in the provinces, but its memory never disappeared entirely.

There were two intervals in Egypt's long history when the pharaoh's powers were seriously diminished, in 2200–2100 B.C.E. and in 1650–1570 B.C.E. The second of these time periods is known to have been triggered by the invasion of the mysterious *Hyksos* people, who crossed the Sinai peninsula and entered the Nile delta. The causes of the first breakdown remain unclear, but it was not the result of invasion. In both cases, a new, native Egyptian dynasty appeared within a century and reestablished strong government. The monarchy's grip upon the loyalties of the people was sufficiently strong that it could re-form the government in the same style with the same values and officials as before.

What enabled the pharaoh to retain such power over his subjects for so long? For almost two thousand years, the belief in the divinity of the king (or queen—there were at least three female pharaohs) persisted, as did the conviction that Egypt was specially favored and protected by the gods. This was the result of the happy situation that Egypt enjoyed through climate and geography. Nature provided, as nowhere else, a perpetual abundance, making

The Instruction of the Vizier to His Son

Most of the documents we have from ancient Egypt are prayers and chronologies of the pharaohs. But some more personal writings also survived; they include contracts, wills, some letters, and collections of wise sayings that were thought important to preserve. Among the latter is a collection of parchment scrolls known as the Instruction from the important official Ptah-hotep to his presumably teenaged son. It was composed in the twenty-fifth century B.C.E., but its words could be applied to many a father-son relationship today.

Then he said to his son:

Let not your heart be puffed up because of your knowledge; be not confident because you are a wise man. Take counsel with the ignorant as well as the wise. The full limits of skill cannot be attained and there is no skilled man equipped to his full advantage. Good speech is more hidden than the emerald; but it may be found among maidservants. . . .

Justice is great, and its appropriateness is lasting; it has been shaken since the times of him who made it [i.e., since the beginning of the world], but there is punishment for him who passes over its laws. It is the right path. . . . Wrongdoing has never brought its undertaking into port. It may be that fraud gains riches, but the strength of justice is that it lasts. . . .

If you are a man of standing and have founded a household and produce a son who is pleasing to god, if he is correct and inclines toward your ways and listens to your instructions, while his manners in your house are fitting, and if he takes care of your property as it should be, then seek out for him every useful action. He is your son . . . you should not cut your heart off from him. But a man's seed [children] often creates enmity. If he goes astray and transgresses your plans and does not carry out your instruction, so that his manners in your household are wretched, and he rebels against all that you say, while his mouth runs on in the most wretched talk, quite apart from his experience while he possesses nothing [i.e., he doesn't know what he is talking about], you should cast him off; he is not your son at all. He was not really born to you. Thus you should enslave him entirely, according to his own speech. He is one whom the gods have condemned in the very womb. . . .

SOURCE: J. B. Pritchard, ed., *Ancient Near Eastern Texts*, 3d ed. © Copyright Princeton University Press, 1969. Reprinted by permission.

Egypt the only place in the known world at that time to export grain surpluses. Furthermore, for three thousand years of civilized life, Egypt was only rarely touched by war and foreign invasion. For a very long time, until the Empire period, no army—that great eater of taxes—was necessary.

The Old Kingdom, Middle Kingdom, and New Kingdom

It has long been customary to divide Egypt's ancient history into dynasties (a period of monarchic rule by one family). In all there were thirty-one dynasties, beginning with the legendary Menes and ending with the dynasty that fell to the Persian invaders in 525. The greatest were those of the pyramid-building epoch and those of the Empire, around 1500–1300 B.C.E. The dynasties are traditionally grouped into three kingdoms: Old, Middle, and New.

Old Kingdom

The *Old Kingdom* (3100–2200 B.C.E.), which extended from Menes to the First Intermediate Period, was ancient Egypt's most fertile and successful era. During these nine hundred years, both form and content were perfected in most of those achievements that made Egypt great: art and architecture, divine monarchy, religion, social and economic stability, and prosperity. The pharaohs were unchallenged leaders who enjoyed the willing loyalty of their people. Later developments were almost always only a slight variation on the pattern established during the Old Kingdom or, in some cases, a deterioration from the Old Kingdom model.

■ This agricultural scene was found in the cemetery of Sheik Abd-al-Qurnah and dates to the fifteenth century B.C.E. The work comes from Mennah as the Scribe of the fields and estate inspector under Pharaoh Thutmosis IV.

Middle Kingdom

The *Middle Kingdom* (2100–1600) followed the First Intermediate Period with five hundred years of political stability and the continued refinement of the arts and crafts. The country under pharaoh's rule was extended up the Nile to the south. Trade with neighbors, including Mesopotamia and Nubia, gradually became more exten-

sive. The condition of the laboring poor seems to have gradually worsened. Religion became more democratic in its view of who could enter the afterlife, and a small middle class of officials and merchants began to make itself apparent.

New Kingdom

The **New Kingdom** (1550–700) is also called the *Empire,* although the name really belongs only to its first three centuries. The New Kingdom began after the defeat of the Hyksos invaders in the 1500s. It lasted through the years of imperial wars against the Hittites and others in Mesopotamia, which ended with Egyptian withdrawal. Then came long centuries of weakness and decline that ended with Egypt's conquest by foreigners.

The Empire was an ambitious experiment in which the Egyptians attempted to convert others to their lifestyle and government. The experiment did not work well, however; apparently because no one else was able to understand the Egyptian view of life or wanted it to be imposed on them. The Empire did not last because of both military reverses starting around the time of Akhnaton (1300s B.C.E.) and internal discontent. By 1100 the pharaoh again ruled only the Nile valley.

During their last three hundred years of independent existence, the Egyptians were frequently subjected to foreign invasion, both over the Sinai desert and from the

■ An example of early hieroglyphics from the Old Kingdom, Fourth Dynasty, evolved into less distinctive pictographs over the centuries.

■ **Egyptian Hieroglyphics.** The Rosetta Stone was discovered by French scientists accompanying Napoleon's army during its occupation of Egypt in the 1790s. It contains three versions of the same priestly decree for the second century B.C.E.: hieroglyphic Egyptian, demotic (cursive) Egyptian, and Greek. By comparing the three, the brilliant linguist Jean Francois Champollion was able in 1822 to finally break the code of hieroglyphic symbols and commence the modern study of the Egyptian language.

Hieroglyphics, (sacred carving,) were pictographs which could convey either an idea, such as "man," or a phonetic sound, by picturing an object which began with a strong consonantal sound. The word for "owl," for example, began with the consonant "m" sound in spoken Egyptian, so a picture of an owl could be used to indicate that sound. This beginning of an alphabet was not fully developed, however, and the use of hieroglyphics, which began as far back as 3000 B.C.E., gradually faded out after Egypt lost its independence in the sixth century B.C.E. The complete repertory of 604 hieroglyphic symbols is now deciphered, enabling the reading of many thousands of ancient inscriptions.

south by way of the great river. Before the Persians arrived in 525, others such as the Kushites (Ethiopians) and the Nubians (Sudanese) had repeatedly invaded—a sure sign that the power of the god-king over his people was weakening. But even after the Persian conquest, which marked the real end of ancient Egypt's existence as an independent state (all the way until the twentieth century!), the life of ordinary people in fields and orchards saw no marked change. Only the person to whom taxes were paid was different; the lifestyle and beliefs of the inhabitants were by now so deeply rooted that no foreign overlord could alter them.

✤ CULTURAL ACHIEVEMENTS

The wealth of the pharaoh and the willingness and skill of his people allowed the erection of the most stupendous monuments put up by any people or government anywhere: the *pyramids and temples of the Old Kingdom.* Visitors have marveled at these stone wonders ever since.

The Great Pyramid of Khufu (Cheops), located a few miles outside present-day Cairo, is easily the largest and grandest edifice ever built. The pyramids (built between 2600 and 2100 B.C.E.) were designed as tombs for the living pharaoh and were built while he was still alive; they possessed immense religious significance for the Egyptians. Much is still unknown about the pyramids' true purposes, but the perfection of their construction and the art of the burial chambers show Egyptian civilization at its most impressive.

The pyramids were not the only stone monuments erected along the Nile. In the period around 1300, several warrior-pharaohs celebrated the fame of their empire by erecting enormous statues of themselves and their favored gods and even larger temples in which to put them. At the Nile sites of *Karnak* and *Tel el Amarna,* some of these still stand. (Most losses of artistic and architectural wonders in Egypt have been caused not by time or erosion, but by vandalism and organized tomb and treasure robbers over many centuries. All of the pharaohs' tombs discovered to date, except one, have long since been robbed of the burial treasure interred with the mummy of the dead king-god. The exception is the famous King Tutankhamen—King Tut—whose underground burial chamber was discovered in the early 1920s. See the Biography in this chapter.)

Egyptian statuary is distinguished by the peculiar combination of graceful and natural lines in association with great dignity and awesomeness. This awe is reinforced by the art and architecture that surround the great statues, which are designed to impress all onlookers with the permanence and power of the Egyptian monarchy. The Egyptians' mastery of stone is rivaled in Western civilization only by the artistry of the classical Greeks and Romans. And most of this art was apparently created by artists and architects who did not know the principle of the wheel and had only primitive tools and what we would consider very clumsy math and physics!

Other art forms in which Egypt excelled included fresco painting, fine ceramics of all sorts and uses, imaginative and finely worked jewelry in both stones and metals, and miniature sculpture. When upper-class Egyptians died, hundreds of small statues would be buried with

■ This figure of Selket, one of the female deities in the Egyptian pantheon, was probably the result of a commission by a grateful devotee. Selket was the goddess who healed bites and wounds.

their mummified remains. The Egyptians believed that what had been precious to a person in earthly life would also be desired in the next (a belief shared by the people of Mesopotamia), so they interred statues representing the person's earthly family and friends. Music and dance were also well developed, as we know from their lively portrayal in thousands of paintings and statuary groups depicting the life of the people of all ranks from the nobles to the poorest peasants. Egypt's artistic heritage is exceeded by few, if any, other peoples of the Western tradition.

✤ RELIGION AND ETERNAL LIFE

Egypt's religion was almost infinitely polytheistic. At least three thousand separate names of gods have been identified in Egyptian writings, many of them the same deities but with different names over the centuries. Chief among them were the gods of the sun, *Amon* and *Ra,* who were originally separate but later combined into one being. Other important deities included **Isis,** goddess of the Nile and of fertility; **Osiris,** god of the afterlife; their son, *Horus,* made visible in the ruling pharaoh; and *Ptah,* the god of all life on earth.

The Egyptians believed firmly in the afterlife. Originally, it seems to have been viewed as a possibility only for the upper class; but gradually, the afterlife was democratized, and by around 1000 B.C.E, most Egyptians were believers in a scheme of eternal reward or punishment for their *ka,* which had to submit to Last Judgment by Osiris. "Ka" referred to the life-essence which could return to life, given the correct physical preparation, even after the death of the physical body.

Mostly, it seems, they expected reward. Egyptians thought of eternity as a sort of endless procession by the *ka* of the deceased through the heavens and the gods' abodes there. In the company of friends and family, watched over by the protective and benevolent gods, the individual would proceed in a stately circle around the sun forever. There was no need to work and no suffering. Such was heaven; the notion of hell as a place for the evil to pay for their sins came along in Egypt only during the New Kingdom, when things had begun to go sour.

The priests played an important role in Egyptian culture, though they were not as prominent as in several other civilizations. At times, they seem to have been the "power behind the throne," especially when the king had made himself unpopular.

In the reign of the young and inexperienced **Akhnaton** (1367–1350), the priests opposed a unique experiment: the pharaoh's attempt to change the basic polytheistic nature of Egyptian religion. Why the young Akhnaton

■ The Egyptians' love of music and feasting is evident in this fresco from a tomb near Thebes. The emphasis on the eyes of the female figures was one of the many conventions that the anonymous artists were obliged to follow.

(aided by his beautiful wife Nefertiti) chose to attempt to introduce a monotheist cult of the sun god, newly re-named Aton, we can only guess. The pharaoh announced that Aton was his heavenly father and that Aton alone was to be worshiped as the single and universal god of all creation. The priests naturally opposed this revolutionary change, and as soon as Akhnaton was dead (possibly by poison), they denounced his ideas and went back to the old ways. This attempt at monotheism is a great novelty in ancient civilization, and it was not to be heard of again until the emergence of Judaism five or six centuries later.

✦ EGYPT'S PEOPLE AND THEIR DAILY LIVES

The Egyptian population was composed overwhelmingly of peasants, who lived in the villages that crowded along the Nile. Most were free tenant farmers who worked on the estate of a large landholder or government official, who had been granted the land as payment for services to the crown. Each village followed a similar pattern: the huts were set close together within the village, and the fields lay outside. Several adults lived in each hut. Each day the peasants would go out to work in the fields, care for the irrigation works, or tend the animals.

Besides farmers, many small merchants and craftsmen lived in the villages. But Egypt had *no real cities* as in Mesopotamia, where neighborhoods were filled with spe-cialized wholesale and retail markets, and dozens of crafts were practiced in hundreds of workshops. Egypt's capital cities, like Memphis, Tel el Amarna, and Thebes, were really royal palaces and pleasure grounds for the wealthy, not commercial centers. The common people had nothing to do with the capitals except for occasional huge labor projects. *Trade and commerce* were of relatively minor importance in Egyptian history and for a very long period were treated as a monopoly belonging to the government's officials. A small middle class existed by consent of the government officialdom.

As the centuries passed, daily life changed remarkably little. *Slavery* was originally rare, but increased during the period of the Empire when professional soldiers became necessary and prisoners of war became common. As in Mesopotamia, slavery was most often the result of owing debts to a landlord or committing a serious crime. A kind of *serfdom*—lifelong restrictions on one's mobility—also came into existence in later Egypt. Free tenant families were gradually turned into serfs, probably because of debt, and then had to work the land on a system of sharecrop-ping that ensured that they remained in their village.

All in all, however, the common people of Egypt were better off more of the time than the commoners in almost any other ancient society. They were usually free, had enough to eat, lived in one of the world's easiest and most healthful climates, did not have to pay heavy taxes until fairly late in the history of Egypt, and were usually ruled

King Tutankhamen

The pharaoh Tutankhamen (r. 1347–1339 B.C.E.) died at the age of eighteen without having done anything of consequence during his short reign. The world probably would never have noted him had not the British archaeologist Howard Carter stumbled on his grave three thousand years later. The burial site of the young king became one of the most spectacular archaeological finds of the twentieth century. For eight years, Carter salvaged its magnificent treasure, classifying and restoring more than five thousand objects, including a beautiful golden death mask, a gilded throne, statues, vases, and hundreds of artifacts made of wood covered in gold leaf and decorated with gems. A magnificent stone sarcophagus held the luxurious coffin, richly wrought in pure gold. The treasure offered scholars and the public a glimpse of the wealth of the ancient Egyptians and their Nile kingdom.

The son-in-law of Queen Nefertiti and King Akhnaton, due to an arranged marriage, Tutankhamen came to the throne around 1347 B.C.E. at the age of nine, soon after the controversial reign of Akhnaton, the reformer who had attempted to impose a monotheistic religion. Since Akhnaton had no surviving children, Tutankhamen rose to the throne while still very young.

After his accession, the young monarch ruled Egypt through a regency of senior officials. He remained with his court at Tel el Amarna, the city founded by Akhnaton, for only one year; under the influence of the priests, he moved back to the old capital, Thebes and changed his name from the original Tutankhaton to Tutankhamen as a token of his attachment to the traditional sun god, Amen (or Amon).

On the priests' advice, he issued a proclamation restoring the ancient cults and ordering his father-in-law's name and deeds to be removed from the monuments. He repaired and reconstructed the old temples, recast the statues of the various gods, and even prohibited the people from speaking the name of Akhnaton. He also reestablished the feastdays that had been abolished and eliminated the last vestiges of monotheism. All these actions made him a favorite of the priests, who had been outraged at Akhnaton's actions.

Tutankhamen died suddenly in 1339 from unknown causes. In 1968, British doctors determined that he had died not of tuberculosis as had been previously thought, but from a sharp blow to the head, either accidental or murderous. During the next dynasty, his name, along with those of other pharaohs,

by a relatively just and effective government with honest officials. They even had hopes of pleasing the gods and attaining heaven. Compared with the fate of many others, that was not a bad prospect!

✤ EGYPT AND MESOPOTAMIA: CONTRASTS

The two great early centers of civilized life—Egypt and Mesopotamia—were situated fairly close to one another and experienced some cross-cultural stimuli at times. But their differences were notable and permanent. Egypt enjoyed enormous stability; life was highly predictable; tomorrow was today and yesterday under very slightly changed circumstances. Mesopotamia was frequently sub-

ject to violent change; not only were invasions or war commonplace, but the kings—who were men, not gods—were often challenged by rebels and curtailed in their power by rivals.

Egypt was protected from outsiders for a very long time by natural barriers and could pick and choose among the cultural influences that it wanted to adopt. Mesopotamia was a crossroads between barbarism and civilization, and between barbarian and barbarian. New ideas, new techniques, and new beliefs were introduced by invasion, trade, and simple curiosity.

Egypt had been a unified nation as long as anyone could remember. The Egyptians viewed the world as consisting of the Egyptian people and the rest, whom they

was also removed from the official list of Egyptian kings.

The young monarch was buried in the Valley of the Kings. There is clear evidence that his tomb, like others in the region, was robbed soon after it was completed. Apparently, the criminals were either caught or frightened off, for the treasure remained almost intact. The tomb was never molested again. Two hundred years later, the architects of the tomb of Ramses VI, excavating just above that of Tutankhamen, ordered the workers to dispose of their waste limestone down the slope, thus completely covering the earlier tomb. The rock chips hid the tomb entry for three millennia, until November 4, 1922, when Carter uncovered the steps leading down to the entrance gallery and the actual burial chamber beyond it.

No other archaeological discovery has received so much

publicity. During the following decade, hundreds of articles appeared in the international press. Many of them were written for literary or popular consumption and had little or no scientific value. Many played up the "curse of the pharaohs," pointing out that more than twenty persons connected at sometime or other with the unsealing of the tomb had died under somewhat mysterious circumstances in the 1920s and 1930s. The thousands of visitors who flocked to the site constantly interrupted Carter's scientific work.

The publicity, however, greatly stimulated interest in Egypt and its ancient history. Many additional archaeological digs were undertaken in the Middle East and Central America, as well as in Egypt, supported by public interest in the new field. All in all, Tutankhamen's relics gave the young king far more fame than anything he did in his lifetime.

■ **The golden deathmask of King Tut.**

regarded as inferiors who had little to teach Egypt. This feeling persisted long after the time when it was clearly no longer true and contributed much to the Egyptians' eventual vulnerability to outside forces. As their ability to resist foreign invaders declined, the Egyptian governing class took refuge in a false sense of superiority in culture.

Mesopotamia was a melting pot: repeatedly, large groups of outsiders would arrive with sufficient power to force their ideas and beliefs upon the conquered people, at least for as long as they needed to strike roots and change some elements of the previous civilization. Stagnation could not occur; challenge was on the daily menu. In Egypt, the sense of superiority seems to have eventually become a sort of "defense mechanism" that prevented

the rulers from seeing the truth and choked off badly needed reform. They viewed change as subversive and successfully resisted it for a long time—so long as to make successful adjustment to necessary change almost impossible.

Of these two early civilizations, Mesopotamia proved to be the major cradle of later Western traditions and beliefs. For all its long life and success, Egypt was something of an island in space and time, with relatively little permanent influence on its neighbors or on future generations. In the next chapter, we will look at some of those neighbors in the Near East, and particularly at two peoples who eventually conquered Egypt, the Assyrians and the Persians.

Summary

The Nile valley produced a civilized society as early as any in the world, thanks to a unique combination of favorable climatic and topographical factors. Long before the emergence of central government under a god-king called pharaoh, the farmers along the river had devised an intricate system of irrigated fields that gave Egypt the enviable asset of a surplus of food. The unification of the villages was accomplished about 3100 B.C.E., giving rise to the high civilization of the Old Kingdom and its awesome monuments celebrating the linkage of Egypt and the protective gods. Two thousand years of prosperity and of isolation from contacts with others except on its own terms allowed the pharaoh's government to assume a superiority that, although originally justified, gradually became a clinging to tradition for its own sake. When Egypt faced the challenge of repeated foreign invasions after about 1000 B.C.E., the divine kings lost their stature, and the uniquely static civilization of the Nile fell under the sway of once disdained aliens from the east and south.

Test Your Knowledge

1. Which of these adjectives would you *not* associate with Egypt?
   a. Stable
   b. Predictable
   c. Poor
   d. Isolated
2. The geographical status of Egypt destined the country to be
   a. vulnerable to repeated invasions.
   b. a crossroads of travelers through the ages.
   c. almost self-contained.
   d. divided into many natural regions.
3. The key element of Egypt's government was the
   a. pharaoh's efficient police.
   b. code of royal law.
   c. popular respect for the king.
   d. powerful military establishment.
4. Slavery was widespread in Egyptian society only
   a. before the founding of the New Kingdom.
   b. before the founding of the Old Kingdom.
   c. after the founding of the New Kingdom.
   d. after the founding of the Old Kingdom.
5. The pharaoh Akhnaton promoted
   a. a return to the traditional beliefs.
   b. the worship of the new god Aton.
   c. the conquest of the Middle East by Egypt.
   d. major agricultural reforms.
6. Which of the following was *least* likely to have occurred in Egypt from 3000 to about 1000 B.C.E.?
   a. A social rebellion against the government
   b. A drastic change in the prestige of various Egyptian deities
   c. An invasion from outside Egypt
   d. An attempt to extend rule over non-Egyptians
7. A chief difference between Egypt and Mesopotamia was their relative
   a. dependence on irrigation farming.
   b. importance of city life and commerce.
   c. degree of democratic government.
   d. vunerability to attack from outsiders

Identification Terms

Akhnaton	*Hyksos*	*ka*	Osiris
Horus	Isis	New Kingdom	pharaoh

Bibliography

Edwards, I. E. S. *The Pyramids of Egypt,* 1976. Covers the whole topic of pyramid building.

Frankfort, H. *Ancient Egyptian Religion,* 1948. By the grand master of Egyptology in this century.

Gardner, A. *Egypt of the Pharaohs,* 1966. Very readable; covers the political and military events primarily.

Hawkes, J. *King of the Two Lands,* 1966. A historical novel of Egypt by a distinguished archaeologist.

———. *Life in Mesopotamia, the Indus Valley, and Egypt,* 1973. The work of a much admired writer. Good on comparisons among the three places and their societies.

James, T. G. H. *Pharaoh's People: Scenes from Life in Imperial Egypt,* 1984. Interesting and worthwhile.

Michalowski, K. *Art of Ancient Egypt,* 1969.

Montet, P. *Everyday Life in Egypt in the Days of Ramses II,* 1958. An interesting contrast to the James book which looks at the same epoch.

Redford, D. *Akhnaten, the Heretic King,* 1984.

White, J. *Everyday Life in Ancient Egypt,* 1963. A worthwhile study.

ASSYRIA, PHOENICIA, AND PERSIA

The Near East between the Nile valley and the Sumerians soon became a region of cultural overlap and interchange. First one people and then another would take command of a portion of the region for a century or more, only to fall under the sway of the next onslaught of newcomers. In southern Turkey, Syria, and Lebanon arose kingdoms whose very names are sometimes forgotten, but whose contributions to the ascent of civilization in this region are not. In this chapter, we look at two of these less populous civilizations of the Near East who have some claim to fame.

With the coming of the Persian armies in the sixth century B.C.E., the ebb and flow of power in Mesopotamia and Egypt took a decisive turn. This chapter concludes by examining the largest and most potent empire that the region had yet seen—that of the Iranian-Persians.

✤ THE ASSYRIAN EMPIRE

The Assyrians have already been introduced in Chapter 2 among the several successors to the Sumerians in Mesopotamia. They were a warrior tribal group who entered history around 900 B.C.E. as challengers to other Semites who were attempting to establish control over the Tigris valley from the south. The Assyrians' chief town, **Nineveh,** lay in the upper valley of the Tigris, and their chief god was the very fierce **Assur,** from whom the people derived their name. By 800 B.C.E., through their own ferocity and cunning in war, the Assyrian kings had conquered much of the Tigris-Euphrates region and were fighting the Babylonians for the southern portion (see Map 4.1). The Assyrians displayed great talent in two closely related areas, *military prowess* and *efficient administration.* Anyone who resisted them and lost suffered a terrible fate: wholesale slavery, execution, pillage, and rape.

By this epoch the horse and the chariot had come into wide use in warfare. (It is believed that the chariot was introduced to warfare by the Hyksos invaders of Egypt in the 1500s). For a couple of centuries, leather-clad warriors armed with short swords had fought from chariots drawn by two or three horses. The chariots would split the loose ranks of the enemy footsoldiers, and the momentum of the horses combined with the raised platform gave the swordsmen an almost irresistible advantage over opposing infantry.

The early Assyrian kings took away this advantage, however, by fielding tightknit infantry formations with

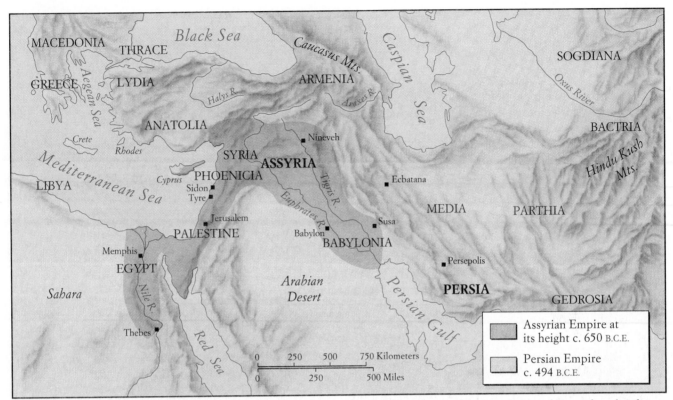

⊙ **MAP 4.1 The Assyrian and Persian Empires.** Although the Assyrians subdued most of the Near East and Egypt for a brief time, the later Persian empire was much more extensive, reaching from Egypt to the borders of the Indus valley. Most of this huge area was held through a network of tributary kingdoms whose rulers regularly acknowledged Persian overlordship.

long spears and swords, protected on the flanks by bands of horsemen who engaged the enemy charioteers while they were still far off. The Assyrian infantry were heavily armored and so disciplined they would stand up to a chariot charge without breaking. The Assyrians were also experts in siege warfare, and no enemy fort could hold for long against their artillery of stone-throwing catapults and rams. Once conquered, the enemy was closely supervised and any effort to spring free of the Assyrian yoke was immediately suppressed. The chronicles left by the Assyrians delight in telling of the huge piles of dead left by the triumphant armies of kings such as Assurbanipal and Esarhaddon who reigned in the seventh century B.C.E. (see the Document in this chapter).

■ The extraordinary naturalism of the animal anatomy and the sense of motion depicted here contrast with the traditional rigidity of the Assyrian potrayal of human figures. Here the king conducts a royal hunt for lions that have long since disappeared from the Near East.

King Tiglath-Pileser's Boast

The Assyrians were undoubtedly the most hated of all the ancient conquerors in the Near East. Emerging from barbarism in what is now northern Iraq during the twelfth century B.C.E., they expanded in waves southward and westward. At its height in the seventh century, the empire stretched from Egypt to Iran.

An Assyrian king exercised absolute power and ruled as the great god Assur's deputy on earth. The kings gloried in the most effective and well-equipped army of early times and used that force to crush any rebellion of their numerous civilized subjects. The following excerpt from an Assyrian inscription relates the proud exploits of king Tiglath-Pileser in the eleventh century B.C.E.:

> Assur and the great gods who have enlarged my kingdom, who have given me strength and power as my portion, commanded me to enlarge the territory of their country, putting into my hand their powerful weapons, the cyclone of battle. I subjugated land and mountains, cities and their rulers, enemies of Assur, and conquered their territories. With sixty kings I fought, spreading terror and achieved a glorious victory over them. A rival in combat, or an adversary in battle, I did not have.
>
> . . In the beginning of my reign five kings . . . with an army of 20,000 . . . whose power no king had yet broken and overcome . . . trusting to their strength rushed down and conquered the land of Qummuh.* With the help of Assur my lord, I gathered my war chariots and assembled my warriors; I made no delay, but traversed Kashiari,† that almost impassable region. I waged battle in Qummuh with those five kings and their twenty thousand soldiers, and accomplished their defeat. Like the Thunder, I crushed corpses of their warriors in the battle. I made their blood flow over into all the ravines and over the high places. I cut off their heads and piled them at the walls of their cities like heaps of grain. I carried off their booty, their goods, and their property beyond all reckoning. Six thousand, the remainder of their troops who had fled before my weapons and thrown themselves at my feet, I took away as prisoners and added to the peoples of my country (i.e., slaves).
>
> At this time I marched also against the people of the land of Qummuh, who had become unsubmissive, withholding the tax and the tribute due to Assur, my lord. I conquered Qummuh to its whole extent, and carried off their booty, their goods, and their property. I burned their cities with fire, destroyed, and devastated them.

This delight in enumerating the destruction caused by their armies is a distinctive mark of the Assyrian kings. Many ancient warriors were not shy about recounting how many enemies they had overcome and how many slaves they had captured. But no one else quite matched the chest beating of the Assyrians.

*Qummuh or Commagene is a region along the upper Euphrates River.
†Kashiari is a hilly region in Mesopotamia.
SOURCE: J. B. Pritchard, ed., *Ancient Near Eastern Texts,* 3d ed. © Copyright Princeton University Press, 1969. Reprinted by permission.

But less than a century later, Nineveh was in total ruins ("not a stone upon a stone" asserts the Old Testament), and the Assyrians were swept from the pages of history as though they had never existed. According to the Old Testament, the Assyrians were perhaps the most hated people in ancient history. Only their expertly calculated plans for "divide and conquer" and mass deportations of subject peoples enabled them to remain in power as long as they did. At one point their empire reached from the upper Tigris to central Egypt. It was governed from Nineveh by a network of military commanders who had no mercy for rebels and held large numbers of hostages for the good behavior of the rest of their people. Finally, the Assyrians' many enemies and rebellious subjects, led by the Chaldees of New Babylon, united against their oppressor and took full revenge for the atrocities that the Assyrians had visited upon them. When they captured Nineveh in 612 B.C.E., the victors even salted the fertile irrigated lands that ringed the city to prevent the site from ever being inhabited again. It was indeed forgotten until the middle of the nineteenth century when Nineveh's ruins were unearthed by some of the earliest archaeological expeditions to the Middle East.

Remarkably, the Assyrians combined their cruelty and delight in slaughter with a sophisticated and genuine appreciation for all forms of pictorial and architectural art. Their numerous statues, shrines, reliefs, and frescoes are famous for their imagination, realism, and skill in execution. Much of what we know about the Assyrians comes from this artistic heritage, for their former subjects tried to erase all mention of the Assyrian epoch from the historical record after their overthrow.

❧ THE PHOENICIANS

Another small people who made big waves were the Semitic Phoenicians, who originally inhabited a strip along the coast of what is now Lebanon. From their port towns of Tyre and Sidon, the Phoenicians became the greatest maritime traders and colonizers of the ancient Near East. Their trade in luxury wares such as copper and dyes took them through the Mediterranean and into the Atlantic as far as the coast of Britain (Cornwall). Here they obtained the precious tin that could be mixed with copper to form bronze, the main metallic resource before 1000 B.C.E. The Phoenicians also apparently spread the art of iron making to the Greeks and westward into Africa. They also established a whole series of colonies in the western Mediterranean, in Spain, and in North Africa.

■ In the middle of the nineteenth century, archaeologists from several European countries (later from the United States) began the time-consuming excavation of several important Mesopotamian cities. One of these cities was Nineveh, the capital of the Assyrians, which had been destroyed by their enemies in 612 B.C.E.

Some of these became major states, and one of them, the rich city-state of Carthage, became the great rival to Rome until its final defeat around 200 B.C.E.

But the Phoenicians' most notable contribution came in a quite different field. This small people was the first to use a *phonetic alphabet,* a system of twenty-two written marks ("letters"), each of which corresponded to a specific sound of the oral language and could be used in writing whenever that sound was desired. The Phoenicians' alphabet, which emerged around 1000, was a definite advance over the nonalphabetic systems devised by the Sumerians and also over the hieroglyphs of the Egyptians. Hieroglyphs were a highly pictorial form of writing that eventually included abstract and phonetic meanings, but never developed into a true alphabet as we saw in Chapter 3.

By the time the Assyrians emerged, the Phoenicians were in decline as an independent state, and they were absorbed into the Assyrian and succeeding empires but retained their importance as great traders and seafarers until the rise of Greece in the 600s B.C.E. The Greeks improved the Phoenician alphabet, added signs for the vowels, which the Phoenicians did not have, and thereby created essentially the same alphabet (though in a different letter form) that we use today.

■ This marvelous carved ivory plaque of a lion attacking a young man dates from eighth- or ninth-century B.C.E. Phoenicia.

✤ The Persians

In olden times, present-day **Iran** was called Persia. Between 500 B.C.E. and 500 C.E., its inhabitants—the Persians—were the most powerful and most significant of the many different groups in western Asia.

Like the Hittites before them, the Persians were an *Indo-European*–speaking people who migrated south from the central Asian steppes into the Middle East. Actually, several related groups, collectively termed Iranians, moved south. The two most important were the **Medes and the Persians.** They entered Iran, the huge area between the Caspian Sea and the Indian Ocean, around 1000 B.C.E. When they arrived, they were nomads and herders, who knew nothing of agriculture or the civilized crafts and techniques.

The Iranians did have large numbers of horses, however—they had pioneered in domesticating the horse—and their skill at using horses in battle gave them a decisive advantage over their neighbors. The Persians were among the first to use wheeled horse-drawn chariots in war; both their soldiers and their horses wore extensive body armor, made first of leather and later of iron. Eventually, through both war and trading contacts with their Mesopotamian neighbors to the west, they learned the basics of agriculture and civilized life.

The Persians had settled in a country with a peculiar geography. Iran is mostly a high, arid plateau, surrounded on the north, west, and east by high mountains and on the south by the Indian Ocean (see Map 4.1). Between the plateau and the sea is one of the most terrible deserts on the globe, forcing nomads from central Asia to go either east into India or west into Mesopotamia. On the India or east side of the mountains, the monsoons bring enough rain to create a series of fertile oases at the foot of the mountains, and here agriculture has flourished. For a long time, the country has been a natural divide for travel from east to west, from the eastern Mediterranean to China and India, and vice versa. Later, it became the great exchange point between the Arabic-Muslim world and the Hindu.

■ The mastery of stonework was not limited to Egyptian masons, but some may have been brought to the palace site at Persepolis to assist in its construction in the fifth century B.C.E.

When the majority of long-distance trade moved either in small coastal boats or in land caravans, Iran and the Iranians were able to play a considerable role in world affairs.

The Persian Empire

In the mid-sixth century B.C.E., the Persians united under a brilliant warrior king, *Cyrus the Great,* and quickly overcame their Iranian cousins and neighbors, the Medes. In a remarkable series of campaigns, Cyrus created what was by far the largest empire yet seen in history. In thirty years (559–530), he extended his domains from the borders of India to the Mediterranean coast. By 525 his son and immediate successor, Cambyses, had extended the empire to include part of Arabia and the Nile valley. Notably, the main Persian capitals were at Persepolis and Ecbatana in Iran, not in Mesopotamia; the gradual decline of Mesopotamia's importance can be dated to this time.

The Persians' achievement was to be very long-lasting. Cyrus had a concept of imperial rule that was new and different. He realized that many of his subjects, like the Babylonians, were more advanced in many ways than his own Persians and that he should learn from them rather than trying to dominate and terrorize them. Accordingly, his empire became a sort of umbrella, sheltering many different peoples and beliefs under the *"King of Kings"* at Persepolis.

The Persian subjects mostly retained their own customs, laws, and religious beliefs; their appointed supervisors only interfered when the central government's policies were threatened or disobeyed. The Persians were the first to build good roads over long distances and excellent communications were now possible, enabling the King of Kings to work his will over the huge area under his control. The Royal Road reached from Susa to Sardis near the Mediterranean coast in Turkey—about as far as from New York to Minneapolis. Mounted on swift horses, the royal post riders could cover this distance in a week.

In the furthest provinces (**satrapies**), the local kings and chieftains were kept in power after conquest by Persia, so long as they swore obedience to the central authority, paid their (relatively light) taxes, and gave aid and comfort to the Persians when called upon. Religion was totally free, and all sorts of beliefs flourished under Persian rule, from the Hebrews to the fire worshipers of the Indian borderlands.

Darius I (522–486) was the third great Persian ruler (see the Biography in this chapter). During his reign, standard weights and measures were introduced, along with a stable coinage in gold and silver and a calendar based on the Egyptian model that was commonly used throughout the Near East until the coming of the Muslims. The Persian law code was also an advanced and refined distillation of earlier codes from Mesopotamia and Egypt.

Zarathustra (Zoroaster)

Like all other early peoples, the Iranians were polytheistic and had many deities personifying water, fire, the moon, the stars, and the like. The fire god was particularly important, and his worship was led by priests called *magi.* The Iranians' chief god, however, had long been **Ahura-mazda,** god of the sun's light and creator of all life on earth.

Early in the seventh century, a prophet arose among the Persian Iranians, whose name is given as **Zarathustra** or **Zoroaster**—we know virtually nothing of his life. Zarathustra, whose teachings were not written down until much later in a book of scripture called the Avesta, apparently believed he had been called by the gods to cleanse and elevate the previous religion. The faith he preached won many converts during his lifetime and is now known as *Zoroastrianism.* It is based on the idea that *two principles are in eternal conflict* on earth: good and evil, truth and lies. Good was represented by the sexless **Ahura-mazda** and evil by its twin, **Ahriman** (a close equivalent to the Christian Lucifer).

Humans, as the possessors of free will, could and indeed must choose between the two gods, serving one and defying the other. In an afterlife, individuals would be made responsible for their choice. They would stand before a divine tribunal and have to answer for their lives on earth. Evil could not be undone, but could be balanced by good deeds. If the balance was positive, they would enjoy Heaven; if negative, Hell awaited them after the final victory of Ahura-mazda over Ahriman. The role of the priests was very important, for they determined proper conduct and proper worship. Fire continued to play a significant role in ritual, and a sacred fire was at the heart of the worship of Ahura-mazda. For a time, the Zoroastrian religion became the state cult of imperial Persia. Even after Alexander the Great had defeated the Persians, and their first empire had crumbled (see Chapter 11), the prophecies of Zarathustra continued to attract many followers among the peoples of the Near East.

The numerous similarities between Zarathustra's doctrines and Judaism and Christianity are not coincidental. The Last Judgment that all souls must undergo, the

King Darius I of Persia

Darius I, the third in the series of great Persian rulers that began with Cyrus, lived from 550 to 486 B.C.E. The Greek historian Herodotus tells us that Darius came to power in 522 B.C.E. in a very unusual way. The previous ruler, Cambyses, had left no surviving sons. Seven contenders to the throne after Cambyses' death agreed they would mount their horses at sunrise; the rider whose horse neighed first was to be the new king. According to the legend, Darius won the contest by riding his stallion close to a tethered mare! In reality, he probably earned the crown by quelling a rebellion.

For several years, the eastern provinces of the huge empire defied him, and he had to impose his rule by force. When he finally secured peace, he reorganized his domain by dividing it into twenty provinces (*satrapies*) and appointing resident governors and vice-governors in each. While these officials had considerable freedom, special officers visited regularly to protect the interests of the central government in Sardis.

Darius wanted to rule justly and well. He closely followed the conservative views of his predecessors Cyrus and Cambyses. Ceremonial life became very important. The King of Kings could be approached only on special occasions. Men of differing ranks dealt with one another in accord with strict protocol. Zoroastrianism became the equivalent of an official religion, but local faiths were allowed to continue undisturbed.

The Persians did not have a standing army, but each satrapy was expected to supply a quota of troops when required. This meant that the Persian army, though enormous, was neither well-coordinated nor reliable on the battlefield, because the soldiers sent by the various regions spoke different languages and had different traditions of combat.

The king built magnificent royal cities, among them Persepolis in the center of his realm. He built roads to encourage commerce and enable his orders to be quickly transmitted to every satrapy. To foster seaborne trade, he reconstructed a former canal that the Egyptians had dug from the Nile to the Red Sea.

But Darius could not change Persian prejudices. They despised trade and regarded commercial dealings as incompatible with their religion. Shops were hidden away in obscure places. There were few centers of industry among the Persians, who depended on other peoples and on their many thousands of slaves to carry on any necessary industry. War and conquest brought them luxuries in tribute from the new subjects. But to obtain them, Persia had to continue to expand.

After consolidating his political power, Darius turned to his calling as war leader. He captured rich Babylon after a siege lasting twenty months; he then conquered Thrace and defeated the Scythians far to the east, on the Caspian shores. The empire now reached from the Aegean Sea to the Indus River. But then came a stunning reversal. The rich Greek trading city-states on the shores of present-day Turkey were under Persian rule; when they attempted to rebel; Athens came to their aid. Outraged, Darius launched an expedition against the Greek mainland, but suffered a significant defeat by the Greek *phalanx* at Marathon (see Chapter 9). Immediately, Darius began to plan a second expedition to punish the upstarts and conquer all of Greece, but he died before he could accomplish his ends. His son and successor Xerxes would make the attempt a few years later—to his and Persia's sorrow.

eternal bliss of Heaven or the eternal torments of Hell, and the responsibility humans bear for using free will entered first Jewish and then Christian belief. Through Zarathustrian preaching and its converts in the eastern Mediterranean, the image of an all-powerful God who allowed humans the freedom to choose good or evil entered the mainsprings of Western religious culture.

Zarathustra's teaching that Ahriman was in some way closely bound up with the flesh, while Ahura-mazda was a noncorporeal deity of the spirit would haunt Christianity for ages and reappeared again and again in various Christian sects. The most famous of these sects was medieval Manichaeism, which originated in the Middle East and spread throughout Christian Europe. It taught that the flesh and everything it touches is essentially evil, the province of Satan. Many people think that the puritanical element in Christianity is largely the product of this offshoot of the Zoroastrian creed.

In Persia itself, the religion of Zoroaster was almost extinguished after the Muslim conquest in the 600s C.E. The Parsees of the region around Bombay, India, are the major center of the cult in modern days. They take spiritual guidance from the holy Avesta. This collection of poetry, prayers, and moral stories is one of the first attempts to unite *religion,* the worship of the immortal gods, with *ethics,* a code of good conduct for mortals.

Summary

The Assyrian empire lasted only a brief time, but it was important in that it brought several peoples for the first time under the scepter of a single ruler. The Assyrians' ruthlessness and brutality brought them into disrepute, and when their empire was toppled in the seventh century B.C.E. by a coalition of enemies, most traces of it were wiped away in its Mesopotamian homeland. One of the Assyrians' conquests in the eastern Mediterranean was Phoenicia, whose people are remembered for their maritime explorations and colonization and for taking the first major steps toward a phonetic alphabet.

For over two hundred years, from the conquests of Cyrus the Great to the coming of Alexander the Great, the Persian empire brought relative peace, stability, and progress to much of the Near East. Learning from their more advanced subjects, the imperial governors allowed substantial freedom of worship, language, and custom, while upholding superior justice and efficient administration. Trade and crafts flourished throughout the immense empire. From the preachings of Zarathustra emerged a new, highly sophisticated ethics that was elevated to a state religion.

Cyrus's successors generally continued his work of intelligent and tolerant civilizing, but eventually made the mistake of biting off more than they could chew. Two of them, Darius and Xerxes, attempted to invade the European mainland for no good reason except to extend their power and salve their wounded egos. The attempt would cost them dearly, as we will see when we discuss Greek civilization in Chapter 9.

Test Your Knowledge

1. The Phoenicians concentrated their talents on
   a. development of weaponry.
   b. maritime trade and exploration.
   c. devising new styles of literature.
   d. agricultural advances.
2. The outstanding contribution of the Phoenicians to world history was
   a. the marine compass.
   b. the phonetic alphabet.
   c. the invention of coinage.
   d. the howitzer.
3. The key to Assyrian success in empire building was
   a. cultural superiority.
   b. respectful treatment of the conquered peoples.
   c. the bravery of the individual soldier.
   d. effective military organization.
4. The overthrow of the Assyrians was accomplished by
   a. an internal palace plot.
   b. a coalition of their enemies led by the Babylonians.
   c. the Egyptian and Hittite armies.
   d. a general rebellion of the slaves.

5. The pair of adjectives most closely describing the Persians is
   a. Indo-European and nomadic.
   b. Indo-European and Iranian.
   c. Semite and barbarian.
   d. Neolithic and pastoral.
6. The creator of the Persian empire was
   a. Zoroaster.
   b. Xerxes.
   c. Cyrus.
   d. Ahura-mazda.

7. Which of the following is the correct chronological sequence of empires?
   a. Assyrian, Persian, Hittite, Sumerian
   b. Persian, Hittite, Sumerian, Assyrian
   c. Sumerian, Hittite, Assyrian, Persian
   d. Hittite, Assyrian, Sumerian, Persian

Identification Terms

Ahriman	Assur	Medes/Persians	satrapies
Ahura-mazda	Iran	Nineveh	Zoroaster/Zarathustra

Bibliography

Boyce, M. *Zoroastrians: Their Religious Belief and Practices,* 1979.

Countenau, G. *Everyday Life in Assyria and Babylon,* 1954. An identical title was issued by H. W. F. Saggs in a revised edition in 1987.

Frye, G. *The Heritage of Persia,* 1963. More concise and easier to read than Olmstead's large work, as is the next entry.

Ghirshman, R. *Persia: From the Origins to Alexander the Great,* 1964.

Olmstead, A. T. *History of the Persian Empire,* 1948. The place to find all the answers, including those to questions you never thought to ask.

Saggs, H. W. *The Might That Was Assyria,* 1984. Probably the best single work in English on this topic; perhaps more detail than students may wish.

Sandars, N. *The Sea Peoples,* 1978. A standard work on the Phoenicians.

Starr, C. *Early Man,* 1968. Also treats the Assyrian empire.

THE HEBREWS

1900s B.C.E.	Hebrews leave Mesopotamia
c. 1250 B.C.E.	Exodus from Egypt
c. 1000 B.C.E.	Hebrew kingdom established
late 900s B.C.E.	Kingdom divided into Samaria (Israel) and Judea (Judah)
722 B.C.E.	Assyrians conquer Samaria
586–539 B.C.E.	Babylonian Captivity
c. 530s–330s B.C.E.	Judea under Persian rule

Of all the people we have discussed thus far, the Hebrews are the smallest in number, but the most influential in terms of their impact on later Western civilization. What we know of them is derived in large part from the "poetic history" of the Old Testament. In recent years, the Old Testament's stories have been partially borne out by modern archaeological evidence, and it is clear that many events and stories previously regarded as mythological have a strong basis in fact. These range from the siege of Jericho by Joshua to the prophecies of Hosea about the punishments the Hebrews would suffer if they did not turn to God. The Exodus led by Moses, the kingdom under Saul and his successors, the battle of David against the Philistines—these and other biblical episodes are the history of a unique people, the God-fearing Twelve Tribes.

✦ HEBREW ORIGINS

The Hebraic tradition of a certain Abraham leading his people out of the wilderness and into the land of Canaan refers to what is generally now accepted as historical fact: certain nomadic, primitive Semitic tribes departed from someplace in northern Mesopotamia in the twentieth century B.C.E. and wandered for some time through what is now Saudi Arabia. By the 1500s B.C.E., they were established in Canaan, the southern part of Palestine (see Map 5.1). Here they came under imperial Egyptian rule, and a good portion of the Twelve Tribes went off—perhaps voluntarily, perhaps as coerced slaves—to live in the Nile delta.

We know that in the thirteenth century B.C.E. many semicivilized peoples were moving about the Mediterranean region. The so-called Sea Peoples raided and sometimes settled in areas reaching from the Nile to Lebanon; the Etruscans entered the Italian peninsula and established a kingdom; and the Indo-European invaders known as Dorians invaded the Greek mainland. The Hebrews' **Exodus** from Egypt under their legendary leader Moses occurred during the same century. The exact reasons for the Exodus are not clear; it is entirely possible that the Old Testament story of brutal treatment by the pharaoh is true. In any case, under Moses, the Hebrews resolved to return to the "land of milk and honey," the Promised Land of Canaan, whose memory had been kept alive by their leaders in Egypt.

Escaping pharaoh's wrathful pursuit (the story of the parting of the Red Sea), the Hebrews wandered for many

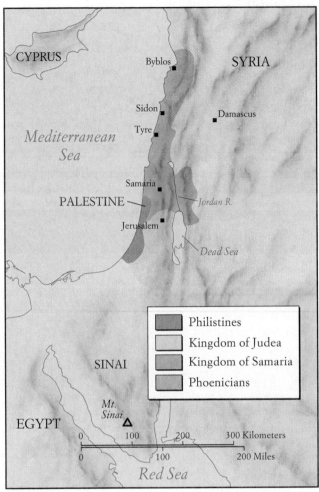

Jerusalem, especially the Temple, the Hebrews' great civic and religious monument. During his reign, the Hebrews became a fairly important factor in Near Eastern affairs, serving as intermediaries between Egypt and the Mesopotamians. But many of his subjects hated Solomon because of his heavy taxes and luxurious living (see the Biography in this chapter); when he died, there was a revolt against his successor, and the Hebrew kingdom split in two: *Judea* and *Samaria*, or, as they are sometimes called, Judah and Israel.

Judea, which was centered on Jerusalem, was the home of the two tribes that remained true to Solomon's line; the other ten gravitated toward Samaria to the north. Although ethnically very close, the two kingdoms were hostile to one another. As time passed, Samaritans and Judeans (or Jews as they eventually came to be called) came to look on one another as different peoples. Their differences arose primarily because of differing religious beliefs, but also because Judea came under the shadow of a briefly revived Egyptian empire, while Samaria fell to the successive conquerors of Mesopotamia, especially the Assyrians. (The first definite date in Hebrew history is the battle of Karkara in 852 B.C.E., when the Samaritan Ahab came to the assistance of his Syrian ally against

● **MAP 5.1 Ancient Palestine and the Jewish Kingdoms.** The kingdoms of Judea and Samaria (Judah and Israel) divided the region once occupied by the Philistines and Canaanites prior to the Jews' return to the Promised Land.

■ The poetry of the Old Testament is strikingly exhibited in the story of the battle between the young hero David and the Philistine Goliath. The battle of the two individuals stands for the generations of struggle between the Jews and the Philistines for control of southern Palestine.

years until they encountered the **Philistines,** who were already settled in Palestine. At first the Philistines were militarily superior, but after many trials of strength, the Hebrews succeeded in pushing them back. By around 1000, the Hebrews had set up their own small kingdom, with Saul as the first king. Saul carried the war to the Philistines, and his work was carried on by his lieutenant and successor, David. David (the victor over Goliath of the Philistines) was a great warrior hero, and he was successful in conquering Jerusalem, which then became the Hebrews' capital.

His son, **Solomon** (r. 970–935 B.C.E.), was the greatest king of the Hebrews. Solomon expanded and beautified

King Solomon

According to the Old Testament, three thousand years ago King Solomon (died c. 935 B.C.E.) ruled the Hebrew tribes with wisdom and justice. The stories of his reign are rich with anecdotes and moral homilies. They also contain many religious and literary traditions that conflict sharply with the historical truth. Solomon's wisdom and justice were in fact conspicuous by their absence.

The son of King David and his fourth wife Bathsheba, Solomon succeeded his father, despite the existence of an older surviving son. His mother, with the help of the prophet Nathan, persuaded the old king to recognize Solomon as his heir shortly before his death. Several years later, Solomon secured the throne by eliminating his rival.

Under the guidance of counselors, the young monarch established a form of absolute monarchy. Ignoring Hebrew tradition, he subordinated everything to the splendor of his court, adopting a style of life hitherto unknown to the Hebrew rulers but attractive to many people. The Canaanites, defeated by David but long allowed to go their own way, were now reduced to slaves and forced to work for Solomon's government.

Under Solomon's hand, the city of Jerusalem grew in commercial importance in the Near East. Its residents, formerly impervious to foreign influences, became wealthy and attracted to other lifestyles as a result of expanding contacts with outsiders. Solomon was able to extend his dominions into Mesopotamia and northern Egypt by marrying foreign brides, including the daughter of the pharaoh.

The king also built magnificent palaces and changed the dress of his courtiers. In place of the simple quarters that had sufficed for David, Solomon constructed a large royal home whose size and fittings rivaled those of the Persians. The famous Temple of Jerusalem, constructed of stone and cedarwood and decorated inside and out with gold, be came a wonder of the ancient world. Visitors from many countries came to marvel and to ask Solomon for solutions to their problems, for the king was reputed to have great wisdom. The little nation of Israelites, so long isolated and ignored, became commercially versatile and sophisticated.

Having neither aptitude nor desire for war, Solomon built massive forts at strategic points to protect

Assyrian invaders.) Israel-Samaria was wiped out as an independent state by the Assyrians in 722, but Judea survived Assyrian and Babylonian conquests and internal upheavals until it was absorbed into the Roman Empire in the first century B.C.E.

✤ JEWISH RELIGIOUS BELIEF AND ITS EVOLUTION

From the time of the kingdom of Saul, a great god known as *Yahweh* (Jehovah) was established as the Hebrews' chief deity, but by no means the only one. In Samaria, Yahweh was slowly relegated to an inferior position, as other gods such as the famous "Golden Calf" and Baal of the Phoenicians took equal billing. But in Judea, Yahweh's cult gradually triumphed over all rivals, and this god became the *only* deity of the Jews of Jerusalem.

This condition of having a single god was a distinct oddity among ancient peoples. **Monotheism** was so rare that we know of only one pre-Jewish experiment with it—that of Akhnaton in Egypt. Some of the Hebrews were living in Egypt during Akhnaton's reign, and it is possible that the pharaoh's doctrines penetrated into Jewish consciousness. Zarathustra's doctrine of dualism between two almost equal deities who wrestled over the souls of men undoubtedly had much to do with the later forms of Hebrew belief, but just how they are related is a subject for argument, in part because we do not know when Zarathustra lived and preached.

The Judean Jews, under the influence of a whole series of great prophets including Amos, Hosea, Ezekiel, and

his domains. Walled cities arose on the sites of primitive towns; Jerusalem became impregnable. He divided his kingdom into twelve districts and made each responsible for the court's expenses for one month each year. He collected tolls from the expanding overland trade and assessed heavy taxes on his subjects to pay for his projects and his personal luxuries.

Solomon did a considerable amount of religious writing, and several of the lyrical passages of the Old Testament (notably, the Song of Solomon) are attributed to him. But in spite of this devotion to his faith, his extravagances were much resented, and they exacerbated the split that was already developing between Judea and Samaria-Israel. During Solomon's reign Judea received commercial advantages and paid few taxes. The northern ten tribes became indignant, and were threatening to sever their relations with Jerusalem and Judea even before Solomon's death. When the king died in 935, the Hebrew tribes split and formed the two separate, rival kingdoms of Judea and Israel, lessening their ability to rule their satellite peoples and exposing themselves to foreign threats. The vassal kingdoms that David had painfully conquered were lost, and the trading empire that Solomon had labored to create for forty years was destroyed forever. "Vanity of vanities, all is vanity. . . ."

■ **The Wailing Wall.** The last remnant of Solomon's Temple.

Isaiah, came to believe themselves bound to Yahweh by a sacred contract, the **Covenant,** given to Moses at the time of the Exodus. The contract was understood to mean that if the Jews remained constant in their worship of Yahweh and kept the faith he instilled in them, they would eventually triumph over all their enemies and be a respected and lordly people on earth. The faith that Yahweh desired was supported by a set of rigid rules: the Ten Commandments given to Moses by Yahweh on Mount Sinai, from which eventually came a whole law code (the *Torah*) that governed every aspect of Hebrew daily life.

The Jewish faith was one of the earliest attempts to formalize an ethical system and to link it with the worship of supernatural deities. **Ethics** is the study of good and evil and determining what is right and wrong in human life and conduct. Yahweh's followers gradually came to regard him as an enforcer of correct ethical actions; those who did evil on earth would be made to suffer, if not in this world, then in the one to come. In itself, this belief was not unusual, for other religions had made at least some moves toward punishment of evildoers. The laws of Yahweh, however, also assured that the good would be rewarded—again, if not in this life, then in the eternal one to come.

How did people know whether they were doing good or evil? One way was by following the laws of Yahweh; increasingly, though, they could also rely on the knowledge of what is right and what is wrong that Yahweh imprinted in every heart or conscience. The laws were the Ten Commandments given to Moses, as elaborated by the centuries-old procession of prophets sent to the Jews and by the wisdom of the anonymous authors of the Old Testament. These laws and interpretations were peculiarly

■ According to Jewish tradition, Moses climbed the rocky peak of Mount Sinai during the Hebrews' journey from Egypt to the Promised Land. There Yahweh gave the prophet the tablets of stone upon which the Ten Commandments were inscribed, to guide Jewish ethical conduct and form the Covenant between Yahweh and his Chosen people.

the Jews' property, given them as a mark of favor by their lord and protector Yahweh. But all men and women everywhere were believed to have been given conscience, and insofar as they followed conscience, they were doing the Lord's work and possibly gaining eternal salvation.

✤ Jewish Beliefs and Relationships

More than most, the Jews divided all humanity into "we" and "they." This was undoubtedly the result of their religious tradition, whereby they had been selected as the Chosen. Jews looked upon non-Jews as distinctly lesser breeds, whose main function in the divine plan was to act as tempters and obstacles that the pious must overcome. In their preoccupation with the finer points of the Law laid down by Moses and his successors, the Hebrews deliberately segregated themselves from other peoples. Intermarriage with pagans was tantamount to treason and was punished by immediate expulsion from the community. Ancient Judaism was never open to converts.

Economic Situation

Although their religious beliefs would have immense influence on Western civilization, in economic affairs and politics, the Jews were at best minor players on the Near Eastern stage. They had never been very numerous, and the split between Israelites and Judeans weakened both. The military victories over the Philistines had allowed the united kingdom to take tribute from the conquered, which eased the Hebrews' own tax burdens. With the rise of Assyria, however, both Israel and Judea had to engage in numerous, expensive wars. Both suffered economically as a result and became relatively insignificant backwaters under the direct or indirect rule of powerful neighbors. Neither Samaria nor Jerusalem ever became an important international trading or commercial center, although the latter city was located along the overland travel routes between Egypt and the Middle East.

When the kingdom was founded under Saul, most Hebrews were still rural herders and peasants. They lived in a fashion indistinguishable from that of Abraham; the nuclear family (parents and children) was the basic unit of society, with the father enjoying very extensive rights over his wife and children. Over the next half millennium, many Hebrews made the transition from rural to town life. As many people shifted from subsistence farming to wage earning, social tensions dividing rich and poor began to appear. The strong solidarity that had marked the Hebrews earlier broke down, and the prophets of the eighth through fifth centuries remind us that exploitation of widows and orphans and abuse of the weak by the strong were by no means limited to the despised "Gentiles" (all non-Jews).

The Old Testament

In the first five books of the Old Testament or *Torah,* the Hebrews laid down fundamental laws for human conduct as Yahweh revealed them through his prophets. The Book of Leviticus is the third book of Scripture, and it prescribes for the Jews the proper course one must follow toward neighbors and the whole Jewish community:

> When you reap the harvest, you must not reap your field to its very edge, neither shall you gather the gleanings. And you shall not strip bare your vineyards, neither shall you gather the fallen grapes. You shall leave them for the poor and the sojourner. I am the Lord, thy God.
>
> You shall do no wrong in judgment; you shall not be partial to the poor or bow to the mighty, but in righteousness only shall you judge your neighbor.
>
> When a stranger sojourns among you in your land, you shall do him no wrong. The stranger who sojourns with you shall be to you as the native among you, and you shall love him as yourself. . . .

One of the most beloved of all the Old Testament verses is Psalm 8, in which the anonymous author celebrates the great love of Yahweh for his chosen people, giving them dominion over his creation and all the creatures it contains:

> . . . what is Man, that thou are mindful of him,
> and the son of Man, that thou dost care for him?
> Yet thou hast made him little less than a god,
> and dost crown him with glory and honor.
>
> Thou hast given him dominion over the works of thy hands,
> thou hast put all things beneath his feet,
> all sheep and oxen,
> and also the beasts of the field,
> the birds of the air, and the fish of the seas. . . .
>
> O Lord, our God,
> how majestic is thy name in all the Earth!

SOURCE: *Revised Standard Version of the Bible,* © 1946, 1952, 1971 by the Division of Christian Education of The National Council of Churches of Christ in the U.S.A. Used by permission.

Slavery was fairly common among the Hebrews, though not so common as it would be later among the Greeks and Romans. Both Gentile and Jew could be enslaved, usually for debt or for crime. Hebrew slaves were infrequent, however, because they had to be released from their condition on the Sabbath Year (the seventh year) without payment, which of course reduced their value. Both Gentile and Jewish slaves were protected by numerous provisions of the Jewish law (the Torah and Talmud), which limited the jobs they could be put to and the hours they might work, among other things. Owners who physically abused their slaves were to be punished. Manumission (freeing) was common, especially for Hebrew slaves.

Social Customs

Hebrew society was patriarchal in every respect. According to the Old Testament, a husband/father even had life and death authority over his wife and children, but this was certainly no longer true by the 500s B.C.E.

Marriage and divorce reflected the patriarchal values of the society. The married state was strongly preferred, and in fact, bachelors were looked upon as failures and shirkers. Young men were to marry by no later than age twenty-four and preferably by twenty. Girls were thought ready for marriage at puberty, roughly about age thirteen. As in every ancient society, marriage was arranged by the parents, usually with a good deal of negotiating about the dowry or bride-price.

As we noted earlier, endogamy (marrying one's own) was the universal rule; marrying outside one's religion was extremely rare. A man could have several legal wives and an unlimited number of concubines, but as in other societies, only the wealthy could afford this practice. The wife married into the husband's family and moved into his house. The property she brought into the marriage remained hers, however, and could be removed again should her husband divorce her for any reason but unfaithfulness.

Divorce was easy enough for the husband, but very unusual for a wife to initiate. Women caught in adultery could be killed, but were normally divorced and sent back to their father's home. Infidelity by the husband was a crime only if committed with a married woman.

Children were the whole point of marriage; the continuation of the family was the primary duty of both husband and wife. The oldest male child received the lion's share of the inheritance, but the other boys were not shut out. The girls, on the other hand, received nothing beyond their dowries, because through marriage they would be joined to another family, which would care for them. The education of all children was carried on within the family circle; literacy was uncommon among the country folk but not so among the urbanites. As in every other aspect of life, the devout Jew conceived of education along religious lines, and the Torah and Talmudic commentaries were the only texts in use.

Jewish arts and sciences were relatively undeveloped compared to their more sophisticated and richer neighbors. Excepting the Old Testament's poetry, the Jews produced very little of note in any of the art forms; the representation of living things was thought to be sacrilegious and was banned. But the Jews' religion and the philosophy and ethics that it spawned are a permanent part of Western civilization. Both Christianity and Islam are in several ways direct offshoots of Judaism.

✤ LATER JEWISH HISTORY: 600–100 B.C.E.

In the centuries after the fall of the monarchies of Samaria and Judea, the Jews' conception of Yahweh changed in several significant ways, and these changes are linked to their political relations with others. After losing their independence to the Assyrians and later to the Babylonians and Persians, the Jewish people went through a long spiritual crisis. Their hope for a triumph over their enemies was not realized. Indeed, quite the contrary happened: the *Babylonian Captivity* (586–539 B.C.E.), when thousands of Jews were taken off to Babylon as hostages for the good behavior of the rest, was a particular low point. Many of them never returned, having been seduced by the "Great Whore" Babylon into the worship of false gods. Those who returned after release by the Persians under Cyrus (see Chapter 4) were the "tried and true," who had been tested and had survived.

During this period when the books of the Old Testament were being written and assembled by scribes, the image of Yahweh took on clearer lines. Not only was Yahweh the only god, he was the *universal* god of all, that is, whether or not the Gentiles worshiped him, he was their judge and would reward or punish them (mostly the latter) as they conformed or not to the demands of conscience.

God was a *just* god, who would reward and punish according to ethical principles; but he was also a *merciful* god who would not turn a deaf ear to the earnest penitent. His ways were mysterious to men on earth, such as Job, but they would someday be seen for what they are: righteous and just.

God was an *omnipotent and omniscient* master, who could do whatever he desired, always and everywhere. There were no other opposing forces (gods) who could frustrate his will; but in his wisdom, Yahweh had granted his creature Man free will, and allowed the principle of evil to arise in the form of the fallen angel, Lucifer/Satan. Man could ignore conscience and the Law and choose evil, in the same way as Zarathustra had taught. If he did, he would face a Last Judgment that would condemn him to eternal punishment and deprive him of the fate that Yahweh desired and offered: salvation in blessedness.

Finally, Yahweh gradually came to be a *personal* deity, in a way in which no other ancient god had been. He could be prayed to directly, he was observant of all that

■ The "Dead Sea Scrolls" were found by an Arab shepherd boy in 1946. The copper scrolls have been largely deciphered in recent years and have proven a rich source for knowledge of Jewish society and customs around the first century C.E.

affected a man's or a woman's life. His actions were not impulsive or unpredictable; he wanted Man not as a slave but a friend. The relationship between God and Man is meant to be one of mutual love. In a sense, God needed Man to complete the work of creation. Yahweh, the God of the Jews, by about the second century B.C.E. was a quite different being than had ever been envisioned elsewhere by the priests and their faithful.

The promise to preserve the Jews as a people that Yahweh had given Moses was what held the Judean Jews together after the Assyrian and Babylonian conquests. But inevitably, some of them, including many of the learned men (*rabbis*) came to think of this promise as one aimed not at simple preservation, but of counterconquest by the Jews of their enemies. Instead of being a contemptible minority in the empires of the mighty ones, the Hebrews would be the mighty and make the others bend to *their* will.

In this way grew the hopes for a **messiah,** a redeemer who would take the Jews out of their humiliations and make them a people to be feared and respected. In this manner, the message of the Lord speaking through the great prophets was distorted into a promise of earthly grandeur rather than what was intended, a promise of an immortal salvation for those who believed. When the person Christians came to view as the messiah (Christ) finally came and spoke of his kingdom "which was not of this earth," there was disappointment and disbelief among many of his hearers.

The kingdom of Samaria/Israel was ended by a failed rebellion against the Assyrian overlords, resulting in the scattering of the populace far and wide, and the eventual loss of them to Judaic belief (the first **Diaspora** = scattering). Judea, however, survived under the Assyrians until the defeat of the latter in 612. It then fell under Babylonian overlordship, and the ill-fated attempt to throw off this yoke led to the crushing defeat by King Nebuchadnezzar in 586 and the ensuing Babylonian Captivity. The great temple of Solomon was demolished.

Becoming one of the provinces of the Persian empire after 539 B.C.E., the Judeans continued under Persian rule until Alexander the Great toppled the King of Kings in the 330s. They had profited from the Persians' tolerant policies to rebuild the temple and continue the development of the Hebraic theology. They then lived with more or less stability under the successors of Alexander until into the second century before Christ, when they were oppressed by an unwise ruler and were briefly successful in regaining political independence under the **Maccabee Brothers.**

By the time of the Roman conquest of the Near East, in the first century before Christ, some of the Jewish leaders had become fanatical, believing in the protection of mighty Yahweh against all odds. These *Zealots* were unwilling to bend before any nonbeliever, however powerful he might be. This was to cause the tension between the Jewish nation and the Roman overlords that eventually resulted in war and the Second *Diaspora,* the forced emigration of much of this small people from its ancestral home in the land of Israel (modern Palestine) to all corners of the great Roman Empire.

Wherever the Jews went, they took their national badge of distinction with them: the unerring belief in their quality as the Chosen and their peculiar vision of the nature of God and his operations in the mind and hearts of humans. This was a vision of the relationship between the deity and his creature Man that no other people had: mutually dependent, ethical, just but also merciful on the Lord's side; submissive but not slavish on Man's side. It was the relationship between a stern but loving father and an independent, sinful, but dutiful child. The mold for the evolution of Christianity had been formed. All that was needed was the appearance of the long-rumored messiah who would fulfill the promise that the Chosen would enter glory, some day.

Summary

Under Abraham, the Twelve Tribes of the Hebrews wandered out of Mesopotamia and entered Palestine sometime in the middle of the second millennium B.C.E. Coming under the pharaoh's rule, they then left Egypt in the Exodus led by Moses about 1250 B.C.E., seeking the land of milk and honey they had once possessed in Canaan.

Overcoming the Philistines after a long duel, the Jews under Saul set up a monarchy that collapsed and broke into two parts in the 900s. The larger segment, Samaria or

Israel, gradually fell away from Judaism and was dispersed by Assyrian conquest; the smaller part, Judea with its capital Jerusalem, stayed true to Yahweh and survived as a province of other empires into Roman times.

What distinguished the Jews from dozens of other tribal kingdoms in the Near East was their monotheistic religion and their linkage of a universally potent God with ethical standards and immortal salvation for the believer. Their vision of an omnipotent, just, and merciful Lord who would one day send a messiah to lead the Hebrews to glory would be the cement that held this small people together. It was a vision unique to them, and through it they would make vital contributions to later civilization.

Test Your Knowledge

1. The tribes of the Hebrews are thought to have originated in
   a. Israel.
   b. Persia.
   c. Mesopotamia.
   d. Arabia.
2. The Covenant of the Hebrews with their god Yahweh
   a. was given to Moses during the Exodus from Egypt.
   b. had nothing to do with individual conduct, only group survival.
   c. was a contract that was allowed to lapse.
   d. guaranteed each believing Hebrew immortality.
3. The people who conquered Samaria in the eighth century B.C.E. were
   a. Babylonians.
   b. Assyrians.
   c. Egyptians.
   d. Hittites.
4. The first king of the Hebrew kingdom founded after the Exodus was
   a. David.
   b. Saul.
   c. Solomon.
   d. Isaiah.
5. Belief in the messiah among Jews of the first century B.C.E. was focused on
   a. hope for a statesman who would lead the Jews to a new homeland.
   b. expectation of a military leader against the Romans.
   c. finding a political leader who would assert Jewish supremacy.
   d. a hermit who rejected society, such as John the Baptist.
6. The critical factor in the Jews' vision of God by the first century B.C.E. was
   a. the link between the deity and humans' ethical conduct on earth.
   b. the belief that God was all-powerful in human affairs.
   c. the belief that God was supreme over all other deities.
   d. the hope for an eternal life given by God to those he favored.
7. The Jews' belief that they were the Chosen People was solidified and more narrowly defined
   a. after the Assyrian conquest.
   b. after the Babylonian Captivity.
   c. with the Roman overlordship.
   d. with the conquest of Canaan.

Identification Terms

Covenant	Exodus	messiah	Philistines
Diaspora	Maccabee Brothers	monotheism	Solomon
ethics			

Bibliography

Bright, J. *A History of Israel,* 1981. As near as one can come to a standard American treatment.

Davies, W. D., and L. Finkelstine, eds. *The Cambridge History of Judaism,* 1984–87. The first volumes to appear of what will be a standard history.

de Vaux, M. R. *Ancient Israel,* 1965. A good survey, strong on social history.

Gray, J. *The Canaanites,* 1964. A history of the major people inhabiting Palastine before the Hebrews.

Harden, D.B. *The Phoenicians,* 1962. This text deals with the interrelations between Jews and their northern neighbors.

Schwartz, L. W., ed. *Great Ages and Ideas of the Jewish People,* 1956. A good introduction to the biblical Jews.

Shanks, H. *Ancient Israel: A Short History from Abraham to the Destruction of the Temple* (1988). Can be recommended.

Wumbrand, W., et al. *The Jewish People: 4000 Years of Survival* (1967). Less detailed than *The Cambridge History* but brilliantly illustrated.

INDIA'S BEGINNINGS

c. 2500–1900 B.C.E.	Mohenjo-Daro and Harappa flourish
c. 1500 B.C.E.	Invasion of Aryans
c. 1500–500 B.C.E.	The Vedic epoch
563–483 B.C.E.	Life of the Buddha
326 B.C.E.	Invasion by Alexander the Great
320–232 B.C.E.	Mauryan dynasty

Until fairly recently it was believed that the civilization of India had been founded only some two thousand years ago, far later than China, Egypt, or Mesopotamia. But in the early twentieth century, archaeologists found that a highly advanced, urbanized civilization had existed since the middle of the third millennium B.C.E. in the valley of the Indus River in what is now Pakistan. The discovery of this new chapter in world history is a dramatic story, and much of the detail is still being pieced together. Enough is known, however, to whet our appetite to know much more, especially about the possible contributions of this civilization to one of the world's leading religious beliefs, Hinduism.

✣ INDUS VALLEY CIVILIZATION

As in Mesopotamia and Egypt, the earliest Indian civilization was located in the valley of a great stream. The *Indus River* flows south and west from the foothills of the Himalayan range, the world's loftiest and most forbidding mountains. The Himalayas are the highest of several ranges that separate India and Pakistan from Tajikistan and China (see Map 6.1).

In the 1850s, when India was still under British colonial rule, a railway was extended across the Indus. During the construction, the British engineers noticed that the local workers were bringing in large quantities of stone and brick from somewhere nearby. When the engineers inquired, they learned that the local residents had "always" gone to a certain site, where huge piles of these materials were easily unearthed. The engineers notified the authorities, and the sites were put under archaeological supervision, which has continued ever since.

The major "dig" is at a place in modern Pakistan called **Mohenjo-Daro,** about three hundred miles upstream from the mouth of the river. Some years later, another major site was located, four hundred miles further up the river at Harappa. In between these large ruins are dozens of smaller sites being slowly uncovered by first British and now Pakistani and Indian experts. In terms of area covered, this is by far the largest ancient civilization ever found.

Mohenjo-Daro and Harappa

What exactly is being uncovered? At Mohenjo-Daro archaeologists have found the remnants of large, carefully

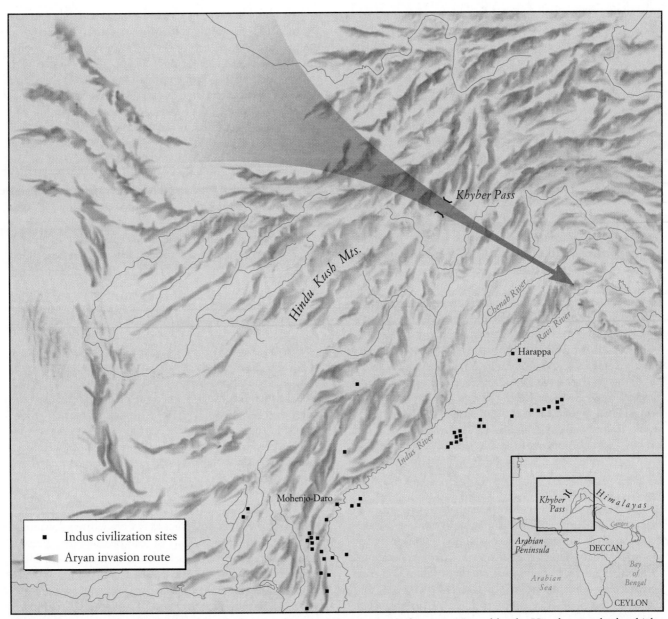

● **MAP 6.1   The Indian Subcontinent.** India is a very large and diverse geographic entity. Ringed by the Himalayas and other high mountains to the north and northeast, the usual routes of contact with other peoples have been from the northwest and by sea from both eastern and western directions.

constructed walls and the city they enclosed. The city was more than three miles across and probably housed more than 100,000 people at some time in the distant past. Now, little remains except the brick with which it was built, buried underground by the passage of time, storms, vandalism, and decay. Many smaller towns and villages have also been found under the dust of centuries, scattered along the Indus and its several tributaries in western India.

The cities and villages were built of fired brick and were carefully planned. The streets ran at right angles, like William Penn's grid plan of Philadelphia, and they were of two widths. The main thoroughfares were thirty-four feet wide, large enough to allow two large carts to pass safely and still leave room for two or three pedestrians. The smaller avenues were nine feet wide. Many of the buildings had two or even three stories, which was unusual for residences in the ancient world. They were built of bricks that are almost always of two sizes, but only those two. The interior dimensions of the houses were almost identical; a sewage canal ran from each house to a larger canal in the street that carried off household wastes. Small statues of gods and goddesses, almost always of the same size and posture, are frequently found in the house foundations.

All this regularity suggests a government that was very powerful in the eyes of its subjects and probably gained its authority from religious belief. Some experts on Indus civilization believe that it was a theocracy, in which the priests ruled as representatives of the gods. In no other way, they think, could the government's power have been strong enough to command uniformity over a period of centuries, as happened in Mohenjo-Daro and Harappa.

Both cities also contain monumental buildings situated on a citadel, which were probably a communal granary and the temples of the local gods. An interesting discovery at Mohenjo-Daro was the "Great Bath," a pool and surrounding cells that clearly existed for ritual bathing. Some have suggested that the emphasis on purification by water in present-day Hinduism may go back to these origins. Harappa differs from Mohenjo-Daro in building style and other details, but the similarities are strong enough that the two cities and the surrounding villages are believed to constitute one civilization.

For their food, the cities depended on the irrigated farms of the surrounding plain, which was very fertile. Like the people of Egypt, the ordinary people apparently enjoyed a high standard of living for many generations. Objects found in the ruins indicate that trade was carried on with Mesopotamia at least as early as 2000 B.C.E. and also with the peoples of southern India and Afghanistan. Although a good many works of art and figurines have been found, the occasional writing has not yet been deciphered. Its 270-odd characters are different from all other known scripts and have no alphabet. Our inability to decipher the writing as well as the long period when this civilization was forgotten have hindered scholars' efforts to obtain a detailed knowledge of these people. We still know next to nothing about their religion, their government, the social divisions of the people, and their scientific and intellectual accomplishments. Much is still shrouded in mystery and perhaps always will be.

One thing now seems clear: the cities and villages were prosperous, expanding settlements from at least 2500 to about 1900 B.C.E. Around 1900, for reasons still only guessed at, they began a long decline, which ended with the abandonment of Mohenjo-Daro about 1200 B.C.E. and Harappa somewhat later. Some evidence indicates that landslides changed the course of the lower Indus and prevented the continuation of the intensive irrigation that had supported the cities. Some people think that the population may have fallen victim to malaria, as the blocked river created mosquito-ridden swamps nearby. Others think that the irrigated land gradually became alkaline and nonproductive, as happened in lower Mesopotamia. Whatever the role of natural disasters, it is certain that the decline of the Indus valley was accelerated by an invasion of nomads called *Aryans,* who descended into the valley from Afghanistan and Iran around 1500 B.C.E.

✤ THE VEDIC EPOCH

The Aryans were one of the earliest horse-breeding people of ancient Asia, and their aggressive ways were the terror of other civilizations besides that of the Indus valley. It is thought that they overwhelmed the civilized Indians in the valley and set themselves up as a sort of master group, using the Indians as labor to do the farming and trading that the Aryan warriors despised as inferior. As we noted, their conquest of the more advanced peoples may have been aided by natural disasters that had weakened the economy severely.

Our knowledge of the Aryans comes largely from their **Vedas,** very ancient oral epics that were written down only long after the Aryan period, so the pictures they present may be deceptive. We know that the Aryans were Indo-European speakers, who worshiped gods of the sky and storm and made impressive use of bronze weaponry and horse-drawn chariots in battle. (Apparently, the Indus valley people knew the horse only as a beast of burden and were at a disadvantage against the Aryan chariots.) The *Rigveda,* the oldest and most important Veda, paints a picture of a war-loving, violent folk, led by their *raja,* or chieftain, and their magic-working priests.

In time, the Aryans extended their rule across all of northern India to the Ganges valley. Gradually, they abandoned their nomadic ways and settled down as agriculturists and town dwellers. They never conquered the southern half of India, and the southern culture still differs from that of the north in some respects as a result.

✦ THE CASTE SYSTEM

The Vedas describe a people who believed they were the natural masters of the inferior Indians and who wished to underline their differences by dividing all of society into four classes. The two highest classes, those of priests and warriors, were reserved for the Aryans and their pure-blooded descendants. The priests were **brahmins** and originally were superior in status to the warriors, who were called *kshatrija* and evolved over time from warriors to governors. The third class, the *vaishya,* was the most numerous and included free farmers and merchants. In the fourth and lowest class were the unfree, the serfs, or *shudra.*

Over the course of the Vedic Age, these four classes evolved into something quite different: each class came to be separated into a series of socioeconomic groups or *castes.* A caste is a group into which one is born and which dictates most aspects of life; it confers a status that cannot be changed. Each caste has special duties and privileges, many of which are shown by the style of clothing one wears, the food one eats, and by one's social contacts with other people. A high-caste Indian had very little contact with the lower castes and none with the lowest of all, the **pariah,** or outcastes. Perhaps a seventh of Indian society still falls into this last, miserable category—the untouchables—whose members until very recently were treated worse than animals. A caste differs from a class in that a class can be changed during one's lifetime and is more closely associated with a person's economic status than with birth. Class is a relatively simple concept; caste involves a large number of factors, including geographic area, education, and religious practice, as well as means of making a living.

The caste system founded by the conquering Aryans is one of the two most important factors in India's long history (the other being the Hindu faith). It grew ever more refined and more complex as time passed. The Aryans themselves eventually were absorbed through intermarriage with upper-caste Indians, but the stratification of society by birth that they began persists to the present day. When the British arrived in the eighteenth century there were thought to be more than three thousand separate castes and subcastes in India! Although the number has sharply declined since then, there are still hundreds of castes and the belief that one is born into a group that is fixed by age-old traditions and allows no change is still very strong in rural India.

Throughout Indian history, caste has had the effect of preventing change, particularly social change. Why? Com-

■ Relatively, few works remain to indicate the creative talents of the Harappan peoples. This small male torso, composed of red limestone, displays an anatomical realism that tantalizes the modern viewer with its sophistication.

bined with the beliefs of Hinduism (see the next section), caste made it next to impossible for someone born in a low caste to climb the ranks of social power and privilege. It also limited political power to the uppermost ranks, in much the same way as the aristocracy monopolized power in medieval Europe. Caste discouraged or prohibited innovation by those in lower castes. Meanwhile those on top were very content to have things go on forever as they were. Under the caste system, India became a *highly stratified and immobile society.*

✦ HINDUISM

The religion of the overwhelming majority of Indians is Hinduism, the fourth largest religion in the world with about 500 million adherents. Hinduism is both more and less than a religion as the West understands that term: it is a "way of life," a philosophic system, a model for art, and the basis of all Indian political life in the past. But it is not

The Laws of Manu

The Laws of Manu are an ancient compilation of teachings from Hindu India. **Manu** was a being simultaneously human and divine from whom devout Hindus could learn what was needed for perfection and the attainment of *moksha*. The attitude of the Laws of Manu toward the lower castes and women are especially revealing. (Note: the *shudra* are the lowest of the original four castes of India established during the Aryan epoch.)

- That place where the shudra are very numerous . . . soon entirely perishes, afflicted by disease and famine.
- A Brahmin may confidently take the goods of his shudra, because the slave cannot have any possessions and the master may take his property.
- A Brahmin who takes a shudra to wife and to his bed will after death sink into Hell; if he begets a child with her, he will lose the rank of Brahmin. The son whom a Brahmin begets through lust upon a shudra female is, although alive, a corpse and hence called a living corpse. A shudra who has intercourse with a woman of a twice-born caste [i.e., a Brahmin] shall be punished so: if she was unguarded he loses the offending part [his genitals] and all his property; if she was guarded, everything including his life.
- Women . . . give themselves to the handsome and the ugly. Through their passion for men, through their unstable temper, through their natural heartlessness they become disloyal toward their husbands, however carefully they may be guarded. Knowing their disposition, which the lord of creation laid upon them, to be so, every man should most strenuously exert himself to guard them. When creating them, Manu allotted to women a love of their bed, of their seat and of ornament, impure desire, wrath, dishonesty, malice, and bad conduct . . .
- It is the nature of women to seduce men in this world; for that reason the wise are never unguarded in the company of females. For women are able to lead astray in this world not only the fool, but even a learned man, and make of him a slave of desire and wrath.

But the exhortations of Manu are not completely one-sided:

- Reprehensible is the father who gives not his daughter in marriage at the proper time [i.e., puberty]; reprehensible is the husband who approaches not his wife in due season, and reprehensible is the son who does not protect his mother after her husband has died.
- Drinking spirituous liquors, associating with wicked ones, separation from the husband, rambling abroad, sleeping at unseasonable hours, and dwelling in houses of other men are the six causes of ruin in women.

SOURCE: D. Johnson, ed., *Sources of World Civilization,* Vol. 1. © 1994, Simons and Schuster Publishers.

---

a rigid set of theological doctrines that must be believed in order to find truth or to be saved in eternity.

The Hindu faith is a product of the slow mixing of the Aryan beliefs with those of the native Indians, over a thousand years from 1500 to about 500 B.C.E. Its most basic principles and beliefs are:

1. The nonmaterial world is the real and permanent one.
2. The soul must pass through a lengthy series of existences, being reincarnated (*samsara*) in accord with its *karma*.
3. **Karma** is the tally of good and bad committed in a given life. Good *karma* results in a birth into a higher caste in the next life.
4. One must strive for good *karma* through following the code of morals prescribed for one's caste, called **dharma,** as closely as one can.

The impersonal gods *Brahman,* giver of life; *Shiva,* the creator and destroyer; and *Vishnu,* the preserver; dominate an almost endless array of supernatural beings. Most Hindus are devotees of either Shiva or Vishnu as the foremost deity, but worship them in a huge variety of rituals.

When a person has lived a very good life, death will lead not to another reincarnation, but to final release from the great Wheel of Life. This release is **moksha,** and it is the end for which all good Hindus live. Moksha is often compared to the heaven of the Western world, but it differs in one all-important respect: moksha is the end of individuality; the individual soul is submerged into the world-soul. A good analogy would be a raindrop, which, after many transformations, finds its way back to the ocean and is dissolved therein.

Vedic Hinduism was highly ritualistic; the priestly caste—*brahmins*—had power by virtue of their mastery of ceremonies and their semimagical knowledge of the ways of the gods. Gradually, the masses of people became alienated from this ritualism and sought other ways to explain the mystery of human existence. In the fifth century B.C.E., two new modes of thought gradually became established in India: *Jainism* and *Buddhism.* Jainism is very limited in appeal. It is less a religion than a philosophy that emphasizes the sacredness of all life (see the Document in Chapter 20). In modern India, it has a small number of high-caste adherents representing perhaps 2 percent of the total Indian population. In contrast, Buddhism is one of the great religions of the world; it has adherents in all south and east Asian nations and includes several sects.

✤ BUDDHISM

Buddhism began in India as an intellectual and emotional revolt against the emptiness of Vedic ritualism. Originally an earthly philosophy that rejected the idea of immortal life and the gods, it was turned into a supernatural belief soon after the death of its founder, the Buddha.

Siddartha Gautama (563–483 B.C.E.), an Indian aristocrat, was the Buddha, or *Enlightened One,* and his life is fairly well documented (see the Biography in this chapter). As a young man, he wandered for several years through the north of India seeking more satisfying answers to the riddle of life. Only after intensive meditation was he finally able to come to terms with himself and human existence. He then became the teacher of a large and growing band of disciples, who spread his word gradually throughout the subcontinent and then into East Asia. Buddhism eventually came to be much more important in China and Japan than in India, where it was practically extinct by 1000 C.E.

■ One of the great trinity of Hindu deities, Shiva is sometimes portrayed as a male, sometimes as a female. Shiva is the god who presides over becoming and destroying, representing the eternal flux of life.

Teachings of the Buddha

The Buddha taught that everyone, regardless of caste, could attain **nirvana,** which is the Buddhist equivalent of Hindu moksha: release from human life and its woes. Nirvana is attained through the self-taught mastery of oneself: the gods have nothing to do with it, and priests are superfluous. The way to self-mastery lies through the *Four Noble Truths* and the **Eightfold Path,** which the Buddha laid out in his teachings.

Touched by a singular ray of enlightenment as a middle-aged seeker, the Buddha preached that human life can only be understood in the light of the Four Noble Truths he had experienced:

1. All life is permeated by suffering.
2. All suffering is caused by desire.
3. Desire can only be finally overcome by reaching the state of *nirvana.*
4. The way to *nirvana* is guided by eight principles.

The Eightfold Path to *nirvana* demands right (or righteous, we would say) ideas, right thought, right speech,

The Buddha

Siddartha Gautama (c. 563–483 B.C.E.) was the pampered son of a princely Indian family in the northern borderlands, near present-day Nepal. A member of the *kshatrija* caste of warrior-governors, the young man had every prospect of a conventionally happy and rewarding life as master of a handful of villages. Married young to a local aristocrat like himself, he dedicated himself to the usual pursuits— hunting, feasting, revelry—of his class and time.

But in his late twenties, a notable change occurred in this routine. According to a cherished Buddhist legend, on successive excursions he encountered an aged man, then a sick man, and finally a corpse by the roadside. These reminders of the common fate set the young man thinking about the nature of all human life, in a (for him) novel fashion. Finally, he abandoned home, wife, and family and set out to find his own answers. In the already traditional Indian fashion, he became a wandering ascetic, begging a handful of rice to stay alive while seeking truth in meditation.

Years went by as Siddartha sought to answer his questions. But for long he found no convincing answers, neither in the extreme self-denial practiced by some, nor in the mystical contemplation recommended by others. At last, as he sat under the bodhi tree (the tree of wisdom) through an agonizingly long night of intensive meditation, enlightenment reached him. He arose, confident in his new perceptions and began to gather around him the beginnings of the community known as Buddhists ("the enlightened ones").

From that point on, the Buddha developed a philosophy that was a revision of the ruling Vedic Hindu faith of India and, in some important ways, a denial of it. By the Buddha's death, the new faith was firmly established, and some version of his teaching would gradually grow to be the majority viewpoint before being extinguished in the land of its birth.

What was the essence of the Buddha's teachings? Like every other ancient founder of philosophies or religions, we have nothing directly from his pen, but only the collected reminiscences of his early disciples to guide us. These disciples soon disagreed among themselves as to what the master had taught or its proper interpretation. But all Buddhists of whatever school accepted the Four Noble Truths and the Eightfold Path as the means of overcoming the tribu-

right action, right living, right effort, right consciousness, and right meditation. The person who consistently follows these steps is assured of conquering desire and will therefore be released from suffering, which is the ultimate goal of human life.

The heart of the Buddha's message is that suffering and loss in this life are caused by the desire for an illusory power and happiness. Once the individual understands that power is not desirable and that happiness is self-deception, the temptation to pursue them will gradually disappear. The individual will then find the serenity of soul and the harmony with nature and fellow human beings that constitute true power and happiness.

Buddhism quickly spread among Indians of all backgrounds and regions, carried forth by the Buddha's disciples during his lifetime. Much of the popularity of Buddhism stemmed from its *democracy of spirit.* Everyone, male and female, high and low was able to discover the Four Truths and follow the Eightfold Path. No one was excluded because of caste restrictions or poverty.

Soon after the Buddha's death, his followers made him into a god with eternal life—a thought foreign to his own teaching. His movement also gradually split into two major branches: *Theravada* and *Mahayana* Buddhism.

Theravada (Hinayana) means "the narrower vehicle" and is the stricter version of the faith. It is particularly strong in Sri Lanka and Cambodia. Theravada Buddhism emphasizes the monastic life for both men and women and takes a rather rigorous approach to what a good

lations of earthly existence. The Buddha taught that suffering is universal among human beings; that it is caused by desires generated by weakness and incomprehension; that these desires must be understood and rejected; and that the Eightfold Path provides the way to triumph over them.

In the original Buddhism, little attention was given to the role of the supernatural powers in human life or to reincarnation. The gods were thought to exist, but to have minimal influence upon an individual *karma,* or fate. Gods could not assist a person to find what Hindus call *moksha* and Buddhists *nirvana,* or the state of release from earthly life and its inherent suffer-

ing. But in time, this changed among the majority, or Mahayana Buddhists, who came to look upon the Buddha himself and other *bodhisattvas* as divine immortals who could be called upon for spiritual assistance.

How this development would have been received by the Buddha during his own lifetime is not hard to guess; his rejection of supernatural deities was well known. But it remains true that the very breadth of Buddhist doctrines, which range from simple repetitive chants to the most refined intellectual exercise, have allowed a sizable proportion of humankind to identify with this creed in one or another of its forms. Buddhism today has the third largest membership of all faiths.

person who seeks *nirvana* must believe. It claims to be the pure form of the Buddha's teachings and rejects the idea of the reincarnation of the Master or other enlightened ones (*boddhisattva*) appearing on earth.

Mahayana Buddhism is much more liberal in its beliefs and views the doctrines of the Buddha as a sort of initial step, rather than as the ultimate word. The word *Mahayana* means "the larger vehicle," reflecting the belief that there are many ways to salvation. Its faithful believe that there are many buddhas, not just Siddartha Gautama, and that many more will appear. Monastic life is a good thing for those who can assume it, but the vast majority of Mahayana Buddhists will never do so and do not feel themselves disadvantaged thereby. Mahayana adherents far outnumber the others and are found in Vietnam,

China, Japan, and Korea. Unlike the history of the Jewish, Christian, and Muslim sects, the two forms of Buddhism take a "live and let live" attitude toward one another, just as the various types of Hinduism do.

✤ KING ASHOKA AND BUDDHISM'S SPREAD

Ancient India came into direct contact with the West for the first time when Alexander the Great invaded with his army of Greeks (see Chapter 9). After Alexander's retreat, the Hindu lands were briefly united by King Ashoka (269–232 B.C.E.). He is beloved by all Indians, who regard him as the most noble political figure of the premodern era.

■ The bronze statuette of a dancer awaiting her turn shows the skill of the Mohenjo-Daro sculptors. It is one of the few surviving metal works.

model for later rulers to which they often aspired but rarely reached.

After Ashoka's death, his weak successors began to give up what he had gained, both in terms of defense against invaders and in internal affairs. Wave after wave of barbarians entered India from the northwest (over the famous Khyber Pass) in the first century B.C.E. Most of them adopted Indian civilization and the Buddhist faith,

■ **The Lions of Sarnath.** The Lions of Sarnath were created by king Asoka to symbolize the proclamation of Buddhism to the world. Sarnath was the site where Siddhartha Gautama first preached. The lions have been adopted by the modern republic of India as the official symbol of state.

Ashoka was the third and last of the *Mauryan dynasty,* who ruled over much of present-day India in the century from the departure of Alexander to 232 B.C.E. His significance stems in part from the fact that he introduced religious tolerance into public and private life after becoming a devout Buddhist in the middle of his reign. This step allowed the Buddhists to play an important role in Indian life for the next several centuries, although they gradually died out, overcome by a renewed and rejuvenated Hinduism.

For the first few years of his rule, Ashoka was a great warrior, but he changed into a peace-seeking and compassionate man after winning the bloody battle of Kalinga. The last twenty years of his reign were perhaps the most prosperous and contented period in all Indian history. He improved the public administration he had inherited from his grandfather Chandragupta, founder of the Mauryan dynasty, and made it considerably more humane. Ashoka saw himself as the responsible father of the Indian people and exerted himself for their welfare. In so doing, he set a

but the political unity of India disintegrated. It was revived for two centuries by the *Gupta dynasty* in the 300s and 400s C.E. During this time, the literature of *Sanskrit,* the classic language of both Hindu and Buddhist India, flourished. Linguists believe Sanskrit is the source of much of the Indo-European language family. We will revisit the course of Indian history under the Gupta kings in Chapter 20.

✤ INDIA AND CHINA

Most Indian connections with the outer world have been westward, across the same routes through the passes of Afghanistan that invaders followed again and again. From the west came the Aryans, then the Greeks under Alexander, then the Persians in the early centuries C.E., and eventually the Afghan and Turkish Muslims. In between, a whole series of "wild men" such as the White Huns and many others streamed southward through the mountain passes. Most of these intruders, even the savage horsemen from the central Asian steppes, eventually enriched Indian culture in one way or another.

In contrast, early India had remarkably little cultural interchange with China, its powerful neighbor to the east.

The main reason for this lack of contact was apparently the extreme difficulty of crossing the Himalayas and the very sparse population of the Tibetan plateau behind that range. The mountains ringing northern India had no easy passes leading eastward, nor did the jungles of Burma allow passage in the premodern era. Despite the immense cultural gifts that the two great nations could have given one another, they had little contact even into modern days.

The one really significant export from India to China was Buddhism. Starting in the first century C.E., word of the new doctrine penetrated across the mountains. By the sixth or seventh century C.E., much of the educated class in China had taken up one or another form of Buddhist thought. The Chinese also passed Buddhism on to Korea and Vietnam. Through Korea, Buddhism entered Japan and transformed that nation as well. In fact, the adoption of Mahayana Buddhism by the Chinese has been called the *most far-reaching single cultural exchange in history,* transforming East Asian religion and philosophy over the centuries between roughly 400 and 1000 C.E. The next chapter will look at the beginnings of China's uniquely long-lived civilization.

Summary

Civilized life is now known to have arrived in India much earlier than previously believed. By 2500 B.C.E. people of the Indus River valley had developed irrigated fields and good-sized towns that traded widely with both the surrounding villagers and distant neighbors to the west. These towns seem to have been governed by a priesthood, but information on their history is still sparse. The civilization was already in decline, possibly from natural causes, when it fell to Aryan nomads, who instituted the beginnings of the caste system.

In the thousand years following the Aryan conquest (1500–500 B.C.E.), the Hindu religion was gradually constructed from a combination of Aryan belief and the Indus valley faith. When this ritualistic Hinduism was challenged by other, more ethically conscious doctrines such as Buddhism and Jainism, it gave way. Buddhism, in particular, became an international religion and philosophy, as several variants took root throughout East Asia.

Although arts and sciences flourished, the cultural and political unity of India was only sporadically enforced by a strong central government. Many invasions from the northwest kept India in a frequent state of political fragmentation, with religious belief rather than government the cement that held its people together and gave the basis for their consciousness of being a nation.

Test Your Knowledge

1. The first civilization in India
   a. was the result of Chinese colonization.
   b. extended over only a small area.
   c. is not yet understood in terms of origins and development.
   d. was made up of small villages.
2. The excavation of Mohenjo-Daro indicates that India's earliest civilization
   a. had a strong central government.
   b. was governed by merchants.
   c. had little if any commercial contacts with other civilized lands.
   d. had no dependence on irrigation agriculture.
3. The decline of the Indus valley civilization occurred because of
   a. a shift in trading routes.
   b. reasons that are not known.
   c. invasion and conquest by barbarians.
   d. sudden changes in climate.
4. Which of the following is *not* a variety of Indian religion?
   a. Jainism
   b. Vedic
   c. *Shudra*
   d. Buddhism

5. The evolution of Indian castes came about because of
   a. economic necessities.
   b. the application of Vedic beliefs to Indian realities.
   c. the rationalization of a social system built on privilege.
   d. climate and geography.
6. In Indian society after the Aryan conquest, the highest social group was that of the
   a. priests.
   b. warriors.
   c. tillers of the soil.
   d. educated.
7. The Laws of Manu show a society in which
   a. there were no essential differences between male and female.
   b. there was a strong sense of social justice.
   c. children were not valued.
   d. women were considered a source of temptation.
8. *Karma* is a Sanskrit word meaning
   a. the soul.
   b. release from earthly life cycles.
   c. the uppermost caste in Hindu society.
   d. the tally of good and bad acts in a previous life.

Identification Terms

brahmin	*karma*	*moksha*	pariah (outcaste)
dharma	Manu	*nirvana*	Vedas
Eightfold Path	Mohenjo-Daro		

Bibliography

Basham, A. L. *The Wonder That Was India,* 1959. With its many photos and maps, this is the best possible introduction to the Indus valley civilization. More up-to-date but not necessarily more readable are D. P. Agrawal, *The Archaeology of India,* 1982 and S. F. Mahmud, *A Concise History of Indo-Pakistan,* 1988.

Burtt, E. A. *The Teachings of the Compassionate Buddha,* 1955. Recommended for those interested in what this religion has to say to modern men and women.

Chandhuri, N. C. *Hinduism: A Religion to Live By,* 1979.

Eliot, C. *Hinduism and Buddhism,* 1954. A three-volume work intended for the serious student.

Humphreys, C. *Buddhism,* 1962 and *The Wisdom of Buddhism,* 1979. Two studies by a leading Western interpreter of Buddhism. Both are meant for beginners.

Radhakrishnan, S. *The Hindu View of Life,* 1926; many reprints. Focuses on Hindu religion and philosophy.

Thapar, R. *History of India,* 1966. A fine work by one of the best Indian historians. There is a good chapter on the Aryan society at the time of the conquest/penetration.

Wheeler, R. E. *Civilization of the Indus Valley and Beyond,* 1966. Looks at the excavations of Harappa in the twentieth century.

ANCIENT CHINA TO 500 B.C.E.

c. 1700–c. 1000 B.C.E. Shang dynasty

c. 1100–c. 750 B.C.E. Zhou dynasty: unified empire

c. 750–c. 400 B.C.E. Later Zhou dynasty

551–479 B.C.E. Life of Confucius

c. 400–225 B.C.E. Era of Warring States

The most stable and in many ways the most successful civilization that history has known began in China in the second millennium B.C.E. It continued in its essentials through many changes in political and social leadership, meanwhile subjecting an enormous area and many different peoples to "the Chinese way." The Chinese educated classes, who considered themselves the hub of the universe, formed the most cohesive ruling group the world has ever seen; in them, scholarship and artistic sensitivity were combined with great administrative abilities. Much of China's permanent culture was already firmly established by about 500 B.C.E., and it would change only very slowly.

✤ EARLIEST CHINA: THE SHANG ERA

About the time the Aryan invaders arrived in the Indus valley, the Neolithic farming villages along the central course of the **Yellow River** were drawn into an organized state for the first time (see Map 7.1). This state was the product of military conquest by a people closely related to the villagers, the **Shang.** The Shang replaced the villagers' earlier political overseers, but otherwise introduced little if any cultural change. (Note: The Shang dynasty may have been preceded by another, the Hsia, which is mentioned in the ancient histories as the first of the Chinese ruling groups. But unlike the Shang, the Hsia have not been confirmed by archaeological evidence.)

Like other Chinese, the Shang and the people they conquered were members of the Sino-Tibetan language group and the Mongoloid or "yellow skinned" race. Other members of these groups include the North American Indians and the Turks. The society the Shang took over was already well on the way to civilized life. The villagers were making advanced stone tools and bronze weapons. Farming had long ago replaced hunting and gathering as the mainstay of the economy. The villagers had several types of domesticated animals and were growing wheat on the fertile soil that the north wind blows into the valley from Mongolia. In later days, the vast plain on both sides of the river would be China's breadbasket, but life was never easy for the inhabitants of the Yellow River valley. Unlike the floods of the Nile, the floods of the Yellow River were tremendously damaging and had to be controlled by extensive levees.

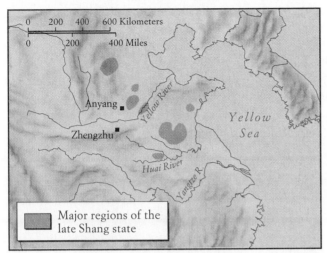

● **MAP 7.1 Shang Dynasty China.** The chief areas of Shang civilization have been located in the North China plain on either side of the Yangtze river.

The central valley of the Yellow River was the cradle of Chinese civilization, but another river would play almost as important a role in China's later history: the **Yangtze.** This great stream is much tamer than the Yellow and runs far to the south through a warmer and wetter landscape. By about the fifth century C.E., it was the center of China's rice culture. Eventually, the rice of the Yangtze became even more important than the wheat of the Yellow River valley. The plains along the two rivers and the coastal area between their deltas were the most densely populated and most important regions of ancient China.

Of all the ancient civilizations, China was the most isolated from outside influences, being even more isolated than Egypt. Both agriculture and metalworking apparently originated independently in China. No connections with either Indian or Mesopotamian arts and sciences are known until much later, after the civilization along the Yellow and Yangtze Rivers had developed its own characteristics.

Most of what we know of the Shang era comes from archaeology rather than history, as Shang writings were not numerous. Several rich grave sites have been excavated starting in the 1920s. Shang society was strictly hierarchical. At the top was a powerful king with his warrior court. War was a commonplace, and warriors were favored in every way, much as in feudal Europe. On a level below the warriors were many skilled artisans and a growing class of small traders in the towns. In the countryside lived the great majority, the peasants in their villages. Already by Shang times, the silkworm was being cultivated, and silk was produced for export to India.

Scholars are not sure whether the early Chinese had a formal religion in which all participated; many experts think that the upper class believed in one set of gods while the majority worshiped another.

Several fundamental aspects of Chinese life are already visible in the Shang epoch:

1. **The supreme importance of the family.** More than any other culture, the Chinese rely upon the family to serve as a model for public life and the source of all private virtue.
2. **The reverence shown to ancestors and the aged by the young.** The Chinese believe that experience is far more important than theory and that the young must learn from the aged if harmony is to be preserved and progress achieved.
3. **The emphasis on this world.** No other civilization of early times was so *secular* in orientation. China never had a priestly caste, and the government always subordinated religious affairs to earthly, practical tasks.
4. **The importance of education, particularly literacy.** No other culture has made the ability to read and write so important for success. The ancient Chinese written language was extremely complex (it has since been simplified). Years of hard study were required to master it, but once it was acquired, it opened the doors to both wealth and power.

In the eleventh century B.C.E., the Shang rulers seem to have faced internal conflicts that weakened the dynasty, and somewhat later they fell to the **Zhou** (Chou), a related but barbarian group from further west. The Zhou would be the longest-lived and most influential of all the Chinese ruling dynasties.

Writing

The *written language* was so important in China that something must be said about how it differed from other languages and how it developed (apparently without input from non-Chinese sources.) Like most languages, Chinese was originally pictographic, but it soon developed a huge vocabulary of signs that had no picture equivalents. These characters are called *ideographs,* or ideas-in-signs. An ideograph with several parts can take the place of as many as seven or eight words in most languages, conveying whole descriptions or actions in one sign. Some ideographs were derived from certain common roots, but others were not connected in any way, which made learning them difficult. All in all, students had to memorize about 5,000 ideographs to be considered literate. Understandably, literacy was rare, and those who knew how to read and write entered a kind of elite club that carried tremendous prestige.

The earliest writing beyond pictography dates to the Shang era around 1500 B.C.E. It is found on **oracle bones,** animal bones and shells, which were used to divine the wishes of the gods. By the end of the Shang period around 1000 B.C.E., histories and stories were being written, some of which have been preserved. Thus, although writing emerged considerably later in China than in Mesopotamia or Egypt, it developed quickly and had a richer vocabulary and more conceptual refinement than any other written language before the first century C.E. In addition, the written language was immensely important in unifying the Chinese. China has dozens of spoken dialects, which are mutually unintelligible, but it has only one way of writing.

Art and Architecture

The greatest artistic achievement of the ancient Chinese was undoubtedly their bronze work. Craftsmen in the late Shang and early Zhou periods turned out drinking cups, vases, wine vessels, brooches, and medallions, whose technical excellence and artistic grace were stunning. Metal technology in general was quite advanced in early

■ **Oracle Bone.** On the flat surface of bones such as this, Shang sages incised the earliest surviving examples of Chinese ideographs. The messages are questions addressed to the gods, and the sages read the answers by examining the patterns of cracks in the bones after hot irons had been pressed against them.

■ **Ritual Vase.** Few if any peoples have rivaled the Chinese in their devotion to detail in the plastic art forms. This ritual vase in the form of an elephant is a beautiful example.

China. Besides bronze, cast iron and copper were widely used for both tools and weaponry.

The Shang buildings that have been partially unearthed by modern archaeologists are impressive in both size and design. The upper class built large palaces and strong forts around towns like Anyang and Zhengzhu (Chengchu) in the middle reaches of the Yellow River plain. The distinctive style with pagoda-type roof lines and diminishing upper stories was developed at this time, although it was carried out much more elaborately later. Most of the art forms of modern China had their roots in very early times.

⚜ THE ZHOU DYNASTY

During the nine hundred years that they ruled, at least in name, the Zhou greatly extended China's borders. Where the Shang had been content to rule a relatively restricted segment of north-central China on either side of the Yellow River, the Zhou reached out almost to the sea in the east and well into Inner Mongolia in the west. We know much more about the Zhou era than the Shang because an extensive literature survives. Much history was written, and records of all types from tax rolls to lists of imports and exports are found. The dynasty falls into two distinct phases: the unified empire, from about 1100 to about 750, and the Later Zhou, from about 750 to about 400 B.C.E. The earlier period was the more important. The Later Zhou dynasty experienced a series of constant

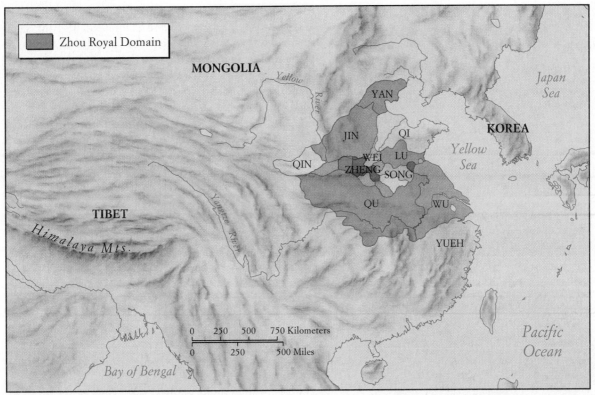

● **MAP 7.2 The Era of Warring States.** By the 500s B.C.E., the domain of the Zhou dynasts had become only a minor state surrounded by autonomous principalities.

provincial revolts until, finally, the central government broke down altogether (see Map 7.2).

One of the novelties of the Zhou period was the idea of the **mandate of heaven.** To justify their forcible overthrow of the Shang, the first Zhou rulers developed the idea that "heaven," that is, the supernatural deities who oversaw all life, gave the chosen earthly ruler a mandate, or vote of confidence. So long as he ruled well and justly, he retained the mandate, but it would be taken from him if he betrayed the deities' trust. A ruler who failed to protect his people from invaders or failed to contain internal revolt had betrayed this trust. Thus, if a Chinese ruler fell to superior force or a successful conspiracy, it was a sign that he had "lost the mandate" and deserved to fall. This marvelously self-serving theory—it was used to justify innumerable conspiracies and rebellions—was to be highly influential in Chinese history.

The first Zhou kings were powerful rulers, who depended mainly on their swords. The royal court employed hundreds of skilled administrators, and it is in the Zhou era that the faint beginning of a professional bureaucracy can be seen. China led the world in this development, as in so many others. As the centuries passed, however, a feudal society developed, in which the kings delegated more and more of their military and administrative duties to local aristocrats. These men stood to gain from the acquisition of new territory, and they did so at every chance. As a result, China expanded, but at the same time the control of the royal government weakened. By the 500s, the local aristocrats were in command of much of the empire, and by 400, the central power had broken down completely—one of the few times that has happened in China.

Culture and Daily Life under the Zhou

Although the Zhou rulers eventually failed to keep the nation together, their era saw great advances in every area of arts and crafts. *Bronze work,* exemplified in all manner of vessels and statues, reached an apex of perfection; much of it was produced using the "lost wax" method of casting into molds. This allowed great delicacy of form and design. *Iron* came into common use for tools and utensils, as well as weapons.

■ **A Bronze Vessel.** The form of bronze casting known as *cir perdue* (lost wax) was used by the Zhou dynasty artists; it enabled them to achieve a fine detailing of the surface.

Wars were common also, and the use of the war chariot led to a technical breakthrough of the first rank: a *horse harness* that allowed the horse to pull with the full strength of its shoulders and body without choking. This type of harness transformed the value of horses, not only in warfare but as beasts of burden. Only much later did other civilizations recognize and copy this fundamental change.

Agriculture was advanced by the invention of the iron-tipped plow, which allowed much more land to be tilled than could be plowed with the previous wooden plow. Iron blades of various sorts, sickles, and knives also increased agricultural production and allowed the growth of large cities like Loyang, the capital of the Later Zhou. The evidence we have suggests that Chinese peasants were moderately prosperous and rarely enslaved at this time.

Although their life was undoubtedly hard, it was not miserable. Zhou peasants were in more or less the same economic situation as Egyptian peasants; that is, they were sharecropping tenants with some rights and were protected from grasping landlords by a respected government.

In the *literary arts,* most of the classics that have been taught to Chinese children ever since originated in the Zhou era. The earliest surviving books stem from the 800s B.C.E., much earlier than any books that survive from other civilized centers. Professional historians, employed by the court, wrote chronicles of the rulers and their achievements. Poetry makes its first appearance in Chinese letters during the early Zhou, beginning a tradition of sensitive, perceptive nature poetry that continues to the present day. *Calligraphy* also began at this time, and officials were expected to master this art form as a qualification for office. *Silk* was already a major item of luxury trade in the Zhou era; traces of Chinese silk have been unearthed from as far away as the Greek city-states of the classical age.

✣ CONFUCIUS AND THE CONFUCIAN PHILOSOPHY

China's greatest single cultural force, the historical figure Kung Fu-tsu (551–479) or *Confucius,* appeared toward the end of the Zhou era. The son of an aristocratic family that had lost its money, he had every reason to expect a fine career in the growing cadre of bureaucrats serving the local lords. He wandered throughout China's eastern provinces, looking for a position which would reflect his merits. Instead, he became a teacher of the sons of the aristocrats and through these disciples found a far greater fame than any official could hope to achieve. When he died, he thought himself a failure; but within two centuries he was the most famous philosopher of his nation, and within four centuries he had become a master teacher to all educated Chinese. For twenty centuries Confucius was the most respected name in China, the molder of Chinese education and the authority on what a true Chinese should and should not do (see the Biography in this chapter).

After Confucius's death, his disciples collected his sayings in a book of wisdom called the *Analects.* Confucius's interests were centered on the relations between individuals, and especially between the citizenry and the governor. He had little inclination to wonder about humans' relationship with God or about the afterlife. In Confucius one sees most clearly why the Chinese are called a secular people.

The great model for Confucius's politics was the Chinese family. In his view, the state should be like a well-run family: the father was the undisputed head, each person had his or her special rights and duties, and the wisdom of the aged guided the young. The oldest male was responsible for protecting and guiding the others, who owed him absolute obedience even when he was wrong.

Confucius insisted on *gentility*—that is, courtesy to all, justice, and moderation—as the chief virtue of the public man. He taught that the rich and the strong should feel a sense of obligation toward the poor and the weak. A gentleman was made, not born. An aristocrat might not be a gentleman, while a lowborn person could learn to be. Much of the true value of education was in learning to be a gentleman, and for that reason education must be open to all who had the talents to make use of it. The proper calling of a gentleman was government. He should advise the ruler and see to it that government policies were fair and promoted the general welfare. The effective ruler was like a good father to his people and would make constant use of the talents of his gentlemanly advisers. Such a ruler would retain the mandate of heaven.

This philosophy of public service by scholarly, virtuous officials was to have enormous influence on China. Rulers came to be judged according to whether or not they made use of the Confucian prescriptions for good government. A corps of officials educated on Confucian principles and believing him to be the Great Teacher came into existence; these **mandarins,** as the West later called them, were the actual governing class of China for two thousand years.

■ The Chinese mastery of saying much with little in their arts is demonstrated here. These comic wood figures date from the early Zhou.

■ **Warriors.** These clay statuettes of imperial army men date from approximately the third century B.C.E. Their upraised hands once held spears and swords.

Confucius
551–479 B.C.E.

The most revered of all Chinese statesmen and philosophers was Master Kung, or Kung Fu-tzu, who is known as Confucius in the West. As a lasting influence upon a nation, he has no match in world history. During his long lifetime (551–479 B.C.E.), he acquired a devoted group of followers who gave educated Chinese their moral and ethical landmarks for two thousand years. Confucianism has, of course, evolved considerably over the centuries, and no one now knows precisely what the Master's original thoughts may have been. But by reading what his disciples said about him and about their own understanding of his message, we can appreciate his greatness and his importance in the life of the Chinese people.

Confucius was born into an impoverished but aristocratic family in the state of Lu at the time when the Zhou empire was falling apart and the Era of the Warring States was beginning. Given a good education, the young man set out to find a suitable place for himself in the world. His ambition was to acquire a post in the government of his home state, which would allow him to exert a real influence for good and to assist the princely ruler in providing wise and benevolent rule.

Frustrated by the intrigues of his rivals in Lu, where he briefly obtained a post in the ministry of justice, Confucius was forced to seek a position elsewhere. But in the neighboring states, too, he was disappointed in his quest, never securing more than minor and temporary positions before running afoul of backbiting competitors or speaking his mind when that was a dangerous thing to do. He had to return to Lu to earn his living as a teacher, and for the rest of his life, he subsisted modestly on the tuition fees of his wealthier students. Confucius accepted this fate with difficulty; for many years he continued to hope for appointment as an adviser to the prince and thus to translate his beliefs into government policy. Only gradually did he realize that by his teaching he could have more influence upon the fate of his people than he might ever attain as a minister to a trivial and corrupt ruler. By the end of his life, his fame had already reached much of China's small educated class, and his students were going out to found schools of their own, reflecting the principles the Master had taught them.

Confucius taught that all human affairs, public and private, were structured by the Five Relationships: father and son, husband and wife, elder and younger

One of the unfortunate and unexpected results of this system was the tendency of most rulers to interpret Confucian moderation and distrust of violence as an *endorsement of autocratic rule* and resistance to change. The rulers naturally tended to see in Confucius's admonition that the state should resemble a well-run family a condemnation of revolt for any reason. In time many of the Confucian-trained bureaucrats came to agree and to believe that the status quo was the natural and proper way of doing things. The insistence that harmony was the chief goal of politics and social policy sometimes was twisted into an excuse for stagnation; it led to a contempt for the new and a fear of change, which from time to time in China's long history have led to acute problems.

✤ RIVALS TO CONFUCIUS

In the later Zhou period, two rival philosophies arose to challenge the Confucian view. Neither was as successful in capturing the permanent allegiance of the educated classes, but both were sometimes seized on as an alternative to the Great Teacher.

Daoism

Daoism (Taoism) is a philosophy centered on Nature and following the Way (*Dao*) it shows us. It was supposedly the product of a teacher-sage called **Lao Zi** (*Lao-tzu*), who purportedly was a near contemporary of Confucius, but may be entirely legendary. The book attributed to him, the

brother, ruler and official, and friend with friend. The fact that three of these relationships are within the family circle shows the Confucian emphasis on the family. He believed it to be the model and building block of all other social or political arrangements. This emphasis continues in Chinese life to this day.

Confucius was not so much an original thinker as a great summarizer and rephraser of the truths already currently embraced by his people. He did not attempt a complete philosophical system and was not at all interested in theology or what is now called metaphysics. Rather, his focus was always on the relation of human being to human being, and especially on the relation of governor to governed.

Two of the sayings attributed to him in the *Analects* will give the flavor of his teaching:

Tsi-guang [a disciple] asked about government. Confucius said: "Sufficient food, sufficient armament, and sufficient confidence of the people are the necessities."

"Forced to give up one, which would you abandon first?"

"I would abandon armament."

"Forced to give up one of the remaining two, which would you abandon?"

"I would abandon food. There has always been death from famine, but no state can exist without the confidence of its people."

The Master always emphasized the necessity of the ruler setting a good example:

Replying to Chi Gang-tsi who had asked him about the nature of good government, Confucius said, "To govern is to rectify. If you lead the people by virtue of rectifying yourself, who will dare not be rectified by you?"

famous **Book of Changes** (***Dao de Jing***), was probably written by his followers much later.

Unlike Confucius, Daoism sees the best government as the least government, and the people as being inherently unable and unwilling to govern themselves. The responsibility of the ruling class is to give the people the justice and good administration that they are unable to devise for themselves. In so doing, the rulers should follow the Way of Nature, as it is perceived through meditation and observation. All extremes should be avoided, even those meant to be benevolent. The truly good ruler does little except *be*; excessive action is as bad as no corrective action.

Daoism has taken so many forms through the centuries that it is almost impossible to provide a single description of it. Originally, it was a philosophy of the educated classes, but it eventually degenerated into a superstition of the peasants. Yet for many centuries, it was a serious rival of Confucius's ideas and was often adopted by Chinese seeking harmony with the natural world and escape from earthly conflicts. This dichotomy was summed up in the saying that the educated classes were "Confucian by day, Daoist by night"; that is, in their rational, public lives they abided by Confucian principles; in the quiet of their beds, they sought immersion in mysterious, suprarational Nature.

Dao De Jing of Lao Zi

Confucian philosophy was by no means universally accepted in ancient China; it had to overcome several rival points of view among the educated class and was only partly successful in doing so. Among the ordinary people, Daoism was always stronger because it lent itself more readily to personal interpretation and to the rampant superstitions of the illiterate.

The **Dao de Jing** or "the way," is a collection of sayings attributed to Lao Zi (Lao tzu), who supposedly lived in the sixth century B.C.E. Like much Chinese philosophy, the essence of the Dao de Jing is the search for balance between opposites, between the *Yin* and *Yang* principles. Unlike Confucianism, Daoism puts little faith in reason and foresight as the way to happiness; instead, it urges its followers to accept the mystery of life and stop striving for a false mastery. It delights in putting its truths into paradox.

Chapter II

- It is because every one under Heaven recognizes beauty as beauty, that the idea of ugliness exists.
- And equally, if every one recognized virtue as virtue, this would create fresh conceptions of wickedness.
- For truly Being and Non-Being grow out of one another;
- Difficult and Easy complete one another;
- Long and Short test one another;
- High and Low determine one another.
- The sounds of instruments and voice give harmony to one another.
- Front and Back give sequence to one another.
- Therefore the Sage relies on actionless activity,
- Carries on wordless teaching. . . .

Chapter IV

- The Way is like an empty vessel
- That yet may be drawn from

- Without ever needing to be filled.
- It is bottomless; the very progenitor of all things in the world.
- In it is all sharpness blunted,
- All tangles untied,
- All glare tempered,
- All dust smoothed.
- It is like a deep pool that never dries.
- Was it, too, the child of something else? We cannot tell.

Chapter IX

- Stretch a bow to the very full
- And you will wish you had stopped in time;
- Temper a sword edge to its very sharpest,
- And you will find that it soon grows dull.
- When bronze and jade fill your halls
- It can no longer be guarded.
- Wealth and position breed insolence
- That brings ruin in its train.
- When your work is done, then withdraw!
- Such is Heaven's Way.

Chapter XI

- We put thirty spokes together and call it a wheel;
- But it is on the space where there is nothing that the utility of the wheel depends.
- We turn clay to make a vessel;
- But it is on the space where there is nothing that the utility of the vessel depends.
- We pierce doors and windows to make a house;
- But it is on these spaces where there is nothing that the utility of the house depends.
- Therefore, just as we take advantage of what is, we should recognize the utility of what is not.

SOURCE: *The Way and Its Power: A Study of the Dao de Qing.* A. Waley, editor, translator © 1934.

Legalism

Legalism was more a philosophy of government than a philosophy of private life. It was popularized in the **Era of Warring States** (c. 400–c. 225 B.C.E.) between the collapse of central Zhou dynastic authority (around 400 B.C.E.) and the rise of the Qin emperor in the 240s. The general breakdown of authority that characterized this period provided the motivation for Legalist ideas.

The Legalists were convinced that a government that allowed freedom to its subjects was asking for trouble. Legalism was a rationalized form of governmental ma-nipulation. It was not so much a philosophy as a justifica-tion for applying force when persuasion had failed. The basis of Legalism was the conviction that most people are inclined to evil selfishness, and it is the task of government to restrain them and simultaneously to guide them into doing good, that is, what the governors want. This task is to be accomplished by controlling people even before their evil nature has manifested itself in their acts. In other words, the Legalists advocated strict censorship, pre-scribed education (differing by class), and immediate crushing of any signs of independent thought or action.

Summary

The civilization of China originated in the northern plains near the Yellow River in the second millennium B.C.E. Under the first historical dynasties of the Shang and the Zhou, this agrarian civilization displayed certain charac-teristics that were to mark China for many centuries to come: reverence for ancestors, the tremendous impor-tance of the family, and the prestige of the educated. Fine arts and literature were cultivated in forms that persisted: bronzeware, ceramics, silk, historical literature, and nature poetry.

The breakdown of central government that ended the long Zhou dynasty and introduced the Era of Warring States demanded further definition of basic values, and these were given by the three great schools of practical philosophy that arose between 500 and 250 B.C.E.: Confu-cianism, Daoism, and Legalism. Of these, the most signifi-cant for later Chinese history was the secularist, rationalist thought of Confucius, the Sage of China for the next two thousand years.

In a later chapter, we shall investigate how the Chinese government and state were definitively formed in the second and first centuries B.C.E. But Chinese culture, as distinct from the state, was already shaped by 500 B.C.E. and would not change much until the modern era. The emphasis on the family, the respect due to elders, the subordination of women to men, the focus on this life on earth rather than on a life to come, and the lofty position of the educated were already deeply rooted in Chinese society long before the Romans had established their empire.

In the next chapter the focus returns to the West, specifically, to the cradle of much of later Western civili-zation, the society of classical Greece.

Test Your Knowledge

1. China's geography
   a. isolated it from other civilizations.
   b. was semi-tropical.
   c. is much like that of Mesopotamia.
   d. made it a natural marketplace and exchange point.
2. The Shang dynasty was established in northern China at roughly the same time as the
   a. rise of the Assyrians.
   b. Aryan conquest of northern India.
   c. beginnings of Sumerian civilization.
   d. first dynasty in Egypt.
3. The craftsmen under the Shang are best known for their
   a. fine ceramics.
   b. wood carving.
   c. bronzes.
   d. stonework.

4. After seizing power from the Shang, the Zhou rulers adopted
   a. a theory of government justifying their action.
   b. a militarized dictatorship.
   c. a theocracy where the priests had true powers.
   d. a democracy.
5. A significant long-term advantage of the Chinese style of writing is its
   a. easiness to learn.
   b. independence of regional dialects.
   c. effective use of an alphabet.
   d. great complexity.
6. Early Chinese religious thought is noteworthy for
   a. its insistence on the existence of only two gods.
   b. its emphasis on devotion to the spirits of the ancestors.

c. its superstition about heaven and hell.
   d. its clear theology.
7. In many aspects of philosophy, Chinese thought generally aimed
   a. at attaining union with the immortal gods.
   b. at inspiring loyalty and fear in the common people.
   c. at teaching myths and magical formulas.
   d. at attaining harmony and avoiding disorder on earth.
8. Daoist political views emphasized that
   a. people get the government they deserve.
   b. people are naturally evil and that government must restrain them.
   c. people should be enslaved to ensure peace.
   d. people should be left to their own devices as much as possible.

Identification Terms

Book of Changes (*Dao de Jing*)
Era of the Warring States

Lao-zi
oracle bones
mandarin

mandate of heaven
Shang dynasty
Yangtze River

Yellow River
Zhou dynasty

Bibliography

Creel, H. G. *The Birth of China,* 1967. A good introduction to Chinese history.

———. *What Is Taoism,* 1959 and *Confucius and the Chinese Way,* 1960. Outstanding explanations of these religions/philosophies by one of the best interpreters of early China to English speakers.

Fairbank, J. K., et al. *East Asia: Tradition and Transformation,* 1973. Deals with both Japan and China.

Goldschmidt, D. L., and J. C. Moreau-Gobard. *Chinese Art* (1962). Includes many first-rate photos of early Chinese paintings and bronzework.

Karlgren, B. *The Chinese Language,* 1949. Makes this obscure topic come alive and demonstrates how important a single written language was for Chinese history.

Liu, Z. *Ancient India and Ancient China,* 1988. Sheds light on both nations in early times.

Loewe, M. *Imperial China,* 1965. Its early sections are a good place to begin with Chinese history.

Schirokauer, C. *A Brief History of the Chinese and Japanese Civilizations,* 1989. Shorter than Fairbank et al., *East Asia,* but not better.

Smith, B. *China: A History of Art.* Many photos of early Chinese paintings and bronzework.

Sullivan, M. *The Arts of China,* 1984. Has good illustrations and a wide range.

Waley, A., trans. *Analects,* 1938. A very readable translation of the Confucian *Analects.*

———. *Three Ways of Thought in Ancient China,* 1956. An easy introduction to the meaning and differences among Confucianism, Daoism, and Legalism.

CHAPTER 8

ORDINARY LIVES IN THE ANCIENT PAST

EARNING A LIVING
FAMILY AND INDIVIDUAL RELATIONS
WOMEN: THEIR STATUS IN SOCIETY
Marriage and Motherhood
Sexual Life
EDUCATION OF CHILDREN

This chapter deals with the ancient civilizations between c. 3000 and 500 B.C.E. studied in the earlier chapters.

In recent years, many historians of ancient civilizations have shifted their attention from the traditional accounts of the doings of kings and generals to those of average men and women. This history "from the bottom up" is a challenging task; the ancient records and chronicles tell us little about the lives of ordinary people. What is known has had to be reconstructed from the scraps of information available. Much will always remain unknown, of course. Much else can be guessed at, but lacks certainty.

In the following pages, we will look at three distinct, but related aspects of the four chief centers of early civilization: Mesopotamia, Egypt, India, and China. One aspect will be basic economics: how ordinary persons were employed and how they secured themselves (if indeed they could) against the universal fear of famine and misery. Another will be family relations: parent and child, man and wife, individual and kin. Then we will look at the status of women, both within the home and outside it. Marriage and divorce, differences between free women and slaves, and the clash between patriarchal tradition and the aspirations of talented women will be given special attention. Comparisons and contrasts among these ancient societies will be drawn wherever enough information is known.

✤ EARNING A LIVING

All early civilizations had an advanced center (town, city) that drew its necessities from a surrounding countryside subject to it. This model seems to have been universal, differing only in the size and complexity of the urban areas.

The largest and most differentiated cities were those of Mesopotamia, some of which may have had populations in excess of 100,000. The ancient Indus civilization also developed large cities, but Egypt and China were originally much more agrarian in nature. There the normal living environment was the farmers' village rather than the town.

Many different trades and business were conducted in these cities and villages, although the variety was by no means as great as in a modern society. The most common occupation, by far, was tending and tilling the land—*farming*. The land was worked variously with sharecroppers, free peasants, or slave labor. What was grown varied considerably, of course, depending on the climate and terrain, tradition, and knowledge. But everywhere some type of grain was the essential crop. Bread was indeed the "staff of life."

The land itself was sometimes leased and sometimes owned by the individual family; more often, it was the collective possession of the entire village and was rotated about from family to family according to the changing needs of each generation. Most commonly of all, the land was not divided into plots with exact boundaries, but was sown and harvested through the communal effort of the whole village or clan. The crops were then divided up according to both tradition and need.

It is now thought that both agriculture and the domestication of animals began quite independently in different places at differing times (see Chapter 1). Both these activities certainly began in the Neolithic Age in the Middle East, the Nile valley, and East Asia. For example, pigs and chickens seem to have been domesticated first in Southeast Asia, and horses almost certainly were first domesticated in central Asia. Sheep and goats as herd animals are western Asian in origin. The first of all tamed animals was probably the dog, which has been "man's friend" since before the Neolithic Age.

The vast majority of people at this time drew their livelihood either from the land directly, as farmers and herders, or indirectly, as carters, wine pressers, millers, or any of the dozens of other occupations that transformed agrarian products into food and drink and delivered them to the consumer. As we know from both historical and archaeological evidence of many kinds and from many places, commerce was also primarily concerned with trade in foodstuffs, grain above all. It is very easy for us to forget just how much of the time and energy of the early civilizations went into the pursuit of sufficient caloric intake! Three square meals a day were often the exception and rarely to be taken for granted by the ordinary person.

Not all occupations involved farming or foodstuffs. A few of the many nonagrarian occupations required education and a degree of formal training: scribes, bookkeepers, and the priesthood, for example. Although each civilization had some learned occupations, they varied in prestige and in the number of persons who practiced them.

In China, the difficulty of the written language meant that many years of careful practice were necessary before one was recognized as educated. Even a good-sized village might not have a single inhabitant who could read and write. In Egypt, on the other hand, we know that most villages had scribes, who could handle the secrets of hieroglyphics. Vedic India, for its part, was an almost entirely oral culture, and writing was insignificant in Indian cultural life until well into the first millennium C.E.

Finally, Mesopotamian city dwellers seem to have been literate to an unusual degree and took writing for granted as a normal part of daily life.

Many other occupations did not require literacy, but they did demand a lengthy period of apprenticeship. Most of these occupations were found in the towns. They included metalworking, leather work, jewelry-making, all types of ceramics, fine and rough carpentry, masonry, and other building trades. Besides these skilled jobs, there were shopkeepers, their clerks and errand boys, casual laborers available for any type of manual task, and a large number of trades connected with the production of clothing and textiles. Many people were also involved in the preparation, distribution, and sale of food, whether in shops or eating places such as taverns and street booths. One crucial task was something we in the twentieth century United States rarely think about: the obtaining of a regular supply of water. This was one of the most important tasks of women and children everywhere and took great amounts of time and labor.

Some civilized centers employed more of one type of labor than others, but overall there was a rough parity. Most jobs were in very small-scale enterprises; these were usually family owned and staffed, with perhaps two or three paid or slave laborers. *Slavery* was less common in some places than others, as we have already mentioned; but in all ancient societies except early Egypt and China, slaves made up a sizable portion of the working population and sometimes performed much of the particularly unpleasant or dangerous work (mining, serving as galley rowers, and handling the dead, for example). Such jobs were also often reserved for criminals or the pariahs of society, as in Vedic India.

Whether people were free or slaves often made little difference to their standard of living. Slaves were usually not maltreated by private owners. The free man or woman rarely knew abject misery in Egypt and Mesopotamia, it seems, although we have little information on which to base an opinion for many centuries. In India, China, and Persia, the harvests were less reliable, and the specter of famine appeared from time to time. In addition to the weather and the threat of natural catastrophes, people had to worry about war and epidemic diseases; nothing could be done about either except headlong flight. Even if all else went well, heavy taxes could be imposed without warning or recourse; for the ordinary person, evasion was very difficult.

Many modern authorities believe that everywhere the main cause of human misery has been *overpopulation*. Where too many mouths are competing for a resource

■ Threshing the village grain.

that is scarce either because the supply is too small or because it is too poorly distributed, the results are much the same: social deprivation and anarchy. But as a continuing problem, overpopulation is a modern dilemma. In all of the ancient civilizations we have looked at thus far, overpopulation was a rarity. When it occurred, it was soon corrected by migration, famine, or disease, and supply and demand were brought back into balance.

All in all, though life in many areas could indeed be short and miserable, it is difficult to show that it was any worse, in a material sense, for Everyman and Everywoman in the ancient world than it was until a century or two ago. The basic economic institutions of the early civilized societies may appear primitive to us, but they worked quite well in providing their inhabitants with a degree of security and predictability and the necessities of human existence.

✤ FAMILY AND INDIVIDUAL RELATIONS

The near universal arrangement of ancient civilization was a **patriarchy,** exercised through an extended family or group of families (clan) living in close proximity. All four of our early centers were strongly patriarchal in nature, just as their hunting and gathering predecessors had been. (There is some evidence of a very early period of **matriarchy** in Neolithic China.) The move toward female-centered religions, which accompanied the development of agriculture, was reversed, according to some opinion,

when the beast-drawn plow was introduced. To control the heavier plow, the strength of a male was necessary.

Civilization had the effect of distributing powers formerly held tightly by one or a few individuals in the precivilized era. Within the tribe or clan, the leadership was fragmented as the clan became divided into specialized labor groups. Soon the **nuclear family** emerged as the fundamental unit of society although the **extended family** (uncles, in-laws, and other relatives) was still important.

The patriarchal system meant that the father was the undisputed head of the nuclear family and its lawgiver as well. He continued to have substantial power over his married children as well as over his unmarried sons and daughters. This power was clearest in the Judaic tradition but it was also the case among peoples as different as the Chinese and the Persians. When, for example, a Mesopotamian wife divorced her husband, the dowry she brought into the marriage reverted to her father, and if she had been the victim of her husband's illegal acts, the recompense (in money) was paid not to her, but to her father.

Children of both sexes were traditionally the property of their fathers and only incidentally attached to their mothers. The earliest natural scientists thought the father's semen was the fundamental source of a child's life and nature, while the mother's womb functioned as a carrying bag only. Among the Chinese, the *yin-yang principle* identified the female as the passive element and the male as the active, creative one.

Although all civilizations we have thus far studied gave pride of place to the father, none applied this principle so systematically as the Chinese. In ancient China, the father was accorded absolute obedience by children and grandchildren, while the mother supposedly never raised her voice in contradiction to her husband. A widow owed the same obedience to her father and sons. This arrangement remains the ideal in modern China, although one can question whether it is still a reality; there is no scarcity of reports of independent Chinese wives within the four walls of the home in modern times. But without a doubt, the principle of male superiority and female inferiority was adhered to and implemented systematically throughout Chinese history. For Confucius, whose teachings formed the basis of Chinese education for 2,300 years, women scarcely existed; he mentions them rarely and only in the context of male activity. As late as the seventeenth century, Chinese philosophers debated whether the female was fully human.

Wives everywhere were in either their father's or husband's power after marriage. In Hammurabi's law, the husband was the owner of his wife as well as his children and could pawn or sell her to settle a debt. This situation

The Eloquent Peasant

This story, whose author or authors are unknown, was probably written during the Middle Kingdom and certainly appears to have enjoyed widespread popularity at that time. It is debatable whether it was intended as a purely literary composition or was written primarily to illustrate the principles of ma'at and the workings of simple justice in Egypt under the pharaohs.

There once was a man named Khunanup, who was a peasant of the Wadi Natrun [salt field], and he had a wife named [Maryet]. . . . [Khunanup, while journeying through the country is cheated by a man named Djehutinakte, who illegally takes away his asses, and then has him beaten. When Khunanup protests, he is threatened with death] . . . And the peasant spent a period of ten days appealing to Djehutinakte, but he paid no attention to it.

So the peasant went to Ninsu to appeal to the High Steward Rensi . . . "O High Steward my lord, greatest of the great, guide of everything, if you go down to the Lake of truth, you shall sail on it with a fair breeze. . . . your ship will not lag . . . the current shall not carry you off, you shall not taste the evils of the river, you shall not see the face of fear, the darting fish shall come to you . . . because you are a father to the orphan, a husband to the widow, a brother to her who is divorced, a garment to the motherless . . . who destroys falsehood and fosters truth . . . I am heavy-laden; examine me, for see, I am in a loss." . . . [Amazed at the peasant's boldness, persistence and the articulate manner in which he appealed his case, Rensi reported this to pharaoh.] . . . "I have found one of these peasants who is really eloquent; his goods have been stolen, and see, he has come to appeal to me

about it." And His Majesty said: "As you wish me well, make him linger here without replying to anything that he has said. . . . And let his speech be brought to Us in writing. . . . But make provision for his wife and children. . . . Further, make provision for the Peasant himself." . . .

. . . [Khunanup returns to appeal for justice to Rensi no less than nine times, becoming increasingly frustrated, so that he begins to lose his sense of caution and to criticize Rensi for his apparent failure to live up to ma'at.] . . . "Do not speak falsehood, for you are great. . . .

"See, you are a wretch of a washerman, rapacious in injuring a friend. . . . See, you are a ferryman who ferries [over] only the possessor of a fare, a straight-dealing man whose straight-dealing has been cut off . . . see, you are the head of a storehouse who does not permit the needy man to pass . . . see, you are a purveyor whose joy is to slaughter . . . why, pray, do you not hear?" . . . And he [Rensi] caused two apparitors [servants] to attend to him with whips, and they belabored all his limbs therewith. . . .

[Despite the beating, Khunanup persists, and Rensi finally makes a judgment in the peasant's favor, sending a detailed record of all the proceedings to pharaoh.] . . . and it pleased him more than anything which was in this entire land. . . . Then Rensi . . . caused two apparitors to go to [fetch] Djehutinakte. . . . An inventory was made of [all his goods] . . . and Djehutinakte's [house was given to the] peasant, [together with] all his [goods].

SOURCE: Simpson, The Literature of Ancient Egypt. (1972), pp. 31–49. Used by permission.

was not modified for hundreds of years, and then only for the worse! We know less about the legal rights of wives and husbands in India and China in this earliest period, but there is no reason to think that women had any more rights than in Mesopotamia.

Adultery was always considered the worst of all possible offenses between husband and wife because it put the children's parentage under a cloud of doubt and thus undermined the family's continuity. Punishment for wifely adultery was frequently death, not only for her but for her lover if he was caught. It is important to note that adultery as a legal concept was limited to the wife's acts. The husband's sexual activity with slave girls or freeborn concubines, as he might see fit, was taken for granted. The "double standard" has existed since the beginnings of history.

In any society until modern days, the usual and fundamental *value of children* was economic, not emotional. Affection toward the small child was common and often encouraged, but the underlying source of that affection was the knowledge that if it lived to maturity, the child represented what we now term social security for the parents. In most families, children of either sex were also an important source of labor; the family was an economic unit, and children had well-defined roles to play in it. Only the wealthy could manage without their child's labor in the home, the shop, or the fields.

The principle of **primogeniture,** that the first-born legitimate male child took precedence in various ways over other children, was generally accepted. Older brothers had rights of inheritance over younger and were more likely to be given the father's social distinctions, where these were inheritable. Male children were normally more valued than female, if only because the daughters had to be given some type of dowry in order to obtain a husband.

In some societies, infanticide by abandonment, or **exposure** seems to have been commonly practiced. Historians are engaged in an ongoing debate as to whether infanticide was a deliberate form of population control practiced by the entire society, a measure resorted to only by the desperate poor, or simply a way of getting rid of unwanted females. Certainly, a large number of the prostitutes and tavern girls in the Roman era were picked up as abandoned babies and raised to their later professions by brothel keepers. What seems to us a shocking, heartless crime was, in fact, not considered an offense at all but a matter of private conscience.

✤ WOMEN: THEIR STATUS IN SOCIETY

Recently, there has been much comment on the fact that the history of ancient civilization has been written by and about men. Women play roles within this story only insofar as they are related to or used by the male actors. We know something about queens, royal concubines, and great poetesses, but very little at first hand about ordinary daughters, wives, and mothers. What we do know has been filtered through male consciousness, and we cannot be sure how that has affected the facts we are told. Certainly, there is a difference between the way women themselves see their lives and the way they are seen by the men around them.

In any case, historians generally agree on some categorical statements about the women of ancient Mesopotamia and Egypt:

1. In the very earliest stage of civilization, women shared more or less equally with men in social prestige and power.
2. This egalitarianism was undermined and overturned by the coming of militarized society (armies), the heavy plow in agriculture, and the establishment of large-scale trade.
3. The trend toward patriarchy and male dominance in public affairs of all sorts proceeded at varying speeds in different societies, but was impossible to reverse once it started.

Ancient law codes from Mesopotamia show a definite break between about 2000 B.C.E. and 1000 B.C.E., with Hammurabi's code being a transition. In the earliest codes (and to a lesser degree in Hammurabi's), the female enjoys extensive rights; by about 1200, she is an object ruled by men. By the era in which the Old Testament was written (700 B.C.E. on), she scarcely exists as a legal or political entity, but has been subordinated to men in every way.

The Judaic Yahweh was very definitely a male lawgiver, speaking to other males in a society where women

■ This drawing of a granary at Mohenjo-Daro shows the working activities of both men and women. The bull carts are similar to those still in use in India today.

■ This photo shows how little the task of weaving has changed in Western Asia over three thousand years of civilization.

counted only as the relatives and dependents of men. The nomadic background of the Twelve Tribes of Israel is evident here, for nomads have a universal tendency to subordinate females and to consider them the possessions of their men. In the Old Testament, even when a Jewish woman acts in a self-assertive fashion, the point of her action is to secure some advantage or distinction for her menfolk, and not on her own behalf. Judith slays Holofernes not to avenge herself, but to secure the safety of her people. The reward of the heroine is not leadership, to which she never aspires, but an honorable place in the folk memory.

Because of the lack of historical documentation, the general position of women in the earliest Indian civilizations is unclear. Scholars have detected a few signs of equality or even a matriarchal society. With the arrival of the Aryan nomads, female status began a descent that continued in Hindu culture. According to Hindu tradition, the Laws of Manu, the mythical lawgiver, established the proper relation between the sexes once and for all: the woman was to serve and obey the male (see the Document in Chapter 6, page 60). Gradually, the rituals of *sati* (widow's suicide) and *purdah* (isolation from all nonfamily males) became established. The degree of female subordi-

nation varied according to caste. In the upper castes, women were subordinate to their men, but not to the extent that was expected in the Jewish or Chinese traditions, for example. The female *dharma* in all castes, however, was to care for her husband and her sons and honor her parents.

In China the male was always superior to the female in the public arena, and proper observance of religious customs (ancestor "worship") depended on him. It was through his blood that the family was preserved, and he was the equivalent of priest as well as ruler. The good wife was defined as the mother of male children who would keep the family name alive and honor the dead in the proper fashion.

In all four civilizations, most of the routine occupations were open to women as well as to men. Women could engage in business in their own name (but normally under a male relative's supervision). They could be priests, scribes, or tavern keepers, as well as housewives. But their proportional representation in the high-level jobs was much smaller than men's, and in all types of employment, they were normally acting under male supervision or as a man's agent or deputy. Very rarely did a woman operate completely independently. For a woman from an upper-class family, working outside the home was unheard of, unless she became a priestess or took a similar position that brought honor with it.

Female slaves were everywhere, both inside and outside the home. Free women and slaves often worked side by side. Some occupations were dominated by free persons, others by slaves, but most had room for both. Even relatively poor families had a domestic slave or two, who helped with housework and child care and often had a secure place within the household. These slave women had frequently been sold into slavery by destitute parents, who undoubtedly were correct in believing that their daughters would have a longer life expectancy as a slave than as a free person. The painful tradition of selling daughters into slavery persisted in China until well into the twentieth century.

Many house slaves were purchased to serve as a **concubine,** or "second wife," to the master of the household. This practice was particularly common in childless marriages, when the husband began to worry about his lack of posterity. The offspring of such arrangements were generally treated as legitimate. The husband in a childless marriage normally was encouraged by his wife to take another woman, because the continuation of the family name was as crucial to her as to him—it had become her name at her marriage. If this second wife did not produce male children, the husband often adopted a son from among his clan relations.

Marriage and Motherhood

Marriage and motherhood were, of course, the chief concerns of females everywhere. In all ancient civilizations, the production of male posterity was the chief duty of a good wife. Marriage was always arranged by the two families—something so important could never be left to chance attraction. A great many of the clay tablets dug up in the Mesopotamian ruins deal with marital contracts. Some of them were made when the bride and groom were still babies. Such early arrangements were especially common for girls, who normally were considerably younger at marriage than their husbands. The age of menarche (onset of menstruation) seems to have been about fourteen on average in West Asia; girls were considered capable of bearing children, and therefore marriageable, at age twelve in China and India. One must distinguish, however, between a formal betrothal, or engagement, and the beginning of cohabitation, that is, sharing bed and board, which came later—perhaps years later.

Marriage usually involved the exchange of "bride money" and a dowry. Bride money was a payment by the groom's family to the bride's family as specified in the marital contract; the dowry was also specified in the contract and was paid by the bride's family to the groom when the couple began to cohabit. The dowry remained in the husband's control as long as the marriage lasted; when the wife died, the dowry was distributed among her children, if she had had any.

Divorce and lawsuits arising from it were frequent in Mesopotamia, as the tablets attest. Most divorces were initiated by husbands, who were disappointed by childless wives or were sexually attracted to another woman and did not wish to or could not support the first wife as well. The lawsuits came as a result of the wife or her father protesting the lack of provision made for her support or the husband's attempt to retain her dowry. Then as now, the lawyers must have relied on divorce proceedings for a substantial part of their income.

Of all the ancient civilizations, the Chinese wife's lot was probably the hardest. Wife beating was taken for granted among the ordinary people, as it would be for many generations. Divorce at the wife's request was rare, though it could be granted for abandonment or criminal action. One of the most admired women in Chinese folklore was a wife who defied her own family's wishes to stay with a husband who was utterly worthless. Virginity

before marriage and submissive loyalty afterward were the great virtues for a woman.

In China as in most places, *the wife moved in with her husband's family* and became a part of it. The mother-in-law was the jealous supervisor of the household, living with the young couple (or couples) who shared the home or the compound of connected houses. China's folk literature is filled with stories about the mean-hearted persecution of young wives by sour mothers-in-law. The older women had the approval of society: they were acting, supposedly, as protectors of their son's honor and property. This is one more instance of the female who can only assert herself as the agent of the male, in this case, her son.

Sexual Life

The *sexual nature* of the society was more openly discussed in some of the ancient civilizations than others. In China's early literature, sex is treated discreetly, if at all. In contrast, the people of the Near and Middle Eastern centers had little inhibition by modern standards, while the artistic and literary records of ancient India display an absolute joy in the body's sexual powers. Since children and the continuity of the family were the real reasons for marriage, the marital bed was an honorable and even sacred place, and what took place there was in no way shameful. But the male and female had desires that went beyond the creation of children, and these were also nothing to be ashamed of, for these desires were implanted in humans by the all-wise gods. The result was a fundamentally different sexual attitude than we commonly find today. In the Near East, the rites of the "Sacred Marriage" between a god and his high priestess, celebrating the fertility of the earth and of all creatures on it, were central to religious practice. In both the Near East and India, orgies were frequently included in the ceremonies honoring the gods and goddesses.

In India, the female was often seen as being more sexually potent than the male. This conviction, it is now argued, arose from men's fears about the "devouring woman," represented in Hindu art by the ferocious goddess of destruction, Kali. Some equivalent of the devouring woman, who is sexually insatiable and physically overpowering, is found in several ancient religions whose rites were developed by men (as kings and priests). It is notably absent from those that arose during a period of female predominance (matriarchy), or when the sexes were more or less equal in public affairs. The tensions between the sexes are thus reflected in differing views of the sexual instinct and its satisfaction from earliest times.

■ This sketch depicts the organized walled cityscape of Mohenjo-Daro. Houses had open-air central courtyards, and many street intersections had public wells.

Every ancient culture insisted that brides should be virgins; this was one of the reasons for the early marriage of women. Although many literary and folk tales describe the horrible fate that awaited a woman who lost her virginity before marriage, it is still quite clear that love-making between young unmarried persons was by no means unheard of and did not always result in shame. Loss of virginity was looked upon as damage to the family's property rather than a moral offense; as such, it could be made good by the payment of a fine. Punishment for seducing a virgin was less severe than for adultery or rape. Some authorities believe that the early stages of civilization in all areas were more tolerant of nonvirginal marriage for women than were later ones. If premarital relations were followed by marriage, very little fuss was made.

Prostitution was commonplace from very early times in all civilizations and was one of the most profitable employments of female slaves. Married and unmarried males were expected to make use of their services, which were available in every price range. Originating in many places as an element of a religious festival, the so-called temple prostitute soon had counterparts in the taverns found in every town. Women employed in taverns (or "public houses" as they are still called in Great Britain) were normally available for commercial sex. Prostitutes were definitely inferior in social standing to other women, free or slave, but they did possess certain legal rights and were protected to some slight degree from abuse by clients or pimps, as testimony in lawsuits from the Near East as early as 2000 B.C.E. and beyond demonstrates.

⚜ EDUCATION OF CHILDREN

Our information about the rearing of children is limited, but it is sufficient to make some points with certainty. Girls were treated very differently from boys and were given much less opportunity to advance beyond the fundamentals. Only a small proportion of the population, mostly in the urban areas, received any type of formal training.

A *male's education* depended entirely upon his social class. If he was born into an aristocratic or wealthy family, he would usually receive a basic education from a live-in tutor or be sent to "school" under the aegis of local wise men. If he showed promise, even a boy in a poor family might be sent to such a school by the collective sacrifices of his kinfolk or fellow villagers. A talented young man might undertake higher studies as the protégé of a priest, an official of the king, or a childless man who wished to adopt the pupil (by no means rare). In the Near East and Egypt, this higher study might be focused on mathematics, astrology, or theology; in China and Japan, it would more likely deal with philosophy, music, or etiquette.

Female education usually aimed at preparing the girl to meet the demands of the household. Spinning and weaving were necessary arts in every civilized society, even where slaves did the actual work. Most wives were expected to keep some sort of elementary budget, and a lower-class wife was frequently as involved in the shop or trade as her husband. We have many indications that both in Egypt and in the Mesopotamian cities women were employed as scribes and officials on occasion and that some women rose to high governmental office. (There were at least three female pharaohs; and we know that a queen of the Near Eastern Palmyra rose from slavery.) But these were clear exceptions to the rule and almost always resulted from prior relationships with powerful men.

Girls were invariably instructed in the household arts by their mothers, mothers-in-law, or older sisters before marriage. There were no schools for girls, nor were girls accepted into the male schools so far as is known. For the few girls who were deemed worthy of literacy, tutors were employed.

Summary

The social history of ancient times reveals sharp differences between the classes and between the sexes. Civilized living accentuated the chasm between rich and poor while multiplying the ways in which the two groups could be kept separated in daily life. The great majority worked with their hands, and most of them lived in a rural setting, working on the land in one way or another. While the villages continued to have only one class, the towns were increasingly stratified among the wealthy few, the less wealthy who were slightly more numerous, and working people of various skills who formed the majority.

The condition of women also varied according to class, but the female generally deferred to the male in every sphere of public life. Religion, commerce, government, the arts and sciences, and ownership of property were all dominated by the male in all four civilizations we examined. Females were cherished largely in relation to their fertility and the assistance they provided to males in the daily labor of life. While marital affection and romantic passion were by no means excluded, both sexes perceived the common lot of women in terms of willing, permanent subordination to a series of male overseers and protectors.

Test Your Knowledge

1. Which of these would most likely be able to read and write?
   a. A Jewish farmer
   b. A Mesopotamian craftsman
   c. An Indian shopkeeper
   d. An Egyptian villager
2. Slavery in ancient societies was most often the result of which combination of possibilities?
   a. Commission of crime and personal violence
   b. Prisoner of war and debt
   c. Blasphemy and defiance of the gods
   d. Debt and rebellion
3. The most common example of different standards of punishment for the same offense in ancient society was the handling of
   a. treason against the throne.
   b. adultery in marriage.
   c. theft of others' property.
   d. blasphemy against the gods.
4. Women's participation in ordinary trade and business was normally
   a. possible only in exceptional cases, where no males were available.
   b. a routine affair with full equality with males.
   c. common in the lower-status occupations, usually under some male supervision.
   d. common in the lower-status occupations, usually as independent agents.
5. In most societies that we know much about, the wife
   a. moved in with her husband's family as a junior member of the household.
   b. moved in with her husband, but lived apart from the rest of his family.

c. set up independent housekeeping with her husband apart from both families.

d. determined where the new couple would live.

6. As a general rule, the education of the two sexes in ancient times

a. was similar in the subjects taught and the methods employed.

b. was sharply divided by gender, with both boys and girls being systematically instructed.

c. was rarely undertaken by any formalized system of instruction.

d. was very limited for most girls and was the exception for boys of the lower classes.

7. Farming or tending animals was the normal way of making a living

a. for everyone in every ancient society.

b. for most people in most societies.

c. for those people who had access to irrigation.

d. for those who were not someone's slaves.

8. The usual fashion for educating a female child was

a. to send her off to a tutor.

b. to teach her necessary skills at home.

c. to have her compete with other females for a place in a school.

d. to charge her older brother with her instruction.

Identification Terms

concubine

exposure

nuclear and extended families

patriarchy

primogeniture

Bibliography

Beyond the items listed at the end of Chapters 2–7 for specific civilizations, the *Everyday Life* series is a superior source of information on how people ate, worked, dressed, and so on in a given epoch or locale. Some are much more easily digested than others: browse through them to discover what is useful.

Loewe, M. *Everyday Life in Early Imperial China* 1968.

Potter, K. H. *Guide to Indian Philosophy,* 1988. Casts light on many other topics besides formal philosophy.

Romer, J. *Ancient Lives: Daily Life in the Egypt of the Pharaohs,* 1984. A fine account of village life.

Saggs, H. W. F. *The Greatness That Was Babylon,* 1962 and *Everyday Life in Babylonia and Assyria,* 1987. Both look at society and its structures in the ancient Near East down to about the first century C.E.

Zhongshu, W. *Han Civilization,* 1982. Adds some detail on agriculture and architecture to Loewe's picture of early China.

PART 2

CLASSICAL MEDITERRANEAN CIVILIZATIONS

500 B.C.E.–500 C.E.

The use of the word *classical* to identify this thousand-year-long epoch requires a brief explanation. In the eastern Mediterranean and the East and South Asian river valley civilizations, the period from about 500 B.C.E. saw an impressive expansion and development of several branches of culture, especially philosophy, the arts, and language. The monuments and methodologies created then served as benchmarks for many centuries for the Mediterranean, Indian, and Chinese peoples; some have endured to the present day.

The two other early centers of civilization—Mesopotamia and the Nile valley—did not undergo similar expansion during this period, however. In Egypt, the heritage of two thousand years of cultural and political sovereignty was eroded by invaders from both Asia and Africa. After about 500 B.C.E., Egypt was under foreign masters and became ever more peripheral to the world's affairs. Somewhat similar was the fate of Mesopotamia, where ecological damage intensified the negative effects of the Persians' decision to locate their chief cities elsewhere.

A hallmark of the classical age was the larger territorial size of the civilized societies and their more pronounced cultural attractions for the nomadic barbarians on their fringes. Urban centers were both more numerous and more important. Economic sophistication was evident in the expanded long-distance trade for the more numerous upper classes and in the more refined instruments of payment and credit employed by the merchants. Social strata were more differentiated and more complex than in the ancient age, and social tensions more evident. Wars were fought on a much larger scale and provided the impetus for much development of government.

Knowledge of the natural world (that is, science) made great strides in certain fields, but remained paltry in many others. Technology, on the other hand, remained primitive in an age of easy access to slave labor. Supernatural and salvationist religions, especially Christianity, came to play an ever-increasing part in daily life after about 300 C.E. in the Mediterranean basin.

In this part of our book, we look at the classical civilization of the Mediterranean and western Europe, established first by the Greeks and then expanded and modified by Romans. (The classical age in South and East Asia will be the subject of much of Part 3.) Chapters 9, 10, and 11 outline the history of the Greeks from the Mycenaeans' rise to civilized life to the creation of the kingdoms after Alexander. Although we note the Greeks' debts to their Mesopotamian and Egyptian predecessors, our emphasis is on the remarkable two centuries between 500 and 300 B.C.E. Then follows the story of the rise, triumph, and decline of the Roman *imperium* between c. 500 B.C.E. and 400 C.E. This occupies Chapters 12, 13, and 14. Chapter 14 also examines the establishment and effect of early Christianity on Roman society. Chapter 15 provides a comparative look at daily life and work in the Hellenic, Hellenistic, and Roman cultures.

	Law and Government	Economy
GREEKS	Evolution of written law begins with Draco and Solon's reforms in the sixth centure B.C.E. Although property still outweighs personal freedoms, there is noticeable shift toward primacy of individual citizens. Strong differences still between enslaved and free, and alien and citizen in this wholly patriarchal society. Mass political activity within the framework of the polis is encouraged by democratic reforms of early fifth century in Athens. Sparta emerges as Athens' opposite pole after conquest of Messenia, and the Pelopponesian War prepares the way for Macedonian take-over in late fourth century. The polis ideals die out under alien rule and Hellenistic monarchies are established, which then fall to Roman overlords.	Small farms, pasturage, and home-crafts were at all times the backbone of the Greek economy. Relatively few natural resources. The absence of large fertile areas restricted the growth of plantation-like estates. Overpopulation became major problem by 600s B.C.E. and was solved by largescale emigration and creation of colonies by many poleis. In Hellenistic period, numbers of Greeks go into Middle East and Egypt as favored immigrants. Much inter-city and interregional trade, as well as with Egypt and eastern Mediterranean basin. Strong maritime orientation evident at all times. In pre-Common Era there was not much socioeconomic stratification among free persons, though slavery was common. Under Roman rule, Greece diminishes in economic importance and poverty is widespread.
ROMANS	Evolution of Roman law and government forms particularly marked over this millennium. Beginning with usual class-based justice and oral law, Roman republic produces written codes by fifth century B.C.E. and eventual balance of noble-commoner powers. The Punic wars and resultant imperial outreach corrupt this balance, however, and bring about social problems which cannot be solved peacefully. Augustus's administrative reforms answer most pressing needs for civic peace and stability for next two centuries, while law continues evolution on basis of equity and precedent until final distillation in *Corpus juris* of Justinian. The central government's authority sharply weakened in west by transfer to Constantinople and then destroyed by successive Germanic invaders after 370s C.E. Eastern provinces remain secure.	Small peasants were original citizenry, but after the Punic Wars are increasingly overshadowed by hordes of slaves and unfree immigrants from Africa and the eastern Mediterranean. Italy became dependent on food imports. Plantations and estates replaced farms, while the urban proletariat multiplied. After about 200 C.E., the western provinces were losing ground to the richer, more populous East, a process hastened by the Germanic invasions. Socio-economic reforms of Diocletian and Constantine (295—335 C.E.) do not stop declining productivity of Western provinces and resultant vulnerability to invaders.

CLASSICAL MEDITERRANEAN CIVILIZATIONS

Peoples: Greeks and Romans

Religion and Philosophy	Arts and Culture	Science and Technology
Greeks of Classical Age were founders of philosophy as a rational exercise. They also explored most of questions which have occupied Western philosophy in metaphysics, ethics, and epistemology. Religion was conceived of as a civic duty more than as a path to immortality. Lack of fear of the gods and of their priestly agents particularly striking. Gods seen as humans writ large, with faults and virtues of same. Theology and ethics sharply separated; the educated class turned to philosophy as a guide to ethical action. "Man the measure." After c. second century B.C.E., religion-philosophy divergence ever stronger as masses turned to mystery religions.	Classical Age brings brilliant flowering of both literary and plastic arts, giving many models for later Western civilization. Particular mastery of sculpture, architecture, poetry of several formats, drama, and history. In Hellenistic period, Roman overlords generally adopt Greek models for their own literature and sculpture, thus spreading them throughout western Europe. Greeks are patriarchal to point of misogyny in their public and private culture.	In the Classical Age, Greeks profited from their extensive contacts with Mesopotamia. Physical science was generally subordinated to philosophy in the broad sense, of which it was considered a branch. In Hellenistic period, physical sciences were selectively advanced, especially mathematics, physics, and medicine. At all times, little or no interest in technology apparent. Scientific knowledge was pursued for its own sake rather than for possible application.
Romans adopted notions of the supernatural and immortality from the Etruscans and Greeks, modifying them to fit their own civic religion. No connections between theology and ethics until advent of mystery religions, including Christianity. Christianity originally adopted to sustain faltering imperial rule, soon became the equal or even senior partner of the civil regime.	Art was of high technical quality, but lacked creative imagination in contrast to Greeks and Egyptians. Artists generally content to follow models from abroad in both plastic and literary forms. Exceptions: some minor literary genres, mosaic work, and architecture. Public life not so patriarchal as Greece but more affected by class divisions.	Roman science advanced only slightly from Hellenistic heritage. No interest in technology outside the engineering skills, which were a Roman specialty (road building, bridges, use of brick and cement, fortifications). As with Greeks, abundance of slaves argued against search for labor-saving techniques and devices.

THE GREEK ADVENTURE

c. 2000–c. 1100 B.C.E.	Mycenaean era
c. 1900–c. 1300 B.C.E.	Minoan civilization on Crete
c. 1100–c. 800 B.C.E.	Dark Age
c. 800–c. 300 B.C.E.	Hellenic Civilization
c. 500–c. 325 B.C.E.	Classical Age

The small, rocky peninsula in the eastern Mediterranean Sea called Greece proved to be the single most important source of later Western civilization. In this unpromising landscape emerged a vigorous, imaginative people who gave the later European and Western world a tradition of thought and values that is still very much alive.

The history of the ancient Greeks can be divided into three epochs: (1) The *Mycenaean* age lasted from c. 2000 B.C.E. to the conquest of the Greek peninsula by invaders in the 1100s. (2) The *Hellenic* period extended from the age of Homer to the conquest of the Greek city-states by the Macedonians in the mid-300s. It includes the Classical Age, when Greek philosophical and artistic achievements were most impressive. (3) The final period of Greek predominance was the *Hellenistic* Age, which lasted from c. 300 B.C.E. to the first century C.E.; during this age, Greeks interacted with eastern peoples to produce a hybrid culture that was extraordinarily influential upon the arts and science of both Western and Asian civilizations. This chapter will look at the political and social aspects of the Mycenaean and Hellenic periods, while Chapter 10 will focus on intellectual and artistic developments. Chapter 11 will examine the Hellenistic era.

✦ THE MYCENAEAN ERA

More than most societies, Greece was shaped by its *geography.* It is the tip of the European mainland that gradually sank beneath the Mediterranean many tens of thousands of years ago, leaving only the tops of a high mountain range as islands in the Aegean and eastern limits of the Mediterranean. Greece has very little suitable land for large-scale farming, no broad river valleys, and no level plains. No place in modern Greece is located more than 80 miles from the sea; dozens of protected harbors and bays can be found all along the coast. From a very early time, the Greeks became expert sailors, and ships and shipping have been a major part of their livelihood since ancient days. The mountains of the peninsula make overland travel very difficult, and it has almost always been easier to travel and trade by sea than by land.

Greek geography encouraged political fragmentation; the people in each valley and river basin developed their own sense of patriotism and identity, much as the people of our own Appalachians did. Greeks grew up thinking of themselves first as residents of a given place or town and

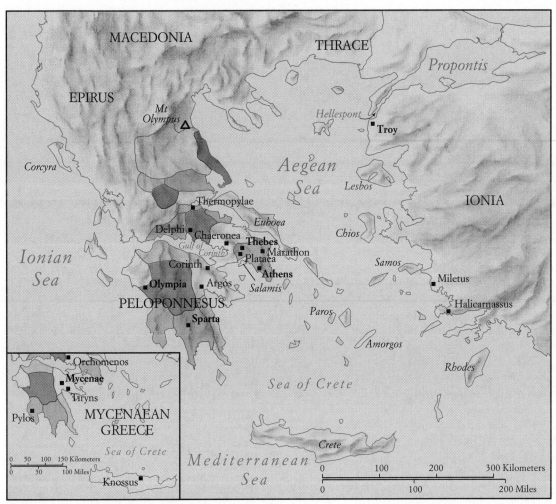

● **MAP 9.1 Early Greece.** At the height of Greek power, there were more than 200 independent *poleis,* many of them on the numerous islands of the Aegean Sea and the Ionian coast. A few were entirely urban; most combined a town with surrounding rural agricultural areas.

only secondarily as Greeks sharing a common culture and language with the other inhabitants of the peninsula.

The *first Greeks* to enter the peninsula came around 2000 B.C.E. as wandering nomads from the eastern European plains. By around 1600 they had become semicivilized, and some of them lived in fair-sized towns, notably *Mycenae* on the eastern side of the Peloponnesus (see Map 9.1). The people are known as the **Mycenaeans,** and the first few hundred years of Greek civilization are called the Mycenaean Age.

Our knowledge of this period comes largely from archaeological excavations and from the ***Iliad*** and the ***Odyssey,*** two epics of ancient Greece written by the

magnificent poet Homer in the eighth century B.C.E. The *Iliad* deals with the Mycenaeans' war against the powerful city-state of Troy, and the *Odyssey* tells of the adventures of the hero Odysseus (Ulysses) after the war (see the Document in this chapter). For a long time, historians believed that the Trojan War was simply a fiction created by a great poet about his ancestors. But thanks to archaeology, we know that there actually was a Troy and that it was destroyed about the time that Homer indicates— around 1300 B.C.E. Whether it was destroyed by the Greeks or not, we do not know, but there is no reason not to believe so. Ancient Troy, now a great pile of rubble, was situated on a hill commanding the entrance into the straits

Odysseus and the Cyclops

The Homeric hero Odysseus (Ulysses) served as one of the chief role models for the ancient Greeks. He embodied the qualities of craftiness and effective action that the Greeks considered most commendable in a man. The second of the ancient epics, the *Odyssey,* tells how the hero survived a perilous ten-year voyage home after the Trojan War. Living by his wits, he managed to extricate himself from one deadly situation after another until he was finally able to return to his family at Ithaka.

One of Odysseus's most formidable challenges came when he and his shipboard companions found themselves at the mercy of the dreadful one-eyed giant, the Cyclops. The Cyclops invited the sailors to land on his island and then entertained himself by dismembering and devouring the Greeks two at a time. Then the sly Odysseus devised his counterblow:

I, holding in my hands an ivy bowl full of the dark wine stood close up to the Cyclops and spoke out:

"Here, Cyclops, have a drink of wine, now you have fed on human flesh, and see what kind of drink our ship carried. . . ."

Three times

I brought it to him, and gave it him, three times he recklessly drained it, but when the wine had got into the brain of the Cyclops, then I spoke to him, and my words were full of beguilement. . . .

[The Cyclops falls asleep.]

I shoved the sharp pointed beam

underneath a bed of cinders, waiting for it to heat. . . .

when the beam of olivewood, green as it was, was nearly at the point of catching fire and glowed, terribly incandescent, then I brought it close up from the fire and my friends about me stood fast. . .

They seized the beam of olive, sharp at the end, and leaned on it into the eye [of the now sleeping giant], while I from above, leaning my weight on it

twirled it. . . and the blood boiled around the hot point, so that the blast and scorch of the burning ball singed all his eyebrows and eyelids, and the fire made the roots of his eye crackle. . . .

He gave a giant, horrid cry and the rocks rattled from the sound. . . .

[The now blinded Cyclops attempts to capture the Greeks by feeling for them, but they escape his wrath by suspending themselves beneath sheep that walk past him to the waiting boat.]

When I was as far from the land as a voice shouting carries, I called aloud to the Cyclops, taunting him:

"Cyclops, in the end it was no weak man's companions you were to eat by violence and force in your hollow cave, and your evil deeds were to catch up with you, and be too strong for you, ugly creature, who dared to eat your own guests in your own house, so that Zeus and the rest of the gods have punished you."

SOURCE: Excerpts from pages 146, 147, 149, from *The Odyssey of Homer* by Richard Lattimore. Copyright © 1965, 1967 by Richard Lattimore. Copyright Renewed. Reprinted by permission of Harper Collins Publishers, Inc.

of the Dardanelles. Much evidence indicates that the Greek towns, led by Mycenae, were engaged in commercial rivalry with Troy throughout this period and may well have made war upon their nearby enemy.

The Mycenaean civilization was inspired by the model of one of its trading partners and rivals: Crete. This large island supported an urbanized civilization of its own, dating back to at least 1900 B.C.E., when the Greeks on the mainland were still nomads. Historians and archaeologists call the Cretan culture Minoan after Minos, the mythical king of Crete. The Minoan towns, led by the town of *Knossos* on the northern coast, were evidently masters of a wide- ranging trade empire, including Greece, by about 1600 and had much to do with the civilizing of the Greeks.

■ This photo shows the extent of the massive heap of debris that now marks the site of Troy. It was originally excavated by the German amateur archaeologist Heinrich Schliemann in the 1870s.

The Minoans taught their pupils too well in some ways, however, and around 1400 the warlike Mycenaeans were able to turn on their teachers and destroy much of the island settlements, aided by either volcanic explosions or earthquakes. By about 1300 the high civilization of the Minoan Cretans was in ashes, and the island ceased to play an important role in Mediterranean affairs.

The Mycenaeans themselves seem to have engaged in extensive internal warfare among the competing towns. These civil wars weakened them sufficiently that they fell to a new wave of barbarians from the north, the *Dorians.* From about 1100 B.C.E. to about 800, the Greek peninsula declined, so much so that this period is called the *Dark Age.* Not only did arts and crafts decline, but even the ability to write seems to have been largely lost during these centuries. Whether the Dorians are to blame or whether, as many experts think, the Mycenaeans simply fought one another to mutual exhaustion is unclear. What is clear is that the achievements of the Mycenaeans were forgotten and the formerly urban civilization reverted to a rural, much less sophisticated one.

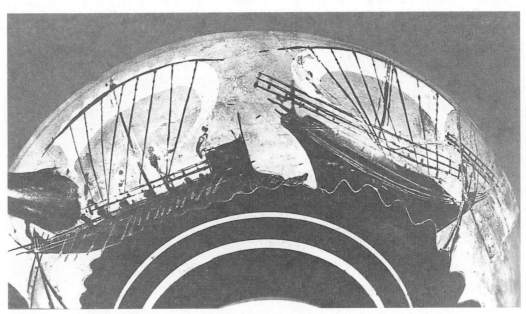

■ Greek merchant ships like the one painted on this vase c. 540 B.C.E., carried vessels containing oils, wines, and other merchandise to cities throughout the Mediterranean. Note the sharp ram on the prow of the vessel on the left, indicating its use as a warship when needed.

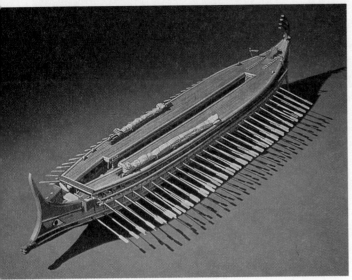

■ This reconstruction of a Greek trireme was built after study of contemporary vase paintings. It bears the three rows of oars that give the boat its name. Greek students volunteered to build the trireme in the 1980s.

✤ EARLY HELLENIC CIVILIZATION

Starting about 800 B.C.E., the Greek mainland slowly recovered the civilization it had created during the Mycenaean era. It then went on to far greater heights during its *Classical Age* (500–325 B.C.E.).

During the Dark Age, the peculiarly Greek institution of the **polis** gradually developed. In Greek, *polis* means the community of adult free persons who make up a town or any inhabited place. In modern political vocabulary, the word is usually translated as "city-state." A *polis* could be almost any size; classical Athens, the largest, had almost 300,000 inhabitants at its peak, while the smallest were scarcely more than villages. At one time the Greek mainland and inhabitable islands (all told, about the size of Maryland) were the home to more than two hundred *poleis*. Each thought of itself as a political and cultural unit, independent of every other. Yet each *polis* also thought of itself as part of that distinct and superior family of peoples calling themselves "Greek."

The *polis* was much more than a political and governmental unit; it established a frame of reference for the entire public life of its citizens and for private life as well. Not everyone who lived in a *polis* was a citizen; there were many resident aliens, who were excluded from citizenship, as were the numerous slaves. Women were also entirely excluded from political life. Basically, only free males of twenty years of age or more possessed full civil rights. That meant that as much as 80 percent of the population might be excluded from political life because of their gender, age, or social status.

Each *polis* had more or less the same economic design: a town of varying size, surrounded by farmland, pasture, and woods that supplied the town with food and other necessities. In the town lived artisans of all kinds, small traders and import-export merchants, intellectuals, philosophers, artists, and all the rest who make up a civilized society. Life was simpler in the countryside. Like all other peoples, the majority of Greeks were peasants, woodcutters, and ditch diggers of whom formal history knows very little except that they existed.

✤ ATHENS AND SPARTA

The two *poleis* that dominated Greek life and politics in the Classical Age were Athens and Sparta. They were poles apart in their conceptions of the "good life" for their citizens. Athens was the center of Greek artistic and scientific activity and was also the birthplace of political democracy. Sparta was a militaristic, authoritarian society that held the arts and intellectual life in contempt. Eventually, the two opposites came into conflict, and interestingly, it was the artistic, philosophic, and democratic Athenian *polis* that provoked the war that ultimately ruined Athens.

In general, four types of government were known to the Greeks:

1. A *monarchy* is rule by a single person, a king or equivalent (either sex) who has the final word in law by right. Most of the *poleis* were monarchies at one time or another, and many of them apparently began and ended as such.
2. An *aristocracy* is rule by those who are born to the leading families, whether or not they are particularly qualified in other ways. Aristocrats are born to the nobility, but not all nobles are born aristocrats.
3. An *oligarchy* is rule by a few, and almost always the few are the wealthiest members of society. Many *poleis* were ruled by wealthy landlords whose land was worked by tenant farmers.
4. A *democracy* is rule by the people as a whole, almost always by means of majority vote on disputed issues. Voting rights are limited to citizens, and in the Greek *poleis,* this meant freeborn adult males.

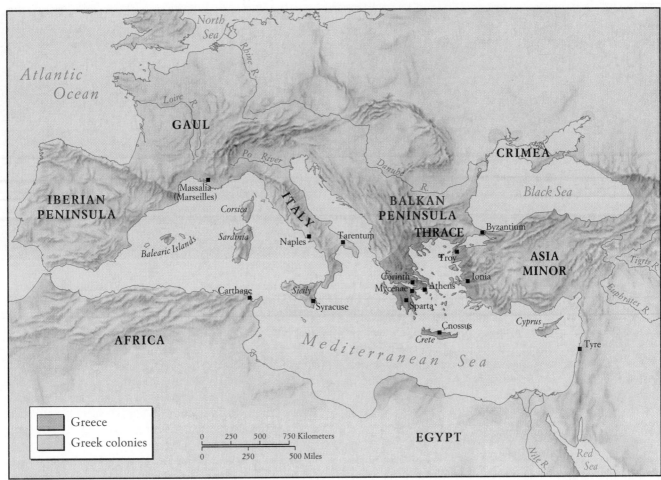

⊙ **MAP 9.2   The Greek World in the Classical Age.** In the seventh and sixth centuries B.C.E., many of the *poleis* suffered from overcrowding and encouraged colonists to emigrate around the Black and Mediterranean Seas. Some of these colonies, such as several on the island of Sicily and in southern Italy, became more prosperous and powerful than their home cities in Greece proper.

Additionally, the Greek word *tyranny* originally meant rule by a dictator who had illegally seized power. That person might be a good or bad ruler, a man or a woman.

Early Athens

Athens went through all these forms of government in the period after 750 B.C.E., when we know something definite about its history. The original monarchy was gradually forced aside by the aristocrats, who ruled the *polis* in the seventh and early sixth centuries. The aristocrats gave way in the 500s to oligarchs, some of whom were nobly born and some of whom were rich commoners. The most important oligarch was **Solon.** When the city faced a social and economic crisis, the other oligarchs gave him supreme power to institute reforms to quell the discontent. Solon responded by establishing a constitution that struck a balance between the desires of the wealthy few and the demands of the impoverished masses. Neither group was satisfied, however, and the contest soon resumed.

Eventually, an aristocratic tyrant named Pisistratus succeeded in making himself the sole ruler and made certain important concessions to the common people to gain their support for his plan to start a new monarchic dynasty with his sons as his successors. But the sons were not nearly as clever as their father and were swept from power by rebellion in 510 B.C.E.

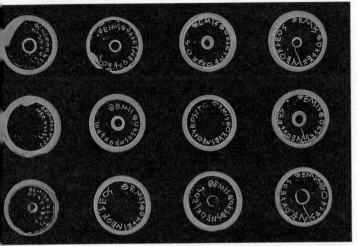

■ These fragments of broken pottery were the ballots used by fourth-century Athenians as they decided whether or not to exclude (ostracize) one of their fellows from citizenship in the polis. Included are the ostraka shards of Pericles and Thucydides.

The winner of the ensuing free-for-all was **Cleisthenes,** an aristocrat and the true founder of the Athenian democracy. Cleisthenes believed that the people should have the last word in their own government, both because it was just and because he believed it was the best way to keep civil peace.

Athenian Democracy

Cleisthenes (ruled 508–494 B.C.E.) in effect gave away his tyrannical powers to a series of political bodies that were unprecedentedly democratic in character: the *ekklesia, boule,* and *deme.* The *ekklesia* was the general "town meeting" of all free male Athenians, who had an equal voice in the great decisions of the *polis.* All could speak freely in an attempt to win over the others; all could be elected to any office; all could vote at the meetings of the *ekklesia* in the center plaza of Athens below the Acropolis hill.

The *boule* was a council of 500 citizens who were chosen by lot for one-year terms. It served as a day-to-day legislature and executive, making and implementing policy under the general supervision of the *ekklesia.* The *boule* supervised the civil and military affairs of the *polis* and carried out many of the functions of a modern city council. All male citizens could expect to serve at least one term on it.

The *deme* was the basic political subdivision of the *polis;* it was a territorial unit, something like a modern precinct or ward, but smaller in population. Each *deme* was entitled to select a certain number of *boule* members

and was represented more or less equally in the officers of the *polis.*

To enforce the will of the majority, Cleisthenes introduced the idea of *ostracism,* or the "pushing out" of a citizen who would not conform to the will of the majority. An ostracized person lost all rights of citizenship for a certain length of time, normally for ten years. So attached were the Greeks to their *poleis* that many preferred to kill themselves rather than submit to ostracism.

Of all the Athenian political institutions, *democracy* has attracted the most attention from later history. Americans tend to think of political democracy as a natural and normal way to govern a state, but in actuality, until the twentieth century, democracy was a very abnormal system of government. It was talked about a good deal but was not put into practice outside the West and in only a limited way within it. A great many countries still give only lip service to the idea of democracy, and sometimes not even that. The idea that the ordinary man was capable of governing himself wisely and efficiently was quite daring when it was introduced. After democracy failed in Athens, as it did after about a century, it was so discredited that after the fourth century B.C.E., it was not resurrected until the eighteenth century C.E.

How many other *poleis* became democracies at some time is not clear; under the strong pressure of democratic Athens, probably quite a few did adopt democratic governments between 500 and 400 B.C.E. But even within Athens (as well as everywhere else), there was *strong resistance to the democratic idea* that did not cease until democracy had been abandoned and condemned as "the rule of the mob." Ultimately it was the democratic leadership in Athens that created the conditions that allowed the opponents of democracy to win out.

Spartan Militarism

By about 500 B.C.E. Sparta differed from Athens in almost every possible way, although the two were originally similar. The Spartan *polis,* located in the southern Peloponnesus about eighty miles from Athens, was a small city surrounded by pastoral villages. As the population grew in the 700s, the Spartans engaged in a bloody territorial war with their nearest Greek neighbors, the Messenians, and finally won. The defeated Messenians were reduced to a state of near slavery (*helotry*) to the Spartans, who from this point on became culturally different from most other Greeks. The most striking example of their divergence was their voluntary abdication of individual freedoms.

During the 600s the Messenians rebelled again and again, and as a result of these **Messenian Wars,** the Spartans made themselves into a nation of soldiers and helpers of soldiers so that they could maintain their privileged position. Unlike other Greeks, the Spartans held the arts in contempt and rejected individualism as being unworthy of them. Public life was expressed in total obedience to the state, which was headed by a group of elected officers called *ephors* under the symbolic leadership of a dual monarchy. This strange combination seems to have worked very satisfactorily into the 300s.

Sparta's economic needs were largely met by the captive Messenians, who were terrorized into submission. They worked the fields and conducted the necessary crafts and commerce under close supervision. The Spartans themselves devoted their energies to the military arts; male children entered a barracks at the age of seven and were allowed only sufficient free time thereafter to ensure that another generation of Spartan warriors would be born of Spartan mothers.

One might think the other Greeks would detest such a regime, but on the contrary, most Greeks admired the Spartan way of life, especially its self-discipline, sacrifice, rigid obedience, and physical vigor. Even many Athenians thought the Spartan way was superior to their own and envied the single-minded purpose displayed by the Spartans in all their public affairs. The Spartan army was so large and so feared that after about 600 Sparta rarely had to use it in war. Sparta actually became a peaceable *polis* and directed all of its attention to keeping the political status quo within its own borders and, so far as possible, outside them. Despite its military nature, Sparta was a conservative and nonaggressive state.

✦ THE PERSIAN WARS

Throughout the early fifth century B.C.E., the foreign policy interests of Athens and Sparta more or less coincided, as both were primarily concerned with maintaining their independence in the face of foreign threats. These threats originated from Persia, which had expanded rapidly in the 500s, as we described in Chapter 4. By 490 B.C.E., the Persian emperor Darius I was faced with spreading rebellion among his subjects, Greeks on the Turkish coast (Ionia). When he attempted to subdue them, Athens went to their aid. Determined to punish the Athenians for their boldness and wishing in any case to expand his domains still further, Darius sent an army across the Aegean Sea to the Greek mainland. Aided by brilliant generalship, the Athenians were waiting and defeated the Persian expedition at the *battle of Marathon* in 490. Thus, the First Persian War ended with an Athenian victory.

■ This vase painting shows the Greeks' basic military formation; the phalanx. Sixteen columns of heavily armored men marching eight deep attacked the enemy with their spears of graduated length forming a wall of iron. Having broken the enemy formations, the Greeks dispatched them with their short swords or maces.

Pericles

c. 495–429 B.C.E.

One of the great figures of democratic politics, the Greek general and statesman Pericles (c. 495–429 B.C.E.) is also a prime example of the dangers of the imperial vision. Desiring to bring his fellow Greeks into a mutually supportive and prosperous defensive alliance against Persia, by the end of his career he was viewed as the chief villain of an imperialist scheme to reduce all Greeks to Athenian subjects.

Pericles was born into an aristocratic Athenian family and received a traditional education in rhetoric under Anaxagoras, a leading philosopher. Committing himself to the emergent democratic party in the hurly-burly of *polis* politics, he rose quickly to prominence. At the age of thirty-two, he became chief magistrate (the equivalent of mayor). For the next thirty-three years, Pericles was the leading political figure in Athens, a feat that speaks volumes not only about his abilities, but also about his sensitivity to popular opinion in a city where every free male saw himself as a co-maker of policy.

In power, Pericles showed himself sincerely committed to the extension of democracy, though he was not above using a bit of demagoguery to retain his grip on popular affection. By appealing to the emotions of the populace he reformed the political and judicial systems to allow greater participation by the ordinary citizen. He instituted a system of paying jurors and established new courts to hear criminal cases, thus lessening the powers of the aristocratic judges. He raised the payment citizens received for attending the great debates in the *agora* in the town's center where questions of policy were decided. By paying for jury duty and attendance at the assemblies, Pericles ensured that ordinary men could take time off from work to participate. Pericles himself was a master orator, and his speeches were deemed masterpieces of effective rhetoric. Only one has come down to us: the famous Funeral Oration given near the end of his life to commemorate the Athenians who had fallen in the war.

Ten years passed before Darius's successor, Xerxes, could find time to take up the challenge. The Second Persian War (480–478 B.C.E.) was fought on both land and sea and resulted in an even more decisive Greek victory. This time not only Athens, but several other Greek *polei* assisted the defensive effort. Spartan troops lived up to their fame at the *battle of Thermopylae* in 480 and again at the decisive defeat of the Persian force at *Platea* in 479. The Athenian navy completely routed the larger Persian fleet at *Salamis* and established Athens as the premier naval force in the eastern Mediterranean. The Greeks had turned back the attempts of the Asian empire to establish a universal monarchy over the entire Mediterranean basin. It was a crucial turning point for Western civilization.

✤ THE PELOPONNESIAN WAR

The Greeks' victory in the Persian Wars did not lead to inter-Greek harmony, however. Athens used its new prestige and growing wealth to form a group of unwilling satellites (the Delian League) among the nearby *poleis*. The democrats, led by the great orator **Pericles,** were now in command and were responsible for bringing Athens into conflict with Corinth, one of Sparta's Peloponnesian allies (see the Biography in this chapter). Corinth asked Sparta for help, and when the Spartans warned the Athenians to back down, Pericles responded with war.

Athens was embarked on an imperial adventure, with the goal of extending its authority over not only Greece but the surrounding coasts as well. With its very strong navy, Athens believed that it could hold off the land-based Spartans indefinitely while building up its alliances. These allied forces would then be able to challenge the Spartan army on Sparta's home territory.

For a long while, the **Peloponnesian War** (431–404 B.C.E.) was an intermittently fought deadlock. Neither side was able to deal the other an effective blow, and long truces allowed the combatants to regain their strength. But after Pericles died in 429, the Athenian democrats

Under Pericles, Athens became the center of the extraordinary intellectual and artistic life that is always associated with the term "Classical Age." The immortal temples on the Acropolis were erected in this period, as were many of the monuments and statues that we know only through fragments or legends of their splendor. This was the age of the tragic drama of Aeschylus and Sophocles, the heroic sculpture of Polyclitus, the philosophic explorations of Socrates, and the histories of Herodotus and Thucydides. All of these creative talents spent most or part of their lives in Periclean Athens.

But in relations with other Greek city-states, Pericles was not so fortunate. It was he who transformed the Delian League from a defensive alliance against the Persians into an instrument of Athenian empire building. It was he who spent the forced contributions of the other members of the league on the beautification of Athens and the expansion of its

navy, which was then used to blackmail the other Greeks into submission to Athens' will. And finally, it was Pericles who refused to take the warnings of the Spartans seriously when they sought to protect their allies against Athenian aggression.

After a series of short conflicts and truces in the 450s and 440s, the long-gathering storm broke out between the two leading cities, Athens and Sparta, and their various allies. The Peloponnesian War (431–404 B.C.E.) wrecked all hopes of peaceable unity. It ended in a decisive defeat for Athens and for the Peri clean policy of expansion, even though its author had died many years earlier in 429.

The age of Pericles was a time of glorious achievements and stunning defeats. This epoch saw the summit of Greek classical achievement in the arts, but also the beginning of the decline of Athens and all Greece into mere provinces of new and alien empires. The Greeks would remain in this condition until modern times.

argued among themselves while the antidemocratic forces within the *polis* gained strength. An ambitious attempt to weaken Sparta by attacking its allies on Sicily was a disaster for the Athenians. Finally, in 404 the Spartans obtained effective naval aid (from Persia!) and defeated the Athenians at sea. After that, it was a simple matter for their large army to lay siege to Athens and starve it into surrender.

The Peloponnesian War ended with a technical victory for Sparta, but actually this long civil war between the leading Greek cities was a loss for all concerned. Sparta was not inclined or equipped to lead the squabbling Greeks into an effective central government, and defeated Athens was torn between the discredited democrats and the conservatives favored by Sparta.

❧ THE FINAL ACT IN CLASSICAL GREECE

After the Peloponnesian War, the Greeks fought intermittently among themselves for supremacy for two genera-

tions. Whenever a strong contender emerged, such as the major *polis* of Thebes, the others would band together against it; once they had succeeded in defeating their rival, they would begin to quarrel among themselves, and the fragile unity would break down once again. To outsiders observing these incessant squabbles, the Greek *poleis* seemed highly unstable. The Greek passion for independence and individuality had degenerated into endless quarrels and maneuvering for power with no clear vision of what that power should create.

To the north of Greece were a people—the Macedonians—whom the Greeks regarded as savage and barbarian, although they were ethnically related. *Philip of Macedonia,* the ruler of this northern kingdom, had transformed it from a primitive society into an effectively governed, aggressive state. One by one he began to absorb the northern Greek *poleis,* until by the 340s he had made himself the master of much of the mainland.

After much delay, the Athenians finally awoke to the danger and convinced Thebes to join with them against the menace from the north. In the *battle of Chaeronea* in 338 B.C.E., the Athenians and Thebans were defeated by Philip's forces, however. The former city-states became provinces in a rapidly forming Macedonian empire. Chaeronea was the effective end of the era of Greek independence and of the Classical Age's great triumphs of the spirit and the arts, which we will examine in Chapter 10. From the latter part of the fourth century onward, Greeks were to be almost always under the rule of foreigners.

Summary

The Greeks were an Indo-European nomadic group who entered the Greek peninsula around 2000 B.C.E. and were gradually civilized, in part through the agency of the Cretans. By 1200 the Greeks had developed to the point that they were able to conquer their former overlords and mount an expedition against Troy. Following the coming of the Dorian invaders, Greece entered a Dark Age of cultural regression. This period ended around 800, and the Greeks began their ascent to high civilization that culminated in the Classical Age from 500 to 325 B.C.E.

Throughout the Classical Age, the democratic *polis* of Athens was the political and cultural leader of the more than two hundred city-states, which contended with each other for preeminence. Athens evolved through the various types of Greek government to achieve a limited but real democracy in the early fifth century. Through its commercial and maritime supremacy, it became the richest and most culturally significant of the *poleis*.

Victory over the Persians in the two Persian Wars led democratic and imperialist Athens to attempt dominion over many other city-states. Its main opponent was militaristic and conservative Sparta, and the two came to blows in the lengthy Peloponnesian War, which ended with a Spartan victory in 404. The real winner, however, proved to be the semibarbaric Macedonians, whose king Philip succeeded in imposing his rule over all Greece at the battle of Chaeronea.

Test Your Knowledge

1. The *polis* was a
   a. warrior-king.
   b. community of citizens.
   c. commercial league of merchants.
   d. temple complex.
2. Which of the following was *not* a form of classical Greek government?
   a. Monarchy
   b. Hierarchy
   c. Oligarchy
   d. Democracy
3. In early Greece, a tyranny was rule by
   a. the professional military.
   b. a small group.
   c. a person who had illegally seized power.
   d. a person who was evil and vicious.

4. The founder of the Athenian democracy was
   a. Solon.
   b. Cleisthenes.
   c. Pisistratus.
   d. Plato.
5. The critical factor in transforming Sparta from an ordinary *polis* to a special one was
   a. the war of the neighboring Messenians.
   b. the invasions by the Persians.
   c. the war against Athens.
   d. its commercial rivalry with Athens.
6. The Peloponnesian War is best described as
   a. a struggle between Athens and the rest of Greece.
   b. the start of an era of Spartan overlordship in Greece.

c. the discrediting of the Athenian democracy as leader of Greece.
d. the establishment of Persian influence in Greece.
7. Athenian women were thought to be
   a. suitable only for marriage and then seclusion within the home.

b. the collective sexual property of all free Greek males.
c. unsuited for any public political role.
d. the more talented of the two sexes.

Identification Terms

aristocracy
Cleisthenes
Iliad

Messenian Wars
Minoans
Mycenaeans

Odyssey
oligarchy
Peloponnesian War

Pericles
polis
Solon

Bibliography

Bury, J. B., and R. Meiggs. *A History of Greece to the Death of Alexander,* 1975. One of the best general works on Greek history.

Cartledge, P. *Sparta and Lakonia,* 1979. An introduction to Spartan politics and government.

Fine, J. *The Ancient Greeks,* 1984. Another good general history.

Hornblower, S. *The Greek World 479–323 B.C.,* 1983. A good introduction to politics and government.

Iliad and *Odyssey.* Both are available in several readable translations, notably those in the Penguin Book edition.

Jones, A. H. *Athenian Democracy,* 1957. Deals with classical politics and government. An expert's book for students.

Just, R. *Women in Athenian Law and Life,* 1988. One of many recent books on the Greek female and family relations.

Lazenby, J. F. *The Spartan Army,* 1985. Looks at the institution that was so admired by the Greeks.

Meiggs, R. *The Athenian Empire,* 1972. A modern look at the Peloponnesian War.

Mueller, M. *The Iliad,* 1984. Good background on the Trojan War.

Pomeroy, S. B. *Goddesses, Whores, Wives and Slaves,* 1975. Another well-known book on Greek women and family relations.

Thucydides, *History of the Peloponnesian War.* A major work of ancient history that has come down to us intact. Written by a participant in the war.

HELLENIC CULTURE

776 B.C.E.	First Olympic Games
c. 600–c. 500 B.C.E.	Pre-Socratic philosophers
470–399 B.C.E.	Socrates
c. 427–347 B.C.E.	Plato
384–322 B.C.E.	Aristotle

The Greek contribution to the creation of Western civilization is equal to that of the Jews and the Christians. In addition to the concept of democratic government, the Greek achievement was exemplified most strikingly in the fine arts and in the search for wisdom, which the Greeks called *philosophy.* In both areas, the Greeks developed models and modes of thought that have retained their validity and still provide inspiration today. The overall achievement of the Greeks during their great age is summed up in the term *Hellenic culture,* and we turn now to look at its specific aspects.

✤ PHILOSOPHY: THE LOVE OF WISDOM

The Greek word *philosophy* means "love of wisdom," and the Greeks themselves used it to mean the examination of the entire spectrum of human knowledge and not just the narrower fields of inquiry, such as the rules of logic, to which it is limited today. The ancient Greeks can legitimately be called the originators of philosophy. Of course, other peoples before them had attempted to work out the nature and meaning of human existence, but none pursued their studies so systematically with as much boldness and imagination, as the Greeks starting in the sixth century B.C.E.

Greek philosophy can be divided into two periods: the Pre-Socratic period and the Classical Age. The first period extends from the earliest surviving philosophical writings around 600 B.C.E. to the life of Socrates (470–399 B.C.E.). The second period extends from Socrates through about 300 B.C.E.

Pre-Socratic Philosophy

The Pre-Socratic philosophers devoted themselves mainly to investigations of the origin and nature of the physical world. They were less concerned with the determination of truth or how to distinguish between good and bad than philosophers would be in the Classical Age and later. The very first philosopher whose writings have survived (in very fragmentary form) is *Thales of Miletus,* who lived around 600. During the 500s came a group of thinkers who attempted to analyze the physical nature of the world and make it intelligible. Some of their ideas have had a lively influence on philosophy ever since, and some of their general concepts, such as the atom as the fundamental building block of nature, have been proven correct in modern times.

The greatest contribution of the Pre-Socratics was the concept of law in the universe. Unlike any previous thinkers, these Greeks believed that what happened in the physical cosmos was the result of laws of causation and thus understandable and predictable on a purely natural level. They did not deny the gods or the powers of the gods, but they did not look to the gods as the normal and usual causes of phenomena. Instead, they conceived of what we now call "natural law"—a set of phenomena in nature that, when properly understood, explain why certain things occur.

Two of the greatest of the Pre-Socratics were *Anaximander* and *Hippocrates*. Anaximander was the father of the theory of natural *evolution of species*—long before Darwin ever dreamed of it. He also thought the physical universe had no limits; he conceived of it as boundless and constantly expanding, much as modern astronomers do. Hippocrates is best known as the founder of scientific medicine, but curing people was really only incidental to his intellectual interests. First and foremost, he wished to teach men to observe the life around them. He was the first great **empiricist** in the natural sciences; that is, he arrived at his general theories only after careful and prolonged observation of the world that could be weighed and measured.

Socrates, Plato, and Aristotle

Socrates (470–399 B.C.E.) was the first philosopher to focus on the ethical and epistemological (truth-establishing) questions that have haunted the thoughtful since the dawn of creation. Like most of the Classical Age figures, he concentrated his efforts on the human being, rather than on physical nature. He was more interested in "How do I know?" than in "What is to be known?"

Socrates believed that intellectual excellence could be acquired; his method when working with his young Athenian disciples was to engage in systematic questioning, so that they would take nothing for granted. Everything should be fearlessly examined and justified before it could be taken for truth. This is the essence of the Socratic method, which has been employed by teachers ever since. Our knowledge of Socrates comes not from him directly, but from the numerous works of his pupil and admirer, **Plato** (427–347 B.C.E.), who joined his master in Athens a few years before Socrates' suicide. Socrates, Plato tells us, was accused of poisoning the minds of the youth of Athens by his irreverent questions, a practice that greatly irritated the conservative elders of the *polis*. Brought to trial, he was found guilty and given the choice of exile or suicide. A true Greek, Socrates chose suicide rather than being outcast from his chosen community.

Plato defended his teacher from the unjust accusation, but nevertheless was a very different thinker than his predecessor. Plato tried above all to solve the problem of how the mind can experience and recognize Truth (see the Document in this chapter). He concluded that it cannot, beyond a certain superficial point. Beyond that, he ventured into an analysis of politics as it should be (in the *Republic*) and as it existed (in the *Laws*). Plato was an antidemocrat, and his arguments have often been used by conservatives and monarchists ever since. During his lifetime Greece was in constant turmoil, which probably had considerable influence on his strongly conservative political views.

Aristotle was a pupil of Plato (who founded the first *Academy* in Athens), but he too was a very different man from his teacher. Aristotle is the nearest equivalent to a universal genius that Greece produced. His interests

■ Plato tells us that his master Socrates was considered extraordinarily ugly, but his mastery of logic and beauty of expression made all those who heard him forget everything else about him.

Plato's Metaphor of the Cave

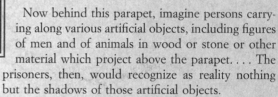

Of the great trinity of Greek classical philosophers, Plato distinguished himself by wrestling with the eternal question: how does the human brain penetrate appearances to attain Reality? Our impressions of the outer world originally are entirely dependent upon sensory data, what can be touched, or smelled, or seen and heard. How, then, can we formulate ideas that go beyond the specific detail of particular objects that the senses perceive? Or is there any idea, beyond the specific object? Could there be an abstract Idea of, say, a chair? Or only of *this* chair, with rounded legs and a straight back made of walnut wood? Most particularly, are there Ideals of Truth, Beauty, and Goodness that lie behind the weak and unstable versions of those virtues that human experience can conceive of?

Plato thought that such abstractions existed and were far more perfect in their nature than any specific sense-perceptible version of them. But he also believed that the large majority of people were unable to apprehend such Ideals in anything like their pure forms. Few men and women possessed the mental powers and the desire to allow them to penetrate beyond mere appearances into Truth and Reality.

Seeking to convey his meaning, Plato came to write the Metaphor of the Cave, which has remained one of the best-known philosophical anecdotes in history. Most people, he said, were like prisoners condemned to existence in a dark cave. They peered constantly through the dim light trying to make out what was happening around them:

> Imagine the condition of men living in a cavern underground, with an entrance open to the daylight and a long passage entering the cave. Here they have been since childhood, chained by the leg and by the neck, so that they cannot move and can see only what is directly in front of them. At some higher place in the cave, a fire burns, and between the prisoners and the fire is a track with a parapet built in front of it, like a screen at a puppet show which hides the performers while they show their puppets. . . .

> Now behind this parapet, imagine persons carrying along various artificial objects, including figures of men and of animals in wood or stone or other material which project above the parapet. . . . The prisoners, then, would recognize as reality nothing but the shadows of those artificial objects.

Our sense impressions, unenlightened by wisdom, deliver us into a prison of ignorance, where men mistake blurred shadows for reality.

Plato further says that if a prisoner were released and forced to go out into the unaccustomed sunlight, he would, of course, be blinded by the light and utterly confused. But this would change as he became accustomed to his new condition; his inability to see this huge new world would gradually cease:

> He would need, then, to grow accustomed before he could see things in the upper world. At first, it would be easiest to make out shadows, and then the images of men and things reflected in water, and later on the things themselves. After that, it would be easier to watch the heavenly bodies and the skies by night, looking at the light of the moon and stars rather than the sun and the light of the sun in daytime. . . .

Plato drew his conservative political and social conclusions from these beliefs about the nature of Reality and human ability to perceive it. He thought that relatively few people would ever be released from the cave of ignorance and shadow-play. Those who did attain to the upper world of Truth and slowly and with difficulty worked through the ever-higher, more accurate stages of Reality should be given the leadership positions. They deserved to be leaders not only because they merited power and prestige, but because they—and not the masses who remained in the cave—were able to make proper choices for the welfare of the whole society. Plato, who lived through the Peloponnesian War, remained a convinced antidemocrat all his life.

Source: F.M. Cornford translation, *The Republic of Plato,* 1941. By permission of Oxford University Press.

included practically every field of science yet known, as well as the formal analysis of thought and actions that we know as philosophy in modern times.

Most of what he wrote has survived and can fill a whole shelf of books. His best-known works are the *Politics, Physics,* and *Metaphysics,* but he was also a first-rate mathematician, an astronomer, the founder of botany, and a student of medicine. So great was his renown in the medieval world that both European Christians and Arab Muslims referred to him simply as the Master. The Christian scholars thought of him as a sort of pagan saint, who lacked only the light of the Revelation as outlined in their scripture, while the learned Muslims thought of him as the greatest natural philosopher and man of science the world had yet produced.

Greek philosophy was marked at all times by the strong sense of self-confidence that the philosophers brought to it. The Greeks believed that humans were quite capable of understanding the cosmos and all that lived within it by use of reason and careful observation. In that sense, the Greeks were the world's first real scientists. They were not overawed by the gods, but created the gods in their own image and never resorted to supernatural powers to explain what could be explained by law. The wisdom the Greeks sought in their "love of wisdom" was that which was reachable by the unaided human intellect.

✤ GREEK RELIGION

Not all Greeks by any means were able to find the truth they needed in philosophy. Probably, the large majority of people were not exposed to or were quite unable to follow the reasonings of the philosophers. They turned instead to religion. But Greek religion was rather different from the religions we have discussed earlier. Like most of the other peoples we have discussed, the Greeks were polytheistic. Their gods included Zeus, the father figure; Hera, the wife of Zeus; Poseidon, god of the seas; Athena, goddess of wisdom and also of war; Apollo, god of the sun; and Demeter, goddess of fertility. From early times, however, the Greek gods were less threatening and less powerful than other peoples' gods. The Greeks never created a priestly class or caste, but used their priests only as informal leaders of loosely organized services. After about 500 B.C.E., the priests and priestesses receded more and more into the background, while many of the gods themselves became symbolic. Even the great deities whom all Greeks recognized were not taken too seriously by the educated. They were certainly not feared in the way that the Sumerians feared their gods or the Jews feared Yahweh.

It is important to understand that Greek religion was very different from our modern ideas of what religion involves. It was not revealed to humans by a supernatural authority. It did not stem from a Holy Book. It made no attempt to impose a system of moral conduct upon the faithful. The Greeks never had a centralized ecclesiastical authority or a hierarchy of priests. Greek religion after the fifth century was largely a series of rituals, something like our American celebration of the Fourth of July. Participating in the rituals was an act of *polis* patriotism as much as worship and had little or nothing to do with ethics and morality of private life.

In addition to greater deities whom all Greeks recognized, each *polis* had its own local deities. The cults of these local gods were forms of civic celebrations in which everyone joined, even those who did not believe in the existence of supernatural forces or immortal life. The Greeks did not believe that the gods controlled human destiny in any detailed fashion. Behind and above the gods was an impersonal, and unavoidable Fate, which could not be successfully defied by either humans or gods.

The Greeks were usually on good terms with the heavens. They did not offer bribes as the Mesopotamians did; they did not prostrate themselves before the altars in the manner of the Egyptians. Nor did they accept priestly admonitions about conduct. Normally, the Greeks did not engage in speculation about the afterlife and saw no reason to fear it. As with the Confucians, it was *this world* that engaged the Greeks' attention and provided their frame of reference for good and evil.

By the opening of the Classical Age, most of the educated class apparently did not believe in immortality anymore, if indeed they ever had. For them at least, philosophy increasingly took the place of religion. The acts of the gods came more and more to be viewed as myths, stories that served a useful moral purpose in educating the people to their duties and responsibilities as good citizens of the *polis* and as good Greeks.

✤ THE ARTS AND LITERATURE

The classical Greeks gave at least three major art forms to Western civilization: (1) the *drama,* a Greek invention that originated in the 600s, presumably in Athens, as a sort of pageant depicting scenes from the myths about the gods; (2) *lyric poetry,* originating in the pre-Classical era and represented best by the surviving fragments from the work of **Sappho,** a woman who lived on the island of Lesbos in the 600s; and (3) *"classical" architecture,* most notably the temples scattered about the shores of the Mediterranean by Greek colonists, as well as the Acropolis in Athens. Besides these art forms, which they originated, the Greeks excelled in epic poetry (the *Iliad* and *Odyssey*); magnificent sculpture of the human form and face at a level of skill not previously approached; dance, which was a particular passion for both men and women; fine ceramic wares of every sort; and painting, mainly on ceramic vessels and plaques.

The particular strengths of Greek pictorial and architectural art were the harmony and symmetry of the parts with the whole; the ability to depict the ideal beauty of the human form, while still maintaining recognizable realism in their portrayals; and the combination of grace and strength so that they balanced each other in vital tension. The models established during the Classical Age have remained supremely important to artists of the West ever since. Most plastic forms of European art are derived from these models, at least until the twentieth century.

◼ This much-imitated bronze statue is probably a Roman replica of the Greek original. It captures the dedication of the classical artist to anatomical accuracy combined with physical perfection.

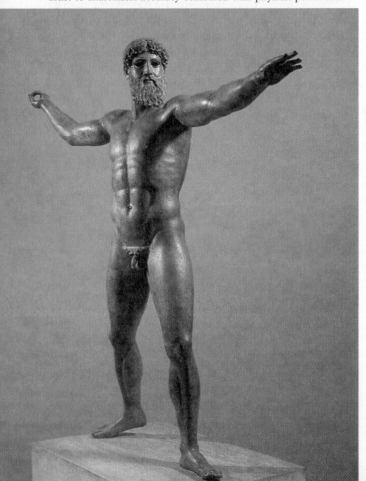

Most Hellenic art was anonymous. The artist worked as a member of the *polis,* contributing what he did best to the benefit of his fellow citizens just as others contributed by paying taxes or working on the roads. We do know that the main Athenian temple, the **Parthenon,** was erected by order of Pericles during the Peloponnesian War and was intended as a shrine to Athena, the patron goddess of the city. Within the Parthenon stood an enormous marble statue of Athena by Phidias, the most famous of all the Athenian sculptors. Most of the outer structure of the Parthenon is still intact (though under severe stress from air pollution in modern Athens), but the interior and its contents have long since been destroyed (mainly by a great explosion when the building was used as a powder depot by the Turks in the seventeenth century).

Greek *literature* took several distinct forms: poetry of all types was very highly developed from the time of Homer (eighth century) onward. The outstanding names besides Sappho are Hesiod, Euripides, Aeschylus, Sophocles, Aristophanes, and Pindar. Most of these were dramatists as well as poets. The great trio of Euripides, Aeschylus, and Sophocles created the tragic form, while Aristophanes is the first noted comic playwright.

The *drama* was one of the Greeks' most popular arts, and the plays that have survived represent possibly one-hundredth of what was written in the fifth and fourth centuries. Playwrights and actors were originally amateurs, but soon became professionals. Every citizen was expected to take part occasionally in the dramatic productions, which soon came to be a central element in the numerous civic celebrations that marked the life of the *polis.*

Dance and music were intensely cultivated, both by professionals and amateurs. There is abundant mention of both in Greek literature of all types, as well as in Greek painting and sculptural representations. The god Dionysius was particularly connected with orgiastic out-of-doors dancing, accompanied by reed and string instruments, which celebrated the god's triumphant return from the dead. His cult was also instrumental in creating the first drama.

The Greeks evidently learned much of their skill in ceramics and metalwork from the Egyptians and the Minoans, but improved on their models. Greek ceramics were in great demand throughout the Mediterranean world, and Greek ships were frequently loaded with wine jugs, olive oil vessels, and other household utensils made from clay, as well as fine work. Craftsmanship was highly prized by the Greeks, and much of the Athenian population evidently worked for the export trade, making objects of clay, metal, leather, and wood.

✤ SOCIAL RELATIONS IN THE CLASSICAL AGE

The average Athenian was a laborer, small artisan, merchant, or slave. The freeman and his family generally lived very simply. He made a modest income working for others or for the *polis* (all *poleis* usually had an ongoing public works program) or as an independent shopkeeper. His wife normally worked inside the home, performing the usual domestic duties; she also generally had considerable control over the children's education.

Outside the home in public life, the women were very much inferior to men, except for the trained and educated entertainer-prostitutes, called **hetairai,** who were uniquely respected and allowed to do as they pleased. Few men could afford their services, however, and the usual Greek household seems to have been much like the modern one: husband, wife, and children. Wives could divorce their husbands and had control over any property they brought into the marriage. Nevertheless, it was very definitely a male-dominated, even a misogynous, society (see Chapter 15).

Homosexuality seems to have been relatively common, at least among the educated, and to have been looked upon as a tolerable, though somewhat disreputable, practice. It was viewed as particularly disreputable for the older man, because he was sometimes led to ignore his family responsibilities by a younger lover. From the glancing attention paid to the subject in the surviving literature, it is impossible to know how common such relations were, what the nonhomosexual majority thought of them, or indeed much else regarding the sexual practices of the time (see Chapter 15).

It has frequently been remarked that Athenian democracy was built on and supported by a large population of slaves; this is true, but it may not be as damning as it seems at first. Certainly, slaves were numerous (perhaps 30 percent of the total population); enslavement was something that could happen to both Greeks and foreigners and usually occurred as the result of debt. Slaves were normally not abused by their masters, and many slaves were prized workers and craftsmen who worked for pay but were not free to go off at will to other employment. The economic life of the *polis* always centered on freemen, not slaves, and the kind of plantation agriculture that depended on coerced labor was not found in Greece due to the unpromising terrain. The individual slaveholder

■ **The Conversation.** This glimpse of ordinary affairs is unusual for Greek art in that it portrays females who have no visible connection to the more often depicted male life. It is a product of the third or recent century B.C.E.

Oedipus Rex

Greek classical tragedy was built upon the conviction that an inexorable Fate had the final word in the life of human beings. Fate might be evaded or even defied for a time, but sooner or later, its commands would be obeyed. In this view (which it seems all educated Greeks held), Man himself assured the punishments and retributions that descended upon him by reason of his fatal moral shortcomings. One of the most compelling renditions of this principle is told in the three plays of the fifth-century B.C.E. Athenian playwright Sophocles that tell the story of Oedipus.

Oedipus was the son of King Laius of the city-state of Thebes. Because the oracle of Apollo had prophesied that this boy would one day kill his father and disgrace his mother, King Laius ordered his newborn son to be taken out to a hillside and left to die of exposure. Unknown to the sorrowing parents, a shepherd happened by and rescued the child, taking him to the court of Polybius, the king of neighboring Corinth, who was childless. Brought up as the heir to Corinth's throne, Oedipus was told of the prophecy one day and fled the city, as he loved Polybius and thought him to be his natural father. Wandering through Greece, Oedipus happened to encounter Laius on the road. As a result of a foolish argument over precedence, the hot-tempered Oedipus killed his true father. Some days later, he came to Theban territory and challenged the monster Sphinx who had terrorized the city for many months, devouring anyone who could not solve her riddle: "What goes on four feet in the morning, two at noon, and three in the evening?" Oedipus replied: "Man, in life's three stages."

As a prize for freeing the city, Oedipus was married to the widowed queen Jocasta, his own mother, thus fulfilling the prophecy of years ago. With Jocasta he raised two sons and two daughters before the blind seer Tiresias reluctantly revealed the awful secret. In horror and shame, Jocasta committed suicide. Oedipus in despair blinded himself with the pins of her brooches and was driven from the palace by public outrage to a life of exile. Only his daughter Antigone accompanied him.

The story is told in the play *Oedipus Rex,* which was first produced in Athens about 429 B.C.E. at the height of the Peloponnesian War and the same year as the death of Pericles. The story of the unhappy ex-king is continued in Sophocles' *Oedipus at Colonus.* Colonus is a place near Athens where Antigone helps her father comprehend what has happened and prepare for death. Antigone herself is the protagonist of the final play in the Oedipus cycle, in which the heartbreaking tragedy of a man who thought he might triumph over Fate by his wisdom and willpower is brought to an end.

The moral that Sophocles wished to teach is that intelligence and will alone are not sufficient for a good life. Compassion and consideration, qualities that Oedipus lacked until his last days but then learned from his daughter, are more important. Antigone, the faithful daughter who overcomes her revulsion and elects to share her father's misery, is the real hero of the piece.

usually did not own more than one or two men or women and used them more as servants and assistants than as laborers. Slaves did not enjoy civil rights in politics, nor could they serve in the military. Only in the *polis*-owned silver mines near Athens were slaves abused as a matter of course, and these slaves were normally criminals, not debtors.

Most of the Greek population lived in the villages, where the vast majority of people were, of course, simple farmers and herders. In theory, they were free and politically equal to the townsmen. It is difficult to determine how much attention these rural people paid to the public affairs of the town, how often they participated in the *ekklesia* and *boule,* or whether were elected to public office. Certainly, though, they could not participate to the same extent as the townsmen.

Politics was basically an urban pursuit, as it would remain until a century or two ago everywhere. Education was also basically an urban phenomenon, and most of the country people must have been illiterate. Still, the general level of education among the Greeks of the Classical Age was remarkably high and was not approximated again in the Western world until very much later. Neither the Romans nor the medieval Europeans came close.

❖ SPORT AND THE GOLDEN MEAN

The Greeks were the first people to look upon the nurture of the physique (the word itself is Greek) as an important part of human life. They admired a healthy body and thought it was a duty to cultivate its possibilities. As part of this effort, they organized the first athletic events open to all; the most important was the great pan-Hellenic festival known to us as the *Olympic Games*.

According to the records, the first Olympics were held in 776 B.C.E. and were held every four years thereafter in the small *polis* of Olympia on the west coast of the Peloponnesian peninsula. The games were originally more a religious festival than a sports event, but soon became both. The best of the Greek athletes competed for their hometowns in footraces, chariot drives, the discus throw, weightlifting, and several other contests. Prizes were limited to honors and a crown of laurel leaves. The games lasted for about a week and were immensely popular; they served an important function as a sort of patriotic reunion for people from all over the Greek world. After the Macedonian conquest, the games soon declined and then ceased altogether for many centuries until they were revived in the late nineteenth century.

The ideal of the **golden mean,** the middle ground between all extremes of thought and action, was a Greek specialty. They distrusted radical measures and tried to find that which embraced the good without claiming to be the best. They believed that the man who claimed to have the perfect solution to a problem was being misled by **hubris,** a false and blinding overconfidence. The gods were "setting him up," as we might put it, and disaster was sure to follow. The wise man always kept this in mind and acted accordingly.

This by no means should be seen as a sign of humility. The Greeks were not humble by nature, but were quite willing to take chances and to stretch their intellectual powers to the utmost. They believed passionately in the potential of the human being. But they did not defy Fate or the gods without expecting to be punished. The great tragedies of Sophocles are perhaps the most dramatically effective expression of this expectation, particularly the trilogy about the doomed Oedipus and his vain struggle to

■ This sheet gold death mask of Mycenaean king was unearthed by Heinrich Schliemann, first of the archaeologists of the Peloponnesus. He believed it was the mask of Agamemnon, commander of the Greek forces at Troy; later research indicates that this was not the case.

avoid the fate that lay in wait for him (see the biography on the opposite page.)

❖ THE GREEK LEGACY

The dimensions and lasting importance of the Greeks' bequest to Western civilization cannot be overemphasized. When the *poleis* fell to the Macedonians, this bequest was retained, though in diluted forms. When the Macedonian world was then itself overtaken by the all-conquering Romans a couple of hundred years later, the new masters adopted much of the Greek heritage with great enthusiasm and made it their own. In this way, the Greek style and the content of their art, philosophy, science, and government gradually infiltrated into much of Europe. In the process, though, parts were lost permanently, and much of it was radically altered by other views and conditions of life.

The mixture of Greek with non-Greek produced a peculiar form of civilization that spread through much of the Mediterranean and the Near East after the Macedonian conquest and during the Roman era. We will look at this civilization in the following chapter and see that it was very different from Hellenic civilization in many ways, but never severed all connections with the original Greek model.

Summary

Hellenic culture represents a high point in the history of the Western world. The two centuries embraced by the Classical Age produced a series of remarkable achievements in the fine arts and in the systematic inquiry into humans and nature that we call philosophy. In some of these affairs, the Greeks were building on foundations laid by others including the Egyptians and the Phoenicians; in others, such as drama and lyric poetry, they were pioneers. In philosophy, the mighty trio of Socrates, Plato, and Aristotle defined most of the questions that the Western world would ask of the universe ever since. In drama, Aeschylus, Sophocles, and Euripides played the same pathbreaking role. Poets such as Sappho and Pindar, sculptors as Phidias, and the mostly unknown architects of the Classical Age created monuments that remain models of excellence and sensitivity.

In all of their efforts, the Greeks' intellectual fearlessness and respect for the powers of reason are strikingly apparent. They believed, as they said, that "Man is the measure" and that what could not be understood by the mind was probably best left alone as being unworthy of their efforts. Their legacies in intellectual and artistic activities rank with those of their predecessors, the Hebrews, in religion and with their successors, the Romans, in government and law.

Test Your Knowledge

1. Sophocles and Euripides are two of the greatest Greek
   a. dramatists.
   b. poets.
   c. sculptors.
   d. painters.
2. The Cave Metaphor in Plato's writings refers to
   a. the need of humans to have a place of refuge from their enemies.
   b. the ability of humans to form a community.
   c. the difference between reality and falsely understood images.
   d. the importance of a stable homeplace for an advanced society.
3. Slavery in classical Greece was
   a. common and harsh.
   b. nonexistent.
   c. rare.
   d. common and usually mild.
4. The Athenian women who enjoyed the most free lifestyles were the
   a. aristocrats.
   b. mothers.
   c. unmarried girls.
   d. entertainer-prostitutes.
5. Greek religion was
   a. dominated by a powerful priesthood.
   b. the same from one end of the country to the other.
   c. greatly varied in its forms.
   d. dominated by fear of the afterlife.
6. The pre-Socratic philosophers sought most of all to explain the
   a. human capacity to reason.
   b. motion of the stars.
   c. composition and laws of the natural world.
   d. reasons for the existence of good and evil.
7. Which adjective is *least* appropriate for the classical Greeks?
   a. Intimidated
   b. Rational
   c. Proud
   d. Curious

Identification Terms

Aristotle

empiricist

golden mean

hubris

hetairai

Parthenon

Plato

Sappho

Socrates

Bibliography

Bulfinch, T. *Mythology.* A classic work that tells the stories of mythology in a most entertaining way.

Burkert, W. *Greek Religion,* 1987. Deals with Classical Age religion and philosophy.

Dodds, E. R. *The Greeks and the Irrational,* 1951. A controversial study that sees the Greeks as a supremely passionate people.

Finley, M. I., ed. *Slavery in Classical Antiquity,* 1960. A good source for Greek slavery.

Kitto, H. D. F. *The Greeks,* many editions. A brief study that is very lucid and easily digested.

Lawrence, A. W. *Greek Architecture,* 1983. A standard treatment of the subject with many illustrations.

Osborne, R. *Demos,* 1985. See for slavery and Athenian society in general.

Pinsent, J. *Greek Mythology,* 1969. A clear overview of the Greeks' beliefs about the gods and the way different classes of society perceived them.

Richter, G. M. *Sculpture and Sculptors of the Greeks,* 1971. A richly illustrated treatment of painting and sculpture.

Sansone, D. *Greek Sport,* 1988. An illustrated work dealing with sport and its place in Greek life.

HELLENISTIC CIVILIZATION

336–323 B.C.E.   Alexander the Great's campaigns
c. 300–50 B.C.E.   Hellenistic Age

The new style of civilized life created by the Greeks of the Classical Age is called *Hellenism.* After the Greeks' fell to the Macedonian barbarians in 338 B.C.E., Hellenism in a diluted form was spread into the East and Egypt by the conquerors. This altered form of Hellenism is known as *Hellenistic* culture or civilization. It retained many of the values and attitudes of the classical Greek *polis,* but it also dropped many in favor of the very different values and attitudes of the eastern kingdoms and empires.

✣ ALEXANDER AND THE CREATION OF A WORLD EMPIRE

After the battle at Chaeronea, which brought him mastery of Greece, King Philip of Macedonia was assassinated and his twenty-year-old son, Alexander, succeeded to the throne. In his thirteen-year reign (336–323 B.C.E.), Alexander conquered most of the world known to the Greeks and proved himself one of the most remarkable individuals in world history (see the Biography and Document in this chapter).

At the time of his death, Philip had been organizing a large combined Macedonian-Greek army with the announced purpose of invading the huge Persian empire. After swiftly putting down a rebellion in Thebes, Alexander continued this plan, and crossed the Dardanelles in 334 with an army of about 55,000 men (very large for the times). In three great battles, the young general brought down the mightiest empire the world had yet seen, the empire of Darius III of Persia, who was slain by his own troops after the third and decisive loss at *Gaugamela* in present-day Iraq (see Map 11.1).

After conquering Egypt, Alexander invaded the Persian heartland and then proceeded eastward into the unknown borderlands of India. After spending five years marching up and down the Indus basin and the wild highlands to its north (present-day Pakistan and Afghanistan), his remaining troops finally mutinied and refused to go farther. In 324 Alexander led his exhausted men back to Persia. A year later, he died in Babylon at the age of thirty-three. The few years of his reign would have a lasting effect on much of the world's history.

A Mixed Culture

Alexander the Great (as he was soon called) founded the largest empire yet seen in history, but it fell apart almoston

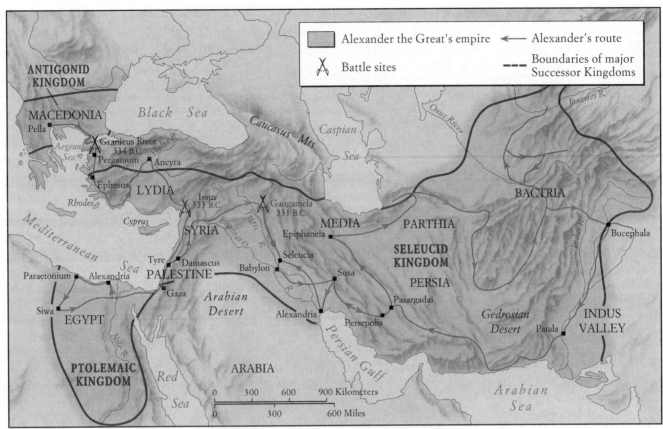

● **MAP 11.1 Alexander's Empire and the Successor Kingdoms.** The huge area conquered by Alexander between 334 and 324 B.C.E. was too large to control from a single center. It quickly broke down after the conqueror's death into regional kingdoms under several of his generals.

the day of his death. He left an infant son by his last and favorite wife Roxana, but the child became a mere pawn as Alexander's generals struggled to succeed him as sole ruler. (The son was eventually put to death at age sixteen by one of the contestants.) Finally, the exhausted combatants tired of the civil war and split up the vast territories conquered by Alexander into a whole series of kingdoms, each ruled by one of Alexander's generals. Collectively, these successor states are called the *Hellenistic kingdoms.*

Everywhere Alexander led his armies, he founded new cities or towns, many of which bore his name. He then recruited Greeks from the homeland to come and establish themselves as a ruling group in the new cities and encouraged them to follow his own example and intermarry with the locals. Tens of thousands of Greeks took up the invitation, leaving overcrowded, impoverished Greece to make their names and fortunes in the new

countries now under Greco-Macedonian control. Inevitably, they brought with them the ways of thought and the values they had cherished in their native land. As the conquerors, the Greeks could and did impose their ideas upon the Asiatics and Egyptians with whom they had contact or intermarried. The result was Hellenistic culture, a *mixed culture* that blended Greek and Asiatic attitudes. As the conquerors, the Greeks first tried to reconstruct the *polis* mode of government and community in their new homes, but quickly found that this was impossible. The easterners had no experience of the *polis* form of government and did not understand it; they had never governed themselves, but had always had an all-powerful king who ruled through his officials and generals. Soon the Greeks themselves adopted the monarchical form of government. Thus, instead of the small, tight-knit community of equal citizens as was typical of the *polis* of the Classical Age, a Hellenistic state was typically a large

Alexander the Great
356–323 B.C.E.

In the midst of his fantastic campaign of world conquest, Alexander the Great lost his dearest friend and companion Hephaestion. The young man had died of a fever, and Alexander was overcome with grief. He cut off all his hair, refused to eat, and executed the physician who had failed to save his friend. Then he sacrificed an entire enemy tribe to honor Hephaestion's memory. In the funeral pyre that consumed the remains of the dead warrior, Alexander also burned many articles of gold and silver, works of art, jewels, fine garments, and oriental spices worth millions. This spectacular display was not a unique occurrence in Alexander's life. Hundreds of similar stories about this extraordinary individual have been told through the centuries.

Alexander the Great was perhaps the most renowned of all the world's military heroes. He possessed an active imagination and a lively curiosity, both of which were stimulated by the tutoring of Aristotle himself. The young king possessed a talent for practical matters and a wonderful gift for command. He achieved his most brilliant victories against great odds. But he also committed errors of judgment in his dealings with subordinates. The suspicion of disloyalty was enough to ensure speedy death, and from the accounts of several eyewitnesses, we know that innocent men died because of Alexander's unjustified rages.

During an era when no distinction was drawn between myth and history, he was hailed in his lifetime as a god. People accepted his extraordinary feats as the work of supernatural forces. How else could his achievements be explained?

Born in Macedonia in 356 B.C.E., Alexander became the kingdom's ruler at the age of twenty after his father Philip was murdered. Contin-

kingdom in which a bureaucracy governed at the king's command. The inhabitants, whether Greek or native, were *no longer citizens, but subjects*—a very different concept.

It is worth noting that although Alexander never conquered India's heartland, the Greek invasion also had lasting effects upon the Indians. It introduced them to the Western world, and from this time onward, there were trade contacts between India and the eastern end of the Mediterranean. The invasion also disrupted the existing political balance and paved the way for the conquering Mauryan dynasty, including the great Ashoka. Finally, the Greek models introduced into Indian arts at this time were to have lasting impacts.

⚜ HELLENISTIC CITIES

During the Hellenistic Age, a true *urban civilization,* in which the towns and cities were far more important than the more numerous rural dwellers, came into existence for the first time since the decline of the Mesopotamian cities. The life of the Hellenistic kingdoms was dominated by large cities such as Alexandria in Egypt, Antioch in Syria, and Susa in Persia. Like modern cities, Hellenistic cities

uing with his father's plans, Alexander subordinated the quarreling city-states of Greece to "barbarian" Macedonia and crushed a rebellion by Thebes and Athens. Soon afterward, in 334 he began his assault on the mighty Persian empire with a Greek-Macedonian army of 55,000. He occupied Asia Minor and Egypt after catching the Persians unprepared for his lightning attacks. Then, at Gaugamela in the Persian heartland, he defeated emperor Darius III decisively, and all the lands of the great empire were at his feet.

In 327 he extended his reach to the Indus valley in distant India, where he engaged the forces of the Hindu ruler and defeated them despite their use of war elephants. He had pledged to go to the ends of the earth, but the weary Greeks finally refused to go on and forced him to return to Persia. Worn out by a life of constant excess, Alexander died a short time later in 323. Deified by his Macedonian veterans, he was supposedly buried in a casket of solid gold in Egyptian Alexandria, greatest of the several cities he founded or renamed after himself. His remains have never been located.

Alexander the Great's intents and policies have been the subjects of much debate from his own day forward. Some think that he intended to create a world empire in which all peoples would be equal—a sort of world federation. There is no doubt that his efforts to reconcile Greeks with Asians offended many of his Greek and Macedonian followers. When Alexander himself adopted some Asian customs, many of his men protested so vehemently that the new ceremonies had to be dropped.

During his Asian campaign, Alexander was faced with several such mutinies from officers and men who thought that he was too lenient with a beaten enemy. They did not appreciate Alexander's vision, nor his habit of making the local prince and princess practically the equal of the conquering commanders. Alexander himself married many Asian women in an attempt to establish lasting ties; the last was Roxana, who bore him his only son.

Alexander's imprint on history is only partly the result of his military genius. He also spread Hellenic culture to much of the East through his conquering armies. He was the beginner of the Hellenistic civilization, the blend of Greek and eastern ideas and institutions that dominated western Asia and the Mediterranean for the next several centuries. But his empire fell apart almost immediately, and his attempt to found an Alexandrine dynasty collapsed in intra-Greek wars for dominance. Eventually, the all-conquering Romans took over much of what had once been Alexander's empire in the eastern Mediterranean and Asia. They proudly saw themselves as continuers of the Alexandrine tradition of glorious conquest.

were centers of commerce and learning with great museums, libraries, and amusement halls. Some of them had more than 500,000 inhabitants drawn from a vast variety of ethnic backgrounds. Most of the people in these cities were free, but there were also many slaves. Slavery became more common in the Hellenistic era than it had been in the Classical Age—another example of the eastern tradition dominating the Greek. Even the free majority felt little sense of community, largely because they came from so many different social and ethnic groups. On the contrary, the feeling of alienation, of being apart from others in the psychic sense, was very common. Many city people were peasants who had fled from the civil wars after Alexander's death; many others were former prisoners of war who had been uprooted from their homes and forced into the cities. They had little in common with their neighbors except that they were all the subjects of the powerful rulers.

Originally, the Greeks were the governing class of the cities, but gradually they were absorbed by the larger group that surrounded them. The Greek language remained the tongue of the cultured, but in most other respects, the eastern way of life and thought won out. In the arts, a hybrid of classical Greek and traditional eastern

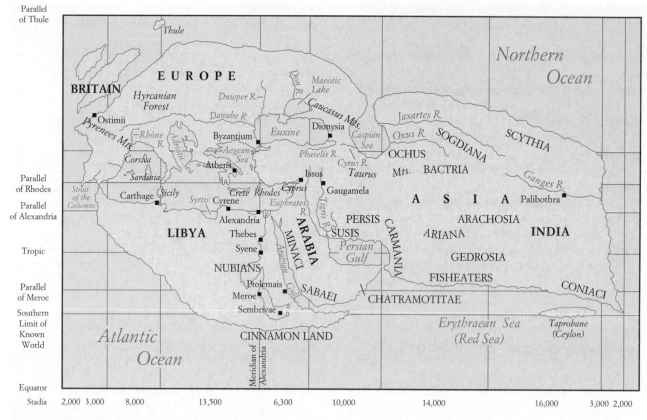

◉ MAP 11.2   The World According to Erathosthenes. This is the first world map that bears substantial relation to the globe as modern people know it. It was drawn by the Greek Erathosthenes in the third century B.C.E., relying on reports by mariners and other travelers and on his own observations.

forms and content came into existence. Hellenic forms became a thin veneer, covering the underlying Syrian, Egyptian, or Persian traditions. Some of the new forms were truly excellent, but later ages have deemed most of them a deterioration from what the Greeks had achieved during the Hellenic period.

✤ GREEKS AND EASTERNERS IN THE HELLENISTIC KINGDOMS

The civil wars after Alexander's death resulted in the formation of three major "successor kingdoms," each ruled by a former Greek general who had fought his way into that position (see Map 11.2):

1. **The Ptolemaic kingdom of Egypt.** A general named Ptolemy succeeded in capturing Egypt, the richest of all the provinces of Alexander's empire. There he ruled

as a divine king, just as the pharaohs once had. By the 100s B.C.E., the many immigrant Greeks and the Egyptian upper class had intermixed sufficiently to make Egypt a hybrid state. Many Greeks adopted the Egyptian way of life, which they found very pleasant. Meanwhile ordinary Egyptians remained exploited peasants or slaves.

2. **The Seleucid kingdom of Persia.** The Seleucid kingdom, which was the successor to most of the once mighty empire of Darius III, reached from India's borders to the shores of the Mediterranean in Lebanon. It was founded by a former general named Seleucus, and like Ptolemaic Egypt, it lasted until the Roman assault in the first century B.C.E. Many tens of thousands of Greek immigrants came here as officials, soldiers, or craftsmen, and the contact between the locals and Greeks was very extensive in the western parts of the kingdom, especially Syria and Turkey. The

Plutarch: *Parallel Lives*

One of the most colorful characters of ancient history, Alexander of Macedonia is known to us through several eyewitness accounts. The best biography of all, however was written by a Greek citizen of the Roman Empire who lived several hundred years after Alexander. Plutarch wrote his *Parallel Lives* to provide the youth of Rome with examples of both Greek and Roman heroes for them to emulate. It has been a favorite ever since.

In the following selection, Plutarch tells a famous anecdote of the hero Alexander's boyhood at his father Philip's court:

> Philonicus the Thessalian brought the horse Bucephalus to Philip, offering to sell him for thirteen talents of silver; when they went into the field to try him they found him so very vicious and unmanageable that he reared up when they endeavored to mount him and would not suffer even the voices of Philip's attendants. Upon which, as they were leading him away as wholly useless, Alexander, who stood nearby, said "What an excellent horse do they lose for want of boldness to manage him! . . . I could manage this horse better than the others do."

Philip, who was a harsh father, challenged his son to prove his boast:

> Alexander immediately ran to the horse and taking hold of his bridle turned him directly toward the sun, having, it seems, observed that he was disturbed by and afraid of the motion of his own shadow. . . . Then, stroking him gently when he found him begin to grow eager and fiery, he let fall his upper garment softly, and with one nimble step securely mounted him, and when he was seated by little and little drew in the bridle and curbed him so, without either striking or spurring him. Presently, when he found him free from all rebelliousness and only impatient for the course, he let him go at full speed, inciting him now with a commanding voice and urging him also with his heel. Philip and his friends looked on at first in silence and anxiety, till seeing him turn at the end of the course and come back rejoicing and triumphing for what he had performed, they all burst out into acclamations of applause; and his father, shedding tears of joy, kissed Alexander as he came down from the horse and in his exultation said "O my son, look thee out for a kingdom equal to and worthy of thyself, for Macedonia is too little for thee!"

Philip was indeed so impressed that ". . . after this, considering him [Alexander] to be of a temper easy to be led to his duty by reason, but by no means to be compelled, he always endeavored to persuade rather than command or force him to do anything. . . . " Soon after, Philip sent for the most famous of all teachers in Greece of the time, the philosopher Aristotle, to act as tutor for this son who was so clearly destined by the gods for greatness.

kingdom was too large to govern, however, and began to lose pieces to rebels and petty kings on its borders as early as the 200s. By the time the Romans were assaulting the western areas, most of the east was already lost.

3. **The Antigonid kingdom.** This kingdom was also founded by a general, who claimed the old Macedonian homeland and ruled part of what had been Greece as well. The rest of Greece was divided among several leagues of city-states, which vied with each other for political and economic supremacy, until both they and the Macedonians fell to the Romans in the middle 100s B.C.E.

⚜ RELIGION

In form and content, the Hellenistic religions that evolved after the conquests of Alexander were different from both the Greek religion of the Classical Age, and the earlier religions of China and India. In form, the new religions were frequently modeled on Greek beliefs; worship was often conducted outdoors, and the priests played a relatively minor role and were accorded little prestige. In content, however, eastern contributions far outweighed those of the Greeks. Despite the prestige of the conquering Greeks, the worship of the traditional Greek gods such as Zeus and Athena soon died out completely in the East.

■ The cult of Isis was one of the most popular mystery religions in the Hellenistic world. This fresco from Herculaneum in Italy depicts a religious ceremony in front of the temple of Isis. At the top, a priest holds a golden vessel while below him another priest leads the worshipers with a staff. A third priest fans the flames at the altar.

As you will remember, participation in the cults of the traditional Greek gods did not imply belief, an ethical viewpoint, or even an emotional attachment to the gods. The rites were essentially civic ceremonies, rather than a moral guide to living well or a promise of salvation. As such, they held no appeal to non-Greeks, who neither understood the patriotic meaning of the ceremonies nor found any satisfaction in their moral or emotional "message." As time passed, instead of the natives adopting the Greek religion, the Greek immigrants turned more and more to the native religions, which were allowed full freedom under Greek rule. These religions *did* offer some promise of eternal life or earthly prosperity; they provided some concrete emotional support; and they also responded to human longing for security and a guide to right and wrong.

In the second century B.C.E., these eastern religions became immensely popular among many of the eastern Greeks, especially the lower classes. Three of the most important were the cults of Isis, goddess of the Nile and renewal; Mithra, god of eternal life; and Serapis, the Egyptian god of the underworld and the judge of souls. All three shared certain characteristics, which allow them

to be called **mystery religions.** They demanded faith rather than reason. To believers, who followed the instructions of the priests, they promised eternal life. Life would overcome death, and the afterworld would be an infinitely more pleasant place than this one. These deities were universal gods, who had jurisdiction over all people everywhere whether they recognized the god or not. The stage was being set for the triumph of the greatest of the mystery religions, Christianity.

✦ PHILOSOPHY: THREE HELLENISTIC VARIETIES

The mystery religions were especially appealing to the less educated and the poor. These people were the most likely to suffer the terrible alienation and desperation that were often part of life in the cold, impersonal Hellenistic towns. For them, the promise of a better life in the next world became the true reason for living at all.

The better educated upper class was more inclined to look askance at such "pie in the sky" and turn, instead, to philosophies that seemed more realistic and did not demand a difficult leap of faith. An additional reason was the search for some other all-embracing concept of community as the *polis* ideal faded.

Three philosophies in particular attracted the Hellenistic Greeks. The first to appear was **Cynicism,** which emeged as an organized school in the middle 300s but became more popular later. Its major figure was the famous **Diogenes,** who reportedly toured the streets of Athens with a lantern in full daylight, searching for an honest man. Cynicism has come to mean something very different from what it signified originally. In his teachings, Diogenes called for a return to absolute simplicity and a rejection of artificial divisions, whether political or economic. Cynicism was the opposite of what is now called materialism. Relatively few people could adapt themselves to the rigid poverty and absence of egotism that the Cynics demanded, but the philosophy nevertheless had a great impact upon Hellenistic civilized life, in much the same way that St. Francis would later influence thirteenth-century Christianity.

The second philosophy was **Epicureanism,** named after its founder, **Epicurus,** who taught at his school in Athens during the early third century B.C.E. (After the Macedonian conquest, Athens continued to be the undisputed intellectual center of the Greek world for many years despite its loss of political importance). Like cynicism, the word *Epicurean* has undergone a major transformation of meaning. Epicurus taught that the principal good of life was *pleasure,* which he defined as the avoidance of pain. He was not talking about physical sensation so much as mental or spiritual pleasure and pain. He believed that inner peace was to be obtained only by consciously rejecting the values and prejudices of others and turning inward to discover what is important to you. Epicureanism resembles Buddhism in certain respects, and some feel that this is no coincidence, as Epicurus may have had knowledge of the Indian philosophy, which was spreading rapidly in the East during this period. Epicureanism led to political indifference and even withdrawal, as it said that political life led to delusive excitement and false passion: better to ignore the public affairs of the world, and focus on finding your own serenity.

The third philosophy, **Stoicism,** was the product of a freed slave, a Phoenician named **Zeno** who had been brought to Athens around 300 B.C.E. The name *Stoicism* came about because Zeno taught at the *stoa,* a certain open place in the city's center. Although Epicureanism attracted many converts, it was Stoicism that captured the largest following among the Hellenistic population. Zeno emphasized the *brotherhood of all men* and disdained the social conventions that falsely separated them. He taught that a good man was obliged to participate in public life to help the less fortunate as best he could. Whether he was successful or not was not so important as the fact that he had tried. The Stoics (again, the word has undergone a huge change in meaning from ancient times to the present) thought that it was not whether you won or lost, but how you played the game that mattered. Virtue was, and had to be, its own reward.

The Stoics made popular the concept of an overarching *natural law* that governed all human affairs. One law for all, which was implanted in the brain and heart of all humans by the fact of their humanity, was the Stoics' guiding principle. This concept was to gain a following among the Romans after they came into the eastern Hellenistic world; Stoicism eventually became the chief philosophy, by far, of the Roman ruling class. It was a philosophy of noble acts, guided by lofty ideals of what a human being could, and should be. It strongly emphasized the necessity of service to one's fellows and the recognition that all are essentially equal under the skin.

❖ SCIENCE AND THE ARTS

The common belief that Greek science had its heyday during the Classical Age is erroneous. Science did not really come into its own until the Hellenistic period. The most important areas of inquiry were *biology, physics,* *math, astronomy,* and *geography.* The medical arts were particularly prominent during this period; the third and second centuries B.C.E. produced a number of major contributors to medical knowledge and theory.

The Greek habit of rational and logical thought was especially useful in the sciences. Aristotle, who had been the tutor of the young Alexander, insisted on the necessity of careful *observation of phenomena* before attempting to explain their causes. His successors at the Lyceum, the famous school he founded in Athens, proceeded along those lines and obtained worthwhile results in several fields. The biggest single center of science was in the great city of Alexandria, Egypt, where many "research centers" were established and supported by the very rich Ptolemaic kings. The world's largest library and museum were there.

One of the chief stimuli to scientific work was the new exposure of the Greeks to the Babylonian mathematicians and astronomers/astrologers, thanks to the conquests of Alexander. The work in *astronomy* done at this time would stand without serious challenge until the sixteenth century C.E.! Among the outstanding astronomers were Aristarchus of Samos (310–230 B.C.E.) and Hipparchus of Nicaea (260–190 B.C.E.). Aristarchus proposed a heliocentric model of the universe in which the earth revolved around the sun. **Heliocentrism** was attacked by Hipparchus and others, however, and in the second century C.E., a later astronomer named Ptolemy picked up the theory of a geocentric universe (that is, centered on the earth); this became the standard wisdom of astronomy for the next 1,500 years, until Copernicus questioned it.

The most important figures in *geography* were the Greek **Eratosthenes** (c. 276–c. 194 B.C.E.). and Strabo (c. 64 B.C.E.– c. 23 C.E.). Eratosthenes calculated the circumference of the earth very accurately, and his data provided the first reliable maps of the globe. (see Map 11.2.)

In *physics,* the outstanding researcher was **Archimides** (c. 287–212 B.C.E.), who was equally important in mathematics. In the third century B.C.E., Euclid, an Egyptian Greek, produced the most influential math treatise ever written, the *Elements of Geometry.* All of these scientists profited from the work done by Mesopotamian, and especially Babylonian, scholars during the previous three centuries; now in the Hellenistic Age, the Greek world was brought into contact with the knowledge of the Middle East.

It is worth noting that most of Hellenistic science was not driven by the desire to ease men's burdens or to save labor. The Greeks in general were not interested in the practical aspects of science, which we now call technology. Many of their discoveries and experimental results were allowed to be forgotten because no one saw any need to transform these theoretical breakthroughs into practical applications for daily life. The physical experiments performed by the brilliant Archimides are a good example: neither he nor his fellow scientists ever tried to apply his findings to ordinary work tasks.

The reasons for the Greeks' lack of interest in practical applications of science are not clear. One factor seems to have been the Greeks' contempt for manual labor. They seemed to think that hard labor was fitting only for beasts, not for human beings. Then, too, labor-saving devices were not much in demand in the Hellenistic period for there was an abundance of labor available for all tasks—slaves, who were much more numerous now than they had been earlier.

By about 200 B.C.E., Hellenistic science had begun a slow decline. Astronomy was being replaced by astrology, and the initial advances in physics and math were not being followed up by Greeks or non-Greeks. Only in

medicine were some significant advances made, notably by the so-called Empiricists, doctors who were convinced that the answer to the ills of the body was to be found in the careful analysis of diseases and their physical causes. Building on the work of the great Hippocrates, these men were able to identify a good part of the body's anatomy, including the circulation of the blood and the functions of the nerves, the liver, and other vital organs. Medical knowledge would not reach so high a level again in the West until the end of the Middle Ages.

Art and Literature

The fine *arts* in the Hellenistic world were generally modeled on the art of the Hellenic Age, but tended to be more realistic. They also lacked some of the creative vigor and imagination that had so marked Greek art in the earlier period, and they sometimes tended toward a love of display for its own sake—a sort of boastfulness and pretentiousness. The Hellenistic Age was a time when many individuals were becoming immensely rich through trade or manufacturing, and they wanted to show off their new wealth. Adorning their homes with works of art or sponsoring a piece of sculpture and the like for the community allowed the new rich to indulge their desires.

A chief hallmark of Hellenistic art was the new emphasis on the individual artist as creator. In this epoch, for the first time, the name of the artist is almost always found on a work of art. Not only did many artists sign their works, but we even hear of architects who took money for their plans, rather than being satisfied by the honor of the community. This emphasis on the individual is another aspect of the decreased sense of community and the growing alienation that we discussed earlier in this chapter.

Much more *literature* has survived from the Hellenistic Age than from the Classical Age. Unfortunately, the Hellenistic Age produced many second-rate, but few first-rate talents. Both artistic inspiration and execution seem to have declined; there were many imitators, but few original thinkers. The main centers of literature were in Alexandria, Rhodes, Pergamum, and other eastern areas rather than in Athens or Greece itself.

The same was generally true of the *plastic arts;* great sculpture and buildings were more likely to be created in the East than in Greece, in large part because the richest cities of the Hellenistic Age were to be found there, along with the wealthiest inhabitants. In imagination and execution, much Hellenistic sculpture and architecture were very impressive; indeed, they were much superior to the

■ Hellenistic artists were often intent on producing both a realistic portrayal and on demonstrating their technical mastery. Both intentions are fully achieved in this life-sized statue of an old woman.

literary works. The absolute mastery of stone that was already established by the artists of the Classical Age continued and even developed further. Such great works as the *Laocoön, The Dying Gaul,* and the *Old Woman* show an ability to "make the stone speak" that has been the envy of other ages. But even in sculpture, there was a great deal of copying of earlier forms and an abundance of second-class work.

✤ THE HELLENISTIC ECONOMY

Hellenistic civilization was much more urban than Greece had been during the Classical Age. The Hellenistic economy was characterized by large-scale, long-distance enterprises. Big cities such as Pergamum, Alexandria, and Antioch required large-scale planning to ensure that they would be supplied with food and consumer necessities of all types. Manufacturing and commerce were common and also were large scale; trade was carried on in all directions, even with China and Spain. The upper classes became very wealthy indeed.

The goods traded included ceramic housewares, olive oil, wine, and, perhaps most commonly, grain. They were carried by land and sea to all corners of the Near and Middle East and most of coastal Europe, as well as to India. A contract, written in what is now Somalia in Africa, has survived. It was signed by a Greek from Greece, a Carthaginian from North Africa, and a black from the African interior. In this era, the Greeks really came to the fore as tireless and daring mariners of the world's seas.

Outside the cities and towns, the economy depended as ever on farming and related activities such as fruit growing, timber, beekeeping, and fishing. The plantation system of agriculture, based on large gangs of unfree labor, was introduced wherever it could flourish. Consequently, the Hellenistic economy depended more heavily on slavery than had been the case in previous civilizations. For the first time, large groups of people were pulled into lifelong slave status, which was hereditary and passed on to their children. In many places, small farmers were forced into debt, and the family farms that had been typical of earlier Greece gave way to some form of bondage to a large landlord.

In Ptolemaic Egypt, the old system went on without change: small sharecroppers tilled the land for the great

■ This marvelous statue, now in the Louvre in Paris, portrays Nike, the Hellenistic goddess of victory. Unfortunately, the head was lost in ancient times.

landlords, except now the lords were mostly Greeks, and the exploitation was more severe. Egypt was the wealthiest of all the successor kingdoms, and the Ptolemaic dynasty, which ruled Egypt for three centuries until it fell to the Romans, was the envy of the other Hellenistic kings. Cleopatra was the last of these Greek-Egyptian monarchs.

In the next three chapters, we will see how the unimportant and provincial city of Rome became the inheritor of the Hellenistic East. We will also look at the way the Romans altered Hellenistic culture until it became a specifically Roman civilization.

Summary

The Hellenistic Age is a convenient, though deceptively simple label for a widely varying mix of peoples and ideas. For about three centuries, from the death of Alexander to the Romans' coming into the East, the physical extent of the Mediterranean and western Asian cultures, that is, the world of the Western heritage, increased dramatically. This period also saw the first large-scale contacts between the civilization of the Mediterranean basin and those of East Asia, mainly India but also China.

Rome was a part of the Hellenistic Age, and through it, the civilization of the Mediterranean was passed on to Europe in later years. The philosophies and religious thought of the Hellenistic world eventually became the basic lenses through which the entire European continent (and its North American offspring) would perceive the world of the spirit. Our cultural debts to these Greco-Eastern forebears are beyond easy measure.

Test Your Knowledge

1. *Hellen istic* means a
   a. blend of Greek and eastern ideas and forms.
   b. blend of Greek and Roman ideas and forms.
   c. purely Greek style later transferred to Rome.
   d. mixed style limited in extent to Europe.
2. Compared to the classical Greek economy, the Hellenistic economy depended
   a. more on slaves.
   b. less on slaves.
   c. more on free labor.
   d. more on the inventiveness of resident alien craftsmen.
3. Which of the following does *not* describe the Egypt of the Ptolemies?
   a. A backwater in the sciences
   b. A very wealthy government
   c. Ruled by a supremely powerful pharaoh
   d. A highly centralized political and economic authority
4. The scientific interests of the Hellenistic period
   a. were limited to math.
   b. led to an industrial revolution.
   c. were limited to agriculture.
   d. had little connection with technology.
5. In public affairs, the Epicureans insisted

   a. on active participation by their followers.
   b. that all politics and governments were equally corrupt.
   c. that democracy was superior to all other types of government.
   d. on indifference to government.
6. The Greek immigrants to Hellenistic Asia were usually
   a. resented and resisted by the local authorities.
   b. given favored official and financial positions.
   c. poverty-stricken workers and craftsmen.
   d. eager to mix with the native populations.
7. In the Hellenistic period, the sociopolitical unit replacing the classical *polis* was the
   a. village.
   b. city.
   c. province.
   d. family.
8. Which of these adjectives is the *least* appropriate description of Hellenistic society and customs discussed in this chapter?
   a. Alienated
   b. Stratified
   c. Urban
   d. Communal

Identification Terms

Archimedes	Epicureanism	heliocentrism	Stoicism
Cynicism	Epicurus	mystery religions	Zeno
Diogenes	Eratosthenes		

Bibliography

Bowman, A. K. *Egypt after the Pharaohs,* 1986. Deals with the mixing of Greek and eastern cultures in Egypt.

Green, P. *Alexander the Great,* 1970. One of many biographies of Alexander. Well illustrated and readable.

Hadas, M. *Hellenistic Culture: Fusion and Diffusion,* 1959. A difficult but informative study of the mixing of Greek and eastern cultures.

Hamilton, J. R. *Alexander the Great,* 1973. Another readable and well-illustrated biography.

Lloyd, G. E. *Greek Science after Aristotle,* 1973. Deals with the development of the natural sciences in the Hellenistic Age.

Long, A. *Hellenistic Philosophy,* 1986. Examines the three major philosophies in detail.

Pollitt, J. *Art in the Hellenistic Age,* 1986. Shows how art forms reflect the mixing of Greek and eastern traditions.

Rose, H. J. *Religion in Greece and Rome,* 1959. An examination of Hellenistic religions.

Tarn, W. W., and G. T. Griffith. *Hellenistic Civilization,* 1966. A good introduction.

Walbank, F. W. *The Hellenistic World,* 1981. Perhaps the best general history for students.

THE ROMAN REPUBLIC

c. 750–500 B.C.E.	Etruscans rule Rome
c. 500–27 B.C.E.	Roman Republic
300s–200s B.C.E.	Conquest of Italy
264–201 B.C.E.	The Punic Wars begin Roman expansions outside Italy
100s B.C.E.	Expansion into the eastern Mediterranean basin
50s–30s B.C.E.	Crisis of the late Republic: the two Triumvirates

The successor to the Greek and Persian civilizations in the Mediterranean basin and the Near East was Rome, the Italian city-state that grew to be the most feared power in the East and West alike. It is important to remember that although Rome is usually called the successor to Hellenistic Greece, early Rome and Greece actually overlapped in time. Chronologically, Rome emerged during almost the same era as Athens and Sparta, but did not become important until much later. This chapter will look at the initial stages of Rome's growth, the era of the Roman Republic, which lasted until almost the first century C.E.

✤ ROMAN FOUNDATIONS

Rome is situated about halfway down the western coast of the Italian peninsula, where one of the country's very few sizable rivers, the Tiber, flows through a good-sized fertile plain before emptying into the sea. This river and the plain (*Latium*) were the reason early settlements were located here, and it is only in modern times that their significance to the city's prosperity has faded.

Very early Italy and the Italians are even more a mystery than Greece and the Greeks. We do know that Indo-European peoples settled central and south Italy at least as early as Minoan days (about 1500 B.C.E.), reaching a high degree of Neolithic culture. They developed farming and villages, but lagged seriously behind the peoples of the eastern Mediterranean, and the Near East. Among other things, there is no sign that they had a written language until as late as 700 B.C.E.

About 800 B.C.E., three peoples from the East began to enter Italy first as colonists and then as rulers of various segments of the peninsula. These were the *Etruscans,* the *Greeks,* and the *Phoenicians.* Each of these civilized groups contributed substantially to Italian development, and the first two had a decisive effect on Roman civilization's early forms.

We know very little about the **Etruscans** except that they came into Italy around 800, probably by following a route along the northern Adriatic Sea, and were already highly civilized at that time. They established a series of small city-states in the northern and central areas of the peninsula, ruling over the native Italians by virtue of their superior weaponry and organization. They left a small amount of writing, but it has never been deciphered, so we have no historical record in the strict sense. We do know that Etruscan kings ruled over early Rome from about 750 to about 500 B.C.E.; during that time, they brought civilized life to the Romans. The pictorial record left by the Etruscans, mainly in recently rediscovered underground tombs, make it clear that the early Romans derived much of their religious beliefs, art forms, and architecture from the Etruscans.

One thing the Etruscan upper classes prized, but which the Romans came to hold in contempt, was physical comfort. According to Roman sources that may be unreliable, the Romans eventually were able to defeat the Etruscans because they were soft and could not stand up to the rigors of war as long as their rivals. After the Roman victory, the Etruscans gradually fade from history, absorbed by their former subjects and others.

In the long run, the Greeks had even more influence upon Roman attitudes and manners than did the Etruscans. Whereas the Romans viewed the Etruscans as rivals and defeated enemies, they regarded the Greeks as the one people who were superior to themselves in some ways, namely, in culture, imagination, and in commerce. The early Romans were very much impressed by the Greek migrants who had settled in southern Italy during the 700s. The Romans were awed by the Greek towns and cities, by the Greeks' skills in organizing and governing, and by their experience in the great world outside Italy.

Overcrowding at home and the Greek love of adventure had caused these colonists to leave their homes in Corinth, Thebes, and other Greek cities and settle in Italy. They soon transformed southern Italy into a prosperous and commercially advanced civilization, but found they had to fight both the Etruscans and the Phoenicians to hold onto it. True to Greek tradition, they made the job much harder by fighting among themselves. By the 500s, *Carthage* (present-day Tunis), the great colony founded by the Phoenicians on the coast of North Africa, was vying with the Greeks for control of the rich island of Sicily. At the same time, the Etruscans were pushing down from their bases in northern Italy.

Phoenician influence on Italian events came through Carthage, although this great trading city had become independent of its mother country by 700. Before the rise of Rome, Carthage was the most powerful force in the western Mediterranean. It sent ships as far away as Britain and the North Sea, as well as into the Nile, and had founded colonies of its own all over the coasts of Spain and France. The Carthaginians fought the Greek cities of southern Italy to a draw until the Romans were able to take advantage of their mutual exhaustion to conquer both of them.

■ The vivid quality of Etruscan statuary is one of our few sources of knowledge about these people, who were the forerunners of the Romans in central Italy.

According to ancient Roman tradition, Rome was founded by the twin brothers Romulus and Remus, legendary descendants of the survivors who fled burning Troy after the Trojan War. By 753 B.C.E., the population had grown to the point that the settlement could be considered a town; it had walls and its own government. Modern historians agree that the city-state of Rome was founded at approximately that date. According to Roman history written much later, the town was under Etruscan rule until 509 B.C.E. In that year, a peaceable rebellion ousted the last Etruscan king, and the city was thenceforth ruled by a combination of the Senate and the people—in the original Latin, the *Senatus et populus.*

The Senate was composed of the upper class, the **patricians** (from the Latin *patres* or "fathers"), who made up perhaps 5–10 percent of the total population and had had considerable power even under the king. The **plebeians** or commoners, composed the other 90 percent and were represented in political affairs by delegates to the General Assembly whom they elected by wards within the city and by so-called tribes outside it. Originally, the General Assembly was to be as powerful—perhaps more so—than the Senate, which had only advisory powers. But soon after the foundation of the Roman Republic, the Senate had obtained decisive power while the Assembly became a seldom-summoned rubber stamp.

The executive was a small staff of officials who were elected by the Senate and Assembly for short terms. The chief executive power resided in two *consuls,* who were elected from among the members of the Senate for one-year terms that could not be repeated. Each consul had a veto power over the other, an indication of the Romans' fear of permanent dictatorship. When one consul was in the field as leader of the republic's forces, the other was the head of the civil government at home. Below the consuls in authority were the *censors,* who were also always drawn from the ranks of the senators. The censors were originally tax assessors, but later came to have the power to supervise the conduct and morals of their fellow senators. The Roman bureaucracy also included a few other offices, which were dominated by the patricians until a series of plebeian revolts or threats to revolt opened them up to the commoners.

At the beginning of the republic, the patricians controlled all important aspects of politics and government and did not hesitate to exploit the plebeians. For two centuries, the plebeians struggled to attain equality; in the process, their most effective weapon was the threat to lay down their arms rather than defend the city. Their most important gains were the adoption of the **Law of the Twelve Tables,** the first codified Roman Law, in 450 B.C.E.; the expansion of their political influence in 367 after threatening a revolt; and finally, the enactment of the Hortensian Law (named after the consul of the day) in 287, which expanded the powers of the Assembly, making it supposedly equal to the Senate.

By about 250, the Roman political structure had obtained a nice balance between the aristocrats (patricians) and the common people (plebeians). The chief officers of the plebeians were the **tribunes,** who were representatives of the various tribes. There were about ten tribunes, and they had great power to speak and act in the name of the common Romans. At first, the tribunes were chosen from the common people, and were true representatives of the plebeians. Later, however, after about 200, the tribunes were offered membership in the Senate, and as they sought to become censors and consuls, they came to identify increasingly with the interests of the patricians. This development was to be fateful for the republic.

After the passage of the Hortensian Law in 287, the Roman political community remained essentially democratic in structure for about two centuries. Plebeians and patricians had equal voting rights and supposedly equal access to office. But in practice, the government was not really democratic. Democracy failed in Rome, just as it had in Athens. When a crisis arose, the Roman Republic and democracy died an inglorious death.

✦ ROME'S CONQUEST OF ITALY

Under this mixed government of aristocrats and commoners, the Roman city-state gradually and painfully became the master of Italy. Down to about 340, the almost constant wars took place in a strip of land along the west coast. The Romans led a federation of tribes living in the plain of Latium, first against the Etruscans and then against other Italians (see Map 12.1).

Little by little, the Romans made gains. Although Rome suffered a devastating invasion by Celtic tribes called Gauls in 390, by 340 or so the Romans and their Latin allies were the rulers of most of central Italy. When the Latins attempted to revolt, the Romans crushed them. Next the Romans turned their attention to the Samnites, a group of Italic tribes in the south and east of the peninsula. The war against the Samnites was lengthy and very difficult, but proved significant, for during this conflict the Romans perfected their military organization and created the myth of Roman invincibility.

The surrender of the Samnites in 282 B.C.E. brought the Romans into contact with a new enemy—the Greek city-states of southern Italy, who were supported by *Pyrrhus,* a powerful Greco-Macedonian general. After a couple of costly victories, Pyrrhus was defeated. Rome now inserted itself into the ongoing struggle between the Greeks and the Carthaginians in Sicily. It would be only a matter of time before the two great powers of the western Mediterranean engaged in a contest for supremacy.

During these almost continuous conflicts, the Romans learned how to assure that yesterday's enemies became today's friends and allies. A pragmatic and flexible people, the Romans very soon realized that their original practice of humiliating and enslaving the conquered was counterproductive. Instead, they began to encourage the subject populations to become integrated with Rome—to became "good Romans" regardless of their ethnic or historical affiliations. The Romans gave partial *citizenship rights* to the conquered Italians as long as they did not rebel and agreed to supply troops when Rome called. This arrangement was advantageous to the conquered because it eased their tax burden, assured them of Roman assistance against their own enemies, and gave them wide-ranging powers of self-government. Some of the conquered were eventually allowed to become full citizens, which meant they could run for office and vote in Roman elections,

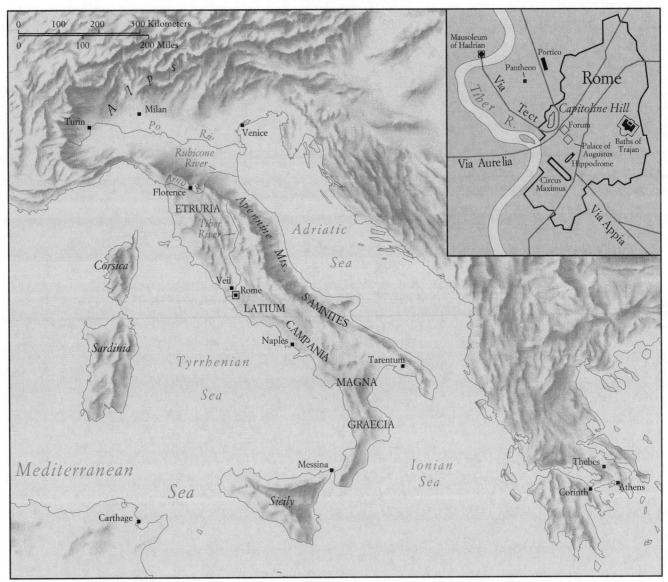

⦿ **MAP 12.1 Ancient Italy.** The Italian peninsula was invaded innumberable times in history. The native Italic peoples of the north and center were taken over by the more civilized Etruscans in the tenth to eighth centuries B.C.E. Rome itself was probably founded by the uniting of several villages under a single government in the eighth century, as Roman legend states.

serve in the Roman army and bureaucracy, and have protection for property and other legal rights that were not available to noncitizens. The upper classes of the conquered Italians and Greeks were eager to Latinize themselves and thus to qualify as full citizens. They achieved this by intermarrying with Romans, adopting the Latin language, and accepting the basic elements of Roman custom and law.

⚜ THE PUNIC WARS

Although the Romans were almost constantly at war between 500 and 275 B.C.E., these conflicts were generally defensive in nature or were responses to the calls of allies for help. In these wars, the Romans were dealing with peoples who were similar to themselves and whose conquered lands were adjacent to Roman possessions.

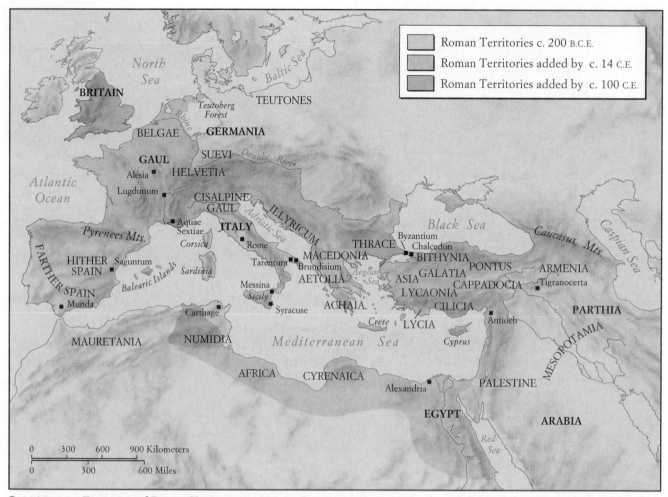

● **MAP 12.2 Expansion of Roman Territories to 100 C.E.** Rome's empire was created not by plan, but by a series of wars which had little or no relation to one another. Roman influences were permanently barred from central Europe after the massive defeat in the Teutoburg Forest in 9 C.E. and the establishment of the Rhine and Danube borders thereafter. In Asia, the Romans created a series of client kingdoms which relieved them of having to station large numbers of troops there.

Not until the First Punic War (264–241 B.C.E.) against Carthage, did Rome more or less openly embark on imperial expansion. With that war, Rome became an empire in fact, though it retained the laws and politics of a democratic city-state. This created internal tensions that ultimately could not be resolved; the result was bloody civil war.

The two wars against mighty Carthage were decisive in Rome's rise from being a merely Italian power to becoming the center of a great empire. The first war broke out over the question of dominance in Sicily. It lasted for more than twenty years until both sides were almost exhausted and made a reluctant peace. In this war, Rome for the first time developed a navy, which was necessary to counter the large Carthaginian fleets.

The First Punic War ended with the surrender of Sicily and Sardinia to Rome, but Carthage was far from completely subdued. During the ensuing twenty-year truce, it built up its forces, especially in the large colony of Spain. There, the brilliant general **Hannibal** amassed a large army (50,000 men), which successfully crossed the Alps in mid-winter and descended on Italy (see the Biography in this chapter).

Hannibal won battle after battle against the desperate Romans, but lost the war. Finally, after ravaging Italy for fifteen years (218–203), Hannibal was forced to return to Carthage to defend the city against a Roman counterinvasion. The decisive **battle of Zama** in 202 was a clear Roman victory, and Carthage was forced to give up most of its extensive holdings in Africa and Spain. These were made into new provinces of what by now was a rapidly growing empire (see Map 12.2). The **Punic Wars** determined that Roman, and not Carthaginian, culture and civilization would control the Mediterranean basin for the foreseeable future.

✣ THE CONQUEST OF THE EAST

Victorious in the Punic Wars, the Romans at once turned their eyes eastward. Rome's eastward expansion was somewhat surprising, because until this time the Romans had shown very little interest in the East and had tried to stay out of the continuous quarreling of the Hellenistic kingdoms. The Roman upper classes were much influenced by Greek culture and Greek ideas, which they had encountered in conquering the prosperous colonies in southern Italy, but they had shown no interest in actually taking over the Greek homelands.

But in the 190s, immediately after the Punic Wars, ambitious consuls did just that by taking sides in an internal Greek struggle. Within a very short time, the Greco-Macedonian kingdom was under Rome's control.

The other Hellenistic kingdoms around the eastern edge of the Mediterranean were also soon defeated by the Roman armies, and could have been at once made into Roman provinces. But there was strong opposition to this from some senators, who thought that the society being created by military conquests was far from what Roman traditions honored. A seesaw struggle between conservatives, who wished Rome to remain a homogeneous city-state, and imperialists, who wanted expansion (and wealth!), went on for about a century (150–50 B.C.E.). The conservatives were fighting for a lost cause, however. By the latter date the question had become which of the imperialist groups would eventually triumph in the constant maneuvers for supreme power.

The conquest of the East was executed by an outstanding military machine. It was composed mainly of infantry, which was recruited from all male citizens. In the early republic, only property holders were allowed citizenship, and only citizens could bear arms. The commanders were all patricians, while the plebeians served in the ranks. Service was for an indefinite term, and as the wars multiplied in the fourth and third centuries B.C.E., many citizens were away from their homes for lengthy periods. The effects were ruinous for many simple peasant-soldiers, who could not tend their fields adequately and had no other source of income (because army service was considered an honor, soldiers were not paid).

As early as the mid-300s, military needs were great enough that a group of permanent commanders called *proconsuls* was created; they were responsible for given areas of newly conquered lands. The custom of electing commanders annually fell into disuse, as it was clear that men of talent would be needed for more than a year. In this way, a group of men who were both politically potent through their connections in the Senate and militarily potent through their command responsibilities came into existence. So long as they continued to regard the Senate and the consuls whom the Senate elected as their rightful superiors, all went well. But it was inevitable that an ambitious commander would come along who would look

■ **Street Scene at Pompeii.** A tremendous volcanic explosion buried the thriving Roman city of Pompeii in 79 C.E. with such suddenness as to preserve much of the masonry and even many mummified bodies under the ash. This scene of the Via della Abbondanza shows the result of a century's excavation work.

Hannibal
247–183 B.C.E.

Although the Carthaginians left few historical records, we know a little about the life of their greatest leader through the comments of his enemies, the Romans. Hannibal, son of the general Hamilcar Barca, was born in 247 B.C.E. in Carthage, the imperial city-state on the coast of North Africa opposite Sicily. When still a boy, Hannibal was taken on campaign by his father, who led the Carthaginian forces in Spain against Rome's allies in the First Punic War. Hannibal swore eternal enmity to Rome, an oath he carried out to his dying day, in 183 B.C.E.

At the end of the twenty-year truce after the First Punic War, Hannibal was ready. From his Spanish base, he set out in 218 with an army of approximately 50,000 and 58 African elephants. Crossing over the low Pyrenees and through the coastal plain of Mediterranean France in the autumn, Hannibal was intent on invading Rome's home grounds. The Roman leaders, despite warnings, did not believe that anyone would be so foolish as to attempt a crossing of the Alps in winter, elephants or not. They underestimated their opponent. An attempt to cut Hannibal off before he reached the mountains failed. We do not know what route Hannibal's army took to cross the snow-covered Alps into northern Italy. Certainly, though, it was an extraordinarily difficult, even suicidal undertaking. Avalanches were a constant threat, and the icy footing and fierce winter weather took the lives of many horses and elephants. As many as 10,000 soldiers were lost as well. But their leader's iron will never wavered.

Finally, the army reached relative safety in the Po River valley, still intact and soon in good fighting trim. Now the difficulties were on the Roman side, as the leaders in the capital tried to recover from their surprise. The vassal tribes of Italy were soon put to flight by the battle-hardened Carthaginians, and Hannibal's cavalry proved too much even for the Romans. In several battles in 217–216 B.C.E., the Romans were routed, notably, at Cannae in central Italy. There, despite being outnumbered by many thousands, Hannibal inflicted the worst defeat Rome had ever suffered. Reportedly, the rings plucked from the hands of dead Romans after the battle filled three large sacks.

---

first for personal advancement and only later or never to the welfare of the state. Such men began to appear regularly after the First Punic War, which created opportunities to get rich in the new territories won from Carthage. These opportunities redoubled after the Second Punic War. By then, Rome was rapidly developing a professional army that would look to its field commanders and not to a distant Senate as its legitimate director.

✤ ROMAN GOVERNMENT IN THE LATE REPUBLIC

All through this imperial expansion, Rome's government had remained technically that of an ethnically homogeneous city-state, with traditional powers neatly allocated between the senatorial upper class and the masses. By the end of the second century, the real Rome had deviated far from this ideal, and the strains were beginning to show (see the Document in this chapter).

Many poverty-stricken ex-farmers flocked into the city, seeking any kind of work and ready to listen to anyone promising them a better existence. Many of them had served in the army for years and were then discharged only to find that their lands had been seized for debt or confiscated through the maneuvers of wealthy speculators. The new landowners created great estates that were worked by the vast quantities of slaves, which the Roman overseas conquests were bringing into Italy.

The members of the new urban *proletariat* were citizens with votes, and they were ready to sell those votes to the highest bidder among the upper-class demagogues who wanted power. They were also ready to follow any general who promised them a decent living in his army of long-serving veterans; men would serve out their time and

But Cannae was Hannibal's high tide; for reasons that are still obscure, he failed to follow up his victory with a direct attack on the panicked city of Rome. Instead, he allowed his army to become bogged down for years in central and southern Italy, fighting Roman allies. In Sicily and Spain, the reviving Romans used their navy to attack Carthaginian colonies and force their surrender. At home in Carthage, the leaders were growing tired of the costly war and told Hannibal that they could supply him no longer. The Romans intercepted reinforcements under the command of Hannibal's brother and hurled the brother's decapitated head into Hannibal's camp one night.

For the next several years, Hannibal sought to bring Rome to terms by ravaging much of Italy. At last, the Roman general Scipio (later Scipio *Africanus*) turned the tide decisively by invading Carthage's home territory in 204. Recalled to defend his city, Hannibal was defeated at Zama in 202; Carthage was forced to surrender most of its colonies and its fleet and to pay massive reparations. Rome was now supreme throughout the western Mediterranean. Many years later, the still defiant Hannibal engaged in one last plot to overthrow the hated Romans. The plot was discovered, and he poisoned himself rather than face extradition and certain death in Italy.

then be given a good mustering-out pension or a bit of land to support themselves in old age. That land could easily enough be taken from the victims of new Roman-incited wars around the Mediterranean and in what is now Western Europe.

Starting about 150 B.C.E., Roman public life thus became a complex struggle between those upper-class individuals who saw the growing need for social and political reform and those who were against reform either because they could not understand the need or because they advocated a full revolution rather than just reform. The outstanding reformers were the two **Gracchi brothers,** who were elected tribunes in the 130s and 120s and attempted to help the proletariat. The Gracchi recognized the land problem—the forcing of the peasants-soldiers off their ancestral lands—as the fundamental error of the Roman system and attempted to remedy it by dividing the

large state-owned lands in the provinces among them. This outraged the conservatives, and the brothers were murdered for their pains.

A different sort of approach to the land problem was made by *Marius,* a few years later. This former consul saw his chance for fame in a war against African rebels, and had himself reelected consul for six terms—a "first" that was to became a commonplace within a couple more decades. Marius also abolished the property qualification for his soldiers, thereby opening the way for a professional, volunteer army composed of men who had nothing to lose and would follow any leaders who made sure that they got plunder and pensions. More and more, the Roman military was becoming a force for instability and a potential base for all who had political ambitions.

The harsh soldier-consul *Sulla* took advantage of the changes Marius had made in the army to force reforms on

Sallust on the Decline of the Roman Republic

The historian Sallust (86–35 B.C.E.) wrote tellingly of the moral decline that he saw in the later republic. Ultimately, this civic laxness and indifference to virtue opened the path for one would-be dictator after another. Sallust saw the turning point as the final defeat of Rome's great rival, Carthage. When Carthage was finally destroyed, Rome's corruption began in earnest. Although Sallust may have idealized the early days of Rome, there is little doubt that by the first century B.C.E., the Roman state had fallen on evil days.

> ... when Carthage, Rome's rival in her quest for empire, had been annihilated [in 146 by the Third Punic War], every land and sea lay open to her. It was then that fortune turned unkind and confounded all her enterprises. To the men who had so easily endured toil and peril, anxiety and adversity, the leisure and riches which are generally regarded so desirable proved a burden and a curse. Growing love for money, and the lust for power which followed it, engendered every kind of evil. ... Avarice destroyed honor, integrity and every other virtue, and instead taught men to be proud and cruel, to neglect religion, and to hold nothing too sacred to sell. ...
>
> Ambition tempted many to be false, to have one thought hidden in their hearts, another ready on their tongues. ... At first, these vices grew slowly and sometimes met with punishment; later, when the disease had spread like a plague, Rome changed; her government, once so just and admirable, became harsh and unendurable.

Reflecting on the result of this decline in civil propriety, Sallust relates the story of a recent attempt at usurpation of power, the conspiracy of the senator Catiline in 63 B.C.E.:

> In spite of two senatorial decrees, not one man among all the conspirators was induced by the promise of reward to betray their plans, and not one deserted from Cataline. A deadly moral contagion had infected all their minds. ... The city populace were especially eager to fling themselves into a revolutionary adventure. There were several reasons for this. To begin with, those who had made themselves conspicuous anywhere by vice and shameless audacity, those who had wasted their substance by disgraceful excesses, and those whose scandalous or criminal conduct had exiled them from their homes—all these had poured into Rome, till it was like a sewer. ... Young men from the country, whose labor had barely kept them from starvation had been attracted by the private and public doles [welfare payment] available at Rome, and preferred an idle city life to such thankless toil. These, like the rest, stood to gain by public calamities. ... The whole truth is that all disturbers of the peace in this period put forward specious pretexts, claiming either to be protecting the rights of the people or to be strengthening the authority of the Senate. But this was mere pretence; in reality, every one of them was fighting for his personal aggrandizement. Lacking all self-restraint, they stopped at nothing to gain their ends. ...

SOURCE: Sallurts, tras. by S. A. Handford, *The Jugurthine War: The Conspiracy of Cataline*, Penguin Classics. © S.A. Handford, 1963. Reprinted by permission.

an unhappy Senate through military intimidation. He made himself dictator in 83 B.C.E. and packed the Senate with new men, most of them wealthy foreigners from the provinces who had no experience with patrician responsibilities. Sulla instituted several beneficial reforms as well, but because he effected them through brutal force, his overall reputation in Roman history is negative. He instigated civil war against his enemies and killed thousands while trying to save the faltering republic's government. Most of his well-intentioned reforms were abolished as

soon as he died in 78, and the government reverted immediately to open or covert warfare of group against group.

The Triumvirates: Julius Caesar and Octavian Caesar

The final collapse of the republican system was brought on by the patrician general and politician **Julius Caesar** (died 44 B.C.E.), who saw that it was unsuited for governance of a far-flung empire and tried to change it. He maneuvered and conspired with others who were also discontented with the Senate leadership to form an alliance known as the *First Triumvirate* (rule of three). The other members were the wealthy speculator Crassus and the brilliant general Pompey.

During the 50s B.C.E., Caesar made his reputation by conquering the semicivilized Gauls in what is now France, which he turned into a Roman province of great potential. His ambitions fully awakened, he now wished to become consul and use that powerful office to make basic changes in the structure of government. He was opposed by his former ally Pompey and the large majority of the Senate, who viewed him as a dangerous radical. Armed struggle broke out between Pompey and Caesar (Crassus had died) in 49, and after a hard fight, Caesar emerged as the victor.

Returning to Rome in triumph, he made himself dictator and fully intended to start a royal dynasty. He subordinated the Senate entirely to himself and initiated several major reforms of the existing system, including even the Roman calendar. But, in March 44, he was assassinated by

■ **A Roman Physician at Work.** Roman medicine was superior to most of its predecessors. Many Greeks and Egyptians were imported to teach the natives the healing arts. Here a Roman doctor attempts to clean a hero's leg wound.

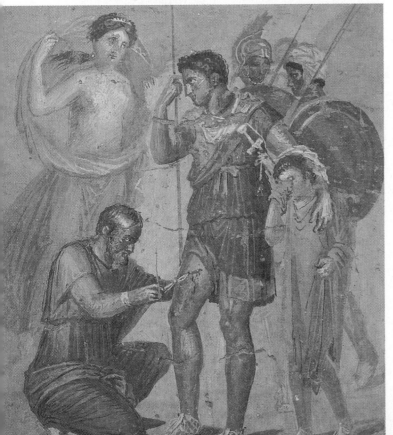

two conservative senators. His only surviving male relative was his grand-nephew, *Octavian Caesar,* whom he had adopted as a son (a common Roman practice) and made his political heir. But Octavian was only eighteen when Caesar died; he had had little political experience and lacked military prowess, so it appeared very unlikely that he would ever fill the office of his adoptive father.

When the senatorial assassins of Julius Caesar could not agree on what should be done to restore the republic, Octavian, Lepidus, and the successful general **Mark Antony** formed an alliance known as the *Second Triumvirate.* The three allies crushed the assassins and then divided the empire: Antony took the East and Egypt, Octavian Italy and the West, and Lepidus Africa. Octavian soon showed himself a gifted politician, but he stood in the shadow of Mark Antony. Lepidus had no independent political hopes and could be ignored. Antony soon made himself unpopular in Rome by apparently succumbing to the charms of the Ptolemaic queen of Egypt, Cleopatra, and maltreating his noble Roman wife and her influential family. Octavian cleverly built his political strength in Italy and acquired much experience in handling men. When the test came, he was ready. The Roman navy in particular was behind him and suspicious of Antony's plans.

In 32 B.C.E. Octavian maneuvered Antony into declaring war against him, thereby threatening to renew the bloody civil wars that had thoroughly alienated the Roman populace by this time. The victory of Octavian's forces at the **battle of Actium** in 31 B.C.E. marked the effective beginning of the Roman Empire.

❧ ROMAN CULTURE IN THE REPUBLIC

Although the Romans always considered the Greeks inferior to themselves in matters of government and war, they generally admired the Greeks' cultural achievements, especially in the arts. But the Romans were less familiar with the Greek culture of the Classical Age (fifth and fourth centuries B.C.E.) than with the Hellenistic culture of the southern Italian Greeks. This culture was less specifically Greek and more cosmopolitan and therefore more easily adapted to others' needs.

In general, the Romans borrowed heavily from the Greek heritage in philosophy, the sciences, and the arts, but that does not mean that they had no native culture. Their own genius and inclinations lay more in the fields of law and administration than in the realm of imagination or the fine arts. In the practical aspects of life, the Romans had few equals. They were always willing to experiment until they found a winning combination or at least one that was acceptable to the majority of citizens. At the same time, they never failed to make elaborate bows to tradition and to insist that they were following in the footsteps of the past when, in fact, they were making changes.

Roman law developed much more fully in the empire than in the republic and will be treated more extensively in the next chapter. One of the greatest Roman achievements, though, was the development of a system of law with the flexibility to meet the needs of peoples as diverse as the Britons and the Syrians. Law and a system of government that combined effective central control with wide local autonomy are the best-known Roman gifts to later Western civilization.

The Latin language evolved rapidly and brilliantly as the republic expanded its contacts with others. *Roman literature* began in the third century B.C.E. when poetry of some excellence, history of a rather inferior sort, and drama modeled on the Greeks began to appear. During the republic's last century, *Cicero, Julius Caesar, Terence, Polybius, Cato,* and *Lucretius* were major contributors. The best days of Roman literature, however, were still ahead.

In the *plastic arts,* the early Roman sculptors and architects worked from both Etruscan and Greek models to produce something specifically Roman by the end of the republican era. Roman portrait sculpture, especially the busts that were produced in numbers, are amazingly realistic and seem "modern" in a way that other ancient art does not. The architectural style favored in the republic was strongly reminiscent of the Greek temple, but also incorporated arches and circles, as in the cupola roofs and semicircular altars, to a much greater degree.

✦ Roman Religion and Philosophy

The religious convictions of the Romans during the republican era centered on the state and the family hearth. Toward the state, the Roman patricians felt an almost personalized attachment, a sense of duty, and a proud obedience to tradition handed down from generation to generation. Toward the family and its symbol, the hearth, the Romans felt the same attachment as most ancient peoples, with the honor of the lineage being of the usual importance to them.

Roman religion was a matter of mutual promises: on the gods' side, protection for the community and survival for the individual; on the human side, ceremonial worship and due respect. Priests existed in Rome, but had relatively little power and prestige among the people. It was a

■ The Roman preference for realism and exactitude in their pictorial arts is shown by this bust of who is assumed to be Emperor Macrin. Although their techniques were generally dependent on classical Greek models, the Roman soon progressed beyond their original desire merely to imitate.

religion of state, rather than of individuals, and it was common for Romans to worship other gods besides those of the official religion. Most of the mystery religions of the Hellenistic world eventually were taken up by Rome.

The gods of the Roman state were taken from both Etruscan and Greek sources, mainly the latter. Chief among them was Jupiter, a father figure similar to the Greek Zeus. Also important were Apollo, Neptune (Poseidon), Hercules, Venus (Aphrodite), Minerva (Athena), and Mars (Ares). Like the rituals of the Greeks, the worship given to these deities was more like a present-day patriotic ceremony than a modern church service. Even less than among the Greeks were the civic gods looked to for ethical guidance or to secure personal immortality by passing a last judgment. The Roman notion of an afterlife changed from person to person and from age to age during Rome's long history. In broad terms it resembled that of the educated Greek: the existence of an afterlife was an open question, but if it did exist, one could know nothing about it through the gods.

Roman philosophy was entirely a product of Greek models, and there was no native Roman creed. In philosophy, the Romans showed great interest in Stoicism and found Epicureanism less appealing. Ideally, and in their own musings about the good life, educated Romans believed that service to the state and the community was the highest duty and that the only way to ensure against the disappointments of earthly life was to renounce the pursuit of wealth and power and live a life of modest seclusion. But few Romans did that! As a people, they were very much attuned to the delights of wealth and power and very much willing to make great efforts to get them.

Roman society was marked by this generalized tension between what it asserted as its highest values and what Romans actually did, given the chance. More than most, Romans were caught between the demands of tradition and the desire to excel in new ways. A people who made much of military virtue, they also insisted on the autonomy of the individual's conscience. A people who were very conscious of the concept of justice and the rule of law, they also had many moments of blind rage when they exerted sadistic power over others.

Summary

From minuscule beginnings, the Roman city-state fought its way forward and outward during the centuries when Greece was sowing the seeds of Western secular culture. The peculiar balance of political power between aristocrats and commoners that the Roman Republic established could last as long as Rome remained a socially and ethnically homogeneous state and extended its rule only to its neighbors in the Italian peninsula. This situation ended with Rome's success in the Punic Wars of the third century B.C.E., when the city-state became in effect, but not yet in name, an empire.

The failure of the republic's political structure to adapt to the demands of imperial rule led to civil war and constant upheaval during the last century of its existence. Reformers as varied in motive as the Gracchi, Marius, and Sulla attempted in vain to find a solution during these unstable years. Julius Caesar tried to establish a monarchy, but was cut down by his conservative enemies. After another decade and a brief war, his adoptive son Octavian had better success and ended the republic.

Roman republican culture and art forms were largely based on Greek and Etruscan models, with the Greeks of the Hellenistic Age being particularly important. In form and contents, philosophy and religion resembled the Greek originals from which they were largely derived. Somewhat more innovation was shown in architecture, the plastic arts, and prose during the late republican epoch.

Test Your Knowledge

1. The peoples who exerted the greatest influence on early Rome were the
   a. Etruscans and Hittites.
   b. Greeks and Egyptians.
   c. Greeks and Etruscans.
   d. Egyptians and Etruscans.
2. Chief executive authority in the Roman Republic was exercised by
   a. a king.
   b. two consuls.
   c. four praetors.
   d. ten tribunes.
3. Roman law is notable for its
   a. egoism and arrogance.
   b. brutality and vengeance.
   c. gentleness and mercy.
   d. practicality and flexibility.
4. The first breakthrough in the plebeians' struggle to achieve legal equality with the patricians came with
   a. a revolt against the Etruscan king.

b. the establishment of the Senate.

c. the election of the consuls.

d. the Law of the Twelve Tables.

5. The decisive change in the political nature of Rome from a homogeneous city-state to an empire came after the

a. conquest of Greece.

b. triumph of Octavian Caesar over his partners in the Second Triumvirate.

c. attainment of supreme power by Julius Caesar.

d. winning of the wars against Carthage.

6. The first province to be added to the infant Roman empire was

a. Gaul.

b. Carthage.

c. Sicily.

d. Spain.

7. The Roman state religion consisted mainly of

a. ritual and ceremony.

b. prayer for personal salvation.

c. theological discussions.

d. emotion-charged public devotions.

8. The cultural influences most prominent in late republican Rome came from

a. the Etruscans.

b. the Egyptians.

c. the Greeks.

d. the Persians.

Identification Terms

Actium (battle of)

Etruscans

Gracchi brothers

Hannibal

Julius Caesar

Law of the Twelve Tables

Mark Antony

patricians

plebeians

Punic Wars

tribunes

Zama (battle of)

Bibliography

Adcock, F. E. *Roman Political Ideas and Practice,* 1959. Clear and always to the point.

Gelzer, M. *Caesar, Politician and Statesman,* 1968. An informative biography.

Harris, W. V. *War and Imperialism in Republican Rome,* 1979. A broad treatment of Rome's expansion.

Heurgon, J. *The Rise of Rome to 264 B.C.,* 1973. Examines the Roman military establishment in clear detail.

Huzar, E. G. *Marc Antony,* 1987. A biography of an important late republican figure.

Lazenby, J. F. *Hannibal's War,* 1978. See for Hannibal and the Punic Wars.

Ogilvie, R. M. *The Romans and Their Gods,* 1970. An introduction to Roman religion.

Richardson, E. *The Etruscans: Their Art and Civilization,* 1964. An illustrated handbook to the influences of this rather mysterious people upon early Rome.

Scullard, H. H. *Festivals and Ceremonies of the Roman Republic,* 1981. Explains how the Romans viewed their supernatural overseers and assistants.

Sherwin-White, A. N. *The Roman Citizenship,* 1973. A standard study of politics in the late republic.

Syme, R. *The Roman Revolution,* 1984. Another major study of late republican politics.

Note:

Social and economic affairs are covered in the bibliography for Chapter 15.

THE ROMAN EMPIRE

31 B.C.E.–180 C.E.	*Pax Romana*
31 B.C.E.–14 C.E.	Augustus Caesar
14–68 C.E.	Julio-Claudian emperors
69–96 C.E.	Flavian emperors
96–180 C.E.	Era of the Five Good Emperors
161–180 C.E.	Marcus Aurelius

Empires have had varied histories. Some have lasted only a generation, others for many centuries. From the ruins of the Roman republican political order arose a government that has served the Western world as a model of imperial rule ever since. For two and a half centuries, Rome maintained peace and relative prosperity throughout western Europe and the Mediterranean basin. Striking a balance between the power of a central policy-making group in Rome and provincial officers drawn from all the peoples of the empire, the Roman system proved successful in a variety of circumstances. Only when external enemies were aided by internal chaos after 250 C.E. did the system begin to waver. As late as the fifth century C.E. it was still operating well in some places in the west and throughout the eastern half of the empire.

✤ THE AUGUSTAN AGE

Octavian's defeat of Mark Antony and Cleopatra at Actium in 31 B.C.E. had made him master of the Roman world; the question was, how would he respond to this opportunity? Like his predecessor Julius Caesar, Octavian knew that basic reforms were necessary if the Roman Empire was to survive.

Augustus's Reforms

Octavian's method was to *retain the form, while changing the substance.* Knowing the Roman hatred of kings and their respect for tradition, Octavian pretended to be simply another elected consul, another *pontifex maximus* (high priest of the state religion), and another general of the Roman legions. In reality, he became consul for life, his priestly duties were crowned with semidivine status, and his military resources overshadowed all possible rivals. He enlarged the Senate, packing it with loyal supporters who would vote the way he wanted. He made a great show of working with the Senate, while giving it enough busywork to keep it out of mischief. Meanwhile he made all real policy decisions. He cut the army's size by half, while retaining all key military posts under his direct control.

Early in his reign Octavian accepted the title *Augustus* ("revered one") from a grateful Senate. The title denotes superhuman powers, and it is as *Augustus Caesar* that he is best known. Knowing the Romans' dislike of anything reminiscent of kings, he would not hear of the title

imperator (commander) as it implied sole authority (later Roman rulers lacked Augustus's concerns, however, and assumed the title *imperator,* from which we derive the word *emperor*). Instead, he preferred to be called ***princeps*** ("first citizen"), and his rule is often called the Principate. It lasted from 27 B.C.E., when he was elected consul for life, until his natural death in 14 C.E. In those forty years, Augustus placed his mark on every aspect of public affairs and was so successful overall that his system lasted for the next two and a half centuries without fundamental change. Augustus created a type of constitutional monarchy that was suited to contemporary Roman realities; to many it long remained the model of what Roman government *should* be.

In *government and constitutional matters,* Augustus kept the republican institutions intact. Supposedly, the *Senatus et populus* together were still the sovereign power, and the consul was simply their agent. In practice, however, Augustus had the final word in everything important through his control of the military and the Senate. His steadily increasing prestige with the commoners also helped him. Ordinary Romans were tired of the rebellions, civil wars, and political assassinations that had become commonplace in the last decades of the republic. Augustus was strong enough to intimidate any would-be trouble-makers among the Roman nobility and became immensely popular among the common people as a result.

In *social policy,* Augustus recognized the problems presented by the huge numbers of propertyless, impoverished citizens, especially in the cities. He therefore provided the urban poor with a form of welfare. The poor received basic food rations from the state treasury, supplemented by "gifts" from the consul from his own resources. This annual dole of grain and oil became a very important means of controlling public opinion for Augustus and his successors. He also instituted huge public works programs, both to provide employment and to glorify himself. Projects were carried out all over the empire, but especially in Rome itself. Many of the Roman bridges, aqueducts, roads (the famous, enduring Roman roads), forts, and temples that have survived were products of the reign of Augustus or were started by him and completed later.

Augustus also attempted to institute moral reform and end the love of luxury that had become characteristic of the aristocratic class during the late republic. By his own simple life with his wife Livia, he set an example of modest living. He also tried to discourage the influx of slaves because he believed that the vast number of slaves being imported into Italy represented luxury and, as such, threatened the simple traditional lifestyle. But none of

■ This picture shows a bronze figure of a Roman legionary in full dress at the time of the height of the empire in the second century C.E. The soldier's cuirass is constructed of overlapping metal bands.

these moral reform attempts proved successful over the long run. His imperial successors soon gave up the struggle. Augustus also tried to revive the faith in the old gods and the state religion by conscientiously serving as high priest and resurrecting some ancient ceremonies that had been neglected or forgotten. Here, too, he was unsuccessful in the long run, as the educated classes turned from supernatural religion toward philosophy, and the masses sought something more satisfying emotionally than the ceremonial state cult.

In *foreign policy,* Augustus gradually came to recognize that Rome had overextended itself through its conquests, although he himself added several territories during the first thirty years of his reign. Not all of his military ventures were successful, however. The northern frontiers in Germany and the Low Countries had long been a problem that Augustus resolved to solve by conquering the fierce tribes who lived there. This foray ended in spectacular failure: in 9 C.E. the Germans ambushed and exterminated a Roman army that had pushed eastward into the Teultoburg forests of what is now Belgium. The entire German province was thereby lost, and the borders between Roman and non-Roman Europe were henceforth the *Rhine and Danube Rivers*. After Augustus, Rome's only significant territorial gains were in the British Isles and in present-day Romania. To govern this vast empire, Augustus reformed the administration so that the outermost provinces, including Spain, Mesopotamia, and Egypt, were either put directly under his own control as "imperial" provinces or turned over to local rulers who were faithful satellites of Rome. Most of the army was stationed in the imperial provinces, enabling Augustus to keep the military under his control.

Augustus initiated other reforms in *military matters* as well. The army had become so large as to be unwieldy, so he reduced its size by more than half, to about 250,000 men. The army was made thoroughly professional and used extensively as an engineering force to build roads and public works all over the provinces. Augustus also located his armies where they could effectively counter against rebels and invasions. The army was made up of twenty-eight legions, each with about 6,000 highly trained and disciplined infantry. These were supported by cavalry and by a large number of auxiliaries, taken from the non-Roman populations of the provinces.

The Roman citizen volunteers who made up the legions served for twenty years and were given a mustering-out bonus sufficient to set them up as small landowners or businessmen. The legionaries were highly mobile, and a common soldier often served in five or six different provinces before retirement. The auxiliaries served for twenty-five years and were normally given citizenship on retirement. In and around Rome, Augustus maintained his personal bodyguard and imperial garrison, the **Praetorian Guard.** Containing about 10,000 men, it was the only armed force in Italy. Whoever controlled its loyalty had a potent lever for political power in his hand.

Augustus also reorganized the Roman navy and used it effectively to rid the Mediterranean of pirates who had been disrupting shipping. For the next two hundred years, the navy protected the provinces and Italy from any naval threat. Not until very recent times were the seas around Europe as safe as in the first and second centuries. A river navy on the Rhine and Danube supplemented the army's extensive system of forts to defend the empire against surprise attacks from the barbarian east and north.

Peace and Prosperity

With Augustus's reign, Rome and its now completed empire entered upon five generations of peace and prosperity, a time when even ordinary citizens found protection under the law and had prospects for a still better future. Literature and the arts flourished, supported by generous subsidies from the state treasury and commissions provided by a new class of very wealthy men who were proud of their achievements and wished to celebrate them. Augustus set the tone by *encouraging the arts* in public buildings of all sorts and providing financial support for many of the outstanding literary figures of his time.

The **Pax Romana,** the Roman peace, was the greatest of Augustus's achievements. It allowed, for example, Syrian merchants to move their goods safely from Damascus to Alexandria; from there, Egyptians would transport the goods to Gibraltar; from there, the goods would go on to Cornwall in Britain, where they would be exchanged for tin ore that would then be brought back to a bronze foundry in Damascus. Under the Pax Romana, people throughout the empire lived under a common concept of peaceful order, expressed and upheld through laws that were as valid in London as in Vienna or Barcelona (all of these cities were founded by the Romans). The provinces were supervised by governors appointed in Rome, but were allowed considerable freedom of action in local affairs while being protected by Roman garrisons. For two and a half centuries, the Western world from Syria to Spain and from Bristol to Belgrade was unified and generally peaceful—a record that has not been approached since.

Much of our second-hand knowledge of this record comes from a series of historians, the most important of whom for early Roman history is **Livy.** Livy lived during the age of Augustus, and his history unfortunately was much influenced by his desire to remain in the *princeps's* good graces. Most of Livy's long *History of Rome,* has been lost; what remains tells us what the Romans of Augustus's time thought about their history, but not many of the facts themselves. What can be truly known of Roman republican history has been derived from archaeology more than historiography. Rome later produced several historians who wrote with more veracity than Livy about the first three centuries C.E.

The Succession Problem

One important problem that Augustus was unable to solve was that of succession to his office and powers. Having only a daughter (the scandalous Julia), he adopted her husband, Tiberius, as his son and co-ruler. He thus set an example that would be followed by most of his successors: a combination of *heredity,* meaning succession by blood, and *co-option,* meaning succession by designation of the ruler. But this method often resulted in chaos, and was at times disregarded in favor of heredity alone.

Tiberius was an effective ruler, though by no means the equal of Augustus in popularity or ability to manipulate the Senate. Whereas Augustus had been deified (declared a god) by a grateful Senate almost immediately after his death, Tiberius was much resented. He was followed by other members of the family of Augustus (the *Julio-Claudians*) until 68 C.E., when the succession system experienced its first crisis. The unpopular Nero committed suicide in 69 and was replaced by the *Flavian* emperors from 69 to 96. They based their right to rule simply on having imposing military force behind them. Even though they were effective and wise rulers, an ominous precedent was set that would come back to haunt Rome in the third century.

❧ UNIFICATION OF THE EMPIRE

The successors of Augustus continued his work in bringing together the very diverse peoples over whom they ruled. Gradually, the Latin language became the common denominator of higher culture in the western half of the empire, while Greek continued to serve that function in the east. The imperial government used both languages equally in its dealings with its subjects.

Unification was also assisted by the gradual development of a large bureaucracy for the first time in Roman affairs. This added greatly to the previously minimal cost of government, but also provided many visible ways to reward useful provincials and encourage them to follow a pro-Roman policy. As long as the empire was prosperous, the increased costs of the bureaucracy were bearable.

The imperial government became increasingly centralized. The freedoms of the cities of the ancient East were curtailed by directives and governors sent out from Italy or selected from the romanized locals. In the western half of the empire, the Roman authorities founded many **municipia;** these were towns with their surrounding countryside that formed governmental units similar in size and function to our own counties. The municipal authorities were partly appointed by Rome and partly elected from and by leading local families. The provincial governor (usually an Italian given the job as political patronage) was responsible for their good behavior. He was backed by a garrison commander who had wide-ranging authority in matters both military and civil.

Everywhere, the government became open to non-Italians, as soon as they romanized themselves sufficiently to become citizens. (Citizenship was eventually granted to all freemen by a popularity-seeking emperor in 212.) From the time of the emperor Hadrian (the 120s C.E.), half the members of the Senate were of provincial origin. Men of talent could rise swiftly to the highest offices regardless of their ethnic background. Religious differences were ignored, so long as one was willing to make the very undemanding ceremonial tributes to the official Roman

■ A favorite amusement of the Roman crowd during the empire was combats between professional warriors called gladiators, or between men and beasts such as lions. These combats were held in the Roman Coliseum during holidays and were immensely popular. Both men and beasts were expected to battle until death.

gods (Jupiter, Neptune, and the like). Most individuals had no difficulty combining this state cult with the more intimate, traditional religions of their preference.

One of the chief contributors to Roman unification was *Roman law.* Many types of law originally existed within the borders of the empire, but they gradually gave way to the system that the Romans had hammered out by trial and error during the republic and that continued to be developed in the empire. The basic principles of this legal system were (1) the notion of *precedent* as co-equal to the letter of the law; (2) the belief that *equity* was the goal of all law; and (3) the importance of *interpretation* in applying the law to individual cases.

The Romans had various codes of law. One originally applied only to citizens; another applied only to aliens and travelers on Roman territory. During the early empire, the law code that governed relations between citizens and non-Romans, known as the **jus gentium** ("law of peoples"), gradually came to be accepted as basic. The rights of citizens and noncitizens, of natives and aliens, came to be seen as worthy of protection by the Roman authorities. These rights were not equal, but they were recognized as existing. This concept paved the way for what we call international law, and it gradually took Roman law far beyond the usual concepts of "us against you" that other peoples employed when dealing with foreigners.

Later, in the third and fourth centuries, the Romans evolved the idea of *natural law,* the idea that all humans, by virtue of their humanity, possess certain rights and duties that all courts must recognize. As the Romans adopted Christianity, this natural law came to be viewed as the product of a God-ordained order that had been put into the world with the creation of Adam.

✤ LIFE IN THE ROMAN EMPIRE'S HEYDAY

We have a great deal of information about the *economic and cultural life* of the empire in the first and second centuries C.E. Much of our knowledge has been obtained through archaeology, and every year new "digs" are started in some part of the former Roman domains.

Trade and manufacturing enjoyed a considerable boom (see Map 13.1). Trade was conducted mainly within the borders of the empire, but also extended beyond them to India, Africa, and even China (this was small in volume and was conducted through Asian intermediaries). Italy itself became more and more dependent on imports from other parts of the empire, mainly from the East where the levels of skills far exceeded those of the West. In the East (meaning from the Adriatic to Mesopotamia and Egypt)

lived the bulk of the population and the majority of the urbanites; here, too, were the sophisticated, civilized traditions of the Hellenistic world. Increasingly, the balance of intra-imperial trade shifted to favor the East. Even the skilled slave labor in Italy came almost exclusively from eastern sources.

Most Roman subjects were, as always, workers on the land. But much of this land was now owned either by the imperial government or by wealthy absentee landlords. Small free farmers were a declining species by the second century. They were replaced not so much by slaves as by sharecropper-tenants, who were still free in most of the empire, but would not long remain so. *Slaves* were common in all parts of the empire, but their number stabilized in the first century C.E. The number of slaves stopped increasing because prisoners of war were no longer coming in once the empire ceased expanding and because widespread prosperity meant fewer people were enslaved for debt.

By the 300s, however, in the Italian and Western European countryside, the lifestyle exemplified by the *villa,* or country estate of the wealthy, was steadily gaining at the expense of the impoverished small farmers. More and more people were tempted or coerced into giving up their independence in order to obtain regular income and protection against rapacious tax collectors. This trend, too, would be a source of future trouble as the imperial defenses weakened.

Another trend in the early empire was the increasing social *stratification,* particularly in the towns of Italy. The rich were more numerous and more distinct as a group than ever before, and the poor were both more numerous and more miserable. In the preserved ruins of Pompeii and the excavated areas of several other Italian towns, we see many multistory tenements. Here lived the unfortunates who did not have steady work or a protector from the propertied class. Wealth seems to have become the main qualification for public office.

Everywhere the early empire saw a major expansion of urban life and its values. The Romans founded numerous towns; some like Carthage were revivals of old towns, but most were quite new. Many of them were the direct descendants of Roman military forts. Perhaps half of the cities of modern Europe west of the Rhine-Danube frontier are Roman foundations.

These towns supported a *large middle class* of merchants, skilled artisans, clerks, and administrators. They were well educated in public and private schools where they studied the disciplines made popular by Hellenistic culture: literature, rhetoric, some math, history, and phi-

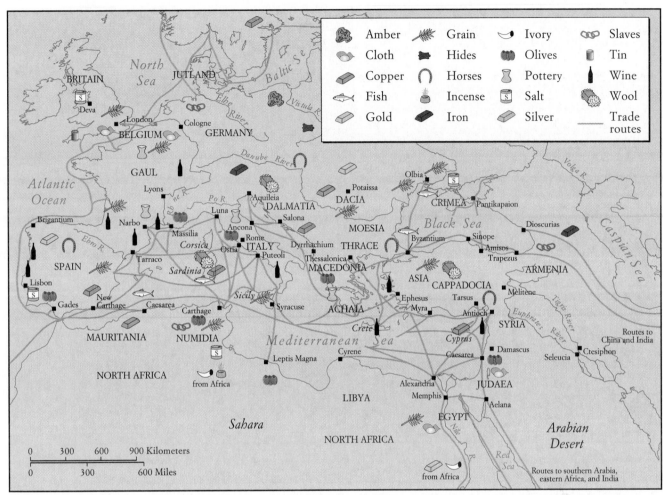

⦿ **MAP 13.1　Products of the Roman Empire c. 200 C.E.** The Romans traded extensively both within and without their borders. Some of the more important items carried are displayed in this map.

losophy of various types. Both Greek and Latin literature flourished in the early empire, although the cultural differences represented by the two languages were causing increasing difficulties after about 300 C.E. The move of the capital to Constantinople accentuated this. In general, though, the Romans were very successful in creating a *single, unified vision* of what life was about—and how it should best be lived—that was accepted from Britain to Egypt and from Spain to Romania.

✤ THE ARTS AND ARCHITECTURE OF THE EARLY EMPIRE

All of the arts flourished under the early emperors, who poured public and private money into celebrations of

their military triumphs and what they proudly termed the "Roman mission," that is, spreading civilization. Some of these monuments were in stone and concrete, such as the triumphal Column of Trajan telling the story of the conquest of Romania; some were in paint and ceramics, such as the great Golden House of Nero; and some were vast public works like the Roman *Forum* and the *Coliseum.* The Coliseum was built in the first century and is still one of the most impressive outdoor theaters of the world. Map 13.2 shows the location of many of the other monuments of imperial Rome.

Rome and several other cities (Antioch, Damascus, Alexandria, Athens, Marseilles) saw a great burst of building, which called for a mastery of masonry and engineering design unapproached even by the Greeks in

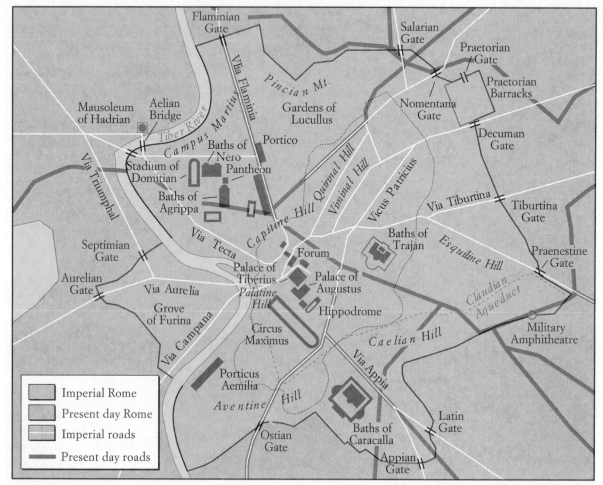

● **MAP 13.2 The Imperial City.** This map shows the outlines of the public areas in the center of Rome and a few of the transportation arteries that served it.

its imaginative boldness and endurance. In addition to buildings, the Romans constructed roads in all directions, harbors, aqueducts and sewage works, bridges, and fortifications. None exceeded the Romans' abilities to get things done—and done right. A great many of these structures are still in use today 1,600 years later.

Literature

The great age of Roman literature came at the end of the republic and during the first century of the empire. **Virgil** (70–19 B.C.E.) was without doubt the greatest of the Roman poets. His masterwork was the *Aeneid,* the story of Aeneas, a royal refugee from burning Troy. The *Aeneid* follows him through many adventures until he lands in

Italy and, by implication, becomes the founding father of Rome. *Horace, Ovid,* and *Catullus* were the other leading poets of the Augustan period. Although their work still shows some traces of the Greek models, all four authors developed a style that can accurately be called original. In their hands, the Latin language became an extraordinary instrument, capable of extreme directness and concentration of meaning. Its clarity and accuracy made it into a rival of Greek for both literary and scientific expression.

The historian *Tacitus,* the satirist *Juvenal,* and the prose storytellers *Pliny the Elder, Petronius,* and *Suetonius* were among the more notable writers in Latin in the first and second centuries. After about the middle of the second century, the quality of Latin literature began to slacken.

Art and Architecture

In the plastic and pictorial arts such as painting, ceramics, mosaics, and sculpture, the Romans were generally content to elaborate, if only slightly, on models drawn from the Hellenistic East. Perhaps the single most impressive triumph of the Romans in this area was the extraordinary portrait sculpture that has been mentioned earlier; it is also noteworthy that with few exceptions, the superb "Greek" statues in the world's museums are Roman copies of originals long since disappeared. In architecture, the Romans' affinity for grand size and their skills in masonry combined to give magnificent expression to public works and buildings. They were the first people to master the large-scale domed roof and the uses of the arch.

Philosophy

How best to live was a question that preoccupied imperial Romans. Perhaps the greatest of the emperors after Augustus was **Marcus Aurelius** (r. 161–180 C.E.) who left a small book of aphorisms called *Meditations,* which has been a best-seller ever since (see the Document in this chapter). Marcus settled on a pessimistic Stoicism as the most fitting cloak for a good man in a bad world, especially a man who had to exercise power. This was a common feeling among upper-class Romans, and it became ever more popular in the third and fourth centuries as difficulties multiplied. Like Marcus Aurelius, Roman Stoics were often opponents of Christianity because they rejected external prescriptions for morality and insisted that each person is responsible for searching and follow-

■ **Roman Ruins in North Africa.** The huge arch and palace was erected by the emperor Trajan in the early second century C.E. to commemorate his victorious reign. The Timgad Arch still stands in Algeria, North Africa.

ing his own conscience. *Seneca,* another Stoic and the most moving of the Roman moralists, had a somewhat different way of looking at things. The new note was that

■ **Roman Lady at Her Toilette.** This mosaic from the ruins of Pompeii shows the luxury surrounding a wealthy woman in the seconed century C.E. Female slaves assist at the dressing table while others bring refreshments.

The *Meditations* of Marcus Aurelius

Marcus Aurelius (121–180 C.E.) was perhaps the greatest of all the Roman rulers, in the sense of moral grandeur. As the last of the Five Good Emperors who ruled in the second century C.E., he inherited an empire that was still intact and at peace internally. But on its eastern borders, the first of the lethal challenges from the Germanic tribes materialized during his reign (161–180), and he had to spend much of his time organizing and leading the empire's defenses.

Even during his campaigns, his mind was tuned to the Stoic philosophy, which the Roman upper classes had acquired from the Greeks. In his *Meditations* he wrote a personal journal of the adventure of a life consciously lived. His book, which was never meant for publication, has lived on into our day because of its nobility of thought and expression.

Begin each day by reminding yourself: today I shall meet with meddlers, ingrates, insolence, disloyalty, ill-will and selfishness—all of them due to the offenders' ignorance of what is good and what evil. But I have long perceived the nature of good and its nobility, the nature of evil and its meanness, and also the nature of the culprit himself, who is my brother . . . therefore, none of those things can injure me, for no one can implicate me in what is degrading. . .

Never value the advantages derived from anything involving breach of faith, loss of self-respect, hatred, suspicion, or execration of others, insincerity, or the desire for something which has to be veiled or curtained. One whose chief regard is for his own mind, and for the divinity within him and the service of its goodness, will strike no poses, utter no complaints, and crave neither for solitude nor yet for the crowd. . . .

Hour by hour resolve firmly, like a Roman and a man, to do what comes to hand with correct and natural dignity, and with humanity, independence, and justice. Allow your mind freedom from all other considerations. This you can do if you will approach each action as though it were your last, dismissing the wayward thought, the emotional recoil from the commands of reason, the desire to create an impression, the admiration of self, the discontent with your lot. See how little a man needs to master, for his days to flow on in quietness and piety; he has to observe but these few counsels, and the gods will ask nothing more.

Men seek for seclusion in the wilderness, by the sea, or in the mountains—a dream you may have cherished only too fondly yourself. But such fancies are wholly unworthy for the philosopher, since at any moment you choose you can retire within yourself. Nowhere can man find a quieter or more untroubled retreat than in his own soul; above all, he who possesses resources in himself, which he need only contemplate to secure immediate ease of mind—the ease that is but another word for a well-ordered spirit. Avail yourselves, then, of this retirement, and so continually renew yourself. . . .

Marcus Aurelius's links with the Greek philosophers are evident from this brief excerpt from Book IV of the *Meditations:*

Time is a river, a violent torrent of things coming into being. Each one, as soon as it has appeared, is swept away; it is succeeded by another which is swept away in turn. All that happens is as natural and familiar as a rose in Spring, or fruit in Summer. Such like are diseases and death, calumny and treachery, and all else which gives fools their joys and their sorrows.

SOURCE: Excerpt from Marcus Aurelius *Meditations,* trans, Maxwell Staniforth, © 1964, Penguin Classics. Reprinted by permission of Penguin, Ltd.

of humane compassion, a belief that all shared in the divine spark and should be valued as fellow creatures.

The *Roman character,* insofar as one can sum up a whole people's character, leaned toward the pragmatic. They admired the doer more than the thinker, the soldier more than the philosopher, and the artisan more than the artist. The Roman educated class could and did appreciate "the finer things"; they admired and cultivated art in many media and many forms and spent lavishly to obtain it for their own pleasure. But they did not, generally speaking,

Jesus of Nazareth

c. 6 B.C.E.–c. 30 C.E.

In the final centuries of the Roman Republic, several religions arose in the eastern Mediterranean that shared certain fundamental features. They insisted that there was a better life to come after the earthly existence and that some individuals had the potential to share in that life; they also maintained that it was necessary to follow the teaching of a mythic hero-prophet in order to realize that potential. These were the "mystery" religions, whose truth depended upon an act of faith by the believer, rather than simple attendance at a priestly ceremony.

Christianity was by far the most important of the mystery religions of the Roman Empire. Its founder was not a mythic hero such as the Egyptian Osiris or the Greek Cybele, but a real historical person, Jesus of Nazareth, later called by his followers the *Christos,* or Messiah. Jesus was born in the newly Romanized province of Judea, the former Kingdom of Judah and home of the two tribes of Israel that had stayed true to the Mosaic Law and the belief in being the Chosen of Yahweh.

Of Jesus' early life until he entered on his preaching career about age thirty, we know next to nothing. His life and work are known only through the recollections of his followers, written in the half century after his death. In this he strongly resembles most of the other founders of the world religions, whose message and example passed through many hands and tongues before reaching an agreed-upon form and content. The Christian disciples who wrote the books of the New Testament did not think it relevant to Jesus' work to tell us of his boyhood or his youth, or the intellectual context in which he grew up.

It is reasonably sure that Jesus was born to a woman and a man—Mary and Joseph—who were quite ordinary, practicing Jews of undistinguished status prior to the miraculous selection of Mary as the mother of the Messiah. For many years thereafter, the family (Jesus may have had at least one half-brother, the apostle James) led an obscure life in the region of Galilee, probably in the town of Nazareth. We know that the Zealots, who opposed Roman rule by militant acts were strong in this region, but they seem to have had no effect upon Christ.

Around 26 C.E. Jesus was introduced into the teachings of John the Baptist, one of the numerous wandering sages of the day who were "stirring up" the people and making difficulties for the Roman officials, led by the *procurator,* or governor. In that same year, Pontius Pilate was appointed to the post. He was an average official, mainly concerned with making money out of his position and keeping the subject population sufficiently quiet so as not to create difficulties for himself and his reputation back in Rome.

During the next few years, a group of lower-class Jews attached themselves to Jesus, seeing in him truly the Son of God and the long-awaited Messiah, as he claimed to be. Most of the time, Jesus followed the precepts of Jewish law and tradition quite closely, and he repeatedly said that he did not intend to found a new religion. By so doing, he assured himself of a platform in the synagogues and was allowed to preach without interference for a time. But his bold insistence on the spirit, rather than the letter of the law, and his flat statement that though he was the Messiah, his kingdom was not of this world brought him into ill repute among the leaders. Before long, his message of faith in God, hope in his mercy, and love of one's fellow man was being seen by the high priests and rabbis as revolutionary. They carried their complaints to Pontius Pilate and induced him to let them crucify Christ as a potential enemy of Roman rule as well as the Mosaic Law.

The Sermon on the Mount gives us the most coherent and concise overview of Jesus' message. It is a message of tolerance, justice, and humility, of turning the other cheek and keeping the peace. It is also an exhortation to remember how brief and unimportant worldly renown and worldly goods are when compared to the prospects of Eternal Life. In so doing, Jesus differentiated himself and his doctrines from all other mystery religions, in which the prospect of eventually triumphing over those outside the religion and reveling in the "good things" of the world was a major motivation for keeping the faith. Already by the Resurrection three days after his crucifixion, the small cadre of believers in Christ the Messiah felt they were distinguished from other Jews and were the possessors of a sacred truth. Led by the apostles, they prepared to carry out their heavy responsibility to "make smooth the path of the Lord" on earth.

■ This model from the Museo della Civilta' Romana shows the complex nature and urban sprawl of ancient Rome.

provide that sort of intense, sustained interest that led to superior taste and to the inspiration of superior and original works of art, such as the Greeks possessed in abundance. The early empire's successes in several fields were magnificent and long-lasting; but they were not rooted in an original view of earthly life or a new conception of humans' duties and aspirations.

The really new elements in Roman culture were originated and nurtured by a new sect that was steadily finding more adherents in the empire in the second and third centuries: Christianity. In the next chapter, we look at what the Christians believed and what they achieved in a faltering society.

Summary

The early Roman Empire (27 B.C.E.–180 C.E.) was built upon the constitutional and administrative foundations laid down in the reign of the first emperor, Octavian Augustus Caesar. For two centuries, it functioned quite well as a political and economic organism, even though the capital city saw occasional outbursts of civic upheaval or palace coups as in Nero's time. Law and order were established securely in an area that reached from Scotland to North Africa and from Spain to the Iranian borderlands. External raiders were kept at bay without creating a huge bureaucracy and expensive armies; internal malcontents were isolated or put down without much trouble. Though not original contributors in philosophy or the arts, the Romans found their triumphs in the construction of a system of law and government that was flexible enough to serve vastly different subject peoples. Indeed, it served them so well that the statement "I am a Roman" remained a badge of honor and a claim to justice and respect for more than five centuries. Governmental responsibilities were divided between the center and the provinces and municipalities in such a way as to provide many outlets for talent and to allow a general inculcation of a sense of patriotism.

The economy of the empire generally prospered, creating a large middle class of merchants and landowners. But in the cities a growing proletariat, or working class, underlined the huge differences between poor and rich. The eastern half of the empire was clearly overshadowing the west by the third century. Slavery was common, as was a sharecropping dependency on large landholders in the countryside. Literature and architecture flourished, though both depended on Greek models and Greek ideas, as was also true of many of the plastic arts.

Test Your Knowledge

1. In 27 B.C.E. Octavian Caesar began to organize a new government for Rome that was a
   a. republic.
   b. dictatorship.
   c. democracy.
   d. constitutional monarchy.
2. A major problem that confronted Augustus was that the Roman army
   a. had lost its will to fight.
   b. was much too large.
   c. no longer had any contact with Roman culture.
   d. was under the control of the Senate.
3. Virgil's *Aeneid* is a(n)
   a. history of the decline and fall of Greek civilization.
   b. plea for tolerance and justice for the Christians.
   c. argument for pacifism.
   d. explanation of Rome's origin.
4. Augustus's successor and Rome's second emperor was
   a. Diocletian.
   b. Tiberius.
   c. Caligula.
   d. Julius Caesar.
5. Roman official cults
   a. insisted on unwavering belief in doctrine.
   b. were religions of ritual without emotional content.
   c. despised the non-Italian subjects of the empire.
   d. sometimes demanded human sacrifices.
6. Within the Roman sphere, which of the following centuries could appropriately be described as a period of peace and security?
   a. Sixth century B.C.E.
   b. First century B.C.E.
   c. Second century C.E.
   d. Fourth century C.E.
7. Which of the following was *outside* the Roman Empire's borders?
   a. Austria
   b. Greece
   c. Denmark
   d. England

Identification Terms

imperator	Marcus Aurelius	*Pax Romana*	*princeps*
jus gentium	*municipia*	Praetorian Guard	Virgil
Livy			

Bibliography

Benko, S. *Pagan Rome and Early Christianity,* 1985. A comprehensive study of Roman philosophy and pagan religion.

Campbell, J. *The Emperor and the Roman Army, 31 B.C. to A.D. 235,* 1984. Useful study of the military.

Duff, J. W. *Literary History of Rome from the Origins to the Close of the Golden Age,* 1953. A survey of Roman literature.

Gernsey, P., and R. Saller. *The Roman Empire,* 1987. A good general account of politics and administration.

Grant, M. *The Army of the Caesars,* 1974. This and Watson below are the most accessible studies for students interested in the imperial army, its personnel, weaponry, and organization.

Liebeschutz, J. *Continuity and Change in Roman Religion,* 1979.

Macmullen, R. *Paganism in the Roman Empire,* 1981.

Rostovtzeff, N. *The Economic and Social History of the Roman Empire,* 1957. The standard treatment of Roman economic and commercial life. A great book on a huge topic.

Schulz, F. *Classical Roman Law,* 1951. A good introduction to the principles guiding the Roman jurists.

Toynbee, J. M. *Art of the Romans,* 1965. A short study of how Roman art strove to fulfill certain civic ideals.

Watson, G. R. *The Roman Soldier,* 1969.

Wells, G. *The Roman Empire,* 1984. A good general study of politics and administration.

ROME'S DECAY AND TRANSFORMATION

After 180 C.E. Rome's power and purpose began to decline rapidly. Several of the outer provinces were invaded in the mid-200s, and the empire was wracked by internal troubles that threatened to bring it down entirely. A last attempt was made to maintain the old pagan order, but it soon collapsed in civil wars. Out of these wars at the beginning of the fourth century came a renewal and a realignment based on Christian religious belief and absolute monarchy. Despite this renewal the West could not be effectively defended against the Germanic barbarians, and the removal of the capital to Constantinople only underlined what was already apparent: the day of the Roman *imperium* in the West had passed.

The idea of universal Christian monarchy was to live for another thousand years in the Byzantine Empire until it was finally extinguished by the Turks. The former western provinces, however, gave birth to a new civilization: early medieval Europe, where Roman pagan culture, Christianity, and Germanic government were slowly and unevenly melded together.

❧ INTERNAL UPHEAVALS IN THE THIRD CENTURY

After the unfortunate reign (180–193) of the corrupt and incompetent Commodus, son of Marcus Aurelius, the central government fell into the hands of generals and usurpers for almost a century. Agriculture, which had always provided the livelihood of most Romans, came increasingly to be dominated by large estates employing unfree labor. Cities declined in size and importance as civil wars among the generals reduced one urban center after another to ashes or strangled its commerce. Some of the provinces were relatively untouched by these conflicts, particularly in the East, and this fact reinforced the ever clearer *dominance of the eastern half of the empire over the western.*

In the half century between 235 and 284, Rome had twenty emperors, eighteen of whom died by violence. This was the Age of the **Barracks Emperors.** An ambitious commander who had the momentary support of a legion or two might attempt to seize power in Rome itself or in one or another of the provinces. Those who had the allegiance of the Italian garrison, the Praetorian Guard, were the most powerful at any given moment, and the guard was easily bought with promises of booty.

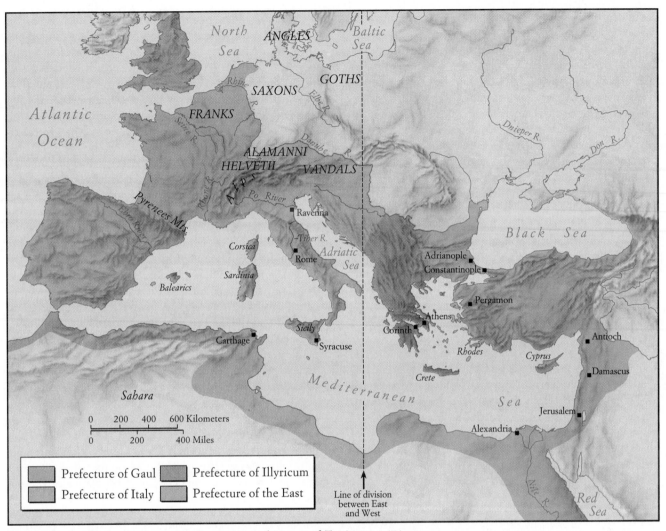

● MAP 14.1 **The Later Roman Empire: Gains and Losses of Territory to 476 C.E.**

Ordinary citizens were not involved in these struggles for raw power, of course, but suffered the effects in many ways. Respect for imperial authority disappeared, the courts of law were overruled by force, bribery and corruption of officials became commonplace, and the long-distance trade that had sustained much of Roman prosperity was badly disrupted. For a time in the mid-200s, the total collapse of society and government seemed inevitable to many, as the army disintegrated into an undisciplined mass of adventurers and their ambitious leaders.

⚜ BARBARIANS AT THE GATES

It was Rome's bad luck that the period of the Barracks Emperors coincided with the first really serious challenges from the barbarian tribes beyond its borders. In the late third century, the great *Wandering of the Peoples* from Asia and eastern Europe slammed into Rome's outer provinces, from the Low Countries all the way to the Balkans (see Map 14.1). When these tribal peoples reached the river frontiers, they found large gaps in the defenses, caused by the army's dissolution into a series of private forces. Sometimes peaceably and sometimes by force, the newcomers crossed into the civilized areas in groups both small and large.

The mainly Germanic invaders were sometimes neutralized by offering them wholesale entry into the Roman military as auxiliaries. Rome had followed this practice for five centuries, using it as a means to reward loyal new subjects. But the newcomers were still quite ignorant of Roman law and culture and were unreliable. By accepting them, the Roman army in several western provinces was "germanized," rather than the auxiliaries becoming good Romans as they had in the past.

Almost miraculously, the last few general-emperors in the 270s were able to beat off the barbarian attacks and manipulate the various tribes and nations into fighting one another more than the Romans. Rome gained breathing space that was utilized by the last of the Barracks Emperors, *Diocletian,* to reorganize the badly wounded system.

⚜ RENEWAL OF THE EMPIRE UNDER DIOCLETIAN AND CONSTANTINE

Under Diocletian (r. 294–305), a capable general who had fought his way to supreme power, the fiction created by Augustus Caesar that he was merely first among equals was finally buried. From now on, the emperor was clearly the absolute ruler of a subservient *Senatus et populus;* his bureaucrats were his instrument to effect his will, rather than agents of the Roman people. He brooked no opposition, not because he was a tyrant, but because he saw that if the empire was to survive, something new must be tried immediately.

To make the huge empire more governable, Diocletian divided it into western and eastern halves and underlined the clear dominance of the East by taking that half for his personal domain. The other he gave to a trusted associate to rule from Rome. Each of the two rulers appointed an assistant, who was to follow him in office when he died or stepped down. By providing the emperors with clear and experienced successors, this system, called the **Tetrarchy** (rule of four), was supposed to end the civil wars. It failed as soon as Diocletian retired (305 C.E.), but the political reorganization of the empire into two halves remained.

Diocletian also attempted to revive the economy by lowering inflation, which had been rampant since the early Barracks Emperors. He issued the first governmental "price ceilings" on consumer goods in Western history (which failed, of course). He attempted to restore the badly damaged faith in the value of Roman coinage, whose gold and silver contents had been steadily and surreptitiously reduced. He also increased the tax burden and insisted that the tax collectors were personally responsible for making up any arrearages in their districts. The net result was to make taxes more hated than ever and the tax collectors' posts almost unfillable.

Constantine the Great (r. 313–337), Diocletian's successor to supreme power after an eight-year civil war, generally continued these policies and increased the restrictions on personal freedoms that the central government was steadily imposing. Under Constantine, it became nearly impossible for people to change their place of residence or occupation. The measures were aimed especially at the free peasants, who were being forced into

■ **Trajan's Column.** The Roman army was thoroughly trained and equipped in accord with precise regulations issued by the central government. The soldiers' discipline in battle usually won the day against most foes. Here the campaign of the second century C.E. emperor Trajan is memorialized.

debt by big landlords and therefore often ran away or flocked into the towns.

Along with these measures, Constantine continued the changes in the nature of the emperor's office that Diocletian had introduced. Constantine reigned like an Egyptian pharaoh and claimed godlike powers. Others had to prostrate themselves when they entered into his presence, and his word alone had the force of law. All of this was a far cry from the earlier imperial style introduced by Augustus and maintained by most of his successors.

In the 330s, Constantine took the expected step of formally transferring the capital to the East to the site of the old Greek city of *Byzantium*. Perched on the shores of the straits between Europe and Asia in a highly strategic location (see Map 14.1), the new capital was defensible from both land and sea. In time, the city of Constantine or *Constantinople* in Greek, as it came to be called, became the largest city of the Western world.

Greek was the dominant language in the new capital, and Greeks were the dominant cultural force almost from the beginning. The New Rome was no longer a Latin entity, but a hybrid that steadily drew apart from the Italian-Latin-Western world. From this point on, the size and importance of the old Rome began to decline, even though a deputy emperor maintained his government there for another century and a half. The city was ravaged by two barbarian raids (in 410 and 455), which left parts of it in ruins. In 476 a German chieftain pushed aside the boy-emperor of the day, and crowned himself, an event that is conventionally taken as the end of the Roman *imperium* in Western Europe.

✤ CHRISTIANITY

The story of *Jesus of Nazareth* (c. 6 B.C.E.–29 C.E.) and his message of salvation to his fellow Jews is sufficiently well known that only the historical context will be given here. Jesus Christ, whom about half of the world's population assert to be the Son of God and Redeemer of Mankind, was born to a Jewish couple of very ordinary family and background. He was born during the reign of Augustus Caesar, about a generation after Pompey had incorporated Judea into the growing Roman Empire. According to the New Testament of the Christian Bible, Mary, Christ's mother, had been selected by an omnipotent God to be the vessel through which his son would gain human form, lead his fellow humans out of the wilderness of their sins, and show them the path to eternal salvation.

A few years after Jesus' birth (the original Christmas Day), the Romans chose to take direct control of Judea from the satellite kings, such as Herod the Great (40–4 B.C.E.) who had ruled in their name. A series of Roman procurators, or governors, were then appointed. They relied heavily on the advice of the rabbis in dealing with what they considered a fanatical and religiously obsessed people. Jesus grew up in this tense atmosphere, but we know nothing about his actual childhood and youth. The New Testament stories about him begin with his entry into public life at about age thirty. He wrote nothing at all (that has survived), and as with other great religious leaders, our knowledge of his life stems from the recollections of his disciples compiled years later.

During the last century B.C.E., the Hellenistic mystery religions (see Chapter 11) had become widely popular in the eastern empire. Egyptian, Persian, Greek, and Italian cults promising power and immortality appealed to the lower ranks of a population that was steadily being divided into economic haves and have-nots. The Jews were not immune to this appeal and subdivided into several factions that held different views of the deliverer—the messiah promised to them long ago. The Sadducees were strict traditionalists, who looked to the yet unknown messiah as a liberator from Rome (and all others), but rejected the belief in an afterlife and even, perhaps, belief in a merciful Yahweh. The Pharisees, who apparently dominated the high council, the *Sanhedrin,* were more liberal in their interpretations and eager to make some accommodation with the pagan Roman culture. The uncompromising Zealots, on the other hand, were ready to follow their messiah into physical battle with the Roman occupiers.

None of these factions nor the Essenes, a group who insisted upon withdrawing from a corrupt world, were receptive to the pacifist and provocative message of love and forgiveness that Jesus preached between 26 and 29 C.E. To the Sadducees and Pharisees, Jesus' admonition to stop confusing the letter of the law with its spirit was an attempt to seduce the Jews, who had survived and remained a distinct nation only because of their unbending adherence to their Mosaic laws. Zealots wished to fight; they had no empathy with a prophet who asked them to "render unto Caesar the things that are Caesar's," that is, to accept the legitimate demands of their Roman overlords.

Meanwhile the Roman administrators must have regarded Jesus as a special irritant among an already difficult people. The Jews' peculiar religious doctrines were of no concern to the Romans, but Jesus' preaching and challenges to the traditionalist rabbis did create difficulties in governing. In the most literal sense, Jesus was "stirring things up." As a result, when the Jewish leaders in the

Sanhedrin demanded that the Roman procurator, Pontius Pilate, allow them to punish this disturber of the peace, he reluctantly agreed, and Jesus was crucified on Golgotha near Jerusalem.

For a couple of decades thereafter, the Christian cult spread slowly in Judea and was nearly unknown outside it. This situation changed as a result of two developments: First, the Jewish Roman citizen **Saul of Tarsus** (c. 6–67 C.E.) was miraculously converted to Christianity on the road to Damascus and began to preach the gospel to the Gentiles (non-Jews) as the apostle Paul. Then the fanatical elements among the Jews rebelled against their Roman overlords in the **Jewish War** (67–70 C.E.) After some unexpected difficulties, the Romans won and decided to punish this troublesome people by dispersing them in what is known as the **Diaspora** (actually, the Second Diaspora; the First Diaspora had occurred centuries earlier at the hands of the Assyrians). One result of this forced eviction from Judea was the establishment of Jewish exile colonies that became breeding grounds for Christianity throughout the eastern Mediterranean basin and soon in Italy itself. Spurred by the strenuous efforts of the apostle Paul, the Christian doctrine was spreading steadily, if not spectacularly, among both ex-Jews and Gentiles by the end of the first century.

The Appeal of Christianity

What was the appeal of the new religion? First, it distinguished itself from all the other mystery religions by its *universality*. All persons were eligible for full membership and admittance into its secrets: men and women, Jew and Gentile, rich and poor, Roman and non-Roman. Second, Christianity offered a message of *hope and optimism* in a Hellenistic cultural world that appeared increasingly grim to the aspirations of ordinary people. Not only were believers promised a blessed life to come, but the prospects for a better life on this earth also appeared to be good. The Second Coming of the Lord and its accompanying Last Judgment, when the just would be richly rewarded and the evil punished according to their deserts, were thought to be not far off. Thirdly, Christians were far ahead of their rivals in the *spirit of mutuality* that marked the early converts. To be a Christian was to accept an active obligation to assist your fellows in any way you might; it also meant you could count on their help and prayers when needed. Lastly, Christianity featured an *appeal to idealism* that was much more powerful than anything its rivals offered; it emphasized charity and unselfish devotion in a way that had strong appeal to people weary of a world that seemed to be dominated by the drive for wealth and power.

The Gospels ("good news") of the four evangelists Mark, Luke, Matthew, and John were the original doctrinal foundations of the faith. They were written and collected in the late first century C.E., along with the letters of St. Paul to the communities of Christians he had founded in the eastern Mediterranean. By the second century, a written New Testament had appeared that was accepted by all Christians and largely superseded the Old Testament of the Jews in their eyes.

■ This fresco shows Christ with his twelve disciples, calling the soul of a deceased Christian to the Last Judgement. By the third century, when this scene was painted, Christianity was winning converts throughout Roman society.

Christianity's Spread and Official Adoption

Slowly, Christian cells sprang up in the major towns all over the Mediterranean basin. The story of *Peter the Apostle* coming to Rome shortly after the death of Christ may well be factual; certainly, several disciples, spurred on by Paul, left the strictly Jewish environment in which the religion had begun and "went out into the world" of Roman pagan culture. Paul himself is thought to have died a martyr in Rome under the emperor Nero. Missionaries were also pushing beyond the boundaries of the empire at a relatively early date; according to legend, St. Andrew preached to the Slavs, for example, and St. Thomas reached the Indian coast as early as the middle of the first century.

By the early fourth century, it has been estimated that about 10 percent of the population of the East had become Christian and perhaps 5 percent of the West. In this situation, the emperor Constantine (whose mother Helena was a Christian) decided to end the persecution of Christians that had been going on at intervals since Nero's time. In 313 he issued the *Edict of Milan,* which announced the official toleration of Christianity and signaled that the new religion was favored at the imperial court. Constantine himself seemingly became a Christian only on his deathbed in 337; but from this time on, all emperors in East and West, with the exception of Julian (361–363), were Christians. In 381, the emperor *Theodosius* took the final step of making Christianity the *official* religion of the empire. From then on, other faiths were persecuted by the authorities.

Constantine's Motives

Why did the suspicious and warlike Constantine decide to stake his own fate, and possibly the fate of the empire, upon a new religion that had distinguished itself by its pacifism and its intolerance of other faiths, in particular, of the traditional Roman state cult? As the story has it, Constantine became convinced that the Christian God had aided him in a crucial battle, but historians suspect that something more was behind such a momentous decision. It is difficult to determine the emperor's true motives, however. Although he did not make Christianity the state religion, he definitely favored it and encouraged its spread. Probably, he expected this move would assist him in shoring up a wounded political system by creating a new unity of belief between governors and governed. He enjoyed playing an active role in settling thorny theological questions, notably at the Council of Nicaea. Certainly, too, he

recognized the growing support that Christianity was attracting among those who counted in Roman society.

For a long time, however, Constantine's personal commitment to Christianity was partial and questionable; he continued to use the title *pontifex maximus,* which was identified with the old state paganism, to his death. And he made no attempt to outlaw the cults that competed with Christianity, even allowing new temples to be built to the old gods. At the same time, he had his sons educated by Christian tutors, and many of his closest official advisers were known to be Christians. Whatever Constantine's vision of the faith may have been, by the end of his quarter-century reign, it would have been very difficult to reverse what he had done in bringing Christianity up out of the catacombs and into the light of official favor.

Constantine's action would both aid and hinder the new religion. Of course, giving Christianity a favored status and putting the resources of the secular government behind it aided its growth. Soon Christians were a majority in the cities; the countryside appears to have been much slower to adopt the new creed (see Map 14.2). At the same time, Constantine's decision ensured that the Christian church would be linked with the state and the wishes of the state's governors. Church councils would soon find that civil questions would sometimes override purely religious considerations. Compromise between the concerns of the religion and those of the state was considered essential, if both religion and the state were to survive.

Early Church Organization and Doctrine

Until Constantine, occasional persecutions had forced the Christians sometimes to hide their beliefs and worship in private. Now they came out into the open and organized their church on Roman civil models. In each community of any size, *bishops* were elected, and they in turn appointed priests on the recommendation of the local faithful. The early Christian emperors made the fateful decision to allow the bishops to create their own courts and laws (canon law) for judging the clergy and administering church property—a decision that later led to great friction between kings and bishops.

Several bishops claimed that they were the direct spiritual descendants of Jesus' twelve disciples and therefore possessed special authority. They included the bishops of Rome, Antioch, Jerusalem, and Alexandria, among others. The bishop of Rome claimed to be first among

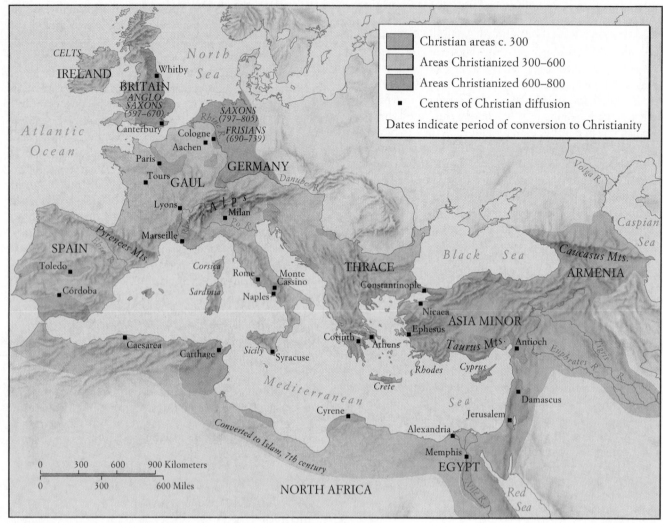

MAP 14.2 Spread of Christianity, 400–750 C.E. The kingdom of the Franks was the first of the Germanic states to accept Roman Christianity, around 500 C.E.

equals through the doctrine of *Petrine Succession*. According to this concept, the bishop of Rome was the direct successor of Peter, whom Christ had pronounced the "rock (*petros*) upon which I build my church," and therefore succeeded Peter as the preeminent leader of the church.

The early church experienced many serious disputes about theology. Heated arguments about the nature of Christ, the relation between members of the Holy Trinity, the nature of the Holy Spirit, and similar topics broke out repeatedly, especially in the East, where the majority of Christians lived for the first three or four centuries C.E. After the Edict of Milan, the efforts to settle these disputes led to two developments: (1) the council of

bishops became the supreme arbiter in matters of faith, and (2) the civil and religious authorities established a close and permanent relationship.

The first council was the **Council of Nicaea,** which was held in 325 during the reign of Constantine in present-day Turkey. It was attended by more than three hundred bishops. Some of the decisions of the council were implemented by the secular government, thus bringing the second new principle into play. From this time onward, the Roman emperors in East and West saw themselves as possessing executive powers within the Christian community—a development that led to conflict when the emperor and bishops had differing opinions on the civic implications of theological issues.

Justinian and Theodora

The emperor Justinian I (r. 527–565) was the first eastern Roman emperor since Constantine the Great to undertake an aggressive policy of attacking the "barbarians." By Justinian's time, the invaders had overthrown Roman authority everywhere in the West and were constantly threatening the East. Unfortunately for Justinian, what we know of him as a person and a ruler is largely dependent on one source, Procopius's *Secret History,* which is most hostile (see this chapter's Document). Very unusually for a Roman emperor, Justinian was apparently much influenced by his imperial consort, Theodora, and she is therefore treated equally with Justinian.

Justinian came to the throne a few years after his scandalous marriage to Theodora, and for the first decade or so, he pursued reforms and great projects of state with considerable success. One of his first steps was to appoint a commission to revise and codify the empire's code of law. Some earlier rulers had tried to end the confusion caused by conflicting laws passed centuries apart, but still in force. These efforts had failed, mainly because they were only partial remedies. Justinian's commission, on the other hand, succeeded brilliantly with its *Corpus Juris Civilis* of 534, which presented the Western world with a fully integrated, uniform set of principles, as well as a comprehensive set of statutes for applying those principles. The *Corpus Juris* has served as the basis of most Western law codes ever since.

In 532 the center of Constantinople suffered extensive damage during the so-called Nike riots before they were suppressed (Procopius says that Justinian was ready to flee like a coward, but the determined and cold-blooded Theodora persuaded him to stay and fight it out). As a result, the city's monuments had to be rebuilt, and Justianian took full advantage of the opportunity. The largest and most impressive Christian church in the world, the Hagia Sophia (Holy Wisdom) cathedral was his creation. Adorned now with Muslim minarets, it still stands in midtown Istanbul.

In the 530s, the gifted general Belisarius carried out much of Justinian's plan to retake the western Roman Empire from the Germans and others who had overrun it during the previous two centuries. First, the imperial army took North Africa from the Vandals, then Sicily and southern Italy from the Ostrogothic king. Unable to hold Rome, Belisarius set up headquarters in Ravenna in the Po valley, where he and his successors engaged in a long struggle with the Goths for possession of the peninsula of Italy. A little later, Spain was briefly recaptured from the Visigoths.

But all these military enterprises came at a huge cost. Taxes had to be increased radically for the much larger army, and popular discontent mounted at home. The Persians, recovering from past defeats, now went on the attack on the eastern frontier, while from the north, the migrating Slavs and Avars came down the Danube valley into Roman territories with sword in hand.

Theodora helped her husband get through these strenuous days more or less successfully. She had a sure touch for the popular approach and was better liked by ordinary people than the emperor himself. Her dubious background (see the Document) was apparently no handicap once she became empress. There is considerable evidence that Justinian listened carefully to her in matters of religious policy and in some matters of personnel. She was featured prominently in the official artworks of Justinian's reign and even later. Though her influence was surely less than Procopius would have us believe, she stands out as a woman of power in an era when that was very rare.

Meanwhile the pagan culture did not just roll over and die with the Edict of Milan. Many educated Romans could not bring themselves to adopt the new faith, which they regarded as a mixture of base superstition and a sort of cannibalism (the Eucharist), the same objections that had been raised about Christianity in earlier centuries.

The challenges paganism presented to Christianity contributed to the rise of a school of Christian explainers of sacred doctrine, or **apologists,** in the 300s. The most important of these *Fathers of the Church,* as they are called, were **Augustine** and Ambrose, the bishops of Hippo (North Africa) and Milan, respectively. These men, assisted by others, delineated in detail what Christians had to believe, what they could not believe, and why. Their writings are the secondary foundation of the Christian faith, as the Gospels of the New Testament are the primary one. St. Augustine has been especially influential in molding belief, and his *Confessions* and *The City of God* have possibly been the most important repositories of Christian teaching after the Gospels themselves.

By the early fifth century, the Christian faith was giving the tottering Roman Empire a new cast of thought and a system of morality and ethics that challenged the old beliefs in myriad ways. After Theodosius's reign, the imperial government was a Christian entity, so Christians could actively support it and perhaps even defend it against its external enemies. But if this worldly empire fell, it was no tragedy; it was only the otherworldly kingdom of the Lord that should count in Man's eyes. By thus shifting the focus to the next world, Christian doctrine made it easier to accept the sometimes brutal and painful ending of the Roman Empire. Some must have welcomed its collapse, believing that the empire exemplified the inherent weakness of all earthly institutions when compared to the majesty of the Lord. Others believed in the imminent Second Coming of Christ, when worldly life would end in anarchy and the just would receive their reward; the more signs of collapse, the better, in this view.

Christianity did not so much sweep aside pagan culture as amalgamate itself with the earlier tradition until it dominated. The pace of the process varied from one place to another. Only slowly did many Christians acquiesce to the idea of blending Christian and pagan world-views and realize that there was something to be learned from the Roman secular environment while they awaited the Last Judgment. By the time they had arrived at this realization, however, much of that secular world had already been hammered to pieces.

✣ Germanic Invasions

Marcus Aurelius had mounted a campaign against the Germanic tribes on the other side of the Danube and had pushed them back, but this was the last success Rome had against the Germans. Commodus lost the advantage, and the Germans began to organize themselves more effectively, as they learned Roman military tactics. Soon they were applying steady pressure on the Rhine and Danube frontiers.

During the 200s, as the imperial succession was increasingly determined by rebellion and assassination, the troops in the provinces began to look to their local commanders rather than Rome as the source of authority. These troops and even their commanders were increasingly Germans, who had been taken into the Roman army because of a general shortage of manpower and the Romans' mistaken hope that the Germans, like many of their predecessors among Rome's subjects, would become rapidly romanized.

The chief Germanic tribal confederations facing the Romans in the third century were the *Franks* along the lower Rhine; the *Helvetii* and *Alemanni* in present-day Switzerland and southern Germany; the *Goths* from eastern Germany to southern Russia; the *Vandals* in Austria; and the *Saxons,* in the Netherlands. All of these, at various times, tested the Roman borders. Some ground was lost permanently, but Diocletian and others managed to check the invaders, or bring them peaceably into the empire by allowing them special privileges and/or auxiliary status in the army.

After the capital was moved to Constantinople, however, the western provinces were sacrificed to the Germans, who by this time were being pushed from behind by various Asiatic peoples. The ravaging invasion of the Huns, an Asiatic nomadic people who suddenly appeared in the 440s and pillaged their way through Italy, confirmed the Romans' decision to more or less abandon the West. The Huns dispersed after the death of their warrior leader, Attila, but the vulnerability of the West had been demonstrated, while the East was still intact. With the survival of the empire at stake, it was clear that the East had the better prospects, so the Roman rulers acted accordingly. Although they maintained close contact with Rome and the western provinces for a long while, the center of the empire's gravity had shifted decisively.

In the fourth and fifth centuries, the Germanic tribes roamed through the western provinces more or less at will. Replacing the demoralized Roman officials with their own men, the Germanic war chiefs began to create rough-and-ready kingdoms:

1. The *Franks* established the core of the French kingdom in the fifth century.
2. The *Saxons* set up a kingdom in northern Germany from present-day Holland eastward.
3. The *Angles* and *Saxons* invaded and conquered England in the fifth century.

4. The *Vandals* invaded Roman North Africa, established a kingdom there, and from it made the raid on Rome itself (455), which gave their name to history.
5. The *West Goths (Visigoths)* took over Spain.
6. The *East Goths (Ostrogoths)* took over most of Italy itself.

In these Germanic kingdoms, Roman customs and ideas were overlain by the invaders' native concepts. The Germans were a seminomadic tribal people; probably originating in Scandinavia, they had wandered far and wide in continental Europe from the Netherlands to Russia. Along the route, during the last centuries B.C.E., they picked up farming, but preferred the life of the hunter and herder when possible. Pushed westward by the Huns and other Asiatics, they came into contact with expanding Rome in the last century of the republic. The Roman historian Tacitus tells us that his fellow citizens regarded the Germans as a barbarian people who possessed many admirable qualities, such as bravery in war, hardiness, and fierce loyalty to their leaders.

What we know of the very early Germans derives entirely from Roman sources, for they left no writings of their own and, in fact, had no written language until they learned Latin from the Romans. They spent much time fighting one another, and the Romans encouraged this inclination to keep the Germans weak. But once they learned to band together, the outer defenses of the Roman Empire came under frequent attack from a fierce and determined foe. Like other barbarians that have attacked more civilized societies, the Germans were trying to obtain for themselves the more comfortable and richly varied life that civilization offered. Many of them eventually adopted at least a thin veneer of civilization and were accepted into Roman society. Many converted to Christianity after the empire became Christian.

By the 500s, the western half of the empire was an administrative and sometimes also a physical ruin. Germanic kings and nobles had generally supplanted Italian or other romanized officials as the rulers. Open warfare, piracy, and general insecurity were common. Under such conditions, Roman traditions and the Roman lifestyle gradually disappeared except in a handful of cities, whose walls kept them relatively secure. Even in the cities, manufacturing and trade dwindled, as the population shrank.

In some places, German masters and their Roman subjects got along quite well as soon as the actual conquest was completed. The German ruling groups were anxious to imitate their far more cultured subjects and intermarried with them from the start. In southern France, for example, the transition from Roman province to Germanic kingdom was accomplished practically without destruction or friction, as far as we know. In other places, it was a very different story. London and Bath, which had thrived under the Romans, became little more than ghost towns under the very warlike Angles and Saxons. Rome itself was devastated by the Vandal raids and had become a forlorn outpost of the Christian power based in Constantinople.

✤ THE EASTERN ROMAN EMPIRE

The *Byzantine Empire,* as the eastern half of the Christian world is usually known (from *Byzantium,* the Greek name for the town Constantine renamed for himself), proved to be an extraordinarily resilient competitor among the several barbaric and civilized rivals for supremacy in the eastern Mediterranean. The Arab Muslims (see Chapter 16) would come to be the most dangerous of these, after the Byzantine Greeks had engaged in long wars with the neighboring Persians that weakened both.

As already noted, after the transfer of the government to Constantinople, it soon became clear that the western provinces were expendable, while the East would be defended. In the mid-500s, however, the ambitious emperor *Justinian* made a concerted effort to recover the

◼ This fresco of Christ at the Last Judgment by Michelangelo is one of the glories of Byzantine art, which was almost exclusively religious in nature.

Procopius's *Secret History*

The appetite of most people for the "inside story" or a juicy bit of gossip about the lives of celebrities did not begin in the twentieth century. One of the most renowned examples dates from the Byzantine Empire in the sixth century, when the powerful emperor Justinian attempted to reconquer much of what had been lost to the Germans in the West. His chosen tool was the general Belisarius, who took on a young man to become his secretary in 527. This young man, Procopius, later wrote a *History of the Wars of Belisarius* that made him famous. He had a prestigious position in the government and presumably knew many of the leading figures in Constantinople on a close personal basis.

Sometime about 550, Procopius wrote his *Secret History,* a short work that is far better known to modern readers than the *Wars.* The *Secret History,* which was not published until much later, is a scandal sheet, an account of rumors and underhanded doings of all sorts that, according to Procopius, took place in Justinian's court. Procopius was especially scathing on the personal character of the emperor and his empress Theodora. True or not (most of the stories are found solely in Procopius), his tales make for interesting reading.

On Justinian's character:

Justin's nephew, Justinian, ran the whole government and was responsible for evils to the Romans of a kind and magnitude such as no man before ever heard of. He readily advanced to the wicked slaughter of man and to the seizure of property to which he had no right, and it was nothing to him if many tens of thousands of men perished, even though they had done nothing to deserve it. . . . No Roman whatever succeeded in escaping from this man—he fell like a disaster from heaven over the whole race and left no one whatever untouched. Some he killed without cause, others he left contending with poverty, more wretched than the dead, praying to him to release them from their present troubles even by cruel death. . . .

This emperor, then, was dissembling, treacherous, false, secret in his anger, two-faced: a clever man, well able to feign an opinion; one who wept not from joy or from sorrow but on purpose, at the right moment to suit the present need. He was always deceiving. . . . He was an unreliable friend; an enemy who would not keep a truce; a passionate lover of murder and of money.

On Theodora, whom Procopius seems to have despised, and about whom we know relatively little except through the *Secret History:*

. . . As soon as she grew and matured, her mother put her on stage and she became a prostitute at once, what used to be called a "whore." She could not play the flute or the harp and she had not even trained in dancing; she simply sold her beauty to all comers, putting her whole body to work. . . . She was very witty and full of jokes and became famous for it at once. The girl had no shame and no one ever saw her embarrassed. She would undertake shameless services without hesitation, and she was the sort of girl who would joke and laugh out loud when she was being beaten. . . .

She never even expected that any of the men she was with would make the approach; instead, she approached them herself, with laughter and clowning, shimmying her hips at everyone, especially if they were young boys. There was never such a slave to pleasure of every kind. . . .

In this way, then, the woman was born and reared and became notorious in the eyes of many prostitutes as well as of all mankind. When she came to Byzantium [Constantinople] for the second time, Justinian fell passionately in love with her and at first associated with her as his mistress, though raising her to the rank of patrician. So Theodora managed to acquire enormous power at once and also a considerable amount of money. As happens with all who are passionately in love, Justinian thought nothing sweeter than to give every kind of present and money to his mistress. The state served as fuel for this love affair. With her he set about still further destruction of the people, not only in Byzantium but throughout the Roman empire. . . .

Because it was impossible for a man of senatorial rank to marry a prostitute . . . he forced the emperor [i.e., the still ruling Justin] to revoke the laws by another law, and after this he lived with Theodora as his wife and made marriage to prostitutes possible for all the others. . . . And not many days later, Justin died of sickness after a reign of nine years, and Justinian together with Theodora got the imperial power for himself.

SOURCE: *Procopius* edited by Averil Cameron, © Washington Square Press. Reprinted by permission of Pocket Books, a division of Simon and Schuster, Inc.

West (see the Document and Biography in this chapter). His general Belisarius defeated the Vandals and reunited North Africa with Constantinople; a few years later, part of Italy was retaken from the Ostrogoths. Justinian's dream of re-creating the empire was ultimately a failure, however. Within just two generations, almost all the reconquered areas had fallen to new invaders. The effort had exhausted the Byzantines and would never be attempted again.

From the early 600s, the Byzantine Empire was under more or less constant attack for two centuries. During this period, it lost not only the western reconquests, but also most of its own outlying territories, first to Avars and Persians and then to Arabs and Slavs. Much of the empire's Near Eastern territory was lost to the first, explosive surge of the Arab armies. The besieging Muslims nearly succeeded in taking Constantinople in 717, when the desperate defenders used "Greek fire", a combustible liquid, to beat them off at sea. While the imperial defenders were occupied, their tributary Slavic subjects in the Balkans (Bulgars, Serbs) established independent states that soon became powerful enough to threaten the Greeks from the north.

In the long term, the most outstanding achievement of the Byzantine rulers was the *Christianization of eastern Europe.* By the 700s, the missionaries of the western empire, supported by the bishop of Rome (the pope), had made many converts among the Germanic tribes and kingdoms, but they had not yet ventured into eastern Europe, which was unromanized and still barbaric. Thus, in eastern and southeastern Europe, the field was open to the Byzantine missionaries.

The Byzantine missions to the Slavs of eastern Europe met with remarkable success. Beginning in the 800s, Greek monks moved into the nearby Balkans and then to the coast of the Black Sea and Russia. Their eventual success meant that Russia, Romania, Serbia, Bulgaria, and, of course, Greece itself would look for centuries to Constantinople rather than Rome for their religious and cultural values, their laws and their literature, their styles of art and architecture, and, thanks to their ethnically organized churches, their very sense of nationhood.

The conversion of the Slavs to the Greek rite was a crucial and permanent turning point in European history. The split that originated in the political rivalry between Rome and Constantinople (see Chapter 18) gradually deepened and was reflected in the cultural and religious differences between Greek and Latin and between the leaders of the two churches, the Byzantine patriarch and

■ After the move from Rome, the government devoted much money and energy to making the new capital impregnable from both sea and land. On the land side, a series of gigantic walls were erected, which protected the city from all attacks until 1453.

the pope. After many years of alternating friction and patched-up amity, the rift culminated in *the division of Christianity between West and East.* In 1054, a headstrong pope encountered a stubborn patriarch in Constantinople who refused to yield to the pope's demands for complete subordination in a matter of doctrine; the two leaders excommunicated one another in a fit of theological egotism. Their successors have not been able to overcome their differences to the present day. The Greek Orthodox or Eastern rite Christians of Russia and eastern Europe look to their own national churches in communion with the patriarch in Constantinople (now Turkish Istanbul) for religious guidance. The Roman pope still commands the doctrinal obedience of the worldwide body of Roman Catholics.

One other enormously influential result of Byzantine initiative should be mentioned in even this brief survey: the sixth-century distillation of Roman law that was undertaken by the emperor Justinian and passed on to posterity as the **Corpus Juris.** On this foundation rested most Western medieval and early modern law codes, and its basic precepts (see Chapter 13) are operative to the present day.

Summary

The Germanic invasions of the third and fourth centuries found a Roman pagan society that was already breaking apart under the burdens of heavy taxes, declining productivity, and instability at the top. The demoralization summed up by the phrase "Barracks Emperors" could not be stopped by the reforms of Diocletian and Constantine in the early 300s C.E. Constantine attempted to make Christianity a rallying point for an imperial revival, but it could not halt the constellation of forces that were laying waste to the western provinces. In moving the government to Constantinople, Rome's rulers tacitly admitted that much of the West was indefensible. The decision to play from their strength in a time of crisis was a wise one.

The Germanic tribes took note of Rome's weakness and acted accordingly. From the Hunnic invasion in the mid-fifth century onward, savage or semicivilized groups marched across the former borders almost at will. The Roman provincial armies were engaged in plundering one another's territories more often than defending against invasion. Commands from the central government in far-off Constantinople were ignored.

Christianity spread rapidly after winning the favor of Constantine and his successors. By 381, Theodosius made it the official religion. But Christianity had inherited a state that was no longer capable of enforcing its commands through much of its territories, and the Christians' concerns remained focused on the world-to-come as they passed under the alien rule of Germanic kings. In the eastern empire, attacks came from all sides after the failed attempt to recover the western provinces. The conversion of the Slavs and some other peoples to Greek rite Christianity was that government's outstanding contribution to Western civilization.

Test Your Knowledge

1. Which of the following does *not* help explain the appeal of early Christianity?
   a. Encouragement of military valor
   b. Sense of supernatural mission
   c. Receptivity to all potential converts
   d. Promotion of a sense of community among its adherents
2. Christianity became a universal faith in large part due to the efforts of
   a. the Roman officials in Judea.
   b. the apostle Paul.
   c. the apostle Peter.
   d. the Zealots.
3. The reforming emperor who created the Tetrarchy was
   a. Commodus.
   b. Constantine.
   c. Diocletian.
   d. Augustus.
4. Which is *not* true of the Byzantine Empire?
   a. It was a Christian state.
   b. It was under attack through much of its history.
   c. Its culture and political offices were dominated by Greeks.
   d. It never attempted to regain the lost provinces in the West.
5. Emperor Diocletian
   a. reorganized the territory of the empire into two halves ruled by two co-equal officers.
   b. made himself into a prime minister of a new, cabinet-style government.
   c. fought his rival Constantine for supremacy until he was killed.
   d. abandoned the western half of the empire to the barbarians and moved to Constantinople.
6. The emperor Theodosius (380–390 C.E.) is important to Christian history for
   a. his final persecution of Christians.
   b. making Christianity the official religion.
   c. beginning the practice of intervening in internal church affairs.
   d. moving the church headquarters to Constantinople.

7. The decision to move the capital to Constantinople was justified
   a. by a vision given to the emperor Constantine before battle.
   b. by weighing military and economic factors.
   c. by the lack of a good harbor at Rome.
   d. by the defeat of Rome's armies.

8. Which of the following was *not* accomplished by Justinian?
   a. Reconquest of North Africa for a time
   b. Reconquest of France for a time
   c. Reconquest of Spain for a time
   d. Composition of a new code of law

Identification Terms

Apologists	Council of Nicaea	Diaspora	Saul of Tarsus
Augustine	Corpus Juris	Jewish War	Tetrarchy
Barracks Emperors			

Bibliography

Balsdon, J. P. V. *Life and Leisure in Ancient Rome,* 1969. An enlightening book on ordinary affairs in Rome.

Barnes, T. D. *The New Empire of Diocletian and Constantine,* 1978. Analyzes the attempt to salvage the faltering empire in the late third and early fourth centuries, as does MacMullen below.

Benko, S. *Pagan Rome and Early Christianity,* 1985.

Bridge, A. *Theodora: A Portrait in a Byzantine Landscape,* 1984. A highly entertaining look at a controversial figure.

Frend, W. H. *The Rise of Christianity,* 1984. A good study of Christianity's rise.

Grant, M. *The Fall of the Roman Empire: A Reappraisal,* 1976. See this and Jones below for different explanations for the collapse of the Roman Empire.

Jones, A. M. *The Decline of the Ancient World,* 1966.

MacMullen, R. *Constantine,* 1988.

Mango, C. *Byzantium: The Empire of New Rome,* 1980. A good survey of Byzantine affairs. See also Runciman below.

Mattingly, H. *The Man in the Roman Street,* 1972. Deals with ordinary people in ancient Rome.

Musset, L. *The Germanic Invasions: The Making of Europe* A.D. *400–600,* 1975. Looks at the Germanic barbarian invaders in some detail, as does Wallace-Hadrill below.

Runciman, S. *Byzantine Civilization,* 1956.

Stenton, F. *Anglo-Saxon England,* 1971. Deals with the Germanic invaders in a particular country.

Wallace-Hadrill, J. M. *The Barbarian West,* 1967.

Wilken, R. L. *Christians as Romans Saw Them,* 1984. An interesting variation on the theme of the persecutions.

ORDINARY LIVES IN THE CLASSICAL AGE

c. 600–c. 300 B.C.E.	Classical Greek and early Roman republican civilizations
c. 300 B.C.E.–200 C.E.	Hellenistic civilization in the East
c. 200–27 B.C.E.	Late Roman Republic
27 B.C.E.–180 C.E.	Roman Empire's flourishing

This chapter looks at the activities and attitudes of people living in the Greek and Roman civilizations between 500 B.C.E. and 500 C.E. The topics we discussed in Chapter 8 will be considered again here: how people earned a living, women's place in society, what constituted moral and immoral acts, sexual relationships, and how children were treated and educated. Again, the reader is cautioned that what we know about these topics is partial at best and is almost always limited to the upper classes. In this epoch, history still refers to the lives and acts of the few.

✤ EARNING A LIVING

Greece and the Roman Republic

Farming, fishing, and herding were still the means of keeping body and soul together for the majority. In Greece and Italy, only a small portion of the total area is good farmland. Greece was a country of small farmers, who had to expend a great deal of labor to make a living from the stony, unrewarding soil. Many pastured a few goats and sheep as well, and both olives and wine grapes were important supplements to grain farming. The food supply was a major factor regulating the Greek population and promoting the extensive emigration throughout the Mediterranean basin during the sixth and seventh centuries B.C.E.

The Greek *polis* was usually a small place, and its inhabitants were generally racially and culturally homogeneous. The center of the *polis* was a town of moderate size, with a population of 10,000 to 20,000 as a rough average. It supported all of the usual urban trades and crafts. Here culture and politics were matters of wide concern, debated about and participated in by most adult persons.

Wealthy and educated Greeks, who formed a minority of the population, thought of manual labor as being beneath the dignity of the free and assigned as much of it as possible to their slaves. But the majority could not afford to keep slaves and had to do the work themselves. Athens, the center of the *polis* of Attica, was exceptional in that perhaps as many as half of its total inhabitants were slaves. Many of these men and women were employed directly by the state, and most of the rest were domestic servants of all types, rather than productive workers. Most Greeks active in the labor force were free men and women, working for themselves or for a wage in small-scale enterprises.

Machinery of even primitive design was a rarity, and a Greek or Roman woman spent a majority of her waking hours, from childhood to old age, preparing the next day's bread and porridge, carrying water, spinning and weaving cloth, and in general performing the same routine tasks that occupied her predecessors in the East and in Egypt. In the countryside, women did much the same jobs as men, though we know little about the rates of pay or other details.

From the consistent attention given to textile production in classical literature and art, it is clear that a large part of a woman's life—young or old, married or single (spinsters)—was spent on this task. Among most peoples throughout history, spinning and weaving have been specifically female tasks—no male would be caught doing these jobs, which were identified as "woman's work," just as warfare was "man's work." (The legend of the Amazon female warriors was just that—a legend.) As the Greeks became maritime traders, the production of cloth for sale throughout the Mediterranean and Black Sea basins increased dramatically, quite apart from the demand from the domestic markets. Leather, ceramics, and metal weap-

■ The Roman upper and middle classes had a highly developed domestic architecture. All interior space centered on an opening called the atrium, which allowed light and air into the abutting rooms. This style of architecture is still common in countries with a Mediterranean climate.

■ **Apartment House in Ostia.** Roman dwellings were normally made of brick like this apartment house in the port of Rome, Ostia. They were frequently four or more stories tall and extremely overcrowded by modern standards. The residents shared sanitary and kitchen facilities with many others.

onry were major exports, engaging the efforts of a number of craftsmen in several *poleis.* Imports included grain, timber, and some luxuries. Both exports and imports were carried by the constantly expanding fleets of Athens and other trading towns. Probably a higher proportion of people were engaged in the import-export business in classical Greece than in any previous civilization, and the proportion grew in the Hellenistic Age.

The Hellenistic Kingdoms and the Roman Empire

In the Greek-ruled kingdoms of the East, the cities dominated and exploited the countryside. While the *polis* ideal of citizenship grew dim in these multi-ethnic territories, economic segregation between rich and poor grew more marked. Slaves increased in numbers and in importance to production. Widespread slavery had the effect of seriously depressing the income and security of the free, thereby essentially preventing them from exercising their rights of citizenship. The poor are rarely able to afford the luxury of political participation.

Large enterprises that produced for a wide market became more numerous, an indication of the increased *economic interdependency* of the Mediterranean lands. Some of these enterprises in the Seleucid, Persian, and Egyptian kingdoms, especially, were manned entirely by slaves, who often were highly skilled. The increased technological capacity and larger markets enabled these large enterprises to supplant the small-scale businesses of the classical Greeks.

The conquests of Alexander paved the way for *material wealth* unheard of by the classical Greeks. Although the Greek/Macedonian overlords were eventually pushed out or absorbed by the eastern peoples, they retained their business contacts. Silk from the East, for example, now entered the western world as perhaps the most valuable single item of trade. The Chinese monopoly on silk production for export would not be broken until the sixth century C.E., and then only insignificantly. Not until modern times would Europeans understand how to produce silk in quantity as fine as the Chinese version.

Trade with the East was conducted by the traditional overland caravans (the Silk Road to China) and also by new sea routes. The Hellenistic achievements in science had repercussions for navigation and mapmaking, which received considerable attention during the first centuries B.C.E. and C.E. Alexandria in Egypt became a major center of scientific endeavor, much of which was devoted to geography and mapping the heavens.

Agricultural production seems to have risen during the Hellenistic Age. Most of the Mediterranean countries now had agricultural exports, with the major exceptions of Greece and Italy. Thanks to the fertility of the Nile valley, Egypt remained the richest single area in the western world, both under the Ptolemies and later as a province of the Roman Empire. Slave labor was widely employed on plantationlike farms, but small subsistence farmers, living in their ancestral villages, were still the norm during Rome's rise to preeminence.

During the five hundred years (100 B.C.E.–400 C.E.) of Rome's empire in Europe, the methods by which the poor made a living changed very little from earlier days. Farming or herding animals remained the paramount occupation in the countryside. The urban population grew considerably, especially in the west where the Romans introduced an urban culture for the first time. In the towns, the number of people—both men and women—engaged in skilled or semiskilled labor increased steadily. But the real growth of urban population came from the influx of country people who had lost their land and their livelihood. They came to town hoping for a better life, but many ended up as beggars.

Impoverishment was particularly dramatic in Italy. As outlined earlier, the Roman citizen militia of the early republic was changed radically by the ongoing wars. Farmer-citizens were away from home for years, fighting one enemy or another. Instead of being rewarded, many were taken advantage of by wealthy speculators, who bribed or coerced their way to large-scale estate ownership. The new estates were staffed by slaves from the

■ **Girl Spinning.** This fresco from the first century C.E. shows a young woman at probably the most common household task outside the kitchen: spinning fiber from a hand spindle into thread.

conquered lands. The increasingly corrupt Senate, itself full of these speculators, made no effort to stop this practice. By the time of the Gracchi (130 B.C.E.), the small peasants who had formed the backbone of Italian society were a rarity. The "land question" had become Rome's primary social problem—and it was not resolved.

The dispossessed country folk flooded into the towns, above all into Rome, where citizens could sell their votes, if nothing else. The formerly honorable relationship of "patron" and "client" now came to mean the dependency of a beggar upon his master and almsgiver. Persons with nothing but the clothes on their back held themselves ready to be of service to some ambitious man: politically, as a voter, and economically, as casual labor. By the end of the republic, the "Roman mob" was in full flower, living off the handouts of their various patrons, demoralized and in poverty. Other cities had similar problems, though Rome attracted the bulk of this new **proletariat**—people without sources of income except the daily sale of their labor.

It is to Augustus Caesar's credit that he understood the necessity of linking this unstable mob to the anchor of

Roman imperial government. He and his successors did this by the combination of *panem et circenses* ("bread and circuses"). By giving the mob a minimal supply of free food and entertaining it with gladiatorial combats, chariot races, and frequent spectacles, the emperors instilled a commitment to Rome's prosperity and success in much of the lower classes.

But Augustus also transformed the role of the central government, turning it into a massive public works agency, not only in Italy but throughout the far-flung empire. By so doing, he and other early rulers reduced the urban unemployment that had been one of the chief unsettling factors of the late republic's politics. He also banned the importation of slaves into Italy and put the army to work as a huge engineering contractor in the outer provinces. These government measures helped to steady the Roman economy, while the maintenance of peace and order for most of two centuries encouraged the expansion of private trade and commerce throughout the empire.

✤ GENDER RELATIONS

Greece in the Classical Age

The degree of freedom accorded women in classical Greek society has been a topic of intense debate in recent years. Perhaps what this really says is that we know much more about the Greeks' preferences and prejudices than we do about any other early society (thanks to the large amount of surviving literature by Greek authors). Historians agree that women were generally excluded from any effective exercise of political and economic powers and that the Greeks were the originators of *misogyny*, the pervasive distrust and dislike of women by men. The philosopher Thales once said that he was grateful to Fortune for three reasons: that he was born a Greek and not a barbarian, that he was born a man and not an animal, and that he was born a man and not a woman. An authority on Greek women says that they "neither had nor sought political power, but worked through their husbands or fathers or sons."* Any women who took political action did so "only under certain closely defined conditions, and unless they [did] so at least ostensibly on behalf of a male relative, they and those around them [came] to a bad end." The great tragic heroines such as Electra,

*M. R Lefkowitz, "Influential Women," in *Images of Women in Antiquity*, ed. A. Cameron and A. Kuhrt [Detroit, 1983], p. 49.

Antigone, and Medea and the mythological heroines such as Cassandra and Artemis, are examples of women who came "to a bad end."

Greek males' treatment of the other sex exhibits some interesting variations. Another modern scholar notes that the antifemale prejudice exhibited in later Greek literature is not present in the Homeric period. The women of Sparta were quite free and equal with their menfolk. Spartan women allegedly shared the sexual favors of their men, regardless of marriage. The men were so frequently away in the field or in barracks that both they and the government saw this practice as essential to Sparta's survival. Since our knowledge of Sparta comes exclusively from non-Spartan sources, it is impossible to know if this very unusual attitude was actual fact or another example of the antidemocratic Athenians' admiration for their powerful neighbor.

In contrast, we have a good deal of definite information about Athens. Respectable Athenian women were limited to the home and could make only rare public excursions under the guardianship of servants and slaves. Their work was closely prescribed for them: management of the household and supervision of children and servants. Within the four walls of the home, one or two rooms were reserved for their use; in multistoried houses, these rooms were normally upstairs, but in any house, they would be in the back away from the street. This was the Greek equivalent of the Muslim *harem* or the Hindu *purdah,* and it fulfilled the same purpose: keeping women, as the valuable possession of men, away from the prying eyes of nonfamily members and all sexual temptations. Poor urban women undoubtedly had more freedom to leave the home and enter the workplace unescorted, as did rural women who had a great many essential tasks to perform daily, some of them outdoors.

Even in the age of democracy (fifth century B.C.E.), Athens was not a happy place for the ambitious woman. Not only was she excluded from politics, but she was also legally and customarily inferior to men in terms of property holding, custody of children, marriage and divorce, and business enterprises. A freeborn, native Athenian woman was recognized as a citizen. But her citizenship was very different from that enjoyed by males; its main advantage was that citizenship could be passed on to (male) children through her. Aristotle's attitude was typical. In his *Politics,* he states that the male is by nature superior and the female inferior; the one rules, the other is ruled: "silence is a woman's glory."

In *family and sexual matters,* the Athenian woman must have suffered a good deal of frustration. Marriage, of

The *Satires* of Juvenal

Among the many sharp-tongued commentators on the vice and follies of the Romans, Juvenal stands out. Few details of this second-century author's life are known, but his *Satires* have remained a favorite source of information about the daily lives of Romans who were his contemporaries. Sixteen of these free verse poems have survived, although he probably wrote many others. In the following selections from the *Third Satire,* the poet gives free rein to his feelings about the trials and miseries of life in the Big City by pretending to let his friend Umbricius speak:

> Since there's no place in the city,
> He says, "For an honest man, and no
>   reward for his labors,
> Since I have less today than yesterday,
>   since by tomorrow
> That will have dwindled still more, I
>   have made my decision. I'm going
> To the place where, I've heard
>   Daedalus put off his wings,
> While my white hair is still new, my old
>   age in the prime of its straightness,

> While my fate spinner still has yarn on
>   her spool, while I'm able
> Still to support myself on two good
>   legs, without crutches.
> Rome, good-by! Let the rest
>   stay in the town, if they want to....
> What should I do in Rome? I am no
>   good at lying.
> If a book's bad, I can't praise it, or go
>   around ordering copies.
> I don't know the stars; I can't hire out
>   as assassin
> When some young man wants his
>   father knocked off for a price; I
>   have never
> Studied the guts of frogs,* and plenty of
>   others know better
> How to convey to a bride the gifts of
>   the first man she cheats with.
> I am no lookout for thieves, so I
>   cannot expect a commission

course, was a contract arranged by the two families, and as in earlier civilizations, its overriding purpose was to ensure that the male lineage would be continued. Marriage seems to have been the only respectable status for an adult female; there is no information on the frequency of spinsterhood excepting a handful of virgin priestesses.

Prostitution was common in classical Greece. The upper rank of women who engaged in it were equivalent to the *geisha* of modern Japan; they were well-educated, well-paid performers, who amused their clients in many nonsexual fashions as well as the essential acts of their trade.

It is thought that male *homosexuality* or *bisexuality* was originally a product of Sparta and its militaristic society, which brought youths together for long periods without women. But this interpretation is open to much question, and certainly, homosexuality existed among the Greeks

long before Sparta's transformation and also existed in other parts of classical Greece—notably, Athens. We know from the writings of several of the philosophers that the Greeks themselves differed sharply about the morality and general advisability of same-sex attraction. Plato has one of his spokesmen (in the *Symposium*) say that in both Athens and Sparta public attitudes on the topic are "complicated."

Wives occasionally found themselves in competition with "boyfriends" for the attention of their husbands; in such situations, they had no more legal grounds to complain than if the man was sleeping with a female slave or a prostitute. Classical society looked upon the homosexual relationship between older, experienced males with younger, inexperienced males as potentially the most elevating form of **paideia** (education) possible for the younger person. The fact that it undoubtedly did not

On some governor's staff. I'm a useless
   corpse or cripple.
Here in town the sick die from
   insomnia mostly.
Undigested food, on a stomach
   burning with ulcers,
Brings on listlessness, but who can
   sleep in a flophouse?
Who but the rich can afford sleep and
   a garden apartment?
That's the source of infection. The
   wheels creak by on the narrow
Streets of the wards, the drivers
   squabble and brawl when they're
   stopped,
More than enough to frustrate the
   drowsiest son of a sea-cow.
When his business calls, the crowd
   makes way, as the rich man,
Carried high in his car, rides over
   them, reading or writing,
Even taking a snooze, perhaps, for the
   motion's composing.
Still, he gets where he wants before we
   do; for all of our hurry

Traffic gets in our way, in front,
   around and behind us.
Somebody gives me a shove with an
   elbow, or two-by-four scantling.
One clunks my head with a beam,
   another cracks down with a beer
   keg.
Mud is thick on my shins, I am
   trampled by somebody's big feet. . . .
You are a thoughtless fool, unmindful
   of sudden disaster,
If you don't make your will before you
   go out to dinner.
There are as many deaths in the night as there are
   open windows
Where you pass by; if you're wise, you
   will pray, in your wretched devotions, that
People may be content with no more
   than emptying slop jars."

*Frogs were often used for reading the omen, that is, fortune-telling.

SOURCE: Translation by R. Humphries. *The Satires of Juvenal* © by Indiana University Press, 1958.

always work out that way, but sometimes led to the same emotional dead end as a heterosexual romance might, was apparently accepted without special comment. Lesbianism was apparently accepted by some Greek males as easily as male homosexuality. But others found it a matter for ridicule and contempt, even when they had no problems with the male variety. We have very little direct evidence on this; the topic was avoided in the comedies and other dramas, which were otherwise so forceful and direct on human follies.

The Hellenistic Age

Based mainly on literary sources, historians generally agree that women's overall status gradually rose in the Hellenistic and Roman eras, though this statement applies more to the upper classes than to the lower ones. Several of the Hellenistic kingdoms were ruled by queens, and the incidence of female writers slowly increases from the very low levels of the classical age (Sappho is one of the very few known before 300 B.C.E.).

One modern author thinks that the rise in female status can be summarized best by contrasting the goddess Athena with the Hellenistic Aphrodite. Both were outstanding figures: Athena was the goddess of wisdom and patron of the Athens *polis;* Aphrodite was the goddess of love. But Athena was a very manlike female and was even portrayed regularly as a warrior. The myths depict her as saying that she feels like a man feels and that she believes all great virtues are transmitted through the male. Aphrodite, on the other hand, was very much a woman and was not confused as to which side of the gender line she stood upon! She delighted in defeating men who contested her in the war between the sexes.

In the Hellenistic cities, upper-class women played an active role in business affairs, and the older prohibitions about leaving the family home seem to have faded. By the time of the Roman dominion, women in the East sometimes held positions of importance in politics, such as the queen Cleopatra, the last of the Ptolemys in Egypt. Priestesses such as the female oracles at Delphi were accorded semidivine status by their male adherents and their fellow citizens.

The *rights of married women* definitely increased. They were no longer regarded as the property of husbands and fathers, but as independent legal personages. In this highly law-conscious society, female status was best revealed by property rights. Dowries were protected from greed and/or stupidity on the husband's side; no "second households" were permitted (though casual affairs with slaves or prostitutes went on as before). Divorce could be obtained on preordained grounds by either party. When the husband was at fault, he had to return the dowry. But communal property, that is, goods obtained since the start of the marriage, would remain with the husband. Women also had more opportunities for education in this age. The founder of the Epicurean philosophy, for example, admitted females to his school on the same criteria as males. Even physical exercise, always a justification for segregating males and females in classical Greece, was now opened to some females as well. Illiteracy was the rule for women outside the urban upper classes, but was somewhat reduced.

Roman Custom

In Roman times, the most characteristic earmark of the female's status was the far-reaching authority of the father over his daughter and indeed, over all his *familia,* defined as wife, children, grandchildren, and household slaves. This **patria potestas** (literally the "power of the father") extended even to life and death, though the exercise of the death penalty was very rare. This power had originated in the early republic and was reflected in the first Roman code, the Law of the Twelve Tables of 450 B.C.E. It lasted well into the empire, in theory if not in practice.

The *lex Julia* of 18 B.C.E. was enacted by Augustus Caesar to shore up the crumbling morality of the Roman aristocracy; it continued to give the father authority to kill an adulterous daughter (and also the adulterer, if he was caught red-handed). The unfortunate emperor was forced to apply the law against his own daughter Julia, whose escapades were a constant mockery of her father. In any event, he settled for exile rather than death as her penalty.

All Roman law was primarily concerned with the protection of property, and the laws concerning women clearly show that they were considered the property of the male head of the *familia.* It is worth noting that the father's powers exceeded those of the husband. For example, if a wife died without leaving a will, the property she left reverted not to her husband, but to her father as head of the *familia* she had come from.

A woman who passed from her father's control and was not under that of a husband was termed **sui juris** ("of her own law"). This status was quite unusual. Women who were neither married nor possessing *sui juris* had to be under tutelage; that is, a male relative was legally responsible for her.

Roman Marriage and Divorce

Roman girls married young by our standards, and betrothal was often much earlier still. By age twenty, most females were married, and marriage at age thirteen was not unusual. The girl's consent was not necessary, and the young wife usually (not always) passed under the **manus** ("hand") of her husband. The details of who controlled what property were spelled out in a marriage contract. Unlike many other civilizations, the Roman widow was expected to remarry if she could, and she was normally then *sui juris,* legally equal to her new husband in terms of control over property. Marriage between close relatives was prohibited as incest; interestingly, the Egyptian habit of marrying one's sister was carried on under Roman rule, regardless of this prohibition.

Divorce of wives by husbands was quite common among the upper classes. Augustus, scandalized by the habits of some of his colleagues, decreed that a man catching his wife in adultery must divorce her or be considered her procurer and be punished himself. Divorce was much harder to obtain for a woman, and sexual impotence was one of the few grounds accepted. Because marriage was considered a *consensual union* rather than a legal obligation of the spouses, the lack of continued consent was itself grounds for its dissolution. This is the source of the modern divorce by "irreconcilable differences."

Abortion was common throughout the republican era. The birthrate among the Roman nobility had sunk so low at the time of Augustus that he strongly encouraged having more children. But abortion was legal until the first century C.E., and when it was declared a crime, it was because the act affected the property of the father of the fetus—a typical Roman viewpoint. Infanticide by exposure also continued, but no one knows how common it may have been, nor whether it favored the male over the female child, as is frequently assumed. A large proportion of slaves and prostitutes originated as girl babies picked up "from the trash heap," as the Roman saying went.

Law and Morality

The Romans used the legal term **stuprum** to refer to a wide range of crimes and other behavior that was not illegal, but was considered undesirable. Rape and female adultery were two of the most serious offenses in the empire; both were punishable by death, though actual prosecutions seem to have been few.

Homosexual acts were not illegal, though many considered them immoral and even depraved. Homosexuality does not appear to have been as widespread in Rome as it had been in Greece, although it was certainly not unusual among the upper classes. We have no way of knowing its true frequency or what the population as a whole thought about it.

Prostitution was also not itself illegal, but it carried with it **infamia,** meaning disrepute and shame for the practitioners. Prostitutes were expected to register with the local authorities, and they paid heavy taxes on their earnings. Nevertheless, they were not criminals, but were simply engaged in business and were so treated. Brothel keeping in Roman times, as earlier and later, was one of the more dependable sources of wealth for the (generally female) proprietors. The girls were mostly slave born, but some were free, and some were even married. Dress and hairdos indicated their profession: showy and revealing togas were their trademark. (In Roman times, only men wore the toga in respectable circles; women dressed in a long robe or cloak.)

Female Trades

Women worked in all trades not requiring the heaviest labor. Textile trades were still the most common occupation for women of all classes, slave and free. Midwives, many physicians, scribes, and secretaries were female. Wet nurses were always in heavy demand; normally, they were country dwellers who cared for the children of urban mothers, either on a live-in basis or by taking the infant to the farm for a year or two. Personal servants, hairdressers, nannies, and masseuses (a Roman passion) were always women.

Entertainers of all sorts—acrobats, clowns, actresses, musicians, dancers—were in high demand. They were often female and frequently combined their stage talents with a bit of prostitution on the side. The tradition that female *artistes* are sexually available continues in Mediterranean folklore to the present day.

✤ SLAVE AND FREE

The number of slaves climbed sharply in the first century B.C.E., as the legions took over one province after another and made off with the human booty. Just as important, the number of debt slaves rose as the Italian countryside came to be dominated by large estates (*villas*).

The slaves brought back as war booty were often more educated and better skilled than the native Italians, and slaves from Greece, in particular, brought high prices in the market. Augustus tried to protect the free citizens by banning the importation of additional slaves into Italy, but his measures were evaded and later revoked. Slaves undercut the price of free labor in some parts of the empire. In the eastern empire, which had a long tradition of slavery, this apparently did not happen. This could be one of the reasons for the slow but steady tilt of economic power in

■ This tender rendition of a young girl daydreaming over her studies is marked by a sentiment not often encountered in Roman painting.

favor of the East and against the West, whose effects we have seen in Chapter 14.

Roman slavery was harsher than had been the case earlier. The large merchant fleet and the navy were dependent on galley slaves, often criminals. The extensive Roman mining industry also depended on slave labor, because this job was so dangerous that few freemen could be lured into it.

Slave families were broken up and sold to the highest bidders. Slaves could own no property of their own; nor could they inherit or bequeath property. The children from a marriage of slaves were automatically the property of the parents' owners. Rape of another's slave was considered a damage to the slave owner, not to the woman, and was paid for accordingly. The rape of a slave by his or her owner was not an offense at all. Despite such treatment, by the third and fourth centuries C.E. free persons were increasingly selling themselves into *voluntary slavery,* which promised them a better life than freedom could. Sometimes, too, the self-sale was a dodge to avoid the tax, which a free person had to pay, but a slave did not. It is not possible to know which motive predominated.

✤ CHILDREN AND EDUCATION

We know a bit about Roman attitudes toward young children in the educated class, but not much otherwise. First and foremost, the male child as the continuer of the *familia* was important, and much attention was devoted to his education, sometimes at a school, more often by a live-in tutor. Strict demands for achievement were placed upon him from the earliest years; the *patria potestas* was applied here to enforce obedience and learning. External display of affection between adult and child was apparently very rare; in this, the Romans were quite different from the Chinese, say, who were not adverse to a show of sentiment.

As in classical Greece, which served as the model in so many ways, the education of males revolved around future public service. Learning was acquired for a communal purpose; it was designed to advance the welfare of the state (in the Roman case) or the *polis* (in Greece). Therefore, the most important subjects to master were law and the principles of government. Rhetoric and philosophy were also needed by all men of affairs. Science and the fine arts were secondary; they were viewed as personal matters, possibly important to the individual, but only incidental to the community.

Females continued to be educated along domestic housekeeping lines, but were gradually given increased freedom to enter the "great world" of male concerns. They could do this through advanced studies and larger political responsibilities. Hence by the second century C.E., it was no longer absurd for a middle-class Roman girl to study mathematics or philosophy or to become an instructor in one of the arts—all careers that had been closed to even upper-class Greek females. The segregation of the sexes so marked in classical Greece was being largely overcome in Roman theory and, to some extent, in practice.

Summary

Between the Classical Age of Greece and the dissolution of the Roman Empire eight hundred years later, a marked evolution of social structure took place. One aspect of this change was the trend toward urban life with its accompanying dislocations and psychic strains on the population at large. Another was the greater prominence of merchants, traders, businessmen, and professionals. Peasants and laborers who still constituted by far the largest segment of the population began to recede into the background. Slaves became more common, but were treated considerably worse than earlier. Free individuals were under economic pressures that were hard to resist; by the end of the Roman imperial period in the West, the beginnings of hereditary serfdom were clearly visible.

The status of the female generally improved from its earlier low point in classical Athens. Women gained some freedoms in arranging their own social and economic fates, though men still controlled every important aspect of public life. The male also controlled his female dependents in a legal sense, and this was particularly true of the Roman father. Greek misogyny was remedied to some extent, however, by the Romans' sensitivity to the value of the female as property of the male. Changing sociocultural attitudes in the late empire reflected the changing political and cultural realities of a declining *imperium.*

Test Your Knowledge

1. Educated Greeks generally believed that manual labor
   a. should be engaged in as a healthy remedy for too much thinking.
   b. was fit only for the unfortunate and slaves.
   c. was an absolute necessity for proper living.
   d. was something that only the Spartans could do well.
2. The condition of women in classical Greece is best summed up by saying
   a. they had more or less equality with males of the same social status.
   b. they had few rights or duties outside the home.
   c. they often held leading positions in the *polis.*
   d. they were respected only after they had married and produced children.
3. The *patria potestas* of Roman law was
   a. the power to produce legitimate children.
   b. the right to be accepted as a Roman citizen.
   c. the power of a father to do what he chose with his family.
   d. the power of the law to define who was the father of a child.
4. As a generalization, upper-class women of the Hellenistic Age
   a. were invisible figures in the background of public affairs.
   b. had less prestige than women had enjoyed in Hellenic times in Greece.
   c. were almost all concubines and rarely married.
   d. were able to gain a considerable measure of public prestige.
5. Slavery after about 100 B.C.E. was usually
   a. harsher and more common than had been the case earlier.
   b. a temporary condition that was easily passed through.
   c. a punishment for serious crimes against the state.
   d. reserved for non-Italians.
6. For Roman women, divorce was
   a. as easily obtained as for men.
   b. an absolute impossibility because of *patria potestas.*
   c. granted only for cases of homosexuality in the husband.
   d. difficult but obtainable on a few grounds.

Identification Terms

infamia	paideia	proletariat	*sui juris*
manus	*patria potestas*	*stuprum*	

Bibliography

Note: Because much more written history survives, we have considerably more choices in trying to reconstruct the daily lives of ordinary Greeks and Romans than was true of the earlier civilizations.

Balsdon, J. P. V. *Roman Women,* 1975. See also his book in the Chapter 14 Bibliography.

Bradley, K. R. *Slaves and Masters in the Roman Empire,* 1988. A good overview of this topic.

Carcopino, J. *Daily Life in Ancient Rome,* 1956. A deservedly famous classic, written for students at the undergraduate level.

Dover, K. *Greek Homosexuality,* 1978. A standard work.

Garlan, Y. *Slavery in Ancient Greece,* 1988.

Golden, M. *Children and Childhood in Classical Greece,* 1990. The latest work on this subject.

Humphrey, J. *Roman Circuses and Chariot Racing,* 1985. Will give the student some understanding of how important these mass entertainments were to the Roman way of life.

Keuls, E. *The Reign of the Phallus,* 1987. An interesting, if much-attacked work on the politics of sexuality in Greece.

Lacey, W. K. *The Family in Classical Greece,* 1984.

MacMullen, R. *Roman Social Relations AD 50 to AD 284,* 1981. More detailed and broader than Bradley above.

Pomeroy, S. *Women in Hellenistic Egypt,* 1984. Discusses the lives of women from all social classes.

Sherwin-White, A. *Racial Prejudice in Imperial Rome,* 1967. Covers a special topic.

EQUILIBRIUM AMONG POLYCENTRIC CIVILIZATIONS

500–1500 C.E.

Prior to about 500 C.E., contacts among the centers of advanced civilized life were limited and tenuous; usually, they were made through intermediate, less-developed societies. Rome, for example, had only the most sparing contacts with China, and they were all indirect. Its contacts with Hindu India were more direct but still very limited. Even India and China had very little contact with one another despite their geographic proximity. Thanks to the mountain walls and the deserts that separated them, few Chinese and still fewer Indians dared that journey.

After 500, however, entirely new centers of civilization emerged, quite detached from the original west Asian and Mediterranean locales. In sub-Saharan Africa, urban life and organized territorial states were emerging by about 800 C.E. Earlier, the Mesoamerican Indians and the Muslims of Asia and northern Africa had achieved a high degree of city-based civilization, the former developing independently of all other models and the latter building on the ancient base in western Asia. As one example of many, commercial relations between Mediterranean Christians and the Hindu/Buddhist regions became closer and more extensive. Both overland and by sea, the Muslims of the eastern fringe of the Mediterranean were the essential mediators between these distant centers and profited from the middleman role.

In the West, this entire thousand-year epoch carries the title "Middle Age." But this term has no relevance to the rest of the civilized world, of course, and should be avoided when speaking of any culture other than the Christian Europeans. In Europe, the Middle Age began with the gradual collapse of the Roman West under the assaults of the Germanic tribes and ended with the triumph of the new secularism of the Renaissance and the final expulsion or assimilation of the Mongol invaders in Russia.

In Asia, this millennium was an era of tremendous vitality and productivity—the south and east Asian Classical Age—which was briefly interrupted by the Mongol conquests of the thirteenth century. But the Mongols were soon assimilated or expelled by their Chinese/Turkic/Persian subjects. At the end of the period in Asia, a reinvigorated Islam extended its conquests in both southern Europe and Africa under the aegis of the Ottoman Turks. In 1500, the Ottoman sultan was in Constantinople, and his armies were menacing the Christian bastion of Vienna. An observer would have been hard put to guess which of the two great contesting religions/polities—Christianity and Islam—would emerge as the determinant of world history in the next century.

In the still isolated America, throughout this period a series of ever more skilled and more populous Indian societies arose in the middle latitudes of the continent and along its western fringe. They were mysteriously (to us) dispersed or overcome by later comers, until the most advanced and skilled of all fell prey to the Spanish conquistadors.

Chapters 16 and 17 deal with the rise of Islam and its culture. The next two chapters outline the painful establishment of medieval European Christianity and its kingdoms, giving particular attention to the church and to the three major groups in Christian society: warriors, worshipers, workers. Chapters 20 through 24 look at the stable and technically advanced south and east Asian societies and the slowly emergent civilizations of the Americas and Africa. The first of this series surveys India's flourishing Hindu and Buddhist cultures; the second looks at China in the great age of Confucian order and prosperity. Then comes Japan as it evolved from an adjunct of China and Korea into cultural and political sovereignty. Sub-Saharan Africa's immense variety is then examined, as parts of the continent emerge into historical light. Finally, Chapter 24 surveys the chief actors in the pageant of pre-Columbian America.

Part 3 ends with Chapters 25 through 27, which are devoted successively to the daily lives of the non-Western peoples in this epoch and then to the European decline in the later medieval age and the recovery termed the European Renaissance.

	Law and Government	Economy
EUROPEANS	Roman institutions are transformed by Germanic admixtures; government evolves slowly from the imperial model through feudal decentralization to the monarchies of the late medieval age. A struggle occurs between papacy and monarchs for supremacy within the new kingdoms. Law degenerates badly in the early period, begins comeback on Roman model in high medieval centuries. Faint beginnings of bureaucracy appear at end of period.	Peasant farmers continue to make up large majority, but by end of this period, citydwellers become numerous and economically important in western Europe. Economy increasingly mixed between agrarian and nonagrarian occupations. Feudal serfdom in west diminishes and is all but ended by labor shortage resultant from Black Death of fourteenth century, but is on the rise in eastern states less affected by plague. Long-distance trade resumes and seeks new directions by end of period, which also sees rise of capitalism and sophisticated credit/investment devices.
EAST ASIANS	A thousand year-long golden age for China, which recovers from a second period of disintegration in late 500s and prospers during the ensuing Tang and Song periods. Law and bureaucratic mandarin government operate generally to good effect for peace and stability, particularly in the south where nomads cannot easily reach. Japan selectively emulates Chinese system, but imperial court never exerts control over nation in like fashion to China; feudal nobility resists bureaucratic system, and negates it entirely in later part of this period by erecting the shogunate. Mongol conquest in thirteenth century interrupts, but does not severely damage the Chinese "mandate of heaven" monarchy which resumes under vigorous new Ming dynasty in 1300s.	Farming continues as support for huge majority, but in China, especially, the cities' growth during Tang and Song is impressive, with towns with populations over one million. Very active domestic trade, but only limited contact with foreigners (Europeans and Indians) in both nations until 1500s. The sudden end to the Chinese maritime expedition of the fifteenth century shows power of government over economy in contrast to the West.
HINDUS	Written law exceptional in this oral civilization. Government exercised by tiny minority of high-caste warriors, confirmed by the brahmin priests. Villages govern themselves with little contact with central or regional authorities excepting taxation. Central government is the exception, due to frequent nomadic invaders from the north.	Village fieldwork is norm throughout Indian history for the majority. Domestic and external trade with Southeast Asia and the Muslims is important in the cities. Colonial outreach to Southeast Asia and Pacific islanders is very strong in south India. Cotton cloth, spices, precious metals exported.

500–1500 C.E. EQUILIBRIUM AMONG POLYCENTRIC CIVILIZATIONS

Peoples: *Europeans, East Asians, Hindu, Muslims, Sub-Saharan Africans, Americans*

Religion and Philosophy	Arts and Culture	Science and Technology
Roman papal Christianity gradually superimposed upon west and central Europe through missionary activity in 500–800s. East Europe and Russia brought into Byzantine Orthodox orbit in 800–1000s. Politico-religious divisions between East and West reach climax with formal schism between Constantinople and Rome in 1054. Eastern Orthodoxy is closely associated with the state and falls under royal or imperial dominion especially in Russia. Roman clergy, on the other hand, often in conflict with Western kings after the papal reform in the tenth and eleventh centuries.	Greco-Roman models were lost to northern and central Europe after Roman collapse. After centuries of relative crudity of form, the Gothic architectural style takes root and rapidly spreads in twelfth and thirteenth centuries, giving stimulus to associated plastic arts for church and civic building decor. In the Renaissance, Gothic is supplanted by a neo-classicism based on rediscovered Greek and Roman ideas of beauty. Vernacular literature also comes to replace Latin after 1300s in popular literature. Painting, sculpture, architecture, and metalwork profit from novel techniques and ideas. Secularism and individualism apparent in Renaissance art and civic culture.	Natural sciences stagnate or worse until late medieval period. After universities are founded in 1200s, advances in humanities occur but little in science. Technology attracts some interest, especially after devastation of Black Death, but few breakthroughs occur except in agriculture, where three-field system, horse collar, use of animal manure, and better plows appear.
In China Buddhism rivals and then blends with Confucian tenets among educated. Peasantry continues ancestor worship and Daoism. In Japan, Buddhism enters from Korea in sixth century, subdivides into several noncompetitive sects, and strongly affects national religion of Shinto. Neither country produces a clergy or much theology; ethics are derived from nonsupernatural sources in both. Warrior creeds becomes increasingly dominant in feudal Japan. Philosophy is Buddhist based in both and focuses on questions of daily life rather than abstract ideas. Zen particularly popular in Japan after 1100s.	Landscape painting, porcelain, bronzes, inlaywork, silk weaving, and several forms of literature (notably, poetry and the first novels) are highly developed in both nations. Japanese take numerous Chinese forms, alter them to suit Japanese taste. Some art forms, such as Zen gardens and No drama for the Japanese and jade sculpture and porcelain for the Chinese are peculiar to each nation. Upper class life allows more freedom to Japanese women than to their counterparts in China.	Both science and technology highly developed in China throughout this period. Many inventions produced, including gunpowder and printing with movable type. Japanese not so active in these areas, depend heavily on Chinese importations but produce exceptional metalwork.
Vedic Hinduism is transformed in response to Buddhist challenge and gradually recaptures almost all of Indians' allegiance while Buddhists disappear. Both religions accept multiple nature of truth, contrasting with both Christians and Muslims. Strong ethical tone, exemplified in the Upanishads in Hinduism, teachings of Mahavira among Jains, and the Eight-fold Path of Buddha.	Art forms emphasize interweaving of gods and humans and mutual dependency. Much Indian art lost due to climate and repeated invasions. Literature is oral until very late. History almost nonexistent in the period. Much sculpture in stone and metal of high quality. Indian artistic influence felt throughout southeast Asian mainland and Indonesia.	Selective scientific advances. Math is particularly strong (zero concept, decimal system, much algebra). Pharmacy and medicine also well developed. Excellent metalwork. Technology is dormant.

	Law and Government	Economy
MUSLIMS	Law is wholly derived from words of the Qur'an as interpreted by *ulema* and the *kadi*. Government is also derived directly from the doctrines of the Prophet. The caliph is head of state and head of religion, as well as commander in chief. No separation of any type between religion and state. Only believers are full citizens; others are excluded from office holding.	A mixed economy, often urban based. High levels of sophistication in trade and finance. Mercantile activity of all types strongly encouraged, built on previous eastern civilized life. Wealth open to all, Muslim and infidel. Enormous variations in relative prosperity of Muslim groups, dependent on previous history and regional economy.
AFRICANS	Law is almost always customary until arrival of Muslim traders/conquerors. Government is based on tribal affiliations, ranging from semidivine monarchs with cadres of officials, to practically family-level autonomy from all exterior authority. Large areas never organize formal governments but remain "stateless societies."	Varied lifestyles, dependent on changing climate and terrain. Much nomadism; agriculture important in northern savanna and coastal plains. Long-distance trade from south to north across desert supports large-scale governments beginning in eighth century Ghana. Gold, slaves, and salt major trade items. Active commerce across Indian Ocean to Arabia and points farther east.
AMERICANS	General absence of writing meant reliance on customary law. Government is generally a monarchy of limited powers, with a large group of royal kin sharing in prestige and income from taxes. Priesthood always powerful, sometimes dominant. Conquest of neighbors is usual means of constructing imperial control over large areas. Causes of decline of these governments seldom known or knowable.	Only major ancient civilizations not located in river plain or valley and not dependent on irrigated farms. Both Mexican and Peruvian centers depended on agricultural surplus generated by new crops. Most subjects were farmers, but a few large urban areas (Tenochtitlan, Teotihuacan, Cuzco) appeared in time.

500–1500 C.E. EQUILIBRIUM AMONG POLYCENTRIC CIVILIZATIONS

Peoples: Europeans, East Asians, Hindu, Muslims, Sub-Saharan Africans, Americans

Religion and Philosophy	Arts and Culture	Science and Technology
Religious belief is basic organizing principle of public life. No priesthood, but the *ulema* wise men advise caliph and make policy. Strongly exclusivist, monopolistic in regard to truth. Muslim faith clashes head-on with the similar Christianity. Initial pressure to convert soon dropped by the conquering Bedouin. Split between Sunni and Shi'a destroys Islamic unity and adds to political struggles in Middle East.	Art of all types strongly impacted by Qur'anic prohibition of human "counterfeits" of God's work. Architecture, interior decor, landscaping are particular strong points in plastic arts, as are poetry, stories, and history in literature. Respect for ancient achievements of Greeks in both art and philosophy. Strongly patriarchal society.	Sciences initially and for a long time are fostered by Arab willingness to learn from Greeks and Persians. But by 1300 science is languishing in comparison with West. Technology is selectively introduced, especially in maritime affairs and, for a time, in war. Muslims are frequently first beneficiaries of Hindu and Chinese breakthroughs.
Animism is universal until arrival of Muslims after about 700. Slow conversion of sub-Saharan elite begins then. Christianity isolated in Ethiopia after fourth century. In parts of Africa, distinct two-level religious society forms with Muslims ruling over the animist majority.	Art was entirely devoted to religion or quasi-religious purposes, few of which are understood today. Fine bronzes and carvings in parts of sub-Saharan west and in southeast. Nok terra-cotta work oldest surviving art (seventh century). The wholly oral culture produced no literature in this era.	Science and technology stultified in contrast with other parts of globe. Lack of written languages hampers retention and exchange of complex information. Introduction of Arabic in Muslim areas of continent only partial help in alleviating this.
Religious belief usually unknown in detail. The gods are often fearful, demonic rulers of the afterworld. Strongly resembles aspects of Mesopotamia, with human sacrifice on large scale in at least some of the ruling groups (Aztec, Maya). No apparent connections between religion and ethics.	Much pre-Columbian artwork survives. Art served theology and cosmology. Extraordinary relief sculpture in central America. Architecture (pyramids) highly developed in both Peru and Mexico. Symbolism of much pre-Columbian art unknown to us.	Technology highly developed in certain fashions, notably handling of large stone masses in buildings and fortifications. Mayan mathematics and complex but accurate chronology are other examples. Mastery of hydraulics at Tenochtitlan, Incan road building over very difficult terrain in Andes necessitated basic science knowledge, but no written records exist.

ISLAM

---

c. 570–632   Life of Muhammed
641   Conquest of Persian empire completed
661–750   Ummayad dynasty at Damascus
711–733   Conquest of Spain/Muslims defeated at
              Tours
750–1260   Abbasid dynasty at Baghdad

In the Arabian town of Mecca, late in the sixth century an individual was born who would become the founder of a religion that now embraces about one-fifth of the world's population. Muhammed created a faith that spread with incredible speed from his native land throughout the Near and Middle East. Carried on the strong swords of his followers, Islam became a major rival to Christianity in the Mediterranean basin and to Hinduism and Buddhism in East and Southeast Asia. Like these faiths, Islam was far more than a supernatural religion. It also created a culture and a civilization.

✤ THE LIFE OF MUHAMMED THE PROPHET

The founder of Islam was born into a people about whom little was known until he made them the spiritual and political center of a new civilization. Arabia is a large and sparsely settled peninsula extending from the Fertile Crescent in the north to well down the coast of Africa. Mecca, Muhammed's birthplace, was an important interchange where African goods coming across the narrow Red Sea were transferred to caravans for shipment further east. Considerable traffic also moved up and down the Red Sea to the ancient cities of the Near East and the Nile delta. For these reasons, Mecca was a much more cosmopolitan place than one might at first imagine, with Egyptians, Jews, Greeks, and Africans living there, alongside the native Arabs. Long accustomed to trading and living with civilized foreigners, the Arabs in towns were using a written language and had a well-developed system of tribal and municipal government. In such ways, the Arabs of the cities near the coast were far more advanced than the Bedouins (nomads) of the vast interior.

Mecca itself was dominated by several tribes or clans; one of the most important was the Qur'aish, the clan into which Muhammed was born about 570 (see the Biography in this chapter). The first forty years of his life were uneventful; he married a rich widow and set himself up as a caravan trader of moderate means. The marriage produced one daughter, Fatima. Around 610, Muhammed began to talk about his mystical experiences that took the form of visits from a supernatural messenger. He went into the nearby desert, where he went into long trances in which he was allowed to speak with the angel Gabriel and others about the nature of life and the true appreciation of the Almighty. For years he dared speak of these visions only to his immediate kin.

Finally, he began to preach about his visions in the street, but soon ran into the condemnation of Meccan authorities, who supported a peculiar form of worship centered on the magical qualities of the **Ka'aba,** or Black Stone. Muhammed was forced to flee Mecca in 622, which came to be known as the year of the **Hegira** ("Flight") and is the first year of the Muslim calendar.

Muhammed fled to the rival city of Medina, where he found the support he had vainly sought in Mecca. After a few years, he had enough followers to begin a kind of trade war against the Meccan caravans and to force the city fathers there to negotiate with him on spiritual matters. He gained support among the Bedouins and by 630 was able to return to Mecca as master. By his death two years later, already a good part of the Arabian peninsula was under Islamic control. A **jihad,** a war of holy conquest, was under way.

⚜ ISLAMIC DOCTRINE

What was this message that Muhammed preached that found such ready acceptance? The doctrines of Islam (the word means "submission") are the simplest and most readily understood of any of the world's major religions. They are laid out in written form in the **Qur'an,** the sacred writ of the Muslim world, which was composed a few years after the Prophet's death from the memory of his words (see the Document in this chapter). The basic ideas are these:

1. There is but one God, *Allah,* who rules over all whether they acknowledge him or not.
2. The last and greatest Prophet of Allah is Muhammed.
3. Allah expects all to conform to his will, which will be shown to them in the sacred Qur'an dictated to Muhammed.
4. There will be a Last Judgment, when souls will be consigned to an eternal heaven or hell.
5. All men are brothers in Allah's eyes and have a responsibility to care for one another both spiritually and physically.

The specific rules for demonstrating that one is conforming to the will of Allah (and is thereby a good person) were equally simple and direct. The good man (or woman, though all of Muslim doctrine was posited on the absolute dominion of the male over the female) does the following:

1. Signifies his voluntary submission by praying at five specified times daily.
2. Keeps to a set of dietary rules prescribed in the Qur'an.

3. Makes the pilgrimage (the *Hajj*) to the holy places at least once in his lifetime.
4. Meets his obligations to the Muslim poor and unfortunate by money or work.
5. At all times and places acknowledges the glory and righteousness of the one, true God, Allah.

This strict monotheism was undoubtedly influenced by the Jews and Christians with whom Muhammed had contact in Mecca. Many other aspects of the Muslim faith also derive in some degree from other religions, such as the regulations against pork and against the use of tobacco and other stimulants that alter the God-given nature of man. But the Muslim creed is not just a collection of other,

■ In this thirteenth century miniature from Baghdad the *hajj,* or pilgrimage is depicted in its glory.

Muhammed

c. 570–632

The founder of the second largest religion in the world was born into poverty around 570 C.E. in the market town of Mecca, in central Arabia. Of his early life we know next to nothing, as he apparently considered it immaterial, and his early disciples followed his views. Even after he had become a notable person, we have practically no personal information about him, and the sacred book of Islam, the Qur'an, gives us few clues as to the human nature of the Prophet. A member of the clan of the Qur'aish, Muhammed was orphaned at six and entrusted to his uncle. Sometime about 590 he entered the service of a wealthy widow, Khadija, who had a thriving caravan trade into the interior. Later, he married her and continued the business with such success that he became a respected member of the Meccan community. With Khadija he produced a daughter, Fatima, his only surviving child and the wife of Ali, one of Islam's most notable early warriors.

About 610, at the age of forty, the devout Muhammed began to retire to the surrounding desert for periods of fast and prayer. Here, he had visions, in which an angel commanded him to heed the divine messages he would be given and preach them to the world as the final Prophet of the Lord. A deeply religious person, Muhammed was frightened at the prospect of this stunning responsibility, and it was not until many other visions had come to him that he began public preaching about 617. At the time, the Arab Meccans adhered to a kind of animism centered on the miraculous qualities of the Black Stone, preserved in the shrine of the *Ka'aba* in the center of the town. Muhammed's new faith attacked this belief, by asserting that the sole and supreme Lord (*Allah*) demanded much different and more specific commitments than mere pilgrimages to visit the *Ka'aba*.

So long as Muhammed was protected by the influential head of his clan, he remained safe from the hostility his preaching aroused in the Meccan establishment. But this changed in 619 when a new clan chief arose, who saw the new doctrine as dangerous to his own social and financial position. Muhammed was forced to flee and take refuge in Medina, Mecca's commercial rival. Muslims see this flight (*Hegira*) as beginning a new era in human history and use it as the first year of their calendar, conforming to the Christian year 622.

In Medina, Muhammed was able to surround himself with a core group of dedicated converts; supported for commercial reasons by the leaders in the town, he organized and led a small army to attack Mecca. Though repulsed at first, he gradually won over enough Meccans to make the resistance of the rest impossible and entered the city without force of arms in 630. Only two years later, he died, but not before the faith he founded was already sweeping over most of Arabia and preparing to enter the mainstream of Near Eastern and African life.

Muhammed was able to achieve what he did for various reasons. He preached a straightforward doctrine of salvation, ensured by a God who never failed and whose will was clearly delineated in comprehensible principles and commands. Secondly, those who believed and tried to follow Muhammed's words (as gathered a few years after his death in the Qur'an) were assured of reward in the life to come; this included all of those who lost their lives attempting to spread the faith, regardless of their previous conduct.

Lastly, Muhammed's preaching contained large measures of an elevated, yet attainable moral and ethical code. It deeply appealed to a population that wanted more than the purely ritualistic animist doctrine could give them, but were repelled by the internal conflicts of Christendom or unsympathetic to the complexities of Judaism. His insistence that he was not an innovator, but the completer of the message of the Jewish and Christian prophets and gospel writers was also of great significance in the success of his religion among the eastern peoples.

previous beliefs by any means. It includes many elements that reflect the peculiar circumstances of Arabs and Arabia in the seventh century C.E.

✤ ARABIA IN MUHAMMED'S DAY

Much of the interior of the Arabian peninsula was barely inhabited except for scattered oases. The Bedouin tribes that passed from one oasis to the next with their herds were at constant war with one another for water and pasture. The virtues most respected in this primitive society were those of the warrior: bravery, hardiness, loyalty, and honor.

The Arabs' religion prior to Muhammed involved a series of animistic beliefs, such as the important one centering on the *Ka'aba* stone. *Animism* means a conviction that objects such as rivers, trees, or stones possess spirits and spiritual qualities that have direct and potent impact on human lives. In the coastal towns, these beliefs coexisted side by side with the more developed religions of Judaism, Christianity, and Zoroastrianism.

In towns such as Mecca, commerce had bloomed to such an extent that many Arabs were being corrupted by this newfound wealth, at least in the eyes of others who were perhaps not so fortunate in their affairs. Traditions were being cast aside in favor of materialist values. The cultural gap between town Arab and Bedouin had widened to such an extent that it threatened to become irrevocable. Worship of the *Ka'aba* had degenerated into a business proposition for the merchants of Mecca, who profited greatly from the many thousands of Arabs from the interior who made annual processions there. Superstitions of the most nonsensical sort abounded, which made the Arabs contemptible in the view of the foreign traders who dwelt among them.

From this standpoint, Muhammed's religious message was the work of a reformer, a man who perceived many of the problems facing his people at a given time in their social and cultural development and responded to them. The verses of the Qur'an contain many references to these problems and propose solutions. For example, the condition of women in pre-Muslim Arabia was apparently very poor. They were practically powerless in legal matters, had no control over their dowries in marriage, and could not have custody over minor children after their husband's death, among other things. In his preaching, Muhammed took pains to change this situation and the attitude that lay behind it. Though he never said that women were equal to men, he made it clear that women are not mere servants of men; that they do have some inherent rights as persons, wives, and mothers; and that their honor and physical welfare should be protected by the men around them. Indeed, the status of women in early Muslim teaching is relatively elevated; it is actually higher and more firmly recognized than the status accorded women in the contemporary Christian culture of the Latin West or the Greek East.

This example is only one of many differences between Islam and the other cultures of the period. Islam was far more than just a copy of other beliefs that had touched the lives of Arabs of the time.

✤ THE *JIHAD*

One of the unique aspects of Islam in its earliest days was the *jihad,* the war for conversion of the unbeliever. Taking part in a *jihad* was the highest honor for a good Muslim, and dying in one assured a direct ticket to heaven. The appeal of the *jihad* seems to have been based on several aspects of Arabic culture. The desert Bedouins were

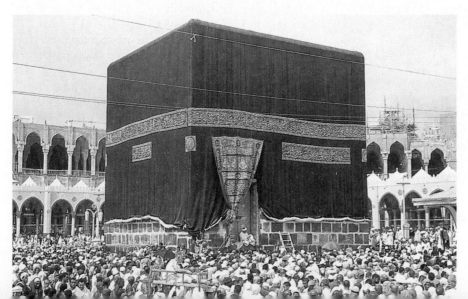

■ In this courtyard assemble hundreds of thousands of worshippers during the Muslim holy days each year. The Ka'aba is the cubicle of stone in the center. It contains a piece of black meteorite worshipped by the Arabs before their conversion to Islam.

The Qur'an

The Qur'an is not only the bible of the Muslims, it is also an elaborate and poetic code of daily conduct. As the literal word of God, the holy book is held by all devout Muslims to be the unfailing source of wisdom, which, if adapted to the changing realities of daily life, can be as usable in the twentieth century as it was in the seventh when it was written. Now translated into every major language, the Qur'an was long available only in Arabic, one of the world's most poetic and subtlest languages. This circumstance both helped and hindered the religion's eventual spread. Some excerpts from the Muslim holy book follow:

The *Jihad*

Fight in the cause of God against those who fight against you, but do not begin hostilities. Surely, God loves not the aggressors. Once they start the fighting, kill them wherever you meet them, and drive them out from where they have driven you out; for aggression is more heinous than killing. But fight them until all aggression ceases and religion is professed for the pleasure of God alone. If they desist, then be mindful that no retaliation is permissible except against the aggressors.

Do not account those who are slain in the cause of God as dead. Indeed, they are living in the presence of their Lord and are provided for. They are jubilant . . . and rejoice for those who have not yet joined them. . . . They rejoice at the favor of God and His bounty, and at the realisation that God suffers not the reward of the faithful to be lost.

Piety and Charity

There is no piety in turning your faces toward the east or the west, but he is pious who believeth in God, and the last day, and the angels, and the scriptures, and the prophets; who for the love of God disburses his wealth to his kindred, and to the orphans, and the needy, and the wayfarer, and those who ask, and for ransoming. . . .

They who expend their wealth for the cause of God, and never follow what they have laid out with reproaches or harm, shall have their reward with the Lord; no fear shall come upon them, neither shall they be put to grief.

A kind speech and forgiveness is better than alms followed by injury. Give to the orphans their property; substitute not worthless things of your own for their valuable ones, and devour not their property after adding it to your own, for this is a great crime.

Women's Place; Marriage

Ye may divorce your wives twice. Keep them honorably, or put them away, with kindness. But it is not allowed you to appropriate to yourselves any of what you have once given them . . . no blame shall attach to either of you for what the wife shall herself give for her redemption [from the marriage bond].

Men are superior to women on account of the qualities with which God hath gifted the one above the other, and on account of the outlay they make from their substance for them. Virtuous women are obedient, careful, during the husband's absence, because God hath of them been careful. But chide those for whose obstinacy you have cause to dread; remove them into beds apart, and whip them. But if they are obedient to you, then seek not occasion to abuse them.

Christians and Jews

Verily, they who believe and who follow the Jewish religion, and the Christians . . . whoever of these believeth in God and the Last Day, and does that which is right shall have their reward with the Lord. Fear shall not come upon them, neither shall they be grieved.

We believe in God and what has been sent down to us, and what was sent down to Abraham, Ishmael, Isaac, Jacob and their descendants, and what was given Moses, Jesus and the prophets by their Lord. We do not differentiate between them, and are committed to live at peace with Him.

SOURCE: T.B. Irving, trans. *The Quran: Selections*, 1980.

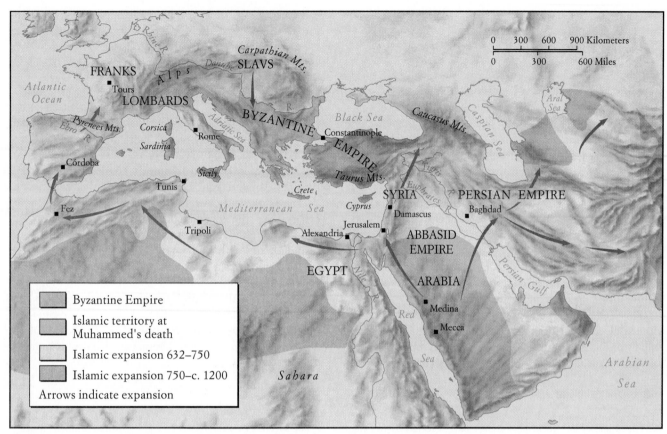

⦿ **MAP 16.1 Spread of Islam.** The lightning-like spread of the new faith throughout a belt on either side of the equator is evident in this map. About one-third of the world's populations known to the Christians converted to Islam in the space of a long lifetime, 630–720 C.E.

already a warlike people, who were ready to die for their beliefs. Much evidence also indicates that they faced an economic crisis at the time of Muhammed, namely, a severe overpopulation problem that overwhelmed the available resources. Under such conditions, many were willing to risk their lives for the possibility of a better future. They saw Muhammed as a war leader as much as a religious prophet and flocked to his army from the time he returned to Mecca.

Once the *jihad* was under way, another factor favored its success: both of the major opponents of Islam, the Byzantine Greeks in Constantinople and the Persians, had been fighting each other fiercely for the previous generation and were mutually exhausted. Neither was in any condition to resist this new, fanatical attack. As a result, by 641, only nine years after the death of the Prophet, all of

the huge Persian empire had fallen to Arab armies and much of the Byzantine territory in Asia (present-day Syria, Lebanon, and Turkey) as well (see Map 16.1). In place after place, the defenders of the Byzantine provinces put up only halfhearted resistance or none at all, as in Damascus. The religious differences within Christianity had became so acute in these lands that several varieties of Christians preferred to surrender to the "pagan" Muslims than continue to live under what they regarded as the wrong-thinking emperor and his bishops. This was true not only in Syrian Damascus, but also in several Christian centers in North Africa and Egypt, which were in religious revolt against the church in Constantinople and in Rome. Thus, the *jihad* succeeded so well not only because of the abilities of the Arabs but also because of the divisions among their opponents.

❧ THE CALIPHATE

The First Period to 661

Muhammed had been both religious and temporal ruler over his faithful; he never considered dividing the two powers. He was priest, king, and general, and so also were his successors.

The first **caliph** (successor to the Prophet) was one of Muhammed's generals, Abu Bakr, who was elected by his colleagues, as were the next three caliphs. Abu Bakr died soon after his election, however, and was succeeded by another general, Omar, who ruled Islam for ten years and was the real founder of the early Muslim empire. His Arab armies pushed deep into North Africa, conquering Egypt by 642. At the same time, he invaded Persia and the Byzantine territory in the eastern Mediterranean. By the time of Omar's death in 643, mounted Arab raiders were penetrating into extreme western India.

This lightning expansion came to a short halt because of a brief civil war for mastery within the Muslim world, which brought Ali, husband of Fatima and the son-in-law of Muhammed, to the fore. Ali was the last "orthodox" caliph for a long time, and his assassination by a competitor in 661 marked the end of the first phase of Muslim expansion.

The Ummayad Dynasty, 661–750

The first four caliphs had been elected, but three of the four died by murder. At this point, since the elective system had clearly failed, the system of succession became in fact a dynasty, although the elective form was preserved. From 661, two dynasties ruled Islam: the Ummayad to 750, and then the Abbasid from 750 to 1260.

The **Ummayad** dynasty was initiated through the murder of Ali by the governor of Syria, Muawiya, and this was to prove fateful. Ali's supporters claimed that because of his family ties with Muhammed and because the Prophet had designated him as a leader, Ali had been the rightful caliph. These supporters of Ali were known as **Shi'ites,** and they formed a significant minority within Islam that continues to the present. They believed that only the blood descendants of the Prophet should become caliph, and they looked upon the Ummayad dynasty as murderous impostors.

■ **The Dome of the Rock.** This great edifice, erected by Muslims in the late seventh century, has been used by three religions as a sacred place of worship. According to legend, it is built on the spot where Jesus died.

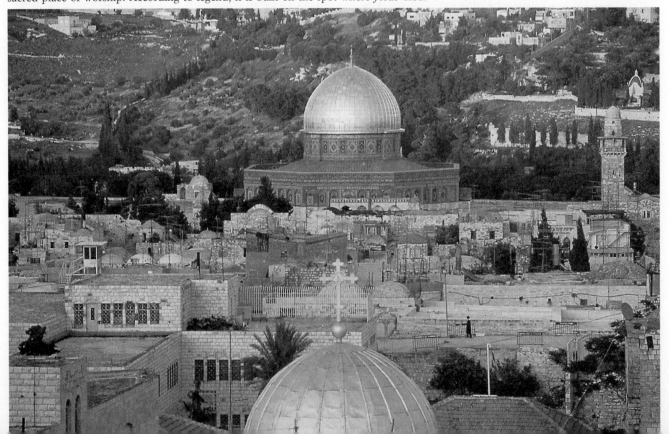

The supporters of Muawiya and his successors were known as **Sunni,** and they constituted the large majority (currently, about 90 percent) of Muslims at all times. They accepted the principle that the succession should go to the most qualified, regardless of blood connections with the Prophet. They believed that this is what Muhammed desired, and they rejected the claims of the Shi'ites that the family of Muhammed had been the recipients of some special enlightenment in spiritual matters.

The division of Islam between Shi'ite and Sunni was to have decisive effects on the political unity of the Muslim world. Most members of the Shi'ite minority were concentrated in Persia and the Near East, but they had support in many other areas and were always a counterweight to the policies of the Sunni central government. From their ranks came many of the sects of Islam.

Muawiya proved to be a skillful organizer and statesman. He moved the capital from Medina (where Muhammed had established it) to his native Damascus, where he could be more fully in charge. He made the office of caliph more powerful than it had been before and also laid the foundation for the splendid imperial style that would characterize later caliphs in great contrast to the austerity and simplicity of the first days. Muawiya made clear the dynastic quality of his rule by forcing the reluctant tribal leaders to accept his son as his successor. The caliph under the Ummayads was normally the son or brother of the previous ruler.

The Ummayads continued the advances to east and west, though not quite so brilliantly and rapidly as before. To the east, Arab armies penetrated as far as western China before being checked and pushed deep into central Asia (to Tashkent in Uzbekistan). Afghanistan became a Muslim outpost. In the west, the outstanding achievement was the conquest of Christian Spain between 711 and 721; at least part of Spain would remain in Muslim hands until the time of Christopher Columbus. The Arab horsemen actually penetrated far beyond the Pyrenees, but were defeated in 733 at *Tours* in central France by the Frankish leader Charles Martel, in one of the key battles of European history. This expedition proved to be the high-water mark of Arab Muslim penetration into Europe, and soon afterward they retreated behind the Pyrenees to set up a Spanish caliphate.

In the 740s the Ummayad dynasty was overthrown by rebels, and after a brief period of uncertainty, the **Abbasid** clan was able to take over as a new dynasty. One of their first moves was to transfer the capital from unfriendly Damascus to the entirely new town of **Baghdad** in Iraq, which was built for that purpose.

The Abbasid Dynasty, 750–1260

The Abbasid clan claimed descent from Abbas, the uncle of Muhammed, and for that reason were more acceptable to the Shi'ite faction than the Ummayads had been. They were also careful to appease the Sunni majority.

The Abbasids also differed from the Ummayads in another important way. Whereas the Ummayads had allowed an Arab elite to monopolize religion and government, the Abbasids opened up the faith to all comers on an essentially equal basis. Although Arab officials attempted to retain their monopoly on important posts in the central and provincial administration, Persians, Greeks, Syrians, Berbers, Spanish ex-Christians, and many others gradually found their way into the inner circles of Muslim authority and prestige. In every area, experienced officials from the conquered peoples were retained in office, though supervised by Arabs. Through these non-Arab officials, the Abbasid administration incorporated several foreign models of government. As time passed, and more natives chose to convert to Islam, the Arab upper class was steadily diluted by other ethnic groups. It was they who made Islam into a *highly cosmopolitan, multiethnic religion and civilization.* Like the doctrines of Islam, the community of believers was soon marked by its eclecticism and heterogeneity, consisting of a wide variety of cultural traits.

During the Abbasid caliphate, the powers of the central government underwent a gradual but cumulatively severe decline. Many segments of the Islamic world broke away from the political control of Baghdad. Spain became fully independent; Egypt almost so. Even with the cement of a common faith, the empire was simply too large and its peoples too diverse to hold together politically and administratively. Nevertheless, the Muslim faith was strong enough to bind this world together, permanently, in a religious and cultural sense. With the sole exception of Spain, where the Muslims were always a minority, those areas captured at one time or another by the Islamic forces after 629 remain Muslim today—and those areas reach halfway around the globe, from Morocco to Indonesia.

✤ CONVERSION TO ISLAM

Contrary to widespread Christian notions, *Islam normally did not force conversion.* In fact, after the first generation, the Arab leaders came to realize the disadvantages of mass conversion of the conquered and discouraged it. By the time of the Ummayads, conversion was looked upon as a special allowance to deserving non-Muslims, especially those who had something to offer the conquerors in the way of talents, wealth, or domestic and international prestige.

No effort was made to convert the peasants or the urban masses. Life in the villages went on as before, with the peasants paying their rents or giving their labor to the new lords just as they had to the old. When and if they converted, it was generally due to specific local circumstances rather than to pressure from above. Centuries passed before the peasants of Persia and Turkey accepted Islam; in Syria and Lebanon, whole villages remained loyal to their Christian beliefs during ten centuries of Muslim rule.

Intermarriage between Muslim and non-Muslim was strictly prohibited, a restriction that was supposed to preserve the ruling group indefinitely. In fact, Muslims had very little social contact with non-Muslims, although the two groups did mix together in business transactions, administrative work, and even, at times, intellectual and cultural interchange (especially in Spain).

The Muslims did not view all non-Muslims the same way. Instead, non-Muslims were categorized according to what the Qur'an and Arab tradition taught about their proximity to spiritual truth. The *Jews and the Christians* were considered particularly meritorious because both had progressed some way down the Way of Truth and had possessed holy men (like Jesus of Nazareth) who had tried to lead them onward. The Zoroastrians were viewed in much the same way. All three were classed as *dhimmis,* or "Peoples of the Book," and were thought to have risen above what Muslims regarded as the base superstitions of their many other subject peoples.

The *dhimmis* were not taxed as severely as pagans were, and they had legal and business rights denied to others. In some areas of the Muslim empire, the *dhimmis* outnumbered the Muslims themselves. Restrictions on the *dhimmis* were generally not severe, and in many places there is good evidence that they prospered. They could worship as they pleased and elect their own community leaders. Their position was certainly better in every way than that of either Jews or Muslims under Christian rule.

■ Although the Islamic peoples have no sacred priesthood, men called *imams* are appointed to positions of leadership and are responsible for leading the faithful in daily prayer. In former days they called the devout to the mosque five times daily from one of the minarets. Today, tape recordings perform this service.

✤ EVERYDAY AFFAIRS

In the opening centuries of Muslim rule, the Muslims were a minority almost everywhere outside Arabia, so they had to accustom themselves to the habits and manners of their subjects, at least to some degree. Since the Bedouin Arabs had little experience with commerce and finance, they were quite willing to allow their more sophisticated subjects considerable leeway in such matters. Thus, Christian, Jewish, or pagan merchants and artisans were generally able to live and work as they were accustomed to doing without severe disturbance. They managed economic affairs not only for themselves, but also for the ruling Arabs. This gradually changed as the Bedouin settled down to civilized urban life, but in the meantime the habit of using the conquered "infidels" to perform many of the ordinary tasks of life had become ingrained.

Somewhat similar patterns could be found in finance and routine administration; the conquered subjects were kept on in the middle and lower levels. Only Muslims could hold important political and military positions, however. The Bedouin maintained an advantage over the neo-Muslim converts as late as the ninth century, but

Greek, Syrian, Persian, and other converts to Islam found their way into high posts in the central government in Baghdad under the Abbasids. And in the provinces, it was very common to encounter native converts at the very highest levels. With the native peoples playing such a large role in affairs, it is not surprising that economic and administrative institutions came to be an amalgam of Arab and Greek, Persian, or Spanish customs.

Society in the Muslim world formed a definite social pyramid with the descendants of the old Arab clans on top, followed by converts from other religions. Then came the *dhimmis,* other non-Muslim freemen, while the slaves were at the bottom. All five classes of society had their own rights and duties, and even the slaves had considerable legal protections. Normally, there was little friction between Muslims and non-Muslims. Different courts of law had jurisdiction over legal disputes depending on whether Muslims or non-Muslims were involved. All non-Muslims were taxed heavily, although, as we have seen, the burden on the *dhimmis* was less than on other non-Muslims. Despite their role in economic affairs, it was always clear that the non-Muslims were second-class citizens, below every Muslim in dignity.

As this suggests, *religion* was truly the decisive factor in Muslim society. Like Christians and Jews, but even more so, good Muslims believed that a person's most essential characteristic was whether he adhered to the true faith—Islam. The fact that all three faiths—Christianity, Judaism, and Islam—believed in essentially the same patriarchal, strict but forgiving God was not enough to bridge the differences between them. Rather, it seemed to widen them. No one, it seems, hates as well as brothers.

Summary

The surge of Islam from its native Arabia in the seventh century was propelled by the swords of the *jihad* armies. But the attraction of the last of the Western world's major religions rested finally on its openness to all creeds and colors, its ease of understanding, and its assurance of heaven to those who followed its simple doctrines. The Prophet Muhammed saw himself as the completer of the works of Abraham and Jesus, the final messenger of the one God. His work was assisted by divisions among the Christians of the Near East, by economic rewards to the Muslim conquerors, and by the momentary exhaustion of both Byzantium and Persia. Already by the middle of the 600s, the new faith had reached Egypt and the borders of Hindustan; by the early 700s, the fall of Spain had given it a foothold in Europe. Not only was this the fastest spread of a creed in world history, but it would go on spreading for many years to come.

The political leadership of the faith was held by the caliphs, at first by the Ummayad dynasty at Damascus, then by the Abbasids at their new capital at Baghdad. The unity of Islam was split as early as the first Ummayad caliph by the struggle between the Sunni majority and the Shi'ite minority, the later of which insisted that blood relationship with Muhammed was essential for the caliphate.

The upshot of the Muslim explosion out of Arabia was the creation of a new civilization, which would span most of the world by the twelfth century and be carried into Christian Europe in the fourteenth. In the next chapter, we will look at the cultural aspects of this civilization in some detail.

Test Your Knowledge

1. Muhammed's religious awakening came
   a. as a result of a childhood experience.
   b. in his middle years, after a vision.
   c. in response to the Christian conquest of Mecca.
   d. after an encounter with a wandering holy man.
2. Which of the following is *not* necessary for entry into eternal bliss according to the Qur'an?

   a. Frequent and regular prayer to Allah
   b. Fasting at prescribed times
   c. Passing a Last Judgment
   d. Taking arms against the infidel
3. Which of the following statements about Islamic belief is *false?*
   a. A Last Judgment awaits all.

b. The faithful will be guided by the Qur'an to salvation.

c. Mortals must submit to the will of the one all-powerful Lord.

d. The divinity of Jesus is beyond doubt.

4. The farthest reach of Muslim expansion into Europe was at
   a. Palermo.
   b. Tours.
   c. Córdoba.
   d. Gibraltar.

5. The conflicts between Sunni and Shi'ite Muslims centered on the
   a. divinity of Muhammed.
   b. authenticity of Muhammed's visions.
   c. location of the capital of the Islamic state.
   d. importance of blood kinship to Muhammed in choosing his successor.

6. The basis of all Muslim political theory is
   a. a person's religion.
   b. the wealth possessed by a given group of citizens.

c. the social standing of an individual.

d. the historical evolution of a given social group.

7. Which of the following cities was never the capital of Islam?
   a. Baghdad
   b. Damascus
   c. Cairo
   d. Medina

8. In Islam, the social prestige and position of the Arab Bedouins
   a. varied according to their wealth.
   b. was sometimes below even that of slaves.
   c. was at the top of the pyramid.
   d. was above the *dhimmi*, but below that of converts.

9. The *dhimmi* in early Muslim societies were
   a. Christians and Jews who had not converted to Islam.
   b. the merchants.
   c. the original Arabic believers in Islam.
   d. non-Arab converts to Islam.

Identification Terms

Abbasids	*Hegira*	Qur'an	Sunni
Baghdad	*jihad*	Shi'ite	Ummayads
caliph	*Ka'aba*		

Bibliography

Andrae, T. *Mohammed: The Man and His Faith,* 1970. A reliable biography. See also Rodinson below.

Denny F. *An Introduction to Islam,* 1985. Fulfills what the title promises.

Donner, F. M. *The Early Islamic Conquests,* 1986. Looks at the reasons for the rapid expansion of the religion and the concept of the *jihad,* so often misunderstood in the West.

Kennedy, H. *The Prophet and the Age of the Caliphates,* 1986. A good survey of the spread of Islam to the Seljuk era.

Lewis, B., ed. *Islam and the Arab World,* 1976. As good an introduction to the topics covered in this chapter as exists. Excellent illustrations. The same author's *The Arabs in History,* 1961, is focused more sharply on the Arabian peninsula.

Nutting, A. *The Arabs: A Narrative History from Mohammed to the Present,* 1964. Written especially for beginners.

Qur'an. Many translations are available. Perhaps the best for students is that of N. J. Dawood, 1990.

Rodinson, N. *Mohammed,* 1971.

Mature Islamic Society and Institutions

The consolidation of Islamic civilization took place during the period from the founding of the Abbasid dynasty in 750 C.E. through the degeneration of that dynasty in the tenth century. After a nearly complete breakdown of the unity of the Baghdad caliphate in the eleventh and twelfth centuries, the Mongols and then the Ottoman Turks took over the leadership of Islam and infused it with new vigor.

Even after all semblance of central governance of the vast empire had been destroyed, a clear unity was still visible in Islamic culture and lifestyle, whether in the Middle East, India, or Spain. Conflicts with other civilizations and cultures (African, Chinese, Hindu, Christian) only sharpened the Muslims' sense of what was proper and necessary for a life pleasing to God and humans. At its height, Islamic civilization was the envy of its Christian neighbor and enemy, with achievements in the sciences and arts that could rival even those of the Chinese.

✦ The Caliphate in Baghdad

We have seen how the Abbas clan seized power from the Ummayads, and transferred the capital to the new city of Baghdad in the 760s. This city quickly became one of the major cultural centers of the entire world, as the Abbasids adorned it with every form of art and encouraged its educational establishments with money and personal participation. They also further developed the Ummayad institutions of government.

In Baghdad, governing powers were exercised by an elaborate, mainly Persian bureaucracy. This was headed by a **vizier,** a kind of prime minister for the caliphs who had enormous powers. Many of the other officials were eunuchs, who were thought to be more likely to be devoted to the government because they could have no family interests of their own. In the provinces, the *emir* or governor was the key man. His tax collecting responsibility was crucial to the well-being of the Baghdad government. Rebellions normally started in the provinces and were led by independent-minded emirs.

The major institutions of the central government were the **ulema,** or high court for religious matters; the *diwan,* or financial board; and the *kadi,* or local judge who had jurisdiction in all disputes involving a Muslim. The *ulema* operated to gradually bring into existence the **sharija,** or sacred law, based on the words of the Qur'an. The *sharija* involved far more than religious or doctrinal matters; in the Muslim view, religion entered into many spheres of what we consider civil and private life, so that the decisions of the *ulema* and the applications of the *sharija* affected almost all aspects of public and private affairs.

Unlike the Western world, the Muslims' sacred book remained the basis of all law, and hence of all administration and government, to a very late date. The Qur'an was still the fount of all legal knowledge into modern times, and for some Islamic fundamentalists, it still is (for example, in Iran since the revolution of 1979–1980, Libya, and Saudi Arabia).

The *Muslim army* in the Abbasid era was very international in composition. Many of the soldiers were slaves, taken from all the conquered peoples but especially from the Africans and Egyptians. They were well trained and equipped, and their commanders came to have increasing political power as the caliph became weaker. Some contemporary estimates of the army's size are incredibly large, running up to hundreds of thousands in the field at one time (which would have been a logistical impossibility for the time). Still, there is little doubt that the Abbasid forces were the most impressive of the era and far overshadowed the Europeans' feudal levies and the Byzantines' professional soldiery. Abbasid raids into Afghanistan and western India established footholds that were gradually expanded by later Muslim forces.

✦ LITERATURE AND THE NATURAL SCIENCES

The Arabic language became an important source of unification in the Muslim world, spreading into its every part. Because the sacred book of the Qur'an could only be written in Arabic, every educated Muslim had to learn this language to some degree. The Arabs also came to possess a cheap and easily made writing medium—paper (picked up from the Chinese, as so much medieval technology would be). A paper factory was operating in Baghdad as early as 793, providing a great stimulus to the making of books and the circulation of ideas.

The university was also a Muslim creation. The world's oldest still functioning higher educational institution is the University in Cairo, founded in the ninth century by Muslim holy men as a place of religious study. Long before the names of Aristotle and Plato were known in the Christian West, the Muslims of the Middle East had recognized the value of classical Greek learning and acted to preserve and expand it. In the academies of Baghdad and other Muslim centers, students of philosophy and the various sciences congregated and debated the writings of the Greek masters. The Muslims especially revered Aristotle, whom they regarded as the greatest teacher of all

■ The University of Cairo is the oldest seat of higher learning in the world still operating in its original site. The modern university has a student body of approximately 50,000, many of whom are adults studying part-time.

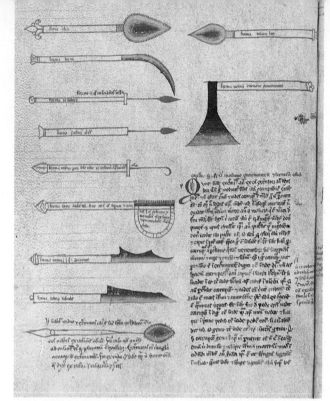

Surgical Instruments. Islamic medicine was so far ahead of medieval European practice that despite the enmity between Christianity and Islam, Arab doctors were frequently invited to spend time teaching in Europe. The Muslim practitioners were particularly adept at eye surgery and amputations.

Rushd **(Averroës)**; and al-Zahrawi, a surgeon and medical innovator.

✤ THE ARTS IN THE MUSLIM WORLD

Because the Qur'an prohibited the representation of the human figure as blasphemous to the creator Allah, the Muslims had to turn to other motifs and developed an intricate *geometrically based format for the visual arts.* The motifs of their painting, ceramics, mosaics, and inlay work—in all of which the Muslim world excelled—were based on garlands, plants, or geometric figures such as triangles, diamonds, and parallelograms. The Muslims produced no sculpture beyond miniatures and, for a long time, no portrait painting.

In architecture, the Muslims, especially the Persians, developed a great deal of lastingly beautiful forms and executed them with great skill. The "most beautiful building in the world," the *Taj Mahal* in India, is a thoroughly Muslim creation. The use of domes, reflecting pools, and landscapes of great precision and intricate design was common in public buildings such as mosques, the Muslim church. Great wealth and a love of luxury were earmarks of Muslim rulers throughout the world of Islam, and it was

time. They passed on this esteem for Aristotle to their Christian subjects in Spain, who in turn transmitted it to the rest of Christian Europe in the twelfth and thirteenth centuries.

In the sciences, the Muslim contribution was selective, but important. In the *medical sciences,* the world of Islam was considerably ahead of any Western civilization. Pharmacology, physiology, anatomy, and, above all, opthamology and optical science were special strong points. In *geography* Arabic and Persian writers and travelers were responsible for much new information about the known and the hitherto unknown world. In *astronomy and astrology,* the Muslims built on and expanded the traditions of careful observation they had inherited in the Near East. In *mathematics* they developed and rationalized the ancient Hindu system of numbers to make the "Arabic numbers" that are still in universal use. They also introduced the concepts of algebra and the decimal system to the West. Some of the most important figures in Muslim science were Ibn Sina (Avicenna), a physician and scientist of great importance to medieval Europe (see the Biography in this chapter); the philosophers al-Rindi and **Ibn**

Arabic Calligraphy. The beauty of written Arabic is rivalled only by the Oriental scripts. Several different styles evolved in different places and times, quite as distinct as the various alphabets of the Western world. Below is an eleventh century Persian script.

Avicenna
980–1037 C.E.

The Persian Muslim Avicenna (Ibn Sina in Arabic) was an outstanding example of the Islamic philosophers and men of science who did so much to preserve classical learning in an epoch when the Christian West was unable to appreciate it. His compilation *The Book of Healing* is the closest thing to a comprehensive encyclopedia of the medical arts attempted until modern times. In its several hundred pages, it dealt with many topics in addition to the medical sciences, embracing logic, rhetoric, and all the natural sciences as well.

Avicenna spent his entire life in Persia, mainly at the court of one or another of the several Muslim potentates who divided the country. Most of the time he served as court physician, an honored post. His handbook on clinical medicine, entitled *The Canon of Medicine,* is probably the most famous single work on healing ever published.

Avicenna was a child prodigy. At the age of ten, he had already memorized the Qur'an and soon outgrew all his teachers. By the time he was twenty-one, his reputation as a scholar was known throughout Persia. Despite his brilliance, his career was often tempestuous due to the violent changes in dynasties that Persia experienced in the eleventh century. More than once,

Avicenna was even imprisoned for a brief period as punishment for having served at the court of the defeated party. But each time he was able to regain his position, thanks to his distinction as a learned man and his practical abilities in the healing arts.

Avicenna was largely responsible for the revived interest in the philosophy of Aristotle that began to percolate into the Christian world (via Spain) in the late eleventh century. Through him the West was able to rediscover the Greek explorations of both the natural and the spiritual worlds and eventually to link them with the teachings of the medieval Christian scholars. His *Book of Healing* was partly translated into Latin in the twelfth century, and the entire *Canon of Medicine* somewhat later. The latter work replaced that of Galen as the standard medical text for several centuries.

As a court official, Avicenna was obliged to accompany his prince on military campaigns. On one of these, he fell ill from exhaustion and died despite his own treatment. Only his enormous physical strength allowed him to live as long as he did, while continuing a schedule of medical work, teaching, and writing that would have killed most men much earlier.

---

considered a mark of gentility and good manners for a ruler to spend lavishly on public and private adornments.

Calligraphy was a special strength of the Muslims, whose Arabic script is the product of esthetic demands as much as the desire to communicate. As in ancient China, a beautiful script was considered to be as much a part of good breeding as beautiful clothing. Arabic lettering was incorporated into almost every form of art, generally as quotations from the Qur'an.

Arabs developed storytelling to a high art and are generally credited with the invention of *fiction,* that is, stories told solely to entertain. The most famous book of stories in the history of the world is **The 1001 Nights** (also called **The Arabian Nights**), which was supposedly created by a courtier at the court of **Harun al-Rashid,** one of

the greatest of the Baghdad caliphs in the early ninth century. Poetry was also a strongly cultivated and very popular literary art form, especially among the Persian Muslims (see the Document in this chapter). The quatrains of *Omar Khayyam,* a twelfth-century Persian, are famous throughout the world.

✤ MUSLIM CIVILIZATION AT ITS APEX

Muslim civilization flourished most brilliantly between about 900 and about 1200. After the latter date, relatively little original work was forthcoming, and it is no coincidence that the devastating invasion of the Mongols occurred then. At its height, Islam was the most lavish and innovative civilization of the world, rivaled only by China,

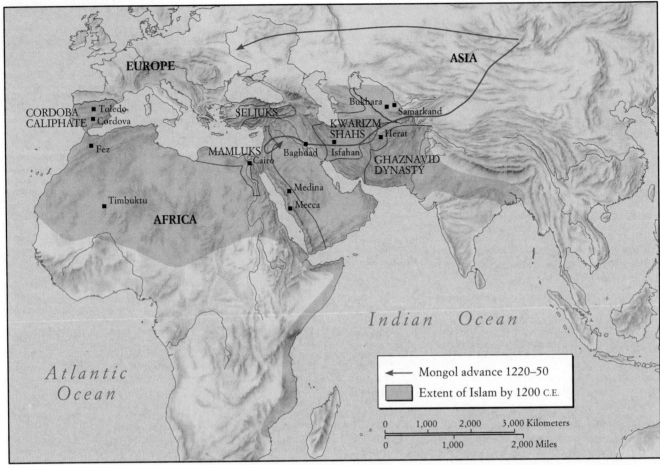

● **MAP 17.1 Islamic Domains, c. 1200 C.E.** By this time the Baghdad caliph's hold on territories beyond Arabia and Iraq was minimal, if it existed at all. Persia and Egypt, as well as Spain and Afghanistan were autonomous under their own shahs and caliphs. African Muslims had never had direct contact with Baghdad.

with which it had extensive commercial and some intellectual contacts. The Muslim world at this time extended from the Atlantic to the Pacific, and Muslim traders were found on every continent and on every sea of the universe known to them at the time (see Map 17.1).

Islam provided a precise place for every person in its social scheme without severely limiting freedom of movement. Believers could move without hindrance all around a huge belt of settlements on either side of the equator, from Spain to the Philippines. Travelers could journey to distant lands, secure in the knowledge that they would be welcomed by their co-religionists and would find

the same laws and prejudices, the same literary language, and the same conceptions of justice and truth that they had known at home. Wherever they were, all Muslims knew they were members of a great community, the Muslim *umma*.

The cities of this world were splendid and varied. *Córdoba* in Spain was a city of about a million people in the tenth century; its ruling class was Muslim, from the North African Berber people, but its inhabitants included many Jews and Christians as well. Anything produced in the East or West could be purchased in the markets of Córdoba. The same was true of *Baghdad,* which had an

The *Memoirs* of Usama ibn Munqidh

The Arab Usama ibn Munqidh lived in Christian-ruled Palestine over 90 years. A well educated Muslim gentleman, he had many friends among the Franks (the Muslim term for all Westerners) and made many insightful comments about them in his *Memoirs*. The following excerpts deal with his wonderment at Frankish medical lore and at their incredible absence of jealously about their women:

They brought before me a knight in whose leg an abcess had grown; and a woman afflicted with imbecility. To the knight I applied a small poultice until the abscess opened and became well; and the woman I put on a diet and made her humor wet. Then a Frankish physician came to them, and said, "This man knows nothing about treating them." He then said to the knight, "Which would thou prefer, living with one leg or dying with two?" The latter replied, "Living with one leg." The physician said, "Bring me a strong knight and a sharp ax." A knight came with the ax. And I was standing by. Then the physician laid the leg of the patient on a block of wood and bade the knight strike his leg with the ax and chop it off with one blow. Accordingly he struck it—while I was looking on—one blow, but the leg was not severed. He dealth another blow, upon which the marrow of the leg flowed out and the patient died on the spot.

He then examined the woman and said, "This is a women in whose head there is a devil which has possessed her. Shave off her hair." Accordingly they shaved it off, and the woman began once more to eat the ordinary diet—garlic and mustard. Her imbecility took a turn for the worse. The physician then said, "The devil has penetrated through her head," He therefore took a razor and made a deep cruciform incision on it, peeled off the skin at the middle of the incision until the bone of the skull was exposed, and rubbed it with salt. The woman expired instantly. Thereupon, I inquired whether my services were needed any longer, and when they replied in the negative, I turned home, having learned of their medicine what I knew not before.

One day a Frank went home and found a man with his wife in the same bed. He asked him, "What could have made thee enter into my wife's room?" The man replied, "I was tired, so I went in to rest." "But how," asked he, "didst thou get into my bed?" The other replied, "I found a bed that was spread, so I slept in it." "But," said he, "my wife was sleeping with thee!" The other replied, "Well, the bed is hers. How could I have therefore prevented her from using her own bed?" "By the trust of my religion," said the husband, "if thou shouldst do it again thou and I would have a quarrel."

SOURCE: "The Memoirs of Usamah," excerpted from *The Islamic World* edited by McNeill, Waldman, 1973. Reprinted with permission of Oxford University Press.

even larger population and featured the most lavish imperial court of all under caliph Harun al-Rashid and his ninth-century successors.

Commerce was particularly well developed in the world of Islam, and the exhortation in the Qur'an to "honor the honest merchant" was generally observed. The Muslim faithful saw nothing wrong in getting rich, and in contrast to both Christians and Buddhists, they considered a wealthy man to be the recipient of God's blessings for a good life. The rich had an obligation to share their wealth with the poor, however. Most schools, hospitals, orphanages, and the like in Muslim areas are to this day the result of private donations and foundations, the **vakf,** which are very commonly included in Muslim wills.

⚜ SOCIAL CUSTOMS: MARRIAGE AND THE STATUS OF WOMEN

The Qur'an allows but does not encourage a man to marry up to four wives if he can maintain them properly. The marriages may be either serial or simultaneous; there is no limit on the number of concubines he can have. In practice, though, few Muslims had as many as four wives; and fewer still could afford concubines. The children of a legal wife had precedence over those from a concubine in inheritance, but the children of the concubine, if acknowledged by the father, were also provided for in law and custom.

Many households kept at least one slave (sometimes the concubine). *Slavery* was very common, but usually not very harsh. Most slaves worked in the household or shop, not in the fields or mines. It was common for slaves to be freed at any time for good behavior or because the owner wished to assure Allah's blessing. Most people fell into slavery for the usual reasons: debts and bad luck.

The household was ruled absolutely by the man, whose foremost duty toward it and himself was to maintain honor. Muslim society was dominated by honor and shame; feuding was endemic, and every insult had to be avenged. In the law of the Qur'an, women were granted many rights—far more than they had had in pre-Islamic Arab society—though how many of these were actually put into practice is difficult to know. One sign of women's inferior status was the **harem,** the secluded part of every well-to-do Muslim house that was reserved for them and their children; here they were safe from the insulting eyes of strangers. Shut up in the *harem* with little to do, the various wives and concubines often occupied their time trying to devise ways to win the favor of the master of the household and advance their own status and that of their children. Sexual jealousy was one of the main hinges around which the society revolved, and the relationship between the sexes was apparently even more one-sided and tension filled than in other civilizations. Some emirs and caliphs spent so much time in the *harem* that the word came to mean a kind of illicit government by women, who ruled their lords by sexual intrigues. In later Muslim history, the *harem* system had ruinous effects on the administration and government of the empire. Given the powerlessness of women in these circumstances, it isn't difficult to envision that the pursuit of distinction and prestige through highly personalized means seemed desirable to them.

Women were not to be seen or heard outside the house in theory and often in practice as well. This seclusion of women and their total inaccessibility prior to marriage

■ **Townscape of Grenada.** This striking view of one of the strongholds of the Spanish Moors shows the remnants of the medieval walls and the castle sitting on its hill below the high mountains of southern Spain.

contributed to the relative frequency of male homosexuality in the Islamic world, where it became even more common than it had been in ancient Greece.

✤ THE DECLINE OF THE ABBASIDS AND THE COMING OF THE TURKS AND MONGOLS

Despite all their efforts, the Abbasids were unable to restore the political unity of the empire they had taken over in 750. Even great caliphs like Harun al-Rashid, who was well known in the West, could not force the Spaniards and the North African emirates to submit to their rule. Gradually, during the 800s, almost all of the African and Arabian possessions broke away and became independent, leaving the Abbasids in control of only the Middle East. More and more, they came to depend on wild Turkish tribesmen, only some of whom had converted to Islam, for their military power. It was inevitable that the Turks would turn on their weak masters and make them into pawns.

In the mid-1000s C.E., a new group of Turks, known as **Seljuks** blasted their way out of Afghanistan into Iran and Iraq. In 1055 they entered Baghdad as victors. Keeping the Abbasid ruler on as a figurehead, the Seljuks took over the government for about a century, until they, too, fell prey to internal rivalries. The central government ceased to exist, and the Middle East became a series of large and small principalities, fighting one another for commercial and territorial advantage.

Into this disintegrated empire exploded a totally new force out of the east: **Chinghis Khan** and the *Mongols.* Chinghis started out as a minor tribal leader of the extremely primitive Mongols. In the late twelfth century, he was able to put together a series of victories over his rivals and set himself up as lord of his people. Leading an army of savage horsemen in a great campaign, he managed to conquer most of central Asia and the Middle East before his death in the early 1200s.

His immediate successor as Great Khan (the title means "king") was victorious over the Russians and ravaged about half of Europe before retiring in the 1230s. But a few years later, the Mongols felt themselves ready to settle accounts with the Seljuks and other claimants to the Baghdad throne. They took Baghdad in an orgy of slaughter and rape—eyewitnesses claimed that some 800,000 people were killed! In this gory debacle, the Abbasid caliphate finally came to an end and was replaced by the Mongol Khanate of central Asia.

Summary

Muslim civilization was an amalgam of the many civilizations that had preceded it; it was eclectic, taking from any forebear anything that seemed valuable or useful. In the opening centuries, the civilization was dominated by the Arabs who had founded it by military conquest. But it gradually opened up to all who professed the true faith of the Prophet and worshiped the one god, Allah.

Much of the territory the Arabs conquered was already highly civilized, with well-developed religions. The Arabs therefore contented themselves with establishing a minority of rulers and traders and intermarrying with the natives as they converted to Islam. Based on the easy-to-understand principles of an all-embracing religious faith, Muslim civilization was a world into which many streams flowed to make up a vast new sea.

Test Your Knowledge

1. Which of the following cities was *not* a center of Muslim culture?
   a. Cairo
   b. Constantinople
   c. Córdoba
   d. Baghdad
2. The impression given by the Arab Usama about Crusader medical knowledge is that
   a. the Muslims had a lot to learn from the West.
   b. the Muslims should send their best students to Europe.

c. the Franks were delighted to be able to study Muslim technique.

d. the Franks were too stupid in their practice to learn anything useful from them.

3. The common Muslim attitude toward trade and mercantile activity was

a. that they were best left to the "infidel."

b. that nothing was morally or ethically wrong with them.

c. reluctant acceptance of their necessity.

d. condemnation as temptations to evildoing.

4. Many Muslim scholars especially revered the work of

a. Gautama Buddha.

b. Aristotle.

c. Confucius.

d. Socrates.

5. Muslim knowledge significantly influenced the West in all these areas *except*

a. philosophy.

b. law.

c. medicine.

d. mathematics.

6. The major area from which Muslim culture entered Christian Europe was

a. Greece.

b. Spain.

c. Italy.

d. Russia.

7. The *Canon of Medicine* was the work of

a. Aristotle.

b. Avicenna.

c. Harun al-Rashid.

d. Averroës.

Identification Terms

Averroës	Harun al-Rashid	*Sharija*	*ulema*
Chinghis Khan	Ibn Rushd	*1001 Nights*	*vakf*
harem	Seljuk Turks	(*The Arabian Nights*)	vizier

Bibliography

Ashtor, E. *A Social and Economic History of the Near East in the Middle Ages,* 1976. Just what its title indicates.

Cambridge History of Islam, vols. 1 and 2, 1970. Perhaps the handiest collection of work on every aspect of Islamic culture, but is sometimes too specialized for student use.

Dunlop, D. M. *Arab Civilization to AD 1500,* 1971. An excellent collection dealing with many facets of this world, including the achievements of women.

Haddawy, H., trans. *Arabian Nights,* 1990. A recent translation that stands out.

Lapidus, I. *Muslim Cities in the Later Middle Ages,* 1967. A standard introduction to the wealth and variety of those urban societies. See also the same author's *A History of Islamic Societies,* 1988.

Lewis, B. *The Arabs in History,* 1968.

Morgan, D. *The Mongols,* 1986. An interesting presentation of Mongol history.

Musallam, B. F. *Sex and Society in Islam,* 1983. Discusses women in Islamic society.

Nasr, S. H. *Science and Civilization in Islam,* 1968.

Rice, D. T. *Islamic Art,* 1975. See for explanations of how the Islamic peoples adapted art to their supernatural ends and pioneered new forms and methods to do so.

Yarshater, E. *Persian Literature,* 1988. An illuminating discussion.

Watt, W. *History Islamic Spain,* 1965.

EARLY MEDIEVAL EUROPE

The slow breakdown of Roman authority and order in the western half of the empire took most of the fourth and fifth centuries C.E. Some parts of the West were almost untouched by the invasions; others were ravaged again and again until there was little of value left to seize or burn. But everywhere, the old order of provincial governments was swept away and replaced with Germanic kingdoms, independent of one another and of Constantinople. In most of these, violence and uncertainty of lawful power produced a Dark Age lasting from the sixth through the eighth centuries.

The Frankish king Charlemagne made a huge effort to restore what had once been, but his revived "Roman Empire" soon collapsed into fragments beset by invasions and internal rivalries. Not until 1000 C.E. was there much evidence of a return to civilized society and stable government.

❖ GERMAN INVASIONS AND ROMAN COLLAPSE

One by one, Rome's western provinces fell to the successive invasions of German tribes. By the end of the 400s, all of the western empire had been taken over: England by the Angles and Saxons; France by the Franks and Burgundians; Spain by the Visigoths; Italy itself by the Ostrogoths; and North Africa by the Vandals.

The Roman cities and towns that had been built on trade and commerce went into rapid and permanent decline. Many of them became ghost towns, or nearly so. The cities and towns were, of course, the obvious targets for the invaders. With their walls and watchtowers, they controlled the countryside roundabout, and it was within them that the goods of civilized living were to be found. Once thriving urban centers like Vienna, Frankfurt, Bath, and Lyons became semideserted backwaters for the next several centuries. Their merchants and artisans fled to safer places, abandoning their businesses to save their lives. The laborers and apprentices fell victim to one marauding band or another or fled altogether to the quieter villages.

❖ BEGINNINGS OF FEUDALISM

In the countryside, a process that had begun during the later empire accelerated dramatically. This was the establishment of large estates or **manors,** which were almost entirely self-sufficient and had little to do with the towns. The manor normally began as a *villa,* the country hideaway of a wealthy Roman official in quieter days. As order broke down and the province could safely ignore the central government, some of these officials became the equivalent of Chinese warlords, maintaining private armies to secure the peace in their own localities. Frequently extorting services and free labor from the villagers nearby, they evaded the central government's controls and taxes. These men grew ever more wealthy and powerful and began to acquire the peasants' lands through bribery, intimidation, and in trade for the protection they offered.

When the invasions began and provincial order broke down entirely, these estate holders simply took over the basic elements of government altogether. In return for physical protection and some assurance of order in their lives, the peasants would often offer part of their land and labor to the "lord" for some period, perhaps life. In this way was born both the European *nobility* (or a large part of it) and the medieval *feudal system* of agricultural estates worked by bound laborers. The serfs of later days were the descendants of these men and women who were desperately seeking protection in a world of chaos and danger.

As the cities and towns declined, more and more people found themselves in these manorial villages, dependent on and loosely controlled by the Roman or German lord and his small band of armed cronies. Life became much simpler, but it was more a daily struggle for survival than a civilized existence. The skills and crafts of Roman days fell into disuse, for there was little demand for them in this rough and brutal world. Trade in all but the barest necessities over the shortest distances became rare. Neither the roads nor the waters of western Europe were safe from marauders and pirates, and the Roman transport network fell into disuse. Literacy, that foundation stone of all education, declined sharply. Only the clergy had much need of writing, and many of the priests and monks in the seventh and eighth centuries would do well to read or write more than their names.

⚜ THE CHRISTIAN CHURCH IN THE DARK AGE

So backward did much of society become that it was once usual to refer to the centuries between 500 and 800 as the "Dark Age" in Europe. This name refers as much to the lack of documentation as to the ignorance of people living then. Not only have many documents perished through vandalism, but relatively few records were kept in the first

■ This illustration from the *Tres Riches Heures* or "Book of Hours," of Jean, Duke of Berry depicts the month of June. As seen here, men and women worked side by side to reap this duke's hay.

place—it is difficult to think of the future when one's daily life is hard and often dangerous.

The Christian clergy in the Dark Age were more often than not illiterate in the official Latin language of the church and knew their church history and doctrines only by hearsay. Many a bishop could not write his sermon. The immoral conduct of some clergy gave rise to scandal, and the prohibition against taking wives or concubines was widely ignored. Church offices were bought and sold like so many pounds of butter in many places. Rome was far away and could be easily ignored in churchly affairs, as it was in civil ones. Besides, the pope himself in this era was a Roman nobleman who rarely gave much attention to things spiritual.

In some countries, notably the German lands east of the Rhine, the bishops were more or less forced by the king to take on secular and even military duties as the king's lieutenant. The churchman was very often the only educated person in the area and the only one who had some concept of administration and record keeping. The combination of civil and religious duties was, however, often injurious to the latter; the bishop or abbot (the head of a monastery) often devoted more time and energy to his secular affairs than to his spiritual ones. Such conduct did not enhance the prestige and authority of the church as a moral force. All too frequently, important clergymen bribed their way into their position with the intention of using it as a means of obtaining wealth and/or influence in political matters. Their ecclesiastical duties played little or no role in these considerations. In the circumstances, it is more remarkable that some clergy *were* good and gentle men who tried to follow the rules than that many were not.

■ The conversion of Clovis, King of the Franks, to orthodox Christianity was an important factor in gaining support from the Pope of the Frankish kingdom. In this illuminated book, the *Grandes Chroniques de France,* bishops and nobles watch as Clovis is baptized.

Having said all that, it is still true that the Christian church was the only imperial Roman institution that survived the Germanic onslaught more or less intact. The church was changed, usually for the worse, by German custom and German concepts; but it did survive as recognizably the same institution that had won the religious allegiance of most Roman citizens in the fourth century. All the education that was available in early medieval Europe was supplied by the church, which also operated whatever charitable and medical institutions existed. When the higher concepts of Roman law were recovered in Europe, the church adopted them first and spread them to secular life.

By the end of the seventh century, after the majority of the German kings were converted, the church had become the paramount influence on the beliefs of Europeans, both about this world and the world to come. The *Age of Faith* had opened, and the church's teachings and preachings about the nature of humans and their relations with God were to have tremendous influence on every facet of human affairs, an influence that did not diminish noticeably for about a thousand years.

❧ GERMANIC CUSTOMS AND SOCIETY

The Germans who streamed into the former Roman provinces and gradually asserted their control over them were at first starkly differentiated from their subjects (see Map 18.1). Most of them wanted to be "Roman," as they understood that term; they certainly did not hate or despise the Roman population or think themselves culturally superior. But they brought with them a large number of habits, beliefs, and values that were not at all like those of the conquered. It would take centuries for the two peoples to come to resemble each other and for the two cultures to blend together to form the new culture that we call medieval.

From the comments of the Romans who observed them, we know that the Germans had a highly personalized concept of government. Authority was exercised by an *elected leader*. He received the sworn loyalty of his warriors, who were organized in small bands (the *comitatus*). The leader's authority only applied in time of war; in peacetime, the Germans remained essentially large families led by the oldest male, each of whom was a little king in his own right. If the war leader was defeated or the warriors were dissatisfied with his leadership, he could be deposed. The male warriors considered themselves equals; there was no hierarchy below the chief and apparently *no permanent offices* of any sort.

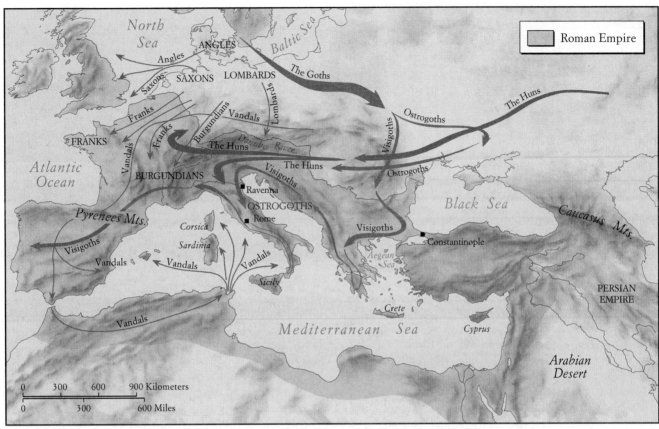

⊙ **MAP 18.1 Barbarian Migrations in the Fourth and Fifth Centuries** C.E. This map shows the movements of the major of Germanic and Asiatic invaders of Rome's empire.

Before entering the Roman Empire, most of the tribes had led a nomadic existence, and once in the empire, they at first had little appreciation of town life. For many years, the new Germanic kings had no fixed residences, but traveled continuously about their kingdoms "showing the flag" of authority and acting as chief justices to resolve disputes. Gradually, this changed to the extent that the king had a favorite castle or a walled town named for him where he might stay for part of each year.

Very slowly also, the idea made headway that the subject paid tribute and gave loyalty to the *office* of king, rather than to the individual holder of the crown. This last development resulted from Roman influence, and its contribution to peaceable transfer of power and stable government was so clear that all the tribal leaders sooner or later adopted it. The church authorities helped in this by preaching that the crown itself was a sacred object and that its holder was a sacred person, ordained by an all-wise God to exercise civil powers over others.

Germanic Law

Germanic law was very different from Roman law and much more primitive. Germanic law derived from custom, which was unwritten and allowed for no fine points of interpretation. Law was the collective memory of the tribe or clan as to what had been done before in similar circumstances. It allowed for little or no flexibility in application, at least over the short run; it did not inquire into motivation, but looked simply at the result.

The Germans used trial by fire and by water to determine guilt in criminal cases where the evidence was not clear-cut. In some capital cases where the two parties were of equal rank, they sometimes reverted to the extreme measure of trial by combat to get a verdict. As in ancient Mesopotamia, the object of a trial was to ascertain whether damage had been done to an individual and, if so, how much compensation the victim was owed by the perpetrator. As in Hammurabi's Code, the court, which was the general meeting of the elders of the clan or village, acted as a detached referee between the opposing parties.

The ultimate object of Germanic law was preventing or diminishing personal violence, which endangered the whole tribe's welfare, rather than rendering justice to the victim. The guilty party, as determined by the assembly, was punished by the imposition of a money fine, or **wergeld,** which was paid to the victim as compensation. In this way, the blood feuds that would have wrecked the tribe's ability to survive were avoided and the honor of the victim maintained.

German Religion and Conversion

The Germans had strong religious beliefs when they entered the Roman Empire, but we do not know much about their religion because the Christians rooted it out thoroughly after the Germans converted to Christianity. Originally, the Germans were animists, who saw spiritual powers in nature and in certain natural objects, such as trees. Their chief gods were sky deities, such as Wotan and Thor, who had no connections with either an afterlife or ethical conduct but served as enforcers of the will of the tribe. The Germans had no priests, no temples, and little, if any, theology.

The various tribes within the old Roman Empire converted to Christianity between about 450 and 700, while those beyond the empire's borders converted somewhat later. Last of all were the Scandinavians, some of whom were still pagans as late as 1100. The *method of conversion* was similar in all cases: after much negotiation, a small group of priests, perhaps headed by a bishop, secured an invitation to go to the king and explain to him the Christian gospel. If they were fortunate (rarely!), conversion of the king, his queen, or important nobles was achieved on the first try.

The Germans' reasons for accepting Christianity were almost always a combination of politics, desire for trade with Christians, and recognition of the advantages that Christian law could give the ruler in his efforts to create a stable dynasty. Occasionally, the German would also be sincerely convinced of the truth of the gospels and the prospects of immortality. After conversion and baptism (the outward sign of joining the Christian world), the new Christian would exert pressure on family and cronies to join also, and they, in turn, would exhort their dependents. When much of the upper class was converted at least in name, and some native priests were in place, the

nation was considered to be Christian, a part of the growing family of ex-pagans who had adopted the new religion.

It generally took decades for the faith to filter down to the common people, even in a formal sense. Centuries might pass before the villagers could be said to have much knowledge of church doctrine and before they would give up their most cherished pagan customs. Medieval Christianity was in fact a hodgepodge of pagan and Christian images and beliefs. Most priests, whether native or foreign, were satisfied if their faithful achieved a very limited understanding of heaven and hell and the coming Last Judgment. More could not be expected.

Female Status

The status of women in pre-Christian Germanic society is a subject of much debate. According to some Roman sources, women who were married had very considerable freedom and rights, more so than Roman matrons did. Although it was a warrior society, an extraordinary amount of attention seems to have been paid to the rights of mothers and wives, in both the legal and the social senses. The legal value (*wergeld*) of women of childbearing age was much higher than that of women who were too young or too old to have children, reflecting the view we have found in other ancient societies that women's chief asset was their ability to perpetuate the male family's name and honor.

The Romans admired the Germans' sexual morality; rape was a capital crime when committed against equals, as was adultery by a woman. Both concubinage and prostitution seem to have been unknown. In some cases, the widows of prominent men succeeded to their husband's position, a phenomenon the Romans found remarkable. After the Germans became Christian, there are many instances of queens and princesses exercising governmental power, and exercise of managerial powers by noble women was routine in their husband's death or absence (see the Biography in this chapter).

⚜ CHARLEMAGNE AND THE HOLY ROMAN EMPIRE

The greatest of the Germanic kings by far was Charlemagne (Charles the Great), king of the Franks (768–800) and the first Holy Roman Emperor (800–814), although the word *holy* was not actually used until the twelfth

Blanche of Castile
1187–1252

The powers of women in a patriarchal society naturally depended very much on their birth; noblewomen could do things forbidden to commoners. But in the violent and strongly patriarchal society of the European Middle Age, all women were under some constraints imposed by law and custom. Occasionally, an exception to the rule appeared, a woman who was in every way the equal of her male associates in terms of exercising public power. Blanche of Castile (1187–1252), queen of France, is a good example.

Blanche was a granddaughter of the most famous queen of the entire Middle Age, Eleanor of Aquitaine, and the niece of the unfortunate John of England. Selected by her grandmother as a suitable match, she was married to the heir to the French throne, Louis, at the age of twelve. Her bridegroom was a ripe thirteen! This was not unusual for royal or noble marriages; the legal age of maturity was twelve for females, fourteen for males, conforming to current ideas on mental and moral development. Such a marriage would not be consummated until later, when puberty had been reached at about sixteen for males, fourteen for females.

Blanche gave birth to her first child—of a total of twelve—when she was seventeen. Of the twelve, five lived to adulthood—a relatively high percentage for the time. The oldest surviving boy became the saintly King Louis IX, patron saint of the French kingdom. He and his mother remained extraordinarily close throughout their lives.

Blanche had a forceful temperament. At the age of twenty-eight, when her father-in-law, King Philip Augustus, refused to send money to her husband for one of the latter's feudal wars, Blanche swore that she would pawn her two children to get the needed cash. Philip decided to put up some funds after all.

In 1223 Philip died, and Louis succeeded him as King Louis VIII. Only three years later, he himself died, leaving his queen as the guardian of his twelve-year-old heir, Louis IX. Blanche thus became not only queen, but ruler. Although not unheard of in medieval Europe; it was very unusual for a woman to exercise royal powers. Louis apparently knew and appreciated the qualities of his young wife; she did not disappoint his expectations.

Several of the great barons who had sworn feudal vows to their dead king considered themselves released from them in the absence of an adult male successor. For the next three years, Blanche showed both courage and a mastery of diplomacy in fighting down repeated challenges to the boy-king and her own regency. Later, she organized French resistance to an invasion mounted by King Henry III of England. The English action was supported by rebel nobles in Brittany and Normandy who feared the extension of royal power. At the head of her own army, Blanche faced the rebels down, and the English departed.

Louis IX, a deeply pious person, was content to leave much of the task of governing to his mother even after he had attained his majority. Mother and son had a mutual appreciation that lasted until her death and was undisturbed even by Louis's marriage in 1234. Blanche herself selected Louis's bride, thirteen-year-old Marguerite of Provence, but Joinville, Louis's contemporary biographer, tells us that the mother-in-law was jealous of the young girl and took pains to assert her dominant position: "[Louis] acted on the advice of the good mother at his side, whose counsels he always followed."

Life must have been difficult for young Marguerite, who found that the only way she could be with her husband without his mother was to accompany him on a long-promised crusade against the Muslims in the Holy Land in 1248. During the king's lengthy absence, Blanche again served as regent, and she was the reigning authority in France when she died, at age sixty-five, in 1252. Like her more famous grandmother Eleanor, she was a woman who knew how to handle the levers of power in a masculine age.

century. The kingdom of the Franks had been in a favored position since its founder, **Clovis,** had been the first important German ruler to accept Roman Christianity, in or around 500. (France still prides itself on being "the first daughter of the Church.") The line of Clovis (the **Merovingians**) had been pushed aside in the 700s. Charlemagne became king through the aggressive action of his father, a high official of the last Merovingian who seized power and established the **Carolingian** dynasty. An alliance with the pope in Rome did much to cement the new King's shaky legal position. Charlemagne himself earned the papacy's lasting gratitude by crushing the Lombards, a Germanic people who had settled in northern Italy and were pushing south, threatening Rome. In return, he was solemnly recognized by the pope as rightful king.

For thirty years (772–804), Charlemagne was at war with one or another pagan German neighbor: Lombards, Saxons, and Burgundians. He also led expeditions against the Spanish Moors, as the Muslims in Spain were called. His persistence was rewarded by the gradual establishment of by far the largest territorial unit under one rule since Roman times and by the granting of the title *Holy Roman Emperor* (HRE) by Pope Leo III himself.

Charles's new empire was an attempt to revive the Roman order in Europe, this time under the auspices of the church, which would act in close cooperation with the civil powers. According to medieval theory, the secular government and the ecclesiastical establishment were the two arms of one body, directed by one head (Christ). To these theorists, Charlemagne's coronation by Leo in the papal city on Christmas Day 800 was looked upon by all who witnessed it to be the greatest event since the birth of Christ. They saw it as a means of rejuvenating the faded idea of harmony between the works of God and the works of humans on earth.

The Byzantine emperor in Constantinople was not pleased, to put it mildly. But he could do little to hinder or change what was happening in the West; he had his hands quite full with the Muslims at home. In fact, it was because of the Byzantine government's inability to defend Rome from the Lombards that the pope had turned to the Franks in the first place.

What Charlemagne thought of his new honor is not known; apparently, he was less than overwhelmed, because he stopped using the title during his lifetime. He went on to divide up his territories among his sons, as was usual with Frankish kings but inconceivable to Roman emperors. The later history of the title of Holy Roman Emperor shows that even its mostly German holders regarded it largely as an honor, an adjunct to the title of "king" from which *real* power flowed.

Carolingian Renaissance

Charlemagne's claims to fame stem more from his brave attempts to restore learning and stable government to Europe than from his position as the first emperor. Thanks to his military campaigns (in which a great deal of blood flowed), he controlled much of western and central Europe by 800 (see Map 18.1). From his capital city of Aachen in northern Germany, he then tried to break the rule of might and institute that of right in his realm. He revived the Roman office of *comes,* or count, as the representative of the king in the provinces. He started the **missi domenici,** special officers who checked up on the counts and others and reported directly to the king. Knowing that most people were touched more directly by religion than by government, Charlemagne also concerned himself with the state of the church. Many of his most trusted officials were picked from the clergy, a practice that would lead to problems in later days.

Charles admired learning, although he had little himself (supposedly, he could not sign his name!). From all parts of his domains and from England, he brought men to his court who could teach and train others. Notable among them was **Alcuin,** an Anglo-Saxon monk of great ability, who directed the palace school for clergy and officials set up by the king. For the first time since the 400s, something like higher education was available to a select few. Charlemagne funded the creation of dozens of new monasteries, where many monks devoted much of their time to laboriously copying ancient manuscripts. The monastic *scriptorium* was the equivalent of a printing shop for creating new libraries.

A new script was also devised, making the Latin much more readable; several new editions of the Bible and the works of the Church Fathers were produced, and by Charlemagne's orders, the Benedictine Rule for monastic institutions was spread throughout his territories. Not a devout man himself (according to the two contemporary biographies that have survived—see the Document in this chapter), he still respected and encouraged piety in others. At his orders many new parishes were founded or given large new endowments.

But all Charlemagne's efforts were insufficient to turn the tide of disorder and violence. His "renaissance" was short-lived, and his schools and governmental innovations were soon in ruins. The times were not ripe for them; at

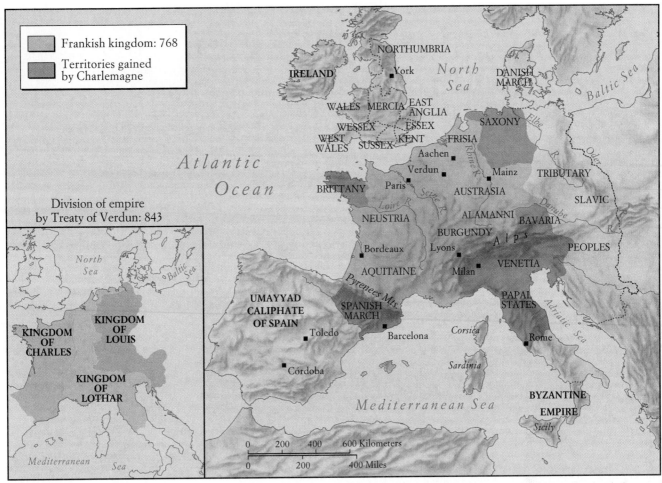

● **MAP 18.2 Charlemagne's Empire.** Charlemagne intended for the territories of the first Holy Roman Empire to be divided among his three sons. However, two died before their father, so the entire realm passed to Louis. Louis then repeated his father's plan and divided the empire among three sons: Louis, Lothar, and Charles.

the first crises, they collapsed, and the darkness descended again.

⚜ DISINTEGRATION OF THE CAROLINGIAN EMPIRE

Charlemagne eventually bequeathed his empire to his only surviving son, Louis the Pious, a man who was unfit for the heavy responsibility. Louis's own sons, whom he made subrulers early in his reign, constantly maneuvered for supreme power, and Louis seemed helpless against them. By the time of his death in 840, the prestige of the imperial title had been greatly reduced.

By Louis's will, the empire was divided among the three sons: Charles, Lothar, and Louis. Charles received France; Lothar, the midlands between France and Germany reaching down into Italy; and Louis, Germany. Fraternal war immediately ensued. The **Treaty of Verdun** in 843, which established the peace, is one of the most important treaties in world history, for the general borders it established still exist today, 1,150 years later (see Map 18.1). When Lothar died a few years later, the midlands were divided between the survivors, Charles and Louis.

First, the grandsons of Charlemagne had fought one another and divided the unified empire; then, in the late ninth century, it was attacked from outside from three directions: the *Vikings* swept down from the north, the *Magyars* advanced from the east, and the *Muslims* attacked from the Mediterranean (see Map 18.2). In the ensuing chaos, all that Charlemagne had been able to do was

The Biography of Charlemagne

The monk Einhard was a German, born around 770 to a minor noble family that educated him as well as possible in those stormy days. In the 790s he went to join the school founded by Charlemagne and administered by Alcuin in the Carolingian capital at Aachen. There Einhard came to admire King and Emperor Charles very much and was for many years one of his foremost officials and advisers. After Charlemagne's death in 814, Einhard stayed on as adviser to his son, Louis the Pious.

After Charles's death, Einhard found time to write the most famous biography of the Christian Middle Age. Very brief and easily read, the *Life of Charlemagne* is our chief source of information about the character of the greatest of all medieval kings.

Chapters 18 and 19: Private Life

At his mother's request he married a daughter of the Lombard king Desiderius but repudiated her for unknown reasons after one year. Then he married Hildegard, who came from a noble Swabian family. With her he had three sons, Charles, Pepin, and Louis, and as many daughters... he had three more daughters with his third wife Fastrada.... When Fastrada died he took Liutgard to wife....After her death he had four concubines....

For the education of his children, Charles made the following provisions ... as soon as the boys were old enough they had to learn how to ride, hunt, and handle weapons in Frankish style. The girls had to get used to carding wool and to the distaff and spindle. To prevent their getting bored and lazy he gave orders for them to be taught to engage in these and in all other virtuous activities. Of his children, only two sons and one daughter died before him: Charles, the oldest, and Pepin, who he had made king of Italy; and the oldest daughter, Rotrud, who had been engaged to marry the emperor Constantine in Greece.... When his sons and daughter died, Charles reacted to their deaths with much less equanimity than might have been expected of so strongminded a man. Because of his deep devotion to them he broke down in tears.... For Charles was by nature a man who had a great gift for friendship, who made friends easily and never wavered in his loyalty to them. Those whom he loved could rely on him absolutely.

He supervised the upbringing of his sons and daughters very carefully.... Although the girls were very beautiful and he loved them dearly it is odd that he did not permit any of them to get married, neither to a man of his own nation nor to a foreigner. Rather, he kept all of them with him until his death, saying he could not live without their company. And on account of this, he had to suffer a number of unpleasant experiences, however lucky he was in other respects. But he never let on that he had heard of any suspicions about their chastity or any rumors about them....

---

extinguished, and government reverted back to a primitive military contract between individuals for mutual defense.

The *Vikings or Norsemen* were the most serious threat and had the most extensive impact. Superbly gifted warriors, these Scandinavians came in swift boats to ravage the coastal communities, then flee before effective countermeasures could be taken. From their headquarters in Denmark and southern Sweden, every year after about 790 they sailed forth and soon discovered that the Franks, Angles, and Saxons were no match. In 834, a large band of Vikings sailed up the Seine and sacked Paris. Seventy years later, they advanced into the Mediterranean and sacked the great city of Seville in the heart of the Spanish caliphate.

By the late 800s, the Vikings were no longer content to raid; they came to conquer. Much of eastern England, Brittany and Normandy, Holland, and Iceland fell to them. In their new lands, they quickly learned to govern by intimidation rather than to plunder and burn; taxes took the place of armed bands. They learned the advantages of literacy and eventually adopted Christianity in place of their northern gods. By about 1000, the Vikings had footholds ranging from the coast of the North Sea to the eastern Mediterranean and had become one of the

Chapter 22: Personal Appearance

Charles had a big and powerful body and was tall and well-proportioned. That his height was seven times the length of his own foot was well known. He had a round head, his eyes were unusually large and lively, his nose a little longer than average, his gray hair attractive, and his face cheerful and friendly . . . his voice, though clear, was not as strong as one might have expected from someone his size. His health was always excellent except during the last four years of his life, when he frequently suffered from attacks of fever . . . he continued to rely on his own judgment more than that of the physicians, whom he almost hated because they ordered him to give up his customary roast meat and eat only boiled. . . . Charles

■ The Pope Crowns Charlemagne, 800 C.E.

was also fond of the steam of the natural hot springs. He swam a great deal and did it so well that no one could compete with him. . . .

Chapter 24: Habits

Charles was a moderate eater and drinker, especially the latter, because he abominated drunkenness in any man, particularly in himself and in his associates. . . . After his midday meal in the summer he would eat some fruit and take another drink, then remove his clothes just as he did at night, and rest for two or three hours. His sleep at night would usually be interrupted four or five times and as soon as he awoke he got up. . . .

Chapter 25: Studies

Charles was a gifted speaker. He spoke fluently and expressed what he had to say with great clarity. Not only was he proficient in his mother tongue (Frankish) but he also took trouble to learn foreign languages. He spoke Latin as well as his own language, but Greek he understood better than he could speak it. . . . He also tried his hand at writing, and to this end kept writing tablets and notebooks under his pillow in bed. . . . But since he had only started late in life, he never became very accomplished in the art.

SOURCE: Einhard: Vita Caroli Magni, *The Life of Charlemagne.* Translated by Evelyn Scherabon Firchow and E. H. Zeydel. University of Miami Press. Coral Gables, FL, 1972.

most capable of all the European peoples in government and administration, as well as the military arts.

The *Magyars* were a different proposition. They were an Asiatic people, who swept into the central European plain from Russia as a horde of horsemen. As such, they were the next to last version of the Asiatic invasions of western Europe, which had begun as far back as the Huns; this resemblance earned their descendants the name *Hungarians* in modern nomenclature. The Magyars arrived in Europe at the end of the ninth century and for fifty years fought the Christianized Germans for mastery. Finally, in a great battle in 955, the Magyars were de-

feated; they retired to the Hungarian plains where they gradually settled down. In the year 1000, their king and patron saint, Stephen, accepted Roman Christianity, and the Magyars joined the family of civilized nations.

The *Muslims* of the Mediterranean were descendants of North African peoples who had been harassing southern Europe as pirates and raiders ever since the 700s. In the late 800s, they were successful in wresting Sicily and part of southern Italy from the Italians and thereby posed a direct threat to Rome. But the Muslims were checked and soon settled down to join the heterogeneous group of immigrants who had been coming to southern Italy for a

■ This reproduction of an actual Viking ship shows the type of swift boats used by the Norsemen to ravage the coastal communities and then flee before effective countermeasure could be taken by the victims.

■ Pastoral life in medieval Europe required the work of men, women, and children. This painting of a farmyard in April is from Da Costa's "Book of Hours."

very long time. The Muslims' highly civilized rule was finally disrupted by the attacks of the newly Christian Vikings, who began battling them for mastery in the eleventh century and eventually reconquered Sicily and the southern tip of the peninsula from them.

The Invasions and the Growth of Feudalism

The invasions fragmented governmental authority, as the royal courts in France and Germany were unable to defend their territories successfully, particularly against the Viking attacks. Consequently, it fell to local strongmen to defend their own areas as best they could. Men on horseback had great advantages in battle, and the demand for them rose steadily. Thus, the original **knights** were mercenaries, professional warriors-at-horse who sold their services to the highest bidder. What was bid normally was land and the labor of those who worked it. In this way large tracts passed from the king, technically the owner of all land in his kingdom, into the possession of warriors who were the lords and masters of the commoners living upon these estates.

The invasions thus greatly stimulated the arrival of the professional army and the feudal military system in northern Europe, which felt the brunt of the attacks. Any headway Charlemagne had made in restoring the idea of a central authority was soon eradicated. The noble, with control over one or more estates on which manorial agriculture was practiced with serf labor, now became a

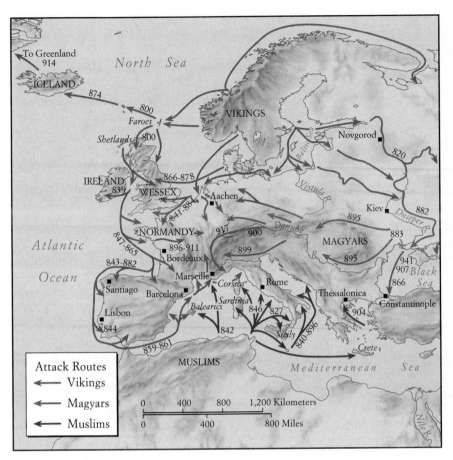

● MAP 18.3 Ninth-Century Invaders. Of the three invaders of Christian Europe, the fierce Vikings were the most enterprising and had the most widespread impact. Their conversion to Christianity and adoption of civilized life were crucial to the High Medieval period of prosperity that began in the twelfth century.

combined military and civil ruler for a whole locality. The king remained the object of special respect, and the sacred powers of the royal crown were acknowledged by all. But day-to-day administration, military defense, and justice were all carried out by the feudal nobles and their hired men-at-arms.

Summary

The collapse of Roman order in the fourth and fifth centuries left western Europe prey to the Germanic tribal leaders who set up one "kingdom" after another by right of conquest. A Dark Age of violence and ignorance ensued from which relatively little documentation has survived. In time, the efforts of missionaries from Rome showed results, as the Germanic warriors set up governments of a rough-and-ready sort. By the 700s, these had become stabilized and Christianized, at least in the upper classes.

The most important of the early medieval rulers was Charlemagne, the first Holy Roman Emperor as well as king of the Franks. His attempts to restore the ancient empire went astray almost as soon as he was dead, and the renaissance that he promoted also proved ephemeral. New invasions by Vikings, Magyars, and Muslims and the chaotic conditions they created in Europe were too much for the highly personal system of government that Charlemagne had established. It collapsed and was replaced by a highly decentralized administration based on agrarian manors and local military power in the hands of a self-appointed elite, the nobility.

Test Your Knowledge

1. The bishops of which country were most susceptible to royal pressure to take on civic duties?
   a. Germany.
   b. France
   c. England
   d. Spain

2. Blanche of Castile was unusual in early medieval times because
   a. she actually exercised royal powers.
   b. she was appointed regent for a young child-king.
   c. she had selected a wife for her son.
   d. she was married before reaching puberty.

3. All of the following were German tribes *except* the
   a. Gauls.
   b. Lombards.
   c. Franks.
   d. Ostrogoths.

4. The first Holy Roman Emperor was
   a. Pippin I.
   b. Richard the Lionhearted.
   c. Charlemagne.
   d. Louis the Pious.

5. The biographer of Charlemagne tells us that the king
   a. cared greatly about the manners of his courtiers.
   b. enjoyed the company of his daughters.
   c. despised physical exercise.
   d. read and wrote a great deal.

6. The decisive advantage held by the Vikings in their raids on Europe was
   a. overwhelming numbers.
   b. superior weapons.
   c. great courage.
   d. mastery of naval tactics.

7. The primary reason for the quick collapse of Charlemagne's empire after his death was the
   a. fierceness of the subject peoples.
   b. low morals of the clergy.
   c. lack of stable governmental institutions.
   d. poor quality of his successors.

8. The Treaty of Verdun in 843
   a. divided Europe between Muslims and Christians.
   b. created the kingdom of the Franks.
   c. was a compromise between Eastern and Western Christianity.
   d. divided Charlemagne's empire into three states.

Identification Terms

Alcuin
Carolingians
Clovis
knights
manor
Merovingians
missi dominici
Treaty of Verdun
wergeld

Bibliography

Note: Some of the bibliography in Chapter 14 will serve here as well, as we look at the introduction of Germanic institutions and Christianity into the former provinces of the western half of the Roman *imperium.*

Barraclough, G. *The Crucible of Europe: The Ninth and Tenth Centuries in European History,* 1976. Discusses the invasions of the ninth century.

Bronsted, J. *The Vikings,* 1970. See for the Vikings' role in the invasions of the ninth century.

Bullough, D. *The Age of Charlemagne,* 1965. See for Charlemagne and his empire.

Burns, C. D. *The First Europe,* 1948. Takes a positive view of these early centuries as a time of creative force.

Dawson, C. *The Making of Europe,* 1953. Emphasizes the role of the Christian church and clergy.

Duby, G. *The Early Growth of the European Economy,* 1974. Covers economic and commercial topics.

Einhard. *Life of Charlemagne* (many editions). A classic thumbnail sketch.

Fichtenau, H. *The Carolingian Empire,* 1972. Takes a critical view of the emperor and his ambitions.

Painter, S. *The Rise of the Feudal Monarchies,* 1957. Looks at the period after 1000 C.E.

Riché, P. *Daily Life in the World of Charlemagne,* 1978. A lively survey of the life of the people in the earlier Middle Age.

Strayer, J. *Western Europe in the Middle Ages,* 1982. A fine survey of the whole period, with a very good bibliography.

Veyne, P., ed. *A History of Private Life,* vol. 1, 1987. A survey of daily life. See especially the article by M. Rouche (p. 411ff).

AFRICA TO THE FIFTEENTH CENTURY

300s–700s C.E.	Kingdom of Axum
600s–700s C.E.	Muslims conquer North Africa
c. 900s C.E.	Origins of Sudanese kingdoms/trans-Saharan trade
c. 900s–c. 1400s C.E.	Great Zimbabwe
1200–1450 C.E.	Kingdom of Mali
c. 1300s C.E.	East African city-states founded

The chief characteristic of Africa's history is its variety. Africa is a huge continent with many different climates and topographies. Each of these produced civilizations or proto-civilizations, embracing different races of people. Before the Europeans came, Africa was almost entirely isolated from the rest of the inhabited world except for Egypt in its northeastern corner and the Mediterranean coast. Little has been known of African history until recent days, and much still remains obscure. The tropic climate of many areas and the lack of written languages combine to create lengthy periods when almost nothing at all is known about humans' activities. Here and there, however, archaeology, art objects, and travelers' accounts illuminate this obscurity and provide evidence of centers of a high civilization in various regions.

❖ AFRICAN GEOGRAPHY AND CLIMATE

Africa is shaped like an inverted saucer with a coastal lowland giving way to highlands and mountain ranges that dominate the interior. Much of the continent is a series of vast plateaus that can be reached only after dangerous and laborious journeys from the coast. Where the great rivers of the interior plateaus break through the ring of mountains, tremendous waterfalls and rapids block human transport and travel. The continent lacks harbors on most of its perimeter, on both the Atlantic and Indian Ocean sides, while a heavy surf makes the open beaches unusable by small boats.

All in all, geography has not been kind to Africa for purposes of settlement or development. It has remained isolated from the world for a much longer period than one would suppose, given its proximity to Europe across the narrow and normally quiet Mediterranean Sea and its attachment to the Near East via Egypt.

Part of the reason for Africa's isolation is climatic. The continent is divided into five climatic and vegetative *zones* (see Map 19.1):

1. The *Mediterranean and extreme southern coasts,* with temperate weather and good soil.
2. The *Sahel-Sudan,* or the dry, treeless steppes that cross Africa north of the bulge.
3. The *deserts,* of which the enormous Sahara is the chief but not the only one.
4. The *rain forest,* which extends on either side of the equator in the west and center.

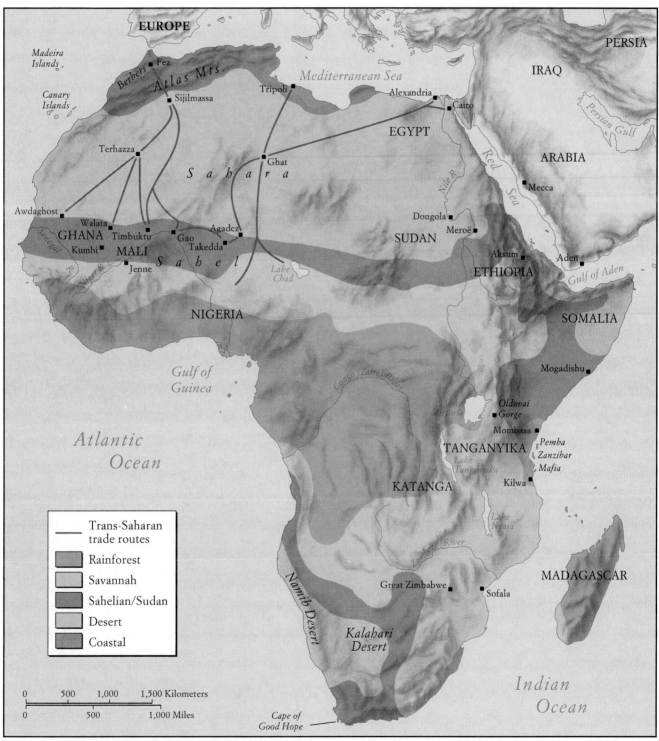

⬤ **MAP 19.1   The Continent of Africa.** Africa has a highly diverse geography and climate. This map shows five major subdivisions.

■ Where great rivers of the interior plateaus break through the ring of mountains, tremendous waterfalls such as Victoria Falls prevent human transport and travel.

5. The **savanna,** the grassland regions of the interior plateaus.

The various peoples of Africa developed different "ways of life" depending on the zone where they lived. The Mediterranean region was really a part of Europe, and Egypt, as noted, was a land to itself in its isolated Nile valley. In much of the center and west of the continent, the rain forest's unsuitability for agriculture prevented development almost to the present. In the desert regions, nomadic pastoral life on a small scale was the only possible lifestyle, and vast areas were left uninhabited. The dry Sahel also could support only a pastoral economy. Only the savannas of the north and the eastern plateaus could sustain crop agriculture.

⚜ THE PEOPLES

The peoples of Africa are also very diverse. In the coastal strip along the Mediterranean dwelled Egyptians and **Berbers,** later joined by Arabs after the Muslim expansion. Along the eastern coasts and inland plateaus were Abyssinians (Ethiopians), Nubians, and various Bantu-speaking peoples who seem to have come in a great prehistoric migration from their original homes in the west of the continent.

In the far south and southwest, the original settlers were the Bushmen or Khoisan, who in much reduced numbers still survive in a hunting-gathering culture in the Kalahari Desert. To the north of them in the center of the African forest belt lived the Pygmies. They, too, still practice a hunting-gathering life, though only a quarter million or so Pygmies survive today. Finally, in the huge bulge of Africa below the Sahara lived, and still live today, an assortment of tribes and language groups.

In general, Africa south of the Sahara has been primarily Negroid in composition for millennia. North of the Sahara, it has primarily a mixture of peoples derived from Gothic, Arab, Roman, and several other stocks.

⚜ EARLY SOCIETIES

The key elements in the development of civilization normally are the availability of agricultural land and iron tools. In Africa, these elements were closely associated. Most of the land suitable for agriculture in Africa is in the savanna south of the Sahara and the Nile valley, with only bits and pieces elsewhere. Archaeology reveals that agriculture was practiced in some places in Africa as early as anywhere in the world, perhaps several thousands of years B.C.E. But most of the continent did not develop agriculture, and where it did appear, it was unable to advance very much for a very long time due to the shortage of iron ore and/or lack of knowledge of how to smelt it.

For centuries, iron seems to have been limited to the Sudan (the huge region south of the Sahara, reaching from Lake Chad to the mountains of Ethiopia), where it presumably was introduced through trade contacts with the Egyptians. Only as late as about the first century B.C.E. did the use of iron spread into the forest belt below the Sudan, where it was carried by Bantu migrants.

■ The Sahara was never totally impassable, but until the introduction of the camel in the early Christian era, crossing it was very difficult. The camel was able to make the north-south crossing a feasible undertaking for commerce.

Bantu Expansion

The **Bantu** speakers, a people of West Africa, were the chief agents and the chief beneficiaries of the spread of iron working. For reasons unknown, they started to migrate south and east in the first centuries C.E. and used their iron weaponry and tools to dominate the less developed people they encountered. Eventually, the Bantu greatly enlarged their numbers by conquest and absorption and created a series of tribal kingdoms stretching across central and eastern Africa until, by the 1500s, they had reached the east coast (present-day Tanzania). Very little is known about this lengthy process, as the Bantu had no written language and built few monuments of any sort until relatively late. Only when they arrived on the coast and built or took over the existing port cities do we know much more than that they had migrated and created kingdoms dependent on agriculture and trade in the interior.

Ethiopia

The *Ethiopians* converted early (fourth century) to Christianity, which was brought to them by missionaries from the Nile. The Ethiopian *kingdom of Axum* had much contact with the Roman world through ports on the Red Sea, and its kings were proud of achieving a level of civilization equal to that of the Roman Christians. The kings' powers were impressive, and northeastern Africa in the fourth through eighth centuries was under either Egyptian or Ethiopian cultural and political sway.

In fact, Ethiopia and Egypt were quite similar because the Ethiopian church was an offshoot of the Coptic Church in Egypt. This branch of Christian belief (it differed from the orthodox variety in insisting that Christ had a single divine nature rather than being simultaneously man and God) was very much linked with civil government. The Ethiopian king at Axum was also head of the church, and the bishops were his chief councilors of state.

During the Muslim conquests in the seventh and eighth centuries, Ethiopia was protected by its impassable mountains, but the Muslim advances left it cut off from the rest of the Christian world. We know very little about Ethiopian history between the eighth century and the eighteenth except chronologies of the kings and that they carried on incessant warfare against the neighboring Muslim states. Church and government sank into a mutually supportive isolation that lasted until the present century. Ethiopian Christianity became even more esoteric, producing a rite and a clergy that are unlike any others in the world.

The Sudanese Kingdoms

The Sudanese kingdoms were a series of states that were formed starting around 900 in the bulge of Africa. Here, iron tools enabled agriculture to advance and provide for a rapidly growing population and an active trade across the Sahara with the Berbers and Arabs to the north. **Ghana,** the first of these kingdoms, lasted for about two centuries before it fell apart. It was created by the Soninke

al-Bakri: Ghana in the Eleventh Century

The Arab and Berber Muslims are our chief sources of knowledge about sub-Saharan affairs until as late as the fifteenth century C.E. One of them was al-Bakri, a great Muslim geographer who lived in the eleventh century. Although it is unclear whether he himself ever visited Africa, he was much interested in the continent and wrote extensively about West Africa where by his day animist and Muslim Africans were living together in many towns. The following excerpt is from al-Bakri's account of the society of Ghana, the name for both the place and the king of a large empire in what is today Mali and Nigeria:

> The city of Ghana consists of two towns situated on a plain. One of these towns, which is inhabited by Muslims, is large and possesses twelve mosques, in one of which they assemble for the Friday prayers. There are salaried imams and muezzins, as well as jurists and scholars. In the environs are wells with sweet water, from which they drink and with which they grow vegetables. The king's town is six miles distant from this one, and bears the name al-Ghaba. Between these two towns there are continuous habitations. The houses of the inhabitants are of stone and acacia wood. The king has a palace and a number of domed dwellings, all enclosed with a city wall. In the king's town and not far from his court of justice is a mosque where the Muslims who arrive at his court pray. Around the king's town are domed buildings and groves and thickets where the sorcerers [sha-
> mans] of these people, men in charge of their religious cult, live. In them too are the idols and the tombs of their kings. . . .
>
> All of them shave their beards, and the women shave their heads. The king adorns himself like a woman, with necklaces around his neck and bracelets on his forearms, and he puts on a high cap decorated with gold and wrapped in a turban of fine cotton. He sits in audience or to hear grievances against officials. . . . Behind the king stand ten pages holding shields and swords decorated with gold, and on his right are the sons of the [subordinate] kings of his country, wearing splendid garments and their hair plaited with gold. . . . When the people professing the same religion as the king approach him, they fall on their knees and sprinkle dust on their heads, for this is their way of greeting him. As for Muslims, they greet him only by clapping their hands.
>
> Their religion is paganism and the worship of idols. When their king dies they construct over the place where his tomb will be an enormous dome of wood. Then they bring him on a bed covered with a few carpets and cushions, and place him beside the dome. At his side they place his ornaments, his weapons, and the vessels from which he used to eat and drink, filled with various kinds of food and beverages.

SOURCE: N. Levtzion and J. F. P. Hopkins, eds., *Corpus of Early Arabic Sources for West African History* (Cambridge: Cambridge University Press, 1981), pp. 79–80. Reprinted with permission of Cambridge University Press.

people in the tenth century and had extensive dealings with the Muslims across the great desert. The *ghana* was the title given to the king, a sacred being who ruled through a network of subchieftains in an area that at one point reached the size of Texas. Kumbi, the capital city, was so impressive that the sophisticated Muslim geographer al-Bakri spent some time describing it in a well-known travel and sightseeing guide of the eleventh century (see the Document in this chapter).

The Muslims, both Arabic and Berber, were very influential in Ghana and, for that matter, in all of the Sudanese kingdoms that followed. The peoples of the Sudan were animists, but they had little difficulty converting to the Muslim religious doctrines preached by Arab missionary-merchants from the Mediterranean region. Like the Christian Europeans earlier, the missionaries concentrated their efforts on the upper class, usually in the towns where trade flourished. Soon animist masses and Muslim ruling groups coexisted in these states without apparent friction. The Muslims introduced their concepts of law and administration, as well as religious belief. Animist kings often relied on Muslim advisers for political and administrative advice.

After Ghana fell to the Berbers in the eleventh century, its tribally oriented segments made war upon one another until one was powerful enough to intimidate its neighbors into submission. This was the kingdom of **Mali,** which lasted from about 1200 to about 1450. Mali was larger and better organized than Ghana, but it too had a sacred king who ruled with the help of his chieftains. The adoption of Islam by the upper class, led by a powerful king, assured good relations with the trans-Saharan Berbers, who were essential to the economic prosperity of the kingdom.

The governments of both Ghana and Mali relied heavily upon the taxes imposed on the trans-Saharan traders in vital commodities: *gold, salt, and slaves.* Although the king had other means of support for his extensive and expensive court, these taxes made the wheels go round, so to speak. These Sudanese kingdoms were first and foremost the products of a strategic trading position that allowed them to monitor the movements of goods from sub-Saharan Africa to North Africa (and on to both Europe and the East).

African *gold* was essential to Roman and medieval European commerce, as well as to the Muslim world. Gold was rare in Europe, but was found in large quantities in parts of sub-Saharan Africa controlled by Mali.

Salt was almost as prized as gold in the ancient world. Though it was a necessity, supplies were limited in most areas except near the sea, and it was difficult to transport without large loss. This made salt highly valuable, and the African mines on either side of the Sahara were a major source.

Slaves were a common item in the African markets long before the beginnings of the Atlantic slave trade by the Europeans. As in every other part of the world, slavery was an accepted practice in Africa, both for debt and other reasons. Being captured in raids by enemies was reason enough for enslavement. Huge numbers of black slaves passed northward through Ghana and Mali, bound for collection points on the Mediterranean coast. From there they were traded all over the known world. Neither African nor Muslim culture had any moral scruples about slave trading or possession.

The kingdom of Mali expanded by military conquests in the thirteenth century, until it came to dominate all of West Africa. Early Africa's most noted ruler, the far-traveled **Mansa Musa** ruled from 1312 to 1337 and extended the kingdom as far north as the Berber cities in Morocco and eastward to include the great mid-Saharan

■ This fourteenth-century mud brick mosque at Jenna is one of the most striking traces of Muslim influence in the western Sudan.

trading post of **Timbuktu** (see the Biography in this chapter). Perhaps eight million people lived under his rule, at a time when the population of England was about four million.

Like his predecessors, Mansa Musa became a Muslim, and in 1324 he made the pilgrimage to the holy places in Arabia. His huge entourage laden with golden staffs and plates entered Muslim Cairo like a victory procession and made an impression that became folklore. He distributed so much gold as gifts to his hosts that reportedly a terrific inflation ensued that disturbed the Egyptian economy for a generation.

Thanks to Mansa Musa's enthusiasm and determination, Islam gained much ground in West Africa during his lifetime. Thereafter, the religion gradually passed through the upper classes to the common people. The Muslim presence in sub-Saharan Africa has been growing slowly for many generations. It has had almost the same impact there as Christianity did in the Germanic kingdoms. African law, social organization, literature, and political institutions all stem from it.

Mansa Musa

r. 1307–1332

Because of the African tradition of oral literature and history, we have practically no written sources from that continent until the occasional accounts by Muslim traders appear in the twelfth century. One of the first sub-Saharan African rulers known to us in any detail is Mansa Musa, king of Mali (r. 1307–1332) and grandson of the founder of that kingdom, the famous warrior Sundiata.

Mansa Musa ruled a kingdom that had been penetrated by Arab trader/missionaries for over fifty years; the ruling group was already converted to Islam. Caravans from North Africa and the upper Nile valley traveled to the major towns of Timbuktu and Walata, where they exchanged their goods for the slaves and gold of Mali.

In 1324, at the height of his powers, Mansa Musa decided to obey the precept to make the *hajj* to Mecca and the holy places of Islam. He did so in a style that endured in the Muslim world's mythology for centuries. According to Egyptian accounts, he arrived in Cairo accompanied by a retinue of soldiers, courtiers, and slaves. One hundred camels carried almost a ton of gold dust in their packs; five hundred slaves each carried a staff of gold weighing six pounds!

Staying in Cairo before journeying on to the holy cities across the Red Sea, Mansa Musa spent and gave away so much gold that its price in Egypt declined to a record low and stayed down for a generation! Mali soon became known to the Christian world as well as the Muslim as "the land of gold" and began to appear regularly on the maps of the time with that appellation. The reputation of the country as a source of great wealth was established, and the fame of its king penetrated every mercantile network.

Mansa Musa returned from Mecca with several talented men from the Muslim East, who settled in Mali and contributed to the development of that society. In Timbuktu a Muslim *madresh* (religious school) gradually became a university, similar to the great Muslim center in Cairo. The king was a devout man, and his dedication to Islam resulted in an expansion of education in general. According to a later visitor, Timbuktu had more bookstores than any other type of mercantile establishment and as many scholarly resources as any other city in the Muslim world.

Under Mansa Musa, Mali reached its maximal territorial limits, stretching from the lower Gambia River on the bulge of West Africa well into present-

The East African Coastal Cities

The East African city-states also had a large hand in the gradual civilizing of the continent. Trade between the ports of Southeast Africa and India had been carried on since the first centuries C.E., both by Indians and by Roman ships that were built in Egypt and traveled down the Red Sea to the Indian Ocean. But the real entry of these places into history came after the Muslim advances of the seventh and eighth centuries. Then, a number of Arab traders settled in colonies all up and down the east coast, where they acted as middlemen between the peoples of the interior and the Arabs sailing down from the north.

Arabs and native peoples steadily intermarried, and the children of these unions were raised as Muslims, while many native peoples opted to convert to gain credibility as business partners. Persian and even Indonesian Muslims also came to the East African coast, adding to the melting pot of cultures there, with Islam serving as the one binding thread. By the fourteenth century, just before the appearance of the European explorers, a series of small kingdoms or city-states were established; some of these sophisticated, commercial states were controlled by the Bantu and some by colonies of Arabs ruling over the locals.

The slave trade was even more extensive in East Africa than in the Sudan. It was highly profitable to send slaves north and east into the Muslim territories where blacks were a novelty that would bring a high price. Some were taken as far as Southeast Asia. Ports like Mombasa, Kilwa, and Mogadishu (in present-day Kenya, Mozambique, and

day Nigeria to the south and east. This expansion was accomplished through a standing royal army, which overwhelmed its tribal neighbors. Berber and Arab traders crossing the difficult Saharan trade routes were obliged to seek Mansa Musa's protection. All merchandise sold in his kingdom carried a "sales tax," which went to the royal court. A royal bureaucracy composed of Muslim blacks administered the tax and judicial systems, apparently without challenge.

Most of the world's supply of gold in the fourteenth century came out of Mali. It supported a notably successful Arab-black mercantile empire that endured for two generations after Mansa Musa's death in 1332.

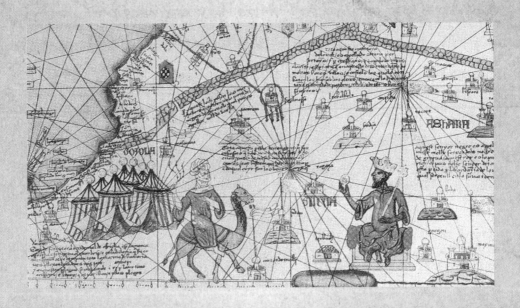

Somalia, respectively) had a rich trade in slaves, gold, ivory, animal skins, amber, and other highly desirable luxuries. When the Portuguese came at the end of the fifteenth century, they were amazed at the wealth and opulent lifestyles in these cities, among the upper class at least.

The culture and language of these cities are termed **Swahili,** a Bantu word meaning "mixed." The Swahili language has ever since been a sort of *lingua franca,* a common ground for communication among all black and Arabic East Africans.

South Africa

South Africa has a moderate climate and much good agricultural soil, which allowed it to develop under the Bantu-speaking peoples who reached it around the 700s. Reports by shipwrecked Portuguese sailors in the early 1500s indicate that Bantu speakers and Bushmen were living either in agricultural villages or in a hunting culture all across the tip of the continent. Archaeology reveals that iron had come into use as early as the fifth century C.E. Nevertheless, development seems to have been slow, and agriculture did not replace hunting as the normal source of food until around 1500, shortly before the Europeans first appeared.

The chief center of early civilized life in southern Africa was **Great Zimbabwe.** Today the ruins of what was once a large capital city and fortress can be seen in the present-day nation of Zimbabwe on the eastern side of the Cape of Good Hope. Great Zimbabwe was not discovered until 1871, and unfortunately, we know nothing of its history.

Nevertheless, its massive walls and towers make it the most impressive monument in Africa south of the pyramids. Apparently, it was built in the tenth and eleventh centuries by kings whose wealth and power rested on control of rich gold mines. The city flourished as a cultural and trading center until the fifteenth century, when it fell into decline for reasons not known. Perhaps the population exceeded the limits that a backward agriculture could supply, and the city was gradually abandoned; perhaps military conquest was threatened or achieved by enemies of the king—we cannot know.

❧ GOVERNMENT AND SOCIETY

The early African states were universally organized on the principle of kingship; they had no bureaucracies, but depended on the loyalties of subkings and chieftains to work the king's will. The king was a war chieftain, a member of a family or a lineage that enjoyed great prestige or was even thought to be sacred. He acted as intermediary between the living and the dead and was thought to be able to discern the wishes of the tribal ancestors through magic. His will was undisputed, unless and until he demonstrated himself to be incompetent in controlling his underlings. Then, he might be turned out or even killed.

The basic unit of society was not the family but the *clan or lineage,* a much larger unit supposedly descended from a common ancestor. Clans lived together in compounds that spread to make up a village. Within the village, it was customary for particular families to specialize in a trade or a business.

Several clans made up a tribe, and the tribe was the keystone of all government. Religion and government were closely linked, as in all early societies, but we know very little about the exact practices. Religious sacrifices were demanded before any important action was taken; they were generally led by the king in his capacity as high priest. Animism was universal before the influence of Islam began to be felt in the ninth century.

Arab travelers' accounts tell of the "shocking" freedom (to Muslims, at least) of women in African society in the tenth through thirteenth centuries. There was no attempt to seclude women or to restrict them from business dealings. Nevertheless, no women seem to have had access to the world of political power. When some of the African states fell under the sway of Islam, the public status of women declined. In a few instances, however, *matrilineal descent* (children taking the mother's clan name) and even *matrilocality* (husbands moving after marriage into the wife's family) provided exceptions to this rule.

❧ AFRICAN ART

In the absence of written languages, art was necessarily visual and plastic, and the sculpture and inlay work of all parts of sub-Saharan Africa have lately been much in demand in the Western world. Perhaps the most famous are the *Benin bronzes* from the West African kingdom of

■ These ruins of Great Zimbabwe in Africa are the most impressive monument south of the Great Pyramids in Egypt.

Benin, one of the successors to Mali. The highly stylized busts and full-length figures in bronze, gold, and combinations of metal and ebonywood are striking in their design and execution; obviously, they are the product of a long tradition of excellence. Many of these pieces were vandalized by Benin's enemies during the constant warfare that marred West African history; many others were carried off as booty by the early Europeans and have since disappeared. Enough remain, however, to give us some appreciation of the skill and imagination of the makers.

The same is true of the *wood sculptures* of the Kanem and Bornu peoples of central Sudan, who assembled a large kingdom between the twelfth and fifteenth centuries that lasted in one manifestation or another until the eighteenth century. The *ivory and gold work* of the Swahili city-states is also remarkable and is much appreciated, especially by Middle Eastern buyers. Some Muslims, unfortunately, looked upon this infidel artwork depicting human figures as a mockery of Allah and destroyed much of it, either in place in Africa or later in the countries to which it was transported.

⚜ EARLY EUROPEAN IMPRESSIONS

Unfortunately for the Africans' reputation, the Europeans arrived on the African coast at about the same time that the most potent and most advanced of the sub-Saharan kingdoms collapsed or were in decline. The causes of decline are not easily identified, but largely involved a lethal combination of internal quarrels among the nobility who served the king and conquest from outside, generally by other blacks or sometimes by Muslims. As a result, the European explorer-traders perceived the kingdoms as subservient and backward, an impression that was reinforced by the relative ignorance of the Africans in military matters and by the readiness of the African leaders to sell their people into slavery—a practice that had been commonplace for a thousand years, but which Christian teaching had by that time forbade in Europe.

The Europeans (largely, the Portuguese in the first century of contacts) concluded that the Africans were retarded in their sensitivity and degree of civilization and that it would not be wrong to take advantage of them. The Africans were perceived as not quite human, so what would have been a despicable sin against God and humanity had it been done back home in Lisbon was quite forgivable—perhaps not worth a second thought—here. Early attempts to convert the Africans to Christianity were quickly subordinated to business interests by the Portuguese and never attempted at all by their successors.

The tendency to see Africans as a source of profit rather than as fellow human beings was soon rationalized by everything from biblical quotations to Arab Muslim statements reflecting their own prejudices. The Portuguese attitude was shared by the Dutch, English, and other Europeans who came into contact with the Africans, often as slavers. The basis of European (and later American) racism directed against the dark skinned is to be found in these earliest contacts and the circumstances in which they were made.

Summary

Africa is a continent of vast disparities in climate and topography. Much of its interior remained shut off from the rest of the world until very recently, and little was known of its history either from domestic or foreign sources. While the Mediterranean coastal region and Ethiopia came to be included in the classical Christian world, the great Saharan desert prevented Christianity from reaching the African heartland. The Bantu-speaking inhabitants of the western forest regions gradually came to occupy most of the continent in the early centuries C.E. aided by their mastery of iron and of advanced agriculture.

In the tenth and succeeding centuries, the region of the savanna lands called the Sudan was the scene of several advanced kingdoms. An active trade across the desert was maintained with the northern Muslim regions. A slave trade was carried on in both western and eastern Africa between Arabs or Berbers and their black African partners. The tribally organized kingdoms were governed by a black Muslim elite in the Sudan and by one of mixed race along the eastern coast. Indeed, the religion and culture of Islam, carried by proselytizing Arab merchants into the interior, were the prime force for government organization in much of pre-European Africa.

Test Your Knowledge

1. Both agriculture and the use of iron in Africa spread
   a. from the Nile valley.
   b. from Arabia.
   c. from south to north.
   d. only after the coming of Islam.
2. An important population movement in Africa around the first century C.E. was the
   a. drift of Bantu speakers from West Africa to the south and east.
   b. movement of the Pygmies from central to northern Africa.
   c. settlement of North Africa by the Tuaregs.
   d. coming of the Portuguese to colonize the coast.
3. By about the fifth century C.E., the population of the western Sudan had increased dramatically as a result of
   a. immigration from the eastern regions.
   b. changes in climate.
   c. increased food production.
   d. the practice of polygamy.
4. Native African religions were
   a. polymorphic.
   b. animistic.
   c. agnostic.
   d. monotheistic.
5. The outside people having the greatest cultural influence on the kingdom of Ghana were the
   a. European colonists.
   b. Muslim Berbers.
   c. Ethiopians.
   d. Egyptian Christians.
6. Trade in slaves in both East and West Africa before the fifteenth century was
   a. commonplace.
   b. limited to extraordinary circumstances.
   c. controlled by the Muslims.
   d. never a large-scale operation.
7. The Swahili city-states were located
   a. on the northern coast facing the Mediterranean.
   b. on the Cape of Good Hope in the far south.
   c. near the Upper Nile.
   d. on the east coast.
8. Mansa Musa was
   a. the outstanding Muslim geographer who described early Africa.
   b. the wealthy African king who journeyed to Arabia on pilgrimage.
   c. the founder of the kingdom of Mali.
   d. the Arab missionary who converted the king of Mali.

Identification Terms

Bantu

Berbers

Ghana

Great Zimbabwe

Mali

Mansa Musa

savanna

Swahili

Timbuktu

Bibliography

Ade Ajaji, J. F., and I. Espie, eds. *A Thousand Years of West African History,* 1972. A good treatment of West Africa.

Bohannon, P., and P. Curtin. *Africa and Africans,* 1971. A very useful review of social institutions in precolonial days.

Davenport, T. R. H. *South Africa: A Modern History,* 3d ed., 1987. A well-recommended treatment of South Africa.

Fage, J. F. *A History of Africa,* 1978. Considered by many the best textbook treatment of the continent in its entirety.

Gemery, H. A., and J. S. Hogendorn, eds. *The Uncommon Market,* 1979. A collection of essays on the slave trade and its effects.

Hiskett, M. *The Development of Islam in West Africa,* 1984. Deals with Islam in the western and Saharan regions.

The Horizon History of Africa, 1971. Treats individual segments of the continent.

July, R. W. *Precolonial Africa: An Economic and Social History,* 1975. A very straightforward, readable account. Somewhat broader is the same author's *A History of the African People* 3d ed., 1980.

Manning, P. *Slavery and African Life,* 1988. Very detailed but provides a complete picture as it is now perceived.

Oliver, R., and G. Mathew, eds. *History of East Africa,* 1963. A well-recommended treatment of East Africa.

Trimingham, J. *Islam in East Africa,* 1974.

THE AMERICAS BEFORE COLUMBUS

c. 1500 B.C.E.–c. 300 C.E.	Olmec civilization
c. 300–c. 1300 C.E.	Mayan civilization
c. 300–c. 1100 C.E.	Toltecs
c. 1100–1500s C.E.	Incan civilization
c. 1300s–1500s C.E.	Aztec civilization

Like Africa, the Americas demonstrate a tremendous range of cultures and physical environments. The first inhabitants came into the Americas much later than humans appeared elsewhere in the world, perhaps as late as 20,000 years ago. They arrived by way of the then-existing land bridge across the northernmost Pacific, now called the Aleutian Islands. Slowly, they made their way down the Pacific coastal plain through North and Central America into the Andes.

By about 7000 B.C.E., the western edge of North and South America was supporting populations of Amerindians, who lived primarily by agriculture. Central and South America are the home of many of the world's basic farm crops, such as maize, beans, and squashes, which are all derived from native plants. By the arrival of the first Europeans in 1492, agricultural techniques were well advanced, and the crops were sufficient to support a very large population that was organized into states with highly stratified social structures.

✤ FIRST CIVILIZATIONS

Olmec Civilization

Uniquely, the earliest American civilizations did not locate in river valleys, but on soils of the elevated plateaus or the tropic lowlands, inland from the Caribbean Sea. The earliest we now know about (through archaeology, only) arose in what is now southern Mexico and bears the name **Olmec.** It existed between 1500 B.C.E. and about 300 C.E., when it was overwhelmed by enemies from the north, who then quickly adopted many features of the civilization they had conquered.

The Olmec were the human foundation of all other Amerindian civilizations in Central America. Olmec pottery and decorative ceramics have been found throughout Mexico and as far south as Costa Rica. Their main site thus far discovered, which is north of Mexico City, consists of a central fortified complex of governmental halls and religious shrines; from here, they ruled over a large number of peasant villages in the surrounding country.

The Olmecs' skill in stonework enabled them to build ceremonial stone pyramids, one of which reached 110 feet high. This Great Pyramid speaks of a degree of civilized organization and a ready supply of labor, which suggests that the Olmecs' agriculture must have been sufficiently advanced to support a large population. The Olmec had a

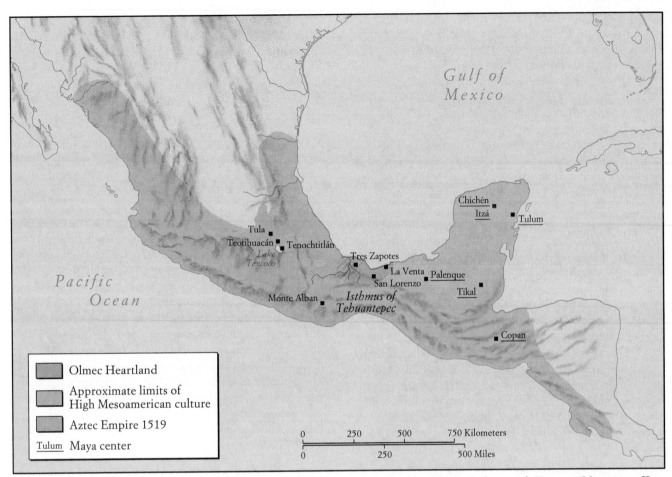

Gulf of
Mexico

Chichén
Itzá
Tulum

Tula
Teotihuacán
Tenochtitlán
Lake
Texcoco
Tres Zapotes
La Venta　Palenque
San Lorenzo
Tikal

Pacific
Ocean

Monte Alban
Isthmus of
Tehuantepec

Copan

Olmec Heartland

Approximate limits of
High Mesoamerican culture

Aztec Empire 1519

<u>Tulum</u>　Maya center

0　　250　　500　　750 Kilometers

0　　　　250　　　　500 Miles

⊙ **MAP 20.1　Mesoamerican Civilizations.** The Aztec empire was at its height when the Spanish arrived. Emperor Moctezuma II had extended Aztec rule to the south into modern Guatemala and Honduras. The Mayan cities of Palenque and Tikal were abandoned in the tenth century for unknown reasons, possibly failure of the food supply.

primitive form of writing and a number system, neither of which is understood, but which enabled them to survey and build a large number of massive edifices. A small elite group, including the priests of the official religion, had great powers, and the ruler was probably a hereditary king/high priest. Unfortunately, more than this is not known.

The Maya

Before or around 300 C.E., the Olmec civilization collapsed. After several centuries, their place as civilized leaders was taken by the Maya, who were the *most advanced* of all the Amerindians, and their mysterious demise as an organized society before the arrival of the Spaniards is a continuing problem for archaeologists and historians. The Maya had a *written language, a calendar, and an understanding of mathematics* that was far more

advanced than European mathematics in the twelfth century. The recent decipherment of some of the Mayan written language has enabled scholars to more accurately reconstruct the events portrayed in the rich pictorial images of Mayan stonework, although much remains obscure.

From about 300 C.E., the whole southern tip of present-day Mexico and Guatemala were governed by a hierarchy of Mayan cities, some of which contained several tens of thousands of people (see Map 20.1). But the large majority of the population were peasant villagers, and the whole population of the Mayan empire may have reached fourteen million—far and away the largest state under one government outside Asia at that time.

The cities seem to have been more religious/administrative centers than commercial/manufacturing centers. Trade was a relatively minor part of Mayan life, and the political and social power rested, as with the Olmec, in the hands of a hereditary elite who were very wealthy. The common folk seem to have been divided into freemen, serfs, and slaves, as in much of the ancient world. Sharp social divisions existed between the elite (who included both priests and artists) and the common people.

Religious belief was paramount in ordering the round of daily life. The ruling class included priests, who had magical powers given them by the gods. They also had access to the underworld, which seems to have been as fearsome as that of Mesopotamia. The jaguar—a species of great cat indigenous to the Americas—was particularly revered. Human sacrifices provided the rulers with companions on their journey to the next world.

For several centuries these cities and their satellite villages prospered; then, for reasons unknown they began to decline, and some had to be abandoned. A revival occurred about 1000 C.E. and lasted until about 1300, when the last Mayan site seems to have been finally abandoned. By the time Cortez arrived in the Valley of Mexico, the Mayan rulers and their achievements had been forgotten.

Their memory has been revived by the recent discoveries of giant basalt heads and whole figures, scattered about in the southern Mexican jungle, along with the ruins of great stone pyramids and temples in the Yucatán peninsula. These sites have now become major tourist attractions, especially **Chichén Itzá,** where a vast complex of Mayan buildings has been excavated. The pyramid form was almost the same as that of Egypt, and the mastery of stonework almost as complete. The Mayan ruins are an American version of Tel Amarna or Karnak, and it is not surprising that some anthropologists are convinced that a link existed between ancient Egypt and Mexico.

The Toltecs

During the same era when the Mayan civilization was reaching maturity, another high culture was appearing in the Valley of Mexico some hundreds of miles west of Yucatán. This was the civilization of the **Toltecs,** an Amerindian tribal federation that became famous among their neighbors both for crafts and for war. Their chief city was at **Teotihuacán,** in the northern part of the valley, and they had a later center at Tula. Historians believe that the populations of these cities may have reached 200,000—far larger than any European city. These cities also featured great religious monuments in the pyramidal form that was found all over Central America.

Around 700 the Toltecs were severely defeated by barbarians from the southwest, and the city of Teotihuacán was destroyed. Tula later replaced it, and the Toltecs managed to restore themselves to supremacy for a few more centuries until the 1100s. Then, they were finally overcome by new nomads, who eventually gave way themselves in the 1300s to the all-conquering *Aztecs.* This later people would build the great city of **Tenochtitlán,** which the Spaniards renamed Mexico.

✤ Aztec Rule in Mexico

In the space of two hundred years, the Aztec people converted themselves from nomad barbarians to the elite of a huge state embracing many millions of Amerindians. It was governed from a city that was the largest in the New World and one of the largest anywhere. These achievements were based on the foundation provided by earlier Amerindian civilizations, but the Aztecs themselves contributed many new characteristics.

The Aztecs were an extremely *militaristic people,* whose lives revolved around conquest. War was their reason for existence; it shaped their religion and imposed a social structure that was unique in America. The chief god was Huitzilopochtli, god of the sun at noon. To keep him in his proper place in the sky, thereby assuring that the crops would have the warmth they needed to grow, the sun had to be fed with human blood. Therefore, the Aztec religion featured frequent *human sacrifices* on altars in the middle of their great city. Some of these ceremonies were stagger-

■ This massive twenty-six ton disc reflects the Aztec view of the universe. The Aztec believed that there had been four previous worlds, and that they were living during the fifth and final one. At the disc's center is the sun god.

■ This mural of Teotihuacan recreates a portion of the huge city which consisted of over 5,000 buildings. Here, the pyramid of the sun is the center of activity.

ing in their bloodiness: thousands of victims, taken from other Indian tribes specifically for that purpose, were sacrificed at one time. Cannibalism was also a part of the ritual. The heart was cut out of a living victim's chest by priests wielding glasslike obsidian knives and then devoured by the Aztec nobility.

Researchers have suggested several explanations for these mass sacrifices. The theory that commands the most support is that it was a form of rule by terror; that is, the Aztec elite, led by their sacred emperor, tried to prevent rebellions by terrorizing the population into submission. According to this idea, the Aztecs were a sort of super-Assyrians, ruling their unfortunate neighbors by fear and random slaughter.

How long such a hateful rule could have lasted had the Spanish not arrived on the scene is an open question; we know from Aztec records that it had lasted about a century before the Europeans arrived in 1519. During that time, it had steadily expanded until it encompassed the center of present-day Mexico from the Atlantic to the Pacific and reached down into the former Mayan lands in Guatemala (see Map 20.2). The last emperor before the Spaniards came had greatly enlarged the domains he ruled.

Aztec Society

We know a good deal about the Aztec state and society, thanks to their pictographic records, some of which the Spanish preserved so they could learn more about their new subjects and control them more efficiently. At the top of the social hierarchy were the officials of the emperor who governed like feudal lords in the provinces conquered by the Aztec armies. They had earned their positions by distinguishing themselves on the battlefield and were rewarded by the emperor with great powers as judges, commanders, and administrators of a highly developed and complex provincial government.

Next came a class of warriors, who were continuously being recruited from the ordinary freemen. They had to prove themselves in battle by taking at least four prisoners for sacrifice. If successful, they were allowed to share in the booty of the Aztecs' constant warfare. The great majority of the Aztecs fell into the next category, ordinary free people who did the usual work of any society. They tilled the fields, carried burdens, built the buildings and roads, and so on. They might also be called for military duty in a pinch and thus shared in the essential purpose of the state.

At the bottom were the serfs, whose rights and duties were very similar to those of the medieval European serfs, and the slaves, who had been captured from other Indians or were victims of debt. If they were not destined for human sacrifice by the priests, Aztec slaves were often able to gain their freedom, and the majority of them actually did so, sooner or later.

The Aztecs also had a very large and powerful class of priests; the highest priests served as advisers to the

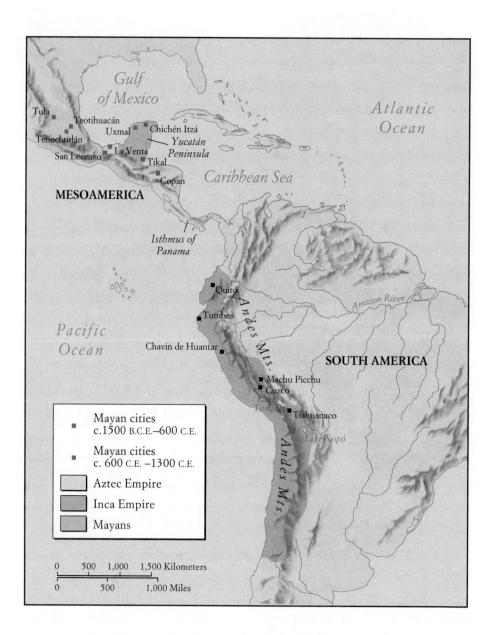

⊙ MAP 20.2 The Mayan, Incan, and Aztec Empires. The relative size of the three best known pre-Columbian states at their maximum extents is shown here.

emperor in his palace. The monarch himself was a quasi-divine person, who was selected by election from among the male members of the ruling family. The emperor at the time of the Spanish invasion of Mexico was *Moctezuma II* (see the Biography in this chapter). He resided with thousands of servants and officials in a palace complex dominating the center of Tenochtitlán (Mexico City), a town built on a lake bed drained by the Aztecs. Its thousands of dwellings were arranged along broad avenues and hundreds of canals; all focused on a huge central plaza, the present-day *Zocalo* in downtown Mexico City (see the Document in this chapter).The city's population is estimated to have been close to half a million,

and an intricate system of irrigation and drainage supplied the inhabitants with water. Among the refinements of Moctezuma's enormous palace were a library and a zoo.

The Aztecs had a fatal weakness, however; they were hated by their subjects. When the Spanish arrived, they soon discovered that the other Indians were willing to join with them to overthrow the Aztecs. In 1519, Hernando Cortez and 500–600 Spanish adventurers from Cuba were led to Tenochtitlán by their Indian allies. The Spanish were astounded at the city's size and beauty. Nevertheless, the empire's days were numbered.

Moctezuma II

c. 1466–1519

The great Moctezuma was about forty years old, of good height and well proportioned, slender, not very swarthy but of the natural color and shade of an Indian. . . . He was very neat and clean, and bathed once every day, in the afternoon. He had many women as mistresses, and he had two *caciquas* for legitimate wives. The clothes that he wore one day he did not put on again until four days later.

So begins the description of the Aztec emperor in the chronicle of the conquest of Mexico by Bernal Díaz de Castillo, an eyewitness.

We know about Moctezuma II, the last elected ruler of the Aztec empire, mostly through the accounts of his opponents. The early Spanish chroniclers sometimes describe Moctezuma as wise and brave, but most of the time they depict him as the brutal leader of a savage people. Modern historians, on the other hand, picture him either as an insecure individual, who was terrified by the supernatural, or as a warrior who overextended himself and proved unable to rise to the demands put upon him when the Spanish arrived.

Born about 1466, Moctezuma was elected to rule by the elders in 1502, when Aztec power was at its zenith. During the seventeen years of his reign, he established a despotic and oppressive government, which governed perhaps as many as fifteen million subjects through force and efficient use of a large army of occupation. Even by the standards of the other leaders of this aggressive people, Moctezuma spent a great deal of energy campaigning to enlarge his inherited empire and quell the rebellions that occurred periodically. Armies were sent on missions as far as present-day Guatemala and Honduras from the Valley of Mexico, the Aztec homeland.

Moctezuma continued the Aztec theocracy, which was organized as a loose confederation of tributary Indian states giving homage to the great city of Tenochtitlán. Fascinated by ceremony, the Aztec rulers separated all citizens and subjects into precise classes. No common folk were allowed to visit the court, and those who wished to see the emperor had to seek permission through an elaborate court bureaucracy. Hundreds of tax collectors, military commanders, accountants, judges, and other officials ran the day-to-day operations of government under the leadership of a supremely important priesthood. The Aztec emperor himself lived in great splendor in a magnificent palace in the center of Tenochtitlán, which was greatly admired by the early conquistadors under Hernando Cortez, who have left us descriptions of it.

Moctezuma's wars against his rebellious subjects created the conditions that allowed the greatly outnumbered Spanish to gain a foothold in Mexico after they landed at Vera Cruz in 1519. And his own religious heritage led him to a fatal hesitancy in dealing with the strangers who rode enormous "deer" (horses) and fired cannons and muskets at their opponents. Believing for a time that Cortez might indeed be the returning god Quetzalcoatl of Aztec legend, Moctezuma feared to confront him directly and tried instead to win his favor by showing him hospitality. Instead of using his huge advantage in numbers to do battle with the Spaniards, the emperor allowed them to take him hostage for the good behavior of his people.

Moctezuma saw too late that these "gods" were only daring buccaneers, whose sole interest was obtaining mastery over the Aztec lands and treasure. When the showdown finally came between the enraged residents of Tenochtitlán and the Spanish adventurers, Moctezuma's death may well have come at the hands of his own people, as the Spanish chroniclers have said.

Bernal Díaz de Castillo: *The Conquest of New Spain*

The long and eventful life of Bernal Díaz de Castillo (?1492–1580) spanned the entire period of the conquest of the Americas. When he was well into his seventies, he set down an eyewitness account of Hernando Cortez's expedition into Mexico (1519–1521); by then he was the last survivor of that expedition. In *The Conquest of New Spain,* Bernal Díaz not only gives us a very exciting account of the entire campaign against Moctezuma II and his successors but provides a unique description of the advanced civilization of the Aztecs and their capital city Tenochtitlán (now Mexico City) in the last years of their imperial glory. Bernal Díaz was no particular friend of the Indians, but it is plain that he was unexpectedly and deeply impressed by what the "savages" were capable of doing. He and the other Spaniards were amazed by the central market:

> On reaching the market place... we were astounded at the great number of people and the quantities of merchandise, and at the orderliness and good arrangements that prevailed, for we had never seen such a thing before.... Every kind of merchandise was kept separate and had its fixed place marked for it.
>
> Let us begin with the dealers in gold, silver, and precious stones, feathered cloaks and embroidered goods, the male and female slaves who are also sold there.... Some are brought there attached to long poles by means of collars around their necks to prevent them from escaping, but others are left loose.

> Next, there were those who sold coarser cloth and cotton goods and fabrics made of twisted thread, and there were chocolate merchants with their chocolate. . . .
>
> There were those who sold sisal cloth and ropes, and the sandals they wear, which were made of the same plant. All these were kept in one part of the market, in the place assigned them, and in another part were skins of tigers and lions, otters, jackals, and deer, badgers, and other wild animals, some tanned and some not. . . .
>
> There were sellers of beans and sage and other vegetables and herbs in another place, and in yet another they were selling fowls and birds with great dewlaps [i.e., turkeys, which the Spaniards had never seen]; also rabbits, hares, deer, young ducks, little dogs, and other creatures. Then there were the fruiterers; and the women who sold cooked food, flour and honey cakes and tripe.
>
> . . . I am forgetting the fisherwomen and the men who sell small cakes made from a sort of weed which they cut out of the great lake, which curdles and forms a kind of bread which tastes rather like cheese. They sell axes, too, made of bronze and copper and tin, and gourds, and brightly painted wooden jars. . .
>
> Some of our soldiers who had been in many parts of the world. . . said that they had never seen a market so well laid out, so large, so orderly, and so filled with people.

SOURCE: Translation by J. Cohen. *Conquest of New Spain,* by Bernal Diza de Castillo, © Penguin Classics Edition, Penguin Ltd.

✤ THE INCA

Another major Amerindian civilization existed far to the south of Mexico. In present-day Peru, in the Andes Mountains that run through the country, an extraordinarily talented people had constructed a militaristic empire, just as the Aztecs had done in Mexico. The title "Inca" really refers to the ruler of this empire, but it is also commonly used to refer to the tribal group that ruled the surrounding peoples and to the empire they created. Their rise to power began about 1200. The peak came just before the Spanish invasion; like the Aztecs, the Inca were under the constant pressure of keeping a large, hostile group under strict control.

This empire rested upon a dramatically increased food supply made possible by agricultural breakthroughs. The Peru Indians learned how to grow new crops and increase the yields of established crops by using fertilizer and metal tools. By so doing, they produced a food surplus big enough to support both a large army and a leisure class that devoted itself to government and religious duties.

Centered on the town of **Cuzco** in one of the high valleys that penetrate the massive wall of the Andes, the

Inca started bringing their immediate neighbors under their rule in the 1200s. By the mid-1400s, they had created a state that rested on the forced labor of the conquered peoples, who are thought to have numbered as many as twelve million. If this number is accurate, the Inca, like the Aztecs, ruled over more people than any European state at the time.

After conquering a new area, the Inca often deported the inhabitants, moving them from their native region to an alien place, where they would be entirely dependent on Cuzco's protection from resentful neighbors—a practice that is reminiscent of Assyrian (and early Roman) techniques of rule. Local chiefs were forced to take full responsibility for the obedience and good behavior of their people under Incan government. The taxes paid by the subjects were collected by an efficient administrative system. The Inca also established colonies among their subjects; the colonists helped to encourage the conquered people to transfer their loyalty to their new masters and also ensured that a military force would be available if needed to suppress a rebellion.

The Inca's impact on their subjects is evident from the linguistic changes that occurred. The variety of unwritten languages that previously existed among the South American Indians was supplanted (along the west coast) by the Incas' **Quechua,** now the official language of most Peruvians along with Spanish.

To unify their lands, the Inca built great roads running north and south both along the coast and in the mountains. They constructed irrigation systems, dams, and canals, and built terraces on the steep hillsides so crops could be planted.

One of the most magnificent achievements of Incan rule was *Machu Picchu,* a city in the clouds of the high Andes, whose ruins were discovered only in 1911 by an American. The Inca accomplished the awe-inspiring feat of moving thousands of huge stone blocks to build the walls of this fortress-city on a mountain top, in the absence of almost all technology (probably even without the wheel). No one knows why the city was built or why it was abandoned.

Incan Government and Society

Like most other ancient and premodern societies, Incan society exhibited sharp class divisions, with a small elite of so-called nobles at the top, under their semidivine king, the Inca, from whom all authority issued. A large army maintained obedience, and most of the rebellions against the Inca were, in fact, fraternal wars in which the rebel leader was a member of the imperial house. The Spaniards under *Francisco Pizarro* used one of these civil wars to great advantage when they arrived in 1533 to rob the gold of Cuzco.

The basic unit of both society and government was the *ayllu,* or clan. A village would normally possess two to four clans, headed by a male in the prime of life to whom all members of the clan owed absolute loyalty; he handled

■ Aztec codices are pictorial representations of rituals and customs of New World peoples. Creation myths, marriage rites, and sacrificial rituals are recorded on these tablets.

■ The Mayan civilization of present-day eastern Mexico was older than the Aztec civilization, but showed many similar characteristics. This seventh century palace at Palenque was uncovered from the jungle in the nineteenth century.

the clan's business dealings with outsiders. After conquering neighboring Indians, the Cuzco emperor broke up the old *ayllus* and replaced them with new ones based on place of residence, rather than common kinship. The head of the new *ayllu* was appointed by the emperor because of good service or demonstrated loyalty. He served the central government in about the same fashion as a feudal baron served the king of France; the ordinary people, organized in these new artificial clans, were his to do with as he liked, so long as they discharged their labor duty and paid any other tax demanded of them by the Inca in Cuzco.

Regimentation was a prominent feature of Incan government, but it also displayed a concern for social welfare that was unusual for early governments. In times of poor harvest, grain was distributed from the government's granaries to the people. Natural disasters such as flooding mountain rivers were common, and a system of central "relief funds" provided assistance for the areas affected. A sort of old-age pension was also in use, enforced by the central authorities. These features of the Incan regime have attracted much attention from modern historians who see in them a tentative approach to the welfare state of the twentieth century.

⚜ FALL OF THE INCA AND AZTEC EMPIRES

These assistance programs were not enough to win the loyalty of the Inca's subjects, however, because just as in Aztec Mexico, the Spaniards found many allies to help them overthrow the Cuzco government in the 1530s. Also, as in Mexico, the Spanish were immeasurably helped by the coincidence of their arrival with Indian expectations of the return of a white-skinned deity, who would be irresistible. Like Moctezuma, the Inca somewhat naively trusted the newcomers. Pizarro's band, which was even smaller than Cortez's, was able to demolish the Inca regime in a very short time in the Peruvian lowlands and valleys, although some of the imperial family and their officials escaped to the high mountains and attempted to rule from there for another thirty years.

The freebooters Cortez and Pizarro were ready to risk everything to win fortune and fame; they used every stratagem and played on every fear among the Indians. Their royal opponents were not used to such dealings and proved unable to counter them effectively. Within two years in both places, the huge wealth and vast territories controlled by the kings fell, like ripe fruit, into the hands of a few hundred bold men.

Summary

The achievements of the Amerindian civilizations are imposing in some respects, but paltry in others. When compared to the works of the Mesopotamian peoples, the Egyptians, or the Chinese, the relative absence of technological breakthroughs, the near absence of written documents, and the small number of permanent monuments make it difficult to get a clear view of the Amerindians' abilities. Also, the physical isolation of the American continent from other centers of civilization assured that the Amerindians did not benefit from outside stimuli—

what they produced was produced from their own mental and physical resources, so far as we can now tell.

Yet, the physical evidence that survives is certainly impressive. That the Inca could govern a huge empire without benefit of writing or the wheel seems to us almost a miracle. Yet it was done. That the Mayan pyramids in southern Mexico could soar upward of three hundred feet without benefit of metal tools or, indeed, any of the technological innovations of the Mesopotamians, Egyptians, and Hindus seems equally incredible. Yet it, too, was done.

The Amerindian civilizations are perhaps the most forceful argument against the diffusion theory of how human progress was effected. Unless the school of thought represented by Heyerdahl is correct, the Amerindians created their own world through their own, unaided, intellectual efforts. What would have been an admirable achievement under any circumstances becomes astounding if the Indians did these things alone.

Test Your Knowledge

1. South America is the home of which of these Amerindian civilizations?
   a. Aztecs
   b. Inca
   c. Maya
   d. Toltec
2. The overridingly important principle of Aztec society and government was
   a. cannibalism.
   b. war and its requirements.
   c. trade and the creation of wealth.
   d. art and excellence in its production.
3. The Aztec society at the time of the Spaniards' arrival
   a. was disorganized, impoverished, and illiterate.
   b. was without social classes.
   c. was tolerant and peaceable.
   d. revolved around the emperor and war.
4. The Aztecs believed that human sacrifices were necessary for the
   a. grain to ripen.
   b. gods to give them victory.
   c. moon to continue its orbit.
   d. rains to fall.
5. Inca civilization owed its origins to

   a. bronze weapons of advanced design.
   b. religious imperialism over neighboring tribes.
   c. agricultural advances that had increased the food supply.
   d. advances in industry and crafts.
6. All the following helped the Inca to build and maintain their empire *except*
   a. the Quechua language.
   b. the reformed *ayllu* or clan organization.
   c. their excellent road system.
   d. wheeled transport.
7. The most advanced, intellectually speaking, of the Amerindian civilizations, was probably that of the
   a. Maya.
   b. Inca.
   c. Toltec.
   d. Aztecs.
8. Moctezuma II was killed
   a. by the Spanish conquerors as an example to the others.
   b. by being starved to death in Spanish captivity.
   c. by a jaguar.
   d. by unknown hands.

Identification Terms

ayllu	Cuzco	Quechua	Teotihuacán
Chichén Itzá	Olmec	Tenochtitlán	Toltec

Bibliography

Katz, F. *The Ancient American Civilizations,* 1972. Smoothly written, this is an excellent introduction to a world that seems very far from our own. Deals with all the major civilizations in the Americas prior to the Europeans.

Von Hagen, C. W. *Realm of the Inca,* 1961 and *The Aztec: Man and Tribe,* 1961. Two of the most readable popular accounts.

On the ancient inhabitants of the Valley of Mexico:

Davies, N. *The Aztecs,* 1973.

Leon-Portilla, M., ed. *The Broken Spears: The Aztec Account of the Conquest of Mexico,* 1961. A special look at the Aztecs.

Weaver, M. P. *The Aztecs, Mayas, and Their Predecessors: Archaeology of Mesoamerica,* 1981. A very good study.

On the Inca in Peru:

Baudin, L. *A Socialist Empire: The Incas of Peru,* 1961. Another excellent scholarly survey.

Cobo, B. *History of the Inca Empire,* 1979.

Lanning, C. *Peru before Pizarro,* 1967.

On the Maya civilization:

Coe, M. D. *The Maya,* 1986.

Sabloff, J. *The New Archaeology and the Ancient Maya,* 1990.

Schele, L., and D. Freidel. *A Forest of Kings: The Untold Story of the Ancient Maya,* 1990.

Stuart, G.E. and G.F. Stuart. *The Mysterious Maya,* 1977. Well illustrated popular account.

INDIAN CIVILIZATION IN ITS GOLDEN AGE

320–480	Gupta dynasty
480 onward	India divided between North and South
c. 500–c. 800	Formative period of caste system
900s–1100s	Anghor Wat (Khmer kingdom) built
late 1100s–1400s	Delhi Sultanate in North India

Under the Gupta dynasty of kings (320–480 C.E.), India experienced a great flourishing of Hindu culture. At about the time that the Roman Empire was weakening, Hindu civilization stabilized. The caste system assured everyone of a definite place in society, and political affairs were in the hands of strong, effective rulers for a century and a half. Vedic Hindu religious belief responded to the challenge of Buddhism, and reformed itself so effectively that it began to supplant Buddhism in the country. Indian merchants and emigrants carried Hindu theology and Sanskrit literature to Southeast Asia, where they merged with native religions and cultures. Long after the political unity under the Guptas ended, India continued to produce scientific advances and technological developments that are still not fully recognized in the West. The invasions of Muslim Turks and others from the northwest redivided India into political fragments, but the essential unity of its Hindu civilization carried on.

✤ THE GUPTA DYNASTY

After the fall of the Mauryan dynasty in the 200s B.C.E. India reverted to a group of small principalities fighting one another for mastery. This was the usual political situation in India, where one invader after another succeeded in establishing only partial control, usually in the north, while the rest was controlled by Indian princes.

Not until 320 C.E. was another powerful native dynasty founded—that of the *Gupta* kings, who ruled from their base in the valley of the Ganges River on the east side of the subcontinent. They overcame their rivals to eventually create an empire over most of India, which lasted until about 500 C.E. when it was destroyed by a combination of internal dissension and external threats. The Gupta dynasty was the last Indian-led unification of the country until the twentieth century. Long after the dynasty had disappeared, memories of its brilliance remained. As time wore on and India remained divided and subject to foreign invaders, the Guptas and their achievements became the standard by which other rulers were measured.

The Gupta period is the first in Indian history for which more or less reliable firsthand accounts have survived. The most interesting is that of the Chinese Buddhist monk *Fa-hsien*, who visited India for a long period around 350 and left a diary of what he saw and did. According to his account, India was a very stable society, well ruled by a king who was universally respected because he brought prosperity and order everywhere. Nevertheless, despite such sources, we know relatively little about Gupta India compared to what we know of other world civilizations of this date. Indians did not begin to keep historical records until very late, so, aside from works such as Fa-hsien's, the main written materials we have are religious poetry and folklore. Even these are quite sparse, for the tradition of both Hinduism and Buddhism was *not literary, but oral.* What was important was memorized, generation after generation, but inevitably with some changes. It was not written down until much later, and then only in the current version, rather than the original. For this reason historians have few definite records to work with in India until perhaps as late as 1500 C.E. and must depend heavily on both archaeology and traveler's reports such as Fa-hsien's.

The arts flourished during the Gupta period, and several models in architecture and sculpture were developed that remained the standards of beauty for a long time. The greatest of ancient India's playwrights, **Kalidasa,** wrote a series of works that remain popular today. He was a major contributor to the upsurge of Sanskrit literature at this time. Sanskrit, the language of the Aryans, was now formally adopted as a sacred literary script.

The Gupta period also produced notable achievements in the sciences. Mathematicians worked out the concept of zero, which enabled them to handle large numbers much more easily; zero is closely associated with the decimal system, which was probably also an Indian invention. The "Arabic numbers" that are used universally today also originated in Gupta India, so far as historians can determine. Indian astronomers also made several breakthroughs in explaining eclipses of the moon and in calculating geographic distances.

The medical sciences developed significantly during and after the Gupta period. Pharmacy, surgery, and diagnosis of internal ills were Indian specialties, and it was not at all unusual for wealthy Muslims from the west to come to Indian doctors for treatment. In this way began the active interchange between the Muslim and Hindu medical men that so profited the Muslims in the period after 850 C.E. and was eventually passed on to the backward Europeans.

✤ POLITICAL FRAGMENTATION: SOUTH AND NORTH

After the fall of the Guptas, India divided at the Deccan plateau into two cultural/political regions, the South and the North (see Map 21.1). Each of these regions was further subdivided into many governmental units, but the units in each region shared enough common features that we can treat each region as a whole.

The *South* was inhabited by dark-skinned peoples whose languages came from the Dravidian language family, which was quite different from the Sanskrit of the North. The South was never brought under Gupta rule, and it was almost untouched by the northern invasions and developed a high culture of its own based on varieties of Hinduism that differed from the northern version. The faith penetrated here later but just as thoroughly. By about 1000 C.E., merchants from southern India were carrying on a lively maritime commerce in every kind of luxury goods and spices with South and Southeast Asia. These migrant adventurers spread as far as Java, carrying Hindu Indian culture with them. They had a deep cultural impact on various Asian peoples that persists to this day. Centuries of close contact with these Indian colonists (and sometimes with the colonists' Indian rulers) have left their mark on the beliefs and lifestyles of Vietnamese, Khmer (Cambodian), Indonesians, and Malays.

The South also saw a great flourishing of Hindu *sculpture and architecture* in the period 300–700 C.E. Both Hindu and Buddhist sects erected many massive stone *stupas,* round temples that stood in the midst of extensive complexes designed for worship and living quarters. In the interiors stood statues of the gods and goddesses and all types of holy shrines. Sculpture, mainly in stone but also in bronze, seems to have been the art form of choice among Hindus during most of their history. Some of their life-size and more-than-life-size work has survived to demonstrate the artists' skills. Even more impressive are the many panels and figures that decorate the exteriors of the *stupa* temples and show us the vigor and life-affirming nature of Hindu art. Much of it was erotic and gave rise to much embarrassment among nineteenth-century British colonial observers. What would have been considered pornographic in a Western context apparently had no such connotations to Indians, either then or now.

Some *painting* has also survived, most notably in the caves of *Ajanta* in the south. But the climate of tropical India is hard on paint, and little has survived, whether indoors or out. Like most architecture and sculpture of India's Golden Age, all paintings were inspired by religious legends and stories, very much as medieval European artworks were. The paintings portray gods good and bad and all sorts of demons taken from the very rich religious folklore.

Military and political affairs were more pressing in the *North.* There the major question was how to defend

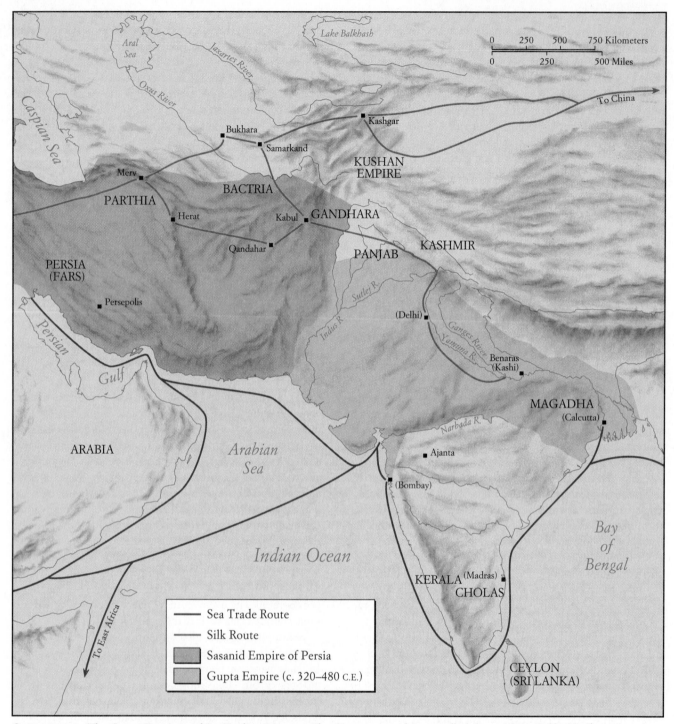

● **MAP 21.1 The Gupta Empire and Its Trading Partners.** The Gupta monarchs controlled the northern half of India and made much of the south into their vassals. Their merchants traded with Persia and Africa as well as the Malayan and Indonesian peoples to the east.

against the repeated and ever-fiercer assaults coming from the region of Afghanistan on the northwestern frontiers. From the eighth century, bands of Muslim raiders and would-be conquerors of the Hindu and Buddhist areas had harassed northwestern India. By the eleventh century, enough of the Turkic tribesmen of central Asia had become Muslims to constitute a fearsome fighting force under the leadership of Afghani *imams*. Defense against these raiders was haphazard despite the common danger. The princes of North India were as divided among themselves as those in the South, if not more so. As a result, the raiders were successful more often than not and were encouraged to attempt full-scale invasions starting in the late 1000s C.E. and continuing throughout the 1100s over the better part of the North.

In the late twelfth century, at the same time that Chinghis Khan was rising to power far to the north, a force of Turks and Afghans rode down into India from their strongholds in the Afghani hills. This time, they overwhelmed the defenders and came to stay. They created the Delhi Sultanate, based in their newly founded capital city at Delhi. This state continued to govern most of northern India for the next three hundred years and ultimately provided the historical foundation for the modern state of *Pakistan*.

Culturally speaking, the contacts between Islamic and Hindu/Buddhist civilizations were important. Indian

■ The candid emphasis on sexual attributes in Hindu sculpture was considered to be justified recognition of a source of human pleasure.

■ The Ajanta caves are beautifully decorated with painting, sculpture, and architectural features dating from second century B.C.E. to 478 C.E. The paintings, which cover the walls, depict many aspects and incarnations of the Buddha.

visitors to Harun al-Rashid's Baghdad trained Islamic scholars at the request of the caliph himself. When he fell seriously ill, Harun was cured by an Indian physician, who was then rewarded with the post of royal physician. Beginning as early as the 800s, many Arab merchants visited the west coast of India. Some of their travel accounts survive and are important sources of Indian history. So many resident Muslims lived in some of the coastal towns as to justify the building of mosques. In addition to carrying cottons, silks, and fine steel swords from India to the world of Islam, these merchants, traders, and other Muslim visitors took back the Indians' knowledge of algebra and astronomy and other cultural achievements.

Muslim conquest induced the final stage of the long decline of Buddhism in India. Much more than Hinduism, Buddhism was a proselytizing religion, like Islam itself, and the two competitors did not get along well. Where the Muslims were able to ignore Hinduism, they attacked Buddhism and its institutions, especially the numerous monasteries that were the heart of the faith. Already weakened by revitalized Hinduism, the Buddhist faith was now, in the twelfth century, wiped out in the land that had originated it. Its strong roots on the island of Sri Lanka, as well as in China, Korea, Japan, and much of Southeast Asia, guaranteed its continued existence, however.

✤ INDIA AND EAST ASIA

From the outset, the historical record in Southeast Asia has been very difficult to interpret largely because few written materials that are more than a few hundred years old survive. In the absence of records from native sources, the Chinese travel accounts mentioned earlier are supremely important, as are the infrequent archaeological remains of buildings and places of worship.

Nevertheless, it seems clear that the rulers of Southeast Asia encouraged Indian colonists because of what they could provide for the locals. Precisely what the colonists could provide or whether it was economic, religious, or artistic in nature is not certain in most cases. We do know that the Indians did not come as conquerors and that they constituted a tiny minority of the population at all times. Thus, it appears that the Indians were invited and that they were viewed as teachers. They were sought by the local ruling class because of their ability and willingness to show the locals some useful things, sell them desirable goods, or discuss attractive ideas. Thus, the Southeast Asians were *highly selective* in adopting Hindu-Indian culture.

Many aspects of that culture did not take root or were rejected outright. The caste system, for a major example, never spread into Asia outside India. Indian culture, though strong among the upper classes, never supplanted the native cultures of Southeast Asia, but mixed with them. Hindu beliefs are so flexible they could be easily absorbed by other systems, especially the animistic religions that were prevalent in Southeast Asia. Hinduism in this area is one of the world's most outstanding examples of *syncretic (mixed) religion and culture.*

The Indians had contacts with both land-based and maritime states to the east. The most important land-based peoples were the **Khmers** or present-day Cambodians. The Khmers had created an independent state as early as 400 C.E. and had extended it until it was a true empire by 800, reaching from the Indian Ocean to the Malay peninsula (see Map 21.2). Indo-Khmer contacts were extensive and fruitful. Buddhism was introduced, as well as Hinduism. The greatest Buddhist temple in the world, **Anghor Wat,** was built by the Khmers in the tenth century. It is still the world's largest building dedicated to religious purposes. Forgotten for seven hundred years after the conquest of the Khmer kingdom by the neighboring Thais, in the last thirty years it has become a major tourist attraction now that it has been reclaimed from the jungle that had buried it.

Hindu-Indian culture was also evident in the great maritime trading empire founded in modern Sumatra, a part of Indonesia, many centuries ago. *Srivijaya* was originally a city-state, but became a multinational empire in the 600s and later. In the eleventh century, a raid

■ The enormous temple at Angor Wat in Cambodia was the spiritual and political center of the ancient empire of the Khmer people. It was buried under jungle foliage for many centuries.

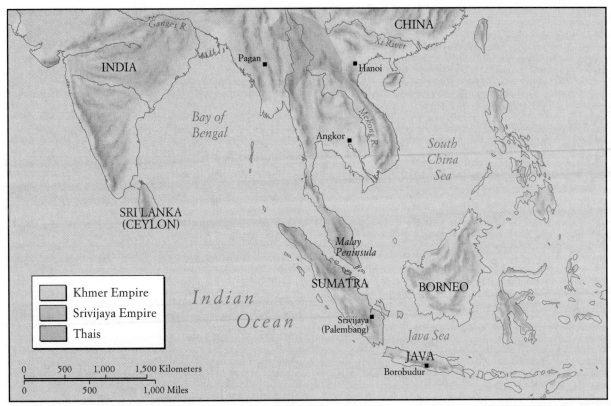

● **MAP 21.2 Southeast Asian Empires.** Of all the governments created to the east of India in the first millenium C.E. the most important were those of the Khmer and Thai peoples on the mainland and the Srivijayan monarchs in the island of Sumatra.

mounted from South India succeeded in capturing the city, and for the next two hundred years, it served as a base for the expansion of Indian commerce in the Indonesian islands. The Srivijayan upper classes became Hindu and through their fleets helped extend the ideas and value system of the religion into many parts of eastern Asia.

✤ HINDU DOCTRINES IN THE CLASSICAL AGE

The doctrines of Hinduism stem from a great mass of unwritten tradition, but also from three written sources: the Vedas, the **Upanishads,** and the **Mahabharata.** The Vedas (see Chapter 6) are lengthy epic poems, four in number, that were originally brought to India by the Aryans and were then "nativized" over many centuries. They deal with the relations between the many gods and their human subjects and relate tales of the god-heroes who created the earth and all that lies in it. The most significant is the **Rigveda,** which was written down in relatively modern times; it contains a great deal of information

about the Aryan-Indian gods and their relations with humans. The chief deities are *Indra* and *Varuna.* Indra, the god of war and revelry, resembles the old Germanic god Thor in several ways. Varuna was the caretaker of proper order in the universe, the first hint of an ethical element in Indian religion. Vedic religion was one of ritual and sacrifice, with priests playing the leading role.

The Upanishads are a series of philosophical speculations, apparently first produced in the eighth century B.C.E.; gradually, they were expanded by a body of poems that deal with the dilemma of being alive on earth as a partial, incomplete being. The Upanishads are a long step forward from the relatively unsophisticated rituals and anecdotes of the Vedas; with them begins the tradition of very involved speculation that became a characteristic of later Hindu thought. The Upanishads deal with the basic questions of finding reality and truth that have perplexed humans since the beginning of time, but in a peculiarly Indian fashion. They dwell on the deceptive nature of the material world and the necessity of getting beyond or behind it in order to confront reality.

An Excerpt from the Bhagavad Gita

Of the myriad Hindu sagas and poems, the Bhagavad Gita is the most popular and the best known among Westerners. It is a part of the larger poem Mahabharata, a tale of the distant and mythical past, when two clans fought for supremacy in India. Just before the decisive struggle, one of the clan leaders, the warrior Arjuna, meditates on the meaning of life. His questions are answered by his charioteer, who is the god Krishna in human disguise. Arjuna regrets having to kill his opponents whom he knows and respects, but Krishna tells him that his sorrow is misplaced because what Arjuna conceives of as death is not that:

> You grieve for those beyond grief,
> and you speak words of insight;
> but learned men do not grieve
> for the dead or for the living.
>
> Never have I not existed,
> nor you, nor these kings;
> and never in the future
> shall we cease to exist.
>
> Just as the embattled self
> enters childhood, youth, and old age,
> so does it enter another body;
> this does not confound a steadfast man. . . .
>
> Our bodies are known to end,
> but the embodied Self is enduring,
> indestructible, and immeasurable;
> therefore, Arjuna, fight the battle!
> He who thinks this Self a killer
> and he who thinks it killed,

> both fail to understand;
> it does not kill, nor is it killed.
>
> It is not born,
> it does not die;
> having been,
> it will never not be;
> unborn, enduring,
> constant, and primordial,
> it is not killed
> when the body is killed.
>
> Arjuna, when a man knows the Self
> to be indestructible, enduring, unborn,
> unchanging, how does he kill
> or cause anyone to kill?. . .
>
> Weapons do not cut it [the Self],
> fire does not burn it,
> waters do not wet it,
> wind does not wither it.
>
> It cannot be cut or burned;
> it cannot be wet or withered,
> it is enduring, all pervasive,
> fixed, immobile, and timeless. . . .
>
> The Self embodied in the body
> of every being is indestructible;
> you have no cause to grieve
> for all these creatures, Arjuna!

SOURCE: *Bhagavad Gita: Krishna's Counsel in Time of War.* B.S. Miller, trans., 1986. Bantam Books.

The Mahabharata is the world's longest poem. It contains about 100,000 lines, relating the exploits of the gods and some of their favored heroes on earth. The most popular part, known by all Hindus, is the **Bhagavad-Gita,** a segment in which the god *Krishna* instructs a warrior, Arjuna, in what is entailed in being a human being who strives to do good and avoid evil to his fellows (see the Document in this chapter).

The supreme deities of all Hindus are **Brahman, Vishnu,** and **Shiva.** Though individuals may worship many gods, all Hindus believe in the paramount importance of these three. In a very general fashion, Hindus are subdivided into the devotees of either Vishnu or Shiva. Brahman is the world-spirit, the source of all life and all objects in the universe. Brahman is roughly equivalent to the Christian God-the-Father, but entirely impersonal.

■ Indian influence is strongly visible in the great complex at Borobudur in central Java where Hindu and Buddhist beliefs merged.

Vishnu is the Preserver, a sort of Christ figure without the ethical teachings. He (or sometimes, she; the Hindu deities are often bisexual) has appeared in nine incarnations thus far in world history, and there will be a tenth. The most popular of all Hindu gods, Vishnu is particularly beloved in the form of Krishna, the instructor and protector of all humans.

The last of the Hindu trinity is Shiva, the Destroyer and also Creator. Shiva is best appreciated as the god of becoming, lord of both life and death. At times he/she is depicted as a beneficient bringer of joy; at other times he is the ruthless and irresistible destroyer, making way for new life to come.

Some of these beliefs, and particularly the position of the priests who interpreted them—the *brahmins*—were challenged by the Buddhists and the Jains (see Chapter 6). By the first century C.E. or thereabouts, Buddhism and Jainism had attracted the allegiance of a large part of the population, as the old Vedic Hinduism proved unable to match the appeal of these religions to persons seeking an ethical and emotionally fulfilling experience (see the Biography in this chapter).

Just as Buddhism gradually evolved into a ritualistic religion after the death of the founder, so did Hinduism respond to the Buddhist challenge by developing a much more formalist and ethical approach to the mysteries of eternal life and the gods who ordained human fate. The Upanishads and the Mahabharata are the embodiment of this response, which changed the old Hinduism into something quite different. This new Hinduism was capable of arousing strong adherence among ordinary souls by giving them a meaningful guide to moral and ethical belief.

Both Buddhism and Hinduism in time evolved into several subdivisions, or sects, which worshiped somewhat differently and had different gods and prophets. All of these are notable for their tolerance toward others; in contrast with the Western religions, they do not assert that there is but one true path to heaven.

✦ THE CASTE SYSTEM

The overwhelming majority of Indians gained their daily bread from farming, perhaps even more so than elsewhere. The villages, not the few towns and cities, were the vital center of Indian life. These villages changed very little over the centuries.

In this period, India was not yet suffering from overpopulation and attendant famine. The average man was a free landowner, who worked a small farm located near his family village, which he had inherited and would pass on to his eldest son. Rice was the most important crop, as in most of southern Asia, and the huge labor demands this crop imposed determined many aspects of life in Indian rural society. The cycle of rice planting and harvesting was the fundamental calendar. Water was crucial for the rice, and the control and distribution of water were the source of immense controversy—and sometimes war. With its emphasis on irrigated agriculture and the resulting impacts on other aspects of life, India strongly resembled ancient Mesopotamia.

By the Gupta period, the caste system was supreme in the villages. At the bottom were the outcastes, or untouchables, who were condemned by tradition to a marginal existence as buriers of the dead, dealers in hides, and slaughterhouse workers. Above them were several dozen varieties of more honorable trades and merchants, each of which was a more or less closed group with its own (unwritten) rules of conduct and religious practice (*dharma*). The system underwent its main development in

Mahavira Vardhamana

540–470 B.C.E.

Not all Indians are Hindus; here and there in that vast subcontinent live small colonies of other believers, some of whom preceded the sixth-century arrival of the Christians in India by many centuries. Foremost among these are the Jains, who are concentrated in the province of Gujarat, particularly among the members of the mercantile castes. Though not numbering more than a few million, they have exercised an influence on Indian spiritual life that far exceeds their numbers.

The Jain religion owes its origins to the work of a sixth-century B.C.E. sage named Vardhamana, later given the title of *Mahavira* or Great Hero. He lived from about 540 to 470 and was thus a contemporary of the Buddha, with whom he seems to have had some personal contact. Both men were members of the *kshatriya* caste and, like others of that warrior-governor grouping, resented the exclusive claims of the *brahmins* to the priestly functions. Animal sacrifice played a major role in the *brahmins'* Hinduism, and both the Buddha and Mahavira rejected it as inappropriate.

Mahavira later took this rejection to its ultimate form: he and his followers made every possible effort to avoid any form of violence to other creatures, even when that nonviolence represented death or danger to themselves. This doctrine of *ahimsa* was the outstanding characteristic of Jainism in Mahavira's day and remains so to the present.

Mahavira's background strongly resembles that of Siddartha Gautama, the Buddha. He was born into a rich family, but began to question the emptiness of his moral life when he was in his twenties. At age thirty, he abandoned his family to become a wandering seeker. Adopting an extreme asceticism (such as the Buddha tried and ultimately rejected), he even dispensed with clothing, preferring to wander naked through the world begging food and sleeping in the open.

After twelve years, he felt he had cleansed himself of worldly ambitions and was qualified to teach others. He preached the Five Great Vows: no killing under any circumstances; no untruth; no greed; total chastity; and no restrictive attachments to any person or object. Certainly, few could maintain these vows fully, but they were meant to be goals that one strived for and did not necessarily attain in one lifetime.

In the present day, Jains often wear gauze masks to avoid inadvertent intake of minute insects and constantly sweep their paths to avoid stepping on some tiny animal or plant. Bathing and moving about in the dark are avoided for the same reason. They set up hostels where they bring sick and aged animals, allowing them to die in peace. And they believe that voluntary starvation is the most admirable death once one has reached a state in which following the Great Vows is no longer possible.

Jainism strongly resembles the other great Eastern faiths in its division of the universe into soul and nonsoul and in the absence of a Creator God from whom humans receive moral instruction or commands. Like Hinduism and Buddhism, Jainism accepts reincarnation and the concept of *karma,* with the accompanying striving for liberation from an earthly existence, *moksha.* Unlike Buddhism, it rejects any form of proselytization and sees other religions as legitimate, but noncompetitive. The emphasis on *ahimsa* is its distinguishing mark, and through that pathway the teachings of Mahavira have had an important effect on Hindu and Buddhist belief. Mohandas Gandhi, the father of modern India and the teacher of worldwide nonviolent political action, is the outstanding modern example.

the period after the fall of the Gupta dynasty, from about 500 to about 800 C.E. By the latter date, most of the many castes we know in modern times were in existence.

The caste was not only a social organization; it also had strong *economic foundations.* For example, while the goldsmiths' caste was high ranking, it was considered desirable to marry into it not so much because it offered social advantages as because it made its large credit facilities available to any of its members. This prospect was so attractive that many people in higher castes would gladly marry off one of their children to a goldsmith. Castes were also *geographic* in nature: the members of a caste that specialized in money lending in Calcutta, for example, were not members of a caste that did the same work in Delhi and could be higher or lower on the caste ladder.

Castes and the caste system were very complex. They were the social cement that held the nation together; yet, at the same time, they created permanent separations between Indians—separations that exist to the present. The modern Indian constitution makes no provision for caste, and all Indians are supposedly equal before the law. Yet the old categories persist, especially in the villages where about 80 percent of the population of modern India still live.

❖ SOCIAL CUSTOMS

For Indians as for most early peoples, blood ties were the basis of social life. The extended family was universal: in-laws, cousins, and second and third generations all lived together under the same roof or in the same compound. Authority was always exercised by the oldest competent male. Polygamy, that is, several wives, was common, as was concubinage for those who could not afford another wife. Children, especially the oldest boy, had an honored place and were often pampered.

Females were clearly and unequivocally subservient to the male. Women were expected to be good wives and mothers and to let the husband decide everything that pertained to affairs outside the house. Marriage was arranged very early in life by the parents of the bride and groom. As in most societies, marriage was primarily an economic and social affair, with the feelings of the individuals being distinctly secondary. Ideally, the girl was betrothed (formally engaged) immediately after coming into puberty, at about age thirteen or fourteen, and given into the care of her much older husband soon after. The reality usually differed, however, as many families began to betroth children as young as one to two years of age to assure they would have proper partners, always within the caste. The actual wedding did not take place until both parties were at least at the age of puberty, however. The wife was to be the faithful shadow of her husband and the bearer of children, preferably sons. A barren wife could expect that her husband would take additional wives to assure the continuance of the family name, much as

among the Chinese. Divorce was very rare among the upper castes; we know little about the others.

There is considerable evidence that in early times Hindu women, at least in the upper classes, had more freedoms than in other ancient societies. The Rigveda, for example, makes no mention of restricting women from public affairs. And some of the numerous sacred texts were composed by women. But later this freedom declined. In the Mahabharata epic, composed about 400 B.C.E., the female's status is generally inferior to any male. The veiling of women among Hindus began with the Muslim conquests in the twelfth century. From that time onward, the Hindu population began to seclude respectable women and treat them as the property of fathers and husbands.

The position of widows was especially pitiful. A widow was expected to be in permanent mourning and never to remarry. She was looked upon with disdain, even by her relatives, and as the bringer of bad luck. No wonder that some women chose to follow their dead husbands into voluntary death through **sati,** the ritual suicide of a wife after the death of her husband, which was so shocking to Westerners. Actually, few widows, even in the priestly castes that were supposed to be a model to others, ever went so far in their devotion. But on occasion, a widow did fling herself into the flames of the cremation pyre, which was the usual way for disposing of bodies in India.

Sexuality

One of the attributes of Hindu culture that is noted by almost all foreigners was its readiness to accept all forms of pleasure that the day might bring. In sharp contrast to Jewish and Christian suspicion of the senses' delights, Hinduism taught that human beings had a positive duty to seize pleasure where they might, so long as *dharma* was not violated. This was particularly the case in terms of sexual matters, which were given prominence in the famous *Kama sutra,* composed sometime before the first century C.E. as a treatise on one of the four spheres of Hindu life.

Prostitutes were as common in Indian life as elsewhere. Many were attached to the temples, where their services were offered to the donors. Others were similar to the Greek *hetairae,* educated and artful women who served the upper class and held a position of general respect. Although the sacred texts denounced prostitution as being unworthy, the attitude of the ordinary man and woman was apparently more flexible. The Indian male's attitude toward women was marked by a very strong duality: woman is both saint and strumpet, to be cherished and to be guarded against. The great goddess Kali, sometimes pictured as a maternal guardian, sometimes as a demonic destroyer, is the classic example.

Summary

India, in its golden, or classical age (which was much longer than the classical age of the Greeks or most other peoples) saw the slow evolution of a civilization that was centered on the quest for understanding the relation between the earthly and the unearthly, between material reality and spiritual reality. Written history is scarce until modern times due to the predominantly oral culture. We know that the Gupta dynasty was a particular high point; after it collapsed in the fifth century C.E., the subcontinent broke up into political fragments, often ruled over by non-Indians.

North and South went their separate ways, though they were still linked by the Hindu faith. Migrants from the South into Southeast Asia established a strong Hindu presence there among the upper classes. In the North, waves of Afghani and other Turkic peoples eventually were able to conquer the natives in the twelfth century and set up a Muslim sultanate at Delhi.

Various subdivisions of Hinduism were continuously evolved by the holy men who gave India's masses their leadership. But as a general rule, their doctrines placed much more emphasis on the spirit and the world to come than was customary in either China or the West. These differences were to be major hindrances to mutual understanding when the West eventually came into extensive contact with the Indians.

Test Your Knowledge

1. Hindus believe that the Vedas
   a. are sacred texts that introduced a caste system of society.
   b. are a remnant of the Aryan days that are no longer relevant.
   c. must be studied in old age.
   d. are forgeries by Westerners.
2. The best known and most beloved Hindu scripture is the
   a. Rigveda.
   b. Upanishads.
   c. Bhagavad Gita.
   d. Sangha.
3. A peculiar facet of Indian civilization was its
   a. lack of interest in mathematics.
   b. avoidance of the pictorial arts.
   c. slowness in producing a literary culture.
   d. strong tendency toward political centralization.
4. The major source of foreign troubles for India has been
   a. its sea frontiers to the east.
   b. its borders with China.
   c. its resident colonies of foreign traders.
   d. its frontier with Afghanistan.
5. Southeast Asians experienced Hindu culture
   a. as a result of Indian conquests.
   b. in a selective and adapted fashion.
   c. mainly among the lower classes.
   d. both a and b.
6. The religion that suffered most severely from the Muslim Turks' invasion of India in the twelfth century was
   a. Christianity.
   b. Hinduism.
   c. Buddhism.
   d. Jainism.
7. The Jains are especially concerned to
   a. avoid killing any creature.
   b. avoid being shamed by others.
   c. spread their religion.
   d. be seen as superior to Hindus.

Identification Terms

Anghor Wat	Kalidasa	Rigveda	Upanishads
Bhagavad Gita	Khmers	*sati*	Vedas
Brahman	Mahabharata	Shiva	Vishnu

Bibliography

Akira H. *A History of Indian Buddhism from Sakyayuni to Early Mahayana,* 1990. A survey of the fortunes of the religion in its first millennium.

Auboyer, J. *Daily Life in Ancient India,* 1965. Covers ordinary life. See also some chapters in Basham below.

Basham, A. L. *The Wonder That Was India,* 1954. Remains very informative for this period, as well as earlier.

Bussagli, M. *5000 Years of the Art of India.* n.d. Perhaps the best illustrated of the histories of Indian art.

Oxford History of India, 4th ed., 1981. A source of general information on India's long history.

Rowland, B. *The Art and Architecture of India: Buddhist/Hindu/Jain,* 1970. The massive impact of Buddhism on Indian art and culture is outlined in Chapters 6–8.

Spear, P., and R. Thapar. *A History of India,* 1966. Covers the period from about the first century B.C.E.

Wales, H. G. *The Making of Greater India,* 1974. Goes into the colonizing and cultural diffusion activities of Indians in Southeast and East Asia.

CHAPTER 22

EMPIRE OF THE MIDDLE: CHINA TO THE MONGOL CONQUEST

The tremendous vitality and flexibility of Chinese civilization in the 1,500 years we examine in this chapter have no match in world history, anywhere. The longest-lived continuous political organism in the world, China was in these years able to combine the stability of an Egypt with the adaptability of a Japan. The government centered on the person of an emperor who, though by no means divine, was able to inspire the loyalty of a great many talented and ambitious servants in his bureaucracy—the world's first based on merit rather than birth. When his regime was working as designed, the life of the common people was about as good and secure as ever seen in the ancient world. Prosperity was widespread; cities thrived under the imperial administration while the villages were secure. When the regime broke down, however, the country fell into anarchy with cruel results for all. But for most of these 1,500 years, anarchy was held at bay, and the arts and sciences prospered.

❖ THE QIN EMPEROR: FOUNDATION OF THE STATE

The last years of the Zhou dynasty (see Chapter 7) were a sad tale of governmental collapse and warring feudal lords. By about 500 B.C.E., effective central government was nonexistent, and a long period of struggle known as the **Era of the Warring States** ensued until 220 B.C.E. It is significant that many of the outstanding philosophical contributions of Chinese thinkers came during this period: Confucian, Daoist, and Legalist. All aimed at restoring proper order to a world gone astray.

The relatively small northwestern state of Qin (Ch'in) adopted the Legalist doctrines wholeheartedly in the mid-200s (see Chapter 7). Guided by them, the Qin ruler managed to reunify the country by a combination of military force and administrative reorganization. The era of feudalism was over, permanently. The general principles which guided Qin rule could still be traced in Chinese government until the twentieth century. Even the name of the country in Western languages comes from Qin.

Although the king of Qin (246–221 B.C.E.) and later **First Emperor** (221–210 B.C.E.) ruled all China only eleven years, he made an imprint that was to last, as he boasted, "ten thousand generations." Shih Huang-di, as he was called, was a man of tremendous administrative gifts and huge personality defects. Both were felt by his subjects. His generalship overwhelmed the rival Chinese

■ **The Great Wall.** Taken in the vicinity of Beijing, this photo shows several of the guard houses/redoubts which were placed at close intervals along the Wall. This section of the fortifications has been reconstructed in modern times.

states. In only nine years (230–221 B.C.E.), the six largest of them fell to Qin armies or surrendered. At once the process of centralization got underway on ruthless Legalist lines. Guided by the minister Li Si (Li Shu), the emperor set out to make his rule irresistible and eliminate the entrenched feudal aristocracy. The country was divided into counties and provinces administered by an efficient bureaucracy. The emperor fixed weights and measures, made the size of the roads uniform so that all carts would fit the ruts, and introduced the first standard units of money. The system of writing was standardized so effectively that it is almost the same in the twentieth century as it was then.

The disconnected fragments of walls put up by various princes in the north and northwest were unified into the first version of the *Great Wall* for defense against the constant series of barbarian invaders from Mongolia. A whole list of other massive public works were started, including the tremendous imperial palace at Sian and the emperor's tomb in which over seven thousand life-sized clay soldiers were buried with him. (They were recently discovered and dug up.) Under Shih Huang-di China expanded to both north and south. The region around Guangzhou (Canton) was brought under his control; it was to be China's premier port for many centuries to come. First contacts were made with the Vietnamese and with several other civilized and less civilized peoples to the west.

■ **Warriors from the First Emperor's Tomb.** The discovery of the tomb of Shih Huang-di, the First Emperor at Sian in 1974 revealed the terra cotta statues of over seven thousand warriors buried with him. Armed with spears, swords, and bows, and presumably meant as a body guard in the next world, each of the warrior statues has individual features taken from living models.

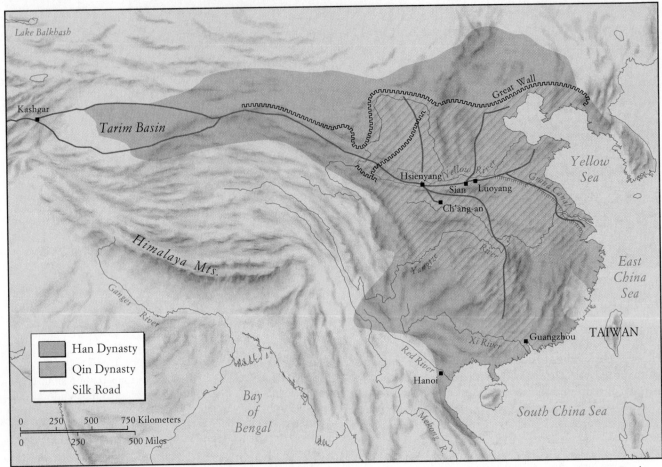

⦿ **MAP 22.1 The Qin and Han Empires.** The Han Empire greatly expanded the borders established by the Qin emperor. By the mid-Han period, China's extent westward reached well into central Asia.

The First Emperor's reign also had its negative side. Convinced of the inherent evil of human nature by his Legalist principles, Shih Huang-di apparently became paranoid and engaged in torture and other harsh treatment of his subjects and officials. He especially hated the doctrines of Confucius, which he regarded as a menace to his style of autocratic rule, and ordered a *burning of the books* in a vain attempt to eradicate the Confucian philosophy from Chinese consciousness, an episode deeply resented by later generations. Shih Huang-di died of natural causes in 210, but the cruelties and heavy taxation that marked the First Emperor's reign assured that his weaker successor would not last long as ruler. His overthrow in 206 was followed by one of the most successful of all the Chinese dynasties, the **Han dynasty,** which lasted until 220 C.E.

Han rule occurred almost simultaneously with the Roman heyday, and these two great empires of the East and West had other similarities as well. Both were basically urban in orientation, though the population remained heavily rural and peasant. Both depended on a nonhereditary officialdom to carry out the distant imperial court's will; both taxed the peasants heavily and made themselves vulnerable to the people's hatred as the central power began to weaken; both collapsed under the combined impact of invading foreign barbarians and widespread internal revolts.

⚜ THE HAN DYNASTY, 202 B.C.E.–220 C.E.

Even more than Shih Huang-di, the Han rulers greatly expanded the Chinese frontiers west, north, and south.

Under them, China took on the geographical boundaries that it has retained ever since except for the much later conquest of Tibet. These conquests brought the Chinese out of their isolation and into contact with the rest of the world for the first time. In the Han period, the Chinese traded with Indians and even Romans, directly and through intermediaries. Chinese commercial contacts soon expanded into cultural influence upon the Japanese, Koreans, and Vietnamese. Everywhere north of India and east of Burma, the "men of Han," as the Chinese called themselves, became the controlling factor in military, political, and commercial life.

The Han dynasts were not revolutionaries in any sense. They kept what the Qin had done to assure the state's existence, while relaxing the strictness and brutality that had made the First Emperor hated. The restrictions against Confucianism were thrown out, and the Han rulers in fact adopted *Confucius as the quasi-official philosopher* of the regime.

This was a changed Confucianism, however, with more emphasis on the obedience owed by the children to the father, that is, by the people to the government. The person of the emperor was given a sacred aura by the renewed emphasis on the "mandate of Heaven," the theory that the gods approved the emperor and all his actions until they showed otherwise. They showed otherwise by allowing the imperial armies to be defeated by the barbarians, by allowing rebels to succeed, or by permitting the provincial administration to break down. In that way, the path was opened to a new dynasty's coming, as the mandate of Heaven was being transferred to more competent hands. Using this logic, Chinese philosophers and political figures maintained the unbroken legitimacy of government, while recognizing the fairly frequent and violent overturns of individual rulers.

Arts and Sciences

Under the Han rulers, *arts and letters* experienced a great upsurge in quality and quantity. *History* came into its own as a peculiarly congenial mode of understanding the world for the Chinese, who are perhaps the globe's most historically conscious people. Records were scrupulously kept, some of which have survived in the scripts of the noted historian Ssu-ma chien and the Pan family of scholars dating from the first century C.E. As a result, we know far more about ancient China than almost any other part of the civilized world insofar as official acts and personages are concerned. History for the Chinese, of course, was the

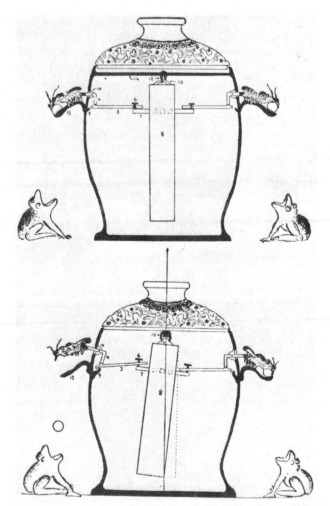

■ **A Chinese Seismograph.** Based on a close description of the original, this sketch shows one of the eight dragons along the outer edge of a bronze vase dropping a ball into the mouth of a ceramic frog below. Inside the vase is a delicately suspended weight which responds to the earthquake by shifting, and thus opening the mouth of the dragon.

record of what the uppermost 1 percent did and thought—the peasantry and other ordinary folk were beneath consideration as a historical force.

Mathematics, geography, and astronomy were points of strength in Han natural science, all of which led directly to technological innovations extremely useful to Chinese society. Some examples include the sternpost rudder and the magnetic compass. The Han period saw the invention of paper from wood pulp, truly one of the world's major inventions. By about the fifth century C.E., paper had come into common usage, paving the way for the invention and use of wood-block printing.

Medicine was a particular interest of the Chinese, and Han surgeons made the first significant advances since ancient Egypt and Babylon, while developing a pharmacology that was more ambitious than even the later Muslim one. It was also during the Han that acupuncture first entered the historical record. Despite the persistence of superstition and folk medicine, a strong scientific tradition of healing through intensive knowledge of the parts of the body, the functions of organs, and the circulation of the blood was established during this period. This tradition has endured and made China one of the permanent world centers of the healing arts.

In the *fine arts,* China continued to produce a variety of metallic and ceramic luxury items, which increasingly found their way into the Near East and even into Rome's eastern provinces. The production of *silk* was both an economic asset of the first rank and a fine art; for nearly a thousand years, the Han and their successors in China maintained this monopoly, until the Byzantines were finally able to emulate them. Bronze work, jade figurines, and fine ceramics were particularly notable among the

plastic arts, while poetry, landscape painting, and instrumental music figured prominently as part of the intellectual equipment of the Chinese educated class.

The Economy, Government, and Foreign Affairs

The Han period also saw major advances in *economic affairs.* Canals were built, and the road system was extended to the south and west, improving communication and commerce. In the Chinese scale of values, merchants did not count for much: they were considered to be more or less parasites who lived off the work of the tillers of the land and had none of the social prestige of the government officials and wealthy landowners. But they were still recognized as vital to the well-being of all and were seldom persecuted or exploited as in some other civilizations. The urban markets were impressive: in both the variety of goods and the number of merchants, they excelled other contemporary civilizations, including Rome.

Iron came into common use during this period, greatly aiding the expansion of *agriculture.* The increased availability of iron allowed new lands in the north and northwest to be plowed. An improved horse harness was developed, enabling Chinese farmers to make much better use of the animal's strength; this idea would not reach the West for another six centuries. Animal fertilizer and crushed bones (phosphate) were applied to the land systematically. Through such methods, Chinese agriculture became the most productive in the world. The peasantry normally produced enough food for a steadily growing urban population, as well as themselves. The horrible famines that came to be common in Chinese history are a later occurrence.

Han government was more complex than anything seen earlier in China. The government functioned through the bureaucracy, whose members were chosen by a written examination on the principles of correct action derived from Confucian teaching. To be eligible to take the final examination in the capital, candidates had to pass several previous tests and be recommended by their teachers at all levels. This *meritocracy* was designed to bring the best talent to the service of the central government, regardless of social origin. A hereditary nobility was not allowed to develop. The **mandarins** (scholar officials) of China were to give generally good service to their country for most of the next two thousand years.

Han China also achieved some notable successes in *foreign affairs.* Again and again, barbarians like the Toba,

■ This strikingly true to life statuette is from the Han Dynasty. It shows the ability of Han artists to work with every day topics with equal skill as they employed in the fine arts.

the White Huns, and others issuing out of the great reservoir of nomads in northern Asia (the present-day Siberian plains) were successful in wresting a piece of the Han domain away, only to be gradually assimilated and become upholders of Chinese civilization. Unlike India and the Middle East, China quickly absorbed its nomadic invaders.

Peaceful contacts were made with India by traders and Buddhist monks; like the devout trader Fa-hsien (see Chapter 20), the Buddhists wished to learn more about the religion in the land of its birth. In the first century C.E., a Chinese trade mission was sent to make direct contacts with the Romans in the Red Sea area. It reported back to the Han rulers that the Westerners had little interest in China. The Chinese attitude that China had what the West wanted but the West had little of interest to the Middle Kingdom became steadily more rooted in the upper classes mind as time wore on. Indeed, this was generally true, at least up to about 1500 C.E. But when this belief was no longer true, it proved very difficult or impossible to change. It then turned into the sort of stagnant defensiveness that would also handicap the Muslim world in the face of the aggressive European challenge.

Even the Han experienced some difficulties on occasion. The enormous building projects started by the emperors, or continued from the Qin period like the building of the Great Wall, imposed heavy burdens on the common people. The bane of all Chinese governments, a rebellious peasantry, began to make itself heard from in the first century C.E. A reforming emperor, who in some ways resembled Rome's Augustus Caesar in his vision of the state, was killed before he could meet his goals. The result was an interval of chaos before order could be restored and the Later Han dynasty established in 25 C.E.

The End of the Dynasty

In time, following the inexorable cycle of Chinese dynasties, the Han broke down into anarchy, with warlords and peasant rebels ignoring the weakened rulers. For a time the Era of the Warring States was replicated; this time, though, there were only three contestants, and the anarchy lasted only 135 years instead of 250. Out of the conflict came two major political divisions: the North, which was dominated by the kingdom of Wei, and the South, which featured various dynasties that took turns fighting one another in supreme power. The dividing line was the Yangtze River, which flows across almost the entire width of China.

During this partial breakdown of central order, the *cultivation of rice* in paddies gradually became entrenched in the South. This development was to be highly important for all later Chinese history, as the grain allowed the Chinese population to expand greatly without putting strains on the economy. A Vietnamese import into South China, rice requires a great deal of hand labor, but produces more caloric energy per acre than any other crop. Rice enabled the population to grow and then provided the work to keep the new hands busy. The South now began to rival and outshine the North in civilized development.

❧ THE TANG DYNASTY, 618–907

The brief Sui dynasty (580–618) was followed by the line of the Tang emperors (618–907) who presided over one of the most brilliant of the epochs of China's long history. Like the Qin earlier, the two Sui rulers had reunified China and gone on to introduce authoritarian reforms which were unpopular but necessary. Failed military expeditions against the northern nomads brought the Sui down in the course of a widespread rebellion. But their Tang successors continued their reforms while avoiding their military misadventures, thus paving the way for a splendid economic and cultural epoch.

The early Tang rulers' primary concern was to improve the state of the peasant tenants, who had fallen into much misery due to the rapacity of their landlords. The landlords had taken full advantage of the collapse of the Han government by shifting the burden of taxation to their tenants, while increasing the rents charged them. The early Tang rulers adopted the *"equal field" system,* whereby the fertile land reverted to the state (that is, the imperial government) upon the death or old age of its peasant cultivator. It was then reassigned to another adult peasant in return for reasonable taxes and labor services. In this fashion peasant needs and resources could be closely matched. For about a century there was a real improvement in the economic lives of the people.

In *government,* the Tang re-created a generally efficient bureaucracy, firmly based on Confucian ethics and the merit system. Although the wealthy and the aristocrats still found ways of bypassing the exams or bribing their way into government service, the Tang system had so much to recommend it that it was still being employed in principle

The Virtuous Officials

The greatest of the classical historians of China, Ssu-ma Ch'ien lived in the early Han dynasty. In the *Annals* (Shih chi) he wrote the entire history of his people. He devoted special care to the events of his own lifetime (c. 150–90 B.C.E.) Ssu-ma Ch'ien was a court historian under the rule of the ambitious emperor Wu who had expanded China's borders at the price of a cruel, Legalist-inspired internal regime.

Ssu-ma Ch'ien regretted the emperor's style of governance, but could not, as court historian, openly oppose it. Instead, he wrote about the virtue of emperors and officials in the distant past, when Confucian principles guided the government and proper attention was paid to the welfare of the people. Some anecdotes from these biographies follow; the first deals with the capable minister Sun Shu-ao, the second with the righteous Kung-i Hsiu, and the third with the relentlessly logical Li Li. All three men served kings of the Zhou dynasty.

The people of Ch'u liked to use very lowslung carriages, but the king did not think that such carriages were good for the horses and wanted to issue an order forcing the people to use higher ones.

Sun Shu-ao said, "If orders are issued too frequently to the people they will not know which ones to obey. It will not do to issue an order. If your Majesty wishes the people to use high carriages, then I suggest that I instruct the officials to have the thresholds of the community gates made higher. Anyone who rides in a carriage must be a man of some social status, and a gentleman cannot be getting down from his carriage every time he has to pass through the community gate."

The king gave his approval, and after half a year all the people had of their own accord made their carriages higher so that they could drive over the thresholds without difficulty. In this way, without instructing the people Sun Shu-ao led them to change their ways.

Three times Sun Shu-ao was appointed prime minister, but he did not rejoice because he knew that it was no more than the natural result of his ability. Three times he was dismissed from the post, but had no regrets, for he knew that his dismissal was not due to any fault of his own. . .

Kung-i Hsiu was an erudite of Lu. Because of his outstanding abilty he was made prime minister. He upheld the laws and went about his duties in a

---

in very modern times. Only the coming of democratic institutions in the early twentieth century ended its reign.

An imperial university originally created under the Han was now expanded to allow about 30,000 students to train for the demanding examinations. Only the very best candidates made it through this rigorous course to sit for the examinations which allocated posts at the central government level. Villagers would pool their resources to allow a talented boy to go to a tutor and support him through the long years of preparation. They knew that if he was successful, he would bring back to the village far more than the cost to train him. Through Confucian ideals of family and the obligations of a gentleman, the official was made conscious of the debts he owed to his native place and would repay them over the rest of his active life.

The Tang also followed the Sui example in attempting to keep the mandarin officials loyal and incorruptible by ordaining that no official could serve in his home district, and no more than once in any place. The Chinese thus anticipated the first European government to put such rules into effect (the France of King Louis XIV) by a thousand years!

For about 150 years, the Tang dynasts were generally successful. In foreign affairs they were active and aggressive in several directions. To the north and northwest, they managed either to win the barbarians' loyalties or defeat their incursions. To the east, the initial era of Chinese-Japanese cultural contacts opened, and the Japanese proved enthusiastic admirers of Chinese culture at this time (see the next chapter). Contact with the Korean kingdoms was less harmonious, but this less numerous people still fell under the powerful magnetism of the splendid civilization based upon the great city of Changan, the Tang capital. The same was true of the Tibetans

reasonable manner, not indulging in needless changes of procedure. . . He stopped men who were receiving government salaries from scrambling for profit in competition with the common people and prevented those on generous stipends from accepting petty gifts and bribes.

Once one of his retainers sent him a fish, but he refused to accept the gift. "I always heard that you were fond of fish," said another of his retainers. "Now that someone has sent you a fish, why don't you accept it?" "It is precisely because I am so fond of fish that I don't accept it," replied Kung-i Hsiu. "Now that I am minister I can afford to buy all the fish I want. But if I should accept this gift and lose my position as a result, who would ever provide me with a fish again?"

Li Li was director of prisons under Duke Wen of China. Once, discovering that an innocent man had been executed because of an error in the investigation conducted by his office, he had himself bound and announced that he deserved the death penalty. Duke Wen said to him, "There are high officials and low officials, and there are light punishments and severe ones. Just because one of the petty clerks in your office make a mistake there is no reason why you should take the blame"

But Li Li replied, "I occupy the position of head of this office and I have made no move to hand the post over. . .I receive a large salary and I have not shared the profits with those under me. Now because of an error in the trial an innocent has been executed. I have never heard of a man in my position trying to shift the responsibility for such a crime to his subordinates!" Thus he declined to accept Duke Wen's suggestion.

"If you insist that as a superior officer you yourself are to blame", said Duke Wen, "then do you mean that I, too, am to blame?"

"The director of prisons", said Li Li, "must abide by the laws which govern his post. If he mistakenly condemns a man to punishment, he himself must suffer the punishment; if he mistakenly sentences a man to death, he himself must suffer death. Your Grace appointed me to this post precisely because you believed that I would be able to listen to difficult cases and decide doubtful points of law. But now since I have made a mistake in hearing a case and have executed an innocent, I naturally deserve to die for my offense." So in the end he refused to listen to the duke's arguments, but fell on his sword and died.

SOURCE: *Han Fei-Tzu: Basic Writing*, translated by Burton Watson. © 1964 by Columbia University Press. Reprinted with permission of the publisher.

in the far west, who were just being touched by Chinese expeditions for the first time. The Vietnamese in the south, on the other hand, steadfastly resisted Chinese attempts to colonize them.

In the mid-700s, the dynasty's successes ceased. An emperor fell under the sway of a beautiful and ambitious concubine and wholly neglected his duties; government was in effect turned over to her family. Unable to bear the situation longer, a general with a huge army rebelled, and the entire country was caught up in a devastating war from which the dynasty, though it put down the rebels, never recovered. Troubles on the northern borders mounted once again; despite the brief intervals of strong rule in the early 800s, the Tang could not successfully solve the internal discontents which finally overwhelmed the dynasty in bloody anarchy and provincial rebellion.

For a half-century China was again divided. Then, one of the northern provincial warlords made his bid. Proving to be more adept as diplomat than as warrior, he was able to induce most of his rivals to join his state voluntarily. The Chinese educated class always favored the idea of a single government center. Unlike Indians and the Middle Eastern peoples, educated Chinese looked upon political fragmentation as an aberration, a throwback to the time before civilization. They saw it as something to be avoided at all costs, even if unity entailed submission to an illegitimate, usurping ruler.

❖ THE SONG DYNASTY, 960–1279

Armed with their newly discovered Mandate of Heaven, the successors to the Tang were able men. The Song rulers systematically promoted the many technical innovations

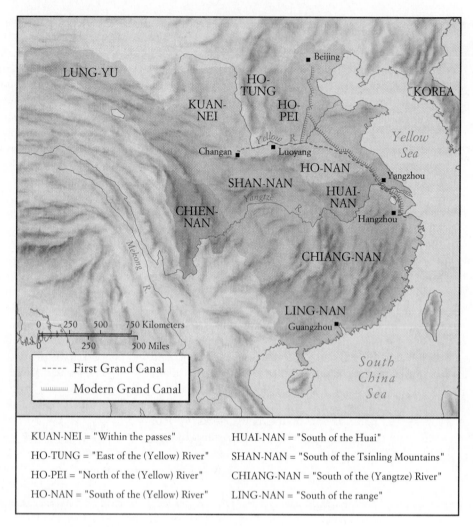

● **MAP 22.2   Tang Dynasty China.**
The Tang Dynasty reached almost the modern boundaries enjoyed by China. Shown here is the maximal extent of the Tang domains.

KUAN-NEI = "Within the passes"	HUAI-NAN = "South of the Huai"
HO-TUNG = "East of the (Yellow) River"	SHAN-NAN = "South of the Tsinling Mountains"
HO-PEI = "North of the (Yellow) River"	CHIANG-NAN = "South of the (Yangtze) River"
HO-NAN = "South of the (Yellow) River"	LING-NAN = "South of the range"

which the Tang period had produced and encouraged others. The most important of these was printing. At first printers used a separate carved wooden block for each page or column of ideographs, but by the eleventh century they had developed moveable wooden type. Labor-saving devices included the water pump and the spiral worm-drive for liquids. Together, they revolutionized the use of irrigation, made mining less difficult and more efficient, and allowed the construction of locks which made canals a more useful form of transport.

Manufacturers were much advanced by the invention of the waterwheel and the forge bellows. The abacus and the waterclock enabled accurate measurement of quantity and of time. Perhaps the best known of all the Tang/Song inventions was gunpowder, which the Chinese used only for pyrotechnic entertainments for a long while, but then adapted to warfare to a minor degree. Strong oceangoing vessels were armed with small rockets, for example, as defense against the frequent pirates. Gunpowder did not play a major role in Chinese military tactics until the 1200s, when it was used against the invading Mongols, who then carried it west to the Muslims and eventually the Europeans.

The Chinese economy reached an enviable state of smooth working and innovative production during this era. A population now estimated at over 100 million by the end of the Song period was supported in decent conditions. The introduction of a new hybrid rice from Annam (Vietnam) helped feed this large population. It was now possible to grow two crops a year in South China, doubling the land's productivity with little additional expenditure of energy or resources. The volume of domestic and foreign trade increased markedly, aided by the development and use of paper money and sophisticated banking and credit operations.

Silk was now joined by porcelain as a major luxury export article. Despite the risk of breakage, it was exported to many lands, including such distant places as the Arab colonies in east Africa. Large ships that used the magnetic compass and the sternpost rudder—both Chinese inventions—were built for the active trade with Japan and Southeast Asia. The itinerant Chinese traders as well as colonies of Chinese peoples throughout Asia have their ancestors in this (Song) period of prosperity.

Avenues of internal trade opened along the massive network of *canals* that linked the South with the North. These have been used ever since to move most of China's bulk goods. Along the canals in central and southern China sprang up a number of large cities, all with more than half a million in population. One of the largest was **Hangchow,** whose delights and splendid vistas were described in wonder by the Venetian visitor Marco Polo in the thirteenth century. Both Hangchow and Kaifeng, the Song capital, had more than a million inhabitants and contained all sorts of amusements and markets for rich and poor. Hangchow was a port and grew in response to market forces and mercantile necessities rather than according to a government plan. As in the Roman Empire, the majority of the people in Song China lived in villages, but the large cities dictated the culture and defined the atmosphere of the empire.

For the most part, the Song continued the government of the Tang period. The bureaucracy they organized worked well for an unusually long period of almost three hundred years in the South. Most decisions had to be made at the top in the capital, many by the emperor himself. By some estimates, only 30,000 officials were needed to govern this large empire (the size of all of Europe), because the habit of obedience and self-discipline was already deeply ingrained in the population.

The generals of the large army were kept under tight control and were not allowed those liberties in the outermost provinces that had often degenerated into warlordism in the past. The rest of society looked down on the military; a popular saying held that soldiers were the lowest types of humans and that good men should not be turned into soldiers anymore than one would waste good iron to make nails. The military ranked even below the merchants, who gained somewhat in prestige during the Song period but still occupied low rungs on the social ladder.

Tang and Song era culture was supremely literary in nature. The accomplished official was also expected to be a good poet, a calligrapher, and a philosopher able to expound his views by quoting the "scriptures" of Confucian and other systems of thought. Skills in painting and music were also considered part of the normal equipment of an educated and powerful man. This was the ideal of the mandarin, the man who held public responsibilities and proved himself worthy of them by virtue of his rich and deep culture. This ideal was often a reality in Tang and later dynastic history.

Under the Song dynasty, China's *control over its East Asian lands was sharply reduced* from the Tang highpoint. The emperors never succeeded in gaining firm control of the northern half of the country. Tibet, Mongolia, and the far western province of Sinkiang were abandoned to the nomads who had continually contested the Han and Tang governments there. Vietnam and Korea were allowed to become autonomous regions, paying the Song a token tribute. The huge northeastern region of Manchuria, always a battleground between nomads and Chinese, broke away entirely.

By giving up territories that were never firmly under China's hand, the Song were able to focus on the heartland, ruling the area between the Yellow and Yangtze Rivers from their capital at Kaifeng. For two centuries the Song rulers and their large armies were able to repel the increasing pressures from the northern and western tribes. But in the twelfth century they weakened. Towards the end of the 1100s, they lost any semblance of control over the far west to the *Mongols;* by the mid-1200s, the Song had been defeated by the descendants of Chinghis Khan and formally gave up the north and center of traditional China to them. The Song were able to hold on for a brief time in the south, but in 1279 there, too, dominion passed into Mongol hands—the first and only time China has been conquered in its entirety by outsiders. The Mongol **Yuan dynasty** thus began its century-long reign (see the Biography in this chapter).

✤ BUDDHISM IN CHINA

The greatest single cultural influence on China during the first millennium C.E. was the coming of Buddhism from its Indian birthplace. The Chinese proved very responsive to the new faith, with all social and economic groups finding something in the doctrine that answered their needs. Buddhism believes in the essential equality of all; the enlightenment of the soul, which is the high point of a

Marco Polo
1254–1324

In the thirteenth century, the Italian city-state of Venice was a notable power not only in the Mediterranean but throughout Europe. Based entirely on its merchant navy, the tiny, aristocratically governed republic became rich from its carrying trade with the Byzantine Empire and the Muslim lands beyond. Venetian ships carried cargoes of silk, spices, precious stones and woods, ivory, jade, Chinese bronzes, and other luxury items for distribution throughout Europe. Their sailors returned with tales of wealth and wonders that awaited the venturesome in the vast Asian distances.

Among those who listened were Niccolò and Maffeo Polo, members of a merchant family. In 1261 they had journeyed as far as the Black Sea by ship and thence overland along the Silk Road to China. The Italians stayed in the court of the Mongol emperor Kubilai Khan for a few years, then returned to Venice by sea. Several years later, they decided to repeat this strenuous journey, this time taking along Niccolò's seventeen-year-old son, Marco (1254–1324). After a tremendous series of difficulties, they succeeded in reaching Kubilai's capital at Beijing in 1275.

Warmly received by the emperor, the Polos settled into a partly commercial, partly official life at the Mongol court. Marco Polo, who quickly mastered Mongol and at least three other Asian languages, proved a particular asset. Enjoying the emperor's full confidence, he apparently traveled extensively as a government official, not only in China proper but also in other East Asian regions of the immense Mongol *imperium* created by Chingis Khan and his successors. These journeys gave him opportunities to observe the customs, agriculture, commerce, and culture of several parts of Asia. He delighted the Khan with the tales and the information that he brought back from each trip, for he had a curious and informed eye and ear.

For more than fifteen years, the Polos stayed on in Beijing. By this time the older men were anxious to return home, but the emperor was reluctant to part with them. In 1292, however, they persuaded him to allow them to depart as guides for a caravan taking a young Chinese bride to the Persian Shah's court. By the time they reached their destination, many members of the caravan had died or been killed, but the princess and the three Polos had survived. From Persia they were able to return to Venice with relative safety and speed, arriving in their hometown after a twenty-three-year absence in 1295.

Marco Polo was now a famous man, and became an admiral in the Venetian navy. During a war with rival Genoa, he was captured and imprisoned briefly. His captors allowed him to pass the time by dictating his memoirs of his years in China, and these were published after Marco's release and return to Venice. The *Description of the World by Marco Polo* soon became a "best-seller" in several languages. It remained the most important source of European knowledge about Asia until the Portuguese explorers reached India in the early sixteenth century. Its detailed observations greatly expanded the very sketchy data brought back by the occasional missionary or merchant who survived the hazards of a central Asian journey. Contemporary readers regarded much of the book, especially the sections on the richness and variety of Chinese urban life, as sheer lies and fantasies and referred to it satirically as "Marco's Millions." He was outraged but could, of course, do nothing. Not until the sixteenth century would his report be validated.

We know almost nothing of Polo's career after his book's appearance. He died in early 1324, leaving a wife and three daughters. A copy of the *Description of the World* accompanied Columbus on his first voyage.

Buddhist life, is available to all who can find their way to it. Unlike Confucianism and Daoism, which are essentially philosophies of proper thought and conduct in this life and possess only incidental religious ideas, Buddhism by the time it came to China, was a supernatural religion promising an afterlife of eternal bliss for the righteous. To the ordinary man and woman, this idea had far more appeal than any earthly philosophy. Another aspect of Buddhism's appeal was that the **Mahayana** version adopted in China was very accommodating to existing beliefs—there was no conflict between traditional ancestor worship and Buddhism in China, for example.

The translation of Sanskrit texts into Chinese stimulated the literary qualities of the language, as the translators had to fashion ways of expressing very difficult and complex ideas. Even more than prose, however, *poetry* benefited from the new religion and its ideals of serenity, self-mastery, and a peculiarly Chinese addition to classic Indian Buddhism—the appreciation of and joy in nature. Chinese arts were very strongly affected by Buddhism for several centuries. Painting, sculpture, and architecture all show Buddhist influences, mostly traceable to India, but some original to China in their conceptions. From about the fourth century onward, China's high-culture arts were strongly molded by Buddhist belief. They not only portrayed themes from the life of the Buddha, but also showed in many ways the religion's conceptions of what proper human life should be.

So powerful was Buddhism's appeal that inevitably a reaction set in against it. In part, this reaction was a political phenomenon; in the 800s the Tang dynasty took steps to curb the worrisome powers of the wealthy Buddhist monasteries. But the reaction was also philosophical and intellectual in the form of *Neo-Confucianism* and a general revival of the Confucian credo. The Neo-Confucians were philosophers who sought to enlighten the world through emphasis on aspects of the master's thought most fully developed by his later disciple, **Mencius** (370–290 B.C.E.). In Neo-Confucianism, love and the responsibility of all to all were the great virtues. Unlike the Daoists and Buddhists, the Neo-Confucians insisted that all must partake of social life; withdrawal and prolonged meditation were impermissible. They also thought that formal education in morals and the arts and sciences was an absolute necessity for a decent life—it could not be left to the "enlightenment" of the individual seeker to discover what his fellow's welfare required. The Confucians' efforts to hold their own against their Buddhist competitors were a major reason why the Song period was so fertile in all philosophic and artistic fields.

Summary

The Chinese government style was molded once and for all by the ruthless Legalist known as the First Emperor in the third-century B.C.E. The Qin dynasty he founded quickly disappeared, but his Han successors built on the foundations he left them to rule a greatly expanded China for four centuries. Softening the brutal Qin policies to an acceptable level, the Han dynasts made Confucianism into a quasi-official philosophy. They also began the merit system of selection of the bureaucracy which would exercise government powers for two millennia.

In the wider view, the five hundred years of the Tang and Song dynasties was the Golden Age of Chinese culture, though there were other vital periods on either side of these centuries. Despite internal dissension at times, the imperial government promulgated and was supported by a vision of proper conduct that was Confucian in essence and very widely held by the educated classes.

In foreign affairs, the long seesaw struggle with the northern nomadic barbarians was finally lost when the Mongols of **Kubilai Khan** were able to defeat the last Song rulers and establish the Yuan dynasty. All of China thus fell under alien rule for the first and only time. Also during the Song, China took on more or less its modern territorial outlines, with its withdrawals from Vietnam, Korea, and Mongolia. Cultural and commercial contacts with Japan were opened, and there was extensive commercial intercourse with the Muslims to the west.

Internally, both the Tang and the Song saw a tremendous development of the economy and its capacity to maintain a rapidly growing and urbanizing population. Thanks in large part to advances in agriculture, in the five centuries under consideration, few, if any, other civilizations could rival China's ability to supply all classes with the necessities of life. A series of technological inventions had immediate practical applications. It was also a period of extraordinary excellence in the fine arts and literature, which were supported by a large group of refined patrons and consumers in the persons of the landowning gentry and the mandarin officials. Buddhist influences were pervasive in both the popular and gentry cultures, rivaling but not overshadowing traditional Confucian thought.

Test Your Knowledge

1. Chinese Buddhism was different from the original conceptions of Sidhartha Gautama in
   a. the rigidity and uniformity of its doctrine.
   b. its insistence on the lifestyle of a hermit.
   c. its supernatural religious quality.
   d. its appeal to only the upper classes.
2. Buddhism found many sympathizers in China because it
   a. offered immortality to all social classes.
   b. was an import from Korea.
   c. came from a civilization that the Chinese regarded as superior to their own.
   d. demanded the rigorous intellectual effort that the Chinese so admired.
3. The Tang dynasty was extremely influential in Chinese history as the
   a. developer of the mandarin system of scholar-officials.
   b. creator of the village democracy.
   c. reformer of the military.
   d. originator of the canal system.
4. Which of the following was *not* a Chinese invention?
   a. The magnetic compass
   b. The waterwheel
   c. Paper from wood
   d. Decimals
5. Which of the following was *not* a requirement for joining the Chinese bureaucracy?
   a. Single-minded dedication to enter its ranks
   b. Extensive formalized education
   c. Connections with the higher social classes
   d. Passing of written examinations
6. The Qin First Emperor attained power by
   a. a palace coup.
   b. playing on the superstitions of his people.
   c. assassinating the previous emperor.
   d. triumph in battle.
7. The Song dynasty was overturned by the
   a. Yuan dynasty.
   b. Korean invaders.
   c. Japanese.
   d. Tang dynasty.
8. Marco Polo served as an official in the service of
   a. the Song emperor.
   b. the Mongol emperor.
   c. an Italian embassy to the Chinese government.
   d. Indian visitors to the Chinese court.

Identification Terms

Era of the Warring States
First Emperor
Han dynasty

Hangchow
Kubilai Khan

Mahayana Buddhism
mandarin

Mencius
Yuan dynasty

Bibliography

The general histories cited in the bibliography for Chapter 7 are still useful in this period: the works by C. Schirokauer and J. Fairbank can be recommended. See also the multivolume Oxford and Cambridge histories of the Chinese state.

Cahill, J. *Chinese Painting,* 1960. A good survey.

Ch'en, K. *Buddhism in China,* 1964.

Fitzgerald, C. P. *Son of Heaven: A Biography of Li Shih-min, Founder of the T'ang Dynasty,* 1933. A fine biography. See also his biography of one of the very few Chinese empresses, *The Empress Wu,* 1968.

Gernet, J. *Daily Life in China on the Eve of the Mongol Invasion,* 1948. A look at an unchanging society in the thirteenth century from a worm's eye view.

Grousset, R. *In the Footsteps of the Buddha,* 1931. A modern version of the journal of a Chinese Buddhist pilgrim visiting India.

Waley, A., trans. Several volumes of poetry translated from the original.

Wright, A. F. *Buddhism in Chinese History,* 1959. A straightforward explanation.

Wu-chi, L. *An Introduction to Chinese Literature,* 1966. A readable introduction to Chinese classical literature with a good bibliography.

JAPAN: AN ISLAND REALM

400s–500s	Yamato state formed
704	Prince Shotoku's Seventeen Point Constitution
710–784	Nara period
794–1185	Heian period
1185–1333	Kamakura shogunate
1336–1573	Ashikaga shogunate

The island nation of Japan emerges from the mists of prehistory in the early centuries C.E., when Chinese travelers begin to report on their adventures there. Geography explains both Japan's receptivity to Chinese influence and its ability to reject that influence when it wished. Japan could adapt foreign ideas and values to its needs without having to suffer military or political domination from abroad. For the first thousand years of recorded Japanese history, until about 1500 C.E., the Japanese state was a successful experiment in the adaptation of imported governmental and cultural institutions to existing customs and the requirements of the native society.

❖ VERY EARLY JAPAN

The Japanese islands (the four main ones are Hokkaido, Honshu, Kyushu, and Shikoku) are situated off the Korean peninsula and Siberia, separated from the mainland by 120 to several hundred miles of open water (see Map 23.1). Together, the islands are about the size of California. Where the original settlers came from is uncertain, but it is clear that the Koreans and Japanese are much closer ethnically than the Chinese and Japanese. The native oral language of Japan is entirely different from Chinese. The written language, which originally borrowed heavily from written Chinese, is still different in many ways.

According to ancient Japanese legends, they are the descendants of the Sun Goddess, who continues to have a special relationship with the country through the person of the emperor. For many centuries, the Japanese thought of the emperor as divine, a status that was only formally rejected by terms of the Japanese peace treaty after World War II. Archaeological data reveal that as early as the third century C.E. a semicivilized society inhabited the southern island of Kyushu and buried their dead chieftains in elaborate mounds with many pottery figures accompanying them to the next world. The first written records do not appear until the eighth century C.E., however; prior to that we must rely on the occasional travel reports of Chinese visitors.

For the most part, Japan has a very mountainous and broken terrain, which helps explain why the process of creating a central government with effective controls was so slow and subject to sudden reverses. The leading clan, the Yamato family, was never able to get real control over

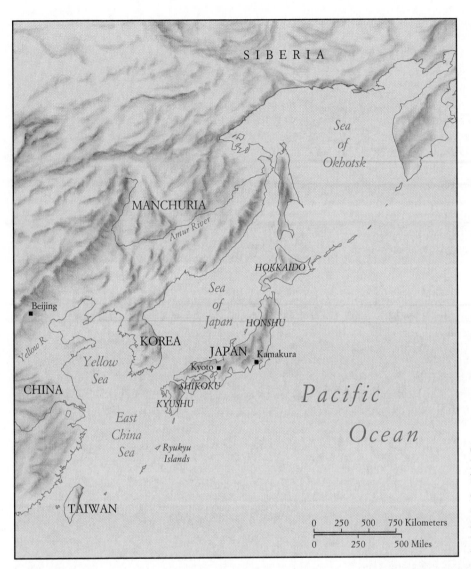

● MAP 23.1 Japan and Its Neighbors. The hundred mile interval between Japan and Korea was not difficult to cross even in ancient times, and Chinese cultural influences came into Japan via Korean intermediaries until direct contacts were established in the seventh century.

the four islands, despite being strong enough to invade southern Korea on several occasions.

During this early period, the *relationship between Japan and Korea* was important for both. There appear to have been invasions in both directions, and many Koreans lived among the Japanese until well into the first millennium C.E. Commerce between the two countries seems to have been lively. Under Korean influences the Japanese moved gradually northward from the island of Kyushu near Korea to Hokkaido, the most northerly and least developed island. From Korea came several major cultural imports, most importantly, Buddhism, which arrived in Japan in the sixth century. From Korea also came powerful Chinese influences. During this era, Korea was subjected to a revitalized Chinese imperialism, as the Tang dynasty succeeded in making their northeastern neighbor into a satellite. Korea adopted the Chinese styles of government, law, and writing and passed them on to the Japanese.

Buddhism and Shinto

The two major religious beliefs of ancient and modern Japan are the import Buddhism and the native Shinto. Buddhism in Japan, as everywhere, proved itself capable of undergoing many mutations and adapting to local

Chronicles of Japan

The introduction of Buddhism into early Japan was one of the two or three most important cultural interchanges in the history of the East Asian peoples. Buddhism arrived in the sixth and seventh centuries from Korea, where it had been introduced by the Chinese. The following brief extract from the so-called *Chronicles of Japan,* which was written sometime in the eighth century C.E. about events in the sixth century, describes the resistance of the native Shinto worshipers and the miraculous nature of the Buddhist symbols.

> King Syong of Pakche [one of the Korean kingdoms] sent. . . an image of the Buddha in gold and copper, several flags and an umbrella, and a number of Sutras. . . saying, "This doctrine is amongst all doctrines the most excellent. But it is hard to explain and hard to comprehend. Even the Duke of Chou and Confucius had not attained to a knowledge of it. This doctrine can create religious merit and retribution without measure and so lead on to the full appreciation of the highest wisdom. . . ."
>
> Syong, king of Pakche, has humbly dispatched a retainer to transmit it to the Imperial Country of Japan, and to diffuse it abroad, and so fulfill the recorded word of the Buddha: "My word shall spread to the East."

One of the clan leaders gladly accepted the image of Buddha for worship, but others resisted:

> The chiefs of the Mononnobe and Nakatomi clans jointly addressed the emperor, saying: "Those who

have ruled our state have always made it their care to worship in spring, summer, autumn and winter the 180 gods [Shinto] of heaven and earth, and the gods of the land and of grain. If just at this time we were to worship in their stead foreign deities it may be feared that we should incur the wrath of our national gods."

The clan which wanted the Buddha among them soon fell victim to a plague which killed many. The anti-Buddhist party at court rejoiced, and the emperor gave order to take off the Buddha statue and dump it into the canal of Naniha. The temple built to Buddha was also burnt so that nothing was left. But at that moment, a sudden conflagration burnt down the Great Hall of the imperial palace, as well.

Thirty-six years later, in 584 C.E., Buddhism was reintroduced, this time successfully, by a certain Mumako Sukune, who found a small Buddhist relic one day:

> By way of experiment, [he] took the relic and placing it on a block of iron beat it with an iron sledgehammer, which he flourished aloft. The block and the hammer were shattered to atoms, but the relic could not be crushed. Then the relic was cast into water, where it sank or floated as one desired. In consequence of this, Mumako Sukune held faith in Buddhism and practiced it unremittingly. He built another Buddhist temple at his house in Ishikaha. From this arose the beginning of Buddhism.

SOURCE: Ni Hong, *The Chronicles of Japan,* Vol. II, edited and translated by W.G. Aston, Harper Collins, UK, © 1956.

---

needs. The special Japanese versions are *Zen, the Pure Land, and the Nichiren sects,* which gradually developed after the introduction of the religion in the sixth century from Korea. Their distinctions became clearer as time passed (see the Document in this chapter and the discussion in Chapter 41).

Buddhism gave Japanese religion a much broader and nobler intellectual content. Its insistence on ethical action and compassion for the weak and unfortunate was as beneficial to Japanese life as it had been earlier in India

and China. In Japan more than elsewhere in Asia, Buddhism emphasized *meditation* techniques. For the more intellectually demanding, Buddhist beliefs could be very complex, but for the majority of Japanese believers, the religion was relatively simple and joyful in its acceptance of things-as-they-are and in its anticipation of happiness in the life to come.

The **Shinto** religion is a native Japanese product, but it is fairly close to Chinese Daoism. The word *Shinto* means "the way of the gods," and the religion combines a simple animism, in which all kinds of natural objects possess a spirit, with a worship of great deities, like the Sun Goddess who are immortal and benevolent, but not perceivable by the human senses. The Shinto legends with which all Japanese are familiar speak of a time when all things, even stones and trees, could speak and interact with humans. But they were forced into silence later and now must evidence their powers through the *kami* or spirits that inhabit them.

Shinto is a basically optimistic, guilt-free view of the world. It has no theology of the gods or sacred book, no heaven or hell or wrathful Yahweh, and no Fall of Adam. Shinto is supremely adaptable, however, and could serve as a sort of permanent underpinning to whatever more advanced, supernatural religion the individual Japanese might prefer. It persists to this day in that role.

⚜ GOVERNMENT AND ADMINISTRATION

The beginning of organized government occurred in the Yamato period in the fifth and sixth centuries C.E. At that time Japan was a collection of noble clans, who ruled over the commoners by a combination of military and economic power familiar to students of feudal Europe. The Yamato, the biggest and most potent of these clans, ruled over a good-sized arable area in central Japan near what is now Osaka. The Yamato claimed direct descent from the Sun Goddess and founded what was to become the imperial family of the Japanese state. This family, or more precisely the dynasty that began with the Yamato kings, has never been overturned. The present-day emperor is considered the direct descendant from the earliest Yamato, though he is no longer a divinity.

Buddhism soon became the favored viewpoint of the Yamato state's upper class, and by the beginning of the seventh century, it was used as the vehicle of a general strengthening and clarification of the role of the central government. In 604, **Prince Shotoku,** a devout Buddhist, offered the *Seventeen Point Constitution,* which is the founding document of the Japanese state. It was not really a constitution in the modern sense, but a list inspired by Buddhist and Confucian doctrine of what a government and a loyal citizenry *ought* to do. It has had great influence on political science in Japan ever since.

The way affairs were being practiced in China was the general model for the Seventeen Points, so to put his constitution into effect, Shotoku sent selected youths to China for a period of study and training under Chinese teachers, artists, and officials. In the seventh century, tens of thousands of Japanese were thus prepared for governmental responsibilities and were also trained in the arts and techniques of Tang China. This was one of the earliest and most impressive examples of cultural transfer from one people to another in history.

The Chinese example had a powerful influence in most public and many private spheres, but it was not overwhelming. The Japanese soon showed they were confident of their own abilities to distinguish what was useful and what was not. For example, they adopted the Tang equal field system, in which land was frequently redistributed among the peasants to ensure equity. But the Japanese soon changed this system to allow an individual to have

■ **A Japanese Temple.** The 1300 year old Horyuji temple complex contains the world's oldest wooden buildings. The five storied pagoda and the neighboring main hall were constructed in the seventh century from trees already three hundred years old.

transferable rights to a parcel of productive land no matter who actually tilled it. Another example was the Japanese approach to bureaucracy. Although they admired the Chinese bureaucracy, they did not imitate it. The concept of *meritocracy was and remained alien to Japanese thinking.* Having competitive exams open to all threatened deep-rooted Japanese social values. Government remained an aristocratic privilege in Japan; the peasants and lower classes were not allowed to attain high posts, regardless of their merit.

✤ THE NARA AND HEIAN PERIODS, 710–1185

For seventy years after the death of Prince Shotoku in 622, Japan experienced anarchy. This was followed by a period of reform, during which the first capital, Nara, was established in central Honshu. Buddhism was especially powerful among the Nara clans, and when a Buddhist monk named Dokyo attempted to use his following in the numerous monasteries to usurp political power, there was a strong reaction against the monasteries. Dokyo also used his position as chaplain to the empress to further his political ambitions. When the empress died he was driven into exile. This experience may explain why in all the remainder of Japanese history there have been only two other female rulers.

The reaction against the Buddhist monks and monasteries did not mean a reaction against the religion itself, which steadily gained new adherents among the educated upper class and soon started filtering down to the common people. In the early ninth century, Japanese visitors to the mainland became acquainted with the Tendai and Shingon sects of Buddhism and took them back to Japan. These sects featured magical elements and promises of salvation to all, which made them highly popular, and they spread quickly. During this period, Buddhism in Japan started a slow but steady transformation from a narrow preoccupation of the court aristocrats to the mass vehicle of popular devotion it would become.

In 794, due largely to the bad experience with the Nara monasteries, the imperial court was moved to a new town called Heian (modern Kyoto), where it stayed until modern times. At this time, the aristocrats checked further Chinese influence by severing relations with the mainland—one of the several episodes of deliberate seclusion with which Japanese history is studded. For about a century, contacts with China and Korea were strictly limited, while the Japanese aristocracy devoted themselves to organizing the government and creating a cultural/

■ The expenses entailed in outfitting a samurai properly were sometimes borne by the daimyo who was his lord. But the two swords carried by the warrior were always his personal property. By the end of the Kamakura era in the 1300s, the samurai were a separate class in Japanese society, a position retained until the late nineteenth century.

artistic style that was uniquely their own. The process lasted several centuries and was more or less complete by about 1200.

Government during the Heian era quickly became a struggle—almost always concealed—between the Chinese model of an all-powerful emperor ruling through a bureaucracy and the kind of rough-and-ready decentralized feudalism that had marked the Yamato state. The feudal aristocrats soon won out. The emperors were reduced to ceremonial figures, accorded great respect but essentially without means of imposing their will. A series of provincial noble families, above all, the *Fujiwara clan,* were able to make themselves the real powers. The Fujiwara ruled from behind the throne by arranging marriages between their daughters and the children of the monarchs and then having themselves nominated as regents. They remained content to dominate indirectly and did not try to displace the ruler.

This system of disguised rule by powerful families at court was to become a recurrent part of Japanese life under the name of the shogunate. The true head of government was the *shogun,* or commander-in-chief of the imperial army. The shoguns stayed in the background, but decided everything that mattered, while the divine emperors conducted the ceremonies.

After this system had worked fairly well for two centuries, it began to break down as rival clans finally found ways to break the Fujiwara monopoly. In the outlying provinces, and especially in eastern Japan, warriors known as *bushi* were experiencing a rise in power and prestige. The *bushi,* or **samurai,** as they are better known in the West, were the executors of the will of the large landholders and the enforcers of public order in a given locality. In their outlook, means of support, and demanding code of conduct **(bushido),** the *bushi* were very similar to the medieval knights of Western Europe. There were, however, some important differences: the samurai's code included no provision for chivalry toward women or for generosity toward a beaten opponent, who expected to die by ritual beheading. This made the samurai a more brutal and menacing figure to the ordinary man and woman.

Using their samurai effectively, the rival clans threw out the Fujiwara regents and then fought one another for supremacy. The house of Minamoto eventually won out and introduced the **Kamakura shogunate.**

✤ THE KAMAKURA PERIOD, 1185–1333

The Kamakura period of Japan's medieval history (it was, in fact, a Japanese version of the European Middle Age) was marked by the complete domination of the country by the samurai and their overlords in the clan aristocracy. The powers of government at the imperial court in Kyoto declined nearly to the vanishing point. Political leadership at any level depended on two factors: control of adequate numbers of fighting men, and control of adequate **shoen** to support those fighting men.

The *shoen* were parcels of productive land, sometimes including villages. They had originally been created in the early Heian era as support for monasteries or rewards to servants of the emperor for outstanding service. Their critical feature was their *exemption from the central gov-*

ernment's taxing authority. Whereas most Japanese land was always considered the property of the emperor, lent out to his favored servants, the *shoen* and the rights to their use and income, called **shiki,** were strictly private and remained outside normal laws.

A monastery or official who owned *shoen* would often convey them to a more powerful person, who would allow the original owner to continue as tenant under his protection. Thus, the ownership and use system became ever more complex and eventually resembled the European system of feudal vassalage. It was not unusual for a *shoen* to have three to five "lords" who each had some special rights (*shiki*) to the land and its produce. *Shoen* and *shiki* were thus the currency used by the aristocrats to pay their samurai. In this sense and others we noted earlier, the samurai very closely resembled the European knights. But there were enough differences that some authorities see the samurai as quite different from the knights and reject the idea that Japanese society in this era was basically the same as medieval European.

One of the chief differences between Japanese and medieval European government was the **bakufu,** or military government under the shogun, which had no European equivalent. The shogun, always a member of the dominant clan controlling the emperor, was supposedly the executor of the emperor's will as generalissimo of the army. In fact, he was totally independent and the real ruler of Japan. The Kamakura period derives its name from the small town of Kamakura where the shogun of the Minamoto clan resided—quite separate from the imperial court in Kyoto.

Perhaps the most dramatic demonstration of the way the shogun and his *bakufu* organization could lead the nation occurred in the late 1200s, when the feared Mongols under Kubilai Khan prepared to invade the islands (see Map 23.2). Having conquered China in its entirety and all of eastern Asia to Vietnam, the Mongols sought to do what the Chinese themselves had never attempted. Twice, the khan assembled armadas from his bases in Korea and landed on Kyushu where his forces were met on the beach by the waiting samurai. The effectiveness of the Mongols' most potent weapon, their cavalry, was sharply limited by the terrain and by Japanese defenses, including a long wall along the coast that horses could not surmount. The Mongols called off the first invasion after fierce resistance led to a stalemate. The second attack in 1281 ended in a huge disaster when a typhoon (the *kamikaze* or divine wind) sank most of their ships and the 140,000 men upon them. Mongol rule was thus never extended to the Japanese.

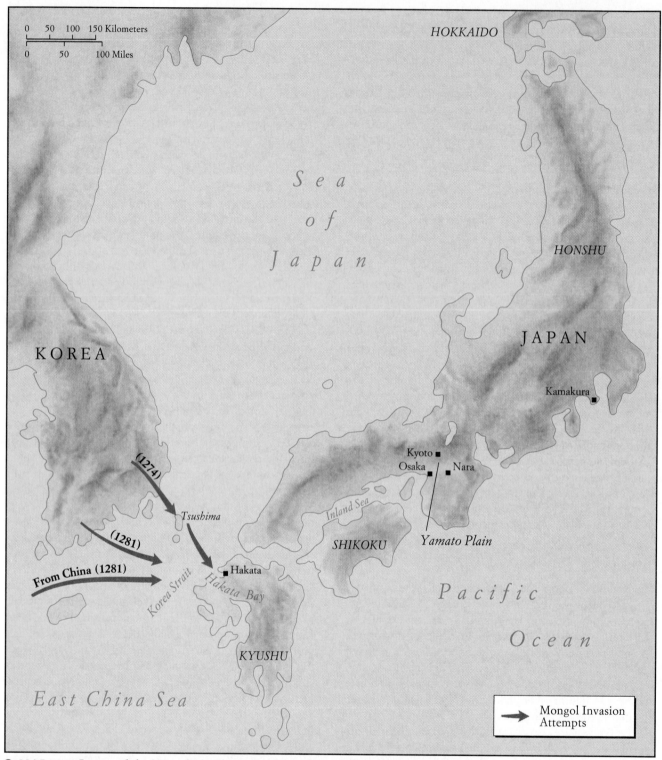

⦿ **MAP 23.2 Japan and the Mongol Invasion Routes in the Thirteenth Century.** From their bases in Korea and northern China, the Mongols mounted two invasion attempts against Japan within a seven year period. Both were repulsed by the samurai gathered at the bay of Hakata, aided by the *kamikaze* wind.

❖ The Arts and Culture in Medieval Japan

The partial severance of relations with China following the establishment of the capital in Heian allowed the Japanese full freedom to develop their own culture. Their *language and literature* shows they were vigorously imaginative. The Japanese and Chinese languages are radically different in both structure and vocabulary; the earliest Japanese writing was a close, but necessarily clumsy adaptation of Chinese. This script was used in the eighth-century *Chronicles of Japan (Nihongi)* and the *Records of Ancient Matters (Kokiki),* the first Japanese books. In the Heian period, it was simplified and brought into closer conformity with oral Japanese. The gradual withdrawal from Chinese vocabulary and modes of expression forced the court authors to invent literary models and expressions of their own. Japanese writers thus evolved two syllabaries, written signs that were based on *phonetics,* rather than being ideographs or pictographs like Chinese, and could therefore be used to match the syllables of the spoken language—in other words, the beginnings of an alphabet.

The world's first *novel,* the famous **Tale of Genji** by the court lady Murasaki Shikibu, was written in the early eleventh century and tells us a great deal about the manners and customs of the Japanese aristocracy of the day (see the Biography in this chapter). It reveals a culture of sensitive, perceptive people, who took intense pleasure in nature and in the company of other refined persons. The impressions left by the *Tale of Genji* are furthered by the other classic court tale of this era, Lady Sei Shonagon's *Pillow Book,* which was a collection of anecdotes and satirical essays centered on the art of love. Neither of these works owes anything to foreign models. The fact that their authors were women gives some indication of the high status of females among the educated class.

Prose was considered the domain of females, but *poetry* was for everyone; everyone, that is, in the tiny fraction of the population that partook of cultured recreations. In the eighth century a collection of poems entitled *Ten Thousand Leaves* was printed.

In *fine arts,* Japanese painting in the Heian era exhibited a marvelous sense of design and draftsmanship. Scenes from nature were preferred, but there was also a great deal of lively portraiture, much of it possessing the sense of amusement that marks many of Japan's arts. The well born were expected to be proficient in dance and music, and calligraphy was as revered as it was in China.

Great attention was given to the cultivation of beauty in all its manifestations: literary, visual, plastic, and psy-

■ **A Japanese Landscape.** Japanese painting strives for a harmonious balance between the works of man and Nature and this balance is revealed in this sixteenth century work. While natural objects are given much space by the artist, the painting's focal point is the house and the human figure within it.

chic. Men as well as women were expected to take pains with their appearance; both used cosmetics. (Blackened teeth were the rage among Heian court ladies!) A refined sense of color in dress was mandatory. Both sexes cried freely, and sadness was very much a part of life. The

Lady Murasaki

c. 976–1026

In the eleventh century, a Japanese noblewoman, whose very name is uncertain, wrote the world's first work of literature that can be called a novel. The *Tale of Genji,* written between 1015 and 1025, is a long, fascinatingly detailed account of the life of a courtier at the Kyoto imperial palace and his relations with women there.

About the life of the author, we know only some fragments. She was born into an official's family, a member of the large and powerful Fujiwara clan that long occupied a major place in Japanese affairs. Shikibu, as she was named, probably received the minimal education customary for even high-class Japanese women. Presumably, she did not know Chinese, which was the literary language of well-educated males in this epoch. She was married to another official at age twenty; her husband died soon after, leaving his widow with a young daughter. For some years, Shikibu retired to a chaste widowhood in a provincial town. In 1004, her father received a long-sought appointment as governor of a province and used his influence to have his widowed daughter made lady in waiting to the empress Akiko in Kyoto.

From 1008 to 1010, Lady Murasaki (as she was now known at court) kept a diary, which was translated and published not long ago. But her major effort in her years with the empress in the extremely refined Kyoto palace was the *Tale of Genji.* In fifty-four books or chapters, which together are more than twice as long as Tolstoy's *War and Peace,* Lady Murasaki depicts the panorama of Japanese upper-class life in the ceremony-filled, ritualistic court of the emperor and his consort.

Prince Genji (Shining One) is a fictional character, but presumably was drawn closely on an actual one. Stricken by the death of his mother to whom he was greatly attached, the young man comes to court to forget his sorrow. Popular with both sexes for his gallantry and charm, he engages in a series of love affairs with the court women, in which he displays both his amorous character and his artistic refinement. In a setting where manners are everything, Genji is supreme. But his escapades with the ladies lead to trouble with jealous husbands and suitors and Genji is banished from the court. He soon obtains forgiveness and returns, only to fall deeply in love with the commoner Murasaki, whom he makes his wife. But she dies young and childless: heartbroken, Genji soon follows her in death.

The action now shifts to Genji's son and grandson by a former marriage. These two are in competition for the same girl, Ukifune, who feels committed to both in different ways. Depressed and ashamed, Ukifune attempts suicide but fails, and she decides to salvage her life by renouncing the world and entering a Buddhist monastery. The competing father and son are both deprived of what they want and are left in bewildered grief at their unconsummated love. The novel ends on a note of deep gloom.

The psychological intricacies of the story have fascinated Japanese readers for nine hundred years, and for most of that very long time, *Genji* has been the touchstone by which all other Japanese novels have been measured. The novel was first translated into English in the 1930s by Arthur Waley. Of Lady Murasaki's last years, we know nothing.

Buddhist insistence on the transitory quality of all good things—the reminder that nothing is permanent—was at the heart of this aristocratic culture. Life was to be enjoyed, not to be worried about or reformed. The wise saw this instinctively and drew the proper conclusions. The Japanese would never have been so crude as to exclaim "Eat, drink, and be merry for tomorrow we die"; their message was more "take pleasure in the flight of the butterfly, for tomorrow neither it nor you will be with us."

Buddhist Evolution

Two Buddhist sects, the Pure Land and the Nichiren, made many converts during the Kamakura period. Both emphasized the salvationist aspect of the religion and the possibility of attaining *nirvana* through faith alone. The founder of the Pure Land sect, Honen (c. 1133–1212), insisted that the Buddha would save those souls who displayed their devotion to him by endlessly repeating his name. The Nichiren, who took their name from their thirteenth-century founder, held a similar belief in the mystical power of chanting devotional phrases and also emphasized the immortality of the soul. The Nichiren differed from all other Buddhists in being highly nationalistic and insisting that they alone had the power to lead the Japanese people on the righteous path.

Zen Buddhism, on the other hand, insisted on strenuous meditation exercises as the only way to purify the mind and prepare it for the experience of *nirvana*. Rising to prominence in the thirteenth century like the Pure Land and Nichiren sects, Zen was to become the most influential of all forms of Buddhist worship in Japan. It was the preferred form for the samurai, who found its emphases on self-reliance, rigorous discipline and anti-intellectualism fit closely with their *bushido* code. Interestingly enough, Zen also underlay much of the Japanese interpretations of beauty and truth, and remained a powerful influence on the visual arts. The famous rock gardens, for example, are a physical rendition of Zen principles of simplicity and restraint. Far outnumbered in adherents by both Pure Land and Nichiren, Zen became the favored belief among the upper class, and has been the form of Buddhism peculiarly identified with Japan in foreign eyes.

⚜ THE ASHIKAGA SHOGUNATE, 1336–1573

The expenses of summoning a huge army to repel the Mongols in the 1280s proved fatal to the Minamoto clan. Despite their desperate efforts, they lost their hold on power. In 1336 the Ashikaga clan succeeded in establishing themselves in the shogunate, a position they continued to hold until the late sixteenth century.

The Ashikaga shoguns ruled from Kyoto as the head of an extended group of **daimyo,** nobles who much

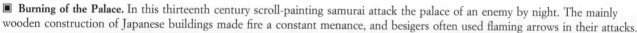

■ **Burning of the Palace.** In this thirteenth century scroll-painting samurai attack the palace of an enemy by night. The mainly wooden construction of Japanese buildings made fire a constant menace, and besigers often used flaming arrows in their attacks.

resembled the dukes and counts of feudal Europe in their lifestyle and powers. Some were much more powerful than others, and at times they were practically independent of the shogun. The most trusted vassals of the reigning shogun were entrusted with the estates surrounding Kyoto, while the outer provinces were rife with rebellion and conflicts among the *daimyo*. The Ashikaga period is one long and bloody tale of wars among the nobility and between groups of nobles and the shogun. For long periods all semblance of central authority seemed to have broken down in Japan. The imperial court was shoved still further into the background and did not play an independent political role at all through this era. All concerned gave verbal respect and honor to the reigning emperor, but these phrases were not accompanied by any devolution of power.

Cultural institutions reflect the increasing attention given to the warrior in this age. The new forms of popular Buddhist worship and the literature of the Kamakura epoch glorified the simple, straightforward virtues of the soldier in sharp contrast to the subtleties and playfulness of the earlier *Tale of Genji* and other stories of the court society. In the period embraced by the Kamakura and Ashikaga shogunates, 1200–1500, Japanese art forms made a definitive turn away from the emulation of Chinese models and became fully nationalized.

Contacts with China

Contacts with Song China were resumed and continued to be close throughout the Kamakura and Ashikaga shogunates, especially in trade. The Chinese especially desired the very fine Japanese steel for swords, which rivaled the "Damascus blades" for which European knights paid a fortune. Japan, in turn, received much from China including the habit of tea drinking, which led to a whole subdivision of Japan's domestic culture, the tea ceremony. The coming of the Mongols interrupted this commerce, but it soon resumed. Many goods were exchanged by force or illegally. Japanese pirates and smugglers gave the early Ming dynasty (1378–1664) so much trouble that for a time, the Chinese rulers actually attempted to withdraw their coastal populations and make them live inland.

Summary

Like the early history of several other Asian societies, the earliest period of Japan's history is shrouded in mists. The lack of written sources until the eighth century C.E. forces us to rely on archaeology and occasional mentions in Chinese travel accounts. Unlike China and many other lands, the Japanese never experienced a military conquest from outside that unified them under a strong central government. Instead, real power was exercised by feudal lords organized loosely in clans who dominated specific localities rather than nationally. The imperial court, located successively in Nara, Heian, and Kyoto, was essentially a symbol of Shinto religious significance and a cultural center rather than a government.

Japan's relations with China were close and intense through most of its early history, but were punctuated with briefer periods of self-willed isolation. In the broadest senses, most of the models of Japanese culture can be traced to Chinese sources; often these came through Korea into Japan. Among Japan's notable borrowings from China were Buddhism, writing, and several art media and forms. But in each instance, the Japanese adapted these imports to create a peculiarly native product.

Test Your Knowledge

1. Very early Japanese history is best summarized as
   a. a complete mystery until the Tang dynasty in China.
   b. unknown except for sporadic Chinese reports.
   c. well documented from native sources.
   d. dependent on the reports of Japan's early invaders.

2. The first Japanese government we know of was organized by the
   a. Yamato clan.
   b. Shinto monasteries.
   c. Buddhist monks.
   d. Heian emperors.

3. Shinto is best defined as
   a. a belief in the infallibility of the emperor.
   b. the original capital city of Japan.
   c. the native religion of the Japanese.
   d. the most important of the Buddhist sects in Japan.
4. The chief original contribution of the Japanese to world literature was the
   a. novel.
   b. epic.
   c. short story.
   d. essay.
5. A shogun was
   a. the high priest of the Shinto temples.
   b. a samurai official.
   c. an illegal usurper of imperial authority.
   d. a general acting as political regent.
6. In the Japanese feudal system, a *shoen* was
   a. an urban commercial concession.
   b. a property outside imperial taxation and controls.
   c. the preferred weapon of the samurai.
   d. land owned by a free peasant.
7. Which of the following best describes the relationship of China and Japan through 1400 C.E.?
   a. Japan was a willing student of Chinese culture.
   b. Japan selectively adopted Chinese models and ideas.
   c. Japan was forced to adopt Chinese models.
   d. Japan rejected Chinese pressures to conform.
8. In Lady Murasaki's tale, Genji is
   a. a samurai warrior who has no time for love.
   b. a betrayed husband of a court beauty.
   c. a romantic lover of many court ladies.
   d. a wise peasant who avoids courtly snares.

Identification Terms

bakufu	Kamakura shogunate	samurai	*shoen/shiki*
bushido	Prince Shotoku	Shinto	*Tale of Genji*
daimyo			

Bibliography

Bowring, R., trans. *Tale of Genji,* 1988. A good recent translation.

Coulborn, R., ed. *Feudalism in History,* 1956. See E. O. Reischauer's chapter on Japan.

Craig, A., and E. O. Reischauer. *Japan: Tradition and Transformation,* 1989. A widely used textbook covering the entire sweep of Japan's history.

Duus, P. *Feudalism in Japan,* 1976. Examines decentralized politics in its Japanese variant.

Kidder, J. E. *Japan before Buddhism,* 1959 and *Early Buddhist Japan,* 1972. Two good introductions for the student.

Kitagawa, J. M. *Religion in Japanese History,* 1966. Deals with the differences between Shinto and Buddhism and how they have been accommodated.

Morris, I. *The World of the Shining Prince: Court Life in Ancient Japan,* 1964. Deals with Genji and his environment by examining artistic life at Kyoto.

Reischauer, E. O., and J. Fairbank. *East Asia: The Great Tradition,* 1960. A detailed survey.

Schirokauer, C. *A Brief History of Chinese and Japanese Civilizations,* 2d ed., 1989. A good introduction.

Suzuki, D. T. *Zen and Japanese Culture,* 1959. A standard treatment.

CHAPTER 24

ORDINARY LIFE AMONG THE NON-WESTERN PEOPLES

KEEPING BODY AND SOUL TOGETHER

MALE AND FEMALE

MARRIAGE AND DIVORCE

EDUCATION AND ITS USES

RELIGIOUS BELIEFS AND MORALITY

c. 500 B.C.E.–1500 C.E.	Agricultural basis of life everywhere but interior Africa and areas possessing too little rainfall
c. 500 C.E.–1500 C.E.	Urban life becomes common in Mesoamerica, East Africa

In the last several chapters, we have examined the evolution of the civilizations beyond the boundaries of Europe and the Mediterranean through, roughly, the fifteenth century. By the end of the 1400s, each of these civilizations—African, Amerindian, Indian, Chinese, and Japanese—had begun to feel the insistent desires and demands of the Europeans. But for the most part, the coming of the European explorers and traders led to only minimal change in the accustomed patterns of living of the masses. Their religions, laws, and customs were untouched or only grudgingly gave way except in parts of the Americas, where the Indians were rapidly eliminated or submerged. Even there, however, the ordinary routines of life generally persisted, only under a different master. This chapter will give a brief sketch of how these non-Western commoners lived, in the same fashion as Chapters 8 and 15 did for the ancient and Greco-Roman worlds.

❖ KEEPING BODY AND SOUL TOGETHER

Throughout the civilized world, agriculture had to a large degree supplanted hunting and gathering. The latter mode continued to supply a substantial part of the daily diet only in regions of Africa, which were blessed with more protein-bearing game than any other part of the globe. But even in Africa, in the savanna of the midcontinent where the empires of Ghana and Mali were centered, crops and gardens were at least as important as hunting.

In East and Southeast Asia by the fifteenth century, the growing of basic food grains—notably, rice—had been refined by many hundreds or even thousands of years of practice. All able-bodied males and females were normally expected to work the land in some capacity, their own or someone else's as the case might be. The Asian village, whether Chinese, Indonesian, or Indian, was a very tightly knit socioeconomic organism, perhaps even more so than most village cultures. Depending on custom, the crops raised, and local ecology, land was variously in the hands of peasants with small holdings, tenant farmers, sharecroppers, or collectives embracing all village families. Any combination of these was also possible. Large estates worked by gangs of landless peasants were unknown or exceptional; most people had some direct stake in the cultivation of nearby farmland they considered their own or worked as long-term tenants.

In Africa clan-demarcated villages depended on both crops and gathering for their food supply; hunting was a favored but subsidiary resource, especially in the grasslands where big game abounded. Females were by immemorial tradition the main farm labor; they tended the gardens and prepared the food. In some regions, such as present-day Kenya and Tanzania, the pastoral lifestyle predominated, and agriculture was very limited. The same was true of the Sahel and the Sahara, where there was too little rainfall for agriculture. But in the more settled and urbanized areas, farming supplied Africans, as all other peoples, with the essentials of life and represented the usual work.

In the Americas the Spaniards discovered a large number of foods, which were then introduced into the European diet. These included maize, potatoes, manioc, several types of beans, squashes, and sugarcane. Most or all of these had been cultivated by the Amerindians. From the accounts of the conquistadors and the early missionaries, it seems clear that the large majority of the Indians engaged in agriculture and that hunting and gathering food was rather exceptional except for specialties such as berries and certain wild fruits. The Spaniards with Cortez were astonished at the variety and abundance of the food grown for the population of Tenochtitlán by the surrounding regions of Mexico.

Thus, in the non-Western areas including the Muslim lands, agriculture in one form or another was by far the most common occupation, just as it was in the West. Climate and terrain were always the controlling factors. In some areas where climate and soil conditions were particularly favorable, such as southern China or the islands of Southeast Asia, tilling the land seems to have been the almost universal occupation and to have been engaged in by both sexes, with male and female chores clearly

■ **Rice Paddies.** This modern photo could have been taken a thousand years ago in any of the south and east Asia lands that depend on rice culture. The terraces are critical for maximal yields and water control.

delineated. Where agriculture was more difficult or less important, its tasks were assigned to one gender or the other, usually the female.

Nonagrarian modes of work were the same as in the West. The handful of educated rural people generally engaged in some sort of trading, served as officials with land-holding privileges, or were members of the clergy. The urbanites, more numerous in most Asian and American societies than in Africa, often engaged in a skilled trade or were artists, scribes, or merchants of some importance.

For most people, of course, ordinary physical labor (porters, cleaners, carters, and the like) was the usual means of staying alive in the towns, just as working with

■ **An Indian Bullock Cart.** In most of Asia and Africa, cattle are the usual means of moving heavy items or human beings any distance. Horses are too fragile and too expensive for this type of work, and motorized transport is not available. The construction of this cart has not changed appreciably in two thousand years.

animal and hoe was in the countryside. China was the most urbanized non-Western society, Africa the least so. The Muslim towns of West Asia and North Africa probably had the highest degree of literacy and thus the most nonagrarian occupations, but, of course, no data on such topics are available until recent times.

✛ MALE AND FEMALE

It is impossible to generalize accurately about the relative prestige, powers, or social position of males and females; any rule has too many exceptions. Having said that, we can observe that the female remained always in the male's shadow in public life and could not act publicly except as a reflection of a male's needs or desires. This summary of male-female relations would probably apply most definitely to China and less so to other societies, particularly those of sub-Saharan Africa and Buddhist Asia. As time passed, Muslim Asia became more like China, but this statement must also be qualified by noting that conditions varied from region to region and time to time.

In a stable society that did not face military threats from outside, the role of females, at least those in the upper class, might be enhanced. Where political-military challenges were frequent, however, males were usually in total command. China is the great exception here; despite its isolation and military potency, the tradition of female subordination went very deep. It was reinforced by Confucian teachings, but certainly did not originate with them.

In the Americas we have very little information except the sketchy reports of an occasional missionary father or other European observer. Upper-class Aztec women seem to have had some private rights and freedoms that many sixteenth-century European women might have envied, but the destruction of the Aztec written sources makes it impossible to know for certain. Certainly, the Spanish witnesses give no indication of female governors or high officials, and the major deities that have been identified are male. The absence of written sources in the Mayan and Incan empires limit our knowledge about.

In Africa, the female's status varied somewhat between Muslim and non-Muslim areas. As we have seen, Arab travelers remarked on the laxity of African restrictions on women in public, an indication that females played important roles in social intercourse of all sorts. This continued even after the upper class had accepted Islam; sub-Saharan African women were never as thoroughly isolated and subordinated as women in the Middle Eastern societies. Among the non-Muslim majority, women presumably

held an even more prominent place; nothing in the animist faith of the majority would exclude females from an honorable or significant place in the clan or family. Nevertheless, formal leadership in these hunting-gathering societies was reserved for the males, as was the norm in all societies where that mode of supply prevailed.

We have noted elsewhere the rigid subordination of the female in Confucian China. This inferior condition was ameliorated somewhat by the widespread adoption of Buddhism, a religion that emphasized the basic equality of men and women in cultivation of the Eightfold Path and encouraged the creation of *sangha* (monastic communities) of women as well as men. The Japanese also responded to this impulse after Buddhism was introduced in the sixth century, and upper-class Japanese women were encouraged in unusual freedoms by the refined court culture that Lady Murasaki described in her eleventh-century classic. How much of this freedom percolated down to the peasant mass is problematic, however; certainly, very few of Murasaki's subtleties were experienced or dreamed of in the villages.

✛ MARRIAGE AND DIVORCE

Everywhere, the joining of young persons in marriage was a familial or clan-dictated affair that gave some, but not very much, weight to personal preferences. In Hindu India, the bride and groom often had no direct knowledge of one another prior to the consummation of the marriage, even though they might have been betrothed for years via family contacts and contracts. Everywhere, a bride price or dowry or both had to be carefully calculated and paid, both to signify the serious nature of the marital arrangement for the families involved and to show the partner (and society at large) that he or she had entered into a respectable relationship of social equals.

Did these careful arrangements mean there were little or no marital friction or divorce? Hardly. Early societies had a substantial amount of the same types of marriage problems that afflict men and women today: jealousy, money, adultery, ill treatment, and so on. Physical abuse of the spouse was tolerated in some societies, but not in others. Wife beating was commonly seen through a caste or class filter: what was allowed to the peasant was condemned in the noble.

As in the West, *adultery* by the woman was taken very seriously, but for different, nondoctrinal reasons. [There seems to have been little moral outrage about female extramarital escapades except in the Islamic regions.] In Africa and Asia, it was the potential for doubt about the

Ibn Batuta's Impressions of West Africa in the 1300s

Much of our knowledge of medieval East and West African cultures is derived from accounts of foreigners traveling through these regions. One of the most compelling of these narratives is that of the Moroccan Arab *qadi* (a Muslim judge-theologian), Muhammad Ibn Batuta (1304–1369?), who journeyed as far afield as India, Sumatra, and central Asia.

Ibn Batuta's brief account of the Swahili cities of East Africa offers some insights into what struck an outsider as being of significance. His account of the empire of Mali in the western Sudan provides a detailed description of what he considered to be the more positive and negative aspects of Malian culture. Of particular note is his shock, devout Muslim that he was, at the rather unorthodox sexual practices of the people and the enhanced status enjoyed by women, compared to the practice in the Arab world.

I embarked at Mogadishu for the Swahili country with the object of visiting the town of Kilwa in the land of the Blacks. We came to Mombasa . . . they have fruit trees on the island, but no cereal, which have to be brought to them from the mainland. Their food consists chiefly of bananas and fish. The inhabitants are pious, honorable and upright, and they have well-built wooden mosques. . . . Kilwa is a fine and substantially-built town, and all its buildings are of wood. Its inhabitants are constantly engaged in military expeditions, for their country is contiguous to that of the heathen Blacks. The sultan at the time of my visit . . . was noted for his gifts and generosity. . . . I have seen him give the clothes off his back to a mendicant who asked for them. . . .

Their women [those of the West African empire of Mali] are of surpassing beauty and are shown more respect than the men. The state of affairs amongst these people is indeed extraordinary. Their men show no signs of jealousy whatever; no one claims descent from his father, but on the contrary from his mother's brother . . . *these* are Muslims, punctilious in observing the hours of prayer, studying books of law, and memorizing the *Koran.* Yet their women show no bashfulness before men and do not veil themselves. . . . Any man who wishes to marry one of them may do so, but they do not travel with their husbands, and even if one desired to do so her family would not allow her to go. The women there have "friends" and "companions" amongst the men outside their own families, and the men in the same way have "companions" amongst the women of other families. A man may go into his house and find a wife entertaining her "companion" but he makes no objection to it. . . . One day, at Walata, I went into the qadi's house . . . and found him with a young woman of remarkable beauty. . . . I was shocked and turned to go out, but she laughed at me . . . and the qadi said to me "Why are you leaving? She is my companion." I am amazed at their conduct. . . .

The Blacks possess some admirable qualities. They are seldom unjust, and have a greater abhorrence of injustice than other people. . . . There is complete security in their country. Neither traveller nor inhabitant in it has anything to fear from robbers or men of violence. . . . On Fridays, if a man does not go early to the mosque, he cannot find a corner to pray in, on account of the crowds. . . . Among their bad qualities . . . the women servants, slave-girls, and young girls go about in front of everyone naked. . . . Women go into the King's presence naked . . . and his daughters also go about naked. Then there is their custom of putting dust and ashes on their heads, as a mark of respect. . . .

SOURCE: "Travels of Ibn Batuta," excerpted from The *Islamic World* edited by McNeill, Waldman, pp. 274–277, 1973. Reprinted with permission of Oxford University Press.

parentage of a child that disturbed people. Since proper honor for the ancestors was of crucial importance in these societies, knowing *who* was a genuine link in the family chain and thus had a claim to receive honor was essential. Incidentally, what constituted adultery was broader than the sexual act itself. Compromising the family honor and the linkage of generations was possible even without physical contact.

Polygamy was the norm among all non-Western societies. Only the Christian West chose to see monogamous

Fourteenth Century Muslim Customs: Ibn Batuta's *Travels*

Muhammed ibn Abdallah ibn Butata was an extraordinary traveller who left his home in Tangiers to make the holy pilgrimage *haji* to Mecca and kept on moving through the Islamic world for the next quarter-century or so. After returning, he wrote a voluminous memoir of his adventures and the sights he had seen, known as the *Travels of Ibn Batuta* in the West. In the following excerpt he tells of the Maldive Islands, an outpost of Muslims in the Indian Ocean where he functioned for a brief time as a *qadi* or judge.

The people of the Maldive Islands are upright and pious, sound in belief, and sincere in thought; their bodies are weak, they are unused to fighting, and their armour is prayer. Once when I ordered a thief's hand to be cut off, a number of those in the room fainted. . . In each island of theirs, there is a beautiful mosque, and most of the buildings are made of wood. They are very cleanly and avoid filth; most of them bathe twice a day to cleanse themselves, because of the extreme heat there and their profuse perspiration. They make plentiful use of fragrant oils such as oil of sandalwood. . .

All, high or low, are barefooted; their lanes are kept swept clean and are shaded by trees, so that to walk in them is like walking in an orchard. In spite of that every person entering a house must wash his feet with water from a jar kept in a chamber in the vestibule, and wipe them with a rough towel of palm matting he finds there.

Their womenfolk do not cover their hands, not even their queen does so, and they comb their hair and gather it at one side. Most of them wear only an apron from their waists to the ground, the rest of their bodies being uncovered. . . .

When I held the qadiship there, I tried to put an end to this practice and ordered them to wear clothes, but I met with no success. No woman was admitted to my presence unless her body was covered, but apart from that I was unable to effect anything.

It is easy to get married in these islands on account of the smallness of the dowries and the pleasures of the women's society. When ships arrive, the crew marry wives, and when they are about to sail they divorce them; it is really a sort of temporary marriage. The women never leave the country.

When I was appointed, I strove my utmost to establish the prescriptions of the Sacred Law. There are no lawsuits there like those in our land. The first bad custom I changed was the practice of divorced wives staying in the houses of their former husbands, for they all do so until they marry another husband. I soon put that to rights. About 25 men who had acted thus were brought before me; I had them beaten and paraded in the bazaar, and the women put away from them. Afterward, I gave strict injunctions that the prayers were be observed, and ordered men to go swiftly to the street and bazaar after the Friday services; anyone whom they found not having prayed I had beaten and paraded.

SOURCE: "Travels of Ibn Batuta" excerpted from *The Islamic World* edited by McNeill, Waldman, pp. 274–277, 1973. Reprinted with permission of Oxford University Press.

marriage as a sacrament that possessed moral value and imposed standards of conduct. Polygamy was usually a function of social and economic standing, rather than the expression of a personal desire (let alone sexual need). Multiple wives, in other words, were the expected consequence of a man's high income and status in the community. If additional wives could not be supported properly, they were neither expected nor permitted. This rule was most specific in the Muslim countries, where the Prophet had been quite clear on the obligations of a husband toward his spouse.

In animist Africa, on the other hand, polygamy was the universal rule, regardless of wealth. Taking younger wives as a man matured was considered a natural and desirable way to expand the clan and its relative importance. The offspring of these unions were considered the responsibility of the females, collectively and without distinction, thus reinforcing the prevalent African custom of seeing the clan or the tribe, rather than the family, as the basic unit of social life.

Divorce was common enough that every society developed some definite rules to regulate it. Grounds varied, but all peoples and religions acknowledged the impossibility of keeping a marriage together when one partner found living with the other intolerable. Like marriage, divorce was viewed not as a question of resolving legal status, but rather as a matter of finding a viable compromise between the inclinations of the individual and the demands of the larger community. In some cases, the wife simply abandoned her husband and returned to her parents' home, or the husband commanded his wife to remove herself from his bed and board. More often all the parties involved had to follow specific traditional steps before some authority, such as a council of village elders, would issue directives about the division of property and future obligations.

In some instances, a divorced wife was considered an outcast with no further prospects of marriage, but this seems to have been the exception. More often, if she was still young, a previous marriage had little negative effect upon her desirability as a wife and might even enhance it if she had borne healthy children. Responsibility for the physical welfare of the minor children (age fifteen and younger) almost always remained with the mother and her female relatives; but parental custody was normally vested in the father as head of the family or keeper of the lineage. In the few matriarchal family systems we know of, responsibility was joined to custody on the mother's side, and the father played a lesser role.

✤ EDUCATION AND ITS USES

Education was sharply defined by gender. Boys of the upper classes were given at least a smattering of literacy and rhetorical instruction in the Muslim and East Asian worlds, either through the Muslim *medresh* or by tutors. The more promising students went on to higher institutions such as the great university in Cairo or the medical research academies. In China, both the sons of the gentry and the occasional peasant boy of exceptional promise were tutored in Confucian philosophy and the arts so they could gain access to the mandarin bureaucracy. In both India and Africa, formal schooling outside the home was

■ **Village in the Sudan.** The style of housing as well as construction material varied markedly throughout the habitat of nonWestern populations. In this African village, the walls of the huts are of mud and wattle, covered by a sharply angled roof of long grass thatch. The interiors are both well-ventilated and cool.

■ **Woman Harvesting Grain.** This Bangladeshi woman is cutting the family grain plot by means of a knife; the process is typical of the huge expenditure of hand labor normally necessary for the most routine tasks in most of the nonWestern world.

unknown, and that also appears to have been the case in America. In these societies, young men acquired the information that was deemed important by emulating the older generation.

For girls everywhere, literacy was not considered important even among the upper class; there were, however, exceptions, such as the Japanese court ladies whom Lady Murasaki so carefully observed. Female education was usually limited to practical instruction in the domestic economy and, among the upper class, to social graces as defined by the male. In Islam, even this aspect was slighted in favor of absolute subordination and passivity.

Outside the Islamic world, the link between education and civil or religious *power* was most pronounced in China and its Confucian satellites in Korea and Indochina. Where Buddhism in its Mahayana form was potent, this link was diminished by the insistence on achieving spontaneous enlightenment and the role of the *boddhisattvas.* In Japan, formal education was certainly prized, but was not essential for the exercise of power in government. Power in sub-Saharan Africa was largely attributable to ancestry and the belief in the sacred nature of the chieftaincy, as created and reinforced by shamans and other quasi-supernatural individuals. The same was true, so far as can be discerned, in the Americas.

For most people, education was associated with attaining or retaining social status—"earning a living" as we would say. It was limited to an apprenticeship in a trade or observing an older model—a father or elder brother for boys, a mother or elder sister for girls. In the more advanced areas such as the Middle East, India, or China, where religion and several millennia of tradition reinforced the high status of the educated minority, occupational mobility was minimal. Only with extraordinary talent or luck could an individual shift from one social stratum to a higher one. In Hindu India, this difficulty was reinforced by caste restrictions, which grew constantly more complex and refined.

All in all, *downward mobility* was probably more common than upward, as a couple of years of scant crops or floods or any of the myriad potential disasters for a farmer could drive him deeply into debt. But as in the West, the village kinship network and the sense of collectivity cushioned the blow for many. All peasants knew that tomorrow they might need what they offered to a neighbor or kinsman today. They withheld it at their peril.

In much of the non-Western world after about 1000 C.E., the relatively static quality of the village economy and the society it supported contributed to the ignorance of math-based science and technology. These subjects were not considered relevant or useful for the governing classes. Exceptions can, of course, be found from time to time, but on the whole, this attitude was a significant cause of the shift of power from East to West that begins to be visible about 1400. In both East Asia and the Muslim countries, formal education continued to focus upon the legal, the literary, and the artistic spheres, while in the West these subjects were increasingly challenged by mathematical and physical disciplines. Nor did any non-Western societies experience a rise in literacy such as that associated with the Protestant sects' insistence on Bible reading.

❧ Religious Beliefs and Morality

Regardless of educational background, the masses of men and women in any civilization are greatly affected by religious belief or the philosophies inspired by religious beliefs. In the non-Western world, such beliefs were as potent as Christianity was in the West. Here we note some differences between these non-Western faiths and those of the West.

Only in the Judeo-Christian West and to a limited degree in the Islamic regions was the *link between theology and morality* taken for granted. In East Asia, Africa, and the Americas, worship of the gods (often conceived of as ancestors) was only distantly, if at all, related to standards of public conduct or private acts. Even among Muslims, the absence of a formal priesthood guaranteed the slow and only partial development of a theology that could be translated into a guide to morals.

Another distinguishing feature of the Eastern religions when compared with the West or Islam is their universal reluctance to develop a supernatural revelation for the behavior and salvation of the faithful. This was true of the varieties of Buddhism, Hinduism, the animist, ancestor-centered belief of the sub-Saharan Africans, and the Daoist nature worship of China. Confucian China essentially rejected the supernatural as irrelevant to human morality. So far as can be determined now, the religions of the Americas also did not attempt to link the codes of morality they employed with theological speculations or revelation.

What constituted righteous living and acceptable public conduct in all these societies was primarily dictated by social and economic factors, rather than theology. Experience over long periods had shown that a certain mode of action or a certain set of values or convictions contributed to private and public harmony and mutual prosperity. Insofar as possible, the institutions and cultural activity of a given people were then adapted to inculcating and reinforcing these modes of action, beginning with the informal education of children at their parents' knees. Rarely did a formal education, conducted by an officially recognized priesthood, constitute the channel for ascertaining right from wrong. This latter approach was a peculiarly Jewish and Christian tradition that was emulated to some extent by orthodox Islam.

The insistence on viewing morals from the standpoint of the *community's welfare* rather than the attainment of individual salvation is another hallmark of the non-Western religions or philosophies. Although both Jewish and Christian teaching have sometimes emphasized the necessity of finding a balance between individual and social welfare, the Eastern faiths have always been more consistent in refusing to permit the individualism that the West has embraced.

In the absence of supernatural sources for doctrine, the Eastern faiths have also been less fearful of heresy and much *more tolerant of doctrinal variation* over time and place. This tolerance has led in places to what appears to Western eyes as a chaos of differing, but not competitive, beliefs. The non-Western civilizations see no problems in this situation; on the contrary, their tolerance has at times been strained by what appears to them to be Judeo-Christian arrogance and doctrinal presumption.

Summary

In the non-Western societies, earning a living revolved around agriculture in some form, just as it did in the West. Only here and there in Africa and the steppes of Asia was sufficient game or pasture land available to support a hunting or pastoral lifestyle for large numbers. In the urban sectors of the populations, merchants and artisans were present in some degree. Before 1500 urbanization was highest in coastal China and the Muslim societies of West Asia, while sub-Saharan Africa lagged in this regard. Male and female patterns generally followed those already encountered in the West. Females were subordinated in public affairs almost everywhere and in every epoch; although exceptions could be found in non-Muslim Africa and possibly among the highest strata in East Asian societies. The ascendancy of males was normally in direct relationship to the violence and instability of the society, which in turn were often determined by its relative isolation from competitors.

Marriage was a matter for the family or clan, more than for the individuals involved. Nevertheless, this did not preclude affection and respect between partners. Where these were lacking, divorce followed specified rules just as in the modern West. Children normally were the responsibility of the mother and were sometimes shared with other wives of the same man, as in Africa.

Education was a function of social class or caste. Boys usually received more extensive and formal training than girls; in most societies literacy was rare for either sex. Social mobility was rarely procured by educational achievement except in China.

Religious beliefs in the non-Western world differ in several fundamental ways from the Judeo-Christian tradi-

tions and values. The absence of an official priesthood gave more scope to deviations from the mainstream. Heresies were more likely to find acceptance than to be proscribed, and the welfare of the community played a larger role in religious belief than it did in the Western tradition of individual salvation attained through individual efforts.

Test Your Knowledge

1. From what we know now, it is most accurate to say that the female in the non-Western world
   a. was generally more prominent in public affairs than in the West.
   b. was often in control of public affairs.
   c. was generally worse off than in the West in the same epoch.
   d. cannot be generalized about in terms of public prestige or prominence.
2. The usual form of male-female marital relationship in the non-Western world was
   a. polygamy.
   b. monogamy.
   c. polyandry.
   d. informal and unstable.
3. As a general rule, the mobility of labor in non-Western societies was
   a. more often down than up.
   b. easily set in motion by technical progress.
   c. dependent on the wishes of the lower classes.
   d. probably easier in rural areas than in urban settings.
4. Which of these societies did *not* take the relation between theology and morality for granted?
   a. Judaism
   b. Christianity
   c. Islam
   d. Buddhism
5. The primary function of marriage in African and East Asian societies was to
   a. enrich the bride's family as recompense for her lost labor.

   b. produce male children to continue the lineage of the husband.
   c. provide an outlet for the sex drive that did not threaten the social order.
   d. assure the happiness of the couple.
6. The society described by Lady Murasaki in her *Tale of Genji*
   a. was typical of only a very small fraction of the Japanese population.
   b. could have been common among the Japanese population at the time.
   c. was surely the product of her imagination.
   d. was based on military prowess of females as well as males.
7. What is known of non-Western habits of divorce indicates that
   a. the woman was always considered the guilty party and treated accordingly.
   b. the man had to provide for his divorced wife as well as for a second bride.
   c. the children were generally turned over to the husband's family for supervision.
   d. maintenance of children and the divorced wife varied from place to place and case to case.
8. Both coastal China and western Asia were
   a. strongly subject to Muslim influences.
   b. supported by a pastoral economy.
   c. more urban than most other areas.
   d. very isolated from foreign contacts.

Bibliography

Many of the works cited in previous bibliographies dealing with the non-Western peoples will be useful here. Authors of works which are particularly relevant include R. Thapar and A.L. Basham for India; J. Gernet and J.K. Fairbank for China; E.O. Reischauer for Japan; J. Fage, and R. Oliver, and P. Bohannon for Africa; and H.W. Von Hagen for the Americas.

The *Everyday Life in. . . .* series, most translated from the original French are often very informative, though the quality and coverage are uneven.

Chang, K.C. *Food in Chinese Culture*, 1977 is an entertaining look at eating habits among people with the widest culinary experience in the world.

Dunn, C.J. *Everyday Life in Traditional Japan*, 1969 is a good example of the series.

Shinnie, M. *Ancient African Kingdoms*, 1966 gives some of the flavor of daily affairs.

Smith, H. *The World's Religions*, 1991 is an excellent introduction to all of the major religions of East and West in their conceptual essences.

Sovstelle, J. *Daily Life of the Aztecs on the Eve of the Spanish Conquest,* 1961 is probably the best single book on the topic. He has also written on the Olmec.

Spence, J. *The Death of a Woman Wang*, 1986 gives a unique account of the daily affairs of an ordinary woman of 17th century China.

Waley, A. has brought a most extraordinary man to life in his *The Poetry and Career of Li-po*, 1958 a biography of one of the greatest and most quoted of Chinese poets.

THE HIGH MEDIEVAL AGE

The European community that emerged from the trials and troubles of the Dark Age was built on personal status. All people had a place on the social ladder, but their specific rung depended on whether their function was to fight, to pray, or to work. The great majority, of course, fell into the third category. But occasionally they could leave it by entering one of the other categories. The church was open to entry from below and grew steadily more powerful in both the spiritual and the civil spheres. Its claims in worldly matters brought it into increasing conflict with the kings and emperors, a conflict that hurt both sides. And despite the resistance of both church and nobles, the royal courts gained more and more prestige and power. The High Middle Age (c. 1000–1300 C.E.) saw the faint beginnings of the modern state and society.

✤ THE WORKERS

The majority of people were *peasants* who worked on and with the land. Perhaps 90 percent of the population in Western Europe, and more in Eastern Europe, worked the fields, orchards, and woodlots for a (generally hard) living. Their lives were filled with sweaty labor, but this work was far from continuous. For six months of the year or so, they were restricted by climate and habit to their huts and villages. Then they spent a great deal of time on farm and household chores and literally "sitting about." Even during the growing season, from about April to the autumn harvest, many holidays and village festivals interrupted the drudgery.

What the modern world calls labor discipline—that is, the custom of reporting to a given place at a given time daily, prepared to do a given job in a specified manner—was almost unknown. Work was a communal responsibility in large part; people worked with others in a rhythm dictated by the needs of the community and ancient traditions. These traditions left much room for rest and recreation.

The Feudal Serf

The work on the large manors, which (as we saw in Chapter 18) became dominant in Western Europe, was performed by millions of *serfs*. By the year 1000, serfs had replaced *slaves* in most places in Europe. Slavery virtually disappeared because the Christian church was opposed to the enslavement of fellow Christians, and gradually this

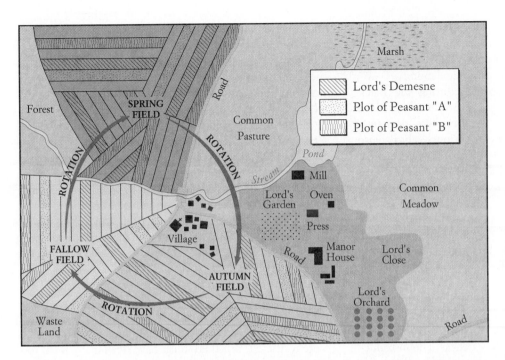

● **MAP 25.1 A Medieval Manor.** The divisions between lord and peasants are shown in this sketch of a typical manor. Note the extent given over to fallow and thus unproductive; note also the lord's demesne holdings which had first call on the peasants labor.

viewpoint prevailed. Since almost the entire continent had been converted to Christianity by 1100, there were few non-Christians left who could be enslaved. Black slaves from Africa were occasionally purchased from Moorish traders, but they were so expensive that they were viewed as curiosities and kept in noble households rather than used for labor. In some places and at some times, serfdom differed little from slavery in practice. Legally, however, a *serf could not be bought or sold* as a slave could, and no one questioned that a serf was a human being with God-given rights and a soul equal in the eyes of Heaven to any other person.

Nevertheless, serfs were in some important measure unfree. They were bound by law and tradition to a given place, normally a farm village, and to a given occupation, normally farmwork, under the loose supervision of their lord (*seigneur, Herr, suzerain*). The actual supervision was generally exercised by a steward or some other overseer appointed by the lord. Beyond this general statement, it is difficult to give a specific description of serfdom because conditions varied so much by time and place. Conditions in, say, tenth-century France were not the same as in eleventh-century Spain or England. In general, however, serfs were bound to perform labor services for their lord and to pay certain "dues" and taxes to the lord, which were set by tradition and by sporadic negotiations. Only rarely were these conditions written. The labor took myriad forms, but usually included work on the **demesne,**

the part of the agricultural land of the estate which belonged to the lord directly. The remainder of the estate's cultivable land (most of it in most cases) was normally given out to the serfs for their own use (see Map 25.1). They did not own it outright, however, but had only a *usufruct* right (that is, a right to use the land, which was still owned by the lord). Serfs who fell into the lord's bad graces could lose their plots.

Serfdom usually became a *hereditary condition.* People usually had become serfs because they fell into debt or because they offered themselves and their land to a local strongman in exchange for his protection during a period of disorder. In bad times, it was always safer to be the ward of some powerful person than to try to stand alone.

Although serfs were born into an unfree condition, it was not unusual for them to gain their freedom. The most common way was simply to run away from the lord's manor and start a new life in freedom elsewhere, normally in a town. "Town air makes free" was an axiom of medieval lawyers; people who could prove they had resided in a town for a year and a day were usually considered legally free, whatever their previous condition may have been. Many other serfs gained their freedom with the lord's permission. Some were freed of further obligation by the lord's will; others were rewarded for good services; still others worked their way out of serfdom by paying off their debts. After the eleventh century freedom could also be won by volunteering to open new lands, particularly in the Low Countries (where dikes were constructed and land was reclaimed from the sea) and in Eastern Europe, where much uncultivated land still existed and lords were anxious to gain new labor.

After the tremendous loss of life during the Black Death (see Chapter 26), the serfs who survived were in a strong bargaining position with their masters, and serfdom in Western Europe in the traditional labor sense became less onerous. Peasant tenants still had to meet certain dues and minor obligations, but the old hardships and treatment like slaves were over.

Medieval Agriculture

Manorial agriculture made steady, though unspectacular progress during the High Middle Age. Productivity, which was formerly very low (perhaps a 3:1 ratio for return of grain from seed), improved with the invention and introduction of the *iron-tipped plow* in the twelfth century. Because it could till heavier soils, this implement opened up whole new regions to grain production. The introduction of the *horse collar,* which was padded to allow the horse to pull a much heavier burden, was another major advance. Horses were expensive, and difficult to handle and keep fit, but they were so much more flexible and faster than oxen that their widespread use amounted to an agricultural innovation of the first importance—similar in impact to the introduction of tractors. The systematic use of animal manure as fertilizer also improved productivity, although this practice remained the exception.

The productivity of medieval agriculture was limited because one-third to one-half of the cultivated land was left **fallow** (unseeded) each year. This practice was necessary because it was the only way the land could recover its nutrients in the absence of fertilizer. Every farmer had a piece or a strip of land in both the cultivated and the fallow segments of the manor, which were rotated from year to year.

Famines were common in years when the harvest was poor; reserves were at best sufficient for one bad harvest, and the miserable state of transportation and roads made it difficult to move foodstuffs. It was not unusual for people to starve in one area, while there was a surplus 100 or 150 miles away.

Urban Workers

The urban workers were not yet numerous and were sharply divided by social status. At the top were the *craftsmen and shopkeepers.* Some of them were highly skilled and enjoyed a solid economic livelihood; they could often afford to educate their children in the hope of advancing them still further. These people benefited from the *guild system* (see Chapter 26), which restricted competition and assured that their socioeconomic status would be secure.

Below these fortunates were the semiskilled and casual laborers. These men and women worked for others and had few prospects of becoming independent. Many of them lived a hand-to-mouth existence that may have been harder than the lives of the bulk of the manorial peasants. They were often the victims of changed economic conditions (like a new trade route) or local famines.

Finally, the towns were filled with marginal people who never had steady work. They begged or moved on to more promising places, "living on air" in the meantime. Historians have estimated that as many as one-fourth of the population of seventeenth-century Paris fell into this category. The number in medieval days was smaller, because the towns were still relatively small and residence rights were restricted. But there must have been many then, too.

⚜ THE WARRIORS

The European nobility of the Middle Age constituted perhaps 2 to 3 percent of the population on average, though their numbers varied from country to country and region to region. Their rights stemmed generally from **patents,** royal documents that granted them or their ancestors the status of noble and certain privileges that went with that status.

What type of privileges did they have? The privileges could be almost anything imaginable: economic, political, or social, but above all, they were social. The nobles were thought to be of a different nature than the commoners. They spoke mostly to one another, married other nobles, held exclusive gatherings, and enjoyed an altogether different lifestyle than ordinary people, be they well-off or poor.

Like serfdom, noble status was hereditary, so nobles were generally born noble. Nobility was thus a *caste* that was more or less closed to outsiders. In medieval times, it was rarely possible to buy one's way into the nobility, although the practice became common later. Women were equally as noble as men, if they were born into the caste. They could not become noble by marriage, however, while men occasionally could. In any event, it was very unusual for either male or female nobles to marry beneath their position.

Like serfdom, nobility varied so much that it is impossible to generalize accurately beyond a few facts. Not all nobles were wealthy, though many were. The only type of wealth that was meaningful was land. By the 1300s it was not so unusual to find impoverished nobles who were anxious to have their sons marry rich commoners' daughters. Many once-noble families sank out of sight, pulled down by their ineptitude in business, their mortgages, or their hugely wasteful lifestyle. Their places were taken by newcomers from below, who had obtained a patent for themselves in some way or another (perhaps as a reward for distinguished military service).

Nobles were always free; they could not be bound as an inferior to another. But they were also normally **vassals** of some person of superior rank to whom they owed feudal loyalty and specific duties. These duties were military in nature or had begun as military and were later changed into something else. The superior person to whom service was owed was called the vassal's **suzerain.** He (or she) gave something of value to the vassal in return, perhaps political advantage, protection, or administration of justice. The details of a medieval noble's life were dictated by this system of mutual obligations.

Not only were the nobility free, but they were also the sole political factor in medieval life. The king depended on his nobility to run the government and administration. In some countries, churchmen who were not noble by birth also held some offices, but the secular nobles were everywhere the decisive factor in government at all levels from the royal court to the village.

A noble's rank more or less determined his job; there were basically five *ranks of nobility,* ranging downward from duke to count to marquis to baron to knight. Each country had its variations on this scheme. The knights were semi-noble in that their status was solely for their own lifetimes and was not hereditary; their sons might be ennobled by the king, but they had no claim to nobility by birth. Knights were by far the most numerous of the nobility and the least prestigious.

The nobles originally claimed their preferred status by virtue of being professional soldiers, policemen, and judges. They protected the other members of society, upheld justice, ensured that the weak were not abused by the strong, and guarded public morals. That, at least, was the nobles' story! In fact, nobles were often noble because they were successful brutes and pirates, who possessed stronger arms than their neighbors and intimidated them into submission. Alternatively, they bought their way into the king's favor or married their way upward.

In any case, the nobles looked upon themselves and their fellows as the orderers and defenders of society through the command of both God and king and their own sense of honor. *Honor* was a particularly important aspect of their lives, and every person was supremely conscious of its obligations. Honor meant spending a year's income on the marriage of a daughter or on a

■ **Armored Knights in Formation.** This Spanish painting illustrates the elaborate armor worn by thirteenth century Christian Knights in their battles against the Moors. Heavy swords and battle axes made such protection a necessity.

proper costume for a court function. Honor meant fighting duels over alleged insults from other nobles and refusing to fight them with commoners. Honor meant living as a nobleman should: as though he had a huge income, while holding money in contempt.

Female nobles frequently held positions of some power in public life. Queens were generally considered to be a political misfortune, but this did not prevent a few women from attaining that rank. More frequently, widows of royal husbands served as regents as did Blanche of Castile (see the Biography in Chapter 18). The widows were usually expected to seek another husband and defer to his advice. Some did, and some did not!

In private life, many noblewomen exerted a strong influence on their husbands or ran the household themselves, as we know from many historical records. They were responsible for the day-to-day management of the estates; when their husband was absent, which was frequent, they moved into his shoes in matters of commerce and even warfare. There are records of duchesses and abbesses who did not hesitate to resort to arms to defend their rights.

But first and foremost, like all medieval women outside the convents, a noblewoman was expected to produce legitimate children to assure the continuity of the (male) family name and wealth. A barren noble wife was in a highly unenviable position; sterility was automatically attributed to the woman, but divorce was next to impossible due to the church's opposition. Hence, sonless fathers sometimes turned to concubines in their search for posterity. A bastard so produced would have only very limited rights, even if he was acknowledged, but for some desperate fathers this was better than nothing. The legal ramifications of bastardy, especially the ability to inherit titles and property, were a preoccupation of medieval lawyers.

✣ The Worshippers

The men and women who worshiped were less numerous than the fighters, but they also filled a social niche that was just as important. In an age of faith, when no one doubted the reality of heaven, hell, or the Last Judgement, when a soul would be sent to either, those who prayed for others were considered to be absolutely essential. They included both the *parish clergy and the regular clergy, or monks,* but since the monks were both more numerous and more important than the parish clergy, the following applies particularly to them.

The chief difference between monks and parish priests was that the monks lived somewhat apart from the world in communities called *monasteries.* The monastery has had a long history in the Christian world. The first ones were founded in the fourth century in Egypt, but the most important monastic institutions were those founded by the Italian St. Benedict in the sixth century. His **Benedictine Rule** for monastic life was the most widely observed in the Middle Age, although several others were also in use by the High Middle Age (the Trappist and Cistercian rules, for example).

The Benedictine monks believed a mixture of *manual and intellectual work* was best for a pious and contemplative life. The monks operated extensive farms, which they sometimes leased out to peasants in part. They were also good craftsmen, and the abbey house or main center of the monastery was a workshop filled with bustling activity. But the monks never forgot that their main responsibility was prayer, and their intercession with God on behalf of their fellows was at all times the center of their lives. From early morning to night, the Benedictine monks set aside hours for prayer and contemplation. They also sometimes ran schools for the more talented peasant youth, some of whom were invited to join them in the monastic life.

Monks and nuns (in the convents that were the close equivalent of the monasteries but designed for females) normally came from the aristocracy until the twelfth or thirteenth century, when they became increasingly middle class in origin. They were very often the younger sons or daughters of a noble family, who had little hope of inheriting property sufficient to maintain them in proper style. Their parents therefore put them into a religious institution at the age of twelve or so. Sometimes, the child was miserable in the religious life and left it sooner or later without permission. More often, a compromise was arranged, and the unhappy monk or nun was allowed to leave without the scandal of an open rebellion.

The wealth of the monasteries was considerable. European Christians customarily remembered the church in their wills, if only to assure that masses would be said for their souls in that way-station enroute to heaven called purgatory. Noble sinners often tried to escape their just deserts at the Last Judgement by leaving the local monastery or convent a large bequest on their deathbed. Since most of the charitable institutions of the Middle Age were connected with and run by the clergy, it was natural to leave money or income-producing property to the church. In these ways, the property controlled by the church, and above all by the numerous monasteries, grew to tremendous figures. Historians reckon that, as late as the fifteenth century, the property controlled by the church institutions outweighed that controlled by the Crown and nobles together.

This involvement with the business world and large amounts of money often had deleterious effects on the spiritual life of the monks and the nuns. Too often, monastic policy was made by those who oversaw the investments and the rents, rather than the most pious and self-sacrificing individuals. The monasteries repeatedly fell into an atmosphere of corruption, fostered by the indifference of some of their leaders to religious affairs and their close attention to financial ones.

Despite this tendency, the monks and nuns generally did much good work and fulfilled the expectations of the rest of society by their devotions and their actions on behalf of the poor. It should be remembered that medieval government was primitive, and the social welfare services that we expect from government did not exist. Instead, the church institutions—monasteries, convents, cathedrals, and parish churches—supplied the large majority of the "welfare" for the aged, the poor, and the helpless. The clergy founded and managed the hospitals, orphanages, and hospices, using funds contributed by the faithful or generated by the church business and rental income. Then as now, money was used for good ends as well as bad ones.

The New Clerical Orders

In the thirteenth century, **heresies** ("wrong belief") became much more widespread in the church than ever before. Regular crusades were even mounted against the heretics at times. In southern France, a crusade was mounted against those who insisted that there were two divinities, one who was Good and another who was Evil. This throwback to the age-old Zoroastrian beliefs (see Chapter 4) had come into Christian Europe from the East centuries earlier and had great appeal to those who tended to look upon the flesh as the province of the devil and the spirit as the province of God. These crusades literally meant to stamp out heresy by killing the heretics. Brutal force was their hallmark. To a pair of saintly young priests, this was not the Christian way; they sought a different approach.

St. Francis of Assisi was a young Italian who believed in and practiced a life of total poverty and total service to his fellows (see the Biography in this chapter). A magnetic personality, he was able to attract many others to his mission by his death in 1226. He thus founded the Franciscan Order of wandering monks, who begged for their food and shelter and preached the gospel of Christ to all who would listen. Orginally devoted to Francis's ideal of poverty, the order gradually changed as it expanded after his death to became a major branch of the priesthood. Though it became more conservative and less dedicated to poverty, it always retained something of Francis's ideals.

St. Dominic, a contemporary of Francis of Assisi, was a young Spaniard who wanted to reform the clergy in a different way. He wanted especially to convert the heretics back to the true faith by showing them the error of their ways calmly and peaceably. The Dominican Order was therefore an intellectual group, who specialized in lawyerly disputation and preaching. Dominicans were the outstanding professors of law and theology in the early universities of Europe, and they would later take the lead in the Inquisition in Spain against suspected heretics.

In their different ways, both Franciscans and Dominicans attempted to elevate the spiritual life of the clergy and, through them, the people of Europe. They attempted to bring about the reforms of the church that the papal court was ignoring. But their efforts were dulled with the passage of time and checked by a clerical hierarchy that did not want to hear of its failures and corruption or think about how to change.

✦ THE ECONOMIC REVIVAL

Starting in the eleventh century, the towns of Europe, so long stagnant or semideserted, began a strong revival. Some entirely new cities were founded, including Berlin, Moscow, and Munich. Mostly, however, the eleventh- and twelfth-century revival saw the renaissance of older sites under the influence of *(1) increased trade, (2) a more peaceful environment, and (3) a higher degree of skills and entrepreneurial activity.*

The basic reason for the resurgence of the towns was the *rising volume of trade.* After centuries of stagnation, Europe's merchants and moneylenders were again looking for new fields to conquer. The increasing ability of the royal governments to assure a degree of law and order within their kingdoms was a key factor in this increased trade. Others included the steady rise in population, the ability of the townsmen to purchase their liberties from the feudal nobles (see the Document in this chapter), and the reappearance of clerical and professional people.

In Western Europe, trade approached levels it had last reached in the fourth century. (In this context, "western" means Europe westward from midway across Germany, including Scandinavia and Italy.) Merchants found that a stable coinage and financial techniques such as checks and

Liberties of Lorris

In the town charter of the small city of Lorris in northern France are to be found the essence of the "liberties" that the medieval bourgeoisie gradually gained from a reluctant aristocracy, using the king as their protector. The charter of Lorris was granted by King Louis VII in 1155. By this time, the towns had fully recovered from the long centuries of decay and lawlessness after Rome's fall. Most of the rights deal with economic regulations and taxes because the feudal nobility were most likely to apply pressure in these areas. The third liberty illustrates the difference between the professional fighters, the knights, and the conscripted bourgeoisie, who dreaded warfare and feared the professional warriors. The knights who had aspirations of becoming landlords themselves, were usually willing to go to war at any time for their lord and to remain in the field as long as the lord desired. The eighteenth liberty is a good example of the rule that runaways would be free from serf status if they could remain in a town and out of trouble for a year and a day.

The charter of Lorris:

2. Let no inhabitant of the parish of Lorris pay a duty of entry nor any tax for his food, and let him not pay any duty of measurement for the corn [grain] which his labor, or that of his animals may procure him, and let him pay no duty for the wine which he shall get from his vines.

3. Let none of them go on a [military] expedition, on foot or horseback, from which he cannot return home the same day[!].

5. Let no one who has property in Lorris lose any of it for any misdeed whatsoever, unless the said misdeed be committed against us or our guests.

15. Let no man of Lorris do forced work for us, unless it be twice a year to take our wine to Orléans, and nowhere else; and those only shall do this work who have horses and carts, and they shall be informed of it beforehand....

18. Whoever shall remain a year and a day in the parish of Lorris without any claim having pursued him thither, and without the right [of remaining] having been forbidden him by us or by our provost [equivalent of sheriff], he shall remain there free and tranquil.

33. No man of Lorris shall pay any duty because of what he shall buy or sell for his own use on the territory of the parish, nor for what he shall buy on Wednesdays at the town market.

35. We order that whenever the provost shall be changed in the town, he shall swear faithfully to observe these customs; and the same shall be done by new serjeants when they shall be instituted.

Given at Orléans, in the year of our Lord 1155.

SOURCE: O. Johnson, *World Civilization*, p. 364.

---

letters of credit, which they learned from the Muslims, increased their commercial opportunities.

The obvious locations for markets were the strategic, protected places that had been market centers in Roman days. Old municipal centers, such as Cologne, Frankfurt, Innsbruck, Vienna, Lyon, and Paris, which had been almost abandoned in the sixth and seventh centuries, began to come back from the grave. These urban communities underwent a fairly steady revival beginning about 1000 C.E. They once again became what they had been under the Romans: commercial and manufacturing centers with some professionals and administrators, often in the employ of the church. Nevertheless, cities and towns

were not yet very large or numerous. By the twelfth century, for example, Cologne's population reached 30,000, which was large by medieval standards. The largest cities were Paris, Florence, and Venice, which had populations somewhere under 100,000 each in the twelfth century.

A number of developments helped to create a *more peaceful setting* for economic activity after the tenth century. One was the increased power of the church to enforce its condemnations of those who fought their fellow Europeans or engaged in random violence against the lower classes. As the church became a major propertyholder, it began to use its influence against those who

■ **Medieval Shopping Scene.** The bourgeoisie were generally occupied with buying and selling of goods. This painting shows the commercial district of a French thirteenth century town. From left to right, tailors, furriers, a barber, and a grocer are visible at work. Dogs were a constant sight in all medieval towns.

Violators were subject to spiritual sanctions, including excommunication, and to civil penalties as well in most areas.

The *Crusades* also contributed to peace by giving young nobles an outlet to exercise their warlike impulses in an approved form. Starting with the First Crusade in 1096, tens of thousands of aggressive younger sons of the nobility went off to Palestine or Eastern Europe to fight the pagans and make their fortune (they hoped).

Finally, the renewed application of Roman law led to the use of legal procedures as a substitute for armed action in disputes. Interest in the *corpus jurisprudentiae* began in the international law university founded at Bologna in the eleventh century. Roman law, which had always been retained to some slight degree in the church's administration of its internal matters, was now gradually reintroduced into secular affairs as well. The legal profession was already well developed in the twelfth century.

In part as a result of the first two factors, people began to develop *greater skills* and engage in more *entrepreneurial activity*. As trade and commerce increased and the threat of violence declined, it made sense for people to develop more skillful ways to make goods and provide services. As these skills became apparent to the potential users and buyers, entrepreneurs came into existence to bring the providers of skills and the users together. Along with entrepreneurs came real estate speculators (medieval towns were notoriously short on space), investment bankers (who usually started out as moneylenders), and a host of other commercial and financial occupations that we associate with "doing business." Some of these people succeeded in becoming quite rich, which was their main interest, and they displayed their success in fine townhouses and good living.

destroyed property through war and plunder. The *Peace of God* and the *Truce of God* were now enforced across most of the continent. Under the Peace of God, noncombatants, such as women, merchants, peasants, and the clergy, were to be protected from violence. The Truce of God forbade fighting on Sundays and all holy feast days.

■ **Moneylenders at Work.** This miniature from a fifteenth century manuscript shows the street booth of a moneylender in the town of Lucca, Italy. The moneylender exchanges different currencies from visiting merchants.

St. Francis of Assisi
1182–1226

The man called Francis of Assisi has long been one of the most attractive of the medieval saints to modern eyes. His message was very clear and simple: "Where there is hate, give love; where there is insult and wrongdoing, grant forgiveness and offer hope. Bestow happiness where there is sorrow, and give light where there is darkness." No one lived this highminded creed better than its originator.

Francesco (Francis) de Bernadone (1182–1226) was born the son of a wealthy cloth dealer in the prosperous town of Assisi in northern Italy. Though he apparently had no formal schooling, he was very quick intellectually and early in life was taken into his father's business. He was a member of the "gilded youth" of the town, drinking heavily, getting involved with loose women, and generally enjoying himself as rich, carefree adolescents have always done. His life seems to have been an ongoing party.

But in 1202 he opted to join the local freebooters (*condottieri*) and was taken prisoner during Assisi's squabble with the city-state of Perugia. He spent a year in captivity, a sobering experience. Two years later, ill with fever, he underwent a visionary experience that permanently changed his life. Faced with death, he came to feel that he had been spared for a purpose that he must discover. He renounced his family's wealth and began to dedicate his time to the service of God and the poor.

He visited the lepers and outcasts of the town and practiced a stringently simple life, begging his food. Wherever he was permitted, he preached to anyone who would listen a message of poverty, austerity, and, above all, love for every creature. Braving the inevitable ridicule, he called on his listeners to renounce their fortunes, sell their possessions, and give the proceeds to the poor around them. For his text, Francis took the word of Jesus to his apostles: "Take nothing for the journey, neither staff nor satchel, neither bread nor money." Trusting fully in the Lord, Francis demanded and practiced absolute poverty and the rejection of all material property.

Some people were touched by the power and sincerity of his preaching and joined him. In a relatively brief time, he had a band of followers, the "Little Brothers of Francis," and came to the attention of Pope Innocent III. Though suspicious at first, Innocent eventually recognized Francis's sincerity and moral stature. He received the papal blessing and was ordained a deacon (a priest with limited powers). His followers, called friars, were allowed to preach where they chose and to solicit the support of good Christians everywhere.

Francis died quite young, but not before he had almost single-handedly made substantial changes for the better in contemporary Christian practice. His example inspired many thousands to reject the materialism that had plagued the thirteenth-century clergy, especially the monastic orders. The Franciscans (who soon had a female auxiliary of nuns) always rejected the idea of the monastery, preferring to live and work among the people as helpmates and fellow sufferers.

Francis of Assisi felt a very strong bond between himself and all other beings. He addressed the birds and the beasts, the sun and the moon and the stars as his brothers and sisters. Once he preached a sermon to the birds, and the legend says that they responded by gathering round him. He did much to instill a love of God's natural world in his followers and should be called one of the Western world's first, and most attractive, ecologists.

Bourgeoisie and Jews

Many people in the towns were what we now call upper-middle-class professionals: doctors, lawyers, royal office-holders, and, first and foremost, merchants. These were the **bourgeoisie,** the people who lived within the *bourg* or *burg,* which was a walled settlement meant to protect life and property.

The towns and their inhabitants were by now becoming a major feature of the political and social landscape, particularly in northwestern Europe and northern Italy. In the thirteenth and fourteenth centuries, kings discovered that their surest allies against feudal rebels were the propertied townsmen. The towns were the source of a growing majority of the royal tax revenue, even though they contained only a small fraction (perhaps 10 percent) of the European population. The majority of the villagers' taxes disappeared into the pockets of the noble collectors and their agents, while the towns paid their taxes directly to the royal treasury.

By now, the townsmen were no longer dependents of the local lord; having purchased a charter from the throne, they had the privilege of electing their own government officials and levying taxes for local needs. Their defense costs (town walls were very costly to build and maintain) were borne by the citzenry, not put into the hands of the nobles. The towns often had the privilege of deciding citizens' casees in their own municipal courts; appeal went to the king's officials, not to the local nobleman.

Initially, *Jews* provided several of the financial services in medieval cities and in the countryside, too. But by the thirteenth century they were being rivaled by Christians, who no longer paid much attention to the church's official distaste for usury, or the taking of money for the use of money (interest). The Jewish population had come to Western Europe from the Mediterranean Jewish colonies of the Diaspora. They lived completely segregated from the Christian majority in small urban areas of a block or two called **ghettos.** Most places prohibited Jews from owning land, so they had little choice but to take up financial and mercantile pursuits.

Until the thirteenth century, anti-Semitic attacks on the Jews were relatively rare, but in that century, the kings of both England and France denounced and expelled the Jews on pretexts and seized their property, and the era of sporadic *pogroms,* or anti-Semitic mob actions, began. At this time, the Jews began to migrate from Western to Eastern Europe. The Eastern European states such as Poland and Hungary were more hospitable than the West this juncture. These states badly needed the Jews' experience in trade and finance, which the native populations were almost entirely lacking.

✣ ROYAL KINGDOMS AND THE FORMATION OF STATES

The revival of the towns and the growth of urban populations were important factors in the steady strengthening of the royal governments against the nobles' claims and feudal fragmentation. The foundations of the modern states of England, France, and Germany can be traced back to the thirteenth and fourteenth centuries.

A *state* is a definite territory with generally recognized boundaries and a *sovereign government.* It recognizes no superior sovereignty within its own borders. It suppresses violence among its subjects in the name of law and defends those subjects from outside oppressors and internal criminals. The state exercises its powers through a group of officials, courts, police forces, and an army.

England and France

England was a pioneer in creating a state. Since the fifth century when the island was conquered by the barbarian Angles and Saxons, it had been divided among a series of tribal kingdoms that fought one another and the invading Vikings. In the late eleventh century, the recently unified Anglo-Saxon kingdom had been invaded and conquered by William (the Conqueror), the formidable duke of Normandy, who had a weak claim to the English throne that the English nobility had not recognized. By right of conquest of what he considered a bunch of traitors, William proceeded to organize a *new type of kingdom,* in which the king alone was the source of final authority. Prior to this, the kings of feudal Europe were always being reminded of their dependency on the voluntary collaboration of their nobles in national affairs. Now William could ignore these claims and establish a cadre of noble officials who were all drawn from his supporters. A tangible sign of his power was the incredibly thorough and detailed **Domesday Book** (1080), which was prepared as a royal census for tax purposes.

William's successors were not all so clever or determined as he, but by the middle of the twelfth century, the earmarks of a modern state were faintly visible in England. It had, among other things, a loyal corps of royal officials, a system of courts and laws that was more or less uniform from one end of the kingdom to the other, a royal army that looked only to the king, and a single national currency.

France developed a little more slowly. In the early twelfth century, France was still a collection of nearly independent duchies and counties whose feudal lords looked only reluctantly and occasionally to the king in Paris for policy and leadership. Some of the French lords, like the count of Anjou and the duke of Normandy, could buy and sell the French king; the royal territory around Paris was a fraction of the size of their lands. Furthermore, the king had no royal army worthy of the name.

This situation began to change in the late twelfth century, when the ambitious **Philip II Augustus** came to the throne and started the process of unifying and strengthening the country. Over the next hundred years, the strength and prestige of the king of France increased relative to his feudal vassals. By the end of the thirteenth century, the king was stronger than any of his nobles and was sufficiently in control of taxation and the military that he could intimidate any of them or even a combination of them. The Crown would experience many ups and downs from this time onward in France, but the outlines of the French state were in place by 1300.

A major difference between the English and French systems of government in the Middle Age (and subsequently) was that the English Crown relied on unpaid local officials, who were rewarded for their service by social privileges and legislative powers (in the Parliament created in the thirteenth century). The French, on the other hand, created a royal bureaucracy, staffed by highly trained and highly paid officials, who were responsible only to the king and kept clear of local ties. The *English system* allowed for a maximum of local variations in administration and justice, although the entire kingdom conformed to the *common law* that the kings had gradually imposed. Each English county had its own methods of tax assessment, types of taxes, and voting rights, as did Scotland and Wales. The *French* bureaucrats carried out the same duties in the same fashion from one end of France to the other, but were not able to overcome the large linguistic and customary differences that distinguished Brittany from Normandy or Provence from Anjou. Until the Revolution of 1789, France remained more a series of semi-autonomous countries than a single nation. Thus, England was held together by its laws and the Parliament that made them, whereas France was unified by the Crown and its officials.

The German Empire

The modern state that we know as Germany was created only in the late nineteenth century. For many hundreds of years before that, its territory was an agglomeration of petty principalities, kingdoms, and free cities. This had not always been the case, however. In the Early and High Middle Ages, Germans had generally lived under one powerful government headed by an emperor who claimed descent from Charlemagne.

But this state failed and broke up for a specific reason. In the eleventh century, the emperor and the pope in Rome became embroiled in a long, bitter struggle over who should have the right to "invest" bishops in Germany, that is, to select the bishops and install them in office. This *Investiture Controversy* ripped the empire apart, as one noble after another took the opportunity to pull clear of the central government's controls. Another factor weakening the empire was that emperors succeeded to the throne

■ **A Prospect of Carcassonne.** The best preserved walled medieval town in France, Carcassonne shows how important protection from enemy armies and marauders was in the Middle Age. Most West European towns once possessed such walls but demolished them later in order to expand.

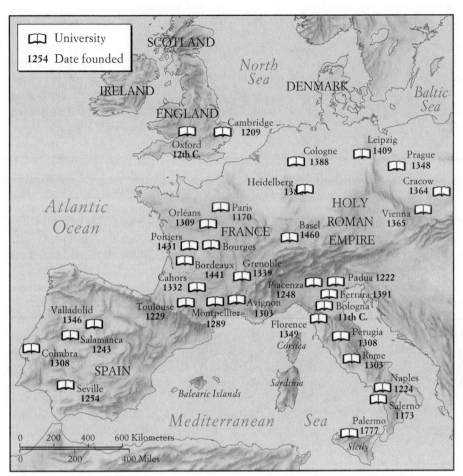

MAP legend:
- University
- 1254 Date founded

SCOTLAND

North Sea

DENMARK

IRELAND

ENGLAND

Baltic Sea

Cambridge 1209

Oxford 12th C.

Cologne 1388

Leipzig 1409

Prague 1348

Heidelberg 1386

Cracow 1364

Atlantic Ocean

Orléans 1309

Paris 1170

HOLY ROMAN EMPIRE

Vienna 1365

Poitiers 1431

FRANCE

Basel 1460

Bourges

Bordeaux 1441

Grenoble 1339

Padua 1222

Cahors 1332

Piacenza 1248

Ferrara 1391

Valladolid 1346

Toulouse 1229

Avignon 1303

Bologna 11th C.

Montpellier 1289

Florence 1349

Corsica

Perugia 1308

Salamanca 1243

Coimbra 1308

SPAIN

Rome 1303

Seville 1254

Balearic Islands

Sardinia

Naples 1224

Salerno 1173

Mediterranean Sea

Palermo 1777

Sicily

0   200   400   600 Kilometers
0   200   400 Miles

● MAP 25.2 Centers of European Learning. After centuries of little advancement or even retrogression, European culture and learning picked up markedly after 1100 C.E. Shown here are several of the major centers of the High Medieval Age.

through election by a small group of nobles and bishops. Prospective candidates engaged in all sorts of maneuvering and conspiracy and were even willing to barter away much of their power in order to gain votes. Civil wars among the nobility were common at the death of each emperor.

In 1152, the noble electors finally tired of this exhausting sport and agreed on a strong leader in Frederick Barbarossa, who tried his best to reunify the Germans. But his claims to rule in northern Italy brought him into conflict with the Italian city-states and the pope in Rome, and he threw away what he had accomplished toward German unity by his costly and vain expeditions into Italy.

Later, in 1212, his grandson Frederick II became the elected Holy Roman Emperor of the German Nation (the official title of the German king) and opted to settle in Sicily, which he made into one of the leading states in contemporary Europe. But in the process, he almost ignored his transalpine possessions, and the Germans looked upon him as almost a foreigner rather than their rightful king. By the time he died in 1250, imperial authority in Germany was severely weakened and would not recover. Instead of becoming the dominant state of late medieval Europe as its destiny seemed to be, Germany gradually broke up into several dozen competing feudal domains and independent cities. Not until the middle of the nineteenth century did Germany make up the ground that it had lost in the thirteenth.

⚜ MEDIEVAL CULTURE AND ARTS

The appearance of more effective central governments in Europe during the twelfth century went hand in hand with the rising wealth of the urban population. Wealth meant a more lucrative base for taxes levied by the royal Crown and by the church. To manage that wealth properly and to levy and collect the taxes, both institutions needed trained personnel who could plan and oversee the work of others. It is no accident that the *first European universities* appeared at this time (see Map 25.2).

The First Universities

The very first were in Italy. In the towns of Bologna and Salerno, specialized academies devoted to *law and medicine,* respectively, gradually expanded and attracted students from all over Europe. Slightly later, in 1200, the University of Paris was founded by a royal charter; there students studied law, philosophy, and Christian theology.

Much of the university curriculum was devoted to commentaries on the semisacred books of the Greek Classical Age. Pagan authors such as Aristotle had long been forgotten in the Christian West, but were now being recovered for study through the Muslims, especially in Spain, where the Christian majority had lived for centuries under Muslim rule. Unlike the people in the West, the Muslims were quite aware of the value of the Greco-Roman classics and had preserved and studied them ever since conquering the Greek lands in the East.

The greatest teacher of the twelfth and thirteenth centuries was St. Thomas Aquinas. In his *Summa Theologica,* he managed to use the arguments of Aristotle to prove the existence of the Christian God. Other great medieval teachers included Albertus Magnus and Peter Abelard, who used reason to teach the truths of faith in an age that was still ruled by universal belief in Christian doctrines.

The *students* at the universities were drawn from all strata of society, but most were apparently from the middle classes or the poor, who sacrificed much to attend their classes. Many lived on the edge of starvation much of the time, but saw a university degree as a passport to a better social position and therefore worth the sacrifice. Many students supplemented their meager funds from home by serving as tutors to the children of the wealthy or as teachers in the "3 R" schools maintained in many towns.

Tension between town and gown was common. Students frequently rioted in protest against the greed of their landlords or the restrictions imposed by town officials. Females were unknown in medieval universities, either as students or teachers. The course of study for a degree in theology (one of the favorites) usually lasted five years, law the same, and medicine somewhat longer. Lectures were the standard approach to teaching, with stiff oral examinations when the student felt ready. It is remarkable how little the basic methods of university education have changed over seven hundred years.

Gothic Architecture

The *Gothic style* of architecture and interior design came to be the norm in Europe during the thirteenth century. The first important example of Gothic architecture, as far as we know, was the abbey church of St. Denis, which was built outside Paris in the mid-twelfth century. It was such an artistic success that the style spread rapidly throughout Western Europe. The Gothic style's basic elements include a flood of illumination through windows and portals designed to throw the sunlight into every corner; an abundance of decoration, inside and out; and the use of arches, buttresses, and complex vaulting to support a sharply vertical, towering architecture.

The great Gothic cathedrals of the thirteenth and fourteenth centuries that were built from Italy north and west to England were expressions not only of building and artistic skills, but of the deep and unshakable faith of those who constructed and used them. The cathedrals were also rich *pictorial teaching devices,* meant to instruct a still largely illiterate population in the mysteries and lessons of Christianity. Enormously expensive, they were built over generations of time with donations of all classes and the contributed labor of many hundreds of artisans. Each town strove to outdo its neighbors in the splendor of its cathedral. Many of the cathedrals were destroyed by fire at one time or another and were rebuilt. They could take fifty to a hundred years to build or rebuild, and many were not completed until modern times.

Vernacular Literature

Until the end of the thirteenth century, all serious writing between educated persons was normally in Latin, the language of the church everywhere in Western Europe and the most highly developed vocabulary and grammar of the day. In the fourteenth century, however, the common people's oral languages (the *vernacular*) began to be used for the first time as vehicles of literature, such as poems, plays, and elementary readers for children. The most important of these early works was Dante Aligheri's *Divine Comedy:* written in Italian, it is one of the great poetic epics of world literature. Somewhat later came the first important work in English: Geoffrey Chaucer's *Canterbury Tales,* which presented a panorama of English society. In the ensuing years, authors writing in the German, French, and Spanish vernaculars also scored artistic breakthroughs in literature. By the end of the fourteenth century, Latin was no longer the automatic choice of the educated for communicating what they held important.

Summary

The High Middle Age was a period of substantial advances for the Europeans, who came back from the long centuries of instability, violence, and ignorance that followed the decline of the Roman Empire. Three segments of society were recognized: the workers, the warriors, and the worshippers. The first were by far the most numerous, but the other two had important roles to fill in government and society. Town life revived after 1000 C.E., especially in the western parts of the continent, where traders, bankers, and artisans of all types began to congregate in the former ghost towns left by the Romans. By the thirteenth century, towns and cities could be found with upward of 80,000 inhabitants. Cities such as Paris, Bologna, and Oxford had universities, and fine goods from the East were obtainable in urban markets across Europe.

In the wake of growing population and increasing government stability, traders began to develop long-distance markets in basic goods. Peace was by no means universal, but the invasions had ceased and many of the riotous noblemen were diverted into the Crusades against the heathen in the Near East or in Eastern Europe. The professions, particularly law, were also reviving, encouraged by the church and its strong interest in a law-abiding environment. Europe had finally emerged from the shadow of Rome's collapse and was developing a new culture all its own. Noteworthy examples included the magnificent architecture and art of the Gothic style and the literary use of the vernacular languages.

Test Your Knowledge

1. A social group ignored by the original medieval divisions of humanity was the
   a. peasantry.
   b. merchants.
   c. monks.
   d. soldiers.
2. A basic distinction between European slaves and serfs was that slaves
   a. could be sold to another person.
   b. could be severely beaten.
   c. had to work much harder.
   d. could be judged and punished by their master.
3. Which of the following statements about a medieval manor is *false?*
   a. It was normally an economically self-sufficient unit.
   b. It was normally headed by an official of the church or a noble.
   c. It was normally dependent on the labor rendered by unfree peasants.
   d. It was normally a politically independent unit.
4. Members of the medieval nobility
   a. did not have any special legal status.
   b. were uninterested in military affairs.
   c. generally inherited their position.
   d. were limited to males only.
5. The usual path to becoming a monk was to
   a. be handed over by one's parent to a monastery's care.
   b. retire to a monastery in middle age.
   c. enter a monastery after being widowed.
   d. be conscripted into an order from a quota of recruits.
6. Noblewomen in the Middle Age
   a. were strictly confined to domestic duties.
   b. generally married men younger than themselves.
   c. often carried large managerial responsibilities.
   d. played no role in political life.
7. A major difference between England and France was
   a. England's insistence on a strong royal government.
   b. France's royal dependency on officials who volunteered their duties.
   c. France's use of a corps of royally appointed officials in the provinces.
   d. England's attempts to hold the king responsible for the defense of the whole realm.
8. Which of the following was *not* a vital ingredient in the making of medieval European culture?
   a. The Greco-Roman artistic heritage
   b. Roman state paganism
   c. Christian theology
   d. Germanic customs

Identification Terms

Benedictine Rule

bourgeoisie

demesne

Domesday Book

fallow land

ghetto

heresies

patent of nobility

Philip II Augustus

vassals/suzerain

Bibliography

Barraclough, G. *The Origins of Modern Germany,* 1963. A good survey.

Duby, G. *Rural Economy and Country Life in the Medieval West,* 1968 and *The Chivalrous Society,* 1977. See the former for the manor and peasant life and the latter for essays on aristocratic life.

Dunbabin, J. *France in the Making, 843–1100,* 1957. An introduction to early French history.

Ennen, E. *The Medieval Town,* 1979. One of the best summaries of medieval town life. Discusses who lived in the towns and how they lived between 1000 and 1300.

Ferruolo, S. C. *The Origins of the University,* 1985. Deals with an important part of medieval culture.

Ganshof, F. *Feudalism,* 1961. The standard explanation of European feudalism.

Gimpel, J. *The Cathedral Builders,* 1961. See for Gothic art and cathedrals.

Gold, P. S. *The Lady and the Virgin,* 1985. Deals with images and reality of upper-class women in twelfth-century France.

Hallam, E. M. *The Domesday Book through Nine Centuries,* 1986. Explains how this survey was made and its importance to later English history.

Haskins, C. *The Renaissance of the Twelfth Century,* 1927. A fine study.

Landes, D. *Revolution in Time: Clocks and the Making of the Modern World,* 1985. Examines the concept of time and how it was spread through a largely illiterate population.

Macaulay, D. *Cathedral: The Story of Its Construction,* 1973. Fascinatingly written.

McNeill, W. H. *Plagues and People,* 1976. Discusses how disease affected medieval society.

Stuard, S., ed. *Women in Medieval Society,* 1976. A collection of essays on women from different backgrounds.

Taylor, H. O. *The Medieval Mind,* 1987. Examines medieval intellectual history.

LATE MEDIEVAL TROUBLES

Starting about 1000 C.E., European civilization was revitalized and flourished during several centuries of expansion and consolidation. In the fourteenth century, however, a series of unprecedented disasters sharply reduced the population and caused a decline in the economy that continued for about 150 years. The feudal governing system and the agriculturally based economy reeled under great blows: the Black Death, the Hundred Years' War, and the labor shortage they created.

The leaders of the Christian church became embroiled in one scandalous affair after another: the shameful degradation of the pope in the Babylonian Captivity in France and then the Great Schism. Though the challenge to papal authority embodied in the Conciliar Movement was crushed, the popes never regained their previous moral authority, and the way was prepared for the eventual Protestant revolt.

✤ DISASTERS OF THE FOURTEENTH CENTURY

The problems that became manifest in fourteenth-century Europe had their origins in earlier days. By 1300 the population had been steadily growing for two centuries, aided by the new land that had been put into production, several major technical breakthroughs in agriculture, and the unusually benevolent climate, which brought warmer temperatures and appropriate amounts of rain. These happy circumstances came to an end in the early fourteenth century. Most good land was already being used and the technology to exploit the marginal lands (swamps, marshes, hillsides, and the like) did not exist. The climate reverted to its long-term pattern, and no new innovations appeared to improve yields.

As a result, local famines became commonplace in parts of Europe; those who did not starve were often physically weakened as a consequence of poor nutrition over many years. Europe had too many mouths to feed, and the balance was about to be restored through the natural disasters of famine and disease and the man-made disaster of war.

The Black Death

The **Black Death** of the mid and late fourteenth century is the most massive epidemic on record and by far the most

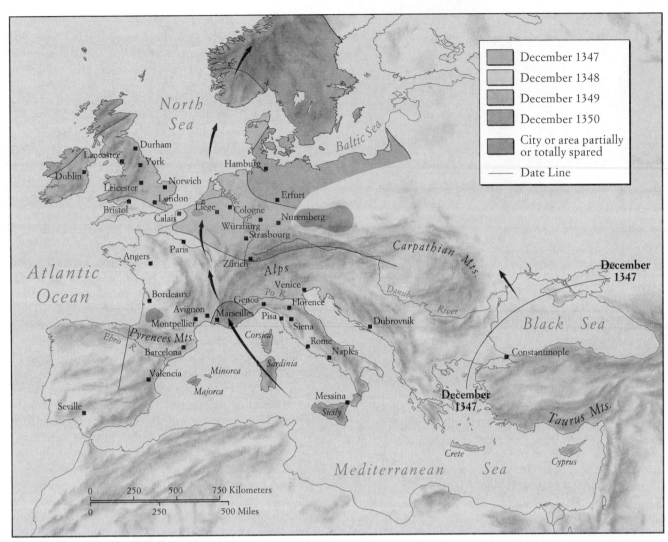

⊙ **MAP 26.1   Spread of Black Death.**

lethal in European history. A form of bubonic plague common in Asia but previously unknown to Europeans was carried to the Mediterranean ports by Italian trading ships in 1346–1347. The plague bacillus was spread by fleas living on rats, and the rats were then (as now) everywhere humans lived. Within two years, this usually fatal disease had spread all over Western Europe and within two more, it had spread from Sweden to Syria and from Russia's western provinces to Spain (see Map 26.1). Hundreds of thousands of people died in the first years of the plague. To make matters worse, it came back again to some parts of Europe during the 1360s and 1370s, sometimes killing one-third or even one-half of the populations of towns and cities within a few weeks.

No one had any idea of how the disease was spread or what countermeasures should be taken. Fourteenth-century European medicine lagged behind the expertise in several other parts of the world, but even had the Europeans been on the same level as the Muslims in Spain or the Chinese, they would have been unable to halt the spread of the bacilli or prevent fleabites. Since the human body lacked any immunity to the disease, a high death toll was virtually inevitable: death came in about two cases out of three, with the hardest hit being the old and the young. City dwellers died in vast numbers because the crowded conditions aided the spread of the disease. Those who could escape fled into the countryside, but often they carried the disease with them.

■ **The Black Death.** A late medieval painter captures the dismay and despair of the victims of the plague. Note the swelling of the neck of the falling man, one of the most common signs of infection. Above, a devil and an angel battled in the sky, as Saint Sebastian (with the arrow-pierced body) pleads for Christ's mercy on the sufferers.

Italy, England, and the Low Countries were the most savagely hit, as these were the most urbanized areas. Debate continues on just how many Europeans died from the plague, but historians believe that as many as one-fourth of the English population did, over a period of a few years. Individual cities, such as Venice, Florence, and Antwerp, suffered even more; some cities were practically depopulated for a generation.

The *economic* consequences of the plague are not easily traced and do not lend themselves to generalizations. Even governments were affected: with fewer taxpayers left alive, tax revenues declined sharply; public works such as the cathedrals had to be stopped for a time. Some places experienced a shortage of labor that was not relieved for at least two generations. In the towns, which had been overcrowded, the plague reduced the excess population, and the survivors enjoyed better health and work security.

Wages for the surviving craftsmen and common laborers rose sharply despite vain attempts to impose wage and price controls. Merchants and traders found fewer consumers to buy their goods, however, and the volume of trade declined.

Peasants who were still bound in serfdom, those who had to pay high labor rents, and those who were otherwise dissatisfied with their lords took quick advantage of their strong bargaining position—or tried to. France, England, and Germany experienced *peasant revolts* against their lords. The peasants invariably lost these armed confrontations with the well-trained and well-armed nobles, but in the longer run, the settlements made between lords and peasants favored the freedoms and economic security of the peasants. Serfdom, which was already weak in Western Europe, died as a result of the plague. The mobility of labor increased as a result. Much land that had been previously worked had to be abandoned and reverted to waste.

The *psychic consequences* of the plague are clearer and can be detected for the better part of a century after 1347. During the late fourteenth and fifteenth centuries, all types of European Christian art reveal a fascination with death. The figure of the Grim Reaper, the reminder of human mortality and the waiting Last Judgment, became a major motif in pictorial and sculptural art. The Dance of Death, a scene in which skeletons link arms with the living revelers, also appeared frequently. The grave is always present in the background, and morbidity is in the air.

Most Christians believed that a wrathful God had given earthly sinners a horrible warning about what awaited the world if morals and conduct were not improved. Many people joined penitential societies, and some engaged in flagellation (self-whipping). It was at this time that Christianity took on much of the burden of *guilt and shame* that distinguishes it from other major religions.

The Hundred Years' War: 1337–1453

Even before the outbreak of the Black Death, another European disaster was underway: the Hundred Years' War. This conflict between England and France, or more accurately, between the kings and nobles of England and France, started because of *a dynastic quarrel.* The two countries had been intimately associated since the twelfth century, when the descendants of William the Conqueror in England had also been the greatest nobles in France, controlling the duchies of Normandy and Aquitaine and the county of Anjou. At a later date, a weak English king had accepted French claims of suzerainty over him, mak-

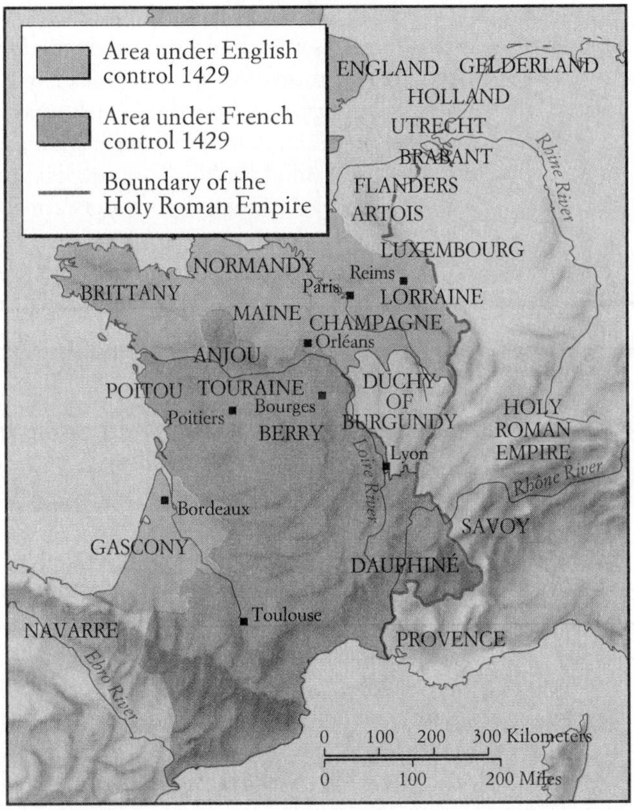
Area under English control 1429
Area under French control 1429
Boundary of the Holy Roman Empire
ENGLAND
GELDERLAND
HOLLAND
UTRECHT
BRABANT
FLANDERS
ARTOIS
Rhine River
LUXEMBOURG
NORMANDY
Reims
Paris
LORRAINE
BRITTANY
MAINE
CHAMPAGNE
Orléans
ANJOU
POITOU
TOURAINE
DUCHY OF BURGUNDY
Poitiers
Bourges
BERRY
HOLY ROMAN EMPIRE
Lyon
Loire River
Rhône River
Bordeaux
SAVOY
GASCONY
DAUPHINÉ
Toulouse
NAVARRE
PROVENCE
Ebro River
0 100 200 300 Kilometers
0 100 200 Miles

◉ **MAP 26.2 The Hundred Years' War.**

ing himself a dependent of the King of France. Determining who was entitled to what under medieval law kept dozens of royal lawyers busy for generations. In the end, what mattered was who could put more soldiers in the field at a given time, and in 1337 the English King Edward III decided to have a full-scale showdown with what he perceived to be a very weak French monarch, Philip VI.

Recent interpretations of the causes of the war have stressed *economic factors.* English prosperity largely depended on the trade with the towns of Flanders across the Channel, where the large majority of woolen cloth was produced using wool from English sheep. English control of the French duchy of Flanders would assure the continuance of this prosperity and would be popular in both Flanders and England.

Questions of *feudal allegiance* also contributed to the conflict. The French kings had been trying for generations to increase their powers of taxation at the expense of their feudal vassals in the provinces. Many French nobles saw the English claim as advantageous to themselves, because they thought an English king's control over the French provinces would inevitably be weaker than a French king's. So they fought with the English against their own king, saying that the English claim was better grounded in law than Philip's. The war turned out to be as much *a civil war* as a foreign invasion of France.

The course of the war was very erratic. Much of the 116 years it lasted actually saw no fighting; several truces were signed, when one or both sides were exhausted. The conflict took place entirely on French soil, mostly in the provinces facing the English Channel or in the region of Paris. The major battles included *Crécy* in 1346 where the English archers used their longbows effectively against the French (the English may have used a few cannon as well); *Poitiers* in 1356, where the English captured the French king and held him for ransom; and **Agincourt** in 1415, where the English routed the discouraged French a third time.

By the 1420s, several monarchs had led the forces on both sides, and the war had long since lost its original personal element. At this point, it had become a matter of national survival to the French, who found themselves being pushed back to the walls of Paris (see Map 26.2). At this juncture appeared the patron saint of France, *Joan of Arc.* This peasant girl who said she had been told by God to offer her services to the embattled (and ungrateful) Charles VII routed the English and their French allies at Orléans in 1429 and changed the trend of the war, which now began to favor the French. In the ensuing twenty years, France recaptured almost all of the lands lost to the English invaders during the previous hundred. In 1453, the costly and sometimes bloody struggle finally ended with the English withdrawal from all of France except the port of Calais on the Channel.

Consequences of the Hundred Years' War

Though originally popular among the *English,* the war eventually came to be seen as a bottomless pit swallowing up taxes and manpower. The costs of maintaining a large army of mercenaries in France for decades were enormous, and even the rich booty brought home from the captured French towns had not been enough to pay for the war. In addition, the war had disrupted England's commerce with continental markets.

The power and prestige of Parliament had increased, however. Since its origins in the thirteenth century, Parliament had met only sporadically. Now, in 37 of the 40 years between the beginning of the war in 1337 and Edward III's death in 1377, Parliament was in session. The king

■ **Joan of Arc.** This miniature of the patron saint of France is one of the few that has survived. Dressed in armor, she was an extraordinary female figure in this age of male warriors.

was always looking for money, and Parliament had to be consulted for the necessary new taxes. As a result, by the end of the war, Parliament was a determining voice in matters of taxation and other policy.

France did not experience a similar parliamentary development. The French kings allowed regional assemblies to meet in the major provinces, but they avoided holding a *national* assembly, which might have attempted to negotiate with the Crown on national issues and policies. This difference between the two countries would become more significant as time wore on. France followed the path of most European monarchies in transferring power steadily *to* the royal officials and *away from* the nobles and burgesses of the towns, who would have been representatives to a parliament. England strengthened the powers of its parliament, while checking those of its king.

The Hundred Years' War effectively *ended chivalric ideals and conduct* in Europe. Warfare changed dramatically during the course of the war; no longer were the heavily armored horsemen the decisive weapon in battle. The infantry, supported by artillery and soon to be armed with muskets, were now what counted. Cavalry would still

play an important role in warfare for four hundred years, but as an auxiliary force, as they had been originally for the Romans. With the introduction of gunpowder, war ceased to be a personal combat between equals. Now thanks to cannon, you could kill your foe from a distance, even before you could see him plainly. The new tactics also proved to be great social levelers. Commoners armed with longbows could bring down mounted knights. The noble horseman, who had been distinguished both physically (by being *above* the infantry) and economically (a horse was expensive to buy and maintain), was now brought down to the level of the infantryman, a commoner who could be equipped for a fraction of what it cost to equip a horseman. The longbow and cannon at Crécy had initiated *a military revolution.*

❧ PROBLEMS IN THE CHURCH

The fourteenth century was also a disaster for the largest, most omnipresent institution in the Christian world: the church. Whether a devout Christian or not, everyone's life was touched more or less directly by the church. The church courts determined whether marriages were legal and proper, whether orphans had rights, whether contracts were legitimate, and whether sexual crimes had been committed. In the church, the chief judge was the pope, and the papal court in Rome handled thousands of cases that were appealed to it each year. Most of the lawyers of Europe from the twelfth through the fourteenth century were employed by and trained by the church. As a result, the clergy came to have a more and more legalistic outlook.

Probably the greatest medieval pope, **Innocent III,** reigned from 1198 to 1216. He forced several kings of Europe to bow to his commands, including the unfortunate John of England, Philip II Augustus of France, and Frederick II, the German emperor. But in behaving much like a king with his armies and his threats of war, Innocent had sacrificed much of the moral authority he derived from his position as head of the church on earth.

Later thirteenth-century popes attempted to emulate Innocent with varying success, but all depended on their legal expertise or threat of armed force (the papal treasury assured the supply of mercenaries). Finally, Pope *Boniface VIII* overreached badly when he attempted to assert that the clergy were exempt from taxes in both France and England. In the struggle of wills that followed, the kings of both countries were able to make Boniface back down: the clergy paid the royal taxes. It was a severe blow to papal prestige.

A few years later, the French monarch actually arrested the aged Boniface for a few days, dramatically demonstrating who held the whip hand if it should come to a showdown. Boniface died of humiliation, it was said, a few days after his release. His successor was handpicked by Philip, the French king, who controlled the votes of the numerous French bishops.

The Babylonian Captivity

The new pope was a French bishop who took the name Clement V. Rather than residing in Rome, he was induced to stay in the city of **Avignon** in what is now southern France. This was the first time since St. Peter that the head of the church had not resided in the Holy City of Christendom, and to make matters worse, Clement's successors stayed in Avignon as well. The **Babylonian Captivity,** as the popes' stay in Avignon came to be called, created a great scandal. Several of the Avignon popes after Clement were quite good and conscientious administrators. Nevertheless, everyone except the French viewed them as captives of the French crown and unworthy to lead the universal church or decide questions of international justice. How could the popes be evenhanded guardians of Christian property and morality if they were under French control?

In 1377 one of Clement's papal successors finally returned to Rome, but died very soon thereafter. In the ensuing election, great pressure was put on the attending bishops to elect an Italian, and one was duly elected, who took the name *Urban VI*. Urban was a well-intentioned reformer, but he went about his business in such an arrogant fashion that he had alienated all his fellow bishops within weeks after the election. They therefore proceeded to declare his election invalid because of the pressures put upon them and elected another Frenchman, who took the name *Clement VII*. He immediately returned to Avignon and took up residence once more under the benevolent eye of the French king. The bullheaded Urban refused to step down. There were thus two popes, and doubt as to which was the legitimate one.

The Great Schism

The final episode in the demeaning decline of papal authority now began. For forty years, Christians were treated to the spectacle, a great schism, of two popes, denouncing each other as an impostor and the Anti-Christ. Europeans divided along national lines: the French, Scots, and Iberians supported Clement; the En-

■ **A Medieval Copyist at Work.** Thousands of monks labored at the tedious job of copying books for medieval libraries. This example comes from Spain in the thirteenth century.

glish and Germans preferred Urban (largely because his sentiments were anti-French). Neither side would give an inch, even after the two original contestants had died.

The **Great Schism** hastened the realization of an idea that had long been discussed among pious and concerned people: the calling of a council, a universal conclave of bishops to combat growing problems within the structure and doctrines of the church. The *Conciliar Movement* was a serious challenge to papal authority. Its supporters wished to enact some important reforms and thought that the papal government was far too committed to maintaining the status quo. Its adherents, therefore, looked for a theory of church governance that would allow them to circumvent papal obstructionism. They found it in the doctrines of *Marsiglio of Padua*. Marsiglio was an early fourteenth-century author whose tract, the **Defensor Pacis (Defender of the Peace)**, argued that the entire church community, not the pope, had supreme powers of doctrinal definition. This community would be expressed in the meetings of a council, whose members should include a number of laypersons and not just clerics. Marsiglio was excommunicated for his troubles, but his ideas fell on fertile ground and were eventually picked up by other fourteenth-century figures such as the English theologian **John Wyclif.**

Wyclif went much farther than Marsiglio and in some ways can be considered a major forerunner of the Protestant revolt. He believed that the clergy had become corrupt and that individual Christians should be able to read and interpret the word of the Lord for themselves. His doctrines were popular with the English poor, and they were emblazoned on the banners of the greatest uprising in English history, the revolt of 1381, which very nearly toppled the Crown (see the discussion later in the chapter). The rebels were called Wyclifites, or **Lollards,** and their ideas about the ability of ordinary people to read Scripture for themselves were to be spread to the Continent within a few years.

The scandal of the Schism aroused great resentment among Christians of all nations, and intense pressure was brought to bear on both papal courts to end their quarrel. Neither would, however, and finally a council was called, at Pisa in Italy in 1409. It declared both popes deposed and elected a new one. But neither of the deposed popes accepted the verdict, and so instead of two there were now three claimants!

A few years later, from 1414 to 1417, a bigger and more representative council met in the German city of Constance. The council had three objectives: to end the schism and return the papacy to Rome, to condemn the Wyclifite and other heretics, and to reform the church and clergy from top to bottom. The *Council of Constance* was successful in its first goal: a new pope was chosen, and the other three either stepped down voluntarily or were ignored. The council achieved some temporary success with its second goal of eliminating heresy, but the heresies

it condemned simply went underground and emerged again a century later. As for the third objective, nothing was done; reforms were discussed, but the church leaders made sure no real action was taken.

Additional councils were held over the next thirty years, but they achieved little or nothing in the vital areas of clerical corruption. The popes who had resisted the whole idea of the council had triumphed, but their victory had come at a very high price. The need for basic reform in the church continued to be ignored until the situation exploded with Martin Luther.

❧ SOCIETY AND WORK IN LATE MEDIEVAL EUROPE

We have already mentioned the upsurge in *peasant rebellions* that followed the Black Death and pointed out that all of them were crushed. Nevertheless, in the long run, the peasants did succeed in obtaining more freedoms and security.

One of the most spectacular rebellions was the **Jacquerie** of 1358 in France, which shocked the nobility, as the peasants raped and looted, burned castles, and even destroyed chapels. The nobles took a heavy revenge, but the French and Flemish peasants were by no means through. Revolts occurred again and again throughout the 1300s and early 1400s in parts of France. In England, the Lollard rebellion of 1381 was an equal jolt to the upper classes and the king. One of its leaders was the priest John Ball. His famous couplet would be shouted or mumbled from now on: "When Adam delved and Eva span / Who was then the gentleman?" ("Delved" means plowed, and "span" is old English for spun.) The causes of the rebellion were complex and varied from place to place. But almost all England was involved, and in an unusual development, the peasants were joined by a large number of artisans and laborers in the towns. These urban workers had been impoverished by a rigid guild system that prevented newcomers from competing with the established shops and kept pay rates very low for all but the workers at the top. The conjunction of urban and rural discontent not only came very near to stripping the English nobles of their customary privilege, but also shook the Crown itself. The revolt was, therefore, suppressed all the more savagely. But as in France, the general trend could not be mistaken: the peasants were no longer mere serfs, and the town laborers no longer hapless victims of the nobles and the rich guildsmen.

The *guilds* controlled what was made, for what price, and by whom. First formed in urban areas in the 1200s,

■ **The *Jacquerie.*** This brilliant illustration exemplifies the usual end of a peasant rebellion in the fourteenth century; the nobles massacre their challengers and throw them into the river, cheered on by the ladies in the left background.

Holy Maidenhood

In the Middle Age literacy was still uncommon among the ordinary folk, so we cannot know very much about their life at first hand. But sometimes a beam of light illuminates it. A good example is *Holy Maidenhood,* by an anonymous author of the thirteenth century. Probably a cleric, he attempts to induce young women to enter the nunnery by arguing against marriage and all its consequences:

> Look around, happy maiden, if the knot of wedlock be once knotted, let the man be idiot or cripple, be he whatever he may be, thou must keep to him. Thou sayest that a wife hath much comfort of her husband, when they are well consorted, and each is well content with the other. Yea; but 'tis rarely seen on earth. . . .
>
> [On childbearing]: Consider what joy ariseth when the offspring in thee quickeneth and groweth. How many miseries immediately wake up therewith, that work thee woe enough, fight against thy own flesh, and with many sorrows make war upon thy own nature. Thy ruddy face shall turn lean and grow green as grass. Thine eyes shall be dusky, and underneath grow pale; and by the giddiness of thy brain thy head shall ache sorely. Within thy belly, the uterus shall swell and strut out like a waterbag; thy bowels shall have pains, and there shall be stitches in thy flank. . . . All thy beauty is overthrown with withering.
>
> After all this, there cometh from the child thus born a crying and a weeping that must about midnight make thee to waken, or her that holds thy place, for whom thou must care [i.e., a wet-nurse]. And what of the cradle foulness, and the constant giving of the breast? to swaddle and feed the child at so many unhappy moments. . . . Little knoweth a maiden of all this trouble of wives' woes. . . .
>
> And what if I ask besides . . . how the wife stands that heareth when she comes in her child scream, sees the cat at the meat, and the hound at the hide? Her cake is burning on the stove, and her calf is sucking

all the milk up, the pot is running into the fire, and the churl [manservant] is scolding. Though it be a silly tale, it ought, maiden, to deter thee more strongly from marriage, for it seems not silly to her that tries it. . . .

MEDIEVAL MEDICINE

Medieval medical lore often sounds fantastic to modern audiences, but modern research has sometimes found that the folk medicine of Europe and other areas of the world has definite clinical value. A certain female physician of the eleventh or twelfth century named Trotula reportedly compiled the handbook from which the following interesting recipes were taken:

Chapter 43: A Treatment for Lice

> For lice originating in the armpits and in the pubic hair, we mix ashes with oil and anoint those parts. For general lice around the eyes and head, we make an ointment sufficient strong to expel them: take of aloes one ounce, white lead five ounces, olibanum and bacon with its grease, the bacon finely chopped. Pulverize the other ingredients and make an ointment with the grease. . . .

Chapter 55: Against Deafness

> For deafness take the cooked fat of fresh caught eels, juice of caprifolium, juice of Jove's beard [both are flowering weeds], and a handful of ant eggs. Grind, strain, and mix them with oil and cook. After cooking add vinegar or wine to make it more penetrating. Pour into the sound ear, and stop up the defective ear, letting the patient lie partly on the sound ear. In the morning he must be careful of drafts. . . .

SOURCE: Cited by Joseph and Frances Gies in *Women in the Middle Ages* (Barnes and Noble: NY, 1980).

the guilds were very strong by the fourteenth and fifteenth centuries, and their scheme in which a worker advanced from apprentice to journeyman to master as his skills developed was almost universal. Many journeymen never took the final step upward, however, because the guild restricted the number of masters who could practice their trade in a given area. The guilds aimed at ensuring economic security for their members, not competitive advantage. The members fixed prices and established conditions of labor for employees, length of apprenticeships, pay scales, examinations for proving skills, and many other things. The labor shortages caused by the Black Death actually prolonged and strengthened the monopoly aspects of the guild system. In some European cities, the guilds were the chief determinants of economic activity until the nineteenth century.

The towns were terribly overcrowded, at least until the Black Death. The breathing space the reduced populations provided enabled many towns to engage in the first instances of *urban planning*. Many medieval towns emerged from the crisis of the Black Death with open spaces, parks, and suburbs that made them more attractive. (*Suburb* originally meant a settlement outside the walls of the town.) Again and again, a cramped city found it necessary to tear down the old walls and build new ones further out; this series of defensive earthwork and masonry walls is still quite perceptible in the maps of some modern European cities.

Inside the town walls or just outside, many types of skilled and semiskilled workers plied their trades, generally in home workshops employing one or two workers besides the family members. Factories, or mass employment places of production, were still in the distant future. Machines of any type independent of human or animal energy were unknown. Even water- and wind-powered mechanisms, such as waterwheels and windmills, were relatively rare.

The Role of the Church and Clergy

Whether in a village or a great city, the church was much more than a place of worship. It was also an informal gathering point, a place for business dealings, and a social center. The three great events of ordinary lives were celebrated in the church: birth (baptism), marriage, and death (funeral). News came first to the church, lovers met in its shadows, ceremonies of all kinds, both secular and religious, were held there. Its bells rang out the news and announced emergencies; popular festivities and the equivalents of town meetings were held there after the Mass. The church was in every way the heart of the community throughout the Middle Ages and into modern times.

Just as the church was the focal point of everyday life, the parish priest was an important man in the village community, where the majority lived. Even if he was ignorant and illiterate, the priest was respected as the representative of an all-powerful, all-seeing lord and final judge. Few, indeed, would attempt to defy or even ignore him in the round of daily life.

Gothic cathedrals (see Chapter 25) remained the most impressive examples of medieval art, combining architecture, painting, sculpture, inlay and carving, stained glass, and (in the church services) music and literature. The late medieval Gothic churches are some of the supreme examples of the ability to project a vision of life into concrete forms. Few, indeed, would attempt to defy or even ignore him in the daily round of life.

Late Medieval Art

Gothic cathedrals (see Chapter 25) remained the most impressive example of late medieval art forms, combining architecture, painting, sculpture, inlay and carving, stained glass, and (in the church services) music and literature. The Gothic churches are some of the supreme examples of the ability to project a vision of life into concrete artistic format.

In the frescoes and alter screens done to decorate the churches' open places, the increasing refinement of European painting is noteworthy, especially from the fourteenth century onward. Experimentation with perspective and more psychological realism in the portrayal of human faces is visible in Italian and Flemish work, particularly. Metalworking still lags behind the achievements of the Chinese and the Muslims, but the gap is being narrowed, and will be overcome by the fifteenth century.

A change in the sponsorship of artwork is also gradually coming about. Most of the artwork of the High Middle Age had been directly commissioned by the church or by individual nobles and kings. The large majority of formal art was done for the church as an institution or for individual clergy who had the wealth and the taste to indulge themselves while allegedly glorifying God.

Toward the end of the medieval period, the members of the commercial class in the towns were at times wealthy enough to begin to play the role that had been monopolized by the nobility and clergy: *patrons of the arts*. In the fifteenth century, rich bankers or doctors began to commission portraits, although this was still not a common practice. Most art was still the province of the two privileged classes, the churchmen and the warriors. Everyone in the medieval town may have contributed to the

Margherita Datini
1360–1423

The discovery of hundreds of letters preserved by accident for five hundred years in a residence in Prato, Italy, allows us to participate in many of the life events of a medieval Italian woman named Margherita Datini. Margherita was the wife of a wealthy merchant, Francesco Datini, for over thirty-five years, and during that time Francesco's frequent business trips made it necessary for the couple to communicate by letter.

The Datinis met in 1376, when he was almost forty and she was sixteen. Such an age difference was not uncommon in upper-class marriages of the period, though Datini was remarkable in not demanding a dowry from his bride's family. Margherita was an orphan, the daughter of a minor nobleman who had been executed in one of the incessant civil wars that wracked the northern Italian city-states; his property had been confiscated by the winners. Francesco was also an orphan, having lost both parents to the Black Plague. But he had been very successful as a merchant in Avignon, serving the papacy of the Babylonian Captivity era. In 1382, the Datini household moved to the ancestral home in Prato, a textile town near Florence.

Datini, always the good businessman, decided to erect a real mansion on a lot he owned in the center of town, and there he and Margherita lived out their long and generally happy lives. The Datini house still stands; it is now a museum housing the archive they left. The Datinis experienced one great sadness: Margherita was unable to conceive, so they had no legitimate offspring. (Francesco had at least two illegitimate children and probably more.) Every classic remedy against barrenness was put into play; *nothing* worked, not even the poultices of ghastly contents and the belts ornamented with prayers to St. Catherine.

Margherita's main tasks were the management of the large house and its several inhabitants. About eleven persons resided with the couple, four of whom were female slaves purchased at various times from Venetian merchants who obtained them in Constantinople or in Venice's trading posts on the Black Sea. The others were servants, who were free to leave if they desired. All, slaves and servants, were treated well as members of the *famiglia,* the household. In addition to these live-in persons, several more servants came and went daily, so the lady of the house was constantly overseeing or instructing someone.

A few years after arriving back in Prato, Francesco's business as a cloth merchant and importer had grown so much that he opened a branch office in Pisa and a retail establishment in Florence. The separations these endeavors required persuaded Margherita to learn to read and write, which for an upper-class wife was by this time neither unexpected nor absolutely necessary. In her frequent letters to her absent husband, she expresses many familiar concerns: he spends too much time away, he is probably unfaithful, and he gives his businesses more attention than his home. But good feeling is evidenced as well: Francesco clearly respected his wife's growing accomplishments as an educated woman; he was proud of her, while she was affectionate to him and wished she could see more of him. She even took care of his illegitimate daughter Ginevra as though Ginevra were her own.

When the plague returned in 1399, the Datinis pledged that they would endow a Prato charity if they survived. When Francesco died at the age of seventy-five in 1410, his wife was the executor of his will and followed his wishes by giving most of his large estate to the poor and orphans. The slaves were all freed and the servants well provided for, as were the surviving illegitimate children. Margherita herself survived thirteen more years, to age sixty-three, and is buried in Prato's St. Maria Novella churchyard, where the visitors to her former home can view her last resting place.

building of a new church, but the portrait sculpture over the main portal still depicted the bishop, and the front pew was reserved for the local baron.

⚜ MEDIEVAL SCIENCES

In later medieval Europe, scientific studies improved somewhat from the very low conditions of theory and practice in the early period. But despite some advances, overall the sciences did not fare as well as the arts. The introduction of Arabic numbers did make *math* faster and easier. The Hindu/Arab invention of *algebra* was becoming known to Europeans; with it, they became much more adept at dealing with unknown quantities. Some faint beginnings of *chemistry* can be detected. These took the form of *alchemy,* the search (begun by the Muslims) for the magical substance that would transform base metal into gold and silver. *Geography* made considerable progress, borrowing heavily from Muslim cartography and knowledge of the seas. Most educated people already believed the world was a sphere, for instance, before Portugese voyages proved that it was. But except in anatomy, *medicine and surgery* made very little headway beyond what the Muslims and Greeks already knew. The main European medical center was at Salerno, which depended heavily on teachers from the Muslim countries. *Physics and astronomy* would only advance after the 1400s. Biological sciences were still in their infancy, the social sciences were not yet heard of, and botany and zoology were basically where the third-century Greeks had left them.

Part of the problem in the sciences was the insistence of the universities now multiplying throughout Europe (see Map 25.2 in Chapter 25) that scientific knowledge was not as important as the arts and humanities. In places like Oxford, Paris, Salamanca, and Heidelberg, the majority of the teachers specialized in theology, classical languages, and rhetoric, rather than biology, physics, or mathematics. The science that the modern world takes for granted as a major source of truth did not yet exist.

Perhaps the most important advances in science in the later medieval period are to be found not in the answers, but in the questions posed by such scholars as *Albertus Magnus and Roger Bacon,* of Paris and Oxford, respectively. Both were seeking new ways to collect data about the natural world and pioneered what we now call the "experimental method" of ascertaining truth.

As we observed in Chapter 25, the teachings of *Aristotle* held pride of place in the humanities and natural sciences. Now familiar to Christians from his Muslim admirers in Spain and Sicily, he became almost as dominant in European thought as he had been in Muslim studies. His theories about the form of the cosmos, the revolution of the planets, and the nature of matter were considered the last word on the subject, even though they sometimes clashed with what could be observed. This reverence toward authority was characteristic of the Middle Age and was sometimes a severe obstacle to the introduction of new knowledge.

The clash between new and old was especially clear in the branch of philosophy called metaphysics. In the thirteenth century, the learned Thomas Aquinas had bridged the chasm between classical and Christian doctrines in his *Summa Theologica* (*The Highest Theology*). This book became the standard work for Catholic theology into modern times. Its subtle and complex reasoning, however, was distorted by the "schoolmen," or *scholastics,* priests and university teachers who tried to ignore or undermine ideas that challenged tradition, especially church-approved tradition. Originally pioneers of a new rationalism that was very much needed in Western thought, the scholastics gradually became fossilized. By the 1400s they had become a retarding force in education, committing themselves to verbal tricks and meaningless hairsplitting. By so doing they transformed the philosophy of the great Aquinas from the most subtle explanation of God's universe available to Christians into an exercise for theology students.

Summary

The later Middle Age (fourteenth and fifteenth centuries) was a mixed scene of cultural advances, social violence, economic and military disasters, and religious strife. The fourteenth century was a particularly disastrous epoch. The Black Plague carried off perhaps one-fourth of the population to an early death and thereby created a shortage of labor that impeded Europe's recovery for generations. Peasants seized the chance to escape serfdom, sometimes to the extent of rebelling openly against their lords. Such revolts were put down mercilessly, but the days of serfdom in the old sense were over from Germany westward.

In the towns the new bourgeoisie continued to gain prestige and wealth at the expense of the nobility, while having to defend their position against the rising discontent of the urban workers. The guilds, which were originally intended to protect the livelihood of the master artisans, increasingly became closed castes of privilege.

The Hundred Years' War dealt a heavy blow to the French monarchy, which was rescued from disintegration only through Joan of Arc. The war also ended the domination of the field of battle by noble horsemen and signaled the coming of modern gunpowder war. The Babylonian Captivity and the Great Schism marked the onset of a decline in the papacy that was not to be reversed until after Luther's challenge. The major weapon in the papal arsenal, the moral authority of the Vicar of Christ, was rapidly being dulled as pope after pope gave more attention to politics and power than to matters of faith.

Test Your Knowledge

1. Which of the following battles was a victory for the French in the Hundred Years' War?
   a. Crécy
   b. Orléans
   c. Agincourt
   d. Poitiers
2. Which one of the following was *not* a consequence of the Black Death in European affairs?
   a. Severe labor shortage
   b. Preoccupation with death and guilt
   c. Heightened sensitivity to the natural world
   d. Increased readiness to rebel against the peasants' lords
3. John Ball was the leader of
   a. a movement to strip the upper classes of their privileges.
   b. the movement to make church councils superior to the papacy in defining doctrine.
   c. the Jacquerie in France.
   d. an English army in France which introduced gunpowder to warfare.
4. During the Babylonian Captivity, the pope became the creature of the
   a. Holy Roman Emperor.
   b. Roman mob.
   c. French crown.
   d. German nobles.
5. The result of the Council of Constance was to
   a. eliminate all would-be popes and elect a new one to end the Great Schism.
   b. set an example of conciliar supremacy over the pope.
   c. make great reforms in the spiritual life of the church.
   d. move the papacy from Rome to a new home in Avignon.
6. The usual reaction of the nobles to peasant rebellions was to
   a. crush them and take bloody vengeance.
   b. blame the urban classes for inspiring them.
   c. negotiate a compromise at the expense of the Crown.
   d. free their remaining serfs and gain peace.
7. Which of the following did Margherita Datini *not* experience in her lifetime?
   a. Raising the illegitimate daughter of her husband
   b. Losing her father by execution
   c. Being frequently separated from her husband by business
   d. Raising two healthy sons

Identification Terms

Agincourt (1415)

Avignon

Babylonian Captivity

Black Death

Defensor Pacis

Great Schism

Innocent III

Jacquerie

Lollards

Wyclif (John)

Bibliography

Aston, M. *The Fifteenth Century: The Prospect of Europe,* 1968. Reviews the social consequences of the plague in lively style; illustrated.

Cipolla, C. *Before the Industrial Revolution: European Society and Economy, 1000–1700,* 1976. An outstanding survey that discusses, among other topics, the difficulties of producing sufficient food and other products.

Ferguson, W. K. *Europe in Transition, 1300–1520,* 1968. Focuses on the interrelations between the plague and the new spirit of the Renaissance.

Hay, D. *Europe in the Fourteenth and Fifteen Centuries,* 1966. See for the broad picture of political and social developments.

Mollat, M., and P. Wolff. *The Popular Revolutions of the Late Middle Age,* 1973. Deals with peasant revolts and their suppression.

Oakley, F. P. *The Western Church in the Late Middle Ages,* 1980. Surveys the problems of the church.

Perroy, E. *The Hundred Years' War,* 1965. A comprehensive survey.

Renovard, Y. *The Avignon Papacy, 1305–1403,* 1970. Looks at the Babylonian Captivity.

Runciman, S. *The Fall of Constantinople, 1453,* 1965. A marvelous account of the Ottomans' long-sought victory over their Christian opponents.

Tuchman, B. *A Distant Mirror,* 1982. A vivid, exciting story of the calamities besetting Western Europe in the fourteenth century; uses a French nobleman as the protagonist.

Ziegler, P. *The Black Death,* 1969. A very readable account of the plague.

THE EUROPEAN RENAISSANCE

1300s	Renaissance begins in Italy
1400s	Renaissance spreads north of Alps
1461–1483	Reign of Louis XI of France
1471–1509	Reign of Henry VII Tudor of England
1480	Russians led by Moscow oust Mongols
1500s	New Monarchies; new concept of state
1511	Third Rome idea broached in Russia

Beginning in the fourteenth century, a new spirit manifested itself in Europe among the educated classes. Later called the Renaissance, or rebirth, it was mainly an urban phenomenon and was restricted to the uppermost segment of society. There were in fact two distinct Renaissances: first, a change in economic and social conditions, and second, an artistic and cultural movement that was founded on that change. The Renaissance also differed substantially south and north of the Alps. In the south (Italy), the spirit of the age was secular and anticlerical; in the north (Germany), there was a more pronounced concern for religious reform and less emphasis on the assertion of individual excellence.

❖ THE ITALIAN CITY-STATES

The Renaissance began in the northern Italian city-states such as Florence, Venice, Milan, and Pisa, which by counterbalancing the claims of the papacy against those of the Holy Roman Emperor had succeeded in becoming independent of both (see Map 27.1). These cities were rich due to both trade and finance. Genoa and Venice dominated the Mediterranean trade routes with the East and Africa; Florence was the center of the skilled metal and leather trades and controlled the textile trade of much of Europe on both sides of the Alps. In the fifteenth century, the huge wealth of the papal court made Rome once again a major center of culture and art.

More and more in the late Middle Age, Italians were leading the way in innovations—scientific, artistic, and economic. Italians were the leading bankers, mariners, scientists, and engineers of Europe; the rest of Europe increasingly looked to Italy for what was new and sent their sons there to study. Even the devastation of the Black Death, which wracked the Italian cities, could not crush them. In a remarkably short time—by the early fifteenth century—they had returned to their prior positions of leadership.

The city-states of the fourteenth and fifteenth centuries were *princely oligarchies;* that is, a small group of wealthy aristocrats, headed by a prince with despotic power, ran the government. No commoners, whether urban workers or peasants outside the city gates, enjoyed even a hint of power. In fact, a huge gap existed between the ruling class

● **MAP 27.1 Renaissance Centers.** The Renaissance was an international phenomenon, but it left stronger traces in South and Northwest Europe then elsewhere. Like most cultural innovations after 1200 C.E., it was closely aligned with the political and social positions of an urban middle class.

of merchants, bankers, and traders and the rest of the population, whom they regarded with a detached contempt. It was possible to rise into the ruling clique, but difficult: the key was money.

⚜ THE RENAISSANCE ATTITUDE

The wealthy in an Italian city were highly educated and very much aware of and proud of their good taste in the arts. Led by the prince, the members of the oligarchy

■ **Equestrian Statue by Donatello.** This was the first successful attempt to cast an equestrian statue since Roman days, and marked a significant breakthrough in artistic achievement for the Renaissance. The statue stands in the main square of Padua.

spared no pains or money to assert their claims to glory and sophistication in the art of living well.

What did "living well" mean to these individuals?

1. **Individualism.** Men and women of the Italian Renaissance believed that the age-old Christian emphasis on submerging one's fate within the general fate of the sons and daughters of Adam was wrong. They wished to set themselves apart from the masses and were supremely confident that they could. They despised Christian humility and encouraged a new pride in human potential. A thirst for fame and a strong desire to put their own imprint upon the contemporary world were at the heart of the psychology of these Renaissance figures.

2. **Secularism.** The focus of the Italian upper classes shifted steadily away from the eternal to worldly affairs. The life to come receded into the background—sometimes, it was pushed off stage entirely. The here-and-now became the critical factor in determining acts and thoughts. The acquisitive instinct was sharpened, and few thought it wrong to pursue riches. Increasingly, people viewed life as an opportunity for glory and pleasure, rather than as a transitory stage on the way to eternal bliss or everlasting damnation. *Man was the measure* of what life had to offer.

3. **Revival of classical values.** The ancient civilizations of the Greeks and especially the pagan Romans became the focus of artistic and cultural interest. Led by notable scholars such as **Petrarch** and *Lorenzo Valla,* the thinkers and writers of the fourteenth and fifteenth centuries looked back to pre-Christian Mediterranean culture for their values and standards.

They were not anti-Christian so much as pro-pagan in their admiration for the achievements of Plato, Aristotle, Virgil, Terence, and countless other contributors to the pre-Christian intellectual world. The collection and careful editing of the ancient texts that had somehow survived (many through Muslim caretakers) became an obsession. What the modern world possesses of the Greco-Roman past is very largely the work of the Renaissance.

There were, of course, variations of degree in these attitudes. Even in Italy, there were many sober upholders of the medieval viewpoint, who insisted that humans were made for God only and that the new emphasis on pleasure and self-fulfillment could lead only to disaster. Many of the scholars who paged through the Roman manuscripts were devout Christians, looking for holes in the arguments of their opponents or for proof of the pagans' search for God.

But, in general, the Italian Renaissance was devoted to the *self-realization of Man* as a being whose earthly life was the only sure one he had. It rejected the Middle Age as a dark interlude, which had lasted all too long, between the light of the Classical Age and the rebirth now beginning.

❧ THE NORTHERN RENAISSANCE

North of the Alps, the Renaissance was also a powerful force, but with a rather different character than in Italy. Carried to Germany and the Low Countries by students returning from study with the great Italian artists and writers, the new spirit underwent a sort of sea change as it came northward, becoming *more pietist and less pagan, more reformist and less self-centered.*

The term **humanism** is often applied to the northern Renaissance and its leading figures. The humanists were aware of the corruption of society and wished to remedy it by nonrevolutionary means through reforms grounded in ancient Christian teachings. The Renaissance in this context meant a serious, pious attempt to return the church and lay society in general to a purer state; it was an acknowledgment of all Christians' duties and responsibilities toward themselves and their fellow humans. The humanists believed nevertheless that much could be learned from the Classical Age, and that the great pagan philosophers and teachers such as Epicurus and Cicero had invaluable messages for the present day.

In the north as well as in Italy, there was great confidence in the powers of the intellect to find the truth and to bring about necessary reform. The use of *reason, rather than dogma,* was an important article of faith for humanists everywhere. They believed that if people could be brought to see the good, they would pursue it. The trouble with the world was that the good was everywhere obscured.

Thomas More's **Utopia** is an excellent example of northern humanism. The book was meant as a satire and a lesson for society. The people of Utopia (Greek for "no place") are properly considerate of one another; they do not seek wealth because they see no rewards in it. Their education continues throughout their entire lives rather than being limited to a few childhood years. All individuals are absolutely equal, and they live by reason rather than passion and ignorance. It was a radical message: More was saying that *society,* not the individual evil person, was responsible for the sorry state of the world. Adam's sin was not enough to explain humans' plight; the very way people lived with one another must be reformed—and by humans themselves.

The best-known and most noble-minded of all the northern humanists was the Dutch Desiderius **Erasmus,** who lived in the late fifteenth and early sixteenth centuries; by his death, his works were being read throughout Europe. His *Praise of Folly* was a scorching indictment of the so-called wisdom of the world and a plea for a return to simple virtues. Even more influential was his new, carefully researched edition of the New Testament, with his commentaries and introduction.

Erasmus's work has two basic themes: the inner nature of Christianity and the importance of education. By the inner nature of Christianity, he meant that the true follower of Christ should emulate Christ's life, not what the theologians have tried to make out of his gospels. Erasmus condemned the empty formalism that was so common in the church of his day. In so doing, he was one of the most important forerunners of the Protestant Reformation, though he absolutely rejected Protestantism for himself and condemned Luther's arrogance.

■ **Death and the Miser.** Hieronymous Bosch was the sixteenth-century master of the grotesque and the damned. Here he shows what happens to the treasure of a miser.

Northern *painting and sculpture* also differed from the artistic achievements of the south. Northern art is more overtly religious and avoids the lush sensuousness that marks much Italian art. The outstanding exponents of the northern Renaissance in art were the *Flemish portraitists* of the fifteenth century such as Van Eyck, Memmling, and Bosch. The Germans of the Rhine valley and Bavaria were also very active in both painting and sculpture. Some of the most accomplished woodcarvings of any age were produced in southern Germany and Austria during this era. These, too, display little of the delight in the flesh or the interest in experimentation of the Italians. In general, *architecture* followed the same pattern. Variations on the Gothic continued to be the standard in the north, and northern architects made no effort to imitate the revived classicism so popular in Italy.

✤ FAMILY LIFE AND EDUCATION OF CHILDREN

Our knowledge of family life in the Renaissance comes largely from the upper classes, as is usual for premodern history. Men continued to marry quite late, in their thirties and forties, after securing their inheritances. Women were normally much younger at marriage, so there were many widows. Marriage to a rich or moderately well-off widow who was still young enough to bear children was a desirable step for a man. Dowries were expected in every case, in the middle and upper classes, and among the poor in the countryside as well. A girl without a suitable dowry was practically unmarriageable.

Families were often large, especially among the well-to-do. The household might include children from a prior marriage, spinster sisters or elderly widows, servants, and perhaps the husband's illegitimate offspring. We know from surviving records that an Italian merchant's household might easily include as many as twenty persons, including servants. Wealthy households were of a similar size throughout most of the rest of Europe.

The woman of the house was expected to run this establishment with vigor and economy. If her husband was away (a business trip might last six months or longer), often she was entrusted with full authority. A woman had to be literate to handle these tasks, and all wealthy families had private tutors for their daughters.

In general, however, women did not fare well during the Renaissance as a social group. In fact, the position of upper-class women actually seems to have declined; they no longer enjoyed the liberties afforded upper-class women during the Middle Age. Middle-class women probably had greater responsibility for the management of household and business affairs and played a role almost equal to that of their husbands. Middle-class families could afford fewer paid staff and household servants, so wives had to contribute more directly to the well-being of the family. As in the medieval period, the wives of artisans and merchants often were essential partners of the males, whose work could not be performed without them. Of working-class women, we as usual know relatively little, but we can assume that the male-dominated, patriarchal society went on without essential change. In both town and country, women had to do hard physical work as a matter of course. Spinning and weaving were the particular domain of the female, as well as care of rural livestock. In the towns, records show that women performed just about every task that men did: butchering, baking, metalwork, dyeing cloth, and all the handwork trades that they had been doing throughout the medieval period. The separation of work by gender had not yet begun.

Education varied for the sexes, as was customary. In the towns, men were educated for an active career in commerce or a craft. Beginning about age seven, they attended a boarding school for a few years and then were apprenticed to an appropriate firm or craftsman. Literacy was very common by this time among the urban population, but still very uncommon in the countryside where most lived. The peasant's son who received any education at all was still the exception, and the peasant woman who could spell out her name was a rare catch.

For girls of the upper and middle classes, education usually meant some study in the home under the supervision of a live-in or outside tutor; very frequently, the tutor was a seminary student who was trying to keep body and soul together until ordination. Their education focused on literacy in the vernacular with perhaps a bit of Latin, music making, and the domestic arts. Marriage was taken for granted as the fate of most young women; the alternative was a convent, which had little appeal. Intellectual women now had many more opportunities to express themselves in written forms, including history, poetry, religious tracts, and other formats. But their gender was still a severe obstacle to being taken seriously.

The *treatment of young children* was slowly changing among the upper classes, but not yet among the lower. Any family that could afford to do so would send a newborn baby to a peasant wet nurse; she would keep the child until it was past the nursing stage—about two years (at times longer, and sometimes without any contacts with the parents!). When the children returned to their parents' house, they were put under the exclusive care of the mother and, perhaps, governesses. In wealthy homes, the father rarely had much to do with his children until they reached the "age of reason" (age seven), when he would take charge of their education.

The usual attitude among the upper classes was that very young children were of interest to adults only because they represented the continuation of the family line. After reaching age seven or so, they became more worthy of attention not only because they had survived the most dangerous age, but also because they were now becoming persons with recognizable traits and personalities. Beating and other severe punishments were applied less often than in earlier centuries, but were still common enough, as we know from many diaries.

We know less for certain about the lower classes because of the absence of sources. Probably, babies continued to get little love and cherishing for the sensible reason that the parents could expect that about half of their offspring would die before reaching their seventh year. After that age, they were treated somewhat better, if only because they represented potential labor.

✤ THE POLITICAL SCIENCE OF RENAISSANCE EUROPE

The political theory of the Middle Age was based upon a strong monarchy, blessed and aided by a powerful and respected clergy. The favorite image for government was a man wearing a crown with a cross in his left hand and a sword in his right. But in the Hundred Years' War and other late medieval conflicts, that image suffered serious damage. In country after country, the feudal nobility took advantage of the confusion to reassert themselves and again decentralize political power.

This state of affairs was reversed in the fifteenth and sixteenth centuries. The monarchs, now armed with a new theory of authority, denied the nobles' claims of autonomy and subdued their frequent attempts to rebel. The new basis of royal authority was not church and king in partnership, but the king as executive of the state. What was new here was the idea of the state.

The Theory of the State

The state in Renaissance thinking was an entity that existed independently of the ruler or the subjects. It possessed *three essential attributes: legitimacy, sovereignty, and territory.*

- *Legitimacy* meant that the state possessed moral authority in the eyes of its subjects. It had a right to exist.
- *Sovereignty* meant that the state had an effective claim to equality with other states, and that it acknowledged no higher earthly power over it.
- *Territory* is self-explanatory; the state possessed real estate that could be precisely bounded and contained certain human and material resources.

The royal personage was the executive agent of the state, and he had every right to use whatever means he deemed fit to assure the state's welfare and expansion. In the fifteenth-century monarch's view, assuring the welfare of the state was about the same as assuring the welfare of the society in general. These so-called new monarchs were intent on one great goal: *power.* To be the proper servants of the state, they felt they must be the masters of all who might threaten it. And that meant being masters of intrigue, deceit, and intimidation. Renaissance politics was a rough game.

All of the Renaissance political theorists spent much time on the relationship between power and ethics, but none had the impact of a young Italian with great ambitions, Niccolò **Machiavelli.** In his extraordinary treatise on politics entitled *The Prince* (1516), Machiavelli described power relations in government as he had experienced them—not as they *should be,* but as they *were in fact.* He thought that human beings are selfish by nature and must be restrained by the prince from doing evil to one another. In so doing, the prince could and should use all means open to him. He must be both the lion and the fox, the one who is feared and the one who is beloved. If it came to a choice between fear and love, the wise prince will choose fear as the emotion he wishes to arouse in his subjects (see the Document in this chapter).

Royal Governments

France

France recovered much more rapidly than might have been expected from the devastation of the Hundred Years' War (fought entirely on French territory). The very unpromising monarch who owed his throne to Joan of Arc's help, Charles VII, turned out to be one of the cleverest and most effective of kings (1422–1461). He created the first truly royal army and used it against those who tried to assert their independence. He also gained much better control over the French clergy, particularly the appointment of bishops.

Machiavelli, *The Prince*

In the year 1513, the Florentine official and diplomat Niccolò Machiavelli (1469–1527) was arrested for treason and subjected to torture. Although he was soon released, his ambitions for power and wealth lay in ruins. Reluctantly retiring to his country estate, Machiavelli devoted much of his remaining life to writing a series of theoretical works on politics and the eventful history of his native Florence. But he is best remembered for his handbook on the art of governance, *The Prince,* the masterwork of Renaissance political literature, which was printed a few years after his death.

Machiavelli's denial that common morality should influence a ruler's politics in any way and his insistence that violence and deceit can be justified in the name of good government have earned him a sinister reputation. To the present day, the adjective *Machiavellian* carries a cynical connotation of taking unfair advantage and using deception to gain one's ends. Yet the author, who had had every chance of observing what he wrote about, was just describing the actual practices of the Italian rulers of his day—and of many wielders of power since then.

> I say that every prince ought to wish to be considered kind rather than cruel. Nevertheless, he must take care to avoid misusing his kindness. Caesar Borgia* was considered cruel, yet his cruelty restored Romagna, uniting it in peace and loyalty.... A prince must be indifferent to the charge of cruelty if he is to keep his subjects loyal and united.... Disorders harm the entire citizenry, while the executions ordered by a prince harm only a few. Indeed, of all princes, the newly established one can least of all escape the charge of cruelty, for new states are encumbered with dangers.

> Here a question arises: whether it is better to be loved than feared, or the reverse. The answer is, of course, that it would be best to be both loved and feared. But since the two rarely come together, anyone compelled to choose will find greater security in being feared than in being loved.... Men are less concerned about offending someone they have cause to love than someone they have cause to fear. Love endures by a bond which men, being scoundrels, may break whenever it serves their advantage to do so; but fear is supported by the dread of pain, which is always present....

> I conclude that since men will love what they themselves determine, but will fear as their ruler determines, a wise prince must rely upon what he, not others, can control. He need only strive to avoid being hated. Let the prince conquer his state, then, and preserve it; the methods employed will always be judged honorable, and everyone will praise him. For the mob of men is always impressed by appearances, and by results; and the world is composed of the mob....

> How praiseworthy it is, that a prince keeps his word and governs by candor, rather than craft, everyone knows... yet, those princes who had little regard for their word, and had the craft to turn men's minds, have accomplished great things, and in the end, they have overcome those who suited their actions to their pledges....

*Caesar Borgia was the illegitimate son of Pope Alexander VI and one of the most ruthless Italian noblemen of the day.

SOURCE: Niccolò Machiavelli, *The Prince,* translated by Luigi Ricci, as revised by E. A. Vincent 1935, Oxford University Press. Used by permission.

Charles's policies were followed, with even greater cleverness, by his son Louis XI, the "Spider King" as he was called by his many enemies. Louis was especially effective at gaining middle-class support—and tax money—against the claims of the feudal nobles. He also significantly expanded the size of the royal domain: that part of the country under the direct control of the Crown. Louis is credited with laying the foundation for the dimensions the French state attained under the great Bourbon kings of the seventeenth and eighteenth centuries.

● **MAP 27.2   Europe, the Near East, and North Africa in the Renaissance.** The political divisions of the Mediterranean basin and Europe in the fifteenth century.

England

England took more time to establish a centralized monarchy than had France. The strong rule of the early Norman kings ended with weak or unlucky individuals such as John the First (and Last!). In 1215 John (r. 1199–1216) had had to accept the *Magna Carta* from his rebellious nobles. Over the centuries, this Great Charter was gradually transformed from a statement of noble privilege against a king to a doctrine that held that the monarch like all others was bound to obey the laws.

The Hundred Years' War further weakened the royal powers and strengthened Parliament, as we have noted. By the mid-fifteenth century, Parliament had become the preserve of semi-independent barons and earls, who held the purse strings and drove hard bargains with the king in the wake of the lost war. The nobility added to the turbulence by carrying on a civil war over the succession to the throne; called the **Wars of the Roses,** the conflict lasted fifteen years (1455–1471).

Three late fifteenth-century kings (Edward IV, Richard III, and Henry VII) gradually threw the balance of internal power in favor of the Crown. Of these, the most important was *Henry VII,* the founder of the Tudor dynasty and a master of intimidation and intrigue. He enlisted the aid of the middle classes and the clergy, both of whom were exhausted by the squabbles of the nobles, and made sure that none of the troublemakers had an opportunity to revive the civil disturbances. Henry not only rebuilt the powers of the royal crown, but also avoided foreign wars, which would have meant going back to the noble-dominated Parliament to beg for funds. By the time he died in 1509, the English royal government was in firm control of the state.

The Holy Roman Empire (Germany)

The great exception to the recovery of royal powers in the fifteenth century was the German kingdom, technically still the Holy Roman Empire of the German Nation. Here there was no central power to recover; it had been destroyed in the medieval struggles between emperor and pope and the struggles between emperor and nobles, which then ensued.

The *emperor was elected,* rather than succeeding to the throne by hereditary right. The seven electors, who were all German princes and bishops, could and did negotiate with the various candidates to strike deals aimed at preserving noble autonomy. As a result, Germany had no centralized government in the fifteenth century. The emperor was only the first among equals, and sometimes not even that. He did not have a bureaucracy, a royal army, a national parliament, or the power to tax his subjects. The Holy Roman Empire was really a *loose confederation* of principalities, dukedoms, and even free cities, which were almost always squabbling among themselves. All real power was in the hands of the aristocrats and the churchmen.

Among the candidates for the throne, the **Habsburgs** had most often been successful. This princely family had its home in Vienna, Austria. In the late fifteenth and early sixteenth centuries, a series of extraordinary events propelled them into a position of great international strength for the first time. Thanks to a series of lucky marriages and the unexpected deaths of rivals, by 1527 the Habsburg territories had trebled in Europe and also included the huge overseas empire being rapidly conquered by Spain, which was now under a Habsburg ruler. It appeared that for the first time since Barbarossa the Holy Roman Emperor would be able to assert real authority. But the prospects of establishing royal rule in Germany were not realized: the division between Catholic and Protestant frustrated all efforts to unify the nation until the late nineteenth century.

Russia

Russia was a brand new entrant, or rather a newly rediscovered entrant, on the European scene in the late fifteenth century. The huge expanse of territory east of Christian Poland and Hungary was practically unknown to West Europeans after its conquest by the Mongols in the mid-1200s (see Chapters 16 and 21). Almost all cultural contacts between Russians and both the Latin and Byzantine Christian worlds had been severed by the primitive Asiatic tribesmen. The latter's adoption of the Islamic faith in the fourteenth century deepened the chasm that separated them from their Russian subjects.

The "Mongol Yoke" that lay upon Russia for almost two and a half centuries (1240–1480) caused a cultural retrogression of tremendous import. Prior to its coming, the Russian Principality of Kiev had entertained close relations with Christian Europe and especially with the Orthodox Christian empire in Constantinople from which it had received its religion, literature, and law. Situated on the extreme eastern periphery of the Christian world, Russia had nevertheless felt itself and been considered a full member of the European family.

After the arrival of the Mongols, this situation changed radically. In an effort to escape Mongol taxes and cruelties, the clergy and people of Russia sought to isolate themselves and had become vulnerable to all the ills that isolation entails. Ignorance and superstition became rife, even among the diminished number of the formally educated; the levels of technical and theoretical skills declined. Literacy all but disappeared among the laity.

In the absence of a native independent government, the Russian church came to play a particularly vital role in keeping the notion of a national community alive. The church of Rome had been rejected as heretical ever since the split in 1054. After Constantinople was seized by the Turks in 1453, the belief grew in Moscow that this had been God's punishment for the Greeks' waverings in defense of Orthodoxy. Now, Russia itself was to become the fortress of right belief: the **Third Rome**. As a Russian monk wrote to his ruler in 1511: "Two Romes, [i.e., Christian Rome of the fourth century, and Constantinople,] have fallen, but the Third [Moscow] stands and there will be no fourth." Russia's government and church saw themselves as the implements of divine providence that would bring the peoples of Europe back to the true faith and defeat the infidels, wherever they might be.

By the late fifteenth century, the Mongols had been so weakened by internal conflicts that the prince of Moscow defied them successfully in 1480 and asserted his independence. Already under Mongol rule, Moscow had become the most powerful Russian principality by a combination of single-minded ambition and consistent good luck. Soon the prince of Moscow had extended his rule to all parts of the nation and had taken to calling himself tsar (Caesar in Slavic) of Russia.

A tsar had far more power than any other European ruler of the day. Indeed, a tsar's powers were so impressive as to raise the question whether Russia was still a European state or whether, under the Mongols, it had become an Asiatic despotism where the will of the ruler was automatically law of the land. Western European ambassadors and traders sent to Moscow in the sixteenth century felt that they had entered upon truly foreign ground. They found themselves in a society that had no middle class and seemed untouched by the technical and psychological developments of the Renaissance. Its superstition and passivity were appalling, and its subservience toward its prince was striking to Western eyes.

✤ ART AND ITS PATRONS

The most visible and historically appreciated form of Renaissance culture is its art, and Italy was the leader in every field. A tremendous creative outburst took place in Florence, Rome, Venice, Milan, and a dozen other city-states during the fifteenth and sixteenth centuries.

In *painting,* great talents such as *Titian, da Vinci, Michelangelo, Botticelli,* and *Giotto* led the way to an unprecedented abundance of innovative compositions. All of them opened their studios to teach others, so that a wave of experimentation in the visual art forms swept across Italy and northward into Europe beyond the Alps. One of their great achievements was the mastery of perspective, which was first accomplished by Giotto in the early fourteenth century. He also led the way to a new realism in portraits. In *sculpture,* the universal genius of Michelangelo was accompanied by *Donatello, Cellini,* and *Bernini,* to mention only some of the better known names (see the Biography in this chapter). Both Renaissance sculpture and painting broke sharply from their medieval forerunners. Artists now saw the human figure as a thing of superb animal beauty quite apart from its spiritual considerations or destiny. They revived the classical ideal with a vengeance, but now combined it with a better understanding of human anatomy and a better sense of how to represent it.

Michelangelo was a leader in *architecture* as well. He designed much of the vast new St. Peter's Cathedral for one of the popes. Other leading architects included *Bramante, da Vinci,* and *Brunelleschi.* The basic architectural style of the Renaissance was an adaptation of the classical temple, with its columns, huge domes, and lofty facades. The Gothic style was now dismissed.

The spirit of this art, in whatever form, was quite different from that of medieval art. Renaissance art was intended to show the artist's mastery of technique. It was experimental: new ideas were tried in all directions, and old ideas were put into quite new forms or media. The huge bronze doors of the Florentine cathedral cast by Ghiberti were something quite new: nothing like that had been attempted previously. With their twelve reliefs depicting the life of Christ, the doors were a brilliant success.

Art was also unashamedly used to display the wealth of the individual or group who had commissioned it, rather than their piety (as in medieval times). The patron was normally depicted somewhere in the painting as part of a crowd; so were his family and sometimes the artist.

The *artist as a respected member of society* was also a Renaissance novelty (one that has generally not been

■ **Thomas More.** The force of character of Sir Thomas More, English statesman and humanist, comes through strongly in this great portrait by Hans Holbein the Younger. The chain of office worn by More shows that the painting was made between 1529 and 1533, when he was the lord chancellor of king Henry VIII prior to More's execution for resisting Henry's divorce and remarriage to Anne Boleyn.

Benvenuto Cellini
1500–1571

In modern terms, a "Renaissance man" is a person who can do everything, or many things, with flair and great competence. One of the best examples was Benvenuto Cellini, the Florentine artist, political figure, warrior, and author. Although he excelled in many fields, his memory is preserved mainly through the pages of his *Autobiography,* one of the few that have come down to us from so early a date with such rich detail.

The autobiography covers Cellini's life from early youth to the year 1558, when he apparently was intent on withdrawing from the world to become a monk, a plan he never carried out. It shows us a man who epitomized the public figure of the Italian Renaissance: violent, passionate, egotistic, and very conscious of talent and honor. At the same time, Cellini depicts a man who was sometimes overwhelmed with sincere religious emotion and trembled at the thought of answering for his multitude of sins. Many are his boasts, but he is aware that some are hollow and that whatever his own accomplishments, others stand above him.

Cellini was the premier goldsmith of his age, but few of his works have survived. He was apprenticed early to a goldsmith in Florence, but had to leave the city clandestinely in 1516 because of a streetfight, one of the many instances of the exaggerated sense of honor Cellini displayed all his life. Fleeing to papal Rome, he stayed mainly in that city for the next twenty years and was a favored recipient of papal commissions in the 1520s. Cellini was present at the plundering of Rome by troops of the Constable de Bourbon, one of several French invaders of the papal territories in the sixteenth century. According to the *Autobiography,* Cellini played an important role in defending the pope's Castel Sant'Angelo against the invaders and was himself the slayer of the constable with a chance shot from his primitive gun. (We know that the constable indeed died storming the walls of Rome; whether he was killed by Cellini's shot remains a mystery.)

A few years later Cellini probably regretted his valor on the pope's behalf. The bastard son of Pope Paul III was responsible for imprisoning the artist on a false charge of theft of papal jewels. After many months in a dungeon, Cellini escaped, breaking his leg in the process, and was then recaptured. Finally, he was released after the intervention of King Francis I of France, who appreciated Cellini's great gifts and wanted him to work in Paris.

From 1540 to 1545, Cellini resided in Paris, supervising a studio executing royal commissions. According to him, these were the happiest years of his life. But in 1545 he opted to return to his native Florence, where the Medici family desired his services as a goldsmith. There he finished his best-known sculpture, the magnificent *Medusa,* as well as a portrait bust of Duke Cosimo, head of the Medici family and ruler of Florence.

The *Autobiography* describes many conflicts with Cellini's Medici patrons and with other artists of the age. Some were lethal, and Cellini does not hesitate to tell of the men whom he has seen fit to kill because of offenses against his honor. He conveys to us the dangers and challenges of a violent age, when intrigue and falsity were taken for granted in public life. The *Autobiography* also tells us of the great admiration Cellini entertained for Michelangelo and for the ancient Romans, whom he acknowledged to be his superiors and his heroes. Better than any other source, Cellini's egotistic, boastful, and forthright memoirs show us the trials and rewards of a Renaissance artist and public figure.

imitated since!). Several of the leading figures of the art world were very well rewarded in money and prestige; they could pick and choose among their patrons and did not hesitate to drive hard bargains for their talents.

Leonardo da Vinci was one of the richest men of his time and lived accordingly; so did Michelangelo and *Raphael,* both of whom enjoyed papal esteem and commissions for the Vatican palaces and libraries.

Artistic *patronage* was limited to a smaller group than had been true earlier. The princes and the oligarchies around them were a tiny fraction of Italian society, but they provided most of the artists' commissions. Only rarely would an artist work without a specific commission in the hope of finding a buyer later. Artists who were not good enough or famous enough to secure commissions worked for others in their studios as anonymous helpers. Many of the great paintings of the Italian Renaissance were only sketched and outlined by the famous artist: his unknown helpers finished out the brushwork.

Artists dealt with their patrons as equals; it was not at all unusual for a secure artist to refuse a lucrative commission because of a disagreement with his patron. For the most part, the patrons respected talent and allowed the artists to execute their work much as they pleased. The idea of *artistic genius* came into currency at this time; the artist was thought to possess a "divine spark" or other quality that ordinary souls lacked and therefore should be allowed to develop his talent without too much restriction.

✤ THE RENAISSANCE CHURCH

Much Renaissance literature engages in satire of the Christian clergy and focuses attention on the corruption and indifference that had become common in the higher ranks. These attacks are clearly directed at the personnel of the church, not its basic doctrines. At a time when increasing educational opportunity outside the church was giving birth to an urban group well read in nonreligious literature, the open immorality of some clergy and the ignorance and selfishness of others gave rise to continual scandal. Many priests were still illiterate; many monks had long since forgotten their vows of poverty and chastity. It was not at all unusual for a bishop never to set foot in his diocese because he preferred to live elsewhere. It was equally common for the abbot of a monastery to have produced a couple of illegitimate children with his "housekeeper."

In any Italian town the political and financial interests of the local clergy often nullified their moral leadership. It was this conduct that embittered many of the leading figures of the Italian Renaissance and turned them into raging anticlerics, while in the transalpine regions to the north the clergy normally preserved themselves from such accusations.

The example came from the top. Some of the fifteenth- and sixteenth-century popes were distressingly ignorant of their religious duties and too mindful of their money and privileges. The Italian noble families who controlled the papacy and the papal court were involved in ongoing struggles for political domination of the peninsula and tended to treat the papacy as part of their worldly intrigues. They regarded the increasing calls for reform as the mumblings of malcontents, which could be safely ignored. Only with the emergence of the Lutheran challenge after 1517 would they slowly realize their error.

■ A modern view of St. Peter's in Rome.

Summary

A rebirth of secular learning derived from classical authors began in fourteenth-century Italy and spread north in ensuing years. The Renaissance produced not only the greatest art of the Western tradition since Greece, but also the foundations of the modern state. That those foundations were laid along the lines of Machiavelli's *Prince* rather than the lines of the Christian humanists and moralists, such as More or Erasmus, would prove fateful. In most of Europe, the fifteenth century saw a significant rise in monarchic powers and prestige. English and French kings fashioned effective controls over their unruly nobles. The Russian tsar also emerged as a strong ruler. Only in Germany and Italy was there no progress in the consolidation of central government. Individualism and secularism made strong advances among the educated, while the moral prestige of the clergy continued to sink amid demonstrations of corruption from the papal court and other higher clergy. The arts flourished under the stimuli of new wealth in the cities and a governing class that placed great store on patronage and fame. Painting and architecture witnessed notable experiments and successful new talents.

Test Your Knowledge

1. During the fifteenth century, the territory now called Italy was
   a. under the firm control of the Holy Roman Emperor.
   b. broken into several political units centered on cities.
   c. finally brought under the monopolistic control of the papacy.
   d. split in allegiance between Rome and Florence.
2. A novel new element in Italian city-state politics during the Renaissance was
   a. preferring fear to love as a basis of authority.
   b. a professional army.
   c. an absolute monarchy.
   d. the organization of a taxation agency.
3. One of the pecular features of Russian Orthodoxy was the belief that
   a. Russians would be the political masters of all Europe.
   b. all Russians would be saved eternally.
   c. Moscow was destined to be the Third Rome.
   d. the sovi was nonexistent.
4. Which of the following *least* fits the Renaissance worldview?
   a. Ambition
   b. Arrogance
   c. Confidence
   d. Caution
5. Titian and Van Eyck were both Renaissance
   a. architects.
   b. painters.
   c. political theorists.
   d. churchmen.
6. The basic message of More's *Utopia* was that
   a. personal wealth is the only sure path to social reforms.
   b. education cannot reduce human sinfulness.
   c. social institutions, not individuals, must be reformed first.
   d. people are inherently evil and cannot really be changed.
7. Which of the following statements about Renaissance secularism is *false*?
   a. It was vigorously opposed by church leaders.
   b. It was a by-product of a changing economy.
   c. Most persons held to the basic tenets of Christian teaching.
   d. It encouraged the acquisition of material things.
8. The Renaissance in northern Europe differed from that of Italy by being
   a. less secular.
   b. more artistic.
   c. less serious.
   d. inferior in quality.

Identification Terms

Erasmus

Habsburg dynasty

humanism

Kievan principality

Machiavelli

Petrarch

secularism

Third Rome

Utopia

Wars of the Roses

Bibliography

Benesch, O. *The Art of the Renaissance in Northern Europe,* 1965. A well-illustrated introduction.

Ferguson, W. K. *The Renaissance,* 1940. A brief, lively account of what the term *Renaissance* meant.

Hale, J. R. *Renaissance Europe: The Individual and Society, 1480–1520,* 1971. Surveys the social aspects of the Renaissance in all of Europe; broader than the title might suggest.

Hay, D. *The Italian Renaissance,* 1977. A gem for students' use; concise and very readable.

Herlihy, D. *The Family in Renaissance Italy,* 1974. A good introduction.

Huizinga, J. *Erasmus of Rotterdam,* 1952. The standard biography.

King, M. L. *Women of the Renaissance,* 1991. An introduction to women in the Renaissance.

Maclean, I. *The Renaissance Notion of Women,* 1980.

Marius, R. *Thomas More,* 1984.

Martindale, A. *The Rise of the Artist in the Middle Ages and the Early Renaissance,* 1972. Well illustrated with an extensive bibliography.

Martines, L. *Power and Imagination: City States in Renaissance Italy.*

Phillips, M. M. *Erasmus and the Northern Renaissance,* 1956. The leading figure of the northern Renaissance.

Woelfflin, H. *Classic Art: An Introduction to the Italian Renaissance,* 1968.

PART 4

DISEQUILIBRIUM:
THE WESTERN EXPANSION
1500–1800 C.E.

Within fifty years on either side of the year 1500 C.E., a host of events or processes contributed to an atmosphere of rising confidence in the power of European governments and their supportive institutions. In the political and military realm, the Mongol Yoke in Russia was lifted; the Turks, victorious at Constantinople, failed in an attempt to seize Vienna and central Europe; the Hundred Years' War had ended and the French recovery commenced. The economy had recovered from the ravages of the Black Death, and maritime trade had increased significantly, as had the sophistication of commercial instruments. The shameful derogation of the papal dignity brought about by the Babylonian Captivity and the Great Schism had ended. The worst of the peasant *jacqueries* had been put down, and a peaceable transition from feudal agrarianism for peasant and noble seemed possible, at least in the West.

But aside from these general developments, the period around 1500 is usually heralded as the beginning of the Modern Era due to two specific complexes of events: the rejection of traditional authority manifested in Protestantism, and the voyages of discovery that revealed the possibilities of the globe to Europeans' imagination—and greed. Both of these complexes contributed, in very different ways, to the expansion of Europe's reach and authority that took place in the next three hundred years, until Europeans began to claim a prerogative to decide the fates of others as almost a God-given right. This tendency was particularly striking in the American colonies, where the native Indians were either obliterated or virtually enslaved by their overlords. But it was also the case, though in a much more limited way, for East and south Asia, the coast of Africa, and the island or Arctic peripheries of a world that was much larger than anyone had formerly supposed.

The difference between 1500 and 1750 in this regard might well be illustrated by comparing the Aztecs' Tenochtitlán, which amazed the envious Cortez, with the sleepy, dusty villages to which Mexico's Indians were confined later. Similarly, one might compare the army of the Persian Safavid rulers of the early sixteenth century that reduced the mighty Moghuls to supplicants for peace with the raggedy mob that attempted—in vain—to stop a handful of British from installing themselves on the Khyber Pass three centuries later. The West, whether represented by illiterate Spanish freebooters or Oxfordian British bureaucrats, seemed destined to surpass or be invincible against what one unrepentant imperialist called the "lesser breeds."

Part 4 examines the massive changes that were slowly evidencing themselves in European life: the Reformation and its effects; the struggle between royal absolutism and the constitutional principle; the widening gap between Western and Eastern Europe; and the scientific advances of the seventeenth and eighteenth centuries. The part concludes with an examination of the Enlightenment and the Atlantic Revolutions.

The voyages of discovery of the fifteenth and sixteenth centuries and the resultant Columbian Exchange are the subject of Chapter 28. In Chapter 29 the successful Lutheran and Calvinist challenges to the papal church and their permanent effects on Western sensibilities are considered. Chapters 30 and 31 examine the absolutist idea and its motivation in religious warfare and the desire for stability; the differences in the social and economic structures of Western and Eastern Europe are also considered. Chapter 32 discusses both the revolution in thinking about the natural world that began in the sixteenth century and its spillover effects upon the general intellectual atmosphere of the eighteenth century, which was called the Enlightenment in Europe. Chapters 33 through 35 complete this section by examining the political and economic phenomenon of liberalism and its contribution to the political revolutions of the late eighteenth century. The French rebellion against the *ancien regime* is considered in detail; its ending is denoted by the rise of Napoleon. The essentials of the Bonapartist empire are outlined, and then attention is devoted to the painful, but briefly successful effort to put the old Europe back together.

	Law and Government	Economy
EUROPEANS	Law and government based on class, but emerge from religious wars as increasingly secular. Absolutist monarchy the rule, with few exceptions (England, Holland). Nobles and landlords rule free peasants in West, serfs in East. State and church still intertwined; religious tollerance considered dangerous to public order by most governments.	Economy continues to diversify, with strong capitalist character especially in Protestant nations. Urban middle class becomes prominent in business and commerce. Growing number of impoverished people, with abject serfdom common east of the Elbe River. Machine industry begins in later eighteenth century in western Europe.
WEST ASIANS	Government continues along traditional Qur'anic lines and law follows the *sharija*. Ottomans bring Muslim international empire to its apex in sixteenth century, but cannot sustain the momentum after 1700. Safavid dynasty in Persia has two hundred years of glory but exhausts itself between Ottoman and Mughal rivals in Turkey and India.	Further evolution of highly commercialized, complex trade among Muslim countries and between them and the non-Muslims. Slavery remains common, mainly from African sources. Wealth generated from gold mines in West Africa, spices from East Asia, and carrying trade between India/China and the West via Mediterranean.
SOUTH AND EAST ASIANS	Western presence not yet decisive but steadily more apparent. Much of South Pacific island territories under Western colonial administration since 1500s. Japan originally welcomes Westerners but then shuts itself off in *sakoku*. China continues as imperial dynasty ruling through mandarins after Manzhou replace the Ming in 1600s. India's north and center unified under the Mughal dynasts, with European colonies beginning to occupy the coasts after 1700.	Japan prospers and advances in *sakoku* isolation; China has last great age under early Qing before humiliation at European hands: north and south brought firmly together by extensive trade. Mughul India still well-organized, prosperous country, with much commerce with Southeast Asia and islands. Merchants and craftsmen multiply, but everywhere the agrarian village is the mainstay of the economy.
AFRICANS	Coming of Europeans to coasts as slavers generally has little immediate effect on African law and tribal government. On east coast, Arab-African trading cities (Zanzibar, etc.) prosper but Great Zimbabwe declines. Tribal warfare increases after introduction of firearms and large-scale slaving in west. Interior tribes barely affected by Europeans throughout period.	Slaving disrupts some established trade patterns in west, making some of the coastal states (Dahomey) more powerful, undermining others (Hausa, Songhay). Agriculture spreads, aided by introduction of new crops from the Americas and South Asia. Bantu areas in east and south develop extensive trade with Arab and Portuguese coastal towns.
AMERICANS	Iberian law and establishment of viceroyalties of Spain and Portugal by mid-1500s. Natives subordinated to small minority of whites. Highly centralized colonial governments committed to mercantilist system and discouragement of autonomy. Temporary reversal of these policies in later 1700s.	Mercantilism enforced until the 1700s, with colonial artisans and manufactures obstructed by Madrid. Mining and plantation agriculture dominant large-scale economic activities. Large majority of population living in agrarian subsistence economy.

1500–1800 C.E. DISEQUILIBRIUM: THE WESTERN EXPANSION

Peoples: Europeans, West Asians, South and East Asians, Africans, Americans

Religion and Philosophy	Arts and Culture	Science and Technology
Christian unity broken by Protestant Reform. Papal church severely challenged, but regains some of lost ground in seventeenth century. Churches become nationalistic and theology more narrowly defined. Skepticism and secularism on rise after 1700, leading to increased religious tolerance by end of eighteenth century. Enlightenment dominates intellectual affairs after c. 1750.	Renaissance continues in plastic arts; great age of baroque architecture, sculpture, and painting in Catholic Europe. Neoclassicism of eighteenth century led by France. Vernacular literature flourishes in all countries. Western orchestral music begins. First professional authors. First signs of democratization of the arts.	Physical, math-based sciences flourish in "Scientific Revolution" of seventeenth century. Science replaces Scripture and tradition as source of truth for many educated persons. Technology becomes much more important. Weaponry enables Western domination of all opponents, agriculture enables population explosion of eighteenth century, beginnings of Industrial Revolution manifested in England.
Ulema and Islamic tradition resist accumulating evidence of Western superiority, attempt to ignore or refute it on doctrinal grounds. Religious orthodoxy severely challenged in various parts of empire (Sufi, Shi'a, etc.), becomes increasingly defensive. Last major surge of Islamic expansion into Asian heartland (Mughal India).	High point of Islamic art forms under Ottoman, Safavid and Mughal aegis. Architecture, ceramics, miniature painting, and calligraphy are some particular strengths.	Sciences neglected; original mental capital derived from Greek and Persian sources now exhausted and no new impulses discovered. Technology also lags, with almost all new ideas coming from West rejected as inferior. By end of period, Westerners moving into preferred posts in commerce of Ottoman and Mughal empires (capitulations, East India Company).
Religious beliefs experience no basic changes from the prevalent Buddhism (China, Japan, southeast Asia); Hinduism (most of India, parts of southeast Asia); Islam (north India, Afghanistan, East Indies); and Shinto (Japan). Christianity briefly flourished in Japan until its suppression by Tokugawa shoguns in 1600s, but makes little headway in China and India.	Superb painting, drawing on porcelain, bamboo, and silk in China and Japan. Calligraphy is major art form. *Kabuki* and *No* plays in Japan, novels in China. Poetry of nature. India: Taj Mahal, frescoes, enamel work, and Mughal architecture are high points.	Sciences throughout Asia falling rapidly behind Europe by end of this period. Exceptions in medicine, pharmacy. China adopts defensive seclusion from new ideas under mandarin officials. Technology lags also, as overpopulation begins to make itself felt at end of period, further reducing the need for labor saving.
African native animism continues unchanged by European "factories," which have no interest in missionary work, but Muslims make steady progress in sub-Saharan conversions, reaching into Congo basin by period's end.	High point of Benin bronze work and masks. Oral folk beliefs in place of literature. Wood carving and gold-work are chief media.	Sciences and technology remain dormant in absence of writing and formal education systems. Some adaptation of European technology by west coastal states in weaponry and ironwork.
Catholicism makes somewhat deeper impression on Indians, but religion remains a mixed cult of pre-Christian and Christian beliefs, supervised by *criollo* priesthood and Spanish hierarchs.	Church remains major sponsor of arts in formal sense, but folk arts derived from pre-Columbian imagery remain universal. Baroque churches are center of social life. Little domestic literature, but secular Enlightenment makes inroads into small educated class by mid-eighteenth century.	Science and technology totally dependent on stagnant mother-country, have no importance to illiterate masses. Enlightened monarchs of later 1700s make some improvements, but these are temporary and partial.

A LARGER WORLD OPENS

mid 1400s	Portuguese begin voyages of exploration
1492	Christopher Columbus reaches Americas
1498	Vasco de Gama arrives in India
early 1500s	Trans-Atlantic slave trade begins
1519–1540	Spanish conquer Aztecs and Incans
1522	First circumnavigation of globe completed
1602	Dutch East India Company founded

The unparalleled overseas expansion of Europe in the later fifteenth and early sixteenth centuries opened a new era. Motives for the rapid series of adventuresome voyages ranged from Christian missionary impulses to the much more common desire to get rich. Backed to varying degrees by their royal governments, Portuguese, Spanish, Dutch, French, and English seafarers opened the world to European commerce, settlement, and eventual dominion. Through the Columbian Exchange initiated in 1492, the New World entered European consciousness and was itself radically changed by European influences. The overseas conflicts generated by the claims of the explorers and merchant-adventurers soon became intertwined with the struggles generated by the Protestant Reformation and brought Europe into multifaceted warfare between 1580 and 1715.

✤ MARITIME EXPLORATION IN THE 1400s

The Vikings in their graceful Long Boats had made voyages across the North Atlantic from Scandinavia to Greenland and on to North America as early as 1000 C.E. But the northern voyages were too risky to serve as the channel for European expansion, and Scandinavia's population base was too small. The Vikings' tiny colonies did not last. Four hundred years later, major advances in technology had transformed maritime commerce. The development of new sail rigging, the magnetic compass and the astrolabe, a new hull design, and systematic navigational charts enabled Western seamen, led by the Portuguese, to conquer the stormy Atlantic. Their claims to dominion over their newly discovered territories were backed up by firearms of all sizes. Most of these inventions were originally the products of the Chinese and Muslims; the Europeans had found them in the traditional interchange ports of the eastern Mediterranean and then improved upon them.

By the end of the fifteenth century, the map of the eastern hemisphere was gradually becoming familiar to Europeans. Knowledge of the high culture of China was current by the early 1400s; overland traders, mostly Muslims, had established an active trade with that country via the famous Silk Road through central Asia. Marco Polo's great adventure was well known even earlier, after the appearance of his book about his many years of service to Kubilai Khan.

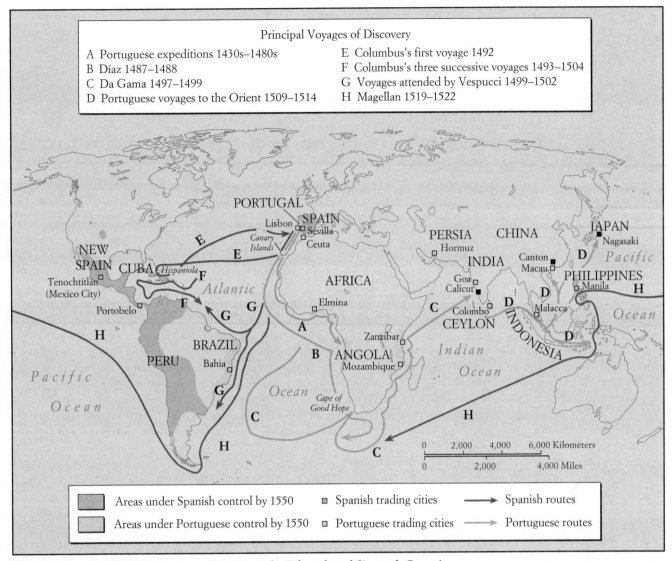

Principal Voyages of Discovery

A Portuguese expeditions 1430s–1480s
B Díaz 1487–1488
C Da Gama 1497–1499
D Portuguese voyages to the Orient 1509–1514

E Columbus's first voyage 1492
F Columbus's three successive voyages 1493–1504
G Voyages attended by Vespucci 1499–1502
H Magellan 1519–1522

Areas under Spanish control by 1550 — Spanish trading cities — Spanish routes
Areas under Portuguese control by 1550 — Portuguese trading cities — Portuguese routes

◉ **MAP 28.1 Spanish and Portuguese Voyages in the Fifteenth and Sixteenth Centuries.**

Most of Europe's luxury imports came from China and India, while the Spice Islands (as they were called by Europeans) of Southeast Asia were the source of the most valuable items in international exchange (see Map 28.1). But in the fourteenth century, this trade was disrupted, first by the Turkish conquest of the eastern Mediterranean, and then by the breakup of the Mongol empire, which had formed a single unit reaching from China to western Russia. Security of transit across Asia was threatened, as was the Europeans' profitable interchange of goods with the Arabs and Persians. In 1453 the great depot of eastern wares, Constantinople, fell into the hands of the Turkish Muslims. Europeans now became much more interested than ever before in finding a direct sea route to the East that would allow them to make an "end run" around the hostile Turks.

⚜ OVERSEAS EMPIRES
Portuguese Pioneers

In the middle of the 1400s, insignificant and impoverished Portugal took advantage of its geographical position to begin the rapid phase of European expansion. Under the guidance of the visionary *Prince Henry the Navigator*

Alfonso De Albuquerque
1453–1515

Tiny Portugal was for a century in the very forefront of European exploration and conquests in the East. Starting in the epoch of Henry the Navigator, Portuguese daring secured a series of "openings" to the wealth of East Asia. By the end of the 1540s, the flag of the Lisbon court was waving over a chain of ports reaching from Mozambique to the China Sea.

The chief architect of this brief-lived but amazing empire was the explorer, administrator, and warrior Alfonso de Albuquerque (1453–1515). An illegitimate relation to the dynasty in Lisbon, he spent his youth at the court of Alfonso V and then served that prince's successor John II. Albuquerque set out for the first time to the East in 1503 and was rewarded the next year by command of a part of a flotilla that sailed for India in 1506 under the great seaman Tristan da Cunha. Separating from the main fleet, Albuquerque raided the Arab settlements on the east African coast and then crossed much of the Indian Ocean to the Persian Gulf. Here he temporarily captured the port of Hormuz, halfway up the gulf and one of the most active trade centers in the Muslim world. Proceeding on to India's western coast, he attempted to make good his authority to supersede the previous governor, Almeida. But this wily opponent threw Albuquerque into jail, and he was only able to regain his freedom after some months by the arrival of the Portuguese grand admiral.

Once Almeida was recalled, Albuquerque undertook a series of maritime raids and conquests that remain among the most remarkable of the Age of Exploration. He secured the important town of Goa on India's western coast, then went on to the Straits of Malacca in Southeast Asia, which controlled all sea traffic from the west to China and the Spice Islands. After a severe struggle against vastly more numerous Muslim fleets, Albuquerque was able to gain control of Malacca for Portugal. On the voyage back to Goa, his ship went down, and the admiral nearly lost his life as well as all the fortune he had captured. In Goa, he established Portuguese rule so solidly that this colony remained under Lisbon's control until 1960.

Among the last of the great admiral's exploits was an attempt to conquer the gateway to the Red Sea, the port of Aden, in 1513–1514. He failed to overcome the city's strong defenses, but became the first European to sail into the Red Sea. Egyptian opposition prevented him from setting up a secure post there, however. According to some reports, he for a time entertained a scheme to force the Egyptians to surrender by diverting the Nile from its course.

In 1515, Albuquerque again sailed up the Persian Gulf and reconquered Hormuz, this time permanently, for Portugal. His reward was bitter: on the homeward voyage to Goa, his ship encountered one newly arrived from Portugal, which carried the new king's command that Albuquerque resign his governor-general's post and turn it over to his rival and enemy, Soarez. Perhaps this humiliation, which was totally undeserved, was the cause of Albuquerque's sudden death at sea. He was buried at Goa, which remained the center of the maritime empire he founded for the next two centuries.

The story goes that King Emmanuel, discovering too late his mistake in dismissing his faithful and brave governor, heaped great honors upon Albuquerque's only survivor, his son Alfonso. But the best testimonial to Albuquerque's wisdom and justice is that both Hindus and Muslims used to go to his tomb in Goa as a place of refuge and a gathering point for protests against abusive or unjust Portuguese officials in later days. A magnificent seaman, who frequently led his tiny fleets of five or six caravels against flotillas that outnumbered him by ten to one, Albuquerque was also a skilled and farsighted administrator. His goal was not to crush the natives, but to induce them to accept the Portuguese as solicitous overlords and protectors. The capital of New Mexico is the one remembrance of him in the New World.

(1394–1460), the Portuguese sponsored a series of exploratory voyages down the west coast of Africa and out into the ocean as far as the Azores (about one-third of the distance to the Caribbean). In 1488 the Portuguese captain **Bartolomeo Díaz** successfully rounded the Cape of Good Hope; a few years later, Vasco da Gama sailed across the Indian Ocean to the west coast of India. Trying to go down the west African coast, the captain Alvarez Cabral got blown all the way across the Atlantic, making landfall in Brazil, which he promptly claimed for Portugal. By 1510, Portuguese flags were flying over Goa in India and **Macao** on the coast of China (see the Biography in this chapter).

The Portuguese empire was really only a string of fortified stations called "factories," from which the Portuguese brought back shiploads of the much sought-after spices, gold, porcelain, and silk from their trading partners in East Africa and the Southeast Asian mainland and islands. The Portuguese paid for these imports initially with metalwares, cloth, and trinkets and later with firearms and liquor. The Lisbon government was the initiator and main beneficiary of this trade, because Portugal's small upper and middle classes were unable to come up with the money necessary to outfit ships for the expeditions.

The era of Portuguese leadership was brief; the country was too poor and its population too small to maintain this fantastic network. By the late 1500s, the Dutch had already forced Portugal to give up some of its overseas stations. Then in 1580 Portugal was incorporated into Catholic Spain, which gave the Dutch and English Protestants an excuse to attack the Portuguese everywhere. Eventually, Portugal was left with only a few trading posts scattered along the African and Indian coasts and in the Far East.

The Spanish Empire in the Americas

The newly unified Spanish kingdom was close behind and in some areas simultaneous with Portugal in the race for empire building. A larger domestic resource base and extraordinary finds of precious metals enabled Spain to achieve more permanent success than its Iberian neighbor. The Italian visionary *Christopher Columbus* was able to persuade King Ferdinand and Queen Isabella of his dream of a shortcut to the "Indies" by heading *west* over the Atlantic, which he thought was only a few hundred miles wide. The first of Columbus's Spanish-financed voyages resulted in the discovery of the American continents. He made three more voyages before his death and

■ **A Portuguese Galleon.** Ships like these opened the trade routes to the East and to Brazil and the Caribbean for the Lisbon government in the sixteenth and seventeenth centuries. In their later days, two or three rows of cannons gave them heavy firepower as well as cargo space.

was still convinced that China lay just around the horizon of the Caribbean Sea. By then, the Spanish crown had engaged a series of other voyagers, including **Amerigo Vespucci,** who eventually gave his name to the New World that Columbus and others were exploring. In 1519–1521, the redoubtable **Hernan Cortez** conquered the Aztec empire in Mexico. Soon Spanish explorers had penetrated north into what is now California and Arizona, and by the 1540s most of northern South America as well as all Central America and the Caribbean islands were under Spain's control.

Perhaps the greatest of these ventures was the fantastic voyage of **Ferdinand Magellan.** Starting from Spain in 1519, his ships made the first circumnavigation of the globe; a few survivors (not including the unlucky Magellan) limped back into Sevilla in 1522 and reported that, yes, the world was indeed round. Most educated people already thought so, but Magellan's voyage proved that the earth had no real ends, and that it was possible to go around the southern tip of the New World into the more or less familiar waters of East Asia.

■ **A Slave Ship.** Some of the slave ships were able to transport up to 800 Africans at a time, of whom fully 15–20% would die at sea or shortly after off loading in the Caribbean or Brazil. Their sea-quarters were crowded and unsanitary to a terrible degree, and the captain's fear of rebellion kept them under lock below decks most of the voyage.

Like the Portuguese, the Spaniards' motives for exploration were mixed between a desire to convert the heathen to the papal church and thus gain a strong advantage against the burgeoning Protestants (see Chapter 29) and the desire for wealth. It is often difficult to tell which motive was uppermost; sometimes, however, as in the cases of Francisco Pizarro in Peru and Cortez in Mexico, it is somewhat easier. By whatever motivation, by the middle of the 1500s, Spanish adventurers had created an empire that reached nearly around the world. By the terms of the royal charters granted to Columbus and his successors, the Spanish Crown claimed the lion's share of anything of value found by the explorers. Indian gold and silver thus poured into the royal treasury in Madrid. Those metals, in turn, allowed Spain to become the most powerful European state in the sixteenth and seventeenth centuries.

Unlike the Portuguese, the Spanish frequently came to stay at their overseas posts. Whereas the Portuguese were primarily interested in quick profits from the trade in luxury items from the East, the Spanish noble explorers were usually accompanied by priests, who set up missions, and by a number of lowborn men (later women, also), who were prepared to get rich more slowly by taking land and workers from among the native population.

Finding that the cities of gold and silver, or the *El Dorados*, were mirages except in Mexico and Peru, the Spanish immigrants gradually created agricultural colonies in much of Central and South America, using first Indian and then black labor. Some of these workers were more or less free to come and go, but an increasing number were slaves, imported from Africa. The Spanish colonies thus saw the growth of a multiracial society—blacks, Indians, and whites—in which the whites held the dominant positions from the outset. The dominance of the whites was to assume increasing importance for the societies and economies of these lands both during their three hundred years as colonies and later as independent states.

The African Slave Trade Opens

The African slave trade commenced in the fifteenth century. When the Portuguese ventured down the West African coast, they quickly discovered that selling black houseslaves to the European nobility could be a lucrative business. But the slave trade remained very small scale through the 1490s and only began to grow when slaves started to be shipped across the Atlantic. By the mid-1530s, Portugal had shipped large numbers of slaves to the Caribbean and to its own colony of Brazil, and the trans-Atlantic trade remained almost a Portuguese monopoly until into the next century. At that time, Dutch and then English traders moved into the business and dominated it through its great expansion in the eighteenth century until its gradual abolition.

Few European women traveled to the Americas in the early years of colonization, so the Spaniards often married Indian or black women or kept them as concubines. As a result, **mestizos** (the offspring of Indians and whites) and **mulattos** (the children of Africans and whites) soon outnumbered Caucasians in many colonies. The same happened in Portuguese Brazil, where a huge number of African slaves were imported to till the sugarcane fields that were that colony's chief resource. Here, the populace was commonly the offspring of Portuguese and African, rather than the Spanish-Indian mixture found to the north.

Dutch and English Merchant-Adventurers

When Portugal's eastern trade began to falter, the Dutch Protestant merchants combined a fine eye for profit with religious prejudice—the Portuguese were after all minions of the pope and the Spanish king—to fill the vacuum. Controlling their own affairs after the failure of the Spanish Armada in 1588 (hitherto in the sixteenth century the Netherlands had also been under Spanish control), the bourgeois shipowners and merchants of the Dutch and Flemish towns quickly moved into the forefront of the race for trade. By the opening of the seventeenth century, Amsterdam and Antwerp were the major destination of Far Eastern shippers, and Lisbon had fallen into a secondary position.

The Dutch had no interest in converting the natives or settling in exotic places. They wanted to accumulate wealth by buying shiploads of goods at low prices from eastern suppliers and selling the goods at very high prices in Europe. Many of the Asian suppliers were Muslims, and their relationship with the Catholic Portuguese had been strained. They preferred to deal with the Dutch Protestants, who were simply businessmen with no desire to be missionaries. If the suppliers were reluctant to sell, the Dutch "persuaded" them by various means, usually involving Dutch superiority in naval gunnery. All of the Europeans at times dealt brutally with their eastern hosts and partners, but the Dutch were probably the most ruthless because they were restricted by neither their home government nor religious scruples.

The Dutch focused on the East Indies spice and luxury trade, but they also established a "settler colony" in New Amsterdam across the Atlantic, and several island colonies in the Caribbean. These colonies were less attractive to the ambitious Dutch and were eventually surrendered to other powers, such as England. New Amsterdam became New York at the close of the first of two naval wars in the seventeenth century that made England the premier colonial power along the East Coast of the future United States.

It is remarkable that such a small nation (Holland did not possess more than 2.5 million souls at this juncture) was able to carry out this vast overseas enterprise at the very time it was struggling to free itself from its Spanish overlords. A chief reason for the Dutch success was the *East India Company;* founded by the government in 1602, the company had a monopoly on Dutch trading in the Pacific. The company proved to be an enormous bonanza for its stockholders and eventually took over the Portuguese spice and luxury trade from the East. The traders were usually temporary partners. A partnership would be set up for one or more voyages with both cost and profits split among the shareholders. The traders hired captains and crews who would be most likely to succeed in filling the ship's hold at minimal cost, whatever the means or consequences. Somewhat later, the traders' attention shifted from importing spices and luxury goods to the alluring profits to be made in the trans-Atlantic trade in African slaves.

The *English colonial venture* was slow in getting started. When the Portuguese and Spaniards were dividing up the newly discovered continent of America and the Far Eastern trade, England was just emerging from a lengthy struggle for dynastic power called the War of the Roses. Starting in the 1530s, the country was preoccupied for a generation with the split from Rome under Henry VIII and its consequences (see Chapter 29). Then came the disappointing failure of Raleigh's Lost Colony on the Carolina coast in the 1580s. Only in the early 1600s did the English begin to enter the discovery and colonizing business in any systematic way. Like the Dutch, the English efforts were organized by private parties or groups and were not under the direction of the royal government. The London East India Company is a good example; despite its name, it soon gave up attempts to penetrate the Dutch monopoly on East Indian luxuries and devoted its attention instead to commerce with Indian cotton and tea.

At this juncture, the East Asian colonial trade was not important to the English, who directed most of their energies in Asia at India. (The only important English station in Southeast Asia was the great fortress port of Singapore at the tip of the Malay Peninsula, which was not acquired until the nineteenth century.) After two victorious wars against the Dutch in the 1650s and 1660s, the English were the world's leading naval power, although the Dutch still maintained their lead in the carrying trade to and from Europe.

English colonies in the seventeenth century were concentrated in North America, and an odd mixture they were. The northern colonies were filled with Protestant dissidents who could not abide the Anglican church regime: Puritans, Congregationalists, and Quakers. Maryland was a refuge for persecuted Catholics. Virginia and the Carolinas began as real estate speculations; they were essentially get-rich-quick schemes devised by nobles or wealthy commoners who thought they could sell off their American holdings to individual settlers at a fat profit. Georgia began as a noble experiment by a group of philanthropists who sought to ban slavery.

Elsewhere, the English were less inclined to settle new lands than to make their fortunes pirating Spanish galleons or competing with the Dutch in the Far Eastern and, later, the slave trade. What the Dutch had stolen from the Portuguese the English stole in part from the Dutch. This was equally true in the New World, where the Dutch challenge to Portuguese and Spanish hegemony in the Caribbean was superseded by the English and French in the eighteenth century.

The colonial empire of *France* parallels that of England. Relatively late in entering the race, the French sought overseas possessions and/or trade factories throughout the world to support their prospering domestic economy. From Canada (as early as 1608, one year after Jamestown in Virginia), to the west coast of Africa (as early as 1639) and India (in the early eighteenth century), the servants of the Bourbon kings contested both their Catholic coreligionists (Portugal, Spain) and their Protestant rivals (Holland, Britain) for mercantile advantage and the extension of royal powers. Thus, the French, too, reflected the seventeenth-century trend to allow state policies to be dictated more by secular interests than by religious adherences, a process we will examine in detail in Chapter 30.

Mercantilism

During this epoch, governments attempted to control their economies through a process later termed **mercantilism.** Under mercantilism, the chief goal of economic policy was a *favorable balance of trade,* with the value of a country's exports exceeding the cost of its imports. To achieve this goal, the royal government intervened in the market constantly and attempted to secure advantage to itself and the population at large by carefully supervising every aspect of commerce and investment. The practice reached its highest development in seventeenth- and eighteenth-century France, but was subscribed to almost everywhere.

As for colonial policy, mercantilism held that only goods and services that originated in the home country could be (legally) exported to the colonies and that the colonies' exports must go to the home country for use there or reexport. Thus, the colonies' most essential functions were to serve as captive markets for home country producers and to provide raw materials at low cost for home country importers. Portugal, Spain, and France practiced this theory of economics rigorously in their colonies, while Holland and England took a more relaxed approach in theirs.

Europeans and Non-Europeans

Historians agree that the European impact on the native cultures of the Western Hemisphere and on the peoples of the Far East, sub-Saharan Africa, and the Pacific Rim was enormous in some areas, but much less so in others. The natives quickly learned that it was not profitable to confront the Europeans by arms, because the Europeans would generally win. The Europeans' guns, more advanced methods of rigging sails and designing hulls, better discipline in battle, and generally higher levels of military training assured them of success in almost all engagements on land or sea (especially at sea where the cannon of the European ships could sink the more numerous Muslim,

■ **Mining at Cerro Rico.** This contemporary sketch shows the enormous labor involved in getting silver ore out of the Spanish mines in the New World. The Spanish overseer at the base of the ladder supervised perhaps as many as 50 Indian slaves.

Hindu, or Chinese vessels before they could come close enough to be a menace).

In the trading colonies the Portuguese, Dutch, and English were usually content to deal with and through the native leaders they encountered. Usually, the Europeans set up coastal factories and interfered little with existing laws, religion, and customs unless they felt compelled to do so to gain their commercial ends. Such interference was rare; in West Africa, for example, the competing Dutch, English, and French interests in obtaining slaves seems to have helped several native kings extend their governmental and military powers.

Spain's American settler colonies and Brazil were quite different. There the Europeans established *encomienda* estates on which first Indians and later Africans were forced to reside and labor. Although the *encomiendas* were soon abolished, the exploitation of the helpless by their Iberian overseers continued unabated on the rice and sugar plantations, which replaced gold and silver mines. Perhaps it is most accurate to say that in the settler colonies of the western hemisphere the natives were extensively and sometimes disastrously affected by the arrival of the whites, but in the rest of the world, including sub-Saharan Africa, the Asian mainland, and the South Pacific islands, the Europeans were less disruptive to the existing state of affairs. Sometimes native governments even succeeded in using the Europeans to their own advantage, as in West Africa and Mughal India. This would remain true until the nineteenth century, when the European impacts multiplied, became more profound, and changed in nature so as to subordinate the natives in every sense.

Racism's Beginnings

Blacks came into European society for the first time in appreciable numbers during the fifteenth century, and with them came the first faint signs of white racism. The black slaves from Africa, who were brought to Europe through Muslim channels, were mostly novelties for the rich and were kept as demonstrations of wealth or artistic taste. Some free blacks lived in Mediterranean Europe where they worked as sailors, musicians, and actors, but they were not numerous enough for the average European to have any firsthand contact.

Many whites thought of blacks in terms dictated either by the Bible or by Muslim prejudices imbibed unconsciously over time. The biblical references were generally negative; black was the color of the sinful, the opposite of light in the world. "Blackhearted," "a black scoundrel,"

and "black intentions," are a few examples of the mental connection between the color black and the evil and contemptible. The Omani Arab slave traders in East Africa who supplied some of the European as well as the Asiatic market were another source of prejudice. They were contemptuous of the non-Muslim blacks on the Zanzibar coast whom they ruled and with whom they traded in human flesh. The traders' point of view was easily transferred to their Italian and Portuguese partners in the trade.

✛ THE COLUMBIAN EXCHANGE

The coming of the Europeans to the New World resulted in very important changes in the resources, habits, and values of both the Indians and the whites. Among the well-known introductions by the Europeans to the Western Hemisphere were horses, cattle, sheep, and goats; iron; firearms; sailing ships; and, less tangibly, the entire system of economics we call capitalism.

But the **Columbian Exchange** had another side: a reverse flow of products and influences from the Americas to Europe. Educated Europeans after about 1520 became aware of how huge and relatively unknown the Earth was and how varied the peoples inhabiting it were. This knowledge came as a surprise to many Europeans, and they were eager to learn more. The literature of discovery and exploration became extraordinarily popular during the sixteenth and seventeenth centuries.

From this literature, Europeans learned, among other things, that the Christian moral code was but one of several; that the natural sciences were not of overwhelming interest or importance to most of humanity; that an effective education could take myriad forms and have myriad goals; and that viewpoints formed by tradition and habit are not necessarily correct, useful, or the only conceivable ones. Initially just curious about the earth's other inhabitants, upper-class Europeans gradually began to develop a certain tolerance. This tolerance slowly deepened in the seventeenth and especially the eighteenth century as Europe emerged from its religious wars.

Contacts with the Americas also led to *economic changes in Europe.* Some crops such as sugarcane and rice that were already known in Europe but could not be profitably grown there were found to prosper in the New World. Their cultivation formed the basis for the earliest slave plantations in the Caribbean basin.

In addition, a series of *new crops* were introduced to the European diet. Tobacco, several varieties of beans and peas, squashes, rice, maize, and others stemmed originally

Bartolomé de Las Casas's Report on the Indies

Bartolomé de Las Casas (1474–1567), a Dominican priest who had been a conquistador and slaveholder in the Caribbean in his youth, turned his back on his former life and devoted himself to protecting the Indians under Spanish rule. In his *Brief Relation of the Destruction of the Indies* (1522), he began an uncompromising campaign to expose the horrendous treatment meted out by his fellow Spanish to the native populations of the New World. So graphic and terrible were his accounts that foreign powers hostile to Spain (notably, England) were able to use them for centuries to perpetuate the so-called Black Legend of the viciousness of Spanish colonialism.

Of the Island of Hispaniola

The Christians, with their horses and swords and lances, began to slaughter and practice strange cruelties among them. They penetrated into the country and spared neither children nor the aged, nor pregnant women, nor those in childbirth, all of whom they ran through the body and lacerated, as though they were assaulting so many lambs herded into the sheepfold.

They made bets as to who could slit a man in two, or cut off his head at one blow . . . they tore babes from their mothers' breasts by the feet, and dashed their heads against the rocks. Others, they seized by the shoulders and threw into the rivers, laughing and joking, and when they fell into the water they exclaimed, "boil the body of So-and-so!. . . ."

They made a gallows just high enough for the feet to nearly touch the ground, and by thirteens, in honour and reverence of our Redeemer and the 12 Apostles, they put wood underneath and, with fire, they burned the Indians alive.

They wrapped the bodies of others entirely in dry straw, binding them in it and setting fire to it; and so they burned them. They cut off the hands of all they wished to take alive, made them carry them pinned on to their bodies, and said "Go and carry these letters," that is, take the news to those who have fled to the mountains. . . .

I once saw that they had four or five of the chief lords [Indians] stretched on a gridiron to burn them, and I think there were also two or three pairs of gridirons, where they were burning others. And because they cried aloud and annoyed the Captain or prevented him from sleeping, he commanded that they should be strangled; the officer who was burning them was worse than a hangman and did not wish to suffocate them, but with his own hands he gagged them, so that they should not make themselves heard,

---

from American or Far Eastern lands. First regarded as novelties—much like the occasional Indian or black—they came to be used as food and fodder. The most important was the *potato,* which was initially considered fit only for cattle and pigs, but was gradually adopted by northern Europeans in the eighteenth century. By the end of that century, it had become the most important part of the peasants' diet in several countries. The potato was the chief reason European farms were able to feed the spectacular increase in population that started in the later 1700s.

So much additional money was put into circulation from the Mexican and Peruvian silver mines that it generated massive *inflation.* The Spanish court used the silver to pay army suppliers, shipyards, and soldiers, and

from their hands, it went on into the general economy. Spain itself, it should be noted, suffered most in the long run from the inflation its bullion imports caused. Spanish gold and silver went into the pockets of foreign suppliers, carriers, and artisans rather than into domestic investments or business. This would prove fateful in the next century.

In a period of inflation, when money becomes cheap and goods or services become dear, people who can convert their wealth quickly from money to goods and services are in an enviable position, whereas those whose wealth is illiquid and cannot be easily converted are at a disadvantage. As a result, in sixteenth-century Europe, the landholders—many of whom were nobles who paid little attention to money matters—lost economic strength,

and he stirred up the fire until they roasted slowly, according to his pleasure. I know this man's name, and knew his relations in Sevilla. I saw all the above things and numberless others.

And because all the [Indian] people who could flee, hid among the mountains and climbed the crags to escape from men so deprived of humanity . . . the

Spaniards taught and trained the fiercest boarhounds to tear an Indian to pieces as soon as they saw him. . . . And because sometimes, though rarely, the Indians killed a few Christians for just cause, they made a law among themselves that for one Christian whom the Indians might kill, the Christians should kill a hundred Indians. . . .

■ **The Conquistadors Arrive.** This Aztec painting shows a skirmish between the Spaniards on horse and their Indian allies, and Aztec defenders. The Indians are armed with obsidian-edge swords capable of cutting off the head of a horse at a single blow.

SOURCE: Translation by F.A. McNutt. *A Very Brief Account of the Destruction of the Indes*, by Bartolome de las Casas, pp. 312–319, H. Clark Co., Cleveland, 1909.

while the middle classes, who could sell their services and expertise at rising rates, were at an advantage. Best off were the merchants who could buy cheap and hold before selling at higher prices. But even the unskilled or skilled workers in the towns were in a relatively better position than the landlords; wages rose about as fast as prices in this century.

Estate agriculture, where serfs paid token rents in return for small parcels of arable land, was dealt a heavy blow. Prices rose for everything the noble landlords needed and wanted, while their rents, sanctioned by centuries of custom, remained about the same. Unaware of the reasons for the economic changes and unable to anticipate the results, many landlords faced disaster during the later sixteenth century and could not avoid

bankruptcy when their mortgages were called. Many of them had been living beyond their means for generations, borrowing money wherever they could with land as security. Much land changed hands at this time, from nobles to peasants or to the newly rich from the towns. Serfdom became impractical or unprofitable. Already weakened by long-term changes in European society, it was abolished in most of Western Europe.

The Fate of the Amerindians

By far the worst human consequences of the European expansion were the tragic fates imposed on the native Indians of the Caribbean and Central America in the first century of Spanish conquest (see the Document in this chapter). Although the Spanish Crown imposed several regulatory measures to protect the Indians after 1540, little could be done to inhibit the spread of epidemic disease (measles and influenza, as well as the major killer smallpox) in the Indian villages. As a general rule, the immune systems of the Indians were unable to cope with the diseases brought by the newcomers, while the Spaniards were much less affected by the Indian maladies. (Which continent is responsible for the appearance of syphilis is much argued.)

Smallpox was a particular curse; the population of Mexico, which was perhaps 25 million at the coming of Cortez, was reduced to 2 million only sixty years later, largely as a result of smallpox epidemics. On the Caribbean islands, no Indians remained after a generation of Spanish occupancy. The same story repeated itself in the viceroyalty of Peru, where as many as 80 percent of the native population died in the sixteenth century. Only in modern times have the Indians recovered from this unprecedented disaster.

Summary

The explosive widening of Europe's horizons in the early sixteenth century, both literally in the geographic sense and figuratively in the psychological sense, was one side of the Columbian Exchange. A series of colonial empires were created, first by the Portuguese and Spanish and then by the Dutch, English, and French. The original objective of the government-funded explorers was to find new, more secure trade routes to the East, but soon their motives changed to a mixture of enrichment, missionary activity, and international prestige.

The establishment and maintenance of colonial empires led to much conflict among the home countries and exacerbated the ongoing religious warfare between Catholics and Protestants. In time, the religious component diminished and disappeared from these conflicts, and the secular political one predominated. The import of great quantities of precious metals, created hitherto unknown inflation and promoted the rise of the business/commercial classes. The discovery of customs and values that were quite different from those of Europeans contributed to the beginning of a new attitude of tolerance. The overseas expansion added new foods to the European diet.

For the non-Western hosts, the European colonial and commercial outreach had mainly negative consequences, although circumstances varied from place to place. The most devastating effects were certainly in Spain's American colonies, where the indigenous peoples were almost wiped out by disease and oppression. In West Africa, the slave trade sometimes decimated but also sometimes strengthened the extant African units, while in East Africa and the Asian mainland, the European trading presence had overall little effect at this time.

Test Your Knowledge

1. The fifteenth- and sixteenth-century voyages of exploration were stimulated mainly by
   a. European curiosity about other peoples.
   b. the determination to obtain more farming land for a growing population.
   c. the individual explorers' hopes of enrichment.
   d. the discovery that the Earth was in fact a sphere without "ends."
2. Which of the following was *not* proved by Magellan's epic voyage?
   a. The world was more compact than had been believed.
   b. The globe was indeed spherical.
   c. A sea passage existed south of the tip of South America.
   d. The islands called "Spice Lands" could be reached from the East.
3. Which of the following reasons was *least* likely to be the motive for a Dutch captain's voyage of discovery?
   a. A desire to deal the Roman church a blow
   b. A search for personal enrichment
   c. A quest to find another lifestyle for himself in a foreign land
   d. The intention of establishing trade relations with a new partner

4. What is the correct sequence of explorer-traders in the Far East?
   a. Spanish, English, French
   b. Spanish, Portuguese, Dutch
   c. Dutch, English, Spanish
   d. Portuguese, Dutch, English
5. The sixteenth-century inflation affected which group most negatively?
   a. Landholding nobles
   b. Urban merchants
   c. Wage laborers
   d. Skilled white-collar workers
6. Which proved to be the most important of the various new foods introduced into European diets by the voyages of discovery?
   a. Maize
   b. Rice
   c. Potato
   d. Coffee
7. Which of the following nations was most actively committed to converting the natives of the newly discovered regions to Christianity?
   a. Spain
   b. Holland
   c. England
   d. Portugal
8. Duke Albuquerque was instrumental in
   a. defeating the Indians of Goa and bringing them under Portuguese dominion.
   b. bringing the first Christian missionaries to China.
   c. bringing Brazil under the flag of Portugal.
   d. opening the way into the Persian Gulf for Europeans.

Identification Terms

Columbian Exchange	Macao	mercantilism	mulatto
Cortez (Hernan)	Magellan (Ferdinand)	mestizo	Vespucci (Amerigo)
Díaz (Bartolomeo)			

Bibliography

Boxer, C. R. *The Portuguese Seaborne Empire, 1415–1825,* 1969. The best account of the achievement of tiny Portugal.

Cipolla, C. M. *Guns, Sails, and Empires,* 1965. A fascinating account of technical progress and its effects on human relationships in an age of exploration.

Crosby, A. W. *The Columbian Exchange: Biological and Cultural Consequences of 1492,* 1972. The most important book on this subject in the last generation.

Curtin, P. *The African Slave Trade,* 1969, and J. L. Watson, ed., *Asian and African Systems of Slavery,* 1980, are among the most interesting and authoritative treatments.

Díaz de Castillo, B. *The Conquest of New Spain,* translated and edited by J. Cohen, 1988. The best of the conquistador accounts.

Elliot, J.H. *The Old World and the New,* 1970 considers the mutual impacts of the discoveries.

Fernandez-Armesto, F. *Columbus,* 1991. The most recent biography, reflecting new information.

Innes, Hammond. *The Conquistadors,* 1969. A lively rendition, which is also sympathetic.

Kirkpatrick, F. *The Spanish Conquistadores,* 1968 is a standard work on the opening of the Caribbean and Central America.

Parry, J. H. *The Age of Reconaissance,* 1981. The classic account of the early voyages. Wonderfully clear prose.

———. *The Discovery of South America,* 1979. Tells how new discoveries affected the Europeans. Excellent illustrations.

———. *The Establishment of European Hegemony 1415–1715,* 1961 is a short treatment.

Sale, K. *Conquest of Paradise,* 1990. Highly critical of the Spanish policies.

Tracy, J.D. *The Rise of Merchant Empires; Long Distance Trade in the Early Modern World 1350–1750,* 1990 is an anthology treating various empires and locales.

Wolf, E. *Europe and the People Without History,* 1982 is critical of the Westeners' arrogance in dealing with others.

Wright, S. *Stolen Continents,* 1995. The discovery of America, from the points of view of the Aztecs, Inca, and North American Indians.

THE PROTESTANT REFORMATION

The split in Christian belief that is termed the Protestant Reformation brought enormous consequences in its wake. Its beginning coincided with the high point of the era of discovery by Europeans. Taken together, these complexes of events provide the basis for dividing Western civilization's history into the premodern and modern eras around the year 1500.

What the opening up of the vast trans-Atlantic and trans-Pacific worlds did for the consciousness of physical geography in European minds, the Reformation did for the mental geography of all Christians. New continents of belief and identity emerged from the spiritual voyages of the early Protestants. Luther and Calvin worked not only a reformation but also a transformation of the church and its members.

✤ LUTHER AND THE GERMAN NATIONAL CHURCH

The upheaval called the *Reformation of the early sixteenth century* had its roots in political and social developments as much as in religious disputes. The long-standing arguments within the Christian community over various points of doctrine or practices had already led to rebellions against the Rome-led majority on several occasions. To name only a few of the major affairs, in thirteenth-century France, fourteenth-century England, and fifteenth-century Bohemia, religious rebels (the official name is *heretics,* or wrong thinkers) had battled the papal church. Eventually, all of them had been suppressed or driven underground.

But now, in sixteenth-century Germany, *Martin Luther* (1483–1546) found an enthusiastic reception for his challenges to Rome among the majority of his fellow Germans. The disintegration of the German medieval kingdom had been followed by the birth of dozens of separate, little principalities and city-states, like Hamburg and Frankfurt, which could not resist the encroachments of the powerful papacy in their internal affairs. Unlike the people in unified and centrally governed France, England, and Spain, the German populations were systematically milked by Rome and forced to pay taxes and involuntary donations. Many of the German rulers were becoming angry at seeing the tax funds they needed going off to a foreign power and sometimes used for goals they did not support. These rulers were eagerly searching for some excuse to challenge Rome. They found it in the teachings of Luther.

Luther was a monk who had witnessed at first hand the corruption and crass commercialism of the Roman *curia.* When he returned to the University of Wittenberg in Saxony, where he had been appointed chaplain, he used his powerful oratory to arouse the community against the abuses he had seen, especially the church's practice of selling *indulgences*—forgiveness of the guilt created by sins—rather than insisting that the faithful earn forgiveness by prayer and good works.

In 1517, a major indulgence sales campaign opened in Germany under even more scandalous pretexts than usual. Much of the money raised was destined to be used to pay off a debt incurred by an ambitious noble churchman, rather than for any ecclesiastical purpose. Observing what was happening, the chaplain at Wittenberg decided to take his stand. On October 31, 1517, Luther announced his discontent by posting the famous *Ninety-five Theses* on his church door. In these questions, Luther raised objections not only to many of the papacy's practices such as indulgence campaigns, but also to the whole doctrine of papal supremacy. He contended that if the papacy had ever been intended by God to be the moral mentor of the Christian community, it had lost that claim through its present corruption.

Luther's Beliefs

Luther had more profound doubts about the righteousness of the papal church than merely its claims to universal leadership, however. His youth had been a long struggle against the conviction that he was damned to hell. Intensive study of the Bible eventually convinced him that only through the freely given grace of a merciful God might he, or any person, reach salvation. The Catholic church taught that men and women must manifest their Christian faith by doing good works and leading good lives; if they did so, they might be considered to have earned a heavenly future.

Martin Luther rejected this. He believed that faith alone was the factor through which Christians might reach bliss in the afterlife and that faith was given by God and not in any way earned by naturally sinful Man. It is this doctrine of *justification by faith* that most clearly marks off Lutheranism from the papal teachings.

As the meaning of Luther's statements penetrated into the clerical hierarchy, he was implored, then commanded to cease. Instead, his confidence rose, and in a series of brilliantly forceful pamphlets, he explained his views to a rapidly increasing audience of Germans. By 1520 he was becoming a household word among educated people and even among the peasantry. In 1521 he was *excommunicated* by the pope for refusing to recant, and in the same year, he was declared an outlaw by Emperor **Charles V.**

The Catholic emperor was an ally of the pope but had his hands full with myriad other problems, notably the Ottoman Turks. Charles had no desire to add an unnecessary civil war to the long list of tasks he faced. He took action against Luther only belatedly and halfheartedly, hoping that in some way an acceptable compromise might be reached.

Threatened by the imperial and papal officials, Luther sought and quickly found the protection of the ruler of Saxony, as well as much of the German princely class. They saw in his moral objections to Rome the excuse they had been seeking for advancing their political aspirations. They encouraged Luther to organize a national church free from papal overlords.

With this protection and encouragement, Luther's teachings spread rapidly, aided by the newly invented printing press and by the power and conviction of his sermons and writings, which were written in German (rather than the traditional Latin). By the mid-1520s, Lutheran congregations, rejecting the papal authority and

■ **Martin Luther.** This contemporary portrait by Lucas v. Cranach is generally considered to be an accurate rendition of the great German church reformer in mid life.

condemning Rome as the fount of all evil, had sprung up throughout most of Germany and were appearing in Scandinavia as well. The unity of Western Christianity had been shattered.

✤ CALVIN AND INTERNATIONAL PROTESTANTISM

It was not Luther the German peasant's son, but *John Calvin* (1509–1564) the French lawyer who made the Protestant movement an international theological rebellion against Rome. Luther always saw himself as a specifically German patriot, as well as a pious Christian, and his writings and translations of the Scriptures were written in a powerful idiomatic German. (Luther's role in creating the modern German language is roughly the same as Shakespeare played in the development of English.) Calvin detached himself from national feeling and saw himself as the emissary and servant of a God who ruled all nations. Luther wanted the German Christian body to be cleansed of papal corruption; Calvin wanted the entire Christian community to be made over into the image of what he thought God intended. When he was through, a good part of it had been.

Calvin was born into a middle-class family of church officeholders who educated him for a career in the law.

■ **John Calvin.** This Flemish portrait of the "pope of Geneve" in his younger days depicts Calvin in a fur neckpiece. This bit of bourgeois indulgence would not have been worn by an older Calvin.

When he was twenty-five, he became a Protestant, inspired by some Swiss sympathizers with Luther. For most of the rest of his life, Calvin was "the pope of Geneva," laying down the law to that city's residents and having a major influence upon much of the rest of Europe's religious development.

Calvin believed that the papal church was hopelessly distorted. It must be obliterated, and new forms and practices (which were supposedly a return to the practices of early Christianity) must be introduced. In **The Institutes of the Christian Religion** (1536), Calvin set out his beliefs and doctrines with the precision and clarity of a lawyer. From this work came much of the intellectual content of Protestantism for the next two hundred years.

Calvin's single most dramatic change from both Rome and Luther was his insistence that *God predestined souls;* that is, a soul was meant either for heaven or hell for all eternity. But at the same time, the individual retained free will to choose good or evil. The soul destined for hell would inevitably choose evil—but did not have to! It was a harsh theology; Calvin believed that humanity had been eternally stained by the sin of Adam and that the majority of souls were destined for hellfire. Despite its doctrinal fierceness, Calvin's message found a response throughout Europe, and by the 1540s, Calvinists were appearing in Germany, the Netherlands, Scotland, England, and France, as well as Switzerland. Geneva had become the **Protestant Rome,** with Calvin serving as its priestly ruler until his death in 1564.

Calvinism and Lutheranism Compared

What were some of the similarities and differences between the beliefs of Luther and Calvin (who never met and had little affection for one another)? Luther believed that faith alone, which could not be earned, was the only prerequisite for salvation; good works were encouraged, of course, but they had little or no influence upon the Last Judgment. Calvin demanded works as well as faith to indicate that a person was attempting to follow God's order on earth.

Later Calvinists saw their performance of good works as a mark that they were among the Elect, the souls predestined for heaven. The emphasis in some places and times shifted subtly from doing good works as a sign of serving God to believing that God would logically favor the members of the Elect. Therefore, those who were "doing well" in the earthly sense were probably among the Elect. From this, some later students of religion saw Calvinist beliefs as the basis for the triumph of the capitalist spirit in certain parts of Europe. In effect, God could rationally be expected to smile upon those who did his bidding in this life as well as the next.

Second, Luther saw the clergy as civic as well as spiritual guides for mankind. He believed in a definite hierarchy of authority within the church, and he retained bishops, who maintained their power to appoint priests. In time, the Lutheran pastors and bishops became fully dependent on the state that employed them, rarely defying it on moral grounds. *Lutheranism became a state church,* not only in Germany but also in Scandinavia where it had become dominant by the mid-1500s. In contrast, *Calvin insisted on the moral independence of the church from the state.* He maintained that the clergy had a duty to oppose any immoral acts of government, no matter what the cost to themselves. In conflicts between the will of God and the will of kings, the Calvinist must enlist on the side of God.

More than Lutherans, the Calvinists thought of the entire community, lay and clerical alike, as equal members of the church on earth. Calvinists also insisted on the power of the congregation to select and discharge pastors at will, inspired by God's word. They never established a hierarchy of clerics. There were *no Calvinist bishops,* but only presbyters, or elders, who spoke for their fellow parishioners. The government of the church included both clerical and lay leaders; the combination gave its pronouncements great moral force.

By around 1570, Calvin's followers had gained control of the Christian community in several places: the Dutch-speaking Netherlands, Scotland, western France, and parts of northern Germany and Poland. In the rest of France, Austria, Hungary, and England, they were still a minority, but a growing one. Whereas Lutheranism was confined to the German-speaking countries and Scandinavia and did not spread much after 1550 or so, Calvinism was an international faith that appealed to all nations and identified with none. Carried on the ships of the Dutch and English explorers and emigrants of the seventeenth and eighteenth centuries, it continued to spread throughout the modern world.

✤ OTHER FORMS OF EARLY PROTESTANT BELIEF

The followers of a radical sect called **Anabaptists** were briefly a threat to both Catholics and Lutherans, but were put down with extreme cruelty by both creeds. The Anabaptists originated in Switzerland and spread rapidly throughout German Europe. They believed in adult baptism, a priesthood of all believers, and—most disturbingly—a primitive communism and sharing of worldly possessions. Both as radicals in religious affairs and as social revolutionaries, the Anabaptists were oppressed by all their neighbors. After their efforts to establish a republic in the Rhineland city of Muenster were bloodily suppressed, the Anabaptists were driven underground, but they emerged much later in the New World as Mennonites, Amish, and similar groups.

Yet another Protestant creed emerged very early in Switzerland (which was a hotbed of religious protest). Founded by **Ulrich Zwingli** (1484–1531), it was generally very similar to Lutheran belief, although Zwingli claimed he had arrived at his doctrine independently. The inability of Zwingli's adherents and the Lutherans to cooperate left Zwingli's stronghold in Zurich open to attack by the Catholic Swiss. The Protestants were defeated in the battle, and Zwingli himself was killed. This use of bloody force to settle religious strife was an ominous note; it was to be increasingly common as Protestant beliefs spread and undermined the traditional religious structures.

The Anglican Church of England

As was often the case, England went its own way; the English Reformation differed from the Reformation on the Continent yet followed the general trend of European affairs. The English reformers were originally inspired by Lutheran ideas, but adopted more Calvinist views as time went on. However, the Church of England, or Anglican Confession, came to be neither Lutheran, nor Calvinist, nor Catholic, but a hybrid of all three.

The reform movement in England had its origins in the widespread popular resentment against Rome and the higher clergy who were viewed as more the tools of the pope than as good English patriots. As we have seen, already in the 1400s, a group called the Lollards had rebelled against the clerical claim to sole authority in interpreting the word of God and papal supremacy. The movement had been put down, but its memory persisted in many parts of England.

But it was the peculiar marital problems of King *Henry VIII* (1490–1547) that brought the church in England into conflict with Rome. Henry needed a male successor, but by the late 1520s, his chances of having one with his elderly Spanish wife Catherine were bleak. Therefore, he wanted to have the marriage annulled by the pope (who alone had that power), so that he could marry some young Englishwoman who would presumably be able to produce the desired heir.

The pope refused, for reasons that were partly political and partly moral. Between 1532 and 1534, Henry took the matter into his own hands. Still believing himself to be a good Catholic, he intimidated Parliament into declaring him the "only supreme head of the church in England"—the **Act of Supremacy of 1534.** Now, as head of the church, Henry could dictate to the English bishops. He proceeded to put away his unwanted wife and marry the tragic Anne Boleyn, already pregnant with his child.

Much other legislation followed that asserted that the monarch, and not the Roman pope, was the determiner of what the church could and could not do in England. Those who resisted, like the king's chancellor *Thomas More,* paid with their heads or were imprisoned. Henry went on to marry and divorce several more times before his death in 1547, but he did at least secure a son, the future King Edward VI, from one of these unhappy alliances. Two daughters also survived, the half-sisters Mary and Elizabeth.

Henry's Successors

Henry's actions changed English religious beliefs very little although the Calvinist reformation was gaining ground in both England and Scotland. But under the sickly and ineffectual boy-king Edward (1547–1553), Protestant views became dominant among the English governing group, and the Scots were led by the powerful oratory of John Knox into Calvinism (the **Presbyterian** church). At Edward's death, it seemed almost certain that some form of Protestant worship would become the official church.

But popular support for Mary, the Catholic daughter of Henry VIII's first wife, was too strong to be overridden by the Protestant party at court. Just as they had feared, Mary proved to be a single-minded adherent of the papal church, and she restored Catholicism to its official status during her brief reign (1553–1558). Protestant conspirators were put to death without hesitation (hence, she is called **Bloody Mary** in English Protestant mythology).

Finally, the confused state of English official religion was gradually cleared by the political skills of Mary's half-sister and successor, *Elizabeth I,* who ruled for half a century with great success while defying all royal traditions by remaining the Virgin Queen and dying childless (see the Biography in this chapter). She was able to arrive at a compromise between the Roman and Protestant doctrines, which was accepted by a steadily increasing majority and came to be called the Church of England. In most respects, it retained the theology and doctrine of the Roman church, including bishops, rituals, and sacraments. But its head was not the pope, but the English monarch, who appointed the bishops and their chief, the archbishop of Canterbury. The strict Calvinists were not happy with this arrangement and wished to "purify" the church by removing all remnants of popery. These **Puritans** presented problems for the English rulers throughout the seventeenth century.

■ **A Calvinist Church.** "Four bare walls and a sermon" constituted the essentials of the Sunday service for followers of Calvin. They believed that the rich interior decor of the Roman churches were an unjustified distraction from worship.

✦ THE COUNTER REFORMATION

Belatedly realizing what a momentous challenge was being mounted, the papacy finally came to grips with the problem of Protestantism in a positive fashion during the 1540s. Pope Paul III (1534–1549) moved to counter some of the excesses that had given the Roman authorities a bad name and set up a high-level commission to see what might be done to "clean up" the clergy. Eventually, the church decided to pursue two major lines of counterattack against the Protestants: a thorough examination of doctrines and practices, such as had not been attempted for more than a thousand years, combined with an entirely novel emphasis on instruction of the young and education of all Christians in the precepts of their religion.

The **Council of Trent** (1545–1563) was the first general attempt to examine the church's basic doctrines and goals since the days of the Roman Empire. Meeting for three lengthy sessions divided by years of preparatory work, the bishops and theologians decided that Protestant attacks could best be met by clearly and conclusively defining what Catholics believed. (Protestants were invited to attend, but only as observers; none did.) As a means of strengthening religious practice, this was a positive move, for the legitimacy of many church doctrines had come increasingly into doubt since the 1300s. But the council's work had an unintended negative effect on the desired reunification of Christianity: the doctrinal lines separating Catholic and Protestant were now firmly drawn, and they could not be ignored or blurred by the many individuals in both camps who had been trying to arrange a compromise. Now one side or the other would have to give in on specific issues, but neither side was prepared to surrender.

The founding of the **Jesuit Order** was the most striking example of the other aspect of the Counter Reform. In 1540 Pope Paul III accorded to the Spanish nobleman Ignatius of Loyola the right to organize an entirely new religious group, which he termed the Society of Jesus, or Jesuits. Their mission was to win, or win back, the minds and hearts of humanity for the Catholic church through patient, careful instruction that would bring the word of God and of his deputy on earth, the pope, to everyone. While the Jesuits were working to ensure that all Catholics learned correct doctrine, the *Index* of forbidden books was created and the *Inquisition* revived to ensure that no Catholic deviated from that doctrine. These institutions greatly expanded the church's powers to censor the writings and supervise the beliefs of its adherents. Both became steadily more important in Catholic countries

Ego fum Papa.

■ **A Protestant View of the Pope.** Clothed in hellish splendor and hung about with the horrible symbols of Satan, the Roman pope is revealed for all to see, in this sixteenth century cartoon.

during the next century, as what both sides regarded as a contest between truth and falsity intensified.

✦ RELIGIOUS WARS AND THEIR OUTCOMES TO 1600

The Counter Reformation stiffened the Catholics' will to resist the Lutheran and Calvinist attacks, which had, at first, almost overwhelmed the unprepared and inflexible Roman authorities. By 1555, the **Peace of Augsburg** had concluded a ten-year civil war by dividing Germany into

Elizabeth I of England
1533–1603

In the late sixteenth century, England became for the first time a power to be reckoned with in world affairs. What had been an island kingdom with little direct influence on any other country except its immediate neighbors across the Channel gradually reached equality with the other major Western military and naval powers: France and Spain. But England's achievement was not just in military affairs. It also experienced a magnificent flowering of the arts and a solid advance in the economy, which finally lifted the nation out of the long depression that had followed the fourteenth-century plague and the long, losing war with France.

The guiding spirit for this comeback was Elizabeth I, queen of England from 1558 until her death in 1603. The daughter of Henry VIII and the ill-fated Anne Boleyn, Elizabeth emerged from a heavily shadowed girlhood to become a remarkable woman. Born in 1533, she was only three years old when her mother was executed. She was declared illegitimate by order of the disappointed Henry and seemed to have little hope of ever attaining the throne. But after her father's death, Parliament established her as third in line to the throne, behind her half-brother Edward and her half-sister Mary. During Mary's reign (1553–1558), Elizabeth was imprisoned for a time, but was careful to stay clear of the hectic Protestant-Catholic struggles of the day. Thus, she managed to stay alive until she could become ruler in her own right.

Elizabeth was an intelligent, well-educated woman with gifts in several directions. She brought to the throne the Tudor concept of strong royal powers and was at all times the true source of authority despite the many handicaps all female rulers faced in this epoch. One of her most remarkable achievements was that she managed to retain her powers without a husband, son, or father in the still very male-oriented world in which she moved.

Her rule began amid many internal and external dangers. The Catholic party in England opposed her as a suspected Protestant; the Calvinists opposed her as being too much like her father Henry, who never accepted Protestant theology. The Scots were becoming rabid Calvinists who despised the English halfway measures in religious affairs. On top of this, the government was deeply in debt, and few expected that the queen would be able to improve its finances.

Contrary to all predictions, Elizabeth showed great insight in selecting her officials and maintained good relations with Parliament. She conducted diplomatic affairs with a caution and farsightedness that England had not seen for many years and found she could use her status as an unmarried queen to definite advantage. Philip of Spain, widower of her half-sister Mary, made several proposals of marriage and political unity that Elizabeth cleverly held off without ever quite saying "No." She kept England out of the religious wars raging in various parts of Europe for most of her forty-five-year reign. But it was in one of these wars, with the disappointed Philip, that she led her people most memorably.

In 1588, after long negotiations failed, Philip sent the Spanish Armada to punish England for aiding the Dutch Calvinists across the Channel (the Netherlands

---

Catholic and Lutheran parcels, but it made no allowances for the growing number of Calvinists or other Protestants.

In the rest of Europe, the picture was mixed by the late 1500s (see Map 29.1). *England,* as we have just seen, went through several changes of religious leadership, but eventually emerged with a special sort of Protestant belief as its official religion. *Scandinavia* became Lutheran in its entirety, almost without violence. *Austria, Hungary,* and *Poland* remained mostly Catholic, but with large minorities of Calvinists and Lutherans who received a degree of tolerance from the authorities. *Spain* and *Italy* had successfully repelled the Protestant challenge, and the counter reform was in full swing. *Russia* and *southeastern Europe* were almost unaffected by Protestantism, being either hostile to both varieties of Western Christianity (Russia) or under the political control of Muslims. In two

at that time were a Spanish possession). The queen rallied her sailors in a stirring visit before the battle, and the resulting defeat of the Armada not only signaled England's rise to naval equality with Spain but also made Elizabeth the most popular monarch England had ever seen.

English colonial efforts now began in serious fashion after three quarters of a century of dormancy. Parliament's good relationship with the Crown promoted trade and the establishment of overseas colonies and trading posts. Commercial banking and the first joint stock companies appeared in London by the end of Elizabeth's reign.

A golden age of English literature coincided with Elizabeth's rule, thanks in some part to her active support of all the arts. Her well-known vanity induced her to spend large sums to ensure the splendor of her court despite her equally well-known miserliness. The Elizabethan Age produced Shakespeare, Marlowe, Spenser, and Bacon. By the end of the sixteenth century, English literature for the first time could hold a place of honor in any assembly of national arts.

Elizabeth's version of Protestant belief—the Church of England—was acceptable to the large majority of her subjects and finally settled the very stormy waves of English church affairs. Although she may not have been beloved by all at the end of her long reign, still "Good Queen Bess" had become a stock phrase that was believed by most people, from barons to peasants.

The Virgin Queen left no direct successor, but in consultation with Parliament, she named her distant cousin James VI of Scotland as her successor just before her death. With her ended the Tudor dynasty of English monarchs. The Stuarts began with James, who ruled as king of both England and Scotland after 1603.

■ **Elizabeth I of England.** The Armada Portrait was painted by an anonymous artist in the late sixteenth century.

countries, however, the issue of religious affiliation was in hot dispute and caused much bloodshed in the later 1500s.

France

France remained Catholic at the level of the throne, but developed a large, important Calvinist minority, especially among the nobility and the middle classes. For a brief time the Catholic monarchs and the Calvinists attempted to live with one another, but in the 1570s religious wars began that threatened to wreck the country (see the Document in this chapter).

After some years the Calvinists found a politician of genius, *Henry of Navarre,* who profited from the assassination of his Catholic rival to become King Henry IV of France. In 1593 he agreed to accept Catholicism to win

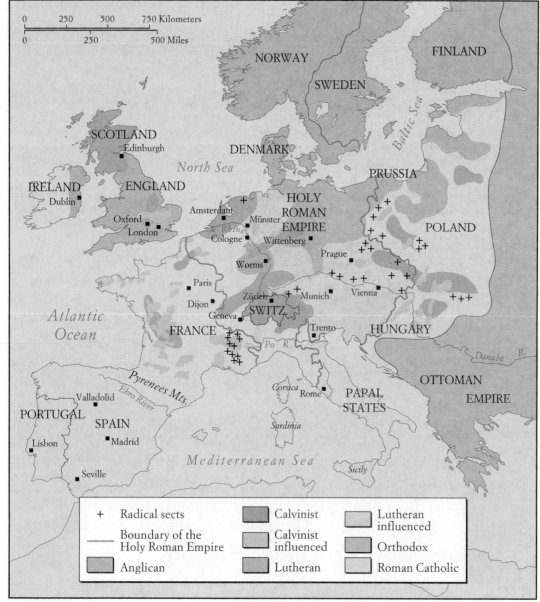

● **MAP 29.1 Catholics, Protestants, and Orthodox Christians in Europe by 1550.** The radical sects included Unitarians in east Europe, Anabaptists in Bohemia and Germany, and Waldensians in France. All of these rejected the idea of a privileged clergy and a priestly hierarchy.

the support of most French ("Paris is worth a mass," he is reported to have said). He became the most popular king in French history. His Protestant upbringing inspired the Calvinist minority to trust him; he did not disappoint them.

In 1598 Henry made the first significant attempt at religious toleration as state policy by issuing the *Edict of* Nantes. It gave the million or so French Calvinists—the Huguenots—freedom to worship without harassment in certain areas, to hold office, and to fortify their towns. This last provision demonstrates that the edict was more in the nature of a truce than a peace. It held, however, for the better part of a century. During that time, France rose to become the premier power in Europe.

The St. Bartholomew's Day Massacre

During the sixteenth-century religious wars in Europe, no battlefield was contested more ferociously by both sides than France. Not only did France contain Europe's largest population, but it lay between the Protestant North and the Catholic South. Though the bulk of the peasantry and the royal family remained Catholic, an influential and determined minority of nobles and bourgeoisie became Calvinists, or "Huguenots."

By 1572, due to the political astuteness of their leader Gaspard de Coligny, the Huguenots were close to a takeover of the French government. However, the queen mother, Catherine de Medici, and the Catholic warlord Henry, duke de Guise, turned the weak-minded King Charles IX against Coligny. The result was a conspiracy that began with Coligny's assassination on August 24, 1572 (St. Bartholemew's Day), and quickly degenerated into a wholesale massacre of the entire Protestant population of Paris: men, women, and children. The death toll is estimated to have approached 10,000; and the streets and alleys reeked of the stench of decaying corpses for weeks afterward.

According to an anonymous Protestant who was among the fortunate few to escape the carnage, vicious cruelties were committed without number, setting the scene for what would become twenty years of intermittent civil war in France:

> In an instant, the whole city was filled with dead bodies of every sex and age, and indeed amid such confusion and disorder that everyone was allowed to kill whoever he pleased, whether or not that person belonged to the [Protestant] religion, provided that he had something to be taken, or was an enemy. So it came about that many Papists themselves were slain, even several priests. . . . Nevertheless, the main fury fell on our people; and to provide better quarry for the murderers, they were permitted to loot and plunder houses, so that by the same means thieves, pickpockets, and other robbers and loafers, always numerous, moved all the more actively against us in the hope of booty. . . .

> No one can count the many cruelties that accompanied these murders. . . . Most of them were run through with daggers or poniards; their bodies were stabbed, their members mutilated, they were mocked and insulted with gibes sharper than pointed swords. . . they knocked several old people senseless, banging their heads against the stones of the quay and then throwing them halfdead into the water [the Seine river]. A little child in swaddling clothes was dragged through the streets with a belt round his neck by boys nine or ten years old. Another small child, carried by one of the butchers, played with the man's beard and smiled up at him, but instead of being moved to compassion, the barbarous fiend ran him through with his dagger, then threw him into the water so red with blood that it did not return to its original color for a long time. . . .

> . . . .[T]he continuous shooting of arquebusses and pistols, the lamentable and frightful cries of those they slaughtered, the yells of the murderers, the bodies thrown from windows. . . . the breaking down of doors and windows, the stones thrown against them, and the looting of more than 600 homes over a long period can only bring before the eyes of the reader an unforgettable picture of the calamity appalling in every way.

SOURCE: Excerpted from *The Hugenot Wars* by Julian Coudy, trans. Julie Kernon, Chilton Press, 1969.

The Spanish Netherlands

The Spanish Netherlands (modern Holland and Belgium) were ruled from Madrid by King Philip II, the most potent monarch of the second half of the sixteenth century. He had inherited an empire that included Spain, much of Italy, and the Low Countries in Europe plus the enormous Spanish overseas empire begun by the voyages of Columbus.

But Philip was a man with a mission, or rather two missions: the reestablishment of Catholicism among the Protestant "heretics" and the defeat of the Muslim Turks in the Mediterranean and the Near East. These missions imposed heavy demands upon Spanish resources, which even the flow of gold and silver out of the American colonies could not fully cover. Although Philip was generally successful in his wars against the Turks, he could not handle a combined political-religious revolt against his officials in the Spanish Netherlands that broke out in the 1560s. The Netherlands were a hotbed of both Lutheran and Calvinist doctrines, and the self-confident members of the large middle class were much disturbed at the Spanish attempt to enforce the Counter Reformation and papal supremacy.

Thanks to Spanish overextension, the revolt of the Protestant Netherlanders succeeded in holding Philip's feared professional army at bay. The wars were fought with ferocity on both sides, each claiming God as their leader and guide. While Philip saw himself as the agent of legitimacy and the Counter Reformation, the Dutch rebels were aided militarily and financially by the English Protestants across the Channel. The English support was due in part to religious affinity, but even more to the traditional English dislike of a great power's control of England's closest trading partners.

In the mid-1580s, the friction came to a head. Philip (who had earlier tried to convince Elizabeth I to become his wife) became incensed at the execution of the Catholic queen of Scots by order of Elizabeth, who had imprisoned this possible competitor for England's throne. With the reluctant support of the pope, Philip prepared the vast *Armada of 1588* to invade England and reconquer that country for the "True Church."

The devastating defeat of the Armada—as much by a storm as by English ships—gave a great boost to the Protestant cause everywhere. It relieved the pressure on the Huguenots to accept Catholic overlordship in France. It saved the Dutch Calvinists until they could gain full independence some decades later. And the defeat of the Armada marks the emergence of England as a major power, both in Europe and overseas.

Spain remained the premier military power long after the Armada disaster, but the country in a sense never recovered from this event. Other fleets were built, bullion from Mexican and Peruvian mines continued to pour into Madrid's treasury, and the Spanish infantry were still considered the best trained and equipped of all the European armies, but the other powers were able to keep Spain in check from now on, until its inherent economic weaknesses reduced it to a second-line nation in the seventeenth century.

✤ THE LEGACY OF THE REFORMATION

The Protestant movement made a very deep impression on the general course of history in Europe for centuries. It is one of the reasons European history is conventionally divided into "modern" versus "medieval" around the year 1500. The religious unity of all Western Europe was irrevocably shattered, and with the end of unity inevitably came political and cultural conflicts. For a century and a half after Luther's defiance of the papal command to be silent, much of Europe was engaged in internal acrimony that wracked the continent from the Netherlands to Hungary. In some countries such as Italy, Spain, and Sweden, one or the other faith was dominant and proceeded to harass and exile those who thought differently. *Separation of church and state was not even dreamed of, nor was freedom of conscience.* These are strictly modern ideas and were not seriously taken up by educated persons until the eighteenth century.

In the Protestant societies, the abolition of the monasteries and convents and the emphasis on vernacular preaching helped integrate the clergy and the laity and thus blurred the class divisions that had been accepted in Europe since the opening of the Middle Ages. Combined with the important roles of the middle-class Protestants in spreading and securing reform, this development provided new opportunities for the ambitious and hardworking to rise up the social ladder.

Some of the other long-term cultural changes that resulted from the Reformation included the following:

1. *Higher literacy and start of mass education.* In much of Protestant Europe in particular, the exhortation to learn and obey Scripture provided an incentive to read that the common folk had never had before. The rapid spread of printing after 1520 was largely due to Protestant tracts and the impact they were seen to have upon their large audiences.

2. *Emphasis on individual moral responsibility.* Rejecting the Catholic assurance that the clergy knew best what was necessary and proper in the conduct of life, the Protestants underlined the responsibility of individual believers to determine through divine guidance and reading Scripture what they must do to attain salvation.

3. *Closer identification of the clergy with the people they served.* Both the Catholic and Protestant churches came to recognize that the church existed as much for the masses of faithful as it did for the clergy—a realization that was often absent previously—and that the belief of the faithful was the essence of the church on earth.

4. *Increase in conflicts and intolerance.* Much of Europe fell into civil wars that were initially set off by religious disputes. These wars were often bloody and produced much needless destruction by both sides in the name of theological truth. Religious affiliation greatly exacerbated dynastic and the emergent national conflicts.

The Catholic-Protestant clashes led to intellectual arrogance and self-righteousness not only in religion but in general among those who wielded power. Open debate and discussion of contested matters became almost impossible between the two parts of Western Christianity for a century or more.

Summary

As much as the discovery of the New World, the Protestant movement gave birth to the modern era in the West. The protests of Luther, Calvin, and many others against what they saw as the unrighteous and distorted teachings of the Roman papacy had immense long-term reverberations in Western culture. The reformers combined a new emphasis on individual morality with assertions of the ability and duty of Christians to read the Gospels and take into their own hands the responsibility for salvation.

Among Calvinists, the material welfare of the Elect on earth was linked to their quality of being saved, a link that would gradually produce what later generations called the "Protestant ethic." The Catholic response was the Counter Reformation, which eventually reclaimed much of the Protestant territories for the Roman church at the cost of an alarming rise in religiously inspired conflict. Europe entered the Modern Age in a flurry of fierce antagonisms among Christians, some of which were to continue for generations and permanently split apart previous communities.

Test Your Knowledge

1. Which of the following practices/beliefs is associated with Calvinism?
   a. The basic goodness of humans
   b. Predestination of souls
   c. Religious freedom for all
   d. Indulgences
2. Henry VIII's reform of English religion occurred
   a. in spite of his children's wishes.
   b. for primarily religious-doctrinal reasons.
   c. for primarily political-dynastic reasons.
   d. at the urging of the pope.
3. The posting of the *Ninety-five Theses* was immediately caused by
   a. Luther's outrage over the ignorance of the clergy.
   b. Luther's conviction that he must challenge papal domination.
   c. Luther's anger over the sale of indulgences.
   d. the tyranny of the local Roman Catholic bishop.
4. The term "Counter Reformation" applies to
   a. a movement in Germany aimed at extinguishing the Lutherans.
   b. the strong resistance of the Roman clergy to real reforms.
   c. a Europe-wide campaign to win back the Protestants to Rome.
   d. the political and military efforts of the German emperor to crush the Protestants.
5. Which of the following countries remained most strongly attached to Rome in the wake of the Reformation?
   a. Scotland
   b. France
   c. The Netherlands
   d. Spain
6. The Edict of Nantes
   a. expelled all Protestants from Catholic France.
   b. gave Protestants in France a degree of official toleration.
   c. brought civic and legal equality to Protestants in France.
   d. ended the war between Catholic France and Protestant England.

7. One of the chief negative effects of the Reformation on Europe was
   a. the lessening of educational opportunity.
   b. the loss of national identities.
   c. the diminished tolerance for variations from official doctrine.
   d. the decreased opportunities for social climbing.

8. The St. Bartholomew's Day bloodshed was
   a. the result of the Catholic fanatics' hatred of Protestants in France.
   b. the revenge of the English Calvinists on the English Catholics.
   c. the upshot of a failed attempt to overturn the Catholic dynasty in Spain.
   d. the slaughter of rebel peasantry in Flanders.

Identification Terms

Act of Supremacy of 1534
Anabaptists
"Bloody Mary"
Charles V
Council of Trent
Institutes of the Christian Religion
Jesuits
Peace of Augsburg
Presbyterians
Protestant Rome
Puritans
Zwingli (Ulrich)

Bibliography

Bainton, R. *Here I Stand,* 1950. Remains perhaps the best biography of Martin Luther.

Bouwsma, W. *John Calvin,* 1988. A good recent biography of the most influential of the Protestant leaders.

Jensen, D. L. *Reformation Europe,* 1990. An excellent survey of the Reformation period.

Kelly, H. A. *The Matrimonial Trials of Henry VIII,* 1975. Another good work on English affairs of state and religion.

McNeill, J. *The History and Character of Calvinism,* 1954. The best survey of what Calvinism meant theologically and as a way of living.

Neale, J. *Queen Elizabeth I,* 1934. Still the best biography of this significant ruler. See also J. Ridley, *Elizabeth I,* 1988.

O'Connell, M. *The Counter-Reformation, 1559–1610,* 1974. A fair-minded balancing of Protestant and Catholic claims as well as a history of the Catholic responses.

Ozment, S. *Protestants: The Birth of a Revolution,* 1992. Also useful for students. The same author's *The Age of Reform, 1250–1550,* 1980, is a very good survey of the conditions in Europe that led to agitation against the papal church.

Youings, J. *Sixteenth Century England,* 1984. Places the English Reformation in the context of English society and culture.

FOUNDATIONS OF THE EUROPEAN STATES

THE THIRTY YEARS' WAR
The Treaty of Westphalia, 1648
Spain's Decline
ROYAL ABSOLUTISM
French Government under Louis XIV
England under the Stuarts: Revolution against
Absolutist Monarchy
POLITICAL THEORY: HOBBES AND LOCKE

In Europe, the seventeenth century saw the birth of modern government. During this century, the powers of government office began to be separated from the person or family of the occupant of the office, creating a group of professional servants of the state, or bureaucrats. Religious conflict continued, but gave way to political-economic issues in state-to-state relations. The maritime countries became steadily more important thanks to overseas commerce, while the central and eastern European states suffered heavy reverses from wars, the Turkish menace, and commercial and technological stagnation.

Royal courts constantly sought ways to enhance their growing powers over all their subjects. These varied from west to east in both type and effectiveness. But by the early eighteenth century, some form of monarchic absolutism was in force in every major country except Britain. In this chapter, the focus will be on the Germanies, France, and England.

✦ THE THIRTY YEARS' WAR

The Thirty Years' War, which wrecked the German states and was the most destructive conflict Europe had seen for centuries, arose from religious intolerance, but quickly became a struggle for territory and worldly power on the part of the multiple contestants. The war began in 1618, when the Habsburg Holy Roman Emperor attempted to check the spread of Protestant sentiments in part of his empire, the present-day Czech Republic or Bohemia, as it was then called. This led to a rebellion, which was put down decisively by the Habsburg forces at the Battle of White Mountain near Prague in 1621. A forced re-Catholicization began. The defeated Protestants did not submit, but found allies among their co-religionists in southern and eastern Germany. From this point, the war became an *all-German civil war* between Lutherans and Calvinists, on the one side, and the imperial armies under the Catholic emperor, on the other. Like most civil wars, it was extremely destructive. By 1635, the war had become an international struggle beyond consideration of religion; the Protestant kings of Scandinavia and the Catholic French monarchy supported the Protestants, while the Spanish cousins of the Habsburgs assaulted the French.

● **MAP 30.1 The Thirty Years' War.** This destructive war had three distinct phases: first, it was an internal challenge to Habsburg Catholic rule by the Bohemian Protestants; second, from 1622 it was an all-German civil war between Lutheran and Calvinists, and the imperial Catholic forces; third, from about 1635 it was an international conflict in which religious affiliation played only minor roles.

The Treaty of Westphalia, 1648

For thirteen more years, France, Holland, Sweden, and the German Protestant states fought on against the Holy Roman Emperor and Spain. Most of the fighting was in Germany, and the country was thoroughly ravaged by both sides, which sent forces into the field with instructions to "forage," that is, to rob the natives of food and fodder, while killing any who resisted.

Finally, a peace, the *Treaty of Westphalia,* was worked out in 1648 after five years of haggling. The big winners were France and Sweden, with the latter suddenly emerging as a major power in northern Europe (see Map 30.1). The losers were Spain and, to a lesser degree, the Austrian-based Habsburgs who saw any chance of reuniting Germany under Catholic control go glimmering. From 1648 on, Germany ceased to exist as a political concept and broke up into dozens, then hundreds of small kingdoms and principalities, some Catholic and some Protestant.

The Peace of Westphalia was the *first modern state treaty*. From start to finish, its clauses underlined the decisive importance of the sovereign state, rather than the dynasty that ruled it or the religion its population professed. The establishment of theological uniformity was replaced by *secular control of territory and population* as the supreme goal of the rival powers.

In religious affiliations, things were left much as they had been in 1618. The principle that had first been enunciated in the Peace of Augsburg a hundred years earlier—*cuius regio, eius religio* (the ruler determines religious affiliation)—was now extended to the Calvinists, as well as Lutherans and Catholics. Northern and eastern Germany were heavily Protestant, while the south and most of the Rhine valley remained Catholic. This division negated any chance of German political unity for the next two centuries.

The Thirty Years' War was an economic disaster for the Germans; plague, smallpox, famine, and the casualties of war may have carried off as many as one-third of the population to an early death! The division of Germany into small states made it all the harder to recover as a nation. For a long while to come, there would be a political and economic power vacuum in the center of Europe.

Spain's Decline

For Spain, the results were almost as painful, though the war was not fought on Spanish territory. The Dutch gained full, legal independence from Madrid, and Portugal, which had been under Spanish rule for 60 years, rebelled successfully in 1640. The war with France was foolishly resumed until Spain was forced to make peace in 1659. By that date, the tremendous military and naval advantages that Spain's government had once possessed had all been used up. Spain was bankrupt, its incoming shipments of overseas bullion were now much reduced, and its domestic economy had seen little or no development for a century and a half.

The Mexican and Peruvian silver had made much of Europe rich in one way or another. But ordinary Spaniards were as poor as ever and perhaps even poorer, because the Spanish nobility and the church were notoriously unproductive users of the vast wealth that went through their hands in the sixteenth and seventeenth centuries. Despite much effort in the eighteenth century to regain its former status, Spain was condemned to a second rank in European and world affairs.

✤ ROYAL ABSOLUTISM

The theory of royal absolutism existed in the Middle Age, but the upheavals caused by the Hundred Years' War in France and England, the Black Death in the fourteenth century (see Chapter 26), and the wars of religion following Luther's revolt had distracted the rulers' attention and weakened their powers. Now, in the seventeenth century, they got back to the business of asserting their sacred rights.

The outstanding theorist of absolutism was a French lawyer, **Jean Bodin,** who stated in a widely read book that "sovereignty consists in giving laws to the people without their consent." Sovereignty cannot be divided; it must remain in the hands of a single individual or one institution. For France, Bodin insisted that this person should be

■ **The Thirty Years War.** In this panorama by Jan Breughel, the horror of war in the seventeenth century is brought home. Turned loose on the hapless peasants and townsmen, the mercenaries who made up the professional armies of the day killed and stole as they pleased.

the French monarch, who had "absolute power" to give his people law. Another Frenchman, Bishop Bossuet, gave a theological gloss to Bodin's ideas by claiming that kings received their august powers from God and that to defy them as a rebel was to commit a mortal sin.

Does this mean that the monarch had to answer to no one or could safely ignore what his people said and felt? No, the king had to answer to his Christian conscience and eventually to his Creator, as did everyone. And any king who attempted to rule against public opinion or the well-meant advice of his councilors was a fool. But the *king was and should be the final source of legitimate authority in politics and law.* Bodin arrived at this theory in part because of the times he lived in; his book was published at the height of the French religious struggles in the 1570s, when it appeared that without a strong, respected monarch France might collapse as a state.

Bodin found his most potent and effective adherent in Cardinal **Richelieu** (1585–1642), the prime minister for the young Louis XIII in the 1620s and 1630s. Richelieu was the real founder of absolute monarchy in France—and most of Europe soon imitated Paris.

Following the murder of the peacemaking Henry IV in 1610, Protestant-Catholic antipathy in France had increased. Henry's widow Marie de Medici was the formal regent for her young son, but was held in contempt by much of the Huguenot nobility, who despised her frivolity and her partisan Catholicism in equal measure. Unable to control the constant intrigues around her, she turned to the strong-minded and talented Richelieu. Despite being a prince of the church, Richelieu believed wholeheartedly in the primacy of the state over any other earthly institution. *Raison d'état* (reason of state) was sufficient to justify almost any action by government. The state represented order, the rule of law, and security for the citizenry; if it was weakened or collapsed, the result would be general suffering. The government had a moral obligation to avoid that eventuality at all costs.

The cardinal set up a cadre of officials *(intendants)* who kept a sharp eye on what was happening in the provinces and reported to the king's ministers. Thus, the faint outlines of a *centralized and centralizing bureaucracy* began to appear: these men were picked for their posts at least partially on merit, were dependent on the central authority for pay and prestige, and subordinated local loyalties and personal preferences to the demands and policies of the center. The cardinal-minister used them to check the independence of the provincial nobles, particularly the Huguenots. He used armed force on several occasions and summarily executed rebels.

■ **The Beast of War.** The seventeenth century was an age of savagery in European warfare, when mercenary armies only loosely controlled by noble amateurs ranged about the countryside ravaging the helpless peasantry. This cartoon illustrates how the "beast of war" was seen by those in its path.

Richelieu was the real ruler of France until he died in 1642, followed a bit later by his king. The cardinal had handpicked as his successor as chief minister another Catholic churchman, Cardinal Mazarin, who had the same values as his master. The new king, *Louis XIV* (1643–1715), was five years old, so the government remained in Mazarin's hands for many years. The young Louis was brought up to believe that kingship was the highest calling on earth and that its powers were complete and unlimited except by God—and perhaps not by him either!

French Government under Louis XIV

Louis XIV had *the longest reign of any monarch in European history,* and the last fifty-four of those years he was his own chief minister, totally dominating French government. He was the incarnation of absolute monarchy, believing in *divine right,* which said that the monarchy's powers flowed from God and that the king's subjects should regard him as God's representative in civil affairs.

The later seventeenth and eighteenth centuries were the Age of France, or more precisely, the Age of Louis

XIV. Not only in government, but also in the arts, the lifestyle of the wealthy and the highborn, military affairs, and language and literature, France set the pace. What Florence had been to the Renaissance, Paris was to the European cultural and political world of the eighteenth century. Once King Louis allegedly said "I am the state," a statement he truly believed. He saw himself as not just a human being with immense powers and prestige, but as the very flesh and blood of France. It is to his credit that he took kingship very seriously, working twelve hours a day at the tedious, complex task of trying to govern a country that was still subdivided in many ways and notoriously difficult to govern. In this task he was greatly aided by a series of first-rate ministerial helpers—the marquis of Louvois, Jean-Baptiste Colbert, Sébastien de

■ **Louis XIV.** This masterful portrait by the court painter Rigaud shows Louis as he would have liked to appear to his subjects. The "well turned leg" was considered to be an absolute essential for royal figures. Louis' wig and his ermine cape were also necessities for a king.

Vauban, and others—each of whom made major contributions to the theory and practice of his chosen field.

Below these top levels, the *intendants* created by Richelieu continued to serve the monarch as his eyes and ears in the provinces. Louis's bureaucrats were the best trained and most reliable servants of their king obtainable; he selected their middle and lower ranks from the middle classes as much as from the nobility. Many latter-day French nobles were the heirs of commoners who were rewarded for outstanding service to King Louis XIV or were given the much sought opportunity of purchasing an office that carried noble status with it.

Louis was steeped in Richelieu's concepts from childhood and was determined to establish the royal throne as the sole seat of sovereignty. To do so, he had to nullify the independent powers of the aristocrats in the provinces, and he did this by forcing them to come to *Versailles,* his magnificent palace outside Paris, where they vied for his favor and he could keep them under a watchful eye. He was generally successful. By his death, the previously potent nobles had been reduced to a decorative, parasitic fringe group, with few real powers and few responsibilities in national government save those granted them by the king.

Louis's *revocation of the Edict of Nantes* in 1685 was a mistake, which led to the loss of a valuable asset: the Huguenots, who despite royal ordinances emigrated *en masse* in the following decade. By allowing them to do so, the king hoped to emphasize the unity of Catholic France; he mistakenly thought that most of the Calvinists had been reconverted anyway and that the edict was no longer needed. Welcomed to Protestant Europe, some 200,000 Huguenots served as bastions of anti-French activity and propaganda against the monarch in the series of wars on which he now embarked.

Wars of Louis XIV

Although Louis kept the peace for the first thirty-five years of his reign, his overpowering thirst for glory led him to provoke four conflicts with England, Holland, and most of the German states, led by the Austrian Habsburgs in the last twenty years. The most important was the final one, the *War of the Spanish Succession (1700–1713),* in which France tried to seize control of much weakened Spain and its empire and was checked by a coalition led by England. The war bankrupted France and was extremely unpopular among the French people by its end. France succeeded only in placing a member of the Bourbon family (the French dynasty) on the Spanish throne,

but under the condition that Spain and France would never be joined together. England, the chief winner, gained control of part of French Canada, the Spanish Caribbean islands, and the key to the Mediterranean, Gibraltar. The war began the worldwide struggle between England and France for mastery of a colonial empire.

Strengths and Weaknesses of French Absolutism

Louis XIV gave all of Europe a model of what could be accomplished by a strong king and a wealthy country. His officials were the most disciplined and most effective that any Western country had seen and were comparable to the Chinese bureaucrats of the same date. Through his personal councilors, the king kept a constant watch on these officials and the country as a whole; anything that happened in the provinces was soon known at Versailles and received a royal response whenever necessary. The palace itself was awe inspiring, serving to reinforce Louis's prestige and power in visible fashion to visiting ambassadors. Versailles, originally a mere hunting lodge for Louis XIII, was made into the largest and most impressive secular structure in Europe. It was surrounded by hundreds of acres of manicured gardens and parks and was large enough to house the immense court and its servants. Its halls were the museums of the Bourbon dynasty and remained so until the Revolution.

But there were also problems. *Finance* was always the sore point for aspiring kings, and Louis spent huge amounts of cash in his quest for military and civil glory. A system of tax "farms," concessions for tax collection in the provinces, did not work well. Begun in the early seventeenth century, the system suffered from a growing disparity between what was collected and what was eventually

forwarded to the court. Pushed by his ministers, the king considered the possibility of introducing taxes on the lands of the church and the nobles, but was dissuaded from this radical step. Instead, taxes on the peasant majority were increased, especially after the wars began.

The financial problem of the monarchy was in fact never solved. Of all European countries, France was the most favored by nature, and its agricultural economy was the most diverse. But the French peasants were slowly becoming aware of the contrasts between the taxes they had to bear and the exemptions of various sorts enjoyed by the privileged orders of the clergy and nobility. When that discontent would be later joined by the resentment of the much enlarged group of middle-class townspeople during the course of the eighteenth century, the potential for revolution would exist.

England under the Stuarts: Revolution against Absolutist Monarchy

At the death of Queen Elizabeth in 1603, the English crown passed by prearrangement to her nearest male Protestant relative, the Stuart King James VI of Scotland, who became *James I (1603–1625) of England.* James was a great believer in absolutism and the divine right of kings and quickly alienated the English Parliament with his insistence that the Crown should have sole control over taxes and the budget. James's lack of respect for English customs, his blatant homosexuality, and his arrogance combined to make him a highly unpopular figure by the end of his reign. His greatest achievement was his selection of a committee of distinguished churchmen who produced in short order the most influential English book ever written: the King James Version of the Bible.

Queen Christina of Sweden
1626–1689

"Far from beautiful, short in stature, pockmarked in face and with a slight humpback. . . ": such was the less than prepossessing description of a woman who would make her mark on her nation and her contemporaries in ways still not forgotten—or forgiven. Christina of Sweden (1626–1689) was the sole surviving child of King Gustavus Adolphus, the warrior-king who died at the head of his Lutheran troops in the Thirty Years' War in Germany. When he died, Christina was only six years old, and a regency led by the upright Chancellor Axel Oxenstierna was established for the next twelve years. Oxenstierna was also the future queen's tutor in things political, and he soon found his charge to be difficult. Prodigal and imperious by nature, the young girl did not take kindly to the wise old man's advice in matters public or private. She was brilliant in intellect and passionate in temperament and found it irritating to listen to those she regarded as her social or intellectual inferiors.

In 1644 she was crowned queen of Sweden, which at that time included most of Scandinavia and had the best army in Europe. Wanting to rid herself of Oxenstierna and knowing that she could not do so as long as the war in Germany raged, she pressured her advisers to end the war as soon as possible. Interfering with Oxenstierna's careful diplomacy, she lost for her country a part of what might have been gained in the peace of Westphalia. Still Sweden emerged from the conflict as a major power, and its twenty-two-year-old queen a major player in the intricate game of high diplomacy. Like the English with Elizabeth a generation earlier, many Swedes thought it unnatural—perhaps foolhardy—to allow the nation's fate to hang on the actions of a mere unmarried woman.

The Swedish estates (clerics, nobles, and commoners) put great pressure upon the queen to marry as soon as possible, but she resisted just as strongly. Raised to believe herself the linchpin of her

---

The England that James ruled was fast developing into a society in which the commercial and professional classes had a great deal of political "savvy" and were becoming used to the exercise of local and regional power. Although the highest level of the government in London was still, as everywhere, dominated by the nobility, the well-off merchants and municipal officials who were represented by Parliament's *House of Commons* were by now insistent on their rights to have final input on taxation and much else in national policy. They were armed with a tradition of parliamentary government that was already four centuries old. They could not be intimidated easily, nor sent home at will.

Another topic of acrid debate between the king and his subjects was the proper course in religious affairs. James had been brought up a Calvinist, but had agreed to adopt Anglicanism as king of England. In truth, he seemed to many to sympathize with Rome, which made the Anglicans nervous and appalled the growing number of Puritans.

It is impossible to say how numerous the Puritans were because Puritanism was more a state of mind than a formal affiliation. Puritans were inclined to accept the

country's fate, she found it difficult to think of herself as only the channel by which a male could steer the ship of state. Disgusted, she was only barely persuaded to withdraw her abdication in 1651 and to appoint her cousin Karl as her potential successor. In 1651 Christina also rejected the Lutheranism of almost all her compatriots and began to neglect the business of state in favor of her personal affairs, including her various lovers from Stockholm's foreign colony.

Her relations with the nobility worsened when she created more than four hundred new nobles in an attempt to gain popularity and thus angered the proud old Swedish families, who began to see her as their enemy rather than their monarch. Friction mounted steadily, and in June 1654 her second offer to abdicate in favor of Karl was gladly accepted. Taking the pseudonym Count Dohna and dressed in her favored male attire, Christina left Stockholm at once and proceeded to Rome, where she spent most of her remaining life. En route, she insulted her fellow Swedes and her upbringing by accepting the Catholic faith and proclaiming herself the ally of the pope. In return, the Roman pontiff welcomed her to his city and saw to her establishment in proper style at a palazzo near the Vatican. Here she spent most of the rest of her life, involving herself with papal politics and with lovers from both the clergy and laity who sought to use this restless, passionate woman for their own ends. Scandal followed her throughout her life, which ended in relative impoverishment and oblivion when she reached the age of sixty-three. Her enemies enjoyed spreading the tale of how she once ordered the summary execution of her Italian adviser when she discovered that he had betrayed her confidence—and made sure that the execution was carried out.

But there were other sides to her nature. In her few short years as queen, Christina had ordered the first general schooling law in Sweden's and perhaps all Europe's history: the act of 1649. Her inteventions in the Diet had resulted in a series of decrees and ordinances that promoted the welfare of the Swedish townspeople and the mining industry, which was so important to the country. She rose daily at 5 A.M. to gain a "quiet time" for her pursuit of scientific and artistic studies.

Above all, though, Christina's authentic fame rests upon her extraordinary artistic taste and her lavish generosity in acting upon it. The queen-in-exile, as she liked to think of herself, was the Roman patroness of the great musicians Alassandro Scarlatti and Arcangelo Corelli, who wrote some of their finest work in her honor; the protector of the gifted architect and sculptor Giovanni Bernini, who crowned his lifework with the plans for St. Peter's Square; and the sponsor of the first opera company in Rome. Her house was a treasure trove of seventeenth-century Italian and Flemish artworks, and at her death her library became an important addition to the Vatican's library, the greatest in all Europe. The small Jewish colony in Rome also owed much to her repeated intercessions to protect them from the anti-Semitic mob.

Left alone and living off the charity of the pope, Christina, the scion of the most potent Protestant power of the seventeenth century, had her last wish fulfilled by being buried in the cathedral of St. Peter's. Her Swedish subjects erected no monuments to her memory.

Calvinist social values: hard work, thrift, and a sober lifestyle that aimed at finding its true rewards in eternity. The Puritans liked to think of poverty as an accompaniment of sin and of wealth and social status as the just rewards of a good Christian, a member of the Elect. The "capitalist ethic" was well rooted in them, and they, in turn, had extensive representation in the business classes of England. In the House of Commons, they were now a majority.

Absolutist king and Puritan Parliament clashed again and again in the 1620s over taxation and religion, and by the time James died in 1625, Parliament was on the point of revolt. James was succeeded by his son *Charles I* (1625–1649), who soon turned out to be as difficult as his father. When the Commons attempted to impose limits on his taxing powers, he refused to honor the ancient custom of calling a Parliament at least every third year. He attempted to bring England into the Thirty Years' War against strong opinion that held that England had no interest in that conflict; he appointed an archbishop of Canterbury, William Laud, who seemed to many to be a sympathizer with popery; and he was at least as stubborn

● **MAP 30.2 Europe in the Seventeeth Century.** After the Thirty Years' War, the Holy Roman Empire was an empty phrase, with an emperor whose powers were nonexistent in the Protestant lands. The Habsburg emperors, always Catholics, were stalemated by the equally Catholic French Bourbons whose country lay between those of the Habsburgs.

as his father had been. Finding that Parliament would not cooperate with him, he sent it home in 1629 and ruled without its advice and consent.

Charles's marriage to a French Catholic princess stirred up much resentment, and many speculated that he himself harbored strong pro-Catholic sympathies. His high-handed attitude toward the Calvinist church and clergy

finally offended his Scot subjects so badly that in 1640 they rose in revolt. Charles needed money—lots of it—to raise an army against them, and that meant he had to impose new taxes, which meant he had to summon Parliament.

Parliament had not met for eleven years, and when the representatives came together, they were in no mood to support an arrogant and unpopular king's demands. Instead, Parliament passed a series of restrictive laws on the royal powers, but the king maneuvered to bypass them illegally. When the increasingly radical Parliament took direct control of military affairs, Charles raised an army of royalist supporters, and this action led directly to the beginning of civil war in 1642.

Civil War: Cromwell's Commonwealth

Britain divided about evenly between supporters of the king (the Anglican clergy, most of the nobility, and most peasants) and supporters of Parliament (the majority of the townspeople, the merchant and commercial classes, the Puritans, and the Scots). Regional and local economic interests often dictated political allegiance. After several years of intermittent struggle, the war ended with Charles's defeat. Parliament then tried the king for treason. He was found guilty after much discussion and executed in 1649.

It was the first and only time that the British had executed their king and the first time since the beginnings of the modern state system that *any* European people had turned so decisively on their legitimate sovereign. The experience was agonizing even for the king's sworn enemies among the Puritans and led to a great deal of debate over where sovereignty resided and how legal process in government should be defined and protected. Over time, the modern Anglo-American ideals of *constitutional government* evolved from this debate.

After the king's execution, Parliament declared that England was a *commonwealth,* that is, a republic with no monarch. Its ruler was the chief of the triumphant Puritan army, **Oliver Cromwell,** who had gained a deserved reputation as a man of iron will and fierce rectitude. During his tenure as *Lord Protector (1653–1658),* there was a comprehensive attempt to eliminate such vices as dancing, drinking, making merry on the Sabbath, and theatrical performances. Such efforts had the predictable result: when Cromwell died, few people wanted to hear more about Puritan government. His rule had also become unpopular because of the high taxes he levied (with the cooperation of an intimidated Parliament) to pay for frequent military expeditions. He put down rebellions against English rule in Catholic Ireland and Calvinist Scotland with bloody force, thereby laying the groundwork for a Great Britain that would include these formerly separate countries as well as England. A maritime war with Holland in the 1650s brought England far along the road to control of the seven seas; a second round ten years later brought the former Dutch colony of New Amsterdam.

Three years before his death, the Lord Protector tired of parliamentary quibbling and instituted a forthright military dictatorship. When Cromwell's weak son attempted in vain to fill his father's shoes, parliamentary negotiations with the exiled son of Charles I were begun. After eighteen months the **Restoration** was completed with the return of *King Charles II (r. 1660–1685)* to his native land.

Restoration and Glorious Revolution of 1688

King Charles II had learned the lessons that had cost his father his head. Charles also wished to exercise absolute powers, but knew when he had to compromise. As he once said, he had "no wish to go on my travels again."

The House of Commons was emerging as clearly the stronger of the two houses of Parliament, and Charles made his peace with the Commons by establishing the beginnings of the *ministerial system.* The king appointed several of his trusted friends to carry out policy, but these men had to answer to parliamentary questioning. Gradually, this informal arrangement became a fundamental part of the English government and was formalized when the party system got underway in the eighteenth century. From it came the modern British cabinet, with its collective responsibility for policy and its reliance on parliamentary votes of confidence to continue its authority as a government.

Charles cared little about religion (his private life was a continual sexual scandal), but many members of Parliament did; and they proceeded to make it legally impossible for anyone but an Anglican to hold office, vote, or attend the universities. The measure was a reaction against the Puritans, Quakers, and Catholics who had caused such turmoil for England over the past quarter century. But this law—the *Test Act*—was too restrictive to be supported by the majority in the long run. It was gradually eased until it was finally abandoned in the nineteenth century.

One aspect of Charles's religious policy helped to create problems for his successor, however. Under a secret arrangement with King Louis XIV of France, Charles was to receive a large annual money payment in exchange for returning England to Catholicism. Although nothing ever came of the pact, the news inevitably leaked out and created a wave of anti-Catholicism that led to a virtual panic. Thus, when it became clear that the childless Charles would be succeeded by his younger brother,

James, who had indeed become a practicing Catholic while in exile in France, the English viewed their new king with a great deal of hostility from the outset.

James II (r. 1685–1688) made things worse by flinging insult after insult at the Protestants in and out of Parliament and by deliberately ignoring the provisions of the Test Act. So long as the king had no Catholic children to succeed him, the English could grit their teeth and wait for the elderly man's death. But in 1688 his young second wife produced a healthy baby son who would be raised a Catholic and would presumably rule Britain for many years. To many, this prospect was too much to bear.

Practically all England rebelled against King James in the *Glorious Revolution of 1688* that ended the Stuart male line on the English throne. James again went into French exile accompanied by his family, while parliamentary committees stepped into the vacuum in London. After brief negotiations, **William of Orange,** the Dutch Calvinist husband of James's daughter Mary, was invited to rule England jointly with his wife. So began the reign of *William and Mary* (1689–1702).

Significance of the Glorious Revolution

The revolution against James Stuart had been almost bloodless; its significance was political, not military or economic. *Sovereignty shifted* from the monarch to his subjects, as represented by their elected Parliament. From now on England was a constitutional state; the king or queen was the partner of Parliament in matters of high policy, both domestic and foreign. William and Mary had accepted the offer of the throne from a parliamentary delegation; what parliamentary committees had given, they could also legitimately take away. The royal pair were never allowed to forget that.

The most concrete result of the Glorious Revolution was the **Bill of Rights,** which was adopted by Parliament in 1689. Its most important provisions spelled out some of the rights and powers of Parliament:

1. Law was to be made only by Parliament and could not be suspended by the king.
2. Members of Parliament were immune from prosecution.
3. The king could not impose taxes or raise an army without prior approval by Parliament.

In addition, the Bill of Rights assured the independence of the judiciary from royal pressures, prohibited standing armies in peacetime, extended freedom of worship to non-Anglican Protestants, and stipulated that the throne should always be held by a Protestant.

The Glorious Revolution was the world's first significant move toward full parliamentary government, but it was definitely *not* a democratic revolution. The great majority of the English and other Britons did not have the vote at any level beyond the village council. That would have to wait until near the end of the nineteenth century. And women of any class would not have political equality in Britain until the twentieth century.

In accord with the 1701 Act of Succession worked out by Parliament and king, Mary's younger sister Anne succeeded William and Mary on the English throne. Like them, she died without surviving children. Now Parliament exercised its new powers under the Act to invite the duke of Hanover, a distant German relative of king James I and the nearest male Protestant relation to the deceased queen, to become King George I (r. 1714–1727). George thus introduced the **Hanoverian dynasty** to Great Britain.

The first two Georges lived mostly in Hanover, could barely speak English, and showed little interest in the intricacies of English political life. Both were content to leave policy making to trusted confidants among the aristocrats and landed gentry who dominated both houses of Parliament. Robert Walpole, the prime minister for more than twenty years (1721–1742), was the central figure in British government and the true founder of the ministerial government that had begun under King Charles II. Under Walpole, the monarchs were manipulated by the parliamentary leadership more and more so that Parliament became the more important force in most aspects of internal policy. While foreign affairs and the military still belonged primarily in the Crown's domain, Parliament was supreme in legislation and finance.

✤ Political Theory: Hobbes and Locke

Two British political philosophers formed the basis of public debate on the nature of government during the tumultuous seventeenth century. **Thomas Hobbes** (1588–1679) thought that the pregovernmental "state of nature" had been a riotous anarchy, a "war of all against all." A strong government was essential to restrain humans' natural impulses to improve their own lot by harming their neighbors. Recognizing this need to restrain the violence, early societies soon gave birth to the idea of the state and to the state's living embodiment, the monarch. The state,

Hobbes, *Leviathan*

Thomas Hobbes published *Leviathan* to provide a philosophical basis for absolutist monarchy that went beyond the conventional idea of "divine right." Much influenced by the events of the day in England—the civil war was raging—Hobbes wished to demonstrate that strong control of the body politic by a monarch was a political necessity. The following excerpts come from the opening section of the second part of *Leviathan,* where the author summarizes his case:

The final cause, end, or design of men (who naturally love liberty, and dominion over others) in the introduction of that restraint upon themselves . . . is the foresight of their own preservation, and of a more contented life thereby; that is to say, of getting themselves out of that miserable condition of war, when there is no visible power to keep them in awe, and tie them by fear of punishment to the performance of their covenants.

For the laws of nature . . . without the terror of some power to cause them to be observed, are contrary to our natural passions. . . . And covenants without the sword are but words, and of no strength to secure a man at all. . . . And in all places where men have lived in small families, to rob and spoil one another has been a trade, and so far from being reputed against the law of nature, the greater spoils they gained, the greater was their honor. . . . And as small families did then; so now do cities and kingdoms, which are but greater families. . . .

It is true that certain living creatures, as bees and ants, live sociably with one another . . . and therefore some man may perhaps desire to know, why mankind cannot do the same. To which I answer

First, that men are continually in competition for honor and dignity, which these creatures are not. . . .

Secondly, that amongst these creatures, the common good differs not from the private; and being by nature inclined to their private, they procure thereby the common benefit.

Thirdly, that these creatures, having not [as man] the use of reason, do not see, nor think they see any fault, in the administration of their private business: whereas among men, there are very many that think themselves wiser, and abler to govern the public, better than the rest; and these strive to reform and innovate, one this way, another that way; and thereby bring it into distraction and civil war.

Lastly, the agreement of these creatures is natural; that of men, is by covenant only, which is artificial; and therefore it is no wonder if there be somewhat else required to make their agreement constant and lasting; which is a common power, to keep them in awe, and to direct their action to the common benefit.

The only way to erect such a common power . . . [is] to confer all their power and strength upon one man, or upon one assembly of men, that may reduce all their wills, by plurality of voices, unto one will . . . as if every man should say to every man, *I authorize and give up my right of governing myself to this man, or to this assembly of men, on this condition, that thou give up thy right to him, and authorize all his actions in like manner.*

And he that carries this power is called *sovereign,* and said to have *sovereign power,* and everyone besides him is his *subject.*

The attaining of this sovereign power is by two ways. One, by natural force . . . the other, is when men agree amongst themselves to submit to some man or assembly of men, voluntarily, in confidence to be protected by him against all others. This latter may be called a political Commonwealth. . . .

SOURCE: *The English Works of Thomas Hobbes,* excerpted from Chapter XVII, vol. 3, edited by Thomas Molesworth.

which Hobbes termed *Leviathan* in his famous book of 1651 was both the creature and the master of Man. The state commanded absolute right of obedience from all; those who rebelled should be crushed without mercy for the protection of the rest (see the Document in this chapter).

Hobbes's uncompromising pessimism about human nature was countered at the end of the seventeenth century by the writings of **John Locke** (1632–1704). In his most famous work, the two *Treatises of Civil Government,* Locke said that all men possess certain natural rights, derived from the fact that they were reasonable creatures. Some of those rights were voluntarily given up to form a government that would protect and enhance the remaining ones: the rights to life, liberty, and property. No prince might interfere with such rights or claim to have one-sided powers to define the citizenry's welfare. Insofar as the government fulfilled its duties, it should enjoy the citizens' support and loyal service; when it did not, it had no claim to their support, and they could righteously push it aside and form a new government.

While Hobbes's words were harsh and shocking to most English people of his time, Locke's message fell on much more fertile ground. His readers, like the author, were members of the middle and upper classes, who possessed properties and freedoms they were determined to protect from the claims of absolutist monarchs. The English Revolution of the 1640s and the events of the 1680s had given them confidence that their views were both correct and workable. Locke's arguments made good sense to them, and he was also to become the most important political philosopher for the English colonials in North America.

Summary

The Thirty Years' War wrecked Germany while providing a forcible resolution to the question of religious wars in Europe. The Treaty of Westphalia, which ended the war, was founded on state interests, rather than religious doctrine or dynastic claims, and from the early seventeenth century on, doctrines of faith took an ever-decreasing role in forming state policy. The Catholic but anti-Habsburg French emerged as the chief beneficiaries of the conflict in Germany. France replaced Spain as the prime force in military and political affairs and, under the long-lived Louis XIV, became the role model for the rest of the aspiring absolutist monarchies on the Continent.

The English Revolution, sparked by the attempts of the Stuart kings to emulate Louis XIV, ended in clear victory for the anti-absolutist side. Led by the Puritan rebels against Charles I, the wealthier, educated segment of the English people successfully asserted their claims to be equal to the Crown in defining national policies and the rights of citizens. These seeds would sprout continuously in the Western world for the next two centuries, especially in the British colonies in North America. Given a theoretical underpinning by philosophers such as John Locke and practical form by the leaders of the Glorious Revolution, the idea of a society that was contractual in its political basis began to emerge, along with the ideal of a state that guaranteed liberty and legal equality for all its subjects.

Test Your Knowledge

1. The message conveyed by Hobbes's *Leviathan* was in brief that
   a. man would find his way to a better future.
   b. man could make more progress once religion was abolished.
   c. man was irredeemably stained by original sin.
   d. man needed a powerful government to avoid anarchy.
2. In its final stage, the Thirty Years' War became
   a. the first religious war in Europe.
   b. a political struggle for additional extra-European colonies.
   c. a struggle between the Roman pope and various Protestant groups.
   d. a struggle between the Habsburgs and Bourbons.
3. The Thirty Years' War began
   a. as a struggle for religious freedom for reformers in Bohemia.
   b. as a contest between Calvinists and Lutherans in Germany.
   c. as a political contest between Germans and French in the Rhineland.
   d. as none of these.

4. *Raison d'état* is most accurately translated as
   a. the power of a duly constituted government to do what it wishes.
   b. a false reason given by a spokesman to justify what the government desires.
   c. an immediate pretext used by a government to justify what it wishes to do.
   d. the state's legal power to make war.
5. Which of the following seventeenth-century English monarchs was most successful in retaining the support of Parliament?
   a. James II
   b. Charles I
   c. James I
   d. Charles II
6. William and Mary came to rule England
   a. at the invitation of Parliament.
   b. as the successors to Cromwell after his death.
   c. as the conquerors of Cromwell's Commonwealth.
   d. as the brother and sister of the next-to-last Stuart king.
7. Which of the following characteristics was *not* true of the government of Louis XIV?
   a. It was based on parliamentary policy-making.
   b. It was Catholic in religion.
   c. It was staffed by many members of the middle classes.
   d. It was highly concentrated in the person of the king.

Identification Terms

Bill of Rights	Hanoverian dynasty	*Leviathan*	Richelieu
Bodin (Jean)	Hobbes (Thomas)	Locke (John)	William of Orange
Cromwell (Oliver)	*intendants*	Restoration (English)	

Bibliography

Aylmer, G. E. *Rebellion or Revolution? England, 1640–1660,* 1986. Interestingly written.

Cipolla, C. *Miasma and Disease,* 1992. A very engaging account of how diseases were perceived and reacted against by seventeenth-century Europeans.

Dunn, R. *The Age of Religious Wars, 1559–1689,* 1979. Probably the best short account.

Goubert, P. *Louix XIV and Twenty Million Frenchmen,* 1966. A survey of French society during the seventeenth century.

Hill, C. *God's Englishman: Oliver Cromwell and the English Revolution,* 1970, and A. Fraser, *Cromwell: The Lord Protector,* 1974, are both reliable aids to understanding what England went through in the seventeenth century and what sort of people the Puritans were.

Jessop, T. F. *Thomas Hobbes,* 1960. Good, short biography.

Kamen, H. *The War of the Succession in Spain,* 1969. Very good on Europe's foreign affairs in the late seventeenth century.

The same author's *Spain 1469–1716,* 1983, is insightful on the causes for the decline of Spanish power.

Laslett, P. *Locke's Two Treatises of Government,* 1970. Both texts in full, with incisive introductions to them.

Lee, S. J. *The Thirty Years War,* 1991.

Lewis, W. H. *The Splendid Century,* 1953. An entertaining and very readable account of French life in the seventeenth century.

Rabb, T. K. ed. *The Thirty Years War,* 1972. Sometimes heavy going, but has generally interesting essays on the meaning of this conflict. Also good is S. H. Steinberg, *The Thirty Years War and the Conflict for European Hegemony 1600–1660,* 1966.

Wolf, J. *Louis XIV,* 1968. The standard, highly readable biography of this king who set the mold for so many of his contemporaries.

EAST EUROPEAN EMPIRES

1533–1584	Ivan IV, the Terrible (Russia)
early 1600s–1613	Time of Troubles (Russia) ended by first Romanov tsar
1640–1688	Frederick William the Great Elector (Prussia)
1682–1724	Peter I, the Great (Russia)
late 1600s–1700s	Habsburgs (Austria) defeated Ottoman Turks
1713–1740	Frederick William I (Prussia)
1740–1786	Frederick II, the Great (Prussia)
1740–1748	War of the Austrian Succession
1740–1780	Maria Theresa (Austria)
1762–1796	Catherine II (Russia)
1772–1795	Poland disappears from map

East Europe was a different society from West Europe. In the seventeenth and eighteenth centuries, three states—Russia, Austria, and Prussia—came to dominate this "other Europe." The colonization that the West was practicing overseas was imitated in the East through warfare and organized settlements of migrants. Unlike the West, large areas of the East were still underpopulated and of little value economically.

The borders of the East European states were extremely unstable due in part to war, political backwardness, and centuries of migrations. This instability both contributed to the rise of absolutist monarchic government and acted against its effectiveness. By the end of the eighteenth century, East Europe had westernized its upper, ruling classes, but deep differences remained between Europe east of the Elbe River and west of that traditional dividing line.

❧ ABSOLUTISM EAST OF THE ELBE

Absolutism began to develop in East Europe at about the same time as in West Europe, but proceeded further in the East and was not disturbed or checked until much later. Part of the reason for this difference was economic, but political and social factors were also important. The gap between East and West in this regard is one of the outstanding characteristics of modern European history.

Absolute monarchy was able to develop more forcefully in East Europe because of the nature of its agrarian economy. *Feudal landlords and their estates lasted much longer* in Russia, Poland, and Hungary than in France, England, and Sweden. The social cleavage between noble lord and peasant serf was perpetuated by the rising profits that the landlords were able to wring from their large estates. The grain necessary for the food supply of the expanding cities of western and central Europe was produced on these feudal holdings—a business that became increasingly profitable for those landlords who could produce the crop cheaply with non-free labor.

The normal struggle between noble landowners and the royal government was resolved in East Europe by a silent compromise: the weak monarchies surrendered full control over the peasants to the landlords in return for the landlords' political loyalty and service to the Crown. As time passed, the once-weak monarchs steadily gained power, and the nobles became their servants, just as the peasant serfs were servants to the nobles. No effective

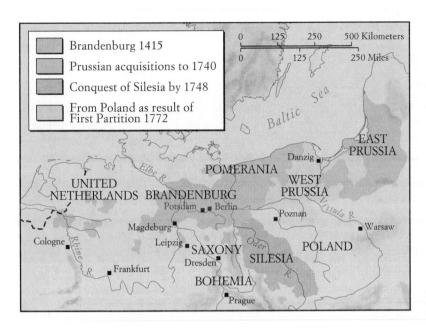

● **MAP 31.1   The Expansion of Prussia, 1640–1772.**

middle-class voice was ever heard; the towns were too few, and the medieval urban populations never gained self-government and economic freedom as in the West. In Russia, Prussia, and Austria, the royal dynasts were gradually able to subordinate all classes and interests to themselves, and the continuity of royal power had become the pivot on which all society revolved by the eighteenth century.

The three states' political constitutions were not identical, however. Russia became the most autocratic by far. The *Romanov* tsar was not beholden to any earthly power in Russian legal theory; his will was law. The power of the Austrian emperor—always a member of the **Habsburg dynasty**—was sharply limited by the high nobility until the later eighteenth century. The Prussian king—a *Hohenzollern*—originally had fewer supreme powers than the Romanovs but more than the Habsburgs. Eventually, the Prussian king was to become the most powerful of the three, and from Prussia came modern Germany. We will look at Prussia first and then at the other two East European dynasties.

⚜ PRUSSIA'S RISE

After the Thirty Years' War, much of Germany was in a state of economic decay and political confusion. The 300-odd German states were divided along religious lines; half were Catholic and half Protestant. Neither trusted the other, and animosities were always present. The famines and epidemics that accompanied the war had killed about one-third of the population, and whole regions almost reverted to wasteland. From this very unpromising situation arose one of the major powers of modern Europe, Prussia-Germany (see Map 31.1).

The rise of the small and commercially insignificant Prussia during the later seventeenth and eighteenth centuries was largely due to the Hohenzollern princes who occupied the Prussian throne from 1640 to 1788. **Frederick William, the Great Elector** (r. 1640–1688), was a man of iron will and great talent. He united his previously quite separate family holdings of Prussia, Brandenburg, and some small areas in western Germany into a single government that was known thereafter simply as Prussia. During his reign, Berlin began its rise from a simple market town to a capital city. A sign of his strength was his victory over the powerful feudal lords in a struggle over who would have the final word in policy making, particularly regarding taxes.

Through such measures, the Great Elector tripled the government's revenues and then spent much of the increase on his prize: a new professional army. Every fourteenth male citizen was a member of the army on active service. No other European country even came close to this ratio. Frederick William only once had to use this force directly against a foreign enemy, its existence was enough to intimidate his many opponents both inside and outside Prussia's borders.

Frederick II's Justification for the Seizure of Silesia in 1740

King Frederick II ("the Great") of Prussia was an outstanding practitioner of royal *Realpolitik*. Despite his undoubted intelligence and artistic sensitivity, he was never inclined to allow legal or ethical niceties to stand in the way of what he regarded as his country's or his own interests. Shortly after ascending to the throne in 1740, he was presented with a unique opportunity when the Austrian emperor Charles VI died suddenly and left his throne to his only heir, his daughter Maria Theresa. Despite the solemn promise given by a predecessor to respect the integrity of the Austrian domains (the "Pragmatic Sanction"), Frederick used his superbly trained army to invade the neighboring Austrian province of Silesia. This act touched off the **War of the Austrian Succession** (1740–1742, 1745–1747) and was a prime cause of the bloody, worldwide Seven Years' War somewhat later.

Two documents from Frederick's pen in 1740 show different sides of his rationale for seizing Silesia. In the first, a letter to King George II of England, Frederick poses as the pious upholder of Prussian claims, international order, and the "real interests" of the helpless Maria Theresa; in the second, an internal memorandum to his cabinet, he states his real views.

1. The House of Austria, exposed to all its enemies since the loss of its head and the total disintegration of its affairs, is on the point of succumbing under the claims of those who openly advance claims to the succession and secretly plan to seize a part . . . . owing to the situation of my territories I have the chief interest in averting the consequences and above all, in preventing those who may have formed the design to seize Silesia, the bulwark of my possessions. I have been compelled to send my troops into the duchy (Silesia) in order to prevent others from seizing it, to my great disadvantage and to the prejudice of the just claims which my house has always had to the larger part of the place. I have no other purpose than the preservation and the real benefit of the House of Austria.

2. Silesia is the portion of the imperial heritage to which we have the strongest claims and which is most suitable for the House of Brandenburg [i.e., Prussia]. It is consonant with justice to maintain one's rights and to seize the opportunity of the emperor's death to take possession. The superiority of our troops, the promptitude with which we can set them in motions, in a word, the clear advantage we have over all other Powers of Europe . . . all this leads to the conclusion that we must occupy Silesia before the winter, and then negotiate. When we are in possession we can negotiate with success. We should never get anything by mere negotiations except very onerous conditions in return for a few trifles. . . .

SOURCE: G. P. Gooch, *Frederick the Great: The Writer, the Ruler, the Man*, 1947, pp. 6–8, Achon Books.

Frederick William also began the understanding between king and nobles that gradually came to dominate Prussian politics until the twentieth century. The Crown handed over the peasants to the noble landlords, who acted as their judge and jury and reduced them to a condition of misery as serfs. In return, the Crown was allowed almost total control over national policy, while the noble landlords' sons were expected to serve in the growing military and civil bureaucracy that Frederick William was creating.

During the reign of the Great Elector and for a long time thereafter, many of the Prussian nobles were not yet resigned to their inferior position as policy makers. But they could not bring themselves to look for help from a likely quarter. In the struggle over constitutional rights and sovereignty, the nobles ignored the third party that might have been able to tip the balance in their struggle against the king: the townspeople. As in the rest of Eastern Europe, the Prussian *urban middle classes were not able to play the same crucial role that they had in Western Europe.* They could not strike a "deal" with either king or nobles to guarantee their own rights. Along with the serfs, the urban middle classes were the big losers in Prussian political affairs for the next two centuries. They had to pay the taxes from which the nobles were exempt and their social and political status was much lower than that of the estate-owning **Junkers.**

After Frederick William's death, his son Frederick I and grandson Frederick William I ruled Prussia until 1740. By clever diplomacy in the War of the Spanish Succession, Frederick I was able to raise his rank from prince to the first king of Prussia, while Frederick William I was even more intent than his grandfather on building the finest army in Europe. He was the real founder of Prussia-Germany's military tradition and its deserved reputation as the most efficiently governed state on the Continent.

During the reign of Frederick William I (r. 1713–1740), Prussia was aptly called "an army with a country." Military priorities and military discipline were enforced everywhere in government, and the most talented young men automatically entered state service, rather than going into business or the arts and sciences. The aristocratic bureaucrats were known far and wide as dedicated, honest, hardworking servants of their king, whether in uniform (which they generally preferred) or in civilian clothing. Separate legal codes applied to civilians and military, and the officer corps became the highest social group in the nation.

The series of determined Hohenzollern monarchs culminated in the eighteenth century with Frederick II, the Great (r. 1740–1786), who is generally seen as one of the most talented and effective kings in modern history. A shrewd judge of people and situations, Frederick was cultivated and cynical, daring and calculating. His artistic inclinations as a youth were so strong as to have him defy his father, and toy with the idea of abdicating his rights to the throne. But a sense of duty combined with unlimited ambition to thrust out this romantic notion. As king, Frederick proved to be one of the most effective in an age of outstanding monarchs. His victories in **Silesia** (see the Document in this chapter) and later in the Seven Years' War enabled Prussia to rise into the first rank of European Powers. Under Frederick's rule, the Prussian economy prospered after the close of the Seven Years' conflict and Berlin became a significant capital. The Prussian territorial gains in Western Germany were brought together under the efficient bureaucracy which Frederick continued to develop. The universal adoption of the potato as a staple enabled the population to subsist on the product of the marginal agricultural land of northeast Germany. Frederick II cleverly associated the Prussian monarchy with a reviving sense of national unity. With him began the "German dualism," the contest between Catholic Austria and Protestant Prussia for leadership of the German-speaking people.

✤ THE HABSBURG'S DOMAINS

Prussia's strong rival for eventual political supremacy over the fragmented Germans was Habsburg Austria. Based in the capital of Vienna, the dynasty ruled over three quite different areas: Austria proper, Bohemia (the present-day Czech Republic), and Hungary (see Map 31.2). In addition, the Habsburgs found allies among the south German Catholics, who sympathized with their Austrian cousins and had strong antipathies toward the Prussian Protestants.

The dynasty had acquired Hungary and Bohemia through lucky marriages in the sixteenth century. At that time, much of Hungary was still occupied by the Ottoman Turks (see the next section); it was liberated by Habsburg armies at the end of the seventeenth century. Though a potentially rich agricultural country, Hungary had been laid waste by the Turks during their long occupation. It was now repopulated by Catholic Germans and others and put under the close control of the Vienna government.

Bohemia was even more valuable. It had been severely hurt by the Thirty Years' War, but had scored a quick comeback. Commerce and manufacturing were more developed here than in any other Habsburg dominion. As a center of the arts and commerce, Prague at this juncture was almost as important as Vienna. It was inhabited almost entirely by Germans and Jews, however. The Czechs were still peasants, ruled over by foreign nobles imported by the Catholic emperor as a result of the native nobles' support of the Protestants in the Thirty Years' War.

The Struggle against Turkey

At the end of the seventeenth century, Austria was being threatened on several sides. Against its southern and eastern flanks, the Ottoman Turks were determined to make one more attempt to capture Vienna. In the west, the French monarch Louis XIV was embarking on the War of the Spanish Succession (1700–1715). Louis's object was to make Spain, including its overseas possessions, an integral part of France and thereby make France the decisive power in European affairs.

The Ottomans' attack on Vienna was beaten off in 1683, and the ensuing war against Turkey went well at first

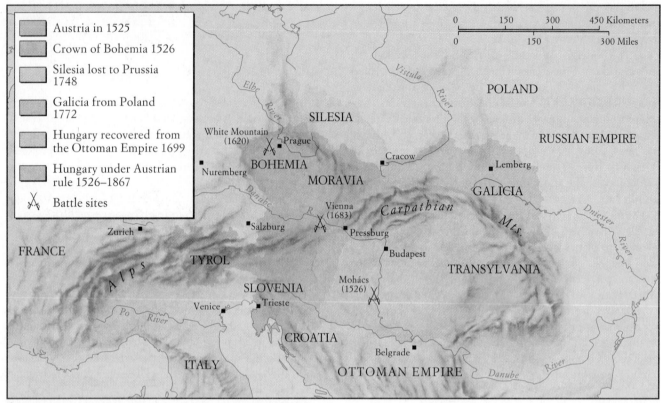

MAP 31.2   The Growth of the Austrian Empire, 1526–1772.

for the Habsburgs. But then it bogged down and allowed the Turks to recoup their strength. The Treaty of Karlowitz in 1699 regained Hungary for the Habsburgs, but did not definitively end the Ottoman menace to Austria. In this conflict, the chief architect of Austrian greatness in the eighteenth century, **Prince Eugen of Savoy,** first won renown. He successfully led the imperial forces against the army of Louis XIV along the Rhine and then returned to the Ottoman front where he won a decisive victory at Belgrade in 1716. From this point on, the Ottomans were almost always on the defensive against the Christian powers opposing them. The threat of a Muslim Turkish invasion of central Europe was eliminated, and Austria under the Habsburgs became a leading power for the first time.

But this new power had a flaw that became apparent with time. Ethnically, the empire of *Austria was the least integrated of all European countries.* It included no fewer than ten different nationalities: Germans, Hungarians, Italians, Croats, Serbs, Slovenes, Poles, Czechs, Slovaks,

and Ukrainians. Most of these peoples were still not nationally conscious and thus were not disturbed at being ruled by nonnatives or being unable to use their native tongues in court proceedings or schools. Nevertheless, as late as the mid-eighteenth century, the Habsburg lands resembled a salad of nations and regions that had little in common except ultimate allegiance to the Habsburg dynasty.

Maria Theresa, the only surviving child of the previous emperor, became the first and only Habsburg female to rule Austria (1740–1780). (see the Biography in this chapter.) She was also the first to introduce some coherence to the Habsburg government. Despite losing Silesia to the Prussians at the outset of her reign, she slowly welded the various provinces and kingdoms into a single entity under a centralized government headquartered in the impressive royal city of Vienna. She and her son *Joseph II* (r. 1780–1790) waged war against the Turks and the Prussians with little success, but did much to modernize the Austrian armed forces and civil bureaucracy. They also made Austria a major force in cultural affairs. Thanks to Russian initiatives (see the next section), Austria even gained some territory from neighboring Poland.

In the nineteenth century, when it gradually became clear that Austria was losing the battle over the future allegiance of the German-speaking people, the Austrians turned east and south to realize their expansionary dreams. In southeastern Europe, they encountered the Turks, who were rapidly sinking into second-level status and would not have been a serious obstacle had they been forced to stand alone. But in the nineteenth century, much of Europe agreed to let the Turks continue to control southeastern Europe (the Balkans), so as to avoid the inevitable conflicts that would ensue if the Turks were pushed aside and replaced by others. Foremost among those contenders were the newly powerful Russians.

❧ RUSSIA UNDER THE TSARS

Russia rose from centuries of oblivion and near-disintegration to attain great power status in the eighteenth century (see Map 31.3). Until the 1200s Russia had been an independent Christian principality based on the city of Kiev, with extensive trading and cultural contacts with both West and Mediterranean Europe through the Baltic and Black Seas. The Russians had been converted to Orthodox Christianity by Greek missionaries in the late 900s and had remained attached to Constantinople in culture and doctrine for the next three centuries.

But in 1241 the fierce, pagan Mongols had conquered the principality of Kiev and settled down to rule the Russians for the next 240 years (see Chapter 27). During that period, Russia's formerly numerous contacts with Europe were almost completely severed or neglected, and the Russians retrogressed culturally. Even their crafts and skills declined. In the sixteenth century, after the Mongols were overthrown, the Kremlin in Moscow was rebuilt in stone rather than wood, but Italian masons had to be brought in because the Russians could no longer handle large-scale projects as they had in the eleventh and twelfth centuries when they built their great churches in Kiev.

In a sense, their governmental institutions also deteriorated as formerly independent Russian princes connived and maneuvered to serve as agents and intermediaries of the Mongol khan, who played them off against each other for almost two centuries. *Moscow,* one of the

● **MAP 31.3   From Muscovy to Russia, 1584–1796.**

Maria Theresa
1717–1780

The only surviving child of Charles VI, the Habsburg emperor of Austria, Maria Theresa was the most remarkable example of an effective female ruler in the history of central Europe. She came to a throne that was visibly shaking on its pedestal and left it at her death one of the most prestigious in Europe. Without any particular philosophy of government or vision of what she wished to achieve, she took a ramshackle collection of territories and gradually molded them into a centrally governed empire. Her major tools were a lively sensitivity to what was possible and what was not and clearheaded determination to improve the moral and material welfare of her subjects.

Born in 1717, she came to the Habsburg throne in Vienna as a young woman of twenty-three and immediately faced a serious threat to her inheritance. Despite having pledged to respect Maria Theresa's right, the bold king of neighboring Prussia, Frederick II, attempted to use a transparent pretext to seize Silesia, the richest of all the Austrian provinces. Like many eighteenth-century statesmen, Frederick (later termed the Great) viewed international affairs as not much different than a general brawl; those who struck first and with the best preparation would win. In this emergency, the young, inexperienced empress resorted to the weapons that she would use repeatedly in the next few years: a direct appeal for aid, combined with a very sharp eye for picking men she could trust to stand by her. All her life she would place loyalty over every other virtue, and it brought her through some difficult and dangerous years.

Austria's major problem in the mid-eighteenth century was that it was only an empire on paper; in reality, Austria was an incoherent heap of kingdoms, duchies, bishoprics, free cities, and other political subdivisions that had practically nothing in common except that all were legally subject to the Habsburg family in Vienna. Before Maria Theresa, other Habsburg regents had attempted to negotiate some uniform arrangement of power sharing between the court and the local authorities. But they had made little progress against the established aristocrats in the provinces who jealously guarded their ancient rights.

After the War of the Austrian Succession (1740–1748), in which she lost Silesia but secured her throne, the empress devoted most of her energies to bringing better order and more efficient controls to the central government. Using her shrewd husband as a chief source of advice, she spent exhausting day-to-day sessions with her councilors working out a more or less rational plan of administration. She was always careful not to push too far or too fast, for the local nobles were just as suspicious of the central government's ambitions as they had been earlier. Over a period of thirty years, she was able to strike the compromises and do the horse trading

---

dozen or so principalities into which Russia was divided after the conquest, came to overshadow its rivals even during the Mongol era.

Shifting alliances between Russians, Mongols, and the briefly potent Lithuanian state on the western borders marked the entire fourteenth century. Taking advantage of a temporary split in the upper rank of the occupying *orda* (horde), one Muscovite prince actually defeated the Mongol cavalry in 1380, but could not follow up his victory. In the fifteenth century the princes of Moscow gained steadily on both their external and Russian rivals. Using every available means from marriages to bribery, the Muscovites brought neighboring principalities under their control as the Mongol grip slowly loosened.

The Mongol Yoke, as the Russians call it, was finally thrown off by bloodless rebellion in 1480. The once fearsome Golden Horde's remnant retired eastward into the Siberian steppe and the Russians re-emerged into European view. The English traders, the German diplomats, and the Greek clerics who now arrived in Moscow, looked upon the Russians as residents of a "rude and barbarous kingdom."

that were necessary to make Austria into a major power.

When all else failed, she was not above trading a bit on the fact that she was a woman in a man's world. She could pretend to feminine "emotionalism" when it served her purposes in a way that her contemporary and rival, Catherine II of Russia, could never bring herself to do. The two were very different in other ways as well. Maria Theresa sought refuge from state affairs in the large family she created with her much-loved Franz (sixteen children!). Her private life was wholly exemplary; a devout Roman Catholic, she became famous in much of Europe for her insistence on creating a Society for the Prevention of Vice that supposedly would watch over the morals of the Viennese. Despite an occasional arrest, the society was soon laughed out of existence.

The most trying years of her life came in her final decade, after she had allowed her oldest son Joseph to become her co-ruler. There was almost constant tension between mother and son in matters both private and public. Joseph had been more or less forced into a second, loveless marriage after the very early death of his adored young wife. As the heir to the throne, he was expected to generate future Habsburgs, but he never quite forgave his mother for insisting on a marriage that never had any chance.

More importantly for Austria, mother and son clashed strongly on governmental matters and on relations between church and state. Joseph II (r. 1780–1790) was a convinced adherent of religious toleration—one of the earliest in the ranks of European monarchs—while his mother believed firmly in the primacy of the Catholic religion for all her subjects. It made little difference to her that many millions of them were members of several other religious denominations. She died knowing that her son and successor was intent on changing many of her most ardently held policies. In the end, many of these changes failed and Joseph died early, a broken man.

■ **Maria Theresa.** This somewhat idealized portrait shows the young queen as she settled into the rigorous routine of government in the 1740s.

In fact, during the 1500s and 1600s few west Europeans gave any thought to Russia or the Russians. Trade relations were eventually established with Britain through the Arctic seas, and later with the Scandinavians and Germans through the Baltic. But beyond some raw materials available elsewhere, and some exotic items such as ermine skins, there seemed little reason to confront the extraordinary challenges involved in trading with this alien society. Militarily and politically it had nothing to offer the West, and whatever technical and cultural progress was made in Russia during these centuries usually stemmed from Western—particularly German and Swedish—sources.

The Russian Tsardom

The Russians were not inclined to welcome Western ideas and visitors except on a highly selective basis. As the Orthodox church had been crucially important in keeping alive national identity during the Yoke, most Russians responded with a fanatical religious Orthodoxy. Their distrust of Western Christians was strong, and it was

■ **A Prospect of St. Petersburg.** The beautiful Neoclassical facades of the government buildings in St. Petersburg were ordained by the eigthteenth-century Russian rulers, notably by Catherine the Great whose winter palace later became the Hermitage art museum.

accentuated by the Pope's failure to prevent the fall of Christian Constantinople to the Turks. The sporadic attempts of both papal and Protestant missionaries to convert the Russian "heretics" contributed, of course, to this distrust and dislike on the Russians' side, while the ill-concealed disdain of the Europeans for their backward hosts in Moscow, Novgorod and other trade markets sharpened native xenophobia (antipathy to foreigners).

The expansion of the Muscovite principality into a major state picked up its pace during the sixteenth century. The brutally effective tsar Ivan IV, the Terrible (r. 1533–1584) encouraged exploration and settlement of the vast and almost unpopulated Siberia, brushing aside the Mongol remnants in a program of conquest which reached the Pacific shores as early as 1639—six thousand miles from Muscovy proper. Soon after, Russia was brought into formal contacts with China for the first time—a fateful meeting and the onset of a difficult relationship along the longest land border in the world.

Culturally, Russia had experienced almost nothing of the Protestant revolt against Rome or the Renaissance, a situation that greatly heightened the differences between it and the rest of Europe. The religious barriers between East and West had become higher and less penetrable. All Russians were Orthodox Christians, united in the belief that Moscow had become the *Third* (and ultimate) *Rome.* They either were ignorant of or rejected the changes Western Christianity had undergone such as the enhanced role of the laity in the church, the emphasis on individual

piety and Bible reading, and the restrictions on the power of the clergy. Protestant doctrines were looked upon either as negligible tamperings with a basically erroneous Roman faith or—worse—Western surrender to the lures of a false rationalism.

Above all, from their Byzantine-inspired beginnings, the Russian clergy had accepted the role of partner of the civil government in maintaining good order on earth. Unlike the papal or Protestant West, the Russian Christian establishment accorded the government full authority over the earthly concerns of the faithful. This tradition had been much strengthened by the church's close support of the Muscovite princes' struggle to free Russia from the Mongols. The high Orthodox clerics saw their role as helper and moral partner of the government in the mutual tasks of saving souls and preserving Russia.

Absolutism in Its Russian Variant

Like the countries of West Europe, Russia adopted a form of divine right monarchy in the seventeenth century. But the tradition of the tsar ruling without consulting his people went much farther back in Russian history and had become part of the accepted political landscape. Already in the sixteenth century, Ivan the Terrible had established a model by persecuting all who dared question his rights. So fearful had been his harassment of his nobles—**boyars**—that many of them abandoned their lands and positions and fled. Those who chose to remain often paid with their lives for nonexistent "treason" or "betrayal." Ivan did not stop with the nobility; he also persecuted the churchmen who dared call attention to his morals or condemned his drunken orgies. He even killed his own son and successor in a blind rage. Whether or not Ivan became clinically paranoid is open to question; mad or not, he bullied and terrified the Russian upper classes in a fashion that would have certainly led to revolt in other countries of the age. But in Russia, no such rebellion occurred.

A *Time of Troubles* in the early seventeenth century threatened the state's existence. The ancient dynasty of Kiev died out, and various nobles vied for the vacant throne. A serf rebellion added to the turmoil, and the Poles and Swedes took advantage of the confusion to invade Russian territory. Nevertheless, recovery under the new **Romanov dynasty** (1613–1917) was fairly rapid. By the middle 1600s, Moscow was pressing the Poles and Swedes back to the Baltic shores and reclaiming some of the huge territories lost to these invaders and to the Ottoman Turks in the far south during the previous fifty years.

Peter I, the Great (r. 1682–1724), is the outstanding example of Russian royal absolutism. There is no question of Peter's sanity; in fact, his foreign policy was one of the shrewdest of his age. But like Ivan IV, he was in no way inclined to share power with any group or institution and believed the fate of the country was solely his to decide. There *were* attempts to rebel against Peter, but they were put down with great cruelty. Nobles and peasants suffered equally at his hands.

Peter was the driving force for an enormously ambitious, partly successful attempt to make Russia into a fully European-style society. He did westernize many Russian public institutions and even the private lives of the upper 2–3 percent of the society. This tiny minority of gentry or noble landowners/officials assisted the tsar in governing his vast country; they were swept up into lifelong service to the state, much against their will. In Peter's scheme, the peasants (five-sixths of the population) were to serve the nobility on their estates and feed the townspeople; the nobles were to serve the government as both military and civil bureaucrats at the beck and call of the tsar; and the tsar, in turn, was the chief servant of the state.

The impact of the human whirlwind called Peter on stolid and conservative Russia is impossible to categorize. He was the first Russian ruler to set foot outside the country and to recognize how primitive Russia was in comparison with the leading countries of West Europe. He brought thousands of foreign specialists, craftsmen, artists, and engineers to Russia on contract to practice their specialties while teaching the Russians. These individuals—many of whom eventually settled in Russia—acted as yeast in the Russian dough and had inordinate influence on the country's progress in the next century.

Peter established a new capital at St. Petersburg to be Russia's long-sought "window on the west," through which all sorts of Western ideas and values might flow. He began the slow, state-guided modernization of what had been a very backward economy; he built a navy and made Russia a maritime power for the first time; he also

■ **The Belvedere in Vienna.** This palace was built by and for Prince Eugene of Savoy, greatest of the Habsburg generals in the wars of the late seventeenth and early eighteenth centuries. It is an example of Austrian baroque architecture.

■ **Peter the Great.** The great reformer/modernizer of backward Russia, painted in the middle years of his reign, 1682–1724. In the background, the Russian navy which the tsar created, and St. Petersburg, his new capital on the Baltic sea.

■ Peter's many domestic opponents saw him as an atheistic upstart and vandalizer of all that the conservative Russians held sacred. Here, Peter clips the beard of a dignified nobel who has refused to pay the tax on beards which the Tsar imposed in his modern evasion drive.

encouraged such cultural breakthroughs as the first newspaper, the first learned journal, the Academy of Sciences, and the first technical schools.

But Peter also made *Russian serfdom even more rigid and more comprehensive;* he used his modernized, professional army not only against foreign enemies in his constant wars, but also against his own peasant rebels. He discouraged any independent political activity and made the Orthodox clergy into mere agents of the civil government under a secular head. His cruelty bordered on sadism, and his personal life was filled with excess. His legacy to later Russia was a very mixed bag of good and bad concepts and practices. Perhaps, as he himself said, it was impossible to avoid every evil in a country as difficult to govern as Russia. He remains *the watershed figure of Russia's long history.*

✣ TWO EASTERN POWERS IN ECLIPSE
Poland

The Polish kingdom had come into existence in the 900s under native Slavic princes who converted to Western Christianity. Under pressure from Germans pushing eastward, the Poles expanded into Lithuanian and Russian/ Ukrainian territory between the twelfth and the sixteenth centuries. In the 1500s Poland reached from the Baltic to the Black Sea, making it easily the largest European state west of Russia. It shared in the West European Christian culture in every way, while rejecting and condemning the Orthodox culture of the Russians. The Polish nobles were numerous and powerful, and they had instituted a system of serfdom over their Polish and non-Polish subjects that was as oppressive as any in the world.

In the 1500s the native dynasty died out, and the Polish nobles successfully pressed for an *elective monarchy* that would give them decisive powers. From then on, the succession to the Polish throne was a type of international auction; whoever promised the most to the noble voters was the winner. As a result, centralized and effective government on a national scale ceased to exist; Poland became a series of petty feudal fiefdoms headed by the great magnate, i.e., large landholder families.

Under the famous *Liberum veto*—perhaps the most absurd technique for governance ever devised—a single individual could veto any proposed legislation of the *sejm* (parliament of nobles). Poland was truly what its proud motto asserted: a "republic of aristocrats." No one else counted; the urban middle classes lost all influence on national policy, and the peasantry had never had any. The king, often a foreigner who had no roots whatever among the Poles, had to be content with being a figurehead, or he could not attain the post in the first place. The clergy was a noble domain. In the 1600 and 1700s, Poland resembled a feudal monarchy of West Europe five centuries earlier. Even the royal army ceased to exist, and the nation's defense was put into the very unstable hands of the noble "confederations," that is, the local magnates and their clients.

This situation was too tempting to Poland's neighbors to be allowed to continue. In the seventeenth century, the kingdom was seriously weakened by rebellions among the Ukrainian peasants and invasions by the Swedes. A long war against the Muscovites for control of the lower stretches of the important Dnieper waterway to the Black Sea had resulted in a decisive defeat. And the Turks had seized and kept the area along the Black Sea coast that had formerly been under Polish sovereignty.

In 1772, the Russian empress Catherine II decided that a favorable moment had arrived to "solve" the problem of a weakening Poland on Russia's western borders. Coordinating her plans with Frederick II of Prussia and Maria Theresa of Austria, she found a transparent pretext to demand Polish subordination. When the nobles attempted resistance, the upshot was the *First Partition,* whereby about a third of Poland was annexed to the three conspirators' lands. The tremendous shock at last awakened a reform party among the aristocrats in Warsaw. Further impetus to reform was provided by the example of the American Revolution and its constitutional aftermath in the 1780s. In 1791, simultaneous with the French Revolution's first constitution but entirely separate in its origins, the nobility produced a remarkably liberal, forward-looking document for future Polish government. Serfdom was abolished, and many other significant reforms were enacted.

Catherine used this "unauthorized" constitution as a pretext for renewed armed intervention. Striking a bar-

■ **The First Partition of Poland.**

gain with an originally reluctant Prussia (but not with Austria), in 1793 the Russian monarch executed the *Second Partition,* which took another very large slice for Russia and Prussia. The Poles in desperation then rebelled in an uprising led by the same Thaddeus Kosciusko who had assisted General George Washington a few years earlier. After a brave fight, the rebels were crushed, and *Poland disappeared from the map* in the ensuing Third Partition of 1795 (Russia, Prussia, Austria).

The Russian tsardom thereby gained another ten million or so inhabitants and a very considerable extension to the west. But the Polish acquisition was to be a costly one in the longer run. Napoleon would capitalize on the Poles' deep resentment to create a satellite duchy, which he used as a launching pad for his invasion of Russia five years later in 1812. The Prussians and Austrians had somewhat more amicable relations with their Poles, but were never able to integrate them effectively.

Throughout the nineteenth century, Polish patriots in and outside the country constantly reminded the world that a previously unthinkable event had happened: an established nation had been swallowed up by its greedy neighbors. Two major uprisings (1831, 1863–1864) were attempted against foreign rule. Finally, in the waning days of World War I, the revolution in Russia and the defeat of the Germans and Austrians allowed the Polish state to be re-created.

Turkey

The other unsuccessful empire in east Europe was Ottoman Turkey. The Turks had invaded the Balkans in the later 1300s and gradually expanded their territory north, west, and east through the later 1500s. After a period of equilibrium of power, they began to lose ground. The decisive turning point came in 1683, at the second siege of Vienna when the Ottoman attackers were beaten off with heavy loss. The surrender of Hungary and Transylvania ensued in the 1690s. At this point, Russia joined with Austria to counter the Turks throughout the eighteenth century, and the fortunes of the Ottomans came to depend on how well the two Christian empires were able to coordinate their policies and armies. When they were in harmony, the Turks were consistently pushed back; but when, as often, the two powers were pursuing different aims, the Turks were able to hold their own.

From 1790 on, the Austrians feared Russian territorial ambitions more than Turkish assault, and ceased to make war on the Ottomans. But in the nineteenth century, the Turks had weakened sufficiently that they were repeatedly defeated by the Russians acting alone. Finally, all the other great powers stepped in to restrain Russia and support the sultan's government in its feeble attempts to modernize and survive.

Why was the Ottoman government unable to adapt effectively to the demands of a modern state and civil society? Certainly, a basic problem was the inability of the Ottoman ruling philosophy or "political science" to devise an effective substitute for military conquest as the reason for government to exist. Thus, when military conquest was no longer easily possible against the Europeans (roughly about 1600), the government no longer commanded the respect and moral authority it had enjoyed earlier.

Furthermore, the entire tradition of the Ottoman state and its governors emphasized the crucial importance of religion as the foundation stone of public life and public institutions. Islam was never intended to be a matter of conscience. This attitude—which grew stronger rather than weaker as time passed—meant that a large part of the population was always excluded from consideration as a creative or constructive force. In southeastern Europe, 80 to 90 percent of the native populace remained Christian everywhere except Bosnia. These were the *raja,* the barely human who were destined to serve and enrich the Islamic ruling minority. A modern society could not be created on such a basis.

In addition, the bureaucracy and military, which had originally served the sultan faithfully and effectively in the conquered lands, became corrupt and self-seeking as time passed. Foremost were the **Janissaries,** the professional soldiers who gradually became a kind of parallel officialdom in East Europe, rivaling and often ignoring the Istanbul appointees in day-to-day government. The Janissaries also blocked every effort to modernize the armed forces of the sultan after 1700 because the changes would have threatened their privileges. For example, they resisted the introduction of modern field artillery drawn by horses because their tradition was to employ heavy siege guns, which could only be moved very slowly and were meant to be used only against immobile targets. The Turks were therefore consistently outgunned in battles in the open field after about 1700 and suffered heavy casualties before they could engage the enemy. The Janissaries' corruption and greed in dealing with their Christian subjects and serfs triggered several rebellions in the Balkans in the eighteenth and nineteenth centuries. Too entrenched to be disciplined by the central government, the Janissaries were finally eliminated by massacre in Istanbul in the 1830s.

Finally, the Ottomans as an economic entity were weakened by corrupt local governors who withheld taxes from the central government and so oppressed their non-Muslim subjects that they rebelled and/or failed to produce. The local officials could justify their failure to forward tax money to Istanbul by claiming that it was needed to combat rebellion or to supervise an increasingly restive subject population. In many parts of the Balkans, the Christian peasants habitually went "into the hills" to evade the Muslim landlords, and this, of course, further reduced the tax funds collected. Banditry was widespread; in some of the more backward areas such as Montenegro, it became a profession. So long as most of the victims were Muslims, supposedly no social stigma attached to it.

For all these reasons, the Ottomans were destined to fall behind their European enemies and were unable to catch up despite sporadic reform attempts by the sultans and grand viziers. The government's problem was not that it was ignorant of what was happening in its domains but that it was unable to correct the situation. In the end, this inability condemned the government in Istanbul to a slow death.

Summary

The East European dynasties were able to grow and foil the occasional efforts to restrict their royal powers because neither of the two major counterforces, the peasant majority and the noble minority, had either the political sophistication or the desire to substitute themselves for the king. Outside Prussia, the townpeople were both too few and too alien (Jews, Turks, Germans) to assert themselves, while the clergy were mainly a part of the machinery of government rather than an autonomous moral force. These factors, while true everywhere to some extent, were particularly noteworthy in the Orthodox lands.

The rise of the Prussian kingdom began in earnest in the mid-1600s when the Great Elector cleverly made his petty state into a factor in the Thirty Years' War, while subordinating the nobility to a centralized government. The Elector's policies culminated in the reign of his great-grandson Frederick II (1740–1786). At this juncture Prussia emerged as a major European power.

The Habsburgs of Austria took a different path. Through fortunate marriage alliances, they gradually created a large empire based on Bohemia and Hungary as well as Austria proper. The weaknesses of this state were partially addressed by the efforts of Empress Maria Theresa (1740–1780), who brought a degree of centralization and uniformity to the government. But the ethnic diversity of the population was to eventually prove fatal to the prospects of the Habsburgs to become the rulers of a united German state.

The turning point in the Russian tsardom's rise to international prestige was the reign of Peter I, the Great. After an obstacle-filled climb from obscurity under the Mongols, the Muscovite principality "gathered the Russian lands" in the 1500s and began to expand eastward. Its Polish, Turkish, and Swedish rivals in the west were gradually overcome in the next two centuries by Peter and Catherine II, the Great. The Russian nobility, once all-powerful, were reduced by the late 1700s to mere servants of the imperial throne. As in Prussia, this collaboration of throne and noble had been secured by giving the estate-owning nobility full powers over the unfortunate serfs and the insignificant townspeople.

Two other would-be great powers in the East had been either swallowed up by their neighbors or reduced to impotence by the late eighteenth century. Poland was made to disappear as a sovereign state by the partitions, and the Ottomans were checked and weakened by both internal and external factors so as to become a negligible factor in European affairs.

Test Your Knowledge

1. Maria Theresa's major achievement for Austria was
   a. to conquer more territories from the Turks.
   b. to bring order into the workings of government.
   c. to defeat the claims of the Prussians to Austrian lands.
   d. to clean up the corruption in society.
2. East of the Elbe, the feudal landlords
   a. maintained or increased their local powers and prestige.
   b. regularly overthrew the royal governments.
   c. suffered a general decline economically.
   d. practically became extinct with the rise of urban life.
3. Which of the following did the Great Elector in Prussia *not* do?
   a. He made a tacit alliance with the landlord-nobles.
   b. He ensured the political and social prestige of the peasants.
   c. He greatly increased the financial resources of the government.
   d. He began the tradition of noble military and civil service to the government.
4. The most valuable province in the Habsburg domains in the eighteenth century was
   a. Hungary.
   b. Austria.
   c. Slovenia.
   d. Silesia.
5. A great difference between Ivan IV, the Terrible, and Peter I, the Great, is

a. the savagery of the first and subtlety of the second.
b. the minimal successes of Ivan and the tremendous ones of Peter.
c. the tender consideration shown to the nobles by Peter.
d. the degree of foreign models and influences apparent in each tsar's policy making.

6. The most striking difference between the absolutist governments in East and West was
   a. the degree of local powers retained by the townspeople.
   b. the ability of the peasants to express their political opinions to the central government.
   c. the coordination of the policies of the official church and the government.
   d. the degree to which constitutions restrained them in their policies.

7. Which of the following was the *least successful* at changing his country's traditions and laws?
   a. Joseph II of Austria
   b. Peter I of Russia
   c. Frederick William, elector of Prussia
   d. Maria Theresa of Austria
8. The foundation of Frederick William's success in establishing strong royal government in Prussia was
   a. his ability to intimidate the rebellious nobles into submission.
   b. his success at waging war against the rebel peasants.
   c. his ability to bribe his enemies.
   d. his tacit bargain with his nobles.

Identification Terms

Bohemia
boyar
Great Elector (Frederick William)
Habsburg dynasty
Janissaries
Junker
Prince Eugen
Romanos
Silesia
War of the Austrian Succession

Bibliography

Artz, F. *From the Renaissance to Romanticism,* 1962. An excellent brief survey of the formal culture of the Europeans in the sixteenth and seventeenth centuries, East and West.

Blum, J. *Lord and Peasant in Russia from the Ninth to the Nineteenth Century,* 1961. The best available survey of Russian serfdom down to its abolition.

Carsten, F. W. *Origins of Prussia,* 1954. Discusses how the Great Elector created a state from a collection of territories.

Coles, P. *The Ottoman Impact on Europe, 1350–1699,* 1968. Tells how the Turks terrified much of Europe for centuries until they lost their military edge.

Evans, R. J. W. *The Making of the Habsburg Monarchy, 1550–1700,* 1982. A detailed summary of how this dynasty flourished and expanded its power.

Kann, R. A., and Z. David. *The Peoples of the Eastern Habsburg Lands, 1526–1918,* 1984. A unique overview of the history of the nationalities and regions comprising the Austrian empire's eastern half.

Massie, R. *Peter the Great,* 1980. A first-rate popular biography that later served as the basis for a TV series seen around the world. Long, but constantly interesting.

McKay, D., and H. Scott. *The Rise of the Great Powers, 1648–1815,* 1983. A general account with much attention to the three great eastern empires.

P. Avrich: *Russian Rebels 1600–1800,* 1972. Just what it sounds like, focusing on the Razin and Pugachev revolts.

Stoye, J. *The Siege of Vienna,* 1964. Gives much insight into why the Turks never recovered from the failed siege of 1683.

Sumner, B. H. *Peter the Great and the Emergence of Russia,* 1962. Good though somewhat outdated in his estimate of the great ruler's impact on his people.

Wandruszka, A. *The House of Habsburg,* 1964. A sympathetic but still reliable survey of this dynasty in its long history.

THE SCIENTIFIC REVOLUTION AND ITS ENLIGHTENED AFTERMATH

The most far-reaching of all the "revolutions" since the agricultural revolution in the Neolithic Age was the change in educated persons' thinking about Nature and its components during the early modern era. This Scientific Revolution became fully evident in the work of the *philosophes,* but its major outlines were drawn earlier, when the focus of European intellectual work gradually shifted away from theology to the mathematical sciences. By the end of the eighteenth century, it had proceeded so far among the educated classes that the new worldview was taken for granted. While the consolidation of royal absolutism was proceeding in most of Europe during the seventeenth and eighteenth centuries, theology's claim to be the summit of intellectual activity had been successfully challenged by the sciences.

✤ THE SCIENTIFIC REVOLUTION OF THE SEVENTEENTH CENTURY

So great were the achievements in science during this epoch that one of the outstanding philosophers of the Modern Age has said that "... the two centuries [that followed] have been living upon the accumulated capital of ideas provided for them by the genius of the 17th century." The natural sciences, that is, those based primarily on observed phenomena of Nature, experienced a huge upswing in importance and accuracy during the seventeenth century. A new style of examining phenomena, the **scientific method,** came into common usage. It was composed of two elements: *careful observation and systematic experimentation* based on that observation. Interpretation of the results of the experiments, largely relying on mathematical measurement, was the final step in achieving new knowledge.

The most significant advances in the sciences came from posing new types of questions, rather than from new data. Different questions led directly to novel avenues of investigation, and those led to new data being observed and experimented with. For example, **René Descartes** (1596–1650), one of the founders of the mathematical style of investigation, wished to take humanity to a higher plane of perfection than ever yet achieved. To do so, he separated the material from the nonmaterial universe completely, insisting that the material world could be comprehended by mathematical formulas that existed entirely apart from the human mind. If that was so, knowledge of these broad laws of number and quantity could provide explanations—hitherto lacking—of observed phenomena. The proper way to understand the material world, then, was to formulate broad generalizations of a mathematical nature and employ these to explain specific events or processes. This approach, in which one went from a general law to a particular example of that law observed by the human mind, was called the **deductive method of reasoning.**

The other method of accumulating knowledge about the natural world was exemplified in the writings of the Englishman *Francis Bacon* (1561–1626). Bacon insisted that contrary to traditional belief, the great majority of the ideas and principles that explain Nature had not yet been discovered or developed, but lay buried, like so many gems under the earth, awaiting uncovering. Like Descartes, he looked forward to a better world, but this world was to be created by the persistent and careful observation of phenomena *without* any preconceived "laws" or general explanations of them, a process that became known as inductive reasoning.

Bacon was not methodical in his science or his reasoning. He was what would now be called a gifted amateur. His close association with the concept of **inductive reasoning** is not really deserved. But his writings did encourage later scientists to practice the **empirical method** of gathering data and forming generalizations. *Empirical* means the evidence obtained by observation through the five senses, which is then worked up into hypotheses (assumptions) that may be subjected to experiment. This Baconian style of assembling knowledge blossomed in the seventeenth century and later became the normal fashion of proceeding in all the sciences.

Background of the Scientific Revolution: Medieval and Renaissance Scholarship

There is no easy answer to why the spectacular advances in natural science occurred in the seventeenth century rather than earlier or later. As with most important changes in the status quo, several factors both material and immaterial came together at that time to encourage more rapid progress than before. But this is not to say that no progress had been under way previously. It is now accepted that the old view of medieval science as a laughable collection of superstitions and crackpot experiments is quite wrong. The medieval universities harbored many people who seriously undertook to widen the horizons of knowledge and had some success in doing so. The long search for magical elements to convert base metal into gold, for instance, did much to found the

science of chemistry. The belief in a potent "touchstone" through which the hidden qualities of a substance would be revealed is another example.

The real problem of medieval and Renaissance science seems to have been its exaggerated reliance on authority, rather than empirical evidence. The great Greek philosophers of science—Aristotle, Ptolemy, Galen, Eratosthenes, and Archimides—were held in excessive reverence as the givers of final truth. The weakening of this reverence for, or intimidation by, the ancients made possible the breakthroughs of the sixteenth and seventeenth centuries.

Aided by the reports of the explorers and voyagers in the New World, scholars accumulated a mass of evidence about Nature and geography that could be ignored only at the risk of retarding the power and wealth of the whole society. Another mass of evidence that partly contradicted what the Greeks had believed was the product of the new instruments. Still more important, perhaps, was the rapid advance in the mathematical capabilities of Europeans. At the beginning of the sixteenth century, European math was still at the same level as in the seventh century; only with the recovery of the Greek and Hellenistic mathematical works could it advance into new areas: *logarithms, calculus,* and *decimals.* By the middle of the seventeenth century, math had become as much a device for theoretical exploration as for counting.

The new math made possible analyses of the physical world that had never before been attempted. It was now possible to measure, weigh, divide, and synthesize the world in ways that seemed to explain the previously inexplicable. New instruments of all sorts (sensitive scales, pressure gauges, microscopes, telescopes, thermometers, chronometers) came along one after the other to assist in this analysis.

The Philosophy of Science

Until modern times, the natural sciences were regarded as a branch of philosophy, rather than a separate intellectual exercise. Already in the Renaissance, math and physics were beginning to establish a place in the university curriculum. Their prestige was still relatively low, and they could not rival medicine, law, or theology in attracting students—but they did begin to form their own rules of data and evidence.

The recovery of the Classical Age scientific treatises by the Renaissance scholars (often working from Arabic translations of the Greek and Latin originals) stimulated European curiosity while simultaneously providing a series of new insights into the makeup of the natural

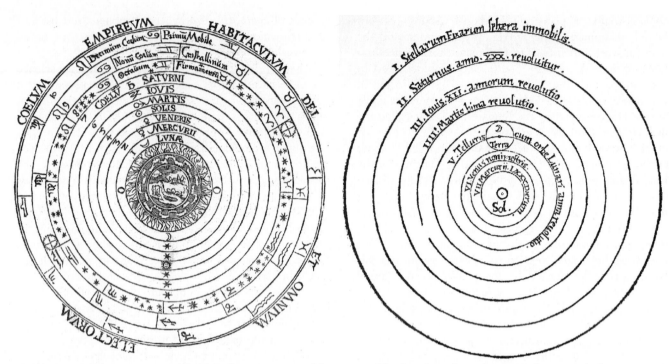

■ **The Two Cosmoses.** Contrasted here are the two visions of the cosmos. The first dates from the sixteenth century before Copernicus' death and shows the geocentric universe. The second is from the first edition of Copernicus' great work and shows the heliocentric universe.

world—insights that contradicted the received knowledge of the medieval philosophers. This progress was sharply interrupted by the wars of religion in the sixteenth century, when the focus shifted away from science to clashing theologies. Only with the exhaustion of those religious antipathies after the Thirty Years' War did scientific endeavors once again become the primary field of intellectual curiosity.

✣ THE PROGRESS OF SCIENTIFIC KNOWLEDGE: COPERNICUS TO NEWTON

Our emphasis on seventeenth-century events does not mean that modern science commenced then. The first solid theoretical advance in knowledge of the natural world came earlier with the *Revolution of the Heavenly Bodies,* the pioneering treatise on astronomy by the Polish scholar *Nicholas Copernicus* (1473–1543). Copernicus cast severe doubt on the generally accepted theory of an earth-centered (**geocentric**) universe, which he criticized as extremely complex and difficult to understand. Copernicus's observations led him to conclude that the earth revolved around a fixed sun, a belief first advanced by

Hellenistic Greek astronomers. A cautious and devout man, Copernicus published his conclusions only in the year of his death. The church ignored his theory at first, though it was ridiculed by both Luther and Calvin. But when **heliocentrism** began to win adherents in large numbers, both Rome and the Protestants officially condemned it as contrary to both Scripture and common sense.

Two astronomer-mathematicians who emerged a generation after Copernicus also deserve our attention. The first was an eccentric Dane, *Tycho Brahe* (1546–1601), who spent much of his life taking endless, precise measurements of the rotation of the visible planets. Using these data, Tycho's student, the German *Johannes Kepler,* (1571–1630), went on to formulate the *three laws of celestial mechanics,* which showed that the heavenly bodies moved in great ellipses (ovals) around the sun, rather than in the perfect circles that had been believed necessary as the handiwork of a perfect Creator. This insight explained what had been previously inexplicable, and made Copernicus's proposals still more persuasive.

In the early 1600s, an Italian professor at Pisa named *Galileo Galilei* (1564–1642) used his new invention of the telescope to rewrite the rules of cosmology as handed down from the ancients. His discoveries strongly supported Copernicus's suppositions that the universe was indeed sun centered and that the *earth was a relatively small, insignificant planet in a huge solar system.* Not only did Galileo's astronomy force a reconsideration of the condemned theory of Copernicus, but his physics contributed to the final overthrow of Aristotle's long reign as master physicist. Through his work with falling bodies and the laws of motion, Galileo came close to discovering the fundamental law of all Nature: the law of gravity. When he died in 1642, the whole traditional view of the physical universe as an impenetrable mystery, created by God for his own reasons and not responsive to human inquiries was beginning to come apart.

Aided by new instruments like Galileo's telescope and by the frequent discovery of new laws in the natural course of things, European thinkers and experimenters were in the midst of revolutionary changes. The horizons that had been in place for many centuries were steadily receding as the seventeenth century progressed. What was still needed was some overarching explanation of the physical world order, which was now being revealed as though through a semitransparent curtain.

The genius of *Isaac Newton* (1642–1727) put the capstone of the new science in place (see the Biography in this chapter). While still a student at Cambridge University, he theorized that there must be a "master key" to the edifice of the universe. In the century and a quarter since Copernicus, a great deal had been discovered or strongly indicated about the laws of Nature. Still lacking, however, was a universally applicable explanation of the most basic property of matter: movement. In the 1660s Newton occupied himself with the study of physics. At that time he evolved his deceptively simple-looking theorem, the most famous in the history of the world: $E = M^2/D.^2$ This was the formula of the law of gravitation, although it lacked mathematical proof. After many more years of research, Newton published his conclusions and their proofs in the *Principia Mathematica* in 1687. The *Principia* was the most influential book on science in the seventeenth century and was soon known from one end of educated Europe to the other.

Newton created a new universe. He saw the physical cosmos as a sort of gigantic clockwork in which every part had its particular role to play and every movement and every change were eventually explained by the operation of law. It was humans' proud duty and privilege to identify those laws and in so doing to penetrate to the heart of the God-created universe.

⚜ RELIGION AND SCIENCE IN THE SEVENTEENTH CENTURY

We have mentioned the churches' condemnation of the teachings of Copernicus and Galileo. Both Catholic and Protestant preachers felt that relegating the earth to a secondary, dependent position in the universe was at least an implied rejection of Holy Scripture (the Old Testament story about the sun standing still at the battle of Jericho, for example). It also downgraded the jewel of God's creation, human beings, who lived on earth and were limited to it. Galileo was threatened with imprisonment if he did not retract parts of what he had published in one of his books on science. He spent his final years under house arrest by order of the pope.

The Roman Catholic church enforced strict censorship through the **Inquisition,** and the Calvinists were not far behind in the areas where they ruled. None of the established churches thought that mere humans should be encouraged to attempt to figure out the rules of God's universe by themselves; to do so was arrogant and presumptuous and was therefore forbidden by every means available to the clergy through the civil powers.

Yet most of the seventeenth-century scientists considered themselves good Christians and made no attempt to rule a divine being out of the universe. Newton himself spent most of his later life in religious speculations and obscure theological inquiries. He was a good Anglican believer until his death. Descartes was a Catholic who saw no conflict between what he taught about the nature of the material world and what he purported to believe about the spiritual one. Quite to the contrary, Descartes, like many scientists, believed that his speculations only pointed more clearly to the existence of a divine intelligence in the universe.

Most ordinary people were unmoved by the revelations of science. The peasants never heard of them, and even urban dwellers were ignorant of them except for the privileged few whose education went beyond the three Rs. The fourth R, religion, generally retained the strong grip upon the daily lives of common folk that it had always had.

But the organized churches and their various doctrines now had a growing rival in the universal search for a persuasive explanation about what human beings could and should know. The church's truth, resting as it did on revelation rather than empirical data, was being challenged—at first only tangentially, but later more and more confrontationally—by the truth of science. And science's truth had potent appeal for human beings weary of the strife of theologians and the claims of priests and pastors. Science's truth had no axes to grind for one party or another. It was not linked to politics or to a social group's advantage or disadvantage. It was self-evident and could sometimes be used to benefit the ordinary person, for example, through technology (though the connections between science and technology were as yet almost entirely undeveloped).

Increasingly, educated people were beginning to wonder whether it was indeed more useful to know whether the Holy Eucharist should be given in two forms than to know how digestion takes place in the stomach or some similar aspect of the new physical science. *Science came to be seen as an alternative to theology* in finding useful knowledge and applying it to society's multiple problems.

In this regard, two of the most important thinkers of the seventeenth century were the Dutch Jew Baruch Spinoza and the devout Catholic Frenchman Blaise Pascal. Spinoza was a great questioner, who after leaving Judaism finally found some measure of peace by perceiving his God in all creation— *pantheism.* His rejection of a personal deity earned him a great deal of trouble, but his thought influenced generations. Pascal wrote his *Pensées (Thoughts)* to calm a troubled mind and produced a work that has ever since been considered one of the greatest of Christian consolations. The fact that Pascal was highly suspect to the French clerical establishment only added to his later fame. His boldness of mind and readiness to challenge any forces to get to the truth were much admired in his own time and even more later.

The Science of Man

The shift in focus from theology to natural science had another, later phase. As the mathematics-based sciences came to be accepted as the sources of much previously unknown truth, the previous relation between natural science and philosophy underwent a gradual but decisive reversal. Philosophy, which had been the more inclusive term, encompassing science itself, now became for many merely a branch of science. Insomuch as an object of thought could not be measured and weighed, it ceased to be worthy of close attention. Such individuals held that *only* what could be determined in its existence by the tools of science was reachable by the intellect and useful to humans. They did not deny that other phenomena that were not reachable by intellectual means existed, but they insisted that these phenomena should have only a secondary place in the hierarchy of values.

Among those phenomena, of course, were religious belief, artistic creativity, wonder, imagination, ethics, and political theory, to mention only a few. None of these could be measured, and none could be brought under uniform and predictable laws. Or could they? In the seventeenth century, a body of thought gradually arose that said these phenomena, too, might be subject to law, analyzable through mathematical computations, and comprehensible in the same as physics. The *Science of Man,* not as an anatomical construct or an example of biological systems, but as a thinker, political actor, and artist, began to form. By the early eighteenth century, this science—which we now call social science—was competing with physical science for the attention of the educated classes.

⚜ THE ENLIGHTENMENT

Following the Scientific Revolution, educated persons' attitudes about the possibilities of human life underwent a kind of sea change. Eighteenth-century intellectual leaders saw no reason why what had been done in the natural sciences could not be attempted in the social and intellectual sciences. They wanted to put history, politics, jurisprudence, and economics under the same logical lenses that had been applied to math and physics. Instead of the sciences being considered branches of philosophy (as had been true since the ancient Greeks), philosophy itself was reduced to a science, as we have already seen. Collectively, these axioms and attitudes laid the groundwork for the so-called *Enlightenment of the eighteenth century.*

Above all, the eighteenth century in Western Europe was distinguished from what had come before by the attitudes that educated persons exhibited about the affairs of everyday life: the atmosphere of their mental life. Two key characteristics marked the Enlightenment: *optimism* and *rationality.* Here optimism refers to the belief that change is possible and controllable in society at large, while rationality refers to the idea that the universe and all creatures within it, especially humans themselves, are comprehensible, predictable, and lawful.

The commitment to a rational view of the universe usually embraced a similar commitment to *secularism,* that is, a downgrading or outright rejection of the importance of supernatural religion. The Enlightenment preferred to see humans as a being capable of creating its own moral code for its own benefit and in accord with the precepts of a rational mind.

■ **The Establishment of the French Academy of Sciences and the Observatory.** Louis XIV sits in the center as the scientists who depend on his support for their work scramble around him to display their achievements.

One might best describe the mind-set of the educated eighteenth-century European (or North American) as the product of the achievements of physical science transferred to the social sphere. In other words, the ways of viewing the world that math and physics had introduced were now applied to the world's social, political, and moral aspects. If physicists could measure the weight of the earth's atmosphere (as indeed they could), then why couldn't historians isolate the exact causes of cultural retardation and determine how to avoid them in the future? Why couldn't criminologists build a model prison and establish a regime there that would turn out completely rehabilitated prisoners? Why couldn't political scientists calibrate various methods of selecting public officials to ensure that only the best were elected?

Formative Figures and Basic Ideas

The two outstanding fathers of the Enlightenment's ideals were the Englishmen *Isaac Newton* and *John Locke.* As we have already seen, Newton was the greatest scientific mind of his age, and Locke was the leading mapper of the political path that England embarked upon with the Glorious Revolution of 1688 (see Chapter 30).

Newton's greatest contribution to science—even more important than the law of gravity—was his insistence on rational, lawful principles in physical Nature. He rejected supernatural causes as an explanation of the natural world; because Nature is rational, human society as part of Nature should be rational in its organization and function.

Locke was as much a psychologist as a political scientist; he set forth his view of the mind in the immensely influential **Essay concerning Human Understanding** (1690). Here he said that the mind is a blank page until experience writes upon it and molds it. Thus, human nature is dynamic and unfixed; it will be formed by controlled external experience. Humans are *not* condemned to repeat endlessly the mistakes of the past. They can and indeed must take charge of their destiny; they can perfect themselves.

More than anything else, this faith in *perfectibility* is the distinguishing innovation of the Enlightenment. For the previous seventeen centuries, the Christian idea of guilt from the sin of Adam as an insuperable barrier to human perfection had been the foundation stone of Western moral philosophy. Now, the eighteenth century proposed to move the house off this foundation and erect it anew. *Progress,* both moral and physical, was reachable and real. The study of history showed how far humans had come and how far they still had to go. The past was filled with error and blindness, but it could be—*must* be—learned from, so that it could light the way to a better future. Thus, the purpose of studying the past history was only to avoid prior mistakes. Looking at the past because of its intrinsic interest was pointless, for it was a tale of error and horror that should never be repeated.

The reformers of the eighteenth century believed that *religion* was generally controlled by those who profited from the continuance of ignorance and was everywhere used as a tool for obscuring the truth. The reformers took an especially harsh view of the Roman Catholic clergy.

Isaac Newton
1642–1727

The man many consider the most distinguished scientist of all history, Sir Isaac Newton, was born on Christmas Day, 1642, in Lancashire, England. Best recognized as the discoverer of the law of gravity, Newton in his own day was equally famed for his work in optics, higher mathematics, and physics. He was a distinct exception to the rule that pioneers are not appreciated in their own countries; his career as both a Cambridge professor and government official under William and Mary was brilliant and adequately rewarded.

Although his father was a farmer with little property, Newton received a fine education. He completed the local grammar school at Grantham, near his home village, with the aid and encouragement of the Anglican vicar, who was a graduate of Cambridge. With this gentleman's recommendation, Isaac won a scholarship to the university in 1661, graduating in 1665 with what would now be called a major in natural science. He wished to go on for the M.A. degree at once, but an outbreak of plague forced the university to close in both 1666 and 1667, and Newton returned home.

During these years at home, the great, groundbreaking work was basically outlined in Newton's mind. The notion that all physical being was, so to speak, tied together by a single principle—that of gravity—took shape in the twenty-five-year old's long studies at his family home in Woolsthorpe. He gradually refined and expanded his theory when he returned to Cambridge, first as an M.A. candidate, then as a professor in 1669. He held this post until his honor-filled retirement in 1701. Although Newton apparently regarded gravitation as a fact as early as the 1660s, he hesitated in publishing his work until 1687. In that year, his *Principia Mathematica,* or *Mathematical Principles of Natural Philosophy,* was finally published in London and soon afterward in most of the capitals of Europe. Rarely has a scientific book been hailed so universally as a work of genius. At the same time, Newton was bringing out fundamentally important work on the spectrum, proving that light was composed of colored particles. His theory remained unchallenged until the wave theory of light transmission was developed in the nineteenth century. Newton is also generally credited

Where the church had obtained a monopolistic position in the state and was the official church, the reformers believed that inevitable corruption had made it a parasite that should be cast off as soon as possible and replaced with freedom of conscience.

In the reformers' view, *education* was the salvation of humankind. It should be promoted at every opportunity everywhere. Insofar as people were educated, they were good. The educated would be unerring seekers of the best that life held, defenders of the helpless, teachers of the misguided, and the consolation of the oppressed.

✤ THE PHILOSOPHES AND THEIR INTERRELATIONS

The Enlightenment was a view of life, a philosophy, and that meant it must have its philosophers. They are generi-

cally known by the French term *philosophes* and included men and women of both thought and action, scientists and philosophers, who were committed to the cause of reform. Despite their intense personal differences, they were united in their desire for progress, by which they meant controlled changes.

Several of the outstanding philosophes were French. Paris, and secondarily London, was the center of the Enlightenment's activities (the Enlightenment was a decidedly urban phenomenon), but the philosophes kept in frequent touch with one another through a network of clubs and correspondents that covered the map of Europe (see Map 32.1). They included the Frenchmen Voltaire (François-Marie Arouet), Baron Montesquieu, Denis Diderot, and Jean-Jacques Rousseau; the English and Scots David Hume, Adam Smith, and Samuel Johnson; the Germans Josef von Sonnenfels, Gotthold Lessing, and

with being the co-discoverer of the calculus, along with his rival Gottfried Leibniz. The two men were working quite independently, and their quarrel over who was first became one of the Scientific Revolution's less appetizing anecdotes.

Newton was at least as interested in alchemy as in physics and optics. He thought that fundamental truths about the nature of the universe could be obtained through alchemy, a belief widely shared at the time in educated circles. A century later, the modern science of chemistry emerged from such experiments.

In his later years, Newton's dedication to Old Testament studies and theology surpassed his scientific interests. Newton was a master of Greek and Hebrew and spent much energy on his researches into the Old Testament prophecies.

Highly placed friends in the government of William and Mary secured his appointment as warden of the royal mint in 1696, a lucrative post that Newton was very grateful to have. In 1703 he was elected president of the Royal Society, the premier scientific post in England, and was reelected every year thereafter until his death. In 1705 the queen knighted Sir Isaac for services to his country as well as to the realm of science. At eighty-five years of age, Newton died, heaped with honors and substantial wealth. After a state funeral, he was buried in the walls of Westminster Abbey.

Although later research has overturned a good deal of what Newton thought to be basic and unchanging truth about the physical universe, much also remains unchallenged. His modesty was legendary; on his deathbed he is supposed to have said, "If I have seen farther than others, it is because I have stood on the shoulders of giants." The famous story of the falling apple just may be true; no one will ever know.

August Ludwig von Schlözer; and the Italians Lodovico Muratori and Cesare Beccaria; but the list could be made as long as one wants. The Americans Thomas Jefferson, Benjamin Franklin, and John Adams belong as well—the Enlightenment had no territorial boundaries, though it was much narrower and shallower in East Europe than in the West. The East lacked the refined urban middle class that produced a great many of the philosophes.

Chronologically, one can say that their first major achievements date from the 1730s and that the period ended with the French Revolution. The high point of reform activity was in the 1770s and 1780s, when various governments experimented with or fully adopted one after another of the favored ideas of the philosophes.

Beyond reform, it is difficult to find a common denominator in these ideas because the philosophes themselves were difficult to categorize. Some of them were the first public atheists, while the majority were at least outward Christians and some were quite pious clergymen. Muratori, for example, was a priest. Most believed constitutional monarchy was the best form of government, while others were uncompromising republicans.

In the physical sciences, some believed unreservedly in the Baconian procedure of going to the sense-perceptible data (empirical science); others rejected all knowledge that was not reducible to mathematics, and still others classified quantifiable knowledge as inherently inferior. Some were hopeful of gradual improvement in human affairs (ameliorationism); others were convinced that nothing important could be accomplished without radical, even revolutionary changes in society.

The philosophes did not hesitate to argue with one another as well as with their conservative opponents. Much of the literature of the later eighteenth century

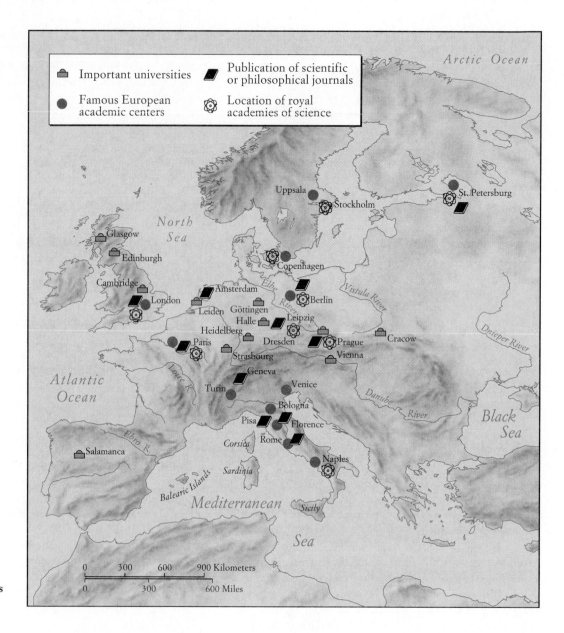

● **MAP 32.1   Centers of the Enlightenment.**

consists of pamphlets and newspapers arguing one or another favorite idea. In a society where literacy levels made wide distribution of printed matter a paying proposition for the first time, the philosophes made full use of the available channels to get their various messages out into the public.

Common Goals of the Philosophes

Although they differed on specific details, the majority of the philosophes agreed on many general points. For one

thing, they universally acclaimed the idea of *a balance of governmental powers between executive and legislature* as presented in Baron Montesquieu's famous **Spirit of the Laws** (1748), perhaps the most influential of a century of very influential books on government. In it, the French aristocrat argued for the careful division of powers to prevent any one branch from becoming too strong and dictatorial. He thought that of current governments, the British example came closest to perfection in that line (he did not really understand the British system, however), and his ideas had great impact on the makers of both the U.S. and the French Revolutions.

■ **The Wheelwrights' Trade.** One of the lasting values of the *Encyclopedie* was the exact illustration by copper engravings of the various trades and handicrafts of the eighteenth century. Pictured here are five steps in the making of carriage wheels.

The constitutional limitation of monarchic power was considered an absolute essential of decent government. The brilliant Voltaire (1694–1778) in particular, led the charge here, as he had a good deal of personal experience with royal persecution in his native France before becoming such a celebrity that kings desired his witty company. He, too, admired the British system of assuring civil rights and condemned the French lack of such safeguards.

The philosophes also agreed that *freedom of conscience must be assured* at least for all varieties of Christians, if not Jews and atheists as well. "Established" or tax-supported churches should be abolished, and no one faith or sect should be identified with governmental powers (as was the case in all European countries at this time). The First Amendment to the U.S. Constitution was the first example of the separation of religion and government in Western history. It was much applauded by the philosophes.

All persons should enjoy *a fundamental equality before the law*. The philosophes saw this as a basic right that no government could take away or diminish. In line with this principle, punishments were to be blind to class distinctions among criminals; the baron would be whipped just like the peasant. Meanwhile those who had talent should have *increased possibilities for upward mobility*. This did *not* mean that the philosophes were democrats; almost all of them agreed with the majority of educated persons that humans should definitely not have equal social and political rights.

Most philosophes viewed the *abolition of most forms of censorship* as a positive step toward the free society that

they wished to see realized. Just where the lines should be drawn was a topic of debate, however; some of them would permit direct attacks on Christianity or any religion, for instance, while others would not.

The philosophes also agreed that the cause of most misery on earth was ignorance, not evil intentions or sin. They were thus picking up a thread that had been running through the fabric of Western intellectual discussion since the Renaissance: that the main causes of Man's inhumanity to Man were to be found in ignorance, and that in a good society, such ignorance would not be tolerated. This view led the philosophes to call for *state-supervised education* through the elementary grades as perhaps the most important practical reform for the general benefit.

In addition to censorship, the philosophes were not in agreement on several other broad areas of public affairs. Some would have abolished the barriers to social equality, so that all government posts would be open to commoners; others feared that this would guarantee the rule of the mob. A few, like the Marquis de Lafayette, became republicans; most thought that monarchy was a natural and necessary arrangement for the good of all. Thus, the philosophes never sought or found a single voice to enunciate their hopes.

Economic Thought: Adam Smith

The outstanding figure in eighteenth-century economic thought was undoubtedly the Scotsman *Adam Smith* (1723–1790). In his **Wealth of Nations,** which was published

■ **Dual Portraits: Voltaire and Rousseau.** Two faces of the Enlightenment are shown here. Voltaire's knowing half-smile suited the man who wrote the savagely satirical *Candide,* while Rousseau's moral seriousness comes across in this portrait of the author as a young man.

in 1776 and soon became a European best-seller in several languages, Smith put forth the gospel of *free trade and free markets.* Smith is often described as saying that the smaller the government's role in the national economy, the better, and that there is no economic problem that a free market cannot solve to the benefit of all. *Laissez faire* (Let them do what they will) was supposedly his trademark. But this is a vast oversimplification of Smith's ideas; in reality, he acknowledged that government intervention in one form or another was necessary for society's well-being in many instances.

Smith is rightly credited with being the father of free enterprise as that term is used in the modern West. In *The Wealth of Nations,* he laid out in persuasive detail his conviction that an "unseen hand" operated through a free market in goods and services to bring the ultimate consumers what they wanted at prices they were willing to pay. Smith criticized mercantilism, the ruling economic wisdom of his time, for operating to the disadvantage of most consumers. As in so many other instances, his doctrines followed the Enlightenment's underlying conviction that *the sum of individual liberties must be collective well-being.* Whether this is true, seen from the perspective of the twentieth century, is debatable; to the eighteenth century, it was a matter of faith.

Educational Theory and the Popularization of Knowledge

One of the least orthodox of the philosophes, Jean-Jacques Rousseau (1712–1778) was the most influential of all in the vitally important field of pedagogy and educational philosophy. His book *Emile* (1762) outlined in detail what was wrong with the education of youth and how it might be corrected. Rousseau was a maverick in believing that children can and *must* follow their inherent interests in a proper education, and that the teacher should use those interests to steer the child in the wished-for directions. Rousseau was also a maverick in strongly criticizing the prevalent belief that progress meant achieving more consumption and a better material life through mastery of science and exploitation of Nature. On the contrary, Rousseau thought that progress must involve improvements in the moral and ethical life of the people and had little to do with material prosperity.

Rousseau had little following in his own lifetime, but his ideas had a strong impact upon some of the revolutionary leaders a few years later and gained more adherents in the nineteenth century. He is now regarded as the founder of modern pedagogical theory and is probably the most important of the philosophes to the twentieth century.

Prison in Eighteenth-Century Russia

Reform ideas penetrated into nearly every aspect of life during the later eighteenth-century Enlightenment. Every institution of society, including the criminal justice system, fell under the relentless scrutiny of the philosophes. The Italian aristocrat **Cesare Beccaria** (1738–1794) in his epoch-making *On Crimes and Punishment* established criminology as a legitimate field of study and called in question the rational basis for a legal system that aimed at retribution rather than rehabilitation.

The English reformer John Howard (1727–1790) approached this question with the fervor of an evangelist and the exact observation of a good journalist. Howard became famous for his extensive travels to prisons and jails in every part of Europe; everywhere he went he wrote firsthand descriptions depicting the filthy, degrading, and brutal conditions in the prisons. Among his visits was a trip to St. Petersburg to see the prisons under Catherine II, the Great, who had abolished the death penalty and most forms of investigative torture early in her reign. But this is not to say that criminals did not die in Russian jails.

While in St. Petersburg in 1781, Howard interviewed the chief of the city police about the administration of the much-feared knout as a form of correction:

> The knout whip is fixed to a wood handle a foot long and consists of several leather thongs about two feet in length, twisted together, to the end of which is fastened a single thong of a foot and one half, tapering towards a point, and capable of being changed by the executioner when too much softened by the blood of the criminal.
>
> [A conversation with the executioner] "Can you inflict the knout in such a manner so as to occasion death in a short time?" "Yes, I can." "In how short a time?" "In a day or so." "Have you ever so inflicted it?" "I have." "Have you lately?" "Yes, the last man

who was punished with my hands by the knout died of his punishment." "In what manner do you thus render it mortal?" "By one or more strokes on the sides, which carry off large pieces of flesh."

[Howard continues:] August 10, 1781. I saw two criminals, a man and a woman, suffer the punishment of the knout. They were conducted from prison by about fifteen hussars and ten soldiers. When they arrived at the place of punishment the hussars formed themselves into a ring round the whipping post. The drum beat a minute or two, and then some prayers were read, the attending populace having taken off their hats. The woman was taken first, and after having stripped her roughly to the waist, her hands and feet were bound with cords to the post, made for that purpose; a man standing before the post and holding the cords to keep them tight.

A servant attended the executioner, and both were stout men. The servant first marked his ground, and then struck the woman five times on the back. Every stroke seemed to penetrate deep into her flesh. But his master, thinking him too gentle, pushed him aside, took his place, and gave all the remaining strokes himself. . . . The woman received twenty-five, the man sixty . . . both seemed but just alive, especially the man, who yet had strength enough to receive a small donation with some sign of gratitude. They were conducted back to prison in a little wagon. I saw the woman in a very weak condition some days later, but could find the man no more.

On January 21, 1790, the indefatigable Howard died while making a return trip to Russia, having contracted cholera while ministering to the sick. Along with Beccaria, he will be remembered as a major contributor to the movement for more humane treatment of prisoners and the accused.

SOURCE: James Baldwin Brown, *Memoirs of Howard*, edited by Richard H. Ward and Austin Fowler. AMS Press © 1973.

In the mid-eighteenth century, Europeans were able to profit for the first time from the popularization of science and intellectual discourse that had come about through the Scientific Revolution. The upper classes developed a passion for collecting, ordering, and indexing knowledge about the natural world and humans' relations with it and with each other. The century also saw the initial attempts to make science comprehensible and accessible to the masses.

The most noted of these was the immensely successful French ***Encyclopedie,*** which contained thirty-five volumes and thousands of individual articles on literally everything under the sun. Its general editor was *Denis Diderot* (1713–1784), assisted by Jean d'Alembert, who saw the work through in fifteen years (1751–1765) against enormous odds. Contributors to the *Encyclopedie* (the first of its kind) included the outstanding intellectuals of Europe, including Voltaire. The articles were often very controversial, and their "slant" was always in the direction favored by the more liberal philosophes. Not the least valuable part of the enterprise were the numerous volumes of illustrations, which are the greatest single source of information on early technology. The *Encyclopedie* sold more than 15,000 copies, a huge number for the day, and was found on personal library shelves from one end of Europe to the other, as well as in the Americas and Russia.

✤ Ideals of the Enlightenment: Reason, Liberty, Happiness

Reason was the keyword in every philosophical treatise and every political tract of the Enlightenment. What was reasonable was good, what was good was reasonable. Reason was derived from Nature by the observation of what was natural. Nature and natural were favored expressions of all the philosophes, and to contravene Nature was the worst of sins. The philosophes took for granted that the reasoning faculty was humans' highest gift and that its exercise would, sooner or later, guarantee a decent and just society on earth.

Liberty was the birthright of all, but it was often stolen away by kings and their agents. Liberty meant the personal freedom to do and say anything that did not harm the rights of another person or institution nor threaten the welfare of society. The French Marquis de Condorcet and the Scot David Hume took this concept to the conclusion that no one owed allegiance to a government or society that denied liberty.

Happiness was another birthright of all humans. They should not have to defer happiness until a problematic eternity; it should be accessible here and now. In a reasonable, natural world, ordinary men and women would be able to engage in what one of the outstanding philosophes called "the pursuit of happiness" (The Declaration of Independence by Thomas Jefferson).

All of the ideals of the philosophes and their numerous followers flowed together in the concept of *progress.* For the first time in European history, the belief that humans were engaged in an ultimately successful search for a new state of being here on this earth crystallized among a large group. The confidence and energy that were once directed to the attainment of heaven were now transferred to the improvement of earthly life. Not only was the individual perfectible, but collective perfectibility would result in a transformed human life for all. Progress was inevitable, and it was the individual's proud task to assist in its coming.

The Enlightenment was, then, an unintentional intellectual training ground for the coming explosion at the end of the eighteenth century. In its insistence on human perfectibility, the necessity of intellectual and religious freedoms, and the need to demolish the barriers to talent that everywhere kept the privileged apart from the nonprivileged, the Enlightenment spirit served as a forerunner for something far more radical than itself: the revolution.

✤ The Audience of the Philosophes

The Enlightenment was not by any means a mass movement. Its advocates, both male and female, felt most at home amid the high culture of the urban elite. There were probably more fans of the acid satire of Voltaire in Paris than in all the rest of France and more readers of Hume in London than in all the remainder of the British Isles. It was an age of brilliant conversationalists, and the hostesses who could bring the celebrated minds of the day together were indispensable to the whole movement. In the "salons" of Madame X or Madame Y were heard the exchanges of ideas and opinions that were the heartbeat of the Enlightenment.

The movement rarely attempted direct communication with the majority of the people, who in France and elsewhere remained outside the social circles of the philosophes. Most were still illiterate and could not absorb this highly language-dependent message. Others, especially among the peasants, rejected it as atheist or antitraditional. Only the upper strata—the educated professional and merchant, the occasional aristocrat and liberal-minded clergyman—made up the audience of the philosophes, bought the *Encyclopedie,* and were converted to the ideals of progress, tolerance, and liberty. The majority of these would undoubtedly have been appalled by the prospect of revolution, and they had no sympathy for the occasional voice that considered violence against an evil government acceptable.

Summary

In the sixteenth century, the Renaissance scholars' rediscovery of classical learning and its methods produced an acceptance of empirical observation as a method of deducing truth about the physical world. This new attitude was responsible for the Scientific Revolution, which was at first confined to the physical sciences, but inevitably spread to other things. Inductive reasoning based on observation and tested by experiment became commonplace in the educated classes. Mathematics was especially crucial to this process, and several new forms of math evolved to support it.

A century later the confidence that the method of science was adequate to unlock previously incomprehensible mysteries had spread to the social sciences: the Science of Man. The same overreaching law that governed the rotation of the planets operated—or should operate—in politics and government. When that law was finally under-

stood, all would fall into place, and the earth would cease to be out of joint and filled with friction.

The conviction that progress was inevitable and that humans were good and wanted good for others was the product of a relatively small but very influential group of *philosophes* in France and other countries. They were the leaders of a significant transformation of Western thought that was gradually embraced by most members of the educated classes during the course of the eighteenth century. This transformation is termed the Enlightenment. The philosophes were obsessed by reason and the reasonable and saw Nature as the ultimate referent in these respects. A phenomenon of the urban, educated classes, the Enlightenment made little impact on the masses, but prepared the way for middle-class leadership of the revolutions at the end of the eighteenth century.

Test Your Knowledge

1. The source of the major elements of medieval European thought in the physical sciences was
   a. Augustus Caesar.
   b. Aristotle.
   c. Virgil.
   d. St. Augustine.
2. Developments in which two sciences were at the heart of the advances of the sixteenth and seventeenth centuries?
   a. Physics and astronomy
   b. Math and chemistry
   c. Math and medicine
   d. Biology and chemistry
3. Kepler's great contribution to science was
   a. his theory of the creation of the universe.
   b. the three laws of celestial mechanics.
   c. the discovery of the planet Jupiter.
   d. his theory of the geocentric nature of the universe.
4. Which of the following did *not* make his fame as a natural scientist?
   a. Galileo
   b. Spinoza
   c. Copernicus
   d. Brahe

5. Newton's conception of the universe is often described as
   a. an apparent order that cannot be comprehended by humans.
   b. an incoherent agglomeration of unrelated phenomena.
   c. a mirage of order that exists only in the human mind.
   d. a machine of perfect order and laws.
6. By the end of the seventeenth century, educated Europeans were generally
   a. ready to abandon the search for a more intelligible natural science.
   b. considering applying the scientific method to the study of humans.
   c. impelled toward atheism by the conflicts between religion and science.
   d. abandoning Bacon's empiricism for Descartes's inductive reasoning.
7. Which of the following was particularly interested in reforming education?
   a. Rousseau
   b. Diderot

c. Hume
d. Voltaire

8. The Enlightenment is best described as a phenomenon that
   a. was generally limited to an urban, educated group.
   b. was found more or less equally throughout Christendom.
   c. reached quickly into the consciousness of most people.
   d. was generally favorable to the idea of an official religion.

Identification Terms

Beccaria (Cesare)

deductive method of reasoning

empirical method

Encyclopedie

Essay concerning Human Understanding

geocentric/heliocentric

inductive reasoning

Inquisition

scientific method

Spirit of the Laws

Wealth of Nation

Bibliography

Anderson, M. S. *Europe in the Eighteenth Century,* 1987. A general survey of political and cultural trends and a good place to start research on almost any eighteenth-century topic.

Andrade, E. *Sir Isaac Newton,* 1974. A short biography of the most famous of the early scientists.

Butterfield, H. *The Origins of Modern Science,* 1951. A classic readable account of how science came to be what we now understand it to be.

Chisick, H. *The Limits of Reform in the Enlightenment: Attitudes toward the Education of the Lower Classes in France,* 1981. A very interesting examination of its topic.

Darnton, R. *The Business of Enlightenment: A Publishing History of the Encyclopedie, 1775–1800,* 1979. Fun to read and tells a great deal about the philosophes. The same author's *The Great Cat Massacre and Other Episodes in French Cultural History,* 1984 is equally good.

Gay, P. has written several books on the Enlightenment and is one of the most readable of authors who deal with cultural history.

Hampson, N. *A Cultural History of the Enlightenment,* 1968. A brief, fact-filled survey of how society was affected. On the same lines is F. Artz, *The Enlightenment in France,* 1968.

Hill, B. *Eighteenth Century Women, An Anthology,* 1984. A good survey of women's lives in various social classes.

Jacobs, M. *The Cultural Meaning of the Scientific Revolution,* 1988. Helpful to the student.

Koestler, A. *The Sleepwalkers,* 1959. An enthralling study of how the great breakthroughs in early science were made.

Rosen E. *Copernicus and the Scientific Revolution,* 1984. Shows how astronomy and physics were transformed and what the effects of that transformation were.

Spencer, S. ed. *French Women and the Age of Enlightenment,* 1984. A good insight into the salons and other contributions made by women.

LIBERALISM AND THE CHALLENGE TO ABSOLUTIST MONARCHY

THE LIBERAL CREED

THE AMERICAN REVOLUTION, 1775–1783

RESULTS OF THE AMERICAN REVOLUTION
IN EUROPEAN OPINION

1756–1763	Seven Years' War (French and Indian War)
1765	Stamp Act
1773	Boston Tea Party
1775	Fighting begins at Lexington and Concord
1776	Thomas Paine, *Common Sense* Declaration of Independence
1781	Articles of Confederation
1789	U.S. Constitution

Among the long-term consequences of the Scientific Revolution and the subsequent Enlightenment was the mental attitude called liberalism. It took strong root in the Anglo-Saxon countries, where it was also fostered by the events of 1688 and the English Bill of Rights.

The political revolutions in America and France at the end of the eighteenth century were quite different in course and outcome, but they were linked by a common origin in the belief in the inherent freedom and moral equality of men. This belief was at the heart of liberal politics and economics and could not be reconciled with the existing state of affairs in either the American colonies or France.

In America, the more radical colonists' discontent with their status grew to the point of rebellion in the 1770s. The term *rebellion* is usually associated with starving workers or mercilessly exploited peasants. On the contrary, the American Revolution was led by a prosperous middle class, who had nothing against their government except that it was located in London.

✤ THE LIBERAL CREED

Liberalism was born in the form that the modern world knows in the late eighteenth century. Its roots go back much further, to the Protestant Reformation and the seventeenth-century political philosophers in England. The basic principles of liberalism are (1) the liberty of the individual in religion and person and (2) the equality of individuals in the eyes of God and the laws.

Liberals were especially noticeable in France and England, much less so in central, southern, and eastern Europe. They believed in the necessity of *equality before the law and freedom of movement, conscience, assembly, and the press.* They considered censorship both ineffective and repressive, and they despised the inborn privileges accorded to the aristocracy. They thought that a state religion was almost inevitably corrupt and that individuals should have the power to choose in which fashion they would serve their God.

Liberals originally did not believe in equality for all in political or social matters but only in legal and economic concerns. They subscribed to what we would now call "the level playing field" theory; that is, that all people should have the opportunity to prove themselves in the competition for wealth and the prestige that come with it. Those who were weaker or less talented should be allowed to fail, as this was nature's way of allowing the best to show what they had to offer and keeping the best on top.

The liberals of the eighteenth century reflected the general optimism of the Enlightenment about human nature. Like most of the philosophes with whom they were in fact interchangeable, the liberals believed that the good would inevitably triumph and that humans would recognize evil in whatever disguises it might assume for the short term. They believed that rational progress was possible and—in the long run—certain. They believed that education was the best cure for most of society's problems.

In matters of government, they sympathized with John Locke and Baron Montesquieu, who thought that the powers of government must be both spread among various organs and restricted by a *checks and balances* system in which the legislative, judicial, and executive powers were separated. Liberals believed that representative government operating through a property-based franchise was the most workable and most just system. *They mistrusted total democracy,* which they thought would lead to rule by the "mob" of uneducated and easily misled. They rejected aristocracy (even though there were many liberal nobles) as being outmoded, a government by the few for the few. They were willing to have a monarchy, so long as the powers of the monarch were checked by a constitution of laws and by free judges.

In the liberal view, the *legislature should be the most powerful branch* of government; it should be elected from among the "solid citizens," that is, from among the liberal sympathizers: educated and well-off commoners, professionals, merchants, and the lower ranks of the nobles. They all believed that the government of eighteenth-century England should be the model for the world; they admired its mixture of parliamentary and royal powers, with Parliament holding the whip hand in matters of domestic policies. They thought England after the Glorious Revolution had achieved a happy blend of individual freedoms within proper limits, with the responsible and forward-looking elements retaining political and social dominance.

⚜ THE AMERICAN REVOLUTION, 1775–1783

On the other side of the Atlantic, the British American colonies were strongholds of liberal thought and sympathy. Men like George Washington, Thomas Jefferson, James Madison, Benjamin Franklin, and many others were ardent supporters of the liberal view. They had read Locke and Montesquieu and digested their ideas; and they had much less fear of democracy than the home country, because the masses of desperate poor who might threaten the continued leadership of the middle- and upper-class liberals in Europe were not present in America. In fact, the three million or so free colonists were probably the best-off large group of individuals in the world at this time.

The American Revolutionary War began with a routine dispute between the British government and its subjects over taxation. Winning the **Seven Years' War** (French and Indian War), which lasted from 1756 to 1763 in North America, had cost the British government a considerable sum, while the American colonists had contributed very little to meet those expenses. The necessity of maintaining a much larger standing army to garrison America meant that London would be faced with a budgetary drain for the foreseeable future. Therefore, Parliament imposed a series of new taxes on the colonists, most notably, the **Stamp Act of 1765;** it created such a furor, however, that

■ **July 4, 1776.** This well known painting by the American John Trumbull shows Jefferson as he presented his final draft to the Continental Congress in Philadelphia.

it was quickly repealed. The **Navigation Acts,** which had been very loosely enforced until now, were tightened and applied more rigidly to colonial commerce.

These British demands fell on colonists who had become thoroughly accustomed to having their own way in most political and economic affairs. The American colonies had the highest per-capita income in the Western world in 1775, and they paid among the lowest taxes. They were the great "success story" of settlement colonies, and they had achieved this condition without much guidance or interference from the London government. The Americans were used to a high degree of democracy in local and provincial affairs; many now felt they were being unduly pushed about by the ministers of King George III, and they resolved to let their feelings be known.

The *Boston Tea Party* of 1773 was a dramatic rejection of the right of the Crown to change the terms of colonial trade in favor of British merchants. When the British replied to the illegal acts of the Bostonians by sending troops and closing Boston harbor while giving the royal governor much expanded powers, the clash came much closer. One act led to another as the stakes were raised on both sides; finally, in April 1775 the "shots heard round the world" were fired in Lexington, and the War for Independence was on.

At the outset, the moderate faction in the Continental Congress, which the rebels summoned to provide political

■ **The Tea Party in Boston, 1773.** This contemporary engraving shows the colonists, emptying cases of tea into the Boston harbor in order to express their contempt for the new excise-tax laws imposed by Parliament. Their disguise as Indians neither fooled, nor was intended to fool anyone.

leadership, was in control; they demanded "no taxation without representation" and other, mild slogans upholding the alleged rights of Englishmen. But by 1776, a more uncompromising group, led by Patrick Henry and Jefferson, had assumed the leadership role. This group wanted nothing less than independence from Britain, and in the *Declaration of Independence* Jefferson wrote their program and battle cry (see the Document in this chapter). The great popularity of the radical pamphlet *Common Sense* by the newly arrived **Thomas Paine** showed how inflamed some tempers had become (see the Biography in this chapter).

Not all the colonists agreed by any means. Many remained true to the Crown, and these Loyalists were later either maltreated by their fellow Americans or chose to emigrate. The conflict was as much a civil war as a rebellion; even families were split. Washington's troops froze during the savage winter at Valley Forge, while in nearby Philadelphia most of the populace enjoyed their comforts under British protection.

The military outcome was eventually dictated by three *factors favoring the rebels:* (1) the logistic effort needed to transport and supply a large army overseas; (2) the aid provided by the French fleet and French money; and (3) the only halfhearted support given by the Parliament in London to the war.

By 1779, it was clear that the second-rate British commanders had no plans worth mentioning and could not put aside their mutual jealousies to join forces against Washington. Even if they had, the many London sympathizers with the Americans, both in and out of Parliament, would negate any full-fledged war effort. Under the **alliance of 1778,** the French supplied the Americans with much material aid, some manpower, and, above all, prevented the British navy from controlling the coasts. The defeat of General **Lord Cornwallis** at Yorktown in 1781 spelled the end of armed hostilities, and the Peace of Paris officially ended the war in 1783.

⚜ RESULTS OF THE AMERICAN REVOLUTION IN EUROPEAN OPINION

We are accustomed to thinking of a revolution as necessarily involving an abrupt change in the economic and social system. But this was not the case in America in 1783. The existing political, economic, and social circumstances of the citizenry, whether white or black, were scarcely changed by independence. The War for Independence had been won, but this was not at all the same as a

Thomas Paine
1737–1809

Of all those who might be called the liberal instigators of the American Revolution, Tom Paine must take pride of place. When he came to the colonies in 1774, he was an unknown English acquaintance of Benjamin Franklin; two years later, he was one of the foremost figures in America. But at that point his extraordinary public career was just beginning.

Paine was born into rural poverty in 1737 and had to leave school at age thirteen to go to work to supplement the family's meager income. For the next quarter century, he failed at everything he tried, from seaman to schoolteacher. His first wife died a year into their marriage in 1760; he married again in 1771, only to separate in bitterness three years later. His appointment as excise collector (a hated post among the people) in 1762 was revoked because of an improper entry in his records. Although he managed to be reinstated in 1766, he remained under a cloud and was dismissed again in 1774 for reasons that are unclear. At this juncture, friends introduced him to Franklin, who had come to London to represent the North American colonies before Parliament.

Paine arrived in Philadelphia in late 1774 and began writing for Franklin's *Pennsylvania Magazine.* A few months later, he became editor of the magazine. His contributions were marked by a gift for rhetoric and a radical turn of mind on public issues.

In early 1776, his pamphlet *Common Sense* appeared; the work immediately became a best-seller in the colonies and was reprinted in several European countries as well. Paine had a way with memorable phrases; *Common Sense* made a powerful argument not only against colonial government, but also against the person of George III as a "hardened, sullen Pharaoh." In a mere seventy-nine pages, the pamphlet gave discontented Americans both abstract arguments and very concrete objections against being ruled by a distant, uncaring, and allegedly tyrannical monarch.

General Washington and other leaders at once recognized Paine's merits and his potential to assist in the revolutionary cause. Between 1776 and 1783, he produced the papers known collectively as *The Crisis:* "These are the times that try men's souls . . ." with references to "the summer soldier and the sunshine patriot . . . ."

In 1787 Paine returned to England for a short visit. Delays kept him until 1789 and while there, he was swept up in the initial liberal euphoria about the French Revolution. He wrote the *Rights of Man* (1791) to defend the Revolution against the increasing number of English critics. Having to flee England, Paine went to France and was elected to the Convention of 1793 despite being a foreigner. But here his independent attitude also made him an uncomfortable ally, and he was imprisoned for almost a year during the Terror. Released by the intercession of the American minister James Monroe, Paine wrote *The Age of Reason* (1794), a pamphlet denouncing revealed religions, especially Christianity, and challenging people to exercise their capacity to find a morality independent of faith.

When Paine finally returned to America in 1802, he was astonished and depressed to find that the outrage over his attack on religion had overwhelmed all gratitude for his services in the Revolution. Former friends like the Adams family avoided him, and the children in his adopted town of New Rochelle, New York, taunted him. After several years of living as a social pariah on his farm, he died in 1809 and was denied the burial in a Quaker cemetery he had requested. A final bizarre note was added when a project to take his remains back to England failed because of the bankruptcy of one of the principals, and the coffin, which was seized as an "asset," disappeared forever.

The Declaration of Independence of 1776 and the Declaration of the Rights of Man and Citizen of 1789

The political principles and ideals of the liberal Enlightenment operated on both sides of the Atlantic. The American Declaration of Independence and the French Declaration of the Rights of Man and Citizen were products of individuals who had studied the same authors and were committed to the same visions of government's proper role. The French document was aimed at generic reform of a monarchy that had neglected its duties to its people; the American declaration was intent on dissolving political ties with what the colonists considered an unjust and alien government. For that reason, and because a fifteen-year interval of increasingly radical thought had intervened in France, the Declaration of the Rights of Man is more specific, but both display liberalism in its most persuasive and attractive guise. The similarities between the U.S. Bill of Rights of the Constitution of 1789 and the simultaneous Declaration of the Rights of Man are also immediately evident.

The Declaration of Independence of 1776

...We hold these truths to be self-evident, that all men are created equal, that they are endowed by their Creator with certain inalienable rights, that among these are life, liberty, and the pursuit of happiness. That to secure these rights, governments are instituted among men, deriving their just powers from the consent of the governed. That whenever any form of government becomes destructive of these ends, it is the right of the people to alter or to abolish it, and to institute new government, laying its foundation on such principles and organizing its powers in such form, as to them shall seem most likely to effect their safety and happiness ....

The Declaration of the Rights of Man and Citizen of 1789

The representatives of the French people, organized in National Assembly ... recognize and proclaim, in

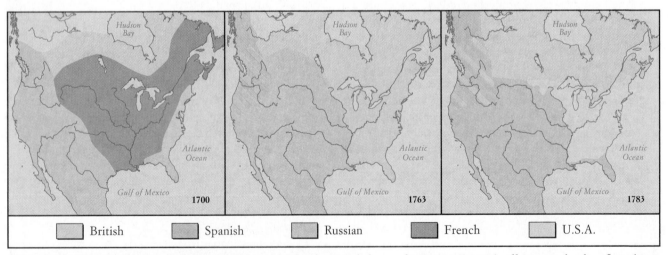

British   Spanish   Russian   French   U.S.A.

● **MAP 33.1   North America's Possessors, 1700–1783.** The changing balance of power in Europe's affairs was closely reflected in North America in the eighteenth century.

the presence and under the auspices of the Supreme Being, the following rights of man and citizen:

1. Men are born equal and remain free and equal in rights. . . .
2. The aim of every political association is the preservation of the natural and inalienable rights of man; these rights are liberty, property, security, and resistance to oppression;
3. The source of all sovereignty resides essentially in the nation; no group, no individual may exercise authority not emanating expressly therefrom;
4. Liberty consists of the power to do whatever is not injurious to others; thus the enjoyment of the natural rights of every man has for its limits only those that assure other members of society the enjoyment of those same rights; such limits may be determined by law.
5. The law has the right to forbid only actions which are injurious to society. Whatever is not forbidden by law may not be prevented, and no one may be constrained to do what it does not prescribe.
6. Law is the expression of the general will. . . . All citizens, being equal before it, are equally admissible to all public offices, positions, and employments, according to their capacity, and without other distinction than that of virtues and talents.
7. No man may be accused, arrested, or detained except in the cases determined by law, and according to the forms prescribed thereby. . . .
10. No one is to be disquieted because of his opinions, even religious, provided their manifestation does not disturb the public order established by law.
11. Free communication of ideas and opinions is one of the most precious of the rights of man. Consequently, every citizen may speak, write, and print freely, subject to responsibility for the abuse of such liberties in cases determined by law.
13. For maintenance of the public force and for the expenses of administration a common tax is indispensable; it must be assessed equally on all citizens in proportion to their means.
17. Since property is a sacred and inviolate right, no one may be deprived thereof unless a legally established public necessity obviously requires it, and upon condition of a just and previous indemnity.

SOURCE: John H. Stewart, *A Documentary History of the French Revolution* (Macmillan, 1979).

revolution. The American Revolution was slower to manifest itself and did so only by degrees after 1783.

At the outset, the thirteen former colonies were recognized as a sovereign nation, equal to any other; all the territory west of the Appalachians to the Mississippi was open to the new nation (see Map 33.1). For the first time, a major state of the Western world would have a *republican form* of government with no king and no established church: Most of the (white male) citizens would be entitled to vote and to hold office. They would enjoy freedom of religion, be fully equal before the law, and have no economic restrictions imposed on them by birth, residence, or circumstance. The establishment of *that* form of government and *those* freedoms was the American Revolution, not the severance of ties with London.

A few years after independence, the ex-colonists acknowledged the severe shortcomings of the 1781 Articles of Confederation, which had been their first try at bonding the states together, and set themselves the task of creating a workable, permanent system of government. The outcome of the effort, the *U.S. Constitution of 1789,* is now one of the oldest constitutions in the world; it was drafted by men raised in the liberal traditions of the eighteenth century. They wished to create a system that would allow free play to individual talent and ambition and protect individual rights, while still asserting the primacy of the state. They believed in *freedom of opportunity,* while *rejecting political and social equality.* They believed in equality before the law and in conscience, but like Locke, they believed in the sacred rights of property. The framers of the Constitution under which Americans still live were conservatives in their approach to the life of the society, but liberals in their approach to the life of the individual person.

More than the successful war, the U.S. Constitution made a huge impact on educated European opinion. It demonstrated for many that a large number of men could create a moderate system of self-government with

■ **Marquis de Lafayette.** This somewhat idealized portrait of Lafayette shows him in the uniform of a French lieutenant general after his return from America.

elected representatives, but without an aristocracy or a monarch at its head. Many European liberals had informed themselves in detail about the United States; some of them even came to fight in the rebellion (the French Marquis de Lafayette, the Poles Casimir Pulaski and Thaddeus Kosciusko, and the German Baron von Steuben). They were an effective propaganda apparatus. And they were seconded by the equally effective work of Americans like Franklin, Jefferson, and the Adamses, who resided in Europe as officials of the new country.

Naturally, the American innovations received the most attention in France. The rebellion had many friends in enlightened society, including some in the government at Paris who welcomed this weakening of the British winner of the Seven Years' War. Many French officers had been in the country and had contact with the leading American figures and their programs. The drawing rooms of the Parisian elite were filled with talk about America. Some of it was negative: the crude Americans would soon see that government must be either by the king and his responsible officials or by the mob; no third way was possible, given human nature. But much of the talk was enthusiastically favorable. More and more men of high social standing came to be convinced that the present French monarchic system was in terrible need of reform, and they looked to some aspects of the American experiment for models of what they wished to introduce at home.

Summary

Liberal politics was the product of beliefs dating to the Protestant Reformation and the seventeenth-century English revolution against absolutism. Its fundamental principles asserted the equality and liberty of individuals in both the moral and the legal sense. Liberals believed that all were entitled to the opportunity to prove their merits in economic competition, but they generally rejected social and political equality as impractical for the foreseeable future.

The British colonies in America were strongholds of liberalism, and those convictions led directly to the rebellion against British rule in 1775. Thanks in part to French military and financial aid and the lukewarm support of the war effort by Parliament, the rebellion was successful; the American Republic was born, the first large-scale experiment in liberal politics. Although the War for Independence was won, the true American Revolution took longer to develop. Its paramount expression came in the Constitution of 1787–1789, which made a deep impression upon educated Europeans, particularly the French adherents of reform.

Test Your Knowledge

1. To liberal-minded Europeans, the success of the American Revolution meant above all that
   a. force is most important in political affairs.
   b. democracy should be introduced to their own governments.
   c. the best aspects of the Enlightenment were being implemented.
   d. Americans were more aggressive than other Westerners.

2. Eighteenth-century liberals thought that
   a. all men should have equal opportunities.
   b. all individuals should have basic necessities guaranteed to them.
   c. men and women were essentially equal in talents and abilities.
   d. social and cultural position should be about the same for all.

3. In matters of religion, eighteenth-century liberals normally believed that
   a. there should be an officially designated and supported faith.
   b. all individuals should have freedom to believe as they saw best.
   c. the government must have authority over religion because of its connection with politics.
   d. all humans were naturally inclined to evil and sinfulness.

4. An important reason for the democratic spirit among the North American colonists in the era before 1776 was
   a. the natural inclinations of colonials toward equality for all.
   b. the total absence of the social divisions commonly found in Europe.
   c. the habit of religious tolerance in the American traditions.
   d. the absence of masses of poor people who might have threatened social revolution.

5. Which of the following individuals played no military role in the success of the American War for Independence?
   a. Baron von Steuben
   b. Casimir Pulaski
   c. Marquis de Lafayette
   d. Tom Paine

6. The impact in Europe of the American Revolution can best be summarized as
   a. important and influential among the educated classes everywhere.
   b. important in Great Britain but not acknowledged widely elsewhere.
   c. minimal except among a handful of liberals.
   d. important in a military but not a political sense.

7. Which of the following was *not* a reason for American victory in the Revolutionary War?
   a. The division in Parliament about the conduct of the war
   b. The military mediocrity of the British commanding officers
   c. The better equipment of the American forces
   d. French aid to the rebels.

8. The essence of Baron Montesquieu's theses on government is that
   a. power should clearly be concentrated in the executive.
   b. lawmaking powers should be shared between the federal and state levels of government.
   c. elections should be guaranteed to be held within short time periods.
   d. powers should be divided among three branches of government.

Identification Terms

alliance of 1778	Lord Cornwallis	Paine (Thomas)	Seven Years' War
Common Sense	Navigation Acts	Republican government	Stamp Act of 1765

Bibliography

Bailyn, B. *The Ideological Origins of the American Revolution,* 1967. A standard work.

Calhoon, R.M.: *Loyalists in Revolutionary America,* 1973.

_____ : *Revolutionary America,* 1976 is a short introduction to the events of 1763–1787.

Higgonet, P. *Sister Republics: Origins of the American and French Revolutions,* 1988. A comparative study of much value.

Maier, P.: *From Resistance to Revolution,* 1972 looks at the influence of the radical thinkers among the rebels against Britain. The same author's *The Old Revolutionaries,* 1980 portrays five of the leading American patriots.

Mill, J. S. *On Liberty.* A mid-nineteenth-century tract, which though somewhat difficult has never been superseded as the platform of the classic liberal in the political arena.

Morgan, E. S. *The Birth of the Republic, 1763–1789,* rev. ed. 1977. A good short overview. The same author has written *Inventing the People: The Rise of Popular Sovereignty in England and America,* 1988.

Palmer, R.R.: *Age of the Democratic Revolution,* 1981 is a deservedly classic interpretation of the political and constitutional importance of the events in the former colonies.

Warren, C.: *The Making of the Constitution,* 1947 is especially adapted to student needs.

Wood, G. *The Creation of the American Republic, 1776–1787,* 1972. Speaks to our point in this chapter that the war in America was not revolutionary in any but the international sense.

THE FRENCH REVOLUTION

The watershed of modern political history is the upheaval, called the French Revolution, that struck France and then all of Europe in the last years of the eighteenth century. More than what had happened in the American colonies a few years earlier, the unrest in France challenged every tradition and shook every pillar of the establishment. During its unpredictable and violent course evolved the ideas of democracy, equality, and personal liberty, which the Revolution originally stood for, but later betrayed. What started as a French aristocratic rebellion against taxes became the milepost from which all modern political and social developments in the Western world are measured.

✤ THE BACKGROUND

The Revolution of 1789 in France was triggered by a dispute over finances and taxation between monarch and subjects, just as the American Revolution was. But the tax question was superficial; it could have been remedied, if the deeper problems of the royal government in Paris had not been not so intense and so complex.

Since the death of the "Sun King" Louis XIV in 1715, the quality of French officialdom had been in decline. Louis's immediate successor was his great-grandson (he had outlived both his son and grandsons), *Louis XV,* a young boy. During his youth, actual power had been exercised by a group of nobles who used the opportunity to loosen the controls put upon them by the former regime. Intent mainly on personal luxuries, they abused their newly regained freedom. Corruption and bribery began to appear in the courts and in administrative offices where it was previously not tolerated. The middle-class professional officials who had been the heart and soul of Louis XIV's bureaucracy were passed over or ignored in favor of the aristocrats who occupied the highest offices, supposedly by right of birth.

By nature, Louis XV was not suited to the demands of governmental reform. He was intelligent, but lazy and preferred play to work. Mostly, he delegated power to cronies and careerists and refused to involve himself if he could avoid it. France was so rich a country by nature and its population so prosperous in comparison with most others that it could seemingly weather almost any incompetence in the governing circles.

But the tax problems could not be put off indefinitely. During the mid-eighteenth century, France engaged in a series of costly wars against Britain overseas and against Austria and then Prussia on the Continent (War of the Austrian Succession 1740–1747, Seven Years' War 1756–1763). And the French were not rewarded with victories. Taxes had to be increased, but from whose pockets? The middle classes and the peasantry were already paying too much, while the church (the greatest single property owner in France) and the rich nobles were paying next to nothing, claiming ancient "exemptions" granted by medieval kings.

In a daring novelty, Louis instructed his finance minister, a commoner by birth, to raise money from the nobility by means of a token tax on land. This set off a storm of protest, and the king backed down in the face of both noble and clerical opposition. During the Seven Years' War, he tried again, but again had to back down after a few years. The nobles steadfastly refused to acknowledge their taxable status, and the church insisted that it would make only occasional "donations" to the government at its discretion. By the time of Louis XV's death in 1774, the government was already on the verge of bankruptcy, unable to pay its military forces on time and forced to go to several moneylenders (notably, the Rothschild family) to meet current accounts.

Louis XV was succeeded by his weak-minded and indecisive grandson *Louis XVI* (r. 1774–1792). A sympathetic and decent person, Louis XVI was in no way qualified to lead an unstable country that was rapidly approaching a financial crisis. Specifically, he could not be expected to limit the vast expenditures that were wasted on the maintenance and frivolities (such as the amusements of Queen Marie Antoinette) of the royal court. Nor would he take an effective stand against the rising pretensions of the nobility. These latter, acting through their regional assemblies—the *parlements*—claimed to be the true defenders of French liberties.

This was the situation when the French decided to enter the American rebellion on the side of the colonials in order to get back at the British in North America and perhaps reclaim what they had lost in the Seven Years' War some years earlier (that is, Canada and the Mississippi valley). The expenses of this effort were very high for France. And by now, much of the entire budget had to be funded by borrowed money at rates of interest that rose higher and higher because of the justified fear that the government would declare bankruptcy and refuse to honor its outstanding debts. Half of the revenues had to be paid out just to meet the interest due on current accounts. No one knew when or whether the principal could be repaid.

Faced with the refusal—once more—of the nobles and the clergy to pay their share, the king reluctantly agreed to the election of an assemblage that had been forgotten for 175 years: the *Estates General,* or parliament of all France. No Estates had been called since 1614, for after that time first Richelieu and then Louis XIV had embarked on absolutist government. Now the principles of absolutism were in retreat; not the peasants or the townsmen, but the nobles and clergy had rebelled against the Crown's authority. Not the weak king, but the Estates would decide how taxes would be reformed and how much each would pay in the future. The nobles and clergy were determined to ensure that it would not be they who suffered.

⚜ CONSTITUTIONAL MONARCHY

According to tradition, the members of the delegations to the Estates General would be elected from their own estates. There were *three estates, or orders of society: the First Estate was made up of the clergy; the second consisted of the nobility, and the third included everyone else.* Rich or poor, rural or urban, educated or illiterate, all people who were neither in the church nor of the nobility, which meant about 97 percent of the population, were in the Third Estate. And tradition further held that each estate voted as a bloc, so that only three votes would be cast on any issue. Since the two "privileged" estates could always form a majority against the commoners, they were assured of retaining their privileges if they stayed together.

Calling of the Estates

The first two estates, the privileged, made up about 3 percent of the total population of France. The nobles and higher clergy lived a life apart from the great majority; they had their own customs and their own entertainments. They looked upon the commoners with contempt and, sometimes, fear. They controlled most high offices and held a very large share of the property in France—about 40 percent of the real estate and an even higher share of income-producing enterprises of all sorts.

The nobles and clergy dominated every aspect of public life except commerce and manufacturing. They were the exclusive holders of political power above the local level; they were the king's powerful servants and concession holders, and they had every social privilege imaginable. Some of the representatives of the First and Second Estates were youthful, liberal-minded individuals who sympathized with the demands for reform. Their

■ **A French Cartoon from 1792.** In this engraving the enraged peasant finds himself unchained, and reaches for his weapons while the shocked priest and noble recoil in horror.

assistance was crucially important to the success of the Revolution.

The *Third Estate* was represented mainly by lawyers and minor officials; a very few delegates were peasants, but there were virtually no representatives from the vast mass of illiterate laborers. The Third Estate's major complaints were the legal and social inequalities in the kingdom and their own lack of political representation (see the Document in this chapter). The Estate's guiding principles and its political philosophy were taken straight from the liberal Enlightenment.

In the spring of 1789, the Estates General convened at Versailles, the site of the royal palace and government outside Paris. The First and Second Estates were each represented by about 300 men; the Third Estate was allowed double representation. Immediately, a dispute arose over voting: the Third Estate demanded "one man, one vote," which would have given it the majority when joined with known sympathizers from the others. The

■ **The Fall of the Bastille.** This anonymous artist's sketch illustrates the events of July 14, 1789 when a Paris mob stormed the royal prison in Paris and released the handful of prisoners in it.

What Is the Third Estate?

The original ideals of the French Revolution were moderate and primarily concerned with eliminating the special privileges of the church and the nobles. By the 1780s, the large majority of the French populace understood more or less clearly that they were being severely disadvantaged by the various exemptions and concessions that the 3 percent of the population belonging to the privileged classes held.

No one better expressed the sentiments of the middle classes (the *bourgeoisie*) at this time than the priest Emmanuel Sieyès (1748–1836). In a pamphlet entitled *What Is the Third Estate?* he identified the commoners and their demands in a fashion that propelled him to national prominence. Abbé Sieyès made a special point of refuting the traditional claims to privilege by the nobles, based on their supposed generic abilities to govern well.

The plan of this book is fairly simple. We must ask ourselves three questions:

1. What is the Third Estate? Everything.
2. What has it been till now in the political order? Nothing.
3. What does it want to be? Something. . . .

. . . Only the well-paid and honorific posts are filled by members of the privileged order. Are we to give them credit for this? We could do so only if the Third Estate was unable or unwilling to fill these posts. We know the answer.

Nevertheless, the privileged have dared to preclude the Third Estate. "No matter how useful you are," they said, "no matter how able you are, you can go so far and no further. Honors are not for the likes of you. . . ."

. . . Has no one observed that as soon as the government becomes the property of a separate class, it starts to grow out of all proportion and that posts are created not to meet the needs of the governed but of those who govern them? . . .

Who is bold enough to maintain that the Third Estate does not contain within itself all that is needful to constitute a complete nation? It is like a strong and robust man with one arm still in chains. If the privileged order were removed, the nation would not be something less, but something more!

What then is the Third Estate? All; but an "all" which is fettered and oppressed. What would it be without the privileged order? It would be all; but free and flourishing. Nothing will go well without the Third Estate; everything would go considerably better without the two others. . . .

SOURCE: Excerpted from Sieyès, *What Is The Third Estate?* translated by M. Blondel, reprinted with permission of Greenwood Publishing Group, Inc., Westport, CT. (Praeger 1964).

other two estates refused, and the king was called upon to decide. After attempting a show of force, Louis XVI caved in to the demands of the Third Estate. A number of renegades from the privileged then joined with the Third Estate to declare themselves the *National Constituent Assembly,* and on June 20, 1789, they resolved not to disperse until they had given the country a constitution. In effect, this *was* the French Revolution, for if the Assembly were allowed to stand, the old order of absolutist monarchy was ended.

The National Assembly and Its Constitution

What the National Assembly wanted was a constitutional monarchy like England's. But the king's hope to reestab-lish control and the refusal of most of the high nobility and clergy to go along with the Assembly's project made a confrontation unavoidable. The confrontation came in the summer of 1789, with the **storming of the Bastille** (the royal prison in Paris) as the beginning. From here on for the next several months, the Parisian mob played a major role in the course of political events, the first time in modern history that the "underclass" asserted direct influence on government. The moderates and conservatives who dominated the Assembly were forced to listen and heed the demands of the poor, who staged a series of bread riots and wild demonstrations around the Assembly's meeting place.

On **August 4, 1789,** the nobles who had joined the Assembly made a historic voluntary renunciation of their

Maximilien Robespierre
1758–1794

The most dreaded name in all France during the Terror of 1793–1794 was that of the leader of the Committee of Public Safety, Maximilien Robespierre. A small figure with a high-pitched voice, he had come to the forefront during the National Assembly in 1790–1791 as an advocate of uncompromising democracy. His power base was the Society of Jacobins in Paris, which took him as its leader from the time of the king's bungled escape in 1791. Again and again he demanded the establishment of a republic and the removal of the king from the scene.

Robespierre was the driving force behind the steady radicalization of the Legislative Assembly in 1792 and its successor, the Convention. He engineered the declaration of the republic in August 1792 and justified the horrific massacre of imprisoned nobles and clerics in September as a necessary step in preparing France to defend its revolution against the menacing conservative powers on its borders. Attacked by his enemies in the Convention as a would-be dictator, he defied them to find any stain upon his patriotism and his selflessness in the revolutionary cause.

His election to the Committee of Public Safety in July 1793 meant a sharp turn toward even more shocking measures. In the fall he led the Convention into the Republic of Virtue, an attempt to supplant Christianity and indeed all religion in France. Patriotism would henceforth be measured by devotion to reason and the people, rather than to God and king. The names of the days and the months were changed to rid them of all overtones of gods and saints; the calendar was totally revised, and the counting of the years began all over again with the declaration of the republic in 1792 being Year One. Churches were renamed Temples of Reason, and the Catholic clergy subjected to both ridicule and bloody persecution. Much of this went far beyond what Robespierre intended, but he was powerless to stop the frenzy that he had helped set loose among the *sans-culottes* and the provincial Jacobins. The *sans-culottes* were the lower-class workers and artisans; the name literally means "without breeches," reflecting that the *sans-culottes* wore long trousers rather than the knee breeches of the middle and upper classes.

In 1794 Robespierre found it necessary to eliminate even his co-workers in the committee and the

■ **Female Patriots, 1790.** A club of women discusses the latest decrees of the revolutionary government, while a collection plate is set up for the relief of those families who have suffered in the cause.

feudal rights, which effectively ended serfdom and the nobility's legal privileges in France forever. A little later, the Assembly adopted the **Declaration of the Rights of Man and Citizen,** which went much farther than the almost simultaneous first ten amendments—the Bill of Rights—of the American Constitution.

By late 1789, the king and queen were virtual prisoners of the Parisian mob, and the National Assembly was hard at work on a constitution. The Revolution was becoming radical in its revisions of the previous order.

In 1790, the Assembly adopted the **Civil Constitution of the Clergy,** meaning the Catholic clergy in France. This allowed the state to confiscate the church's property and made the priests into agents of the emerging new government—paid by it and therefore controlled by it. This very radical act was a misreading of the country's temper, as the majority of the French were still good

Convention for being lukewarm supporters of the Revolution. He felt himself destined to cleanse the ranks of all who would falter on the road to perfection. In June he pushed the notorious Law of 22 Prairial through an intimidated Convention (Prairial was the name of the month in the revolutionary calendar). This allowed kangaroo courts all over France to issue the supreme penalty with or without substantive evidence of hostility to the government. In the summer of 1794, thousands of innocents were guillotined, either because they were anonymously denounced or simply because they were members of a "hostile" class such as the nobles. This was the height of the Terror. Robespierre justified it in a speech saying that since the Terror was but an inflexible application of justice, it was indeed a virtue and must be applauded.

■ **Robespierre.** An anonymous eighteenth century portrait.

In July 1794, the increasingly isolated Robespierre rose in the Convention to denounce the backsliders and the hesitant; in the past, such speeches had foretold another series of arrests by the People's Courts. This time, by prearrangement, the Convention shouted him down and arrested him. On the following day, July 28, he was guillotined amid sighs of relief and curses.

The dictator's character still arouses controversy. To some, he was the pure and selfless servant of the *menu peuple*, the little people who had made the Revolution and were ready to carry it through to a total re-creation of France. To others, he was the personification of evil and of the excess into which human beings are carried when they attempt to replace God with Man in defining morality and compassion.

Catholics and rallied to the support of the church's continued independence. The pope in Rome condemned the Civil Constitution; with the resistance against it began the counterrevolution. By 1791, the new constitution had been completed. It provided for powers to be shared between king and parliament along the English lines, but with even stronger powers for the parliament. A national election for this new Legislative Assembly was ordained.

❖ REVOLUTIONARY TERROR

The conservative governments of Europe were closely watching what was happening, of course, and were determined to restore Louis XVI to his rightful powers with armed force. The counterrevolutionary war began in the summer of 1792 when France in an ill-considered move declared war on Prussia and Austria. Combined with the

■ **The Levee on Masse.** In 1792, the National Convention created a new, massive army composed of volunteers from all classes and later conscripts. Here, citizens enthusiastically sign up while receiving money payments for their enrollment.

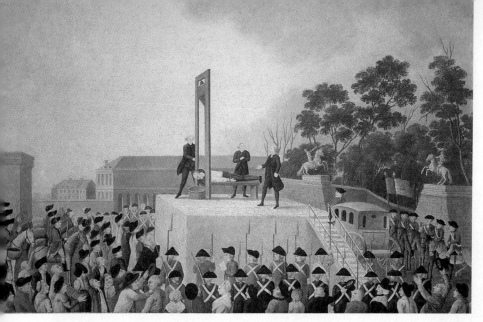

■ **The Execution of Louis XVI.** In January 1793, Louis XVI went to his death by guillotine in Paris. He was accused of treason to the revolutionary government of France by reason of his attempted flight. This painting is by an anonymous artist and witness.

earlier attempt of Marie Antoinette and Louis to flee the country, the war changed the internal atmosphere at a blow. Until 1792, the moderates, who wished to retain the monarchy and to avoid any challenge to the rule of property, had been in control. Now the radical middle-class element called the **Jacobins** (their original headquarters was in the Parisian convent of the Jacobin order of nuns) took over the Legislative Assembly. The moderates were soon driven into silence or exiled.

The Jacobins and Their Goals

The Jacobins were determined to extend the Revolution, to put the "common man" into the driver's seat, and to guarantee the eradication of aristocratic privileges and royal absolutism. They brushed aside the Legislative Assembly and called a National Convention, elected by universal male suffrage, into being. In Paris, a self-appointed Commune established itself as the legal authority. By early 1793, the war emergency encouraged the Jacobins to institute a *Reign of Terror* against all enemies within the country. This was the first known mass purge of people on account of their beliefs or suspected beliefs in history. Over the next year or so, between 25,000 and 40,000 victims were guillotined, and many tens of thousands more were imprisoned or exiled by the extraordinary Courts of the People, which were everywhere.

Among the early victims of the Jacobin Terror was the king. Held as a prisoner since his foiled attempt to escape, he was given a mock trial for treason and beheaded in January 1793. Marie Antoinette followed him to the guillotine in October. The killing of the king and queen was an enormous shock to the many Europeans who believed in liberal ideals and had seen the first stage of the Revolution as their implementation. From 1793 on, the educated classes of Europe were sharply divided between friends and enemies of the Revolution, with more and more tending toward the latter camp as the atrocities of the Terror were recognized. What had started as a high-principled campaign for justice, liberty, and progress had degenerated into a bloodbath.

The Reign of Robespierre

After September 1792, France was no longer a monarchy, but a republic. The executive power was exercised by a **Committee of Public Safety** with dictatorial authority. Under it, France became an egalitarian society, governed by the decrees of a small group. In the conservative provinces, the people rose in open revolt against the excesses in Paris, but the revolt was crushed mercilessly. Eventually, the Terror struck too many and too indiscriminately to be tolerated further. Maximilien **Robespierre** and Georges-Jacques **Danton,** the two leaders of the committee, fell out among themselves; Danton lost and was executed. By July 1794, fear of Robespierre's unpredictable acts of vengeance had become so great that the National Convention mutinied against him; within a couple of days, he fell from revolutionary chieftain to beheaded corpse. His measures and those of his colleagues were simply too radical for most French and especially the majority living in the traditional, Catholic provinces outside Paris (see the Biography in this chapter).

The years 1793–1794 were the height of the Revolution. The Jacobins produced many ideas and techniques of power that were new and would be imitated in revolutions to come over the next two centuries. They insisted:

- That all men were legally and politically equal—*Egalité*.
- That they were free—*Liberté*.
- That they were, or should be, brothers—*Fraternité*.

They elevated reason and patriotism to entirely new heights, making these faculties into virtues that were supposed to supplant the old ones of religion and subservience. They recognized no neutrality, nor would they tolerate neutrals; those who were not supporters of the People's Revolution were necessarily its enemies and would be treated accordingly. These were novel and shocking thoughts to the conservative forces inside and outside France. In the years of the Jacobin Revolution, early socialist, nationalist, and secularist philosophies and convictions also began to come to light. The nineteenth century would see their extensive development.

The Jacobins also started the **levee en masse** (*conscript army*) to defend the Revolution. They used that army so effectively that the French were on the offensive from 1794 onward against the coalition of Prussia, Austria, and eventually Britain and Holland as well. And they completed the *wholesale confiscation and distribution of land* to the peasants, thereby eliminating one of the major causes of complaint in pre-1789 France. The nobility and the church had lost their economic bases. They would never get them back.

✤ REACTION AND CONSOLIDATION

The machinery of terror was dismantled after the execution of Robespierre, as the fear had become too great for most French, even radicals, to live with. In place of the Jacobin-led poor who had greatly influenced government policy till now, the provincial middle classes and the wealthy came again to the fore. They chose several of their own to form a new government, called the **Directory,** because the top officials were five directors. They created a much more conservative-minded assembly, derived largely from the propertied classes.

The Directory

The Directory lasted about five years, during which France was able to settle down somewhat internally, while continuing to fight a series of wars against the opposing coalition. This period is called the **Thermidorean reaction** against the excesses of the Terror (the name came from Thermidor, one of the months in the new French calendar). It was marked by a great deal of corruption in public office, by the removal of the radical minority from influence, and by a general truce with the Catholic clergy and the peasants who were supporting them. It can best be understood as a "breathing space" that was desperately needed by a society that had been torn from its hinges by the events of 1789–1794.

The Coming of Napoleon

The five directors were soon squabbling among themselves, and the original wave of support for them vanished as they proved incapable of meeting the demands of the urban poor, particularly in Paris, for a better life. For a few years the directors were able to contain the discontent by force and by playing to the large majority of the French people, the peasantry. The peasants had gotten what they most wanted—land from the church and nobility. Now they were satisfied and wanted no more radical experiments.

Until 1798, the foreign war went well for France (see Map 34.1). A young general named *Napoleon Bonaparte* distinguished himself in the campaigns against the Austrians which forced the Austrians to make a losing peace with France. In 1798, however, Russia joined the anti-French coalition, and Britain remained an enemy that would not give in. Napoleon persuaded the directors to send him with a large army to Egypt to cut off the British commercial route to the East and thus induce this "nation of shopkeepers" to make peace. The Egyptian campaign of 1798–1799 was a disaster for France, but Napoleon saved his reputation by returning home secretly and letting his subordinates take the eventual blame. His ambitious wife, Josephine, and his friends had told him that the time was ripe to brush aside the unpopular civilians and take command in France. In November 1799 he acted on their advice.

A new era was about to begin, led by a thirty-year-old general who had come out of nowhere four years earlier to begin a military career of legendary brilliance. This half-Italian Corsican was originally a strong supporter of the Revolution, but had trimmed his sails in time to retain the Directory's confidence and become its leading military figure. He was a rising star, filled with a confident sense of destiny backed by an immense talent.

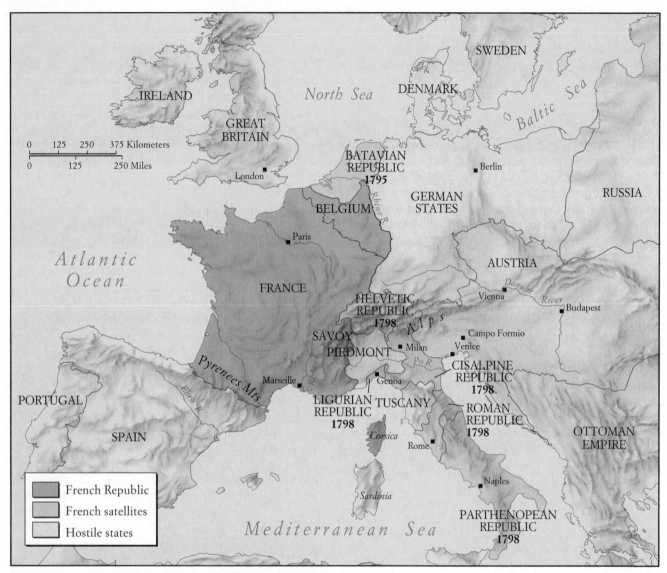

◉ **MAP 34.1 The French Republic, Its Satellites, and Hostile States in 1799.**

Summary

The problems of the French monarchy in the later eighteenth century were manifold. Despite natural advantages of climate and terrain, the country was riven by discontent, and the government was near bankruptcy. Inspired by the Enlightenment's ideas and the example of the North Americans, many people in the middle and upper classes were insistent that the weak and directionless regime of King Louis XVI must change. In 1789 their insistence finally overcame the stubborn selfishness of the nobility and the reluctance of the king and brought about a bloodless revolution in favor of constitutional monarchy. Within two years, however, this movement was turned into a radical social upheaval by the Jacobins and their supporters among the Parisian mob and an important part of the bourgeoisie.

The Jacobin Reign of Terror totally transformed France and the structure of French society, creating an egalitarian dictatorship in the name of the common people. Much of the support for these measures was generated by the war against conservative Europe that began in 1792. After it exceeded the tolerance of even its original supporters, the Jacobin dictatorship was overthrown in 1794, and a consolidation under the Directory was begun. The more radical and antiproperty features of the Terror were eliminated, and the war was prosecuted for a time with success. But popular disgust with the corruption and personal aggrandizement of the directors enabled the most successful of the generals, Napoleon Bonaparte, to sweep aside the civil authority and install himself in sole power in late 1799.

Test Your Knowledge

1. The trigger for the outbreak of revolution in France was
   a. the nobles' refusal to pay their share of taxes.
   b. peasant unrest caused by landlord abuses.
   c. an armed rebellion by outraged middle-class tax-payers.
   d. the assassination of the king.

2. One distinctive reason for the outbreak of revolt in France rather than elsewhere in Europe in 1789 was
   a. the existence of a monarch claiming absolutist powers.
   b. the wide impact of the theories of the Enlightenment on educated persons.
   c. the very poor financial situation of the government.
   d. the existence of an officially supported church and clergy.

3. The opening phase of the Revolution saw the establishment of a
   a. republic.
   b. military dictatorship.
   c. representative democracy.
   d. constitutional monarchy.

4. The two privileged estates in France were about 3 percent of the population but owned
   a. 10 percent of the land.
   b. 20 percent of the land.
   c. 40 percent of the land.
   d. 80 percent of the land.

5. The Third Estate in France consisted of
   a. the peasants.
   b. the urban dwellers of all types.
   c. the nonprivileged.
   d. the children of the nobles who had no right of succession.

6. Which of the following does *not* describe the administrators of the Reign of Terror?
   a. Mainly urban-based middle-class people
   b. Fearful of a conservative counterrevolution
   c. Unsympathetic toward the Catholic church and clergy
   d. Rural landowners and their clerical accomplices

7. The National Assembly was composed of
   a. the delegates of the Third Estate joined by sympathizers from the other estates.
   b. the Jacobins.
   c. the designated members of the first two estates joined by some of the third.
   d. the Paris mob.

8. Abbé Sieyes wrote a much-read pamphlet in 1789 that
   a. attacked the whole idea of the monarchy in France.
   b. defended the rights of the Third Estate.
   c. demanded the separation of church and state
   d. urged the immediate introduction of a proletarian dictatorship.

Identification Terms

August 4, 1789

Bastille (storming of)

Civil Constitution of the
Clergy

Committee of Public Safety

Danton (Georges-Jacques)

Declaration of the Rights of
Man and Citizen

Directory

Jacobins

levee en masse

Robespierre (Maximilien)

Thermidorean reaction

Bibliography

Cobb, R. *The People's Armies,* 1987. The tale of the first *levees en masse* creating the modern conscript army.

Connelly, O. *The French Revolution and the Napoleonic Era,* 1991. A constantly interesting account.

Dickens, C. *A Tale of Two Cities.* An exciting and more or less historical account of how British liberals reacted to the Terror of 1793.

Doyle, W. *Origins of the French Revolution,* 1981, and its earlier and differently angled companion piece by J. Lefebvre, *The Coming of the French Revolution,* 1947, are both invaluable.

Hampson, N. *Terror in the French Revolution,* 1981. A thorough and highly readable account of Robespierre and his associates.

Hufton, O. *The Poor in Eighteenth Century France,* 1974. The best exposé of the problem of poverty amid plenty; it explains how the French situation differed radically from that of the Americans.

Jones, P. *The Peasantry in the French Revolution,* 1988. Tells how far the peasants supported the Jacobin ideas and ideals.

Jordan, D. *The King's Trial: Louis XVI vs. the French Revolution,* 1979. A compelling and very readable story of the unfortunate king who could not quite comprehend what was happening to him and to his country.

Levy, D. G. et al., eds. *Women in Revolutionary Paris, 1789–1795,* 1979. A collection of documents that show how active the poor women of Paris were in the years of rebellion.

Palmer, R. *Twelve Who Ruled,* 1941. Has not been surpassed as a study of the Jacobin leadership.

Robiquet, J. *Daily Life in France under Napoleon,* 1963. One of the *Daily Life* series.

Schama, S. *Citizens,* 1989. Challenging in length and ideas, but well worth the effort.

THE BONAPARTIST EMPIRE AND THE PEACE OF VIENNA

THE NAPOLEONIC SETTLEMENT
FRENCH DOMINION OVER EUROPE
NAPOLEON PRO OR CON
THE TREATY OF VIENNA
OVERALL ESTIMATE OF THE VIENNA
SETTLEMENT

1796–1809	France conquers Spain, Portugal, Italy, Austria, Prussia, Holland
1799	Napoleon becomes First Consul
1804	Napoleon takes title of emperor
1812	Napoleon invades Russia
1814	Napoleon abdicates/exiled to Elba
1815	Napoleon returns: Hundred Days, Battle of Waterloo, exiled to St. Helena
1815	Treaty of Vienna
	Quadruple Alliance (Austria, Prussia, Russia, Britain)

For a decade and a half, the figure of Napoleon Bonaparte overshadowed every other on Europe's stage. The *Grande Armée* he brilliantly led carried the message of the Revolution by force into every part of the continent but Russia. In time, it spread throughout the world, not so much by arms as by the visions it created. Under Napoleon, however, the message was very different from that of the Jacobins and their dreams of uncompromising equality. Radical political and social change was no longer desired nor permitted; as the emperor declared, "the revolution is completed." Bonapartist policy assured that society would retain definite restraints while encouraging talent and ambition to rise. After Napoleon's defeat in 1814, that bourgeois vision of the proper society lived on in western Europe. The efforts of the reactionaries to eliminate it through the Vienna peace treaties were strenuous, but ultimately in vain.

✤ THE NAPOLEONIC SETTLEMENT

As the corruption mounted and the wars went badly, the Directory had become very unpopular. Finding very little resistance, Napoleon and his army accomplices pulled off the **coup d'état of 18 Brumaire (November 1799),** which made Napoleon **First Consul** of France, holding civil and military power in his ambitious hands.

From 1799 until 1804, Napoleon pretended to obey a new constitution that was concocted by his agents in the "tame" legislature he allowed to stand. He suppressed all political opposition and solidified his already high standing with the public by carrying out a series of acts, called collectively the *Napoleonic Settlement.* It embraced the following:

- Establishing the *concordat* with the papacy in 1801. This agreement pacified the French clergy and the peasants by declaring that Catholicism was the semi-official religion, but also pleased the strong anticlerical party by making the Catholic church and clergy a part of the state apparatus and putting them under strict controls.
- Creating administrative and judicial systems that have lasted in France until the present-day. Napoleon created a highly centralized network that went far to unify the formerly diverse provinces and regions with the capital.
- Granting legal title to the peasants for the lands they had seized.
- Giving the country new civil and criminal codes of law (the **Civil Code of 1804**).

- Putting the national currency and finances in good order.
- Establishing social peace by allowing the exiles to return if they agreed to support the new France, crushing royalist plots to return the Bourbons, and also crushing the radical Jacobin remnants.

✤ FRENCH DOMINION OVER EUROPE

In 1804, Napoleon did what everyone had expected and crowned himself monarch of France. He took the formal title of emperor, for by then France controlled several non-French peoples. His intention was to found a Bonaparte dynasty that would replace the Bourbons. As long as his wars went well, he was so popular at home that he could raise vast conscript armies and levy heavy taxes through a legislature and bureaucracy that were completely his creatures. And the wars went well for France for several years.

Napoleon was perhaps the greatest military mind the modern era has produced. He devised and led one victorious campaign after another against European conservative powers between 1796 and 1809. French armies conquered *Spain, Portugal, the Italian peninsula, Austria (three times), Prussia, and Holland,* all of which were either incorporated into France directly, made into satellites, or neutralized. He also defeated a Russian army sent against France and was on the verge of invading England when his defeat in a major sea battle at *Trafalgar* off the Spanish coast in 1805 put that plan to rest forever.

Coalitions against Napoleon came and went, but his implacable enemy was Britain. Except for a few months in 1802, the English refused all offers to make peace and went on fighting France almost uninterruptedly for twenty-two years (1793–1814), both in Europe and overseas, on land and at sea. The British actively supported the Spanish guerrilla war against Napoleon, which began in 1808 and was eventually successful; they also fought on the Continent in the final battles against the dictator. Mostly, however, they supported others with money, naval protection, and diplomacy. While the fight against France took on the character of an international crusade for "legitimacy" (meaning no revolutionary usurpation of government), the British also saw it as a way of maintaining a *balance of power* on the European continent.

Napoleon's relations with Russia were always edgy, even when the Russian government agreed to adopt a pro-French and anti-British stance after its defeat at French hands in 1807. By 1810, Napoleon was convinced that the tsar, **Alexander I,** was preparing hostilities again and would form an alliance with the English. From his base in France's Polish satellite, Napoleon planned an invasion that would eliminate any threats from Russia. In the summer of 1812, the invasion began with a huge army of 600,000, including Frenchmen, their coerced allies, and some volunteers.

Napoleon's *campaign in Russia in the winter of 1812* is one of the epic stories of modern war. Unable to gain a decisive victory over the main Russian army despite a very bloody clash at Borodino, the French pushed onto the steppes, occupied Moscow, and waited for peace offers from their presumably beaten foe. But no overtures came from Tsar Alexander, who was residing far to the north in St. Petersburg. Confident that he could outwait his opponent, Alexander prepared his counterblow: the Russian winter.

Only belatedly did the French realize that they had fallen into a trap. But by then, Moscow had been burned down around them, food and fodder had run low, and the first snows of an early winter found them 800 miles from

■ **The Eve of Austerlitz.** Perhaps Napoleon's most brilliant victory, Austerlitz, was the key to the French mastery of Europe in 1805–1806. This painting by Francois Lejeune shows the emperor (in white trousers at center) making final arrangements for the coming day's attack.

Retreat from Moscow

Napoleon's Russian campaign marked the death knell of the emperor's aura of invincibility and inspired the final European coalition that destroyed him. But although many accounts of alliances, conferences, and battles have come down to us, only a very few accounts of the experiences of the ordinary people caught up in these great events have survived.

One of the most straightforward and unsophisticated (and for that reason, most evocative) accounts is the diary of Jakob Walter, a nineteen-year-old Westphalian stonemason conscripted into the *Grande Armée* of Napoleon. He was one of those fortunate enough to survive the disaster in Russia that began with the retreat from Moscow in the fall of 1812. The following excerpts relate some of the terrible sufferings that occurred as the French withdrew through hostile country in freezing weather without adequate supplies:

. . . At Smolensk, horses were shot and eaten. Because I could not even get a piece of the meat, and my hunger became too violent, I took along the pot I carried, stationed myself next to a horse that was being shot, and caught up the blood from its breast. I set this on the fire, let it coagulate, and ate the lumps without salt.

While we tarried two days at Smolensk the Russians advanced and awaited us at Minsk. Everyone

hastily fled. Cannons were thrown into the river. The hospitals were nearly all left to the enemy, and, as commonly rumored, they were set afire and burned with all their inmates. This is more credible when one considers the treatment (we gave) to captive Russians. Whole columns of captives were transported past us, and anyone who lagged behind because of weakness and fell back as far as the rear guard was shot in the neck so that his brain crashed down beside him. . . .

When we came near the Beresina river, there was a place where Napoleon ordered his horses to be unharnessed, and where he ate. He watched his army pass by in the most wretched condition. What he may have felt in his heart is impossible to surmise. His outward appearance seemed indifferent and unconcerned about the wretchedness of his soldiers; only ambition and lost honor may have made themselves felt in his heart; and although the French and the allies shouted into his ears many oaths and curses about his own guilty person, he was still able to listen to them unmoved.

. . . We came to a half-burnt village away from the road, in which a cellar was found beneath a country mansion. We sought for potatoes, and I also pressed down the broad stairway, although the cellar was already half-filled with people (who were also searching for food). When I was at the bottom of the steps, the screaming began from right under my feet. Every

friendly territory. The long, agonizing retreat that commenced in October (too late!) claimed the lives of two-thirds of the *Grande Armée* by starvation, freezing, and combat before the survivors stumbled onto friendly Polish soil (see the Document in this chapter). Foreseeing the disaster and wishing to be on the scene when the news arrived in France, the emperor abandoned his troops midway and hurried on to Paris.

Napoleon's major weapon was irretrievably broken despite his frantic efforts to raise another army in France during the spring of 1813. The culminating **Battle of the Nations at Leipzig in 1813** ended in French defeat at the hands of Russian, Prussian, and Austrian forces. Occupied

Europe was gradually freed of French troops and governors, and in March 1814 Bonaparte was forced to abdicate. After twenty-three years, the wars ignited by the French Revolution were finally over.

⚜ NAPOLEON PRO OR CON

The debate over Napoleon's greatness as a leader and statesman has occupied the French and others for almost two centuries. Opinions divide nearly as sharply now as during his lifetime. While some see him as a man of genius and the founder of a progressive, stable social order, others see him as a dictator whose visions for society were

one crowded in, and none could get out. Here people were trampled to death and suffocated; those who wanted to stoop down for something were bowled over by those standing, and had to be stepped upon. When I reflected on the murderous shrieking, I gave up pushing into the cellar, thinking: how will I get out again? I then pressed flat against the wall so that it afforded me some shelter and pushed vigorously. . . .

In the village of Sembin . . . there was a burned house, under which there was a low, timber-roofed cellar with a small entrance from the outside. Here again, as potatoes and the like were being hunted for, the beams suddenly fell in, and those who were inside and were not entirely burned up or suffocated were jumping about with burning clothes, screaming, whimpering, or freezing to death in terrible pain.

SOURCE: Jacob Walter, *Diary of a Napoleonic Foot Soldier*, editor 1991 edition Marc Rarff, Bantam Doubleday Dell.

■ **The Burning of Moscow, 1812.**

always subordinate to his concern for his own welfare and glory.

There can be little doubt that he was an able administrator and selector of talent. In those crucial capacities, he came closer to the ideal "enlightened despot" than any other ruler of his day or earlier. In contrast to earlier French governments, his government was for years efficient, able, popular, and relatively honest. Men of ability could move upward regardless of their social background. Though not a revolutionary himself, *Napoleon kept the promises that the Revolution had made* to the peasants and to the middle classes. He confirmed, though he may not have originated, many of the liberals' favorite measures, such as the disestablishment of the Catholic church, equality before the law, and the abolition of privilege by birth. His codes provided a modern, uniform basis for all French law, both civil and criminal (though the subordination of women was kept very much intact). His administrative reforms replaced the huge mishmash that had been the French bureaucracy with a thoroughly rational centralized system; now power was concentrated in the government in Paris, which appointed and oversaw the provincial and local officials.

But the imperial regime developed more than a few blemishes as well. After about 1808, the *government was a dictatorship* in which individual liberties depended on

Napoleon's wishes. No political parties were allowed, and the legislature was at all times a sham; the press was so heavily controlled that it became meaningless; political life was forced underground; an internal spy system had informants everywhere.

French policies in the occupied or satellite territories that made up the Napoleonic empire (see Map 35.1) were often harsh even when enlightened, and patriots who opposed French orders were executed without mercy. The non-French populations were steadily exploited; they were expected to pay taxes, furnish conscripts for the armies, and trade with France on terms advantageous to the French. Napoleon also strongly promoted the nationalist spirit that had been so important to the early years of the Revolution, as long as the subject peoples accepted the absolute leadership of Paris. When they did not, they were regarded as traitors to Napoleon's rule and dealt with accordingly, as the Prussian liberals learned to their dismay when they attempted to reject French overlords after Prussia's defeat in 1806. There is also no doubt that as time went on, *Bonaparte became increasingly cynical and indifferent* to the welfare of the masses.

■ **Napoleon Leading His Troops.** This magnificent if imaginary scene of Napoleon Crossing the Alps was created by J.L. David to give the French a vision of their emperor they could not forget.

■ **Sketch of the General Napoleon.** In this unfinished sketch, the great French painter J.L. David (1748–1825) captures the likeness of the "man of destiny" before he seized power.

Perhaps, after all is said, the question of Napoleon's greatness comes down to how much one values glory. For many French, then and now, *la gloire* is a priceless asset, and under Napoleon France reached the zenith of armed power and the respect it necessarily generates. For others, the oppressive aspects of his internal regime far outweigh its glories, and his memory outside France remains tainted by the fact that in bringing a version of the Revolution to the rest of Europe, he tried to accomplish through force what can succeed only through voluntary imitation.

⚜ THE TREATY OF VIENNA

With Napoleon exiled (in luxurious circumstances) to the island of **Elba** in the Mediterranean, the allies returned France to the Bourbon dynasty, in the person of the old and feeble **Louis XVIII,** a brother of the last king. He issued a Constitutional Charter that struck a middle ground between the extremes of liberal government and conservative reaction. The allies meanwhile went to Vienna to try to work out a general settlement of the extremely complex issues that the two decades of war had created. Originally, France was not invited, but the brilliant and slippery **Talleyrand,** foreign minister to Louis XVIII, used his talents to assure that France received an

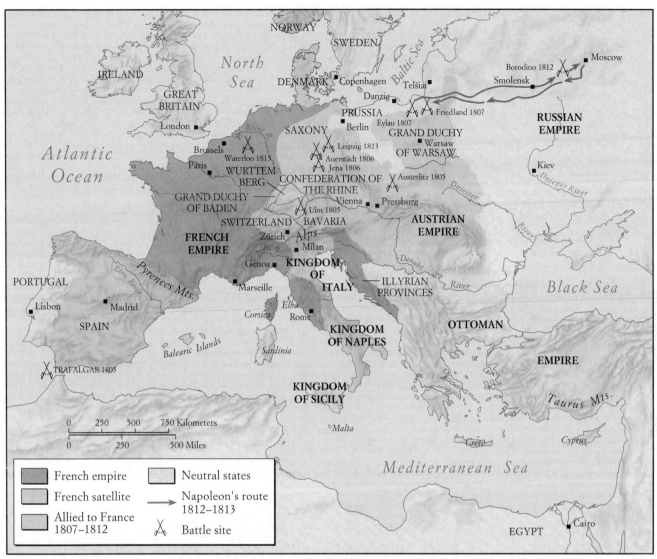

⊙ **MAP 35.1 The Napoleonic Empire in 1810–1813.** Except for Britain and Russia, Napolean controlled almost all of Europe by 1810, either directly through incorporation into his empire, or by coerced alliances.

equal seat at the bargaining table (see the Biography in this chapter).

In the midst of the discussions came the news in February 1815 that Napoleon had fled Elba, landed in southern France, and issued a call to all his followers to renew the war. They responded with enthusiasm in the tens of thousands. The *Hundred Days campaign* nearly succeeded, but ended in total defeat for the Bonapartists at **Waterloo.** This time, Napoleon was shipped off as a prisoner of war to a rock in the South Atlantic, St. Helena, where he lived out the remaining six years of his

life. Years later, his body was brought back to Paris and given a glorious reburial in the building called Les In-valides, which is now a major tourist attraction.

In Vienna, the "Big Four" victors—Austria, Prussia, Russia, and England—were busy working out the political and territorial outlines of a new Europe. Actually, the conservative powers, led by Austria's **Prince Clemens von Metternich,** hoped to reconstruct the old Europe but found that was impossible. Too much had happened since 1789: too many hopes had been awakened, borders changed, kings removed, and constitutions issued. In the

Talleyrand
1754–1836

Maurice de Talleyrand-Périgord, prince of Benevento, diplomat extrordinaire, and foreign minister of France under five different regimes, was born in 1754 the second son of a high noble family. As was customary for that time and that class, his upbringing was turned over to a nurse and a governess, while his mother and father were in constant attendance at the royal court. When Talleyrand was five, a fall from a chest of drawers injured his foot and lamed him for life. It also deprived him of the career in the army that would normally have been his lot; when he was thirteen, he was sent to a seminary against his will, and he never forgave the parents who sent him nor the church that he was supposed to serve.

Consecrated bishop of Autun in 1789, he at once joined with the moderate members of the Third Estate in the deliberations of the Estates General at Versailles. In general, he endorsed the state's confiscation of the church's property, the Civil Constitution of the Clergy, and the subordination of the religious establishment to the government. For these opinions, he was excommunicated by the pope and spent the rest of his long life as a layman.

Talleyrand's demonstrated administrative and diplomatic abilities caused the National Assembly to name him as a special emissary to Great Britain in 1792. But the Revolution's radical turn later in 1792, especially the execution of the king and queen, frightened Talleyrand, who remained all his life an adherent of constitutionalism and tolerance. Expelled from Britain after the war broke out, he went to the United States (whose society he did not care for) for two years and then returned to France under the Directory in 1796. He served as foreign minister both for the Directory and for Napoleon, whose triumphant takeover in 1799 Talleyrand had a hand in preparing.

For the next eight years, Talleyrand was the most important man in France except for the emperor himself. He constantly tried to tame Napoleon's ambitions and to work out a permanent peace between France and the rest of Europe. He was convinced that Bonaparte's cynical disregard of the interests of other powers would not succeed in the long run, although it

---

years since, Europe had passed a great watershed in political and social history. The "Old System" of European government and society (*l'ancien régime*) was like Humpty-Dumpty after his fall—it could not be reconstructed.

After nearly coming to blows on the thorny question of what should happen to Poland—a state that had been gobbled up by its neighbors and partially re-created by Napoleon—the four victors hammered out a series of agreements that collectively gave Europe its political borders for the next hundred years. They were guided in their work by some underlying principles:

1. *Legitimacy in government.* Kings were restored to their thrones, and radical constitutions written by pro-French revolutionaries were thrown out or rewritten to reflect more conservative themes. Revolutions would henceforth be suppressed by international collaboration.

2. *International cooperation to maintain peace.* The victors (and soon also France) formed an alliance with regular meetings of foreign ministers. The Quadruple Alliance lasted for only a decade, but its principles of international responsibility for peace guided diplomatic meetings throughout the century from 1815 to 1914.

3. *Discouragement of nationalism and liberalism in politics.* The conservative forces saw both nationalism and liberalism as evils brought by the French radicals to Europe; neither was recognized as a legitimate demand of the citizenry.

4. *Balance of power.* No single state would be allowed to dominate the Continent as had France under Napoleon.

Within the framework created by these general principles, each of the four chief victors had its own agenda:

was sustained at the moment by superior force. But he could not get his master to see things in this light, and after the peace of Tilsit in 1807, Talleyrand resigned his ministry. He remained a member of the Imperial Council of State, however, and still possessed some influence with Napoleon until the disastrous decision to invade Russia in 1812. Supposedly, he then told Napoleon, "It is the beginning of the end," an opinion that the emperor interpreted as treason. The two last saw each other in early 1814, when Napoleon abdicated and the defeated French began negotiations with the allies.

Talleyrand's career in international diplomacy now resumed with a flourish, as he was able to induce Tsar Alexander I of Russia to support the return of the Bourbon family to the throne of France in the name of the sacred principle of "legitimacy." He was also crucial to the decision to allow France to come to the Congress of Vienna as an almost equal member rather than as a defeated enemy. Talleyrand's skill at protecting French national interest at Vienna became legendary. He was rewarded by being appointed France's foreign minister once again in 1815, this time by the restored Bourbon Louis XVIII. Shortly afterward, he resigned the post, however, preferring to retire to a life of ease and social activity at his country mansion.

He was by now immensely rich, having taken full advantage of many opportunities to increase his wealth during the Napoleonic era. His many enemies in Paris claimed that he had acquired his money by illegal means, and the accusations were at least partly true: he had taken part in schemes to manipulate the nation's finances for his own advantage more than once. Apparently, a man who took his patriotic duties to the nation very seriously and who was energetic in their execution saw no moral problems in making himself wealthy by means that verged on illegality, if not clearly so.

In 1830, the old man emerged briefly into the political limelight once again as a supporter of the "Citizen King" Louis Philippe, who took the throne after the July Revolution in that year. Louis wished to make him foreign minister once more, but Talleyrand preferred to be ambassador to London, where he negotiated the treaty that made England and France formal allies for the first time in centuries. In 1834, he resigned his post and returned to France to die. In his final weeks, he reconciled himself to the Catholic church and died with honors showered upon him as one of the greatest statesmen of the age. He had terminated a loveless marriage in 1815 and left no heirs.

- *Russia,* under the visionary Tsar Alexander I (1801–1825), had been the main force in the final military defeat of the French and now for the first time played a leading role in European affairs. Alexander had originally sympathized with liberalism and constitutionalism, but came to think better of it after the struggles with Napoleon began. After 1817, Russia became a force for the status quo. Under Alexander's successor, Nicholas I (1825–1855), the country became a bastion of reactionary and antiliberal forces.

- *Austria* under the astute diplomat Prince Metternich, who served as foreign minister from 1809 until 1848, also took a leading role in the reconstruction. Metternich was convinced that nationalism and popular participation in government would ruin the multinational state of Austria and then all of Europe. He fought these ideas with all his considerable skill and energy, and because he stayed at the helm of Vienna's foreign policy for almost forty years, he became the outstanding example and main voice of European conservatism until 1848. Austria stagnated intellectually and scientifically, however, as conservatism turned into first reaction and then paralysis. As Metternich himself put it by the 1830s, "Austria is not governed, it is administered." That is, there was no policy at the top except to hang on.

- *Prussia* originally tended toward liberalism and carried out internal reforms under a group of statesmen (Karl vom Stein and Karl August von Hardenberg) who admired the constitutional phase of the French Revolution but hated Napoleon's dictatorship. But, after the defeat of the French, the Prussian king Frederick William III asserted his distaste for constitutional government and succeeded in turning back the political clock for a generation. Prussia came out of the wars with France strengthened and expanded, with improved technology and an aggressive entrepreneurial class. By the 1830s, it had the best educational system in Europe and was in a position to contest Austria for the lead in pan-German affairs. This contest would become more intense as time went on.

- *Great Britain* was clearly the leading naval power and one of the strongest military forces in Europe by 1815. But the British primarily wanted to concentrate on their business interests to take advantage of the big lead they had established since 1780 in the race to industrialize (see the next chapter). The British always felt uncomfortable on the same side of the table as Tsar Alexander and Metternich, and by 1825 they had abandoned the alliance system. Having helped establish the balance of power on the Continent, they retreated into *splendid isolation* for the rest of the nineteenth century, involving themselves in Europe's affairs only when they deemed their commercial and business interests endangered. After about 1825, the British government tended more and more toward liberal ideas, especially in economics, where the English manufacturers became the vanguard of the free trade philosophy (see the next chapter).

These four powers plus France would be the molders of Europe's destinies for the rest of the nineteenth century. Italy was not yet formed into a single power and would in any case remain in the second tier in international affairs. Spain subsided into a third-rank state, especially after losing its empire in the western hemisphere early in the nineteenth century. Turkey was "the sick man of Europe," increasingly powerless to protect its European possessions. Already in the early nineteenth century, the Scandinavian countries had adopted the neutral course that they would henceforth maintain.

❖ OVERALL ESTIMATE OF THE VIENNA SETTLEMENT

During the nineteenth century, the treaty making at Vienna was criticized on many grounds. The aristocratic negotiators meeting in their secluded drawing rooms *ignored the growing forces of popular democracy, national feeling, liberalism, and social reform.* They drew up territorial boundaries in ignorance of and disregard for popular emotions and restored kings to their thrones without citizenry support. The treaty makers were a small handful of upper-class men, contemptuous of the ordinary people and their right to participate in politics and government.

All these criticisms are more or less true. Yet, if success is measured by the practical test of enduring peace, it would be hard to find another great international settlement as successful as the treaty of Vienna of 1815. The borders it established endured without serious challenge for fifty years until the German and Italian petty states were unified into two great powers. With the single exception of the Franco-Prussian conflict of 1870, Europe did not experience an important, costly war until the outbreak of World War I in 1914. The great multilateral conflicts that had marked the late seventeenth and all of the eighteenth centuries were avoided, and Europe had three generations of peaceable economic expansion.

The Vienna Treaties were followed by a century of general progress for the middle classes and toward the end, at least, for the common people as well. That this was not the original intent of the peacemakers is beside the point. Any judgment of the treaties must consider that the massive social and economic changes witnessed by the nineteenth century were successfully accommodated within the international relationships established in 1815.

■ **The Congress of Vienna, 1815.** Each of the major participants in the Congress of Vienna is pictured here. Metternich is the figure in white trousers, sixth from the left among the standees, while the sly Talleyrand waits for his chance, seated fourth from the right.

Summary

Bonaparte's genius in military matters is undisputed and was frequently proven in a series of wars with all of Europe. Whether he properly used his talents to benefit society as a whole is another question and still arouses sharp debate. The conquering Napoleonic armies carried the propaganda and the principles of the French Revolution to most of the Continent, but the unwanted presence of the French often meant that it was nationalism that made the most memorable impression on the natives. At home, Napoleon presided over a settlement that was acceptable to almost all, and it created the modern French state and government.

Once the French were defeated, the four chief victorious powers, led by Austria, attempted to restore Europe to its previous state under the slogan of legitimacy and the sacredness of historical rights. This task was impossible in several respects because too much had changed that could not be reversed, and the governments grudgingly accepted those changes. On the whole, however, the principles of legitimacy and conservatism were enforced for a generation, and the general outline of the Vienna political settlement held up for a century.

Test Your Knowledge

1. Napoleon came to power in 1799 because of the
   a. public reaction against the Terror of the Jacobins.
   b. complete anarchy in France after Robespierre's fall.
   c. threat of the counterrevolutionaries.
   d. unpopularity of the Directory.
2. The battle at Trafalgar
   a. assured French domination of most of the Continent.
   b. frustrated a potential French invasion of England.
   c. knocked the Russians out of the anti-French coalition.
   d. made it necessary for France to sell the Louisiana Territory to the United States.
3. The Hundred Days campaign ended with Napoleon's
   a. retreat from Russia.
   b. defeat at Waterloo.
   c. escape from exile in Elba.
   d. surrender of Paris.
4. Which of the following did Napoleon *not* preside over in France?
   a. The signing of a *concordat* with the Vatican
   b. The creation of a new administrative system
   c. The enactment of uniform legal codes for the whole country
   d. The elimination of the Catholic clergy's influence on French opinion
5. The chief conservative powers at the Vienna peace conference were

   a. Prussia, Russia, and Austria.
   b. Prussia, Russia, and Britain.
   c. Austria, Russia, and France.
   d. Russia, Prussia, and France.
6. Which country of post-1815 Europe does the phrase "splendid isolation" apply to most directly?
   a. Great Britain
   b. France
   c. Russia
   d. Turkey
7. Which of the following was least considered in the negotiations at Vienna?
   a. The right of forcibly deposed monarchs to regain their thrones
   b. The right of working people to determine their form of government
   c. The right of states to adequate territory and resources for defense
   d. The right of nations to be governed by one of their own
8. That France was able to quickly gain a place in the deliberations of the great powers after Napoleon's defeat was due primarily to
   a. the negotiating skills of Talleyrand.
   b. the respect for the Bourbon king.
   c. the size of the French armies even after 1815.
   d. the rapid expansion of French foreign trade.

Identification Terms

Alexander I

ancien régime

Battle of the Nations
(Leipzig, 1813)

Civil Code of 1804

coup d'état of 18 Brumaire
(November 1799)

Elba

First Consul

Louis XVIII (Bourbon
dynasty)

Metternich (Prince Clemens
von)

Talleyrand (Maurice de
Talleyrand-Périgord)

Waterloo

Bibliography

Bergeron, L. *France under Napoleon,* 1981. Covers all aspects of French society under the emperor with a light but learned touch.

Doyle, W. *The Oxford History of the French Revolution,* 1989. Very strong on both the revolutionary and the imperial periods. It is divided into convenient segments.

Geyl, P. *Napoleon: For and Against,* 1949. A famous collection of views never surpassed for readability and stimulus.

Herold, J. C. *The Age of Napoleon,* 1968. A lively account.

Markham, F. *Napoleon and the Awakening of Europe,* 1954. Focuses on the impact of the revolution on national feeling, both in and outside France.

———. *Napoleon,* 1963. One of the best biographies of the great leader. Another good one is V. Cronin, *Napoleon Bonaparte,* 1972. His military campaigns are well treated in D. Chandler, *The Campaigns of Napoleon,* 1966.

Nicholson, H. *The Congress of Vienna,* 1946. A witty and thoughtful history of the nineteenth century's most famous political conclave.

PART 5

INDUSTRY AND WESTERN HEGEMONY

1800–1920

The nineteenth century was the period *par excellence* of European imperialism and its economic facilitator, industrial development. During this century, there was no area of the globe that Europeans could not reach, influence, arbitrate, and remold, either directly or through their acculturated intermediaries. During this time, two worlds were rapidly forming: the industrialized Western world and the traditional agrarian-based world of everyone else. By the end of the century, "Western" had come to include North America, but not yet Latin America or Japan, though both were moving into the West's wake.

A Europe-wide population explosion was a chief factor in setting off the waves of technological improvements, new financial resources, and economic reorganizations that together make up the industrial production mode. By the Napoleonic wars, Britain had seized a firm lead in industry and finance that would not be overtaken by its closest competitors until near the end of the century. The non-Western world was relegated to the position of raw material supplier and potential market for the surplus generated by the industrial countries.

To secure this dependent relationship, a second wave of imperial expansion, more rapid and more politically inspired than the first, rolled out over Asia and Africa in the late nineteenth century. It was thrust forward by varied impellers: military strategy, economic aspirations, the "white man's burden," and fear of falling behind the competitors.

On the eve of the West's fratricide in World War I, it seemed to be the high noon rather than the sunset of imperialism. When the smoke of battle had lifted, the extent of the physical and financial damages to Europe became clear at once, but the political and moral changes induced by a war in which no European country was a winner emerged only very slowly. Among the later casualties was the image of the irresistibility and omniscience of the whites in the nonwhite world.

Chapters 36 and 37 begin this section with a detailed look at the process of industrializing production and the social changes that accompanied it. In Chapters 38 and 39, the West remains the focal point, with an examination of the mature national states, including the new Italy and Germany formed in the 1860s.

The non-Western world takes center stage in Chapters 40 through 44 with serial commentary on, first, East Asia and then the Muslims, sub-Saharan Africa, and Latin America through the end of the nineteenth century. The different responses to Western imperialism by the peoples of these three continents receive extensive consideration. In Chapters 45 and 46, the mature industrial society of the West is examined, with emphasis on the workers' responses to the Second Industrial Revolution. Finally, Chapter 47 is devoted to the causes and course of World War I and its disputed settlement.

	Law and Government	Economy
EUROPEANS	After French Revolution, law is based on secular viewpoint rather than religious authority. Government becomes steadily more sophisticated, bureaucracy is universal in advanced societies. Colonial imperialism revives in mid-century and is extended to Asia and Africa by armed force and economic activity.	Industrialization develops throughout this period, with deep regional variations of pace and impacts. By 1920 northern and western Europe far more industrial than east and south. Capitalist structures and processes are challenged by newly organized Marxist groups in most countries. Mechanized, factory-based mode of production replaces handwork after Second Industrial Revolution.
WEST ASIANS AND AFRICANS	Both Muslim and African regions subordinated increasingly to Western imperialism. Islamic states in Middle East reduced to satellites or taken over entirely by Europeans. The Ottomans are helpless to defend their interests and empire crumbles. African interior penetrated after 1840 by various imperialist missions and by private individuals; "scramble" for Africa completed by 1890s.	Economy of West Asia heavily damaged by rise of Atlantic maritime trade and by the continuing decline of Muslim empires. Machine industry is still unknown at end of period, and huge technological gap has opened between West and Muslim worlds. Africa less affected, partly because of lower levels of international trade and contacts, and the lower intensity of European interest in Africa after abolition of trans-Atlantic slaving.
SOUTH AND EAST ASIANS	Tokugawa shogunate and Manzhou dynasty continue in Japan and China throughout most of the period. Both encounter Western penetration and aggression after 1840 but respond in sharply different fashions; the Meiji Restoration in Japan is very successful but Manzhou China collapses into anarchy. The Mughals in India also fail to deal with West successfully and are eliminated as governors by both Hindus and Europeans. Southeastern Asia and Pacific islands are mainly appropriated by British and French colonialists in second half of century.	China begins to feel overpopulation problem in early part of period, while Japan continues to prosper and urbanize. The urban population and particularly the merchants in both countries gain prestige and some power in government, while the peasantry sinks. After Meiji Restoration (1867) Japan rapidly industrializes and soon is leading economic power in Asia. China attempts economic reforms but cannot overcome mandarin traditionalism. India enters urban age and selective industrial development as the major British colony.
AMERICANS	After 1825 both North and South Americans are independent peoples pursuing different goals in government and law. North Americans continue their heritage of constitutional and representative government within the republican form; South Americans also adopt republican form but are unable to translate it into effective constitutional government. Criollos continue to rule as before over the mestizo majority. The United States pioneers in universal enfranchisement of whites and basic democratic forms, while the slavery question has to be decided finally by a bloody war.	After unspectacular but steady growth to 1860, North America's industrial economy, propelled by largescale immigration, explodes after the Civil War. By 1920, the United States is the most potent industrial nation in the world. Latin America receives relatively little immigration and little capital investment until the early twentieth century; industry is minimal and the overwhelmingly agrarian society is still controlled by a relative handful of wealthy families.

INDUSTRY AND WESTERN HEGEMONY 1800–1920

Peoples: *Europeans, West Asians and Africans, South and East Asians, Americans*

Religion and Philosophy	Arts and Culture	Science and Technology
The Enlightenment and French/American Revolutions attack official churches and the link between state and church. Secularist philosophies become widely accepted and after Darwin, traditional Christianity is seen as anti-scientific by many educated persons. A philosophy of progress based on the advance of science becomes popular.	Major achievements in all the plastic and pictorial arts. Neoclassicism followed by Romanticism and Realism as leading schools of art and literature. Late nineteenth and early twentieth centuries especially significant for innovations. Beginnings of mass culture facilitated by rapidly changing technologies.	Physical and biological sciences' spectacular advances is rivaled toward end of this period by innovations in the social sciences. Technological breakthroughs multiply, utilizing new energy sources. Positivism is ruling philosophy, challenged at end of nineteenth century by destructions of Newtonian physics and by antirationalist trends in the arts.
Nadir of Muslim religious and cultural vitality. Secularism rejected by traditionalists who dominate society. Toward end of period some signs of revival via Arab nationalism. Both North and sub-Saharan Africa dominated by Western cultural influences and Christian missionaries exert significant influence on the non-Muslim areas.	Art forms both in Muslim and animist regions stultify or become imitative of previous work. Still some fine artisanry produced in Persia, Ottoman Empire, and the few parts of Africa where the machine products of West have not yet penetrated. Reduced wealth and a sense of impotence contribute to the decline of creativity.	This period is the nadir of Asian science and technology as compared with West and with North America. Occasional attempts to remedy through modern education are blocked by religious fundamentalism and by anti-Western feelings of Muslim populace.
Muslims and Hindus peaceably contest for allegiance of northern Indians under Mughal rule while both religions see the rise of strong minority sects. In China and Japan, Buddhism in several forms blends with Confucian and Dao beliefs (China) and Shintoism (Japan). Neo-Confucian philosophy in China also influences Japanese. Christian missionary efforts in all three countries bring relatively minor returns.	In China and Japan the later eighteenth century was a high point in both pictorial and literary arts. Luxury items of bronze, porcelain, silk, and jade enjoy enormous prestige in West. Mughal arts extraordinarily cosmopolitan and reach high degree of excellence as political powers wane.	Until 1867 Japan continues to lag the West but then rapidly closes gap in sciences and technology. China resists Western ways and does not develop the scientific outlook or sufficient Western contact to make much difference. The traditional Muslim and Hindu views of life hinder India's progress in this respect although a few upper-caste individuals respond to British examples and westernize.
Secularism triumphs in the founding law codes of both Americas, although Catholicism is the religion of state in all but name in most of Latin America. In the United States, the separation of church and state is taken farther and becomes generally accepted. The United States and Canada share in the general debate over the place of religion versus science that Darwin has begun. In Latin America, the anticlericalism of most of the European intellectuals is carried to an extreme.	Both Americas are still essentially dependents of the European art forms and fashions throughout most of the period. Only in folk art or in the figure of an occasional eccentric can a native genius be discerned. Signs of rebellion against this are multiplying at the end of the nineteenth century, and the early twentieth century sees a definite change toward cultural autonomy, especially in the United States.	In North America in the later part of the period, the physical sciences and their accompanying technology make major advances, while still lagging the most developed parts of Europe. By 1920 the gaps had been closed in almost all fields. In Latin America, the gaps were widening except for the tiny minority of educated and well-off people. A key difference in the two continents can be found in the educational systems and the place of the sciences within them.

EUROPE'S INDUSTRIALIZATION

1700s	Increase in trade, population, and agricultural production
1760s–1820s	First Industrial Revolution in Britain/steam power
c. 1815–c. 1860s	Industrialization of Belgium, northern France, Western Germany
1830	First railroad
late 1800s	Second Industrial Revolution/use of electricity

The ending of the Napoleonic wars allowed the changes that had been taking place in England's economy to emerge more clearly into view. Even during the conflict, the factory and its large-scale production techniques had become more common.

The Industrial Revolution that gripped Europe in the nineteenth century was a direct outgrowth of the Scientific Revolution, and like that earlier event, this was not really so much a revolution as a gradual accretion of new knowledge and techniques. The Industrial Revolution was made possible by another "revolution": the transformation of agriculture that took place at the same time. Stimulated by several developments, England was the leader in both of these transformations, and the rest of Europe only slowly and unevenly fell into line behind the English.

❧ PREREQUISITES FOR INDUSTRIAL PRODUCTION

Historians have identified several factors that are necessary for an economy to engage in large-scale industrial production. All of these were present in England by the late eighteenth century.

1. *Upsurge in world trade.* The large and expanding market for European goods and services created by the new colonies was matched by the large volume of exports from those colonies destined for European consumption. From Eastern ports flowed a stream of tea, coffee, and cacao as well as spices, exotic woods, Chinese jades, porcelain, and above all, silk. From the American colonies came not only Spanish bullion but also the sugar, rice, and dried fish that added variety to European tables and tobacco and dyes as well.

   In the eighteenth century, French overseas trading grew more than tenfold; and the English were not far behind. Intra-European trade also grew spectacularly, as the colonial goods were often re-exported to third parties. All of this increase reflected much *higher demand* from consumers and also higher demand for the basic needs of commerce: maritime equipment and boats and "trade goods" for the natives.

2. *Rising population.* The increased demand for imports from the colonies was due in large part to the rapidly rising population of most of the Continent and England. Although the precise reasons for this rise are still in dispute, it is clear that the death rate fell and the

birth rate rose in Europe after 1750. As a result, the English population, for instance, quadrupled in a century—a phenomenon never before recorded in history.

3. *Increased flow of money.* Commercial expansion required additional capital; money was needed to finance the purchase of goods until they could be resold. Many individuals tried to profit from the rising consumption by building new factories, port facilities, and warehouses—all of which required money or credit. Capital was raised by the expanding stock markets, partnerships and speculations, and the bullion of America. The bullion came from Spanish colonies, but quickly passed out of Spain into the other European countries to become part of the money stock.

4. *Experienced managers and entrepreneurs.* By the later eighteenth century, several pockets of entrepreneurial expertise could be found, primarily in London, Antwerp, Amsterdam, and other cities of northwestern Europe. All these places had already had two centuries of experience in colonial trade. Now they were the home of numerous individuals who had had experience in organizing and managing fairly large enterprises. These people knew how to calculate risks, how to spread them, and how to use the corporation and insurance to minimize them. They knew how to raise capital, secure credit, and share profit. They were relatively open to new ideas and new technology that promised good returns on investment.

⚜ AGRARIAN IMPROVEMENTS

If industrial society was to be successful, Europe's farmers would have to produce sufficient food to feed the growing urban labor force. To assure this production, the crop yields had to be increased. Everywhere in seventeenth-century Europe, croplands were tended in much the same way and with much the same results as in the Middle Age. The ratio of grain harvested to seed sown, for an important example, was still only about 3 or 4 to 1, which was far too low.

The most important single step toward modernizing farming was the change from *open fields to enclosures,* which enabled individual proprietors to cultivate their lands as they saw fit. Now individuals could vary their crops as they wished without having to conform to what the rest of the village did. These new enclosed fields were capable of producing two crops yearly, while only a third rather than the traditional one half lay fallow. The enclosed field system originated in Holland, which had the

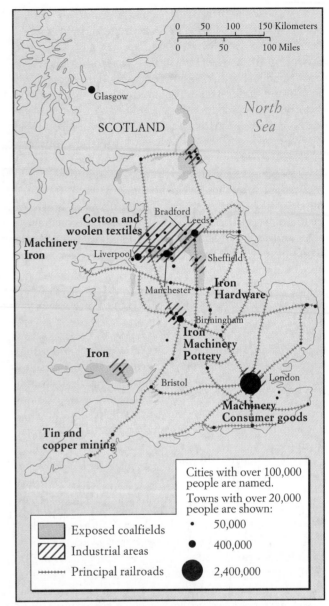

⊙ **MAP 36.1 Britain's Industrial Revolution.** The fastest pace in industrial development was in the North of England where coal and textile production combined to create strong attraction for laboring immigrants.

densest population in all Europe and consequently the most precious land. The Dutch also pioneered many other new techniques that improved crop yields including the use of *manure fertilizer, rotation* between root crops such as potatoes and seed crops such as wheat, the use of *hybrid seeds,* and *land drainage.*

From Holland the new agrarian practices spread quickly to Britain, where they were systematically applied by some big landowners and their tenants who were producing for the markets of the growing towns. As it became apparent that landowners using the new methods and crops could make profits equal to those of the industrial manufacturer but at much less risk, many landlords took up the new idea of *market farming*. Thus, the Western world saw the advent of agrarian capitalism, in which reducing unit costs and raising the volume of production were just as important as in industry.

Without these improvements in agriculture, the huge numbers of laborers required by industry and commerce in the nineteenth century might not have become available; and they certainly could not have been adequately fed. Not only were they fed, but they were fed considerably better than ever before.

✤ The Method of Machine Industry

Industrial production is aimed at *lessening the unit cost of production through improved technology*. The changes that occurred in the late eighteenth and early nineteenth century took place not so much because new products were in demand, as because industrialized technology allowed the production of familiar products in greater quantity and at lesser cost.

For example, one of the chief early products of industry was underclothing for men and women. There was nothing new about its design, raw material, or general method of production. What was new and revolutionary was the much lower price for a shirt or underpants when those items were woven on a machine—a power loom—from textiles that had been spun by machine from flax or cotton that had been cleaned and deseeded by machine. The factory owner could sell to wholesale outlets at much lower unit prices because five machine-made shirts could be produced for the cost of one previous handwoven shirt. The wholesaler could then place those five shirts with a single retailer because the price was so low the retailer could be sure of disposing of all five quickly. Men and women who had previously not worn underclothing because of its high cost now were able and willing to buy several sets.

Most early industrial products were simply variations of previously handworked items that had been adapted to a mode of production that used machines for all or part of the process. These products included clothing and shoes, lumber, rough furniture, bricks, coal, and pig iron. Sophis-

ticated or new products came only gradually. They appeared well into the second generation of industrial society, when inventors and entrepreneurs had developed a clearer vision of what could be accomplished with the new machinery.

The Factory

The **factory system** was a very important aspect of new industry. Before the eighteenth century, it was unusual for a single employer to have more than a handful of workers on the payroll directly. Very often, people took in some type of raw material, such as rough bolts of cloth, and worked it up into a finished consumer product in their own homes, working on their own schedules, and being paid when they had completed the task assigned. This was commonly called the *"putting out" system* because the same entrepreneur put out the raw material, found the parties who would work it, and collected the finished product for sale elsewhere. He bore the risks and made all the profits, while the workers received a piecework wage. Most clothing, draperies, shoes, kitchenware, and table utensils were made this way in early modern days, and the wages earned were a very important part of the income of many families.

In the new factory style of production, an entrepreneur or a company of them gathered together perhaps hundreds of individual workers under one roof and one managerial eye; they were paid on a single payscale and worked under tight discipline on a single, repetitive part of the production process. The shift to factory production was a true revolution in work, and it was as important in changing lifestyles in the Western world as the industrial products themselves were (see the Document in this chapter).

No longer did the individual workers function as partners of the employer and have a good deal to say about the conditions and pay they received. No longer would workers have much to say about how their skills would be employed, the nature of what they were making, or where it would be sold or to whom. All those decisions and many others were now fully and exclusively in the hands of the employer, the *capitalist entrepreneur* who controlled the factory (or mine, or foundry, or railroad).

✤ England: The Initial Leader in Industrialism

Several reasons assured England the early lead in the industrial production of goods and services:

1. Already in the early eighteenth century, *the English were the Western world's most experienced traders and entrepreneurs.* The English colonies were spread around the world, and the North American colonies were the biggest markets for goods outside Europe. The English national bank had existed as a credit and finance institution since 1603, rates of interest were lower than anywhere else, and the English stock markets the world's largest and most flexible.

2. *The population was sharply increasing.* As mentioned earlier, the English population rose about 15 percent per decade throughout the eighteenth century, generating a huge increase in demand and an equally huge increase in the potential or actual labor supply.

3. *"Steam is an Englishman."* The key to industrialization as a mechanical process was a new source of energy: steam. And the English pioneered the inventions that made steam engines the standard form of mechanical energy during the nineteenth century. All over the world, English steam engines opened the path to industrialized production of goods.

4. *English agriculture underwent its own "revolution."* The improvements in agricultural production during the eighteenth century made it possible not only for the farmers to feed the rapidly growing urban sector but for them to do so with fewer workers in the fields. The excess rural population then migrated from the countryside, contributing to the growth of the urban sector.

5. *England controlled much of the two basic raw materials of early industry: coal and cotton.* The English coalfields were large and easy to access; they provided the fuel for the new steam engines and used those engines extensively to produce coal more cheaply than anywhere in Europe. Cotton came from India, now an English colony, and from the North American colonies; it was carried to Europe almost entirely in English ships, and the finished cloth was exported to the rest of Europe without effective competition for a century.

■ **Isambard Kingdom Brunel.** This jaunty figure was the outstanding engineer of ironwork in the mid century. He designed several famous bridges in addition to *The Great Western* steamship whose anchor chain he is standing in front of here.

6. *England had the most favorable internal transport system.* The geography and topography of England made the country ideal for moving goods to market. Not only were there few natural obstacles to travel and transport, but the river system, connected by canals in the eighteenth century, made transportation cheaper and safer than elsewhere.

■ **Opening of Royal Albert Bridge.** Named in honor of Queen Victoria's husband, this span was a design by I. K. Brunel and one of the triumphs of the transport revolution spawned by industrialization.

Smith on Labor Specialization

One of the outstanding results of early industrialization was the specialization of labor. Tasks that previously had been performed by two or three individual craftsmen working at their own pace and in their own sequence were broken up by the early factory operators into distinct phases, each with its own machine-supported applications by individual workmen.

Adam Smith (1723–1790) anticipated these results in his epoch-making book *Concerning the Wealth of Nations* . . . , written in 1776 when the Industrial Revolution's impacts were just barely discernible in Great Britain. Smith provided the economic and philosophical bases of liberalism, as that word was used in the eighteenth and nineteenth centuries. In the following excerpt, he considers the division of labor, using a trade that but rarely receives attention in economic histories.

CHAPTER I: Of the Division of Labor

. . . To take an example, therefore, from a very trifling manufacture; but one in which the division of labor has been very often taken notice of, the trade of the pin-maker; a workman not educated to this business (which the division of labor has rendered a distinct trade), nor acquainted with the use of the machinery employed in it (to the invention of which the same division of labor has probably given occasion), could scarce with his utmost industry, make one pin in a day, and certainly could not make twenty. But in the way in which this business is now carried on, not only the whole work is a peculiar trade, but it is divided into a number of branches, of which the greater part are likewise peculiar trades. One man draws the wire, another straightens it, a third cuts it, a fourth points it, a fifth grinds it at the top to receive the pin-head; to make the head requires two or three distinct operations; to put it on is a peculiar business, to whiten the pins is another; it is even a trade by itself to put them into the paper; and the important business of making a pin is, in this manner, divided into about eighteen distinct operations, which in some manufactures, are performed by distinct hands, though in others the same man will perform perhaps two or three of them.

I have seen a small manufactory of this kind where ten men only were employed . . . they could when they exerted themselves make among them about twelve pounds of pins per day. There are in a pound upwards of four thousand pins of a middling size. Those ten persons, therefore, could make among them upwards of forty-eight thousand pins in a day. Each person, therefore, making a tenth part of forty-eight thousand pins, might be considered as making four thousand, eight hundred pins in a day. But if they had all wrought [i.e., worked] separately and independently, and without any of them having been educated to this peculiar business, they certainly could not each of them have made twenty, perhaps not one pin in a day; that is, certainly, not the two hundred and fortieth, perhaps not the four thousand eight hundredth part of what they are at present capable of performing, in consequence of proper division and combination of their different operations.

As a result of these advantages, it was natural for England to take the lead in industry (see Map 36.1). In the generation between 1740 and 1780, England produced a variety of mechanical inventions (including Richard Arkwright's *spinning machine,* called the **spinning jenny,** and Samuel Crompton's *mule,* which made yarn or thread). By 1800 these machines had been joined by others including the *cotton gin,* invented by an American Eli Whitney, and Edmund Cartwright's power loom. Together, these inventions revolutionized the production of cotton cloth. Machines that still used water or animal power were now quickly replaced by the perfected steam engines designed by **James Watt and Matthew Boulton** (see the Biography in this chapter). Cheap and reliable steam power became the standard energy source of the Western world's machines for the next hundred years.

England became the source of new technology, patents, and products for most of that period as well. Engineers of all sorts, bridge builders, railroad and tramway developers, and mining superintendents—in short, all types of the

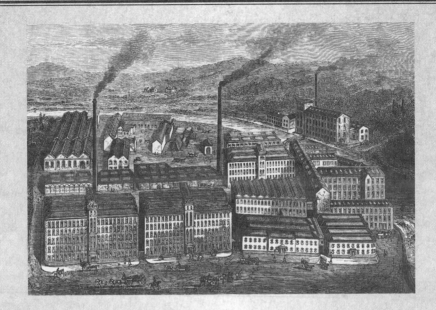

In every art and manufacture, the effects of the division of labor are similar to what they are in this very trifling one; though, in many of them, the labor can neither be so much subdivided, nor reduced to so great a simplicity of operation.

In Chapter VII, Smith went on to condemn the mercantilist habit of discouraging imports and to make a plea for free trade in the international marketplace:

To give the monopoly of the home market to the produce of domestic industry, in any particular art or manufacture, is in some measure to direct private people in what manner they ought to employ their capital, and must, in almost all cases, be either a useless or a hurtful regulation. If the produce of domestic can be brought there as cheap as that of foreign industry, the regulation is evidently useless. If it cannot, it must generally be hurtful.

It is the maxim of every prudent master of a family never to attempt to make at home what it will cost him more to make than to buy. The tailor does not attempt to make his own shoes, but buys them of the shoemaker. The shoemaker does not attempt to make his own clothes, but employs a tailor. . . .

What is prudence in the conduct of a private family can scarce be folly in that of a great kingdom. If a foreign country can supply us with a commodity cheaper than we ourselves can make it, better buy it of them with some part of the produce of our own industry employed in a way in which we have some advantage. . . .

SOURCE: Smith, Adam. *Concerning the Wealth of Nations.*

nineteenth century's burgeoning technical aristocracy—were England's contribution to the industrial world.

✤ SPREAD OF THE INDUSTRIAL REVOLUTION

From England the new processes spread only slowly during the eighteenth and early nineteenth centuries. No other country had England's peculiar combination of advantages, but there were also other reasons for this slowness. A major factor was England's attempt to treat industrial techniques as state secrets; the English government strictly prohibited the export of any process or machine design that could help another country rival England. For a time, the government went to the extreme of prohibiting the emigration of skilled workers! Needless to say, these restrictions could not be effectively enforced, and the theoretical knowledge of machines and technology spread into northern Europe and the U.S. after about 1815.

James Watt
1736–1819

James Watt was the engineer who made the steam engine into a practical source of industrial power. Although Watt did not invent the engine, his version was the first to use the potential of steam power efficiently. His work was crucial in bringing the Industrial Revolution into being.

Watt was born in Greenock, Scotland, in 1736. He educated himself by studying instruments, working with all types of mechanical devices, and building small machines. He was highly proficient in practical mechanics from early boyhood.

In 1757 the University at Glasgow hired him as an instrument maker. There Watt worked with a Newcomen engine, an earlier version of a machine that used steam power, and was able to make several basic improvements. First, he saw the advantage of a separate condensing chamber and designed a more efficient system of condensing the steam back to water. Then he invented a mechanism that increased the speed of the piston in both directions. He also insulated the engine parts. The upshot was an engine that performed more efficiently and more cheaply. A few years later Watt was able to devise a method of gears and wheels that allowed the vertical motion of the piston to be translated into rotary motion, such as in grindstones.

In 1774 Watt entered into an enormously successful partnership with Matthew Boulton, the owner of an English foundry. Within a few years, the Watt-Boulton engine had set an entirely new standard for steam power in Britain; it was cheaper, lighter, more flexible, and far more efficient in its use of fuel and in its applications to industrial tasks.

By the 1780s, British textile factories were employing large numbers of the new engines to revolutionize the manufacture of cotton goods of all types. As a result, textiles became much cheaper and more easily obtained than ever before. Steam engines were widely used for pumping water out of mines, for driving large saws in sawmills, and for other types of repetitive, straightforward motion that had formerly been done by backbreaking human labor or, in some cases, by the water wheel.

Watt continued to experiment with other applications of steam power most of his long life. He invented a double-acting engine powered by steam that was much more efficient than the usual single-direction piston. He also experimented with the design of a screw propeller for boats and a machine for reproducing statues by casting in a mold. His patents for the separate condenser and the application of the piston to rotary motion made Watt a moderately wealthy man, but he reinvested most of his earnings into further experiment.

George Stephenson took the Watt engine, put it on wheels and wooden tracking, and designed the earliest form of locomotive, which was used to pull coal cars in mines. From this gradually evolved the railroad. In 1829 Stephenson's **Rocket** bested several other competitors to become the engine for the first rail line in the world, constructed in 1830 between Manchester and Liverpool. For many years, the locomotive was simply a Watt engine laid on its side and mounted on a wheeled platform with gears and levers connecting the piston in its cylinder to the drive wheels below.

Already by the end of the Napoleonic Wars in 1815, Watt engines were to be found everywhere in British factories and mines. A year earlier, the first steam-driven printing press had been put to work for the *Times* in London. Despite the efforts of the English government, the patents and other design secrets worked out by Watt and Boulton were quickly exported overseas, and steam power spread almost as rapidly on the Continent and in the United States as in Britain. Engineers of all nations continued to improve and refine the engine, and new uses for steam power followed one after another each year. When James Watt died in his eighty-third year, he could look with satisfaction upon a world that his engine was transforming.

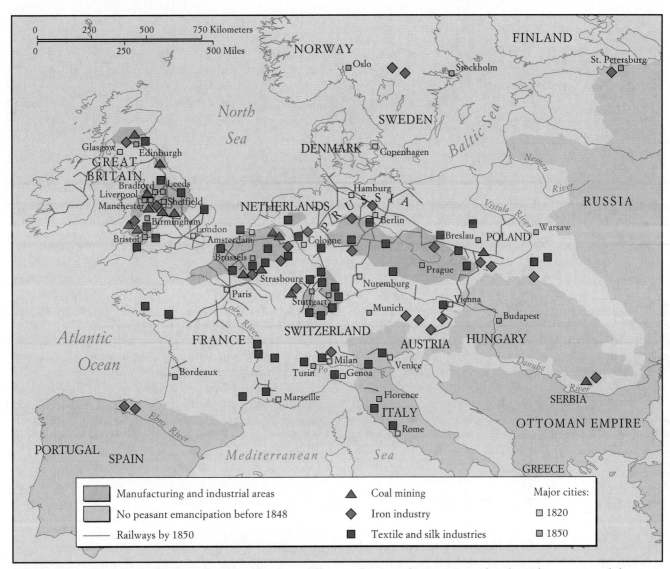

⦿ MAP 36.2 The Spread of Industry by 1850. The sharp differences between the countries with industrial resources and those without are shown on this map. There is also a notable correlation between industry and the peasantry's freedom from landlords' controls.

Another factor retarding non-English industrialization was the long Napoleonic wars, which disrupted the normal communications and commerce between the Continent and England for most of the quarter century between 1793 and 1815. After the wars, much of Europe was too impoverished or too unstable to encourage the importation of new processes or machines. It would take another generation before even the more advanced areas of western Europe could rival Britain.

By about 1830, the areas on the Continent closest to England had begun to industrialize part of their productive capacity. *Belgium and northern France* began to use steam power first in coal and textile production, the same industries that had initiated the use of steam in England. By the 1860s, industrial techniques had spread to the Rhine valley, especially the Ruhr coal and iron fields, as well as to parts of northern Italy and the northern United States (see Map 36.2). Nevertheless, even as late as the

■ **Rail Station.** This magnificent 1862 illustration by the British painter W. Powell Frith captures the bustling activity of a Victorian era station and the crowds who were glad to board the "iron horse."

1860s, *eastern Europe, Russia, and Iberia as well as most of Italy were almost untouched* by the industrial lifestyle and industrial production. These regions all lacked one or more of the important factors that had to come together for industrialization to proceed. Some areas, such as eastern Europe and the Balkans, were still untouched well into the middle of the twentieth century. Industrialization was not automatic or inevitable, and large parts of the non-Western world are still only superficially and partially industrialized.

⚜ EARLY INDUSTRIAL SUCCESSES

The first industries to feel the full weight of industrial processes were *cotton textiles and coal mining.* Both of these were highly labor-intensive and were peculiarly able to use the new steam engines to replace tedious, hand labor. Cotton production in England rose geometrically during the late eighteenth century. Previously, cotton cloth had been a luxury good used only by the rich for tapestries and upholstery; now cotton clothing became commonplace. Production of raw cotton in India and the southern United States became a major branch of agriculture.

From cotton the revolution in spinning and weaving spread to wool, and parts of England and Scotland became vast sheep ranges, as former agricultural lands were converted to pastures, which brought in more profit. Meanwhile the huge increase in coal production provided a great boost for the *iron industry,* which now used coal in lieu of less efficient and more costly charcoal. British iron production rose from 68,000 tons in 1788 to 260,000 in

1806. It kept on climbing at almost the same pace throughout the nineteenth century.

As the steam engine's capacity increased and the addition of gears, belts, and flywheels expanded the uses to which it could be put, all kinds of products felt the impact of the Industrial Revolution. Instead of having to locate near flowing water as in the past, flour milling, timber sawing, and other industries requiring simple repetitive motion could be located near the labor supply or the raw material source.

In the preindustrial age, most manufacturing was carried on in rural areas, preferably near a navigable river where a dam could be built to supply energy for a water wheel. Now new mills and foundries could be built on the edge of existing towns, where labor, transport, and housing were already in place. The urban nature of much new industry was, of course, a major reason for the rapid growth of many towns into cities, and cities into metropolises.

⚜ RAILROADS

One of the most spectacular results of steam was the railroad. Again, Britain led the way, but in this instance, the new invention spread very rapidly. The first commercial use of steam railroading was in 1830, when a line connected Liverpool and Manchester, two of the newly important British industrial towns. By the 1840s lines were underway in most countries of the old and new worlds, including Russia and the United States.

Most early rail lines were built by private companies. But railroads were costly, and the large debts the owners incurred were often more than the lines could sustain during the frequent downturns in the economic cycle. As a result, many railroads went bankrupt and were taken over by the government. By the 1860s, most railroad lines were in government hands.

The steam locomotive was the heart of a railroad. Yet the locomotive's mechanics were so simple that only a few years after the first one was mounted on its track, it had reached a state of perfection that hardly changed over the next century. Bigger and slightly more efficient locomotives were built, but they were essentially the same machine as the famous *Rocket* of the Liverpool-Manchester line.

The *railroad dramatically reduced the costs of shipping and personal travel*. It also greatly increased the security of moving goods and people long distances. By as early as 1850, trains were steaming along in excess of fifty miles per hour—a speed that seemed almost diabolical to many onlookers. By that year it was possible to travel from London to Edinburgh overnight in safety and comfort. Twenty years earlier, the same journey had taken four or five jolting, banging days in a stagecoach. And the train cost less as well. The railroad had an impact on the first half of the nineteenth century similar to the impact of the automobile on the first half of the twentieth—another "revolution"!

✤ PHASES OF THE INDUSTRIAL REVOLUTION

Industrial work and lifestyles did not develop rapidly as a one-time occurrence at the end of the eighteenth century. The changes that began then have continued to the present day, but can be divided into certain discernible stages:

- The *First Industrial Revolution,* which occurred from about 1760 to 1820, was marked by the predominance of Britain, the central importance of a new supply of energy from steam, and the production of textiles and coal and iron in the factory setting.

■ **The Rocket, 1829.** This engraving shows George Stevenson's locomotive as it traveled across the English countryside in 1829. Essentially a steam boiler laid on its side with pistons and wheels, the Rocket quickly outdistanced its stagecoach competitors between Liverpool and Manchester.

- The *Second Industrial Revolution* began in the later part of the nineteenth century in western Europe and produced modern applied science or technology. The chemical and petroleum industries came to the fore in this phase, and a new source of energy was developed—electricity. The national leadership shifted gradually from Great Britain to Germany (after its formation in 1871) and the post–Civil War United States.

In our own time, we have witnessed a very rapid spread of industry into many less developed countries. At the same time, the older industrial countries in the West have moved on to a "postindustrial" society, in which the production of goods in factories and their transport by railroad has given way in importance to the provision of services and information relying on electronic transmissions. We are, in fact, living through a Third Industrial Revolution.

Summary

Industrial methods of producing goods via machinery entered European life gradually in the mid-eighteenth century, with England as the leader. The English had several natural advantages and social characteristics that enabled them to expand their lead over the rest of the world until well into the nineteenth century. This First Industrial Revolution was largely dependent upon two related changes: the increase in agrarian production and the rapid rise in population and attendant demand for consumer goods. Without these, the factory system of concentrated labor under single management and discipline would not have been feasible.

The industrial system spread quite slowly at first due to the wars and to the difficulty of replicating the English advantages. By the mid-nineteenth century, however, industrialization had spread into much of northern and western Europe and the United States. Coal mining and textiles were two of the initial industries to be affected, and the steam engine became the major energy source for all types of industry. The railroad, introduced in the 1830s, soon effected massive change in the transport of goods and people and contributed to the success of the industrial system in substantial ways. A Second Industrial Revolution commenced in the late nineteenth century fueled by petroleum and electricity, and a Third Revolution is currently underway in the provision of services rather than goods.

Test Your Knowledge

1. Which of the following was *not* a factor in England's leadership in industrialization during the later eighteenth century?
   a. A rapidly growing population
   b. Familiarity with the principles of finance and credit
   c. The government's commitment to stable currency and interest rates
   d. Thorough government supervision of the economy's trends and patterns
2. James Watt was the inventor of
   a. an entirely new form of mechanical energy.
   b. the power loom for weaving.
   c. an improved and more flexible form of steam-driven engine.
   d. a device for raising water from flooded mines.
3. Development of competitive industry on the Continent was delayed by
   a. the Napoleonic wars and their attendant disruption of trade.
   b. a sustained labor shortage due to war losses.
   c. the upper classes' contempt for profit making.
   d. lack of suitable and basic natural resources.
4. The basic aim of industrial production is to
   a. provide more employment opportunities for the labor force.
   b. allow a greater variety of jobs.
   c. lower the unit cost of production.
   d. discipline and organize the labor force more efficiently.
5. The chief driving force for the Industrial Revolution in eighteenth-century England was
   a. the threat of being overshadowed by France in the world economy.
   b. the invention of an improved source of energy.
   c. the creation of the British overseas colonial empire.
   d. the encouragement of the British government.
6. The first major industry to feel the impact of industrial production was
   a. lumbering.
   b. textiles.
   c. grain farming.
   d. paper making.
7. The example used by Adam Smith to demonstrate specialization of labor was
   a. coal mining.
   b. textile spinning.
   c. pin making.
   d. shipbuilding.

Identification Terms

Matthew Boutton   Manchester   spinning jenny   James Watt

factory system   *Rocket*

Bibliography

Cameron, R. *A Concise Economic History of the World,* 1989 is one of those books whose titles are exactly fulfilled in the text. Its treatment of early industrialization is clear and very useful.

Deane, P. *The First Industrial Revolution,* 1965 is also good, as is *The Industrial Revolution* by C. M. Cipolla, 1973, which looks at Europe generally but with focus on Britain.

Evans, E. G. *The Forging of the Modern State. Early Industrial Britain 1783–1870,* 1983 is a standard appreciation of the beginnings and development of industrial life.

Landes, D. *Unbound Prometheus: Technological Change and Industrial Development in Western Europe from 1750 to the Present,* 1969. Probably the best single treatment of the whole topic of industrialization; clearly written and easy to follow for students who have no background in economics.

Pollard, S. *Peaceful Conquest; The Industrialization of Europe 1760–1970,* 1981 is very useful in its earlier chapters to give an idea of how the British inventions migrated.

Taylor, P. ed. *The Industrial Revolution: Triumph or Disaster?,* 1970, is a discussion of positive and negative aspects.

Taylor, G. R. *The Transportation Revolution 1815–1860,* 1951 looks at the US but its conclusions are applicable anywhere in the West.

Tilly, L., and J. Scott. *Women, Work, and Family,* 1978 is a survey of the female workforce in early industrial society. It is an updating of I. Pinchbeck's *Women Workers and the Industrial Revolution,* 1930, a pioneering study.

THE SOCIAL IMPACTS OF EARLY INDUSTRY

---

c. 1750	Europe enters "population explosion"
1750–1850	Change in premarital relationships/ Children more prized by parents
1800–1850	Urbanization of northwestern Europe/First Industrial Revolution completed in Britain, gets underway in western and central Continent

Lifestyles of ordinary people altered substantially during the transition from a preindustrial to an industrial society. The change was gradual in most cases and only really remarkable over a generation or more. But taken all in all, the lives of many Europeans changed more in the century between 1750 and 1850 than they had in all preceding centuries together.

This chapter will take an extended look at four areas of social transformation during this period: family and gender relations, occupations, urbanization, and living conditions. Much of this material is relatively new as an object of formal history, and this "new social history" has become one of the major research fields for historians everywhere. Their findings are constantly changing previous ideas and frequently show that innovations formerly presumed to be the result of industry actually began earlier.

❧ CHANGES IN SOCIAL RELATIONS

During the later eighteenth century in Britain and France (where the records are best preserved), a change in social habits and relationships became apparent. The causes of this change are not well understood, but they seem to be linked with the arrival of science as a competing primary source of knowledge with religion and with the philosophy of the Enlightenment as it trickled down into popular concepts.

The beginnings of the Industrial Age accelerated changes that had already begun. The mutual stimuli afforded to industry by science, and vice versa, became ever more intense. Eventually, an industrial lifestyle made itself apparent, quite different from what had gone before. It was long believed that one of the changes effected was a new structure of the family. This belief is now being reexamined.

The Structure of the Family

For most people, the family they are born into is the most important social institution in their lives. Historians once assumed that for many centuries before industrialization, the European family had a standard structure, which varied little. This family, so it was thought, was characterized by an extended kin-group living under one roof, high rates of illegitimate children, and early universal marriage. Now, however, researchers have established that this *stereotype of the preindustrial family is false;* the characteristics that were assumed to be commonplace were in fact very uncommon during the preindustrial centuries.

Instead, it is now clear that major changes in the family structure took place beginning in the middle of the eighteenth century *before* industry became common. Three changes were particularly noticeable:

- A lowering of the average age of marriage from the previous 27 for both men and women to about 22 for women and 23.5 for men by 1850.
- A sharp increase in the bastardy rate, beginning in the towns but soon also becoming common in the rural areas where the majority of the population lived.
- A steady increase in the previous low number of aged persons (over 60) who lived on to see their grandchildren and share their homes with two younger generations.

The Place of Children

Until the eighteenth century, only the very wealthy or the nobility could afford to give much loving attention to infants or very young children. The reason was simple: The mortality rate for infants and children was so high that it discouraged people from putting much financial or emotional "investment" into them. In many places, three of five children of ordinary people normally would die before age ten, and another would die before age twenty.

Diseases of every type hit children (and the aged) harder than others; in times of famine, young children were often the first victims; and household and farm accidents of a lethal nature were an everyday affair among children (we hear of children drowning in the farm pond or the well, being kicked by a horse, cut by sharp tools, or burned to death). In those days when medical care for rural people was nonexistent, even minor burns or slight infections would often result in death, weeks or months later.

Therefore, the usual *attitude toward the infant* was a mix of indifference with a good deal of realistic caution about its prospects. Most peasants and workers viewed children below age seven or so as debit factors; they demanded time-consuming care and feeding without being able to contribute anything to the family resources. Only after they had become strong and rational enough to do adult work were they looked on as assets. The urban classes and the wealthy could afford to take a more relaxed attitude toward children's work, but their emotional relations with the young child were about as distant as the peasant's. Urban children died as readily and as unpredictably as rural children. It only made "biological sense" to restrict maternal love and paternal pride to those

■ **Manchester England at Mid-Century.** This moody portrait of the outstanding industrial town in Britain conveys the uncompromising ugliness of the environment created by the early factories.

old enough to have a good chance of a long life. And for most people, the point of having children at all was to provide a primitive form of social security. Children were expected to see to it that their parents did not suffer the ultimate indignity of a beggarly old age or have to throw themselves on the charity of others when ill or disabled.

At some point between 1750 and 1850, a change began, as parents began to show what we now consider normal parental love and tenderness toward newborn and young children. This change occurred first in the better-off segment of society and then seeped downward into the lives of the majority. Why did it happen?

The answer is complex, but several factors can be identified: the declining child mortality rate, which gradually increased the chances that a child would survive; the rising numbers of middle-class people who did not need children's labor, but valued them for their own sake; and the influence of educational reformers like *Jean Jacques Rousseau, Johann Heinrich Pestalozzi, Friedrich Herbert,* and others. These reformers insisted that children should be given more humane education and treated more like unformed, responsive individuals than as contrary creatures whose naturally evil ways must be corrected by strict discipline. Another influence on the attitudes of adults toward young children was the introduction of *general public instruction in state-supported schools,* which began, as already noted, in the mid-1700s. Clearly, children worthy of being educated at parental tax expense were valuable for more than just serving as attendants in their parents' old age (for which the children needed no education).

Relations between Men and Women

The premier event of most people's social lives was, of course, *marriage*. And marriage among the rural folk and most urbanites was still a *contract between two families,* rather than the result of individual erotic attraction. But this too changed during the eighteenth century in Europe. Not only did people marry at an earlier age as the century progressed, but social relations among the young also became considerably freer. Premarital sex had always been tolerated among the peasants, as long as it was followed by marriage. It was even considered normal in that it assured both families that the young man could make the young woman pregnant; the wedding date was set once pregnancy ensued, not before!

In the later eighteenth century, however, *premarital sex without marriage plans* seems to have occurred with increasing frequency. Both sexes, in countryside and town, were able to "get away with" behavior that previously the full weight of social opinion would have prevented. Why this happened is a subject of some debate among historians. Some say that a psychological sea change occurred after 1750 that allowed new freedoms in the sexual sphere. Others, the majority, say that the young people simply seized the increasing opportunities that a *more mobile society* gave them to get together outside the watchful eyesight of pastors, parents, and elders.

For most women, marriage was still the main career option, but demographic changes made it impossible for a number of women to marry. Although the number of males and females is about equal at birth, females begin to outnumber males after about age twenty-five; and this discrepancy was larger in the past than now because males were affected disproportionately by accidents and violence. Consequently, there were fewer eligible males than females in the age cohort most likely to marry. *Many women were never able to marry.* These "spinsters" were common in all social strata except the very highest, and they were often taken shameless advantage of by their married relatives, who forced them to work as child watchers, laborers, maids, and seamstresses in return for minimal room and board.

Since children were generally considered an absolute necessity for a good marriage, a single female who was beyond childbearing age was a near-hopeless case. Only one thing could improve her chances: if she were rich, she might attract some ambitious young man as a husband. The well-off widow who was courted by a series of younger men who had their eyes on her money is a stock figure of eighteenth- and nineteenth-century folklore. In return for giving the woman a respected place in society, her husband became the master of her money and expected to find his sexual pleasures, and possibly children, elsewhere.

⚜ OCCUPATIONS AND MOBILITY OF INDIVIDUALS

The ordinary work of ordinary men and women was changing during the latter part of the eighteenth century. This change steadily picked up momentum as new industrial towns began to emerge in Britain and northern Europe.

Whereas most people previously had worked directly with and on the land (farming, tending orchards, fishing, timbering, shepherding), by the 1750s the number of people engaged in urban occupations and nonmanual work was gradually increasing. As methods of agriculture on the large estates improved, they could reduce the number of farm laborers they employed; the so-called **Enclosure Movement** in Britain also forced a good number of independent farmers off the land. They could escape poverty only by moving away to a new life as wage earners in the towns.

Some small minority of these ex-farmers had the intelligence, drive, and luck to take up nonmanual work, perhaps as bookkeepers, salesclerks, or schoolteachers (for which the only real qualification was semiliteracy). Any who could make their way into these occupations would move upward in the social scale and find the opportunity to better themselves by imitating the manners and ideas of the socially superior classes.

But ex-peasants could also get ahead in many other ways. They could apprentice themselves to a skilled craftsman for a number of years or take any of the new opportunities for manual work now opening, such as building canals or railroads. The rapidly increasing overseas commerce of the eighteenth and early nineteenth centuries extended the horizons of ambitious youths, a good many of whom had left their ancestral villages because they saw only too clearly what a miserable future awaited them there. Some of them ended up in one or another of the American colonies, but many more stayed at home, unable to bring themselves to take the leap into the dark that emigration entailed.

As there were, of course, absolutely no government provisions to aid the needy, the threat of unemployment and of literal starvation was often very real (see the Document in this chapter). Many young men spent years teetering on the edge of the abyss, before they had

A Navvy's Life on the Tramp

The anonymous author of this piece was born about 1820 in England. When he left home at about twenty years of age, he was already well acquainted with hard work. Like tens of thousands of other young men, he went "on the tramp," taking pickup laboring jobs with farmers or railroad gangs. He would do streetcleaning or any other unskilled work he could find. Many men (and a few women) who could not find a suitable place for themselves in the home village, pursued this life for years, sometimes even into old age.

Family and Earliest Work

My father was a labouring man, earning nine shillings a week in the best of times [about the equivalent of $135 currently] .... There was a wonderful large family of us—eleven was born, but we died down to six. I remember one winter, we was very bad off, for we boys could get no employment, and no one in the family was working but father. He only got fourteen pence a day to keep eight of us in firing and everything. It was a hard matter to get enough to eat.

The first work I ever did was to mind two little lads for a farmer, I drawed them about in a little cart, for which I got my breakfast and a penny a day. When I got older, I went to tending sheep. I was about seven year old then. . . .

On the Tramp

After I left home I started on the road "tramping" about the country, looking for work. Sometimes I'd stop a few weeks with one master, then go on again, travelling about; never long at a time in the one place. I soon got into bad company and bad ways, and at times it would come over my head that I thought more about the devil than I thought about the Savior; but still I kept wandering on in that long lane, and found no end to it.

This is the way we'd carry on. Perhaps I'd light on an old mate somewhere about the country, and we'd go rambling together from one place to another. If we earned any money, we'd go to a public house [tavern], and stop there two or three days, till we'd spent it all, or till the publican turned us out drunk and helpless to the world. Having no money to pay for a lodging, we had to lie under a hedge, and in the morning we'd get up thinking, "What shall we do?" "Where shall we go?" And perhaps it would come over us, "Well, I'll never do the like again."

We'd wander on till we could find a gang of men at work at some railroad or large building; sometimes they would help us and sometimes they would not. Once I travelled about for three days without having anything to eat. We'd always sooner take a thing than ask for it, and the devil kept on tutoring me to steal, till at last, seeing some poor labouring man's victuals lying under a hedge, I jumped over and took them. I thought to myself at the time, "I'll never get so low again, but always keep a shilling in my pocket, sooner than get to this pitch."

. . . [W]hile I was in Yorkshire I met with a young gentleman who had a fine house of his own, but would spend all his time in the beer-shop. One day he saw me there and called out, "Well, old navvy," he says, "can you drink a quart of ale?"

'Thank you, sir," says I.

"Well, if you will stop along of me, I'll keep you in drink, as long as you like to sing me songs," says he.

"Master," says I, "I'll have you! I do like my beer."

. . . I stopped with him a fortnight drinking Yorkshire ale at 6 pence a quart, while he drank rum and brandy, and soda water between whiles. But at the fortnight's end I had to run away. I could not stand it any longer. He'd have killed me with it if I'd gone on.

It was not long after this that I got sent to prison. I was working at Hastings, when we struck [went out on strike] there. The ganger [foreman], he came up and then he upped with his fist and knocked me down; and as fast as I got up he hit me down again. . . . They come and ta'en us the next day, and had us locked up in Lewes Gaol; two of us got two months, and the other one one month. We was all very happy and comfortable there, though we were kept rather short of victuals. There they learnt me to spin mops, and it was there that I got hold of most of my scholarship. . . .

SOURCE: *Useful Toil,* "Life of a Navvy," p. 55, edited by J. Burnet, © 1984, Penguin Classics. Reprinted by permission of Penguin, Ltd.

sufficiently mastered a trade, established themselves in business, or inherited some land to farm, so that they could set themselves up as the head of a family household.

Female Occupations

For young women, the choices were considerably narrower. They could stay at home, hoping for a successful marriage to a local youth of their own class, or they could go into "service"; that is, they could join the millions of teenaged daughters of peasants and laborers who left home to become servants. The *prevalence of servants* is hard for twentieth-century Americans to imagine; practically every household, even relatively poor ones, had one or more. It was not at all unusual for a poor farmer's house to harbor one or two servant girls as well as a male laborer or two, and no middle-class or upper-class house in the nineteenth century was without its servant staff, mainly females from rural families who came to town to seek work. Sometimes the servants were related by blood or marriage to the household; sometimes not.

Many of these young women left their employers after shorter or longer periods of service, having found a suitable marriage partner with whom to "set up" a household. But many others stayed for life; they remained unmarried, contributing part of their meager wage to support the old folks in the village. Some of these servant women practically became members of the family and were cared for in their old age; many were turned out like so many used-up horses when they became too old to work.

By the early nineteenth century, when *factory work* had become fairly common in Britain, young women also had the option of taking a job tending a machine. The very *earliest factories were often staffed by entire families,* working together just as they had earlier in the home. But increasingly, young women and children replaced the male adults and family units in the unskilled jobs such as cotton spinning and mechanical weaving. The owners of the textile and shoe mills found that young women would work for lower wages than young men commanded and were more reliable. Many country girls preferred factory jobs, where they could be with their peers and have some freedom in their off hours, to going into service with its many restrictions.

⚜ THE MIGRATION TO THE CITIES: URBANIZED SOCIETY

Throughout the Western world, a massive flight to the cities began in the eighteenth century and continued through the twentieth century. Most of the migrants from the countryside were young people in the prime of life. The precise reasons for this **urban migration** varied considerably from place to place and era to era, but three motives underlay it everywhere:

- *Human curiosity and the desire for change.* The young in every culture are more open to change and more eager to embrace it than their elders. When it became relatively easy to move about and experience new things, new places, and new people, young people took advantage of the changed conditions.
- *The desire to improve economic and social status.* The variety of occupations that the towns offered, the opportunity to gain at least a minimal education, and the belief that talent and ambition had a freer field in the town than in the ancestral village inspired many persons to move.

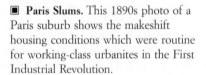 **Paris Slums.** This 1890s photo of a Paris suburb shows the makeshift housing conditions which were routine for working-class urbanites in the First Industrial Revolution.

- *The desire to find better marital partners.* Young women in particular, whose prospects of finding a husband in their village were tightly restricted by their families and their social standing and who could not easily rebel, took the opportunity to search elsewhere.

Beyond these human motivations, we should note the objective economic fact that by the nineteenth century the shift from a rural to an urban majority was, for the first time in history, sustainable. The gradual spread of commerce and long-distance communications and financial credit arrangements allowed towns to grow regardless of the local food-producing capacity. Bristol in England, Lyon in France, Brussels in Belgium, and Oslo in Norway, to cite some examples at random, no longer depended on the ability of the agricultural region close by to supply their daily bread and meat. They could, and did, get their supplies from Canada, Denmark, or wherever it was most convenient. This change, too, was a sort of revolution.

Urban Growth

In the eighteenth century, this urbanization of society was advancing rapidly: London's population rose from 700,000 in 1700 to about one million in 1800; Berlin tripled in size to about 175,000; Paris rose from about 300,000 to 500,000 in the same period. In every country, the number of towns with populations between 10,000 and 25,000 grew considerably; these towns served as important administrative, cultural, and economic centers for the provinces.

It was in these smaller towns that the bulk of the new industry and manufacturing was concentrated as the Industrial Revolution gradually got under way. Land was cheaper there than in the great metropolises, and the smaller towns were usually closer to the raw material sources. Manchester, the English textile center, had a population of about 7,000 in the 1740s; by 1790 the population had risen to about 25,000, and it gained at least 50 percent every decade for the next half century.

Population growth continued at a high rate throughout the nineteenth century, and in western and northern Europe, most of these people eventually resided in urban places, either by birth or by migration. The census of 1851 showed that for the first time, a majority of the people in England lived in an urban setting (that is, in places with more than 5,000 population). About 25 percent of the population of France and Germany lived in urban areas, but the percentage was lower in southern and eastern Europe where industry was not yet established.

■ **The Flower Girl.** "That girl seems to know you, George!" says the suspicious wife as the flower girl recognizes a customer of her other wares. Prostitution was widespread in the early Industrial Age.

Urban Classes and Lifestyles

In the eighteenth-century towns, social classes were quite distinct, as they had always been. At the top, dominating politics and setting the cultural tone was the *nobility*. In some places, particularly in the West and Scandinavia, the aristocrats increasingly intermarried with wealthy commoners—bankers, merchants, officials of the self-governing cities—and together they formed the governing group.

Beneath them, but gaining in power and prestige was an *upper-middle class,* or classes, who included less-wealthy merchants, tradesmen, and professionals. These well-educated, upwardly mobile men and their families constituted what the French called the *bourgeoisie.* Many of them opposed the pretensions of the nobles and their wealthy allies and were on a collision course with the aristocratic governors, a collision that finally exploded in the French Revolution at the end of the century.

Below the bourgeoisie were the *lower-middle classes,* composed of clerks, artisans, and skilled workers, some of whom were independent shopkeepers. They were desperately afraid of falling back into the class from which they had emerged: the workers who labored in semiskilled or unskilled jobs for an employer. The lower-middle classes mimicked their social betters among the bourgeoisie, a class to which they might ascend with luck, time, and good marriages.

This lower-middle class, more than the still relatively small and fragmented working classes, generated most of the social discontents that marked the late eighteenth and early nineteenth centuries. Only in the later nineteenth century, when the industrial working classes had become much larger and more important in the social structure did they begin the various movements that would create the modern urban society.

✤ DIET AND NUTRITION

During the later eighteenth century, at the same time industrialization was beginning, the diet and health of ordinary citizens were gradually transformed. For many centuries, European common people had been accustomed to depending on an uneven mix of grains, cheese, sporadic meats and fowl, and seasonal fruits to maintain life. Much depended on local weather and local harvests; the season determined what provisions would be available for human consumption. In late winter and spring, the supplies put away at harvest would begin to run short, and hunger became a constant companion to much of the population.

Local famine was a commonplace through the early eighteenth century everywhere. In such times, it was not unusual for grain to be rotting in barns fifty miles or so from where people were starving for lack of it. Transport networks for bulk goods were primitive or nonexistent in the more backward regions; only the towns commanded a more or less sophisticated supply system, with stored reserves and emergency powers over the population in times of crisis. In the countryside, every decade or so in one part of Europe or another, people starved in large numbers.

By the end of the century, famines had become a rarity, and Europeans were in fact eating considerably better than ever. What happened to change the situation? First, water transportation was much improved, as were the roads, which had formerly been in an abysmal condition. Second, new and more productive agricultural methods, seeds, and crop rotations had increased food production in western Europe while in eastern Europe the spread of serfdom allowed an increasing amount of grain to be exported to the west. Third, the diet of Europeans had improved a great deal. The potato had become a staple for the poor, and its nutritional value was exceptional. Milk and dairy products were considerably more common, but

still viewed with suspicion by many. Meat and fish, always desired but too expensive to be enjoyed by the poor, were coming to be a standard part of the diet of all but the very poor by the end of the century.

Changing diets had a basic impact on health. The diet of the rich was excessively dependent on protein (meat) and carbohydrates (sweets, fats), with a shortage of vitamins. With the coming of new foods from the colonies like potatoes, maize, beans, and squash, this protein-loaded diet became more balanced. For the poor, the possibility of a better diet had a more dramatic effect; the potato in particular meant the difference between life and death for many hundreds of thousands of northern Europeans who came to depend on it as much as they did on bread. In the latter part of the century, citrus fruits and exotic vegetables began to show up on the tables of the middle and upper classes, adding another dimension to the diet. These were the products of the semitropical colonies, as was sugar from cane, which now replaced honey and other natural sweeteners.

✤ PUBLIC HEALTH

Although the lives of ordinary people were improving in several respects, in many areas conditions were hardly better at all. For example, though diet was generally improving, *medical and surgical conditions* showed very little change over the century. Being admitted to a hospital was still almost a death warrant, and the poor would absolutely refuse, preferring to die at home. Doctoring was very much a hit-or-miss proposition, with primitive diagnosis backed up by even more primitive treatment. Surgery was a horror, with no pain deadener but whiskey. Amputations were the last resort in many cases, and the resultant wounds frequently became infected and killed the patient if shock had not already done so.

Doctors and pharmacists still did not receive formal training in schools of medicine; the trainees did an apprenticeship with a doctor, who may or may not have known more than his apprentice. All sorts of quacks were active, bilking the public with their "Electrical Magnetic Beds" and "Elixirs of Paradise," and both the educated and the uneducated had a very low opinion of doctors.

Medical facts now taken for granted were unknown: the functions of many of the internal organs, germ theory, the dangers of infection, and fever treatment were still guesswork or not known at all. The *mentally ill* were just beginning to be given some treatment besides the traditional approach, under which violent patients were locked up and others were kept at the family home. All in all, the treatment of the human mind and body when they fell ill was hardly improved over what the Romans had done two thousand years earlier. Some would say it was worse.

⚜ HOUSING AND SANITATION

The most urgent problem facing the industrial towns in the early part of the nineteenth century was sanitation. In the rows of cheap rental housing (hastily built largely by the mill and factory owners as an additional source of income), overcrowding to an incredible degree was commonplace. Even the most basic sanitary facilities were largely missing. Ventilation of interior rooms was nonexistent, and all types of infectious disease ran rampant. Tuberculosis (TB, consumption) rapidly became the number one cause of death in nineteenth-century Britain; it bred in the damp, unventilated back rooms and spread easily through the workers' homes where several people crowded into every room.

Privacy was impossible for the working class to obtain; illegitimacy and incest were constant menaces to family security. In report after report to the British Parliament in the 1830s and 1840s, shocked middle-class investigators noted that sleeping five and six to a bed was common, that boys and girls in their teens were frequently forced to sleep together for lack of space, and that greedy landlords regularly extracted the maximal rent by allowing several poverty-stricken families to share the same tiny apartments.

Similar conditions were soon found on the Continent as industry spread. For many years, civic authorities were either unable or unwilling to tackle the huge tasks of assuring decent living conditions for the poorer classes. (Recall that the poor did not yet have the vote anywhere.) Despite the relative youth of the new urban populations, towns and cities normally had a higher death rate than birth rate. Only the huge influx of new blood from the villages kept the towns expanding.

⚜ LIVING STANDARDS

As the Industrial Age began, the *gap between the living conditions of the European rich and poor became wider* than ever before in history. The aristocracy and the handful of wealthy commoners lived a luxurious and self-indulgent life. The higher nobility and court officials were expected to have squadrons of servants, meals with fourteen courses and ten wines, palaces in the towns and manors in the countryside, and personal jewelry whose value was equal to the yearly incomes of a whole province of peasants. As yet, the rich were not at all reluctant to be

identified as rich—on the contrary, great wealth was thought to be a reward for merit and might be displayed as a badge of honor.

The lifestyle of the urban middle classes was much more modest, although some of the richest, such as bankers, might have six times the income of the poorer aristocrats. Secure in their solid townhouses, the members of the middle classes entertained modestly if at all and concentrated on their countinghouses, investments, shops, businesses, and legal firms. They devoted much attention to their families. The wife was expected to be a thrifty, farsighted manager of the household, and the husband was the source of authority for the children and the bearer of the most precious possession of all, the family honor.

For most people in urban areas, material life was gradually improving, but the lower fringes of the working classes and the many beggars, casual laborers, and wandering peddlers and craftsmen were hard put to keep bread on the table and their children in clothes. Poverty was perhaps never so grim in European cities as in the early nineteenth century, when it became more visible because of the much increased numbers of poor. As industrial work began to become common in the towns, the uprooted ex-peasants who supplied most of the labor often experienced a decline in living standards for a while, until they or their families found ways to cope with the demands of the factory and the town lifestyle. This decline could last for a first generation of migrants; only their children benefited from the often painful transition.

■ **Textile Mill Workers.** This early photo shows the noisy and dangerous conditions of work in a mid-nineteenth century mill. The many exposed machinery parts were constantly jamming, often at the expense of a worker's daily wages.

George Gordon, Lord Byron
1788–1824

The triumph of the Industrial Age also saw a vigorous reaction against it in the **Romantic Movement,** which seized upon much of Europe during the middle years of the nineteenth century. Beginning in Britain, this movement first attacked the excessive faith in rationalism that characterized the later eighteenth-century Enlightenment. By the 1820s it had become a rejection of the narrow moneygrubbing that many believed had come into British urban life with the Industrial Revolution. A recognition of the power of the emotions and of the impenetrable mystery of life came to be seen as essential elements of all the arts, but particularly the art most given to expression of feeling—poetry. Among the British Romantic poets, George Gordon, Lord Byron took the first place through not only the magnificence of his verse but also the enormous publicity his unconventional life generated. Several of the finest Romantic poems are from his pen, but Lord Byron's place in history has also benefited from what would now be called successful media exposure.

Born to a dissipated and irresponsible father and a loving but unbalanced mother, Byron's early years were very unstable. He was lamed by a clubfoot that grew worse under the attentions of a quack doctor who tried to heal the boy with painful braces. His erratic schooling was successful at least in arousing a love of literature and encouraging his inclination to write. At age sixteen, he fell in love with Mary Chaworth, a slightly older girl whose tantalizing cold-blooded attitude toward her teenage admirer, Byron later said, was the turning point of his emotional life. From this time on, this handsome and passionate man became involved in a steady procession of short- and long-term affairs with women of all descriptions. There is much evidence of sexual ambivalence as well in his relations with men both in Britain and abroad.

Byron's poetic efforts begin to see the light of day in 1807, when he was a student at Cambridge. His gifts were equally apparent in his lyrics and in his satires of his detractors, which could be savage. In 1809 he entered the House of Lords (his father had been a minor noble) and soon took off for a two-year visit to the Continent, despite the Napoleonic wars then raging. Most of his time was spent in Greece, a place and a people for whom he developed a lasting affection.

The major literary product of his trip was the magnificent *Childe Harold's Pilgrimage,* which became the rage of all London and made Byron's reputation overnight. The long poem beautifully caught the moods of the growing reaction against conventional manners and values, personified in the autobiographical Childe Harold. The magnetic Byron now took advantage of his notoriety to enter into one sexual affair after another, an "abyss of sensuality" as he himself put it, enhanced by both wine and drugs.

Seeking perhaps some stable influence, in early 1815, he suddenly married a rich young woman, but the marriage went awry almost as soon as it com-

❧ LABOR REFORMS AND URBAN IMPROVEMENTS

To the credit of the British aristocrats who still controlled Parliament, as early as the 1820s, after the war emergency had passed, a number of reform proposals to aid the working classes were introduced, and by the 1830s some of the worst abuses in the workplace were attacked. The **Factory Acts** of 1819 and 1833 limited the employment of young children and provided that they should be given at least a little education at their place of work. (Still, it was entirely legal for a nine-year-old to put in eight-hour workdays and for a thirteen-year-old to work twelve hours a day, six days a week!)

Women and boys under the age of ten were not permitted to work in the mines after 1842. Until then, much of the deep underground work, which was highly dangerous and exhausting to anyone, was done by women and young children. In most textile manufacturing, physical strength was not as important as quickness and endurance. Women and children were paid much less than men demanded, and their smaller size allowed them

menced. Only a scant year later, his wife was hurrying back to her parents and requesting legal separation despite her just-born daughter. After some unpretty squeezing of his in-laws for money, Byron agreed to sign the separation papers; in those days this was tantamount to an admission of guilt. His social reputation was now destroyed, not only by the scandalous separation but also by dark hints, never denied and much later confirmed, that he had committed incest with his half-sister, Augusta Leigh. In 1816, he left to visit his friend, the poet Shelley, in Switzerland. He never set foot in Britain again.

For the final seven years of his life, Byron was mainly in Italy, where he wrote much of his finest work, including the *Don Juan* epic as well as several of his poetic dramas. The Italian years were made happy by his permanent attachment to the young Teresa Guiccioli, the love of his life who finally released him from the aimless philandering he had engaged in for fifteen years.

In 1823, the Greek's rebellion against their Turkish overlords attracted Byron's attention, and he hastened to Greece to put his money and energies into the cause. He contracted a lethal fever and died in his adoptive country in 1824. Throughout the rest of the century, his reputation grew, not only as a poet but as the literary symbol of the brave but doomed individual who challenges the destiny of ordinary souls and must eventually pay for his temerity by defeat and death. Denied the honor of burial in Westminster Abbey because of his shocking escapades, Byron finally received a memorial stone in the abbey floor in 1969. His beloved Greeks had acted much earlier to memorialize him in their own country.

■ **Byron as the Giaour.** This portrait was painted in 1813, shortly after Lord Byron returned from his tour of the Near East.

to move about in the crowded machine halls with more agility than men. Boys as young as seven years of age were regularly employed in twelve- or thirteen-hour shifts until the passage of the 1833 act.

Little was done to reform sanitation in worker housing until the 1860s. In 1842 a pioneering report by **Edwin Chadwick** on the horrible conditions in the slums and how they might be corrected through modern sewage and water purification systems began to draw attention. But not until the great cholera scare of 1858, when London was threatened by a major outbreak of this lethal waterborne disease, was action taken. Then the upper and middle classes realized that although epidemic diseases such as cholera might originate in the slums, they could and would soon spread to other residential areas. At about the same time, the restructuring of the sewer system allowed Paris for the first time to manage its waste disposal problem. Led by the two capitals, the provincial city authorities soon began to plan and install equivalent systems. By the end of the century, European city life was again reasonably healthy for all but the poorest slum dwellers.

Summary

The social change introduced by the industrial process took many forms. Overall, industrialization probably had more impact on men and women than any other development since agriculture replaced hunting and gathering. This chapter examined the impact of industry on four areas: family relations, occupational mobility, urbanization, and diet. The family was changed by a decreasing age of marriage and a sharp rise in illegitimacy. Children came to be valued as creatures worthy of love in their own right. A number of new occupations were opened to both men and women in factories and mills as industry spread, while the traditional servant jobs multiplied in the expanding cities and towns.

Living standards varied from an unprecedented opulence among the rich to an actual decline in the conditions of recent urban migrants. Slums appeared in the new industrial quarters, which were horribly lacking in basic sanitation and privacy. Nevertheless, to the working classes, the attractions of the towns were manifold and irresistible, particularly for those who sought a better life than the traditional social and economic restrictions that the villages allowed. A richer and more varied diet even for the poor gradually made itself felt in better health. By the end of the nineteenth century, sanitation and workers' living conditions had visibly improved.

Test Your Knowledge

1. Around the mid-eighteenth century, the European population
   a. began to rise as a result of declining mortality and rising birthrates.
   b. began to stabilize after a century of steady increase.
   c. tapered off from the sharp decline that had marked the sixteenth and seventeenth centuries.
   d. began to rise as a result of medical breakthroughs against epidemics.

2. Formerly, historians erroneously believed that in premodern Europe
   a. the average age at marriage was in the early thirties.
   b. the average life span was no more than twenty-five years.
   c. daughters shared equally with the sons in inheriting land.
   d. there was a great deal of illegitimacy.

3. Marriage in preindustrial European society is best described as
   a. a contractual relation formed mostly by economic and social aspirations.
   b. a contractual relation that conformed closely to biological drives.
   c. an economic relationship between two individuals.
   d. a stratagem to "cover" the sexual activities engaged in by the young anyway.

4. An important function of children in preindustrial society was
   a. to serve as security for their parents in old age.
   b. to elevate themselves socially and thus to honor their parents.
   c. to bring grandchildren into the world for the gratification of their parents.
   d. to pray for the departed souls of their deceased parents.

5. In the early industrial period, the most common employment for a female
   a. involved prostitution at least part-time.
   b. was as a domestic household servant.
   c. was in one or another "white-collar" jobs.
   d. was to substitute for a man temporarily.

6. The governing class in the cities of the eighteenth century was composed of
   a. the hereditary aristocracy.
   b. the aristocracy and the wealthiest commoners, who had intermarried.
   c. the military commanders responsible to the royal government.
   d. the masses of urban commoners who had obtained the vote.

7. As a generalization, living standards in late eighteenth century towns

a. saw a huge differentiation between top and bottom, perhaps the most ever.

b. were roughly similar to conditions in the countryside for the mass of people.

c. were worse than they would ever be again for the laboring poor.

d. were much better than ever before in European history.

8. Diet and nutrition in the later eighteenth century

a. were steadily worsening for the poorer classes.

b. were favorably affected by the trade with the colonies.

c. were about the same for the poor and the rich.

d. were undermined by the frequent famines.

Identification Terms

Chadwick (Edwin)

Enclosure Movement

Factory Acts

Romantic Movement

urban migration

Bibliography

Bridenthal, R., and C. Koontz. *Becoming Visible: Women in European History,* 1976 and several later editions. A selection of articles and very good bibliography on the changing role of women as mothers, wives, and workers. See also volume 2 of B. Anderson and J. Zinsser, *A History of Their Own: Women in Europe from Prehistory to the Present,* 1988, which has a huge bibliography.

Heilbroner, R. *The Worldly Philosophers,* 1967. An introduction to economic liberalism as it appeared in the nineteenth century.

McKeown, T. *The Modern Rise of Population,* 1976. Has a lot to say about the changes induced by better nutrition and sanitation after the late eighteenth century.

Mayhew, H. *London Labour and London Poor,* 1851 (many reprints). A classic journalistic account of the lives of the ordinary poor people in the early years of the Industrial Age. A fascinating series of vignettes of street life. Highly recommended.

Moraze, C. *The Triumph of the Middle Classes,* 1966; E. Gauldie, *Cruel Habitations: A History of Working-Class Housing, 1790– 1918,* 1974; and G. Himmelfarb, *The Idea of Poverty: England in the Early Industrial Age,* 1984. All are very readable accounts of certain aspects of industrial society in the nineteenth century.

Pinchbeck, I. *Women Workers and the Industrial Revolution,* 1930. A pioneering study of females. See also P. Robertson, *The Experience of Women: Pattern and Change in Nineteenth Century Europe,* 1982, for a survey of female public and private life.

Shorter, E. *The Making of the Modern Family,* 1975. A controversial—some would say outrageous—essay.

Taylor, A. J., ed. *The Standard of Living in Britain in the Industrial Revolution,* 1975. A collection of important articles on the pros and cons of industrial life for the masses of workers.

Taylor, G. *The Transportation Revolution, 1815–1860,* 1968. Looks at the effects of steam-driven transport.

EUROPE IN IDEOLOGICAL CONFLICT

1815–1850	Economic liberalism, conservatism, nationalism, and socialism emerge
1830	July Revolution (France): Louis Philippe (1830–1848)
1848	Revolts in France, Austria, Prussia, Italy
1849–1850	Failure of revolts/conservatives regain control

The *ancien régime* of pre-1789 Europe could not be brought back despite the efforts of the conservative leaders. But in countries other than France, a great many of the political, legal, and social reforms that the French Revolution had brought or attempted to bring could be delayed or even temporarily reversed. In France itself, however, the changes since 1789 were too popular to be ignored in the post-1815 settlement. And even outside France the forces unleashed by the economic changes that had been taking place in England—the First Industrial Revolution, as it has come to be called—were going to remake the society of western Europe by the mid-nineteenth century. The revolts of 1848 were the direct result of the political and economic changes set in motion by industrialization and by the ideas of 1789.

✤ THE DUAL REVOLUTION: LIBERAL POLITICS AND INDUSTRIAL ECONOMY

Much of the history of the past two centuries, especially in Europe, has been a reflection of a sustained dual revolution in politics and economics. The political revolution was highlighted by events in the United States between 1775 and 1789 and in France between 1789 and 1814, which we looked at in earlier chapters. In the first example, a republic of federated states was born, committed to political democracy and the legal equality of all citizens. In the second, the ancient class distinctions and privileges given the highborn were declared extinct, and the way upward was opened to all who had the talent and ambition to tread it.

The economic revolution was slower and less spectacular, but it was at least as important over the long run. It was generated by the changes in industrial production that took place in the second half of the eighteenth century, particularly in Britain; by the conquest of space through the railroads; and by the immense growth of population in Europe and the United States, which provided formerly undreamed of markets for consumer products.

The two revolutions fused together after 1815, reinforcing one another in all kinds of ways. Two examples will suffice:

1. In the 1790s, during the period of the Directory in France, a tiny group of conspirators put forth the first "socialist" ideas, although they did not use that term. Their ideas of eliminating property-based distinctions and sharing equally the products of human labor got

nowhere; the leaders were put to death as pernicious agitators of the poor. A generation later, when the horrible working conditions produced by early industrialization had joined with the political beliefs of liberal democracy, another group of thinkers arose in Britain and France who were determined to change "the system" and to replace the abuses and exploitation of early capitalism by the humane ideals of equality and mutual care. This was the origin of an organized political effort to introduce socialism.

2. The eighteenth-century political revolution was guided by the middle classes—the lawyers, teachers, and merchants—on their own behalf. They had little, if any, sympathy with democracy as we now understand that term. Later, in the post-1815 period of reaction, the more perceptive members of the middle classes recognized that without the active assistance of much of the laboring classes, they could not gain and hold power against the aristocracy. The industrial laboring classes were growing rapidly, but lacked leadership from within their own ranks. Instead, "renegades" from the middle classes became more or less radical democrats and helped the industrial laborers to find their rightful voice in the political arena. During the later nineteenth century, a partnership grew up between the middle-class reformers and the laboring class voters, which brought about substantial improvement in the condition of ordinary people.

We have already explored the fundamental principles of liberal thought (see Chapter 33). Inspired by the philosophical concepts of Locke, Montesquieu, and others, middle- and upper-class reformers believed that so long as law and custom prevented most people from enjoying certain fundamental liberties and rights, the human race would fail to fulfill its high destiny.

These liberal sons and daughters of the Enlightenment everywhere formed a *"party of reform,"* dedicated to changing the traditional, class-based system of political representation. By 1815 much had been achieved in those respects in America and France, but the conservative reaction after 1815 nullified some of those gains everywhere in Europe. Only in France and England was much of the liberal political agenda retained. Here, men of property had the vote, all men were equal in the eyes of the law, and royal powers were sharply curtailed by written laws that could not be easily manipulated. Parliaments in both countries, like Congress in the United States, were responsible to the voters, rather than to the king, and freedom of conscience was more or less guaranteed.

The Free Enterprise Gospel

Another side of the liberal philosophy focused on freedoms in the marketplace and the rebellion against the traditional restrictions imposed by mercantilism. In contrast to political liberalism's gradual evolution, economic liberalism grew directly from the work of Adam Smith whose ideas were mentioned in Chapter 32.

What did Smith's adherents want?

- *Laissez faire.* If government would only let them alone (*laissez faire*), the merchants and manufacturers of every nation would produce goods and services to meet the demands of the market most efficiently and economically.

- *Free trade.* The existing mercantile system of quotas, licenses, and subsidies should be eliminated as quickly as possible, and the most efficient producers should be allowed to trade with anyplace and anyone who desired their goods at prices that the free market would set.

- *The less government, the better.* As the first two conditions suggest, the economic liberals despised governmental controls of any sort in the economy (even though Smith himself made certain important exceptions to *laissez faire*); they believed that the free market alone would provide proper guidance for policy decisions and that it was government's task simply to follow these guidelines as they revealed themselves over time. Any interference in the economy they condemned as an obstruction to the prosperity of the nation; the famous "unseen hand" of the free market should be allowed to do its beneficial work for all.

In early nineteenth-century England, economic liberalism, often called *Manchester liberalism* because of its popularity with the cotton-mill owners in Manchester, provided the employers of industrial labor with an excuse for the systematic exploitation of the weak. Drawing on theorists like *Thomas Malthus* (*An Essay on Population,* published in 1798) and *David Ricardo* (*The Iron Law of Wages,* published in 1817), the Manchester liberals were able to demonstrate that the poor would always be poor due to their excessive birthrate and other moral faults, and that it was the duty of the well-off to protect their material advantages by any means they could. Since sympathizers with this line of thought came into control of the British House of Commons after the electoral Reform Act of 1832, the government was largely unsympathetic toward the idea of social protection of the lower classes. Only in the 1870s and later did a number of reformers emerge

The Ruined Abbey. Caspar David Friedrich (1774–1840) was the best known of that school of painters who saw Nature as a mysterious and somewhat ominous force. His *Abbey in the Woods* displays the early nineteenth century fascination with ruins.

who rejected this heartless attitude and busied themselves with the improvement of the lot of the poor majority.

✦ CONSERVATISM IN POST-NAPOLEONIC EUROPE

The liberals were by no means the sole players in the political field after 1815. Supported by the wave of anti-Napoleonic patriotism, conservative forces registered a strong effect for at least a generation. In eastern Europe, the conservative wave lasted much longer. Conservatism in the first half of the nineteenth century meant one of two things: *moderate conservatism,* an attempt to take the liberal ideas of the day and adapt them to the service of the traditional institutions of monarchy, established religion, and class-based distinctions, or *reaction,* a total rejection of the ideas of the American and French Revolutions and a determination to turn the clock back.

Moderate Conservatism

Moderate conservatism was a response to the excesses of the Jacobins in France. It was supported by a large percentage of ordinary Europeans who had been appalled by Robespierre's radicalism and then angered by Napoleon's arrogance and his economic exploitation of non-French Europeans. The clergy, both Catholic and Protestant, were the leaders of moderate conservatism in much of the Continent. The more enlightened aristocrats, who could see what would happen if turning the clock back were to be adopted as state policy, also contributed to moderate conservatism; they wished to avoid revolutions in the future by making some concessions now to the masses.

Conservatives of all stripes believed that an official religion was a necessity for instilling proper respect for law and tradition; they could not imagine a state in which church and government were separated by law. They supported a constitution, but rejected political democracy as being the rule of the mob. They believed that only those who had a stake in society, evidenced by property, could and would take on the burdens of self-government with the requisite seriousness and respect for legal procedure. They thought that just as differences in talent would always exist, so also should differences in privilege. Some conservatives rejected the idea of privilege by birth; others embraced it as the best way to assure a responsible group in continuous command of the ship of state.

In economics, the moderates generally favored the continuation of government controls in trade (especially foreign trade) and industry. They thought that Smith was well-meaning but wrong, and that without such supervision, the national welfare would only be harmed by selfish and greedy entrepreneurs.

Since many of the nonclerical conservatives were either wealthy or had prospects of becoming so, any drastic change in the existing economic system would almost certainly harm their interests. Much of their wealth was tied up in inherited land, and they were not happy watching financial speculation, commerce, and manufacturing replace land as the primary source of large income.

Reaction

Reactive conservatism was the rule in large parts of Europe, namely, Prussia, Austria, and Russia, where few if any concessions were made to the new social structures being created by the changing economic conditions. This led to explosive pressures, which eventually burst forth in the upheaval of World War I and its revolutionary aftermath. In Prussia and Austria, the reactionary conservaties ruled for a generation after 1815; they denied a constitution; retained the established church, whether Catholic or Protestant; and maintained strict class distinctions in justice, taxation, and voting rights. Both countries maintained a form of serfdom as well. Neither the French nor the American examples found an effective following here until the explosion of 1848.

In Russia, which meant not only the Russian ethnic groups but also much of what is now independent eastern Europe, the reactionaries were also in command. Tsar Alexander I had died in 1825 without ever giving his nation the constitutional government that he had toyed with since his accession to the throne twenty-five years earlier. He was followed on the throne by his younger brother, Nicholas I (1825–1855), a sincere believer in autocracy and a dyed-in-the-wool reactionary. Nicholas's inclinations were reinforced by the botched attempt of a handful of officer rebels (the "Decembrists") to organize a revolution and impose a constitution on liberal lines in December 1825. During Nicholas's reign, Russia was called the *"Gendarme of Europe,"* eager and ready to put down revolutionary change wherever it might rear its ugly head.

✤ NATIONALISM

Besides the struggle between liberal and conservative, another extensive source of conflict was evidencing itself in post-1815 Europe: nationalist feeling. *Modern political nationalism* has its origins in the Napoleonic period, starting in France between 1792 and 1795, when the Jacobins insisted upon the duties imposed on all citizens by patriotism. Later, when the French armies occupied half of Europe, in many lands the patriotic reaction against the occupier contributed to nationalism in the form of a mass emotion generated by the fact of "otherness" between occupier and native.

Nationalism and liberalism went well together in several nations, especially Britain and France. Conservatives, on the other hand, were often split on the question of nationalism. Many conservatives denounced nationalism as a trick exercised by demagogues to fool the common people into supporting revolutionary actions. They could not forget its origins.

Early nationalism was generally a culturally productive phenomenon. It had a definite constructive note to it. To be aware of being French did not mean to reject the Germans or English as inferiors. One could simultaneously strive for the freedom of the individual and the free nation.

Sometime in the 1840s, however, nationalism in much of Europe lost its constructive, tolerant character. This later phase was marked by the negative qualities of national feeling that we in the twentieth century are thoroughly familiar with: "we" versus "they," and right against wrong; nationalism as a zero-sum game in which one person's gain is another's loss and vice versa. This nationalism was characterized by a conviction of cultural superiority over other nations and by a sense of national mission—the belief that one's nation was "bringing the light" to other, less fortunate neighbors. It degenerated to its worst in the Balkans and East Europe, where many distinct peoples lived in mixed communities and regions without clear dividing lines. Here, nationalism soon became an excuse for one war after another in the later nineteenth and early twentieth centuries. World War I exemplified the expression of this type of negative nationalism.

✤ SOCIALISM IN THE PRE-MARX ERA

Usually, the word *socialism* is associated with Marxism and its failed attempt to impose a communistic society in Russia and elsewhere. But that connection did not always exist. As we have seen, the earliest socialists were a handful of conspirators in France in the 1790s. Once they were eliminated, no others arose to take their place until a generation later. None of these individuals had any link with Marx.

What did the early social thinkers wish to achieve? What constituted this phenomenon of socialism? Three chief goals were involved:

1. *A planned economy.* The free market was an entirely wasteful, haphazard way of supplying the needs and wants of most people.
2. *Greater economic equality.* There was too much for the rich, too little for the rest, and too few ways in which that situation could be changed peaceably and fairly.
3. *Ownership of income-producing property by the state rather than private parties.* Only the state was powerful enough to resist the wealthy and ensure that the means of producing wealth were not controlled by a few for their own benefit.

The early nineteenth-century socialists were often later termed "Utopian," because what they wanted allegedly could never be secured so long as human nature remained as it was. But that label (originated by Karl Marx) is inherently unfair to them; what they wanted has been, in large part, achieved by modern societies all over the globe.

Charles Fourier
1772–1837

The most interesting of all the early or pre-Marx socialist theorizers was the Frenchman Charles Fourier (1772–1837). Though perhaps not entirely sane, he nevertheless pinpointed many of the unpleasant truths about modern industrial society seventy-five or a hundred years before those truths were accepted by most.

Fourier was born into a well-off family in a provincial city and received an excellent education, but he lost his property during the French Revolution. He fought for the Napoleonic regime for two years, but ill health forced him to resign his army post. He then began a life of scholarship and propagandizing his ideas.

In 1808 he published, anonymously, his basic work *The Theory of the Four Movements,* in which he explains that human society has been corrupted by the unnatural restraints on passion that we impose on ourselves. Only when those restraints have been lifted will humans achieve their potential. Fourier's focus on the importance of emotions, or passions, and on the necessity of women finding satisfaction in their emo-tional life make him an important forerunner of the feminist movement. However, Fourier's demand that passions be given free expression quickly stamped him as an eccentric and a dangerous challenger to accepted values.

In the economic aspect of this doctrine, Fourier worked out an answer to the blight of early industrialization: the socioeconomic unit he called the *phalanx* (Greek for a military unit). He insisted that individualism and the competition it fostered were the prime cause of social evils. The new society would consist of voluntary associations, where cooperation would be the rule in every aspect of life.

The phalanx envisioned by Fourier consisted of exactly 1,620 persons, equally divided by sex, with sufficient farmland around the common dwelling and workplace—the **phalanstery**—to supply the members with food. Work would be assigned as much as possible by preference, but the dirty tasks would be rotated, and there would be no "high" or "low" occupations. The work would be suited to the natural temperaments of different age and gender groups.

The most influential of the early socialists worked in France. The reform-minded nobleman *Henri de Saint-Simon* (1760–1825) was perhaps the most important of all. He believed that industrialized society had the potential to be the fairest, as well as the most productive, society that the world had ever seen. He believed further that the state, that is, the government, had the positive duty to look out for those who were unable to look out for themselves—the misfits, the incompetent, and the handicapped. Since industrialized production would be so much more lavish than anything previously seen, the *economy of scarcity would be abolished* soon, and it would be no hardship to care for these "welfare cases." Saint-Simon thought that private industry and government must combine in planning this economy of abundance that was surely coming.

Charles Fourier and *Pierre Proudhon* were active later than Saint Simon and had differing views. Fourier was an obsessive theorist of technology and organization; his vision of special, self-contained units of precisely 1,620 persons living and working together was one of the oddities of early social thought (see the Biography in this chapter). Fourier was particularly important as a forerunner of *feminist equality in work and politics* and as the upholder of the demands of the emotional, passionate side of human nature in industrialized society.

Proudhon was the first anarchist; he believed the power of the state must be destroyed if men and women were ever to be truly free and capable of living humane lives. Unlike most socialists, Proudhon was convinced that government was at best a barely tolerable evil; it was always controlled by the wealthy and was almost always the oppressor of the poor. In 1840 he posed his famous question, *What Is Property?* and gave a resounding answer: Property is nothing but organized theft! It has been stolen from the sole creator of value, the worker, by the

For example, young children with their natural affinity for dirt would be assigned to act as public scavengers and garbage collectors! Those who desired could marry, but all could rightfully engage in free sexual expression, which was considered a basic human need. Needless to add, such reasoning did not convince many in a Europe that was still largely controlled by church and censor.

Though he led a very reclusive life, Fourier continued to publicize his theories to his dying day, but never had the satisfaction of seeing them translated into fact. Despite the best efforts of his friends and converts, there was but one French experiment with Fourierism, as the theory was termed by the 1830s. It ended quickly in total failure. Instead, Fourier's most important impact was in the New World. Several American experiments in communal living in the first half of the nineteenth century drew their inspiration and some of their structure from Fourier. Brook Farm, the famous New England venture in an intellectual and communal society, was one of these.

In his later life, Fourier devoted his energies to finding a rich backer, who would supply the necessary capital to establish a phalanstery, or a series of them, under his own supervision. Reportedly, having published an appeal for the equivalent of a million dollars or so in his tiny newspaper, Fourier would go to his office at noon on the appointed day to wait for the unknown benefactor to drop the money in his lap. No matter how many times the benefactor failed to appear, the next time the notice ran Fourier would go in all confidence to wait for the gift.

This sort of unworldliness pervaded Fourierism, as well as its founder, and kept the authorities from becoming too concerned about his challenge to the status quo. Fourier was contemptuous of the competing theories of Saint-Simon and Owen, believing that their failure to appreciate the importance of human passions rendered their whole approach to socioeconomic questions invalid. Although it is beyond dispute that much of his own theory would, if applied, do more damage than good to people, it is still impressive to note how well Fourier understood some of the damage that modern individualistic and competitive societies inflict on their members. While the phalanxes and phalansteries may be condemned without hesitation as unworkable daydreams, the emotional repression, social isolation, and alienation from one's fellow beings that they were meant to counter are also indisputably bad for the human body and soul.

owning class. And it should be taken back—by force if necessary.

In England, utopian socialism's standard-bearer in the early nineteenth century was a businessman, *Robert Owen.* Owen was a remarkable man whose hard work and ambition made him a wealthy mill owner at the age of twenty-seven. He then decided to give much of his wealth and power to his workforce. At his famous cooperative textile mill at New Lanark, Scotland, Owen put his theories into practice and created a profitable enterprise that also provided well for every need of its workers and their families. Although not all of his visions worked out so well (the American experimental community he founded in the 1820s was a quick disaster), Owen remained convinced that industrial production and a decent life for workers were compatible and within reach. His examples were of considerable influence in the later development of socialist theory.

In the 1840s socialism was still very much an idea or theory of outsiders. It was not taken seriously by most people and condemned as against the laws of God and man by most of those who *did* take notice of it. Economic liberals thundered against it as unnatural; political liberals were appalled at the prospect of hordes of industrial workers being admitted into equality in government. All types of conservatives thought it terribly misunderstood human nature. With the advent of a new, so-called *scientific socialism of Karl Marx,* this situation changed drastically. Marxist socialism was to become one of the driving forces of Western civilization in the later nineteenth century (see Chapter 41).

✤ POLITICAL EVENTS TO 1848

In the period just after the Vienna settlement of 1815, European international affairs were relatively calm (see

● **MAP 38.1 Prussia and Austria after the Peace of Vienna, 1815.** The center of the continent was the scene of an increasing rivalry for leadership of the German-speaking peoples. Austria and Prussia both emerged victors in 1815, and both were bulwarks of the reaction against French revolutionary ideas.

Map 38.1). The Quadruple Alliance was easily strong enough to suppress any attempts to overthrow the peace, as long as its members agreed. Revolts by liberals in Spain (1820) and Italy (1822) were quickly squelched, but a nationalist guerrilla war by the Greeks against their Turkish overlords (1827–1830) was allowed to succeed because it was a special circumstance of Christian versus Muslim.

During this decade, the Spanish-American colonies were also allowed to break away from backward Spain, which was too weak to suppress their revolts by itself. First Mexico, then most of South America rebelled against Madrid and were independent states by 1825. Brazil, Portugal's one colony in the New World, also broke away during this same period (see Chapter 45).

The Liberal States: France and Britain

In an almost bloodless revolution in July 1830, *France* threw out its unpopular Bourbon ruler, who had foolishly attempted to install an absolutist government. In his place came the "Citizen King," *Louis Philippe* (1830–1848). Louis gladly accepted from Parliament a moderately liberal constitution, which called him "king of the French," rather than the traditional king of France, and stated that sovereignty lay in the people, not in the throne. This was a novelty in monarchic government.

The **July Monarchy,** as the eighteen years of Louis Philippe's reign are generally called, was a major step forward for both economic and political liberalism. The middle class and especially the new upper class of wealth (not birth) did very well under this government. The rising number of urban poor and industrial workers found very little sympathy from it, however. Troops were repeatedly used to break strikes and to control the populace. Citizen rights were granted and usually observed by the government, but those rights were much more extensive for the well-off than for the majority. Social tensions were steadily building during the July Monarchy and could not be held in check forever. Victor Hugo's great novel *Les Miserables* is the best mirror of this epoch.

In Great Britain, the other country favoring the liberal views, the major fact of political life during the 1820s to 1840s was the rising influence of the middle classes. In 1832, the most important reform of voting rights since the Glorious Revolution was finally passed over the protests of the Conservative Party (**Tories**) by their opponents in Parliament, the Liberals (**Whigs**). This great **Reform Bill of 1832** stripped away many of the traditional political advantages of the landholding upper class of wealthy aristocrats and strengthened the previously weak urban middle classes. Overnight, the House of Commons seats controlled by rotten boroughs (very few voters) and pocket boroughs (controlled by a single family) were eliminated, and the seats thus made free were distributed to urban and industrial districts. Since these latter were controlled by the Liberals, the composition of the Commons changed drastically. The Whigs would remain in charge for the next thirty-five years.

By making Parliament into a more representative national body and giving the vote to a large number of property holders who previously had been denied it, British government diminished the danger of revolution. The British middle classes were assured of a forum—Parliament—in which their voice would be heard and through which they could attain peaceable, orderly change. In the later nineteenth century, these concessions would be extended downward from the propertied classes to the unpropertied, working classes. Revolution and radical socialism never gained much following among the common people for those reasons.

The Reactionary States: Austria, Russia, and Prussia

In the reactionary conservative countries, the story was different. In Austria, Russia, and the Germanies, the rulers spent the generation after Napoleon attempting to hold back all thought of political liberalism. Through censorship, police and military force, diplomacy, and eventually war, they threw a dam across the tide of reform, which held more or less until 1848. The Austrian emperor, the Russian tsar, and the Prussian king rejected the kind of concessions the French and British governments had made to their citizens, with the result that revolt seemed to many thinking people the only hope of bringing these countries into modern political and economic life.

Austria had a special problem in that it was a *multinational society* in a time of increasing national conflict. It was for this reason that Prince Metternich was so determined to wall off Austrian politics from liberal ideas. He saw that whereas liberalism fostered nationalism, the conservative point of view generally disregarded national divisions as irrelevant and looked at people solely in terms of social class. Until 1848, in Austria, one's social background was far more important than one's ethnic group. The governing class was composed of a multiethnic aristocracy, where it mattered not at all whether a person was a Pole, a Hungarian, a Croat, or a German by blood. What counted was birth to one of the "right" families, that is, being an aristocrat.

⚜ REVOLTS

Cross-National Similarities

The revolt that broke out in the streets of working-class Paris in late February 1848 was destined to sweep through Europe from one end to the other during the next year. These revolts of the lower classes against their stepchild position in society, combined with an explosion of nationalist conflicts and assertions of popular sovereignty against kings and emperors, set all Europe aflame (see Map 38.2). Of the major countries, only Britain and Russia were

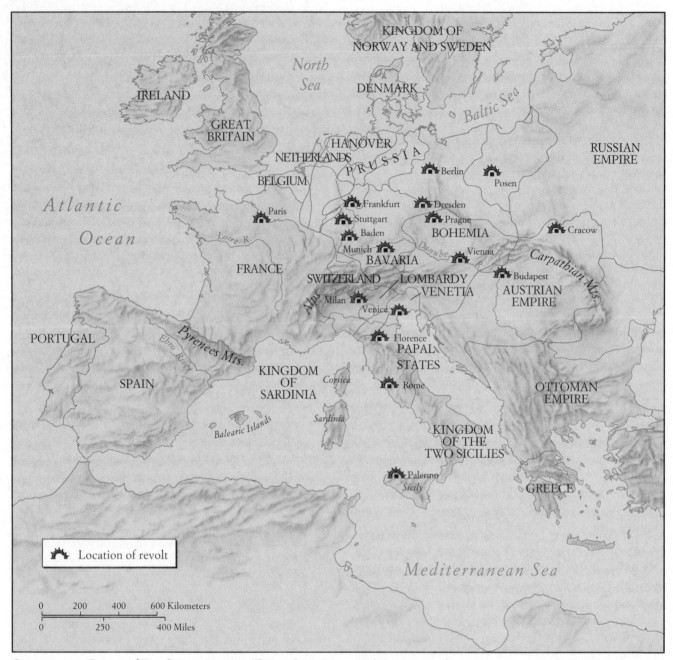

⦿ MAP 38.2 Centers of Revolt in 1848–1849. The revolts in France and German-speaking Europe were primarily political in nature: liberal versus conservative. In south and east Europe the revolts were above all national in nature: native versus alien overlord.

spared, the first because there was no intense dissatisfaction with the government, and the second because the government seemed too strong to be challenged.

The revolts did not have a single cause, and it is impossible to bring them down to a lowest common denominator. Nor did they have the same outcome; in

some cases, the revolutionaries were partly successful (Italian states, Scandinavia); in others (German states, Austria, France), they were defeated in the short term.

Nevertheless, at least *three underlying similarities* can be established. First, the revolts were led initially by middle-class liberals, not by the workers and/or the peasants. Second, the workers soon grew disappointed with the liberals' hesitancy and created their own more violent revolutions against both aristocrats and the middle classes. Third, national divisions contributed to the failure of the revolts throughout central Europe.

Two Phases

In the initial stages, the revolts appeared to be on the verge of achieving political success. In France, the exhausted July Monarchy fell within days, and France was turned into a republic for a few years (see the Document in this chapter). In the German states, several kings and princes were brushed aside by popular assemblies that claimed supreme powers and enacted liberal constitutions. In the Austrian Empire the Hungarians and the Italians declared themselves independent, while the German-Austrians attempted to set up a liberal and constitutional monarchy. In the "Springtime of Nations," as the Germans called 1848, it looked for a while as though the reactionaries had been routed.

But appearances were deceptive. Everywhere, the conservative or reactionary elements were more powerful than they first seemed when taken by surprise. The military generally remained loyal to the monarchies, and the churches rallied round the throne. The peasants remained on the sidelines everywhere, as they could see no common ground with the urban liberals or workers.

When the workers in Paris, Vienna, and Berlin went into the streets to demand decent working conditions and better pay and housing, the liberals got "cold feet." If they

■ **Austrian Revolutionaries.** The fever of revolution swept through Europe in 1848. Here, the artist shows University of Vienna students joining with the liberal bourgeoisie to work out a new constitution for the Habsburg realm.

had to choose between the continued rule of the aristocracy and Crown and radical social change in favor of the masses, the middle classes would take the first alternative every time. They figured, more or less correctly, that time was on their side in their efforts to obtain political power peaceably; if they allowed radical reform of social conditions, on the other hand, they had no way of knowing what would happen in the long run. The liberals, composed overwhelmingly of urban middle-class property holders, were more afraid of some form of socialism than they were of aristocratic privilege and royal absolutism.

■ **Liberty Leading the People.** This often reproduced painting by Eugene Delacroix shows the female symbol of Liberty leading the way in the revolution of 1848. Delacroix was probably the illegitimate son of Talleyrand and was the foremost Romantic painter of his day.

De Tocqueville on Antagonisms among Parisians in 1848

After the revolution of February 1848 had ousted the king and created the Second Republic, the provisional Assembly established National Workshops (*ateliers nationaux*) in Paris to provide work relief for the many unemployed, who were near starvation. In a matter of a few weeks, more persons were registered in the Paris workshops than either the available work or financial resources could accommodate. National elections in April returned an Assembly whose delegates were much more conservative, and steps were undertaken to dismantle the workshops. This led to a vicious confrontation, the "**June Days,**" in which the army, acting in the name of the Assembly, brutally crushed a rising of the Parisian workers. Alexis de Tocqueville (1805–1850), the liberal author and historian, served as a delegate to the Assembly and recorded his impressions of these tragic days:

> The revolution of July [1830, bringing in Louis Philippe] was effected by the people, but the middle classes had stirred it up and led it, and secured the principal fruits of it. The revolution of February, on the contrary, seemed to be made entirely outside the bourgeoisie and against it. . .
>
> From the 25th of February onward, a thousand strange systems came issuing pell-mell from the minds of innovators and spread among the troubled minds of the crowd. Everything still remained standing except Royalty and Parliament; yet it seemed as though the shock of Revolution had reduced society itself to dust. . . . Everyone came forward with a plan of his own. . . .

> These theories were of very varied natures, often opposed and sometimes hostile to one another; but all of them, aiming lower than the government and striving to reach society itself, on which government rests, adopted the common name of Socialism. Socialism will always remain the essential characteristic and the most redoubtable remembrance of the Revolution of February. . . .
>
> Personally, I had no doubt that we were on the eve of a terrible struggle; nevertheless, I did not fully understand all the dangers of that time until a conversation I had with [the novelist] Madame Sand. . . . Madame Sand gave me a detailed and very vivacious picture of the state of the Parisian workers: their organizations, numbers, armed preparations, thoughts, passions and terrible resolve. I thought the picture was exaggerated, but it was not so, as subsequent events clearly proved. . . . "Try and persuade your friends, sir," she said to me, "not to drive the people into the streets by rousing or offending them. . . for if it comes to a fight, believe me, you will all perish!"
>
> . . . [F]or four days more than a hundred thousand men took part in it [i.e., the June Days], and there were five generals killed. . . the insurgents were fighting without a battle cry, leaders, or a flag, and yet they showed wonderful powers of co-ordination, and a military expertise that astounded the most experienced officers.

Results by 1850

In instance after instance, during the years 1848 and 1849, this open or barely concealed split between the middle class and the lower class enabled the conservative forces to defeat the goals of both. The liberals in most places got only a very conditioned increase in political power and the vote; the workers got nothing but bayonets.

1. *France.* The Second Republic lasted but three years (1848–1851), before **Louis Napoleon (Napoleon III)**, nephew of the great Bonaparte, used the power of the republican presidency to which he had been elected in 1848 to declare himself emperor. So began the Second Empire in France, which was to last twenty years.

2. *Prussia.* After a year of wrangling about the exact form and provisions of a liberal constitution for a united Germany, the middle-class **Frankfurt Assembly** dissolved in complete failure. The assembly had offered the crown of all Germany to the conservative Prussian king, but he flatly refused to accept. Led by Prussia, the bulk of the German states reverted to the conservative regimes that had been briefly pushed aside by the revolts. German liberals had suffered a permanent defeat—one they would not recover from for the rest of the century.

... [I]ts [the insurrection's] object was not to change the form of government, but to alter the organization of society. . . .The women took as much part in it as the men. While the men fought, the women got the ammunition ready and brought it up. And when in the end they had to surrender, the women were the last to yield.

It is fair to say that these women carried the preoccupations of the housewife into battle; they counted on victory to bring easy circumstances for their husbands and help them to bring up their children. They loved this war as much as they might have enjoyed a lottery. . . .

When I was getting near [the Assembly chamber] and was already in the midst of the troops guarding it, an old woman with a vegetable barrow stubbornly barred my way. I ended by telling her to make room rather sharply. Instead of doing so, she left her barrow, and rushed at me with such sudden frenzy that I had trouble defending myself. I shuddered at the frightful and hideous expression in her face. . . . In all these little streets we saw smears of blood from the recent fighting, and fighting broke out again there from time to time. For this was a war of ambushes, with no fixed theatre of operations, and it was continually doubling back on its tracks. When you least expected it, you would be shot at from a garret window; and when you got into the house, you would find the gun, all right, but not the marksman; he would have slipped out the back door while you were breaking down the front. . . .

■ **A Parisian, 1848.** A Parisian working man strikes a self-conscious pose holding a banner proclaiming the Republic of France. The Second Republic lasted only four years before giving way to the Second Empire of Louis Napoleon.

SOURCE: Alexis de Tocqueville, *Recollections: The French Revolution of 1848.* Excerpted from Boyer and Goldstein, *Readings in Western Civilization,* vol. 8. University of Chicago Press, 1988.

3. *Austria.* The Austrian emperor, eighteen-year-old **Franz Joseph** (1848–1916), relied on his aristocratic advisers to gradually regain control of the revolutionary situation, which had forced Metternich out and briefly turned Austria into a constitutional and liberal regime. Playing off one nationality against the other, the Vienna government crushed the independence movements of the Czechs, Hungarians, and Italians within the empire and then intimidated the German liberals in Austria proper. By the summer of 1849, reaction was unchecked, and Austria was embarked on a decade of old-fashioned royal absolutism.

4. *Italy.* It is important to remember that as yet there was no unified Italy. It was simply a collection of small kingdoms and the Papal States of Rome. The north was controlled by Austria, the middle was divided between the kingdom of **Sardinia-Piedmont** and the papacy, and the south and Sicily were controlled by the kingdom of Naples. Liberal Italians had long wanted to unite Italy under a central, constitutional monarchy. They favored the Sardinian kingdom as the basis of this monarchy because it was the only state that had a native Italian, secular ruler. Many middle-class Italians, especially those in the northern cities, were anticlerical and antipapal. They viewed the popes as political reaction-

aries and upholders of class privilege. For several of the nineteenth-century popes, this was a fair judgment.

In 1848, anti-Austrian and antipapal riots broke out in various parts of Italy. Sardinia declared war on Austria, believing that Vienna was too occupied with other crises to defend its Italian possessions. This proved to be a mistake; the Austrians were decisive victors, and all thought of removing northern Italy from Austrian control had to be abandoned for a time. Pope **Pius IX** (r. 1846–1875) was so frightened by the Roman mobs that he opposed any type of liberalism from then on. In 1849, it appeared that a united Italy was as far away as it had ever been.

Thus, by 1850 the revolts and attempted revolutions had accomplished very little. Both middle-class liberals and working-class radicals had been defeated by military force or its threat. Yet, within a generation's time, almost all that the middle classes had fought for and even some of the demands of the radicals had come into being in many European capitals. Reaction proved unable to meet the needs of the day, and the necessity to introduce a more or less industrialized economy overrode the objections of the Old Guard. Many of the thousands imprisoned for treason or violating public order from 1849 to 1850 would live to see the day when their governments freely gave the rights they had fought for and been punished for seeking.

Summary

In the era after the Napoleonic wars, Europe divided into liberal and reactionary segments, both of which were attempting to meet the new challenges thrown up by the Americans' successful revolt against their colonial overlord and the French Revolution. Moderate conservatives tried to adapt government to changing conditions, while reactionaries stood firm against the times.

The dual revolutions in politics and economics had gotten underway in the later eighteenth century, but matured in the nineteenth. In politics, the conservatives reluctantly discovered that the French upheaval and its spread by Napoleon's armies had changed traditional relationships so that they could not be successfully reconstructed. Despite the defeat of the French radicals by their own countrymen and the defeat of Napoleon by the rest of Europe, some of the seeds planted by each would

sprout in a generation's time.

The liberal spirit that was forcing its way into prominence by mid-century took a less idealistic form in economics than in politics. The ideas of Adam Smith and others were selectively adopted by the Manchester liberals of the early industrial age and used to justify harsh exploitation of the workers. They were answered by experiments with social reform that attracted little attention because of their utopian nature and quick failure.

The Europe-wide revolts of 1848 mostly failed in the short run, but the forces in society that had touched them off proved too strong to resist in the long run. One reason for the initial failure was the rising sense of nationalism in multiethnic states; another was the divergence between the mainly political goals of the liberal middle classes and the mainly social goals of the workers.

Test Your Knowledge

1. Charles Fourier propagandized for a society structured
   a. in large states with dictatorial leadership of the working classes.
   b. in a military fashion.
   c. in small communities of self-directing workers.
   d. in communities of fellow believers housed in monasteries.
2. Which country was least affected by the revolts of 1848?

   a. France
   b. Great Britain
   c. Italy
   d. Austria
3. Which of following would a moderate conservative be most likely to support?
   a. An officially established church with preeminent rights in education

b. An absolutist monarch ruling with no constitutional restraints

c. A proposal to sever any connections between church and schools

d. A proposal to give poor and rich alike an equal vote

4. Which of the following did *not* have its modern birth in the 1789–1814 era?

   a. Socialism

   b. Nationalism

   c. Egalitarian democracy

   d. Meritocracy

5. The most uncompromisingly radical of Europe's early socialists was

   a. Henri Saint-Simon.

   b. Pierre Proudhon.

   c. Robert Owen.

   d. Charles Fourier.

6. The revolts of 1848 began

   a. in Belgium with an outbreak against Dutch rule.

   b. in Paris with demonstrations against the July Monarchy.

   c. in London with hunger marches in the slums.

   d. in St. Petersburg with protests against the Crimean War.

7. The most important parliamentary political act in nineteenth-century British history was the

   a. passage of the United Kingdom Act.

   b. passage of the Reform Bill of 1832.

   c. decision to exile Napoleon to St. Helena.

   d. passage of the Factory Act of 1819.

8. De Tocqueville believed that the revolt in 1848 was

   a. the product of liberal ideas that poisoned immature minds.

   b. the product of working people who had been provoked beyond limit.

   c. an upper-class plot against the king.

   d. an entirely misguided conspiracy against the throne.

Identification Terms

Frankfurt Assembly (1848)

Franz Joseph of Austria

July Monarchy

June Days (Paris 1848)

Louis Napoleon (Napoleon III)

phalanstery

Pius IX (pope)

Reform Bill of 1832

Sardinia-Piedmont (kingdom of)

Whigs and Tories

Bibliography

Briggs, A. *The Making of Modern England, 1784–1867,* 1967. An excellent study of why Britain was spared upheavals as violent as those on the Continent in the nineteenth century.

Bullen, R., and F. R. Bridge. *The Great Powers and the European State System, 1815–1914,* 1980. An excellent overview of international affairs in Europe after Vienna.

Deak, I. *The Lawful Revolution: Louis Kossuth and the Hungarians, 1848–49,* 1979. An enlightening treatment of the ethnic and national conflicts in the Austrian Empire.

Droz, J. *Europe between Revolutions, 1815–1850,* 1967. A survey, as is A. Sked, ed., *Europe's Balance of Power 1815–1848,* 1979.

Heilbroner, R. *The Worldly Philosophers,* 1967. Has already been mentioned as a good introduction to the economic liberals.

Kissinger, H. *A World Restored,* 1957. A good defense of Metternich and his policies, written by President Nixon's secretary of state. Compare A. J. May, *The Age of Metternich, 1814–48,* 1963, which is not so sympathetic.

Namier, L. *1848: Revolution of the Intellectuals,* 1964. Highly critical of the failure of the liberal leaders in the German-speaking lands.

Stearns, P. *Eighteen Forty-eight,* 1974. Especially good on the social background of the rebellions throughout Europe. This theme is also well treated in P. Robertson, *Revolutions of 1848: A Social History,* 1960.

Wright, G. *France in Modern Times,* 1960. A well-written and consistently interesting study.

CONSOLIDATION OF NATIONAL STATES

After the defeats of 1848, liberals and nationalists were in retreat during the next decade, and conservative statesmen were everywhere in control. But only twenty to thirty years later, many of the goals of the liberals had been reached, and nationalism was already one of the givens of policy making. These years in the late nineteenth century also saw the dawn of the epoch of mass society. The beginnings of modern political democracy were visible in several countries, notably Britain and the post–Civil War United States. In Russia the serfs were freed, and the universal franchise was introduced in several countries. Labor unions were legalized in many places. The Western world was entering the next phase of the dual revolution, that is, the Second Industrial Revolution and the massive social changes that accompanied it.

❖ RUSSIA

Defeat in the Crimea

The first severe failure of the system of international cooperation set up by the Vienna treaties was the *Crimean War (1853–1856)* between Russia on the one side and England, France, and Turkey, on the other. An awkward war that no one wanted, it represented an accidental breakdown of the system. Russian ambitions led Tsar Nicholas I (1825–1855) to demand Turkish concessions in southeastern Europe. Once assured of British and French help, the Turks resisted, for by now they were far too weak to handle the Russians alone. The British and French sent small armies to help the Turks, and the conflict was mostly fought on the Crimean peninsula in the Black Sea.

Militarily, the war was a general debacle for all concerned. The Russian commanders and logistics were even less competent than the allies, so in time Russia had to sue for peace. The *Peace of Paris of 1856* was a drastic diplomatic defeat for St. Petersburg, and for the next twenty years, Russia was essentially bottled up in the south, unable to gain the much desired naval access to the Mediterranean. The Russian Colossus, which had intimidated Europe for a generation, was seen to have feet of clay. No longer could it be expected to play the role of reactionary watchman against revolutionary or even liberal sentiments. Now Russia's attention was occupied by its own internal problems.

The Great Reforms

The military embarrassment in the Crimea hardened the determination of the new ruler, **Tsar Alexander II** (1855–1881), to solve Russia's number one social and economic problem: the question of the serfs. For the previous half century, educated Russians had been debating what could and should be done to bring the almost 50 percent of the population who lived in bondage into freedom and productivity. Various tsars since Catherine the Great had proposed various steps to better the serfs' condition; in the end, little had been done, and the serfs still lived in almost total illiteracy, ignorance, and superstition. Not only were they growing increasingly resentful of their noble landlords and masters, but they were an immense drag on the Russian economy. Living in stagnant poverty as they had for centuries, they had no money to consume anything except what they made or grew themselves; nor could they contribute to the nation's capital for investments.

In 1859, Alexander grew impatient and commanded a quick resolution of the serf problem, based on these principles:

- Freeing the serfs from the judicial and administrative control of their lords and making them legally equal to other citizens with full personal liberty.
- Giving the serfs a substantial part of the estate land that they had previously worked for their master; the landlord would be compensated by government bonds, which would be redeemable by annual payments of the peasants.
- Anchoring the ex-serfs to the land by making them collectively responsible for paying the tax debts of the village and supplying a quota of conscripts for the army.

Over the next two years, a special Court Commission worked out the details, and on February 19, 1861, the most massive emancipation order ever issued by any government *abolished serfdom in Russia.* About 55 million individuals—serfs and their dependents—were directly affected.

Emancipation was only a very limited success. Many serfs were disappointed with their allotted portions of land, which were either small or of poor quality. And instead of outright possession of the land, they received only a tentative title subject to several restrictions imposed by the government. The serfs could not mortgage the land or sell it without permission from the village council *(mir),* which was difficult to obtain. So, instead of creating a class of free, prosperous farmers as the authorities in St. Petersburg had hoped, the emancipation of the serfs

■ **The Crimean War.** The war in the Crimea was the first to be photographed. Here, the English journalist Roger Fenton shows us an officer and men of the Fourth Dragoons in their encampment in 1855. At their side is one of the first military nurses, a colleague of Florence Nightingale.

actually made a good many worse off than before—much like the condition of many of the freed slaves in the U.S. South after the Civil War.

Besides emancipation, Alexander II presided over several other major reforms of Russian public life. These **Great Reforms,** as they are called, included the following:

- *Local government.* The central government reorganized local and provincial authority. It allowed the election of a sort of county commission, called the *zemstvo* board. Originally, the zemstvo boards had few real powers, but they acted as a catalyst of civic spirit and helped the local peasants become aware of what they could do to better their lives. From the zemstvo boards came many of the middle-class reformers and liberals who attempted to avert revolution before World War I by persuading the imperial government to make timely concessions to democracy.
- *Judicial system.* The Russian court system was so antiquated and corrupt (bribing the judge was normal) that it barely functioned. In 1864, Tsar Alexander decreed a complete overhaul, and very soon the courts were on the level of the West European countries. The class of lawyers and judges who emerged played a leading role in politics from then on.
- *Army reform.* In 1873, the conscription, training, length of service, and many other aspects of the Russian army were completely revamped. The army became less a penal institution and more an educational and engineering facility, used by the government to do something about the very low level of rural education. The

maximum service time was set at two years for most youth and less for the educated.

Over the long term, however, what Alexander did not do was more important than what he did. Like several of his predecessors, he did not think the time ripe for Russia to have a constitution, an elected national legislature, or strong local government bodies. Russia remained what it had always been, an *autocracy,* in which the tsar alone decided law and policy and the people were viewed as simply passive recipients of the government's demands. This failure to change the basic governmental institutions was to be a crucial mistake. The continuing autocratic nature of Russian government blocked the way to peaceable political evolution and forced serious reformers to became revolutionaries.

Ironically, it was during the reign of the reforming Alexander II that the *Russian revolutionary movement* became a serious threat. In the 1870s, both socialism and anarchism found their first adherents in the urban *intelligentsia,* the intellectuals and activists drawn mostly from the thin ranks of the professional class. Every variety of revolutionary doctrine was to be found in the Russian underground by the 1890s, ranging from orthodox Marxism through peasant communes to nihilistic terrorism. As late as 1905, however, the absolutist government of the tsar still seemed to be in control over the illiterate peasants and a very small and divided group of socialist workers in the towns. We will look at this situation more closely later, when we examine the Russian Revolution of 1917.

✤ FRANCE: THE EMPIRE OF NAPOLEON "THE LITTLE," 1851–1871

The nephew of the great Napoleon was the winner of the presidential election in France that was held in the wake of the 1848 revolt, which threw out King Louis Philippe and created the Second Republic. Riding on the coattails of his uncle and claiming to be a sincere republican, Louis Napoleon, or Napoleon "the Little" as he was at once nicknamed by his enemies, was the first modern ruler who understood how to manipulate the democratic franchise to create a dictatorship. What he did in France during the 1850s showed the power of modern propaganda when controlled by an individual who knew how and when to appeal to his people.

Within a few months of his election, Napoleon sensed that there would be no effective opposition if he imitated his uncle and made himself Emperor of the French, as **Napoleon III.** This *Second Empire* lasted twenty years, which divide into two distinct segments: until the 1860s, it was an authoritarian regime led by one man's vision; after that, Napoleon gradually liberalized his rule and allowed political opposition. The main reason for the change was his increasingly unpopular foreign policy: a failed colonial adventure in Mexico in 1863–1864, his failure to stop an aggressive Prussia, and his inability to protect the pope from the Italian secularists and nationalists made trouble for Napoleon at home. He had to encourage a tame legislature to share leadership responsibilities by allowing competitive elections.

Internally, Napoleon was more successful in changing the primarily agrarian France of 1851 into a mixed economy with the firm beginnings of industrial development in place by 1870. Paris was the only large industrial city and was regarded as a foreign place by much of the French public, in much the same way as midwesterners in the United States looked upon New York City. But by 1870 capitalist industry was also taking root in many smaller cities, such as Lyon, Marseilles, Nancy, Brest, and Rouen. Britain and Germany were still far ahead of France in industrial development, but at least the French were beginning to make up the difference.

■ **Escape by Balloon, Paris 1870.** In this dramatic photo, the head of the French government, Leon Gambetta, eludes the Prussian blockade of Paris by balloon. Despite Gambetta's efforts to continue resistance, the war was lost through the early mistakes of emperor Louis Napoleon.

KINGDOM OF
PIEDMONT

Kingdom of Piedmont, before 1859

To Kingdom of Piedmont, 1859

To Kingdom of Piedmont, 1860

To Kingdom of Italy, 1866; 1870

● **MAP 39.1 The Unification of Italy.** The diplomatic manuevers and military triumphs of the 1860s were not matched by political integration of two quite different Italies joined in the new Kingdom.

Napoleon and the Second Empire came to a disgraceful finish in the *Franco-Prussian War of 1870* (see below), which was the emperor's last policy miscalculation. Foolishly taking the field, he was captured by the enemy, forced to abdicate, and died in quiet exile in England.

Four years of political struggle followed the defeat as monarchists vied with republicans, conservatives with liberals, and Paris with the rest of France. At the end of the war, the first attempt at socialist revolution had taken place in Paris until it was crushed with great bloodshed by the army. This **Paris Commune of 1871** was very frightening to the majority of the French. From this time onward, the split between the conservative villages of the French provinces and the radical workers and intellectuals of Paris that had originated in the Revolution of 1789 was wide open. It would remain that way for much of the following century.

The internal struggles were ended by the inability of the monarchists (who certainly represented the majority of

the French) to agree on a single candidate. This quarrel enabled those who favored a republic to gradually establish themselves in power. By 1875, the **Third Republic** was more or less in place: it was a liberal state with a strong legislature (the Assembly) and a very weak presidential executive. A confused mass of political parties ranged across the whole spectrum from extreme reactionaries to Marxists and anarchists. About the only thing that most French agreed on during the later nineteenth century was the necessity of someday gaining revenge on Bismarck's Germany and reclaiming the "Lost Provinces" of Alsace and Lorraine.

⚜ THE UNIFICATION OF ITALY, 1859–1870

One of the major changes in the political map of nineteenth-century Europe was the completion of the unification of Italy (see Map 39.1). This had been the goal of two generations of Italian statesmen and revolutionaries, going back to the Napoleonic wars. In the 1860s, unification was thrust through over the opposition of both Austria, which controlled much of northern Italy, and Pope Pius IX, who despised and dreaded a secular, liberal Italy. Austria's opposition could only be ended through warfare; the pope's opposition was never actually ended, but it was made harmless.

The father of Italian unification was the liberal-minded aristocrat Count Camillo Cavour (1810–1861), who became the prime minister of the kingdom of Sardinia in 1852. Based on the industrial city of Turin in northwestern Italy, Sardinia had long been the best hope of those who wanted a united, liberal Italy. It was better known as **Piedmont,** because the center of political gravity in the kingdom had long since moved from backward Sardinia to progressive and modern Turin at "the foot of the mountains." Cavour was a strong supporter of economic progress, and during the 1850s, he built Piedmont into the leading economic force in all of Italy, as well as the major political power. Cavour was a moderate, a believer in constitutional monarchy, and he firmly rejected radical social change. In his king, Victor Emmanuel II, he found an ideal partner, for the king was both supportive and pliable.

Cavour fully realized that Austria would never willingly let go of its Italian provinces and that Piedmont alone was too weak to force it to (as had been demonstrated in 1848). Therefore, a foreign ally was needed, and that ally could only be France. Carefully, he drew the French ruler Napoleon III into a so-called defensive alliance and then provoked a war in 1859. Faced with the French-Piedmont alliance, the Austrians were outmatched and forfeited the large Lombard province to Cavour.

As Cavour had reckoned, after the defeat of Austria, much of the rest of Italy threw in its lot with Piedmont. The newly christened *Kingdom of Italy,* based in Turin, now embraced about half of the peninsula. The rest was divided among the pope, the reactionary Bourbon king of Naples and Sicily, who wished to remain independent, and Austria.

The romantic and popular revolutionary *Giuseppe Garibaldi* now entered the scene and led a volunteer army ("The Thousand Red Shirts") through southern Italy, routing the royal government of Naples and joining Sicily and southern Italy to the Italian kingdom in 1861 (see the Biography in this chapter). A few months later Cavour died, with the job of unification-by-conquest almost done. But severe tensions were building among the Italians themselves.

Two pieces of the picture still remained to be fitted in: the Austrian province of Venetia and the Papal States centered on Rome. Venetia was gained in 1866, as a prize for joining with Prussia in another brief war against Austria. The Papal States, however, were guarded by France, where the Catholic population was insisting that Napoleon III preserve papal liberties. When the Franco-Prussian War broke out in 1870, the French garrison was withdrawn, and the Piedmontese quickly annexed the Papal States, making Rome the capital of the Italian kingdom. The pope was reduced to the status of quasi-prisoner within the Vatican City, a tiny enclave in the center of Rome. The relationship between the kingdom of Italy and the papacy remained frigid until the twentieth century. Not until the dictator Benito Mussolini were formal relations finally established (1929). Papal resentment and condemnation contributed much to the difficulties of the Italian state and discredited it to some extent in the eyes of devout Catholics in Italy and elsewhere.

The new Italy was a very mixed success story. Lacking all important industrial material resources except manpower, Italy was the weakest of the great powers. This country was in most ways really two, quite distinct countries: the industrializing, urban, liberal North and the agrarian, rural, feudal South:

- The *South* (from Rome down) and Sicily were controlled by reactionary aristocrats, mainly absentee landowners whose impoverished peasants still lived in serfdom in everything but name. The church was all powerful and was itself an ally of the aristocracy. The population outside the towns was almost entirely illiterate, superstitious, and quite unaware of anything outside their native region. The South had no modern industry or transport, and no prospects of any.
- The *North* (from Florence up) was controlled by educated wealthy landowners and a large commercial middle class, who lived and worked in good-sized cities like Turin, Milan, and Venice. These towns, which had ties to transalpine Europe, were rapidly industrializing, producing a proletariat who would soon be one of Europe's most fertile fields for socialist ideas. The average income in Milan was three or four times what it was in Palermo, Catania, or Naples. The northerners viewed the Sicilians and the South in general with contempt and despair and refused to regard them as equal fellow citizens of the new state.
- From the start, national politics and national economic policies were controlled by the Piedmontese and other northerners. The South was ignored or given a few

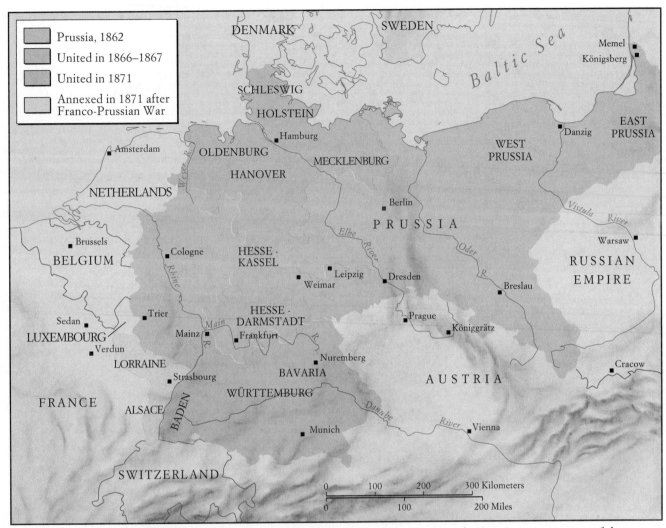

● **MAP 39.2 Unification of the German Empire.** After the battle of Koeniggraetz in 1866 the Austrians were put out of the running for primacy among German-speakers. The surrender of French emperor Napoleon III at the head of his army at Sedan completed the task Bismarck had set himself.

crumbs in the budget to ensure that the party in office could control southern votes. The "national culture," as well as government money, was tilted heavily in favor of the North and would remain that way into the mid-twentieth century. Almost all of the millions of Italian emigrants came from the overpopulated, backward South.

⚜ THE UNIFICATION OF THE GERMANS, 1862–1871

During the same years that the Italians were uniting into one state came the unification of Germany (see Map 39.2). As the new Italy was an extension of the kingdom of Sardinia, so the new Germany was an extension of the kingdom of Prussia. Like Italy, Germany was the product of both diplomacy and war. But here the similarities mostly ended.

The creation of the German Empire, as it was called, was the *most important single development in the later nineteenth century in Europe.* Far more than Italy, Germany was an economic and military powerhouse and the most important military force in the world by the 1880s. Germany would surpass Britain as the foremost industrial power as early as 1890 and would be rivaled only by the United States in the early twentieth century.

Giuseppe Garibaldi
1807–1882

The first half of the nineteenth century saw a protracted campaign for the unification of Italy that ended in seemingly permanent failure in 1849. After the bloodshed of that eventful year throughout Europe, the men and women who dreamed of a single Italian nation were as far from success as ever. One of them was Giuseppe Garibaldi (1807–1882).

Born in Nice on the Mediterranean coast, Garibaldi was a subject of the kingdom of Sardinia, one of the several midget states into which the Italian peninsula was then divided. A dedicated republican, the young man joined an attempt to overthrow the Sardinian king and had to flee for his life to South America in 1835. In Brazil and later, Uruguay, he fought a guerrilla campaign for independence and republican government. Garibaldi was an enthusiastic supporter of Giuseppe Mazzini, the greatest of the nineteenth-century romantic revolutionaries, who saw the brotherhood of man arising from the smoking ruins of monarchy.

In 1848, Garibaldi hastened back to his native land to join the fight against Austria. When this ended in defeat, he briefly sought to establish a Roman Republic on the Mazzini model. Chased from the country by the victorious forces of reaction, Garibaldi lived for a short while in the United States and then decided to return to assist the Sardinian royal government. Garibaldi's change of heart came from his realization that brave words alone would not defeat the enemy's cannon, one had to have more cannons of one's own. In that spirit, Garibaldi reluctantly put aside his republican convictions and became an ally of Count Cavour's diplomacy aimed at making the king of Sardinia, Victor Emmanuel II, the eventual king of united Italy.

In 1859, Garibaldi joined with Cavour in Sardinia (or Piedmont, as the kingdom was increasingly known) against the Austrians. Then he embarked on the crowning adventure of an adventurous life: the conquest of Sicily and southern Italy for the forces of unity. At this time, Sicily and the southern third of the peninsula were governed very poorly by one of the most unpopular monarchs of Europe, Francis II of the house of Bourbon. With his famous One Thousand volunteers (who had been outfitted and trained in the north), Garibaldi succeeded in routing the royalists first in Sicily (at the battle of Calatafimi in June 1860) and then on the mainland (at the Volturno River). These victories against a numerically superior

---

The fashion by which Germany was united would have a dominant influence on the later history of the country. The unification was the conservative, even reactionary realization of the vision of two men: the Prussian king William I (r. 1861–1888) and, more importantly, his chancellor and trusted friend *Otto von Bismarck* (1815–1898). Bismarck was the outstanding European statesman of the entire nineteenth century, and his shadow hung over the German nation until 1945. For good or evil, modern Germany was largely the product of Bismarck's hand and vision.

A Junker aristocrat, Bismarck deeply distrusted liberalism, while remaining a nationalist to the core. Like almost all nineteenth-century patriots, he wished to see the German people united rather than remain fragmented among the sixteen kingdoms and city-states left by the 1815 Treaty of Vienna. Above all, he wanted to complete what many years of Prussian policies had attempted with only partial success: to unify all Germans under the political leadership of Berlin. A chief reason for the failure thus far was the determined opposition of the other major Germanic state: Austria. Austria insisted on a seat in any pan-German political arrangement, and its size and prestige in the early nineteenth century assured it a leading seat if such an arrangement ever came about.

The Prussians resisted Austria's pretensions, because they considered the Austrian Empire not really a German territory at all. Within Austria's borders were more non-Germans than Germans, as we have seen. In 1848, this tension between **kleindeutsch** ("little German," or Ger-

enemy were greatly aided by the support of the oppressed populace for the rebels. Francis II surrendered his capital at Naples and was forced into exile shortly thereafter. All of Italy except the Papal States around Rome and the city itself were now under the control of either Piedmont or Garibaldi.

Now the victorious leader of the "Red Shirts" resisted what must have been a strong temptation to renege on his promise to support the Sardinians and resume his attempt to make the new Italy a republic. Instead, he kept his promise and accepted the monarchy, even when it failed to oust the pope and his French protectors from Rome throughout the decade of the 1860s. Finally, the Franco-Prussian War of 1870 allowed Victor Emmanuel to move his forces into Rome and make it the capital of the united Italy.

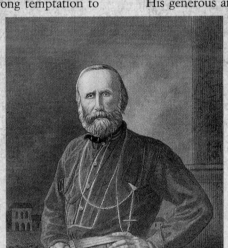

Garibaldi became a delegate to the new Italian parliament, but his true place in history was accorded to him by the Italian people, who regarded him as the chief hero of their long campaign to throw out foreign rulers and native oppressors. By the time of his death, he had become almost an object of worship among the common people of his country.

His generous and fearless nature won the admiration of even his enemies, and his contribution to the Italian *Risorgimento* was just as important as the cunning diplomacy of Cavour. Garibaldi himself attributed much of his passionate determination to the influence of his wife, Anita Ribiero da Silva, whom he met and married while fighting for Uruguayan independence, and who stayed at his side throughout his campaign in Italy until her death in 1849.

mans only) and ***grossdeutsch*** ("big German," or Germans predominantly) did much to wreck the hopes of the constitutionalists and allow the reestablishment of absolutist monarchy in most of the Germanic lands.

Bismarck was a decided *kleindeutsch* adherent, and his policy was to remove the Austrians from German affairs as soon as possible. To this end, he cleverly manipulated the Vienna government into a situation where, no matter what Austria did, it came out looking opposed to German unity. This was notably the case in an otherwise insignificant war against Denmark in 1863–1864. Bismarck then provoked Austria into declaring war on Prussia, so that Austria appeared to be the aggressor in the eyes of the other Germans, who tried to remain neutral. The *Austro-Prussian War of 1866* was over in one bloody battle, won

unexpectedly by the Prussians using their new railway system and repeating rifles. Bismarck was remarkably generous: instead of seeking territory or money damages, he insisted only that Austria withdraw from German political affairs, leaving the field to Prussia.

The capstone of Bismarck's policy for unity was to provoke a third war against the traditional enemy west of the Rhine. The *Franco-Prussian War of 1870–1871* was the result of clever deception by the Prussian chancellor to maneuver the French (under Napoleon III) into becoming the formal aggressor. As Bismarck had reckoned, the other German states could no longer remain neutral in this situation; fevered nationalist opinion forced the governments to join the Prussians, as fellow Germans, against the ancient enemy.

■ **Bismarck and the Young Kaiser, 1988.** The tension between the ambitious young William II and his revered chancellor Bismarck comes through even in this formal photo. William found it impossible to continue his predecessors' warm relations with the old man who had piloted Germany since 1862.

When Prussia (again to the surprise of most experts) quickly pierced the French defenses and besieged Paris, the captured and disgraced Napoleon had to abdicate, and France sued for peace. Bismarck now put forward the Prussian king as emperor of Germany as a wave of national pride swept up almost all German speakers (see the Document in this chapter). The Germans, after all, were the most numerous nation in Europe and had been artificially divided for many centuries. Only the Austro-Germans and the neutral Swiss stayed outside the new empire, which counted 70 million inhabitants and extended from Alsace (annexed from France) almost to Warsaw and from the North Sea to the Alps.

The German Empire was a decidedly conservative state; Bismarck drew up a constitution that replicated that of Prussia. In fact, the empire was just Prussia on a bigger scale. In the *Reichstag,* the national legislature, it was the Prussian delegation that counted, and votes in Prussia were based on property: one-third of the legislators were elected by the top 5 percent of property holders. Ministers were responsible not to the Reichstag, but to the king. Behind everything was the looming, stern figure of Bismarck, by now a national monument. His power would be almost unchallenged for the next nineteen years.

✣ THE MULTINATIONAL EMPIRE OF AUSTRIA-HUNGARY

In the center of the European map stood the huge, backward Austrian Empire. The fourth largest state in population, and third largest in territory, Austria under the guidance of its long-time foreign minister Metternich had played a major role in international affairs for a full generation after 1815. After the national-liberal revolts of 1848 had been crushed, a decade of absolutist rule had ensued under the young *Kaiser* Franz Joseph. Internally,

■ **The Krupp Works, 1912.** One reason for the dramatic rise of Germany's economic and military power after unification was the massive investment in metallurgical engineering. The enormous naval artillery guns equipping the new German fleet are shown here as they come off the assembly line at the Krupp factory in Essen.

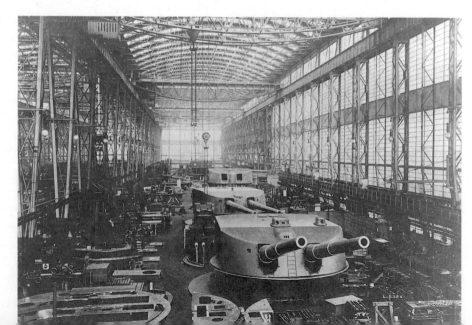

von Treitschke: Speech to Commemorate War of 1870

Heinrich von Treitschke (1834–1896) was the foremost German historian of his day, and also the most glaring example of the excesses of nationalist feeling. As professor of modern history at the University of Berlin (1874–1896), he influenced an entire generation of German leaders. His dislike of modern industrial society encouraged him to hark back to an imaginary Age of Heroes, which found its current reflection in the Prussian soldier and the Iron Chancellor, Bismarck, whom Treitschke idolized. In this speech given to commemorate the twenty-fifth anniversary of the Prussian victory over France in 1870, von Treitschke elaborates on what he believes true Germanness is and how it can be demonstrated:

Dear Colleagues and Fellow Students:

Today's festival recalls to us of the older generation the golden days of our life—the days when the grace of God after battle and tribulation and mourning gloriously fulfilled beyond all expectations the longings of our youth.... Let us turn today from everything that is trivial and regard only the moral forces which operated in the most fortunate of all wars.... "What we needed was a complete, incontestable victory, won solely by German strength, which would compel our neighbors at least to recognize, respectfully, that we as a nation had attained our majority...." France, which had so often fomented and misused our domestic quarrels, all at once found herself opposed by the vital union of the Germans; for a righteous war releases all the natural forces of character, and side by side with hatred, the power of affection. Inviolable confidence bound the soldiers to their officers, and all to those in supreme command.

Those who remained at home also became more generous, broader-minded and affectionate; the seriousness of the crisis lifted them above the selfishness of everyday life. Party strife disappeared, unpatriotic fools were quickly reduced to silence, and the longer the struggle lasted, the more firmly did the whole nation unite in the resolve that this war should restore to us the German Empire and our old lost western provinces.... When the reports of deaths arrived from the West, the fathers and brothers of those who had fallen said "Much mourning, much honor," and even the mothers, wives and sisters had in their heavy sorrow the consolation that their little house owned a leaf in the growing garland of German glory....

At last came the time of harvest. Paris surrendered.... Four great armies were taken prisoners or disarmed, and all the German race had an equal and glorious share in the enormous success. In these last weeks of the war there stepped into the foreground of German history the strong man of whom the troops had so often spoken [Bismarck]. In all historical times the masses of people have always rated character and energy above intellect and culture; the greatest and most boundless popularity was always only bestowed on the heroes of religion and of the sword....

In my youth it was often said, "If the Germans would be German, they will found the kingdom on earth which will bring peace to the world." We are not so inoffensive any longer. For a long time past we have known that the sword must maintain what the sword has won, and to the end of history the virile saying will hold good: *"Bia Bia Bialetai,* Force is overcome by force." [Germany] has offered peace to the Continent not by means of the panacea of the pacifists—disarming—but by the exact opposite—universal arming. Germany's example compelled armies to become nations, nations to become armies, and consequently war to be a dangerous experiment; and since no Frenchman has yet asserted France can recover her old booty by force of arms,* we may hope for some more years of peace.

*von Treitschke meant that France alone could not recover the Lost Provinces along the Rhine; but at the time he spoke, the French had already taken steps to secure allies. See Chapter 47.

SOURCE: Treitschke, *Speech to Commemorate the Great War,* excerpted from Boyer and Goldstein, *Readings in Western Civilization,* vol. 8, p. 461. University of Chicago Press, 1988.

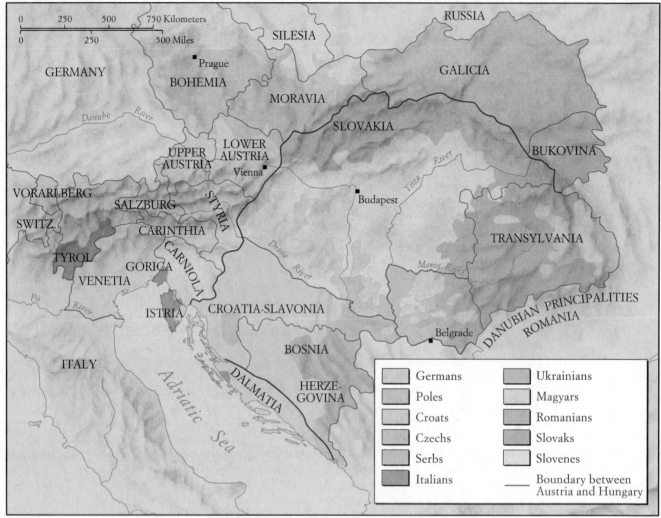

● **MAP 39.3 Ethnic Groups in the Dual Monarchy.** The Austro-Germans and the Hungarian Magyars shared leadership of the empire of Austria-Hungary, but both were in a minority in their respective halves. The *Ausgleich* (Compromise) of 1867 was designed to keep the empire together while assuring their continued political domination.

there had been considerable progress, both economic and cultural, but these successes were nullified by setbacks in foreign policy and by the refusal of the defeated Hungarians to participate in central government. Since the Hungarians were the second largest group in the empire and had a long tradition of self-government, their boycott crippled internal politics.

After the defeats in Italy in 1859 and by Prussia in 1866, the kaiser had to come to terms with the Hungarians. He did so in the **Ausgleich of 1867,** a compromise arrangement that divided Austria into roughly equal halves, Austria and Hungary. Each was independent of the

other in everything except foreign policy, defense, and some financial matters. Each had its own constitution on generally liberal principles. The *Dual Monarchy,* as it came to be called, was a unique arrangement held together by the person of the ruler (emperor in Austria, king in Hungary), the army, the Catholic church, and a supranational bureaucracy and nobility.

The minority peoples composing the empire—Czechs, Slovaks, Croats, Serbs, Italians, and others—were less satisfied (see Map 39.3). Those living in Hungary were now under the domination of the highly nationalistic Hungarians (Magyars), which they strongly resented.

Those in Austria were under the Austro-Germans; for a time, the internal affairs of this half of the Dual Monarchy were more harmonious. But by the 1890s, the national question was heating up here as well, and the fairly liberal, constitutional government was paralyzed by the obstructionist minorities in Parliament. To get anything done, the emperor had to rule by decree. Even the introduction of universal male suffrage in 1907 did not break the deadlock. Austria-Hungary was the prime European example of the negative aspects of nationalism in politics.

✤ THE UNITED STATES ENTERS THE INDUSTRIAL AGE

At its independence from Britain, the United States was still an agrarian society, with its four million inhabitants concentrated along the eastern coast. Skilled tradesmen and master craftsmen were in short supply; 85 percent of the labor force were farmers and their auxiliary helpers and servants. Even in the urbanized areas of New England and the Middle Atlantic region, as late as 1800 there was practically no large-scale commercial production.

Industrial Progress

By the Civil War, this situation had changed markedly. Thanks to steady waves of immigrants from Europe and slaves from Africa, the United States had more inhabitants than Great Britain—about 30 million. A half dozen cities had populations of more than 100,000, and farm labor now made up less than half of the total. The dependence on British engineering and machinery that had characterized the first generation after independence (and made the United States the best customer outside Europe for British exporters) was now entirely gone. American manufacturers and industrial techniques were rapidly proving they could compete throughout the world.

New England was the original center of American industry. Factories making consumer goods such as textiles and shoes, harness and wagons, and metal tools and kitchenware located there to take advantage of both the abundant waterpower provided by the many rivers and the large pool of labor in the overcrowded and poverty-stricken rural areas. New England's expanding population had long since exceeded the supply of reasonably arable farmland. The new immigrants who came by the tens of thousands in the 1830s and 1840s often found they had only two choices: to take the plunge and try the unsettled frontier life in the west or to go to work in a mill or factory. Most chose the latter, believing its rewards were safer and more predictable.

Mill towns like Lowell, Massachusetts, and Bridgeport, Connecticut, became common. They were similar in many ways to those in England but less dreary and unsanitary because of cheaper land and a different building style. Compared to the early industrial towns in Europe where workers for the most part faced exploitation and limited horizons, American towns offered a degree of *social mobility*. Although the myths of Horatio Alger ascents from rags to riches were indeed just myths, Americans probably did have far more opportunities to improve their condition than were available to the working class in Europe. The belief that a relatively high degree of economic equality and opportunity was and must remain open to Americans permanently shaped American political and social ideals.

The Nature of U.S. Industrialization

Two characteristics of U.S. industrialization should be noted. The first was the advantage of not being the pioneer, a characteristic the United States shared with all other industrializing nations outside Great Britain. Americans were able to use British know-how and capital, and they avoided some of the technical and financial blind alleys that the English had experienced in their initial stages. By mid-century, the U.S. entrepreneurs in such vital areas as land and sea transport, iron making, and mining were catching up to or surpassing their teachers, and the U.S. gross industrial product was already as large as that of the rest of Europe outside Britain.

The second characteristic was the "rugged individualist" nature of capitalism in nineteenth-century America. Men like the railroad barons Cornelius Vanderbilt and Edward H. Harriman, the banking wizards John Hay Whitney and John Pierpont Morgan, and the iron makers Andrew Carnegie and Henry Clay Frick came into their own only after the Civil War, when American industry and finance exploded forward. But the tradition of enjoying *total freedom from governmental and public opinion* in one's method of business and use of money was already deeply ingrained and would not be modified until the twentieth century. This tradition stands in contrast to the experiences of both England and the Continent, where either government or a degree of social conscience exercised some controls over the way the early industrialists made and spent their money.

● **MAP 39.4 Europe after 1871.** The unification of the Germanies and of the Italian peninsula had been completed by 1871, but southeastern Europe was still in political flux. Bosnia would soon fall under Austrian occupation and a lost war against Russia would force the Ottomans to recognize the independence of Serbia, Montenegro, Romania, and Bulgaria in 1878. In 1912 the new kingdom of Albania would emerge from the Ottoman empire while Greece and Serbia were enlarged.

⚜ THE MODERN NATIONAL STATE: A MID-NINETEENTH-CENTURY CREATION

We have seen that in the quarter century between 1850 and 1875, great political changes occurred in several major European states: Russia, France, Italy, Germany, and Austria-Hungary (see Map 39.4). These changes were accompanied by sweeping changes in the economy and the structure of society. Toward the period's end, the Second Industrial Revolution—powered by petroleum and electricity—was in full swing, bringing technological advances that had a direct impact upon the everyday lives of everyday people.

What emerged in Europe during these years, was in fact the modern nation-state, in which an ethnic group (the nation) exercises control over a territory (the state) through mass participation in government. Its political-governmental outlines had been initiated in the French Revolution, but were not perfected until the industrial-technical breakthroughs of the late nineteenth century. A host of familiar concepts first came into daily life during this period: mass political parties electing legislatures and executives who were more or less responsible to their voters; mass school systems turning out disciplined, trained minds to take over the technical tasks of a much more complex society and economy; and labor unions representing the rapidly increasing numbers of workers negotiating with the representatives of impersonal corporations. All of these developments were characterized by *a large group, a mass or class, coming into a predominant position,* while the individual receded into the background.

✣ THE NEW IMPERIALISM

The last half of the nineteenth century also witnessed an extraordinary surge in Western activity in the non-Western world. While sub-Saharan Africa was the most spectacular example, much of Asia and the Pacific islands were also the objects of a huge landgrab by the United States and Japan as well as the European powers.

What was behind this sudden burst of imperial expansion? One factor was the conviction in the European capitals that a state must either expand its power and territory or watch them shrink. There could be no standing still in the race for international respect. Another factor was the coming of the oceangoing steamship in the 1860s. With its ability to carry much larger cargoes over much longer distances on a cost-efficient basis, it changed the rules of international maritime trade. Now it became imperative for trading nations to obtain secure refueling harbors. That meant assured military control over a far-flung network of colonial ports.

Third, many statesmen assumed that new colonies would soak up the excess production of industrial consumer goods that was already looming in Europe and the United States. This economic consideration was generally accepted as a rationale for the industrialized nations to secure new markets in what we now term the developing countries.

Lastly, and by no means least, many well-intentioned folk at all levels of American and European society felt that it was, in Rudyard Kipling's phrase, the *"white man's burden"* to "civilize" the Asians and Africans, whether they desired that happy state or not. In other words, what was happening to the non-Western world was not a power play by rapacious foreign exploiters, but an act of duty toward fellow humans who—perhaps without acknowledging it—needed the West's magnanimous aid. The combination of all these factors in varying degrees justified to both government and public the surge of Western military and economic power into the Asiatic and African lands that the following chapters will examine in detail.

Summary

The 1860s and 1870s produced major changes in almost all of the political and territorial maps of continental Europe. The modern nation-state with its mass participatory institutions was coming into existence, although its pace varied from place to place as it faced various obstacles. In Russia, attempts at basic reform fell short because of the reluctance to allow the people a full share in governing themselves. Instead, the reforms resulted in the growth of a revolutionary movement that would blossom in the early twentieth century. In France, the empire of Napoleon III brought progress internally, but failed in foreign policy and was destroyed by the lost war with Prussia. Italy was finally unified in the 1860s, in part voluntarily and in part through conquest by the kingdom of Sardinia-Piedmont. What emerged, however, was two Italies, South and North, that had little in common.

The German chancellor Bismarck was the most successful of the statesmen who attempted to realize national "destiny." Unified by war and nationalist fervor, Germans entered into a Prussia-dominated empire after 1871 and immediately became the most potent military force on the Continent. One of the countries the new empire surpassed was Austria-Hungary, a former rival now split by conflicting nationalisms. In the United States, steady industrial growth on a regional level in New England was greatly expanded on a national scale after the Civil War. By the end of the century, the American economy rivaled Germany's for leadership of the industrial world, while Britain fell back. In the last half of the century, the West engaged in a new imperialism that was particularly focused on Asia and Africa and transformed many areas previously untouched by modern politics and economic developments.

Test Your Knowledge

1. The biggest single problem in mid-nineteenth-century Russia was
   a. how to defend the enormous borders against simultaneous attacks.
   b. how to make the tsar's government more efficient.
   c. how to bring the serfs into the national economy.
   d. how to bring the military into the modern technical age.
2. The Paris Commune was
   a. an attempt to impose a socialist regime under Karl Marx on France.
   b. an imaginative attempt to introduce democracy through popular vote.
   c. an uprising against the conservative government that had lost a war.
   d. a kind of new religion prompted by anti-Christian radicals.
3. Cavour's role in unifying Italy was that of
   a. the diplomat-statesman.
   b. the rabble-rousing tribune of the people.
   c. the military commander.
   d. the right-hand man of the pope.
4. The crucial question for Bismarck as Prussia's chancellor in the 1860s was
   a. how to strengthen the army.
   b. how to crush the socialists' opposition.
   c. how to unite the German people politically.
   d. how to strengthen the constitutional rights of the citizens.
5. The Franco-Prussian War represented first and foremost
   a. a major shift in the European balance of power.
   b. a victory of a land power over a naval one.
   c. a lesson to would-be autocrats like Napoleon III that the citizens' will cannot be ignored in modern politics.
   d. the rising powers of the socialists in dictating policy to government.
6. The most serious problem facing nineteenth-century Austria was
   a. the constant rebellions of the peasantry.
   b. the friction among the various nationalities.
   c. the pressure against its borders from the rising power of Germany.
   d. the lack of continuity at the top, that is, on the throne.
7. Garibaldi's contribution to Italy's unity is best described as that of
   a. the militant romantic.
   b. the calculating politician.
   c. the religious prophet.
   d. the financial wizard.

Identification Terms

Alexander II of Russia

Ausgleich of 1867

Cavour (Camillo)

Great Reforms in Russia

kleindeutsch versus *grossdeutsch*

Napoleon III

Paris Commune of 1871

Piedmont

Third Republic of France

Bibliography

Baumgart, W. *Imperialism,* 1982. A first-rate study of British and French expansion in the late nineteenth century. See also on this topic B. Davidson, *Modern Africa,* 1989; R. Robinson and J. Gallagher, *Africa and the Victorians,* 1961; M. Edwardes: *The West in Asia, 1850–1914;* and H. M. Wright, ed., *The "New Imperialism,"* 1976.

Clark, G. K. *The Making of Victorian England,* 1962. A good brief introduction.

Cochrane, T. C. *Business in American Life,* 1977. One of the dozens of good books on the rise of business and industry in mid-nineteenth-century America.

Crankshaw, E. *Bismarck,* 1981. A reliable biography of the founder of the modern German state; so is G. Kent, *Bismarck and His Times,* 1978.

Emmons, T. *The Russian Landed Gentry and the Peasant Emancipation of 1861,* 1968. The standard treatment of the abolition of serfdom in Russia. R. Zelnik, *Labor and Society in Tsarist Russia, 1855–1870,* 1971, is very informative.

Macartney, C. A. *The Habsburg Empire, 1790–1918,* 1969. A very well written, detailed history of the problems of the Austrian Empire and the attempts to solve them, which ultimately failed. On this, see also the less detailed A. Sked, *The Decline and Fall of the Habsburg Empire, 1815–1918,* 1989, and A. J. May, *The Habsburg Monarchy, 1867–1914,* 1951, which covers the foreign and domestic affairs of the Austro-Hungarian state.

Smith, D. *Cavour,* 1985. The most recent biography of the Italian statesman. For the context, see Smith's *Italy: A Modern History,* 1969.

Seton-Watson, H. *The Russian Empire, 1801–1917,* 1967, and B. Lincoln, *The Great Reforms,* 1991, deal extensively with the shattering impact of the Crimean War on Russian government and society.

Smith, W. H. C. *Napoleon III,* 1972. Covers the life and affairs of Napoleon III in a readable and comprehensive style.

Stavrianos, S. *The Balkans, 1815–1914,* 1968, and B. Jelavich, *History of the Balkans,* vols. 1 and 2, 1983, are excellent sources of information on southeastern Europe from the late eighteenth century to the present.

Williams, R. *Gaslight and Shadows,* 1957. A fascinating work on the Paris of Napoleon III.

Woodham-Smith, C. *The Reason Why,* 1953. A really good example of how entertaining history can be when written with skill and commitment. It is the story of the Crimean War, that low comedy of military errors.

CHINA FROM THE MING TO THE EARLY QING DYNASTY

The ages of China do not coincide with those of Europe. China had no Middle Age or Renaissance of the fourteenth century. The outstanding facts in China's development between 1000 C.E. and 1500 C.E. were the humiliating conquest by the Mongols and their overthrow by the rebellion that began the Ming dynasty. For over two hundred years, the Ming remained vigorous, providing the Chinese with a degree of stability and prosperity that contemporary Europeans would have envied. But the sustained creative advance in the sciences and basic technologies that had allowed China to overshadow all rivals during the thousand years between the beginning of the Song and the end of the Ming dynasties (600–1600) was slowly drawing to a close. Indeed, China was being overtaken in these fashions by the West, but as late as the eighteenth century, this was hardly evident to anyone. Possessed of an ancient and marvelous high culture, China was still convinced of its own superiority and was far from being forced to admit its weaknesses.

✣ MING CHINA, 1368–1644

The Ming was the last pure Chinese dynasty. It began with the overthrow of the hated Mongols who had ruled China for a hundred years. Founded by the peasant Zhu who had displayed masterly military talents in leading a motley band of rebel armies, the Ming would last three hundred years. Zhu, who took the imperial title **"Hongwu"** meaning the Generous Warrior, was an individual of great talents and great cruelty (see the Biography in this chapter). In many ways his fierce ruthlessness was reminiscent of the First Emperor. He built the city of Nanjing (Nanking) as his capital near the coast on the Yangtze River. His son and successor Yongle was even more talented as a general and as an administrator. During his twenty-two-year reign (1402–1424), China gained more or less its present territory, reaching from Korea to Vietnam and inwards to Mongolia (see Map 40.1). The eastern half of the Great Wall was rebuilt, and the armies of China were everywhere triumphant against their Mongol and Turkic enemies.

In the Ming era, China generally had a good, effective government. One sign of this was the sharp *rise in population* throughout the dynastic period. When the Ming took power, bubonic plague (the same epidemic that was simultaneously raging in Europe, see Chapter 26) and Mongol savagery had reduced the population to about 60

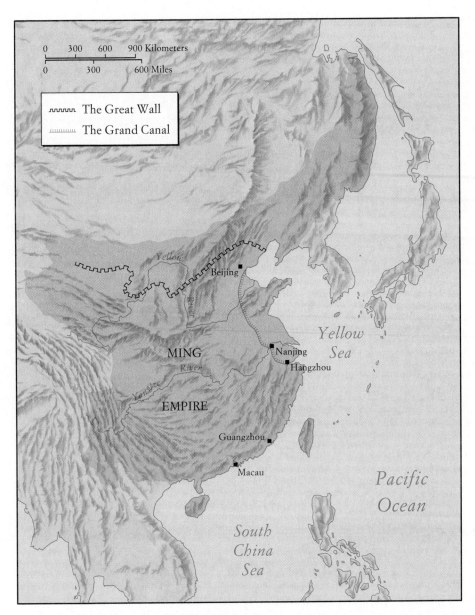

● **MAP 40.1 The Empire under the Ming Dynasty.** By the time of the Ming Dynasty, China had reached its modern territorial extent, with the exception only of Tibet and the far Western deserts. Beijing and Nanjing alternated as the capital cities.

million, the same size it had been in the Tang period, five hundred years earlier. The population rose to perhaps 150 million by 1600—the most dramatic rise yet experienced by any society.

This new population necessitated an equally dramatic rise in food supply. The old center of Chinese food production, the Yangtze basin in south-central China, was not able to meet the demand. A new area for rice cultivation in the extreme south near Vietnam was devel-

oped during the Ming, while some new crops from the Americas such as corn, squash, peanuts, and beans made their way into Chinese fields via trade with the Portuguese and Spanish. Interestingly, the Irish potato, which would become the staple food crop of northern European peasants in the eighteenth century, was introduced into China but did not catch on. Since rice has a greater nutritional value than the potato, this turned out to be a boon for China.

Hongwu, Founder of the Ming Dynasty

–1398

Zhu Yuanzhang (Chu Yuan-chang) was a peasant who ruled China from 1369 to 1398 as the first of the mighty Ming dynasts. The dynasty that he created lasted for over two hundred and fifty years. It was a period of impressive cultural achievement and social stability, though toward its end China was beginning to fall behind the West in military affairs and technology.

The peasant family from which Zhu came died in a plague, and the young boy was reduced to begging to survive. He later entered a Buddhist monastery before rising to command one of the many peasant rebel bands that fought both landlords and the corrupt Mongol (Yüan) rulers in the central government at Beijing. He rose to power swiftly due to his bravery and military ability, and by 1368 he had defeated many competitors and established himself as national ruler.

Zhu gave his government the dynastic name "Ming," or "brilliant," and titled himself the Hongwu emperor. In the traditional Chinese system of identifying emperors, the title of the man was actually the name of the period of his rule. Immediately upon assuming the throne, Zhu sought to remove all traces of the hated Mongol period, the only time when all of China had fallen under foreign control. Those who had adopted Mongol names dropped them, Mongol dress was abolished, and the nomads themselves were driven out of the country and forced back to their ancestral lands beyond the Great Wall by a large and efficient imperial army.

The Hongwu emperor also moved quickly to reestablish the agrarian economy that had suffered much under Mongol rule and to calm the peasant rebels who ravaged the countryside. To do so, he did not hesitate to use the most brutal methods. A later historian described him as combining in his person "the nature of a sage, a hero, and a robber." He could be terrifyingly cruel to his subordinates and those who did not live up to his demands for absolute loyalty. He introduced the practice of holding public beatings of officials who had failed to please him, and some of those unfortunates were beaten to death. But he also realized how much good government in China depended upon the scholar-officials, the mandarins, who had been forced out by the Mongols. He reinstituted the annual examinations for the civil ser vice and insisted that the majority of new officials be selected solely upon their merits. This system lasted without serious change into the twentieth century.

✤ ECONOMIC PROGRESS

Commercial activity steadily increased until it was probably more prevalent in China than in any other country of the world by the 1600s; that is, a larger percentage of the labor force was directly engaged in buying, selling, and transporting goods than in any other land. The merchants remained rather low on the social ladder, but had sufficient money under their collective control to provide them with a comfortable and cultivated lifestyle. Commercial contact with the Europeans started in the early 1500s with the coming of the Portuguese. Originally welcomed, the Portuguese behaved so badly that the Chinese limited them to a single port, Macao. Here the Portuguese obtained luxurious and exotic goods that brought exorbitant prices from European nobles who coveted them for the prestige they lent their possessor. A merchant who could take a single crate of first-class Chinese porcelain tableware back to Europe could make enough profit to start his own firm.

Urbanization and Technology

The Ming period also saw an enormous increase in the number of urban dwellers. Some Chinese cities, serving as marketplaces for the rural majority and as administrative and cultural centers, grew to have several hundreds of thousand inhabitants; a few had more than a million at a time when no European town had a population of even 100,000. In these Chinese metropolises, almost anything was available for money, and all available evidence indi-

Hongwu was an extraordinarily gifted administrator. He was ever mindful of the poor peasants, from whom he himself came. He abolished slavery, which at the time was common for debt. He pushed land improvement schemes and better transportation for peasant crops. Vacant land was opened to anyone willing to cultivate it, and the settlers were exempted from taxes for several years. The emperor sought to curb the growing appetite of the landlord class for more and more land by cracking down hard on the corrupt linkings of officials and landlords.

Government at the center was reorganized to reduce the powers of the emperor's councilors and enhance his own. Confucianism with its reverence for the aged and the teacher was made the official philosophy once again. A drastic example of its application was given the student who dared question his teacher's interpretation of a Confucian dialogue: his head was cut off and placed on a pole outside the classroom as a reminder to others.

Hongwu was particularly alert to the illegitimate influences that the court women sometimes exerted over government. He believed that by taking his hundreds of wives and concubines from only the poorer class he could cut short the unending conspiracies and corrupt "backscratching" among the wealthy relatives of the court women who used their connections at the palace for their own advancement. He also introduced the wholesale use of eunuchs into the emperor's service, as these men were physically incapable of having families. Many of these practices worked well under strong emperors such as Hongwu, but were distorted under the later Ming.

Toward the end of his generation-long reign, the Hongwu emperor allowed his suspicious nature to get the better of him, and when he died in 1398, he was more feared and hated than admired. Still, he performed the same necessary and difficult functions as had the First Emperor of the Qin dynasty many hundreds of years earlier: the building of a solid foundation through brutally direct methods.

cates that the kind of urban poverty that would arise later was still unknown. In general, the villagers and city dwellers of Ming China were decently housed and fed.

Historians have often asked why China with its large, financially sophisticated commercial class and a leadership role in so many ideas and techniques did not make the breakthrough into machine industry. Why, in other words, did the Chinese fail to make the leap from the "commercial revolution" of the later Ming period to an "industrial revolution" of the kind that began in the West a century later? Various answers have been proposed and no single one is satisfactory. The Chinese esteem for artists and scholars and the tendency of such people to place little emphasis on material goods must be part of the explanation. Engineers and inventors were never prominent in

China's culture, even though Chinese science and technology led the world until the 1200s at least. Also, *the Confucian ethic did not admire the entrepreneur.* In the end, we can only attest that China did not experience an industrial-technical breakthrough; if it had, China and not Western Europe would have been the dominant power of the world in the past three centuries.

❧ THE MING POLITICAL SYSTEM

As always since Han times, the Chinese government culminated in the person of an all-powerful emperor who ruled by the mandate of Heaven through a highly trained bureaucracy derived from talented men of all classes and backgrounds. Hongwu, the peasant rebel commander,

Peasant Wisdom

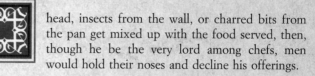

All peoples have words of wisdom and folktales designed to educate their children in the ways of the world. But the Chinese have an extraordinary store, possibly because Chinese civilization has such a long history of successful adaptation to the challenges of the day. The author of the first selections given here lived in the eighteenth century. His name was Yuan Mei, and he was a gourmet at the feast of life.

> Cookery is like matrimony; two things served together should match. Clear should go with clear, thick with thick, hard with hard, and soft with soft. I have known people to mix grated lobster with birds' nests, and mint with chicken or pork!!
>
> Cooks today think nothing of mixing in one soup the meat of chicken, duck, goose and pig. But these chickens, ducks, geese, and pigs doubtless have souls. And these souls will doubtless file complaints in the next world on the way they have been treated in this.
>
> A good cook will use plenty of different dishes. Each article of food will be made to exhibit its own nature, while each dish made will be characterized by one dominant flavor. Then the palate of the gourmand will respond, and the flowers of the soul blossom forth. . . .
>
> A good cook frequently wipes his knife. . . frequently changes his cloth, frequently scrapes his board, and frequently washes his hands. If smoke or ashes drop from his pipe, perspiration from his

head, insects from the wall, or charred bits from the pan get mixed up with the food served, then, though he be the very lord among chefs, men would hold their noses and decline his offerings.

The next selections are from Han Feizi, who lived many centuries before Yuan Mei. Before his death around 233 B.C.E., Han Fei collected some of the folk sayings of his region and passed them on:

> While working in the fields, a farmer saw a rabbit running. It ran into a tree, and was instantly killed. He took the rabbit home, cooked it, and found it delicious. On the second day, he gave up his farming work, and took a seat beneath a tree, to wait for the same thing to happen again. It never did.
>
> A mussel had opened its shell and was sunning itself on the beach when a snipe [a long-beaked shorebird] pecked at it. The mussel quickly closed its shell and caught and tightly held the snipe's beak. The mussel could not get back to the river, nor could the snipe walk away. "If it does not rain for two days, the mussel will be dead," thought the snipe. "If I keep his beak between my shells for two days, soon there will be a dead snipe," thought the mussel. While the mussel and the snipe were angry with one another, and neither one would make any concessions, a fisherman happened by and caught both of them and ate them.

brought militaristic and authoritarian ways to the government he headed. The first Ming ruler divided China into fifteen provinces, subdivided into numerous counties that have survived almost intact into the present day. He made occupations hereditary and classified the population into three groups: peasants, soldiers, and workers. Supposedly, the class people were born into would determine the course of their lives, but this was truer on paper than in reality. China was far too vast and the bureaucracy far too small to allow the theory to be put successfully into practice.

But the emperor's powers during the early Ming were probably greater than ever before. Hongwu created a corps of palace eunuchs, men who had been raised since

boyhood to be totally dedicated servants of the ruler. They served as his eyes and ears, and during periods of weak leadership, the eunuchs often exercised almost dictatorial powers over the regular officials, since they alone had direct access to the emperor. This practice, of course, led to much abuse, and the eunuchs were hated and feared by most Chinese. Curiously, the eunuchs never seem to have attempted to overthrow a legitimate ruler, although some Ming emperors practically turned the government over to their favorites. The corps of eunuchs lasted into the twentieth century, though their powers were much diminished by then.

After a brief sojourn in Nanjing during the rule of the first Ming emperor, the capital city was returned to the northern city of Beijing (Peking) originally built by the Mongols. In its center was the **Forbidden City,** a quarter-mile-square area of great palaces, offices, and living quarters for the higher officials. No ordinary person was ever permitted within its massive walls. The Forbidden City was expanded several times during the Ming, until it came to house more than 20,000 men and women who served the emperor or his enormous official family. Its upkeep and the lavish entertainments and feasts that were regularly put on for thousands were a heavy burden on the whole country.

The Bureaucracy

The basis for entry and success in the bureaucracy remained the same as it had been for the last 1500 years: the Confucian philosophy and ethics. Confucianism grew stronger than ever; many schools were founded solely to prepare boys for the government service exams. These exams, which had been suspended by the Mongols, were immediately reinstated by the first Ming emperor; their essentials would not change until the twentieth century. The exams were administered every other year at the lowest (county) level and every third year at the provincial capitals. Each candidate was assigned a tiny cubicle where he slept and ate when not writing his essays during the three to five days of the examination. Only a tiny minority were successful in obtaining an official post and the distinction it brought.

Unchanged for centuries, the exams influenced all Chinese education and kept what we now call the curriculum to a very narrow range. After basic reading, writing, and arithmetic, most Chinese schooling was aimed only at preparing the student for the civil service examinations. It consisted of a good deal of rote memorization and required very extensive knowledge of the various interpretations of Confucian thought. *Imagination, creativity, and individuality were definitely not desired.* Over the long term, this limited education put China's officials at a distinct disadvantage when confronted with situations that required flexibility and vision. On the other hand, the uniform preparation of all Chinese officials gave the country an especially cohesive governing class; conflicts generated by differing philosophies of government were nonexistent. Until very recent times, civil upheaval and antagonism never occurred *within* the governing class, only *between* it and some outer group (usually provincial usurpers). This unity was very valuable in preserving China from threatened disintegration.

■ This seventeenth century painting shows the examinations for government posts in progress. Despite years of preparation very few candidates were successful at the higher levels.

In the early Ming period, both the government and the great majority of the educated population agreed on the vital principles of a good life and how to achieve it. All officials, from the emperor down to the minor collector of customs in some obscure port, were accepted by the masses as their proper authorities. Unfortunately, this harmony declined in later years, as weak emperors ignored the examples set by the dynasty's founder.

✤ DEALING WITH FOREIGNERS

The Mongols on the northern and northwestern frontiers were still a constant menace after they had been expelled from China proper. Much of the large military budget of Ming China was spent on maintaining the two thousand miles of the Great Wall, large sections of which had to be rebuilt to defend against them. To do this job, a huge army—well over a million strong—was kept in constant readiness. The main reason for moving the capital back to Beijing from Nanjing was to better direct the defense effort.

The rulers at Beijing followed the ancient stratagem of "use the barbarian against the barbarian," whenever they

■ **Woman Bathing Their Children.** This domestic scene is taken from a twelfth-century Song dynasty painting of life in the palace.

could. But twice they miscalculated, and the Mongol tribes were able to put aside their squabbles and unite in campaigns against the Chinese. The first time the Mongols actually defeated and captured the emperor, holding him for a tremendous ransom; the second, they smashed a major army and overran Beijing itself in 1550. Eventually, both incursions were forced back, and the Ming dynasty was reestablished.

With the *Japanese,* relations proceeded on two planes. From the fourteenth century, pirate-traders (there was little distinction) from Japan had appeared in Korean and north Chinese waters. Gradually, they became bolder and often joined Chinese pirates to raid coastal ports well into the south. During the sixteenth century, the Beijing government actually abandoned many coastal areas to the pirates, hoping this tactic would enable them to protect the rest. Since the Japanese could always flee out of reach in their islands, the Chinese could only try to improve their defenses, rather than exterminate the enemy fleets.

Otherwise the Ming period was a high point in cultural and commercial interchange between China and Japan. Direct Chinese-Japanese relations concentrated on trading between a few Japanese *daimyo* and Chinese merchants, a private business supervised by the respective governments. Several of the shoguns of Japan (see the next chapter) were great admirers of Chinese culture and saw to it that Chinese artifacts and ideas were imported regularly.

Meanwhile China's contacts with *Westerners* were limited to a few trading colonies, mainly Portuguese or Dutch, and occasional missionaries, mainly Jesuits from Spain or the Papal States. In the long run, the missionaries were not very successful, though they made enormous efforts to penetrate the Confucian mentalities of the upper-class Chinese officials and adapt Christian doctrines to Chinese psyches. Outstanding in this regard was **Matteo Ricci** (1551–1610), a Jesuit who obtained access to the emperor thanks to his adoption of Chinese ways of thought and mastery of the difficult language. Ricci and his successors established a Christian bridgehead in the heart of China that for a century or more looked as though it might be able to broaden its appeal and convert the masses.

The **Maritime Expeditions** of the early 1400s are a notable departure from the general course of Chinese policy in that they were naval rather than land ventures. Their purpose remains unclear, but it does not seem to have been commercial. Between 1405 and 1433, fleets carrying as many as 30,000 sailors and soldiers traveled as far west as the east coast of Africa. The expeditions were sponsored by the government, and at the emperor's order, they stopped as suddenly as they had begun. The fleets made no attempt to plant colonies or to set up a network of trading posts. Nor did the expeditions leave a long-term mark on Chinese consciousness or awareness of the world outside.

The Maritime Expeditions were a striking demonstration of how advanced Chinese seamanship, ship design, and equipment were and how confident the Chinese were in their dealings with foreigners of all types. Although China possessed the necessary technology (shipbuilding, compass, rudder, sails) to make a success of overseas commerce, the government decided not to use it. The government's refusal was the end of the matter; the mercantile class had no alternative but to accept it because the merchants had neither the influence at court nor the high status in society that could have enabled the voyages to continue. In this sense, the failure to pursue the avenues opened by the expeditions reflects the differences between the Chinese and European governments and the relative importance of merchants in the two cultures.

✤ THE MANZHOU INVADERS: QING DYNASTY

The end of the Ming dynasty came after a slow, painful decline in the mid-seventeenth century. A series of ineffective emperors had allowed government power to slip into the hands of corrupt and hated eunuchs, who made decisions without responsibility for them. Court cliques contended for supreme power. The costs of the multitude of imperial court officials and hangers-on were enormous and could be met only by squeezing taxes out of an already hard-pressed peasantry. Peasant rebellions began to multiply as the government's ability to restrain rapacious landlords declined. Adding to the troubles was the popularity among the governing **mandarins** of an extreme version of scholarly Confucianism that paralyzed innovation.

The Manzhou tribesmen living north of the Great Wall in **Manchuria** had paid tribute to the Beijing emperor but had never accepted his overlordship; when the rebellions led to anarchy in several provinces, the Manzhou saw their chance. The Manzhou governing group sincerely admired Chinese culture and made it clear that if and when they were victorious, the Chinese would have nothing to fear from them. Presenting themselves as the alternative to banditry and even revolution, the Manzhou won the support of much of the official class. One province after another went over to them rather than face continuous rebellion. The last Ming ruler, faced with certain defeat, committed suicide. Thus was founded the last dynasty of imperial China, the Manzhou or **Qing** (1664–1911).

Manzhou Government

In the eighteenth century, when the Qing dynasty was at the apex of its power and wealth, China had by far the largest population under one government and the largest territory of any country in the world (see Map 40.2). China reached its biggest territorial extent at this time. The Manzhou had been close to Chinese civilization for many years and had become partially Sinicized (adopted Chinese culture), so the transition from Ming to Qing rule was nothing like the upheaval that had followed the Mongol conquest in the 1200s.

Many Ming officials and generals joined with the conquerors voluntarily from the start; many others joined as it became apparent that the Manzhou were not savages. High positions in the central government were in fact occupied by two individuals: one Manzhou, one Chinese. Chinese provincial governors were overseen by Manzhou, and the army was sharply divided between the two ethnic groups with the Manzhou having superior status.

Like most new dynasties, the Manzhou Qing were strong reformers in their early years, bringing order and respect for authority, snapping the whip over insubordinate officials in the provinces and villages, and attempting to ensure justice. The two greatest Manzhou leaders were the emperors **Kangxi** (Kang-hsi; r. 1662–1722) and his grandson **Qienlong** (Chien Lung; r. 1736–1795). Their unusually long reigns allowed them to put their stamps upon the bureaucracy and develop long-range policies. Both were strong, well-educated men, who approached their duties with the greatest seriousness. Both attempted to keep Manzhou and Chinese separate to some degree, though the Manzhou were always a tiny minority (perhaps 2 percent) of the population and were steadily Sinicized after the early 1700s by intermarriage and free choice.

Kangxi was the almost exact contemporary of Louis XIV of France and, like him, was the longest-lived ruler of his country's history. From all accounts, Kangxi was a remarkable man with a quick intellect and a fine gift for administration. He was particularly active in economic policy making, both domestically and with the Western visitors who were now starting to appear regularly in Chinese ports. He did much to improve the waterways, which were always of great importance for transportation in China; rivers were dredged, and canals and dams built. After decades of negotiations, Kangxi opened four Chinese ports to European traders and allowed them to set up small permanent enclaves there. This decision was to have fateful consequences in the mid-nineteenth century.

Kangxi's grandson Qienlong was a great warrior and intelligent administrator. He eradicated the persistent Mongol raiders on the western borders and brought Tibet under Chinese control for the first time (see Map 40.2). The peculiar fashion of dealing with neighboring kingdoms as though they were voluntary satellites of China was extended to most of Southeast Asia at this time. Qienlong ruled through the last two-thirds of the eighteenth century, and we know a good deal about both him and his grandfather because Jesuit missionaries were resident in Beijing during this era. Their perceptive reports contributed to the interest in everything Chinese that gripped late eighteenth-century Europe. Voltaire and other philosophes often referred to China's government with admiration.

The Manzhou emperors were unusually vigorous leaders, and the Chinese responded positively to their rule until the middle of the nineteenth century, when their prestige suffered under a combination of Western military intrusions and a growing population crisis. This period is covered in a later chapter.

❦ QING CULTURE AND ECONOMY

No break in cultural styles occurred between the Ming and Qing dynasties. As in earlier China, the most respected cultural activities were philosophy, history, calligraphy, poetry, and painting. In literature, a new form reached maturity in the 1500s: *the novel.* Perhaps inspired by the Japanese example, a series of written stories about both gentry life and ordinary people appeared during the late Ming and Qing eras. Best known are the *Book of the Golden Lotus* and *The Dream of the Red Chamber,* the latter a product of the eighteenth century. Most of the authors are unknown, and the books that have survived are probably a small portion of those actually produced.

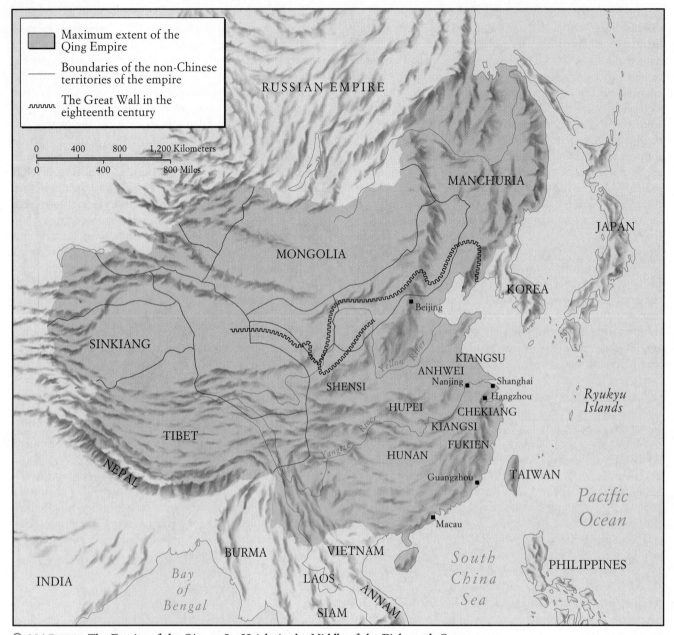

Maximum extent of the Qing Empire

Boundaries of the non-Chinese territories of the empire

The Great Wall in the eighteenth century

● **MAP 40.2   The Empire of the Qing at Its Height in the Middle of the Eighteenth Century.**

Some of the stories are pornographic, a variety of literature that the Chinese evidently enjoyed despite official disapproval.

Porcelain reached such artistry in the eighteenth century that it became a major form of Chinese aesthetic creation. Throughout the Western world, the wealthy sought fine "china" and were willing to pay nearly any price for the beautiful blue-and-white wares brought back by the Dutch and English ships from the south China ports. Chinese painting on scrolls and screens was also imported in large amounts, as were silks and other luxury items for the households of the nobility and wealthy urbanites. The decorative style termed *chinoiserie* reflected Europe's admiration for Chinese artifacts and good taste. The "China Clipper ships" of New England made the long voyage around Cape Horn and across the Pacific in the first half of the nineteenth century to reap enormous profits carrying luxury goods in both directions: sea otter furs from the Pacific Northwest and porcelain, tea, and jade from China.

During the Ming and Qing periods, far more people were participating in the creation and enjoyment of culture than ever before. By the 1700s China had a large number of educated people who were able to purchase the tangible cultural goods produced by a host of skilled artists. Schools and academies of higher learning educated the children of anyone who could afford the fees, generally members of the scholar-official class who had been governing China since the Han dynasty. Developing a sensitivity to beauty, such as the art of calligraphy, was considered as essential to proper education as mastering literacy and math. Painting, poetry, and meditation were considered far more important than physics or accounting. It was in this era (from the 1500s on) that China definitely *lost its lead in science and technology* to the West, a lead that had been maintained for the previous thousand years.

Progress and Problems

Among the outstanding achievements of the Qing emperors were improvements in agriculture and engineering that benefited uncounted numbers of ordinary Chinese. Kangxi, for example, did much to ensure that the south China "rice bowl" was made even more productive and that the Grand Canal linking the Yellow River with the central coast ports was kept in good order. New hybrid rice, a variety derived from Vietnam called Champa, allowed rice culture to be extended and increased yields, which in turn led to an expansion in population.

Internal trade in the large cities and many market towns became ever more important in this era. Although most Chinese remained villagers working the land, there were now large numbers of shopkeepers, market porters, carters, artisans, moneylenders, and all the other occupations of commercial life. Money circulated freely as both coin and paper, the coins being minted of Spanish silver brought from the South American colonies to Manila and Guangzhou (Canton) to trade for silk and porcelain.

All in all, the Chinese in the early Qing period were living as well as any other people in the world and better than most Europeans. But this standard of living was to change for the worse in later days, when for the first time the population's growth exceeded the ability of the economy to find suitable productive work for it. By the nineteenth century, almost all the land that had adequate precipitation for crops had already been brought under the plow. Machine industry had not yet arrived in China (and would not for many years), and trade with the outside world was on a relatively small scale that government policy refused to expand. (China wanted very few material things from the non-Chinese, in any case.) In the nineteenth century, China began to experience massive famines that were the result of too rapid growth in population in a technically backward society without the desire or means to shift to new production modes.

■ **Festival at the River.** This is part of a 33 foot long scroll painted in the Ming dynasty era portraying one of the several civic festivals which marked the Chinese calendar. The emperor's participation in these festivals was an important part of his functions as head of government and holder of the mandate of heaven.

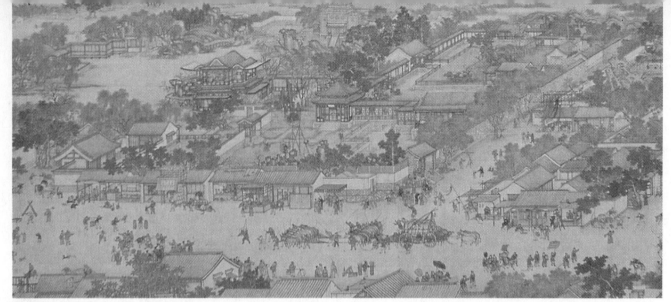

■ **Urban Life in the Qing Dynasty.** This eighteenth century scroll detail shows the Chinese artist's delight in the exact portrayal of everyday life scenes. Compare this with the Festival at the River photo, painted some two hundred years earlier.

Summary

The overthrow of the hated Mongols introduced another of the great Chinese dynasties: the Ming. Blessed by exceptionally able emperors in the early decades, the Ming imitated their Tang dynasty model and made notable improvements in agriculture and commerce. Urban life expanded and the urban bourgeoisie of merchants became economically (but not politically) important. The borders were extended well to the west and north, and the barbarian nomads thrust behind the Great Wall for a couple of centuries.

But in time the Ming's grip on government and people weakened, and the costs of a huge court and army pressed heavily on the overtaxed population. When rebellions began in the northern provinces, they were encouraged by the promises of change offered by the Manzhou people in the northeast. Triumphant, the Manzhou leader began the final dynastic period in China's three thousand years of history, that of the Qing. The Qing emperors of the first half of the dynasty were able men, who in the eighteenth century led China to one of the summits of its national existence. The economy and the fine arts prospered, and overpopulation was not yet a problem. But in science and technology, China now lagged far behind the West, and the coming century was going to be filled with political and cultural humiliations brought on by weakness. China entered the modern age (post–1800) unprepared to handle the type of problems that it now faced: impoverishment, military backwardness, and technical retardation. First the Europeans and then the Japanese would find ways to take advantage of these handicaps.

Test Your Knowledge

1. The last dynasty to be of pure Chinese origin was the
   a. Manzhou.
   b. Song.
   c. Tang.
   d. Ming.
2. The most serious menace to China's stability during the 1300s and 1400s was

   a. the Japanese coastal pirates.
   b. the Mongol tribes in the north.
   c. the conspiracies of the palace eunuchs.
   d. the invasions of the Vietnamese in the south.
3. During the Ming period, Chinese-Japanese contacts were

a. restricted to occasional commerce and raids by Japanese pirates.

b. thriving on a number of fronts, both commercial and cultural.

c. hostile and infrequent.

d. marked by the Japanese willingness to accept China's dominance.

4. The replacement of the Ming by the Manzhou Qing dynasty was

a. caused by a Japanese invasion of China and collapse of the Ming.

b. a gradual military takeover from a demoralized government.

c. carried out by Westerners, anxious to install a "tame" government in Beijing.

d. caused by Western Christian missionaries hostile to the Ming.

5. Which of the following did *not* figure prominently in Manzhou culture?

a. Poetry

b. Landscape painting

c. Theology

d. Fictional narratives

6. During the Ming/Manzhou era, China was ruled by a bureaucracy that

a. was selected on the basis of aristocratic birth.

b. was controlled by a professional military establishment.

c. was dominated by the Buddhist priesthood in most localities.

d. was selected on the basis of written examinations.

7. The outstanding Qing emperors of the eighteenth century

a. learned much of political value from the West.

b. were cruel tyrants in their treatment of the common Chinese.

c. split governmental responsibility between Manzhou and Chinese.

d. tried hard to expand commerce between China and Europe.

Identification Terms

Dream of the Red Chamber Kangxi Maritime Expeditions Qienlong
Forbidden City Manchuria Matteo Ricci Qing dynasty
Hongwu mandarins

Bibliography

Cahill, J. *Chinese Painting,* 1977. On this topic, see also R. Thorpe, *Son of Heaven: Imperial Arts of China,* 1988, which is richly illustrated.

Miyazaki, I. *China's Examination Hell: The Civil Service Examinations of Imperial China,* 1964. A memorable look into what Chinese education emphasized and why.

Naquin, S., and E. Rawski. *Chinese Society in the Eighteenth Century,* 1987. A perceptive overview of a great civilization before its decline.

Ricci, M. *The Journals,* 1953. An edition of the Jesuit's interesting account of life in China in the sixteenth century.

Schirokauer, C. *A Brief History of Chinese and Japanese Civilizations,* 1989. Very helpful and clearly written. E. O. Reischauer, J. Fairbank, and A. Craig, *East Asia: Tradition and Transfor-*

mation, 1973, is a good introduction to both China and Japan. For more detail, try the relevant volumes in the *Cambridge History of China,* 1978–.

Spence, J. *The Search for Modern China,* 1990. Especially recommended for its general account of affairs in the later Ming period. Spence has written a series of major works on China in this period. His *Emperor of China: Self-Portrait of Kang Hsi,* 1974, is a fine biography of the outstanding statesman of eighteenth-century China.

Wakeman, F., Jr. *The Great Enterprise,* 1985. A good analysis of the way the Manzhou emperors attained control of their huge new conquest.

Wang, Chi-chen, ed. *The Dream of the Red Chamber,* 1958. The best short English translation of the classic novel.

JAPAN TO THE MEIJI RESTORATION

1543	First European contacts with Japan
c. 1600	Tokugawa shogunate established
c. 1630s	Christianity suppressed; foreigners expelled/*sakoku* begins
1600s–1700s	Money economy and commercial society develop
1853–1854	Perry opens Japan to trade/*sakoku* ends

Though akin to China in some ways, Japan was very different in many others. The political prestige of the emperor in Kyoto was quite weak throughout early modern times, and Japan became a collection of feudal provinces controlled by clans. In the century between the 1460s and the 1570s, the warrior-nobles—*daimyo*—had engaged in a frenzy of the "strong eating the weak." Finally, a series of military strongmen managed to restore order, culminating in the establishment of a type of centralized feudalism, the *shogunate*.

The first European contacts occurred in the mid-1500s, when traders and missionaries were allowed to establish themselves on Japanese soil. One of the most important trade items brought by the Portuguese was firearms; another was the Christian Bible. Contacts with Europe were complicated by Japanese distrust of the Christian faith and its hints of submission to an alien culture. The shogun eventually decided that this danger was intolerable, and within a generation's time, Japan withdrew behind a wall of enforced isolation from the world, from which it would not emerge until the nineteenth century.

❖ FIRST EUROPEAN CONTACT: CHRISTIANITY

The *Portuguese* arrived in Japanese ports for the first time in 1543, looking for additional opportunities to make money from their active trading with all the Eastern countries. They took Chinese silk to Japan and Japanese silver to China and used the profits from both to buy spices in the South Pacific islands to bring back to Portugal.

One of the first influences from the West to reach the thus-far isolated Japanese was Christianity, which arrived via the numerous Catholic missionaries sponsored by the Society of Jesus. The Jesuit order had been founded to fight Protestantism only a few years earlier, and its missionaries were well educated and highly motivated. For various reasons, a fair number of the Japanese daimyo were sympathetic to the Jesuit efforts and converted to Christianity during the 1550s and 1560s. By the year 1600, it is estimated that 300,000 Japanese had converted; that number would have constituted a far higher percentage of the population then than in modern times.

At this time, the great majority of Japanese were adherents of either Shinto or one of the many varieties of

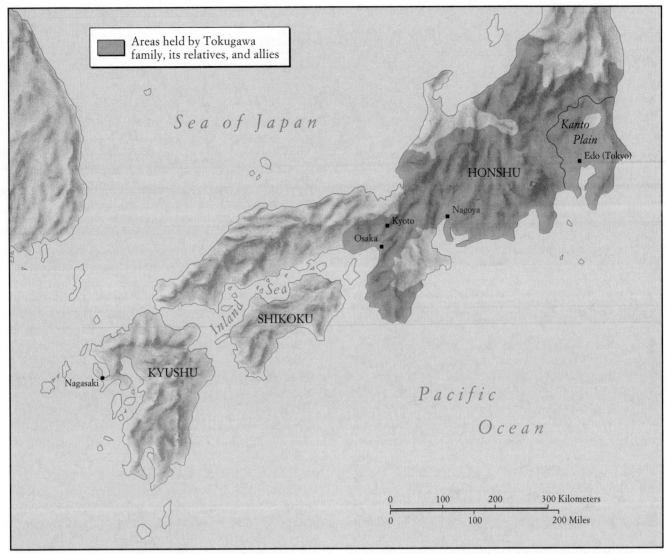

Areas held by Tokugawa
family, its relatives, and allies

Sea of Japan

Kanto Plain

Edo (Tokyo)

HONSHU

Nagoya

Kyoto

Osaka

Inland Sea

SHIKOKU

KYUSHU

Nagasaki

Pacific Ocean

| 0 | 100 | 200 | 300 Kilometers |
| 0 | | 100 | 200 Miles |

⦿ **MAP 41.1 Japan under the Tokugawa Shoguns.** The area nearest Edo (later Tokyo) was tightly held by members of the Tokugawa clan or their closest allies among the daimyo lords. In western Honshu and Kyushu powerful daimyo were neutralized by setting them against one another for imperial favor.

Buddhism. Why the Japanese proved more receptive to Christianity than, for example, the Chinese or the Hindus is impossible to say. One reason, certainly, was the personal example of the Jesuits, led by *St. Francis Xavier,* who greatly impressed their hosts with their piety and learning.

But the success was not long-lived. In the later 1500s, a movement for Japanese national unity led by **Oda Nobunaga** (1523–1582), a feudal lord who had fought his way to regional power, was getting underway. In the 1570s, the brutal Nobunaga succeeded in capturing Kyoto and most of the central island of Honshu, but was killed by one of his cohorts. Following Nobunaga's death, his

lieutenant **Toyotomi Hideyoshi** took over. Aided by the first large-scale use of firearms in Japan, Hideyoshi had visions of Asian, if not worldwide, supremacy. He invaded Korea with a well-equipped army of 150,000 as a first step toward the conquest of Ming China. Repulsed in 1592, he was in the midst of a second attempt when he died in 1598. After a couple of years of struggle among Hideyoshi's would-be successors, the baton was seized by the formidable warrior and statesman, Tokugawa Ieyasu (r. 1603–1616).

Tokugawa ceased the abortive invasion of the mainland and by 1600 had beat down his several internal rivals.

Tokugawa Ieyasu
1542–1616

On March 8, 1616, the shogun Tokugawa Ieyasu died as he had lived: from illness contracted at the storming of the great fortress of Osaka some months earlier. According to his wish, he was buried in Nikko, a beautiful wood ninety miles north of Tokyo. His tomb stands at the end of a long avenue of great gardens. Statues of Japanese heroes, the tombs of many of emperors, and the largest and richest Shinto temples of Japan surround his resting place. The funeral itself was a state occasion; even the seldom-seen emperor traveled to Nikko to honor the shogun. Posthumously, Tokugawa was given the title "Noble of the First Rank, Great Light of the East, Great Incarnation of the Buddha." He had been recognized as one of the most important members of the court aristocracy, the *kuge,* the only humans who could approach the emperor and see him face to face.

Tokugawa Ieyasu (that is, Ieyasu of the Tokugawa clan) was born in 1542. During the last decades of the sixteenth century, he became an ally of Toyotomi Hideyoshi, the most powerful of all the feudal aristocrats who divided the country among themselves. When Hideyoshi died unexpectedly in 1598, Ieyasu and another man were the prime candidates to succeed him. Political maneuvering began at once. Tokugawa assembled a force of 80,000 feudal warriors, while his opponent led a coalition of 130,000. In the decisive battle of Sekigahara in 1600, the two armies collided. Thanks to the treachery of one of the members of the coalition, the outnumbered Tokugawa forces claimed the field. In the next few years, Ieyasu destroyed the coalition's resistance and secured the shogun's office for himself and his second son. (The eldest was forced to commit hara-kiri by his enraged father, who suspected his son of treachery.)

Ieyasu's victory was a turning point of great importance. For the next two and a half centuries, the Japanese were forced to live in peace with one another. This "Era of Great Peace" was marked by the Tokugawa clan's uninterrupted control of the shogunate in Edo (Tokyo), while the semidivine emperor resided in Kyoto and remained the symbolic center of Japanese devotion. The Tokugawa remained in control until the Meiji Restoration in 1867.

Ieyasu was an extraordinarily gifted man. Coming out of the samurai tradition of military training, he was nevertheless able to appreciate the blessings of a permanent peace. He established his court as the capital of real government and carefully redivided the feudal lords' domains throughout the islands so as to assure his control over all of them. He established the daimyo as the officials of his kingdom; they were given considerable freedom to do as they pleased in their own backyards, so long as their loyalty to the shogun was not in doubt. In 1615, Ieyasu triumphantly crushed an attempted rebellion by the heir of the Hideyoshi clan by storming the previously impregnable fortress at Osaka.

Thus began the two and a half centuries of the Tokugawa shogunate, a military regency exercised in the name of a figurehead emperor. Tokugawa "ate the pie that Nobunaga made and Hideyoshi baked" goes the schoolchildren's axiom in modern Japan. He was the decisive figure in premodern Japanese history (see the Biography in this chapter).

✦ THE TOKUGAWA SHOGUNATE

Once in power, Tokugawa continued and expanded the changes in society and government that Hideyoshi had begun. By disarming the peasants, Tokugawa removed much of the source of the rebellions that had haunted Japan during the preceding century. From this time on, only the professional warrior class, the *samurai,* and their daimyo employers had the right to own weapons. The daimyo, who were roughly equivalent to the barons of Europe some centuries earlier, were expected to spend half their time at the court of the shogun where they would be under the watchful eyes of the shogun and his network of informers.

In the early 1600s, the Tokugawa shoguns began to withdraw Japan into seclusion from outside influences.

The chief goal of the Tokugawa shogunate was a class-based political stability, which they successfully pursued for centuries. The shogun controlled all contacts with foreigners and gradually ended them so as to isolate the island empire for over two hundred years. Christian missions were banned in 1614, and Christian Japanese were steadily persecuted after the 1630s. Ieyasu's successors forbade Japanese to travel abroad and prohibited the residence of any foreigners in Japan (with the exception of a handful of Dutch traders in Nagasaki Bay).

Ieyasu and his successors in the 1600s did much to improve and nationalize Japan's economy, particularly among the peasant majority. Some of the barbarous practices retained from ancient days such as the coerced mutilation of the servants and peasants of a dead daimyo were abolished. Bud-

dhism, mixed with native Shinto forms, was strongly encouraged in several versions. The *heimin* or plain folk were divided into three basic groups: farmers, artisans, and traders, in that rank order. Farmers were generally regarded as honorable people, while traders were originally looked down upon as in China. At the bottom of the social scale were the despised *hinin*, who were equivalent to the Indian untouchables; unlike the untouchables, however, the *hinin* were able to rise in status.

In many ways, Tokugawa Ieyasu was the father of traditional Japan; political institutions of the country did not change in any significant way until the late nineteenth century. He lives on in the pantheon of Japan's heroes as a model of military virtue, who reluctantly employed harsh and even brutal measures in response to the overriding needs of the day.

■ **Tokugawa Ieyasu.** This portrait was done after the powerful warrior had assured his position as shogun in 1603.

Earlier, Hideyoshi had had misgivings about the activities of the Jesuits within his domains, and in 1587 he had issued an order, later revoked, that they should leave. After newly arrived members of the Franciscan order attempted to meddle in the shogunate's internal affairs, Tokugawa acted. He evicted the Christian missionaries who had been in the country for half a century and put heavy pressure on the Christian Japanese to reconvert to Buddhism. After Christian peasants supported a revolt in 1637, pressure turned into outright persecution. Death became the standard penalty for Christian affiliation. In a few places, the Christians maintained their faith through

"underground" churches and priests, but the majority gradually gave up their religion in the face of heavy state penalties and their neighbors' antagonism.

At the same time, Japan's extensive mercantile contacts with the Europeans and Chinese were almost entirely severed. Only a handful of Dutch and Portuguese traders/residents were allowed to remain in two ports (notably, Nagasaki, where two Dutch ships were allowed to land each year). The building of oceangoing ships by Japanese was forbidden. No foreigners could come to Japan, and no Japanese were allowed to reside abroad (with a few exceptions). Japanese who were living abroad were

Valignano's *Summario for 1580*

One of the earliest Christian missionaries to Japan was the Italian Franciscan, Alessandro Valignano. An able preacher, Valignano was also an acute observer, and his report to his religious superior entitled the *Summario for 1580* provides a description of the Japanese that is still of interest.

Note how Valignano emphasizes the willfulness and emphasis on freedom of action among the Japanese at this time. This description stands in sharp contrast to the impressions gathered by foreign visitors three centuries later, who describe nineteenth-century Japanese as being highly concerned with conformity and sensitivity to social conventions. Whether Valignano exaggerated or whether the national character indeed was changed by the two and a half centuries of *sakoku* and submission to a stable government of Tokugawa shoguns is a question much debated.

> The people are all white, courteous, and highly civilized, so much so that they surpass all the other known races of the world. They are naturally very intelligent, although they have no knowledge of sciences, because they are the most warlike and bellicose race yet discovered on earth. From the age of fifteen onwards, all youths and men, rich and poor, in all walks of life, wear a sword and a dagger at their side. Moreover, every man, whether a gentleman or commoner, has such complete control over his sons, servants, and others of the household that he can kill any of them on the smallest pretext at any time he likes. . . .
>
> They are absolute lords of their lands, although the highest among them frequently league together for defense against their suzerains, who are thus often prevented from doing as they wish. They think nothing more of killing a man than an animal, so that they will kill a man not only on the smallest excuse but merely to try the edge of their swords. . . .
>
> On the one hand, they are the most affable people and a race more given to outward affection than any yet known. They have such control over their anger and impatience that it is almost a miracle to witness any quarrel and insulting words in Japan, whether with one another or with foreigners. . . . On the other hand, they are the most false and treacherous people. . .for from childhood they are taught never to reveal their hearts, and they regard this as prudence and the contrary as folly, to such a degree that those who lightly reveal their mind are looked upon as fools, and are contemptuously termed single-hearted men. Even fathers and sons never reveal their true thoughts to each other, because there can be no mutual confidence between them in word or deed. . . .
>
> They are a people universally accustomed to living as they wish, for both men and women are brought up in such freedom from childhood that they are allowed to behave as they please, without their fathers checking them in the smallest degree, for they neither whip not scold them. This is particularly so with nobles and gentry, who are so wedded to their own ideas that nobody, however much a servant or a friend he may be, dares to contradict them, whether they want to do good or ill; on the contrary, they try to divine their master's wish and to give advice and counsel in conformity therewith. . .
>
> They hold some horrible sins to be positive virtues and they are taught as such by their bonzes [holy men] and priests [i.e., Shinto or Buddhist], particularly as regards the accursed sin [sodomy] which is allowed free rein to such an extent that it is as unspeakable as unbelievable. Likewise, they have many iniquitous customs and laws so unjust and contrary to natural reason, that it is an exceedingly difficult thing to persuade them to live in conformity with our law. Withal, when they do become Christians. . .since this people is the best and most civilized of all the East, with the exception of the Chinese, so it is likewise the most apt to be taught and to adopt our holy law, and to produce the finest Christianity in all the East, as in fact it already is.

SOURCE: Charles Boxer, *The Christian Century in Japan*, "Sumario of 1580" excerpt. Reprinted with permission of Carcanet Press, Ltd.

forbidden to return. The previously lively trade with China was sharply curtailed. This isolation (called *sakoku* in Japanese history) lasted until the middle of the nineteenth century. It was a remarkable experiment with highly successful results so far as the ruling group was concerned. Japan went its own way and was ignored by the rest of the world.

Shogun, Emperor, and Daimyo

The shoguns continued the dual nature of Japanese government, whereby the shogunate was established at **Edo** (later Tokyo) while the emperor resided in the imperial palace at **Kyoto** and occupied himself with ritual and ceremony as the current holder of the line of the Sun Goddess who had created Japan eons earlier. True power in both a military and a political sense remained, of course, with the Tokugawa shogun. This system continued without important change until 1867. An individual who was always a member of the Tokugawa clan acted in the name of the emperor while closely overseeing some two hundred land-holding daimyo who acted both as agents of the shogun and as autonomous regents in their own domains.

The daimyo were the key players and posed a constant threat to Tokugawa's arrangements. As the major powers on the local level, they could tear down any shogun if they united against him. Therefore, to secure the center, the shogun had to play the daimyo off against each other in the countryside. He did this by constant intervention and manipulation, setting one clan against another in the competition for imperial favor. The shogun controlled the domains near Edo himself or put them in the hands of dependable allies; domains on the outlying islands went to rival daimyo clans who would counterbalance one another (see Map 41.1). Meanwhile the wives and children of the more important daimyo families were required to live permanently at Edo, where they served as hostages for the loyal behavior of the clan. The whole system of supervision and surveillance much resembled Louis XIV's arrangements at Versailles in seventeenth-century France.

Economic Advances

Japan's society and economy changed markedly during the centuries of isolation. One of the most remarkable results of *sakoku* was the great *growth of population and trade.* The population doubled in the seventeenth century and continued to increase gradually throughout the remainder

■ **Arrival of Portuguese.** The sixteenth century arrival of the Portuguese traders was commemorated by Japanese artists in several paintings that have survived. This one shows a large group of Westerners in what must have been outlandish costumes to the host's eyes.

of the Tokugawa period. The closing off of trade with foreigners apparently stimulated internal production, rather than discouraged it, and domestic trade rose accordingly. The internal peace imposed by the powerful and respected government of the shogunate certainly helped. The daimyo aristocracy had an ever increasing appetite for fine wares such as silk and ceramics, and their fortress-palaces in Edo and on their domains reflected both their more refined taste and their increasing ability to satisfy it.

The *merchants,* who previously had occupied a rather low niche in Japanese society (as in China) and had never been important in government, now gained a much more prominent place. Formerly, the guilds had restricted access to the market, but the early shoguns forced them to dissolve, thereby allowing many new and creative actors to come onto the entrepreneurial stage. Even so, the merchants as a class were still not as respected as government officials, scholars, and especially the daimyo and their samurai. Nevertheless, the merchants' growing wealth, which they often lent to impoverished samurai, began to enhance their prestige. A money economy gradually replaced the universal reliance on barter in the villages. Commercialization and distribution networks for artisans invaded the previously self-sufficient lifestyle of the countryfolk. Banks and the use of credit became more common during the later Tokugawa period, and some historians see the growth of a specifically Japanese form of capitalism long before Japan's entry into the world economic system in the nineteenth century.

Peasants and Urbanites

The *peasants,* who, of course, still made up the vast majority of the population, received a good deal of formal respect and protection from exploitation from the Tokugawa government. Agriculture was always considered the most honorable of occupations, but the government's taxes were heavy, taking up to 60 percent of the rice crop. In the later years, the increasing misery of the peasants led to many rebellions against the local daimyo who were their landlords, but these revolts were on a much smaller scale than those that would trouble Manzhou China in the same nineteenth century epoch.

Cities grew rapidly during the first half of the Tokugawa period, more slowly later. Both Osaka and Kyoto were estimated to have more than 400,000 inhabitants in the eighteenth century, and Edo perhaps as many as one million. All three cities were bigger than any town in Europe at that date. The urban population ranged from very rich daimyo and merchants at the top, through many tens of thousands of less fortunate traders, shopkeepers, and officials of all types in the middle, and many hundreds of thousands of skilled and unskilled workers, casual laborers, beggars, prostitutes, artists, and most of the samurai at the bottom. Most Japanese, however, still lived

■ **Samurai, Mounted and Afoot, 1688.** This portrait clearly shows the weaponry of the samurai, including the muskets which had entered the country with the Portuguese a century earlier. Compare the warriors appearance with that of the armored figure in Chapter 23.

as before in small towns and villages; they depended on local farming, timbering, or fishing for their livelihood and were in only occasional and superficial contact with the urban culture. Until the late twentieth century, the rhythms of country life and rice culture were the dominant influence on the self-image and the lifestyle of the Japanese people.

❧ TAMING THE SAMURAI

In the seventeenth and eighteenth centuries, the samurai caste, which had been the military servants of the wealthy daimyo and their "enforcers" with the peasants, lost most of their prestige in Japanese society. Estimated to make up as much as 7 percent of the population at the establishment of the Tokugawa, the samurai had now become superfluous. With the establishment of the lasting domestic peace, there was literally nothing for them to do in their chosen profession, and they were neither allowed to adopt another lifestyle, nor could they bring themselves to do so after centuries of proud tradition. The Edo government encouraged the samurai to do what they naturally wished to do: enjoy themselves beyond their means. Borrowing from the merchants (and often repudiating their debts), the samurai tried to outdo one another in every sort of showy display. After a generation or two, the result was mass bankruptcies and social disgrace. The fallen samurai were replaced by newcomers who were finding they could advance through commerce or through the civil bureaucracy, which, as in the West, was slowly assuming the place of the feudal barons and becoming the day-to-day authority.

Like the European feudal knights whom they resembled in many ways, the samurai lost out to a new class of people—men who did not know how to wield a sword, but were good with a pen. Trained to make war and raised in the **bushido** code of the warrior, most of the samurai were ill equipped to make the transition from warrior to desk-sitting official of the shogun or a daimyo lord. Some of them did so, but the majority seem to have gradually sunk into poverty. Many reverted back to the peasant life of their long-ago ancestors.

❧ TOKUGAWA ARTS AND LEARNING

The almost 250 years of peace of the Tokugawa period produced a rich tapestry of new cultural ideas and practices in Japan. Some of the older ideas, imported originally from China, were now adapted so as to become almost entirely Japanese in form and content. The upper classes continued to prefer Buddhism in one form or another, with a strong admixture of Confucian secular ethics. Among the people, Shinto and the less intellectual forms of Buddhism formed the matrix of belief about this world and the next. Japanese religious style tended to accept human nature as it is without the overtones of penitence and reform that are so prominent in Western thought. As before, there was a very strong current of *eclecticism*, blending Buddhism with other systems of belief and practice.

Literature and Its Audiences

Literacy rates were always quite high in Japan and became still higher in the later years of the Tokugawa period, when perhaps as many as 50 percent of the males could read and write. This percentage was at least equal to the literacy rate in central and southern Europe of the day and was facilitated by the relative ease of learning the phonetic written language (in distinct contrast to Chinese, the source of Japanese writing). Literature aimed at popular entertainment began to appear in new forms that were a far cry from the elegant and restrained traditions of the past. *Poetry, novels, social satires, and Kabuki plays* were the foremost types of literature; by this era, all had liberated themselves from imitation of classical Chinese models. Several were entirely original with the Japanese.

Haiku poems, especially in the hands of the seventeenth-century poet Basho, were extraordinarily compact revelations of profound thought. In three lines and seventeen syllables (always), the poet reflected the Zen Buddhist conviction that the greatest of mysteries can only be stated—never analyzed. Basho's contributions in poetry were matched by those of Saikaku in fiction, also during the late seventeenth century. His novels and stories about ordinary people are noteworthy for their passion and the underlying sense of comedy with which the characters are observed. Saikaku's stories, like Basho's verse, are read today in Japan with the same admiration they have enjoyed for centuries.

Kabuki is a peculiarly Japanese form of drama. It is highly realistic, often humorous and satirical, and sometimes violent in both action and emotions. For its settings, it often made use of the "floating world," the unstable but attractive world of brothels, shady teahouses, and gambling dens. *Kabuki* was wildly popular among the upper classes in seventeenth- and eighteenth-century Japan, and it was not unusual for a particularly successful actor (males played all parts) to become a pampered "star." Actors were often also male prostitutes, just as actresses in

the West often were female prostitutes at this time. Homosexuality was strongly frowned upon by the shogunate authorities, but had already had a long tradition among the samurai and some branches of Buddhism.

Adaptation and Originality

In the *fine arts*, Japan may have drawn its initial inspiration from Chinese models, but it always turned those models into something different, something specifically Japanese. This pattern can be found in landscape painting, poetry, adventure and romance stories, gardens, and ceramics—indeed, in any art medium that both peoples have pursued. The Japanese versions were often filled with a playful humor missing in the Chinese original and were almost always consciously close to nature, the soil, and the peasantry. The refined intellectualism common to Chinese arts appeared less frequently in Japan. As a random

■ **Battles of the Hogen and Heiji Eras, Detail.** The strong resemblance and contrasts between Chinese and Japanese painting traditions can be seen in this detail from a large screen painting. The extraordinary precision of drawing everyday life, such as the woman getting her hair dressed, was common to both peoples.

■ **Himeji Castle.** This relatively late construction, known as the White Egret to the Japanese, stands today as a major tourist attraction. The massive stone walls successfully resisted all attackers.

example, the rough-and-tumble of *kabuki* and the pornographic jokes that the actors constantly employed were specifically Japanese and had no close equivalent in China.

The merchants who had prospered during the Tokugawa era were especially important as patrons of the arts. Again, there is a parallel with the European experience, but with differences. The European bourgeoisie became important commissioners of art two centuries earlier than the Japanese merchants and did so in rivalry with the nobles and church. Japan had no established church, and the bourgeoisie never dared challenge the daimyo nobility for taste-setting primacy. Nevertheless, high-quality painting and woodblock prints displaying a tremendous variety of subjects and techniques came to adorn the homes and collections of the rich merchants. In fact, much of what the modern world knows of seventeenth- and eighteenth-century Japanese society is attributable to the knowing eye and talented hands of the artists rather than to historians. Unlike the Chinese, the Japanese never revered compilers of records. There are no Japanese equivalents of the great Chinese histories.

❧ RESPONSE TO THE WESTERN CHALLENGE

In the later Tokugawa, the *main emphasis of Japanese thought shifted from Buddhist to Confucian* ideals, which is another way of saying that it shifted from an otherworldly emphasis to an empirical concern with this world. The Japanese version of Confucianism was, as always, different from the Chinese. The secular, practical political nature of Confucius's doctrines comes through more emphatically in Japan. The Chinese mandarins of the nineteenth century had little tolerance for deviation from the prescribed version of the Master. But in Japan, several schools contended, unimpeded by an official prescription of right and wrong. Another difference was that whereas China had no room for a shogun, Japan had no room for the mandate of Heaven. Chinese tradition held that *only* China could be the Confucian "Empire of the Middle"; the Japanese, on the other hand, while confident they were in that desirable position of harmony and balance, believed they need not ignore the achievements of other, less fortunate folk.

The significance of this Confucian secularism for Japan is that it helped prepare the ruling daimyo group for the invasion of Western ideas that came in the mid-nineteenth century. The Japanese elite were able to abandon their seclusion and accept whatever Western technology could offer them with an open mind. In sharp contrast to China, when the Western avalanche could no longer be evaded, the Japanese governing class accepted it with little inherent resistance or cultural confusion.

At the outset of the Tokugawa shogunate, the Japanese educated classes were perhaps as familiar with science and technology as were the Westerners. *Sakoku* necessarily inhibited further progress; the Scientific Revolution and its accompanying technological advances did not become part of the cultural landscape in Japan. From the early 1800s, a few Japanese scholars and officials were aware that the West (including nearby Russia) was well ahead of them in certain areas, especially the natural sciences and medicine, and that much could be learned from the Westerners. These Japanese were in contact with the handful of Dutch merchants who had been allowed to stay in Japan and occasionally read Western science texts. "Dutch medicine," as Western anatomy, pharmacy, and surgery were called, was fairly well-known in upper-class Japan in the early nineteenth century, although it did not yet have much prestige.

When the American **Commodore Matthew Perry** arrived with his black ships to forcibly open the country in 1853 and 1854, the Japanese were not as ill prepared as one might assume after two centuries of isolation. Aided by the practical and secular Confucianist philosophy they had imbibed, the sparse but important Western scientific books they had studied, and the carefully balanced government they had evolved by trial and error, the Edo officials, the daimyo, and their subofficials were able to absorb Western ideas and techniques by choice rather than force. Rather than looking down their cultured noses at what the "hairy barbarians" might be bringing, the Japanese had a strong tendency to adopt the attitude: "If it works to our benefit, (or can be made to), use it." Unlike China, the Japanese were decidedly not overwhelmed by the West. On the contrary, they would show themselves to be very confident adapters of what they thought useful to themselves, rejecting the rest.

Summary

The first European contacts with Japan were quite successful from the point of view of the European traders and missionaries, but quickly led to Japanese suspicions that the visitors wished to dominate their hosts. After Catholic peasants rebelled against their overlords, the missionaries were banned, and the Christian religion persecuted as a threat to traditional values.

After a century of unchecked feudal warfare, three strongmen arose in the late sixteenth century to re-create effective centralized government. Last and most important was Tokugawa Ieyasu, who crushed all opposition.

By the 1630s, Japan was rapidly isolating itself from the world under the Tokugawa shogunate. In this variant of feudalism, the daimyo nobility were carefully controlled by the shogun in Edo who ruled from behind the imperial throne. Social changes took place while the feudal political structure remained immobile. While merchants rose in the socioeconomic scale, the samurai (professional warriors) slowly declined.

Overall, the lengthy Tokugawa period was a success for Japan despite its self-imposed isolation (*sakoku*), which was maintained until the 1850s. Population surged and the general economy prospered. The arts, particularly literature and painting, flourished. A small but vital intellectual elite kept in touch with the "Dutch learning" and the outer world. When Perry's expedition broke into Japan's solitude in 1853, the elite were ready to deal with the challenge of Western science and technology in a constructive manner.

Test Your Knowledge

1. The Tokugawa shogun is best described as a
   a. military dictator.
   b. military adviser to the emperor.
   c. chief of government under the supposed supervision of the emperor.
   d. symbolic and religious leader under the emperor's supervision.
2. The early Christian missionaries to Japan
   a. found a very hostile reception.
   b. were mainly Protestants.
   c. made the mistake of trying to conquer the Buddhist natives.
   d. were made welcome and given a hearing.
3. The Shinto faith is best described as
   a. the native Japanese religion.
   b. the Japanese Holy Scripture.
   c. a mixture of Christianity and Japanese pagan belief.
   d. a variety of Buddhism imported from Korea.
4. The government system created by the shoguns in the 1600s
   a. gave ultimate power to the local chieftains called daimyo.
   b. was an imitation of the Chinese system of mandarin officials.
   c. made the daimyo dependent upon the central government.
   d. used the emperor as military chief while the shoguns ruled all else.
5. Which of the following did *not* occur during the Tokugawa period?

a. Japanese thought shifted from Buddhist to Confucian patterns.
b. Japanese formal culture stagnated in its continued isolation from the world.
c. Trade and economic activity generally increased.
d. Internal peace and order were effectively maintained.

6. The *kabuki* drama
   a. specialized in dreamy romantic comedies.
   b. was limited in appeal to the samurai and daimyo.
   c. depicted daily life in a realistic, humorous way.
   d. was an import from China.

7. The reduction of the samurai's influence in public affairs was

a. carried out through government-ordered purges.
b. attempted, but not achieved during the shogunate period.
c. achieved by eliminating internal warfare through a strong government.
d. achieved by encouraging them to become merchants and landlords.

8. Which of the following art forms was an authentic Japanese invention?
   a. Woodblock printing
   b. Kabuki theater
   c. Nature poetry
   d. Weaving of silk tapestry

Identification Terms

bushido

Edo and Kyoto

Haiku

Hideyoshi (Toyotomi)

kabuki

Nobunaga (Oda)

Perry (Commodore Matthew)

Tokugawa (Ieyasu)

Bibliography

Akutagawa, R. *Rashomon and Other Stories,* 1959. A twentieth-century storyteller re-creates medieval Japanese society, including the sketch that served as the basis for the famous movie.

Beasley, W. G. *A Modern History of Japan,* 1973.

Berry, M. E. *Tokugawa Ieyasu,* 1982. A biography of the maker of the Japanese state.

Boxer, C. R. *The Christian Century in Japan, 1549–1650,* 1951, and R. N. Bellah, *Tokugawa Religion: The Values of Pre-Industrial Japan,* 1957, are good treatments of opposing religious viewpoints in premodern Japan.

Cooper, M., ed. *They Came to Japan,* 1981. A series of pieces about Japan and the Japanese by European visitors.

Dunn, C. J. *Everyday Life in Traditional Japan.* 1969. A vivid discussion of social habits and groups in Tokugawa Japan. Highly recommended for giving a "feel" of Japanese lifestyle.

Endo, S. *The Samurai,* 1984. An exciting novel of seventeenth-century Japan and the Franciscan priests who journeyed there to establish trading relations and win converts.

Henderson, H. *An Introduction to Haiku: An Anthology of Poems and Poets from Basho to Shiki,* 1977.

Hibbitt, H. *The Floating World in Japanese Fiction,* 1982. A revealing analysis of the world of *kabuki.*

Keene, D. *An Anthology of Japanese Literature,* 1955, and *Japanese Literature: An Introduction to Western Readers,* 1953. Keene has written a series of very helpful introductions to Japan's literature and these are especially good. More specialized is his *World within Walls: Japanese Literature of the Pre-Modern Era, 1600–1867,* 1973.

Mason, P. *Japanese Art,* 1993. A good review for the thoughtful student. J. E. Kidder, Jr., *The Art of Japan,* 1985, is beautifully illustrated.

Morris, I., trans. *The Life of an Amorous Woman and Other Writings by Ihara Saikaku,* 1977.

Reischauer, E. *Japan: The Story of a Nation,* 1990. A highly readable general history, as is the book by C. Schirokauer mentioned in the bibliography to Chapter 40.

Varley, H. P. *Japanese Culture: A Short History,* 1981.

CHAPTER 42

THE MUSLIM WORLD TO THE END OF THE EIGHTEENTH CENTURY

1200s–mid 1300s	Mongol empire
1300s–1500s	Ottoman Empire expands and flourishes
1500s–1722	Safavid empire in Persia
1500s–mid 1800s	Mughal empire in India
later 1600s	Ottoman decline begins

While Europe was slowly finding its way from feudal disintegration to modern statehood, and East Asian governments were experiencing challenges from both external and internal rivals, the world of Islam in Asia and Africa was undergoing enormous upheavals. Like the East Asian civilizations, the Islamic world did not have a Middle Age. Instead a series of intrafaith wars wracked the West Asian centers of Islamic civilization and contributed much to its slow decline.

In Chapter 16, we looked at the rapid rise of Islam in the tropical zone between Spain and India. Within a remarkably few decades, the Arab Bedouin armies carried the message of Muhammed the Prophet from Mecca in all directions on the blades of their conquering swords. The civilization created by this message and conquest was soon a mixture of Arab, Greek, Persian, Egyptian, Spanish, and others—the most cosmopolitan civilization in world history.

In the thirteenth century, the capital city of Islam was still Baghdad in Iraq, although various segments of the faithful had long since broken off in both a governmental and doctrinal sense. In that century, the Mongols swept into the Islamic heartland in Southwest Asia, devastating all in their path and establishing brief sway over half the world. After their disappearance, the Ottoman Turks gave the faith of the Prophet a new forward thrust. By the later 1400s, the Ottomans had captured Constantinople and were reigning over enormous territories reaching from Gibraltar to Persia. Farther east, the Safavids in Persia and the Mughals in India established Muslim dynasties that endured into the modern age.

❖ THE MONGOL WORLD IMPERIUM

Ethnically speaking, Islam's origins were Arabic and Persian. The Bedouins who conquered Persia in the 640s were quickly absorbed by the much more sophisticated and numerous Persians. Unlike the Arabs, the Persians had long been accustomed to serving as rulers and models for others, and they reasserted those talents after mass conversion to Islam. For two centuries, the message of the Qur'an came through an Arab-Persian filter. In the 900s the religion and culture began to be dominated by a new ethnic group, the Turkic peoples. In the next centuries, the Seljuks who initially took over the Baghdad caliphate and their Mongol successors gave Islam a Turco-Mongol cast that it retained for centuries.

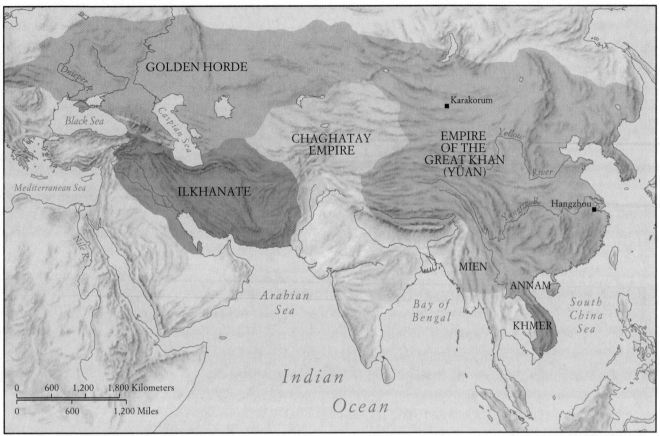

● **MAP 42.1   The Mongol Empire in 1255.** In the early 1200s, Chinghis Khan created the most vast empire ever seen. His sons and grandsons expanded the empire after his death in 1227. Excepting India and the far southeast, almost all of Asia and eastern Europe was under Mongol sway.

The Conquering Khans

The Mongol invasion of what the West calls the Middle East began in the early thirteenth century under the leadership of the fierce Temujin, better known to history as *Chinghis Khan* (1167–1227) (see the Biography in this chapter). As Chapter 17 described, by the mid-thirteenth century, the Mongols had amassed the *largest land empire ever created,* extending from Korea to the Danube in eastern Europe (see Map 42.1).

Everywhere, the invaders distinguished themselves by their exceptional bloodthirstiness toward those who resisted, and everywhere they were despised as cultural inferiors. This was particularly true in China, but also in the Christian and Muslim lands they overran. Many of the conquered territories had been under Persian Muslim rule for centuries and had developed a highly civilized lifestyle.

Cities such as Samarkand, Bokhara, Herat, and Baghdad itself suffered terrible devastation, and some never recovered their former wealth and importance.

The Mongols believed that their great spirit-god, Tengri, had commanded them to conquer the world, and they came very close to doing so. Neither Christians nor Hindus nor Buddhists were able to stop them, and only their defeat at *Ain Jalut,* near Nazareth in Palestine, by an Egyptian commander saved the remaining Muslim lands. Coming two years after the Mongol conquest of Baghdad in 1258, this victory revived Muslim resistance and is one of the handful of truly *decisive battles of world history.*

Along with the destruction they brought, the Mongol hordes also opened some notable possibilities for the traders and merchants among the peoples they had conquered. For about a century, the *pax Mongolica* (peace of

Chinghis Khan
1167–1227

If one measures greatness by area, there can be no doubt at all as to who is the greatest ruler in world history. It is the illiterate son of a twelfth-century Mongol who was named Temujin, but adopted the title of Chinghis Khan in later life. Before his death in 1227, he had come to rule a vast territory from the south Russian steppes to the China Sea. His sons and successors expanded the Mongol empire even farther, until it was easily the largest the world has ever seen.

Temujin was born about 1167 and had to struggle almost from birth against harsh competitors in a harsh land. Mongolia at this time was the home of primitive nomads who warred against one another continuously when they were not assaulting the richer lands of the Chinese and Koreans. By 1200 Temujin had established his claim by right of conquest to be the leader of a confederation of several tribes. A few years later in his capital at Karakorum, he accepted the title of Great King (Chinghis Khan) of the Mongols and imposed a tight military order upon his several hundreds of thousands of followers.

The prime advantage of the Mongols was their ability to cover long distances more rapidly than any of their enemies. Virtually living on their small, hardy ponies, the Mongol warriors combined the tactic of surprise with an uncanny accuracy with the bow and arrow and the ability to use massed cavalry against their mainly infantry opponents. The Mongols would bypass walled strongholds where the cavalry charge would be ineffective and starve them into submission by controlling the surrounding countryside.

Using these tactics, Chinghis Khan conquered much of north China in only two years (1213–1215), then turned west against the Turks and Persians. By his death, all of what is now Central Asia and western Siberia was under Mongol rule. Proud cities such as Bokhara, Samarkand, and Herat, all centers of a high Muslim civilization, were overwhelmed after desperate resistance and their populations massacred or led into slavery. Mosques were turned into stables, and libraries burned. Never had such destruction been seen, and word of an approaching Mongol army was sometimes enough to cause wholesale flight. Russia was spared for a few more years only by the death of Chinghis Khan, which necessitated a great conclave of the other Mongol chieftains.

Chinghis Khan had ruled by installing members of his family in positions of command as he fought his way into western Asia. His sons and grandsons succeeded him and divided the huge empire among themselves. The richest part, China, went to Kubilai Khan, the host of Marco Polo. Gradually, the wild Mongols came to see that the arts of civilized life brought greater rewards than the practice of terror on defenseless subjects. By the later 1200s, many of them had adopted either the Chinese lifestyle as the rulers of that nation or had joined with their Turkic allies to adopt the Muslim religion and Islamic civilization. The vast empire founded by Chinghis Khan broke into pieces by the later 1300s, but not before it had given the world a name that would always strike terror into the hearts of the civilized.

the Mongols) extended for many thousands of miles, all under the supervision of the Great Khan and the relatives and clan leaders he appointed as his subordinates from his headquarters in Karakorum. Goods could be safely transported from the coast of China to the towns of the eastern Mediterranean, so long as a tribute or tax was paid to the khan's agents. It was the first and only time that all of mainland Asia (except southern India) was under the rule of a single power, and a few areas and cities prospered to an unprecedented degree as a result.

Fragmenting Empire

The Mongols had five Great Khans in the 1200s, beginning with Chinghis and ending with the death of Kubilai Khan in 1294; after that the segments of the huge empire went their own ways. The primitive nomadic culture and the Mongols' approach to government (exploitation through conquest) would have made it difficult to maintain their vast empire under a single center, even if much better communications and a much larger pool of loyal officials had been available. Since they were not, the original conquest soon broke up. First China, then Russia and the Middle Eastern lands separated from one another under subkhanates with their own interests. Successive intra-Mongol fights for regional supremacy after 1280 further weakened the power of the dynasty.

The second and third generations of Mongol rulers were more sensitive to their subjects' needs and expectations and included some exceptionally able men. Their adoption of one or another of the three competing religions of Asia also enhanced their prestige for a time at least. *Kubilai Khan* (r. 1260–1294), the host of Marco Polo and the introducer of many new ideas into the closed Chinese universe, favored Buddhism. One of the Middle Eastern khans adopted the Muslim faith in the 1290s and simultaneously began the revival of Persian power and prestige. The Russian-based Mongols (the "Golden Horde") also adopted Islam in the late 1200s, but their conversion had no influence on the Russian people, who remained steadfast in their Eastern Orthodox Christianity.

Gradually, the Mongols' far more numerous Christian (Russia, Near East), Muslim (Middle East, India), and Buddhist (China, Tibet) subjects began to make their presence felt, as they civilized and absorbed their conquerors. By the mid-1300s, the empire was disintegrating into its preconquest component parts, and rebellions against Mongol rulers were multiplying. In China and Persia first (late 1300s), then the Near East and Russia (1400s), Mongol rule became a bad memory, and the former rulers

were either absorbed into the subject populations or retired back into their desolate Central Asian homelands.

✦ THE OTTOMAN TURKS

The Mongols had smashed the Persian center of Islam in the 1250s, leaving the caliph himself as one of the victims in Baghdad. At this time, the all-conquering intruders intended to wipe out the rest of the Islamic states reaching westward to Spain. One of these was the Ottoman principality in what is now Turkey, which took full advantage of the Mongols' defeat at Ain Jalut to maintain its independence.

The Ottomans (the name comes from Osman, their first chieftain) originated as a frontier force, guarding central Turkey from the Greek Christians across the straits in Constantinople. Having converted to Islam in the 1200s, they were famed as fanatical warriors for the *jihad* (holy war against the infidel). By the 1300s, they had established a beachhead in Europe against the weakening Greeks, while simultaneously taking advantage of the destruction of Baghdad and its caliphate to assert themselves as a new dynasty of *sultans* (protectors).

After several failed attempts to capture Constantinople, the great fortress city of the Christians on the western side of the narrow waterway separating Europe from Asia, Sultan Mehmed the Conqueror succeeded in taking his prize. A long siege weakened the defenders' resistance, and the sultan's new bronze cannon destroyed the walls. In 1453, the city finally surrendered. By then present-day Serbia, Bulgaria, and Greece had also fallen to the Ottoman forces. By the mid-1500s, Hungary, Romania, southern Poland, and southern Russia had been added to the sultan's domain, while in North Africa and the Middle East all the Islamic states from Morocco to Persia had accepted his overlordship (see Map 42.2). At this stage, Ottoman military power was unmatched in the world.

Ottoman Government

The apex of Ottoman glory was reached in the reign of **Suleiman the Magnificent**, a sixteenth-century sultan whose resources and abilities certainly matched any of his fellow rulers in an age of formidable women and men (Elizabeth of England, Akbar the Great in India, and Ivan the Terrible in Russia). The government he presided over was composed of the "ruling institution" and the "religious institution." At the head of both stood the sultan. The ruling institution was what we would call the civil government, composed of various levels of officials from

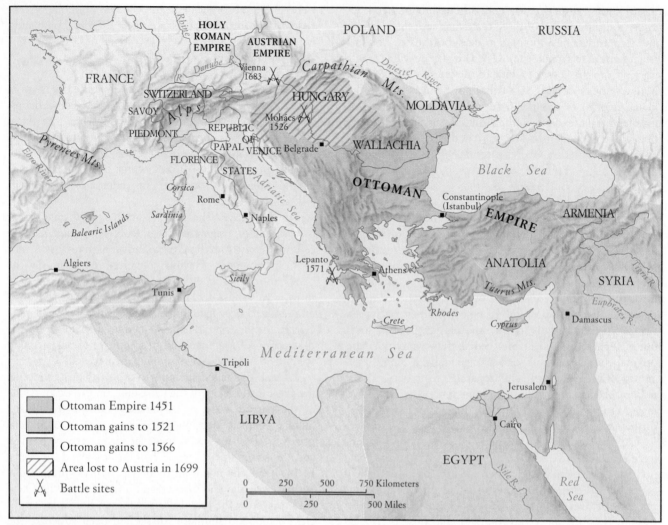

⦿ MAP 42.2 Ottoman Empire's Growth and Decline. At its peak in the later 1500s, the domain of the sultan in Istanbul reached from the Persian Gulf to the Atlantic Ocean. For a short time, the losses in eastern Europe were counterbalanced by advances in the Middle East.

the **grand vizier** or prime minister down. Most members of the ruling institution were originally non-Muslims who had converted to the True Faith. The army, too, was part of the ruling institution.

The religious institution was parallel to the ruling institution. At its head (but below the sultan who appointed him) was the grand mufti; its members were collectively the **ulema** or learned men of the law, which was derived from the holy book of Islam, the Qur'an. The religious institution lent its great moral authority to the ruling institution; it was in effect a junior partner of the government bureaucracy. In the ordinary course of events, conflict between the two was unthinkable.

The Ottoman army was far in advance of the Europeans by virtue of its professionalization and discipline. At its heart were the well-trained and well-armed **Janissaries,** an elite infantry created by conscripting Balkan Christian boys at a tender age, converting them to Islam, and giving them unlimited chances to rise high in both army and government. Some of the most brilliant leaders of the Ottoman state in the sixteenth through eighteenth centuries were these willing slaves of the sultan (as they proudly termed themselves), recruited from the infidel.

The Ottoman state for many years successfully avoided the weakening of the central authority that was inevitable with feudalism by refusing to reward military service with land grants. Instead, the bulk of the standing army was a mobile, permanent corps that could be shifted about throughout the huge empire controlled by Istanbul. The soldiers received salaries paid by the central government and supplemented their pay with pillage taken from defeated enemies. Without local connections and rarely remaining very long in one place, the soldiers were loyal to the central government alone.

As long as the Janissaries, in particular, conformed to this ideal, the Ottoman governmental system operated smoothly and effectively. The provincial authorities obeyed the center or were soon replaced and punished. But after about 1650, when the professional army was able to obtain land and develop the connections to purely local affairs that landholding entailed, a lengthy period of decline commenced.

Non-Muslims under Ottoman Rule

The treatment of the non-Muslims varied over time. In the early centuries of Ottoman rule (1300–1600), official treatment of Christians and Jews ("People of the Book") was generally fair. They were distinctly limited in what we would call civil rights, could not hold office, could not proselytize for converts or bear arms, and suffered many other disadvantages. But they were not forced to convert to Islam and could run their own civil and cultural affairs on the local and even provincial level. They were taxed, but not excessively. Their public life was certainly far better than that of Jews or Muslims living under Christian rule.

The majority of the *Balkan population* was Orthodox Christian. Under Turkish rule, those peasants were almost always decently treated until the seventeenth century; they were allowed to elect their own headmen in their villages; go to Christian services; baptize, marry, and bury their dead according to tradition; and so on. Like other non-Muslims, they were more heavily taxed than Muslims, but were allowed to own land and businesses and to move about freely.

In the course of the seventeenth century, however, the condition of the Balkan Christians deteriorated badly for several reasons, including the central government's increasing need for tax funds, the increasing hostility toward all "infidels" at Istanbul, and a moral breakdown in provincial and local government. "The fish stinks from the head," says the old Turkish proverb; the bad example of the harem government in the capital was having effects in the villages.

By the middle of the eighteenth century, the condition of the Balkan Christians had become sufficiently oppres-

sive that they were looking for liberation by their independent neighbors, Austria and Russia. From now on, the Ottomans had to treat their Christian subjects as potential or actual traitors, which, of course, made the tensions between ruler and ruled still worse.

This is the background of the widespread Western conception of the Turks as perhaps the most inept of all the peoples who have ruled in Europe, a conception that is partially true at best. It applies only to the last century and a half of Ottoman dominion, when imperial rule had effectively broken down into a kind of free-for-all among crudely ambitious provincial authorities and their rebellious Christian subjects.

The Decline of the Ottoman Empire

Suleiman's reign (1520–1566) was the high point of the sultan's authority and also of the efficiency and prestige of the central government. Beginning with Suleiman's son and successor Selim the Sot, many of the sultans became captives of their own viziers and of the intrigues constantly spun within the *harem*. After 1603 the sultans began to allow their sons to be raised within the harem, where they were subject to every conceivable manipulation by scheming eunuchs and ambitious women. This practice proved highly injurious to official morale, and was one of the worst influences on government.

Nevertheless, the empire did not run straight downhill after 1600. Once every few decades, a dedicated grand vizier or a strong-willed sultan would attempt to reverse the decay. He would enforce reforms, sweep out the corrupt or rebellious officials in one province or another, and make sure the army was obedient. But then the rot would set in again. By the end of the 1700s, effective reversal was becoming impossible.

Besides the personal qualities of the sultan, several other factors contributed to the long decline:

1. *Economic.* Starting around 1550, the shift of European trade routes from the Muslim-controlled Near and Middle East to the Atlantic Ocean (and later the Pacific Ocean) was a heavy long-term blow to Ottoman prosperity. Equally, the influx of silver from the Americas undercut the value of the silver from Africa on which the Ottomans had based their trading and financial systems.

2. *Military.* After the 1570s, the Janissaries and other elite units were allowed to marry and settle down in a given garrison, which gradually eroded their loyalties to the central government and allowed them to become local

strongmen with local sympathies. Also, the Turkish cavalrymen were allowed to meet their heavy expenses by becoming landlords over peasant-worked domains (*ciftlik*), which encouraged the same erosion of loyalty to the Istanbul government.

3. *Technological.* From the 1600s, the Ottomans failed to comprehend how Western technology and science were changing. Increasingly, they found themselves unready when confronted in tests of power. They almost always responded by attempting to ignore the unpleasant realities. They failed to acknowledge or give up old ways when the situation demanded change. This characteristic was spectacularly apparent in military sciences, where the once-pioneering Turks fell far behind the West in weapons and tactics.

Strengths and Weaknesses of Ottoman Civilization

The strengths of the Ottomans are most evident during the earlier centuries of their rule, as one would expect, and the weaknesses later. But some of each are clear throughout. Aside from their military merits, their *strengths* included their extraordinary artistic sensitivity in literature, architecture, and symbolic imagery; a commitment to justice for all, no matter how weak; a tolerance for nonbelievers that was unusual for its time; and a literary language (Arabic-Persian in origin) that was truly an international bond as well as being the channel of a rich literature. In economic and administrative affairs, the Ottomans had a far more efficient tax system and better control of their provincial authorities than any European government of the fourteenth through sixteenth centuries. Unfortunately, these institutions were to weaken very much later on.

Among the Ottoman's *weaknesses* were a government that depended too much on the qualities and energy of one or two individuals, the sultan and the grand vizier; a theory of government that was essentially military in nature and needed constant new conquests to justify and maintain itself; an inability to convert the Qur'an-based *sharija* code of law to changing necessities in legal administration; a blind eye to the importance of secular education and to all types of technology; and an overreverence for tradition, which led to stagnation.

From the late 1600s on, the weaknesses of the Ottoman state in Europe rendered it prey to an increasingly aggressive West. First, the Habsburg dynasty in Vienna, then, the Russian Romanovs went on the counterattack against Turkey-in-Europe, driving back its frontiers step by step.

In the Napoleonic era of the early 1800s, the native peoples began to rebel until the Turk's domain was reduced to Bulgaria, Albania, and northern Greece. At that point, about 1830, the external attacks ceased only because the aggressors became wary of one another. The "Sick Man of Europe" was allowed to linger on his deathbed until 1918 only because his heirs could not agree on the division of the estate.

⚜ THE MUSLIMS IN PERSIA AND INDIA

In the sixteenth and seventeenth centuries, the **Sufi** and **Shi'ite** currents, which had existed within Islam for many centuries, became noticeably stronger. The Sufi minority sought a different path to God than orthodox Muslims; they believed in a mystic union with the almighty, sometimes achieved by long sessions of ceremonial dancing that induced a state of hallucination. The "whirling dervishes" described in nineteenth-century Western literature were Sufi devotees. Some of the Sufi of Central Asia adopted the theology of the Shi'ites, who reject all the successors to Muhammed who were not related by blood or marriage to him. In the eighth century, this belief resulted in a major split in Islam between the Shi'ite minority and the **Sunni** majority, who believe that the caliph, or successor to the Prophet, can be anyone qualified by nobility of purpose and abilities. From that original dispute over succession gradually emerged a series of doctrinal differences. Much Islamic history can be best conceived of within the framework of the rivalry between Shi'ite and Sunni.

The Shi'ites took over much of the Persian Muslim state and from that base made frequent wars on their Sunni competitors. In the early 1500s, a leader named Ismail succeeded in capturing Baghdad and made himself *shah* (king). Thus was founded the **Safavid empire,** which lasted for two centuries and was a strong competitor to the Ottomans, who were Sunni Muslims (see Map 42.3). This doctrinal and political rivalry was most vividly apparent in the early seventeenth century, and it reached its height in the reign of **Shah Abbas I** (r. 1587–1629), the greatest of the Safavid rulers.

Shah Abbas was aided in his conflicts with Istanbul by the European opponents of the Turks, who were then at the gates of Vienna. A number of foreigners occupied high positions in his government, as Abbas, like Akbar in Mughal India, strove to avoid favoring any one group within his multiethnic realm. His beautifully planned new capital at Isfahan was a center of exquisite art and artisanry, notably, in textiles, rugs, ceramics, and painting. The Safavid period is considered the high point of the

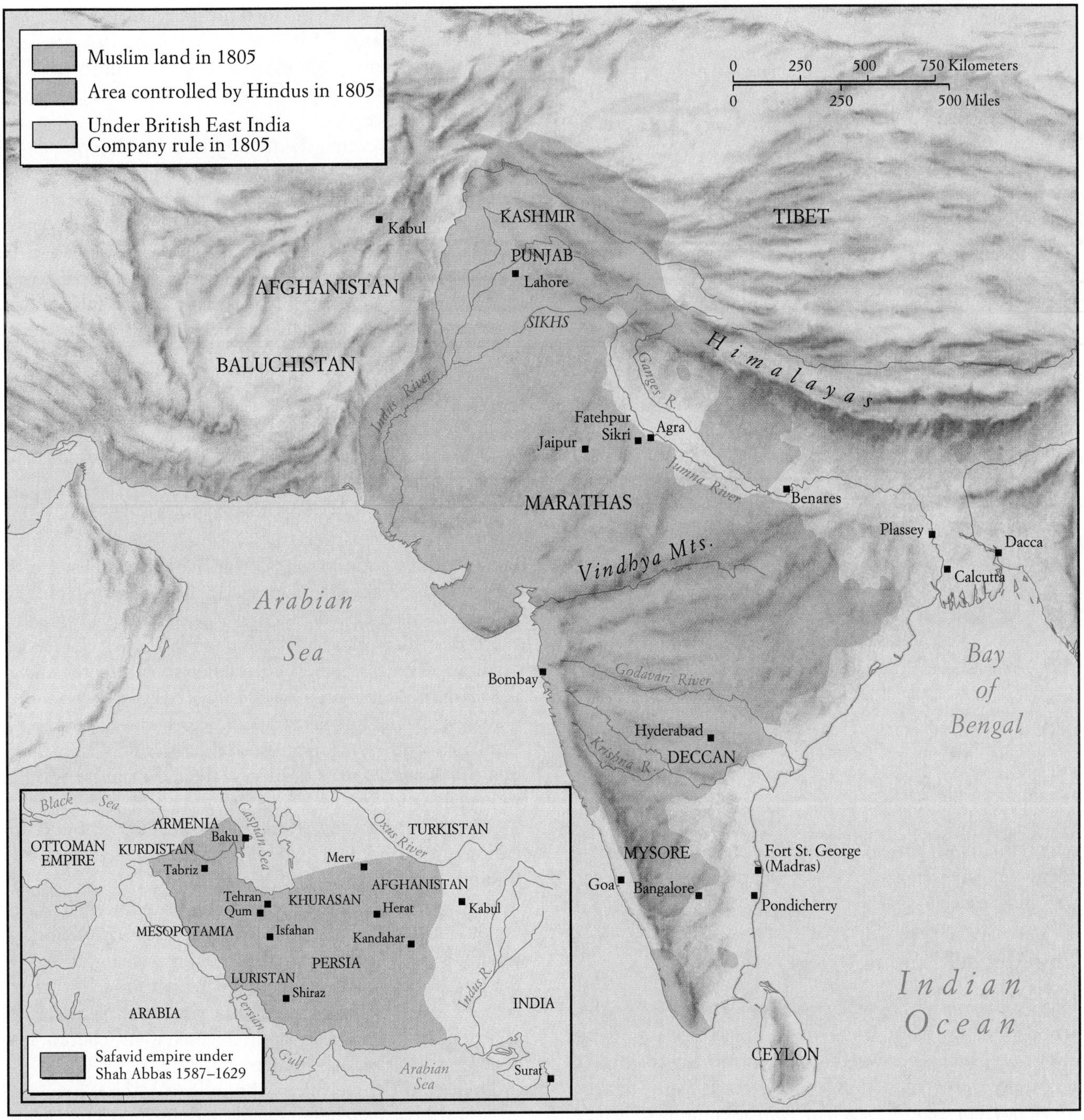
Muslim land in 1805
Area controlled by Hindus in 1805
Under British East India Company rule in 1805
0 250 500 750 Kilometers
0 250 500 Miles
Kabul
KASHMIR
TIBET
PUNJAB
Lahore
AFGHANISTAN
SIKHS
BALUCHISTAN
Himalayas
Indus River
Ganges R.
Fatehpur Sikri
Agra
Jaipur
Jumna River
Benares
MARATHAS
Plassey
Dacca
Vindhya Mts.
Calcutta
Arabian Sea
Bay of Bengal
Bombay
Godavari River
Hyderabad
DECCAN
Krishna R.
MYSORE
Fort St. George (Madras)
Goa
Bangalore
Pondicherry
Indian Ocean
CEYLON
Black Sea
ARMENIA
Caspian Sea
TURKISTAN
Oxus River
Baku
OTTOMAN EMPIRE
KURDISTAN
Merv
Tabriz
AFGHANISTAN
Tehran
Qum
KHURASAN
Herat
Kabul
MESOPOTAMIA
Isfahan
Kandahar
PERSIA
LURISTAN
Shiraz
Indus R.
ARABIA
INDIA
Persian Gulf
Safavid empire under Shah Abbas 1587–1629
Arabian Sea
Surat

◉ **MAP 42.3 Mughal and Safavid Empires.** Most of north and central India were under Mughal rule until the late eighteenth century, when losses to the Hindu Marathas and the English multiplied. The Safavids were crushed by Ottoman and Afgani attacks in the 1720s after two centuries of independent Shi'ite rule.

long history of Persia and the Iranian people. After Abbas, the empire slowly lost vigor and collapsed altogether in the 1720s under Turkish and Afghani attack.

It is worth noting at this point that, like the European Christians, the various subdivisions within Islam fought as much against each other as against the infidel. A common

■ **A Young Safavid Prince Reading.** This early sixteenth century portrait is an example of the harmonic balance of the Persian miniature painters of the Safavid era.

religion is rarely able to counter the claims of territorial, economic, or military advantage in the choice between war and peace.

The Mughal Empire

One of the most impressive Muslim empires was that founded in northern India by a branch of the Turks known as **Mughals** or **Moghuls.** The word is a corruption of Mongol, to whom the Turks were distantly related. Muslims from Central Asia had been attempting to invade India since the 600s, but had been repulsed by the dominant Hindus until the 1200s, when the *sultanate of Delhi* was established by an early band of Turks. Within a century, they controlled much of the Indian subcontinent.

But another onslaught of barbarians from Asia overthrew the Delhi rulers, and the petty Muslim principalities in northern India fought among themselves for a long time

before a leader emerged to unite them. That man was **Akbar the Great** (r. 1556–1605). Akbar was the greatest Indian ruler since Ashoka in the third century B.C.E. Indeed, he was perhaps the greatest statesman that Asia has ever produced.

Akbar has several claims to his title. He splendidly fulfilled the usual demands made on a king to enlarge his kingdom. Under his guidance, the Mughal empire came to control most of the subcontinent. Second, he completely reorganized the central government, developed an efficient bureaucracy to run it, and introduced many innovative reforms in society. Thirdly and most strikingly, Akbar practiced a policy of religious *toleration* that was most unusual in any part of the world. He himself was at least formally a Muslim, ruling a Muslim empire. But he allowed all faiths to flourish and to compete for converts in his lands, and he liked to invite the clergy of several religions to stage week-long debates, in which he actively participated.

Since Hindus made up the majority of his subjects, Akbar thought it particularly important to heal the breach between them and the ruling Muslim minority. His efforts met with very considerable success. He married Hindu princesses, and one of his sons by a Hindu eventually succeeded him. Hindus were given an equal chance at obtaining even the highest government posts. By repealing the high poll tax on non-Muslims, Akbar earned the gratitude of most of his subjects who had had to pay it. The sorrowful peace that existed between Muslim and non-Muslim at Akbar's death was the most sincere tribute to his character.

Midway in his long reign, Akbar decided to build an entirely new capital at Fatehpur, some distance from the traditional royal cities of Delhi and Agra. This palace-city is now a ruin, but its beauty and magnificence were famous throughout the Muslim world. The court library reputedly possessed over 24,000 volumes making it easily the largest collection of books in the world at this time. Akbar's love of learning encouraged sages of all religions and all parts of the Asian world to come to his court at his expense as teachers and students.

None of the three rulers who followed Akbar between 1605 and 1707 matched his statesmanship, and the last of the three, *Aurangzeb* (1656–1707), though a triumphant warrior, was responsible for *reversing the policy of toleration* that Akbar had introduced. This change, in turn, heightened the frictions between the Muslim ruling class and their Hindu, Zoroastrian, Jain, and (a few) Christian subjects. Aurangzeb was a convinced Muslim, and he attempted to reintroduce a distinctly Islamic character to public life. Though his large and efficient army was too big to challenge directly, his rule set the stage for rebellion by the dispossessed Hindus against his weaker successors.

Mughal Culture and Society

Most Indians, whether Muslim or Hindu, were village-dwelling farmers. Most of them were free, but debt slavery was common enough. Cotton was already a major crop, thanks to the Europeans' growing demand for this light, tough fabric that could be dyed a variety of colors and easily cleaned.

India remained a hodgepodge of different peoples, as well as different religions and languages. Besides the civilized Indians, there were still many tribal peoples, especially in the jungled areas of the eastern coast, whom the Mughals did not consider fully human and often enslaved. Many foreigners, especially from the Middle East, came into the country to make their fortunes and often did so at the very luxurious and free-spending courts

■ **Ruins of Fatehpur.** Even after centuries of vandalism, the extent and beauty of the stonework still standing at the palace-city of Fatehpur is impressive. These buildings were built during the reign of Akbar the Great in the early sixteenth and seventeenth centuries.

of the Mughal rulers. The upper class took much pride in funding institutions of learning and supporting artists of all types.

The Muslims had an extensive system of religious schools, while the local brahmins took care of the minimal needs for literacy in the Hindu villages by acting as open-air schoolmasters. Increasingly, the Muslims used the Urdu language (now used in Pakistan) rather than the Sanskrit literary language of the Hindus.

After the Muslim revival led by Emperor Aurangzeb, the governing class was almost entirely Muslim again, and their habits of dress and manners were sometimes imitated by aspiring Hindus. A notable example was *purdah,* the seclusion of women, which was adopted by the upper castes of Hindus. Hindus remained monogamous, however, unlike their Muslim neighbors.

In the *fine arts,* the Mughals made a conscious and successful effort to introduce the great traditions of Persian culture into India, where they blended with the native forms in literature, drama, and architecture. The **Taj Mahal,** tomb of the much-loved wife of the seventeenth-century emperor Jahan, is the most famous example of a Persian-Indian architectural style, but it is only one of many. Much painting also survives from this era and shows traces of Arab and Chinese, as well as Persian and Indian, influence. By this time, the ancient prohibition against reproducing the human form was ignored by Muslim artists, and the wonderful variety of portraits, court scenes, gardens, and townscapes is exceeded only by the precision and color sense of the artists. The quatrains of Omar Khayyam's *Rubaiyat,* which have long been famous throughout the world, held a special appeal for

■ **Palace at Fatehpur.** The palace-city erected by Akbar the Great outside Delhi is now mostly ruins; it was abandoned soon after Akbar's death by his successor as Great Mughal. The lovely design and exquisite stonework are still visible in buildings like this, now cared for by the Indian government as national treasures.

The *Rubaiyat* of Omar Khayyam

Perhaps the most quoted poem in the English language is a nineteenth-century translation of a twelfth-century Persian philosopher, who may or may not have written the original. The *Rubaiyat* of Omar Khayyam is a collection of four-line verses that became associated with his name long after his death in 1122. Edward Fitzgerald, who had taught himself Persian while passing his days as a Victorian country gentleman, published them in the year 1859 in a very free translation. Instantly finding a public, the *Rubaiyat* was reprinted several times during Fitzgerald's life and many more since.

The poem speaks in unforgettably lovely words of our common fate. Death comes all too soon: in wine is the only solace. The verse story, of which only a fragment is given here, opens with the poet watching the break of dawn after a night of revelry:

1

Awake! for Morning in the Bowl of Night
Has flung the Stone that puts the Stars to Flight
And lo! the Hunter of the East has caught
The Sultan's Turret in a Noose of Light.

2

Dreaming when Dawn's Left Hand was in the Sky
I heard a Voice within the Tavern cry,
"Awake, my Little ones, and fill the Cup
"Before Life's Liquor in its Cup be dry."

7

Come, fill the Cup, and in the Fire of Spring
The winter Garment of Repentance fling
The Bird of Time has but a little way
To fly—and Lo! the Bird is on the Wing.

14

The Worldly Hope men set their Hearts upon
Turns Ashes—or it prospers; and anon,
Like Snow upon the Desert's dusty Face
Lighting a little Hour or two—is gone.

15

And those who husbanded the Golden Grain
And those who flung it to the Winds like Rain
Alike to no such aureate Earth are turn'd*
As, buried once, Men want dug up again.

■ **The Taj Mahal.** Perhaps the most perfect blend of architecture and landscape in the world, the Taj Mahal was erected by one of Akbar's Mughal successors as a memorial to a beloved wife.

Mughal poets, who attempted to imitate them (see the Document in this chapter).

Like the Safavids to their west, the Mughals were an exceptionally cosmopolitan dynasty, well aware of cultural affairs in and outside their own country and were anxious to appear well in foreign eyes. European travelers were welcomed. Like Marco Polo's reports about Kubilai Khan's China, the early tales of visitors to the Great Mughal were only belatedly and grudgingly believed. Such cultivation and display of luxury were still beyond Europeans' experience.

✣ INDIA'S RELATIONS WITH EUROPE TO 1800

In the expanding empires of the Safavids in Persia and the Mughals in India, the appearance of European explorers and traders during the 1600s did not create much of a stir.

18
I think that never blows so red‡
The Rose as where some buried Caesar bled;
That every Hyacinth the Garden wears
Dropt in its Lap from some once lovely Head.

19
Ah, my Beloved, fill the Cup that clears
Today of past Regrets and future Fears—
Tomorrow?—Why, Tomorrow I may be
Myself with Yesterday's Sev'n Thousand Years.

20
Lo! some we loved, the loveliest and best
That Time and Fate of all their Vintage prest
Have drunk their Cup a Round or two before,
And one by one crept silently to Rest.

21
And we, that now make merry in the Room
They left, and Summer dresses in new Bloom,
Ourselves must we beneath the Couch of Earth
Descend, ourselves to make a Couch—for whom?

22
Ah, make the most of what we yet may spend,
Before we too into the Dust descend;

Dust into Dust, and under Dust, to lie,
Sans Wine, sans Song, sans Singer, and—sans End!

23
Alike for those who for TODAY prepare,
And those that after a TOMORROW stare,
A Muezzin from the Tower of Darkness cries
"Fools! your Reward is neither here nor there!"

24
Why, all the Saints and Sages who discuss'd
Of the Two Worlds so learnedly, are thrust
Like foolish Prophets forth; their Words to Scorn
Are scatter'd, and their Mouths are stop'd with
Dust.

25
Oh, come with old Khayyam, and leave the Wise
To talk; one thing is certain, that Life flies;
One thing is certain, and the Rest is Lies;
The Flower that once has blown for ever dies.

*Aureate earth . . . ." means once buried, the body is no golden
treasure.
‡ The verb *to blow* means to bloom.

SOURCE: *The Rubaiyat of Omar Khayyam,* translated and edited by
Edward Fitzgerald, first edition, 1859. Used by permission of
Dover Publications.

Actually, the very first European explorers and missionaries in India arrived in the early 1500s, but they had had little interest in creating settler colonies. At that time, the European presence in India was limited to a relative handful of traders in a few ports such as Goa. They had no appreciable influence on Indian life.

The Portuguese were the first Europeans to arrive in India, but were followed by the Dutch, English, and French. By the end of the 1600s, the Portuguese areas had been absorbed by the English, while the Dutch moved on to easier pickings in Indonesia. After some skirmishing on the seas (demonstrating that no non-Western force could hold its own against the European navies), the Mughals had settled into a mutually comfortable relationship centered on luxury trade goods in both directions. The privately owned *British East India Company,* founded in 1603, was given monopolistic concessions to trade Indian goods to the West and bring in a few European items in return.

For a long time, the arrangement worked out quite harmoniously. The East India Company made large profits, and the members of the Mughal upper class were pleased with their access to European firearms, metal, and fabrics. Within the company's handful of port enclaves, all power over both Englishmen and Indians was vested in the English superintendent.

The arrival of the *French* in the 1670s put some strain on English-Mughal relations, as the French were already in competition with London for a colonial empire. Under the brilliant administrator Joseph François Dupleix, the French made an effort to enlist the Indians as allies, not just trading partners. The British then responded similarly. By the 1740s, the frequent wars between Britain and France involved their Indian outposts as well. On the

French side, Dupleix commanded tens of thousands of Indian troops; on the British side, **Robert Clive** was just as active. They fought one another even while the home countries were at peace.

In India as in North America, the *Seven Years' War* (1756–1763) was the decisive round in the contest. British control of the sea proved more important than French victories on land. By the Treaty of Paris in 1763, control of much of India fell into British hands through the East India Company. But Parliament was unwilling to trust such an asset to private hands; in 1773 a statute divided

political oversight between London and the company. In the 1780s, Lord Cornwallis (lately commander-in-chief of the British forces in Virginia) was put in charge of the Indian possessions of the British Crown, and he was followed by others who crushed the occasional Muslim and Hindu attempts to defy British power. Increasingly, those *rajahs* who did not obey London's wishes found themselves replaced by British civil governors. One after another, the many subdivisions of the subcontinent were incorporated into the British-ruled possessions.

Summary

The various Muslim empires and subempires that occupied parts of the Asian continent between 1200 and 1800 were able to hold their own with their Chinese, Hindu, and Christian competitors. Sometimes warring among themselves, they were still able to maintain their borders and prestige for two hundred to four hundred years before a combination of factors acted to weaken them.

After the terrible destruction rendered by the still pagan Mongols, the Muslims of the Middle East converted their conquerors and rebuilt. Chief and most enduring among their states were those of the Ottoman Turks and the Indian Mughals. The Ottomans profited from the destruction of Baghdad by the Mongols to erect their own powerful emirate and then claim the caliph's role by taking Constantinople (Istanbul) for their capital. Under a series of warrior-sultans, they extended their power to the gates of Vienna before weakening internally and being driven back in the 1700s. By the nineteenth

century, the Ottomans had become so weak that they were held upright only by the rivalry of their enemies.

For two centuries, the Shi'ite dynasty of the Safavids reclaimed grandeur for Persia and Iraq, where they ruled until they were brought down by the superior power of their Sunni rivals in Istanbul. The Mughals descended upon Hindu India in the early sixteenth century, and set up one of the few regimes in Indian history that managed to rule most of this intensely varied subcontinent successfully. For over two centuries, Muslim rulers and their majority Hindu subjects got along well enough, especially in the reign of the great Akbar. The wealth of India's exotic trade items lured European commercial interest from the early seventeenth century and stimulated British and French colonial experiments. By the end of the eighteenth century, Britain had turned much of India into its indirectly ruled colony.

Test Your Knowledge

1. Together the Ottoman, Mughal, and Safavid empires,
   a. extended from the Atlantic Ocean to Australia.
   b. included all of Asia except the Japanese islands.
   c. could be termed a united political territory.
   d. extended from the Atlantic to the Ganges River valley.
2. The Muslim rulers of the Safavid dynasty were
   a. the conquerors of Constantinople.
   b. the allies of the Mughals in India.
   c. a Persian Shi'a family.

   d. the first conquerors of Persia for Islam.
3. Shi'ite Muslims
   a. believe the leader of Islam must be descended from the prophet Muhammed.
   b. make up the largest single group of Islamic people.
   c. reject the prophetic vocation of Muhammed.
   d. believe the Qur'an is only partly correct.
4. The most universally revered of all the Indian Muslim rulers was
   a. Aurangzeb.

b. Akbar.

c. Ashoka.

d. Abbas.

5. The original objective of the British East India Company in India was to

a. study native customs.

b. control the spice and cotton trade with Europe.

c. conquer and convert the Hindus to Christianity.

d. colonize southern India for the British Crown.

6. A major source of internal trouble for the Ottoman rulers of the eighteenth and nineteenth centuries was

a. the spreading atheism of most of the Turkish upper class.

b. the professional military units called Janissaries.

c. the missionaries from Europe in the Ottoman cities.

d. the attacks from the Mughal empire of India.

7. Which of the following was *not* accepted by Ottoman theory and practice?

a. The precepts and prescriptions of the Qur'an

b. The function of the sultan as leader of the faithful

c. The favored situation of the Muslims over the non-Muslim subjects

d. The necessity to keep at least one major Christian ally

8. The treatment of non-Muslims in the Balkans under Ottoman rule

a. deteriorated sharply in the seventeenth and eighteenth centuries.

b. improved as the powers of the sultan diminished.

c. tended to become better the farther away they were from the capital.

d. depended entirely on the whims of the ruling sultan.

Identification Terms

Akbar the Great	Mughals (Moghuls)	Shi'ite	Sunni
Clive (Robert)	Safavid empire	Suleiman the Magnificent	Taj Mahal
grand vizier	Shah Abbas	Sufi	*ulema*
Janissaries			

Bibliography

Andric, I. *The Bridge on the Drina,* 1948, and other novels by this Nobel Prize winner tell more than any factual history of the Christian-Muslim interrelationship in the Balkans.

Basham, A. S. *A Cultural History of India,* 1975. Covers the entire Muslim period, before and during the Mughal epoch.

Bernier, F. *Travels in the Mogul Empire,* 1968. An account of a European's experiences in the mid-seventeenth century.

Hansen, W. *The Peacock Throne,* 1972. A fine general history of the Mughals, very readable.

Holt, P. M., A. K. S. Lambton, and B. Lewis. *The Cambridge History of Islam,* vols. 1 and 2, 1970.

Ikram, S. M. *Muslim Civilization in India,* 1964. A standard work on Mughal and other Muslim principalities.

Inalcik, H. *The Ottoman Empire: The Classical Age, 1300–1600,* 1973. A solid scholarly overview of the empire at its height.

Kinross, P. *The Ottoman Centuries,* 1977. Recommended for its many episodes and anecdotes that illustrate Turkish attitudes and origins.

Lewis, B. *Istanbul and the Civilization of the Ottomans,* 1963. Written by a renowned interpreter of the Muslim Arabic world.

Lewis, R. *Everyday Life in Ottoman Turkey,* 1971. Revealing and entertaining.

Lippman, T. *Understanding Islam,* 1992. A good survey of what Westerners can learn from Islam and the Muslim society.

Merriman, R. *Suleiman the Magnificent, 1520–1566,* 1944. Remains the best biography of this world-shaker.

Mujeeb, M. *The Indian Muslims,* 1967. Strong on Mughal culture.

Rizvi, S. A. *The Wonder That Was India,* vol. 2, 1987. A continuation of the well-known work by A. Basham, focusing on the Muslim Indians, especially the Mughals.

Saunders, J. J. *The History of the Mongol Conquests,* 1971. A straightforward account of the tremendous explosion caused by Chinghis Khan. D. Morgan, *The Mongols,* 1986, is more oriented toward the Mongols as people, throwing much light on their culture and habits.

Shelov, J. M. *Akbar,* 1967. A first-rate biography of the greatest Mughal.

Southern, R. W. *Western Views of Islam,* 1962. Enlightening on why the Western world paid little attention to the Muslims after the decline of their military powers.

AFRICA IN THE COLONIAL ERA

1650–1870	Height of Atlantic slave trade
c. 1800–1850	North Africa and many coastal areas brought under European control
1840s	Christian missionaries and explorers begin to move into interior
1880s–1914	Almost all Africa under European control
1880–1898	Mahdi rebellion in Sudan
1899–1902	Boer War in South Africa

Though different in practically every other aspect, Africa and Japan share one important similarity: their long sustained isolation from the European West, even after their respective "discoveries." For centuries interior Africa remained in an isolation that was less self-willed than the result of circumstance. Long after the Europeans had arrived on the coasts in the fifteenth century, they had penetrated very little into the enormous depths of the continent or into the interior life of the people. Slaving had a strong impact on African life in some places, but more often it seems, it did not. The African leaders dealt with the white traders on a more or less equal status, as the whites depended entirely on them to gather not only slaves, but the other exotic goods that the interior tribes produced for export. The Europeans established practically no settlements; their presence was limited to trading posts at wide intervals along the coasts.

Until about 1850, the Arabs and Moors remained the major external influence on sub-Saharan Africa, as had been true for centuries. After that date, the Europeans moved into Africa in an entirely new fashion, as missionaries and governors and, in some places, even as settlers. The previously unmapped interior was rapidly explored. By the end of the century, sub-Saharan Africa had been completely divided up into new European colonies, governed in the spirit of a New Imperialism. (Africa is usually divided into northern, western, southern, and eastern sections. The continent will be reviewed here accordingly.)

❦ WHY THE LONG DELAY IN COLONIZING AFRICA?

In contrast to the Americas and Asia, sub-Saharan Africa long remained free from outside interventions. The chief reason seems to have been the ability of the early Europeans to gain what they wanted without establishing extensive settlements or permanent relationships. What they wanted was slaves and a small list of exotic products peculiar to Africa, which were delivered to them by the local chiefs on the coast in mutually profitable fashion. The Europeans saw no persuasive reason to risk the dangers of a long journey into unknown territory to get what the coastal authorities would deliver—for a price. There was certainly profit enough for all.

The coastal chiefs possessed sufficient authority and knowledge of trading practices to deal with the newcom-

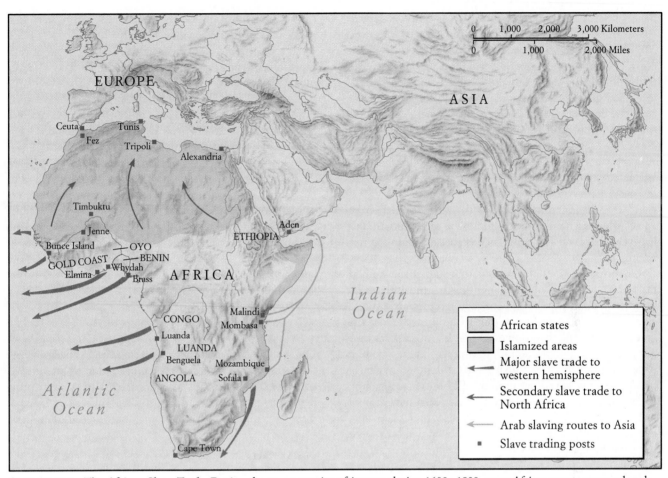

⊙ **MAP 43.1** **The African Slave Trade.** During the two centuries of intense slaving 1600–1800, most Africans were captured and shipped from west African ports across the Atlantic. But millions also went north and east into the Islamic areas.

ers as equals. The European traders did not simply overwhelm the Africans and seize what they wanted, at least not for more than a very short period. And for the entire four centuries of European trading contact with West Africa, the Portuguese, Dutch, British, and French were engaged in competition, which the native leaders at times manipulated to their own advantage.

Also discouraging settlement were the devastating *diseases* that were endemic in much of the interior. Fevers and infections that were unknown elsewhere were commonplace, and the interior was long known as "the white man's graveyard." Adding to the difficulties were the oppressively hot climate and the dangerous animals that ranged in huge numbers through most of the interior.

The *geography of Africa* makes traveling inward from the coast especially difficult. Thanks to the tsetse fly, spreader of "sleeping sickness," no beasts of burden are native to the southern two-thirds of the continent, and the wheel was unknown in sub-Saharan Africa when the Europeans arrived. The interior plateaus drop off sharply to the coastal plains, creating waterfalls that make river transport impossible in much of the continent. Only the Nile, the Niger in the west, and the Congo in the center are navigable for long distances into the interior. All three of these rivers were controlled by substantial states when the Europeans arrived, and the Nile valley was, of course, in Muslim hands.

The Slave Trade and Its Results

No topic in African history is as controversial as the extent and results of the trans-Atlantic slave trade (see Map 43.1). The latest figures, summarized in *A History of Africa* (second edition 1988) by the English expert J. D.

Fage, indicate that a total of *about 10 million human beings were exported from Africa to the New World* in the 220 years between 1650 and 1870, which were the high point of the trade. Another 3.5 million were involuntarily transported from Africa to the Near East and the Mediterranean in the same period. Assuming (on the basis of complex demographic research of the last generation) that the total population of sub-Saharan Africa in 1650 was about 75–80 million and that the population was growing at a rate about 1 percent per year (80,000), then the estimated annual loss through slaving in the peak years of the eighteenth century was about the same as the annual gain. The demographers believe that the population of Africa thus essentially stood still for the one hundred and fifty years between 1650 and 1800 before beginning to rise again.

Of course, these statistics do not mean that slaving had little impact on African populations or that the impact was uniform in all areas. Slaves were gathered primarily in two areas in West Africa: first, Guinea (the underside of the great bulge), and then somewhat later, Angola. In East Africa, where the trade ran northward by sea to the Muslim countries, the impact was still more narrowly focused on the areas that are now Tanzania and Uganda. In large regions of Central and East Africa, slaving was of little or no importance, either because the inhabitants successfully resisted it or because the populations were too small to offer an easy target for capture.

Beside checking the population growth in parts of Africa, the slave trade had other effects, but their precise nature is the subject of much debate, even among Africans. It is indisputable that some West African leaders (chieftains, kings, emperors) were able to reap a solid advantage for themselves and for at least some of their people from the trade. They accomplished this by becoming active partners with the whites in securing new human supplies and by using the proceeds of the trade in ways that increased their powers. In some West African states such as Dahomey and the Ashanti kingdoms (present-day Ghana and Nigeria), for example, the leaders traded slaves for firearms, which they then used to enhance their power and to gather more slaves.

On the other side, it is equally indisputable that slaving and the raids or local wars that it generated were a major cause of the chaotic bloodshed observed and condemned by nineteenth-century Europeans. Particularly in East Africa, where Arab traders had a free and brutal hand in obtaining human cargoes for shipment north, the slaving business resulted in not only massive misery for the captured victims but also the degeneration of a previously stable and prosperous village society.

There seems to have been a clear distinction between traditional African slaving practice, which was primarily meant to enhance the economic and social status of the slave taker, and the commercially driven exploitation practiced by both Europeans and Arabs in the modern era. Although the eyewitness **David Livingstone** may have exaggerated when he estimated in the 1860s that ten lives were lost for every slave successfully delivered to the East African coast, he was probably not too far off. The mortality rates of the trans-Atlantic trade were never quite so high due both to its more efficient organization and the emphasis on males to be used for labor, whereas the Arab trade emphasized females for concubines and houseslaves. Fage estimates 15 percent of those taken perished before landing in the New World; over time, this rate means that more than a million lives were lost.

✣ COLONIAL STATUS

The coming of the Europeans as political overseers rather than simply as coastal traders proceeded in different ways and at different tempos in various parts of Africa during the nineteenth century. The process can best be summarized by region and by governing country (see Map 43.2).

North Africa

In the 1830s, *Morocco* and *Algeria* fell under varying degrees of French influence. Morocco remained theoretically independent under its Muslim Berber king, who was supervised by a "resident-general" appointed by the French government in Paris. Less populous Algeria was made into a colony as early as 1847, and more than a million French eventually settled there. Algeria was the sole African colony where this type of intensive European settlement occurred until diamonds and gold were discovered in South Africa. The native Arabs and Berbers in Algeria were made into second-class citizens, subordinate to the French settlers in every way. Nearly the same process occurred later in neighboring *Tunisia*. Thus, by the later nineteenth century, the whole western half of Africa north of the Sahara (in Arabic, the *Maghrib*) was within the French orbit.

The rest of the Mediterranean coast of Africa was part of the dying Ottoman empire, but the Turks had had very little control over these lands for centuries and could not defend them from European ambitions. The Italians and

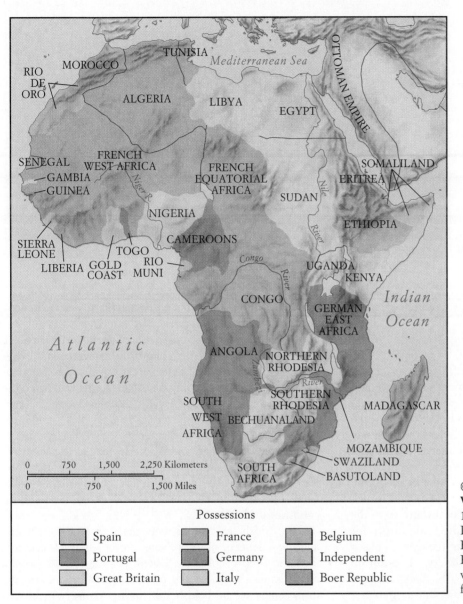

● **MAP 43.2 Africa before World War I.** Following the Scramble of the 1880s and 1890s all of Africa except tiny Liberia in the west and mountainous Ethiopia in the east was brought under European rule. The German possessions were given to either Britain or France following the World War.

Possessions

- Spain
- Portugal
- Great Britain
- France
- Germany
- Italy
- Belgium
- Independent
- Boer Republic

the British eventually divided the rest of the littoral, with the Italians taking over the (then) wastelands of *Libya,* and the British adding *Egypt* and the *Sudan* to their worldwide empire after 1880.

In all these lands, Islam was the religion of the great majority. As the Turks proved themselves unable to act effectively in the face of the Christian "infidels," Islam underwent a fundamentalist revival. Sometimes this revival took the form of armed rejection of the Europeans, most notably in the great **Mahdi rebellion** in the 1880s in the Sudan. The Mahdists were briefly able to set up an

independent state, and in 1885 they even beat off a British expeditionary force sent to punish them. Not until 1898 were they finally crushed by another British force armed with the forerunner of the machine gun. In the crucial encounter outside Omdurman, something like 11,000 Mahdists died but only 28 British! As the doggerel poem went, "whatever else under the sun, remember who has the Gatling gun." The Mahdi revolt and several other fundamentalist plots to throw out the alien whites are strongly reminiscent of the simultaneous Boxer Rebellion in China (see Chapter 51): in each case, as the existing,

■ **The Battle of Omdurman, September 2, 1898.** This engraving shows the British force under General Kitchener massacring the charging fanatics under the Mahdi's leadership. After the smoke cleared, the Mahdists had lost forty times the British casualties.

faltering government was overwhelmed by the foreigners and their hated ways, frustrated men desperately lashed out against them.

West Africa

From the early nineteenth century, the French were also the leading European influence in West Africa (the great bulge), with some British competition in the region of the **Niger River** basin (*Nigeria*) and the Gold Coast (*Ghana, Sierra Leone, Gambia*). In these areas, the slave trade had been the major occupation of Europeans and their African collaborators for centuries. After slaves were banned from British ships in 1807 and from British imperial territory in 1833, the slaving centers moved southward into the Portuguese colony of Angola. Here the trade throve for a time until the American Civil War removed a major destination and the abolition of slavery in Brazil in 1888 the most important one (the U.S. Congress prohibited the importation of slaves in 1808, but they continued to be smuggled into the United States until the Civil War).

In West Africa, the French and British, as well as the Portuguese, had gradually installed colonial systems during the late nineteenth century, as the slave trade was replaced by a new trade based on agricultural exports from Africa and imports of European metal, cloth, and weapons. The three European governments had somewhat different goals for their colonies and administered them in different ways arrived at by necessity and experiment rather than by plan. French possessions were administered from a central office in Dakar and were linked directly with the Paris government. The Africans were given little margin to govern themselves. Strong pressure was exerted on the upper-caste natives to learn French and acquire French manners and values. If they did so, they were considered "black Frenchmen and women." They could then enter the colonial bureaucracy and even become French citizens. Some effort was made to convert the Africans to Christianity, but it met with little success beyond some rote adherence to Catholic doctrine. Very little economic development occurred in these colonies, which were for the most part almost devoid of resources or blanketed by impenetrable forest. Only in this century have modern irrigation works made it possible to develop some agriculture in former French colonies like Mali, Chad, and Mauretania, which are still among the poorest countries in the world.

The British possessions were more favored by nature and experienced more private entrepreneurial activity than the French colonies. Several colonies (Gold Coast, and Nigeria) began as the private lands of a monopoly firm, similar to the British East India Company in India. Sierra Leone began as a refuge for free blacks from the British colonies and from intercepted slave ships after the maritime slave trade was banned in 1807. The British rulers, whether private or governmental, relied heavily on native chiefs to exercise actual day-to-day government under loose British supervision. This system of indirect rule, which was similar to what had been done in British India with the Hindu and Muslim *rajahs* and *nabobs,* was inexpensive for the home country and also gave ambitious natives at least some semblance of authority. Thanks to the palm oil resources and the introduction of commercial peanut plantations by the late nineteenth century, Britain's West African colonies were integrated into the world market and were the most sophisticated and prosperous of all the African colonies. Protestant missions were scattered about in the back country, but had no great effect on the prevalent animism and Muslim beliefs until the twentieth century, when they became substantially more important.

The Portuguese possessions (Guinea in the west, Angola in the southwest, Mozambique in the southeast) were the descendants of much earlier trading posts and were governed entirely from the home country. Natives were excluded from any participation in government and were treated solely as potential labor. As in the French areas, Catholic missions attempted to convert the people to Christianity and to educate the most promising. Enormous numbers of slaves were sent out to Brazil and the Caribbean for many years, and the attitude of the Portuguese administrators was highly influenced by this **Angola-to-Brazil trade.** The rubber and coffee plantations were run like the cotton plantations of the antebellum U.S. South, but without the occasional benevolent paternalism encountered there.

South Africa

The Cape Colony in extreme southern Africa was the other large area, along with Algeria, where whites settled in some numbers prior to the late nineteenth century. As far back as the mid-seventeenth century, Dutch emigrants had come to the Cape, attracted by the pleasant climate and good agricultural conditions. By the time the British took over in 1815 through the Treaty of Vienna, many tens of thousands of **Boers** (*farmers*), as the Dutch called themselves, were living there.

Having been entirely self-governing, the Boers resented British rule. In particular, they resented the British effort to extend the same legal rights to the Africans as were enjoyed by the white Boers. In 1836, the Boers marched northward away from the Cape in the *Great Trek;* once in the interior, they set up an independent state where they could continue the old ways undisturbed: the **Orange Free State.**

For a time, all went well, as the Free State and the British Cape Colony were far apart. British and Boers collaborated in eliminating the ancient Bushman (San) and Hottentot (Khoikhoi) hunter-gathers, pushing them into the Kalahari desert of the southwest. In another joint effort, they crushed the Zulu kingdom. But when diamonds and gold deposits were discovered in the 1880s, the old conflicts rose up again, as the British capitalists led by the redoubtable **Cecil Rhodes** pushed into Boer territory to develop mines and build railroads to serve them.

■ **Portuguese Soldier.** This bronze casting is a seventeenth century Benin portrayal of a Portuguese musketeer in armor and equipped with flintlock weapon. It is one of the few such which have survived to the present in the care of museums.

The result was the *Boer War (1899–1902),* won by the British after a bitter struggle. But the Boers still constituted the backbone of white settlements and commerce in South Africa, and the British had to make concessions to them to maintain a manageable colony. The chief concession, which would become increasingly ominous in the future, was to leave the Boers in control of the economic and social *apartheid* (segregation) that they had always maintained against the black tribal groups who far outnumbered them. The blacks were left with the choice of becoming laborers in the white-owned industries, mines, and farms or remaining in a precivilized, nomadic tribalism on reservations. Politically, the British maintained oversight of the colony from London and Capetown, but the Boers dominated in the *veldt* (rural) villages and towns and elected a majority of the colony's legislature.

Central and East Africa

In the center of the continent, the enormous *Belgian Congo* (present-day Zaire) was a royal plantation, held by a private firm in which the Belgian king held a majority share. Originally explored by Henry Stanley (of Stanley and Livingstone fame), the Congo, a vast area along Africa's second largest and longest river, was an important source of several industrial raw materials, especially copper and rubber.

The Congo resembled Angola and Mozambique in that very few Europeans ever settled there permanently. The main reason for claiming and keeping this jungled kingdom was to exploit its abundant material resources. A great scandal ensued in the early twentieth century when it was gradually revealed how cruel and greedy the royal Congo enterprise was and how little had been done to educate or convert the native peoples to Christianity. Despite many solemn proclamations that European rule would benefit the natives, the final judgment is spoken by a simple figure: the population declined by half in twenty years (1885–1905) of Belgian royal rule!

East Africa felt the most direct impact of the Arab traders who had long preceded the Europeans in slaving and other commerce in African goods. Coastal ports such as Zanzibar and Mombasa were busy for centuries and remained so until the abolition of slavery (1873) and the technology of the Europeans made it impossible for their Muslim Arab rulers to compete.

In these coastal regions, the Bantu tribes had developed a highly civilized lifestyle with an extensive trading network that reached into the interior. The ruling class was a mixture of Arab and African Muslims, while the great majority remained animists. These city-states were commercial in nature, and the illegal slave trade, oriented toward the Red Sea and Persian Gulf destinations, was active here into the late nineteenth and even the twentieth century. (It should be remembered that Muslim law and practice saw nothing wrong with slavery and the slave trade. The idea that slavery was evil was a foreign, Christian viewpoint that the Europeans gradually accepted and then imposed with their guns and officials on Muslim and animist Africans alike.)

✤ THE SCRAMBLE FOR AFRICA, 1880–1914

Except for the French possessions in North Africa, the Europeans did not attempt to disturb the network of tribal kingdoms that existed until the mid-nineteenth century in most of the continent. The Europeans knew no more about the interior in 1840 than their ancestors had known in the fifth century. Not even the basic geography of the river systems was understood, and the quest for the sources of the Nile, which lasted until the 1860s, is one of the great adventure stories of the Victorian era.

From the 1840s onward, this indifference and ignorance changed radically, as Christian missionaries became active in East Africa. The most noted of the nineteenth-century explorers of the interior of the Dark Continent were either missionaries like *David Livingstone* (see the Document in this chapter) or semiprofessional adventurers like *Richard Burton* and *Henry Stanley*. The search for the source of the Nile River was in large part responsible for opening the vast interior of East Africa in the 1860s and 1870s, while the exploration of the Niger and Congo basins did the same in West and Central Africa. Livingstone was the first European to be acknowledged as having crossed the entire African continent, though there is evidence that he was preceded by a half century by a Portuguese explorer. The British journalist Stanley, made famous by his well-publicized search for an allegedly lost Livingstone (1871), went on to become a major African explorer in the 1870s and "opened up" the Congo to colonial status as an agent of the Belgian throne.

By the 1880s, sufficient geographic information was known about the interior to allow the European nations to begin to stake definite claims. Belgium and Germany vied with the British in Central and East Africa. The Portuguese took Angola and Mozambique under firm control at this time. The French cemented their hold on West Africa and parts of the center. Italy took the area around the Horn of Africa and was repulsed when it attempted to add independent Ethiopia to the list. In 1885, all the major European states met at a conference in Berlin to delineate claims and avoid overlapping jurisdictions.

By 1900, all of Africa had fallen under European rule with the exception of mountainous *Ethiopia* and *Liberia,* the small West African country founded by liberated American slaves. No attention whatever was given to native custom or economic relations when the borders of the various colonies were drawn. Tribes were split, and ecological and economic units were shattered by the survey teams sent out from Paris, London, or Berlin. That this disregard for native traditions was a burdensome mistake became clear when the colonial system was dismantled after World War II.

At the completion of the "scramble," perhaps 175 million Africans were under European rule. In sub-Saharan regions, with the exception of some river valleys

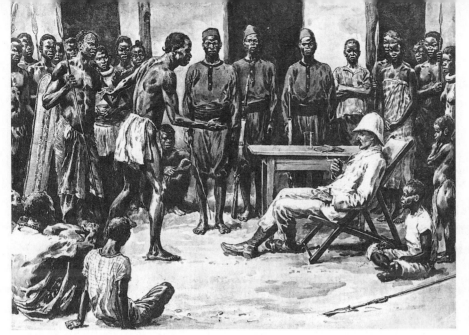

■ **The White Man's Burden.** This engraving from 1895 shows the European concept of civilized administration being brought to the Africans. A district official listens judiciously to the complaint before issuing his decision, backed up if necessary by the native soldiery in the background.

and coastal ports, this rule normally was of the most tenuous sort; huge areas remained unmapped and their populations-if any-were practically undisturbed by the new white chieftains. One of the first tasks of the overlords was to train a native constabulary under white officers to break up the ancient tribal wars and slaving raids. Another was the establishment of district offices, staffed often by young civil servants fresh from the mother country who were given extraordinary responsibilities in maintaining the peace and holding court. In the British colonies it was not unusual to see a twenty-seven- or twenty-eight-year-old, backed by his constables, given life and death authority over a district population of perhaps thirty thousand individuals. Direct challenges were rare; officers could move about freely without fear in the villages, though the nearest European might be a couple of hundred miles distant. Attacks, when they occurred, were almost always motivated either by the breaking of religious taboos or repeated cruelties by the Europeans.

✤ REACTIONS TO EUROPEAN DOMINATION

Although terribly outgunned (literally as well as figuratively), Africans did not passively submit to European overlords. Many African leaders sought to check or defeat the Europeans' encroachments during the nineteenth century. Among the notable struggles were the wars of the Zulu kingdom in South Africa, the fight against the Germans in Tanganyika, and the Ashanti resistance

against the British in the Gold Coast. But like the resistance of the Berber rebels against the French in Algeria and Morocco and the Mahdists in Sudan, these attempts were hopeless. The Europeans' superiority in weaponry and tactics generally won out rapidly and always did so in the long run. One reason was the Africans' fatal willingness to engage in battles in the open field instead of conducting guerrilla-style campaigns. Against the Gatling and Maxim guns and the European artillery, bravery alone was not enough.

Once conquered, the African elites had essentially two choices: to submit and attempt to imitate the manners and values of their new overlords, or to withdraw as far as possible from contact. In the French and British colonies, the native leaders generally chose the first way, encouraged by colonial administrators who sometimes had the real interests of the natives at heart. In the Belgian, Italian, Portuguese, and German colonies, the Africans generally chose the second way, as they were given very little opportunity to do anything else. In some cases, those who withdrew and remained committed to African tradition retained more prestige in the eyes of their people than those who associated with the conquerors and mimicked their manners. The majority, however, believed that the whites' ways were superior, and sought to associate themselves with those who provided access to them.

With the exception of the Congo and the Portuguese colonies, the natives were generally not treated brutally. Many young white males, stationed in the bush far from social contacts with their own race, took local mistresses

Livingstone in Africa

David Livingstone (1813–1873) was perhaps the most sympathetic missionary-explorer the native Africans ever encountered. A man of absolute principle and inherently decent, he delighted in trying to understand as well as convert his flock. His accounts of life in mid-nineteenth-century Africa are among the best of the many explorers' tales. In the following piece, which he wrote for a European audience, he allows an African "rain doctor" the best shots in an argument with a Christian medical doctor like himself on the question of who had the better chance of getting supernatural help.

MEDICAL DOCTOR: So you really believe you can command the clouds? I think that can be done by God alone.

RAIN DOCTOR: We both believe the very same thing. It is God that makes the rain, but I pray to him by means of my medicines, and, the rain coming, it is of course my rain.

M.D.: But we are distinctly told in the parting words of our Saviour that we can pray to God acceptably in His name alone, and not by means of medicines.

R.D.: Truly! but God told us differently. He made black men first, and did not love us, as he did the white man. He made you beautiful, and gave you clothing, and guns, and gunpowder, and horses and wagons, and many other things about which we know nothing. But toward us he had no heart. . . . We never love one another.

But God has given us one little thing, which you know nothing of. He has given us the knowledge of certain medicines by which we can make rain. We do not despise those things which   you possess, though we are ignorant of them. We   don't understand your book [the Bible], but we   don't despise it. You ought not to despise our little knowledge, though you are ignorant of it.

M.D.: I don't despise what I am ignorant of; I only think you are mistaken. . . .

R.D.: That's just the way people speak when they talk on a subject of which they have no knowledge. . . . You . . . may do without rain; we cannot manage in that way. If we had no rain, the cattle would have no pasture, the cows give no milk, our children become lean and die, our wives run away to other tribes who do make rain, and have corn, and the whole tribe would become lost . . . our fire would go out.

M.D.: . . . but you cannot charm the clouds with medicines. You wait until you see the clouds come, then you use your medicine, and take the credit. . . .

R.D.: I use my medicines, and you employ yours; we are both doctors, and doctors are not deceivers. You give a patient medicine; sometimes God is pleased to heal him by means of this medicine, sometimes not—he dies. When he is cured, you take the credit of what God does. I do the same. Sometimes God grants us rain, sometimes not. When he does, we take the credit. When a patient dies, you don't give up trust in your medicine, neither do I when rain fails. If you wish me to leave off my medicines, why continue your own?

M.D.: . . . The clouds usually lie in one direction, and your smoke goes in another. God alone can command the clouds. Only try and wait patiently; God will give us rain without your medicines.

R.D.: Mahala-ma-kapa-a! Well, I always thought white men were wise, till this morning. Who ever thought of making trial of starvation? Is death pleasant, then?

M.D.: Could you make it rain in one place and not in another?

R.D.: I wouldn't think of trying. I like to see the whole country green, and all the people glad. . . .

M.D.: I think you deceive both them and yourself.

R.D.: Well then, there's a pair of us! [meaning both are rogues]

Livingstone goes on to comment: "These arguments are generally known, and I have never succeeded in convincing a single individual of their fallacy, though I tried to do so in every way I could think of."

SOURCE: David Livingstone, Missionary Travels. Excerpted from Perham and Simmons, *African Discovery*, second edition. Northwestern University Press, 1963.

◼ **Railways of Lagos, 1909.** Colonial enterprise in Africa included an attempt to build a Cape to Cairo railway. This British line for transporting of peanuts was built with the labor of native Africans.

and sometimes became much more understanding and sympathetic toward African ways than their superiors in the capital. But anyone who allowed this sympathy to become noticeable ran a strong risk of being reprimanded or dismissed as an eccentric by his white associates.

Of the three types of Europeans with whom Africans now were in contact—merchants, administrators, and missionaries—the latter were most important for African culture. Missionary efforts at basic education in the native languages were responsible for the creation of a small group of educated blacks who came to look upon their own backgrounds as inferior, even primitive. These Africans were the first to be able to communicate in writing in their native tongues; they became the founders of national or regional literatures. A few were eventually sent to Europe for a university career.

These men (there was no education beyond the ABC's—and rarely that—for African females) became conscious of the gap between what the European liberals and intellectuals preached and what the governments practiced in their treatment of the colonial peoples. From their ranks in the early twentieth century were to come the *nationalist leaders* of Africa. They saw that the most telling critique of Western colonial practice was to be found in the classic ideals of the West itself. Like their Asian counterparts, they used the weapons that their Western education delivered to them to free themselves from a sense of their own inferiority and to lead their peoples to independence.

✦ Changes in African Society

By the early twentieth century, the Europeans had completely demolished the traditional division of lands and the commercial and cultural relations among the Africans. The old boundaries based on tribal and ethnic associations had given way to externally dictated boundaries based on European diplomatic agreements and horse trading. In the same fashion, traditional African power relations had been either destroyed or severely altered by the imposition of European-style officials, police forces, and courts, manned either by whites or by their satellite blacks.

Personal relations between masters and underlings varied immensely, sometimes even within the same empire. French officials and black subordinates generally got along well in West Africa, but badly in Central Africa, because of local variations in the French administration. In some instances, the whites and the black Muslim upper class got on well, but both were resented by the black

Dona Beatriz

c. 1675–1706

The kingdom of Kongo was the best-organized and most extensive of all the African states encountered by the Europeans in their early explorations. Extending many hundreds of miles on either side of the great river, Kongo encompassed most of today's Angola and much of the territory of Zaire. The Portuguese, who sent missionaries to the court of Kongo's powerful and wealthy king at the same time as Columbus's voyages to the Caribbean, were delighted at being able to report the conversion of the ruler they dubbed Afonso I (r. 1506–1543) to Catholic Christianity. Afonso collaborated closely with his Portuguese protectors and business partners in a rapidly expanding slave and luxury goods trade. He also was the founder of the only black African dynasty of Christian rulers, which lasted until the defeat and collapse of the Kongo kingdom in the later seventeenth century.

With Kongo's collapse, a variety of visionaries came forward, claiming they could explain why the once mighty kingdom had come to grief and how it could be restored. The most fascinating was a young woman known to the Portuguese as Dona Beatriz, who for two years (1704–1706) was a veritable Joan of Arc for her people. She founded a sect called the Antonians (for St. Anthony), which still has much influence in religious affairs in present-day Zaire.

As described by one of the Portuguese priests resident in Kongo, Dona Beatriz was "about twenty two years old. She was rather slender and fine-featured. Externally she appeared devout. She spoke with gravity . . . foretold the future, and predicted among other things, that the day of Judgement was near." Beatriz believed herself to be the living embodiment of a blend of the ancient animistic beliefs and the Christian religion in which she had been tutored. At the point of death from illness, she had felt St. Anthony (a popular saint among the Portuguese) enter her soul and revive her. He had instructed her to preach to her people, restore the kingdom of Kongo, and punish those who opposed her.

In the next two years, Beatriz succeeded in establishing a doctrine that combined elements of the Christian message with Kongo traditions of worshiping spirits and clan ancestors. She taught that Kongo was the Holy Land, that the founders of Christianity were Negroes, that Christ was born in the Kongo capital city of Sao Salvador, and that the Virgin Mary was the daughter of a Kongo notable. She gave up all earthly goods and lived among the poor, taking St. Francis of Assisi as her model. Her followers wore clothes made from the bark of a fig tree (*nsanda*), which Beatriz taught was sacred.

Antonian belief spread quickly, and the Portuguese authorities and priests took measures to squelch it. They attacked Beatriz as a false prophetess, a heretic who sought to mislead and defraud her people for her own ambitions. Although the priests had to admit that Beatriz was the "enemy of vices, superstitions, fetishism," she rejected the forms of the Catholic church in certain fundamental ways. For one thing, she denounced the use of the cross in church services because it had been the instrument of Christ's death. Europeans were threatened, and priests driven out of the country. Under her inspiration, "little Anthonys" ran rampant in Kongo, persecuting both blacks and whites who adhered to orthodox Christianity.

Beatriz's downfall came suddenly. After long hesitation, the Portuguese-supported king of Kongo, Pedro IV, came to believe she was more a rival than an ally in his struggles to restore his kingdom. Beatriz's claims to be a holy prophet were severely undermined when she gave birth to a child whose father she would not divulge. Mother and infant were arrested and subjected to an interrogation much akin to what happened to Joan of Arc three centuries earlier in France. Beatriz, too, was found guilty of heresy and condemned to death by burning at the stake. Her baby was at her side when the sentence was carried out on July 2, 1706. According to a witness, she died "with the name of Jesus on her lips."

non-Muslim majority who saw them both as exploiters. In colonies with large numbers of settlers, as in British Kenya and South Africa, the whites generally exploited their black labor and established an impenetrable "color line," regardless of central government policies.

Undermining of the Old Ways

Everywhere in the villages where almost all Africans lived, "the old ways" of the natives' culture and institutions lingered on, apparently almost untouched except for the handful of educated, Europeanized blacks. But subtle changes were under way beneath the surface. The tribal chiefs left in place by the Europeans no longer were backed by the universal assent of their villagers, who knew all too well that an unknown European official could overrule them at will. The tribal gods were no longer respected in the same fashion now that some of the tribe's youth were the product of Christian missionary schools. The white man's medicine could save lives that the tribal shaman's magic could not help. In these and other fashions, mostly unintended, the Europeans' coming as permanent overlords had a cumulatively erosive effect on the old ways. Many blacks found themselves adrift between the colonialists' preferred models of belief and conduct and the age-old traditions of African life.

At the beginning of the present century, though Christianity made a slight dent in African animism, the Islamic faith had far more prestige throughout the northern two-thirds of the continent. Urban life was still rare. The great majority of natives lived in villages or in pastoral nomadic societies. Their standards of living were simple, but they generally were not impoverished in any sense, and certainly not in the modern sense of having fewer material goods than was necessary to maintain a decent status in their neighbors' eyes. Illiteracy was nearly universal outside the Europeans' towns and the villages with mission schools.

Economic Changes

Africa proved to be much less an *economic* bonanza than the nineteenth-century imperialists had hoped. On balance, the home governments put at least as much into the colonies as they were able to take out. The hoped-for large markets for excess European industrial products never developed—the natives' incomes were far too small to absorb consumer goods, and it proved impossible to attract private investments into Africa on any scale comparable to what was going into the Americas or even Asia. Only a few of the West African colonies (Gold Coast, Nigeria, Senegal) with their agricultural specialty crops such as palm oil and peanuts were better than a break-even proposition for the home nations.

In a few colonies, the economic impacts on Africans were visible and direct. In British South and East Africa and in Algeria, whole districts were taken from the natives to be used exclusively by the whites. The blacks and Berbers were coerced into providing agricultural labor by the necessity of having to pay new taxes in money. The same system was used to force men to work in the mines; the "Kaffirs" of South Africa's diamond and gold mines were pressured into their dangerous and exhausting work by colonial governments dominated by local businessmen. Like it or not, the Africans were being steadily more involved in the Western-created, Western-dominated economy of trade and cash payments. These economic changes also undermined traditional lifestyles and beliefs.

Only in one or two special situations, notably the mines and rubber of the Congo and the precious stones and minerals of the Cape Colony, did the African bonanza materialize for the home governments and private investors. Cecil Rhodes, the British capitalist and greatest of the private empire builders of the nineteenth century, had envisioned a thorough Europeanization of Africa, driven by railroads and mineral wealth. By 1914, it was already clear that this would not happen, and a degree of disillusion had set in.

Summary

After a long period of isolation, the various regions of Africa experienced more or less the same fate in the later nineteenth century: they became satellites of the European world. Whether coming as explorers, administrators, or missionaries, the whites were armed not only with guns and steam engines, but also with a conviction of cultural superiority that made them irresistible to the politically fragmented and technically primitive blacks. In the three decades between 1870 and 1900, practically the entire continent was divided among the imperialist powers. The British and French took the lion's shares, while Belgium, Italy, Portugal, and Germany picked up smaller portions of varying size. But in general, the imperialist dreams of individual and national wealth from the new colonies were disappointed. Few of the colonies more than repaid the costs of administration.

The Africans superficially held on to much of their basic culture at the village level, even when they had lost all political control of their fate and were forced to provide unskilled labor for the whites. But this was deceptive; over the longer run, the Europeans' demonstrable capacity to work their will upon the traditional leadership eroded the latter's authority and the validity of what it represented. Western religion, education, and economic demands collaborated with military and political power to overwhelm the "old ways" and force the Africans into confrontation with the modern world.

Test Your Knowledge

1. The most widespread, externally introduced religion in sub-Saharan Africa has always been
   a. Catholicism.
   b. Protestantism.
   c. Hinduism.
   d. Islam.
2. In the nineteenth century, most of the northwestern part of Africa fell under the control of
   a. Spain.
   b. France.
   c. Italy.
   d. England.
3. Dona Beatriz believed herself to be
   a. the bringer of a new form of Christianity to her people.
   b. the Mother of Jesus.
   c. the war leader of the Kongo against the Portugese colonists.
   d. the bringer of Islam to the Kongo.
4. Which of the following best summarizes the African reaction to being placed under European colonial rule in the nineteenth century?
   a. The Africans were consistently rebellious and unwilling to do the whites' bidding.
   b. The reaction varied, ranging from free cooperation to rebellion.
   c. The people's reaction varied, but the leaders were usually rebellious.
   d. The reaction varied from rebellion in the North to collaboration in the South.
5. By 1914, the economic results of the New Imperialism in Africa were
   a. disappointing to the home countries, which now regretted their colonies.
   b. disappointing, but generally not admitted as such by the governments or public.
   c. fairly close to the hopes of the imperialist groups.
   d. good for the European public, but negative for the Africans.
6. By 1900, all of the African continent had been colonized by Europeans except
   a. Liberia and Zanzibar.
   b. South Africa and Ethiopia.
   c. Ethiopia and Liberia.
   d. Ethiopia and Egypt.
7. Which of the following would be considered one of the "old ways"?
   a. Mastery of the French language
   b. Taking a Christian name
   c. Buying a house slave
   d. Going to work on a rubber plantation

Identification Terms

Angola-to-Brazil trade

Boers; Orange Free State

Livingstone (David)

Mahdi rebellion

New Imperialism

Niger River

Rhodes (Cecil)

"white man's burden"

Zulu War

Bibliography

Chaudhuri, K. N. *Trade and Civilization in the Indian Ocean: An Economic History from the Rise of Islam to 1750,* 1985. A specialized account of the history of East Africa, with much on the Arab slave trade.

Davidson, B. *African History,* 1968. Still useful though obsolete on the earliest times. Davidson has written extensively on all aspects and periods of African history.

Fage, J., and R. Oliver, eds. *The Cambridge History of Africa,* vols. 1–4, 1977–1985. One of the several multivolume histories that Cambridge University has sponsored on the non-Western world. The same pair have written *A Short History of Africa,* 1986, which is a standard introductory work. It is particularly good on modern times.

Henderson, L. W. *Angola: Five Centuries of Conflict,* 1979. Gives insight into the effects of Portuguese rule in Southwest Africa.

The same theme is explored in A. F. Ryder, *Benin and the Europeans, 1485–1897,* 1969.

Isichai, E. *The Ibo People and the Europeans,* 1973. Deals with the effects of the slave trade in what is now Nigeria.

Morehead, A. *The White Nile,* 1960, and *The Blue Nile,* 1962. Exciting narratives on the topic of European exploration in Africa.

Nicholls, C. S. *The Swahili Coast,* 1971. A standard text on East African city-states.

Pakenham, T. *The Scramble for Africa,* 1991.

Ritter, E. *Shaka Zulu,* 1983.

Robinson, R., and J. Gallagher. *Africa and the Victorians,* 1961. Set a new course in studies of imperial rule.

Shillington, K. *A History of Southern Africa,* 1989. Has many illustrations to accompany a well-written text.

LATIN AMERICA FROM COLONY TO DEPENDENT STATEHOOD

THE COLONIAL EXPERIENCE

The Colonial Administration and Its Goals

The Colonial Economy

Stagnation and Revival in the Eighteenth Century

THE WARS FOR INDEPENDENCE

EARLY POLITICAL AND SOCIAL AFFAIRS

Social Distinctions

Nineteenth-Century Government

THE ECONOMY

Dependency on Foreign Investment

LATIN AMERICAN CULTURE

Exceptions to the Rule

1520s–1810s	Latin America under Spanish/Portuguese rule
1810s–1820s	Wars of independence; slavery abolished in most countries/replaced by peonage
1820s–1900	Domination by landlords; economy dependent on foreign capital and imported industrial products
1910–1920	Mexican Revolution

The arrival of the Europeans in the New World started an enormous exchange of crops and commodities, modalities, and techniques. The beginning and most important phase of this exchange was conducted under the auspices of the Spanish and Portuguese *conquistadores,* who so rapidly conquered the Indian populations in the sixteenth century. For the next three hundred years, most of the newly discovered lands were administered by a colonial system that superimposed Iberian Christian economic institutions, habits, and values upon existing indigenous ones. The form of colonial lifestyle that gradually evolved in Latin America was the product of the native Indians and the imported black slaves, as much as of the whites.

Even after the Central and South Americans gained their independence in the first quarter of the nineteenth century, the hopes of millions for a better life were not realized. Instead, little changed in the lives of the people. No longer ruled by Spaniards from afar, the Indian and mixed-blood masses were ruled equally badly by native-born *criollos* who vied with one another for dictatorial powers. Governments were both authoritarian and unstable; "revolutions" that changed only the personalities at the top made a mockery of politics. The problems of Latin America at the beginning of the twentieth century were at least as intense as they had been a century earlier.

✤ THE COLONIAL EXPERIENCE

We have seen (Chapter 28) that the initial phase of Spanish exploration in the Caribbean was dominated by the search for treasure. The "Indies" of Columbus were reputed to be lands of gold and spices, waiting to be exploited by the first individual who might happen upon them. Within a very few years, however, this image was obliterated by the realities of the Caribbean islands, where gold was nonexistent. The search then shifted to the mainland, and the immediate result was the conquest of the Aztecs in Mexico (1520s) and the Inca in Peru (1530s). Here there was treasure in gratifying abundance, both in gold and even in greater amounts, silver. Indian resistance was broken, and the small groups of Spaniards made themselves into regional chieftains, each with his Spanish entourage. One-fifth (*quinto*) of what was discovered or stolen belonged to the royal government; the remainder could be divided up as the *conquistadores* saw fit.

In this earliest period, until about 1560, the Spanish Crown, which in theory was the ultimate proprietor of all the new lands, allowed the conquerors of the Indians the *encomienda,* or the right to demand uncompensated labor from the natives as a reward for the risks and hardships of exploration. This soon led to such abuses that the priests who were charged with converting the Indians to Christianity (especially the determined and brave Dominican *Bartolomé de Las Casas*) protested vigorously to Madrid, and the *encomienda* was abolished midway through the sixteenth century on paper, though somewhat later in fact.

It should be noted that the Spanish in America have long had an unjustified reputation for cruelty and indifference to Indian welfare. It is true that most of the motley group of fortune seekers who constituted the *conquistadores* had no consideration whatever for the Indians; the Carib Taino tribe, for example, literally disappeared within a generation at their tender mercies. But again and again during the sixteenth century, both the Spanish home government and its agents, the viceroyal councils in the Americas, intervened as best they could to ameliorate and protect the welfare of the natives. The colonial histories of other nations have no equivalent to the flat prohibition of Indian slavery or the precise outline of the rights of the Indians and the duties of the Spanish overlords that were features of the Spanish American administration as early as the 1560s. That these prohibitions were sometimes observed in the breach is also, unfortunately, true. But the general thrust of law, legislation, and instructions to the bureaucracy in New Spain (Mexico) and Peru was definitely more solicitous of humane treatment of the natives than the colonial administrations of France, Holland, or Britain in a later and supposedly more enlightened epoch.

This solicitousness, however could not prevent a demographic disaster without parallel in history. Due in part to a kind of soul sickness induced by their enslavement and subservience, but much more to epidemic diseases brought by the whites and unfamiliar to the Indians, the populations of these civilized, agricultural folk went into a horrific crash (see Chapter 28). In the sixty years after 1520 the Indian population of Mexico declined by 90 percent! In the same sixty years, the Peruvian population was reduced by about 80 percent. Smallpox, measles, and influenza—all unknown in the Americas—were the major killers. By the mid-seventeenth century, the Indian populations had begun to recover, but never did so fully. Latin American populations only reached their pre-Columbian levels in the nineteenth century, when the influx of blacks and whites had created a wholly different ethnic mix.

The Colonial Administration and Its Goals

The Spanish administration in most of the Americas and the Portuguese system in Brazil were essentially similar. Under the auspices of the home government, an explorer/conqueror was originally allowed nearly unlimited powers in the new land. Soon, however, a royal council was set up with exclusive powers over commerce, crafts, mining, and every type of foreign trade. Stringent controls were imposed through a viceroy or governor appointed by the Spanish government in Madrid and responsible solely to it. Judicial and military matters were also handled through the councils or the colonial *audiencia* (court) in each province. There was no hint of elective government beyond the very lowest rung in the traditional communes of the Indian villages.

The colonial administration was dominated by nobles. It was highly bureaucratized and mirrored the home government in its composition and aims. A great deal of paper dealing with legal cases, regulations, appointment procedures, tax rolls, and censuses flowed back and forth across the Atlantic. Throughout the colonial period, most of the top-level officials were Spanish born, rather than native-born *criollos*. From the mid-sixteenth century, the basic aim of the government was to maximize fiscal and commercial revenues for the home country in keeping with standard mercantilist principles. Secondarily, the government wished to provide an avenue of upward mobility for ambitious young men in the administration of the colonies.

Another Iberian institution was as strong as the civil government in the colonies: the Catholic church. Filled with the combative spirit and sense of high mission that were a legacy of the long fight against the Moors, the missionaries were anxious to add the Central and South American Indians to the church's ranks. A church stood at the center of every town in the new lands; all other buildings were oriented around it. The bishops, nominated by the Crown, were as important in the administration of a given area as the civil governors; cultural matters pertaining to both Europeans and Indians were in their hands. In its buildings and artworks, the church left a long-lasting physical imprint throughout the Spanish and Portuguese colonies. The spiritual imprint was even more profound, continuing to the present day.

The Colonial Economy

The major element in the economy of the Spanish colonies was the mining of precious metals. Everything else served that end. (Brazil, the Portuguese colony, was originally a sugarcane plantation, but later also emphasized mining.) The agricultural estates, which were first *encomiendas* and then **haciendas**—rural plantation-villages with at least technically free labor—existed primarily to supply food for the mining communities. Handicraft industries made gloves and textiles, prepared foods and provided black-smithing services for the same market.

Rights to export goods to the Spanish colonies were limited to Spaniards; the goods could be carried only in Spanish ships, which left from one port, Sevilla, twice a year. The tight restrictions on these flotillas were intended to protect the returning treasure from the Americas from pirates and to keep tight control over what was sent to, and taken from the colonies.

The great bonanza of the early years was the "mountain of silver" at Potosí in what is now Bolivia. Next to it came the Mexican mines north of Mexico City. The silver that flowed from the New World to Madrid from the 1540s to the 1640s far overshadowed the gold taken from Mocte-zuma and the Inca in the conquest period. When the volume declined drastically in the 1640s, the Madrid gov-ernment experienced a crisis. Production did not pick up for a century, but thanks to new technology and increased incentives, it reached great heights in the later eighteenth century before declining again, this time for good.

The flow of bullion did not produce lasting construc-tive results in Spain. Much of it flowed on through royal or private hands to enrich the West European shippers, financiers, merchants, and manufacturers who supplied Iberia with every type of good and service in the sixteenth and seventeenth centuries. A good deal wound up in Chinese hands to pay for the Spanish version of the triangular trade across the Pacific: Spanish galleons left Acapulco, Mexico, loaded with silver and bound for Manila, where they met Chinese ships loaded with silk and porcelain, which, after transshipment across Mexico or Panama, wound up in Sevilla and might be reshipped back to the Caribbean. Less than half of the Spanish silver remained in Spanish hands. But this was enough to start an inflationary spiral there that seized all of Europe by the end of the sixteenth century and brought ruin to many of the landholding nobles (see Chapter 28).

Contrary to folklore, the *quinto* (the one-fifth part of imported bullion) never represented the bulk of royal revenues in Spain, which, as in other countries, came mainly from taxes on the citizenry. But it did give the Crown a false confidence in its abilities to do several costly things at once, such as fighting both the Dutch Calvinists and the Ottoman Muslims in the 1570s and 1580s. When

the silver stopped coming in accustomed quantities during the mid-seventeenth century, the royal court was signally unprepared to fill the breach.

Stagnation and Revival in the Eighteenth Century

The later seventeenth century and the first decades of the eighteenth were a period of stagnation and decline in New Spain. Several of the larger islands were captured by the British, French, or Dutch or were taken over by bucca-neers. The mercantilist system imposed by the Madrid government was falling apart, as non-Spaniards ignored the prohibitions against trading with the colonies or took up smuggling in systematic fashion. By now, the colonies could produce the bulk of their necessities and no longer had to import them. The last Spanish Habsburg kings were so weak that local strongmen in Latin America were able to overshadow the *audiencia* and *corregidores* (mu-nicipal authorities) of the viceregal governments. The once-annual fleets were sailing only sporadically, and the total supply of American bullion was down sharply from its high point.

At this juncture, the Spanish government experienced a revival as a new dynasty, an offshoot of the French Bourbons, took over in Madrid in 1701. Especially under King **Carlos III** (1759–1788), who figured among the most enlightened monarchs of the eighteenth century, a policy of thoroughgoing reform was applied to the Indies. A form of free trade was introduced, the navy and military were strengthened, and a new system of *intendants,* re-sponsible to the center on the French Bourbon model, was able to make Spanish colonial government much more effective. Taxes were collected as they had not been for years, and smuggling and corruption were reduced. The two Latin American viceroyalties were subdivided into four: New Spain, Peru, New Granada (northern South America), and Rio de la Plata (Argentina). The officials for these new divisions were drawn almost exclu-sively from the Peninsula, an affront that the people in the colonies did not easily swallow.

The economic reforms were also sometimes painful to the native-born criollos. In a sharp reversal of the previous fifty years' practice, smuggling was almost stopped for a time. With free trade, imports from Europe became considerably cheaper, hurting domestic producers. And the remarkable increase in silver production due to new mining techniques and new discoveries did not flow to the benefit of the locals, but rather to Madrid. All in all, the criollos had some reason to be dissatisfied with the

Bourbon reforms, although these measures undoubtedly did much good for the general population and were responsible for keeping the empire afloat during the eighteenth century.

Finally, the Indian population increased (perhaps doubling) in the eighteenth century, creating an irresistible temptation to both Mexican and Brazilian *hacienda* owners to press this labor force into serfdom in the expanding plantation agriculture. The market for these products was not only the seemingly insatiable demand for sugar in Europe and North America, but the rapidly growing population in the colonies themselves. The foreseeable result was a series of Indian uprisings; one of the most notable was led by *Tupac Amaru,* a descendant of the Inca, in the 1780s. The viceroyal government of Peru was very nearly toppled before the revolt was put down.

The Indians were not the only Latin Americans who were unhappy with the status quo at the end of the eighteenth century. The liberal Enlightenment had proportionately as many adherents in Spanish America as in Europe despite the church censorship. And the success of the North American colonials in throwing out their British overseers did not go unnoticed by the educated class. Finally, the French Revolution added much fuel to the feeling that the monarchies of Spain and Portugal were not the most effective and desirable governors of these lands.

⚜ THE WARS FOR INDEPENDENCE

In the wake of the North American and French Revolutions, one after another of the Iberian colonies in the Americas declared their independence and fought loose from the grip of the mother countries. The revolts against Spain, Portugal, and France were *not uprisings of the common people* against their masters and landlords. On the contrary, with the single exception of the black slaves in French Haiti in 1804, all of the revolutions were led by the native-born whites who formed the elite class. These criollos had become dissatisfied with rule by Madrid and Lisbon because of the grievances just reviewed. But most of all, they were worried that Napoleon's victory over the Spanish and Portuguese monarchies would result in some type of radical, anti-elite reforms in the colonies. To *prevent* such reforms, when Napoleon occupied Spain, various criollo groups proclaimed that they were taking over political leadership in the colonies.

Both Spain and Portugal were far too weak and too preoccupied with their internal affairs after Napoleon's eventual defeat to interfere. The faint hope of the Madrid government that it could find European support for an overseas expedition to "restore order" was put to rest in 1823 when the U.S. president James Monroe issued the **Monroe Doctrine,** backed by the British navy. Latin America was thus acknowledged to be independent, at least in terms of international law. Three of the Latin American warriors for independence were particularly important:

1. **Miguel Hidalgo,** the Mexican priest who started the revolt against Spain in 1810.
2. **José de San Martín,** who liberated Argentina and Chile with his volunteer army.
3. **Simón Bolívar,** who liberated northern South America and is the best known and most revered of the three.

■ **The Independence of Mexico.** This detail of a huge mural by the twentieth-century Mexican painter Diego Rivera clearly shows the artist's commitment to social reform. Most of the figures are easily recognizable actors in the violent history of the country since 1810; only the sweating laborers who support all the rest are anonymous. Note the anti-clericalism in the figure of the gross monk.

Benito Juárez
1806–1872

The popular image of Benito Juárez (1806–1872), the national hero of Mexico and the protector of its independence, stems only partly from his deeds as a political and social reformer. Juárez also planted the seed for a whole series of changes in the national consciousness of his country toward the relative importance of criollo and mestizo values. In a society long known for its aristocratic views, he awakened Mexican nationalism and steered his countrymen toward political democracy. In Mexico, he is considered the spirit and soul of his country and one of the greatest of all the Latin American leaders of the period of early independence.

A contemporary of Abraham Lincoln, Juárez, too, was of humble birth and very poor. The son of Zapotec Indian peasants from the region of Oaxaca, he could not even speak Spanish in his childhood. At the age of three, he lost both father and mother and went to live with an uncle. At twelve he set out on foot to Oaxaca because he had lost one of his uncle's sheep and feared severe punishment. Living with a sister, he was lucky enough to find a Franciscan brother who gave him the rudiments of education. Years later, he succeeded in entering the local Institute of Arts and Sciences to study law and graduated in 1831.

After a few years, Juárez entered local politics and served in the state, and later the national legislatures. In 1841, he was made a judge, and six years later he was elected governor of Oaxaca state. Political differences with the dictatorial government of Antonio López de Santa Anna in Mexico City landed Juárez briefly in jail and sent him into exile in the United States in the mid-1850s. When Santa Anna was deposed, Juárez became minister of justice in the new liberal government, and from that position, he was primarily responsible for the creation of the strongly liberal and reformist Constitution of 1857. All these activities brought him the solid opposition of the conservative elements, notably the entrenched *haciendados,* or great landowners, and the higher churchmen. This opposition led to the War of Reform (1858–1861), where the liberals were able to beat back the challenge of the reactionary groups and preserve the constitution under Juárez's leadership as acting president.

No sooner was the war over than Britain, Spain, and France decided to force Mexico to pay outstanding debts by seizing the country's ports. Although Britain and Spain soon withdrew, the French under Archduke Maximilian and a good-sized army fought their way into Mexico. Despite heroic resistance against the invaders in Puebla (5th of May 1862) and elsewhere, much of Mexico was under the control of the French for several years. Juárez's government retired to El Paso (now Ciudad Juárez), while keeping up the struggle. Finally, the withdrawal of the French and the capture and execution of Maximilian in 1867 ended this major threat to Mexico's independent existence.

Juárez was reelected president, but the years of war against both the dictator Santa Anna and the foreign colonialists had taken a severe toll. The struggle between liberals and conservatives was as fierce as ever and showed no signs of abating after the victory over the French. Like other Latin reformers, Juárez ended his life painfully aware of the difficulties in getting his fellow Mexicans to agree on even the most basic elements of political and social progress. His Indian origins, his commitment to the welfare of the poor masses, and his high-minded dedication to justice and equality have ensured his everlasting memory in Mexico.

In each colony, other men also contributed to the success of the rebellions: Agustin Morelos in Mexico, Bernardo O'Higgins in Chile and Peru, and the Portuguese prince Pedro in Brazil, among many more.

But it should be repeated that, outside Haiti, the revolts were carried through by conservative and/or wealthy men, who had *no interest at all in social reforms or political equality.* Their goal was to enable the colonies to take control of their own affairs by freeing them from the home countries, which were exploiting the colonials, or so the leaders believed. In their disinterest in internal sociopolitical reform, the liberators of Latin America resembled the American revolutionaries of a generation earlier.

✤ Early Political and Social Affairs

The great question in the early years of the revolutions in Latin America was whether the new governments should be *monarchies or republics.* The example of the newly independent United States was well known in Latin America, and many criollos thought that a republic was the only form of government suitable for the new nations (see Map 44.1). But many were fearful of the power of the mob, and especially of the mestizos and blacks. They rejected the sharp break with tradition that a republican form of government necessarily represented; instead, they wanted a monarchy. The struggle between the two schools of thought went on throughout the revolutionary decades of the 1810s and 1820s. Except in Brazil, it was eventually won by the republicans, who placed supreme powers in a legislature elected through a narrowly drawn franchise.

In the constitutions worked out in the 1820s, all legal distinctions among the citizens of the new states were declared void. *Slavery was abolished* in most (but not all) of them. But that did not mean that there were no social class distinctions.

Social Distinctions

The Latin society of the colonial period had already evolved a clear scale of prestige; the "pureblooded" criollos were at the top, various levels of Europeanized mestizos were in the middle, and the non-European *zambos,* or Indians and black ex-slaves were at the bottom. Because people were born into their places on the scale, Latin American society is frequently called a society of *castas* (castes). Status was largely visible at a glance because skin color was an important factor in determining who was who. Although Latin society was relatively free of the legal and political prejudice against the dark-skinned population that the North Americans only partly overcame in the Civil War, the society had a distinct social gradient by complexion that was (and is) taken for granted.

States with numerous pureblooded Indians (most of South and all of Central America) refused to allow them to participate in either political or cultural life and made no effort to introduce them into public affairs for several generations. These restrictions were not necessarily a bad

thing: most of the Indians had neither experience nor interest in government beyond the village or tribal levels.

In free Latin America as under Spain, the towns were the center of everything that was important: politics, administration, cultural events, commerce, and industry. The criollos were disproportionately prominent in the towns. The countryside was inhabited by the bulk of the population: small farmers, farm and pastoral laborers, and many hundreds of thousands of people who had no visible means of support. The absentee landlords lived in town, looked toward Europe, and left daily control of the rural plantations to agents and managers.

For the mestizo and Indian masses, life was a losing struggle against poverty; there was not enough good land, not enough industrial jobs, and not enough enterprise in the ruling group for it to be anything else. Though slavery was forbidden, **peonage** became commonplace on the *haciendas.* Peonage was a form of coerced labor in order to repay real or alleged debt owed to the employer; it was not much different than slavery for the victim and perhaps more lucrative for the master.

Nineteenth-Century Government

The most farsighted and most tragic of the heroes of the early independence era was Simón Bolívar (1793–1847) who struggled through the 1820s to bring the various regions together under a federal constitution modeled on the U.S. Constitution (see the Document in this chapter). He failed, and at the end of his life he declared, "America's ungovernable . . . elections are battles, freedom anarchy, and life a torment." This black depression was the result of seeing one reasonable plan for Latin American union and progress after another fail due to the indifference of the people or sabotage by selfish interest groups.

In most countries, *political affairs* quickly degenerated into a maneuvering for supreme power among a group of **caudillos** (strongmen). The frequent "revolutions" and "manifestos" were shadow plays, disguising the raw greed that impelled almost all of the actors. Only the names of the people in charge changed after a revolution of this nature. When internal affairs seemed to become too dangerous for their continued survival, many *caudillos* would find one excuse or another to divert attention by starting a war with their neighbors. For this reason, much of Latin America was at war over pointless territorial disputes through most of the century.

The main outlines of politics were delineated by the struggle between liberals and conservatives. On the liberal side were those inspired by the French Revolution's

UNITED STATES

Atlantic Ocean

MEXICO
1821

CUBA

DOMINICAN REPUBLIC
1844

JAMAICA

PUERTO RICO

BR. HONDURAS

HONDURAS
1821

HAITI
1804

Caribbean Sea

GUATEMALA
1821

NICARAGUA
1821

EL SALVADOR
1821

COSTA
RICA
1821

PANAMA
1821

VENEZUELA
1821

BR. GUIANA

DUTCH GUIANA

FR. GUIANA

COLOMBIA
1819

ECUADOR
1822

Amazon R.

Pacific Ocean

PERU
1821

BRAZIL
1822

BOLIVIA
1825

PARAGUAY
1811

CHILE
1818

URUGUAY
1828

ARGENTINA
1816

Independent nations

Colonial possessions

1821 Date of independence
as formally recognized
by Britain and the
United States

0   500   1,000   1,500 Kilometers

0   500   1,000 Miles

⦿ MAP 44.1 Latin America in the Early Nineteenth Century. This map shows the changes in colonial possessions from 1800 to 1830.

original goals: the liberty and fraternity of mankind and the abolition of artificial class distinctions. They regarded Bolívar as their leader and thought the proper form of political organization was a federation, exemplified by the United States. Most of the liberals came from a commercial or professional background and were strong promoters of economic development.

The conservatives were generally either landed gentry or had connections with the very powerful Catholic clergy. Like all conservatives, they emphasized stability and protection of property rights first and foremost. They looked upon the Indians and mestizos as wards, who could be gradually trained toward full citizenship but in the meantime must be excluded from political and social rights. The conservatives would support a republic only if their traditional preferences were guaranteed; if not, they could be counted upon to finance and direct the next "revolution."

Everywhere in Latin America, the civil government operated in the shadow of the military, and the frequent dictators almost always came from the army ranks. Government policy was tightly controlled by a small group of wealthy individuals, closely linked with the military officer corps. The prestige of the military man was an unfortunate consequence of the battles for independence—unfortunate, that is, for constitutional process and the rule of law.

Once in a while, a "man of the people" would rise and assert dictatorial rule for a time. Examples are *Juan Rosas* in Argentina and *August Iturbide* in Mexico. Almost always, these individuals soon made peace with the large landlords and other criollos who had traditionally governed. Social reforms were forgotten for another generation, while the *caudillo* became corrupt and wealthy.

The universal *backwardness of the rural majority* was a chief reason for the stagnation of national politics through most of the nineteenth century. Illiteracy and desperate poverty were normal; social castes were fixed from colonial days and did not change. The Indians, blacks, and their zambo offspring remained mostly outside public life, though technically they were free and equal citizens when slavery was abolished (Brazil did not abolish slavery until 1888, when it became the last of the Western Hemisphere countries to do so). Blacks and Indians had more opportunity for mobility in Latin America than in North America, however. Latin American society was willing to consider light-skinned mulattos and mestizos as equivalent to Europeans rather than holding that miscegenation (mixed blood) was an insuperable obstacle to social status. Relative wealth, skills, and education counted for more than blood alone.

✤ THE ECONOMY

Land (the source of livelihood for the great majority of people) was held in huge blocks by a small number of families, who claimed descent from the original *conquistadores*. Sometimes they had land grants from the king to prove it; more often, their ancestors had simply taken over vast tracts from the helpless Indians. Since land was useless without labor, first the Indians, then (in Brazil and the Caribbean) imported blacks were forced to work it as slaves.

Slave agriculture is normally only profitable where *monoculture* plantations can produce for a large market. For this reason, Latin American agriculture came to be based on one or two export crops—an economically precarious system. Originally, the cash crops were sugar and rice destined for the European or North American markets. Later, bananas, coffee, and citrus in the more tropical lands and cattle and wheat in the more temperate climates became the main exports. Almost all the labor of clearing land, raising and harvesting the crop, and transporting it to market was done by hand. Machinery was practically nonexistent into the twentieth century, because with labor so cheap, the landholders had no need for machines.

The size of the *latifundia* (big rural plantations) actually grew after independence. Their owners were practically little kings within the republics. Although these great landowners did not carry formal titles of nobility after independence, they might as well have done so, as they comprised an aristocracy in the truest sense. Mostly of

■ **Buenos Aires Street Scene.** The Argentine capital prided itself on being the "Little Paris" of Latin America. In the early twentieth century the *per capita* income of Argentinians was the highest in South America and the future looked bright.

Bolívar's Proclamation

Flamboyant, idealistic, and moody, the Liberator of Latin America, Simón Bolívar, remains one of history's enigmatic figures. Yet, as this spirited proclamation issued at the height of his campaign indicates, there was nothing hesitant or enigmatic about either his zeal for the cause or his confidence in eventual triumph over all adversities. Put into the magniloquent language prevalent among nineteenth-century Latin politicians, the Proclamation to the People of New Granada (present-day Colombia) was meant to reassure the population of an area that had been temporarily recaptured by Spanish troops under General Morillo. This statement shows little sign of the depressed frame of mind that would eventually afflict Bolívar when he considered the future of the Americas.

> Angostura: August 15, 1818
> Simón Bolívar, Supreme Chief of the Republic of Venezuela and Commander in Chief of her armies and those of New Granada, etc.
> Granadans!
> The army of [Spanish general] Morillo is no more; new expeditions came to reinforce him, but they, too, have ceased to exist. The blood of more than 20,000 Spaniards has drenched the soil of Venezuela. Hundreds of glorious battles fought by the armies of liberation have proved to Spain that the avengers of America are as just as its defenders are noble. An awestruck world beholds with joy the miracles worked by freedom and valor against tyranny and violence. The Spanish empire has pitted its enormous resources against handfuls of men who, though unarmed and barely clothed, were inspired by freedom. Heaven has rewarded our sacrifices, Heaven has applauded our justice. Heaven, the protector of liberty, has granted our prayers and has sent us arms to defend humanity, innocence and virtue. Generous, war-hardened foreigners have come to place themselves under the standards of Venezuela. Can tyrants, then, continue the struggle when our resistance, which has reduced their strength, has augmented ours?
> Spain, plagued by [king] Ferdinand and his murderous rule, approaches her end; her commerce annihilated by swarms of our privateers; her fields deserted, for death has cut off her sons; her wealth depleted by twenty years of war; the spirit of the nation broken by imposts, levies, inquisition, and

European blood, they intermarried with one another exclusively; their sons went into high government office or the army officers' cadres by right of birth. In the nineteenth century, this aristocracy lived very well, in both the material and the intellectual senses. But they inherited the *lack of social responsibility* that also marked their ancestors. They either could not see or would not recognize that the miserable conditions of the majority of their fellow citizens posed a danger to themselves.

Dependency on Foreign Investment

Due to its economic backwardness compared to North America, Latin America remained *dependent* on the United States and Europe throughout the nineteenth and early twentieth centuries (many would say until the present). This did not mean that Latin America was dependent on outside areas just for imports of goods and services it did not produce. In addition, Latin America was becoming increasingly dependent on foreign capital for domestic investment of all types.

The problem was not that Latin America lacked export markets. On the contrary, demand was rising for its raw materials: Bolivian tin, Brazilian coffee and rubber, Chilean copper and fertilizer, Mexico's silver and oil, and Argentina's meat and grain. But instead of providing a general stimulus to the Latin economies, the benefits of these exports were limited to a mere handful of wealthy families, who controlled these resources and either used the profits for their own extraordinarily wasteful lifestyles or squandered them on crackbrain schemes. Little was invested in rational, farsighted ways. No attempt was made to strengthen society by encouraging the poor and the unskilled to become educated, and thus qualify them-

despotism. The most frightful catastrophe is about to overtake Spain!

Grenadans! America's day is come; no human power can stay the course of nature guided by the hand of Providence. Join your efforts to those of your brothers: Venezuela marches with me to free you, as in past years you marched with me to free Venezuela.

Already our advance guard fills whole provinces of your territory with the luster of its arms; and the same advance guard, powerfully aided, will hurl the destroyers of New Granada into the seas. The sun will not have completed the course of its present round through the heavens without beholding in all your territory the proud altars of liberty.

selves to participate in the political process. For that matter, there was no attempt at securing social justice of the most basic sort.

In very many cases, the real beneficiaries of Latin America's raw materials were the foreign investors who supplied the necessary capital to get production underway: American mining corporations, European coffee plantation owners, and British shipping firms. None of their profits went into the pockets of *any* of the natives, let alone the workers.

The rising disparities between the rich handful and the poor majority created an atmosphere of social unrest in much of the continent. At times, the disenchanted were able to find a popular leader (*caudillo*), who frightened the wealthy with his threats to install democratic reform. In every case, either the ruling group was able to bribe and co-opt the *caudillo,* or another army-led "revolution"

forcibly removed him. In some cases when the traditional ruling group did not remove the reformer swiftly enough, the United States acted instead. Examples of U.S. intervention became more numerous in the twentieth century after the Spanish-American War of 1898 brought the North Americans more directly into the Latin world. We will consider these instances in a later chapter.

⚜ Latin American Culture

The prevalent culture of Latin America owes as much to the European background of its original colonists as does the culture of North America. The two cultures differ, of course, in that the ideas and values introduced into Latin America were *Spanish or Portuguese, Roman Catholic, and patriarchal* rather than being British, Protestant, and (relatively) genderless as in the United States.

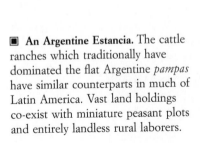

■ **An Argentine Estancia.** The cattle ranches which traditionally have dominated the flat Argentine *pampas* have similar counterparts in much of Latin America. Vast land holdings co-exist with miniature peasant plots and entirely landless rural laborers.

While Iberian culture is supreme on the mainland, the Caribbean islands reflect the African origins of their black populations. The native Indian populations of the islands were exterminated or fled early and have been entirely supplanted by African ex-slaves and mulattos. Thus, the Caribbean culture is very different from the Iberian and is not properly considered a part of Latin America.

From these different roots have developed very different societies. As an example, until recently public life in Latin countries was as much dominated by males as were ancient Greece and the Islamic civilizations. The adoption of the Napoleonic codes of law in these countries contributed to the persistence of the idea that the male is legally and socially responsible for the female. On the contrary, the black ex-slave societies of the Caribbean islands followed the African example of giving females a quasi-equal position in private and—to some degree—public affairs.

The Catholic church was guaranteed a supervisory role in most aspects of public life and private morals. It was from the start and remained an official church, supported by donations and taxes. It had little competition; Catholicism was the religion of the vast majority of the general population and of the entire ruling group. (As in the European homelands, Latin America has simultaneously had a strong tradition of anticlericalism.) The high clergy were automatically men of influence and did not hesitate to intervene in political affairs when they sensed that the church or their own family interests were threatened.

In the nineteenth century, the church was responsible for most educational institutions and practically all social welfare organs. At times, in some places, the church made a sincere effort at lifting the Indians and poor mestizos toward justice and dignity, even when doing so meant

breaking with the ruling group from which much of the higher clergy came. But these episodes were the exception; most of the time, class ties seemed stronger than a sense of obligation to the common people, and the clergy were content to conform to the current ideas of their lay peers.

Cultural stratification is particularly strong in Latin America and has long been an obstacle to national unity. Until the early twentieth century, certainly, the landowner-official group who controlled public life regarded themselves as *Europeans resident in another continent,* rather than as Latin Americans, in the same way the British regarded themselves as British living in Australia or the French regarded themselves as French living in Africa. The elite read European literature, taught their children European languages in European-directed schools, and dressed in current European fashions. When they grew tired of their surroundings, they often spent a year or two in a European capital; many sent their older children to European schools and universities as a matter of course. When asked about family origins, young men and women would say they came from some Spanish town, which their ancestors had left (often as poverty-stricken emigrants) three hundred years earlier! They did not recognize a Latin American culture that was separate and distinct from Iberia. They spent much of their lives attempting to keep up with European culture and trying to replicate it in their alien environment.

A powerful reason for the great difference between Latin and North American social habits in this regard was that the whites in Central and South America perceived *Indian culture as a much greater threat* than did the European settlers of North America. The Indians of Latin America were far more numerous and far more civilized

than their North American cousins. The Spanish and Portuguese conquerors wanted to maintain a sharp distinction between themselves and the natives. This distinction gradually gave way for a large number of ordinary people who intermarried with the Indians and created the mestizo culture that predominates in many present-day Latin countries. But the ruling class rigorously maintained the distinction—they remained at heart Europeans who lived in Peru, Brazil, or Colombia, *not* Peruvians, Brazilians, or Colombians. For them, intermarriage was unthinkable.

Exceptions to the Rule

Chile, Argentina, Uruguay, and Mexico are exceptions to the rule of unchallenged domination by the criollos. In Chile, Argentina, and Uruguay, a surge of European lower-class immigration during the late nineteenth century brought a number of new factors into the political relationships and was accompanied by the systematic destruction of Indian culture. Instead of Neolithic Indians and illiterate descendants of black slaves to deal with, the criollo governors had to adapt to the demands of semi-educated Europeans who could not be so easily intimidated or segregated by color. As a consequence, these countries led the rest of the continent in social reforms and mass politics.

In Mexico, the mestizos were able to maintain sufficient numbers and influence so as to be gradually accepted by the criollos as necessary partners in the political spectrum. This acceptance was strongly advanced by the Mexican Revolution of the early twentieth century, the only genuine popular outbreak in Latin America to achieve a substantial measure of success. These exceptions will be looked at in a later chapter dealing with the Americas in the twentieth century.

Summary

The colonial experience in Latin America was quite different from that in Asia, North America, or Africa. The melding of Iberian with Indian and African cultures proceeded in differing tempos in different places and had achieved distinctive results by the nineteenth century. Nowhere else in the world was such a melding attempted or achieved, and Latin America remains unique as a deep-seated hybrid of Western and non-Western civilizations.

After the flow of American bullion to the Old World tapered off in the mid-seventeenth century, a long period of stagnation and neglect ensued. A century later, the Spanish Bourbons supervised an economic and political revival in Latin America with mixed results. Enough resistance to continued foreign rule was generated among the criollo upper class that the American continent was shaken by the radical ideas of the Enlightenment and the French Revolution. Armed rebellion followed, and by 1825 the colonials had established independent republics that Spain and Portugal could not recapture.

Independence proved easier to establish than to govern, however. Military men and local *caudillos* became the ultimate arbiters of politics despite grand-sounding manifestos and constitutions. An urban elite of absentee landlords maintained power despite numerous "revolutions."

The agrarian and mining economy became dependent on the Western European and North American states. The rural majority lived in agrarian villages or *haciendas* that differed little from serfdom. Little manufacturing could develop due to both the widespread poverty of the internal market and the openness of that market to imports from abroad. By the end of the nineteenth century, Latin America was perhaps tied more closely to foreign economic interests than it had ever been in the colonial era.

The disparities between the governing criollo cliques and the mestizo, black, and Indian masses were underlined by cultural orientations. The members of the upper class considered themselves Iberians and Europeans displaced in a Latin American atmosphere. Exceptions to this rule were the immigrant countries of Argentina and Chile, and Mexico with its Indian majority. In those societies, the criollo group had to make room for political newcomers by the early twentieth century, and mass political movements developed.

Test Your Knowledge

1. Which of following Spanish terms does not apply to Latin American social or ethnic divisions?
   a. Criollos
   b. Menudos
   c. Mestizos
   d. Zambo
2. Which of the following does *not* describe the conditions under which the Latin Americans gained independence?
   a. In the wake of the Napoleonic invasion of Spain
   b. As a result of the Spanish king's intolerable tyranny
   c. As a counter to a feared movement toward radical democracy
   d. Under U.S. assurances of protection against European invasion
3. What of the following is most correct? Racism in the Latin countries has been
   a. wholly contingent on the economic position of the affected person.
   b. expressed as prejudice against the dark skinned but not persecution.
   c. less overt, but more harmful overall than in North America.
   d. divorced from skin color, but reflects religious prejudices.
4. Which was the last country in the Americas to outlaw slavery?
   a. Honduras
   b. Brazil

   c. United States
   d. Mexico
5. The key element in promoting Latin American economic development after independence was
   a. obtaining foreign investments.
   b. establishing political democracy.
   c. training the Indians and blacks to work.
   d. building roads into the interior.
6. The least Indian and most Europeanized of all Latin countries are now
   a. Brazil, Argentina, and Chile.
   b. Mexico, Brazil, and Peru.
   c. Argentina, Chile, and Uruguay.
   d. Chile, Mexico, and Argentina.
7. The Latin criollos of the nineteenth century were interested mainly in
   a. obtaining more land for themselves.
   b. keeping U.S. influences out of their homelands.
   c. assuring the installation of popular democratic government.
   d. maintaining political control against the Indian or mestizo masses.
8. Which of the following does *not* describe Benito Juárez?
   a. A pureblooded Indian
   b. A committed defender of Mexican nationalism
   c. The devout ally of the Catholic clergy
   d. The father of Mexico's constitution

Identification Terms

Bolívar (Simón)

hacienda

Monroe Doctrine

San Martín (José de)

Carlos III

Hidalgo (Miguel)

peonage

zambo

caudillo

Juárez (Benito)

Bibliography

All of the following titles have bibliographies that will assist the inquiring student greatly.

Barman, R. J. *Brazil: The Forging of a Nation, 1798–1852,* 1988. Good overview of how Brazil came to be a sovereign nation.

Bazant, J. *A Concise History of Mexico,* 1978. The best single book in English on this topic for the student.

Burns, E. B. *Latin America: A Concise Interpretive History,* 1986. Just what the title announces; a well-known and authoritative work.

Halperin-Donghi, T. *The Aftermath of Revolution in Latin America,* 1973, and R. Graham and P. H. Smith, *New Approaches to Latin American History,* 1974. Two of the most rewarding studies of the early independence period.

Lynch, J. *The Spanish American Revolutions,* 1986. Perhaps the best short treatment of what happened in the Spanish colonies between 1808 and 1825.

Masur, G. *Simon Bolivar,* 1969. The best biography of the Liberator.

Roeder, R. *Juarez and his Mexico,* vols. 1 and 2, 1947. The standard study of the great Mexican patriot and his times.

Scobie, J. *Argentina: A City and a Nation,* 1971, and J. Mamalakis, *The Growth and Structure of the Chilean Economy from Independence to Allende,* 1976. Two good studies of individual nations that profited from European immigration in the nineteenth century but remained in a dependent relationship.

Tannenbaum, F. *Ten Keys to Latin America,* 1962. A survey of Latin history from the vantage point of ten characteristics of Latin society.

Whitaker, A. *The United States and the Independence of Latin America, 1800–1830,* 1941. Until now the best survey of the relations between North America and the Latin Americans in this period.

ADVANCED INDUSTRIAL SOCIETY

1848	Communist Manifesto
c. 1870s	Second Industrial Revolution begins
1870s–1914	Urbanization increases; labor unions emerge; mass democratic politics emerges; socialism strengthens
c. 1850–c. 1910	Massive emigration from Europe

Throughout the nineteenth century, the West was clearly the dominant factor in world political and military developments. The colonial subordination of much of the rest of the globe to Europe was a reflection of the West's increased lead in technology and economic organization.

In the half-century between 1860 and World War I, Europe itself went through a peaceful change of massive dimensions. As in the eighteenth century, a dual revolution was propelled by a shift in the sources of energy, which then was reflected in social organization and national politics. This Second Industrial Revolution was driven by petroleum and electricity. These two energy sources transformed urban life and made the city clearly the dominant social organism. Urban areas produced new businesses, new organizations of workers, new professions, and new lifestyles. In these decades, socialism became a major force in several countries. As enunciated by Marx, it posed a severe threat from below to the combined aristocratic and bourgeois rule that had become normal in European politics and economics. While the non-Western world was being incorporated into the European colonies, Europeans themselves were emigrating in massive numbers to selected areas of the globe.

✤ THE SECOND INDUSTRIAL REVOLUTION

As in the late eighteenth century, the search for new energy sources was itself a function of population growth and rising demand for consumer goods. Europe's overall population exclusive of Russia rose from 265 million to 401 million in the second half of the nineteenth century (see Map 45.1). Despite the stabilization of the average West European family at 2.5 children at the end of the century, the previous huge increase, combined with a rise in real income, created a large market for consumer goods and services of all types.

With fewer children's hands now necessary for labor, those who were born profited from better public health and nutrition to live longer, healthier lives. They could and did consume more. Goods that were almost unknown in European workers' houses in the early 1800s now became common: mechanically produced footwear and clothes, nursing bottles for babies, gas or electric lighting, and books and newspapers. A definite rise in material standards of living was visible throughout Europe west of Russia.

Adding to this internal market was the rapidly expanding overseas market, both in the European colonies and in the independent nations of America and Asia. The surge of imperial ventures that began in the 1850s brought the hope, if not the reality, of major increases in both the availability of raw materials and the number of potential consumers in the Asian and African marketplaces. The volume of world trade shot upward in the later nineteenth century, and the West controlled that trade entirely. The opening of the Suez Canal in 1869 is one indicator of what was happening in world markets: the volume of goods shipped over long distances (often over the oceans on the now common steamships) was increasing at a geometric rate, and the more developed industrial nations (Britain, Germany, and the United States) were the main beneficiaries.

New Energy Sources

The big lead in industrial production that Great Britain had established in the early nineteenth century gradually narrowed after 1850. Belgium and northern France led in this regard, followed by parts of Germany and Italy. After the unification of those two countries, their industrial growth accelerated sharply. As an important example, Germany's steel and iron production exceeded Britain's by 1893 and was almost double British production by 1914.

Whole new industries sprang up, seemingly overnight. Chemicals, oil fields, steamship building, electrical turbines and machinery, and, toward the end of the 1890s, the automobile industry are outstanding examples. But perhaps the most important of all the new developments was the taming and application of electricity to both industrial and domestic uses.

Electricity had been recognized as a natural phenomenon since the eighteenth century (Ben Franklin!), but no practical use could be made of it then. In the 1870s, this changed dramatically as a result of the work of German, American, and French researchers. The development of generators and transformers allowed direct current to be sent wherever desired cheaply and efficiently, then transformed into easily used, safe, alternating current. The first big power plant was constructed in 1881, and very soon electric power was being used to light streets, power trams, and bring artificial light into hundreds of thousands of city homes and factories. Soon after, electrical machinery was being used in thousands of industrial applications. Electric railways and subway systems were introduced in every major European city. Probably no other invention contributed so much to improving the material life of ordinary people.

■ **A Paris Street Scene.** This view of Montparnasse tramstation was taken in 1900. The regularity of the building facades was one of the results of the massive rebuilding of this former slum undertaken by the government of Louis Napoleon in the 1860s.

Petroleum was the second new energy source. The internal combustion engine, which drew its power from the controlled explosion of gasoline injected into cylinders, was invented in 1876. Although it was clearly an impressive means of applying energy, its full potential was not apparent until the German engineers *Daimler* and *Benz* put the engine on a carriage. Benz's work in the late 1880s is generally credited with the development of the *automobile* as a practical, reliable machine, though literally dozens of other German, French, American, and British experimenters also contributed to its development.

Petroleum and its by-product natural gas were to have many other uses, including lighting, heating, and driving stationary engines and pumps; from petroleum also came a whole range of important new chemicals. Then as now, Europe had very little oil and was dependent on imports from other places. American capital (Rockefeller's Standard Oil) and American exploration and drilling techniques soon led the world in the race for oil production.

The Second Industrial Revolution depended very much on scientific research. The Germans with their well-equipped university laboratories quickly took over the lead in this area and held it without serious competition for many years. Their carefully organized and well-funded research enabled the Germans to dominate European industry after 1870. The British, who were the former leaders, were very slow to realize that the rules of industrial competition had changed; they put little money into research, from either government or private hands. By 1890, Britain was falling steadily behind Germany, and this growing gap had much to do with the rising

⊙ **MAP 45.1 European Population Growth in the Nineteenth Century.** The Italian peninsula and parts of central Europe saw the most dramatic increases in population density during this eighty year period. In some rural areas in these lands, the lack of industry and the poor soils had created an overpopulation crisis which was only controlled by emigration. In the later third of the century, it was a commonplace for most of the younger residents of whole villages and counties to emigrate to the New World. Some intended to return, and did so; but the majority stayed in the new homelands.

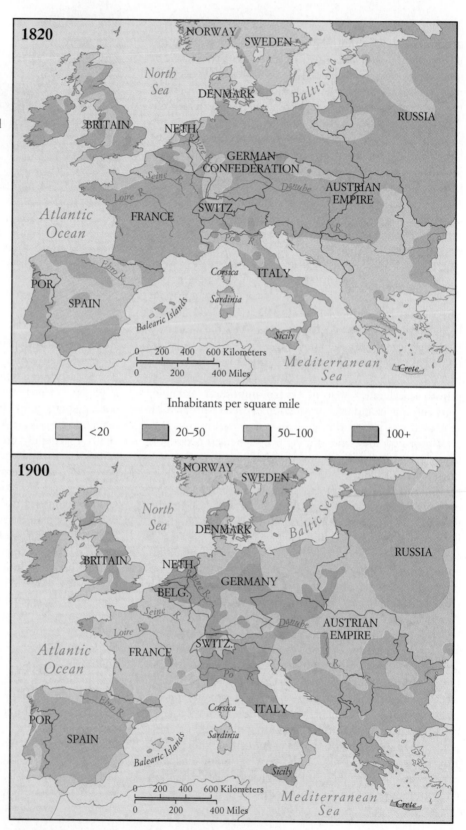

competition between the two countries in political and diplomatic affairs.

New Forms of Business Organization

New forms of business organization assisted the new industrial developments; indeed, they made them possible in several instances. In the First Industrial Age (1760–1860), the standard form of industry had been the private partnership or proprietorship, limited deliberately to a small handful of owner-managers, some of whom might work alongside their employees in the office or even on the shop floor. If and when more capital was needed for expansion, it was borrowed on a short-term basis for specific needs. Partners or stockholders were expected to come up with additional capital on an individual basis; the public was *not* invited in, and the banks were not partners but only facilitators in arranging funds.

In the Second Industrial Age (c. 1860–1920), the **corporation** rather than the small partnership became the standard. And often the corporation was permanently financed by banks, which became part owners of the company. *Joint stock companies,* whose shares were traded on public stock exchanges in every European capital, were formed to raise huge amounts of capital. The shareholders were technically the owners of the company, but in fact, they had little or nothing to say about management policy. The separation of ownership and management was one of the most striking changes in business and commerce of all sorts in the later nineteenth century; it continues to the present.

✤ SOCIAL RESULTS OF THE SECOND INDUSTRIAL REVOLUTION

The Second Industrial Revolution accelerated several trends that had begun during the First Industrial Revolution. Four were particularly important:

1. *Urbanization.* The outstanding feature in European demography throughout the nineteenth century was the rapid growth of urban areas. Britain was the first European country to urbanize; in 1851, the census revealed that more than half of the English people lived in towns and cities. By 1900, Britain alone had more cities with populations of more than 100,000 than there had been on all of the Continent in 1800. At this time, only 22 percent of Americans were urban dwellers.

Industrial jobs located in towns were a major reason for the migration to the cities, but they were by no means the only reason. As we saw in a previous chapter, the ambitions of the more industrious villagers were checked by the limited social opportunities and even more limited economic possibilities available in the rural setting. Their solution was to migrate or, in some cases, to emigrate.

Self-improvement through urban educational facilities was another strong draw; and many young women believed the urban marriage market offered them a better chance to catch a good husband than they would have had at home. Eventually, those who remained in the villages either had no great talents or ambition or had more economic reasons to stay than to leave. Since both of these groups were affected by the same factors promoting growth as were those who migrated, the population of the countryside continued to rise, though not as dramatically as the urban population.

2. *Organization of labor.* After the failure of the 1848 revolutions, the workers on the Continent rarely attempted to gain better conditions by street riots or mass demonstrations against the government. Instead, they took to organizing labor unions, which would fight for improvements in a legal way and attempt to gain government support against abusive employers. In so doing, the continental workers were following the lead of the British, who had attempted to win reforms in their conditions of life and labor through the *Chartist Movement* of the 1840s. Although its short-term goals were frustrated, the movement had initiated a long-term change both in and outside Parliament toward greater democracy and fairer distribution of the country's wealth.

In the 1870s, Great Britain became the first major country to fully legalize labor unions, giving them the right to strike, picket, and boycott. In the 1880s, France took the same course, and in 1890 Germany did also. By the turn of the century, all West European nations except Spain and Portugal had conceded the rights of labor to use all nonviolent means available to it in the struggle for a better life.

3. *Socialism.* The early unions were sometimes socialist in orientation, but sometimes not. By the 1890s, however, the Marxist socialists were close to taking over the labor movement in several key countries. This frightened many employers and their sympathizers in government. The last decade prior to World War I saw many bitter disputes between management and labor all over Europe. Violence was common.

Whether socialist or not, the labor unions never succeeded in gaining the support of most industrial workers. They had very few members among agrarian or service workers (still a majority) who were always much more difficult to organize. But they did give the laboring classes a new and fairly effective way to express their discontents and sometimes win redress for them. By 1914, few workers had to endure the sort of systematically inhumane working conditions that were common during the First Industrial Age. Child labor laws and industrial safety regulations were now common and enforced by both national and local authorities. A few countries had some provisions for worker employment security and pensions (Germany led in these respects). Even worker health and accident insurance was frequently provided by the government, if not the employer.

4. *Mass democratic politics.* A very important effect of industrial life was the coming of mass politics and parties. In the last third of the century, almost all European governments allowed all their male citizens to vote, regardless of property qualifications: Germany in 1871, France in 1875, Britain in 1884, and Spain in 1890. Only Russia, Hungary, and Italy stood firm against universal male suffrage as late as 1905; the Italians conceded by 1912, and the Russians had a mass voting system in place by then, too. Once most males had the franchise, more political parties began to emerge. Prior to that time, the few people who had the vote were property holders, relatively well educated, and generally aware of the issues of national politics. They did not need an organization to get out the vote; they knew very well what was at stake and made voting a major part of their public lives.

Now, the much enlarged number of voters had to be informed of the issues and then organized into groups that would vote. The vehicle for doing this was a mass political party, equipped with newspapers, local organs and offices, speakers, and propaganda material. Most of the new voters were men of the lower, working classes, and the new parties concentrated their efforts on them.

✤ SOCIALISM AFTER 1848: KARL MARX

After the liberal rebels of 1848 failed to gain control of the political process, their difficulties were much analyzed. A chief reason for their failure, all contemporary observers agreed, was the split between the liberal leaders—professionals and intellectuals—and the workers in the cities. This split allowed the conservatives to gain a breathing space after their initial panic and then to mount a political and military counterattack that was successful almost everywhere (see the Document in Chapter 38).

Why did the split between the middle-class liberals and the workers occur? The liberals generally did not want social reforms; they only wanted to substitute themselves for the conservatives in the seats of political power. The workers, on the other hand, were economically desperate and wished to gain for themselves the type of thorough-going change that the French peasants had won in the wake of the 1789 Revolution. When it became clear to the liberals that the workers wanted to go much further than they did, they withdrew to the sidelines or actually joined with the conservatives against the workers, as happened in Vienna, Paris, and Berlin. In the end, *the protection of property meant more than political or social ideals.*

Marxist Theory

One close observer of this development was *Karl Marx* (1818–1883). Marx, a German Jew whose family had been assimilated, grew up in the Rhineland town of Trier (see the Biography in this chapter). He was a brilliant student, and soon after his graduation from the University of Berlin in 1842, he became deeply involved in radical politics. Pursued by the Prussian police, he had to leave his native city and flee to France as a political refugee. There, he came to know his lifelong "angel" and colleague, **Friedrich Engels,** the radical son of a German industrialist. The two men formed a close working relationship that was ideal for Marx, who devoted his entire adult life to research and writing and organizing revolutionary socialist parties.

In 1848, coincidentally just prior to the revolt in France, Marx and Engels published perhaps the most famous pamphlet in all European history: the *Communist Manifesto* (see the Document in this chapter). Marx predicted the coming of a new, revolutionary social order, which he called *Communism,* as an inevitable reaction against the abuses of bourgeois capitalism. When this order would come, he did not predict, but he clearly expected to see communist society arise within his lifetime. It was equally clear that Marx and Engels expected communism would be born in a violent revolution by the industrial workers, the proletariat who had been reduced to abject misery and had little or no hope of escaping it as long as capital ruled.

The proletarian revolution was inevitable; the only questions were the precise timing and how it might be helped along by those persons who understood history and wished to be on the side of progress and justice. Marx

Communist Manifesto

The most inspiring of the nineteenth century's various revolutionary challenges was the manifesto produced by Karl Marx and Friedrich Engels in 1848 as a platform for the tiny Communist League they had recently founded in London. Most later Marxist doctrine appeared in it in capsule form. The following excerpts concern mainly the theory of the formation of classes and the struggle between them in history.

> The history of all hitherto existing society is the history of class struggle. Freeman and slave, patrician and plebian, lord and serf, guildmaster and journeyman, in a word, oppressor and oppressed, stood in constant opposition to one another, carried on an uninterrupted, now hidden, now open fight, that each time ended either in a revolutionary reconstitution of society at large, or in the common ruin of the contending classes. . . .

> The modern bourgeois society . . . has not done away with class antagonisms. It has but established new forms of struggle in place of the old ones.

> Our epoch, the epoch of the bourgeoisie, possesses, however, this distinctive feature: it has simplified the class antagonisms. Society as a whole is more and more splitting up into two hostile camps, into two great classes directly facing one another: Bourgeoisie and Proletariat. . . .

> . . . [T]he bourgeoisie has at last, since the establishment of modern industry and of the world market, conquered for itself, in the modern representative State, exclusive political sway. The executive of the modern State is but a committee for managing the common affairs of the whole bourgeoisie. . . .

> In proportion as the bourgeoisie, i.e., capital developed, in the same proportion as the proletariat, the modern working class, developed; a class of laborers, who live only so long as they find work, and who find work only so long as their labor increases capital. . . .

> Owing to the extensive use of machinery and to division of labor, the work of the proletarians has lost all individual character, and consequently, all charm for the workman. He becomes an appendage of the machine. . . . In proportion, therefore, as the repulsiveness of the work increases, the wage decreases.

> All previous historical movements were movements of minorities. The proletarian movement is the self-conscious, independent movement of the immense majority, in the interest of the immense majority. The proletariat, the lowest stratum of our present society, cannot stir, cannot raise itself without the whole super-incumbent strata of official society being sprung into the air.

> What the bourgeoisie produces above all, are its own grave-diggers. Its fall and the victory of the proletariat are equally inevitable.

> The bourgeois claptrap about the family and education, about the hallowed co-relation of parent and child becomes all the more disgusting, as, by the action of modern industry all family ties are torn asunder among the proletarians, and their children transformed into simple articles of commerce and instruments of labor.

> The Communists disdain to conceal their views and aims. They openly declare that their ends can be attained only by the forcible overthrow of all existing social conditions. Let the ruling classes tremble at a communistic revolution. The proletarians have nothing to lose but their chains. They have a world to win.

> Working men of all countries, Unite!

SOURCE: Excerpted from *The Communist Manifesto* by Karl Marx and Friedrich Engels.

issued an invitation to all righteous persons to join with the ignorant and miserable proletariat in hastening the day of triumph. Once the revolution of the downtrodden was successful in gaining political power, a "dictatorship of the proletariat" (not further defined) was to be created, which would preside over the gradual transformation of the society it ruled.

What was the ultimate goal of Marxist revolution? According to Marx, it was a communist society, in which *private control/ownership of the means of production would be abolished* and men and women would be essentially equal and free to develop their full human potential. For the first time in history, said Marx, the old boast of the Greeks that "Man is the measure of all things" would be

Karl Marx
1818–1883

The critical thing [for the philosopher] is not to understand the world, but to change it!

With this maxim as his polestar, the philosopher Karl Marx became the most notorious, most quoted, and most influential social reformer of the nineteenth and twentieth centuries. The recent demise of that distortion of his ideas called Soviet communism has put his name and reputation under a heavy cloud from which they may never recover. But for one hundred and fifty years, Marx and Marxism provided much of the world's dissatisfied citizenry with what they perceived to be their best hope of better times.

Karl Marx was born into a well-to-do Jewish family in Trier, Germany, which at that time was part of the kingdom of Prussia. He studied at the universities of Bonn and Berlin, where his major interest was philosophy, but his interests soon expanded to include economics and sociology, two sciences that were still in their infancies. By the mid-1840s, he

■ **Karl and Jenny Marx.**

he was slowly shaping his radical critique of contemporary European society by drawing on all three disciplines: German philosophy, English economics, and French social thought.

Prevented by his Jewish background from realizing his original plan of teaching in a university, Marx returned to Trier after graduating from the University of Berlin. In 1842, he opened a small newspaper, the *Rhenish Gazette,* which was dedicated to promoting social and political reform. He soon got into trouble with the conservative authorities and had to flee to escape arrest. He lived briefly in Paris, where he came to know his lifelong supporter Friedrich Engels, son of a wealthy German manufacturer. Engels and Marx collaborated on the *Communist Manifesto,* published just weeks before the 1848 revolutions.

Soon Marx aroused the suspicions of the French authorities, and had to move on. An attempt to use the German uprisings to enter national

fulfilled. A society would be created in which "the free development of each is the condition for the free development of all."

At the time, no government took notice of the *Communist Manifesto;* none of the important 1848 revolutionary groups had heard of it or its authors. But in time this changed. During the 1850s and 1860s, Marx and Engels gradually emerged as two of the leading socialist thinkers and speakers. From his London base (England had the most liberal political association and censorship laws in

Europe), Marx worked on his great analysis of mid-nineteenth century industrial society, *Capital,* (1867–1873), which was published in two volumes. This work was the basis of Marx's boast that his socialism was scientific, unlike the utopian (that is, impractical) socialism of earlier days.

It should be remembered that Marx, like all of us, was a child of his times. The 1840s were the years of the most crude exploitation of the workers by greedy or frightened employers; they were frightened because many of the

politics as a revolutionary leader failed, and again Marx had to flee his native country, this time to London where Engels was ready to help. Marx spent the rest of his life in English exile, living a most bourgeois life in genteel poverty with his German wife and several children.

The world around Marx was in the throes of the first wave of industrialism, and it was not an attractive place for most working people. Horrible air and water pollution were common in the factory towns and in the working-class sections of the cities. Public health was neglected, medical help was re stricted to the well-to-do, and, welfare facilities of any type were almost nonexistent. Women and children worked at exhausting jobs for very low pay, and workers were frequently fired without warning to make room for someone else who agreed to work for less. Neither law nor custom protected the workers' rights against their employer. And among the employers, cutthroat competition was the rule. Government intervention to assure a "level playing field" in the marketplace was unknown. When governmental power was occasionally employed, it was always in favor of the status quo, which meant against the workers.

Marx observed this scene closely and was convinced that the situation must soon erupt in proletarian revolution. The explosion would come first in the most advanced industrial countries, which meant at this time Britain, parts of Germany and France, and possibly the United States. While Engels provided financial assistance, Marx dedicated many years to working out a theory of history and social development that would make sense of the chaos and allow a rational hope of a better world in the future. Eventually, he produced *Das Kapital,* or *Capital,* the bible of "scientific socialism," which was published in the original German in 1867 and translated into most European languages by the later nineteenth century. Almost all the work was done in the Reading Room of the British Library, which Marx visited with clocklike regularity for decades.

At almost the same time, in 1864, Marx actively organized the International Workingmen's Association. This so-called First International lasted only a few years before it collapsed in internal arguments about how the revolution of the proletariat should best be accomplished. Marx was always a headstrong character and was most unwilling to allow others to have their say. Like many prophets, he came to think that any who disagreed with him were ignorant or malicious. Engels was one of the few intimates who remained faithful to the master to the end.

In 1883, Marx died in the same poverty in which he had lived in the London suburb of Hampstead. At his death, the proletarian revolution seemed further away than ever, but the movement was slowly growing. It would make giant strides in several countries in the 1890s, and in far-off Russia, a country that Marx held in contempt for its backwardness, a certain Vladimir Ilich Ulyanov, better known as Lenin, was studying *Capital* with an eye to the Russian future.

smaller businesses were being driven to the wall by the bloodthirsty competition of the free market. As these small business owners desperately looked for ways to lower production costs, they usually tried to save by reducing wages. The result was often an extremely low pay scale for the semiskilled and unskilled workers who made up most of the industrial labor force. Since in this era what Marx called a "reserve army" of unemployed were always ready to work at almost any wage, any workers who complained or tried to organize a strike could be gotten rid of instantly without harm to the employer. The most elementary job security was totally absent. Marx was not alone in believing that this condition would persist until it was changed by militant force.

Marxist Organizations

In 1864, Marx played a central role in creating the **First International,** properly, the International Working Men's Association, in London. This organization had a short life span, falling apart because of internal dissension in 1876. Nevertheless, it served as a central interchange among the budding socialist parties of Europe and gave Marx a good platform for spreading his own brand of revolutionary thought.

When the **Paris Commune** arose in the wake of the lost war with Prussia in 1871, Marx mistakenly thought that the dawn of social revolution had come and enthusiastically greeted the very radical oratory of the *Communards.* The Commune was speedily crushed, but socialist parties came into being everywhere after 1871 and grew steadily over the next decades. By the end of the century, they were the primary voice of the industrial working class. Their common denominator was a demand for radical rearrangement of the existing socioeconomic order. Some of these parties were anti-Marxist in doctrine, preferring either some form of anarchism (see the next section) or wishing to operate mainly through labor unions (a tendency that Marx rejected as mere reformism). But most were Marxist and subscribed to the principles laid out in *Capital* by the master.

The most important socialist parties were in Germany, Austria, Belgium, and France. In southern Europe, the Marxists were outnumbered by anarchists and *syndicalists*; in Britain and the United States, no socialist party had a wide following among the workers; and in Russia, the Marxists were still a tiny exile group at the end of the century.

✛ RIVALS OF MARXISM

Anarchism

In Mediterranean Europe and Russia, the theory of politics called **anarchism** captured many minds. *Anarchism is the rejection of the state* and the powers that the modern state exercises over its citizenry. Anarchists believe that all government is necessarily prone to corruption and that the surrender of authority by the citizen to any institution or party is a general mistake. Only such authority as is necessary to avoid conflict over property or other rights of the citizens should be surrendered, and even then, the least possible authority should be granted and only on a small-scale, localized basis. Anarchists simply do not trust any government to avoid the pursuit of power for its own sake. They believe that sooner or later every government will succumb to the temptation to restrict its citizens' freedoms without just cause.

As a theory of politics, anarchism goes back to the ancient Greeks. The modern founders of anarchism are the Frenchman Pierre Proudhon, whom we have already encountered as a mid-nineteenth century activist, and the Russian **Michael Bakunin** (1827–1876). Bakunin developed the *propaganda of the deed,* the idea that a dramatic, violent act was the most effective way to gather converts for anarchism. The deeds his followers performed were acts of *political terror:* they carried out bombings and assassinations in the hopes of shaking the structures of government from the top down. In the two decades between 1885 and 1905, the high point of terrorism in Europe, about three hundred lives were sacrificed to this belief, including several reigning kings and queens, prime ministers, presidents (including the U.S. president William McKinley in 1901) and assorted generals.

Nowhere did the propaganda of the deed succeed; everywhere but Russia, both governments and popular opinion reacted strongly against the terrorists. Eventually, terror became discredited and was given up as a means of bringing down governments and/or swaying public opinion. After World War I, little was heard of anarchism until the 1960s, when it was briefly revived by French and German university students.

Syndicalism

Syndicalism is a form of political action by the working classes. It is founded on the belief that only the laboring classes and peasants should govern, because only they contribute a substantial asset to society through their work. Instead of the false verbal sparring and make-believe of the political parties of the middle classes, the laborers must create a large-scale association of persons employed in the same type of work. This association, called a *syndicate,* would represent the economic and social interests of the members and confer with other syndicates to find common political means for progress in economics and justice in society. Like anarchism, syndicalism did not wish to abolish private property, but to limit its political power and distribute it more evenly.

Syndicalism was always stronger than socialism in Spain and Portugal and was a strong rival to it in Italy and France. Many working people in these countries condemned the unbounded greed which they saw in liberalism as practiced by the bourgeoisie. Syndical government offered the badly paid and miserably treated working classes and small peasants a way out of this condition without going to the extreme of class warfare and the abolition of private property.

In Great Britain, the labor force was never much attracted to either socialism or its rivals as a solution to the dual problems of concentrated wealth and concentrated poverty. Instead, British workers in the later nineteenth century concentrated on gaining higher pay and better working conditions through a moderate reformism that centered on the right to strike and organize unions. In 1906, the reformist but non-Marxist **Labour Party** was formed, and in the general elections of that year, sent twenty-nine new representatives as delegates to the House of Commons. The new party gradually secured the vote of most union members and much of the liberal middle class. It was able to replace the Liberal Party as the main opponent of the Conservatives after World War I.

Revisionism

In the 1880s, Chancellor Bismarck attempted to crush the appeal of socialism in Germany by an attack on two fronts: first, he outlawed the Marxist socialist party, which had been organized in 1875, claiming that it was a revolutionary group with the destruction of the state as its ultimate aim. Then he tried to show that socialism was unnecessary because the German state itself would look out adequately for the workers' welfare. During the 1880s, a series of new laws instituting unemployment insurance,

■ **Suffragettes.** One of the many late nineteenth century demonstrations for women's voting rights, this one in the United States. In most cases, the Western countries did not grant female suffrage until after World War I.

accident and health protection, and pensions made Bismarck's Germany the most progressive state in the world in terms of social policy.

The attack on the Marxists did not succeed; after a few years, there were more German socialists than ever, and in 1890, the antisocialist law was repealed. The **German Social Democratic Party** (SD) steadily gained votes, attracting not only workers but also the lower middle classes and civil servants. With several newspapers, a tight network of local offices, and an extensive financial base in the German labor unions, the Social Democratic Party set the pace for socialists throughout Europe.

In 1899, a leading Social Democratic theorist, Eduard Bernstein, published a book in which he claimed that the SDs would soon become strong enough to take over the power of the state in peaceful, constitutional fashion. The socialist ideal would then be introduced through the workings of a parliament and government controlled by the Marxists. Thus, the idea of violent revolution was outmoded. According to Bernstein, Marx (who had died sixteen years earlier) had not been able to foresee that capitalism would be so tempered by democracy that the workers would be able to counter it through the ballot, rather than on the barricades. The triumph of social justice could and should be obtained without bloodshed.

This idea was at once denounced by many in the **Second International,** the Europe-wide association of socialists founded in 1889. But the revisionist theory attracted many followers in the more advanced countries, especially in Germany and France. By the coming of World War I, **revisionism** was a strong rival to orthodox Marxism as the true path to the millennium.

■ **The Urban Poor.** This engraving by the Frenchman Gustav Dore (1832–1883) dramatizes effectively the miseries of slum life in the early Industrial Age.

✤ EMIGRATION OVERSEAS

The largest migration of human beings in world history took place from Europe to overseas destinations during the second half of the nineteenth century. In general, the triggers for this movement were economic, but it began with the upheaval of 1848, when tens of thousands of Germans and Austrians looked to America for the freedoms they feared they would never have in their homeland.

From about 2.5 million in the decade of the 1850s, total net emigration from Europe rose each decade until it peaked in the years just before World War I. By then, about 12 million people had left Europe in a ten-year period, a number about equal to the entire population of Scandinavia at that time. The war shut this stream down almost completely, and it never again reached those dimensions. In all, some *60 million Europeans emigrated during the nineteenth century and did not return.* (About one of three emigrants to the United States eventually returned to the home country for reasons ranging from homesickness to deportation.)

Destinations

This river of migrants flowed mainly to the New World, but Australia, New Zealand, and (for Russians exclusively) Siberia were also important destinations. The French colony of Algeria and the British colony of South Africa also attracted emigrants.

In terms of proportionate impact, Argentina was the most dramatic example of immigration in the world; about 3 percent of the total Argentine population arrived

The Dining Hall at Ellis Island. This 1906 photo captures the human faces which poured through the huge New York emigrant facility. By this time, the dominant nationalities were Italian and east European. New York City's population was over one-third foreign born at this era.

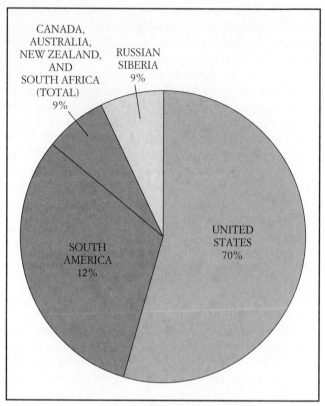

● **MAP 45.2   European Emigrants' Destinations, 1800–1960.** The United States was easily the most preferred destination throughout this century and a half, with South America (mainly Argentina and Brazil) a distant second. Great Britain and Ireland supplied about one third of the total, Italy about 30%, and the rest of Europe the remainder. The ethnic balance shifted steadily from northern and western Europe to southern and eastern as the nineteenth century matured. The peak was reached in the decade just preceding World War I when an average of about 1.2 million emigrated annually, mainly to the United States.

from Europe (mostly Spain and Italy) every year in the early twentieth century—three times the rate that the United States gained from the same source. But the United States was easily the most popular single destination for emigrating Europeans, receiving about 45 percent of the grand total of immigrants worldwide during the nineteenth century.

Why did they leave? First and foremost, they were seeking better economic conditions. The rise and fall of emigration rates corresponded closely to European business cycles. In hard times, more left for the "land of golden opportunities." But a large proportion left because they were dissatisfied with political and social conditions and had little faith that the future held any more promise than the present.

Types of Emigrants

Most emigrants were not the very poor or ignorant; they were people who had been able to save a little or had relatives who were better off and helped them to get a start. Many of them were small farmers who had too little land to ever get much farther up the ladder and feared for their sons' future when that little would be divided again by inheritance. Some were skilled craftsmen, who believed restrictions would prevent them from becoming independent entrepreneurs. Some were educated people who saw no chance of fully using their education in a class-bound society. In the later phases, many were indeed the poor and ignorant; they were assisted by relatives who had emigrated earlier and had managed to establish themselves in their new land. Unmarried young men were the largest single contingent of emigrants, followed by young girls, usually the sisters and fiancées of males already in the new country.

The ethnic origins of the emigrants varied by chronology of departure. The majority of those who left for the New World in the middle of the nineteenth century were from Britain, Ireland, and Germany; in the later decades, they tended to be from eastern and southern European countries. By World War I, the Austro-Hungarians, Russians, Poles, and, above all, the Italians supplied the great bulk of the emigrants.

In the industrial economies of northern and western Europe, the working classes could find reasonably secure factory and white-collar jobs. Hence, they were less likely to emigrate than the unemployed and underemployed peasants and laborers of eastern and southern Europe. As a rule, the more literate and better prepared went to North America or Australia; South America received mainly those with lesser prospects.

Summary

In the wake of the two Industrial Revolutions of the nineteenth century, life changed thoroughly and dramatically for much of the population of western Europe, but less so for people in southern and eastern Europe. These regional differences reflect the relative degree of industrialization they experienced; by the end of the century, eastern Europe and much of Iberia, the Balkans, and Italy were still in a preindustrial state.

In the industrialized areas, constant migrations from country to town created larger and larger cities. Where industry had made little progress, emigration overseas served to relieve the population pressure. The largest mass movement of people in history took place from Europe to the new lands overseas.

For those who remained behind, the status of the working classes improved in both the material and the political sense. A great number of individuals entered the new unions and the new parties. By the beginning of the twentieth century, some degree of democracy, ranging from the full liberties of Britain and Scandinavia to the modest allowances of Austria-Hungary and Iberia, was taken for granted as a normal condition of political life.

Much of what had been dismissed as the empty dreams of radicals in 1848 had become a peaceable reality by 1900 in a large segment of Europe: a state that accepted the laboring masses' rights to the vote, to a degree of economic security, and to perfect equality in the courts and schools. Yet those who believed in true equality for all still had much to accomplish. Following the principles of their leader, Marxist socialists believed they had the answer. But they were opposed by their anarchist and syndicalist rivals, as well as by the property-owning classes, and were split among themselves on the vital question of how to attain power.

Test Your Knowledge

1. The Second Industrial Revolution was generated by
   a. the worker revolts of 1848.
   b. capitalist exploitation of the workers to the maximum extent possible.
   c. industrial chemistry and electrical energy.
   d. mining and iron making.
2. The countries that were in the forefront of the Second Industrial Revolution were
   a. Britain and the United States.
   b. the United States and Germany.
   c. Japan and the United States.
   d. Germany and Britain.
3. The most important of the new forms of business emerging in the late nineteenth century was the
   a. partnership.
   b. proprietorship.
   c. nonprofit company.
   d. corporation.
4. Labor unions first gained the legal right to organize and to strike in
   a. Germany.
   b. the United States.
   c. Britain.
   d. Holland.
5. Which of the following pairs is incorrect?
   a. Karl Marx and scientific socialism
   b. Edward Bernstein and revisionist socialism
   c. Michael Bahunin and syndicalism
   d. Pierre Proudhon and anarchism
6. The bulk of the European emigrants of the nineteenth century were
   a. landless laborers seeking a new start in North and South America.
   b. dissatisfied small farmers, businessmen, artisans, and skilled laborers.
   c. Jews and others fleeing political persecution.
   d. relatively successful shop owners, artisans, and white-collar workers.
7. In the early twentieth century, the country supplying the largest number of emigrants to the United States was
   a. Germany.
   b. Ireland.
   c. Russia.
   d. Italy.
8. Which of the following was *not* something new in the late nineteenth-century?
   a. The corporation as a dominant economic entity
   b. The spread of anarchist philosophy
   c. Emigration to the United States from Europe
   d. Revision of the Marxist plan of revolution

Identification Terms

anarchism	Friedrich Engels	Labour Party	revisionism (Marxism)
Michael Bakunin	First International	Paris Commune (1871)	Second International
corporation	German Social Democratic Party		syndicalism

Bibliography

Berlanstein, L. R. *The Working People of Paris, 1871–1914,* 1985, and E. Weber, *Peasants into Frenchmen: The Modernization of Rural France, 1870–1914,* 1980, are complementary works of importance and authority.

Edwards, S. *The Paris Commune,* 1971. A straightforward account of the bloody class-based uprising.

Erickson, C. *Emigration from Europe, 1815–1914,* 1976. The best single volume work on the topic

Gillis, J. *Youth and History: Tradition and Change in European Age Relations, 1770 to the Present,* 1981. A fascinating survey, focusing on the nineteenth century.

Joll, J. *The Anarchists,* 1964. A survey of what these idealists wanted. See also B. Tuchman's relevant chapter in her work cited below under Social History.

Kraut, A. M. *The Huddled Masses: Immigrants in American Society,* 1982. See also O. Handlin's several books on immigrants to America and their fate here. For immigrants to Latin American countries, see the bibliography in Chapter 58.

Landes, D. *The Unbound Prometheus,* 1969. Remains an excellent introduction to both the First and the Second Industrial Revolutions.

McLellan, D. *Karl Marx: His Life and Thought,* 1974. Probably the best single introduction, but there are many other volumes on the life and action of the greatest of the socialist theorists. F. Mehring, *Karl Marx: The Story of His Life,* 1976, is another good biography.

Milward, A., and S. B. Saul, *The Development of the Economies of Continental Europe, 1850–1914,* 1977. A good textbook on its subject, including all European nations.

Social history is explored from numerous points of view by a host of recent books. Burnett, J. *History of the Cost of Living,* 1969. An eye-opener as to how much was spent by whom on what. J. Laver, *Manners and Morals in the Age of Optimism,* 1966, treats of the various classes' views of what was proper and improper. See also the J. Gillis *Youth and History,* 1981, cited above, as well as P. Stearns, *Old Age in European Society,* 1976, which looks mainly at France.

Tobias, J. *Urban Crime in Victorian England,* 1972. A pioneering effort to reconstruct the incidence and seriousness of crime in London. See also the same author's *Crime and Industrial Society in the Nineteenth Century,* 1967.

Trudgill, E. *Madonnas and Magdalenas,* 1976. An examination of Victorian sexual prejudices and attitudes.

Tuchman, B. *The Proud Tower,* 1963. An extraordinarily readable selection of pieces on various topics in European social history before 1914.

Vicinus, M. *Suffer and Be Still, Women in the Victorian Age,* 1972. Goes far to supplement R. Bridenthal and C. Koontz, *Becoming Visible: Women in European History,* 1976, and B. Anderson and J. Zinsser, *A History of Their Own: Women in Europe from Prehistory to the Present,* 1988 (see Chapter 37).

Walkowitz, J. *Prostitution and Victorian Society,* 1980, provides another look behind the scenes.

Weber, A. *The Growth of Cities in the Nineteenth Century,* 1899. An old but still useful analysis of urban growth. Accompanying it to show the dominant position of the city by the mid-nineteenth century are J. P. McKay, *Tramways and Trolleys: The Rise of Urban Mass Transport in Europe,* 1976, D. Pinckney, *Napoleon III and the Rebuilding of Paris,* 1972, and G. Masur, *Imperial Berlin,* 1970.

CHAPTER 46

MODERN SCIENCE AND ITS IMPLICATIONS

In the West, the eighty years between 1860 and 1940 proved to be one of the most dazzling periods of innovation and change in intellectual history. In the last years of the nineteenth century, it was still possible for sophisticated persons to hold to a Newtonian view of the universe: the physical world was a composition of law-abiding matter, finite in its dimensions and predictable in its actions. Fifty years later, most of the natural sciences and especially physics, biology, and astronomy had been radically changed by some new factual data and many new interpretations of old data. The social, or "soft" sciences such as psychology, sociology, and economics had undergone a similar transformation, although here the novel ideas encountered more resistance because they could not be so easily demonstrated.

Religion, too, experienced striking changes. Long in retreat before advancing secular thought, some Christians believed that their religion was evolving like other human thought and that the Bible was properly subject to interpretations that would differ sharply in various ages and circumstances. But some denominations moved toward an uncompromising insistence on literal interpretation of the Bible as the sole source of God's unchanging truth.

✤ THE PHYSICAL SCIENCES

In the second half of the nineteenth century, the mental frame of reference implied by Science became much more commonplace than ever before. By century's end, educated individuals throughout most of the world accepted the proposition that empirical science was the main source of worthwhile information. Religious revelation, authority, and/or tradition could not compete as legitimate rivals.

In the first half of the present century, the preponderance of Science over competing worldviews became stronger still. Theology and philosophy, which previously had some claim to presenting a comprehensive explanation of human life, became the narrowly defined and exotic preserves of a handful of clerics and academics. In the universities, which had become the intellectual centers of the world, the physical sciences became increasingly specialized while attracting more and more students; meanwhile, armies of scientific researchers garnered the lion's share of academic budgets and prestige. Though fewer and fewer were able to understand the intricacies of the new research, the general public still maintained its underlying belief in the method of Science as the best way of solving human problems, a viewpoint that was weakened but survived even the cataclysms of the two World Wars.

Darwinian Biology

This shift from theology to science and hence from spiritual to material causation had begun with the Scientific Revolution of earlier days (see Chapter 32), but certain nineteenth-century ideas hastened its pace greatly. *Darwinian biology* was by far the most important.

In 1859, the Englishman Charles Darwin published **The Origin of Species,** a book that did for biology what Adam Smith's *Wealth of Nations* had done for economics. The controversy the book set off roiled European and American society for over a generation, but in the end the Darwinian view generally won out over its detractors.

What did Darwin say? Basically, he argued that through a process of "*natural selection,*" the individual species of plants and animals (inferentially including humans) evolved slowly from unknown ancestors. The organisms that possessed some marginal advantage in the constant *struggle for survival* would live long enough to create descendants that also bore those assets in their genes. For example, a flower seed with sufficient "feathers" to float a long distance through the air would more likely find suitable ground to germinate than those with few or none. Slowly over time, that flower type would come to replace others in a given area and survive where others died off.

This is a *mechanical explanation* of Nature's variety and of the evolution of species. It is similar to stating that an automobile moves along a highway because its wheels are propelled by a drive shaft and axles, which are themselves driven by a motor. All true, of course, but it leaves out any mention of a person sitting in the driver's seat and turning the ignition key. Darwin carried Newton's mechanistic explanation of the cosmos into the domain of living things. In so doing, he eliminated the role of an intelligent Creator, or God, who had ordered Nature toward a definite purpose and goal: glorifying Himself and instructing humans. God was superfluous in Darwinian science and, being superfluous, should be ignored.

Darwin carried this theme forward with his 1871 **Descent of Man,** which specifically included humans in the evolutionary process and treated the morals and ethics they developed as the product of mechanical, naturalistic processes, not of an all-knowing and directing God. If it is the ability of our thumbs to close upon our fingers that chiefly distinguishes humans from apes, as some biologists

believe, then it also may be that what some call the human conscience is just a product of evolutionary experience, aimed at physical survival rather than justice and obedience to the will of a Creator-Judge.

Contrary to general impressions, Darwin did not explain *why* natural selection occurs or the factors that caused some variance from the norm (a mutation) that resulted in the survival of one species and the expiration of others. That task was left to an Austrian monk named Gregor Mendel, who worked out the principles of modern genetics in many years of unrecognized labor with vegetables (peas) in his monastery garden. And it should be added that Darwin's work was matched, simultaneously, by the independent research of Alfred Russell Wallace, another English amateur, who never sought or received public notice until after Darwin had taken over the stage.

Physics

In physics the path breakers were **Ernst Mach** (1838– 1916), **Wilhelm Roentgen** (1845–1923), **Max Planck** (1858–1947), and **Albert Einstein** (1879–1955). The fact that all four were educated in German schools is an indication of the emphasis on scientific research in the German educational system (see Chapter 39)—a model

■ **Age of Scientific Progress.** This sketch shows Pierre Curie and the British Sir Richard Krimsky, two eminent chemists, consulting in London on their research into the qualities of radium. Such international collaboration became commonplace in the later 1800s.

Charles Darwin Reflects on *The Origin of Species*

Towards the end of his life, Charles Darwin wrote an autobiographical sketch for his children in which he outlined his feelings about his epoch-making work. The following excerpts are taken from his reflections on the modification of animal and bird species he had observed during his 1836 voyage on the *Beagle* to the Galapagos.

It was evident that such facts as these [i.e. certain species' changes] as well as many others could be explained on the supposition that species gradually become modified; and the subject haunted me. But it was equally evident that neither the action of the surrounding conditions, nor the will of the organisms (especially in the case of plants), could account for the innumerable cases in which organisms of every kind are beautifully adapted to their habits of life—for instance a woodpecker or tree-frog to climb trees, or a seed for dispersal by hooks or plumes. I had always been much struck by such adaptations, and until these could be explained it seemed to me almost useless to endeavour to prove by indirect evidence that species have been modified. . .

I soon percieved that Selection was the key-stone of man's success in making useful races of animals and plants. But how selection could be applied to organisms living in a state of nature remained for some time a mystery to me. In October 1838, that is fifteen months after I had begun my systematic inquiry, I happened to read for amusement 'Malthus on Population,' and being well prepared to appreciate the struggle for existence which everywhere goes on from long continued observation of the habits of animals and plants, it at once struck me that under these circumstances favourable variations would tend to be preserved and unfavourable ones to be destroyed. The result of this would be formation of new species . . .

After many hesitations and delays, Darwin finally decided to publish the book he had been incubating since 1837.

In September 1858 I set to work by the strong advice of Lyell and Hooker* to prepare a volume on the transmutation of species, but was often interrupted by ill health. . . I abstracted the [manuscript] begun on a much larger scale in 1856, and completed the volume on the same reduced scale. It cost me 13 months and ten days hard labor. It was published under the title of the 'Origin of Species' in November 1859. Though considerably added to and corrected in the later editions it has remained substantially the same book.

It has sometimes been said that the success of the *Origin* proved "that the subject was in the air", or "that men's minds were prepared for it". I do not think that this is strictly true, for I occasionally sounded not a few naturalists, and never happended across a single one who seemed to doubt about the permanence of species. Even Lyell and Hooker, though they would listen with interest to me never seemed to agree. I tried once or twice to explain to able men what I meant by natural selection, but signally failed. What I believe strictly true is that innumerable well-observed facts were stored in the minds of naturalists ready to take their proper places, as soon as any theory which would receive them was sufficiently explained. . .

My books have sold largely in England, have been translated into many languages and passed through several editions in foreign countries. I have heard it said that the success of a work abroad is the best test of its enduring value. I doubt whether this is at all trustworthy, but judged by this standard my name ought to last for a few years.

*Eminent British scientists and friends of Darwin.

SOURCE: *Autobiographies: Charles Darwin; Thomas H. Huxley.* Gavin de Beer, ed. Oxford University Press 1974, p. 70–74, 84.

that was gradually extended throughout the Western world.

Mach's several publications in the 1880s and 1890s contributed importantly to the underlying concept of all twentieth-century physics: *the impossibility of applying philosophical logic to physical matter.* Mach believed that scientists could only determine what their intellect and equipment told them about matter, *not* what matter actually was or did. What a later German physicist would call the "Uncertainty Principle" had replaced the Newtonian world machine and *substituted probability for law.*

Roentgen was the discoverer of X rays, by which solid objects could be penetrated by a form of energy that made their interiors visible. His work, published at the end of the nineteenth century, immediately gave rise to experimentation with subatomic particles, especially in the laboratory of the Englishmen J. J. Thompson and **Ernest Rutherford** (1871–1937). Rutherford, who was a pioneer in the discovery of radioactivity and the splitting of the atom, is one of the great names of modern science. His work was materially helped by the simultaneous research conducted by the French radiologist **Marie Curie** (1867–1934) whose laboratory work with radium proved that mass and energy were not separate, but could be converted into one another under certain conditions.

Planck headed a major research lab for many years and revolutionized the study of energy with his *quantum theory,* by which energy is discharged in a not fully predictable series of emissions from its sources, rather than as a smooth stream. Quantum theory explained otherwise contradictory data about the motion of objects and subatomic matter such as electrons and protons.

Then, in 1905, the young Swiss German Einstein published the most famous paper on physics ever, the first of his theories on *relativity.* Einstein insisted that space and time formed a continuous whole and that measurement of both space and time depended as much on the observer as on the subjects of the measurement themselves. He saw time as a "fourth dimension" of space, rather than as an independent concept. Eleven years later, Einstein published his *General Theory of Relativity,* which announced the birth of twentieth-century physics (and the death of the Newtonian model).

Twentieth-century physics differs from the Newtonian conception in several fundamental ways:

- *Uncertainty.* In dealing with some forms of energy and with subatomic particles, modern science does not assume that cause and effect relations are reliable. Strong probability replaces certainty as the best obtain-

■ **The Young Einstein.** This photo was taken about 1902, when Einstein was twenty-three, and yet an unknown dabbler in theoretical physics.

able result. No Newtonian laws apply except in the most crude fashions.
- *Relativity.* The observer's status affects the supposedly independent object observed; some would say that the very fact of observation changes the nature of the object or process observed, so that no "neutral" observation is possible.
- *Interchangeability of matter and energy.* Under specified conditions, Newtonian distinction between matter and energy falls away, and one becomes the other.

These mind-bending novelties have been recognized and acted upon by only a small handful of specialists, mainly in the universities. They have removed modern physics from the comprehension of most ordinary people, even well-educated ones. Physicists tend to resort to a math-based jargon that is hardly intelligible to others but allows them to express themselves concisely. The assumption, so common in the nineteenth century, that physical science would be the key to a fully comprehensible and comprehended universe, in which matter and energy would be the reliable servants of intellect, was dashed by the physical scientists themselves. Their ever more exotic

■ **Thomas Edison in His Laboratory.** The rapid advance of the physical sciences in the nineteenth century was almost immediately translated into technology. One of the outstanding examoles of both scientist and technician was the American Thomas Edison, whose inventions such as the incandescent light bulb were put to profitable use as they issued from his laboratory in New Jersey.

research and its unsettling results widened the previously narrow gap between professional scientists and educated lay people.

This intellectual divorce between the mass of people and the holders of specialized knowledge has become a subject of concern to many observers. The nonspecialists in positions of responsibility are often forced to implement policies involving scientific and technical points that they cannot and do not understand. Statesmen and politicians, for example, rarely comprehend the scientific background of their policies; yet increasingly, the public and even the private lives of citizens in a modern state are affected by these scientific details. The naive optimism of the early proponents of nuclear power plants, who had no understanding of the menace posed by a nuclear meltdown, is a case in point. They were relying on scientific advisers who had every professional interest in seeing the plants built. This dilemma of contemporary politics is not going to be easily solved.

Astronomy

In astronomy the major changes are more recent. The last fifty years have seen fantastic advances and an ongoing debate. The advances were mainly technological: huge new telescopes and radio devices, space vehicles that venture far into the cosmos to report on distant planets, and spectroscopes that analyze light emitted from the

stars. As a result of this new technology, much more is known about the nature of the universe than before. Space probes have revealed that planets such as Mars and Saturn are physically quite different than previously thought, while the moon has become almost familiar territory. The universe is now thought to be much larger than once believed and to contain millions or billions of stars.

Strictly speaking, the debate is not astronomical in character, but rather metaphysical ("beyond physics"). It revolves around how this huge universe was created and how it will develop. The widely supported "big bang" theory holds that the universe originated several billion years ago with a cosmic explosion of a great fireball, which is still flinging fragments of matter—stars—farther out into space. Some think that the expansion will end with a general cooling and dying off of all life-supporting planets; others believe that gravity will gradually slow the expansion and bring all the scattered fragments together again, only to have another big bang and repeat the process.

A third group—Creationists—rejects both of these naturalistic explanations and holds to the Christian tradition that an Intelligent Being created the cosmos and all within it in accord with a preconceived plan. In the same way, a number of respected scientists accept the overwhelming evidence for the slow evolution of humans, but insist that the creation of an immortal soul within *homo sapiens* by a God is a perfectly possible hypothesis.

⚜ THE SOCIAL SCIENCES

The social sciences have human beings, collectively or individually, as their subject matter. They include psychology, sociology, anthropology, economics, and political science. These disciplines were also strongly affected by the waves of new ideas and data produced by the physical sciences in the later nineteenth century. Just as the sciences of the seventeenth-century innovators slowly percolated into the consciousness of historians and political philosophers to produce the Enlightenment, so did the innovations and technological breakthroughs of the nineteenth-century physicists and biologists affect the worldviews of the sociologists and psychologists who followed. The effect was probably most spectacular and controversial in psychology.

Freudian Psychology

Psychology has been radically altered by the widely held modern conviction that its major purpose should be to heal sick minds, rather than merely understand how the mind works. In this century, psychiatry—the healing process—has come to be an important branch of medicine. No one individual has been more crucial to this transformation than *Sigmund Freud* (1856–1939), a doctor from Vienna, Austria who gradually developed a theory of psychiatric treatment called *psychoanalysis* (see the Biography in this chapter).

Freud believed that not the conscious, but the *unconscious is the controlling factor* of the deepest mental life. In effect, he was rejecting the principle of rationality—that is, that men and women are capable and desirous of reasoned acts—on which all previous psychological theory had been built. Psychoanalysis attempts to help the patient to recognize and do something about the distorted impressions of reality that produce social or individual disabilities. It is based on Freud's convictions that the sexual drive is the motor of the unconscious, that childhood events are almost always the source of mental and emotional problems in adult life, and that the eternal struggle between the *libido* or pleasure principle, and the *superego,* which might be translated as conscience, will never be entirely resolved within the human mind.

Freud has had several competitors in explaining the mind's workings and how the sick might be cured. The Swiss *Carl Jung* (1875–1961) was one of Freud's early collaborators, but he broke with the master (as did many others) and founded his own psychological school. It emphasized religious symbolism and *archetypal ideas* shared by all humans in their unconscious as the bedrock of mental activity.

Ivan Pavlov (1849–1936) is considered the founder of the behaviorist school, a widely supported theory that insists that the rewards and punishments given to various types of behavior are the controlling factors of individual psychology. Pavlov's work with dogs in his native Russia before World War I made him famous. His work was supplemented by the Americans *William James* (1842–1910) and *B. F. Skinner* (1904–1990) in the early and middle decades of this century.

Several modern schools of psychology have focused attention on childhood and adolescence. Melanie Klein, Karen Horney, and Anna Freud, Sigmund's daughter, have all contributed substantially to the progress of psychology through their work with younger children.

In recent years, the former sharp division of psychologists into pro- and anti-Freud camps has softened, and while much of his theoretical work is now rejected or discredited from universal application, a good deal more has been accepted as conventional wisdom. When we use terms such as *inferiority complex, Freudian slip,* and *Oedipus complex* in everyday speech, we are paying verbal tribute to the Austrian explorer of the mystery of inner space.

Anthropology and Sociology

Anthropology and sociology may be examined together. Both treat humans as a species, rather than as individuals, and both are new sciences that flourished for the first time in the twentieth century. Anthropology as a scientific discipline is an indirect product of Darwinian biology, though some work was done earlier. It is divided into two basic varieties: physical, dealing with humans as an animal species; and cultural, dealing with humans as the constructors of systems of values. Especially since World War II, great advances have been achieved in extending our knowledge back into prehistoric time. Combining with archaeology and the new subscience of sociobiology, the anthropologists have learned much about the physical and cultural aspects of earlier human life.

■ **The Consultation Room in Freud's Apartment.** This is the famous couch on which Freud's patients reclined while the psychiatrist listened to their "free associations" and took notes.

Sigmund Freud
1856–1939

The founder of modern psychotherapy, Sigmund Freud (1856–1939) is one of the three Germans of Jewish descent who radically changed the physical and social sciences of the Western world in a relatively brief epoch. (The others were Albert Einstein and Karl Marx.) In some ways, Freud's contribution was even more penetrating than the others, as the popularized versions of his ideas and theories have long since become part of the everyday mental equipment of even minimally educated persons.

Freud was born into a nonreligious Jewish household in Bohemia (now the Czech Republic), a province of the Habsburg empire. He entered medical studies at the University of Vienna in 1885 and lived in that city for almost his entire life. At first desiring a career in diseases of the nerves, he became more and more interested in the interlinking of the mind and the body, especially as this was evidenced by hysteria, or the breakdown of certain bodily functions under extreme stress. His attempt to show that the underlying cause of hysteria (almost always found in females) was some type of sexual fear or sexual trauma made him *persona non grata* among his medical cohorts. A few years later, his insistence on the sexuality of infants and small children as well as the sexual meanings of dreams, cemented this rejection.

But Freud was not put off by the disdain of his colleagues. In the decade between 1900 and 1910, he published several major studies in psychology and psychotherapeutic practice that won him international recognition. In this period, he developed his ideas on the possibility of reaching and healing underlying sources of mental anguish by means of free association: encouraging the patient to "talk out" the mental link between outwardly unrelated topics. This came to be called psychoanalysis; the healer's role was to be that of the encouraging listener rather than the active intervenor. Freud insisted that the psychoanalyst be a doctor of medicine who had then gone on to complete an often lengthy self-analysis.

By the mid-1920s, most of the original work in Freud's psychotherapeutic theories had been completed. He remained at the head of the International Psychoanalytical Association and continued his private practice in Vienna, where he had married and raised a family. Most of his later writings are concerned with cultural topics rather than medical ones, including his very famous *Civilization and Its Discontents* and *Moses and Monotheism.*

Sociology also came of age in the late nineteenth century. Unlike most fields of science, it can trace its basic theory to a small handful of brilliant individuals. First in time was **Auguste Comte** (1798–1857), a Frenchman whose philosophical treatise, *The Positive Philosophy,* insisted that laws of social behavior existed and were just as readily knowable as the laws of physical behavior. In this view, humans will advance through three stages of ability to perceive knowledge, culminating in the scientific stage just now being entered. Truth could and must be obtained by the application of *positivism,* by which Comte meant that only empirical, measurable data were reliable and that a philosophy that attempts to identify spiritual, nonmaterialistic forces or values was impossible.

Comte's view of sociology as the culmination of all the sciences inspired many imitators. In the last years of the nineteenth century, the French sociologist Emile Durkheim (1858–1917) and the German Max Weber (1864–1920) were equally important as formative influences, and in his special way, Karl Marx was perhaps the greatest of the nineteenth-century figures who studied the "science of society." Several Americans were also in the forefront of sociology's development, especially in the early twentieth century when American universities took up the discipline with enthusiasm. The underlying premise of sociology seemed to be particularly appealing to American habits of mind: if one knew enough of the laws of social behavior, one could *alter* that behavior in positive and planned ways. This mode of thought fit well with the American optimist view of society as an instrument that might be tuned by human interventions. But in many minds, this optimism was eventually countered by

The antagonism Freud aroused through his insistence on the sexual nature of much human activity was only increased by his equal insistence on the primacy of the unconscious in directing human action. For the same reasons many people were repelled by Darwinian evolutionary theory, Freud's assertions that humans are only sporadically rational and sporadically aware of why they thought or did certain things fell on stony ground, particularly in his native country. Many Austrians thought it no great loss when the "degenerate Jewish manipulator" Freud had to leave Vienna for London in the wake of the Nazi takeover in 1938. Already suffering from a painful cancer of the jaw, he died shortly after arriving there.

Freud is a striking example of the compartmentalization of life that many of the twentieth century's leading scientists have evolved. Promoters of revolutionary change in their professions, their day-to-day life could hardly be more quiet and regulated. Freud married a Viennese woman who was totally devoted to him and her children and who provided him with the very model of a quietly bourgeois family life. One of his daughters, Anna Freud, made a substantial reputation of her own in psychiatry in England.

Sigmund Freud was a pioneer of the huge, dark spaces of the human psyche. Much of what he insisted upon has now been revised or even rejected by the majority of psychiatrists, but it is perhaps no exaggeration to give him the title "Columbus of the Soul."

profound misgivings about the course of human society in the present century.

One offshoot of the Darwinian discoveries in biology was a reexamination of human ethics. More especially, can ethics originate through a particular set of environmental influences? If so, can one type of ethical behavior be promoted over another in some rational manner? Do ethics themselves evolve, or are they instilled by a Superior Being through the directives given in Scripture, as fundamentalist Christians believe?

Herbert Spencer (1820–1903) was the most noted of the upholders of Social Darwinism, a philosophy that held that ethics are indeed evolutionary in nature and that the competition among human beings is the main engine of social progress. As among the plants and animals, the fittest will survive, as a ruthless Nature demands. Though Spencer did not intend such a result, his philosophy of unbridled social competition made it all too easy for the powerful to justify their own position as the proper, even inevitable reward for their superiority. As for the poor or the unfortunate, their misery was the equally inevitable result of their natural inferiority. Social Darwinism was a temporarily fashionable pseudo-philosophy at the end of the nineteenth century, and its adherents have by no means entirely disappeared in the twentieth.

✤ THE MALAISE IN TWENTIETH-CENTURY SOCIETY

With all the triumphs of physical science and the growing acceptance of Science as the most certain path to useful knowledge, many people still felt uneasy about the road ahead. The social sciences were especially linked with this malaise, which became much more tangible after World War I.

In unintended ways, psychology has contributed as much to the *insecurity* and *uncertainty* that cloud modern lives in the West as the revolution in physics has. Both sciences often leave the observer with the feeling that things are not as they outwardly seem. In psychology, the brute instinct is as important as the reason; in physics, matter can suddenly turn into its opposite, nonmatter. Traditional knowledge is no longer applicable or is insufficient; traditional authority has shown itself incompetent to give clear answers to new questions. Freud himself claimed, with a note of ambivalent pride, that his work had finished the destruction of the traditional view of Man begun by the cosmology of Copernicus and continued by the biology of Darwin. While Copernicus had reduced humankind to being residents of a minor planet in a cosmos of millions of similar planets, Darwin had torn down the precious wall of difference between beasts and humans. Now Freud had shown that these human beings did not and could not even control their own acts or perceptions.

One of the prominent features of the social sciences in the twentieth century has been the spread of *cultural relativism*. The nineteenth century's assurance that whatever was the standard in Europe should become the standard of the world's behavior has been largely demolished. Persons raised in Western culture are much less convinced that there is but one proper way to raise small children, inculcate respect for the aged, assign gender roles, and so on than was the case a century ago. An appreciation of the variety of methods that can be applied to solve a generic task, such as instructing the young in what they will need to prosper, has become more common among Western people. It is interesting that this is happening at exactly the time when the rest of the world is imitating the West in many respects. This cultural relativism is another face of the general *abandonment of traditional ethnocentrism* that is an earmark of twentieth-century thought in the West.

⚜ RELIGIOUS THOUGHT AND PRACTICE

During the late nineteenth century, the Christian church came under siege throughout Europe. Both Catholic and Protestant believers found themselves portrayed by numerous opponents as relics from a forgotten medieval age who were against progress, rationalism, and anything modern. Intellectuals, in particular, rejected the traditional arguments of religion and the clergy's claim to represent a higher order of authority than mere human beings. Liberals rejected the stubborn conservatism of the clergy and the peasants who were the church's most faithful followers. Marxists laughed at the gullibility of the believer ("pie in the sky when you die"), while agitating against the churches, which they regarded as tools of the bourgeois class, like other institutions of the modern state.

These varied attacks had very substantial effect. Reportedly, by the 1890s, the English working class had entirely ceased to attend church. In France only a minority of the Catholic peasantry went to hear the priest on occasions other than their wedding day. Like the English and the Germans, the French urban workers were practically strangers to organized religion. In Italy and Spain, where the Catholic church was still an established church, anticlericalism was common in all classes, even though most peasants still supported the church as an essential part of their life.

Positivist science was a strong weapon in the attackers' arsenal. The battle over Darwin's biology was won by the Darwinians by century's end, even though the topic was still acrimoniously debated in some sectors. The long struggle over control of public education was settled everywhere by the coming of state-supported schools in which the religious denominations were excluded or restricted to religious instruction only. Religious belief was removed from the qualifications of officeholders, civil servants, and voters. Everywhere but Russia, by the 1870s Jews and atheists were made fully equal with Christians in law, if not always in practice.

In France, the *Dreyfus case* (1898–1900) aroused terrific resentment against the Roman Catholic hierarchy, which in collaboration with other anti-Semites tried to railroad an innocent man. Among the larger part of the educated and influential classes, *secularism* was taken for granted as the wave of the future in European (and American) civic culture.

Meanwhile, the churches everywhere were struggling to renew themselves and regain at least some of the lost ground. In the United States, the fundamentalist Protestant creeds became strong rivals of the Lutherans, Anglicans, and other, less aggressively evangelical churches. The British Nonconformists (those Protestants who did not "conform" to the Anglican credo, such as Methodists, Quakers, and Unitarians) showed formidable tenacity in their missionary work and the foundation of hundreds of schools. In Germany, Chancellor Bismarck made a major error in attempting to rouse support for his government by attacking the Catholic church. This "*Kulturkampf*" ended in the 1880s with a rout of the Bismarck forces. The church emerged stronger than ever and founded a political party, which was the second largest in the German parliament by 1910. The necessity of meeting the Darwinian challenge and the positivist critics of the Bible made it obligatory for both Catholic and Protestant to reexamine the basis of literal belief in the Creation, and gave birth to a school of Christian Bible exegesis on scientific foundations.

In 1891, the nineteenth-century tradition of papal rejection of all that was new was broken by Pope Leo XIII's major encyclical (papal letter): ***Rerum novarum*** ("About new things"). In this, the pope strongly supported the ideals of social justice for the working classes and the poor, while continuing to denounce atheistic socialism. For the next fifty years, *Rerum novarum* provided a guideline for loyal Catholics who wished to create a more liberal, less exploitative economic order. They frequently found themselves opposed by their co-religionists in positions of power throughout the Western world.

World War I initially dealt a heavy blow to all organized religions. Many members of the clergy in all denominations were caught up in the patriotic hysteria of the early weeks of the war and outdid themselves in blessing the troops and the battleships, claiming "Gott mit uns!" (God's on our side). The ghastly reality of the trenches quickly put an end to such claims. Radical discontent at the endless bloodletting among the troops sharpened the critiques. The clergy were denounced as willing pawns of the various governments that controlled their incomes and status. After the Russian Revolution, Marxist propaganda skillfully intensified these negative feelings both inside and outside Russia.

A small minority reacted differently. They saw the war and the following period of intense political and social upheaval as the inevitable collapse of a godless, mechanistic progressivism that had little of value to offer humans' spiritual nature. In the 1920s and 1930s, both Protestant and Catholic communities experienced a perceptible, though limited *revival of Christian belief.*

A few intellectuals, too, were ready to risk the contempt of their fellows by taking an overtly religious point of view in their speculations in the postwar era. Among them were Paul Claudel and Etienne Gilson in France, Karl Jaspers and Reinhard Niebuhr in Germany, T. S. Eliot in Britain, and Dorothy Day in the United States. They were indeed a tiny minority, but that did not deter them from hoping and working for a Christian renaissance out of the blood and terror of the war. The seeming collapse of the capitalist world in the Great Depression in the 1930s inspired some to turn to religion, while others turned to communism. In some instances, such as the French worker-priests in the mid-1930s, there was a serious effort to blend radical reform and Christian spirituality. As it happened, the revival these various theologians and reformers sought was to come more noticeably after a second Great War had brought Europe to its knees again.

Summary

Advances in the physical sciences multiplied and fed off one another in the second half of the nineteenth century, leading to an explosive ferment in the opening half of the present century. Darwinian biology led the parade of theory and data that together profoundly altered the existing concepts of the physical universe and its creatures, including human beings. The Newtonian cosmology of certainties and irrefutable measurements was overthrown by a New Physics pioneered by German researchers. Somewhat later, astronomy also entered upon a revolutionary era, which had its own impact upon age-old habits of belief.

In the social sciences, the disputed revelations of Freud were equally disturbing to traditionalists, though in quite a different fashion. For many people, human consciousness was overshadowed by irrational forces beyond its awareness, and the soul was reduced to a biochemical entity, if it existed at all. What was left of traditional morality was ascribed to a psyche entangled in its own irrational fears and follies. Sociology and anthropology emerged as accepted disciplines and provided new ways of contemplating humans as a community.

Throughout the nineteenth century, the Christian religion had been assaulted by self-doubt and by persuasive scientific adversaries. Reaction against positivist science had assisted a slight recovery at the turn of the century, increased by the revulsion against the horror of World War I. Nevertheless, the secular tide was still running strongly among the Western educated classes as the twentieth century neared its midpoint.

Test Your Knowledge

1. The Uncertainty Principle refers to modern
   a. psychology.
   b. physics.
   c. history.
   d. economics.
2. Darwinian biology was ultimately based on
   a. Christian theology.
   b. a mechanical view of the cosmos.
   c. a belief in random change in species.
   d. a belief in a kind of deism much like Newton's.
3. Which of the following pairs is *least logically* paired?
   a. Mach and Einstein
   b. Freud and Jung
   c. Marie Curie and Ernest Rutherford
   d. Auguste Comte and Etienne Gilson
4. As a general rule, twentieth-century Christian belief in the Western world
   a. became nearly extinct after World War II.
   b. developed an entirely new view of Christ.
   c. became much stronger as a result of World War I.
   d. recovered some support among intellectuals.
5. Which of the following was *not* embraced by Freudian psychology?

   a. The superego is engaged in struggle against the libido.
   b. The sex drive lies at the bottom of much unconscious activity.
   c. Humans are basically seeking rational answers to their difficulties.
   d. Conscious actions are often reflections of unconscious moods.
6. Which pair fits *most logically* together in terms of their interests?
   a. Durkheim and Weber
   b. Niebuhr and Mach
   c. Jung and Einstein
   d. Darwin and Rutherford
7. Freud's theories of psychology
   a. encouraged the belief in rational planning as an answer to misery.
   b. were taken up most ardently in his home city of Vienna.
   c. were thought to be insulting by many of his colleagues.
   d. were based upon the study of behavior of animals.

Identification Terms

"Big Bang" Theory
Comte (Auguste)
Curie (Marie)
The Descent of Man

Einstein (Albert)
Jung (Carl)
Mach (Ernst)

The Origin of Species
Pavlov (Ivan)
Planck (Max)

Rerum novarum
Rutherford (Ernest)
Spencer (Herbert)

Bibliography

Ambrosius, G., and W. Hibbard. *A Social and Economic History of Twentieth Century Europe,* 1989. A comprehensive survey.

Baumer, F. L. *Modern European Thought: Continuity and Change in Ideas, 1600–1950,* 1977. An excellent introduction to the background as well as to the topics treated in this chapter.

Bowler, P. *Evolution: The History of an Idea.* 1989.

Chadwick, O. *The Secularization of the European Mind in the Nineteenth Century,* 1975, A very incisive study of the changes that put organized churches on the defensive by the later nineteenth century.

Gay, P. *Freud: A Life for Our Time,* 1988. Admiring biography by a well-known intellectual historian. See also S. Wollheim, *Sigmund Freud,* 1971.

Irvine, W. *Apes, Angels, and Victorians,* 1955. A highly literate study of the great debate over Darwinism in England.

Ruse, M. *The Darwinian Revolution,* 1979. A useful and readable introduction.

Stromberg, R. *European Intellectual History since 1789,* 1993. An excellent survey, clear and opinionated. More demanding on the reader but very stimulating is H. S. Hughes, *Consciousness and Society,* 1956.

WORLD WAR I AND ITS DISPUTED SETTLEMENT

Many people would say that the nineteenth century lasted until 1914, when "the lights went out all over Europe" as one statesman put it. And the twentieth century began not in 1900, but in 1918, when by far the bloodiest and most bitter war fought until then finally ended.

World War I was the deathblow to the belief that progress and prosperity were almost automatic. In 1918, much of the youth and political ideals of the Western world lay in ruins on the battlefields and at home. Disillusionment with authorities of all types was strong, and the stage was set for revolution in several countries. From a war that had no true victors in Europe, the United States and Japan emerged as major powers, while the Western image suffered damage that was not easily repaired in Asia and Africa.

❦ THE PREWAR DIPLOMATIC SYSTEM

After defeating France in the short Franco-Prussian War of 1870–1871, the German chancellor Otto von Bismarck knew that the French would be yearning for revenge. Weakening France to the maximum accordingly made good strategic sense. Thus, Germany seized the two border provinces of *Alsace* and *Lorraine,* a move that deprived an industrializing France of its main sources of iron and coal.

The Triple Alliance

Bismarck also wished to keep France isolated, knowing that France alone could not hope to defeat the newly united Germany. Toward that end, he promoted alliances with Austria-Hungary and Russia. These states were engaged in a strong rivalry over the fate of the weakened Ottoman empire, and Bismarck intended to bind them together with Germany as the "swing" partner, so that neither would join France.

For more than twenty years, Bismarck's system worked well: Germany had what it wanted, and peace was preserved because France was indeed too weak to move alone and could not find allies. (Britain in this epoch was practicing "splendid isolation" from continental affairs and in any case had no quarrel with Germany and no friendship toward France.)

When newly unified Italy began to want to play a role in international affairs, Bismarck was able to persuade the

Italians that their desires for colonial expansion in Africa would have a better hearing in Berlin than in Paris. Italy eventually joined Germany and Austria in the *Triple Alliance* of 1882, which said, in essence, that if any one of the three were attacked, the other two would hasten to its aid.

In 1890, however, the linchpin of the system was removed when the old chancellor was fired by the young *Kaiser William II* (r. 1888–1918). William was not a man to remain willingly in the shadow of another. He was determined to conduct his own foreign policy, and did so immediately by going out of his way to antagonize Russia by imposing a new import tariff on grain and allowing a previous treaty of friendship to lapse. As a result, the Russians suddenly showed some interest in negotiating with the French, who had been patiently waiting for just such an opportunity. In 1893–1894, France and Russia signed a defensive military alliance; the pact did not mention a specific antagonist, but was clearly aimed at Germany.

The Anglo-French Entente and the Anglo-Russian Agreement

The cordial relations between Britain and Germany, which had prevailed throughout the nineteenth century, gave way to an unprecedented hostility in the early 1900s for several reasons:

- Few areas of the world were as yet unclaimed by the Western powers, and Germany's imperialists were demanding that Kaiser William carve out a big slice of the remaining areas for establishing colonies before the French and British swallowed them all.

- The unprovoked and one-sided Boer War in South Africa (1899–1902) aroused considerable anti-British feeling among the Germans. These sentiments were quickly reciprocated by the British public.

- Germany's announcement in 1907 that it intended to build a world-class navy that would rival the British fleet, affected relations very badly. The British government and public took this announcement as a deliberate provocation that must be answered.

- The belligerent "sword rattling" in which the impetuous and insecure kaiser indulged during the decade before 1914 was highly unsettling and contributed significantly to the developing tensions. Under William II, the German government often gave the impression that it was more interested in throwing its very considerable weight about than in solving diplomatic crises peaceably.

By 1904, the British had decided that post-Bismarck Germany was a greater menace to their interests than France, the traditional enemy. In that year, Britain and France signed the *Anglo-French Entente* (understanding), which marked the end of the centuries-long hostility between the two countries. Without being explicit, it was understood that Britain might come to the aid of France in a defensive war. Again, no other power was named in the pact, but its meaning was quite clear.

The final step in the division of Europe into conflicting blocs was the creation of a link between Britain and Russia, which had been on opposite sides of everything since Napoleonic days. Here, the French served as middlemen, and in 1907 Britain and Russia signed the *Anglo-Russian Agreement,* which was much like the Anglo-French Entente. Now Germany, Austria, and Italy on the one side faced Britain, France, and Russia on the other. The stage had been set. The action was sure to follow.

✤ THE CAUSES OF THE WAR

Like most wars, World War I had two types of causes: (1) the *proximate cause,* or the event that actually triggered hostilities, and (2) the more decisive *remote causes,* or the trail of gunpowder that led to the explosion.

The proximate cause was the assassination of Archduke Franz Ferdinand, the heir to the Austrian throne, on June 28, 1914, in the town of Sarajevo in Bosnia. Much of former Yugoslavia was then an Austrian possession. Bosnia had come under Austrian rule by international agreement in 1878, following one of several Serbian uprisings against Turkish rule. The transfer from one alien overlord to another had not placated the aspirations of the Bosnian Serbs, who wished to join with the independent Serbian kingdom adjoining Bosnia (see Map 47.1). The archduke had been on an inspection tour and was murdered by a conspiracy of Serbian nationalist youths who had been waiting for such an opportunity for a long time. The conspirators were convinced that the assassination would somehow induce Austria to abandon its Serb-populated possessions. They were, of course, wrong.

The war also had several *remote causes:*

- *Nationalism.* Nationalist sentiment had been rising steadily and growing more lethal, particularly in the enmities it inspired among the various small peoples who inhabited the areas of southeastern Europe held by the Turks. Some of these peoples were the clients of the Austrians, some were the clients of the Russians, and

● **MAP 47.1 The Balkan States, 1914.** The intermixing of several ethnic and religious groups in southeast Europe is a result of many centuries of immigration, conquest, and foreign over lordship. At the eve of World War I, Serbia, Bulgaria, Romania, and Greece were maneuvering for national advantage in the event of the long-awaited collapse of the Ottoman empire.

some had no patron; all were determined to seize as much territory as possible for their own nations when the Ottoman empire finally sank.

• *International imperialism.* Austria, Russia, Britain, France, Germany, and Italy all shared in the frenzy of the New Imperialism of the late nineteenth century. At the time, it appeared that those who were not expanding their territories and populations would be the certain losers in world competition.

• *Weariness of peace.* In all countries, the leaders had forgotten how destructive war could be and how much damage it could do the social fabric of a defeated country. A long generation of peace (1871–1914) had allowed Europeans to forget how quickly war can fan the embers of discontent into revolution and anarchy. In addition, some influential persons in public life were convinced that war was a great ennobler and bringer of progress and that Europe had "suffered" through too many years of peace since 1815. They actually longed for the challenges of war as the ultimate test that would separate the wheat from the chaff.

After a month's ominous silence, the Austrian government presented the government of independent Serbia

■ **Apprehension of Gavrilo Princip in Sarajevo.** The archduke's assassin was seized immediately by the Sarajevo police and rushed into prison before he could be lynched. He died in an Austrian prison from tuberculosis in 1918.

(from which the assassins had obtained their weapons and possibly their inspiration) with a forty-eight-hour ultimatum: acceptance of the conditions would mean in effect the surrender of Serbian independence, while refusal to accept meant war. The Serbs chose war.

Within a week in early August, all but one of the members of the two blocs formed over the past two decades were also at war. The exception was Italy, which reneged on its alliance obligation and instead bargained with both sides for the next several months. Austria-Hungary was joined by Germany, Turkey, and Bulgaria (in 1915); joining Serbia were Russia, France, Britain, Italy (in 1915), and Romania (in 1916). The United States and Greece entered the fray in 1917 on the Entente, or Allied side as it was generally called.

⚜ MILITARY ACTION: 1914–1918

In its military aspect, World War I was almost entirely a European phenomenon, although members of the Allies came from all continents by the time it was over. The battlefronts were (1) the *Western Front* in France and Belgium, which was the decisive one (see Map 47.2); (2) the *Eastern or Russian Front,* which reached from the Baltic Sea to the Aegean, but was always secondary (see Map 47.3); and (3) the *Alpine Front,* which involved only Italy and Austria-Hungary and had no major influence on the course of the conflict.

As so often, the military experts were mistaken, and the generals unprepared. This was particularly true on the Western Front. The experts had thought that thanks to railroads, automobiles, telephones, and radio communications, as well as the use of much heavier cannons and much larger armies than had been seen before, whichever side got the upper hand in the early days would have a decisive advantage. The offense would also have a big advantage over the defense, thought the experts. The war would be won within a few weeks by the superior attacker, just as in a chess game between experts where one player gains the advantage in the opening moves. Just the opposite happened: the *defense proved superior to the offense.* Instead of large numbers of quickly amassed, motorized troops scoring breakthroughs against the enemy, the war turned out to be endless slogging through muddy trenches and hopeless, cruelly wasteful infantry attacks against machine guns while artillery knocked every living thing to perdition for miles around (see the Document in this chapter). Instead of lasting a few weeks, the war lasted four and a quarter ghastly years, with a loss of life far in excess of any other conflict ever experienced.

The Bloody Stalemate

Originally, the Central Powers (as the German-Austrian allies were called) planned to hold off the Russians while rapidly smashing through neutral Belgium into France and forcing it to surrender before its British ally could do much to help. The plan very nearly worked; in late August 1914, the Germans were within a few miles of Paris, only to be permanently stalled along the river Marne by heroic French resistance. Aided now by a British army that grew rapidly, the French were able to contain one tremendous German attack after another for four years.

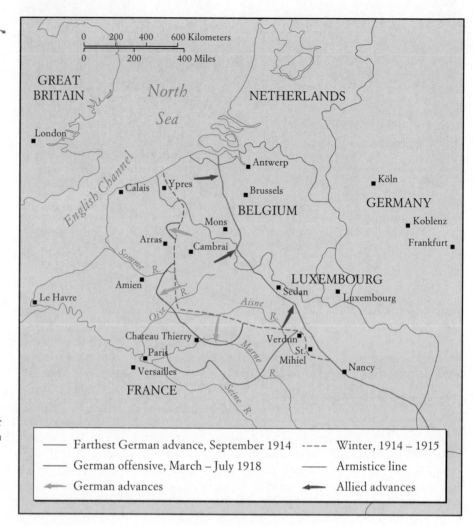

◉ **MAP 47.2   The Western Front in World War I.** Neither the Germans nor the Allies were able to move more than a few miles forward after the initial attack was contained in the Fall of 1914. Artillery, minefields, and machine-guns stopped any assault on the opposing trenches.

Legend:
— Farthest German advance, September 1914
— German offensive, March – July 1918
← German advances
---- Winter, 1914 – 1915
— Armistice line
← Allied advances

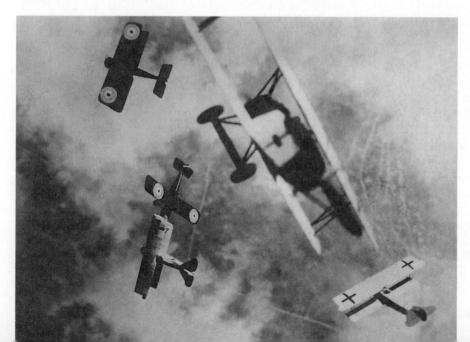

■ **Aerial Dogfight on the Western Front.** Both sides quickly recognized the potential of the airplane for reconnaissance and artillery-spotting. Spectacular dogfights between opposing planes were a daily occurrence.

⊙ **MAP 47.3 The Eastern Front in World War I.** The war in Russia was much more fluid than in the West, but until the collapse of the tsarist government in 1917, neither side could deal a fatal blow. The German High Command accepted a withdrawal to the Brest-Litovsk treaty line in 1918 only because it fully expected to create a satellite state of Ukraine as its eastern outpost.

--·-- Russian advances: 1914–1916

····· Deepest German penetration: 1918

——— Separate peace boundary: 1918

(CRIMEA) Regions of national states

From the English Channel to Switzerland, the battle lines did not move more than a few miles, as millions of men on both sides met their death. The defense of the French fortress city of Verdun in 1916–1917 was the bloodiest slaughter of all; the defenders lost more than 600,000 killed and wounded and the attackers even more.

U.S. Entry and Russian Exit

The long-delayed entry of the United States into the war in April 1917 was vitally important to the Allies. The American decision was triggered by the resumption of unrestricted submarine war by the German High Command. Like airplanes, submarines were a relatively new invention, and as yet, there was no effective counter to them. They were used for the first time as a potentially war-winning weapon by the Germans in 1915 to cut off the flow of war material of all kinds to Britain from its empire and from neutral nations. Strong protests after U.S. ships and American lives had been lost to torpedoes had brought a lull for almost two years during which the United States maintained its formal neutral stance.

In fact, President Woodrow Wilson and most of his advisers had been sympathetic to the Allied cause from

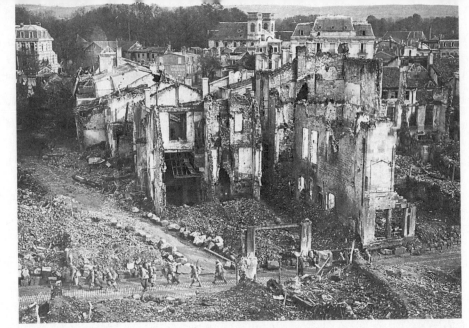

■ **Battle of Verdun.** The utter destruction of Verdun, the fortress city near the German frontier, was the result of a sixteen month-long attack costing both sides over a half-million casualties.

the beginning. Because the public's opinion as to which side was morally right was sharply divided, and because many Americans were recent immigrants from the lands of the Central Powers and had emotional ties to them, Wilson found it politically inadvisable to try to intervene in the war until there was some persuasive reason for doing so. In early 1917, German U-boats sunk several ships carrying American passengers, giving the pro-Allied party in Washington a dramatic and plausible excuse for intervention.

The American entry into the conflict counterbalanced the collapse of the Russian war effort following the revolutions of 1917 (see the Biography in this chapter and Chapter 49) and the terrible losses suffered by the Allies in the Somme River offensive in the summer of 1916. Neither side thought that American troops and materiel would be available in France until much later; they were surprised. The American war industry and military met the demands placed on them by the exhausted British and French. In fact, it was the Americans' ability to deliver large numbers of men and war supplies from U.S. ports during the winter and spring of 1918 that allowed the desperate French to hold on against the final German offensive.

Collapse of the Central Powers

In the fall of 1918, after four bloodstained years of struggle, the Central Powers suddenly collapsed. The Austrians asked for peace without conditions in mid-October; the Bulgarians and Turks had already withdrawn. After years of rigid optimism, the German High Command now concluded that the tide of war was flowing

strongly against it. After Austria's collapse, it advised the Kaiser to accept the armistice conditions that President Wilson had presented some weeks earlier, based on the **Fourteen Points** he had enunciated in a speech in January 1918. In summary, the Fourteen Points looked for a "peace without victors," self-determination for the repressed nationalities, disarmament, freedom of the seas to all, and an international body to keep the peace permanently.

On November 9, 1918, the Kaiser abdicated his throne and handed power to a just-created provisional government. Mainly members of the Social Democratic Party, this government immediately asked for an end to hostilities. On November 11, the long bloodbath came to an end. Everywhere, German troops were still standing on foreign soil, and Germany itself had experienced none of the destruction wrought by war on Allied lands. Those facts were to be very important in future days. They allowed the impression that Germany had been defeated not by foreign troops or war exhaustion, but by the betrayal of some scheming politicians.

✦ THE HOME FRONT

After the outburst of wild enthusiasm that overtook all the belligerent populations in the first weeks of war (and the total failure of the Marxist socialists' hopes for an international general strike), both governments and people came to realize that a long, hard struggle lay ahead. Several steps had to be taken if the demands of this first "**total war**" were to be met. By 1916, all combatants had acted more or less thoroughly to ensure that civilians would

Erich Maria Remarque, *All Quiet on the Western Front*

In his most horrifying nightmare, no one who enthusiastically marched, or cheered on those who were marching into World War I could have foreseen the complete, dehumanizing brutality that the four years 1914–1918 would bring. The German writer Erich Maria Remarque was conscripted into the imperial army soon after the outbreak of the war. In his 1927 novel *All Quiet on the Western Front,* which became an international bestseller, he recounted what he had observed through the experiences of a small group of young German soldiers like himself:

> We wake in the middle of the night. The earth booms. Heavy fire is falling on us. We crouch into corners .... Slowly the grey light trickles into the outpost, and pales the flashes of the shells. Morning has come. The explosion of mines mingles with the gunfire; that is the most dementing convulsion of all. The whole area where they go off becomes one grave. . . .
>
> The dull thud of gas shells mingles with the crashes of the high explosives. A bell sounds between the explosions, gongs and metal clappers warning everyone: Gas! . . . These first few minutes with the [gas] masks decide between life and death: is it tightly woven? I remember the awful sights in the hospitals: the gas patients who in day-long suffocation cough their burnt lungs up in clots.
>
> Killing each separate louse is a tedious business when a man has hundreds. The little beasts are hard, and the everlasting cracking with one's fingernail very soon become wearisome. So Tjaden has rigged up the lid of a bootpolish can with a piece of wire over the lighted stump of a candle. The lice are simply thrown into this little pan. Crack! and they're done for.
>
> We lie under the network of arching shells and live in a suspense. Over us Chance hovers. If a shot comes, we can duck, that is all; we neither know nor can determine where it will fall.
>
> It is this Chance which makes us indifferent. A few months ago I was sitting in a dugout playing *skat;* after a while, I stood up and went to visit some friends in another dugout. On my return nothing more was to be seen of the first one: it had been blown to pieces with a direct hit. I went back to the second and arrived just in time to lend a hand digging it out. In the interval it had been buried.
>
> The brown earth, the torn, blasted earth, with a greasy shine under the sun's rays; the earth is the background of this restless gloomy world of automatons . . . into our pierced and shattered souls bores the torturing image of the brown earth with the greasy sun and the convulsed and dead soldiers, who lie there . . . who cry and clutch at our legs as we spring away over them. We have lost all feeling for one another. We can hardly control ourselves when our hunted glance lights on the form of some other man. We are insensible, dead men who through some trick, some dreadful magic, are still able to run and to kill.

fully support the battlefronts. Among the most important measures they took were the following:

- *Full mobilization of the civilian population.* Unlike all previous wars, World War I did not allow the unarmed masses to remain neutral. Led by Germany but soon imitated by France and the others, the governments insisted that the home front was as vital as the battlefields and that everyone had a role to play in victory.

  The governments made wholesale use of every type of propaganda available: print media, exhibitions, parades, sponsored speaking tours, and so on. Starting in 1915, they indulged in "hate" propaganda. Much of it was deliberate lies; all of it was meant to transform the civil population into a productive machine to fight the enemy. Food was rationed; so were fuel and clothing. All active males aged seventeen to sixty were considered "soldiers in the war for production" and could be ordered about almost like the troops in battle. Even women were pressed into various kinds of unprecedented service as described below.

- *Government control of the economy.* Much more than in any previous war, the governments took command of the entire productive system. Labor was allocated by bureaucratic command; so were raw materials, currency,

Nicky and Sunny

Over the centuries, the European royal families have had considerably more than their share of unusual characters. Indeed, finding a royal personage who had no spectacular eccentricities in appearance or behavior was almost a rare event. But neither Tsar Nicholas II of the Romanovs nor his tsarina, Alexandra, could be considered eccentric. Both were exceptionally handsome specimens, the tsar standing over six feet tall and his wife, the former Princess Alix of Hesse, even more regal in appearance than her husband. With the exception of the hemophilia in Alix's family, neither had a physical or mental handicap of any substance that would present obstacles to a successful reign.

Alix had been the beneficiary of what was considered a very lucky marriage arrangement, brokered by her relatives in Berlin and London. Born in 1872, she was just twenty-two when she was wed to the twenty-six-year-old tsar, who had just succeeded his dead father on the throne. In accord with the usual terms of a Russian noble wedding, she gave up her Lutheran faith and became a member of the Orthodox church, taking the name Alexandra Feodorovna Romanov.

Nicholas II admired his father greatly and was determined to rule in a similar, ultraconservative fashion. Unfortunately for him and for his country, he did not possess his father's personality. Where Alexander III had been blindly self-righteous, Nicholas was hesitant about his course of action. Where Alexander had ignored criticism, Nicholas was confused by it. Nicholas regretted the necessity of using his quite efficient secret police (*Okhrana*) against the revolutionaries; Alexander never regretted anything.

Alexandra soon convinced herself that she was the divinely ordained counterbalance to Nicholas's indecision and softness. For several years after coming to Russia, she remained in the background, content to supervise the rearing of the five handsome children (four girls and a boy) she bore the tsar in the years around 1900. But in 1908 a fateful meeting between Alexandra and the corrupt "holy beggar" Rasputin led to changes that eventually rocked the Russian government's very foundations. In a crisis, Rasputin was able, probably through hypnotism, to arrest the hemophilia threatening the life of the young heir-apparent Alexander. From that moment on, the tsarina came increasingly under Rasputin's influence, and by 1912 "our friend," as Alexandra called him, came to have real power in the appointment of officials and even in domestic policies.

Rasputin's wholly selfish motives served to reinforce Alexandra's natural inclinations in government. In letter after letter to her traveling husband, the tsarina encouraged Nicholas to resist all concessions to constitutional government, liberal ideals, and any-

and imports of all types. New taxes were levied to prevent any excess profit from war contracts. Wage rates and consumer prices were also controlled by government order. All or almost all of these measures were novelties being tried for the first time.

- *Female labor.* Since millions of men were no longer available to the civil economy after 1914, women were induced to fill their places by various means, including high pay, patriotic appeals, and even coercion. Hundreds of occupations that were previously "off-limits" to women were now opened to them, including jobs involving heavy physical labor or considerable authority: women worked as police, tram drivers, truck drivers, bank tellers, carters, and munitions factory labor and held a host of civil service jobs previously reserved for men. Thus, a new world of work opportunity opened for women. After some initial resistance by the labor unions, women were generally accepted as replacements for men and given more or less equal pay. In particular, their ability to do repetitive industrial jobs exceeded male expectations and earned them new respect as productive employees. In every belligerent country, women made up at least 30 percent of the total civilian labor force by war's end—a far higher percentage than in peacetime.

thing smacking of democracy. She despised parliaments and all their works. She is said to have believed that the last truly great Russian leader was Ivan the Terrible; since his time, the rulers of Russia had made entirely too many concessions to the mob and to the rotten intellectuals.

When World War I broke out, Nicholas's government was in serious disarray, caught between the mock constitutionalism adopted after the revolution of 1905 and the basic inclinations of the royal couple and their friends. In 1915, Nicholas made the stupid mistake of leaving St. Petersburg and assuming direct command of the poorly trained and equipped armies. Alexandra, who had come to rely more and more on Rasputin's advice, was left in charge at the palace. The many letters exchanged between the couple (the *Nicky/Sunny* correspondence) show their deep mutual affection, but also demonstrate how weak Nicholas was in contrast to his forceful—and hopelessly wrongheaded—wife. Even the murder of Rasputin by some noble patriots in De-

■ **The Romanov Family in 1905.** The tsarevich (crown prince) is in his mother Alexandra's arms.

cember 1916 did not help matters; the rift between the palace and the hastily reconvoked parliament was by now too deep, and the Romanovs' unpopularity too widespread among the people. The March Revolution of 1917 was inevitable (see Chapter 49).

Under the Provisional Government, the royal family was placed under a loose form of house arrest in one of their homes. When the Bolsheviks took command in November 1917, they were moved to what appeared to be a safe haven in a provincial town. But the entire family was massacred by Lenin's personal order in July 1918, when it seemed that anti-Bolsheviks might free them and use them as a unifying force against the Leninists. Nicky and Sunny went bravely to their graves, according to eyewitness reports that have only become available to us in the last few years. All five of the dead children have now been definitively identified through DNA comparisons, though reports of a surviving daughter (Anastasia) circulated for more than half a century.

As in most wars, the insecurity of life and the desire to accommodate the young men going off to fight resulted in a slackening of traditional standards for both sexes, especially for women. Public demonstrations of affection between the sexes became acceptable even among the "respectable classes." Women insisted on access to some form of birth control as extramarital and premarital sex became more common. Standards of conduct and dress for girls and women became more relaxed—it was even possible to show a bit of leg without automatically being considered "fast" by one's peers. Alcohol consumption by both sexes rose sharply despite attempts to discourage it by all governments (which were concerned about worker absenteeism in the war plants).

Unlike previous wars, so many men were involved and the casualty rates suffered by most belligerents were so high that the slackening of moral restraint during the war had a profound and permanent effect on society. Marriageable men were in short supply for years afterward, and the imbalance between men and women aged twenty to thirty-five influenced what was considered acceptable sexual conduct. After the war it proved impossible to put young men and women back into the tight moral and customary constraints of prewar society.

■ **Female Workers, World War I.** The draining off of males to battlefields after 1914 opened the way for millions of women to enter jobs previously unknown to them. In this 1917 photo, female paper mill workers show they can handle heavy labor.

In addition, the many millions of conscripts in the armies had been torn out of their accustomed and expected "slots" in life. For better or worse, many never returned to their prewar lifestyles. "How're you gonna keep them down on the farm after they've seen Paree?" went the popular song in the United States. That was a relevant question, and not just for Americans.

⚜ PSYCHIC CONSEQUENCES OF WORLD WAR I

Perhaps the most significant of all the consequences of World War I was its effect on the collective European psyche. Three effects in particular stand out:

1. *Political disillusionment.* Even while the war was being fought, many were becoming disillusioned and their mood spread despite intensive propaganda campaigns by all the belligerent nations. As the casualty lists lengthened without any decisive victories for either side, the survivors in the trenches and their loved ones back home came to doubt in the wisdom and effectiveness of their political and military leaders. Men were dying by the millions, but the war goals of both the Allies and the Central Powers remained very unclear. After 1916, the war became a war of brutal attrition; basically, both sides were trying to hold on until the other gave up. When the war ended, disillusionment with the peace was widespread even among the victo-

rious Allies. Some thought it too mild, others too harsh. The losers universally regarded the peace as one of vengeance.

2. *Skepticism toward authority.* This special type of disillusionment was especially common among the veterans back from the battlefields. They regarded the military and political leaders as heartless fumblers who had no concern for ordinary people. But the mood did not stop there, all authority figures were suspect now: the clergy who had blessed each side's cannons, the diplomats who had not been able to prevent the war, and the teachers and professors who had led the foolish cheering at the outbreak of war. None of the old guides could be trusted.

3. *An end to the religion of science and progress.* Before 1914 most educated Europeans assumed that tomorrow would be better than today, and that the next generation would be able to solve most of the problems that still haunted their own generation. They believed material and spiritual progress were inevitable. The war ended that optimism for soldiers and civilians alike. They had seen the mutual slaughter end the way it had begun, with no clear achievement for the victors and with chaos for the losers. As the spiritual and economic costs to all sides became apparent, many people began to doubt whether there had even been any victors. The faith of the European bourgeoisie in liberalism, parliamentary government, social justice, and science looked absurd in 1919, as the smoke of battle cleared and the cemeteries filled. Not progress, but revolution and a kind of vicious nihilism (belief in nothing) were on the day's menu.

The dismay was not universal. Some believed that a triumphant new day had dawned after the carnage of 1914–1918. In the fine arts, a whole series of new ideas and challenging new directions had emerged during or soon after the war. (We will look at them in Chapter 48.) Many nationalists were gratified at the outcome of the war, for the peace negotiations fulfilled many of their dreams and created several entirely new states in eastern Europe. Among them were Yugoslavia, Czechoslovakia, Albania, an independent Hungary and Austria, a reconstituted Poland, and an enlarged Romania.

The feminists were pleased as women gained the vote in almost every country, largely as a result of the promises made by desperate politicians during the war emergency. And the Marxist socialists or communists were filled with surging hopes of a Europe-wide proletarian revolution, brought on by the sufferings of the common people during the conflict and the general rejection of the prewar political order. These hopes were ignited by the success of the revolution in November 1917 and the installation of a Marxist socialist regime in Moscow (see Chapter 49).

✤ THE PEACE TREATIES: 1919–1920

The German surrender was based on acceptance of an armistice offered by the Allies in November 1918. A permanent peace arrangement was worked out in Paris during the first months of 1919. The last of five separate treaties with the losing nations (Austria, Hungary, Bulgaria, and Turkey, as well as Germany) was signed in August 1920.

The popular leader of the victorious Allies was clearly the American president Woodrow Wilson. Most of the European public saw him as a knight in shining armor because of his earlier proclamation of "a peace without victors" and his support of "**open diplomacy.**" But Wilson's popularity did not carry into the closed-door negotiations in Paris. He was soon blocked by the other Allied leaders, who were convinced that the president's slogans and plans were totally unrealistic. *Georges Clemenceau,* the French premier, and *Vittorio Orlando,* the Italian premier, were opposed to a peace without victors, which to them meant political suicide or worse. *David Lloyd George,* the British prime minister, was originally a bit more sympathetic to the American, but he, too, turned against Wilson when the president attempted to make his Fourteen Points the basis of the peace. Each of the European leaders had good reasons for rejecting one or more of the points as being inapplicable or foolish, and they combined against the American on their mutual behalf. The points were eventually applied in a highly selective manner or ignored altogether.

The *negotiations were conducted in secret* (despite Wilson's earlier promises) and involved only the victors. Germany, Austria, Hungary, Bulgaria, and Turkey were each given a piece of paper to sign without further parlays. They were told that if they did not, the war would be resumed. Unwillingly, but without any choice, each signed during 1919–1920. Especially for the Germans, this peace was a bitter pill that would not be forgotten.

Conflicting Principles and Their Compromise

What came out of the Paris treaties?

1. *Territorially.*

   - Germany lost 10 percent of its land and its population to the new Poland and Czechoslovakia. Alsace-Lorraine, the "Lost Provinces" of 1870, went back to France (see Map 47.4).
   - Austria's empire was completely dismantled, a process that had become inevitable during the closing days of the war when each of the major components had declared its independence from Vienna and the last Habsburg ruler had abdicated. The new **Successor states,** as they were called, were Austria, Hungary, Czechoslovakia, Poland, and Yugoslavia. In addition, the former Romania was greatly enlarged.
   - Bulgaria lost some land to Romania, Yugoslavia, and Greece.
   - Turkey's empire was also completely dissolved, and its Middle Eastern lands were partitioned among the Allies: Jordan, Palestine, Iraq, Syria, Arabia, and Lebanon became French or British protectorates. The Turkish core area of Anatolia came under a military dictatorship led by the ex-officer Mustapha Kemal.

2. *Ethnically.* Some of Wilson's plans for self-determination became a reality, but others were ignored. The old multinational empires (Turkey, Austria, Russia) had collapsed and were replaced by states in which one ethnic group had at least a majority. But each of the East European Successor states included a large number of minority groups; some were as much as 30 percent of the total. Czechoslovakia and Yugoslavia were the most vulnerable of the new states in this respect: the Germans living within Czechoslovakia made up close to a third of the population, and the Magyars, Germans, Albanians, and others in Yugoslavia were a strong ethnic counterweight to the dominant Slavs.

   Everywhere, the attempts of the peacemakers to draw up ethnically correct borders were frustrated by either strategic, economic, geographical, or political considerations. The resulting ethnic map between Germany and the new Soviet Russia and between the Baltic and the Aegean Seas looked like a crazy quilt. Protections were formally extended to the minorities by the special treaties that all Successor states were required to sign upon entry into the League of Nations, but nationalist governments soon were ignoring these protections almost without reprimand, for there was no mechanism to enforce them. Minorities were often made the objects of systematic prejudice throughout the interwar era.

3. *Politically.* Germany was tagged with full responsibility for starting the war (**Paragraph 231 of the Versailles Treaty**), which no German could accept as true. This allowed the European Allies (Wilson would not) to claim reparations for wartime damages from the losers. The amount of damages was to be calculated solely by

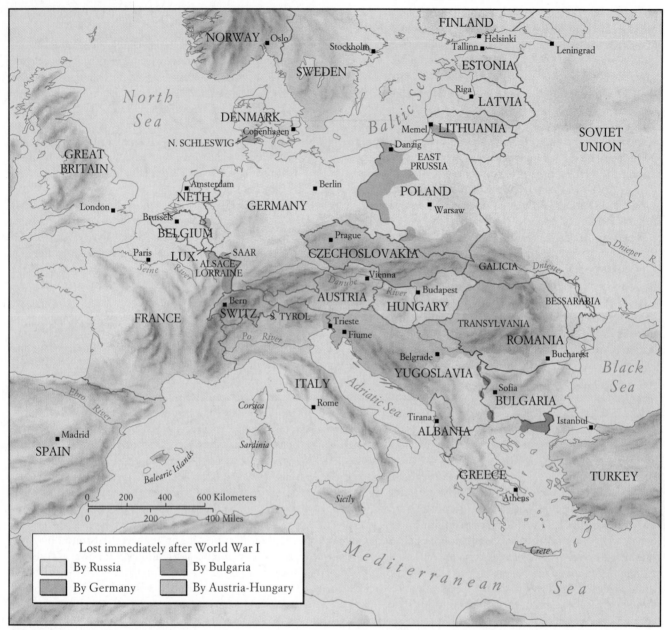

MAP 47.4 Europe after World War I. The war and the peace treaties carved seven entirely new states out of Russia and the Austro-Hungarian empire: Finland, Latvia, Estonia, Lithuania, Poland, Czechoslovakia, and Yugoslavia. Austria and Hungary were separated; Romania, Italy, and Greece were enlarged.

the victors at some future date. The *reparations question* was to be one of the chief bones of contention in international affairs for the next fifteen years, until Hitler came to power and rejected all such claims.

The defeated states and some of the Successor states became republics, having lost their various royal/imperial rulers during the final days of the conflict. The last Habsburg emperor, Charles II, lived out his days in exile. The Hohenzollern Kaiser was gone from Berlin (he died in Dutch exile), and the last Romanov tsar died at Bolshevik orders in 1918. The Turkish sultan was also gone, deposed by the Kemal government, which chose isolated Ankara rather than cosmopolitan Istanbul as its capital. Czechoslovakia, Poland, and the tiny Baltic states were parliamentary republics; constitutional monarchies (Yugoslavia, Romania, Bulgaria, Albania) were also popular. In all of these, democracy was given lipservice and often little more.

4. *Diplomatically.* The Paris treaties created an organ new in world history, a **League of Nations** with universal membership that was to promote peace among all nations and act as a permanent board of mediation when international conflicts arose. The League was Wilson's brainchild, and to obtain it, he had been willing to accept all the injuries that had been inflicted on his ideas by the European statesmen at Paris.

As it happened, despite his best efforts Wilson was not able to sell his fellow Americans on the idea of the League. Because of concern about involving the United States indefinitely in Europe's affairs, the U.S. Senate rejected the Paris treaties in 1919, dealing Wilson a political and physical blow from which he never recovered. (The president suffered a stroke soon after returning from Paris.) The United States eventually made separate treaties with each of the defeated states, duplicating the Paris treaties with the exception of the League of Nations paragraph.

✤ EVALUATION OF THE PEACE TREATIES

Criticism of the peace signed in Paris began as soon as the ink dried. And it came not only from the losing nations, but from a good portion of the victors as well. Some of the victors' complaints came from fear that the losers had been left too well off; many people in France feared that Germany could and would rise once more despite its partial dismemberment and the extraordinary costs of reparations. But some of these concerns arose from the conviction that the peace had been guided by vengeance and that all the high-flown principles of the Allied governments had been ignored in Paris. After all, the peace negotiated in Paris was *not* a peace without victors, nor did it guarantee self-determination, nor did it end imperialism, or any of the other ideals that the Allies had proclaimed.

The most scathing critique came from the young British economist, **John Maynard Keynes,** who believed that the Allies had attempted to impose a "Carthaginian peace" (total destruction) upon Germany that could not succeed and would bring chaos in European affairs. Keynes had enormous contempt for Wilson, and his opinions soon became fashionable among influential people in both Britain and the United States. Both countries regarded the French and Italians as greedy and stupid in their shortsighted fixation on temporary advantage. Some leading British and American opinion makers began to advocate a return to *isolationism,* a retreat from the obligations and goals of the peace treaties. In the United States, the British and French delays in repaying the extensive loans the United States had made to them during the war intensified the disgust with European affairs.

The failure of the Versailles Treaty in the United States was a major turning point in postwar diplomacy. With no commitment to the League, America could and did turn its attention to Europe only when and how it chose for twenty years. And without the assurance of U.S. support through the League, France was left to face a resurgent Germany by itself in the early postwar era. As a result, the French position became more hard-line than ever and drove France and Britain further apart at the very time when close coordination was most necessary.

Perhaps the *worst aspect of the peace* was that it tried to ignore certain political realities. Russia, under the Bolsheviks, was not even invited to send a representative to Paris and so had no access to negotiations that would surely affect its status and future in world affairs. The losing nations, above all Germany, were presented with a *fait accompli* that was intensely disagreeable to them and that they believed was totally unjust. Neither Germany nor Russia, two of the strongest states in the world, was allowed to join the League of Nations for several years. Germany was commanded to disarm almost entirely; yet no machinery was in place to enforce that demand, and none was ever created.

The League was supposed to be not only the enforcer of the Paris treaties, but also the keeper of the peace for the indefinite future. Yet the weak Secretariat had no armed force at its disposal, and the League members never had any intention of creating one. The League's effectiveness was going to depend on the goodwill of the member governments, and some of those governments were filled with anything but goodwill toward their neighbors.

The 1919 treaties were certainly not as harsh as they have sometimes been painted, but they were certainly a long way from the hopes of the Wilsonians and much of the world's population, who were trying to recover from the "war to end wars." As it turned out, the treaties lasted less than twenty years. What Europe had found was not peace, but a short armistice between two terribly destructive wars.

Summary

The system erected by Bismarck to keep France isolated and helpless after 1871 broke down in the 1890s after the impetuous William II took over the direction of foreign policy in Berlin. Within a decade, the blocs that would contest World War I had been formed. When a Serbian nationalist youth assassinated the heir to the Austrian throne in 1914, a general war broke out that, contrary to expectations, lasted for more than four years.

The battlefields where huge slaughters took place were matched in importance by the home fronts, where governments intervened in unprecedented ways to spur the civilian war effort. Women in particular were affected, as the desperate need for labor impelled politicians in all countries to forget prewar restrictions on female activity.

The war aims of all the combatants were poorly understood and never honestly expressed. As the casualty lists soared, a sense of disillusionment and anger toward established authority spread. By war's end, the populations of the defeated Central Powers were on the verge of revolt, while the Russians had already experienced the Bolshevik revolution as the war was being fought.

Even the so-called victors experienced some feelings of revulsion at the disparity between the huge sacrifices demanded and the minimal results gained. This revulsion was strengthened as it became apparent that the "peace without victors" was not to be. The Paris treaties were despised by the losers and satisfied no one with their compromises between the optimistic visions of President Wilson and the hard realities of international and national politics.

Test Your Knowledge

1. The Bismarckian system of alliances for Germany was meant to
   a. restrain Russia and Austria and to isolate France.
   b. allow Austria to expand to the south and east.
   c. encourage peace with France indefinitely.
   d. force Russia to submit to German eastern expansion.
2. The Triple Alliance of 1882, which was renewed through 1914, was composed of
   a. Italy, France, and Britain.
   b. Austria, Russia, and Germany.
   c. Germany, Austria, and Italy.
   d. France, Britain, and Russia.
3. Which of the following was *not* a remote cause of World War I?
   a. Aggressive imperialism practiced by several nations
   b. An inclination toward the "supreme test" of war among some leaders
   c. The belligerent nationalism of the Balkan states
   d. Racial antipathies between colonies and their home countries
4. A chief novelty brought by World War I was
   a. the use of naval blockades.
   b. the desire of the belligerents to gain postwar economic advantages.
   c. the use of conscripts rather than all-volunteer armies.
   d. the massive intervention of government into the war economy in all nations.
5. Which of the following did *not* accompany the wartime use of females in the economy?
   a. Widening of the gap between the wages paid to male and female labor
   b. A demonstration of the women's ability to do many physical tasks
   c. Less male restrictiveness toward female public activities
   d. Less distinction between "male" and "female" jobs
6. In the spring of 1917, two unrelated events changed the course of the war; they were
   a. the failure of the submarine campaign and the entry of Italy into the war.
   b. the success of the socialist revolution in Russia and the first use of conscripts by France.
   c. the toppling of the tsarist government in Russia and the entry of the United States into the war.

d. the collapse of the French government and the entry of Britain into the war.
7. Subsequently, the most serious complaint against the Paris treaties was that
a. they failed to punish the losers severely enough to keep them down.
b. they failed to recognize basic international political realities.
c. they did not give enough national self-determination.

d. they ignored ethnic boundaries entirely when redrawing the map.
8. Tsarina Alexandra was all but one of the following.
a. A firm-willed and energetic woman
b. An opponent of parliamentary government
c. A politically reactionary character
d. A reluctant and timid player in Russian governmental affairs

Identification Terms

Fourteen Points

Keynes (John Maynard)

League of Nations

open diplomacy

Paragraph 231 of the Versailles Treaty

Successor states

total war

Reparations

the Entente

the Central Powers

Bibliography

Each of the nations involved presented lengthy collections of diplomatic documents as well as passionate arguments as to why the outbreak of war was someone else's fault. Seventy years later, the question of war guilt is still debated; this list mentions only a few of the available books.

Falls, C. *The Great War,* 1961. The best short account of the military aspect, but see also B. H. Liddell-Hart, *The Real War, 1914–1918,* 1964. For the generally neglected Eastern Front, N. Stone, *The Fall of the Empires,* 1968, is very good.

Fussell, P. *The Great War and Modern Memory,* 1975. A brilliant résumé of what the war meant to a generation of British survivors and how it shaped their lives thereafter in ways both conscious and unconscious.

Keynes, J. M. *The Economic Consequences of the Peace,* 1920. This attack on the Versailles Treaty was very influential in both Britain and America. Perhaps the most readable of the many accounts of the Versailles negotiations is H. Nicholson, *Peacemaking 1919,* 1938.

Marwick, A. *The Deluge,* 1970. A good social history of the effects of war in Britain. For other countries, see R. Wall and J. Winter, eds., *The Upheaval of War: Family, Work and Welfare in Europe, 1914–1918,* 1988. F. Chambers, *The War behind the War, 1914–1918,* though published in 1939, is still unsurpassed for a summation of the war on the home fronts.

Finally, R. Albrecht-Carrie has put together an insightful anthology entitled *The Meaning of the First World War,* 1965, which deals with several aspects of the war's consequences in society.

Remak, J. *The Origins of World War I,* 1967, and L. Lafore, *The Long Fuse,* 1971, are standard sources for the remote causes of World War I and are short enough to be easily digested.

Tuchman, B. *The Guns of August,* 1962. One of the most brilliant examples of history-as-story.

Winter, J. M. *The Experience of World War I,* 1989. Particularly strong in its pictorial record.

Wohl, R. *The Generation of 1914,* 1979. What World War I meant to the European youth who fought it. On the same topic, see V. Brittain, *Testament of Youth: An Autobiographical Study of the Years 1900–1925,* 1980.

An unforgettable account of the actual fighting is given in A. Horne, *The Price of Glory: Verdun 1916,* 1979, which accurately portrays the horrors of the trenches on the Western Front. J. Romain, *Verdun,* 1939, presents a fictional version based on firsthand experience. E. Remarque's novel *All Quiet on the Western Front,* 1929, and J. Ellis's memoir *Eye Deep in Hell,* 1976, are two of hundreds of personal recollections of this conflict that stress how senseless it seemed to the common soldier.

EQUILIBRIUM REESTABLISHED: THE TWENTIETH-CENTURY WORLD

1920–Present

Part 6 examines the last seven decades from a Western vantage point, but with particular sensitivity to the renewal of polycentrism and pluralism in international politics and interrelationships of all kinds.

In the wake of the disastrous World World I, the central and eastern European nations generally gravitated into various forms of authoritarian government and bade sour farewell to the classical liberal ideals and presumptions about human nature. The legacy of the Enlightenment was found inadequate to the needs of mid-twentieth-century society, particularly after the Great Depression made itself felt in full force after 1930. First formulated by a posturing Benito Mussolini, Fascism in superficially varied forms won popular support and governmental power in several countries.

Britain, France and the burgeoning United States resisted this trend during the interwar period. But after 1930, it was not the liberal democracies, which seemed helpless and exhausted, that seized the imagination and captured the sympathies of many of the world's less fortunate peoples. They turned instead to the novel socioeconomic experiment mounted by a relative handful of Bolsheviks after the 1917 revolution that brought them to power in a war-prostrate Russia. This was indeed unfortunate, because the master Bolshevik from 1930 onward was the cunning and brutal Josef Stalin. Under his aegis, traditional Russia was transformed by the Five Year Plans and the Stalinist aberration of Marxism. Communism's bankruptcy as a viable and humane government would only be gradually and belatedly revealed to its millions of admirers.

The Second World War was the logical upshot of the first; it was catalyzed by the expansionary dreams of Adolf Hitler and his fellow Nazi visionaries. Like World War I, World War II was essentially decided when the American industrial giant entered the war on the anti-Axis side; this time the mistake that led to U.S. involvement was the attack on Pearl Harbor by the Nazis' ally, Japan. The unnatural partnership of democratic Britain, the United States, and Stalinist Russia fell apart immediately after the common enemy was overwhelmed. The Cold War began and lasted for a long and frequently terrifying generation of crises. For a long time, the known world seemed on the verge of becoming divided into the permanent fiefs of the two superpowers, the United States and the Soviet Union.

But western Europe, which had seemed finished in the ruins of 1945, got back onto its cultural and economic feet with American aid and by the mid-1950s was showing an astonishing vitality. Protected by the same American atomic umbrella that allowed Japan to concentrate on internal reform and productivity, the West Europeans marched steadily ahead toward the consumer society once thought of as peculiarly the province of the rich Americans. Meanwhile, their eastern cousins were the unhappy satellites of Moscow and lagged far behind in enjoying the fruits of the workers' labors.

The allegedly revolutionary message of communism was revealed after Stalin's death to be no more than the ideologically enlarged shadow thrown by a crude great power, rather than a new dispensation for humankind. This impression was steadily strengthened in the 1970s and 1980s and was then demonstrated by the abject collapse of the spiritually bankrupt communist regimes at the beginning of the 1990s.

In the non-Western world, the unprecedented process of decolonization went forward with bumps and delays, but encountered no insuperable obstacles in the postwar generation. Either by armed force or moral suasion, the once-subject colonies became newly sovereign nations and took their place proudly in a United Nations Organization that had originally been planned as a great power club. A kind of cultural and political equilibrium among the members of an increasingly polycentric world, between East and West, white and colored, advanced and backward was in the process of being painfully and tentatively reasserted. Using the immense intellectual and moral resources opened to them by Western ideas and ideals, the other three-quarters of humanity are determined to make themselves heard and listened to as this violent and unpredictable century goes toward its end.

Chapter 48 opens this part by reviewing the attempt to make World War I comprehensible to the European consciousness. Chapter 49 is the story of the first generation of Soviet Russian government, from Lenin's coup to the enthronement of Stalin. Chapter 50 puts the totalitarian idea and particularly the Nazi dictatorship under the spotlight. Chapter 51 examines the momentous events in the two chief East Asian powers during the century between 1840 and 1940. World War II is the subject of Chapter 52, which also looks at the strains that quickly broke down the victorious alliance against the Axis. Chapter 53 departs from our usual political-chronological standpoint to review some outstanding aspects of modern culture. The Cold War between the United States and the Soviet Union is the focus of Chapter 54, and it provides the essential backdrop for the strong recovery of western Europe and the creation of the European Economic Community in the 1950s and 1960s. This is followed in Chapter 55 by an examination of the chronology and causation of the decolonizing phenomenon after the war and the staggering problems of the developing countries since the 1950s.

Chapter 56 reviews the history of the countries on the Pacific's western shores and of South Asia since the end of World War II. Africa is the subject of Chapter 57, which looks at the immense difficulties confronting the sub-Saharan states since the euphoria of independence. In Chapter 58 the same problem-oriented survey is made, this time of the Latin American countries throughout this century. In Chapter 59, the focal point is the Islamic community, particularly the Middle East. The collapse of the Marxist regimes in Europe is analyzed in Chapter 60, which also considers the special challenges facing the ex-communist states.

The final two chapters, Chapter 61 and 62, look at some of the phenomena of modern Western and developing societies and at the changing outlines of international relations in the era of atomic weaponry, terrorism, and diminished national sovereignties. The book concludes with a brief address to the student of history at the end of the twentieth century.

	Law and Government	Economy
WESTERNERS	Rise of mass democracy in politics creates new-style party government where money, but no longer birth, plays important role. Law increasingly reflects popular attitudes, as interpreted by party heads. Property rights under attack while civil rights advance. Totalitarian governments appear in many nations after WWI and ensuing Great Depression of 1930s. After WWII, long economic boom allows democratic recovery and stability in West outside Soviet bloc.	Two distinct economic periods: 1920–1945 saw the decline and near-collapse of free market in West, widespread impoverishment of middle classes and agriculturalists; 1945–present has seen a long boom interrupted for several years by oil crisis of 1970s. Japan emerges as leading financial power in 1980s. The European Community becomes economic reality while Soviet bloc stagnates and then collapses. The global economy is rapidly forming under Western dominance.
AFRICANS	Law and government continue on colonial lines until after WWII. Decolonization brings unstable mixture of African traditional law and political structures with European models. Western forms often at odds with precolonial content. Post-independence problems encourage authoritarian single-party governments.	Increasing emphasis on export crops and mining converts some areas to food-deficit regions. Very little manufacturing, even after end of colonial regimes. Increasing international aid in attempt to overcome declining agricultural productivity and dependency on imports of all types. Thanks to large increases in population, most national economies are in crisis by 1990s.
MUSLIMS	Minority attempts to introduce modern Western law, education, and politics are made throughout Muslim world after WWI with minimal success excepting Turkey. After WWII a strong backlash favoring strict fundamentalist Islam develops, led most recently by Iran. Governments of Islamic countries range from a limited Western constitutionalism to undisguised theocracy. Nationalism is a powerful force in all, particularly among Arabs.	Middle East oil is the one major export, generating dependence on international customers. Much effort was exerted to avoid this by using oil funds for varied domestic investments. Arab states and Indonesia relatively successful in doing so, but oil production still remains the key to their prosperity. Poor Muslim countries are very unstable and still are not integrated into world economy constructively.

1920–PRESENT: EQUILIBRIUM REESTABLISHED

Peoples: Westerners (Europeans, North Americans, Japanese, British Dominions), Africans, Muslims, East and South Asians, Latin Americans

Religion and Philosophy	Arts and Culture	Science and Technology
The "post–Christian era." Secularism elevated to formal doctrine in most countries, assisted by rise in influence of Marxism through 1960s. Failure of Marxism in 1980s underlines the crisis of sterility in Western philosophical ideas. Concurrent sharp rise in Western interest in Eastern religion and philosophies.	Art and its audience become fragmented. No recognized models or authority. Much influence from non-Western sources. Abstraction in pictorial arts matched by rejection of traditional models in all other arts among the *avant-garde*. Literature and philosophy either "serious" or popular; no middle ground. Mass cultural forms (TV, movies, music, magazines) often dictated by commercial considerations.	Science becomes defining reference for knowledge and truth. Social sciences (economics, psychology, etc.) rise to prominence. Technology makes enormous strides, removing physical labor as obstacle to almost any task and enabling "information revolution" through computers and electronic apparatus.
Christian missions make inroads into traditional animism in central and southern regions. Islam dominates the north, west, and eastern coast. Most Africans blend one or the other formal doctrines with local animisms. Education for masses begins after 1950, increases after decolonization completed.	Sub-Saharan pictorial and plastic arts become widely recognized for first time, partly due to increased archaeological finds. Modern African artists blend Western training with native motifs and media. Independence brings much greater opportunities for artists, domestically and internationally. Literature continues to be in Western languages, hence limited in audience at home, where oral folklore is still main way of transmitting cultural values.	Physical and social scientists still relatively few and dependent on foreign sources for training, financing, and direction. Higher educational facilities remain oriented toward nonscientific programs and degrees, emulating nineteenth-century colonial culture. Technology imported from West and Japan sometimes has devastating impact on local cultures and economies.
The secularism of some intellectuals and political reformers is sharply opposed by the traditionalists. Only after WWII do the religious fundamentalists learn how to propagandize effectively with a nationalist appeal. Islam in their view is combined with strong rejection of the West's public and private values.	Much increased literacy resulted in revival or first appearance of literature in several Muslim states. Oil wealth of 1970s provided major governmental patronage of arts in Arab states. Nationalism reflected in art forms and revived interest in folk art.	As in rest of non-Western world, physical and life sciences were dependent on Western training and goal setting. This rapidly changed to autonomous science in much of Muslim world since approximately 1970. Emphasis on science and technology in higher education apparently accepted by fundamentalist Muslims as modern necessity.

LINK
6

	Law and Government	Economy
SOUTH AND EAST ASIANS	Former British possessions have generally retained Western outlook on law and government. French and Dutch territories less committed to these ideals. In several, Marxist socialism provided a format for combining nationalism with radical reform. Governments currently range from liberal democratic constitutionalism to oppressive dictatorships. China's mutated Marxism is in a category of its own, combining political censorship with economic and social freedoms.	South and East Asia give a mixed picture of economic progress. In Bangladesh, Sri Lanka, and Burma, the traditional agrarian and poverty stricken economy has barely changed or has gotten worse due to rapid population increase. South Korea, Taiwan, and Malaysia have undergone stunning change in moving toward modern industry and services in the past 30 years. Japan's modified and highly successful free market example has proved influential, but huge China is the X quantity in Asia's economic picture.
LATIN AMERICANS	The fundamental laws continue to be European (Napoleonic codes), and the governmental structures resemble those of the West. The enormous social gap between rich and poor often frustrates the intent of the constitution, however, and makes a segregated legal procedure inevitable. Government often represents only the uppermost minority, though this is slowly changing in most of the continent.	A fully Westernized urban lifestyle is supported for a minority by relatively modern industrial economies. In most of the continent, however, the agrarian and deprived mestizo/mulatto population has made little progress in a century. As in Africa, a very rapid population increase prevents substantial or permanent gains from international investments and loans. Most of Latin America continues as a dependent of the Western nations.

1920–PRESENT: EQUILIBRIUM REESTABLISHED

Peoples: Westerners (Europeans, North Americans, Japanese, British Dominions), Africans, Muslims, East and South Asians, Latin Americans

Religion and Philosophy	Arts and Culture	Science and Technology
Asians have retained their religious and cultural independence of the West, even during the colonial era. Buddhism in its several versions is still the most popular of the mass cults, while Islam and Daoism are major competitors in the southeast and China. India remains Hindu, while secular views gain everywhere among the educated. The superficial cultural phenomena have become increasingly Westernized.	Cultural autonomy in Asia is expressed in the arts now as always. A recognizably non-Western approach is manifested through several regional variations in the fine arts as well as in folklore and artisanry. Literature and philosophy have been deeply affected by Western influences in the last generation, but remain distinct. Higher education now resembles that in the West, with the same emphases in the advanced countries.	The formerly huge gap between the physical and life sciences in South and East Asia and in the West has almost been closed. Technology still lags, largely as a result of shortages of investment funds rather than lack of knowledge or willingness.
Catholicism has split into a reform-minded and a traditionalist party within the clergy as it gradually loses its automatic acceptance among the masses touched by modern secularism. The formal link between state and church is nearly gone. Education is still an unmet need in the mestizo and Indian countries, and literacy rates are still low in them.	Particularly in fiction, Latin American authors have won world acclaim, and the fine arts with some exceptions have also prospered in this century. Formal culture is still restricted to the wealthy and the urban middle class, however. Between them and the rural majority, the cultural chasm still lies open.	Retarded, labor-rich economy has slight connection with technology. The sciences and technology are still heavily dependent on Western and particularly American models and direction. Higher education has been very slow in reorienting itself toward a modern curriculum in these fields, while the mainly foreign-owned companies are not research oriented.

A FRAGILE BALANCE: EUROPE, 1919–1929

World War I had profound and disturbing effects on Europe. The 1919 peace treaties were resented intensely by the losers and did not satisfy the winners. Most of the eastern half of the continent was in continuous upheaval for several years. Russia gave birth to the world's first socialist society in 1917 and then attempted to export its Bolshevik philosophy by legal and illegal channels. Defeated Germany underwent the world's worst inflation, ruining millions. In Italy, Fascism came to power early in the postwar era. International rivalries and rampant nationalism made another conflict appear inevitable. But by the late 1920s, western and central Europe seemed more stable, and the threat of renewed war were more distant. For a few years, it seemed that Europe might weather the crisis that 1914 had set off.

✦ POLITICAL AND ECONOMIC BACKDROP TO THE INTERWAR ERA

The political and economic landscape had changed significantly since the onset of the Second Industrial Revolution in Europe. The sharp increase in the number of workers, their concentration in large industrial plants and in cities, and the advent of universal suffrage meant that politics in the early twentieth century had become democratized in a fashion unthinkable a century earlier. Politics on the national level was now the art of appealing to the interests and prejudices of distinct social groups, but in a way that did not alienate other social groups whose support was necessary for electoral triumph.

Democratization of Politics

All democratically governed societies had turned to *mass political parties* as the fundamental means of determining the popular will. The European nations gave all adult males the vote sometime between 1870 and 1912; the United States had done the same earlier, although racial and property restrictions varied from state to state. These masses of voters were incorporated into modern political life through permanent parties, which now emerged to replace the earlier temporary alliances. Around the end of the nineteenth century, electoral politics in the West took on many of the forms that we still know: the "campaign" led by the chief officer of the party and backed by paid and volunteer organizers; the "platform" of promises by the contending parties; the transfer of power from the hands of the party's legislative officers to the leaders of the executive branch; and the alliances between organized labor and one party or another.

In the United States, and to a lesser degree in Europe, parties ceased to be defined strictly by class; some parties broadened sufficiently to include the working-class *and* members of the middle class, aristocrats *and* intellectuals. (This process really accelerated in Europe only after World War II.) Property alone no longer dictated political affiliation, and the nineteenth-century division into liberal and conservative made less and less sense as cultural experience, secularization, social philosophy, and other intangible factors helped to shape the political inclinations of a given individual. Any parties that continued to represent a single interest group at either end of the social scale were destined to give way to those that welcomed a diverse mix. The only important exception was the Marxists, who claimed a proprietary interest in both progress and the proletariat.

Keynesian Economics

Economic affairs were certainly still important in every person's perception of the proper society. In national economics, the two major innovations of the first half of the twentieth century were (1) the recognition that governments could and probably should intervene to soften the roller coaster of the business cycle and (2) the spread and Russianization of Marxist communism.

John Maynard Keynes (1883–1946), the British economist whom we encountered in connection with his harsh critique of the Treaty of Versailles, proved to be the most influential economic theorist of the century. He insisted that government had the power and the duty to smooth out the violent ups and downs of the business cycle by pumping new money into the credit system in hard times (such as the 1930s). By doing so, the millions of private investors, business owners, and speculators whose collective decisions determined the course of the economy would be afforded the credit they needed to engage in new enterprise. Eventually, the increased tax revenues generated by this stimulus to business, commerce, and manufacturing would recompense the government for its expenditures and enable it to prevent inflation from accelerating too rapidly. A growth economy with some inflation was both attainable and more desirable than the nineteenth-century "boom and bust" cycles that had caused much misery.

Keynes's thought, though admired by some, did not find many adherents among government leaders in Britain or any other part of the world before World War II. President Franklin D. Roosevelt instituted some half-hearted measures on Keynesian lines during the Great Depression of the 1930s, but they had relatively little effect. Only after 1945, with the Labour government in Britain committed to the welfare of the common people, and the Truman administration in the United States committed to avoiding an expected postwar crash, were Keynes's ideas tried in earnest. Since that time, it has become standard procedure for Western governments to counter the economic cycle by "pump priming" in times of unemployment and deflation. Essentially, this means pouring new government expenditures into the economy at a time when the government's income (taxes) is declining. Since increasing taxes during a recession is politically very difficult, a government that follows Keynes's ideas must either borrow from its own citizens (by issuing bonds or treasury notes) or use its powers to inflate by running the money printing presses a bit faster.

The debate as to whether Keynes's ideas actually work continues. Certainly, governments have often abused Keynesian pump priming for the sake of political advantage. And it probably has contributed to long-term inflation, which hits the lower classes hardest. In recent years, free market theory and practice have experienced a significant revival. Examples include the administrations of President Ronald Reagan in the United States and Prime Minister Margaret Thatcher in Britain and, most recently, some of the postcommunist governments of eastern Europe. Such theory rejects the Keynesian view in part and accepts the inevitability of some ups and downs in the national economy.

Marxist Successes and the Soviet Chimera

The other major phenomenon of international economics after World War I was the flourishing of the Marxist gospel among both workers and intellectuals in much of the world. The success of the Russian Bolsheviks (see Chapter 49) in maintaining themselves in power despite civil war and foreign enemies impressed many people in the colonial and less-developed parts of the world. That the inexperienced and supposedly incompetent "Reds" could turn the Union of Soviet Socialist Republics (USSR) into an industrial great power by the 1930s seemed to demonstrate the correctness of Karl Marx's analysis and prognosis of the world's ailments. What had been done in backward, isolated Russia, they reasoned, must and would be done in the rest of the world.

In the early 1920s, new communist parties, inspired and guided by the Russian pioneers, sprang up in every important country and many colonies. From the sitting rooms where intellectuals worried that they would be left behind "on the ashheap of history" to the docks and mines where painfully idealistic communist workers labored, the Marxist belief spread into all social groups and classes. Even some of the hated "bourgeois exploiters" saw the light and abandoned their own class to join the forces of progress and equity.

During the Great Depression of the 1930s, the Marxists made substantial progress not only among the miserable unemployed but also among the many intellectuals and artists who concluded that capitalism had definitively failed, that its day was done, and that the page had to be turned. The Marxist sympathizers delighted in contrasting the millions of out-of-work, embittered men and women in the Western democracies with the picture (often entirely false) painted by Soviet propaganda of happy workers going off to their tasks of "building Socialism in one country" (the Soviet Union) with confidence and dignity. They also contrasted the class warfare in France and Spain in the mid-1930s with the solidarity and equality the propagandists assured them reigned in the Soviet Union.

Since very few sympathizers had the opportunity of seeing for themselves what was going on in the Soviet Union, and those who *did* go were treated to outrageously fabricated displays of prosperity and social welfare by Josef Stalin's minions, the truth about Soviet Marxism was known to only a few. Whenever some honest reporters attempted an accurate description of the first socialist society, they were inevitably shouted down as "rotten bourgeois" or "paid tools of the governing class" and ignored by the closed minds they were trying to reach.

Although only the Soviets were able to sustain a Marxist revolution during the interwar years (several short-lived attempts in eastern Europe in the wake of World War I were put down; see Chapter 49), millions were convinced that sooner or later communism was bound to spread and bring all humankind into the sunlight of a new society. To them, Stalin's Russia was a benevolent pioneer, the guide that would lead the way to this earthly heaven and help bring about their own (inevitable) revolutions. No other doctrine of modern times reached and held so many minds or inspired such diverse groups and individuals. And no other was so cruelly deceptive. Indeed, it proved crueler to its friends than to its enemies.

✤ GERMANY IN THE POSTWAR ERA

Political Problems

The new republican government in Berlin came under fire from large segments of the population from its first day. It had the thankless task of attempting to fill the vacuum left by the military and civil collapse at the end of the war. Very soon the government became the scapegoat for accepting the hated Versailles Treaty, an act that damned it in the eyes of the nationalists and conservatives forever.

Simultaneously, the new government was threatened by Russian-inspired attempts to spread the Bolshevik revolution among the German working classes. But this competition was eventually beaten off. Unlike the Russians, the German workers and peasants were not helplessly exploited by landlords and industrialists, and the majority were not interested in a revolution. In that, they resembled the leaders of the German Social Democratic Party, who had long since adopted "revisionism" and now became the mainstays of the republican government.

In early 1919, the German communists attempted to replicate what their Russian colleagues had done in November 1917. This coup d'état was put down by the German army, which had remained a powerful force under its conservative generals. The generals, who could make or break any civilian government, chose to go along with the Social Democrats rather than risk a communist takeover. This arrangement lasted throughout the 1920s. Although several other attempted revolts inspired by the Communist Party took place in the early 1920s, all were put down without serious trouble by the army.

The menace from the Left was thus contained, but that from the Right became more potent as time went on. In July 1919, the government had adopted a new fundamental law, called the *Weimar Constitution* after the town where it was framed. The constitution was a high-minded, liberal, democratic document. But the government it established was already so tarnished in the eyes of many Germans that neither the constitution nor the state it created was considered truly German and legitimate. As long as economic conditions were tolerable and the menace of a communist coup was acute, the **Weimar Republic** was not in too much danger from the Right. But once these conditions no longer prevailed, the danger was imminent and tangible.

Reparations

The most painful part of the Paris peace to Germany was the insistence of the French (less so the Italians and

British) that Germany bore the full financial responsibility for war damages and therefore must pay reparations. After much delay, the Allies finally presented the full bill in 1921: $33 billion (in 1920 dollars)—approximately Germany's total gross national product for five years! This was supposed to be paid in either cash or goods in annual installments over the next several years.

Paying such sums would have utterly bankrupted a wounded Germany, and the government attempted to reason with the French. But the Paris government would not negotiate. In 1921 and 1922, the Germans actually made most of the required payments, but in 1923 they asked for a two-year moratorium (nonpayment). The French responded by sending troops to occupy Germany's industrial heartland, the **Ruhr** area. The occupying force was instructed to seize everything that was produced, mainly iron and coal. Berlin then encouraged the Ruhr workers to engage in massive nonviolent resistance through strikes.

Inflation and Middle-Class Ruin

The Ruhr occupation set off the final spiral of the inflation that had afflicted the German *Reichsmark* since 1919. The inflation ruined many people in Germany's large middle class, who had been the backbone of its productive society for many years. At the height of the inflation, money was literally not worth the paper it was printed on—one U.S. dollar purchased 800 *million* Reichsmarks in late 1923. A few speculators and persons with access to foreign currencies made fortunes overnight, but most people suffered. People who lived on fixed incomes, as did much of the middle class, were wiped out. Many were reduced to begging and selling family heirlooms to avoid starving. They would not forget.

The inflation was ended by a loan in U.S. dollars to the German national bank, which reassured people that the paper currency had something of value behind it once more. At the same time, in 1924, the **Dawes Plan,** sponsored by a group of American bankers, induced the French to leave the Ruhr, forgo some of the reparations payments, and spread them over a considerably longer time period, if the Germans would resume payments. This agreement held up for a few years (1924–1929), but the psychic and financial damage to the strongest elements of German society could not be made good. They had seen the thrifty turned into beggars while clever thieves became wealthy. They hated the society and government that had permitted such things. From now on, many of them were looking for someone who could

impose order on a world that had betrayed their legitimate expectations.

✤ ITALIAN FASCISM

The peculiar contribution of the first half of the twentieth century to political doctrines was *totalitarianism.* The first example of totalitarian government was **Fascism in Italy.**

Mussolini's Early Career

The Fascist Party was the creation of an ex-socialist named *Benito Mussolini* (1883–1945), the son of a blacksmith who had obtained an education and become a journalist for socialist newspapers in prewar Italy. In 1912, he had become the editor of the major Socialist Party newspaper; from that platform, he regularly denounced all wars in standard Marxist terms as an invention of the capitalists to keep the international proletariat divided

◼ **The Effects of Inflation.** By the early 1920s, the value of the German mark had fallen precipitously. This photograph shows a German housewife using the worthless currency to light a fire in her cooking stove.

Theory of Fascism

Benito Mussolini tried for years to avoid spelling out exactly what the aims of his Fascist movement were and what the good Fascist Party member should believe. He did this in part because he rejected the restrictions such a definition would place on his freedom of intellectual movement, and in part because explaining what Fascism stood for was very difficult (though saying what it was against was relatively easy).

In 1932, however, after seven years of dictatorial powers, Mussolini decided that the time had come. An article entitled "The Political and Social Doctrine of Fascism," signed by Il Duce, appeared that year in the Italian national encyclopedia. The following are excerpts from this article, which is as close as Mussolini ever came to attempting a rationale of his movement:

> ... Fascism was not the nursling of a doctrine worked out beforehand with detailed elaboration; it was born of the need for action and it was itself from the beginning practical rather than theoretical; it was not merely another political party but, even in the first two years, in opposition to all political parties ... a living movement.

Fascism, the more it considers and observes the future and the development of humanity quite apart from political considerations of the moment, believes neither in the possibility nor the utility of perpetual peace. It thus repudiates the doctrine of Pacifism—born of a renunciation of the struggle and an act of cowardice in the face of sacrifice. War alone brings up to its highest tension all human energy and puts the stamp of nobility upon the peoples who have the courage to meet it. All other trials are substitutes which never really put men into the position where they have to make the great decision—the alternative of life or death. Thus a doctrine which is founded upon this harmful postulate of peace is hostile to Fascism. . . .

> Such a conception of life makes Fascism the complete opposite of that doctrine, the base of so-called scientific or Marxian Socialism, the materialist conception of history. . . . Fascism now and always believes in holiness and in heroism, that is to say, in actions influenced by no economic motives, direct or indirect. . . .

and helpless. When World War I broke out, however, he experienced a remarkable change. In the several months of Italian neutrality, Mussolini ceaselessly campaigned for intervention on the side of the Allies; for that, he was kicked out of the Socialists and proceeded to found a nationalist paper. When Italy entered the war in May 1915, he at once volunteered for front-line duty and was wounded in action. He returned to his newspaper, *Il Popolo d'Italia,* and spent the rest of the war denouncing his former pacifist colleagues and demanding that Italy find its overdue respect and national glory in combat.

After the war ended, Italian workers and peasants became extremely discontented with their liberal government. At the Paris peace talks, Italy gained much less than it had hoped; the economy was in critical condition because of the sudden end of wartime contracts and the failure to plan for peace. Immigration to the United States, the traditional haven for unemployed Italians, ended when the United States enacted restrictive laws.

The Bolshevik success in Russia was well publicized by the Socialists, who soon split into moderates and communists, as did every other European socialist party.

Mussolini now came forward as a mercenary strikebreaker and bullyboy in the employ of frightened industrialists and landowners, who were fearful of communism. His party took its name from the ancient Roman symbol of law and order, the *fasces* carried by the bodyguard of the consul. At first very small, the Fascist Party grew by leaps and bounds in 1921–1922 with the secret support of the government itself.

Seizure of Power

In October 1922, Mussolini pulled off a bloodless coup by inducing the weak King Victor Emmanuel III to appoint him as premier. This was grandiosely termed Mussolini's **"March on Rome."** For two years, he ruled by more or

After Socialism, Fascism combats as well the whole complex system of democratic ideology, and repudiates it, whether in its theoretical premises or in its practical applications. Fascism denies that the majority, by the simple fact that it is a majority, can direct human society; it denies that numbers alone can govern by means of periodic consultations [i.e., elections], and it affirms the immutable, beneficial, and fruitful inequality of mankind. . . .

Fascism uses in its construction whatever elements in the Liberal, Social, or Democratic doctrines still have a living value . . . but it rejects all the rest—that is, the conception that there can be any doctrine of unquestioned efficacy for all times and all peoples. Given that the 19th century was the century of Socialism, of Liberalism, and of Democracy, it does not follow that the 20th century must also be a century of Socialism, Liberalism, and Democracy; political doctrines pass, but humanity remains; and it may rather be expected that this will be a century of authority, a century of the Left, a century of Fascism. For if the 19th century was a century of individualism (Liberalism always signifying individualism) it may be expected that this will be a century of collectivism, and hence the century of the State.

■ Benito Mussolini greets the crowd from his office balcony on the occasion of the fifteenth anniversary of the Fascist Party, 1935.

SOURCE: Excerpted from *Mussolini and Italian Fascism*, S. W. Halperin, Encyclopedia Italiano, V. XIV, © 1931.

less legal and constitutional methods; the Fascists were only a small minority in parliament, but their opponents were badly divided. Then, in 1924, Mussolini rigged elections that returned Fascists to a large majority of parliamentary seats. He proceeded to form a one-party state, and by the end of 1926 he had forced the other parties to "voluntarily" disband or had driven them underground (like the communists). Those who protested or attempted resistance were harassed and imprisoned by a brutal secret police.

Mussolini improvised his programs and his ideology as the occasion demanded (see the Document in this chapter). He never bothered about consistency and did not hesitate to shift positions radically if he thought it to his advantage. He had started his political career as a Marxist and pacifist; during the war he had changed to an anti-Marxist, nationalist. Now that he was in power, he became an aggressive imperialist (the "New Rome" was a favored slogan).

Fascist Economic and Social Policies

Fascist economics was a mixture of socialism-without-Marx and laissez-faire. Private property was never disturbed, but the state played a much larger role than heretofore in directing both industry and commerce. The official name of the Fascist policy was *corporatism,* which meant that labor and owners in a given industry were treated as partners under the supervision of the government bureaucracy. It was a type of planned economy, but without the extreme regimentation that the Soviets were engaged in at this time (see Chapter 49). For a few years, it worked reasonably well and avoided or dampened the class struggles that were plaguing much of democratically governed Europe during the 1920s and 1930s.

Until the mid-1930s, Mussolini was genuinely popular. So long as he did not involve Italy in war, a large majority of Italians were fascinated by his undeniable charisma and believed in his efforts to make Italy a major power for the

Gabriele d'Annunzio
1863–1938

The appeal of Fascism in Italy stemmed from many sources; for one man, it was the chance to beat people up without punishment; for another, it was the accumulated resentment at suffering a generation of government without representation. For Gabriele d'Annunzio, the Fascists were the flesh and blood of a philosophy to which he had devoted his life and his art. D'Annunzio was that rarest of men: a poet who at times reached greatness, but possessed the soul of a brute.

Born into a wealthy home, d'Annunzio received a fine education and very early displayed the literary talent that would make him famous. When he was sixteen, he published a collection of verse that raised the critics' eyebrows; two years later, he followed it with another collection, which established him as the leading poet of his generation. *Canto novo* (*New Song*) was a celebration of the senses in a language so vivid and stirring that congratulations rained in upon the young genius. From 1882 onward, d'Annunzio published poems, drama, novels, stories, and literary criticism in such abundance as to become a one-man industry. His first novel—*Il piacere* (*The Pleasure-seeker*)—set the tone for what would follow: the self-centered protagonist tramples all around him (particularly the women who love him), but justifies his actions by telling himself that he stands above the common crowd.

This attitude was made universal in d'Annunzio's autobiographical novels of the 1890s, above all in *The Triumph of Death,* the most famous of them. The hero is a sadistic, selfish exploiter of anyone foolish enough to become attached to him. Women swoon over him, while he uses them and tosses them aside like so many old clothes. Men admire him while despising his arrogance; neither means anything to him. As in most of d'Annunzio's work, there is a hollowness of characterization that is only occasionally overcome by the beauty of the language.

D'Annunzio took much of his novels' action more or less directly from his own life. Though married young to a wealthy noblewoman, he was one of the most distinguished womanizers of the late nineteenth century. In 1894, he established a liaison with the

---

first time (see the Biography in this chapter). He promised action on behalf of the common people, and to some extent he delivered (*autostrade,* pregnancy leaves, vacation pay, agricultural credit for the peasants, and the like). But his price was always total control of the nation's politics.

Many Westerners were impressed and believed that Mussolini had found a way around the terrible socioeconomic problems that surfaced in the interwar years. They thought that Fascism was a not unreasonable compromise: both labor and owners gave up something to get something else that was more important. What they did not know, or would not see, was that political liberties had been entirely sacrificed to a party and its leader ("Il Duce") who ultimately had no vision except his own power. After 1935, when Mussolini started a senseless war of colonial conquest in Ethiopia, even the standard of living of most Italians declined steadily.

✤ EASTERN EUROPE

In the Successor states, parliamentary democracy and constitutional government were facing rocky roads after the war. *Poland,* which had been newly re-created from slices of Germany and Russia, had no democratic tradition and huge economic problems. Its difficulties were compounded by the fact that one-third of its population were not Poles and did not want to be within Polish borders. In the west and north were many Germans, who traditionally regarded the Poles with contempt and were now under Warsaw's rule only by Allied command. In the east were millions of Ukrainians and Jews, separated by religion and national animosities from the host nation. By 1926, **Marshal Józef Pilsudski,** a World War I military hero, had brushed aside the quarreling and ineffectual parliament and established a conservative dictatorship.

great Italian actress Eleonora Duse that lasted many years and received a suitable literary memorial in *Il Fuoco* (*The Fire*) published by d'Annunzio in 1900. He wrote several plays for Duse that she made famous throughout the world despite their minimal artistic value. She believed wholeheartedly in his talents and was able to accept his extraordinary egocentricity without complaint. She financed much of the expense of his princely lifestyle. D'Annunzio's collection of poems entitled *Alcyone* (1904), which is among the finest in the history of the Italian language, was largely inspired by his relations with Duse.

But d'Annunzio was not merely a literary man with a taste for opulence. As World War I approached, he became obsessed with the same taste for violence as a cleansing experience that many of the young Italian intellectuals and artists were displaying. When Italy sat out the early months of the war, he agitated for the nation's immediate entry into the fray, and when Italy did enter, d'Annunzio, like his later hero Mussolini, was among the first to volunteer for the front line. From 1915 to the war's end, he was an active participant, becoming one of Italy's first combat pilots and repeatedly making foolhardy (and well-publicized) flights over enemy territory in a quest for eternal fame. Near the end, he even made the long flight over the enemy capital of Vienna as a taunt to the collapsing Austria.

The poet's most spectacular feat of arms came just after the war's end, however. Disappointed like most Italians with the skimpy gains from their wartime sacrifice, in September 1919 d'Annunzio took 287 fellow romantics to capture the town of Fiume (Rijeka) across the narrow Adriatic. The port had been promised to Italy in a secret treaty designed to bring Italy into the war on the Allies' side, but now was being given to the new Yugoslav state. D'Annunzio's gesture had the desired effect; the peacemakers at Paris threw the question of Fiume back into the undecided category, and eventually it went to Italy.

D'Annunzio was a warm adherent of Mussolini and the Fascist Party from the outset. In 1924, after the Duce was installed as prime minister, he rewarded d'Annunzio with a noble title and a lavish edition of his collected works. The next fourteen years passed much more calmly. The poet-hero died quietly at his retirement home in 1938. Most of his drama and novels and much of his poetry are now totally forgotten.

Hungary had lost more than half of its prewar territory and population, making economic progress impossible even during the good years of the later 1920s. Magyar nationalism was the sole shared rallying point for the Left and the Right. Manipulating the parties and acting as a sort of father figure throughout the interwar era was Admiral Miklós Horthy, a former Austro-Hungarian officer of the Right who insisted on the title of regent (for the deposed Habsburg monarch).

In *Romania,* the prewar constitutional monarchy carried over and provided a facade behind which the two chief parties maneuvered for control. Both were corrupt; neither represented the interests of the vast majority: the impoverished and illiterate Romanian peasantry. Parliamentary government was a series of cynical deals between the parties or between them and the king.

In *Yugoslavia, Bulgaria, and Albania,* similar constitutional monarchies were in place. Parties representing all segments of the population were present, but the small urban bourgeoisie exercised parliamentary control in its own interest and against the peasant majority. This manipulation was facilitated by the several divisions of the populace along ethnic and religious lines, and by the maneuvers of a clique of "patriots" at the royal palace. As a result, by the mid 1930s, almost all of the eastern European states were run by authoritarian dictatorships similar to Poland. In all the East European states but Czechoslovakia, *fear of Bolshevism was intense among the governing classes* even though the industrial workers were so few and the peasants so conservative as to make the Bolshevik appeal very limited. In most of these countries, the native Communist Party was soon outlawed and its mostly urban and proletarian memberships were driven

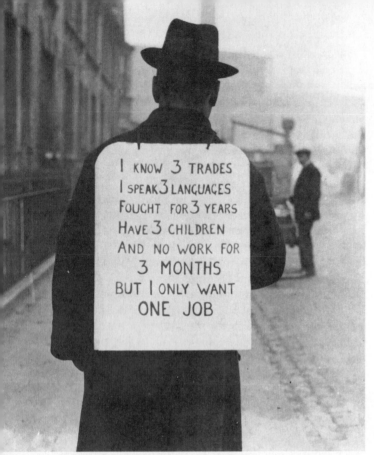

■ **Unemployment in Britain.** The British were unable to solve their continuing unemployment problem, which became evident in the early 1920s as the economy contracted after the war. The wartime transfer of overseas markets and financial power to the United States was a major factor, as was the obsolescence of much English industry.

underground. The one East European state that retained its democratic and constitutional nature throughout the 1920s and 1930s was *Czechoslovakia.* Not coincidentally, it was also by far the most industrially developed.

The most pressing problem of the East European states was that their economies were still based on an *underdeveloped, subsistence agriculture.* Attempts to organize the East European peasantry into a "Green International" (as distinguished from the communist Red International of workers) never prospered. Between 60 and 85 percent of the people of eastern Europe derived an erratic and unreliable livelihood from low-paying agriculture. So long as the world commercial picture was bright and they could export their agrarian products (grain, hides, lumber), the East Europeans could get along. But when the Great Depression of the 1930s began, this picture quickly changed.

Nationalism was the universal blight of the East Europeans. Even the Czechs, who were the most reasonable on

this score, were prone to favor their own ethnic group over the Slovak and German minorities in both official and unofficial ways. Every state east of Germany had a large number of minority citizens, most of whom were living unwillingly under foreign rule. Many of them such as the Magyars in Czechoslovakia and Romania, the Germans in the same states, and the Austrians in northern Italy were vulnerable to **irredentism,** the movement to split away and unite with a neighboring state. The fact that Wilson's promise of material self-determination was only partially fulfilled at Paris aggravated the condition of those who found themselves left outside their national borders. This situation would cause all types of political problems throughout the interwar era in East Europe.

⚜ THE WESTERN DEMOCRACIES

The two major political and social democracies, Britain and France, had several advantages over the central and eastern European states in the 1920s. At least formally, they had been the victors in a war that no European state really had won. Their economies had been hard hit by the war, but not so badly as Germany's, and they had not suffered the outrageous inflation of the losing powers. They had much deeper democratic roots than the other states, and their governments were used to and committed to constitutional processes.

Britain

But this does not mean that Britain and France did not have serious problems. For Great Britain, the most serious were economic: *(1) unemployment and (2) reduced availability of capital.* The British labor force suffered severe and chronic unemployment throughout the entire interwar period for many reasons that were not easily understood. During the war, the United States had replaced Britain as the financial center of the world. The British Empire could no longer be relied on to absorb the products of English mines and factories. Wartime losses had dramatically reduced the earnings of the world's largest merchant marine, and British goods and services were now rivaled or overshadowed by several competitors (notably the United States and Japan) in world markets.

Reduced profits and trade opportunities were reflected in the long decline of capital invested by the British in Britain and around the world. Where once the English led all nations by a large margin in profitable investments such as tramway lines in Argentina, railroads in India, and fishing canneries in Japan, they now often lacked the capital to invest. Furthermore, Britain, which had once been the world leader in technology had slipped behind the United States and Germany in the early twentieth century and was falling even farther behind now.

These conditions of unemployment and reduced capital explain the long depression that gripped Britain early and permanently during the interwar period, when millions were "on the dole" (welfare). One result was the sudden rise of the **Labour Party,** a non-Marxist socialist group, to second place in British politics. The new party displaced the Liberals and was even able to elect a Labour government in 1924 over its Conservative opponent. Labour carried great hopes, but it had no more success than the Conservatives and Liberals in curing the nation's ills. A union-organized general strike in 1926—the first in a democratically governed country—was also a failure. The unemployment rate stayed around 10 percent. No one had a quick answer to what was ailing Britain.

France

In *France,* the economic crisis was not apparent in the 1920s. France had a well-balanced national economy, and German reparations and the return of the rich provinces of Alsace and Lorraine after 1918 helped it. But like the other belligerents, France had been weakened by the loss of 1.5 million of its most productive citizens in the war. And German reparations could only slowly make up for the $23 billion in material damage to French property during the war.

The main economic problem was an invisible one: the steady erosion of the international value of the French franc, which had been one of the most stable currencies. But this decline had no impact on the average French household, and it actually led to an expansion of French exports (they were now cheaper in foreign money) and an influx of tourists, including thousands of American writers and artists who sought escape from provincialism in the capital of world arts.

By the later 1920s, the French economy seemed quite prosperous. The investments in modern industrial technology in the repaired factories and foundries of war-ravaged areas were paying off handsomely in increased profit. Decreased tension with Germany after Locarno (see the next section) allowed more capital to be put into productive, nonmilitary uses. The country was governed by alternating left- and right-of-center coalitions, both of which had fairly wide support.

The United States

In the *United States,* after the passion aroused by the fight over the League of Nations had subsided, a series of conservative Republican administrations (Warren Harding, Calvin Coolidge, and Herbert Hoover) had been content to preside over a laissez-faire domestic economy. Foreign policy questions were overshadowed by the general embitterment over the Europeans' "ingratitude" for U.S. contributions to the victory and the Allies' irritating laxity in repaying their war loans. The extensive social reform crusades of the early twentieth-century Progressives were put aside, and the business of America once again became business.

Nevertheless, fundamental changes were taking place in this decade, although most were unnoticed at the time. The Second Industrial Revolution was now complete. Corporations and the stock market they generated completely dominated both commerce and industry. The consumer economy became much larger thanks to new industrial techniques such as assembly-line production,

■ **General Strike in Britain.** The may 1926 general strike in Great Britain was called by the trade unions to underline their protest at the continued high unemployment rate. One reason it failed was the flexibility displayed by the nonstrikers in meeting the challenge, such as these office workers display in riding to work in a truck.

■ **Lindbergh Prepares for Take-Off.** Colonel Lindbergh became an instant—if reluctant—hero with his first solo flight from New York to Paris in 1927. Shown here just prior to take-off in his all-metal monoplane, the *Spirit of St. Louis.*

retail chain stores, and enormously expanded advertising. Suburban living became popular, and the blurring of traditional class divisions, which had always been an American characteristic, picked up speed. The well-dressed clerk could not be distinguished from the store manager in appearances and tastes. The blue-collar factory hand and the company's stockholders ate the same corn flakes for breakfast and sat in the same grandstand at the baseball game. And the automobile, led by Henry Ford's mass-produced creations, swept the country.

The nation's businesses as a whole profited greatly from U.S. involvement in World War I, while the population had suffered very little damage compared to the European nations. By the early 1920s, the United States had replaced Britain as the Western Hemisphere's leader in technology,

trade, and finance and had become the prime creditor nation in world trade. Only a few pessimists noticed the growing imbalance between production and consumption by the end of the decade or were worried by the indiscriminate speculative activity on the New York Stock Exchange.

✤ INTERNATIONAL RELATIONS

After the failure of the Ruhr occupation, the French spirit of vengeance against Germany gave way to a more cooperative stance. In 1925, the two countries signed the **Locarno Pact,** which was to be the high-water mark of interwar understanding. Locarno allowed Germany to join the League of Nations in return for its promise to accept its frontier with France and Belgium as permanent. Soon afterward, the formerly outlawed Soviet Union was also allowed to join the League.

Much of the credit for the improved state of affairs went to the German foreign minister, Gustav Stresemann, and his French opposite, Aristide Briand. These two found a way to overcome past suspicions and joined with the U.S. Secretary of State Frank Kellogg to propose an international agreement to renounce war as "an instrument of national policy." Since there was no way to enforce this pious hope, more than sixty countries found no problem in signing on to this **Kellog-Briand Pact of 1928.** In the same spirit, a series of conferences and agreements were held toward the goal of limiting armaments worldwide. The late 1920s thus saw considerable hope that the lessons of world war had been learned and that war itself would soon become obsolete.

In the later 1920s, the U.S. government also seemed ready to assume more of the role of international leadership and mediation that Woodrow Wilson had envisioned. The success of the Dawes Plan in ending Germany's inflation and negotiating a schedule for reparation payments led to the *Young Plan* in 1929. Under the leadership of an American banker, this plan substantially reduced the amount of reparations still owed to $8 billion and extended the term of payment to a lengthy fifty-eight years.

By this time, the U.S. president was the internationally experienced Herbert Hoover, a different individual than his immediate predecessors Warren Harding and Calvin Coolidge, neither of whom had ever set foot in Europe. With Washington's tacit blessings, the flow of investment money from the United States to Europe, particularly Germany, was ever increasing as the profits (on paper) from speculating on the bubbling stock market made many Americans feel rich.

✤ ON THE EVE OF THE GREAT DEPRESSION

By 1926, Europe appeared to be en route to full recovery from the economic effects of the war. The Dawes Plan had helped reestablish German prosperity, and the Germans could thus manage their reduced reparations payments to France and Britain. These countries could then begin to repay the large loans they had received from the United States during the war.

For four years, this circular flow of money worked well for all concerned; the booming German economy was the recipient of a great deal of private U.S. investment funds. The East European agricultural products were bought in large quantities by the West European industrial nations. Except in Britain, unemployment was under control as the Second Industrial Age matured and created millions of new jobs even as the older jobs based on the steam engine disappeared.

Even the West's hostility and fear toward Bolshevism cooled, as the Russians ceased to trumpet their confident calls for world revolution and started to behave like reasonable, if somewhat unorthodox, business partners in world trade. It was indicative that by the later 1920s, Soviet diplomats had given up the workers' caps and boots they had donned ten years earlier and returned to formal dress of top hat and tails.

The fear that European workers would gravitate toward Bolshevik Russia had proved to be exaggerated, even though by 1922 every major country had a legal or illegal Communist Party looking to Moscow for guidance. Much communist energy was wasted in fighting the socialists who had refused to join the Communist (Third) International, founded and headquartered in Moscow. Even conservative politicians began to look upon the communists, whether in Russia or at home, as a less urgent danger than they had originally appeared. In the last years of the 1920s, European international relations seemed to be in a healing mode. The wounds of war were closing, and good economic times allowed old enemies to think of one another as potential partners. Hope was in the air.

Summary

During the 1920s, all the belligerent nations attempted to recover from the deep wounds they had inflicted on each other in World War I. In the immediate postwar years, the political situation was extremely unstable in central and eastern Europe, with Russian Bolshevism seeking to expand westward and a series of new states without constitutional stability groping for survival. The Weimar Republic of Germany began its history encumbered with the guilt of signing the Versailles Treaty and presiding over a spectacular inflation, two handicaps that it could never overcome in the eyes of many citizens. In Italy, a demagogue named Mussolini bluffed his way to governmental power in 1922 and then proceeded to turn his country into a quasi-totalitarian state.

In the Western democracies, the search for economic recovery seemed to be successful in France, but less so in a subtly weakened Britain. The United States immediately withdrew from its European wartime activity and devoted itself to domestic affairs under conservative Republican administrations. It enjoyed general prosperity partly as a result of taking the role Britain had vacated in world financial and commercial affairs.

By the end of the decade, international conferences had secured partial successes in disarmament, border guarantees, and pledges of peace. The spread of Bolshevism seemed to have been checked, and the Russians became less threatening. As the decade entered its last year, most signs were hopeful for amity and continued economic progress.

Test Your Knowledge

1. The postwar German state was the product of
   a. a communist coup following the military defeat in the war.
   b. the Allied Powers' intervention and postwar occupation.
   c. a liberal constitution written by the Social Democrats and their liberal allies.
   d. a generals' dictatorship imposed to prevent an attempted communist takeover.
2. The high point for hopes of a lasting peace in the 1920s was
   a. the signing of the Locarno Pact in 1925.
   b. the removal of the French from the Ruhr in 1923.
   c. the entry of Germany into the League of Nations.
   d. the recognition of the Soviet Union by France and Britain in 1921.
3. The nation that suffered most dramatically from inflation after World War I was
   a. France.
   b. Russia.
   c. Germany.
   d. Britain.
4. The Dawes Plan and the Young Plan were
   a. proposals by U.S. financiers to assure Germany's recovery and payment of reparations.
   b. U.S. government plans to carry through the punishment of Germany.
   c. British-French schemes to assure German payment of reparations.
   d. U.S. government plans to try to get the country out of the Great Depression.
5. The only East European state that retained a democratic government during the 1930s was
   a. Romania.
   b. Hungary.
   c. Czechoslovakia.
   d. Poland.
6. The unofficial name of the government set up in Germany after World War I was the
   a. Nazi state.
   b. Weimar Republic.
   c. Fascist Republic.
   d. Bolshevik Republic.
7. Gabriele d'Annunzio
   a. believed in the ideals of Woodrow Wilson.
   b. wanted to show the world the way to peace through pacifism.
   c. believed in the cleansing of society through the ordeal of war.
   d. fought for Italy in World War II.

Identification Terms

Dawes Plan	J. M. Keynes	Locarno Pact	Ruhr
Fascism in Italy	Kellogg-Briand Pact of 1928	March on Rome	Weimar Republic
irredentism	Labour Party	Pilsudski (Józef) of Poland	

Bibliography

Carsten, F. L *The Rise of Fascism,* 1982. A good starting point that might be supplemented by E. Weber, *Varieties of Fascism,* 1964, which is strong on the social aspects of the movement in several countries.

Gay, P. *Weimar Culture,* 1970, and W. Laqueur, *Weimar,* 1972. Both are recommended highly for their literary qualities as well as the exciting subject matter.

On France and Britain, see N. Greene, *From Versailles to Vichy: The Third Republic, 1919–1940,* 1970; C. S. Maier, *Recasting Bourgeois Europe: Stabilization in France, Germany and Italy in the Decade after World War One,* 1975; A. J. Taylor, *English History, 1914–45,* 1965, a witty survey that hits all the bases in incomparable style; and C. Mowat, *Britain between the*

Wars, 1955, which is old but still very useful for its detail on politics.

Seton-Watson, C. *Italy from Liberalism to Fascism,* 1967, and D. Mack Smith, *Mussolini's Roman Empire,* 1976, cover the background and the early years of Italian Fascism. An equally good but different approach is E. Wiskemann, *Fascism in Italy: Its Development and Influence,* 1969. The outstanding biography of Mussolini is D. Mack Smith, *Mussolini,* 1982.

Seton-Watson, H. *Eastern Europe between the Wars,* 1946. Gives as good a summary of what went wrong in interwar East Europe's politics and why, as has been written in English. See also *The Columbia History of Eastern Europe in the Twentieth Century,* 1992. A host of histories of individual countries are available.

Sontag, R. *A Broken World, 1919–1939,* 1971. Perhaps the best of the diplomatic histories of Europe between the wars.

THE SOVIET EXPERIMENT TO WORLD WAR II

One of the chief by-products of World War I was a radical experiment in social organization that was destined to last in Russia for seventy-five years. In 1917, the Russian Marxists took advantage of the disruptions and weaknesses caused by the war to carry out revolution. The first socialist state, the Union of Soviet Socialist Republics (USSR) was born under the watchful eye of a handful of ambitious, visionary men around Vladimir Lenin. Their communist government, which proudly called itself "the dictatorship of the proletariat," was a frightening phenomenon to most of the rest of the world. But everywhere some men and women were inspired by its example and wished to imitate it in their own countries during the interwar period.

✦ THE RUSSIAN REVOLUTIONS OF 1917

By 1917, the imperial government of Russia had been brought to the point of collapse by the demands of total war. Twelve years earlier, an aborted revolution had finally brought a constitution and the elements of modern parliamentary government to the Russian people. But the broadly democratic aims of the Revolution of 1905 had been frustrated by a combination of force and guile, and the tsar maintained a tight grip on the policy-making machinery as the war began.

In the opening years of the war, the Russians suffered huge casualties and lost extensive territory to the Germans and Austrians. Their generals were the least competent of all the belligerents, and the tsar's officials were unable or unwilling to enlist popular support for the conflict. They depended on unquestioning obedience from below to keep the disastrous war going.

As the defeats and mistakes piled up, the maintenance of such obedience became impossible. By spring 1917, the food supply for the cities was becoming tenuous, and bread riots were breaking out. Finally, the demoralized garrison troops refused to obey orders from their superiors. With no prior planning, no bloodshed, and no organization, the **March Revolution** came about simply by the unpopular and confused tsar Nicholas II abdicating his throne. A committee of the *Duma* (the parliament), which had been ignored and almost powerless until now, took over the government of Russia.

The Duma committee, which called itself the **Provisional Government,** intended to create a new, democratic constitution and hold elections as soon as possible. Meanwhile the Allies warmly welcomed the coming of the new government. Allied sympathizers in the United States were especially enthusiastic because the removal of the tsar-autocrat eased the way for the United States to enter the war two weeks later and "make the world safe for democracy."

But the new government was a weak reed on which to attempt to build a democratic society. It had no mandate from the people, but had simply appointed itself. Leadership soon passed into the hands of Alexander Kerensky, a moderate, non-Marxist socialist who was a dynamic speaker but had little understanding of the depths of the people's antiwar mood. The peasants—about 80 percent of the population—were desperately tired of this war, which they had never understood, and which they hated because it was devouring their sons. If peace were not soon achieved, they would refuse to grow and ship food to the cities, and Russian government of any kind must collapse. Kerensky thought that Russia dare not make a separate, losing peace despite the ominous tide of discontent. He believed that only a victorious peace would present Russian democracy with a true mandate from its citizenry, and he was determined to keep Russia in the war.

✣ THE BOLSHEVIKS

The people's extreme war weariness opened the way for the uncompromising Marxists, or **Bolsheviks,** led by the brilliant tactician **Vladimir Lenin** (1870–1924). Before the spring of 1917, Lenin had been a refugee from his native land; for the previous twenty years, he had lived in Swiss and German exile, plotting incessantly for the triumph of the socialist revolution. He was the leader of a movement that had perhaps 100,000 members and sympathizers in the entire Russian imperial population of about 160 million.

Under Lenin's leadership, the Bolsheviks had changed Marx a great deal to make his ideas fit the Russian realities of the early twentieth century. Lenin insisted on a *full-time, professional leadership supervising a conspiratorial, clandestine party.* Unlike Marx, he believed that such a party could hasten the coming of the revolution and that the *peasantry could be led into revolutionary action.* Lenin thought that in a country such as Russia where rural dwellers were clearly predominant (the urban proletariat was at most about 5 percent of the population in 1910), only a movement that galvanized peasant discontent stood a chance of success. Lenin was clear that the vague dictatorship of the proletariat that Marx had talked about

■ **Stalin as a Young Bolshevik.** These police file photos were taken in 1912 or 1913 and show the thirty-four year old Stalin after one of his several arrests as a suspected revolutionary.

Leon Trotsky

1879–1940

Lev Davidovitch Bronstein, better known by far as Leon Trotsky, was born to a prosperous Jewish farmer in southern Ukraine in 1879. Like many other Russian revolutionary figures, Trotsky's career as a radical challenger of the status quo began very early, while he was in high school in Odessa. By 1896 he was already arguing the merits of Marxism with his fellow students, and in 1898 he underwent the traditional coming-of-age ceremony for East European reformers: arrest by the political police.

Exiled to Siberia in 1900, Trotsky escaped two years later and fled abroad where he met Vladimir Lenin and other leaders of the budding Russian Marxist movement. Even in that highly intellectual and aggressive company, young Trotsky stood out by force of character and self-assurance. Opposed to Lenin's version of Marxism, Trotsky later adopted an independent standpoint of his own, refusing to submit to the discipline Lenin demanded of all his followers but not condemning Bolshevism outright. During the short-lived Revolution of 1905, Trotsky had momentary power as chairman of the Petersburg Soviet of Workers. He again was exiled and again escaped to Europe in 1907. From that time until

World War I began, he worked in Vienna and Zurich as a journalist for socialist newspapers. Still opposed in principle to Bolshevism during the early years of the war, Trotsky changed his mind after the March 1917 revolution, which deposed the tsar and allowed all the Marxist exiles to return to their homeland. He now fell under Lenin's powerful personality and joined him as his right-hand man. As chairman of the Military-Revolutionary Committee of the Bolsheviks, Trotsky was second only to Lenin in preparing the October revolution that brought them to power. After a brief stint as commissar for foreign affairs, Trotsky then took over as commissar for war in 1918. His brilliance as a strategist and his ruthlessness in waging a bitter struggle against the Whites were major reasons for the Reds' victory in the civil war that wrecked Russia between 1918 and 1921. A better speaker even than Lenin, Trotsky was not only the creator of the Red Army, but the most prominent single personality within the Communist Party, Lenin alone excepted.

In the struggle for succession to Lenin, which began as early as 1922 (after Lenin's first stroke), Trotsky seemed to most to be the inevitable choice.

---

would quickly become a dictatorship of the Bolsheviks. Within that party, the small group around Lenin, called the Central Committee, would rule in fact.

Lenin versus Kerensky

The Bolshevik leader returned to Russia immediately after the March revolution, when the new government allowed total freedom to all political groups. Through the summer of 1917, Lenin and the Provisional Government under Kerensky dueled for power. The decisive force, however, proved to be neither Lenin nor Kerensky, but the *Soviet* (council) *of Workers and Soldiers* in St. Petersburg, formed spontaneously by urban workers as a counterforce to Kerensky. The chairman of the Soviet was **Leon Trotsky**

(1879–1940), the most dynamic of Lenin's colleagues, and it was he who eventually led the Soviet into the Bolshevik camp (see the Biography in this chapter).

In the short term, the fate of the country necessarily was determined by which group could secure the allegiance of the armed forces. The imperial army had been disintegrating since the spring, with mass desertions commonplace. The peasant soldiers hated the war, and a wide cleft had opened between them and their middle- and upper-class officers. Into this rift Bolshevik pacifist and revolutionary propaganda was pouring and finding a ready audience.

In the belief that only victory could save the country from chaos, Kerensky decided to accede to the demands of his hard-pressed allies in the West and gamble every

But Stalin and others were determined this would not happen and proved to be both less scrupulous and more in tune with Party members' thinking than Trotsky. One step after another forced the civil war hero out of the Party Central Committee, then out of the commissariat for war, then out of the Party, and finally, in 1929, into foreign exile. In 1940, after several moves, Trotsky was slain on Stalin's orders in his final refuge in Mexico.

A tiny, unprepossessing figure with thick glasses, Trotsky was possessed of almost incredible energy and single-mindedness. He was totally un-compromising and totally con-vinced of his own correctness in things political. Like his hero Lenin, he never allowed what the Bolsheviks called "bourgeois sentiment" to interfere with his dedication to a communist tri-umph. Again like Lenin, his force of personality attracted a clique of followers who were en-tirely devoted to him. But he lacked the organizational skills of his master and was never interested in the day-to-day administrative detail that all successful politics requires.

Trotsky became a hero to some because of his unremitting and devastating criticism of Stalin's dic-tatorship, at a time—the 1930s—when few other reformers were willing to see just how repressive Stalin's regime had become. Trotsky believed, as Mao Zedong would later, that bureaucracy was the great enemy of social and political progress, and he con-demned it among communists as well as capitalists. He was a steadfast adherent of "permanent revolution" and the opponent of Stalin's "socialism in one country." He believed that if the communist revolution did not spread, it would inevita-bly degenerate under a dictator such as Stalin. Trotsky's attempt to found an anti-Stalin Fourth International did not get very far, but his charisma and his vivid writings about the Russian Revolution of 1917 have guaran-teed him a place in the pantheon of twentieth-century revolution-aries.

thing on an ill-prepared summer offensive. This was soon turned into a rout by the Germans' counterattack. By September, the enemy was at the gates of St. Petersburg, and the army was visibly collapsing. The cities were on the point of mass starvation, and the peasants were taking the law into their own hands and dividing up the estates of their helpless landlords, much as their French counter-parts had done a century and a quarter earlier.

The October Revolution

By mid-October, Lenin had convinced a hesitant Central Committee that the time for revolutionary action was at hand and that Kerensky's government had lost all valid claim to power in the people's eyes. He insisted that the brilliantly simple Bolshevik slogans of "all power to the Soviets" and "land, bread, peace" would carry the day despite the tiny number of Bolsheviks.

On the evening of October 26, Old Style (November 6 by the modern calendar), the Bolsheviks used their sympathizers among the workers and soldiers in St. Petersburg to seize government headquarters and take control of the city. The *Great October Revolution was a coup d'état* that cost only a few hundred lives to capture a government that, as Lenin had insisted, had practically no support (see the Document in this chapter). In the next few weeks, Moscow and other major industrial towns followed Petersburg by installing Bolshevik au-thorities after varying amounts of armed struggle in the streets.

Lenin's Speech to the Soviet

Immediately after the Bolshevik revolution of 1917 in Russia, on October 27, Old Style (November 7 by the modern calendar), Vladimir Lenin outlined his party's priorities and longer-range goals in a speech to the Petrograd Soviet, which was now under the control of the Bolsheviks and their sympathizers. The uncompromising directness is typical of Lenin's speaking style. He was at this time entirely confident that the workers in the rest of the combatant nations would join Russia in revolt against their capitalist governments, and that peace would come because the workers would refuse to fight their proletarian brothers any longer.

Comrades! The workmen's and peasants' revolution, the need of which the Bolsheviks have emphasized many times, has come to pass.

What is the significance of this revolution? Its significance is, in the first place, that we shall have a soviet government, without the participation of bourgeoisie of any type. The oppressed masses will of themselves form a government. The old state machinery will be smashed into bits, and in its place will rise a new machinery of government created by the soviet's organizations. From now on there is a new page in the history of Russia, and the present, third Russian revolution [i.e., counting the abortive 1905 uprising] shall in its final result lead to the victory of socialism.

One of our immediate tasks is to put an end to the war at once. But in order to end the war, which is closely bound up with the present capitalistic system, it is necessary to overthrow capitalism itself. In this work we shall have the aid of the world labor movement, which has already begun to develop in Italy, England, and Germany.

A just and immediate offer of peace by us to the international democracy will find a warm response everywhere among the international proletariat masses. In order to secure the confidence of the proletariat, it is necessary at once to publish all secret treaties.

In the interior of Russia a large part of the peasantry has said: Enough playing with the capitalists! We will go with the workers!

We shall secure the confidence of the peasants by one decree, which will wipe out the private property of the landowners. The peasants will understand that their only salvation is in union with the workers.

We will establish a real control by labor in production. We have now learned to work together in a friendly manner, as is evident from this revolution. We have the force of mass organization which has conquered all, and which will lead the proletariat to world revolution.

We should now occupy ourselves in Russia in building up a proletarian socialist state.

Long live the world-wide socialist revolution!

For several months, the countryside remained almost untouched by these urban events. The Bolsheviks had never paid much attention to organizing the peasants (despite Lenin's theories) and had few rural sympathizers. In the villages, the peasants took advantage of the breakdown of central government to seize the land they had long craved from the nobles and government officials. For the peasants, the redistribution of land to themselves was the beginning and the end of revolution. Of Marxist theory about collectivization of agriculture, they knew and wanted to know nothing at all.

Lenin moved swiftly to establish the Bolshevik dictatorship, using both armed force and the massive confusion that had overtaken the Russian government after October.

By December large economic enterprises of all types were being confiscated. The first version of the dreaded political police, the *Cheka,* had been formed and was being employed against various enemies. The remnants of the army were being bolshevized and turned into a weapon for use against internal opponents.

✦ CIVIL WAR

Against heavy opposition from his own associates, Lenin insisted that Russia must make peace with the Germans and Austrians at any cost. His rationale proved to be correct: a civil war against the many enemies of Bolshevism was bound to come soon, and the Party could not

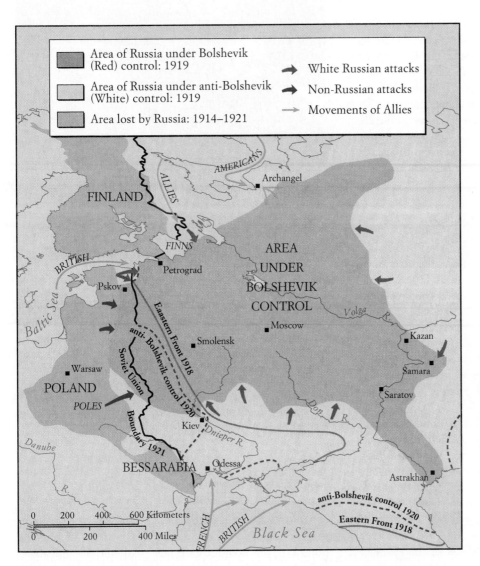

Area of Russia under Bolshevik (Red) control: 1919

Area of Russia under anti-Bolshevik (White) control: 1919

Area lost by Russia: 1914–1921

→ White Russian attacks

→ Non-Russian attacks

→ Movements of Allies

⊙ **MAP 49.1 Russian Civil War, 1918–1921.** The advantage of holding the interior lines of transport and communication, as well as the two leading cities, is apparent in this map of the civil war. The White armies were widely separated geographically and never had unified command or even coordination. By the summer of 1920, the Reds had defeated the Whites and were in control of most of the country.

afford to be still fighting a foreign foe when it did. In March 1918, the Treaty of **Brest-Litovsk** was signed with the Central Powers, giving them huge slices of western Russia either to be maintained as satellites or to be directly incorporated. The collapse of the Central Powers eight months later made this treaty a dead letter. By that time, the Bolshevik "Reds" were engaged in a massive and very bloody civil war, which was to last two and a half years and cause about as many Russian deaths as had occurred in the war between 1914 and 1917.

The Reds won this conflict for several reasons. They were far better organized and coordinated by a unitary leadership than were their opponent "Whites." Despite his total lack of military experience, Trotsky proved to be an inspiring and effective commander-in-chief of the Red Army, which he created in record time. The Reds had a big advantage in that they controlled most of the interior of European Russia, including the major cities of St. Petersburg and Moscow and the rail networks that served them (see Map 49.1). The opposition armies, separated by vast distances from one another, were often at cross-purposes. The Whites were decisively defeated in the propaganda battles, where the Reds played up the White generals' multiple links with both the old regime and the landlords. Personal rivalries also damaged the White leadership.

The intervention of several foreign powers in the civil war also became a Red asset, though it was intended to assist the Whites. In early 1918, fearing that the Bolsheviks would take Russia out of the war and that war materiel meant for the old imperial army would fall into enemy hands, the French and British sent small forces into Russia. Inevitably, these forces clashed with the Reds, and the foreigners (including a small U.S. detachment in the far north) began actively assisting the Whites. Overall, the foreign intervention provided little practical help for the Whites, but gave the Leninists an effective propaganda weapon for rallying support among the Russian people.

✤ THE NEW ECONOMIC POLICY AND INTERNAL STRUGGLES

By the summer of 1921, the Bolsheviks were close enough to victory and confident enough of their ability to intimidate their enemies that they abolished their coercive "War Communism." War Communism was the label for rule at the point of a gun that Lenin had employed since 1918 through the Red Army and the Cheka. It had sustained the Bolshevik rule, but only at great costs. Along with terrible famine and the disruptions of civil war, it had reduced the Russian gross national product to about 20 percent of what it had been in 1913!

In place of War Communism, Lenin now prescribed the **New Economic Policy (NEP),** which encouraged small-scale business and profit seekers, while retaining "the commanding heights" of the national economy firmly in state hands. By this time state hands meant Bolshevik hands. The Communist Party of the Soviet Union (CPSU), headed by Lenin and his colleagues, was in sole control of both economic and political affairs. By 1922, all other parties had been banned, and Russia was fast becoming a totalitarian state.

After being wounded in an attempted assassination, Lenin suffered a series of strokes starting in 1922. After the second stroke, power in everyday affairs was transferred to an inside group of the Central Committee, called the Political Bureau (*Politburo*). This group included Lenin's closest colleagues: Trotsky was the best known and seemed to hold the dominant position within the Party. But when Lenin died in January 1924 without naming anyone to succeed him, a power struggle was already under way.

One of Trotsky's rivals was **Josef Stalin** (1879–1953), a tested party worker since early youth, who was esteemed by Lenin for his administrative abilities and hard work. But at the end of his life, Lenin had turned against Stalin because of his "rudeness" and his contempt for the

■ **Lenin and Stalin: A Faked Photograph.** This photo of the two leaders, purported taken shortly before Lenin's death and used extensively by the Stalinist propaganda machine to show the closeness of their relationship, is known to have been "doctored." Stalin's figure was placed into the photo later. Lenin came to distrust Stalin in his last days, but took only ineffective measures warning the Party against him.

opinions of others. Lenin was too late in reaching this conclusion: Stalin, as the Party general secretary (administrator), had already cemented his position among the hundreds of thousands of new rank-and-file members. Brilliantly manipulating others, Stalin was able to defeat first Trotsky and then other contestants for Lenin's position in the mid and late 1920s. By 1927, he was the leader of the majority faction in the Politburo, and thus of the Communist Party. By 1932, Stalin was becoming dictator of the Soviet Union's entire public life. By 1937, he was the undisputed master of 180 million people.

Why did the others lose and Stalin win? In the 1920s, Stalin was *closer to Russian realities.* A Georgian by birth, Stalin was nevertheless able to comprehend what the average Russian wanted better than any of his rivals. Ordinary Russians viewed Stalin not as a theorist, but as a practical man who was "in touch" with reality and got things done. He was careful to pose as a middle-of-the-road moderate in Party affairs until he no longer needed to do so.

Second, Stalin appealed to the CPSU membership by his theory of *"socialism in one country,"* in which he rejected the orthodox position (which was particularly associated with Trotsky) that worldwide revolution must occur if socialism was to triumph anywhere. Stalin claimed that Russia could go it alone and could build socialism despite the hostility of the encircling capitalists. This argument strongly appealed to both the idealistic young and Russian nationalist pride.

Third, and most important, Stalin was a master of intrigue and deception, who excelled at using divide-and-conquer tactics against his enemies. He used one group to tear down another, then turned against his former allies. And all the time, he managed to make it look as though he were the attacked and not the attacker. All he wanted was peace in the Party; he was willing to do whatever the Party majority asked of him! It was truly a great performance; when it was over, one man held the destiny of a nation tightly in his hand.

By late 1928, under the NEP the economy had made a stunning recovery from the lows of the early postwar era. The peasants were still completely uncollectivized and showed no signs whatever of wishing anything else. Industrial production exceeded that of 1913; foreign experts and industrialists from several countries (including Henry Ford, John D. Rockefeller, Jr., and Hanna Mining Company of the United States) were helping the Russians install modern industry at fat profits for themselves. It appeared that Bolshevism's bark was much worse than its bite. One could, after all, do good business with the Soviets. A few months later, the entire picture changed. At Stalin's command, the **First Five Year Plan** of 1929–1933 was adopted; it would transform the Soviet Union in several ways. The **Second Revolution** had started.

✦ THE FIVE YEAR PLANS

Throughout the 1920s, some Party members had been discontented with the "two steps forward, one step back" philosophy of the NEP. "This is no way to build socialism in our lifetime!" cried the young militants (and the CPSU had plenty of them in the 1920s). In their view, the good proletarian workers in the cities were at the mercy of the reactionary peasants who fed them. The peasants were still the masters of their (private) land and had not shown the slightest inclination to surrender what they had gained in 1917–1918. There had been very little additional investment in industry; Russia was still an overwhelmingly rural, agrarian society, backward in every way compared to western Europe or the United States.

In the fall of 1928, many of the more prosperous peasants decided to hold back their grain until they could get better prices from the state-controlled markets. Stalin used this "betrayal" to start the drive for *agricultural collectivization* and *rapid industrialization,* which would go on at a breath-taking pace until World War II brought it to a temporary halt.

Stalin's policy was intended to kill at least three major birds with one enormous stone. The age-old resistance of private landholders to any kind of government supervision would be broken by massive pressure to surrender their holdings to collective farms run by the state. Then, a huge increase in investment would be allocated to heavy industry and infrastructure to modernize the backward society. Third, the organization and efforts required to achieve the first two goals would enable him to carry out *"a revolution from above."*

Agrarian Collectivization

In 1929, Stalin began his **collectivization campaign** as a way to "win the class war in the villages," that is, the alleged struggle between the poor peasants and those who were better off. The richer peasants (*kulaks*) were to be dispossessed by force, while the poorer peasants were to be forced onto newly founded collective farms under Party supervision.

As many as 10 million peasants are estimated to have died in the collectivization between 1929 and 1933, most of them in an artificially caused famine in 1932–1933. Determined to break the peasants' persistent resistance, Stalin authorized the use of the Red Army as well as armed party militants against the peasant villages. Millions were driven off their land and out of their houses and condemned to wander as starving beggars. Their former land, machinery, and animals were turned over to the new collectives. These enormous farms, which were run like factories, proved to be very inefficient, in part because the peasants heartily disliked their new situation. To this day, agriculture remains a major weakness of the Russian economy.

The collectivization struggle left deep scars, and its costs were still being paid a generation later. Stalin rammed it through because he believed it was essential if the Soviet Union were to catch up to the hostile capitalist states. The backward, conservative peasants must be brought under government control, and their numbers reduced by forcing them to become a new industrial labor force. Both these goals were eventually reached, but at a price that no rational economist could justify.

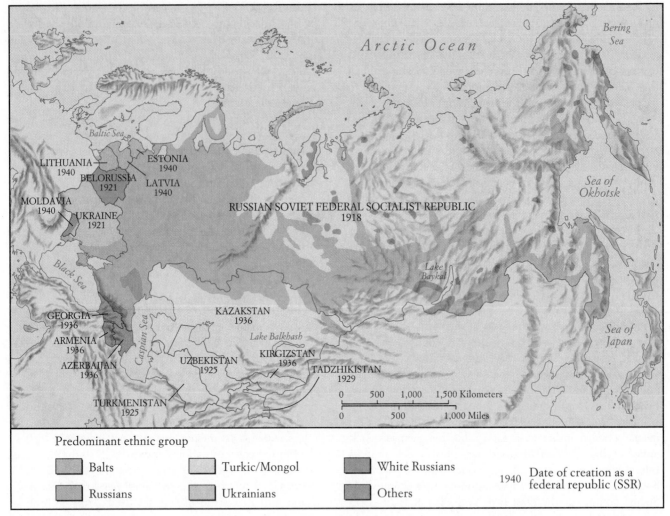

Predominant ethnic group

Balts	Turkic/Mongol	White Russians
Russians	Ukrainians	Others

1940 Date of creation as a federal republic (SSR)

⦿ **MAP 49.2 Ethnic Groups in the Soviet Union.** The ethnic variety of the Soviet state can only be hinted at in this map. At the last census (1981) Russians numbered just over 50% of the total population and entirely dominated the huge Russian Soviet Republic, but had one of the lowest birthrates of any of the Soviet peoples. The Muslim peoples along the southern rim of the USSR had the highest rate of increase.

Industrial Progress

Stalin's second goal was rapid *industrialization*. Here again, the costs were very high, but their justification was easier. Soviet gains in industry between 1929 and 1940 were truly impressive. In percentage terms, the growth achieved in several branches of heavy industry and infrastructure was greater than any country in history has ever achieved in an equivalent period—about 400 percent even by conservative estimates. Whole industrial cities rose up from the Siberian or Central Asian plains, built partly by forced labor and partly by idealists who believed in Stalin

and in communism's vision of a new life. Throughout the economy, "fulfilling the Plan" became all-important, often regardless of quality controls or even need. Untouched by free market realities and constraints, the Soviet managers plunged ahead in a wild race to raise total production.

The new industry turned out *capital goods, not consumer items.* Consumer goods like clothes and baby carriages became more and more difficult to obtain, and their prices rose ever higher throughout the 1930s. When a suit of clothes could be found, it cost the equivalent of four months' wages for a skilled worker. Items such as

The 1930s adulation of the dictator Stalin by the Russian people was partly authentic, partly the result of clever propaganda, and partly advanced by the intimidation of critics. Here is shown one of the innumerable Communist party-directed celebrations of "great Stalin."

refrigerators, automobiles, and washing machines were out of the question for the average family. Even food had to be rationed for a while because of the drop in production caused by collectivization. It is testimony to the extraordinary capacity of the Russian people to suffer in silence that so much was accomplished at such high costs with so little reward for those doing it.

In the West, people who should have known better put aside their critical sense and praised the industrial achievements as though they were the result of a voluntary effort by the Soviet peoples. This was far from the truth; the uprootings and hardships caused by the industrialization drive in the 1930s were nearly as severe as those caused by collectivization in the countryside. And much of the work on the new mines, canals, logging operations, and other projects was performed by Stalin's slave laborers. By conservative estimates, fully 10 percent of the Soviet gross national product was produced by prisoners of the NKVD (one of the several successive names for the Soviet political police).

✤ STALIN'S DICTATORSHIP

The third goal of the Five Year Plans was, in effect, a revolution by Stalin and the Communist Party against the Soviet peoples. In 1928, Stalin was chief of a CPSU that was still an elite organization. It was relatively small (about 6 percent of the adult population) and difficult to join. The proudest boast of a Party member was to be an "Old Bolshevik," someone who had joined before 1917. The Party was tightly disciplined and composed basically of

intellectuals, white-collar personnel, and some workers. It included very few peasants and very few women above the lowest ranks. Many members knew little of Stalin and were totally unaware of the high-level struggles in the Politburo.

Stalin emerged as the Boss (*vozhd*) on his fiftieth birthday in 1929, when a tremendous fuss was made over his role as Lenin's successor. From this time on, no one else in the Soviet hierarchy was allowed to rival Stalin in press coverage or authority. His name was constantly commemorated: songs (literally!) of praise were composed for him, children were named for him, and foreign communists extolled him. From the early 1930s, every Party member lived in Stalin's shadow. He proved a master of Mafia-style politics, never forgetting who had helped and who had hurt him in his climb. Utterly ruthless and devoid of sentimentality, he would have been successful in New York City's Tammany Hall in the nineteenth century or a similar tough-minded organization. Absolutely vindictive toward rivals and enemies (they were the same to him), his character has long fascinated many Russian and foreign analysts. They agree that Stalin was the most powerful single individual in modern world affairs, literally holding powers of life and death over everyone within the Soviet Union and millions outside it.

Although he was not an ethnic Russian, Stalin became a strong Russian nationalist and soon transformed what had been a truly supranational movement under Lenin into a Russian one. To be a communist after about 1929 meant to be the faithful, unquestioning servant of Josef Stalin. He took the international communist organization, called the **Comintern** and based in Moscow, and turned it into an organ of Russian foreign policy until it was formally abolished during World War II. No foreign communists dared to challenge the policies dictated by Stalin's stooges on the governing board of the Comintern, even when, as frequently happened, those policies were directly opposed to the interests of the Communist Party in the foreigners' own country. In the communist world, Moscow alone called the tune. Stalin cultivated an image of mystery. Unlike his fellow dictators, he had no gift for speech making, and he never indulged in the dramatics that Hitler and Mussolini constantly employed in their public appearances. After 1935 he was rarely seen in public and then only under totally controlled circumstances. His offices in the Kremlin were never open to anyone except high-ranking fellow communist leaders. He liked to work at night and did not hesitate to haul his trembling subordinates out of bed at 2:00 A.M. for impromptu conferences.

The Purges

Although Stalin had crushed his high-level opponents by 1933, he still had some opposition in the Party. In 1935, he apparently decided that he must crush those opponents, too, and proceeded to do so in a fashion that shocked the world. Sergei Kirov, the party chieftain in Leningrad, was the only person who could possibly have been a rival to Stalin for CPSU control. He was murdered, probably at Stalin's order, in December 1934. Immediately, various party functionaries were rounded up, and thousands of people were expelled from the Party and sent off to the labor camps in Siberia. The camps had been created as far back as the early 1920s for opponents of the government; until now they had been infrequently used.

A Terrorized Society

Between 1936 and late 1938, Moscow was the scene of a series of *show trials,* where leading Party members were accused of absurd charges of treason and sabotage. Often, the prosecutors were armed with equally absurd "confessions" from the accused. Many leading Old Bolsheviks were condemned to death in this manner; thousands were sentenced to prison camps from which they never returned. Virtually all of Lenin's surviving comrades were disposed of and had disappeared from public sight by 1939.

Neither Russians nor foreign observers at the time could understand the underlying purpose of the trials, nor why hundreds of thousands of ordinary citizens were arrested at the same time for "crimes against the State." It is possible that Stalin was sincerely worried about Party conspiracies and divided loyalties. He may have intended Kirov's murder as a warning to other Party malcontents. But then the whole affair got out of hand, and the NKVD tried to demonstrate its own trustworthiness by mass arrests of "wreckers and spies." Instead of stopping the madness, Stalin then encouraged it because he wished to reconstitute the Party in *his* image and create an organization totally dependent on his favor.

To this day, historians do not agree on an explanation of what happened, and why, during those years. What is known is that between 1935 and the end of Stalin's life in 1953, perhaps 10 million Soviet citizens were banished to prison camps without trial and almost always without proof of violation of current Soviet law. Some of them survived the usual sentence of five to fifteen years; very many did not. It was commonplace for the camp overseers to extend the original sentences, adding five more years for such "offenses" as trading a bit of bread for a pair of socks. Everyone had a close relative or friend who had been spirited away, usually in the night, by the dreaded secret police. These "administrative measures" were conducted completely outside the usual court system, and often the prisoners were never told their crimes, even after serving many years.

At the end, even the members of the NKVD were not safe; in 1938, the NKVD chief Nikolai Yezhov and his entire upper echelon were themselves arrested and condemned. With that, the purge came to an end. Stalin never offered an explanation, then or later.

One thing is certain: if Stalin instituted the **Great Purge** in order to terrorize the Party and Soviet society into complete obedience, he succeeded. Until his death, no one in the Party, military, or general society dared oppose him openly. But once again, the costs had been terrifically high when measured by any humane standards. Whether the Soviets were weakened or strengthened by the purge when the trial by fire came with the Nazi invasion in 1941 is a question still much debated in Russia.

One major difference between the two great Western dictatorships in the twentieth century should be noted: Stalin posed as the champion of the underdog everywhere; his rival Adolf Hitler was the champion only of the Germans. We will see in Chapter 50 that Hitler's narrowly racist ideology had no vision of the transformation of human society whereas Stalin's international communism did. He and his assistants were able to fashion that vision so that a significant portion of the world, from China to Cuba, came to believe it—for a time.

✤ LIFE UNDER THE DICTATORSHIP

Stalin and his associates believed that a *"new Soviet man"* would emerge after a few years of Soviet rule. In this, they were sadly mistaken; the Soviet people continued to be old-style human beings with all their faults. But a new type of society did emerge, and it had both good and bad points.

Possibilities Expanded

On the *good side,* the forced-draft industrialization under the Five Year Plans allowed a very large number of human beings to improve their professional prospects dramatically. Mass education enabled many people to hold jobs and assume responsibilities that they could not have handled or would never have been offered in the old society. Many illiterate peasants saw their sons and daughters obtain degrees in advanced technology, while the new Soviet schools turned out engineers by the millions. Nikita Khrushchev, Stalin's successor as head of the Party, worked as a coal miner in his early years.

Millions of Russian and Soviet women were emancipated from a life that offered them no real opportunities to use their minds or develop their talents. Despite much propaganda to the contrary, the Soviet leaders did not really believe in equality for women, and the highest positions remained overwhelmingly male until the Soviet Union's collapse. But the leaders *did* believe in additional skilled labor, male or female. By the end of the 1930s, most Soviet women worked outside the home. Living standards were very low, and the woman's additional income was crucial for many Soviet families; still, the door to a more varied, more challenging life had been opened and would not be closed again.

A basic "safety net" was established for all citizens. Outside the camps, no one starved, and no one was allowed to die like an animal because of lack of human care. According to the Soviet constitution, every citizen had a right (and a duty!) to a job. Medical care was free, all workers received pensions, and education was open and free to all politically reliable persons. There were truly no ceilings to talent, provided that one was either a sincere communist or paid lip service to the system.

Liberties Suppressed

On the *bad side* were all the drawbacks we have already mentioned as inherent in the Stalinist dictatorship: lack of political freedom, terror and lawlessness, and low standards of living. There were other disadvantages, too: *religious persecution, cultural censorship, constant indoctrination with a simplistic Marxism, and constant interference with private lives.* For a certain time, during the 1920s and early 1930s, many well-meaning people in and outside the Soviet Union were able to rationalize the bad aspects of Soviet life by balancing them against the good. They accepted the Stalinist statement, "you can't make an omelet without breaking eggs." They believed that within a few years, Soviet society would be the envy of the capitalists in the West; then, the glories of developed socialism would be wonderful to behold, and the evils of the transition period would be soon forgotten.

But the terror of the purges of the mid-1930s disillusioned many, and the continued iron dictatorship after World War II discouraged many more. Even the youths, who had been the most enthusiastic members of the Party and the hardest workers in the *apparat,* were disappointed that the enormous sacrifices made during World War II seemed to go unappreciated by the Leader. The CPSU lost its *elan,* and its moral authority as the voice of revolutionary ideals. In the postwar years, it came to resemble just another huge bureaucracy, providing a ladder upward for the opportunists and the manipulators. The only real talent necessary for a successful Party career, it seemed, was to pretend to worship Stalin.

✤ MATERIAL AND SOCIAL WELFARE IN THE INTERWAR SOVIET UNION

Material life under Stalin was very hard. Russians' *living standards* were far worse than those of any other European people. The new industrial cities were plagued by a continuing, unsolvable housing crisis. On average, people were living worse in 1950 than they had in 1930. The typical Moscow apartment housed four adults *per room,* and often they were members of unrelated families sharing a kitchen and a one-floor-down toilet. There was a total lack of privacy in urban apartments, with devastating effects on family living conditions. Until the mid-1950s, certain foods were still rationed—long after the defeated Germans had overcome such shortages.

Social problems were sometimes met head-on by government action, sometimes ignored. The *divorce and*

■ **The Soviet Drive for Literacy.** An undeniable benefit of the Soviet Union to its people was the effective campaign for adult literacy introduced in the 1920s. By the end of the Second Five Year Plan in 1937 most men and women had some capability in reading and writing.

abortion rates shot up in the 1920s in line with the communist-supported emancipation of Russian women; in the mid-1930s, Stalin reintroduced tight restrictions on abortion and divorce and rewarded women who bore many children with cash and medals ("Heroine of Socialist Labor"). The underlying reason for this change in policy was the shortage of labor in Soviet industry and agriculture, both of which were extraordinarily inefficient in their use of labor.

On the other hand, little was done to counter *disease.* Clinics were established for the first time throughout the countryside, but the problems of bad nutrition, superstition about prenatal and postnatal care, and the large Muslim population's distrust of all Western-style medicine were great handicaps to lowering the epidemic death rate or infant mortality.

Alcoholism remained what it had always been in Russia: a serious obstacle to labor efficiency and a drain on resources. Repeated campaigns for sobriety had only limited effects on the peasants and urban workers. Home brew was common despite heavy penalties.

Some common *crimes* were effectively reduced, at least for a time. Prostitution became rare for a while, partly because the original Bolshevik attitude toward sex was quite liberal: men and women were equals and should be able to arrange their sexual activities as they saw fit without interference. Financial offenses, such as embezzlement and fraud, were almost eliminated because opportunities to commit them were almost nonexistent under the new regime. Theft, on the other hand, became very common, as all classes of people frequently had to resort to it to survive. Violence against persons probably increased in the early Soviet period, when civil war, starving wanderers, and "class struggle" were commonplace and provided some cover for personal criminal acts. (The Soviet government was always reluctant to provide accurate statistics on social problems, especially crime.)

Summary

The Bolshevik revolution of 1917 was one of the milestones of modern history. For a long time, millions of idealists considered it the definitive dawn of a new age. No other modern social or economic movement has convinced so many different people that it was the solution to society's various ills.

Lenin's installation of a dictatorship by the Communist Party immediately after the revolution broke the ground for the Stalinist rule of later date. After a hidden power struggle, Leon Trotsky, the presumed successor to Lenin, was overcome by Josef Stalin, who had mastered the art of closed-group infighting better than any of his competitors. In a few more years, he had made himself the master of his country in unprecedented fashion.

In 1928, the introduction of the First Five Year Plan was a Second Revolution, this time by the Party under Stalin's leadership against its own people. The leaders sought to renovate backward Russia by any and all means in their power. Agrarian life was transformed by collectivization of the peasants, and the USSR became a major industrial power. Midway through the decade of the 1930s, the Great Purge of both Party and people began. Probably, Stalin intended it to eliminate any opposition and prepare the Soviet peoples for complete submission to his will.

The material welfare of some large segments of the Soviet populace was helped by the Stalinist policies. The policies improved education, professional opportunities, medical care, and generally allowed the population to live a more modern lifestyle. But, the Soviet peoples paid very high prices for these advantages. They gave up all political and economic liberties, and suffered through a generation of great hardships under the dictatorial rule of the Party and its omnipotent head.

Test Your Knowledge

1. In the early 1920s, Lenin's closest associate and apparent successor as leader of the Soviet Party and state was
   a. Stalin.
   b. Trotsky.
   c. Khrushchev.
   d. Romanov.
2. The Soviet Five Year Plan called for
   a. subordination of the Communist Party to the government.
   b. rapid, forced industrialization.
   c. distribution of the farmlands to the peasants.
   d. war on the Western democracies.
3. By 1921 in Russia,
   a. a large part of the population was in arms against communism.
   b. the majority of Russians had become communists.
   c. a civil war had greatly worsened the damage sustained during World War I.
   d. the economy had almost recovered from wartime damages.
4. During the Five Year Plans, the peasants were
   a. finally liberated from dependence on the government.
   b. ignored by the authorities, who were concentrating on industry.
   c. deprived of most of their private property.
   d. given a major boost in productivity by government action.
5. The Great Purges in Stalin's time started
   a. after an assassination attempt on Stalin himself.
   b. after evidence of a foreign spy ring within the Party.
   c. because of a rebellion of Party leaders against the Five Year Plans.
   d. after the suspicious murder of the Party's number two man.
6. One of the chief rewards for the workers in the new Soviet Union of the 1930s was
   a. improved and expanded housing.
   b. mass educational facilities.
   c. a decisive voice in public affairs.
   d. security of life and property against the state.
7. Which of the following were *not* members of the new communist elite in the Soviet Union?
   a. Artists and writers
   b. Party officials
   c. Medical specialists
   d. Technical managers

Identification Terms

Bolsheviks

Brest-Litovsk Treaty

Collectivization campaign

Comintern

First Five Year Plan

Great Purge

Lenin (Vladimir)

March Revolution

New Economic Policy (NEP)

Provisional Government (Russia)

Second Revolution

Stalin (Josef)

Trotsky (Leon)

Bibliography

A huge literature on the Soviet Union is available, much of which has been seriously marred by ax grinding and propaganda. In the last four or five years, for the first time since 1917, Russian (and other) historians have had free access to many archives formerly out of bounds, and a flood of new and interesting interpretations of Soviet events and personages are appearing.

Conquest, R. *V. I. Lenin,* 1972. A good, though hostile biography meant for students; A. Ulam's *The Bolsheviks,* 1968, is more extensive on Lenin and treats his major associates as well.

Davies, R. W. *The Socialist Offensive: Collectivization of Soviet Agriculture, 1929–30,* 1980. Provides an examination of collectivization. A generally more favorable survey of the Stalin years is given in P. Nettl, *The Soviet Achievement,* 1965, which focuses on the industrial and social transformations of the Five Year Plans.

Koestler, A. *Darkness at Noon,* 1956. The most famous novelistic interpretation of Stalin's purges. On this, see also R. Conquest, *The Great Terror,* 1968, and the brilliant essay by a Marxist, but anti-Stalinist Russian, R. Medvedev, *Let History Judge,* 1972, which looks into many other sins of Stalin as well. The most comprehensive account of the terror under Stalin as it was experienced by ordinary Russians is A. Solzhenitsyn, *The Gulag Archipelago,* vols. 1–3, 1964.

Reed, J. *Ten Days That Shook the World,* 1919. An eyewitness account by a young American who sympathized with Lenin's revolution. It captures the feelings of those who believed a new dawn had come.

Tucker, R. *Stalin as Revolutionary,* 1973, and its sequel, *Stalin in Power,* 1992, are riveting psychological studies of the most powerful individual in world history. See also the very good biography by I. Deutscher, *Stalin: A Political Biography,* 1967 and that by R. McNeal, *Stalin, Man and Ruler,* 1988.

Wildman, E. *The End of the Russian Imperial Army,* 1980. Excellent on the reasons why the tsar's army could not continue the struggle in 1917. R. Massie, *Nicholas and Alexandra,* 1971, is a dramatic biography of the royal pair that is thoroughly historical in nature and very well written.

Wolfe, B. *Three Who Made a Revolution,* 1955. A collective biography of Lenin, Trotsky, and Stalin, especially interesting for the analysis of the conflict between the latter two in the 1920s. A sympathetic account of Trotsky is found in I. Deutscher, *The Prophet Armed, The Prophet Disarmed,* and *The Prophet Outcast,* 1953, a classic biography in three volumes, dealing with events from his youth through his murder by Stalinist agents in 1940.

TOTALITARIANISM: THE NAZI STATE

In the twentieth century, a new form of state organization came into the world—the savage form called totalitarianism. The experts still argue about whether totalitarianism was the result of some peculiar, temporary combination of circumstances in the European political-economic spectrum of the 1920s and 1930s or whether what occurred in those years was a harbinger of things still to come.

The interwar years (1919–1939) saw the rise of several dictatorships in various parts of the world, including Europe. The Soviet Union, Japan, and several Latin American states all embraced one-man rule. With the exception of Stalin's Soviet state, these regimes were not totalitarian in character. In this chapter, our focus is on European dictators. We examine the nature of the totalitarian states they created, focusing on the most aggressive and dangerous one, that erected by Adolf Hitler, the leader of Germany from 1933 until his death at the end of World War II.

✤ TOTALITARIAN GOVERNMENT: ORIGINS

The word *totalitarian* comes from the attempt—more or less successful—to impose *total control* over the public life of a society. Totalitarianism is a twentieth-century phenomenon; before then such an attempt had not been made, in part because it was not technically possible and in part because opinion makers strongly resisted the very idea.

The atmosphere of unquestioning obedience to governmental authority that was a necessary prelude to totalitarianism was a product of World War I. The full mobilization of the civilian population behind the war effort was new in history; no one could escape, at least in theory, from "doing one's bit." As we have seen, the wartime governments took full control of the economy, instituting rationing, allocations to industry, wage ceilings, and price controls. Citizens were expected to sacrifice their personal freedoms for victory, if necessary; the majority readily accepted the government's crude censorship and propaganda.

Six Characteristics

What did the totalitarian state and society mean in practice?

- The traditional boundaries between public and private affairs of citizens were redefined. What had been considered private was now declared public and thus, a matter for governmental concern and control. Even such areas as family relationships and aesthetic values fell into this category.

- The state itself became a symbol of the Leader's will. Government policy was the concrete implementation of what "the people" truly wanted, as interpreted by the Leader.
- The bond between people and Leader was symbolized by the party, a single, mass organization created to form a link between the two. This party embraced all who wished to share in the union between Leader and followers.
- The people were understood to include only those belonging to the majority ethnic group (Italians, Germans, whatever). The others, "aliens," had no inherent rights at all and could be so treated by courts and officials.
- Since the Leader and the people were joined by a mystic bond allowing the Leader to be the sole authentic interpreter of their collective will, there was no need for political competition or discussion. Parliaments and traditional parties could all be eliminated. They were merely selfish interests seeking to confuse the people and negate their true welfare, which lay in the Leader's hands.
- The collective was all, the individual nothing. Individual conscience, affections, and interests were to be rigorously subordinated to the needs and demands of the people and the Leader, as expressed through the party.

Antirationalism

Struggle was the key concept for the totalitarian states. The struggle of the people and their Leader was never completed. Victory was always conditional and partial; another enemy was always lurking somewhere. The enemies were both domestic and foreign ("international Bolshevism," "Jewish conspiracies," "encircling capitalists," and the like), and it was necessary to be constantly on guard against their tricks and destructive ploys.

Action was also essential, though it often lacked any clear goal. Mussolini once said, "Act forcefully . . . the reason for doing so will appear." In other words, don't worry about why something is done; the act of doing it will produce its own rationale in time. Inevitably, this approach often led to contradictory and illogical policies. But reasonable action was not high on the list of priorities. Totalitarian governments often deliberately turned away from reason and cultivated a kind of *antirationalism* as a philosophy. Instincts were raised above logic; the goal was "thinking with the blood," as the Nazis put it.

Such antirationalism was an outgrowth of the late nineteenth century, when a cult of violence appeared among some intellectual fringe groups in Europe. World War I then showed how far civilized humans could descend toward their animal origins. Instead of being revolted by the war, the totalitarian theorists often seized upon those experiences as representing authentic human nature: violent, instinctual, collective.

Benito Mussolini in Italy (see chapter 48) was the first political figure to see what might be accomplished by blending the techniques of wartime government with a mass appeal to national sentiment and the resentments of the masses. In his *Fascisti,* he brought together traditional underdogs of society and gave them a chance to feel like top dogs. The Fascists claimed to be the vanguard of an epoch of national glory, made possible by a radical change in the very nature of social organization and led by a man of genius: **Il Duce** (the Leader).

Fear of communism, frustrated nationalism, and the accumulated resentments of the underdogs made a potent combination, and as we have seen, Mussolini rode that combination into power in the early 1920s. Once he had power, he quickly found ways to increase his popularity by initiating a self-proclaimed crusade for social justice, economic expansion, and imperial glory. Throughout the later 1920s and 1930s, Mussolini was attempting to erect a totalitarian state, but he was to be only partly successful.

✤ THE NAZI STATE: HITLER AND THE THOUSAND-YEAR REICH

The "honor" of creating the most ruthless totalitarian state was divided between the Leftist dictatorship of Josef Stalin in Russia (see Chapter 49) and the Rightist dictatorship of Adolf Hitler in Germany. We have seen that Stalin as leader of the Communist Party attained tremendous power by cynically manipulating an idealistic movement aimed at bringing first Russia and then the world into a new era of equality and freedom. The German dictator had no such visions.

Hitler's Early Career

Hitler was born an Austrian citizen in 1889; he was the only child of a strict father and a loving mother who spoiled him in every way her limited resources allowed. When he was seventeen, he went off to Vienna in hopes of an art career; rejected as having no talent, he survived for the next few years on the fringes of urban society, living hand-to-mouth on money from home. He fully absorbed

Adolf Hitler
1889–1945

Despite many tries, no one has been able to explain satisfactorily why Adolf Hitler's political and social doctrines were so attractive to most German people. During the 1930s, few Germans questioned his anti-Semitic and antiforeigner slogans, his manic nationalism, or his crude and violent ideas for renovating the German nation. Most accepted his rejection of the instinct for peace as a weakness unworthy of a great people. Nazism appeared to be a noble policy and international peace a sign of "democratic decadence." True, the plight of the Germans after World War I and the struggle for survival during the first years of the Great Depression must have contributed to their acceptance of Hitler's views. The orderly world of Kaiser William II had crumbled before their eyes. Germany was forced to yield to Allied occupation of the lands west of the Rhine River and to give up most of its much-honored army and its equipment. Most irritating of all, Germany was forced to accept a peace treaty that branded it as the sole culprit for causing the ruinous war and was required to pay many billions of dollars as compensation to the victors.

The punishment for losing that war was far greater than most had anticipated, and the common people suffered the consequences. Inflation, unemployment, and political turmoil spread. The fear of communism was acute among the middle classes. The old system was thoroughly discredited, and Germans looked for a new messiah. In 1923, one appeared, attempting to take power through a *putsch.* His name was Adolf Hitler.

At the time, Hitler was thirty-three years old. He had served with bravery in the German army during the war and like millions of other front-line soldiers emerged from that experience with contempt for the politicians and the traditional leaders of his people. He was looking for revenge against the "dark forces," which he sensed had thus far prevented him and those like him—the "good Aryan German Volk"—from assuming their rightful place in society and prevented Germany as a nation from reaching its rightful, dominant place in the world.

In Munich, where he had settled, Hitler found his chance at the head of a tiny party of malcontents called the National Socialist German Workers Party:

---

the anti-Semitism prevalent in Vienna at this time, and his constant reading convinced him of the falsity of typical "bourgeois" values and politics. But he despised Marxism, which was the most common hope and refuge of social outsiders like himself. When World War I broke out, Hitler was a young malcontent of twenty-five, still searching for some philosophy that would make sense of a world that had rejected him (see the Biography in this chapter).

Enlisting in the German (rather than the "corrupted" Austrian) army, Hitler distinguished himself for bravery under fire, receiving the Iron Cross. The wartime experience gave him his first idea of his life's purpose. With millions of other demobilized men, he spent the first months of the postwar era in a state of shock and despair, seeing the German socialist government that had replaced the kaiser as the betrayers of the nation. As time passed, he became determined to join those who were aiming to overturn the government.

In 1920, Hitler took over a tiny group of would-be reformers and renamed them the *National Socialist German Workers Party (NSDAP)* or *"Nazis"* for short. Devoting his fanatical energy to the party, he rapidly attracted new members in the Munich area, where he had been living since before the war. In 1923, Hitler, supported by a few discontented army officers, attempted a **putsch in Munich,** but it failed miserably. Arrested for treason, he used the trial to make himself a national celebrity. He was sentenced to five years in prison by a sympathetic judge and used the year he actually served to write his autobiography and call-to-arms: **Mein Kampf (My Struggle).**

The Nazi Program

In wild and ranting prose, *Mein Kampf* laid out what Hitler saw as Germany's present problems and their solutions. It insisted on all of the following:

the Nazis. Rapidly expanding its membership through his mesmerizing ability to capture a crowd, Hitler entered into a half-baked scheme to take over the government in 1923, when the inflation and popular turmoil were at their height. The attempted coup failed with fourteen deaths. Hitler was tried for treason, jailed for a year, and emerged a hero in the eyes of many Germans for attempting to save German honor from the disgrace of the Versailles Treaty and an incompetent and/or traitorous government in Berlin.

From 1924 on, the Nazi movement slowly gained strength, although its results varied in the national and regional elections it entered. Hitler became an ever more skilled manipulator of political propaganda and gathered around him a very mixed band of dreamers, brutes, ambitious climbers, and opportunists. Some of them firmly believed in the Führer and his self-proclaimed mission to save Germany and bring a New Order to Europe; others hitched their wagons to his star without necessarily believing the wild rantings in *Mein Kampf.* Until he came to power, few took his promises to exterminate Jews and communists as anything more than a rabble-rouser's

empty words. They regarded such statements in much the same way as they did the promised thousand-year *Reich* (empire): as a politically useful ploy to attract the ignorant.

Hitler's personality was a collection of contradictions. He proclaimed himself above common morality, yet lived a life of personal restraint. A strict vegetarian and teetotaler, he frowned on the more boisterous and indulgent lifestyle of some of his followers (like the fat hedonist Göring). He was fascinated by the power of the intellect and will, yet held intellectuals in contempt. He would work thirty-six hours at a stretch, yet went into nervous collapse and secluded himself from his officials in several crises. He was perhaps the most murderous power holder of the twentieth century, committing endless atrocities against Germans and other human beings, yet he had a deep reverence for the arts and considerable artistic talent. Perhaps it is in his artistic personality that a hint of the truth lies: when his paintings were exhibited after the war, critics were impressed by his talent for rendering structural accuracy, but noted his inability to sketch the human form.

- *Anti-Semitism.* Hitler wished to eliminate Jews from living at all in "Aryan" Germany. Jews were declared born enemies of all proper German values.
- *Rejection of the Versailles Treaty and German war guilt.* Hitler called the treaty the most unfair in world history, dictated by a (temporarily) strong France against a helpless, tricked Germany.
- *Confiscation of illicit war profits.* This measure was aimed mainly at Jews, but also at non-Jewish German industrialists. This point reflected the Nazis' claim to be socialists (though anti-Marxist).
- *Protection of the middle classes from ruinous competition.* The Nazis made a special show of paying attention to the growing concerns of the shopkeepers and white-collar workers who feared that they were being forced downward on the economic ladder by big business.
- *Land redistribution for the peasants.* Hitler claimed to be protecting the peasants who were being squeezed

out by large landholders and by land speculation schemes.

The basic tenor of *Mein Kampf* and of Nazi speeches and literature in the 1920s was consistent: they proclaimed their hatred for the existing situation in Germany and their determination to change it radically. The socialist government that had accepted the Versailles Treaty and the Weimar Constitution of 1919 was a special target of contempt. The socialists with the help of the Jews had given a "stab in the back" to the brave German army in 1918. Germany must be reborn and once again gain its rightful place! Whatever means were necessary to do this were justified, as only the strong would survive in a jungle world.

After the failure of the Munich *putsch,* Hitler swore that he would come to power by constitutional, legal means. No one could later say that he had acted against the will of his people. From the moment that he was released from jail, he devoted himself tirelessly to organizing, speech making, and electioneering from one end of the country to the other.

Hitler was an extremely gifted rabble-rouser, who quickly learned how to appeal to various groups in language that they could not forget. His mastery of theatrical techniques heightened the effect of his speeches (many of which were recorded); drama and tension were always at a high pitch wherever he appeared. His targets were always the same: Jews, the signers of the Versailles Treaty, the communists, and the clique of businessmen and bureaucrats who supposedly pulled the strings behind the scenes.

Between 1925 and 1929, which were prosperous years for Weimar Germany, the Nazis made little headway among the masses of industrial workers, who remained loyal either to the Social Democrats or the large, legal German Communist Party. But the Nazis did pick up voters among the members of the middle class who had been ruined in the great inflation of 1923 and among the numerous semieducated white-collar workers who saw their relative status slipping in postwar Germany. As late as the elections of 1928, the Nazis received only 2.6 percent of the vote and 12 seats in the *Reichstag.* In comparison, the Communists had 77 seats, and the Social Democrats had 156. The rest of the Reichstag's 500 seats were held by moderate or conservative parties who regarded Hitler as a loose cannon who might possibly be useful against the Left but could not be taken seriously as a politician.

The Great Depression's Effects

The collapse of the German (and world) economy in 1930–1931 set the stage for Nazi political success. In late 1929, the New York Stock Exchange went into a tailspin that had effects on every aspect of finance in the Western world. Germany was particularly affected by the U.S. crisis because for years German industrialists and municipalities had been relying on American loans. Suddenly, this credit was cut off as loans were called in on short notice. As the Great Depression settled on the United States, any prospects of new overseas lending disappeared. Instead, international finance and trade shrank steadily as each nation attempted to protect itself from external competition by raising tariffs and limiting imports.

The results for Germany were horrendous: the number of unemployed rose from 2.25 million in early 1930 to more than 6 million two years later (about 25 percent of

■ This effective appeal to the German populace to choose between the Nazis or Bolshevism was part of the campaign to discredit any moderate solutions to the Depession and its attendant misery.

the total labor force). And this figure does not count involuntary part-time workers or the many women who withdrew from the labor market permanently. In no other country, not even the United States, was the industrial economy so hard hit.

The governing coalition of Social Democrats and moderate conservatives fell apart under this strain. The Reichstag was deadlocked for months. In the vacuum, the old general **Paul von Hindenburg** who had been president since the mid-1920s resorted to the use of the constitution's emergency powers to keep government working at all. A presidential dictatorship was thus established in 1931–1932, which effectively ended Weimar democracy.

Unsere letzte Hoffnung: HITLER

◼ **Our Last Hope, Hitler.** This poster was part of Hitler's unsuccessful 1932 presidential campaign as the National Socialist Party candidate against Paul von Hindenburg.

In the frequent elections necessitated by the collapse of the coalition, the middle-of-the-road parties steadily lost seats to the extremes on Right and Left: the Nazis and the Communists. In an election for the Reichstag in mid-1930, the Nazis won a total of 107 seats, second only to the Social Democrats. As the economy continued downhill, Hitler promised immediate, decisive action to aid the unemployed and the farmers. In another election in early 1932, the Nazis won 14.5 million votes of a total of about 35 million. The Nazis were now the largest single party, but still lacked a majority. Their attacks on the other parties intensified both verbally and, increasingly, in the streets.

The *Machtergreifung* in 1933

As late as 1932, Hindenburg and his conservative, old-line advisers refused to consider appointing Hitler as chancellor (prime minister). To them, Hitler was an upstart, a vulgarian who had no respect for proper conduct. Some of them wanted to give the Nazis a few seats in a new government, but certainly not the leadership—and Hitler would settle for nothing less. He also stood by his earlier promise to gain power legally or not at all. Finally, in a move aimed at moderating Hitler by putting him into a position where he had to take responsibility rather than just criticize, the Hindenburg circle agreed to appoint him chancellor on January 30, 1933. Within eight weeks, Hitler had transformed the government into a Nazi dictatorship. And technically, he had accomplished this **Machtergreifung** or seizure of power by constitutional procedures, as he had promised.

This transformation involved two complementary processes: the capture of legal authority for the Nazis and the elimination of competing political groups. During the national election campaign immediately called by the new chancellor, the Nazis used the burning of the Reichstag building by a mentally ill communist as an excuse to whip up hysteria over an alleged communist revolution. Under the constitution's emergency provision, Hitler introduced the equivalent of martial law and used it to round up tens of thousands of his opponents in the next weeks. After the election (in which the Nazis still failed to gain a simple majority), all Communist and some Social Democratic delegates to the Reichstag were arrested as traitors and hence put out of political action. Finally, in late March, the Nazi-dominated rump parliament enacted the so-called *Enabling Act,* giving Hitler's government the power to rule by decree for four years, or until the emergency had passed. It did not pass for the next twelve years, until Hitler was a smoking corpse in the ruins of Berlin.

The German Communist Party was almost immediately outlawed, and the Social Democrats were banned a few weeks later. One by one the centrist and moderate parties disappeared, either by suicide (dissolving themselves) or by Nazi decree. In mid-1933, the Nazis were the only legal political organization left in Germany. In its various subgroups for women, youths, professional associations, farmers, and others, all proper Germans could find their place. By 1934, about 15 percent of the total population had joined the Nazi Party. The numbers rose steadily thereafter. By the middle of the war, about one quarter of adult Germans belonged, though many joined under

■ **An All-German Party Parade.** A major reason for the Nazi success was the masterly touch of drama accompanying the party's functions. The impression of overwhelming force was fostered by slogans and banners which proclaimed the party's strength in every part of the homeland.

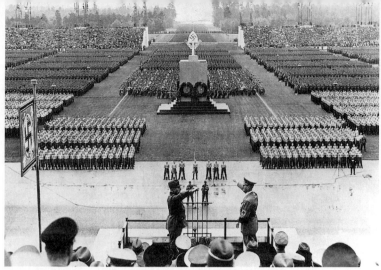

■ **Nuremberg Nazi Rally, 1938.** The massive display of strength and unity so dear to the Nazis was nowhere better on view than at the regular rallied held in the Bavarian town of Nuremberg. In this photo, Hitler takes the salute from his labor union chief before congratulating the 50,000 participants on completing the West Wall along the French border.

severe pressure and contributed nothing except mandatory dues.

Hitler completed the process of consolidating power with a purge within the party itself. This was the infamous **"Night of the Long Knives"** in June 1934, when the paramilitary **Sturmabteilung** (Storm Troopers, SA), who had been very important to the Nazi movement as bullyboys, were cut down to size. Using another of his suborganizations, the new **Schutzstaffel** or **SS,** Hitler murdered several hundred of the Storm Troop leaders. By doing so, he both rid himself of potentially serious rivals and placated the German army generals, who rightly saw in the brown-shirted Storm Troop a menace to their own position as the nation's military leaders.

✦ THE NAZI DOMESTIC REGIME

When the Nazis took power, the NSDAP had an active membership of about one million and probably twice that many supporters who could be counted on to show up for major party affairs or contribute some money. The party was represented in all parts of Germany, which was organized into *Gaue,* or districts under the command of a *Gauleiter* (a district party boss). As under the Weimar government, Prussia was the most important region in Germany, and the brilliant propagandist *Joseph Goebbels* (1898–1945) was Hitler's deputy here. Master of "the big lie," Goebbels directed the Nazi assault against the democratic socialist and communist rivals in the Berlin working

class. Another member of Hitler's small circle of intimates was **Hermann Göring** (1898–1945), the rotund, wisecracking, and entirely cynical pilot-hero of World War I who was generally seen as the number two man in the hierarchy.

Rank-and-file party members were drawn from all elements of the population, but the leaders were normally young men from the working and lower-middle classes who saw Hitler as not only the spokesman for their hopes and resentments, but as someone who could carry them to high office and prestige, if he won. Like the Russian communists, the Nazis were a party of young men who were in a hurry and had no patience with negotiation or gradual reform. They saw themselves not so much as implementers of a revolution, but as the restorers of proud Germanic traditions that had been allowed to decay in the bourgeois Weimar era.

Hitler's policies were designed to make Germany into a totalitarian state, and they did so very rapidly. His right arm in this was **Heinrich Himmler** (1900–1945) the head of the SS and of the *Gestapo,* or political police. Himmler was Hitler's most loyal colleague, and he was charged with overseeing the internal security of the Nazi regime. Himmler's SS operated the concentration camps that had opened as early as 1934 within Germany. And later in the conquered territories, a branch of the SS conducted the Holocaust of the Jews, setting up the slave labor camps and installing a reign of terror against all possible resistance (see the Document in this chapter).

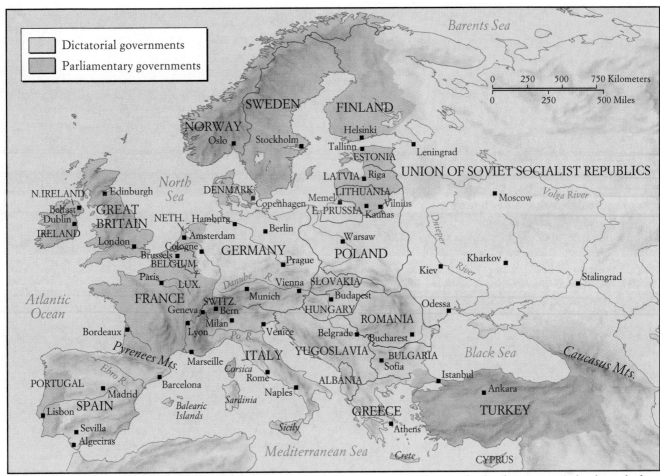

● MAP 50.1 Europe in 1939 at Eve of World War II. Most of Europe was under dictatorial rule of various types by the end of the 1930s. The impact of the Great Depression pushed some of the former parliamentary democracies in to the dictatorship column during the middle of the '30s decade. Only Britain and the Scandinavians kept alive the reality of democratic politics.

The "Jewish Question"

The most horrible of the Nazi policies was *the genocide against the Jews.* For the first time in modern history, a systematic, cold-blooded war of extermination was practiced against a noncombatant people, solely on the basis of race. The war against the Jews went through four distinct phases between 1933 and 1945:

1. From March 1933 to 1935, German Jews were publicly humiliated and excluded from government jobs.
2. In September 1935, the **Nuremberg Laws** prohibiting social contacts between Jews and "Aryans" (persons with no Jewish blood for two generations on both sides of their family) made Jews into noncitizens. The gov-

ernment began to harass Jews constantly and push them into urban ghettos for easier surveillance.

3. In November 1938, new policies made it almost impossible for Jews to engage in public life and business and forbade emigration unless they left all their property in Germany and went as paupers. By this time, many thousands of Jews had been consigned to the camps.
4. At the **Wannsee Conference** in Berlin in 1942, the *Final Solution* for the Jewish "problem" was approved by Hitler. The Jews were rounded up from the ghettos throughout occupied Europe and sent to the death camps in Poland. The Holocaust had begun and would not end until Germany's defeat in 1945. By then, some

Heinrich Himmler, Speech to the SS

Heinrich Himmler was perhaps the most detested—and feared—man in the world, until he died at his own hand in the Nazi collapse in 1945. A totally insignificant looking individual with rimless eyeglasses through which he peered nearsightedly, Himmler was the willing slave of the Führer. In return for his doglike devotion, he was entrusted with the leadership of the SS, the *Schutzstaffel,* or bodyguard of Hitler, which he built up into an elite branch of the German military.

To Himmler was given the responsibility of implementing the "Final Solution" of the Jewish Question, agreed upon at the Wannsee Conference in 1942. The following selection is a partial transcript of a speech given by Himmler to an SS conclave in Poland, on October 4, 1943. Note the peculiar combination of secrecy and an attempt to excite pride in what the concentration camp guards were being asked to do.

I also want to make reference before you here, in complete frankness, to a really grave matter. Among ourselves, this once, it shall be uttered quite frankly; but in public we will never speak of it. Just as we did not hesitate on June 30, 1934,* to do our duty as ordered, to stand up against the wall comrades who had violated their duty, and shoot them, so we have never talked about this, and never will. . . . Each of us shuddered, and yet each one knew that he would do it again if it were ordered and if it were necessary.

I am referring to the evacuation of the Jews, the annihilation of the Jewish people. This is one of the things that can be easily said: "The Jewish people is going to be annihilated" says every Party member. "Sure, it's in our program, elimination of the Jews, annihilation—we'll take care of it." And then they all come trudging in, 80 million worthy Germans, and each one of them has his one "decent Jew." Sure, the others are swine, but *this* one is an A-1 Jew.

*The "Night of the Long Knives" when the SA was eliminated.

Of all those who talk this way, not one has seen it happen, not one has been through it. Most of you know what it means to see a hundred corpses side by side, or five hundred, or a thousand. To have stuck this out and—excepting cases of human weakness—to have kept our integrity, that is what has made us hard. In our history, this is an unwritten and never-to-be-written page of glory, for we know how difficult we would have made it for ourselves if today—amid the bombing raids, the hardships and deprivations of war—we still had the Jews in every city as secret saboteurs, agitators, and demagogues. If the Jews were still situated in the body of the German people, we probably would have reached the 1916–1917 stage by now.

The wealth they had we have taken from them. I have issued a strict order, carried out by SS-Obergruppenführer Pohl, that this wealth in its entirety is to be turned over to the Reich, as a matter of course. We have taken none of it for ourselves . . . whoever takes so much as a Mark of it for himself is a dead man. A number of SS men—not very many—have transgressed, and they will die without mercy. We had the moral right, we had the duty toward our people, to kill this people who wished to kill us. But we do not have the right to enrich ourselves with so much as a fur coat, a watch, a Mark, or even a cigarette or anything else. Having exterminated a germ, we do not want in the end to be infected by the germ, and die of it. I will not stand by and let even a small rotten spot develop, or take hold. Wherever it may form, we together will cauterize it. All in all, however, we can say that we have carried out this heaviest of all our tasks in a spirit of love for our people. Our inward being, our soul, has not suffered injury from it.

SOURCE: Excerpt from "The Holocaust Reader" on *Readings in World Civiliazations,* Lucy Dawidbwicz, editor. © 1976, Behrman House, Inc.

6 million Jews from all over central and eastern Europe had been murdered, starved to death, or otherwise fallen victim to Himmler's henchmen. Of the more than 2 million Jews living in Germany itself in 1933, only a few tens of thousands survived at the close of the war, overlooked or hidden by sympathetic neighbors.

■ **Dehumanizing of the Jews.** The Nazis viewed Jewish-Christian sexual relations as pollution of German blood. The woman's sign reads "I am the biggest pig in the place and get involved only with Jews." The Jewish man's placard says "As a Jewish fellow, I take only German girls to my room." The public humiliation of such couples began immediately after the Nazis came to power in 1933.

Nazi Economic Policy

Economic policy in the Nazi state was a peculiar mixture of a fake "socialism" and an accommodation of the big businesses and cartels that had dominated Germany for a generation. As in Mussolini's Italy, the government's economic policies generated some measure of social reform. Workers and farmers were idealized in propaganda as the true Aryan Germans. But private property remained untouched, and the capitalist process was subjected to only sporadic and selective interference by the government. The labor unions like every other type of public association were fully subordinated to the party and became arms of the Nazi octopus. Strikes were illegal, and the Marxist idea of class conflict was officially declared nonexistent among Germans.

Hitler had come to power partly on the strength of his promises to end the unemployment problem. From 1933 to 1936, he instituted measures that were effective at providing jobs; the huge road construction and public works programs he began in 1934 absorbed a large portion of the pool of unemployed. With rearmament, the military was greatly enlarged, and munitions factories and their suppliers received government orders. Raw materials were rapidly stockpiled; synthetics for the vital raw materials that Germany lacked (petroleum, rubber, tin, and many other exotic minerals) were invented in government-supported laboratories and produced in new factories.

Already by 1936, Hitler was putting Germany on a war footing; the Nazi government was spending money to put people back to work in the same openhanded way as President Roosevelt's New Deal was doing in the United States. But the Nazi program was more successful; it did not have to contend with congressional objections or engage in budget battles with the opposition party. Labor was allocated according to government priorities; government ministries decided what would be imported and exported. In the western border region, a huge "West Wall" was being erected; this system of fortifications would mirror the Maginot Line across the frontier. The *autobahns* (expressways) were crisscrossing the country, creating a system that could move men and materiel quickly in case of war.

By 1937, the number of unemployed was down to 400,000, and a labor shortage was developing. Unmarried women and youths were put into more or less compulsory organizations to relieve the shortfall. In every German village and town, Nazi Youth organizations gave boys and girls age seven to twenty-one a place to get together with their peers for both work and fun while imbibing the Nazi viewpoints. The nation was prosperous, the Great Depression became a dim memory and many millions of Germans were proud of their government and their **Führer.**

Summary

Totalitarianism is a twentieth-century phenomenon that found several homes in Europe after World War I. One experiment with it occurred in Soviet Russia; another in Fascist Italy. But the German Nazi state was the most notable example in terms of its impact upon the remainder of the world and the general revulsion it aroused.

The defeat in 1918, the runaway inflation of the early 1920s, and the weak and unpopular socialist government combined to exert a devastating effect on German national morale. Millions of voters lost faith in liberal democracy and the parliamentary process. The failure of the Social Democrats to assert real leadership and the constant opposition of the German Communists compounded the government's problems in the later 1920s. The onset of the world depression brought on a crisis from which the Nazi Party emerged triumphant in 1933.

The Nazis could soon boast that *der Führer* made good his promises to his people. He had obtained government power legally, and an intimidated legislature gave him dictatorial authority soon after.

By the mid-1930s, rearmament and a vigorous social investment policy had restored German prosperity. The large majority of Germans were quite content with Hitler's guidance; there is little doubt that he would have decisively won any free election he saw fit to hold. His ranting anti-Semitism and harassment of Jews and all opposition elements did not overly disturb the majority, who had found a prosperity and sense of national purpose that were sadly lacking among their democratic neighbors. Not until the shadow of renewed world war fell on the country did some begin to have second thoughts.

Test Your Knowledge

1. The totalitarian state was born
   a. in World War I.
   b. in the French Revolution.
   c. in the pages of *Mein Kampf.*
   d. in the Bolshevik party charter.
2. Which of the following is *not* associated with modern totalitarian government?
   a. Continuous striving toward changing goals
   b. Distinctions between private behavior and affairs of public policy
   c. Subordination of the individual to the state
   d. Leadership exercised by a single semisacred individual
3. Hitler's major intellectual development took place
   a. during his early manhood in Vienna.
   b. as a reaction to the Great Depression.
   c. during his boyhood in rural Austria.
   d. after he formed the Nazi Party in the postwar era.
4. Which of the following did *not* help Hitler in his bid for political power?
   a. His sympathy for Marxist theory and practice
   b. The struggle between the Social Democrats and the Communists in Germany

   c. The ineptitude of the democratic leaders
   d. Massive economic hardship
5. The German chancellorship came to Hitler in 1933 through
   a. legal appointment.
   b. a conspiracy.
   c. an overwhelming electoral victory.
   d. armed force.
6. The Nuremberg Laws
   a. outlawed the German Communist Party.
   b. laid out the details of the Nazi dictatorship in Germany.
   c. detailed who was Jewish and what that meant.
   d. were the formal rejection of the reparations bill from World War I.
7. Which was *not* true of Hitler's government during the 1930s?
   a. Its policy was increasingly anti-Semitic.
   b. It was successful in eliminating German unemployment.
   c. It allowed only one party to participate.
   d. Its economic policy was anticapitalist.

Identification Terms

Final Solution	Hindenburg (Paul von)	*Mein Kampf* (My Struggle)	Nuremberg Laws
Hermann Göring	Il Duce/Der Führer	Munich *putsch*	*Sturmabteilung*/SA
Himmler (Heinrich) and the *Schutzstaffel* (SS)	*Machtergreifung*	"Night of the Long Knives"	Wannsee Conference

Bibliography

A general analysis of Fascist totalitarianism is given in S. G. Payne, *Fascism: Comparisons and Definition,* 1980. See also E. Weber, *Varieties of Fascism,* 1964, which was cited in Chapter 48.

Bullock, A. *Hitler: A Study in Tyranny,* 1964, and J. Fest, *Hitler,* 1974, have each written highly readable and reliable biographies of the Nazi leader.

Craig, G. *Germany, 1866–1945,* 1978. A survey that goes far to illuminate what brought Hitler and his party to power, as well as giving the kernel of Nazi thought and action while he was in power.

Gordon, S. *Hitler, Germans, and the "Jewish Question,"* 1984, and L. Dawidowicz, *The War Against the Jews, 1933–45,* 1975, both give insight into the madness—and its rationalization by the Nazi leadership.

Koehl, R. *The Black Corps,* 1983, and H. Krausnick and M. Broszat, *Anatomy of the SS State,* 1964, are thoroughgoing examinations of the blackshirted elite corps that terrified Hitler's opponents in the concentration camps.

Marks, S. *The Illusion of Peace,* 1976, and R. Sontag, *A Broken World, 1919–1939,* 1971, which was cited in the bibliography for Chapter 48, are good surveys of international relations in Europe in the 1920s and 1930s.

Peukert, D. J. *Inside Nazi Germany,* 1987. Read this analysis of who supported the Nazis, and why, along with the exciting journalistic account in W. Shirer, *Rise and Fall of the Third Reich,* 1964. W. S. Allen, *The Nazi Seizure of Power: The Experience of a Single German Town, 1930–35,* 1971, is a definitive treatment of its subject and very well written.

Stephenson, J. *Women in Nazi Society,* 1975. A fair-minded treatment of its subject, though not entirely reliable.

Watt, D. C. *How War Came,* 1989, A systematic and reliable study of diplomacy just prior to World War II.

CHAPTER 51

EAST ASIA IN A CENTURY OF CHANGE, 1840–1949

CHINA
The Manzhou Decline
Chinese Disintegration after 1895
Chiang Kai-Shek's Regime and Chinese Communism
The Sino-Japanese War and the Maoist Challenge
JAPAN
The Emergence of Modern Japan
Between the World Wars
SOUTHEASTERN ASIA: THE COLONIAL EMPIRES

The explosive development of Western technology and military prowess in the nineteenth century had an impact on East Asia somewhat earlier than elsewhere. By the 1850s, China, Japan, and Southeast Asia had all felt the iron hand of the West in their commercial and political relations with the rest of the world.

China and Japan could hardly have chosen more different ways of dealing with the new situation. Nor could the outcomes have been more different. By the opening of the twentieth century, China was a collapsing government attempting to preside over a society torn by unbridgeable gaps. In contrast, Japan had made itself over in one of the most remarkable self-willed transformations known to history. An aggressive imperialism brought Japan into conflict with a struggling China in the 1930s and later with the West. Meanwhile Southeast Asia had become a group of white-ruled colonies where European values were superimposed on the natives' traditional cultures, producing a bi-level society.

✤ CHINA

The Manzhou Decline

In a real sense, China's modern history begins with the **Opium Wars** (1840–1842). In the eighteenth century, the British East India Company had developed a lucrative trade in Indian opium with south China. The drug had at long last given Westerners an exchange commodity for the luxury goods they imported from China and paid for with precious gold and silver. Previously little known in China, opium became a major public health problem in the coastal cities, and its illegal trade disrupted the empire's finances. After some ineffective protests to the East India officials and the British government, in the 1830s the Chinese finally decided to take strong measures to prevent the drug's importation. The Chinese efforts led to a naval war, which was predictably one-sided, given the huge differences between British and Chinese weaponry and naval tactics.

In 1842, the Beijing government signed the first of the *"unequal treaties"* between a weakening China and the Western powers. The treaties opened up the previously closed Chinese coastal towns to British merchants and consuls. (This was the beginning of the British colony of Hong Kong.) The resident British were subject to British law, not Chinese law. Though not specifically mentioned in the treaty, the opium trade would continue. China had, in effect, lost control of some of its territory and its trade patterns to a foreign power.

The war over the opium trade was just the beginning of frictions between China and the European powers. The treaty with Britain was followed by others with France and, later, with Russia and Germany. All of the treaties were similar; all were extorted from a Chinese government that was still attempting to deal with the West as its ancestors in the sixteenth and seventeenth centuries had dealt with foreigners—as a superior dealing with inferiors. This was so far from reality that it became a bad joke among the Europeans. With the exception of some missionaries intent on bringing Christ to the Buddhist or Daoist Chinese, most Europeans in China in the nineteenth and twentieth centuries were there as imperialist fortune seekers. They were intensely resented by the Chinese, who felt humiliated by their new inability to protect themselves from the "foreign devils."

The Taiping Rebellion

The losses to the European powers, bad as they were, were overshadowed in the 1850s through early 1870s by the *Taiping and Nien Rebellions*. Of the two, the Taiping episode was the more widespread and more disastrous. For more than twenty years and during which the Chinese suffered perhaps twenty million deaths, rebel generals led a motley band of poverty-stricken peasants and urban workers against the Manzhou emperors. The **Taipings'** success in the early years of the revolt brought them wide support from many educated Chinese who were sickened by the government's inability to resist the foreigners. The upheaval was encouraged by several factors:

- Discontent with the corruption and incompetence of the government officials.
- The rapidly worsening problems of overpopulation in much of south China.
- The strong appeal of the Taipings' economic reform proposals.
- The total ineffectiveness of the Manzhou armed forces.

For a few years, the Taipings set up a countergovernment in central China that controlled about half the total area of the country. Their leader, the visionary Hung Hsiu-chuan (who had been exposed to Christian missions and believed himself to be Jesus' younger brother) originally enjoyed sympathy from the West, in part because Hung seemed to want to imitate Western ways. Some thought he was the would-be founder of a Christian China.

But the Taipings also opposed opium smoking and further giveaways of Chinese rights to foreigners. The Western powers thus opted to support the Manzhou government because they knew the government would give them little trouble in the future. At that point, the rebels began to quarrel among themselves, and by 1864, they were breaking up. The government soon defeated them and executed Hung.

The Nien and the Muslim rebels presented almost as fierce a threat to the Beijing emperor. They controlled large areas of the southwest and northwest of the empire and for a time threatened to link up with the Taipings. Total collapse seemed imminent, but the government was unexpectedly saved by a group of provincial officials and landlords, who organized regional armies to take the place of the failed central forces. Most of these men were inspired by the Confucian doctrines of government, which had been forgotten during the recent epoch of rule. Their effort is known as the "late Manzhou restoration" of the 1870s.

Failure of the Late Manzhou Restoration

The new governors were reformers, and their policy of **Self-Strengthening** aimed at giving China the means to hold its own against the foreign barbarians once more. They addressed the peasant problem by instituting land reform measures and encouraging new crops with more nutritive value. Long-neglected public works programs, such as flood control projects on the Yellow and Yangtze Rivers, were taken in hand with good effect. Self-Strengthening attempted to introduce Western methods and technologies, while retaining traditional Confucian values in the Chinese educated class. The examination system was tightened to eliminate favoritism, but candidates were still tested on the Confucian classics. Military and business affairs received much more attention than heretofore, but continued to play a supporting role, rather than being given center stage in Chinese life.

Unhappily for China, this attempt to blend West and East did not work out well; new leaders who could both quote the classics and design a steam-driven factory did not appear. The traditionalist attitudes remained too strong to be overcome among the scholar-officials. The *Empress Dowager Cixi* (1835–1908) was a kind of evil genius of China's government, who pulled the strings for many years in the name of her son and her nephew, both powerless child-emperors. An expert in political infighting, she managed to hold on to power for over a generation (1860–1907). She was not opposed to reform in

Report of Commissioner Li

Li Hongchang (1823–1901) was a key figure in Chinese dealings with the West in the later nineteenth century. He also played an important role in putting down the devastating Taiping rebellion in the 1860s and was later a leader of the Self-Strengthening movement.

The British and French sent ships and troops to help put down the Taipings, giving Li a chance to entertain their commanders and observe their weaponry. His letters and memoranda reveal a clear perception of the nature of Chinese problems, and give his ideas as to their solutions. It will be seen that not all mandarins remained ignorant of the true state of power relations between China and the West, nor of the means by which the West could be matched by China.

Letter to Ceng Kuofan, Li's Superior, February 1863.

I have been aboard the warships of the British and French and I saw that their cannon are ingenious and uniform, their ammunition is fine and cleverly made, their weapons are bright, and their troops have a martial air and are orderly. These things are actually superior to those of China . . . whenever they attack a city or bombard a camp, the various firearms they use are all non-existent in China. Even their pontoon bridges, scaling ladders, and fortresses are all well prepared with excellent technique and marvelous usefullness. All these things I have never seen before. I feel deeply ashamed that the Chinese weapons are far inferior to those of foreign countries. Every day I warn and instruct my officers to be humble-minded, to bear the humiliation, to learn one or two secret methods from the Westerners in order that we may increase our knowledge. . .

Memorandum to Same Individual, June 1863

Of all firearms presently in use, explosive shells can best assure victory, and particularly effective are the long guns to fire them; but unless we use the whole set of foreign machines and employ foreign skilled labor, we cannot start making them. The various arsenals under my jurisdiction cannot yet try to cast

---

principle, but she was also not in favor of it; the only thing that mattered to her was retaining her own position (see the Biography in this chapter).

Due mainly to her footdragging, the Chinese military forces were in poor shape in the war with Japan in 1894–1895. The war was fought over Korea, a traditional no-man's land between Japan and China that Japan was rapidly pulling into its orbit in the 1890s. The Chinese were decisively defeated. Japan annexed Korea and announced that it was replacing China as the most powerful Asian nation (a shift that remained in effect until Japan's defeat in World War II).

Chinese Disintegration after 1895

The defeat by Japan was an even ruder shock to the Chinese leaders than the string of humiliations by the Westerners had been. For many centuries the mandarins had looked upon Japan and the Japanese as pitiable imitators of infinitely superior China. Now modern weapons and armies had been shown to be superior to refined culture and Confucian integrity, even in non-Western hands.

In the wake of the defeat, China again had to submit to a wave of foreign pressure. Russian, German, and British, as well as Japanese, commercial extortions were forced on the Beijing officials, backed by governmental threats. Christian missionaries were granted unprecedented freedoms to attempt the conversion of the mostly unreceptive natives. Coastal enclaves became special spheres of interest for one power or another. The Chinese government conceded that its ancient satellite of Vietnam was now the property of the French colonialists; control of Korea had been surrendered to Japan (over the heads of the Koreans); Manchuria was all but given to the Russians in the north.

The **Boxer Rebellion** (1900) was one answer to this wave of foreign exploitation. The Boxers were a fanatical, quasi-religious society, who believed that they had nothing to fear from bullets. Rebelling at first against Beijing, they

the long guns but we have bought several tons of large and small guns from England and France.

I have learned that when Western scholars make weapons, they use mathematics for reference and exert their energy in deep thinking to make daily increases and alterations. Consequently they can make different weapons every month and every year.

Everything in China's civil and military systems is far superior to the West. Only in firearms is it absolutely impossible to catch up with them. What is the reason? It is because in China the way of manufacturing machines is for the scholars to understand the principles, and the artisans to put them into practice and do the work. In developing their learning the two do not consult each other, hence their achievements cannot keep abreast. The best of the artisans is limited to becoming a head craftsman. Foreigners, however, are different. He who can make a machine that can be used by the nation can become a prominent official and his family for generations can live on the trade and keep their position hereditarily...

Formerly England, France and other nations regarded Japan as a foreign treasury, recklessly making demands upon her. The Japanese emperor and ministers exerted themselves to become strong, selecting brilliant sons and high ministers to learn various techniques in the factories of Western nations. They also bought the machines for making machines, so as to practice manufacturing in their own country. Now they can navigate steamships, and make and use cannon. Last year the British people threatened them ostentatiously and brought up soldiers. And yet the superior techniques of the effective weapons which the British had been relying on had already been shared and mastered by the Japanese. Consequently, they remained steady and undisturbed; and the English, in fact, could do nothing against them... I think that if China wants to make herself strong, there is nothing better than to learn about and use the superior weapons of foreign countries. If we wish [that], there is nothing better than to look for the machines with which to make machines...

We must take warning from what has happened to prevent what has not yet happened. Furthermore, we must investigate thoroughly why it has been so.

SOURCE: Excerpt from Li Hongchang, "A Perceptive Mandarin" in *China's Response to the West: A Documentary Survey* edited by John Fairbanks and S. Y. Teng © 1954 by the President and Fellows of Harvard College. Reprinted by permission of Harvard University Press.

---

changed their mind when the wily old empress joined with them in starting a crusade to cleanse China of the foreign devils. The Boxers had no effective leadership or weaponry. After a few months, an international military force shipped off to China from various European capitals crushed the rebellion and further humiliated the tottering Manzhou dynasty by demanding cash indemnities. The failure of the Boxers convinced even the most conservative leaders that the old, Confucian-based government could no longer be maintained. China had to change or disappear as a state, and a wave of radical reform proposals now came forth from various quarters.

The New China Movement

By the end of the nineteenth century, a small but growing handful of young Chinese had been given a Western-style education, generally through the influence of missionaries who had "adopted" them. The most important of these was the intellectual *Kang Yu-wei* (1858–1927), who

■ **Boxer Rebel Awaits Beheading, 1901.** Surrounded by European troops, Chinese hangmen prepare to behead a captured Boxer.

Empress Cixi
1835–1905

The last effective ruler of the empire of China, the empress Cixi, was an extraordinary woman who defied every cliché of Asian women. Born in 1834 to a provincial gentry family, she was married to the weak Qing emperor Hsien Feng as a child and bore him his only surviving child. When Hsien died in 1861, Cixi took full advantage of her position to have her young son named emperor while she exercised ruling powers in his name. This period, which lasted for twelve years, was the first time Cixi ruled a nation that traditionally despised women who attempted a public role. Two other periods were to follow.

All accounts agree that the empress was a person of more than usual intelligence, but her real strength was her ability to anticipate what others wanted and make sure that they were dependent upon her goodwill to get it. She was a master of everyday psychology, supervising a court and a government that had become so filled with intrigue that every action, indeed almost every word, could carry multiple meanings.

The Qing dynasty had originated outside China in Manchuria. They had come to China as conquerors and insisted for a time on maintaining the signs that they, and not the "men of Han" as the Chinese called themselves, were in charge. But since the Opium Wars (1840–1842), the central government was under severe attack and had shown little imagination in trying to meet the challenge. Foreigners ranging from Christian missionaries to soldiers of fortune had overrun the port cities, turning the Chinese into second-class citizens in their own country. Native rebels, above all the Taipings, had almost overturned Chinese imperial government in the 1860s and 1870s. Much of the blame in the officials' eyes rested squarely on the woman at the head of the imperial court. But blaming her was one thing, removing her was another.

When her young son died in 1875, Cixi managed to have her infant nephew placed on the throne with herself, of course, as regent for the ensuing fifteen years. She outmaneuvered the boy's father, Prince Kung, and eliminated him from the court completely. Even after the nephew came of age and assumed power for himself, most decisions remained in the hands of the empress. When he attempted to put through some badly needed governmental reforms, she removed him and reassumed power herself in 1898. It was she who manipulated the Boxers into becoming her tool for defying the foreign powers that were carving up China.

A determined and intelligent ruler such as Cixi might have been able to bring the tottering Qing

---

argued against the common notion that Confucian philosophy represented an unchanging and unchangeable model of government and society. Kang taught that Confucius himself was a reformer and that reform was a basic ingredient of his philosophy. Kang believed that history was evolutionary, not static, and that history was moving forward in China, as in the rest of the world, toward democratic government.

Kang's ideas were called the New China Movement, and they spread widely among educated people in the 1890s. By 1898 the stage was set for an attempt at revolution from above, similar to that carried out by Peter the Great in eighteenth-century Russia. But this attempt remained just that; it was not successful, and its supporters in Beijing were forced to flee for their lives. For a few more years, under the manipulations of the empress the status quo prevailed; and it was clear that if China were to be changed, it would have to be done from below by the exasperated and desperate people.

The Chinese Republic

An important step toward a new China was the abolition of the Confucian examinations for government office in 1905. This move opened the way for aspiring officials with modern ideas, many of whom had been educated in the West or in rapidly westernizing Japan. The Western-educated liberal **Sun Yat-sen** (1866–1925) was the intellectual leader of an antigovernment reform movement that quickly swept the whole country. Sun was trained as a

dynasty through its crisis, if she had not been so intent upon simply preserving her own position. To do so, she was not above arranging the murder of those who opposed her at court, offering massive bribes, or using government monies for her private ends. The most sensational case was her use of the navy budget to rebuild the Beijing Summer Palace. China's most famous and most awe-inspiring ship was actually a life-size replica made of white marble and resting permanently in a reflecting pool at the palace!

Although not opposed to all reform, Cixi resisted many measures that were needed to modernize the decrepit bureaucracy and military. She played off one group of provincial lords against another with great expertise, so that no single faction could challenge her directly. Even as an old woman of seventy-four, she was not ready to step aside and appointed a distant relative, the infant Pu Yi, as last emperor of China in 1908. A few weeks later, she was dead, and the empire itself was on its deathbed.

■ Dressed in formal court costume, Empress Cixi is shown at the height of her powers around the turn of the nineteenth century.

medical doctor in Honolulu and Hong Kong, and on returning to his country, he gradually became convinced that a revolution from below was the only answer to China's many ills. He took up the cause of reform ("Three Principles") among the overtaxed and impoverished peasantry, believing that China could regain political honor only after a measure of social justice had been established.

The long-awaited revolution against the feeble and incompetent government came in 1911. After Cixi's death three years earlier, the dynasty was so weak that few would defend it when it was challenged. Originally, Sun was called to head the new parliamentary government, but to avoid civil war, the head of the Army, General Yuan Shikai, soon replaced him. The *Republic of China* was formally declared in 1912. The last child emperor was

forced to abdicate and lived long enough to become a supporter of Mao's communist government! For a few years, General Yuan was master of China and intended to become the next emperor. But his dictatorial nature and his failure to stop the Japanese incursions on the coast during World War I made him unpopular, and he died in disgrace in 1916.

For the next decade China was in anarchy, ruled by warlords (local strong men, often ex-bandits) with private armies. More important was the fast growth of fanatical nationalism among the urban classes, particularly the educated youth. Sun was the theoretical leader of this movement, but he was a poor organizer, and the national party he founded, the **Kuomintang,** or *KMT,* split into many factions during the 1920s.

The whole nationalist-reformist phase of China's development in the early twentieth century is called the **May Fourth Movement** because of an incident in 1919 when thousands of Beijing students and youth protested the Versailles Treaty's gift of a part of China to Japan for having participated in the war. The movement had no single leader, and its various subgroups went off in many directions. Eventually, the heightened national feeling and the reform ideas it propagated would provide some of the momentum for the communist takeover after World War II. Mao Zedong himself was one of the outraged students who swore that China would no longer be the pawn of foreigners and capitalists who exploited Chinese backwardness.

Chiang Kai-Shek's Regime and Chinese Communism

Sun Yat-sen's most able and aggressive lieutenant was *Chiang Kai-shek,* who headed the KMT's military branch. After the founder's death in 1925, Chiang moved quickly to take over leadership, while maintaining the liaison with the tiny Chinese Communist Party (CCP) that Sun had established in the early 1920s to assist in modernizing the state. In 1926, Chiang felt himself strong enough to go after the warlords who had made themselves into petty kings in the north and northeast and bring them under effective central control. This Northern Expedition was a success, and several provinces were recovered. Strengthened by this and by the increasing support of Chinese financial circles, Chiang decided to finish off the communists who had displayed disturbing support in Shanghai and a few other coastal cities. In 1927, he conducted a sweeping blood purge of all suspected communists, killing tens of thousands before it was over. The CCP appeared to have suffered an irremediable defeat. Chiang was clearly in control and established himself as the president of a national KMT government in Beijing a few months later.

The Kuomintang government under Chiang (1928–1975) was a barely disguised dictatorship, led by a man who believed in force as the ultimate political argument. He had married a westernized Chinese plutocrat who acted as his intermediary when dealing with Western governments throughout his long career. Madame Chiang was the daughter of immensely wealthy and very conservative business people, and her opinions had great influence. Chiang believed the obstacles to making China into a sovereign, respected state were first the Japanese and then the communists; as time passed, however, that order

■ **Chiang Kai-shek and Madame Chiang.** The newsweekly *Time* selected Chiang and his spouse as "Man and Wife of the Year, 1937." Madame Chiang handled much of the diplomacy of China with the Western powers in this epoch.

began to reverse. The CCP had staged a quick recovery from the events of 1927 and, within a few years, had established a strong base among the peasants in south China.

Knowing that he did not as yet have the strength to challenge the superior weaponry and training of the Japanese, Chiang threw his 700,000-man army against the communists, driving them from their rural strongholds into the famous **Long March of 1934,** an epic of guerrilla war. Under their rising star Mao Zedong, an original force of perhaps 100,000 poorly armed peasants wandered more than 6,000 miles through western China. A year later, the 10,000 or so survivors of starvation and combat barricaded themselves in Shensi in the far northwest near the Mongolian border. Here, during the remainder of the 1930s, they preached the Marxist gospel to the desperately poor peasants around them. In this, they were following Mao's new precept: the Chinese peasants are a true revolutionary force, and no revolution will succeed without them. Mao pursued peasant support in clever and concrete ways. He never spoke of collectivization, but only of justice, lower interest rates, and fair distribution of land. The members of the CCP became village teachers— the first ever in this province—and made sure that the communist army did not behave like earlier Chinese armies and "liberate" what they needed and wanted from the helpless farmers. Soon the peasants were sufficiently impressed with Mao's forces that they began to join them.

The Sino-Japanese War and the Maoist Challenge

We sometimes forget that for four years prior to Pearl Harbor the Japanese and Chinese were engaged in a bloody war. This conflict had actually begun with the Japanese aggression in Manchuria in 1931, but had been sporadic until a minor incident in the summer of 1937 gave the Japanese commanders the pretext they had long sought. After a few months of fighting, the two major cities of Beijing and Nanjing had fallen, and much of coastal China was under Japanese control.

Instead of submitting and becoming a Japanese puppet as expected, Chiang elected to move his government many hundreds of miles west and attempt to hold out until he could find allies. The move inland meant, however, that Chiang was isolated from his main areas of support. Further, in the west the KMT army and officials appeared to the local people as a swarm of devouring locusts. Famine was endemic in this poverty-stricken region, and official corruption was widespread. Much of the KMT army was forcibly recruited, as conscription was equivalent to a death sentence.

Morale deteriorated steadily under these conditions, while Chiang refused to fight the Japanese invader. After the attack on Pearl Harbor, he had decided that Tokyo would eventually be defeated by the Americans, and that the communists under Mao were China's real enemy. Protected in his mountainous refuge, he wanted to husband his forces to use against Mao. When the war ended in 1945, Chiang was the commander of a large, but poorly equipped and demoralized garrison army that had no combat experience and was living parasitically on its own people.

The Maoists, on the other hand, made steady progress in winning over the anti-Japanese elements among the people, especially the peasants. They claimed to be nationalists and patriots as well as reformers, and they fought the invader at every opportunity from their bases in the northwest. Mao set up a local government system that was far more just and more respectful of the peasants than the KMT had been, and he introduced democratic practices that won the communists the support of many of the

intellectuals and the workers. Mao's armed force grew by large numbers during the war years to a total of almost a million men in organized units, plus many thousands of guerrilla fighters behind the Japanese lines. The CCP set up mass organizations with branches in every village for women, youth, educators, and others.

Communist Victory

During the war with Japan, there was little armed conflict between the KMT and the communist forces. Chiang was biding his time until the Japanese had been defeated. At the war's end, his army was about three times the size of Mao's, and he was confident of victory. The civil war broke out soon after the Japanese surrender. The United States at first backed Chiang with supplies and money, but could not counter the effects of years of corrupt KMT rule, inaction, and failure on Chiang's part to appreciate what China's masses wanted. While the KMT armies deserted, the communist forces enjoyed wide and growing support. The superior fighting spirit and military tactics of the Maoists turned the tide decisively in 1948, when Beijing and the big port cities fell into their hands.

By October 1949 all of China was under Mao's control, and Chiang with several hundred thousand KMT men were refugees on the island of Taiwan. Here, they set up a regime that called itself the Republic of China and was recognized as the legitimate government of China by the anticommunist world for some time to come. But "Red" China (properly the People's Republic of China or PRC), with the world's largest population, was now presumably a devoted ally of the Soviet Union under the ruthless communist Mao and was aiming at world revolution side by side with the Soviets.

✤ Japan

The Emergence of Modern Japan

In the mid-nineteenth century, Japan's two centuries of seclusion under the Tokugawa shoguns ended, and the country began to be transformed. The trigger for this was the forceful "opening of Japan" by the American Commodore Matthew Perry in 1853 and 1854; in the name of international commerce, Perry extorted a treaty from the shogun that allowed U.S. ships to dock and do business in Japanese ports. This treaty was soon followed by similar agreements with the European trading nations. With the country divided over whether to allow the "palefaced barbarians" into the ports, a brief civil war broke out

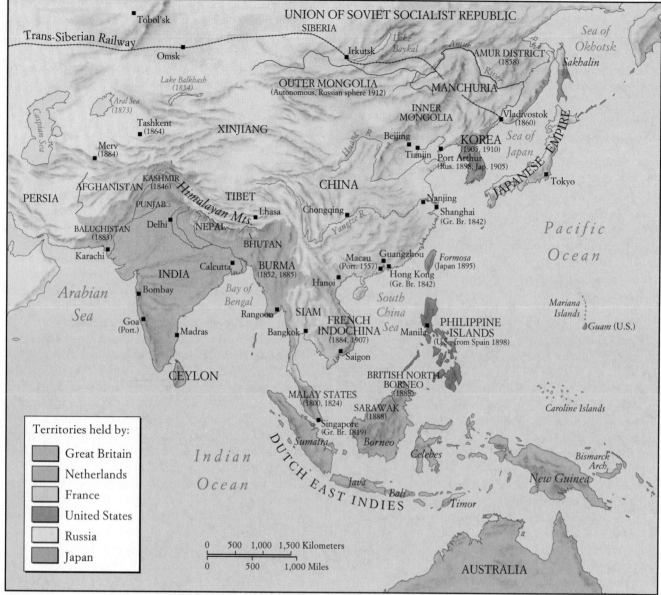

MAP 51.1 East Asian Colonial Territories, 1840–1940. Shown here are the accessions of colonial domains by the West in east Asia during the era of New Imperialism. Only Thailand (Siam) escaped.

among the *daimyo* lords for the shogun's power. During the war, a few resident foreigners were molested. In 1863, a retaliatory attack by Western naval forces revealed how far Japan had fallen behind in the arts of war. Japan seemed on the brink of being reduced to the same helplessness as China. But at this point, a decisive difference emerged. Some of the daimyo and samurai faced the causes and consequences of Japanese impotence squarely:

they decided to *imitate the West as rapidly as possible*. These men engineered the revolt against the shogunate in 1868 that is termed the **Meiji Restoration** because in a formal sense the emperor was restored to the center of political-governmental life and the shogunate was abolished. In control, however, were the powerful daimyo who had seen that the semifeudal shogunate was obsolete and now replaced it with a new style of government. Starting in 1871, one major reform after another came out of the imperial capital in Tokyo (formerly Edo), and all of them were modeled on the West. Unlike their neighbors across the China Sea, the Japanese leaders were willing and able to add up the pluses and minuses of accepting Western ideas and come to definite, consensual decisions about them. Then the reforms were systematically carried out even at the expense of cherished tradition.

Meiji Reforms

The major reforms of the Meiji Restoration included the following:

1. *Military.* The daimyo and samurai were removed in favor of a conscript army with a modern organization.
2. *Financial.* A new national tax system and a new national bank and currency were established.
3. *Agrarian.* Land was redistributed, and ownership was established clearly and securely.
4. *Constitutional.* In 1889, an entirely new constitution was framed by a group of notables. The constitution gave the parliamentary vote to a small electorate and allowed the emperor considerable power over the government elected by the parliament.

By no means did all Japanese support these reforms. The samurai majority were so discontented by their total loss of status (even their precious swords were taken from them in 1876) that they several times attempted to rebel, only to be crushed by the new army. The new tax system, which required money payments to the government, rather than service to the daimyo, reduced many peasants from landowners to tenants. But after twenty years, the reform element in Tokyo was unshakably entrenched.

Students were sent abroad by the hundreds annually to study Western science and Western government. For a time, everything Western was highly fashionable in Japan from pocket watches to Darwinian biology. As elsewhere, the most potent of all the Western influences was the modern sense of *nationalism,* which struck Japanese youth just as strongly as it had Chinese. New political parties sprang up and vigorously contested the seats in the lower house of the Diet (parliament). The constitution of 1889 was modeled after the German constitution authored by Bismarck and reserved decisive powers to the wealthy voters and the imperial ministers. The *emperor was sovereign,* not the people. He was also commander-in-chief of the armed forces, and the ministers answered solely to him, not to the parliament. Only about 5 percent of the male population had the franchise.

At the same time, the Meiji leaders made sure that the ancient regime and the traditional values of the people were held in high esteem. The Shinto faith, which revered the emperor as the quasi-divine leader of his country, was strongly supported by the reformers as part of Japan's heritage. The constitution (which remained in force until 1945) explicitly stated that "the empire of Japan shall be governed by a line of emperors unbroken forever." No attempt was made to throw out what the Meiji reformers thought of as truly Japanese. Rather, the reform consciously—and successfully—aimed at making Japanese of all classes into good patriot-citizens.

Industrial development received much attention from the outset. Government funds were directed to railroad construction, shipyards, mines, and munitions under the supervision of foreign technicians. Later in the 1890s, many of these costly enterprises were sold at bargain rates to combinations of individual investors. Thus began the peculiar Japanese form of government-assisted large corporations called *zaibatsu,* which came to dominate the nation's economy. New banks were founded to provide credit for entrepreneurs, and the internal transport of people and goods was greatly eased by the construction of a dense network of railways. Mountainous terrain and the island geography had caused much of Japan's population to be physically isolated until the early twentieth century; the railroads changed that.

Agriculture became more productive as taxes were paid in fixed amounts of money rather than produce, and peasants were able for the first time to buy and sell land freely. Silk was the big money crop, rising from 2.3 million pounds in 1870 to 93 million in 1929. Japan's mechanization of silk production practically blew the Chinese out of the world market they had previously dominated. Rice production also rose sharply, more than doubling in tonnage produced in one generation's time.

Foreign Successes

The *foreign policy* of Meiji Japan was aggressive and grew more so as time went on. The challenge to "big brother" China in 1895 was a great success. Another success was the gradual elimination of the **unequal treaties** signed with the Western powers in the 1850s and 1860s. Like China, the Japanese authorities had at first agreed to a series of treaties that allowed Westerners to enjoy extraterritoriality. Persistent negotiations reversed this situation by the end of the century, and Japan became the first Asian power in modern times to treat Europeans as equals.

■ **Little Samurai on Parade.** Rituals such as this were very popular during the 1930s as the Japanese military prepared for war with China.

But the big breakthrough for Japanese foreign prestige was the *Russo-Japanese War of 1904–1905.* This war, the first between an Asian and a European nation that ended in victory for the Asians, announced to the world that Japan had arrived as a major power. The takeover of Korea was a major result of the war, and the Japanese nationalists felt cheated that they had not obtained more from the beaten Russians. They would have their chance a few years later, when the Bolshevik revolution made Russia temporarily helpless. After nominally participating on the Allied side in World War I, Japan attempted to seize eastern Siberia from the Soviets. Pressured mainly by the United States, the Japanese agreed to evacuate in 1922, but kept their eyes firmly on the huge border province of Manchuria as a possible field for imperial expansion.

Between the World Wars

The foundation of civil government in Japan was aided substantially by the fact that economic prosperity for the upper and middle classes continued without setback for the entire reign of the first Meiji emperor (1868–1912). World War I then gave the entire economy a boost, but also created severe inflation that caused serious rioting among the working class in 1918. The 1920s and 1930s saw a weakening of party government and a strengthening of the *army in politics,* a factor that Japan had not previously experienced. The career officers often resented their diminished position in Japanese life compared to what the samurai had once had. Considering themselves the most devoted and reliable exponents of all that was good in Japanese culture, they came to hold the civilian politicians in contempt.

In the early and most difficult years of the Great Depression, the officers' ambitions were particularly attracted to resource-rich Manchuria. In 1931, they in effect rebelled against the Tokyo civil government and seized the province from the very weak hands of China. From this point onward, Japan's army was engaged in an *undeclared war against China and also against its own government in Tokyo.* The Chinese war became an open struggle only after 1937, but the war against the party government was already won in 1932. From that year, the military was in effective command of Japan's domestic and foreign policies. Any civilians who opposed the aggressive and self-confident generals and admirals were soon silenced.

In 1936, Japan joined the Hitler-sponsored Anti-Comintern Pact. By 1937, Japan was formally at war with Chiang Kai-shek's government and had close to a million men in China. The alliance with Hitler (and Mussolini) was supposedly strengthened by the signing of the 1940 Tripartite (three-sided) Pact, but the Japanese resented not being informed of Hitler's decision to go to war against the West in 1939. When Germany decided to attack Russia in 1941, the Japanese were again not informed, and they decided to remain neutral despite the provisions of the pact and German anger. The Japanese had, in fact, little to do with their supposed ally throughout World War II. The war in the Pacific was indeed almost entirely separate from the European conflict in timing, motivation, and contestants.

The Japanese *attacked Pearl Harbor* in December 1941 because the Tokyo military command was convinced that war was inevitable if the United States would not go along with Japan's plans for expansion in Asia. Since the U.S. government showed no signs of changing its expressed resistance after long negotiations, the Tokyo general staff wished to strike first and hope that greater willpower would overcome greater resources.

For about eight months it seemed that the Japanese might be correct. Then, with the great naval battles of the mid-Pacific in the summer of 1942, the tides of war changed. From that point on, it was apparent to most observers (including many of Japan's leaders) that the best Japan could hope for was a negotiated peace that would leave it the dominant power in the western Pacific. Those hopes steadily diminished and were finally dashed with the explosions over Hiroshima and Nagasaki in August 1945.

✤ SOUTHEASTERN ASIA: THE COLONIAL EMPIRES

Although China and Japan managed to maintain their formal independence from the Europeans, the Asians in the extreme south and in the Pacific Islands were not so fortunate. In the nineteenth century, all those who had not already become part of a European empire fell under one or another of the great powers, except Thailand, which played off various rivals and thereby retained independence.

In the middle of the century, *Burma,* which had been independent, fell under British rule through war and was united to British India. At the same time, the British possession of *Malaya* and especially *Singapore,* the port at its tip, were experiencing a great economic upsurge. The tin and rubber of interior Malaya attracted much British capital and Chinese labor. By the end of the century, Singapore was a large city serving shipping from around the industrial world. The ruling group was entirely British, but the Chinese dominated trade and commerce, and their wealth enabled them to maintain equality with the Europeans in all except political matters.

The *French possessions* centered on *Indochina,* or Vietnam, Laos, and Cambodia as they are now called. The French had seized Indochina by stages, starting in the 1850s. They took advantage of the differing orientations of the northern and southern Vietnamese, which have long been a hallmark of this people. The people of the north were strongly attracted to Chinese ways, while those of the south were oriented toward the Khmer culture of Cambodia. In 1859, France seized Saigon and a few years later Cambodia. Following a brief war with China in 1885, the French then took over all of Vietnam and Laos.

In time, tens of thousands of French came to Indochina to make their careers and/or fortunes as officials, teachers, rubber plantation owners, and adventurers of all sorts. Like the British in Malaya, the French were able to introduce some beneficial changes into the economy and society, making southern Vietnam, for example, into an enormously fertile rice bowl that exported its product throughout East Asia. Schools were opened in the villages, the practical slavery of women was ended, child marriages were forbidden, and new cash crops (rubber and coffee) were introduced. But as happened everywhere else in Asia, these improvements in social and economic conditions were outweighed in nationalist eyes by the humiliations suffered at the hands of the European conquerors and overlords.

■ **Japanese Advance into Manchuria, 1931.** The artillery pieces are still being horse-drawn, much as in Napoleonic days; but the Japanese army was already an efficient war machine, anxious to demonstrate its prowess against the decrepit Chinese forces.

In *Dutch Indonesia and the Spanish Philippine Islands,* the Europeans behaved from the start as masters while the native peoples had to accommodate themselves to an inferior position in their own countries. The Indonesian islands had been placed under Dutch rule in the early seventeenth century, when bold Hollanders had driven out their Portuguese rivals for the rich spice trade. Since then little had changed: Dutch overlords gradually conquered and replaced native leaders, and a small planter group controlled large estates that produced coffee and sugar at high profits. Despite efforts to assist them, the Indonesian peasants suffered after massive population growth in the nineteenth century turned many of them into landless semiserfs for Dutch and Chinese landlords.

Alone among the Asian lands taken over by Europeans, the Philippines became a nation in which the majority of the population was Christian, and this fact heightened the Filipinos' resentment when Spain still denied them political and social rights. A rebellion against Spanish rule broke out in the late 1890s. It was still going on when the Americans became embroiled in war with Spain and captured the islands (1899–1900).

Since the United States was originally no more inclined to give the Filipinos independence than the Spaniards had been, the rebellion turned against the Americans and persisted for two more years before it was finally extinguished. What had been promoted as a "liberation" became an occupation. Even though American policy became steadily more benevolent and advantageous to the Filipinos and independence was promised in the 1930s, the Philippines had to wait for another decade to pass before attaining sovereignty immediately after World War II.

Summary

China and Japan met the overwhelming challenge of Western intervention in different ways. The Chinese imperial officials, unwilling to leave the false security that Confucian philosophy and many centuries of assured superiority gave them, went down a blind alley of hopeless resistance and denial until they were pushed aside by rebellion and revolution at the beginning of the twentieth century. In contrast, the Japanese upper classes soon recognized the advantages to be gained by selective adoption of Western ways and used them to their own, highly nationalistic ends during the Meiji Restoration of the late nineteenth century.

China's halfhearted and confused experiment with a democratic republic came to an end in World War II, when the corrupt Chiang Kai-shek regime was unable to rally support against either the Japanese or Mao's communists. After a bloody civil war, Mao took Chinese fate in his confident hands.

Japan's civil government was much more stable and successful than China's until the 1930s, when a restive and ambitious military establishment pushed it aside and put the country on a wartime footing with an invasion of China. Then, in 1941, they entered World War II with the attack on Pearl Harbor.

Elsewhere, almost all of East Asia was a European colony until 1945 and was experiencing a buildup of frustrated nationalism among both intellectuals and ordinary folk. This was especially the case after the Asians witnessed the humiliation of Russia by Japan in 1905 and the mutual slaughter of Europeans in World War I. In retrospect, the late nineteenth and early twentieth centuries were the high point of European domination of Asia; after World War II, the tide would turn toward a closer balance in East-West relations.

Test Your Knowledge

1. The bloodiest rebellion in China's history is called
   a. the Boxer Rebellion.
   b. the Nakamura Rising.
   c. the Taiping Rebellion.
   d. the Long March.
2. The "late Manzhou restoration" was
   a. a successful attempt by the bureaucracy to renew itself.
   b. a cultural movement in the late nineteenth century that replaced Western forms with Chinese models of literature and art.
   c. the regeneration of the government by local gentry leaders after the Taiping and Nien Rebellions were put down.
   d. the substitution of a new young emperor for the old empress by the army.
3. The beginning of China's clear inability to withstand outside pressure is found
   a. in the outcome of the Opium Wars.
   b. in the repression of the Boxer Rebellion.
   c. in the defeat at the hands of the Japanese in 1895.
   d. in the concessions in Manchuria to the Russians in 1901.
4. The single most important foreign policy success of post-1853 Japan was
   a. winning the war against China in 1895.
   b. forcing the Boxer rebels to surrender in China in 1901.
   c. winning the war against Russia in 1904–1905.
   d. signing the Anglo-Japanese Treaty of 1902.
5. The Meiji Restoration in Japan saw
   a. the return of the emperor to personal governing power.
   b. a turning away from the West to a renewed isolation.
   c. the reinstallation of the samurai and daimyo to power.
   d. the adoption of Western techniques and ideas by Japan's rulers.

6. Which of the following places was not made into a European colony?
   a. Thailand
   b. Indonesia
   c. Malaya
   d. Burma

7. The most important Asian group in the foreign trade of Southeast Asia was the
   a. Japanese.
   b. Chinese.
   c. Vietnamese.
   d. Indians.

Identification Terms

Boxer Rebellion	May Fourth Movement	Self-Strengthening	Taipings
Kuomintang	Meiji Restoration	Sun Yat-sen	unequal treaties
Long March of 1934	Opium Wars		

Bibliography

A general overview of China and Japan in this period is given in C. Schirokauer, *Modern China and Japan: A Brief History,* 1982, and in E. O. Reischauer, et al., *East Asia: Tradition and Transformation,* 1973. See also the histories of both nations cited in the bibliographies of Chapters 40 and 41.

China

Eastman, L. E. *Seeds of Destruction: Nationalist China in War and Revolution, 1937–49,* 1984. An excellent account of what happened to Chiang Kai-shek's government and army.

Fairbank, J. K. *China: A New History,* 1992. By the master of American Sinology in the twentieth century.

Fay, P. W. *The Opium War,* 1975, and A. Waley, *The Opium War through Chinese Eyes,* 1958, are important to understanding how the Europeans established themselves in China.

Latourette, K. *A History of Christian Missions in China,* 1929. Shows the anti-Christian background of the Boxer Rebellion. See also J. Fairbank, *The Missionary Enterprise in China and America,* 1974, for a focus on the U.S. presence and its effects.

Salisbury, H. A fascinating account of a fiftieth-anniversary reconstruction of the Long March of 1934, accompanying some of the veterans of the original trek.

Schiffrin, H. *Sun Yat-sen and the Origins of the Chinese Revolution.* Explains the desperation of the younger generation of reformers in the late nineteenth century.

Schwartz, B. I. *Chinese Communism and the Rise of Mao,* 1951. Covers the pre-1949 Communist Party of China and its leaders. Other aspects of the early twentieth-century revolutionary ferment are looked at in B. Schwartz, ed., *Reflections on the May Fourth Movement,* 1972.

Snow, E. *Red Star over China,* 1942. A sympathetic account by an American journalist of Mao's peasant republic in Shensi.

Spence, J. *The Gate of Heavenly Peace: The Chinese in Their Revolution, 1895–1945,* 1986. A fine account of how the modernizing movement was shaped by several representative men and women.

Wakeman, F., Jr. *The Fall of Imperial China,* 1975. A standard treatment of the last decades of the empire.

Japan

Kiyooka, E., trans. *The Autobiography of Fukuzawa Yukichi,* 1966. A good view into the transition between traditional and Westernizing Japan in the late nineteenth century. R. Ward, ed., *Political Development in Modern Japan,* is an anthology that surveys post–Meiji Restoration affairs.

Butow, R. *Tojo and the Coming of the War,* 1961. Looks at interwar militarism in Tokyo.

Craig, A. M., ed. *Japan: A Comparative View,* 1979. A controversial and thoroughly interesting book, strong on comparisons between Japan and others.

Dore, R., ed. *Aspects of Social Change in Modern Japan,* 1967, and J. Hunter, *The Emergence of Modern Japan: An Introductory History since 1853,* 1989, are recent and good for political and social overviews. Economic topics are well covered in G. C. Allen, *A Short Economic History of Japan, 1867–1937,* 1972.

Iriye, A. *After Imperialism: The Search for a New Order in East Asia,* 1978. One of the best surveys of Japanese foreign policy in the opening half of the century.

Keene, D., ed. *Modern Japanese Literature: An Anthology,* 1960. Perhaps the best introduction to twentieth-century Japanese novels, stories, and general literature.

Myers, R. H., and M. R. Peattie, eds. *The Japanese Colonial Empire, 1895–1945,* 1984. A recent review of this topic.

WORLD WAR II

For the first fifteen years after the end of World War I, the peace held together. Despite the bitter complaints of the losers, especially the Germans, the Paris treaties were backed up by French diplomacy and the potential application of military force by France and Britain. For a brief period in the late 1920s, the Germans voluntarily adopted a policy of "fulfillment," adhering to the provisions of the treaties.

But with the worldwide economic collapse and the coming of Adolf Hitler to power in the early 1930s, the treaties were once again criticized and an atmosphere of international hostility resumed. The impotence of the League of Nations was quickly evident, and Hitler successfully bluffed his way forward until he felt himself in an invulnerable position to undertake a war of vengeance and conquest.

✤ THE RISE AND FALL OF COLLECTIVE SECURITY

When the French saw the U.S. Senate reject Woodrow Wilson's League of Nations and realized that the British were having second thoughts about their war-time alliance with the French, they hurriedly took independent steps to protect France from potential German revenge. To this end, France signed a military alliance with Poland, Czechoslovakia, and Romania, three of Germany's eastern neighbors. This *Little Entente* assured that if Germany attacked any of the signatories, the others would give assistance. France stayed on good terms with newly Fascist Italy through the 1920s. And the French consistently argued that the League must take unified action against any potential aggressor nation; an attack on one was an attack against all.

Faltering Alliances

Even before Hitler's seizure of power, this collective security, as it was dubbed, was under severe strain. For one thing, the aggressive stirring of international revolutionary hopes by the Bolsheviks meant that Soviet Russia was an outcast; for years, it was not invited to join the League of Nations and was not considered a suitable ally by the capitalist democracies. For another, Japan, a member of the League, totally disregarded the League's disapproval of its invasion of Manchuria in 1931 and got away with the aggression without penalty. The League could only express its moral condemnation; the members never considered punishing Japan militarily or economically. The League's impotence was revealed even more clearly in 1935 in a case that was much closer to European affairs. Hoping to revive his popularity with the Italian people, Benito Mussolini started a blatantly imperialistic war with Ethiopia. He claimed that this practically unknown African territory should be the kernel of a great Italian empire-to-be. The Ethiopians appealed to the League and obtained a vote that clearly branded Italy as an aggressor nation. After much maneuvering, outraged public opinion in France and Britain forced the governments to impose economic sanctions (penalties such as boycotts) on Mussolini. But neither Paris nor London would take potentially decisive measures such as banning oil shipments to Italy, which had no oil of its own. In the end, the Italian invaders were not threatened. The League had been shown to have no teeth and did not play a role in European conflicts thereafter. Collective security had been struck a hard, but not yet lethal blow.

The Spanish Civil War

All hope for collective security was finished off by the Spanish Civil War, which broke out in the summer of 1936. Despite open support for the rebel forces from both Mussolini and Hitler, the Western democracies refused to take sides and declared an embargo on shipments of arms and materiel to both contestants. In the circumstances, this was the same as assisting the rebels led by General Francisco Franco, a Fascist sympathizer, against the legitimate Spanish government.

Spain in the 1930s was a sharply divided nation. Its liberals had recently forced out an ineffectual monarch and declared a republic. But the public remained divided between every variety of Leftist group, moderate democrats, Fascists and even monarchists who pined for a return of the eighteenth century. Franco's rebellion had been inspired by the socialist-communist leanings of many of the republican government's officials and supporters. Like most of the Spanish upper classes, many army commanders were (rightly) afraid that Spain might soon come under a communist government if current trends were not checked. To prevent a communist takeover, they were quite ready to enter into civil war, supported by the Catholic church, much of the peasantry, and most of the middle classes.

Josef Stalin early decided that the Spanish conflict was a golden opportunity for the Soviet Union to gain popularity among the many Western anti-Fascists who harbored doubts about communism as well. The Comintern orchestrated an international campaign to assist the outnumbered and outgunned Spanish Loyalists in the name of a **Popular Front** against Fascism. For two years, the Soviets abandoned their previous propaganda efforts against the democratic socialists in all countries, and for the first time since 1919, socialists and communists were allies. Much Soviet aid was sent to Spain, and some tens of thousands of volunteers from all over the world (including the United States) came to fight with the Loyalists.

But Hitler's and Mussolini's arms and advisers were more numerous and more effective in the long run. By the fall of 1938 the Spanish government's forces were reduced to small areas around the cities of Madrid and Barcelona. In the spring of 1939, the Loyalists surrendered, and Franco established himself as the military dictator of his country for the next generation. Though friendly to the Fascist dictators, he stubbornly defended his freedom of action and never allowed himself to be their tool. Spain sat out World War II as a neutral.

✤ HITLER'S MARCH TO WAR: 1935–1939

Although Mussolini made no effort to conceal his contempt for the Western democracies, it was Germany, much more than Italy, that represented the real danger to the Paris treaties. Hitler had sworn to overturn the Treaty of Versailles even before gaining power, and he proceeded to take Germany out of the League of Nations almost immediately—in 1933.

Whether Hitler intended a major war from the outset of his dictatorship is still much debated. Historians generally agree that he realized that the program he had described in *Mein Kampf* could only be made reality through war, because it entailed a major expansion of German territory eastward into Slavic lands (Poland and Russia). But he seems to have had no concrete plans for war until about 1936, when he instructed the General Staff to prepare them.

In 1935, Hitler formally renounced the provisions of the Versailles Treaty that limited German armaments; this move had symbolic rather than practical importance, as the treaty limitations had been ignored even during the Weimar era. A few months later, he started conscription for a much larger army and the creation of a large *Luftwaffe* (air force). Neither France, which was badly torn between Leftist and Fascist sympathies, nor Britain, in the throes of an economic crisis that seemed beyond the government's ability to cope, reacted beyond a few words of diplomatic dismay and disapproval.

The Reoccupation of the Rhineland

In 1936, Hitler sent a small force into the **Rhineland,** the area of Germany west of the Rhine on the French borders. Under the Versailles and Locarno agreements, the Rhineland was supposed to be permanently demilitarized; to the French, stationing German troops there was a direct threat to their security. But in the moment of decision, France said that it did not want to act alone, and Britain would not support France in an action that might lead to major war. What the British and French did not know was that the German army was more frightened of the consequences of the Rhineland adventure than they were; the General Staff advised Hitler not to try this ploy because the army as yet was in no condition to resist Allied attacks. Hitler insisted on proceeding with his bluff and scored a great psychic and diplomatic triumph over his own generals as well as the French.

From 1936 on, Hitler's policies grew ever bolder. Germany was rapidly re-arming, while France and Britain were paralyzed by defeatism or pacifism among both the general public and the government officials. In Britain, where the English Channel still gave a false feeling of security, many members of the Conservative government leaned toward appeasement and were ready to abandon France. Much of the party leadership was more fearful of a Bolshevik revolution than of a Fascist or Nazi society. Some of the far Right hoped that a Hitler-like figure would rise in Britain and put "order" back into the country. The French, for their part, put all their hopes into the huge defensive network—the Maginot Line—built during the 1920s along their eastern borders, and on their allies in the Little Entente.

Also in 1936, Hitler and Mussolini reached a close understanding, the *Axis Pact,* which made them allies in case of war. This agreement eliminated any hopes the French might have had that if Mussolini had to choose, he would side with France and against Germany.

Anschluss in Austria

Hitler, an Austrian by birth, had always intended to bring about the "natural union" of his birthplace with Germany. The *Anschluss* (joining) was explicitly forbidden by the Versailles Treaty, but by this time that was a dead letter. In Austria, the Nazis had strong support; most Austrians were German by blood, and they regarded the enforced separation from the Reich as an act of vengeance by the Allies. An earlier attempt at a Nazi coup in 1934 had failed because of Mussolini's resistance. Now, in 1938,

Mussolini was Hitler's ally, and the *Anschluss* could go forward. It was completed in March by a bloodless occupation of the small country on Germany's southern borders, and Nazi rule was thus extended to another 7 million people.

Next to fall was the Successor state of Czechoslovakia, a country created by the Versailles Treaty that Hitler had always hated. Linked militarily with France, it contained within its borders 3.5 million Germans, the *Sudetenlander* minority who were strongly pro-Hitler. Under the direction of Berlin, the Sudeten Germans agitated against the democratic, pro-Western government in Prague. Concessions were made, but the Germans always demanded more. After the *Anschluss* in Austria, it appeared only a matter of time before the Germans acted. The attitude of the British government was the key; if Britain supported armed resistance, the French promised to honor their treaty obligation and move against Germany.

Munich: 1938

In September 1938, Hitler brought the British prime minister Neville Chamberlain and the French premier Edouard Daladier to a **conference at Munich,** where they were joined by Mussolini. After several days of threats and negotiations, Hitler succeeded in extracting the Munich Agreements from the democratic leaders. The agreements gave him Czechoslovakia on a platter, although he had to wait a few months before taking the final slice. Chamberlain returned to Britain waving a piece of paper that he claimed guaranteed "peace in our time." One year later, Britain and Germany were at war.

Almost before the ink was dry on the Munich Agreements, Hitler started pressuring Poland about its treatment of its German minority. These Germans lived in solid blocs on the borders with Germany and in the so-called Free City of Danzig (Gdansk) in the Polish Corridor to the sea between Germany and its province of East Prussia (see Map 52.1).

Prodded by British public opinion and the speeches of Winston Churchill in Parliament, Chamberlain now at last moved firmly. In March 1939, he signed a pact with Poland, guaranteeing British (and French) aid if Germany attacked. Hitler did not take this promise seriously, as he knew that the Allies could aid Poland only by attacking Germany in the West. But the French, having put their military in an entirely defensive orientation behind the Maginot Line, were not prepared to go on the offensive. Of more concern to Hitler was the attitude of the other great power in the east, the Soviet Union.

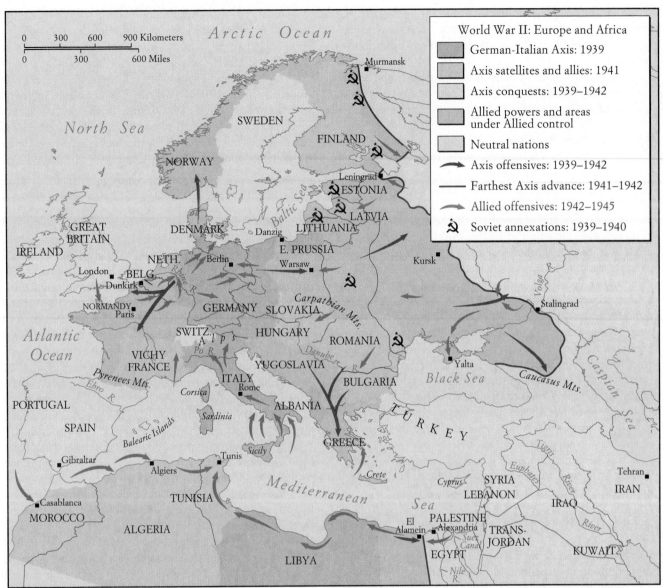

⦿ MAP 52.1 World War II in Europe. In contrast to the first World War 1914–1918, World War II was decided militarily as much or more on the eastern fronts as in the west. Until the war's end, the largest part of Nazi forces was deployed in Russia and occupied east Europe. Civil and military casualties far outstripped those of World War I, again mainly in the east where slave labor was extensively recruited and the extermination camps were located.

The Nazi-Soviet Non-Aggression Pact

At this point, the only convincing threat to Hitler's war plans was the possibility of having to face the Soviet Union in the east and the Allies in the west simultaneously—the two-front war that had proved disastrous in 1914–1918. But even at this stage, neither Chamberlain nor Daladier nor their conservative advisers could bring themselves to ask Stalin to enter an alliance.

In fact, the Russians were equally suspicious of the West's motives as Paris and London were of Moscow. Stalin had not forgotten that the Soviet Union had been excluded from the postwar arrangements and treaties. Nor had he overlooked the fact that when the chips were down, Britain and France had sacrificed their ally Czechoslovakia rather than coordinate action with the Soviet Union, as Stalin had offered to do through Czech intermediaries.

Even so, it was a terrific shock to communists and to all anti-Fascists everywhere to hear, on August 23, 1939, that Stalin and Hitler, whose states were mortal enemies dedicated to one another's destruction, had signed a **Non-Aggression Pact.** By its terms, the Soviet Union agreed to remain neutral in a war involving Germany. In return, in a secret addition to the pact, Hitler agreed that the Russians could occupy the three small Baltic states, eastern Poland, and a slice of Romania, areas that had once belonged to Russia and were still claimed by the Soviets. Both sides affirmed their "friendship." The Non-Aggression Pact made war certain. Hitler no longer had to worry about what Russia might do if he attacked Poland and the Allies came to the Poles' aid as they had promised.

For communists all over the world, the pact represented a 180-degree turn in the party line for which they were entirely unprepared. Hitler, the killer of the German communists, the destroyer of Spanish freedom, and the chief threat to peace, was now the head of a friendly government. The Popular Front died overnight. Many members of the Communist Party outside the Soviet Union dropped out, unable to swallow this latest subordination of truth and others' national interests to the momentary advantage of the Soviets. But Stalin had gained some time; the Soviet Union did not enter World War II for almost two more years. Whether he used the time well is a topic of debate to the present day.

✤ WORLD WAR II

World War II can be divided into three major chronological periods and two geographic areas. Chronologically, the first phase of the conflict saw the German and later the Japanese victories and expansion from 1939 to late 1942. The second phase was the Allied counterattack from late 1942 through 1943, which checked and contained both enemies. The third phase was the steady Allied advance in 1944 and 1945, bringing final victory in August of the latter year.

The European Theater

Geographically, the European theater (including North Africa) was the focus of Allied efforts until the German surrender in May 1945. Then, the emphasis shifted to the Pacific, but the anti-Japanese campaign was unexpectedly shortened by the atomic bombs and Japan's ensuing surrender. The United States, alone among the belligerents, played an important role on both fronts; the Pacific theater was fundamentally a conflict between Japan and the United States. The Soviet Union was drawn into the European war in mid-1941, but maintained neutrality with Germany's ally Japan until the final three weeks. (In the present treatment, the Pacific war will be considered an adjunct of the European theater, as indeed it was for all combatants except Japan and China.)

Phase One: Axis Blitzkrieg

The German *blitzkrieg* machine smashed into Poland on September 1, 1939 (see Map 52.1). Britain and France retaliated by declaring war on Germany two days later. Italy remained neutral for the time being (the Axis Pact did not demand immediate assistance to the other partner.) So did Germany's other ally, Japan, and the United States, Spain, the Scandinavian countries, and the Balkan countries. The Soviet Union remained neutral as well, but moved quickly to occupy the promised segments of eastern Europe in accord with the Non-Aggression Pact.

Poland fell almost at once to the well-trained, well-armed Germans despite brave resistance. The eastern half of the country was occupied by Soviet forces. For several months, all was quiet (the *Sitzkrieg*); then, in the spring of 1940, Hitler struck. France fell to the German tanks (now assisted by the Italians) within a few weeks. Denmark, the Netherlands, Belgium, and Norway had been overwhelmed prior to France. By July, Britain stood alone against a Nazi regime that controlled Europe from the Russian border to the Pyrenees.

For the next several months, the Luftwaffe attempted to bomb England into submission, as many experts feared would be possible with the huge new planes and their large bomb loads. But the Battle of Britain, fought entirely in the air, ended with a clear victory for the defenders. The Channel was still under British control, and Hitler's plans for an invasion, like those of Napoleon a century and a half earlier, had to be abandoned. Just before the fall of France, Churchill had replaced Chamberlain as head of the British government, and he personified the "British bulldog" who would never give up. His magnificent speeches and leadership rallied the British people, cemented the growing Anglo-American sympathies, and played a key role in the Allies' eventual victory (see the Biography in this chapter).

The high point of the war for the Nazis came in 1941, when attacks on Yugoslavia (April), Greece (May), and the Soviet Union (June) were all successful. The Germans gained huge new territories and turned all of eastern Europe and western Russia into either a Nazi satellite (Romania, Bulgaria, Hungary) or an occupied land.

Operation Barbarossa, the code name for the attack on Russia, got off to a tremendous start, as Stalin's government was caught entirely by surprise despite repeated warnings from spies and Allied sources. The Soviets lost huge numbers of men and equipment in the first few weeks. In the first two days alone, some 2,000 Russian planes were destroyed on the ground, and a half million men were taken prisoner by the end of the first month. The Red Army, still recovering from the purge of its officers in 1937–1938 looked as though it had been all but knocked out of the war. At this critical point, Hitler overruled his generals and insisted on diverting many of his forces southward, toward the grain and oil of Ukraine and the Black Sea area, rather than heading straight for Moscow. As a consequence, the Germans were struck by the numbing cold of an early winter before they could take the capital, and Stalin was given precious time to rally and reinforce. The desperate Moscow defenses held through November, and the Germans had to retreat some distance under Russian counterattack. For all practical purposes, the Germans had lost their chance for a decisive victory on the Eastern Front already in the fall of 1941.

Phase 2: Allied Counterattack

In December 1941, the Japanese attack on Pearl Harbor brought the United States into the war against Japan and its allies Germany and Italy. The United States under President Franklin D. Roosevelt was already on the verge of hostilities with Germany, as the U.S. government had taken various steps to help Britain since 1940. As the oppressive nature of the German occupation regime in Europe became known to the American public, opinion began running strongly in support of London and against Berlin. Thus the attack on Pearl Harbor only accelerated a process which was already underway toward the entry of the United States into the conflict.

In many ways the U.S. entry into World War II was similar to its entry into World War I in 1917. Although the American peacetime military was very small and poorly equipped, U.S. industrial resources played the same decisive role they had in World War I. Neither Japan nor Germany had the wherewithal to hold out indefinitely against this power, and in an economic sense, the outcome of the war was decided as early as December 1941.

■ **Ruins of Hamburg, 1945.** The terrible destruction visited upon the German cities by Allied bombing is vividly displayed here. The port of Hamburg was destroyed in two days and nights in 1944 by a huge firestorm set off by incendiary bombs.

But the Allies' eventual victory was far from clear at the time. The Germans had been checked in Russia, but not defeated. Their Italian ally was not much help, but did contribute to the takeover of North Africa and the blockade of the British forces in Egypt. German submarines threatened Britain's supply lines from the United States for the next two years and were defeated (by the convoy system) only after heavy losses.

In the summer of 1942, the Russians were again pushed back hundreds of miles by superior German armor and aircraft. Stalin ordered a "not one step backward" defense of the strategic city of **Stalingrad** on the Volga. Historians agree that the ensuing battle in the fall and winter of 1942 was *the turning point of the war in Europe.* The Nazis suffered the loss of an entire army, which was surrounded and captured; from this point on, they were defending more than attacking.

At the same time, the Western Allies were at last counterattacking. In November 1942, the Americans and British invaded western North Africa, pushing the Germans toward Egypt, while the British army defending the vital Suez Canal attacked westward. In the summer of 1943, the Germans and Italians were driven from Africa, and the Allies landed in southern Italy. After a few months, the discredited Nazi puppet Mussolini fell, and Italy capitulated in September.

A *strategic air war* against Germany was begun at the same time, with waves of U.S. and British bombers attacking the German industrial towns through heavy

Winston Churchill

1874–1965

Each year the American newsmagazine *Time* selects a "Man of the Year" to appear on the cover of the last issue of the year. But a few years ago, *Time* decided that one individual should qualify as Man of the Century. That person was the British statesman, author, artist, and warrior Winston Churchill.

Churchill was born to an American mother and a British aristocratic father in 1874. His father was Lord Randolph Churchill, a stalwart in several Conservative governments of the 1880s. Born to privilege, Winston was a lonely child, unwanted and generally ignored by his very social mother. He was sent to the military academy at Sandhurst and served in India and the Sudan as an army officer. Resigning his commission to have more personal freedom to move about, Churchill covered the Boer War as a correspondent for a London paper. He quickly made a name for himself through his journalistic exploits, especially his escape from Boer captivity.

In 1900, he was elected to the House of Commons as a Tory (Conservative). Four years later, he made the first of several political jumps by joining the rival Liberals and was rewarded by being appointed undersecretary for the colonies in the Liberal government of 1905–1908. Other high posts in succeeding Liberal governments followed, while Churchill developed a solid reputation as an incisive speaker and wily parliamentarian.

But in World War I, as First Sea Lord (that is, secretary of the navy), Churchill suffered a severe blow when the Gallipoli campaign, which he had strongly supported, was an abysmal failure. He was forced out of government for a time, but returned after the war's end to serve in several other posts.

In 1922, he was defeated twice at the polls and then switched back to the Tory side in 1924 as chancellor of the exchequer (minister of finance), a post he held until the Tories were defeated in the elections of 1929. During this period, he strongly upheld the idea of the British Empire and condemned Mohandas Gandhi's campaign for Indian self-government. He also led the opposition to organized labor and the General Strike of 1926. These positions alienated large groups of voters for differing reasons, and after 1929 Churchill was out of office for the entire decade preceding World War II.

During his "exile" in the 1930s, Churchill continued the writing career that had begun with journalism. He wrote a fine biography of his ancestor John Churchill, the duke of Marlborough, and finished his widely admired history of World War I and an autobiography of his early years. But his passion for active politicking could not be satisfied with literary achievement, and he longed to get back into parliamentary action. Churchill was appalled at the inability of the British upper classes to recognize the menace of Hitler and the Fascist movements on the Continent. Again and again, he called on the government to strengthen the country's defenses and to take action against the spread of the Nazi and Italian Fascist aggression. But most politicians regarded him as a "has-been" who could not gracefully accept his defeat

---

antiaircraft fire. How much these attacks contributed to shortening the war is highly debatable; postwar research in Germany indicated that neither the U.S. precision bombing in daylight nor the British nighttime terror bombing did very much damage to the Nazi war effort, at least not until 1945, when the issue had long been decided.

Phase 3: Allied Victory

In Europe, the *tide had turned decisively in 1943*. Italy had surrendered, even though German troops quickly replaced Italians in defending the peninsula against the Allied invaders. Another Allied army landed in the south of France and started pushing northward. In the Balkans,

at the polls and the unpopularity of his views. His refusal to make the least concession to anticolonial feelings also hurt him with the public.

In the fall of 1939, with a major war underway, the government of Neville Chamberlain was forced out by parliamentary vote, and a new prime minister was elected to confront Hitler. Winston Churchill stepped like some fierce, confident bulldog into the seat of power that he had been preparing for since boyhood. Despite the enormous odds, he led Britain through the terrible crisis of 1940–1941, when the country stood alone against the might of Hitler and his Italian ally. For millions of Britons, Churchill was the government, incarnating in his jowly face and stubborn chin the determination not to yield to the enemy's bombs or threats.

In the later years of the war, Churchill along with his American and Soviet colleagues made the final decisions leading to the Nazi surrender in 1945. Almost immediately, he and his party were voted out of office by an electorate that had made enormous sacrifices and now wanted the Labour Party's promised welfare state. Six years later, with the public dissatisfied by Labour's inability to get the economy into high gear, an-

other election returned the Tories and Churchill to power. He governed until his retirement in 1955. The final ten years of his life were dedicated to writing his impressive *History of the English-Speaking Peoples* to go on the shelf next to his magisterial *History of the Second World War* completed earlier. Churchill was known for his biting wit and mental quickness. Once the playwright George Bernard Shaw sent him two tickets to a Shaw premiere. "Bring a friend, if you have one," wrote Shaw on the accompanying note. Churchill returned the tickets with regrets, saying that he could, however, use some for the second performance, "if there is one."

Churchill received almost every honor that his nation could give, but for many years refused a peerage because he wished to remain a member of the more active house of Parliament, the Commons. Finally, in 1953, he accepted a knighthood ("Sir Winston" now became his official name) from the newly crowned Queen Elizabeth, and from then on, he took his seat in the House of Lords. In that same year, he received the Nobel Prize for literature. When he died on January 24, 1965, he was in the eyes of many truly the Man of the Century.

the German occupiers were under heavy attack by partisans (guerrillas) supplied by the Allies. By late 1944, Greece, Yugoslavia, Bulgaria, and Albania had been cleared of Axis forces.

But the main theater of the war in Europe was on the Russian front, where the Germans had the bulk of their forces. Here, the Nazis were forced steadily back, until by

the fall of 1944, they were again on German soil. Poland, Hungary, and Romania had all been freed of the occupiers, and the Red Army became entrenched in those countries, while it pursued the retreating Germans.

The human losses on the Eastern Front were immense. The Nazis had treated the occupied areas with great brutality, taking millions for slave labor in German facto-

■ **The Holocaust: The Extermination Camp at Auschwitz.** After his initial success in the east, Hitler set in motion the machinery for the physical annihilation of Europe's Jews. Shown here is a group of Hungarian Jewish women and children who have just arrived at Auschwitz, a major extermination camp. The picture was taken shortly before their deaths.

ries and mines. Millions more starved to death. The large Jewish populations of Poland, Hungary, and Romania as well as the western Soviet Union were systematically exterminated in the gas chambers of Auschwitz, Belsen, Maidenek, and the other death camps set up by the SS.

Stalin's repeated calls for a *Second Front* in the West were finally answered by the June 1944 invasion across the English Channel by British, American, and Canadian forces (the invasion began on June 6, or **D day**). For the next several months, fighting raged in northern France and Belgium without a decision, but by the winter of 1944–1945, Allied troops were on Germany's western border. The next spring the fighting was carried deep into Germany from both east and west.

On May 1, 1945, a half-mad Hitler committed suicide in the smoking ruins of his Berlin bunker, as the Russians entered the city; several of his closest associates chose the same death, but others fled and were hunted down for trial at Nuremberg as war criminals. Germany's formal surrender—unconditionally this time—took place on May 8. In accordance with previous agreements, the Russians occupied eastern Germany, including East Berlin. The British and Americans controlled the western part of the country.

The Pacific Theater

Japan's Gamble

In the Pacific theater, the naval battles of the Coral Sea and Midway Island in 1942 checked what had been a rapid Japanese advance (see Map 52.2). All of Southeast Asia and many Pacific islands had fallen to the flag of the Rising Sun, and the Japanese were threatening Australia and India by the middle of that year. But by the end of 1942, it was clear that the United States had recovered from the surprise attack on Pearl Harbor a year earlier. The **Battle of the Coral Sea** had nullified the Japanese threat to Australia, and India proved ready to defend itself rather than passively submit, as Tokyo had hoped.

Even with the bulk of the U.S. war effort going toward Europe and the Russians remaining neutral, the Japanese did not have the raw materials or the manpower to keep up with the demands of prolonged conflict over so wide an area. (The Japanese high command knew this, and had counted heavily on the attack on Pearl Harbor to "knock out" American power in the Pacific or at least to make the U.S. amenable to a negotiated peace that would leave Japan in control of the western Pacific.)

In 1943–1944, the United States rolled the Japanese back, taking one island chain after another in bloody fighting. The Philippines were liberated from Tokyo's forces in late 1944 in a campaign led by the American commander Douglas MacArthur, the chief architect of the victory in the Pacific. The Japanese homelands were pummeled by constant bombing from these newly captured island bases.

■ **Refugees Flee Yokohama.** American bombing attacks on Japanese cities began in November 1944. Japan's crowded cities were soon devastated by these air raids. Many refugees took shelter in Yokohama until American bombers devastated the city on May 29, 1945.

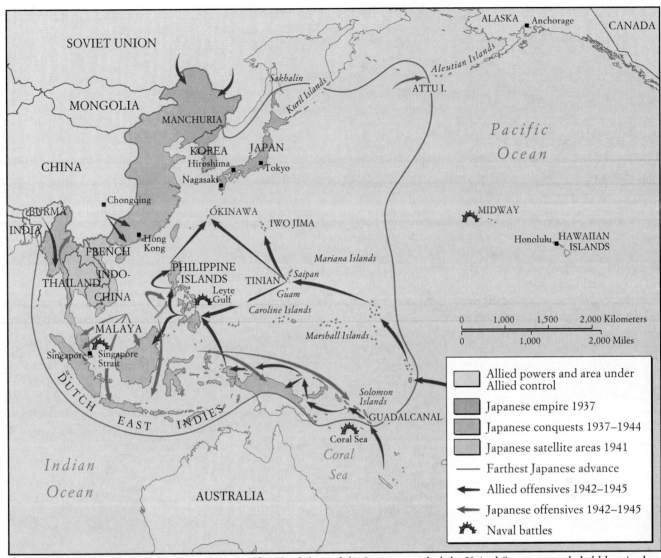

⦿ **MAP 52.2 World War II in Asia and the Pacific.** The failure of the Japanese to deal the United States navy a lethal blow in the first months of the Pacific war meant that the war could not end in victory, as it would be only a matter of time until Washington could summon its far greater resources and drive the Japanese back. From 1943 onward the best Tokyo realists could hope for was a negotiated peace which gave Japan some favored position in China.

Japanese Defeat and Surrender

The end of the Pacific war came quickly after the Nazi capitulation. During 1944–1945, the Japanese occupation forces had been gradually forced from Southeast Asia or had been captured in the Pacific islands. Burma and Indochina had been cleared when the Japanese withdrew voluntarily to return to their homeland. The long war between Japan and China was also now swinging in favor of the communist army under Mao Zedong.

The Americans were preparing for massive casualties in a planned invasion of the Japanese islands when the atomic bombs were dropped on **Hiroshima** and Nagasaki in August 1945. Within a few days, the Japanese government indicated its readiness to surrender, and the formal act was completed on August 15, 1945, with the sole condition being that Emperor Hirohito be allowed to remain on his throne.

Use of the atom bombs has remained a profoundly acrimonious issue. Critics say that the bombing of the two Japanese cities was admittedly aimed against civilians

Excerpts from the United Nations Charter

In June 1945, the victorious Allies sent delegates to San Francisco where for the previous two months the Big Five (the United States, Britain, the Soviet Union, China, and France) had been working out the details of a world organization dedicated to keeping the peace. The resultant charter created the United Nations Organization, later to be headquartered in New York. The United Nations membership roll has risen from the original 51 nations to now include more than 180; practically every state in the world belongs and participates in the annual sessions of the General Assembly. Some also take a role in the Security Council, which is composed of the Big Five permanent members plus ten additional members serving two-year electoral terms.

The United Nations Charter reflects the ideals and hopes of the anti-Axis coalition; certainly, not all their hopes have been realized or even partly attained. But the Preamble still constitutes one of the best statements of what the world *might be* one day:

> We the people of the United Nations, determined to save succeeding generations from the scourge of war . . . and to reaffirm faith in fundamental human rights, in the dignity and worth of the human person, in the equal rights of men and women and of nations large and small, and to establish conditions under which justice and respect for the obligations arising from treaties and other sources of international law can be maintained, and to promote social progress and better standards of life in larger freedom and for these ends to practice tolerance and live together in peace with one another as good neighbors, and to ensure . . . that armed force shall not be used, save in the common interest, have resolved to combine our efforts to accomplish these aims.

Some specific provisions of the charter's 111 articles have been put into operation in the ensuing fifty years; others, like the assumption that the Security Council would have the full support of the members, have proved naive:

CHAPTER 1: Purposes and Principles

Article I

The Purposes of the United Nations are:

1. To maintain international peace and security, and to that end: to take effective collective measures for the prevention and removal of threats to peace, and for the suppression of acts of aggression . . . and to bring about by peaceful means, and in conformity with justice and international law, adjustment or settlement of international disputes or situations which might lead to a breach of peace;
2. To develop friendly relations among nations based on respect for the principle of equal rights and self-determination of peoples, and to take other appropriate measures to strengthen universal peace.
3. To achieve international cooperation in solving problems of an economic, social, cultural, or hu-

---

rather than military targets and cite the huge loss of civilian life (more than 70,000 of a population of about 200,000) in Hiroshima. This was entirely unnecessary, they say, because Japan would soon have surrendered to overwhelming Allied forces in any case. Another school of criticism thinks that the real reason for the bombing was that the U.S. government was looking ahead to the postwar era and wished to intimidate the Soviets.

On the other side, the defenders of President Harry S. Truman and the U.S. high command point out that the Japanese had shown fanatical determination to resist and would have stalwartly defended their home islands. Some estimates at the time thought more than a million U.S. casualties and countless more Japanese might reasonably have been expected before the fighting was over. To avoid these casualties, the atomic attack was entirely justified in their view.

In any case, the sight of the enormous mushroom cloud of an atomic explosion would hover like some ghastly phantom over the entire postwar era. The knowledge that *humans now had the power to entirely destroy themselves* was the most fearsome insight to come out of World War II.

manitarian character, and in promoting and encouraging respect for human rights and for fundamental freedoms for all without distinction as to race, sex, language, or religion.

Article 2

3. All members shall settle their international disputes by peaceful means in such a manner that international peace and security and justice are not endangered.

5. All members shall give the United Nations every assistance in any action it takes ... and shall refrain from giving assistance to any state against which the United Nations is taking preventive or enforcement action.

CHAPTER 7: Enforcement Procedures

Article 42

[The United Nations] may take such action by air, sea, or land forces as may be necessary to maintain or restore international peace and security. Such action may include demonstrations, blockade, and other operations by air, sea, or land forces of Members of the United Nations.

Article 43

All Members of the United Nations in order to contribute to the maintenance of international peace and security, undertake to make available to the Security Council ... armed forces, assistance, and facilities, including rights of passage, necessary for the purpose.

Article 45

In order to enable the United Nations to take urgent military measures, Members shall hold immediately available national airforce contingents for combined international enforcement action. The strength and degree of readiness of these contingents and plans for their combined action shall be determined ... by the Security Council with the assistance of a Military Staff Committee.

Article 47

1. There shall be established a Military Staff Committee to advise and assist the Security Council on all questions relating to the ... employment and command of forces placed at its disposal, the regulation of armaments, and possible disarmament.

2. The Committee shall consist of the Chiefs of Staff of the Permanent Members of the Security Council or their representatives. ...

3. The Committee shall be responsible under the Security Council for the strategic direction of any armed forces placed at the disposal of the Security Council. Questions relating to the command of such forces shall be worked out subsequently.

Article 48

1. The action required to carry out decisions of the Security Council for the maintenance of international peace and security shall be taken by all the Members of the United Nations or by some of them, as the Security Council may determine.

The other balance sheets of the war were almost as terrible. More people died in World War II than in any other disaster in recorded history. The final count will never be known for certain, but it is thought that about 30 million people died as a direct result of hostilities around the world. The most devastating casualties were suffered by the Jews of Europe, followed by the Russians and the Germans. In material categories, much of central and eastern Europe was reduced to shambles by ground or air war, and many parts of Italy and France also suffered severe damage. Many Japanese and Chinese districts were in bad shape from bombings and (in China) years of ground war. Everywhere, the survivors stood on the edge of an abyss; starvation, cold, epidemic disease, family disintegration, and psychic disorientation posed distinct threats to humane life in much of the world.

✦ THE ONSET OF THE COLD WAR

During the conflict, the Allies had not been able to agree on their postwar aims. Between the Western Allies and the Soviets stood a wall of mistrust that had been veiled temporarily, but had by no means been dismantled. As soon as the victory over the Axis powers was secured, the dimensions of this wall were again visible for all to see.

Wartime Alliance and Continuing Mistrust

During the war, three Allied summit conferences (Tehran in 1943, Yalta in 1945, and Potsdam in 1945) had been held. The main concrete results of these meetings were to assure the Soviets of political-military dominion over eastern Europe after the war, to assign parts of conquered Germany to Allied armies of occupation, and to move Germany's eastern border a hundred miles to the west. Moving Germany's border would allow the Soviet border with Poland to be moved west a similar distance, fulfilling an old demand of the Soviets dating back to 1919.

The Cold War between the Soviet Union and the West began as early as 1945. The immediate trigger was the Russians' clear disregard for "free elections and free political life" in the countries of eastern Europe and the Soviet Zone of Occupation in eastern Germany. The fate of the small countries of eastern Europe was of particular interest to both the Western Allies and the Soviets. At the **Yalta Conference** in February 1945, the participants had agreed that free elections would be held as soon as wartime conditions might permit and that Western observers would be allowed to be present even though all of these nations fell under what was conceded to be a Soviet sphere of interest.

Already at the Potsdam Conference, held in July 1945, it was apparent that major problems were arising. From the Russian point of view, the assurance of freedom in any real sense for these nations was unjustified presumption on the West's part. Since 1918, the nations of East Europe had consistently been hostile to the Soviet Union and would undoubtedly continue to be so, given the chance. Therefore, the only freedom for them that the Soviets would agree to was the freedom to choose between various types of Soviet overlordship. The east Europeans could install their own native Communist Party dictatorship, or they could accept the Soviet one—in either case, backed up by the Red Army already on the scene.

From the Western point of view (which increasingly meant the U.S. perspective), Stalin's government was violating the plain meaning of the promises it had made about eastern Europe and eastern Germany. Also, the tiny Communist Parties were being falsely portrayed as the voices of the majority of Poles, Hungarians, and the like by Soviet media, and governments composed of their members were being imposed on anticommunist majorities through rigged elections and political terror.

Both sides were correct in these accusations. The almost inevitable rivalry between the United States and the Soviet Union in the contest for postwar leadership was the basic reason for the Cold War. Which side was indeed the more culpable for the fifteen years of extreme tension that followed is not easily answered except by those who have a doctrinal commitment to Marxism or its capitalist opponents. The following assertions seem in order now:

- Until Stalin's death in 1953 the Soviets were certainly trying to expand their direct and indirect controls over Europe. The large Communist Parties of France and Italy (which consistently obtained more than 25 percent of the vote in postwar elections) were regarded as Trojan horses by all other democratic leaders, and rightly so. These parties had shown themselves to be the slavish followers of Moscow, and if they had obtained power, they would have turned those democracies into imitations of the Soviet Union.
- World revolution was still seen as a desirable and attainable goal by some communists, possibly including Stalin. The progress of the Maoist rebellion against the Chinese government in the late 1940s certainly buoyed these hopes, while greatly alarming American opinion.
- On the other hand, the U.S. military and some U.S. political leaders were almost paranoid in their fears of communism. They were prone to see plots everywhere and to think all communists had exactly the same goals and methods. Like the most fanatical communists, they could not imagine a world where communists and capitalists might coexist. They viewed the U.S. atom bomb as the ultimate "persuader" for a proper world order.

The Original Issues

Several specific issues concerning Germany and eastern Europe during the immediate postwar years brought the two superpowers into a permanently hostile stance:

1. *Reparations in Germany.* The Soviet Union claimed, more or less accurately, that the Allies soon reneged on their promises to give the Russians a certain amount of West German goods and materials, as reparations for war damage.
2. *Denazification of German government and industry.* Again, the Russians were correct in accusing the West of not pursuing the Nazi element very vigorously, as soon as the Cold War frictions began. By 1949, the

Western powers had dropped "denazification" altogether, as an unwelcome diversion from the main issue of strengthening German anticommunism.

3. *The creation of a new currency for the Allied sectors of Germany in 1948.* Without consulting their increasingly difficult Russian occupation "partner," the West put through a new currency (the deutsche mark, which is still in use), which split the former unity of the occupation zones in economic and financial affairs.

4. *The Berlin government and the Berlin blockade in 1948–49.* The Russians showed no interest in maintaining the agreed-on Allied Control Council (where they could be always outvoted) and made East Berlin and East Germany practically a separate administration as early as 1946. In 1948 Stalin attempted to bluff the Western allies out of Berlin altogether by imposing a blockade on all ground access. The Allies defeated the blockade by airlifting food and vital supplies for six months, and Stalin eventually lifted it (see the next chapter).

5. *The country-by-country Soviet takeover of East Europe between 1945 and 1948.* From the moment the Red Army arrived, terror of every kind was freely applied against anticommunists. For a brief time after the war's end, the Communist Parties attempted service to democratic ideals by forming political coalitions with noncommunists. Under Moscow's guidance, these coalitions were turned into "fronts" in which the noncommunists were either powerless or stooges. Protests by Western observers were ignored or denounced. The communists then took the leading positions in all the provisional governments and used their powers to prepare for "free" elections. The elections were held at some point between 1945 and 1947 and returned a predictable overwhelming majority for the Communist Parties and their docile fellow travelers. Stalinist con-

■ **The Big Three at Yalta, February 1945.** This final summit meeting among the three Allied leaders came a few months before the German surrender, and was devoted to arranging the the Soviet Union's entry into the Pacific war against Japan, and the fate of postwar eastern Europe.

stitutions were adopted, the protecting Red Army was invited to remain for an indefinite period, and the satellite regime was complete.

Many other factors could be mentioned, but the general picture should already be clear: the wartime alliance was only a weak marriage of convenience against Hitler and was bound to collapse as soon as the mutual enemy was gone. After 1946 at the latest, neither side had any real interest in cooperating to establish world peace except on terms it could dictate. For an entire generation, the world and especially Europe would lie in the shadow thrown by the atomic mushroom, with the paralyzing knowledge that a struggle between the two superpowers meant the third, and final world war.

Summary

World War II came about through a series of aggressive steps taken by the Fascist and Nazi dictatorships in the later 1930s against what appeared to be the defeatist and indecisive democratic states of western Europe. Hitler quickly recognized the weakness of his opponents and rode his support by most Germans to a position of seeming invincibility in foreign affairs. The remilitarization of the Rhineland was followed by the annexation of

Austria, the cutting up of Czechoslovakia, and finally the assault against Poland in September 1939.

In the first three years of war, the battles were mainly decided in favor of the Axis powers led by Germany. But the Battle of Stalingrad and the defeat of the Axis in North Africa marked a turning point in late 1942. In one sense, the entry of the United States into the war following the Japanese attack on Hawaii was the turning point, even though it took a full year for the Americans to make much difference on the fighting fronts.

By late 1944, the writing was clearly on the wall for both the Germans and the Japanese, and attention turned to the postwar settlement with the Soviet ally. This settlement had not been spelled out in detail during the war because of the continuing mistrust between East and West. As soon as the fighting had stopped (May 1945 in Europe, August 1945 in the Pacific), the cracks in the wartime alliance became plain and soon produced a Cold War atmosphere. East Europe and the administration of defeated Germany were the two focal points of conflict.

Test Your Knowledge

1. Which of the following was *not* a German-instigated step toward World War II?
   a. The occupation of the Rhineland
   b. The invasion of Ethiopia
   c. The seizure of the Sudetenland
   d. The Non-Aggression Pact of 1939
2. A chief reason for Britain's prolonged appeasement of Hitler was that
   a. the British government wanted a counterweight to France on the Continent.
   b. he was seen by some leaders as an anticommunist bulwark.
   c. the British government of the late 1930s was strongly pro-German.
   d. he was seen as a way to tame the East European troublemakers.
3. World War II was started by the Nazi invasion of
   a. France.
   b. Austria.
   c. Poland.
   d. Czechoslovakia.
4. Which of these did *not* occur during the first phase of World War II?
   a. The German *blitzkrieg* against Denmark and Norway
   b. The D-day invasion of France
   c. The loss of the British and French colonies in South Asia
   d. The invasion of Russia and the conquest by Germany of the Balkans
5. The focal point of the Yalta Conference among the Allied leaders in 1945 was
   a. the future of Japan.
   b. the political arrangements in East Europe.
   c. the details of a peace treaty with Germany.
   d. the signing of a peace treaty with Italy.
6. At the Munich Conference in 1938,
   a. Austria was sacrificed to a Nazi invasion.
   b. Czechoslovakia was abandoned by its Western allies.
   c. Soviet Russia was invited to join the League of Nations.
   d. Hitler and Mussolini decided on war.
7. Winston Churchill first became a public figure when he
   a. became the leader of the British government.
   b. was elected to Parliament.
   c. was a journalist in Africa.
   d. was a navy minister in World War I.

Identification Terms

Berlin Blockade	Hiroshima	Non-Aggression Pact of 1939	Rhineland
Coral Sea (battle of)	Munich Conference		Stalingrad
D day		Popular Front	Yalta Conference

Bibliography

The diplomatic and political background to World War II will be found in R. Sontag, *A Broken World, 1919–1939,* 1971, and E. Wiskemann, *Fascism in Italy: Its Development and Influence,* 1969, which were cited in the bibliography for Chapter 48 dealing with the 1920s, and S. Marks, *The Illusion of Peace,* 1967, and D. C. Watt, *How War Came,* 1989, which were cited in the bibliography for Chapter 50.

Carr, R. *The Civil War in Spain,* 1986. A standard history of this conflict, which still reverberates in Spanish life in the 1990s. See also H. Thomas, *The Spanish Civil War,* 1961.

Churchill, W. S. *The Second World War,* 6 vols., 1948–1954. The most elegantly written history by the man who led Britain throughout the conflict. Packed with fascinating detail and highly personal, eyewitness accounts of historic moments from the late 1930s onward to the war's end.

Dallin, A. *German Rule in Russia, 1941–1945,* 1957. Gives a thorough analysis of what Nazi rule of an enemy nation actually meant in terms of its horrors. For the Eastern Front, this should be supplemented by the most memorable "worm's eye" account to come out of the conflict: G. Alzey, *The Forgotten Soldier,* 1965, a young recruit's memoir of his three years in Russia.

Feis, H. *Churchill-Roosevelt-Stalin: The War They Waged and the Peace They Sought,* 1957. A reliable history of the tense relations among the Big Three.

Gilbert, M., and R. Gott. *The Appeasers,* 1963. British foreign policy in the years running up to the war.

Keegan, J. *The Second World War,* 1990. A brilliant military history, rivaled by B. H. Liddell Hart, *History of the Second World War,* 2 vols, 1971. See also the huge crop of more sensational but still accurate works on specific incidents or areas such as J. Toland, *The Last Hundred Days,* 1976, which details the final days of the war, or L. Collins and D. La Pierre, *Is Paris Burning?,* 1965, which tells how the French capital was saved from the fate ordained for it by Hitler.

Kogon, E. *The Theory and Practice of Hell,* 1958. The best book on the Nazi concentration camps.

Michel, H. *The Shadow War: The European Resistance, 1939–1945,* 1972. The story of the undercover war against the Nazi and Fascist occupiers.

Speer, A. *Inside the Third Reich,* 1970. A unique glimpse of how the Hitler regime actually functioned, written by one of the insiders, the minister of economics throughout the war.

Wright, G. *The Ordeal of Total War,* 1967, and P. Calvocaressi and G. Wint, *Total War,* 1972 are good accounts of the worldwide conflicts and how they impacted both the home fronts (Wright) and the other belligerents (Calvocaressi and Wint).

HIGH AND LOW CULTURES IN THE WEST

1880s–1890s	Post-Impressionist painting begins Modernism in the arts
Early 1900s	Modernism in literature, music
1920s	Radio commercialized/movies become major entertainment medium
1930s	Television invented/cheap paper back books
1960s	FM radio/audio tape recordings
1970s	First VCRs and video cameras
1980s	CD recordings/large screen TV

In the present century the arts and their audiences have undergone one more of those radical reorientations which we have termed revolutions when placed in a political or economic context. The twentieth century has been unprecedently receptive to new cultural trends and new ways of communicating both ideas and feeling. Frenetic experimentation has been the hallmark of Western culture since World War I. Many forms have been borrowed from non-Western sources; artists in several media have not hesitated to reject the historical traditions of their art. Popular media, with no traditions to restrict them, have sprung out of the earth like mushrooms, riding a wave of technological innovation.

In painting and literature, especially, an almost complete break with the modalities of earlier times was attempted and occasionally was successful. Such attempts often led to dead ends, however, and the older models were able to hold the allegiance of the audience majority. The century is ending with a distinct gap between the "high" and the "low" cultures, which differ not only in the media employed but also in their content, their aims, and overwhelmingly, their audiences.

✤ FRAGMENTATION AND ALIENATION

If a single keyword to describe twentieth-century Western culture were to be selected, it might well be fragmentation. All authorities agree that never before have so many conflicting approaches to the common problems of human life and art been pursued. Value systems and aesthetic judgments collide head-on with depressing regularity. There often seems to be so little common ground that no lasting consensus is obtainable.

The sense of what is necessary and proper for the fulfillment of ordinary human life, which in the eighteenth and nineteenth centuries was seen as a self-evident proposition by the educated, no longer seems to exist. Artists and writers insist that personal viewpoints, shaped by specific experience, are the only valid points of reference for creative work. The result is frequently an art from which unity of message, form, and technique has been eliminated. What remains often looks like chaos to the observer.

What has happened? Why and how has this fragmentation occurred? Is it harmful to our society, or merely another mode of cultural expression, as legitimate and creative as any other?

The creative arts in this century have been dominated by alienated individuals who are in conflict with their human environment. *Alienation* means to become a stranger and find oneself at odds with the values of your fellows. This is hardly a new phenomenon among artists. Since the beginning of modern times, artists have often felt like outsiders in society, as indeed many were. But in the present century this feeling has deepened, and has become more aggressively expressed. As the Dada movement's manifesto proudly stated, "Art is a private matter; the artist does it for himself; any work of art that can be understood is the product of a journalist" (see the Document in this chapter).

The Dadaists were too extreme to be taken seriously by most but many serious artists also believed that the artist's first duty was always to be true to him- or herself. In practice, this has meant that in painting, fiction, poetry, and to a lesser extent in music and sculpture, those persons working on the innovative frontiers frequently abandoned the forms and even the contents of the classical past. Meterless verse, abstract figures in painting and sculpture, music composed of equal parts silence and dissonance, and stream of consciousness narrative were the essence of their art to many of the most noted twentieth-century practitioners.

The result was frequently all too confusing for much of the previous audience. Artists in all fields found they had to choose between disproportionate sectors of the public when preparing their work. A dual-level audience had arisen: the tiny elite who favored innovators though their art was "difficult"; or the much larger group which included those who visited museums to admire representational paintings, and went to concert halls to hear the works of Bach and Beethoven, and who read poetry that they could understand at first sight. Between the two groups and the artists which each supports there was and is not much communication or shared ground.

Much modern art makes a great many people uncomfortable; the temptation to dismiss the creators as baffling egocentrics, or outright frauds is very strong. Sometimes, no doubt, this suspicion is justified; the fine arts in our times have become in some instances a commodity like any other, exhibiting the usual techniques of clever buyers and sellers.

But this is certainly not always the case. In this century, almost all the arts in the West have experienced a tremendous burst of creativity, such as has not been seen since the Renaissance. In the following paragraphs we will look at a few common characteristics of this explosion, and then at a few of the individual artforms exemplifying them.

✤ MODERNISM

Certain common features of recent Western art and culture can be summed up conveniently in the word Modernism. It carries several implications:

1. *Form was emphasized at the expense of content.* Since many modern artists were convinced that even a sympathetic and knowledgeable audience could not uniformly comprehend what they were saying, they minimized the message (content) and gave full attention to the medium (form). This obsession with form led to novels that shifted narrators and time frame without warning; poetry which seemed much more concerned with the printed format than with the sense of the words; and sculpture that was entirely "abstract", that is, unrecognizable in life, and given such a title as *Figure 19.*

2. *A systematic and determined rejection of the classical models was to be expected.* At no epoch of the past did artists so generally attempt to find new—perhaps shockingly new—ways to express themselves. Not only new technique, but also wholly new philosophies of art were trotted out, following one another in rapid succession from the 1870s (painting), the 1900s (music and dance), to the decade of the 1910s (literature and sculpture).

3. *There was a conscious search for non-Western inspiration.* This was particularly true in the figurative arts—painting, sculpture, weaving, ceramics—where East Asian and African and Polynesian forms had a great vogue.

Modern Painting

Painting has frequently been the pathbreaker in times of change in the high culture. What the eye can see is universal; hence, painted pictures are capable of reaching the largest audiences in the most straightforward fashion. In the 1870s, the **Impressionists** began the long march away from realism and toward abstraction. The Impressionists (working mainly in Paris, which remained the painting capital until the 1950s) were concerned not with realism, which they wanted to leave to the newly invented camera, but with the nature of light and color. In the 1880s and 1890s, center stage went to the *Post-Impressionists,* who focused on mass and line and were daring innovators in their use of color. Several of them (*Paul Cézanne, Claude Monet*) were the pioneers of twentieth-century forms and are revered as the creators of modern classics in painting.

The Dada Artist and His Mission

In the midst of World War I, a tiny group of artists—poets, painters, sculptors—living in neutral Switzerland announced the coming of a final stage in the liberation of art from representational restrictions. They adopted the name *Dada,* variously explained as a French word for hobbyhorse, a nickname for one of their acquaintances, or just nonsense. For a few years, Dada and the Dadaists held a major spot in the international limelight, particularly in Paris and Berlin, the two major art capitals in the Western world. Their total rejection of traditional values in all the arts created a sensation.

One of the founders of Dada was Hugo Ball, a young poet. In a lecture on the Russian artist Wassily Kandinsky at the Galerie Dada in Zurich in 1917, he explained the inspiration of the new movement. It is easy to see how both the war and modern physics and psychology had had an impact on Ball's thinking:

I. The Age

Three things have shaken the art of our time to its depths, have given it a new face, and have prepared it for a mighty new upsurge: the disappearance of religion induced by critical philosophy, the dissolution of the atom in science, and the massive expansion of population in present-day Europe.

God is dead. . . . Religion, science, and morality—phenomena that originated in the states of dread known to the primitive peoples. An epoch disintegrates. A thousand year culture disintegrates. . . . Churches have become castles in the clouds. . . . Christianity was struck down. . . . The meaning of the world disappeared.

Objects changed shape, weight, relations of juxtaposition and superimposition. As minds were freed from illusion in the philosophical domain, so were bodies in the physical domain. . . .

And then came a third element, destructive, threatening with its desperate search for a new ordering of the ruined world: the mass culture of the modern megalopolis.

II. Style

The artists of these times have turned inward. Their life is a struggle against madness. They are disrupted, fragmented, dissevered. . . . The strongest affinity shown in works of art today is with the dread-masks of primitive peoples, and with the plague and terror masks of the Peruvians, Australian aborigines, and Negroes. . . . [The artists] are forerunners, prophets of a new era. Only they can understand the tonalities of their own language. They stand in opposition to society, as did heretics in the Middle Age. . . . They are forerunners of an entire epoch, a new total culture. They are hard to understand, and one achieves an understanding of them only if one changes the inner basis—if one is prepared to break with a thousand year tradition. You will not understand them if you believe in God, and not in Chaos.

[The artist] voluntarily abstains from representing natural objects—which seems to him to be the greatest of all distortions. They seek what is essential and what is spiritual, what has not yet been profaned. . . . They become creators of new natural entities that have no counterpart in the known world. They create images which are no longer imitations of nature but an augmentation of nature, by new, hitherto unknown appearances and mysteries. That is the victorious joy of these artists—to create existences, which one calls images but which have a consistency of their own that is equivalent to that of a rose, a person, a sunset, or a crystal.

SOURCE: Excerpted from Hugo Ball, *Flight Out of Time: A Dada Diary,* translated by Ann Rhines, p. 219, Viking Press, 1974.

At the end of the nineteenth century and the first decade of the twentieth, *Cubism and Abstract art* appeared, again first in Paris. The key descriptor of this new school is "nonrepresentational"; the painter makes little or no attempt to represent external reality as the eye sees it.

Piet Mondrian was perhaps the leading exponent of **Abstractionism.** But the most influential figurative artist of the entire century was **Pablo Picasso,** a Spaniard who chose to live and work in France most of his very long and creative life (see the Biography in this chapter).

During the first decades of the twentieth century, *Expressionism* and other, smaller schools that emphasized the primacy of the emotions through line, color, and composition were the favored ground of the artistic innovators. After World War II, the Americans led by *Jackson Pollock, Hans Koenigsberger,* and others took the lead by combining pure abstraction and new ways of putting the paint on the canvas (sometimes by apparently random splattering). This *Abstract Expressionism* has remained the chief form of modern painting in the second half of the century, though it has a half dozen competitors including its diametrical opposite, a photographic Neorealism. Many attempts to discover profundity in the commonplace and vulgar (Pop Art, Op Art) have also been made in the past fifty years—with limited success.

Modern Literature

In literature the departure from tradition is as sharply defined and uncompromising as it has been in painting. Novelists, playwrights, and especially poets have turned their backs upon the models of narrative and description enshrined by the past. They have experimented with every conceivable aspect of their craft: grammar and meter, characterization, narrative flow, point of view, and even the very language. Some poets and novelists employ what seems almost a private vocabulary, which, like the Red Queen's in *Alice in Wonderland,* means "what I want it to mean."

The inevitable upshot of this fevered experimentation has again been the loss of much of the traditional audience. Modernist poetry, for example, demands so much effort to follow the poet's vision that it is exhausting to most casual readers. Though a poem by Delmore Schwartz may be in every "serious" anthology of twentieth-century verse, it is seldom quoted by lovers of poetry. Instead, their lists of favorites are likely to include any of several poems by Robert Frost. With their familiar English and adherence to traditional rules of poetic construction, Frost's verse is easily understood.

The same is true of novels and novelists. In both style and content, some modern writing is so intent on giving voice to the writer's subjective viewpoints that the essential communication of ideas and events gets lost or is never attempted. It is this *fascination with the self,* at the expense of the reader that "turns off" a large part of the public from modernist fiction.

Two examples among hundreds may be found in the novels of the American Donald Barthelme (b. 1931) and the filmscripts of the Frenchman Alain Resnais (b. 1922).

Though praised highly by critics, their work is appreciated by only a select few who are willing to attempt the hard work of analysis they demand, and who are not deterred by their deliberate obscurity. Time may indeed reveal that Barthelme and Resnais are great artists, but the large majority of the contemporary reading and film-going public seems content to remain happily ignorant of them and their work.

In some instances, the modernists have been rewarded by widespread recognition from the public as well as the critics. The artistry and originality of these authors are undeniable. **James Joyce** (1882–1941), **Samuel Beckett** (1906–1988), **Marcel Proust** (1871–1922), and **Virginia Woolf** (1882–1941) had the creative power to overcome old forms and break new ground. Joyce was the author of two novels that were immediately recognized as marvelously original works. *Ulysses* (1917) and *Finnegan's Wake* (1934) employed the "stream of consciousness" technique to a degree and with an effect never seen before. Joyce succeeded in portraying the ordinary life of an individual

■ **Jackson Pollock, 1951.** The American painter who was the founder and most noted exponent of Abstract Expressionism charged his enormous canvases with raw energy. Splattering apparently random flecks from his brush onto the canvas, Pollock's work convinced most critics that it contained both form and content of genius.

Pablo Picasso

1881–1973

Rare indeed are the artists who can claim to be the originators of an entirely new conception of their art; rarer still are those who can make that claim, and also be the creators of the two most important paintings of an entire century. Pablo Picasso (1881–1973), a Spaniard who lived most of his life in France, could make those claims as a painter, the major art form of his long and productive career.

Picasso studied in Paris in the 1900s after a brief training in Barcelona. At that time Paris was the center of the art world; innovators from every European country and the Americas were eagerly flocking there to join the established painters, sculptors, and authors. From the earliest days of his boyhood, Picasso had known what he wished to do with his life; his pursuit of artistic excellence was single-minded and uncompromising from that period on. In his technical innovation, his tremendously original imagination, and his versatility, he had no peers in this century.

Picasso's painting career went through several more or less distinct phases. In his first years, his so-called Blue Period, he focused on the melancholy lives of the urban poor, using predominantly blue tones. Later, during his Rose Period, which began in 1905, he used a lighter palette of colors to convey more carefree scenes, many taken from life in the circus. He also began his notable works of sculpture at this time.

In 1907, Picasso's *Les Demoiselles d'Avignon* became a sensation, first among his fellow artists and then among the artistic public at large. *Les Demoiselles* was the first major work of Cubism and the signal for an entirely new conception of how the artist might present external reality on canvas. In showing the distorted figures of three young girls, the painting reflected in vivid colors the impressions of African sculptures that Picasso and the rest of artistic Europe had recently experienced. The rigid mathematical basis of Cubism led directly to the abstractionist style, which Picasso himself never joined but which inspired a generation of painters after World War I.

In the 1930s as the war clouds gathered, Picasso refused for years to involve himself directly with political affairs. But in 1937 he surprised the world with a second landmark work, the passionate mural *Guernica* in memory of the agony of that small and previously unremarked Spanish city that had been heavily bombed by Francisco Franco's planes in the civil war. A condemnation of Fascist brutality and war itself, the huge painting was the twentieth century's most remarkable work of artistic propaganda. It now

as experienced by his unconscious mind, as though relating a dream. *Finnegan's Wake* was too abstruse for the public (much of its effect came from a huge series of very obscure puns), but *Ulysses* has become a modern classic.

Beckett's series of plays, written after World War II, were technically so inventive that they found an international audience despite their profound pessimism about humans and their fate. *Waiting for Godot* is his most famous work; others include *Endgame* and *Krapps Last Tape*. Beckett sees human beings as unfortunate worms who sporadically delude themselves into believing that this life holds something besides disappointment and despair. It is a horrifyingly grim picture that this reclusive Irishman paints of humans and all their hopes.

Proust's portraits of upper-class Parisians in the beginning of this century were important not for what he said, but for the way he said it. Proust was a neurotic who lived almost entirely in a cork-lined retreat in his wealthy home, exercising his memory and his imagination to attempt a total recall of the details of life. It is a testament to his success that his multivolume novel *Remembrance of Things Past* is universally accorded a place among the three or four most influential fictional works of this century.

Woolf's fiction, which was written in the early decades of this century, has been highly influential in both matters of style and content. *To the Lighthouse* and *Mrs. Dalloway*, both published in the 1920s, are her most significant

is located in the Museum of Modern Art in New York City.

Picasso settled after World War II in southern France with his third wife and devoted himself to sculpture and ceramics, as well as drawing in several media. His inventive powers were as fresh in his seventies as they had been in his twenties. He became an icon of the modern artist as free spirit. Like many others, his commitment to truth as he saw it led him to an almost childlike faith in the good intentions of those who pretended to agree with him. In the ten years after the war, he lent his name and reputation to the communists in their campaign to dismantle the West's defense capability.

Picasso's genius lay in his ability to see through the conventional forms and beyond them. So strong was his influence that much of what the world calls modern painting is

identified by the signature "Picasso." He was a master of line; much of his postwar work was in graphics rather than paint. With a few strokes of the crayon or pen, he could bring a scene to the viewer complete in every essential. Among his best-known work in this period was the long series on the life of Don Quixote and his faithful Sancho Panza. Picasso was through and through a Spanish artist, but refused to return to his beloved Catalonia (the area around Barcelona) until the tyrant Franco was dead. That meant never, for Franco outlived the artist.

Picasso was survived by several children by various wives and lovers. In the eyes of those near him, he was apparently a failure as both husband and father. He refused to allow anything, even intimate family matters, to come between himself and his chosen work.

works of fiction. She also wrote a pathbreaking feminist tract, *A Room of One's Own* (see the Document in Chapter 61).

⚜ MODERN PHILOSOPHY

Philosophy has not been exempt from the profound changes in traditional thought that mark recent times in the West. Twentieth-century philosophic systems have been divided between those that seek a new basis for human freedom, and those that deny freedom as a myth and insist on the essential meaninglessness of life. Much recent philosophy focuses on the role of language: how it is created, and how it relates to material reality. Behind

this interest is the conviction that the so-called spirit or soul has no existence other than a linguistic one; that is, because we talk about it, it exists.

The *question of existence* itself is the primary concern of **Existentialism,** which has been perhaps the leading school of philosophy in this century. Existentialism, which originated in Europe, rejects the various higher meanings that religion or philosophers have attempted to find in human life and demands that one accept the pointlessness of life. At the same time, most Existentialists, led by **Jean-Paul Sartre** (1905–1980) insist that humans are free to supply their own meaning, and in fact *must* do so. Existentialism blossomed after World War II, when the anguish created by this second bloody conflict within a

■ **Sartre and Simone de Beauvoir.** These two intellectuals established an extraordinary partnership in both their professional and personal lives in the postwar era.

single generation seemed to spell the end of European, and perhaps Western, culture. Seen in historical perspective, Existentialism may be understood as a reaction against the rather naive optimism and faith in Science as the great "fixer" of human problems that marked the late nineteenth century.

Like the arts and literature, twentieth-century philosophy has been strongly affected by the uncertainty and cultural relativism that may be traced to Darwinian and Freudian theory, on the one side, and post-Newtonian physics, on the other. In the present day, most adherents of one philosophic school would not dare accuse their opponents in another school of heresy or attempt to silence them. No one, it seems, has that type of self-assurance any longer in this *culture of probabilities and relative ethics.* This relativism is the other side of the coin of tolerance and sensitivity to others' values that our century has so espoused—or at least pays lip service to.

✤ POPULAR ARTS AND CULTURE

Popular, or low, culture has undergone an explosion in both variety and accessibility. The mass media (television, movies, paperbacks, radio, popular magazines, newspapers, tape and disc recordings) have never had such a large audience as in the late twentieth century—an audi-

ence that transcends the political boundaries that previously fragmented and restricted it. New technology has been largely responsible for this explosion. At the very outset of the century, two inventions were quickly converted to commercial entertainment. The *motion picture* and the *radio,* which were products of the era just before World War I, were developed by Europeans and Americans working independently (Thomas Edison, Guglielmo Marconi, Lumiére brothers, Lee De Forest). After the war, both came into their own as channels of mass communication.

Movies

The "movies" (the more elegant term *cinema* was never accepted in the United States) were first shown in arcades and outdoors. The first narrative film was *The Great Train Robbery* (1903). New York City was the initial home of the motion picture makers, and the American industry was to be the pacesetter of the world cinema for most of the century. By 1920, stars like Charlie Chaplin, Buster Keaton, and Mary Pickford were well established (see the Biography in this chapter), and the studio system, whereby the film creators were financed and thus controlled by distant investors, was already in operation. This uneasy marriage of artistic creativity and hardheaded money making was to be the keynote of the international cinema and particularly of Hollywood, which replaced New York as the center of moviemaking in the United States during World War I. By 1927, the first talking movie was produced (Al Jolson in *The Jazz Singer*), and films were on the way to becoming the number one entertainment medium of the world—a position they retained until the advent of television after World War II.

Radio

Like the movies, radio emerged rapidly from the laboratory to become a commercial enterprise of major importance. The brilliant Italian experimenter Marconi was successful in transmitting signals through the air ("wireless") over long distances in 1901. Two years later, the invention of the vacuum tube enabled voice and music to be carried. The demands of military communications during World War I sped up radio transmission technology and improved receivers. The first radio broadcasts began in the early 1920s. Within a few years, networks of broadcasting stations had been formed by the same combination of creative scientists and entrepreneurs as in the film industry.

In Europe and in other parts of the world, the government normally controlled radio broadcasting. These governments saw in radio the same possibilities for control and influence as were inherent in the postal service and the telephone network. In the United States, however, radio was from the start a commercial venture, and the ever-present advertisements were a standard part of the radio-listening experience.

Radio and movies provided not only entrepreneurs but also politicians and cultural leaders with undreamed of means of reaching a national audience. Many people in positions of power quickly recognized this potential, and the use of both media for *propaganda* as well as commercial and educational purposes was one of the key breakthroughs in the manipulation of democratic societies. The Soviet and Nazi leaders both made adept use of film and radio in the 1930s and 1940s.

But it was probably in the extension of knowledge of what was happening in the world—*the "news"*—that the radio set and the movie screen made their greatest contributions to twentieth-century culture. The radio told and the movie showed your grandparents' generation what was going on outside their own cultural circles in a way that neither books nor newspapers could rival. Not only politics, but also manners, fashion, humor, language, and education were intensely affected. In the interwar period, about two of every five adults went to a movie at least once a week in Britain and the United States—never before had such a large percentage of the population participated in a single form of recreational activity except eating, drinking, and possibly sex.

Music

Music for the masses came into its own in the twentieth century. The technology of Edison's phonograph and its lineal descendants the tapeplayer, compact disc player, and laser were joined to forms of popular music that expressed a great deal more than the simple urge to sing and dance. Since the 1950s, various forms of rock and roll have captured the allegiance of much of the world's youth. The "youth revolt" of the late 1960s was a thoroughly international phenomenon, and its anthems were drawn equally from folk music and rock.

But rock itself was just the latest addition to a parade of musical types that drew from both European and African-American sources in the early twentieth century. The European sources included the artificial folk songs of the Broadway stage and the vaudeville halls. More important was the black contribution—jazz. Jazz was the name given to that mix of gospel song, African rhythms, and erotic blues shouting that was popularized by black musicians in New Orleans and later in Memphis and Chicago. Once introduced into the mainstream white culture via traveling nightclub bands and early radio, jazz was cleaned up and tamed for middle-class consumption on phonographs.

The processing of folk songs and jazz into commercial products began with the "crooners" of the 1920s radio broadcasts. It continued through the swing bands of the 1930s and 1940s, the beboppers of the 1950s, the folk revival of the 1960s, and finally rock and roll. Keeping close pace with the rise of stars like Elvis Presley, the Beatles, the Rolling Stones, and the Supremes was the *stream of mechanical innovations* that made rock music an ever-present accompaniment to most of the rituals of life for Western people under age thirty. The high fidelity stereo system, Walkman portable tapeplayer, FM broadcasting technology, and automobile sound system all are part of this stream. Nowhere is the close relation between mass culture and technology so clear as in the production, distribution, and consumption of popular music.

Television

The powerful impressions left by radio and movies on the popular mind were overshadowed, however, by those delivered by another post–World War II development—

■ **The Ecko Scophony Model 202.** Television was actually available in reasonably good transmission quality in the mid 1930s, but the price of receivers and the very limited broadcasts discouraged potential purchasers. Shown here is a British company's 1936 model, priced at 100 guineas, or about the equivalent of $80,000 in 1995 buying power.

Charlie Chaplin

1889–1977

No one better personifies the huge impact that the motion picture industry had on the world public than Charlie Chaplin. Chaplin was an enormously talented actor, director, composer, and producer of movies that thrilled audiences from Cape-town to San Francisco. He was probably the best-known single name in the world from 1920 to 1960, eclipsing any statesman or general. Born into poverty in 1889, Chaplin began his career alongside his per-former parents in London music halls as an acrobatic clown. He came to the United States in 1913 as one of the dozens of European vaudeville performers who hoped to make their fame and fortune in this country through the booming silent movie industry. By that year, the United States was already on its way to dominating the entertainment film business, although the technical and artistic elements were still mainly in European hands. Since sound films had not yet been invented, it did not matter what language the actors used, only how effectively they could get the plotline across to an audience through strictly visual means. Facial expression and body movement were an actor's capital.

In 1914, Chaplin joined the Keystone Kops and their artistic director Mack Sennett. This most famous of the early Hollywood comedy troupes special-ized in crazy chase scenes and offered Chaplin a great opportunity to show off his own ideas as a comedian. Thus was born the most famous film figure of the century: the "little tramp" swinging his rolled umbrella in baggy pants and flapping coat. His ridiculous flat-footed walk identified him at once as one of the world's eternal underdogs. Yet there was nothing pathetic about this underdog. Often beaten about by the rich and the powerful, the tramp had a wonderful touch for knowing when and how to strike back. He combined the broadest slapstick with a pathos that touched everyone's heart. And always the laughter rolled out from the audience like an irresist-ible wave.

By 1918, Chaplin had dropped his early ten-minute "loops" and started to make feature-length films under his own direction. Joining with such giants as Mary Pickford and Douglas Fairbanks, he formed his own production company (United Art-ists), assuring that he would have complete control of every aspect of film making and distributing. Throughout the 1920s and 1930s, Chaplin scored unparalleled success: *The Gold Rush, The Circus, City Lights, Modern Times,* and his first "talkie" *The Great*

---

television. Invented by Americans and Britons in the early 1930s, TV came into commercial use only after the war. Already by 1950, television had replaced radio as the prime entertainer in the American home, and a few years later, it was threatening to drive the neighborhood movie theaters out of business. Europeans closed the television gap in the 1960s. As with radio, the European govern-ments monopolized the broadcasting studios until private commercial stations were permitted in the 1980s.

More even than films, television shows have the imme-diacy and emotional power of a picture, especially when that picture is edited (that is, manipulated to give a particular effect) by a knowing hand. Television's takeover of the news reporting function on all levels—local, na-tional, international—is striking evidence of how deeply the TV image has penetrated into the Western world's life and thought. Newspapers, which were the chief news medium in the nineteenth century and the first half of the twentieth, are rapidly being converted into bulletin boards for local retail advertisers and human interest storybooks. A newspaper cannot compete with television for quick, colorful reporting of what is happening around us.

✤ MASS CULTURE AND ITS CRITICS

Between the *high culture* of the patrons of art museums, contributors to the Metropolitan Opera, and subscribers to the *New York Review of Books* and the *low culture* of the Elvis Presley cultists, readers of comic books, and fans of

Dictator. (1940). All rank among the best film comedies ever produced.

Chaplin's appeal was truly universal. His pictures were distributed from one end of the world to the other, and they are still shown regularly in the art theater circuit in the United States and in the mass markets of much of the rest of the world. Chaplin's genius lay in his ability to establish an immediate bond with his audience as someone like themselves, but faster in wit and luckier in outcomes. For those purposes, the little tramp character was perfect; always vulnerable but never defenseless, the tramp was the ultimate survivor.

A hardheaded businessman in real life, Chaplin became so wealthy that he did not have to make pictures at all. He clearly was never as comfortable in his talking roles as he had been doing silent pantomime. After about 1936, he made only a small handful of films until his death in 1977. With the single exception

■ The Actor in his favorite role: The Little Tramp

of his hilarious parody of Hitler in *The Great Dictator,* none were as commercially or artistically successful as his earlier films.

In the Cold War hysteria of the 1950s, when Senator Joseph McCarthy was conducting witch-hunts for communists, Chaplin's refusal to become an American citizen (largely for tax reasons) and his naive support of leftist causes made him an easy target for "Red hunting" demagogues. Embittered, he went with his American wife and child to live in Switzerland in 1952, staying there in semiretirement until a triumphant return to the United States twenty years later to receive a special award from the Academy of Motion Picture Arts and Sciences. He was survived by his fourth wife Oona O'Neill Chaplin (daughter of the playwright Eugene O'Neill) and his several children, including the actress Geraldine Chaplin.

the National Football League exists a transition ground whose importance and nature are the subject of much debate. In a famous essay dating from the early 1960s, the critic Dwight MacDonald dubbed this large group of in-betweeners **Masscult.** MacDonald believed that Masscult was a disastrous phenomenon, representing the surrender of the higher to the lower echelon. He thought that the Masscult participants were rapidly losing the ability to tell the real from the phony; they could not distinguish the art and music that came from an authentic artist from that generated by some advertising agency's robots. Better to have honest ignorance, he said, than the tasteless banality of a half-educated flock of pretenders. Authentic culture—the culture that has created the models and set the standards of the world civilizations—has always been an elitist phenom-

enon and always will be. Insofar as it becomes amassed, it declines in value.

Others are not so sure. They argue that Masscult has come about because of the unparalleled degree of education that the Western nations, at least, have enjoyed since World War II; the cultural variety that the late twentieth century has produced; and the openness to experiment and toleration of artistic novelty. In their view Masscult is a praiseworthy reflection of the lower classes' efforts to rise up the ladder of cultural taste. These observers do not deny that Masscult's judgments and preferences are frequently misguided or manipulated. They merely ask when the masses of people ever before had a chance, such as they now enjoy, to educate themselves and refine their taste. In short, they ask MacDonald to give the Masscult

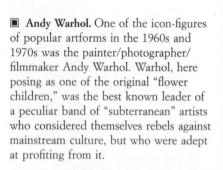

■ **Andy Warhol.** One of the icon-figures of popular artforms in the 1960s and 1970s was the painter/photographer/filmmaker Andy Warhol. Warhol, here posing as one of the original "flower children," was the best known leader of a peculiar band of "subterranean" artists who considered themselves rebels against mainstream culture, but who were adept at profiting from it.

time to mature and develop better taste and surer judgments. Then, the process will be reversed with the low culture being uplifted, rather than the high culture being made banal.

Whichever side of this argument one takes, it is beyond dispute that twentieth-century technology has provided the large majority of the Western world's populations with access to cultural opportunities in an unprecedented fashion. Radio broadcasts, films, television, and cheap paperbacks have been followed by videocassettes and recorders, laser disc recordings, portable telephones, and a seeming unending parade of home entertainment devices that quickly filter down from luxury items to common expectations in the marketplace. We are all now children of the Electronic Age, and the "technological imperative" that was once conceived of as operating only in the science labs has now transformed the consumer market: if it can be done, it will be done! And sold!

Summary

The first half of the twentieth century saw an expansion of cultural opportunities for the masses that has no parallel. New means of communication across distance have joined with new leisure and widespread prosperity in the Western world to allow tremendously widened access to ideas, arts, and news. Commercial entertainment has become one of the chief industries of the modern age and reaches into every level of society with its wares of film, music, sports, and television shows.

Whether or not this trend is truly uplifting the formerly ignorant masses into the lofty realm of high culture is a topic of debate. Some think that the worthwhile has given way to the despicable. The high culture purists have had their position eroded by the Modernist movement in the early part of the century, which permitted artists to forget their former obligation to communicate in easily comprehended ways. By doing so, much literature and pictorial art of a high culture type were removed from the experience of ordinary people. They turned instead to the models of culture being supplied increasingly through commercially driven entertainment media. Such low culture channels have always existed, but could be ignored by the tastemakers until this century, when they have penetrated into so many levels of society as to become what some critics call Masscult.

Test Your Knowledge

1. Modernism in all twentieth-century arts implies, among other things, that
   a. the message of the artwork to its audience should be uniformly understood.
   b. content is more important than form.
   c. the artist cannot be held responsible for differing perceptions of his or her work.
   d. the artist has the duty to attempt something novel.
2. Abstract painting seeks to project
   a. a photographic vision of external objects.
   b. a blueprint for understanding reality.
   c. an internal mood or feeling divorced from external imagery.
   d. a portrait of the artist.
3. The art movement of the early twentieth century that attacked all accepted standards and forms was
   a. Abstractionism.
   b. Cubism.
   c. Dadaism.
   d. Expressionism.
4. "Stream of consciousness" in prose was most memorably employed by
   a. James Joyce.
   b. Samuel Beckett.
   c. Jean-Paul Sartre.
   d. Sigmund Freud.
5. A characteristic of twentieth-century Western art forms has been
   a. a reverence for the great masters.
   b. a timidity in attempting to devise new forms.
   c. an interest in non-Western ideas and forms.
   d. an obsession with propagandizing the audience.
6. Popular music in the mid- and late-twentieth century
   a. has been dominated by the non-Westerners.
   b. has been much affected by technology.
   c. is less important to general culture than it has been in the past.
   d. is more limited to certain ethnic groups than before.
7. Which of the following would *not* be considered a good example of Masscult?
   a. A radio comedy broadcast
   b. A monument to Beethoven
   c. A *People* magazine feature on a new art gallery
   d. A television program on interior decorating
8. The convinced Existentialist believes that
   a. life is hardly worth living as it is devoid of all values.
   b. values are created for others by a handful of strong individuals.
   c. each age creates its own moral values.
   d. each individual must create his or her own values.

Identification Terms

Abstractionism   Impressionists   Picasso (Pablo)   Sartre, J.-P.
Beckett (Samuel)   Joyce (James)   Proust (Marcel)   Woolf (Virginia)
Existentialism   Masscult

Bibliography

Cole, B., and A. Gealt. *Art of the Western World,* 1989. A good summary of what modern Western art has been attempting, and its relative failure with the public.

Eberly, P. *Music in the Air,* 1982. A penetrating review of pop music.

Maltby, R., ed. *Passing Parade: A History of Popular Culture in the 20th Century,* 1989. First-rate selection of items and articles, from CDs to the earliest spy stories.

May, L. *Screening Out the Past: The Birth of Mass Culture and the Motion Picture Industry,* 1980.

Wheen, F. *Television,* 1985. A good short history of the medium.

SUPERPOWER RIVALRY AND THE EUROPEAN RECOVERY

CONFLICT IN THE POSTWAR GENERATION

The Struggle for Germany

NATO and the Warsaw Pact

Grudging Coexistence

From Cuban Missiles to the Invasion of Afghanistan

EUROPE'S ECONOMIC RECOVERY

Factors Promoting Prosperity

European Unity

THE COMMUNIST BLOC, 1947–1980

1947–1949	Marshall Plan and Truman Doctrine/ Blockade of Berlin/NATO and Warsaw Pact
1950s	Western European economies recover
1950s–1990s	Steps toward unifying Europe
1961	Berlin Wall
1962	Cuban Missile Crisis
late 1960s–1970s	Detente in Cold War

As World War II ended, the two great victorious powers were becoming increasingly suspicious of each other's intentions. Leadership in the Western world was passing to the United States from Britain and France for the indefinite future, while in the East, Stalin's Union of Soviet Socialist Republics (USSR) was the engine of a drive to make the world over according to Marx. The two superpowers would have to find a way to settle their differences peaceably or plunge the world into atomic conflict that would leave both in smoking ruins. For the two decades after 1945, the question of atomic war overshadowed everything else in world affairs and dictated the terms of all international settlements. The Cold War became the stage upon which the other vast drama of postwar diplomacy was played: the ending, forcible or peaceable, of the colonial system in the non-Western world. The links between the two struggles were many. In those same decades (1945–1965), Europe staged a remarkable recovery from both the material and the spiritual damages of war. Although most Americans had almost written off Europe as a loss, the nations in the noncommunist two-thirds of Europe were exceeding prewar levels of production as early as 1950. In the next thirty years, they succeeded in progressing far down the road to economic unity, and the ancient hopes of political unification began to seem more attainable.

✤ CONFLICT IN THE POSTWAR GENERATION

Like most other conflicts, the hostility between the United States and the Soviet Union had both proximate and remote causes. The proximate causes were briefly reviewed in Chapter 52: the Soviets' insistence on "friendly" regimes along the western borders of their country and the arguments over the treatment of postwar Germany and the defeated Nazis. But these disputes were only specific reflections of the broader, more remote causes: the friction between two very powerful states, each of which had a tradition of strong nationalism and was convinced its politics and social organization were based on an exclusive truth. The Russians (who were at all times the directing force within the Soviet Union) believed that in Marxism they had found the ultimate answers to the problem of making humans happy on earth; the Americans thought that they had produced a political and economic system that reflected the justified aspirations of all right-thinking people everywhere. The war against Fascism had briefly brought these two nations into the same political bed. Now that it was won, their latent antagonism could inevitably make itself apparent.

The Struggle for Germany

The focus of conflict soon shifted from the elections and governments of the East European countries (which were clearly within the Russian zone of dominion) to defeated Germany, which was "up for grabs" in a political and diplomatic sense. Both superpowers realized that control of Germany meant control of most of Europe; France and Britain were going to be dependents of a foreign power for some time to come, and Italy at this point was both defeated and industrially very weak. Germany was divided into three, then four occupation zones: Russian, American, British, and French. Already in 1946, arguments over industrial reparations from Germany had broken out, the Russians confiscated everything movable in their zone, while the Americans, British, and French soon decided that stripping Germany of its industrial capacity would only bring on political and social chaos and possibly a communist revolution.

In the summer of 1947, the **Marshall Plan** for reconstruction of the European economy was put forth by U.S. Secretary of State George Marshall. It proved to be one of the most successful foreign policy initiatives ever undertaken and was largely responsible for the beginning of the European recovery. The **Truman Doctrine** was also announced in 1947. It committed the United States to defend governments throughout the world when they were threatened by communist-inspired subversion. This policy was a historic departure from the traditional U.S. position of refusing the "entangling alliances" warned against long ago by George Washington. The acceptance of the policy by the U.S. Congress and the public indicated that a decisive change in attitude had taken place since Woodrow Wilson's League of Nations was rejected in 1919. The United States was now prepared, however reluctantly, to shoulder the burdens of what was soon termed "Free World" leadership.

The blockade of Berlin in 1948 (see Chapter 52) was decisive in convincing the Western statesmen that the Soviet Union must be "contained" in eastern Europe, where it had by now created several satellite states. The major key to containment was Germany. Born in September 1949, West Germany (*Bundesrepublik Deutschland*) was a Western ally from the outset; it was larger and more powerful than its Russian-created counterpart, the *Deutsche Demokratische Republik* or East Germany, which came into existence a few weeks later out of the old Russian Zone. Germany, the heart of Europe, was now perhaps permanently divided into two hostile states that mirrored the conflict between the Russians and the Americans.

■ **The Nuremberg Trial, 1946.** Shortly after the German surrender, the Allies put several leading Nazis on trial for "crimes against humanity." The months-long trial was presided over by judges from Russia, the United States, Britian, and France. It resulted in the convictions of all but three of the defendants, who were sentenced to varying terms in prison or to death. Göring, the Number Two Nazi (far left, first row, back to camera), cheated the hangman by taking cyanide.

■ **The Berlin Airlift.** After Stalin blocked all surface routes into West Berlin, the Allies responded by starting an airlift of supplies from their occupation zones in western Germany into the isolated city. Beginning in June 1948, it continued for eleven months until the Soviets allowed overland access again, tacitly admitting defeat.

NATO and the Warsaw Pact

The *North American Treaty Organization (NATO)* was similarly an outgrowth of the East-West struggle. Created in April 1949, it was Washington's solution to the need for an international military organ dedicated to stopping the spread of communism. It originally counted twelve West European and North American members—later increased to 15—who pledged to come to the aid of one another if attacked.

The Soviet answer came with the **Warsaw Pact,** which made the communist states of East Europe military allies. The pact merely formalized what had been true since the series of Marxist takeovers in 1945–1948. All Europe was thus divided into two enemy blocs, along with a handful of militarily insignificant neutrals (Austria, Finland, Spain, Sweden, and Switzerland).

The situation whereby the Continent was more or less at the military mercy of two non-European powers, Russia and the United States, was a definite novelty in history. The traditional powers—Britain, France, and Italy—were in no position to oppose either of the superpowers. Presumably, Germany was not going to be able to play an independent role for many years to come. In the late 1940s and through the 1950s, it appeared that whatever the Europeans might be able to do about their own prosperity, they would remain the junior partners of outside powers in military affairs and diplomacy.

Grudging Coexistence

In 1950, the *Korean War* broke out when South Korea, a U.S. satellite, was invaded by North Korea, a Soviet satellite. Within a year, the conflict had become an international war with the United States providing the leadership in the South, and the Chinese (*not* the Soviets) coming to the aid of their hard-pressed North Korean allies. The fighting ended in deadlock, and a truce was finally signed in 1953.

The master of Soviet affairs, Josef Stalin, also died in that year, and with him died the most aggressive phase of the Cold War. His successors were never so given to paranoia as Stalin had been in his later years. After a behind-the-scenes power struggle that lasted for months, **Nikita Khrushchev** (1894–1971) emerged as Stalin's successor, chief of the Communist Party and the government. Khrushchev, the son of peasants, was very different from the secretive, mysterious Stalin. Though just as convinced that Marxism must inevitably triumph in the whole world, he was generally more open in his dealings with the West and less menacing. He said he believed in *peaceful coexistence with the West,* and challenged the West to engage in economic rather than military competition—a challenge that would turn into a bad joke for the Russians later.

Khrushchev was not about to give up what World War II had brought to the Soviet Union or to release the East Europeans from their bonds to communism, however. In 1956, when the Hungarians rose up in revolt against their highly unpopular satellite government, he sent Soviet tanks to restore order and keep Hungary firmly within the Soviet orbit. The failure of the United States to take any action to assist the "freedom fighters" in Budapest marked the effective end of Washington's propaganda about rolling back the Soviet empire. It was clear that the West had accepted the new borders and the new Soviet-style regimes in East Europe, however much it might denounce their illegality and repression. Since 1949 the Russians had their own atomic weaponry, and in the shadow of the mushroom cloud, the *pax Sovietica* was deemed acceptable.

From Cuban Missiles to the Invasion of Afghanistan

The Cold War continued with the sudden erection of the *Berlin Wall in 1961* by the East Germans to prevent the steady outflow of political refugees. The success of this unparalleled division of a city and a nation perhaps inspired Khrushchev to make an unexpected gamble in an attempt to help his Cuban Marxist ally, *Fidel Castro,* in 1962. Three years earlier, Castro had conquered Cuba with a motley army of insurgents, kicked out the corrupt government, and then declared his allegiance to Marxism. An abortive U.S.-sponsored invasion at the Bay of Pigs had been a total failure; fearing another attempt, Castro asked the Russians for military help. Khrushchev decided to install intermediate-range rockets with nuclear warheads, and the project was well under way when it was discovered by U.S. aerial surveillance over Cuba.

After a few days of extreme tension, the Soviets backed down and removed their weapons when presented with an ultimatum by President John F. Kennedy (see the Document in this chapter). Kennedy allowed Khrushchev some room for maneuver and made some minor concessions on U.S. bases in Asia, along with a promise not to attempt another invasion. Both sides could thus claim to have achieved their goals when the missiles were withdrawn.

The world fright over the **Cuban Missile Crisis** stimulated the nuclear powers to make more serious efforts to reduce the level of hostility. In 1963, they signed the **Nuclear Test Ban**, limiting the testing of weapons in the atmosphere. Under the leadership of Willy Brandt, the West German government after years of resistance moved to recognize the results of World War II and thus to establish better relations with its communist neighbors and with the Soviet Union. This *Ostpolitik* was very successful in reducing tensions in Europe between East and West.

By the mid-1960s, then, the Cold War was less confrontational. The ideology of communist revolution had become a very minor part of the Soviets' baggage in international affairs; it had been replaced by the predictable, selfish interest of a great power with imperialist motives. The Soviet Union was becoming a conservative state—a stable factor in world politics—despite its revolutionary slogans. The best evidence of this shift was the failure of the Soviets to provide military support for the communist side in the Vietnam conflict during the later 1960s (see Chapter 56).

The progress of *detente* (relaxation) between the Soviet Union and the West was marred but not derailed by the Soviet *invasion of Czechoslovakia in 1968,* when that nation attempted to oust its Stalinist overlords through a peaceful revolution. The United States was not inclined to involve NATO in this "internal matter," and communist rule was reimposed without bloodshed. Coming in a year when many Western nations experienced explosive internal frictions between government and citizens, the Czechs' misfortunes were soon forgotten in the West.

■ **The Hungarian Revolt, 1956** The Hungarian people seized the chance to get rid of the highly unpopular Stalinist government in the fall of 1956 and sought to replace it with a Marxist but not Soviet-style regime. After a few days of brave defiance, the revolution was crushed by Soviet tanks in November.

The NATO alliance itself was not so close-knit by this time. Under war hero General **Charles de Gaulle,** France had no sympathy for what he considered the American obsession about the Soviets (see the Biography in this chapter). De Gaulle and many others thought western Europe was no longer seriously threatened by violent communist intervention. The bombastic Khrushchev had been replaced by a tight group of *apparatchiks* headed by Leonid Brezhnev (1906–1982) who showed little commitment to any type of revolution or foreign policy gambles.

The Soviet Union turned inward in the 1970s; its leaders were occupied by the increasing evidence of economic stagnation. The sudden Iranian Revolution (see Chapter 59) at the end of that decade apparently inspired the Soviets' disastrous decision to intervene in Afghanistan, Iran's neighbor, in order to save a pro-Moscow regime. The invasion of Afghanistan ended *detente* and

John F. Kennedy: Speech on Cuban Missiles in 1962

In the fall of 1962, the stunning discovery that the Soviets had secretly deployed nuclear-tipped intermediate-range missiles in Castro's Cuba ignited the most dangerous incident in the generation-long Cold War. Aerial photography of the island during September and October gradually confirmed that Russian engineers were building missile launch sites and bringing in a large number of missiles by ship. If fired, the missiles already transported could destroy much of the eastern United States.

Faced with the cruelest dilemma of any postwar presidency, Kennedy had to frame a response that was absolutely firm, yet restrained and not provocative. A nuclear war might well have been the price of miscalculation. After the Soviets were quietly put on notice that Washington was aware of what was going on, and they had not responded, Kennedy decided it was necessary to "go public" with the news. For some days, the White House continued the agonizing search for the most unambiguous wording, designed to put maximum pressure on the Soviet leader Nikita Khrushchev while giving him an opportunity to retreat without losing face. On October 22, Kennedy made a televised address to a nervous nation and world:

Good evening my fellow citizens.

This government, as promised, has maintained the closest surveillance of the Soviet military build-up on the island of Cuba. Within the past week, unmistakeable evidence has established the fact that a series of offensive missile sites are now in preparation on that imprisoned island. The purpose of these bases can be none other than to provide a nuclear strike capability against the Western hemisphere. . . .

This secret, swift, and extraordinary build-up of communist missiles—in an area well known to have a special and historical relationship with the United States and the nations of the Western hemisphere—in violation of Soviet assurances, and in defiance of American and hemispheric policy—this sudden, clandestine decision to station strategic weapons for the first time outside Soviet soil is a deliberately provocative and unjustified change in the status quo which cannot be accepted by this country if our courage and our commitments are ever to be trusted again by either friend or foe.

. . . All ships of any kind bound for Cuba from whatever nation or port will, if found to contain cargoes of offensive weapons, be turned back.

. . . It shall be the policy of this nation to regard any nuclear missile launched from Cuba against any nation in the Western hemisphere as an attack by the Soviet Union on the United States, requiring a full retaliatory response upon the Soviet Union.

. . . I call upon Chairman Khrushchev to halt and eliminate this clandestine, reckless, and provocative threat to world peace, and to stable relations between the two nations. I am calling upon him further to abandon this course of world domination and to join in an historic effort to end the perilous arms race and to transform the history of Man. He has an opportunity to move the world back from the abyss of destruction, by returning to his government's own words that it has no need to station missiles outside of its own territory, and withdrawing these weapons from Cuba.

Kennedy's words were carefully chosen to assure the Latin American nations that the United States would never abandon them to external force, at whatever cost to itself. This was essential in an era when it appeared that Castro-style Marxism might, under Soviet cover, establish itself on the mainland. At the same time, he reminded Khrushchev and the world that the Soviets were directly violating their own pledges to limit and even slow down the ongoing arms race. After a few horribly tense days, the Russians agreed to dismantle and withdraw their missiles in return for a face-saving pledge on Kennedy's part that the United States would not attempt another invasion of Castro's island.

SOURCE: The Cuban Missile Crisis, Elie Abel, J. P. Lippencott, 1966.

began a general crisis in Soviet government that slowly emerged over the next decade (see Chapter 60).

In the West, the decline of NATO reflected the shift from foreign to domestic policy issues that preoccupied European leaders in the later 1960s. Generated originally by student discontent with the outmoded educational and cultural institutions carried over from the 1930s, protests of every type soon erupted against the governments. These protests reached a peak in 1968, when European disaffection with NATO support of U.S. involvement in Vietnam and with the continuing arms race between East and West reached tidal-wave proportions. Not only was the defense against a fading Marxism becoming superfluous, but to European minds, there were far more interesting and profitable areas to pursue.

✣ Europe's Economic Recovery

The word *renaissance* is not too strong to use in describing the developments in western Europe since 1945. In that year, the Continent was an economic ruin for the most part, and two external powers were contesting for supremacy over what was left intact. By 1965, the West European countries had surpassed every measure of prewar prosperity and were rapidly regaining independence of action in politics.

Factors Promoting Prosperity

What had happened to permit this rebirth? Five factors in particular can be identified:

- *Marshall Plan aid* was remarkably successful in restarting the stalled economies of both the former enemies and the allies. For five years (1947–1951), Austria, West Germany, France, Britain, Italy, and others benefited from this fund of U.S. dollars available for loan. The conditions imposed by supervisory agencies assured a new spirit of collaboration not only between governments but also between government and employers for the benefit of the general public.

- *Social reforms* were enacted immediately after the war to provide benefits for ordinary citizens that they had long sought. Pensions for all, universal medical insurance, family allowances, paid vacations, paid schooling, and other changes all gave the working classes a new sense of being part of the process. Now they felt they had a stake in the success of their country.

- *Effective national planning* provided intelligent direction for the economy without eliminating individual enterprise and its profit reward. The "mixed economy" with some industries and financial institutions directly controlled by the government, some totally private, and many in between came to be the rule from Scandinavia to Portugal.

- *A large, willing labor pool* in most countries allowed employers and entrepreneurs to expand at will when they saw opportunities. The unions, which had generally opposed employers as a matter of principle in the prewar era, now cooperated because governments protected and expanded their rights to a point where they now had a voice in management.

- *Free trade was made general.* The tariff, quota, and license barriers of the 1930s were junked among the NATO countries; the various national currencies were made easily convertible; and international investment was simplified and directly encouraged by Western governments.

- For these reasons, the growth of the West European economies was little short of sensational after the

■ **Postwar Affluence in the West.** The little Morris sedans coming off this British factory assembly-line in the early 1950s showed one aspect of a new phenomenon: mass produced consumer goods for growing markets among the European middle-classes. By the 1960s, the market for new cars had expanded to the laboring class, as well.

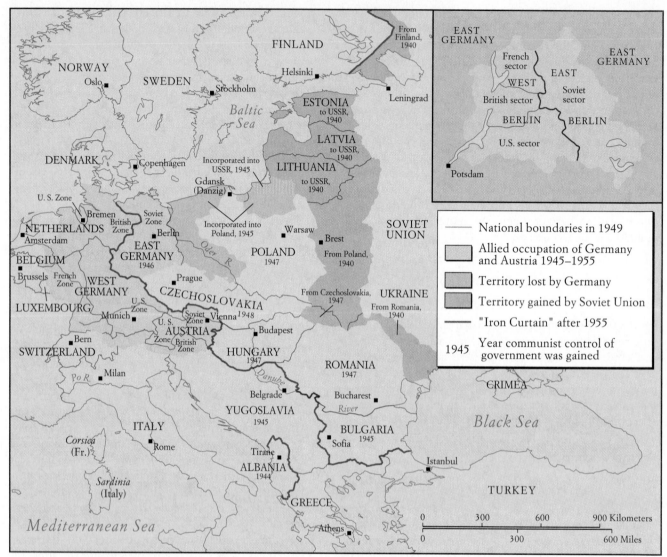

● **MAP 54.1 Cold War Europe, 1945–1990.** The Soviet Union immediately reclaimed those territories in east Europe granted it by the Non-Aggression Pact of 1939, and added half of East Prussia. Yugoslavia was thrust from the Soviet bloc in 1948, and Austria was unexpectedly granted a neutral status by agreement among the occupying nations in 1955. Germany remained divided until the autumn of 1990.

immediate postwar years. West Germany led the way in these "economic miracles" of the 1950s, but France, Italy, and the Benelux nations (Belgium, Luxembourg, and the Netherlands) were close behind. Only Britain did not do very well because of an overly tradition-bound mentality and the breakup of the Commonwealth trading bloc, which had long given British industry a false sense of security from competition.

The *average* rate of growth in West European gross national product during the period 1948–1972 was approximately 4.5 percent per annum—an unbelievable achievement over a full quarter-century. Some nations did much better. And there were no recessions or business crises.

The United States promoted much of this economic development by pouring in new capital first through the

Marshall Plan and then much more through private investment by U.S. companies. By the 1960s, many Europeans were becoming concerned that their economies were being tied too closely to the United States, or that Europe had become a kind of voluntary satellite to the Colossus across the Atlantic. The dollar was so powerful against the other world currencies that it seemed on the verge of becoming the sole measure of value accepted in the financial world.

In retrospect, it is clear that the early 1960s represented the apex of American influence and power in Europe; subsequently, the U.S. preoccupation with Vietnam combined with the erosion of the dollar's value to weaken U.S. moral and financial prestige. President Richard M. Nixon's reluctant decision to allow the dollar to find its own level in the international gold market (1971) immediately demonstrated that the U.S. currency had been overvalued, and the Swiss franc and the German mark began to rise steadily against it. The financial reversal dramatized the slower and more general economic changes that had been taking place under the surface, bringing Europe back into a status of balance with the United States (and far overshadowing the Soviet Union).

European Unity

As the economies of the various West European states recovered and then boomed in the 1950s, the old dream of *supranational union* quickly took on new life. For a couple of generations, some Europeans had looked to the day when the nations would give way to some kind of federation with or without a powerful center. Now at the end of a gruesome war that had been caused in part, at least, by German and French enmity, these visionaries saw their best opportunity ever. With the hoped-for backing of the United States, itself a successful federation, they would turn Europe into a new and peaceable political organism.

The main actors in this movement were the leaders of the Christian Democratic parties in Italy, France, Belgium, and West Germany. These middle-of-the-road Catholic parties had become the leading political forces in their countries immediately after the war. Their leaders in the early 1950s were gifted men, such as *Alcide de Gasperi in Italy, Konrad Adenauer in West Germany,* and *Robert Schuman in France.* They believed that inter-European wars were an absolute disaster and must be avoided through political controls over each nation by some type of international group. Being realists, they thought that the best way to form this political association was to create

economic ties among the potential members, which would grow so strong and all-embracing that an individual government would never consider waging war against its partners. First would come the economic bonds, then the social, and eventually the political ones.

In chronological order, the most important steps in this process of unifying western Europe (communist Europe was for obvious reasons a hostile bystander until the 1990s) were the following:

- 1947: The founding of the *Organization for European Economic Cooperation (OEEC).* The OEEC was the supervisory arm of the Marshall Plan aid to Europe.
- 1951: The founding of the *European Coal and Steel Community.* France, West Germany, the Benelux nations, and Italy agreed to subordinate their individual needs in coal and steel to a supranational council. The system worked splendidly, and the six countries formed the nucleus of the Common Market of Europe.
- 1957: The **Treaty of Rome,** the founding charter of the **European Economic Community (EEC).** The EEC was the fundamental organ for European unity in the past 40 years, and the current European Union evolved from it. The EEC is responsible for the *Common Market,* which now embraces most of Europe's countries in a single, nondiscriminatory economic system. A general success from the start, the EEC was meant to become the vehicle by which Europe would be drawn into social as well as economic integration. It has largely achieved these aims for its original twelve members, which have now expanded to fifteen.
- 1992: The **Maastricht Treaty.** This treaty gave extensive powers to the European Parliament (created in 1957 by the Treaty of Rome) and implemented parts of the 1986 Single Europe Act to facilitate economic and financial intercourse among the member states.

The name of the organization (headquartered in Brussels) that supervises these affairs is now simply the European Union (EU). In 1995, labor, money, credit, raw materials and manufactures, communications, and personal travel flow across the national boundaries of fifteen European states with few, if any, restrictions. By 2000, there will presumably be a single European currency. All noncommunist states except traditionally neutral Switzerland have joined or want to join the EU; several of the former communist states have already applied for membership. Even without those states and the former Soviet Union, the EU contains *the largest, richest, single market in the world—375 million consumers.* It seems probable that the new Europe will overshadow both the United States and

Charles de Gaulle
1890–1969

The first president of the Fifth Republic of France, Charles de Gaulle was easily the most important French statesman of the twentieth century. Born to a devout Catholic family in 1890, de Gaulle went into the officer corps and fought in World War I with distinction before his capture in 1916. While in a German prison camp, he realized that the military was the best field to demonstrate his strongest personal feelings: dedication to the glory of France.

De Gaulle was much impressed by the potential of tank warfare, which had been only lightly and inconclusively used in World War I. In 1934, he published *The Army of the Future,* a call to the General Staff to prepare for a coming war in which mobile units spearheaded by massive tank forces would make the trench warfare of 1914–1918 outmoded. He also called for far more attention to the air force. But the French Army establishment regarded these ideas as radical, and for a time de Gaulle's career was blocked.

When World War II began, de Gaulle finally obtained a post of some importance in the Defense Ministry, but too late to effect the necessary changes. France fell to German armor attacks in 1940, but de Gaulle refused to accept the surrender and fled to Britain. For the next four years, he devoted himself to organizing and leading the Free French, a military and civilian movement of all who wished to continue the fight against the Nazi occupiers. By 1944, several of the colonies were governed by the Free French, and its military units landed with the other Allies on D-Day (June 6, 1944). Paris was liberated from German occupation by a French division.

De Galle's persistence and confidence in the resurrection

■ **Charles de Gaulle and Konrad Adenauer.**

Japan in economic terms and drastically change the relative "clout" between the Old and the New Worlds.

Cast into the shadows by the disasters of the first half of the twentieth century, Europe has reemerged as the most important locale of technical, financial, and commercial power in the world. It has been an amazing comeback.

✦ THE COMMUNIST BLOC, 1947–1980

East Europe, (that is, Poland, Hungary, the Czech and Slovak Republics, Romania, former Yugoslavia, Bulgaria, and Albania), where the communists took over after World War II, developed very differently. Here, the orthodox Marxist program was put into effect, following the lead of the Soviet Union. For several years, the *development of heavy industry and transportation* was the number one priority; labor and capital were placed into heavy industry at the expense of all consumer goods.

This Stalinist phase lasted from the late 1940s to the mid-1950s. As in the Soviet Union, it resulted in a huge increase in industrial capacities and the partial industrial

of a beaten France were matched by his demands that he be treated as an equal by Winston Churchill and Franklin D. Roosevelt. This made for a tempestuous relationship, and sometimes France appeared to be fighting a separate war. Immensely popular among the French people at the end of the war, de Gaulle was elected provisional president in 1945, but when it became clear that the politicians were not so enthusiastic about his authoritarian style, he resigned in a huff after only a couple of months. For the next twelve years he lived in retirement in his native village, waiting confidently for the people's call to lead them "out of the wilderness" of the Fourth Republic's wavering and ineffectual government.

In 1958 in the wake of the French defeat in Indochina and the gathering rebellion in Algeria, the call finally came. A referendum installed him as head of a new government, and another gave strong approval to a new constitution creating the Fifth Republic. De Gaulle then assumed the much-strengthened presidency and gave France ten years of stability and prosperity. He crushed an attempted army revolt on the way to settling the bloody war in Algeria and established a workable relationship with the former colonies in the French Community. Insisting on French equality with the United States, he gradually withdrew his forces from NATO and evolved a remarkable partnership with another stubborn old man, Chancellor Konrad Adenauer of West Germany. The two former enemies had become convinced of the need for a permanent Franco-German alliance if Europe were to find peace. The alliance was created within the framework of the European Community, now the European Union.

In a sense, de Gaulle's success led directly to his ultimate defeat. The wave of discontent against the president began with the famous Parisian student strike of 1968. Thousands of new working-class students had flocked into the few French universities during the prosperous 1960s, only to find themselves practically ignored by a very conservative, entrenched academic system. Supported for a while by the workers, they turned to radical protest in the streets, and although the action was put down by police and army, the public reacted vehemently against the amount of force employed. De Gaulle's government now looked to many to be bankrupt of any constructive ideas. In the following year, when an opportunity came to display displeasure by rejecting a constitutional amendment, it was taken by the same middle-class voters who had so strongly embraced de Gaulle ten years earlier. Reading the results as a rejection of himself, de Gaulle resigned his office in 1969 and again retired to his native Normandy, where he died at age eighty.

Even his most vehement enemies were obliged to acknowledge his role in modern French history, when he had almost single-handedly created the image of a country that may have been temporarily overwhelmed by a brutal enemy, but was far from giving up the struggle. De Gaulle's sense of mission, of being the almost divinely appointed savior of his people, carried over into an obstinacy that made him difficult to work with. But that same obstinacy overcame massive wartime obstacles for the general and gave him the moral authority as president to lead the disunited and cynical French into a better civic life.

---

ization of these previously backward, peasant economies. Urban areas in particular grew by leaps and bounds as the abundant excess labor of the rural areas was siphoned off by the demand for workers in the new industry. As in Soviet Central Asia a generation earlier, whole new towns sprouted out of the fields, built around the new steel plant or the new chemical complex. Agriculture was collectivized and then relegated to permanent stepchild status in the budget.

After Stalin's death in 1953, somewhat more attention was paid to the consumer's needs, although the standard of living in communist Europe lagged far behind that in western Europe at all times. Khrushchev, Stalin's successor, summed up the period between 1955 and 1970 when he called it "goulash communism," communism that would put some meat in the pot. By the early 1960s, it was possible for people with skills and perhaps with good Communist Party connections to live fairly comfortably and to hope for a better future still for their children. Salaries and wages were very low by Western standards, but medical care, and education at all levels were free and rents and food prices were low.

In other words, citizens were guaranteed the basic minimum by the state, but at the price of doing without the freedom of choice in the market and most of the consumer luxuries that were fast becoming commonplace in the West, such as private automobiles, new appliances, roomier apartments, and exotic tourism. In this way, the communist governments more or less satisfied a large proportion of their subjects economically, especially those who had been on the lower end of the social ladder in precommunist days.

In the *1970s,* however, in one communist-ruled country after another, the economic advance halted and went into reverse as far as most consumers were concerned. The Marxist "command economy," which was always struggling with major defects, now showed *increasing signs of breaking down* altogether. Workers' discontents radically increased, and the governments' attempts to placate them with concessions backfired. As periodicals and television reception from the West were legalized and Western tourism increased, East Europeans had a better opportunity to see how miserably they fared in contrast to their Western counterparts.

The "technology gap" between the free and the communist worlds was growing more rapidly than ever before to the huge disadvantage of the communists not only in international economics, but also at home. The average man in Warsaw, Budapest, or Moscow recognized how far behind his society was and how hopeless its chances of catching up were. And the average woman was rapidly tiring of the dubious benefits that communism had given her: a double task inside and outside the home, lower pay than males and "glass ceilings" in her work, declining health care, and other handicaps in both public and private life. In the face of this rising wave of discontent, the rigid old men who were in charge of the Party and government in all of the East European communist lands were paralyzed. They simply did not know what to do, short of abandoning the system to which they had devoted their lives and which had treated *them,* at least, quite well. As the 1970s progressed into the 1980s, all of the European communist countries drifted and stagnated at the top, while the steam was building up below. And, of course, the safety valve of protest—democratic politics and free elections—did not exist.

Summary

The field of ruins that was Europe in 1945 gave birth to new economic and political life in a surprisingly short time. With U.S. aid, but mainly by their own determination and energy, the West Europeans came back strongly and created a stable, prosperous economy by the 1960s. These achievements were guided by governments that were composed either of moderate conservatives, many of them Christian Democrats, or of moderate, non-Marxist socialists.

During the same two postwar decades, the Cold War waxed and waned in accord with U.S. and Soviet initiatives and gambles. So long as Josef Stalin lived, it seemed impossible to find an accommodation that would take the world out from under the atomic mushroom cloud. His successor Nikita Khrushchev proved more flexible despite his gambles in erecting the Berlin Wall in 1961 and the missile adventure in Cuba in 1962. Peaceful coexistence became the slogan of the day, leading to a considerable relaxation (*detente*) in East-West relations by the mid-1960s.

Internally, the East European communist states went through a Stalinist phase of heavy industrial development that transformed these peasant economies into modern, urban-based ones. But the industrial development was not matched by an increase in living standards, and the previous gap between East and West in this respect grew steadily larger in the 1970s. By the early 1980s, the slowdown in the chase for prosperity was noticeable everywhere in the Soviet bloc, and discontent was rising.

Test Your Knowledge

1. The Common Market in Europe was originated by
   a. the Treaty of Versailles in 1919.
   b. the Grand Alliance of the United States, Britain, and the Soviet Union.
   c. the treaty in 1949 that created NATO.
   d. the Treaty of Rome in 1957.

2. The economic "miracle" of West Germany during the 1950s was founded on
   a. a mixed state-and-private economy.
   b. free-market capitalism with few restrictions.
   c. the decision to create a model welfare state.
   d. extensive imports from Britain and the United States.

3. The most dangerous phase of the Cold War's early period (1946–1950) was
   a. during the Russian attempt to blockade access to West Berlin.
   b. the Russian decision to assist North Korea's invasion of South Korea.
   c. the arguments over proper operation of the military government in Berlin.
   d. the Western Allies' attempt to get a democratic government in Poland.

4. Khrushchev emerged as successor to Stalin in the Soviet Union
   a. from the public election held in 1954.
   b. after much backstage maneuvering.
   c. on a platform of anti-Stalinism and more democracy in the Communist Party of the Soviet Union.
   d. because of his wide popular appeal to Russians.

5. What is the correct chronology of these events?
   a. Berlin Wall erection, Berlin blockade, Cuban Missile Crisis, Korean War
   b. Berlin blockade, Korean War, Berlin Wall erection, Cuban Missile Crisis
   c. Korean War, Berlin blockade, Berlin Wall erection, Cuban Missile Crisis
   d. Korean War, Cuban Missile Crisis, Berlin blockade, Berlin Wall erection

6. Which statement about communist Europe's economic progress is most correct?
   a. Much industrial progress from 1945 to 1955, then tapering off to stagnation in the 1970s
   b. Poor results until Stalin's death, then rapid improvement until the 1970s
   c. Gradual change from agrarian to industrial economy during the 1950s and 1960s with a switch to consumer products successfully undertaken in the 1970s and 1980s
   d. A continuous disaster of poor planning and lack of expertise

7. Early postwar leadership in Western Europe was generally held by
   a. socialist parties that severed ties with the communists.
   b. coalitions of communists and socialists.
   c. moderate conservatives in the Christian Democratic parties.
   d. strong conservatives rejecting all aspects of socialism.

8. General Charles de Gaulle
   a. was the United States' most dedicated ally in NATO.
   b. was the founder of the Free French movement in World War II.
   c. was the leader of a coup against the civil government in the 1960s.
   d. was the supreme commander of French forces during the early months of World War II.

Identification Terms

Cuban Missile Crisis	European Economic Community	Marshall Plan	Treaty of Rome
de Gaulle (Charles)	Khrushchev (Nikita)	Nuclear Test Ban	Truman Doctrine
detente	Maastricht Treaty	*Ostpolitik*	Warsaw Pact

Bibliography

On the Cold War's development from 1945 onward, there are a number of reliable histories, including several that take the position that both superpowers were responsible for the initiation of the Cold War and its long continuance.

Kolko, G. *The Politics of War,* 1969. Probably the best known of the "revisionist" accounts that lay the blame for the Cold War more on the United States than on the Soviet Union. W. LaFeber, *America, Russia and the Cold War,* 1985, is a similar attempt. On the other side, Dean Acheson, the secretary of state under Truman, has written *Present at the Creation,* 1969, a strong defense of the policy he helped make. J. Gaddis, *The United States and the Origin of the Cold War, 1942–1947,* 1972, is a balanced account leaning toward making Stalin responsible, while J. Lukacs, *A History of the Cold War,* 1968, berates both sides sharply. A. Ulam, *The Rivals: America and Russia since World War II,* 1971, is perhaps the best summary of the whole picture.

Europe's recovery in the quarter century after 1945 is detailed in several worthwhile books:

Ardagh, J. *The New French Revolution,* 1969. Describes the big changes in France since the war and explains why de Gaulle was so popular for a time.

Barzini, L. *The Italians,* 1970. Fun to read and insightful.

Crouzet, M. *The European Renaissance since 1945,* 1971. Written in a very optimistic mood.

Johnson, P. *Modern Times: The World from the Twenties to the Eighties,* 1983. A vigorously opinionated (conservative) and stimulating history of everything imaginable.

Laqueur, W. *Europe since Hitler,* 1991. A very good survey.

_____. *The Germans,* 1985. Love and hate judiciously balanced.

Marwick, A. *British Society since 1945,* 1982.

Mayne, R. *The Recovery of Europe, 1945–1973,* 1973. Good on economic and diplomatic detail while keeping the big picture firmly in view.

Paxton, R. *Twentieth Century Europe,* 1992. As good as Laqueur but takes in a bigger timeframe.

Postan, M. M. *An Economic History of Western Europe, 1945–1964,* 1967. Lively book, almost makes economics fun to read.

White, T. *Fire in the Ashes,* 1953. A perceptive American journalist visits a western Europe just beginning its recovery.

CHAPTER 55

DECOLONIZATION AND THE "THIRD WORLD"

DECOLONIZATION'S CAUSES

DISMANTLING OF WESTERN COLONIES

THE THIRD WORLD

The Population of the Earth

Misapplied Technology

The fifty years after World War II saw the end of the colonial empires built up since 1500 by the European powers. In the Western colonies, the end came soon after the war. In 1945, many hundreds of millions of Asians, Africans, Polynesians, and others were governed by Europeans from distant capitals. By the end of the 1970s, practically none were still under European rule. These unexpected developments gave birth to the so-called Third World as a counterforce to the superpower blocs of the Cold War years.

In the late 1980s, the last of the colonial powers, the Soviet Union, confessed its inability to coerce continued obedience from its East European and Asian satellites and released them from imposed communist rule. A short time later, the collapse of the Soviet Union itself allowed the emergence of several new independent states and ended the Cold War.

❧ DECOLONIZATION'S CAUSES

The decolonization movement had several major causes. In certain instances, such as *India, Vietnam, and the Philippines*, the rise to independent, sovereign status was the culmination of a generation or more of struggle— sometimes with gun in hand. In other cases, such as *Zaire, Libya, and Iraq* independence came as a more or less sudden "gift" from the home country, often to a population that was quite unprepared for the event. Whatever the individual circumstances, all the independence-seeking colonies profited from some general developments that had occurred during the postwar years:

1. *Nationalism in Asia and Africa.* National pride and a burning resentment of Western dominion were in all cases the driving forces of decolonization. European rule had sown the seed of its own dissolution in the colonies by creating a small, but vitally important native intelligentsia. The products of European-founded schools, these individuals had sometimes obtained higher education in the mother country. There they had learned not only academic subjects, but also to reject the inferior status they suffered at home. They also absorbed Western nationalism and Western techniques of political organization (both legal and illegal). In a few cases such as the Vietnamese **Ho Chi Minh** (1890–1969) in France, they encountered and adopted Marxism as a path to successful revolution and national sovereignty. (See the Document in this chapter.) The

Asian militants' efforts to build a popular following were aided by the repeated humiliations Japan inflicted on European/American armies and navies early in World War II, which revealed that the colonial powers were not invincible.

2. *Loss of European moral authority.* In the nineteenth and early twentieth centuries, most Europeans looked upon their colonies with the sense that they were doing "the right thing," that is, meeting their duties as carriers of the "white man's burden." By the 1950s the conviction that they were destined to rule others had been much weakened by the experiences of the two world wars and by the postwar spirit of egalitarian democracy. The Europeans' self-assurance was gone; they no longer possessed the morale that is always necessary to govern others effectively.

3. *Temporary prostration of Europe after 1945.* After the war until about 1960, Europe's six overseas colonial powers (Belgium, Britain, France, Italy, the Netherlands, and Portugal) were absorbed with repairing the damage caused by the war and/or reforming the low-tech economies and obsolete educational systems they had carried over from the 1930s. The public had no interest in supervising "difficult" colonials or pouring badly needed capital and labor into colonial projects that might never work out. No politician in those countries could hope to gather support by appealing to the voters to build up the colonies!

4. *Opposition to the continuation of colonies in both Allied war aims and U.S. policy.* The stated aims of the United Nations, founded at the end of World War II, were clearly anticolonial. And the United States, which played such a major role in postwar Europe, had always felt uneasy about holding colonies, even its own (it gave the Philippines their promised independence as early as 1946). In light of these facts, the Western countries' more or less voluntary release of their colonies between 1946 and 1962 becomes more understandable. By the latter date, only the Soviet Union was still an important colonial country, holding East Europeans as unwilling satellites and suppliers.

✤ DISMANTLING OF WESTERN COLONIES

Britain led the way by making good on the Labour Party's wartime promise to release *India* from the British Commonwealth as soon as the war ended. The saga of India's rise from colony to partly self-governing possession had played out over the first third of the twentieth century. For many years British governments had grudgingly given

■ **Ho Chi Minh with His Generals.** The leader of the long rebellion against France and then the United States plots his next moves. "Uncle" Ho was an outstanding representative of the large group of Third World nationalists determined to lead their peoples into independence by any means possible after World War II.

ground to the peaceable but persistent movement led by the Hindu Congress Party and its founder, **Mohandas Gandhi** (1869–1948). Gandhi's magnificent ability to reveal the moral inconsistencies in the British position made him an unbeatable opponent, however, and the Labour Party had been gradually won over to his point of view (see the Biography in this chapter). During the war, it promised to release India from the British colonial system as soon as hostilities ended.

In 1945, Labour won the first postwar election, and negotiations with Gandhi and his associate **Jawaharlal Nehru** were begun. It soon became clear that the Hindu leaders could not speak for the large Muslim minority, which demanded separate statehood. The British government, immersed in the severe postwar problems at home, tried in vain to resolve this dilemma. In 1947, independence was granted to India on a ready-or-not basis.

The immediate result was a very bloody civil war, fought by Hindus and Muslims over the corpse, so to speak, of Gandhi, who had been assassinated by a fanatic. From this war came two new states, India and Pakistan (and eventually Bangladesh, the former East Pakistan), which remain hostile to this day and engage in frequent

Vietnam's Declaration of Independence, 1946

Ho Chi Minh remained in Vietnam throughout World War II, organizing and leading the Viet Minh guerrillas against the Japanese occupiers. Many members of the French colonial government had opted to cooperate with the Japanese and had been left in place by the Tokyo authorities. When the end of the war approached, the Japanese garrison ousted the French and took over directly. Ho and his people expected to be treated as allies by the French after the war, but instead were told they must return to colonial status. In September 1945, the Viet Minh leadership made this reply, which draws cleverly on the history of both France and the United States to justify itself. Note that Ho by no means had the "entire Vietnamese people" behind him at this juncture and was hoping to bluff the French and embarrass the Americans with this Vietnamese Declaration of Independence. That independence was achieved only after thirty years of near-continuous fighting.

"All men are created equal. They are endowed by their Creator with certain inalienable rights; among these are Life, Liberty, and the pursuit of Happiness." This immortal statement was made in the Declaration of Independence of the United States of America in 1776. In a broader sense, this means; all the peoples of the earth are equal from birth, all the peoples have a right to live, to be happy, and to be free.

The Declaration of the French Revolution made in 1791 on the Rights of Man and Citizen also states: "All men are born free and with equal rights, and must always remain free and have equal rights."

Those are undeniable truths.

Nevertheless, for more than 80 years, the French imperialists, abusing the standard of Liberty, Equality, and Fraternity, have violated our Fatherland and oppressed our fellow citizens. They have acted contrary to the ideals of humanity and justice. . . .

They have built more prisons than schools. They have mercilessly slain our patriots; they have drowned our uprisings in rivers of blood. . .

In the field of economics, they have fleeced us to the backbone, impoverished our people, and devastated our land. . . .

In the Autumn of 1940 when the Japanese Fascists violated Indochina's territory to establish new bases in their fight against the Allies, the French imperialists went down on bended knee and handed over our country to them. Thus, from that date our people were subjected to the double yoke of the French and the Japanese. Their sufferings and miseries increased. . . .

After the Japanese had surrendered to the Allies, our whole people rose to regain our national sovereignty and to found the Democratic Republic of Vietnam.

The truth is that we have wrested our independence from the Japanese, and not from the French. The French had fled, the Japanese have capitulated, Emperor Bao Dai [a French puppet ruler] has abdicated. Our people have broken the chains which for nearly a century have fettered them and have won independence for the Fatherland. Our people at the same time have overthrown the monarchic regime that has reigned supreme for dozens of centuries. In its place has been established the present Democratic Republic.

For these reasons, we, members of the Provisional Government, representing the entire Vietnamese people, declare that from now on we break off all relations of a colonial character with France; we repeal all the international obligations that France has so far subscribed to on behalf of Vietnam, and we abolish all the special rights that the French have unlawfully acquired in our Fatherland. . . .

We are convinced that the Allied nations which at Tehran and San Francisco have acknowledged the principles of self-determination and equality of nations, will not refuse to acknowledge the independence of Vietnam. . . .

SOURCE: *Selected Works of Ho Chi Minh*, vol. 3 (Hanoi: 1960–62).

border disputes and mutual misunderstandings. It was a shaky beginning to the worldwide movement to end colonial governments.

Elsewhere, however, the British generally managed to avoid the difficulties they had experienced in India. Burma and Sri Lanka (Ceylon) gained their independence in the late 1940s. After considerable negotiation, **Ghana** (Gold Coast) became the first colony in sub-Saharan Africa to be granted self-government. It was then recognized as a sovereign member of the Commonwealth in 1957. Ghana was quickly followed by almost the entire list of British colonies from Malaysia to Belize (British Honduras) in Central America. By the mid-1960s, even such minor colonies as the islands of the south Pacific (Fiji, the Solomon Islands) and the Bahamas were granted either self-government under the Crown or full independence. The only areas once under the rule of the British Crown that have not yet obtained sovereignty are those with very small populations (Bermuda, Falkland Islands), which have asked London for continuing aid and protection.

In *France,* the attitude of the public and government toward retaining the colonial empire underwent a diametrical shift around 1960. This reversal was generated by the unhappy results (for France) of the *Vietnam War* (1945–1954) and the *Algerian War* (1958–1961). Both of these proved lost causes that led to many thousands of French casualties and much discontent at home. In 1958, the war hero General Charles de Gaulle became president of France and almost immediately began to change course on the colonial question. Within four years, most of the former possessions had been granted independence and membership in a French version of the British Commonwealth. The members of this Community remain closely linked with France in economics and culture, but go their

■ **French Troops Prepare for Vietnamese Attack.** The end of the French colonial empire in Asia came at Dien Bien Phu, where the elite paratroops and Foreign Legionaries surrendered to the North Vietnamese after a bloody siege in March 1954.

individual ways in international affairs. On the whole, the French were successful, as were the British, in retaining good relations with their former colonies.

The *Belgians, Dutch, and Portuguese,* on the other hand, were all forced from their Asian and African possessions by a combination of uprisings and international pressure exerted in the United Nations. These small countries had relatively more prestige and wealth invested

■ **Hindu Refugees Fleeing the New Pakistan, 1947.** The interchange of huge numbers of refugees who had been minorities in either the newly independent India or Pakistan was not accomplished without immense misery and loss of life. Here, Hindus and Sikhs fleeing Muslim Pakistan arrive by boxcar-loads in the border city of Amritsar.

Mohandas Gandhi
1869–1948

The worldwide reputation of Mohandas Karamchand Gandhi, the Hindu national and spiritual leader, resulted from his deeds as a nonviolent revolutionary. His acts of defiance against what he considered an unjust colonial government were uniquely successful. He is rightly seen as the father of Indian independence, and his renown and revered place in Indian history are unrivaled. Gandhi was above all else an upholder of human dignity. Believing that all life was precious and should not be wasted, he steadfastly opposed the use of violence, in any cause. His followers titled him the Mahatma, or "great soul." They admired and trusted him with a zeal generally reserved for religious leaders. Even the British colonial government came to recognize and respect his high moral quality and his dedication to his people.

Gandhi was born to a merchant family of medium caste in Porbandar, India, in 1869. All his life he attributed much of his strength of character to his mother, who taught him religious values and spiritual confidence. When he was thirteen he was married in traditional fashion to a distant relative; five years later, he went to England to study law. He returned to India to practice, but after two years, he decided to try his luck in the British colony of South Africa. Here he soon became a leader of the large group of Hindu workers and defended their rights against systematic racial discrimination. During this period, Gandhi changed from being just another ambitious middle-class Hindu to become a man of extraordinary spiritual strength. He gave up Western dress and customs, dressed in the worker's traditional loincloth and homespun shirt, and began a life of complete celibacy.

In 1915, he returned to India and at once became active in the budding Indian national independence movement. But he supported Britain in World War I, counting on London to grant Indians much more self-government after the conflict was over. When this did not happen, Gandhi began his lifelong campaigns of civil disobedience against the injustices of colonialism and the subordination of the Hindus to the British colonial authorities. His most famous act of protest was the Salt March of 1930, which brought him to world attention. Gandhi led hundreds of thousands in a long walk across India to the sea as a protest against a British tax on salt (the one commodity that poverty-stricken Hindus had to buy for money).

After this, Gandhi was in and out of British jails or in London as spokesman for the idea of Indian independence. The bald little man in a loincloth could not be ignored, however much the interwar

---

in their colonies and gave them up reluctantly. The Belgians lost the huge African Congo by threatened rebellion in 1961; the Dutch let go of their Indonesian empire only after prolonged and vain fighting against the nationalists in the late 1940s. The Portuguese gave up their outposts in Africa also under severe pressure from a guerrilla war beginning in the early 1970s.

Decolonization or the "retreat from empire," as it has been frequently called, was a major turning point in world history. Europe (and North America and Japan) continues to exercise great power over the non-Europeans, but this influence is more subtle and is basically economic rather than political and military in nature. It is now inconceivable that a Western country would attempt to install an openly colonial regime in any non-Western land, if only for fear of the penalties it would suffer from its own neighbors. Since the collapse of the Soviet system in the early 1990s, the same can be said of the Russians. Colonialism as an overt political relationship is "history."

✦ THE THIRD WORLD

The largest part of the world's population lives neither in the West nor in the ex-communist countries. Instead, the majority live in what was formerly called the "Third World" of less-developed and scarcely developed countries such as Zaire, Afghanistan, and Bolivia, where the per capita cash income is perhaps one-twentieth of the West's and a basically different set of cultural values and

governments wished he would go away. In World War II, Gandhi refused to support Britain until the government made a definite promise of independence. For this he was jailed again, but was freed in 1944 to take part in the negotiations over India's postwar status. He was a major figure in the conferences of 1946 and 1947 that culminated with the division of India into its Hindu and Muslim portions and the independence of both from European rule.

Because he refused to allow Hindu threats and riots against the minority Muslims, some fanatics considered Gandhi a traitor to the Hindu cause. In early 1948, one of them shot and killed him while he was praying. The entire subcontinent, Muslim and Hindu alike, went into mourning.

Gandhi's example of nonviolent civil disobedience has been followed throughout the world since his death. In the United States, Martin Luther King, Jr., attributed much of

his success in organizing American blacks to lessons learned from Gandhi. But Gandhi's lessons and examples were not always popular or heeded by his own people. His hope that Indians could return to a preindustrial lifestyle, weaving their own clothes and growing their own foods, seemed to many otherwise sympathetic people to be impossible. His protégé and successor to the presidency of the Hindu National Congress Party, Jawaharlal Nehru, strongly disagreed with his mentor on these topics and did not attempt to continue the Mahatma's emphasis on home workshops and the denial of the Industrial Age.

After Gandhi's death, the Congress Party became a normal, faction-filled political organization, rather than the Mahatma's personal instrument to mold Indian national consciousness. But Gandhi is still revered among ordinary Indians and he would unquestionably rank at the head of any list of modern Hindus.

customs reigns. In fact, three-fourths of the 5.5 billion people inhabiting the world in 1990 lived in the less-developed countries. This predominance in numbers has not yet been translated into cultural and economic predominance—and perhaps never will be. But with the global village beckoning in the twenty-first century, we in the West had better prepare to encounter and assist these people if we intend to live in peace. The gap that currently exists between the developed and less-developed countries cannot be sustained much longer without severe frictions.

What is a Third World society? The rapid economic and social development of some nations in recent years makes it imperative to distinguish among these countries that used to be lumped together under that term. Thus,

the following description applies to the less- and least-developed nations:

- *Economically speaking*, it is a society where poverty is the rule, and some form of agriculture still makes up a high proportion (over 50 percent), of the gross national product. Unskilled labor is predominant in both town and country; the industrial and larger commercial enterprises are commonly controlled by or dependent on foreign capital; and industry is most often engaged in unsophisticated processing of raw material, commonly for an export market.

- *Politically speaking*, it is a society where a small elite, often derived from the bureaucracy of the colonial era, controls access to power and wealth. One political party

■ Kwame Nkrumah Dances with Queen Elizabeth, 1957. The queen paid the new nation of Ghana a ceremonial visit shortly after the formal separation of the former colony from Britain. Ghana's independence was the first act in a drama of national emergences which continued in Africa throughout the 1960s.

controls public life, often with dictatorial power; large landholders are the dominant factor in the countryside, overshadowing or intimidating the far more numerous peasants and landless laborers; nationalism is normally carried to the point of mindless chauvinism; and disdain for the colonial past is a patriotic duty that masks many postcolonial failures.

- *Socially speaking,* it is a society where the overpopulation problem is immense and is getting worse each year. Males are still allowed control over females within the family and have far more prestige outside it; education is highly desired and prestigious but often is ill designed for the present tasks; the clan or the extended family is more important than in developed countries; upward mobility is still quite possible but is becoming rarer for the lower classes; and an unhealthy imbalance of town and country is steadily more apparent.
- *Internationally speaking,* it is a society that is in most ways still dependent on the more developed countries—sometimes as much so as when it was formally a colony—though it may be able to use its control of certain natural resources, notably oil, as an effective weapon to defend its interest on occasion. Since independence, it has been

treated by both the West and the former Soviet bloc basically as a pawn to be moved about in accord with their foreign policy designs, and it has likely been materially disadvantaged in some ways by the recent ending of the Cold War.

In the 1960s, under the leadership of **Marshal Tito,** the renegade communist leader of former Yugoslavia, the Third World organized a series of congresses to attempt to work out a common political front. These efforts came to nothing, as it soon became clear that the various Third World countries were as suspicious of each other as of the superpowers. Still, some of the larger and more developed countries such as India, Pakistan, Yugoslavia, Indonesia, and Egypt were able to establish themselves as independent nations which could play off one superpower against the other to further their own goals.

Since the collapse of the Soviet bloc and the discrediting of Marxist economics, some of the less-developed nations have been placed in an awkward position. To a significantly lesser degree can the tension between the rival ideologies of communism and capitalism be turned to third-party advantage in the competition for political and economic power. Additionally, the leaders of the Western world have concluded that the highest priority for international aid programs is to assist the Russians and East Europeans, to avoid chaos as those peoples attempt to make the transition to a free market. Consequently, less aid is available for the less-developed countries.

In some nations, the standard of living has actually declined since they attained independence. Africa is a particularly tragic case. The famine and banditry afflicting much of the **Sahel** (Sudan, Somalia, Ethiopia) in recent years are manifestations of this decline. So are the dictatorships that are the rule in African governments. Where dictators are absent, it is often only because tribal enmities (Somalia), religious differences (Sudan), or a combination of these (Ethiopia) has prevented a single individual or party from seizing power. Almost everywhere, the root causes of these evils are a population that is too large for the available resources, the misuse of poorly understood imported technology, and a terrifying maldistribution of wealth.

The Population of the Earth

In the 1970s a book appeared with the arresting title *The Population Bomb.* Written by a respected biologist (Paul Ehrlich) at an American university, it warned that a time was rapidly approaching when the earth would face massive, prolonged famine. The rate of population growth in the less-developed countries threatened to overwhelm the capacity of the earth to grow food.

Professor Ehrlich's prognosis of early famine proved erroneous; the Green Revolution plus a series of good crop years around the globe actually increased the ratio of available food to mouths. But many believe Ehrlich's basic argument is still valid: inevitably, starvation will come. They point to the examples of the African Sahel in the 1980s, Bangladesh since independence, and many of the Andean populations in South America to assert that the number of consumers is exceeding the available resources. It is just a matter of time, they argue, until the well fed will be using lethal weapons to hold off the starving hordes.

Other observers, however, argue that Ehrlich and similar doomsayers are not taking the so-called demographic transition into account. This transition occurs when parents stop viewing many children as a familial and economic necessity and instead desire a much smaller number of children. Historically, this has occurred when a society becomes industrialized and urbanized; children then become less economically necessary to the family, and a lower mortality rate means that most of those born will live to maturity. Hence, parents no longer need to have many children to ensure that some will survive to care for them in their old age.

Since the three continents (Africa, Asia, and South America) where the large majority of the nonindustrial peoples live are rapidly developing urban and industrialized societies, it was hoped that the birthrates would drop substantially within a generation. This has not happened, however; in Latin America, parts of Asia, and much of Africa, birthrates have remained at levels double or triple Western rates. The "gap" between the present-day medical and technological capacities to preserve and prolong life and the cultural demands to have children early and frequently so that some will survive into adulthood has not closed as swiftly as was hoped. Efforts to lower the birthrate by artificial means (condoms, pills) have worked in some places, but failed in others. The most impressive results have been obtained in communist China through massive government intervention in private life as well as constant propaganda for one-child families. Neither of these measures would be acceptable in most countries.

Yet, some means of controlling the hugely increasing demands of the world's population on every type of natural resource (including privacy, quietude, or undisturbed contemplation) must be found soon, presumably. The human inhabitants of Spaceship Earth are increasing in geometric fashion. The earth's first half-billion inhabitants took perhaps 50,000 years to appear, and the second half-billion appeared over 500 years (1300–1800). But the last half-billion of the 1990 total of 5.5 billion people came aboard in a period of ten to twelve years! The large majority of this last half-billion live in the less-developed countries, where the rate of natural increase—births over deaths without counting migration—is two to four times that of the industrial world.

Misapplied Technology

The developed countries' postwar attempts to assist the former colonies and the Latin American states sometimes compounded the difficulties those nations were already experiencing. In nations with a superabundance of labor, where the economy could not supply more than a few months' paid labor for many citizens, the World Bank and other international agencies frequently promoted industrial projects that actually *lessened* job opportunities. Instead of encouraging the continued use of shovels and baskets or similarly technologically primitive but economically productive means of moving earth, for example, the agencies shipped in bulldozers and large dumptrucks to construct a new dam or mine. In agriculture, a local government's request for modern heavy equipment for plowing or the newest mechanical milking machines for its dairies would be granted, even when the predictable net result for the local labor market would be devastating. The cowherders and other laborers thus thrust out of work only contributed to the problems of the poverty-stricken villages or the overcrowded city slums. This preference for short-term "show" rather than long-term improvement characterized many of the Third World's domestic and internationally funded postwar projects.

Ill-conceived technology also frequently had unfortunate ecological consequences. The Aswan Dam project in Egypt is a good example. Built with Soviet aid in the 1950s, the huge dam and the lake it created radically altered the ecology of the lower Nile. Although the lake (despite tremendous loss from evaporation) supplied tens of thousands of acres with water for irrigation, downstream from the dam the changes were entirely for the worse. A variety of snail that previously had not occurred in the lower Nile waters began to flourish there, causing a massive outbreak of epidemic disease. The schools of Mediterranean fishes that had previously been fed from the flooding Nile delta disappeared; with them went the food supply of many Egyptians and the livelihood of many more who had netted the fish and sold them. The new upstream lands now under irrigation from Lake Nasser could not make up the deficit for the hungry Egyptian peasants because almost all of these lands were devoted to cotton or other industrial crops for export.

All told, the efforts of the Third World nations to achieve industrial and/or agrarian development in the thirty years following World War II were unsuccessful in raising living standards for the masses of people. Some groups did prosper, and some regions did much better than others, notably the western rim of the Pacific Ocean. But in much of Africa and Latin America, the few rich got richer, the many poor stayed poor, and those in between

did not multiply as hoped. The maldistribution of wealth is best displayed by some comparative figures. In the industrialized Western nations, the personal income of the uppermost 10 percent of society is about five times the income of the bottom 10 percent. In the comparatively well-off Mexico, the disparity in income has grown over the past decades, until by the 1990s the upper 10 percent were receiving *twenty-seven times* as much as the bottom 10 percent.

Summary

Decolonization came in the first quarter century after World War II, as the colonial powers realized that economic exhaustion and anticolonial sentiment made it impossible to retain their former possessions in Asia and Africa. Beginning with the difficult and bloody severance of India and Pakistan from the British Empire, the colonial structures were dismantled or toppled by armed revolts between 1947 and 1974.

While the British gave their remaining subjects uncontested self-government and then sovereignty in the 1960s, the French were at first less pliant. First in Vietnam and then in North Africa, they engaged in extended warfare that eventually resulted in defeat and withdrawal. Only then under de Gaulle did they achieve a workable post-

colonial relationship. The French mistakes were imitated by the Dutch, Belgians, and Portuguese, all of whom had to be driven out of their colonies by nationalist rebellions during the 1940s through the 1970s. In the Soviet instance, the attempt to retain satellites persisted into the 1980s.

The Third World that emerged from the postcolonial settlements was a hodgepodge of different states and societies. But to some degree all suffered from generic handicaps in dealing with the First World West and the Second World communist states. Maldistribution of national wealth, misapplication of technological assets, and the overwhelming growth of population were three of the worst.

Test Your Knowledge

1. Which of the following African countries fought a long war against a colonial power and eventually won its independence?
   a. Nigeria
   b. Egypt
   c. Algeria
   d. South Africa
2. The decolonization process went ahead with little violence in most areas of
   a. Southeast Asia.
   b. French North Africa.
   c. French West Africa.
   d. Portuguese South Africa.

3. Which was *not* a strong motivation for the rapid decolonization after World War II?
   a. U.S. opposition to continued colonial administration
   b. The war-caused weakness of most colonial powers' economies
   c. The weakening of Europeans' confidence in their ability to rule others well
   d. The communists' accusations of Western imperialism
4. What proportion of the world's population currently lives in the less-developed countries?
   a. One-half
   b. Two-thirds

c. Three-fourths

d. Four-fifths

5. Which of the following was *not* a factor in lessening the West's attention to the problems of the Third World in recent years?

    a. The collapse of the Second World, that is, the communist bloc governments

    b. The diversion of foreign aid to the former communist lands of Europe

    c. The inability of Third World nations to collaborate effectively in international negotiations

    d. The slowing rate of population growth in most ex-colonial countries

6. One of the prominent identifying factors for a Third World society is a

    a. growing rural and agrarian economy.

    b. steady drain of population into the cities.

    c. reluctance to accept foreign aid.

    d. relatively minor place for the military.

7. The last major colonial power in the traditional imperialist sense was

    a. Portugal.

    b. the Soviet Union.

    c. the United States.

    d. France.

Identification Terms

Gandhi (Mohandas)   Ho Chi Minh   Sahel   Tito (Marshal)

Ghana   Nehru (Jawaharlal)

Bibliography

Fanon, F. *The Wretched of the Earth*, 1968. A searing attack on the Western neo-colonialists, with emphasis on Africa, by a psychiatrist from the Caribbean.

von Albertini, R. *Decolonization*, 1971.

Ward, B. *Rich Nations and Poor Nations*, 1964. Despite its age, a book that is still relevant to world economic divisions. Most often cited as the best overview in English, but not an easy read.

Africa

Achebe, C. *Things Fall Apart*, 1959, and *A Man of the People*, 1966. Two novels of precolonial and postindependence Nigeria by the best-known contemporary African novelist.

Davidson, B. *Let Freedom Come*, 1978. A distinguished Africanist reviews trends and events in independent Africa.

Hargreaves, J. D. *Decolonization in Africa*, 1988.

Horne, A. *A Savage War of Peace: Algeria, 1954–1962*, 1971. The best account in any language.

Iliffe, J. *The African Poor*, 1987. Highly recommended to students wishing to know what the lives of most Africans are like.

Lloyd, P., ed. *The New Elites of Tropical Africa*, 1966. Looks at the "wa-benzi" types that emerged after independence.

Asia

Collins, L., and D. La Pierre. *Freedom at Midnight*, 1975. Vivid account of the coming of Indian independence.

Dahm, B. *Sukarno and the Struggle for Indonesian Independence*, 1969.

Fall, B. *A History of Vietnam*, 2 vols., 1964. A French journalist's enlightening account.

Goldschmidt, A., Jr. *A Concise History of the Middle East*, 1991. Up-to-date except for the most recent events.

Nehru, J. *An Autobiography*, 1972. By a self-anointed visionary and the most important Indian statesman since World War II.

Tinker, H. *South Asia: A Short History*, 1990. One of the few overviews available.

THE NEW ASIA

The two leading Asian powers had both suffered greatly during the war and were temporarily restricted in their international roles while recovering. China and Japan continued to take sharply differing paths to establishing modern societies. China chose the path of revolution and became the world's largest Marxist state; Japan adapted Western ideas and technology to fit its own culture and became the world's leading economic success.

The abolition of the colonial system had its most spectacular effects in Africa, but many areas in Asia had also been in colonial status and were equally intent on gaining full independence. India was the first to do so, followed by the other European possessions in Southeast Asia and the Pacific islands. While World War I had brought relatively minor change to these areas, World War II proved to be the wellspring of major transformations. By the end of the twentieth century, several newly independent states were working their way into the upper ranks of world prosperity by taking full advantage of a changing global economy.

✤ MAO'S CHINA: 1949–1976

The People's Republic of China (PRC) was proclaimed by a triumphant Mao Zedong in the fall of 1949. It entered into a formal alliance with the Soviet Union a few months later. Government and all social institutions were reorganized on Soviet lines, and for the first ten years, the Soviets were both its helpers and its mentors.

The conquest of the world's largest population had essentially been the work of one man—Chairman (of the Chinese Communist Party's Central Committee) Mao, with the help of some brilliant assistants, especially Zhou Enlai. Although Mao had profited from some Soviet arms and economic support and guidance since the 1930s, in its fundamentals Chinese communism was his creation; no one else, not even Stalin, had played much of a role beside him in Chinese eyes. This was to be a critical factor in the years to come.

Mao was convinced that in an agrarian society like China's (about 90 percent of the population were peasants), the correct path to socialism could only lie through a revolutionary peasantry. His experiences in Shensi during the 1930s and 1940s had cemented that conviction, and the fact that the original Communist Party leaders and his advisers from Moscow did not agree did not disturb him. Thus, at all times during his rule, keeping the peasants with him was his chief policy; what happened to the urbanites was of secondary importance. Mao's long and fruitful contacts with the rural folk also seem to have made him increasingly distrustful of intellectuals—a very untraditional attitude for a Chinese leader and one that would have horrendous effects on China in the 1960s.

In its first three years (1949–1952), the regime instituted the basic policies it would employ to assure political and social control indefinitely. In the countryside, land was expropriated from the landlords, and many of them were killed or imprisoned for having supported Chiang Kai-shek in the civil war. The land was first redistributed to the peasants and then in 1955–1957 collectivized as the Soviets had done in their Five Year Plan. Although millions were killed, banished, or allowed to starve in the great famines of 1960–1962, the peasants did not resist as fiercely as in the Soviet Union, in part because of the ancient Chinese tradition of regarding the central government (Beijing) as the legitimate source of authority, and in part because so many poor peasants supported the new arrangements ardently.

The new concept of the *commune* was made the basis of rural production and of government, with disastrous effects for both the agricultural and the industrial economies. The communes were so large (about 25,000 persons) and their responsibilities were so ambiguous that they could not function. Even in good years, food production barely matched the rapidly increasing population due to poor planning and low incentives; when bad harvests came after 1960, mass famine was inevitable. To keep the industrial plant working at all, grain was confiscated from the communes mercilessly, and the peasants starved just as they had under Soviet War Communism. The communes were then abolished, and smaller units created that resembled the traditional villages except that land and work were collectivized.

Industrial expansion was pursued in the same fashion as the Soviets had earlier; heavy industry was emphasized at the expense of consumer goods. A Stalinist Five Year Plan instituted in 1953 produced substantial results in metals, coal, and other basic goods for industry. But Mao was impatient with Soviet models and plans; in 1958 he personally introduced the **Great Leap Forward.** This attempt at overnight mass industrialization was an enormously costly failure (the infamous "backyard steelmaking," for example), and it accelerated the growing gap between the Chinese and their Russian mentors, and especially between Mao and Nikita Khrushchev.

The Russians criticized Mao for foolishly attempting the impossible and also for allowing himself to be made into the sort of Great Father in China that Stalin had been in Russia. Khrushchev had just finished revealing Stalin's true nature to a shocked communist world, and he had no intention of allowing Mao to step up onto the vacant pedestal. On his side, a confident Mao made it clear that while he was no great admirer of Stalin or any other foreigner, he believed that true revolutions demanded a nearly supernatural Leader, with whom the ignorant masses might identify—something that Khrushchev never pretended to be nor was capable of being.

Further, Mao told the Russians that they had been diverted from the authentic Marxist path by their fears of losing what they had in a war with capitalism and that he intended to take their place as spokesman of world revolution. By 1960 the barely concealed *Sino-Soviet conflict* was splitting the communist ranks. The rift worsened and became public at the time of the Cuban Missile Crisis, when the Maoists derided the Soviets' fear of "paper tigers," while Moscow denounced Beijing's stated readiness to plunge the world into atomic war.

Mao had long been convinced that the Soviet revolution had been suffocated by bureaucratization, and he was determined that China would not share this fate. For some years he had been content to remain in the background of domestic policy making, but in 1965 he suddenly called for the **Great Proletarian Cultural Revolution,** an extraordinary upheaval that was meant to, and did turn Chinese society on its head for a number of years. Like Stalin's "second revolution" of 1929, Mao's plan went far beyond

■ **The Little Red Book of Chairman Mao.** Chinese Red Guards mass in Beijing to celebrate the appearance of the Chairman. For many millions during the Great Proletarian Cultural Revolution, the Thoughts of Mao as printed in the famous little red book were a command and an inspiration.

Chinese Lives

In 1985, when Deng Xaioping's government relaxed restrictions on political and economic life, a book of oral histories was published in Beijing. It consisted of interviews with ordinary people of all ages and occupations, who talked about their lives now and in the past. The book was inspired by Studs Terkel's similar works in the United States, entitled *Working* and *American Dreams: Lost and Found.* An excerpt from the English translation of *Chinese Lives* follows:

Her Past: A Sixty-Four-Year-Old Woman Living on a Pension

I am from Fenghua county in Zhejiang province, like Chiang Kai-shek. My father was a peasant. He rented his land from a landlord. When I was 13 [1932] my father sold me as a maid; the landlord took me in lieu of rent. When I was 14, he raped me. That's what happened to most pretty servants.

I was very ignorant then. All I knew was that a girl who wasn't a virgin would never find a husband, or if she did, he would ill-treat her. I was ruined.

That Autumn a girl who lived nearby told me that a labour contractor had come to town to look for girls to work in a silk mill .... I was told I would earn 3 silver dollars a month. I made my mark on a contract agreeing to go that very day.

When we reached Shanghai, the man took me with 3 others to a house where a woman looked us over very thoroughly ....

"From now on I am your Mama and you are to behave yourself," the woman said. I didn't know what this was about so I just nodded. She took out a *cheonsam* and a pair of embroidered slippers and told me to put them on.

"I can't get dressed up in that, I've come to do factory work."

"I've bought you," answered Mama. "There's no factory work here."

I had been sold into a brothel in a well-known red-light district. It was 1933 and I was 14.

A vivid description of "the life" in a Shanghai brothel follows. The woman estimates that in the hard times of the 1930s 30,000 prostitutes were working in that city. She remained there for the next nineteen years. After the communist takeover in 1949, many changes were introduced:

All the brothels were closed in the 1951 campaign. I carried on under cover, working from a coffee bar .... All my earning went on heroin .... In Septem-

political rearrangement. He wished to create a truly new relationship between Party, people, and the exercise of revolutionary power. The attack was aimed primarily at the intellectuals, particularly the CCP's cadres of officials, and they suffered to a devastating extent.

To achieve his main end, Mao was prepared to undertake what seemed an impossible task: to rid the Chinese people of their reverence for tradition. He called on the youthful **Red Guards**—mainly students—to make war on the older generation and its "empty formalisms." Himself a profoundly revolutionary spirit who distrusted all systems, even those he had created, the chairman wished to introduce the permanent, self-perpetuating revolution, which he thought the Russians had given up in return for peace and a fake Marxist society.

For the next three or four years, China experienced barely controlled, officially inspired anarchy. Professors were publicly humiliated; learned doctors were made to scrub the floors in their hospitals; scholars were abused for having foreign language books in their libraries; and Communist Party secretaries were accused of sabotage. Factional fighting of all kinds was allowed and encouraged, sometimes in the streets. The economy, only now recovering from the Great Leap Forward's mistakes, again suffered severe damage; managers and skilled personnel were sent to the villages to "learn the revolution's lessons" as barnyard sweepers or potato diggers. For a time, the only qualification for getting a responsible post was to have memorized the *Thought of Chairman Mao,* immortalized in the "little red book" that tens of millions of Chinese waved daily like an amulet against unknown evils (see the Document on page 728).

In 1969, the anarchy had become so bad that Mao had to call off the Red Guards and put the army in charge of

ber 1952 I was detained by the Security Bureau [police] and ended up in a labor reform school .... When I was first there, nothing put me to shame. Nothing seemed too foul for me to stoop to. We were supposed to study for half the day and work the other half, but as I was an addict, I didn't. Half of our study period was devoted to politics and in the other half we arranged meetings to "remember the bitter past" ... I thought it was all a lot of hot air. The cadres kept telling us that the story about us being sent to the northeast to farm wasteland was only a rumour. The government just wanted us to start new lives ....

She was treated for her syphilis and after a time began to accept the efforts to reform her.

The reform school had a slogan about seeing who could be the first to wash off the filth of the old society and start afresh. It was quite catchy, but I can't remember it now. Have you seen the picture *Stand Up Sisters?* It's all about prostitutes in Beijing before and after the Liberation. It tells our story just the way it was ....

I left in 1956. You had to satisfy certain conditions before you could go. Your political attitude had to be good, you had to be completely clear of syphilis and you had to have learned a trade ....

I have to fill in details about my life on forms sometimes. I used to hate answering questions about employment before Liberation. So I went to ask the factory director's advice and he said it would be all right to put "no regular employment." That was a great weight off my mind .... Everyone needs to keep face.

I hardly met any discrimination at work. Most of my workmates [in a clothing factory] were good to me and treated me like a sister. From time to time I still see a few girls from the reform school. Some of them became workers, some shop assistants, some nurses and some peasants. It closed in 1958. In all, it saved several thousand women ....

In the old society I wasn't a high-class prostitute but I wasn't one of the lowest, either. Of course, we prostitutes were at the bottom of the ladder, anyway. In the New China I've learned that I'm equal to everyone else. Ex-prostitutes like me owe everything to the People's Government ....

As I said, I didn't join any organizations during the Cultural Revolution. Once in those years I went to a hospital and saw the doctor who had cured me. He was scrubbing the floors. A consultant dermatologist! I began to cry. He looked up. I suppose he thought that I was very ill. He put his hand out and asked me what department I wanted. I told him my name but he didn't recognize me.

"Remember the reform school?" I prompted.

Only then did he nod slowly, and walk off. There was no place for good people in those years.

---

everyday affairs. The tensions between China and the Soviet Union had erupted in the **"Amur River War"** as troops stationed on both sides of the frontier sporadically fired on each other. The military chiefs told Mao they could not guarantee what might happen if Russia attacked while the unrest continued. Still, until Mao's death in 1976, the spirit of the Cultural Revolution lived on, especially among the millions of radical youth who thought the demolition of the Communist Party's apparatus and the government's disarray presented a once-in-a-lifetime chance for them to get ahead.

Like the Great Leap Forward and other experiments from above, the Cultural Revolution was a costly setback for China; its effects have been felt for a generation. Many of the leading intellectuals, scientists, writers, and artists who formed the elite of the society were punished unmercifully for alleged sins against the revolution. Most were forced into mines, farms, or some other totally unsuitable occupation, where their spirits were broken and their talents wasted.

Within weeks of Mao's death, the inevitable reaction set in. His ambitious and hated wife and her three closest political associates (*the Gang of Four*) were imprisoned. Individuals who had been falsely accused of treason or other antistate activity began to be rehabilitated (just as occurred twenty years earlier in the Soviet Union when Khrushchev succeeded Stalin). The Cultural Revolution was first partially and then entirely condemned as a mistake. A collective leadership of Party officials moved cautiously but steadily to put Mao's contributions into perspective. In 1980, his portraits, formerly everywhere, were silently removed from all public places. The era of the god-like chairman and his omnipresent Little Red Book was definitely over.

Chairman Mao's Thought

The founder and master of the Chinese Communist Party, Mao Zedong, had a well-developed gift for speaking in the language of the people. From the time he first rose to power in the 1930s, Mao wrote a huge number of speeches and essays, which, taken together, spelled out the peculiarly Chinese way to a Marxist society. He was able to say these things in memorable words:

On the Chinese Revolution and the Communist Party (1939)

In China, it was among the intellectuals and young students that Marxist-Leninist ideology was first widely disseminated and accepted. The revolutionary forces cannot be successfully organized without the participation of revolutionary intellectuals. But the intellectuals often tend to be subjective and individualistic, impractical in their thinking and irresolute in their action . . . . The intellectuals can overcome their shortcomings only in mass struggles over a long period.

Talks at the Yenan Forum on Literature and Art (1942)

I began life as a student and at school acquired the ways of a student . . . . At that time I felt that the intellectuals were the only clean people in the world, while in comparison workers and peasants were dirty. . . . But after I became a revolutionary and lived with the workers and the peasants and with soldiers of the revolutionary army, I gradually came to know them well, and they came gradually to know me well, too . . . . I came to feel that, compared with the workers and the peasants, the unremolded intellectuals were not clean, and that, in the last analysis, the workers and peasants were the cleanest people, and even though their hands were soiled and their feet smeared with cowdung, they were really cleaner than the bourgeois and petty-bourgeois intellectuals.

On the Correct Handling of Contradictions among the People (1957)

The First World War was followed by the birth of the Soviet Union, with a population of 200 million. The Second World War was followed by the emergence of the socialist camp with a combined population of 900 million. If the imperialists insist on launching a third world war, it is certain that several hundred million more will turn to socialism, and then there will not be much room left for the imperialists.

❧ RECENT CHINA

Under *Deng Xiaoping* (b. 1904), an elderly but vigorous pragmatist, the Chinese Communist Party groped its way forward into the vacuum left by Mao's demise. A new spirit of profit making was strongly encouraged by various legal changes and official propaganda. To become rich, or at least well-to-do, was no longer a sin against the state and one's fellow citizens. In Deng's words, China would be *socialist in spirit,* regardless of the semicapitalist economic system it seemed to be adopting. Deng, who had long been associated with the moderate wing of the Party rather than being an obedient Maoist, was particularly interested in establishing better relations with foreign capitalists. Spurred by President Richard M. Nixon's surprise visit to Beijing in 1972, the China-U.S. relationship had grown somewhat warmer since the ending of the conflict in Vietnam. The Soviet adventure in Afghanistan (1979) increased Chinese interest in coming to a better understanding with the other superpower. Hence, in the 1980s, with U.S. encouragement considerable progress was made in opening the country to foreigners and

Speech to the Cheng'tu Conference (1958)

Awed by the professors, ever since we came to the city! [Party members] do not despise the intellectuals, but have an immense fear of them. They are filled with learning, while we are inferior in everything! It is strange for a person to fear the professors while he does not fear imperialism. This mental attitude must be a remnant of the slave system. I cannot stand it any longer!

To a Group of Visiting Frenchmen (1964)

Recently a Japanese merchant came to me and said "I very much regret that Japan invaded China." I replied to him, "You are not being fair. Of course, the aggression wasn't fair either, but there is no need to apologize. If the Japanese had not occupied half of China, it would have been impossible for the entire Chinese population to rise and fight the invader. And that resulted in our army strengthening itself by a million men, and in the liberated [i.e., communist-controlled] bases the population increased to one hundred million." That is why I said to this Japanese merchant, "Should I thank you?"

The Great Leap Forward of China (1964)

We cannot take the old path of technical development followed by various countries of the world, and go at a crawl after other people. We must break with convention and make maximum use of advanced techniques, so that our country can be built into a modern socialist power within not too long an historical period.

Twenty Manifestations of Bureaucracy (1966)

[Bureaucrats] are conceited, complacent, and they aimlessly discuss politics. They do not grasp their work; they are subjective and onesided; they are careless; they do not listen; they are truculent and arbitrary; they force orders, they do not care about reality; they maintain blind control .... They promote error and a spirit of reaction; they connive with bad persons and tolerate bad situations; they engage in villainy and violate the law ... they suppress democracy; they quarrel and take revenge; they do not differentiate between the enemy and ourselves.

Foreword to the Second Edition of *Quotations from Chairman Mao* by Lin Piao (1967)

Comrade Mao Tse-tung is the greatest Marxist-Leninist of our era. He has inherited, defended, and developed Marxism-Leninism with genius, creatively and comprehensively, and has brought it to a new and higher stage.

In 1970, Lin Piao was killed attempting to flee China after an aborted conspiracy against the chairman.

SOURCE: Excerpted from *A Revolution is Not a Dinner Party,* eds. Soloman and Huey, Anchor Press, 1975.

---

democratizing the secretive Communist Party and its iron controls over the populace. But the rapid spread of a critical, questioning atmosphere among the university students eventually frightened the leaders, and in 1989 they cracked down in the infamous **massacre in Tienanmen Square** in the heart of Beijing.

Since that time, China has been isolated diplomatically from the West, as it has long been from the Soviet Union and then from the Yeltsin government in Russia. Attempts by Mikhail Gorbachev and later Boris Yeltsin to unfreeze the Russo-Chinese impasse have made only slow progress.

No basic changes can be expected until both Deng and the clique of elderly comrades he trusts have passed from the scene and a younger generation has taken over in Beijing. Whether this younger group will retain Marxism as the official Chinese ideology is one of the most tantalizing questions of world politics in the mid-1990s. Whether Marxist or capitalist, China has become one of the four most potent international powers. With its aspiring and hardworking population of more than a billion, China will be a major factor in the global economy as well as in Asia in the twenty-first century.

■ **A Single Youth Defies the Tanks.** Just before the 1989 Tiananmen Square massacre a brave (and never identified) young student attempted to make the tanks stop by planting himself in their path. They eventually rolled around him and continued into the great square.

✣ POSTWAR JAPAN TO 1952

The defeat and occupation of the Japanese empire by a foreign force (for the first time in history) was a tremendous shock. But it soon proved to be a constructive shock, which unleashed a great deal of new energy and innovative thinking. Despite heavy damage and loss of life, both military and civilian, during the war, Japan's economy rebounded with unexpected speed and then proceeded to shoot far ahead of anything it had achieved before in industrialization and technology.

The government of occupied Japan was an American affair under the commander-in-chief of Allied Forces in the Pacific, General Douglas MacArthur (1880–1964). Unlike the situation in occupied Germany after its defeat, a native civilian government was allowed to function, but it was reduced to carrying out the directives of MacArthur's staff. In the first two years of the occupation, MacArthur's office initiated radical changes in the traditional Japanese system, culminating in an entirely *new constitution* that established a government similar to the British government. The parliament (Diet) is the most important branch of government, and sovereignty resides in the Japanese people. The emperor is retained but only

as a symbol. Japan "forever renounces war as a sovereign right of the nation," maintaining only a small Self-Defense Force, as it is called.

The constitution and all of MacArthur's many reform decrees in politics and social matters were accepted almost without criticism by the Japanese. Spiritually and materially exhausted by war and defeat, they were in a mood of self-questioning, very unusual for this proudly nationalist and confident nation. They seemed ready to accept a new basis for their social and political organization, and their willingness to change made the Occupation a great success. After a few years, most Japanese regarded the United States more as a friend and protector than as a punitive force.

The war in Korea (1950–1953) was a key element in the elevation of the United States from conqueror to protector. The active support given to the North Korean communist army by Mao's China after 1951 made the U.S. armed forces in South Korea and elsewhere in the western Pacific an indispensable guardian for disarmed Japan. Japanese of all persuasions generally recognized the need for U.S. protection, even though some were disturbed by the U.S.-instigated transformations in their culture.

✣ INDEPENDENT JAPAN

In 1952, the Occupation ended as foreseen, and Japan again became a sovereign state. It signed a treaty of alliance with the United States that extended the U.S. nuclear umbrella over Japan in any future war. In return, the United States was guaranteed the right to have naval and military bases on Japanese soil for the indefinite future. Although minimally opposed at the time, this treaty caused some tensions later, when the Japanese regained their confidence and the Socialist and Communist Parties denounced the treaty as a tool of U.S. imperialism. By then, however, it was clear that Japanese politics tended toward the conservative and that an anti-U.S. position had little appeal.

For the first few years, the Liberal Party was the leading force in postwar politics; in 1955 the Liberals merged with their closest rivals and became the Liberal Democratic Party (LDP). For almost forty years, the LDP formed every Japanese government. Despite the name, it was a conservative party, dominated by the big business interests that have always worked closely with government in Japan. The party reflected the basically conservative instincts of most Japanese over thirty. An homogeneous people who value tradition and group approval, the

Japanese have never shown much interest in social experimentation or political radicalism.

The LDP finally went down to defeat in 1993, when it was to be the culprit in a series of political corruption scandals that rocked the country and the business establishment. Always more an aggregation of financial and economic interests than a political unit, the LDP split into factions and lost out to a coalition of opponents. Economic troubles in the 1990s have kept this coalition unstable without affecting the policies established during the LDP's long reign.

Economic Progress

The *economic success* of postwar Japan is admired throughout the world and even considered as a possible model by the older industrialized states of the West. A combination of external and internal factors contributed to Japan's prosperity through the early 1990s. *Externally,* Japan benefited when the United States assumed the burden of its defense in the 1950s and 1960s; thus, the budgetary expenditures that would have gone into nonproductive weaponry, housing, pensions and so on for the military were saved and could be invested in the civilian economy. The Korean War stimulated Japanese industry in many different ways. Also, during the initial postwar decades, oil was very cheap (Japan is entirely dependent on imported oil), and international credit institutions such as the World Bank and the International Monetary Fund were eager to lend for investment and the acquisition of technology. Japan soon showed itself to be a willing student and a highly reliable borrower.

Internally, Japan had the world's highest savings rate, and the banks reinvested the savings in new industry. The Japanese labor force was disciplined and skilled and had been well educated in one of the world's most effective primary and secondary school systems, which was centrally directed by a government constantly looking for improvements. The Japanese population rose throughout the postwar era, providing a large labor pool as well as a growing internal market. Under strong government urging, labor continued to work with employers rather than take an adversarial position; unions were rewarded by being given extensive powers in the workplace.

Most of all, in the opinion of many, Japan's postwar surge was due to the consistent support of business by the government, which made large sums available for ongoing research and development and aggressively promoted business interests in its diplomacy. The *zaibatsu* combines, which originally were broken up by the Americans, were allowed to reconstitute themselves in a slightly different fashion and with even more political and financial clout. New industrial giants such as Sony and Honda were the product of brilliantly bold entrepreneurs. Industry and government directed a major effort toward expanding foreign trade, and Japanese trade with almost every noncommunist country rose without interruption during the postwar decades. Japanese goods, including electronic products, automobiles, watches, and cameras, conquered the consumer markets of the globe. The "Made in Japan" label, which had been synonymous with cheap imitations in the prewar era, became a symbol of advanced design and the world's best quality. Only in China and the Soviet Union did Japanese exports fail to find a willing market, and this was due as much to Japanese financial caution as to political reasons.

All these factors combined to give Japan the highest rate of growth in gross national product (about 10 percent per annum) in the world during the quarter century between 1950 and 1975. Since then the rate of growth has slowed somewhat and even gone into reverse in the early 1990s. It is still the highest of any developed country over the entire half century since World War II.

Social Affairs

Both rural and urban populations benefited from the postwar surge. After many generations of Buddhist simplicity and restraint, the Japanese have recently become a nation of consumers in the Western sense. Automobiles, television sets, cameras, and all the other manifestations of personal luxury we have become accustomed to are at least equally evident in Japan's cities. The standard of living is about as high as in the United States. But many flaws in the picture of prosperity have recently come to light. Housing for families, for example, remains an acute problem due to the shortage of available land where people wish to live. A well-paid manager working in Tokyo may have a two-hour, nerve-grinding commute because finding an affordable apartment any closer is impossible.

More disturbing to many is the visible erosion of respect for elements of the nation's heritage that has taken place during the last two decades. Some blame this on the Americanization begun in the Occupation years and continued since then by American entertainment media. Others see the lost war itself as the fundamental reason why less respect is shown for the older generation and for all authority. In any case, urban youths in particular are increasingly unwilling to continue the age-old deference to the elderly. They resent having to provide economic support for a generation of older people who can no longer work and take care of themselves, so increasingly these tasks are pushed off onto governmental agencies, as in the West. This unprecedented "war of the generations" as some alarmists have termed it is exacerbated by the housing shortage in the cities, which forces young people to remain in the parental home longer than they desire.

Women in postwar Japan find themselves in a multifaceted struggle to gain economic equality with their husbands and brothers. The constitution gave them legal and political equity, but deliberately failed to alter a system of work and play that firmly separated male and female. In very recent years, Japanese working women have gained some access to jobs that were formerly male preserves, but they still lag behind women in other industrial societies. The glass ceiling in Japan may be the most prevalent and inpenetrable in the world.

As for leisure and play, the ancient habit of allowing men to go places and engage in activities that were quite out of bounds to women has not been seriously challenged to the present day. Company-sponsored visits to geisha bars and nightclubs are still a routine part of white-collar professional life, as is ritualized drunkenness. The wife, on the other hand, usually has undisputed control over the household budget and the handling of the younger children and is the equal of her husband in family decision making. Most Japanese women are quite content with this state of affairs, and divorce rates are relatively low, though climbing.

Japan's example has been an inspiration to other East Asian countries, even those like Vietnam and China, which still subscribe to Marxist principles. Japan's advance to Western levels of material consumption and well-being has been accomplished without sacrificing its national heritage and without overt imperialism.

The **"four little tigers"** of the Pacific Rim—South Korea, Taiwan, Singapore, and Hong Kong—have learned the lessons of Japan well and have recently attained superior growth rates in the drive to establish an electronically driven, information-based economy. They are now being joined by Malaysia, and just behind these five are Thailand and Indonesia. Throughout the western Pacific, rapid economic growth based on a modified free market in goods and services has become the first priority for government, whether Marxist or capitalist in formal ideology. From its backwater status in the early part of this century, industrialized East Asia has become the fastest-growing economy in the world and a vital part of a mutually dependent global interchange.

✤ SOUTH ASIA SINCE INDEPENDENCE
India

Mahatma Gandhi's assassination shortly after India gained its independence left the Hindu masses in confusion and sorrow, but did not interfere with the erection of the new entity's political structure. As leader of the majority Congress Party, Gandhi's close associate and designated heir **Jawaharlal Nehru** (1889–1964) sprang into the breach. Unlike Gandhi, Nehru believed that *Western-style industrialization* was an absolute necessity to avoid social chaos in India, and he set the country firmly on that path during his fifteen years at the government's head. He also believed that India could best live with neighboring Muslim Pakistan by showing it a strong hand that would discourage ill-considered military adventures. In practice this policy meant that India and Pakistan were on a quasi-war footing for the next three decades, largely over the ownership of the rich border province of **Kashmir** where Muslims and Hindus were in close balance.

Nehru dominated Indian politics until his death in 1964 and made his country the international leader of the postwar Third World. He led India toward a moderate *democratic socialism* that owed little to Marx and much to the British Labour Party. A mix of state ownership and free enterprise was worked out that has been relatively successful. For many tens of millions of Indians, living standards have risen in the past half century. But for perhaps 60 percent of the total of 650 million (in the 1990 census), there has been discouragingly little change from the poverty of pre-independence days. The most acute challenge to Indian prosperity, as in so many other developing nations, remains the high rate of population growth. Various governmental campaigns for fewer births have not been very successful in the traditionalist villages where most Indians live.

After Nehru's death, in 1966 his daughter **Indira Gandhi** (no relation to the Mahatma) became the first female prime minister of an Asian state and continued his vision of a modern, industrial India. Her increasingly dictatorial style created conflicts with many Congress Party leaders, however, and she was turned out of office in the 1975 general election, only to return in 1980. These electoral transitions were evidence of the maturity that India—the world's largest democracy—had achieved in its government only a generation after colonial subordination. It was an impressive and heartening performance.

The picture of stability and political consensus has been rudely marred in very recent years by *increased ethnic and religious friction*. In the northwest, the Sikh minority is demanding autonomy for their Punjabi province; its denial by the government of Indira Gandhi was the trigger for her assassination in 1984. In the far south, Tamils and Sinhalese are fighting one another in a nasty but little publicized guerrilla war. Outraged by what he thought was the government's favoritism, a Tamil fanatic killed Indira Gandhi's son and successor, Rajiv Gandhi, in 1991. And in the last several years, recurrent riots between militant Hindus and the Muslim minority have sharpened interfaith mistrust in both India and Pakistan.

Given these deep-seated animosities, it is all the more remarkable that Indian democratic government has held together almost without lapse. The Congress Party, which represents about 80 percent of the Hindu population, has thus far resisted the strong temptation to make itself into a monolithic party in the African style and force the minorities to conform to its will. Within this party, would-be strongmen (or women) have been checked before becoming dangerous. The large, well-equipped army has not meddled in politics, nor have any civilian

■ **Indian Village.** This scene could be replicated in thousands of villages across the subcontinent. It has not changed in any essential way in two thousand years or more. The cattle are given equal consideration as humans for food and shelter.

■ **Indira Gandhi.** The first Asian female prime minister proved herself an adept politician. However, the intense maneuvering required to unite the many factions of the Congress Party became too much for her patience, and her increasingly authoritarian stance defeated her party in national elections in 1975. She returned to power a few years later, and was assassinated in 1984 by Sikh fanatics.

adventurers attempted to gain power by using the military. India's social and economic problems are severe, but its adherence to constitutional and political means to devise solutions is an inspiration to democrats throughout the world.

Pakistan and Bangladesh

When the British withdrew from the subcontinent in 1947, the large Muslim minority demanded separate and sovereign status in a state of their own. The widespread distribution of the Muslim population made it impossible to create this state as a single unit, and Mahatma Gandhi reluctantly agreed to the creation of a bipartite state, West and East Pakistan. All Muslims not already within their borders were encouraged to migrate to them. These new states suffered from severe handicaps: their economies were undeveloped, and they had no infrastructure and very few potential leaders. Together the two Pakistans included about one-fourth of the former British colony's population, but had considerably less than one-fourth of its human and material resources. Under the leadership of Mohammed Ali Jinnah, the two Pakistans were committed from the outset to the supremacy of Islam in public life. This religious emphasis contributed to Pakistan's alienation from Nehru's secular India.

The widely separated states soon discovered that they had nothing in common except Islam, and that was simply not enough to hold them together. With India's assistance,

East Pakistan became the independent nation of Bangladesh in 1971. The distance between them made it impossible for the dominant western half (now just Pakistan) to reassert its power. As measured by gross national product per capita, the overpopulated and flood-prone Bangladesh is about the poorest country in the world. Pakistan is not much farther up the ladder despite a generation of rival Chinese and American foreign aid programs. The burden of caring for 3–4 million Afghani refugees from the civil war in that country has added to Pakistan's difficulties during most of the 1980s and early 1990s. In the circumstances, it is remarkable that Pakistan has managed to retain a commitment to parliamentary rule by civilian politicians (see the Biography in Chapter 61).

⚜ SOUTHEAST ASIA SINCE WORLD WAR II

Stark contrasts can be found in the postwar history of mainland and offshore Southeast Asia. During the middle decades of this century, some areas of the region may have experienced more violence than any other place on earth. Since the expulsion of the Japanese invaders in World War II, insurgents of one stripe or another have challenged the governments of Southeast Asia in several guerrilla campaigns (see Map 56.1). In former French Indochina (that is, Cambodia, Laos, and Vietnam), these insurgencies produced communist governments after long struggles. In Malaya (Malaysia) and the Philippines, guerrillas challenged the governments unsuccessfully in the later 1940s, while in the Dutch East Indies (Indonesia) the campaign for national independence was triumphant. Both Thailand and Burma (Myanmar) withstood significant rebellions in isolated provinces, but these uprisings were more tribal than revolutionary in nature.

The War in Vietnam

The lengthy war in Vietnam began as a nationalist rebellion against the French colonial overlord in the immediate postwar years. Under the Marxist-nationalist Ho Chi Minh, the Viet Minh guerrillas were at last able to drive the French army from the field and install a communist regime in the northern half of the country in 1954. At this point, the U.S. government under President Dwight D. Eisenhower took over the French role in the south, installed an American-funded puppet, and agreed to hold free elections for a national Vietnamese government. But the Americans became convinced that Ho would successfully manipulate any elections, and as a result, none were ever held. In the ensuing Kennedy administration in the early 1960s, the decision was made to "save" the client government in Saigon from a communist takeover by countering increasing guerrilla activity in the south with U.S. ground and air power. Then President Lyndon B. Johnson, who had inherited a small-scale war, was determined to bring it to a successful conclusion and believed that he could do so without crippling the simultaneous War on Poverty in the United States or his effective support for civil rights for the U.S. black population.

He was wrong on both counts. By 1968, half a million U.S. troops were on the ground in Vietnam, and the entire nation was debating the wisdom and the morality of engaging in this faraway, bloody, and apparently unending conflict that appeared on television screens nightly. The War on Poverty had been curtailed by both budgetary and political constraints; the campaign for civil rights had run into African-American resentments and there was decline of white liberal support for a president who continued to slog through the morass of Vietnam.

Johnson in effect resigned the presidency by refusing his party's nomination, and his Republican successor Richard M. Nixon eventually opted to withdraw U.S. forces in the early 1970s under cover of a supposed "Vietnamization" of the conflict. A patched-together peace was signed with North Vietnam's government in 1973 after a year of negotiations, and the South Vietnamese took over their own defense. By 1975, the corrupt and demoralized Saigon authorities had fallen to their communist opponents, and Vietnam was united on standard communist political and economic principles.

Until recently, the country was relegated to a diplomatic limbo by both West and East. The failure of the Soviets to assist their fellow communists in Vietnam fully brought to light the change in the Cold War and the conclusive nature of the break between the Soviet Union and China. In contrast to 1962 when Khrushchev was willing to gamble in Cuba, the Soviet government under Leonid Brezhnev preferred to forgo a foothold in South Asia and a propaganda advantage in the Third World rather than risk a war where Soviet security was not at stake. For its part, China was an active supplier of the guerrillas, but carefully avoided placing its full resources behind the Vietnamese and always kept its distance from possible confrontations with the Americans. After the North Vietnamese had won the war in the south, frictions between the supposed allies reached the point where the Chinese briefly invaded Vietnam and withdrew only after giving a lesson to the recalcitrants in Hanoi. Relations

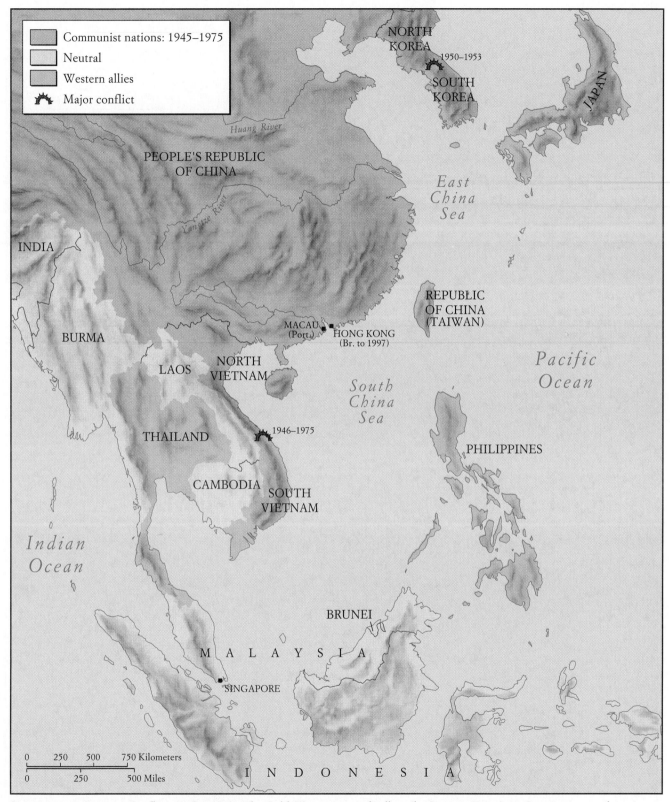

MAP 56.1 Postwar Conflicts in East Asia. The Cold War was sporadically a "hot" one in East Asia. Communism made major gains in the thirty years after the conclusion of World Ward II but was checked in South Korea and the Philippines.

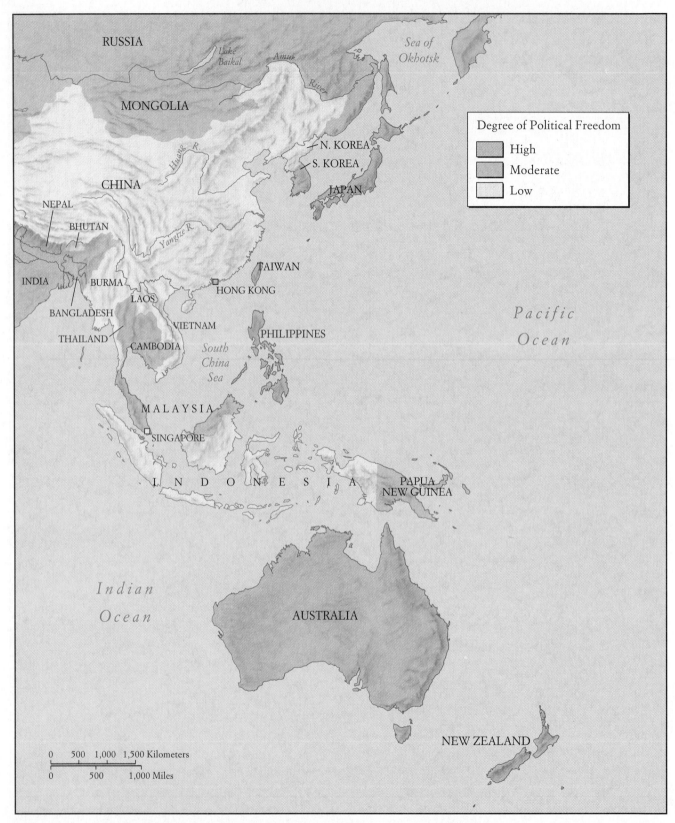

Degree of Political Freedom

- High
- Moderate
- Low

● **MAP 56.2 The Political Spectrum of the New East Asia in 1995.** Degree of political freedom is estimated from reports in the world press 1990–1995. The key nations are Japan, China, and Indonesia, all three of whom have asserted their national interests successfully in the post World War II era while embarking on quite different paths politically.

between the two countries continue to be strained as Vietnam's commitment to Marxism weakens.

Important though the Vietnam conflict was in international affairs, its most striking consequences were probably within the United States itself. Many Americans over age forty formed their views of government, the duty of citizens, and public affairs in general as a result of some type of personal involvement with the issues of the Vietnam War. The 1960s upheavals generated by war protest movements and resistance to what many saw as a wrong-headed and arrogant Washington were second only to the black civil rights movement as a milestone in the domestic affairs of the United States in this century.

Progress and the Promise of Future Prosperity

Other nations of Southeast Asia have been much more successful than the unfortunate Vietnam in escaping the poverty and technological backwardness that have been their lot in modern days. Although they have been handicapped by rapid population growth and a still heavy dependence on agriculture and exports of raw materials in a high-tech world, these obstacles to prosperity are being overcome.

The most successful nations are Hong Kong and Singapore, two city-states with entrepreneurial business as their driving force. Both have had incredible success in finding profitable niches in the evolving global interchange of goods and services. Next come South Korea, Taiwan, and Malaysia, where modern economies have been created by skilled and politically ruthless leaders in the past generation. The authoritarian rule that was the norm between 1950 and 1980 is now being replaced by more open and truly democratic arrangements, as the prosperity created for the rich under the earlier generation filters down and widens choices and horizons (see Map 56.2). Indonesia, the Philippines, and Thailand come next on the ladder of prosperity, while the war-wounded and isolated Burma (Myanmar), Cambodia, and Vietnam bring up the rear.

With relatively abundant resources, high literacy rates, stable village agriculture, and few border conflicts, much of Southeast Asia stands a good chance of now finding the peace and prosperity that have been missing in modern times. The major long-term danger is still excessive population growth and the pressures it puts upon the social fabric, but this threat is not as acute as elsewhere and is partly countered by steady growth in urban and industrial development, which can drain off the rural excess in constructive fashion.

Summary

In the second half of the twentieth century, East Asia has seen two world powers arise, communist China and capitalist Japan. Going sharply divergent ways since they contested one another for predominance in World War II, both nations have come to play important roles in world affairs. In the China, this role has been primarily military and political; in the case of Japan, it has been entirely economic and commercial until the present.

As founder of the Chinese Communist Party, Mao Zedong had tremendous influence after his victory in the civil war in the 1940s. His break with his Soviet mentors ten years later divided communism into hostile camps. It also allowed Mao to follow his own path into a communism that focused on the peasants and the necessity of continual revolution. After his death in 1976, his successors soon rejected this path, and the present leaders are experimenting with an unstable mix of socialism in politics and capitalism in the economy. The radical change in

generations of leaders that lies just ahead puts a large question mark over the entire situation.

In Japan, the economy and society were modernized and westernized under the American Occupation. The American-sponsored constitution allowed a new political culture to take shape that found a wide and positive response in a nation ready to accept change. A sustained partnership between government and business encouraged an unprecedented surge in productivity undisturbed by social or political discontents until very recently. Now one of the world's great economic powerhouses, Japan stands at the verge of decision on its international role in politics and diplomacy.

The Indian subcontinent emerged from the colonial era divided between antagonistic Hindu and Muslim segments. India has shown admirable maturity in retaining democratic politics despite the heavy pressures exerted by ethnic and religious frictions among its several peoples;

but this pressure has been mounting of late, and the economic improvement, while substantial, still lags the population growth in rural villages. Pakistan faces intimidating problems generated by low civil development and by the commitment to hostility with neighboring India.

In Southeast Asia the picture has brightened in recent days after a third of a century of violence and wars. Worst of these was the Vietnam conflict, which also had serious repercussions on the United States internally. Several of the former colonies of Southeast Asia are making a successful transition to the high-tech global economy and have excellent prospects.

Test Your Knowledge

1. What major change in international affairs became fully apparent in the early 1960s?
   a. China and the United States joined forces against the Soviet Union.
   b. China and Japan became allies.
   c. China and the Soviet Union became allies for the first time.
   d. China and the Soviet Union became hostile toward one another.
2. China's attempt to make itself industrially independent of outside aid during the 1950s is called the
   a. Self-strengthening movement.
   b. Red Guard challenge.
   c. China First movement.
   d. Great Leap Forward.
3. Which of the following statements is *not* true of postwar Japan?
   a. It had the world's highest rate of personal savings.
   b. It had the world's highest sustained growth in gross national product.
   c. It had the world's most favorable balance of trade.
   d. It had the world's highest rate of personal consumption.
4. Mao started the Great Proletarian Cultural Revolution because he
   a. believed that China was in danger of imminent attack.
   b. thought that it was the proper time to introduce political democracy.
   c. believed that all revolutions should be constantly renewed.
   d. wanted to forestall the Soviets' move toward coexistence.
5. In very recent years, Japanese working women have
   a. returned to their prewar habits of withdrawing into the home.
   b. been the world's leaders in asserting their political presence.
   c. made some gains in attaining equal pay and opportunity.
   d. finally broken through the "glass ceiling."
6. Japan's postwar political scene has been mainly controlled by the
   a. Socialist Party.
   b. Liberal Democratic Party.
   c. emperor through his political allies.
   d. labor unions.
7. Since independence India has
   a. been a military dictatorship.
   b. maintained a large degree of democracy.
   c. been at war with one or another of its neighbors.
   d. become a single-party, quasi-Fascist society.
8. During the Vietnam War, the Soviet Union
   a. tried to aid the insurgents in every way possible.
   b. consistently tried to bring peace by acting as middleman.
   c. took a passive role rather than assisting the insurgents.
   d. healed the conflict with China in order to assist Ho Chi Minh.

Identification Terms

"Amur River War"
Gandhi (Indira)
Great Leap Forward

Kashmir
Red Guard
Great Proletarian Cultural Revolution

Massacre in Tienanmen Square

Four Little Tigers
Nehru, Jawaharlal

Bibliography

For both modern China and Japan, see the works by Fairbank, Schirokauer, Reischauer, and Spence in the bibliography for Chapter 51. More specific topics are treated in the following:

Japan

Bernstein, G. *Haruko's World: A Japanese Farm Woman and Her Community,* 1983.

Bestor, T. *Neighborhood Tokyo,* 1989. Deals with contemporary urban life.

Buckley, R. *Japan Today,* 1985.

Dore, R. *Shinohata: Portrait of a Japanese Village,* 1978, and *City Life in Japan,* 1982. Interesting accounts of the changes in postwar society.

Hendry, R. J. *Understanding Japanese Society,* 1987.

Heymann, T. *On an Average Day in Japan,* 1992. Interestingly written comparison of Japan and the United States in several social areas.

Kawai, K. *Japan's American Interlude,* 1960. Studies the effects of the American postwar occupation.

Reischauer, E. *The Japanese,* 1977. Very good general history.

Robins-Mowry, D. *The Hidden Sun: Women of Modern Japan,* 1983.

Vogel, E. *Japan as Number One: Lessons for America,* 1977.

China

Cheng, N. *Life and Death in Shanghai,* 1986. A story of what the Cultural Revolution did to ordinary people.

Dietrich, C. *People's China: A Brief History,* 1986.

Fairbank, J. K. *The United States and China,* 1983. Tells the relationship's ups and downs up through the early 1980s.

Hinton, W. *Fanshen: A Documentary of Revolution in a Chinese Village,* 1960. A first-hand account of what happened after the communist takeover.

Karnow, S. *Mao and China: Inside the Cultural Revolution,* 1972. A very good journalist's inside story of the way the Mao-inspired upheaval was tearing China apart.

Meisner, M. *Mao's China, and After,* 1986. A good history written for students.

Morrison, D. *Massacre in Beijing,* 1989. A reaction to the Tiananmen Square events in June 1989.

Schell, O. *To Get Rich Is Glorious,* 1986. A study of Deng's leadership after Mao's death.

White, T., and A. Jacoby. *Thunder Out of China,* 1946. A fine account in journalistic style of the civil war's beginnings.

Whalley, S., Jr. *Mao Tse-tung: A Critical Biography,* 1977. Written immediately after the leader's death, as was D. Wilson, ed., *Mao Tse-tung in the Scales of History,* 1977.

Zhang, Xinxin, and Sang Ye. *Chinese Lives: An Oral History of Contemporary China,* 1987. A fascinating collection by a pair of experienced reporters.

India and Pakistan

Bhatia, K. *Indira Gandhi,* 1974. A good biography.

Freeman, J. M. *Untouchable: An Indian Life History,* 1979, and also K. Bhatia, *The Ordeal of Nationhood.: A Social Study of India since Independence,* 1971. Excellent social histories.

Naipaul, V. *India: A Wounded Civilization,* 1977. A consistently challenging, critical examination of the country of the distinguished novelist's father.

Tinker, H. E. *South Asia: A Short History,* 1990. Provides a good overview of both major states in South Asia.

Wolpert, S. *A New History of India,* 3d ed., 1988. The final part covers the most recent period, since independence.

Southeast Asia

The Vietnam War

Fitzgerald, F. *Fire in the Lake,* 1970. Analyzes why the Viet Cong were able to sustain their costly war effort despite overwhelming U.S. superiority in weapons.

Herring, G. *America's Longest War: The U.S. and Vietnam, 1950–75,* 1979. Told from the American side, but informed about the Vietnamese.

Kahin, G. M. T. *Intervention: How America Became Involved in Vietnam,* 1986. Gives a clear account of this complex situation.

Karnow, S. *Vietnam: A History,* 1983. An exceptionally vivid and fair-minded history that focuses on the U.S. role since the mid-1950s. This book was the companion to the highly respected television documentary on the war, broadcast by PBS.

Other Topics

Legge, J. *Sukarno,* 1972. A good biography of the founder and controversial leader of Indonesia in its early years of independence. See also B. Dahm's *Sukarno and the Struggle for Indonesian Independence,* 1969, cited in Chapter 55.

Rafferty, K. *City on the Rocks: Hong Kong's Uncertain Future,* 1991. Looks toward the 1997 takeover by China.

Sar-Desai, D. R. *Southeast Asia: Past and Present,* 1989. Has good coverage of the twentieth century and particularly post-1945 events.

Steinberg, D. J. *The Philippines: A Singular and a Plural Place,* 1971.

Turnbull, C. M. *A History of Singapore, 1819–1975,* 1977. A comprehensive history of this city-state since the British entered the scene as colonial masters.

Woronoff, J. *Asia's Miracle Economies,* 1986. Looks intensively at the "Four Little Tigers."

AFRICA AFTER INDEPENDENCE

1955–1965	Decolonization much of Africa
1963	Organization of African Unity founded
1960s–1970s	Trend toward dictatorship and one-party states/Cold War interventions by U.S., U.S.S.R., China
1970s–1980s	Overpopulation problem becomes acute; drought, civil wars, AIDS
1990s	More stable, open governments appear in several states/Apartheid dies in South Africa/Muslim fundamentalism gains in northern tier

Africa is now the most problematic area of the world in the most basic terms of the prosperity and perhaps even survival of its peoples. In contrast to East and South Asia, the decolonization process and political independence have signally failed to bring the happy solutions that leaders and much of the general population had counted on thirty years ago. The majority of the continent's fifty-odd countries have undergone major economic and social transitions, and the results so far are not encouraging. Millions have died needlessly from famine, civil wars, and political terror; millions of others have been reduced to misery as refugees.

What is particularly disturbing to both African and non-African observers is that the cycle of deterioration and repression shows no sign of having run its course. With the exception of South Africa, most indicators are still pointing downward for the continent. The hopes of a generation ago have been severely disappointed. Political freedom has brought the African nations only the partial ability to exercise true sovereignty and to satisfy the legitimate demands of their citizens.

⚜ GOVERNMENT IN THE IMMEDIATE POSTINDEPENDENCE YEARS

The decolonization of Africa proceeded very rapidly (and unexpectedly peacefully, for the most part) between 1955 and 1965 (see Map 57.1). About thirty-five states derived from the former European colonies emerged in that decade. Since then, independence has been obtained through armed action in the Portuguese colonies in 1975, the British settler colony of Rhodesia in 1980, and Namibia in 1989.

Aside from resurrecting some African names from the precolonial era (Mali, Ghana, and Zaire, among others), the new states showed remarkably little inclination to try to wipe out the two generations of European presence. The various kingdoms and empires that had been established as recently as the mid-nineteenth century by black and Muslim rulers were not reestablished, nor was a serious effort made to do so. Instead, the colonial borders were continued without change. Where they were challenged by secession, as in Nigeria and Ethiopia, they were defended by armed force.

It often is said that African independence movements were fueled by nationalism, but this term means something different in Africa than elsewhere. Africans were not

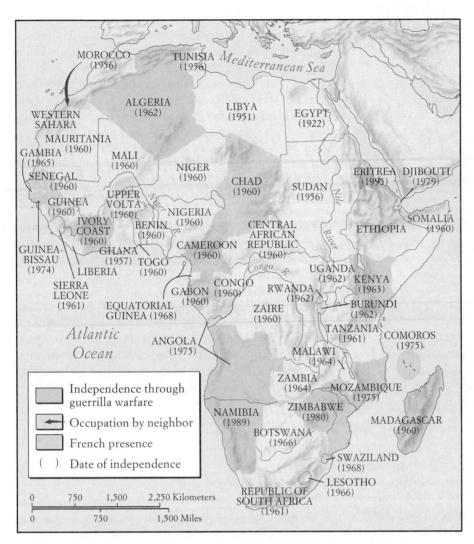

● **MAP 57.1 Africa after World War II.** Independence came with a rush for most African states in the years 1955–1965. Many of them were not prepared for it and lacked a cadre of trained officials to step into the shoes of departing Europeans.

attempting to bind together a distinct people under a single government within a common territory, as the nineteenth-century European nationalists had tried to do. Instead, the African nationalists wanted *modernization and equality with the whites.* African nationalism is not an ethnic phenomenon, but a social and economic one.

A good indication of this is the usual African attitude toward the former colonial powers. The Africans have shown remarkably little bitterness. The Europeans are still welcome, as long as they recognize that the privileges of the past are over and accept that the Africans are in control of foreign policy and internal politics. There was no reaction against European culture, and certainly not against that culture's leading artifacts: money, automobiles, and machines and labor-saving devices of all types.

For the governing classes, assertions of a peculiarly African culture, or **"negritude"** as the literary expression has it, have remained a sporadically modish diversion from the unremitting pursuit of Western material products.

The first years of independence saw a wave of optimism about Africa's prospects and specifically about the intentions and abilities of the native leaders to install democratic parliamentary republics. In several sub-Saharan states (Tanzania, Kenya, Ghana, and Senegal are examples), men of culture and political subtlety were placed at the helm by the first elections. These men were thoroughly familiar with Western forms of government and values; most had been residents of Europe and the United States. In other states (Zaire, Guinea, Angola, Sierra Leone), less known and less subtle leaders asserted

■ **Boys and Mercedes Benz.** The delight in the boys' faces as they admire the car is only a partial counterbalance to the reminder of the vast differences in lifestyles between the "Wabenzi" (the Benz tribe) and the other Africans.

themselves, sometimes through coups against the original elected governments.

The pro-democracy bent disappeared almost immediately. The presidents and prime ministers became dictators within five to ten years of independence, and multiparty systems were replaced by an all-embracing (and completely artificial) "people's union" or "national assembly" single-party states a year or two later. *Ghana,* the first colony to gain independence, is a good example. The Western-educated Kwame Nkrumah (1909–1972) was a popularly elected president in 1957; in 1960 he pushed through a new constitution that made him effectively a dictator, and in 1964 he made Ghana a one-party state.

This sequence of events occurred so regularly as to form a pattern in every part of Africa—Muslim and sub-Saharan, West and East. Why? The answers must be tentative. First, like eastern Europe, pre-independence Africa had no tradition of Western-style political institutions and customs associated with parliamentary give-and-take. In the colonial era, only the British and French had attempted to prepare their colonies for self-government, and the process had barely begun before World War II. When the war ended, the combination of circumstances mentioned in Chapter 55 brought the colonies into a semblance of modern politics with a rush. In most, the "Westminster model" based on British precedents was adopted under European inspiration. But this type of government, based on the interplay of a majority party and a loyal opposition whose voice must be permitted to

be heard, was alien to Africa. On the other hand, Africa did have a strongly rooted tradition of personal leadership and loyalty to a lineage or kin group, which had no place for compromise if certain victory was in its grasp. Political divisions in Africa were often along kin-group lines, or what the West would call "tribalism."

In addition, foreign interests sometimes promoted the removal of a democratically elected regime and its replacement by a group, civil or military, that favored the foreigners. This pattern was most common in nations that were caught up in the Cold War struggles between Russia, China, and the West for control of various parts of the continent. Ethiopia, Somalia, Angola, and Mozambique are examples.

The breakdown of democratic parliamentary government very frequently resulted in the establishment of a *military dictatorship.* The first in sub-Saharan Africa appeared in Ghana in 1966; but such dictatorships were soon endemic from Nigeria to Somalia. Some of the generals have come into power with a vision of what they wished to accomplish; too many have simply wanted power and its accompanying opportunities to get rich. Worst of all have been those who combine the worst features of African tribalism and European terror: the repulsive Jean-Bedel Bokassa in the Central African Republic, Idi Amin in Uganda, and Joseph (Sese Seso) Mobutu in Zaire. The summary given by one Western Africanist is difficult to counter:

> In general, Africa is a misgoverned continent. During the past 30 years the idealism that has characterized various nationalist movements, with their promises of popular self-determination have given way in most states to cynical authoritarian regimes. (J. Ramsay, *Africa,* 4th ed. 1991, Dushkin Publications)

Yet there are some signs a better day is dawning. Popular protests against several of the one-party dictatorships have been increasing in the last five years, and some of them (Zaire, Benin, Ivory Coast) have succeeded in winning the right to establish legal opposition. Only the passage of time will reveal whether this is a trend throughout the continent or only a brief remission in the pattern of authoritarian government.

✤ THE AFRICAN ECONOMY

Postindependence economies in Africa were naturally the outgrowths of colonial era policies. In the interwar years, all of the European powers had encouraged the rise of monoculture plantations, producing crops such as cacao, rubber, coffee, and palm oil for export to the developed world. These plantations were owned and developed by Westerners, but the actual work was done by laborers who were sometimes forced to work on the plantations if they could not pay taxes in cash. In the colonies that possessed sizable mineral resources, such as the Congo, Rhodesia, Angola, and a few others, mines utilizing African labor were similarly owned by Westerners.

Domestic manufactures were relatively scarce, as they were discouraged by the home countries, which exported goods to the colonies. Instead of new products, African enterprises tended to turn out substitutes for imports; that is, a factory might make soap that would otherwise be imported, but not asphalt for paving roads.

The colonial era changed African economics in a number of ways. *Migratory labor,* for example, became more prominent all over the continent; some were attracted to a new area because of money wages or the demands of coerced labor in lieu of taxes. The cash economy introduced along the new railways and river steam ships made it necessary for people who had never seen cash before to earn it, if they wished to buy the new goods introduced by the Europeans. The *emphasis on export crops* meant that a great number of Africans who had previously produced all their own food from their gardens and gathering now had to purchase their food, as they would any other commodity.

As a producer of raw materials, Africa was hit hard by the Great Depression of the 1930s. Prices on the world market dropped much faster for raw materials than for finished manufactures or consumer goods, so African farmers and miners received less for their exports but had to pay more for their imports. With World War II, the market for raw materials revived, and the postwar period until independence was prosperous for African producers. This prosperity was a major reason why Africans and non-Africans alike were optimistic about prospects for the new states. Africa (especially tropical Africa) was thought to be hovering on the verge of an economic "takeoff" period.

Their optimism was disappointed, however, and the takeoff turned out to be a slow crash for most of Africa in the years since independence. For quite some time, the crisis was disguised by international loans and credits. The 1960s saw an influx of foreign aid—mainly through the United Nations and the **World Bank,** but partly from individual countries. Many African nations undertook huge development projects, only some of which made economic sense. "Bigger is better" seemed to be the password: broad four-lane highways were built in capital cities that had only a few thousand cars, big new terminals

■ **African Market.** The people in this marketplace in Burkina Faso are almost all female which is usual in West Africa. The color and bustle of the open-air market is an important facet of life in African towns.

in airports that had five flights on a busy day, and twenty-story government office buildings that towered over cardboard shacks while remaining half-empty.

Huge amounts of aid money were wasted or stolen, both by locals and the foreign contractors, who scented easy pickings and paid the necessary bribes. To a large extent the bribery and waste were products of the Cold War, as the United States and the Soviet Union (and China in some instances) jockeyed for position in a dozen African countries. The United States kept the money flowing to the corrupt and murderous Mobutu regime in power in Zaire because he favored the West. The Soviets were only too pleased to support the Mengistu government in Ethiopia because this tyrannous and bloodstained clique called itself "Marxist-Leninist." Neither side lifted a finger against the insane Idi Amin in Uganda because he was too unstable to be counted upon in the constant maneuvering.

■ **African Urban Contrasts.** The bulk of the immigrants into the African cities have no fixed places of work for months or years after arrival, and live with kin or in shantytowns on the periphery. The new apartment complexes and office buildings are occupied by the relatively fortunate: the educated and those with sufficient "dash" (bribes, connections).

After the oil shock of the 1970s, the African states found themselves slipping rapidly behind. Except for Nigeria and Angola, very few oil wells existed south of the Sahara, and the quadrupling of oil prices in 1973 hit the developing industries and the general citizenry hard. *Inflation* quickly got out of hand. The governments attempted to meet the crisis by redoubling their exports, thus encouraging still more monoculture of cash crops such as cotton and rubber. This in turn discouraged domestic food crops, such as rice and sweet potatoes. By the end of the decade, several formerly self-sufficient countries were importing part of their food. Nigeria, for example, chose to use a good chunk of its oil revenues to pay a subsidy to importers of food, thus keeping food prices low for consumers, but putting local farmers out of business. When the oil bubble burst in the 1980s, Nigeria had far fewer farms to feed its increased population.

The true dimensions of the problem only became visible in the 1980s. Several events coincided to bring this about: the diminishing domestic foodstocks; the very bad drought in Ethiopia, Somalia, and the Sudan; civil wars in the Sudan, Chad, Angola, Mozambique, and Ethiopia; and the sharp reduction in foreign aid flowing into Africa from international bodies and Cold War opponents. The injurious effects of all these were magnified by the continuing rapid increase in population, which was only partly offset by the equally rapid spread of AIDS in several countries.

In the twenty years from 1960 to 1980, in only about 20 percent of African nations, did gross national product (GNP) grow at an annual rate of 2 percent or better, which is considered to be a moderate standard of progress. Nine countries actually had negative growth in this period. In the

1980s, however, the record was still worse. The small farmers and herdsmen who make up a majority in every country in tropical Africa have suffered most from the overpowering changes since independence. Farm output since independence has increased by 2 percent per year at best in most countries, while population growth has averaged more than 3 percent everywhere. One-quarter of sub-Saharan Africans live in what the World Bank calls "chronic food insecurity"—that is, they are hungry.

The *abandonment of traditional diet and work* patterns in the villages has driven many men to seek work in the exploding cities. Increasingly, labor is flowing from the countryside to the towns, which almost never have adequate employment opportunities. People are driven into the streets, as in India or Latin America, where they live by hawking bric-a-brac, cooked food, Coca-Cola, or plastic toys to passersby as poor as themselves. Previously, theft was almost unknown in African society, but it has now become common, as has street violence in the cities. Hunger and deprivation are the reasons.

✤ THE POPULATION BOMB: ROUND TWO

The economic and social problems enumerated here are to a very large degree the result of one overwhelmingly important fact: Africa is producing too many people for the means available to satisfy them. Africa has the world's highest birthrates, averaging 3.3 percent per annum in 1990 (see Map 57.2). In some countries, the rate of population increase has been more than 4 percent. (Most recent figures show some decline in African birthrates.) As yet no African country has made a serious effort to control its overpopulation problem; several governments still

■ **Karaib Dam, Zambia.** Built in 1955–59, the Karib dam supplies energy for the coppermines of Zambia. It creates a lake 175 miles long in the valley of the Zambezi river. Like the similar Aswan Dam on the Nile, it brought with it unforeseen environmental damage as well as industrial and agricultural benefits.

maintain that there *is* no overpopulation problem, only a resource availability problem. But this position cannot be sustained in the face of any serious investigation of *the facts of African ecology.*

For example, only about 10 percent of African surface soil is suitable for any type of crop cultivation. Much of the farming is carried out on marginal land that is subject to repeated droughts, which come in long cycles. Africa has only 8 million hectares (each hectare = 2.47 acres) of irrigated land, versus Asia's 135 million. In exactly the same way as in the Amazon basin, one of Africa's most valuable products is being rapidly diminished: the tropical rainforest. Once the big trees (mahogany, above all) are cut down, the land is next to useless for agriculture and is poor even for pasturage. But the lumber has immediate export value, and that has been a sufficient inducement for governments desperate for revenues and private owners greedy for cash.

The concentration on export crops and timber has seriously disrupted the African ecological balance, and the explosive growth of population has increased the pressures. Nomadic herders in the Sahel, for example, have had to increase their flocks of camels, goats, and cattle, because in a drought cycle, such as was experienced in the 1970s and early 1980s, the animals could not prosper and grow sufficient meat. But these increased numbers put even more stress on the vegetation they browse on and magnify the effects of the drought. As a result, in this area the Sahara is rapidly expanding southward, as the natural vegetation is eliminated.

The popular image of Africa as a vast expanse of jungles and plains filled with lions and elephants is, of course, wildly distorted and always has been. But a great deal of big game is left in Africa in certain regions, and the tourist money that it attracts is a major contributor to some African nations (Kenya, Zimbabwe, and Tanzania lead the list). But as the population has grown in those countries, large regions where lions previously roamed have had to be opened to human habitation. The upshot, predictably, is a *conflict between human and animal uses of the land,* which, again predictably, the animals always lose. That, in turn, harms the tourist trade, reducing the money available to the governments to assist the excess population in the struggle to stay alive.

■ **Famine in Ethiopia, 1985.** The Sahel region and neighboring Ethiopia face consistent famine conditions as the area becomes ever more overgrazed and the desert creeps south. This part of Africa has been a steady recipient of international aid, such as the grain ration these Ethiopian children are awaiting.

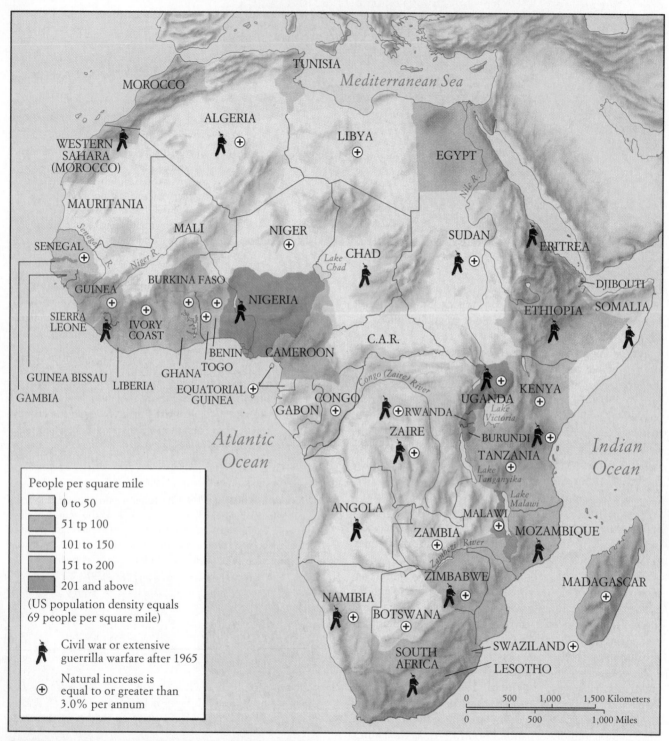

People per square mile

- ☐ 0 to 50
- ☐ 51 tp 100
- ☐ 101 to 150
- ☐ 151 to 200
- ☐ 201 and above

(US population density equals 69 people per square mile)

🕴 Civil war or extensive guerrilla warfare after 1965

⊕ Natural increase is equal to or greater than 3.0% per annum

◉ **MAP 57.2 Present-Day Africa.** The frequent guerrilla wars and rebellions in the past thirty years have sometimes been the result of Cold War manuevering by extra-African powers. But the continent's main obstacle to longterm stability is excessive population growth.

The current surge in African population numbers has constantly produced vicious circles of this sort. The "population bomb" that the ecologists in the 1970s feared would threaten the livability of the entire planet proved to be exaggerated—*except* in tropical Africa where, in some senses, it has exploded. (A prime reason the dire predictions of Paul Ehrlich and his associates have not come true thus far, at least, was the Green Revolution in agriculture. Through a combination of fertilizers and new hybrids, yields of corn, rice, and wheat were greatly increased in much of Asia and Latin America. But this did not occur in Africa, where yields have remained low throughout the postindependence period and probably cannot be raised much.)

✤ Four African States

This section looks at four African nations—Kenya, Algeria, Senegal, and Zimbabwe—which illustrate the troubled internal politics of African states since independence.

Kenya

The Texas-sized East African country of Kenya was a British colony until 1963, when the London-trained sociologist **Jomo Kenyatta** (c. 1890–1978) became the first president (see the Biography in this chapter). Kenyatta had been accused of collaborating with the Mau Mau guerrillas who had begun attacking the British settlers as early as 1951 in an attempt to drive them out. The accusation was groundless, but Kenyatta spent years in jail nevertheless, which made his name known to every Kenyan and made him a folk hero to his Kikuyu tribe, the most numerous of several Kenyan ethnic groups. Kenyatta began auspiciously by assuring the hundred thousand British settlers in the so-called white highlands around the capital city of Nairobi that they were still welcome under African rule. Africanization of land and commerce was pursued and gave many Kikuyu, in particular, a rapid entry into modern and urban living.

But by the early 1970s, Kenyatta had become the effective dictator of a one-party state. He had silenced the major opposition party by jailing its leaders, and within his own party, the Kenya African National Union (KANU), he had even resorted to assassinations. Tribal politics soon displaced the concept of national welfare, and the Kikuyu did not hesitate to oppress their fellow citizens for their own advantage.

Kenyatta's successor Daniel arap Moi has been in command of the country since 1978, and his rule has become steadily more repressive. Barely a shred of democratic government is left, while corruption at the top is rampant and the country's urgent problems are ignored. Possessing one of the most industrialized economies in Africa and some of the best agricultural land, Kenya has gone backward rather than forward in the seventeen years under Moi's dictatorship. An exploding rate of population growth (4 percent per annum, the highest in Africa) has contributed to the country's downward spiral.

Algeria

Algeria has tried to walk the narrow line between democratic politics and a destabilized society. Having waged a fierce and bloody rebellion between 1956 and 1961, the Algerians attained their independence from France in 1962. One-party rule has been in effect ever since; political contests have been carried out within the broad lines of the National Liberation Front (FNL). The massive emigration of the French settlers who had dominated every aspect of life was a blow to the economy in one sense, but it also opened a host of opportunities to ambitious and talented Algerians.

The FNL was a loose umbrella organization founded to pursue the struggle against France and had few specific programs or priorities in place. Individual leaders have had sharply varying notions of which FNL programs should be emphasized, and a power struggle between the rebel leader Ahmad Ben Bella and his former backer, Colonel Hovari Boumedienne, resulted in a bloodless coup by the latter in the mid-1960s. Since then, the government has been a collective with a fair degree of democratic practice until recent years. The windfall from rising oil and gas prices—Algeria is a major producer of both—helped for a time to ease the friction of an otherwise faltering economy. When the oil boom was over in the mid-1980s, hundreds of thousands had to leave Algeria for France to search for employment. Their remittances to the home country are crucial for the domestic economy.

In the last several years, the FNL has clearly lost its popularity and has had to allow opposition parties to appear. Most important among them is a coalition of Islamic fundamentalists who draw support from their coreligionists outside the borders and wish to create a strict Islamic state. Only the decision of the government to cancel scheduled elections in 1992 saved it from a crushing defeat. Since then, the fundamentalists have not hesitated to pursue their goals through indiscriminate terror against the government, which has responded with

Jomo Kenyatta
1890–1978

The history of twentieth-century Africa offers few examples of politicians who have successfully made the transition from colonial-era opposition to independent leaders of a nation. Felix Houphouet-Boigny of the Ivory Coast was one, Sekou Toure of Guinea another, and the Grand Old Man of Kenya, Jomo Kenyatta, a third.

Kenyatta, the son of a poor farmer, had the good fortune to be accepted at a Presbyterian mission school near his birthplace. He was a member of the majority Kikuyu tribe, which would assist his later rise in national affairs, even though Kenyatta was unusual in insisting on the subordination of tribal to national welfare in the campaign for independence. He accepted Christian baptism in 1914, many years after leaving the mission school, and served the British as a laborer during the campaigns against the Germans in East Africa. In the early interwar period, Kenyatta joined the Kikuyu associations that were permitted by the colonial overlords as a beginning of self-government. He became the general secretary of the Kikuyu Central Association in 1928 and the editor of its paper in the following year (the first newspaper published by Africans in East Africa).

At this time, politically minded Kikuyu were primarily concerned with inducing the government to restrain or reverse the large-scale land theft practiced by the whites in the fertile highlands of Kenya, and Kenyatta became a well-known figure in this campaign. He visited London to testify before one of the several investigatory commissions in 1929. In 1931, he was again sent to London by the association, and this time he remained for fifteen years. He married an English woman and had a son by her while studying at the London School of Economics under the famed anthropologist Bronislaw Malinowski. In 1938, Kenyatta published a paper originally prepared for Malinowski, *Facing Mount Kenya,* which created a major stir as a program for eventual African independence. At the end of World War II, Kenyatta, Kwame Nkrumah, and several other Africans in Britain founded the Pan-African Federation, the first association of African nationalities.

Returning to his native land, Kenyatta spent the postwar years organizing the Kenya African National Union (KANU) and serving as the influential head of an African teachers' college. In 1952, the Mau Mau guerrilla/terrorist campaign against the British settlers began in Kenya, the first of its kind on the continent against the colonial powers. Kenyatta, on no evidence of any kind, was hauled up to a biased court, tried, found guilty of treason, and sentenced to seven years

---

bloody repression and a veritable state of siege. More than 10,000 lives have been lost thus far, mostly by the actions of the military-ruled government.

Senegal

Senegal, a West African coastal state about the size of Indiana, became independent in 1960 under the leadership of the renowned poet **Leopold Senghor.** Senghor was an outstanding example of the black intellectuals trained under the French in the early twentieth century who would become pioneers of *negritude* and African nationalism. Islam arrived in Senegal in the twelfth century, and as in most of West Africa, the population is still predominantly Muslim. Unlike much of West Africa, however,

Senegal has clung to multiparty democracy. The associations called **Muslim Brotherhoods,** which have up to three-quarters of a million members, are the backbones of the various political parties.

President Senghor never had to resort to the political strong-arm tactics of most of Senegal's neighbors, and he retired from office in the 1980s a revered figure. He was succeeded in a relatively open election by his protégé Abdou Diouf, who continues the policies initiated by Senghor, but has had increasingly thorny relations with his neighbor The Gambia and with resident Gambians in Senegal who demand autonomy.

Senegal is a good example of an African country that has chosen to remain close to its former colonial master, in this case, France. French is the official language, French

in prison. Refusing compromise offers, he served out his full term, becoming a continentwide symbol of Africa's irresistible surge toward independence. Under international pressure he was freed in 1961 and immediately returned to his work for KANU, looking toward participation in the government of a new Kenya.

By this time, the British authorities had accepted the inevitability of the independence of the former colonies despite the adamant resistance of many white settlers. New constitutions had been effected in the later 1950s that pointed toward autonomy and then independence for the black majority. In 1963, Kenya held national elections for self-government, which were easily won by KANU on a platform of black-white cooperation and moderation. In 1964, Jomo Kenyatta, a vigorous figure in his seventies, had the satisfaction of becoming the first president of a sovereign Kenyan republic, a post he held until his death fourteen years later.

firms and technicians are important throughout the economy, and French troops (the remnant of the famed Foreign Legion) are stationed near the capital city of Dakar as a peacekeeping force. In return, Senegal has benefited from numerous special arrangements that favor members of the French-sponsored *Economic Community of West Africa* in their dealings with France and, through France, with the European Union.

Zimbabwe

Zimbabwe, which is about the size of Montana, emerged in 1980, the fruit of a lengthy and sometimes bloody guerrilla war against the British settlers. The conflict began in 1966, when the settlers defied London's commands and set up their own independent government based on white minority rule; they called their creation Rhodesia. The whites, who constituted only 5 percent of the population, were eventually worn down and entered into negotiations with the guerrillas. In 1980, the state was renamed Zimbabwe, symbolizing the coming of black African rule by evoking the ancient city-state. Robert Mugabe, head of the Zimbabwe African National Union (ZANU) and a leader of the guerrilla war, was elected prime minister in the first national election in which blacks participated as equals. He has taken a relatively moderate approach to the Africanization of white-owned businesses, land, and cultural institutions despite his party's formal commitment to what it terms African socialism. The private sector has been spared wholesale confiscations, and the state has moved cautiously and in limited ways into the economy.

Mugabe has followed the same path as innumerable other African nationalists in looking to establish unity by monopolizing political action. Since the beginning, he has actively persecuted his chief internal opponents. ZANU swallowed the major opposition party by coerced merger (1987) and has frequently threatened to ban the others. Adding to the tensions is the fact that the political map is based on ethnic lines dividing the dominant Shona tribe and the minorities. Resistance to Mugabe has been gradually increasing. He has been hurt internally by the evolution of South Africa away from *apartheid* and into black rule, because he had long been a leader of the anti-apartheid forces internationally and has used that role to justify his often repressive domestic policies.

Economic progress in this quite rich country has been solidly impressive in the years since independence. The farmers who make up by far the largest single occupational group have increased production per acre significantly, aided by government credits and advice. Some industry has been established by blacks and the very small but economically important white minority. Social progress has also been substantial in health and education.

✤ PROSPECTS AT THE END OF THE CENTURY

If one were to listen to the daily news bulletins as the sole source of information, it would be easy to predict that Africa's future would be chaos, famine, and brutality. That has been Africa's fate in the recent past and is presumably what will happen for the indefinite future. This view can be supported by an infinitude of social data. Not only does the continent have the world's highest rates of population growth, but it has most of the world's poorest people. In 1990, the per capita GNP for Mali was $190; it was $155 for Madagascar, $235 for Tanzania, and $200 for Niger. In the same year, U.S. per capita GNP was $16,444. Life expectancies for males and females were 45 and 48, respectively, in Senegal, 42 and 47 in Angola, 45 and 49 in Mozambique, and 38 and 40 in Chad (perhaps the world's lowest). For the United States, they were 74 and 78.

Chad had one physician for every 53,000 residents in 1990. The infant mortality rate in sub-Saharan Africa averages about 125 per 1,000; in the United States, it is about 10 per 1,000. The adult literacy rate in many countries of Africa is below 50 percent overall and is far lower than that among village dwellers. Higher education (postsecondary) is still a rarity, and the large majority of

higher degrees are issued for the traditional specialties such as law, the humanities, foreign literature, and education. Relatively few students are interested in the applied sciences, engineering, or health specialties, which are precisely the disciplines most needed in their countries. These curricula lack prestige unless they can be studied at a foreign university, a dream open to few Africans.

In a different arena, the *internal and international conflicts* afflicting Africa are frightening. Beside the strengthening challenges of the Islamic fundamentalists in the north, almost every country south of the Sahara has some ethnic or tribal group that is acutely unhappy with the state of affairs in the national capital. As of 1994, major civil wars were being fought in at least seven countries. Riots and street demonstrations against the current regimes were taking place in another half dozen. Only in the Republic of South Africa, now making the transition from generations of white-dominated apartheid to majority black rule, is there solid evidence of a new harmony (see the Document in this chapter). The **Organization for Pan African Unity (OAU),** founded in the wake of the independence surge in the 1960s as both a sounding board and a peacekeeper for the continent, has proved ineffectual in the latter role. It has long since become a club of autocrats who never wish to reprimand one of their neighbors for fear that the example might spread to themselves.

All of the African states are more or less deeply indebted to the World Bank and a series of private banks from which they have borrowed large sums over the years. Since the prospect that these monies will ever be returned has grown dim, the lenders now insist on internal economic reform in the guise of so-called **Structural Adjustment Programs (SAPs),** which supposedly will restart stalled African economies and allow increased export earnings. But the SAP goals are contingent on painful governmental measures to reduce inflation, reduce subsidies to exporters, or other steps equally unpopular with the public and/or the wealthy. As a result, the governments have very little incentive to implement them. In the circumstances, the worst SAP of all seems to be the World Bank, which lent the money often in violation of the most elementary business principles.

Yet with all of these negatives, it is still possible to look at the first generation of independent Africa as a learning experience that may produce much of value for the continent's peoples. In several instances, a ray of light is entering the political and economic darkness that has engulfed Africa during the past twenty years. Here are a few examples:

Inaugural Address by Nelson Mandela

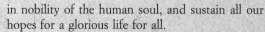

The rise of Nelson Mandela to the presidency of the Republic of South Africa must be one of the more amazing events of recent African history. Imprisoned for twenty-five years as a subversive by the white South African government, Mandela remained the rallying point for all those who believed that the day of apartheid must finally pass.

For his mainly black followers in the African National Congress, Mandela's convincing majority in the first universal balloting ever permitted in South Africa was a day of great elation and a satisfying end to an "extraordinary human disaster." But the white and Coloured (Indian) minorities were naturally nervous about what the future might hold; would Mandela allow his more passionate black adherents to take revenge for their long exclusion from power and from human dignity? Would he remember the humiliations he had suffered both before and during his long imprisonment at the hands of the dominant Afrikaner whites? Or would he attempt to calm the waters stirred by a sometimes bloody electoral campaign and look into the future rather than at the past? His inaugural address of May 10, 1994, was eagerly awaited.

> Today, all of us by our presence here . . . confer glory and hope to newborn liberty. Out of the experience of an extraordinary human disaster which lasted too long must be born a society of which all humanity will be proud.
>
> Our daily deeds as South Africans must produce an actual South African reality that will reinforce humanity's belief in justice, strengthen its confidence in nobility of the human soul, and sustain all our hopes for a glorious life for all.
>
> That spiritual and physical oneness we all share with this common homeland explains the depth of the pain we all carried in our hearts as we saw our country tear itself apart . . . isolated by the peoples of the world precisely because it has become the universal base of the pernicious ideology and practice of racism and racial oppression . . . .
>
> The time for the healing of the wounds has come. The moment to bridge the chasms that divide us has come. The time to build is upon us. . . .
>
> We have triumphed in the effort to implant hope in the breasts of the millions of our people. We enter into a covenant that we shall build the society in which all South Africans, both black and white, will be able to walk tall, without any fear in their hearts, assured of their inalienable right to human dignity—a rainbow nation at peace with itself and the world. . . .
>
> We dedicate this day to all the heroes and heroines in this country and the rest of the world who sacrificed in so many ways and surrendered their lives so that we could be free. Their dreams have become reality. Freedom is their reward.
>
> We understand . . . that there is no easy road to freedom. We know it well that none of us acting alone can achieve success. We must therefore act together as a united people, for national reconciliation, for nation building, for the birth of a new world.
>
> Let there be justice for all. Let there be peace for all. Let there be work, bread, water, and salt for all. Let each know that for each the body, the mind, and the soul have been freed to fulfill themselves. . . .
>
> Let freedom reign! God bless Africa!

■ **A Teaching Hospital in Nigeria.** This modern facility is one manifestation of the much-improved attention to health and hygiene which the independent African states have developed.

- Several of the one-party autocracies established in the 1970s have been forced to surrender power or loosen their grip on it during the past few years. Malawi, Benin, Zaire, the Ivory Coast, and Kenya, among others, have to some extent democratized their politics, thanks to popular protest.

- The end of the Cold War competition for African allies has allowed a measure of sanity to creep back into relations between the First and Second Worlds and the African Third. Fantasts, tyrants, and "kleptocracies" (rule of thieves) are no longer supported on the ground that if "we" don't, "they" will.

- International lenders are no longer willing to put up money for construction of personal or national shrines in the form of steel plants with no markets; international airports with no traffic, and hydropower plants with no customers. New projects now must be rationally justified and be suited to the real needs of the country.

- After many unhappy experiences, African governments have toned down or stopped their previous emphasis on cash export crops and focused instead on family farming to meet the constantly growing domestic food demand.

- There has been a change in attitude encouraged by African governments toward women and their roles in society. African women are receiving active support and being encouraged to make their voices heard not only in politics, but in the working economy and in public affairs generally.

One of the more gloomy and recalcitrant situations is the huge menace of the AIDS epidemic, which started in Africa and has hit that continent much harder than any other part of the world. According to reliable estimates, in parts of tropical Africa about 30 percent of the population is infected with the HIV virus, and already far more people have died from the disease in Africa than in the rest of the world combined. Official countermeasures have been weak and ineffective. In essence, the governments are relying on the developed countries to find a solution and bring it to Africa. In the meantime, AIDS might be the temporary answer—a cruel and drastic one—to the overpopulation crisis.

Africa's future as a human society is impossible to predict. This rich continent, with its immense variety in both natural phenomena and human activities, may continue to suffer from a welter of civil wars, tyrannical politics, and economic hardship internally and peripheral status internationally. But it could be that the first generation of freedom was a period of growing pains and that the twenty-first century will see a recovery from past internal mistakes, followed by a steady rise from neocolonialism to equality in the world community. "Out of Africa, always something new," said the Roman sage Pliny in 65 C.E., and his words remain true today.

Summary

The second largest continent has seen some evil days since attaining freedom from colonial status in the 1960s and 1970s. The fond hopes of political democracy were largely gone to dust within a few years, as single-party or outright dictatorial regimes took power. Where guerrilla wars had been necessary to attain independence, the warriors imposed themselves in the guise of united fronts or similar vehicles of personal power. In other cases, free elections produced the rule of an ethnic or tribal group, whose leadership soon reacted to opposition by creating a dictatorship. In still others, the military reacted to civilian squabbles by brushing them aside. In all instances, the attempt to introduce the Westminster model of parliamentary government has had a rocky path. Corruption has been endemic and has been stimulated by foreign aid and trade arrangements.

In the economy, the new states continued the colonial era's emphasis on cultivating export crops and mining, but added a new dependency on international credits for some ill-conceived "prestige" projects. When combined, these factors made Africa vulnerable to conditions no government could control: famine in the wake of droughts, low raw material prices on the world market, and rising food imports to feed an exploding population. In most African countries, the economy has at best been stalled and has often shown actual losses in GNP during the past decade. In very recent years, there has been an encouraging shift toward economic realism and political toleration. Attacking the overpopulation problem is the continent's most pressing task. What the future holds in both politics and living conditions is impossible to know, but Africa will need both luck and assistance from the developed world to overcome its present handicaps.

Test Your Knowledge

1. Which of the following statements about African nations is false?
   a. They have fewer educational facilities now than before independence.
   b. They all have primarily rural populations.
   c. They are all aware of their impoverished status in contrast to the West.
   d. They have almost all experienced a colonial past.
2. Which of the following was *not* a consequence of post–World War II medical advances in the sub-Saharan regions?
   a. The extension of medical services to many rural areas
   b. Considerably longer life expectancy
   c. Decline in birthrates
   d. Decline in infant mortality rates
3. In terms of the Green Revolution, Africa
   a. benefited more than elsewhere in food supply.
   b. benefited less than elsewhere.
   c. grew no crops that could have benefited from the revolution.
   d. experienced practically no effect because of the nomadic lifestyle of many inhabitants.
4. In Africa, since independence, the most common population movement has been
   a. from the cities to the rural areas.
   b. from the inland cities to the coastal areas.
   c. from the nomadic life to the farm villages.
   d. from the farm villages to the cities.
5. One of the following reasons does *not* apply to the causes for African economic missteps since independence:
   a. Misguided notions of establishing national prestige
   b. Desire for personal enrichment
   c. Desire to spread the benefits to maximal numbers of citizens
   d. Conceiving national progress in terms of imitating Westerners
6. Which of the following countries experienced the most difficult transition from colony to independent nation?
   a. Tanzania
   b. Zaire
   c. Egypt
   d. Ghana
7. Since about 1965, the general trend of politics in Africa has been toward

a. one-party dictatorships.
b. monarchies.
c. socialist states.
d. parliamentary democracies.

8. The career of Jomo Kenyatta can best be summarized as
   a. from terrorist to statesman.
   b. from patriot to terrorist.
   c. from imitator of Europeans to African patriot.
   d. from ignorant native to sophisticated Westerner.

Identification Terms

Kenyatta (Jomo)

negritude

Senghor (Leopold)

World Bank

Muslim Brotherhoods

Organization for Pan African Unity (OAU)

Structural Adjustment Plan (SAP)

Bibliography

In addition to the general histories mentioned in the bibliography for Chapter 43, see also the following:

Burke, F. *Africa,* 1970. A brief and easily digested summary history. Maps and charts help make the story.

Davidson, B. *Let Freedom Come,* 1978, and *The African Genius,* 1969. Davidson has written several studies of tropical Africa since the 1960s; these are among the more notable.

Dwyer, D. J. *The City in the Third World,* 1974. Treats Africa along with Asia and Latin America.

Hafkin, N., and E. Bay, eds. *Women in Africa,* 1977. A broad investigation of the present-day problems of the female African.

Harrison, P. *The Greening of Africa: Breaking Through in the Battle for Land and Food,* 1987. A perhaps all-too-optimistic survey of agrarian problems and their possible solutions.

Iliffe, J. *The African Poor: A History,* 1987. A marvelous work and a very unusual one.

Lipton, M. *Why Poor People Stay Poor: Urban Bias in World Development,* 1977. Highly recommended to help understand why so little has been accomplished for the rural majority.

Patterson, K. *History and Disease in Africa,* 1978. Written prior to AIDS.

Turnbull, C. M. *The Lonely African,* 1962. A case study of what happens when the traditional ideas and communities no longer suffice, but have not been effectively replaced.

LATIN AMERICA IN THE TWENTIETH CENTURY

PERSISTENT DEPENDENCY

NEW AND OLD SOCIAL PROBLEMS

ECONOMIC NATIONALISM

Mexico under Cárdenas

Argentina under Perón

Brazil under Vargas

THE SHARK AND THE SARDINES

THE U.S. ROLE IN RECENT LATIN AFFAIRS

CURRENT ISSUES AND PROBLEMS

Rich and Poor

Changing Styles in Government

In the present century, the histories of the twenty countries making up Latin America have varied sharply in detail but have been generally similar overall. In all cases, the politics and international relationships of the Latin countries have been fundamentally influenced by the economic and social problems they faced—problems that were roughly alike from Mexico to Argentina. All of the countries have also had to come to terms with the United States, the dominant power in the Americas with the ability to intervene in hemispheric affairs at will.

The Great Depression of the 1930s was a decisive turning point for the Latin Americans in a national economic sense, as several countries attempted to recover from their loss of international markets by becoming self-sufficient. Though not completely successful, they did manage a partial escape from the neocolonialism to which they had formerly acquiesced. Since the end of World War II, repeated attempts have been made to introduce more or less radical changes in both the political and economic structures, but with the exception of a failing and unpopular Marxism in Cuba, these efforts have not been supported for more than a few years. Facing immense problems, Latin America awaits a better future.

❖ PERSISTENT DEPENDENCY

The obstacles facing the Latin American countries are similar in many respects, even though their political systems and social divisions are different, in some cases dramatically so. *National economic policy* throughout modern Latin America has aimed at escaping from the basic pattern that has plagued all the countries: they have been exporters of raw materials and importers of manufactured goods. A few countries made significant progress in the middle years of the century, usually in combination with a radicalization of internal politics. For example, in Argentina in the 1940s, the lower classes enthusiastically supported the dictator **Juan Perón** when he attacked both traditional domestic class privileges and Argentina's traditional import dependency on the United States. In the 1930s under President **Lázaro Cárdenas,** the Mexicans actually expropriated U.S. oil firms (with compensation) and withstood the wrath of the Giant to the North until a negotiated agreement was reached.

But in general, the economy of the southern continent (and of its Caribbean outliers) remained nearly as much under the control of external forces as it had always been.

Until well into the twentieth century, the majority of the South American and all of the Central American states remained agrarian societies as they had been since colonial times. They exported bulk quantities of raw materials such as coffee, grain, beef, timber, petroleum, and copper ore; they imported the vital elements of industry and personal consumption such as machinery, steel, automobiles, transformers, and telephone wire. In such an equation, the raw material exporters are always at a disadvantage, because their products can almost always be found elsewhere or replaced by new technologies.

✤ NEW AND OLD SOCIAL PROBLEMS

Socially, by the mid-twentieth century, the Latin American countries were divided into two major groups: the more industrialized and urban states, which included Argentina, Brazil, and Chile (the ABC countries) and, with reservations, Mexico; and the majority, which remained agrarian and rural. In the first group, the migration of much of the population into the handful of major towns accompanied industrialization, and added to the spiritual isolation of the countryside from the highly centralized government. The peasants in their adobe villages or their equivalents in the mine and ranch country saw the capital city as a distant seat of invisible (and parasitic) powers, rather than as a leader addressing national problems. But in the cities, the industrial working class was growing rapidly and began to play a new role in national affairs in the 1930s and 1940s under the guidance of populist politicians.

In the nonindustrial countries, the people remained isolated from the government as they had always been and continued their traditional passivity. The illiterate *mestizo, mulatto,* and *Indio* peasants remained in a very backward condition, dominated in every sense by the landowners and with no hope of the social and economic mobility that the cities offered.

The social and political complexion of a given Latin American country depended largely on the number of its *immigrants* between about 1890 and 1930. In a select group, consisting of the ABC countries plus Uruguay and Costa Rica, immigration from Spain and Italy in particular was large enough to maintain a European flavor of life in the cities and extinguish whatever Indian culture they may have once possessed. At first glance, these countries seemed to have very favorable prospects for extensive and intensive development. With the exception of Brazil, they had little or no history of slavery and its accompanying social distinctions. Race was not a factor. Basic natural resources were generally adequate to abundant, and good farmland was in sufficient supply. In short, these countries seemed to have enough actual and potential wealth to meet their individual population's needs for a long time to come *if* no human-made obstructions to the distribution of that wealth were imposed.

But it was precisely such obstructions that led to much of the social tension in Latin America in the twentieth century. In the ABC countries (less so in Uruguay and Costa Rica), the Creole latifundists and their *caudillo* partners prevented the land from being subdivided for the latecomers in the nineteenth and twentieth centuries. Social discontent in the cities could not be relieved by settling the vast and underdeveloped countryside. Mineral wealth remained in a few, mainly foreign, hands. Industry and commerce were almost as tightly controlled as the fertile lands by the availability of credit. In the absence of a vibrant economy that would act as the rising tide that lifts all ships, these nations attempted to find answers to their social problems in politics. The offered solutions ranged from a demagogic and nationalist populism to total dependency on foreign (meaning mostly U.S.) interests and investment.

Until recently, Latin America's most intractable social problems were in countries such as Colombia, Peru, and Bolivia, where a large Indian or mestizo population continued to present a threat to the Iberian culture of the dominant Creoles. As late as the 1940s, the Creoles responded to the perceived menace by attempting to exclude the natives completely from national affairs.

Now, the ancient chasms between the landowning class and their laborers and between Iberians/Creoles and mestizos have been further complicated by the widening gap between urbanites and rural dwellers. In the last thirty years or so, everywhere in Latin America *the demographic picture has changed markedly:* the cities are growing at an incredible rate, and the *barrios* and *favelas,* the shanty towns that surround every Latin city and often contain more people than the city proper, are the future of Latin society if current trends are not reversed. Overcrowding, unsanitary makeshift accommodations, and the absence of even elementary public services (schools, police, pure water, and the like) are taken for granted in these slums, where some shacks have harbored three generations already. In the meanwhile, the villages and small towns have become even less important in the affairs of the nation than before. Always a disproportionately urban economy, Latin America is becoming a series of huge heads (the cities) weakly supported by anemic bodies.

■ **Mexican Contrasts.** The struggle to house the flood of urban immigrants throughout Latin America is often seemingly hopeless. Scenes like this abound on the perimeters of every city; the new flats in the background will remain out of reach of many.

Unemployment is endemic; no figures are kept because it is impossible to do so, but at least one-third of the adults in the cities have nothing that U.S. citizens would recognize as a steady job. *Income distribution* is as bad or worse now than it ever has been. Even by the standards of the developing world, Latin America has the most skewed distribution of cash income imaginable. A very small group of industrialists, latifundists, and import-export business owners are rewarded handsomely while a very large number of unskilled urban and agricultural workers have next to nothing. In the middle, the number of professionals, white-collar employees, managers, and small business owners is increasing, but usually they are still too few, too unorganized, and insufficiently independent to play an important role in civic affairs and policy making.

⚜ ECONOMIC NATIONALISM

One result of social stratification and continuing economic dependency on foreign nations has been the wavelike rise of radical reform movements with strongly nationalist overtones. Interestingly, the leaders of such protests have often been *military men*. The widespread impression of Latin American military leaders as conservatives who automatically uphold the status quo has become increasingly erroneous. Depending on the circumstances, they have frequently been at the forefront of economic nationalism.

Such movements were especially prominent during the years of the Great Depression and continued to be important into the 1960s. Perón in Argentina, Batista in Cuba in the 1930s, and the MLN in Bolivia in the 1960s were examples of the military in leading roles of reformist parties. **Getúlio Vargas** in Brazil and *Lázaro Cárdenas* in Mexico were civilians who managed either to attract military support or to weld together such a broad coalition that the conservative officers hesitated to interfere.

The reform parties of the mid-century were often strongly influenced by the practice, but not the theory, of a Mussolini-type corporate state, in which all sectors of the population would find adequate representation. The most popular of these broad-based movements appeared in Mexico under Cárdenas in the 1930s and in Argentina a decade later under the Peróns.

Mexico under Cárdenas

The spasmodic and complicated revolution that took place in Mexico between 1910 and 1920 was, as has been mentioned, the only genuine social and political change in the first half of this century. Out of this revolution finally came a single-party government committed to social equalization and redistribution of both wealth and power. In this mestizo country where a small number of *haciendados* had held all power for generations, such goals were unprecedented—and unfulfillable. In the 1920s, the governing party (Partido Revolucionario Institutional or PRI) despite much talk did little to advance social causes. But under the impact of the world depression and the Marxist experiment in Russia, President Lázaro Cárdenas (1934–1940), an Indian by birth, tried to give substance to some of the revolution's slogans. He confiscated and redistributed much land to Indians and peasants in the poverty-stricken north, expropriated foreign mineral firms, and insisted on Mexican sovereignty in every sense. In so doing, he set the pattern of Mexico for the Mexicans, which his less flamboyant successors in office have followed.

Cárdenas's efforts to achieve security and a political voice for the lower classes, however, have generally not been followed, and the gap between the haves and the have-nots in Mexico remains vast. The PRI became an intricate web of established social powers ranging from labor leaders to intellectuals, all of whom expected—and got—a calculated payoff for their support. Despite much criticism and undoubted abuses, particularly corruption at the top, the Mexican system has allowed an increasing pluralism in politics. If the PRI can fulfill its current promises to open the political stage still further, Mexico has good prospects for both stability and democracy.

Argentina under Perón

In Argentina, Juan Perón and his military and industrialist backers in the 1940s were ardent nationalists, who dreamed of making Argentina the dominant power in Latin America—a status for which it seemed destined by its size, natural resources, and European immigrant population. Perón was one of a group of officers who threw out the elected government in 1943 and soon made himself into leader. Perón's well-known pro-German sympathies guaranteed that the United States would oppose him, which all but ensured his election in 1946 on a vehemently nationalist platform. His wife **Eva** (the "Evita" of song and story) was a product of the slums who knew her people intimately. She was always at his side in public, and her personal charisma and undoubtedly sincere concern for the Argentine working classes made her an idol whose popularity among the populace exceeded the colonel's. She was the most important woman in twentieth-century American politics, North or South, and her early death in 1952 was in a sense the beginning of the decline of the movement her husband headed (see the Biography in this chapter).

Perón (or Evita) understood something that eluded most Latin American reformers: to overcome the apathy of the rural dwellers and the tradition of leaving government in the hands of a few, it was necessary to appeal to people in a way that they would respond to, directly and with passion. Such an appeal must concentrate on their many economic and social discontents. Perón played on this theme very effectively, organizing huge rallies of the lower classes and making inflammatory speeches against the "exploiters" while simultaneously, though quietly, assuring the entrepreneurs and big business of government contracts and concessions of unprecedented size. It was a fine balancing act between encouraging the egalitarian desires of the **descamisados** (shirtless ones) and reassuring the rich that nothing unbearable was in store and that anyone else in Peron's place would probably be worse. Perón was helped by the fact that the early years of his era (1946–1955) were a time of profits for raw material producers, of whom Argentina took a place in the first rank. Like Africa in the immediate postindependence era, the Argentine economy prospered mightily, and the bigger pie allowed a bigger slice for all.

In 1954, Perón was confronted by a gradually strengthening democratic opposition. Attempting to keep his support, he allowed the radical-socialist wing of the *Perónistas* more prominence, which alienated his industrial and business support. In that year, he also made the mistake of taking on the Catholic church—which had originally been favorable toward Perónismo—by attacking its higher clergy. In 1955 the military drove Perón into exile.

The colonel had produced few if any real answers to the problems of his country, but the working classes still were devoted to him, and the next two decades of Argentina's volatile history are only comprehensible if one remembers the figure waiting in exile. One military puppet after another attempted to reduce the Perónist nostalgia through persecution or persuasion, but with no success. Perónismo without Perón was the order of the day until 1973, when a discredited military finally allowed a sick, elderly Perón to return. He easily won the following presidential election, but died soon after, and a cynical effort was made to continue Perónismo through the elevation of his politically illiterate second wife to the presidency. Again a desperate military intervened and dismissed the civil government. By then it was already clear that Argentina's problems would not be solved by a renewal of the class conflicts that had plagued the nation for a generation. The potentially richest country in Latin America was still as far as ever from realizing that potential.

Brazil under Vargas

Mexico and Argentina are only two examples of Latin Americans' efforts to solve the dilemmas that a dependent economy and an inflexible, caste-bound social system have forced on them in this century. Brazil under the flamboyant *Getúlio Vargas* (presidential dictator 1929–1945, 1950–1954) had somewhat greater success for a time. Vargas was a demagogue who could rally his fellow citizens to extremes of devotion for a program that was filled with contradictions and illogic. He came to power as the Great Depression began and modeled his government on Mussolini's corporatism. Supposedly, all sectors of the Brazilian populace would join in a common effort to secure industrial development and international respect for the "sleeping giant of the Amazon."

For well over a decade Vargas's nationalist and populist message overcame all criticism, and the support it aroused allowed his program to work reasonably well. Unlike Perón, his international prestige benefited from joining the Allied side in World War II. But he came to the same end as Perón a decade earlier. In 1945, he was deposed by a military *junta,* which feared his concessions to labor and to the small but important Communist Party. Five years later, he was reelected, but committed suicide out of discouragement in 1954. Vargas remains the political idol

Juan and Eva Perón

In the entire history of Latin America, the husband and wife team of Juan and Eva Perón is unique. Colonel Juan Domingo Perón (1895–1974) was an Argentine army officer who became the country's virtual dictator in the middle decades of this century. Eva Duarte de Perón (1919–1952) was his wife and co-ruler until her early death from incurable cancer. To this day, they arouse feelings of love and hate among the Argentine people that have no parallel.

The Peróns rode to power on the wave of nationalism and class antagonism that afflicted many of Latin America's more developed countries in the early twentieth century. Perón was a career officer who joined with a handful of others to oust the visionless political authorities governing Argentina during World War II. Strongly nationalist and generally sympathetic to Fascist ideas of reform, these men were viewed with suspicion by the U.S. government.

■ **Juan and Evita Perón.** This 1951 photo shows the couple acceding to the "demand" of the Argentine people that they run for re-election.

Perón himself was pushed out by his fellow *junta* members in 1945, but massive popular protest organized by his wife got him out of prison and made him the leading candidate for the presidential election of 1946. The U.S. State Department's heavy-handed intervention against him practically assured his election by resentful Argentines.

Evita Perón came from a typically poverty-stricken working-class background. The illegitimate child of a village seamstress and an unknown father, she was raised among ignorance and misery. Guided by an iron determination to make something of herself, she left her mother and went off to the great city of Buenos Aires at age fifteen. The details of her life in the next several years vary depending on who is telling the story. Her enemies delighted in picturing her as a part-time actress who was not overly scrupulous in how and where she made her living. Her admirers picture her as a victim of an unjust and

---

of millions of poor Brazilians who saw in him what Mexicans saw in Cárdenas and Argentinians in Perón: a leader who, whatever his faults, claimed to stand on *their* side of the social and economic barricades. And that was a rarity.

✤ THE SHARK AND THE SARDINES

During the first two-thirds of the twentieth century, the United States repeatedly played a heavy-handed and frankly conservative role in Latin American international affairs. One leader who had experienced at first hand what American influence could do in a small country (Guatemala) called it the relationship of the "shark with the sardines." That may be overstating the case slightly, but there is no doubt that in ways both open and covert, Washington was the court of final appeal for Latin foreign relations and, in some cases, not just foreign relations.

The United States first began to pay close attention to Latin America during the Spanish-American War (1898–1900), which was fought, in part, over the rights of the Cuban people to independence. In the ensuing thirty

brutally oppressive society, who used her intelligence and beauty to lift herself up out of the mud she was born into. In 1943, this strikingly attractive, aspiring minor actress met the equally aspiring Juan Perón, who made her first his mistress and two years later his wife. A year after that, she became in effect his co-president.

Working together, husband and wife imme diately began a program of social and economic reforms that seemed revolutionary to the upper classes who had been accustomed to ruling the country as a private club. Although their bark was frequently more severe than the bite, the program of *Perónismo* did assure the Argentine workers and peasants a considerably enlarged role in politics at the direct expense of the older ruling group. Evita Perón became the equivalent of minister of labor and of social welfare, and from those positions, she built up a huge following among the poor and the ignored. These *descamisados,* or shirtless ones, were the backbone of the Perónist regime for the next ten years.

The Peróns capitalized on the long-smoldering resentment felt by many Argentines against the dependency on foreign nations that had been the fate of all of Latin America throughout the postindependence period. A strange coalition of labor, nationalist intellectuals, industrialists, lower clergy, and much of the military supported the Perónist program in its early years. Each of these elements could gain something from the grab bag of Perónismo.

While Juan Perón concentrated on meeting the industrialists' hopes for greater profits and protection from foreign competitors, his wife used her enormous powers to assist the millions who lived at the bottom of the economic ladder. She led the efforts to establish a public health system and to assure some degree of schooling for every child. Her army of male and female admirers considered her a saint.

Evita's death in 1952 marked the beginning of the Perónist decline. Without her charisma (which her husband had never shared), the cracks in the coalition rapidly surfaced. The higher military became increasingly uncomfortable with Perón's alliance with the Left and with labor. When Perón mounted a campaign against the Roman Catholic clergy, he was excommunicated in 1955. A few months later, he was chased out by a military coup similar to the one he had used to begin his own rise to power twelve years earlier.

For the next eighteen years, Perón lived in exile, while his country went through waves of social unrest and economic decline in the hands of both the old civilian establishment and military *juntas.* Finally, confronted with the demands of the loyal Perónistas, an unwilling military was forced to allow the nearly eighty-year-old Perón to return and be elected president once again in 1973. But the fire was gone, and the old man died a year later without having had the time or, perhaps, the will to again disturb the course of his country's political life. While Juan Perón has become only another name to his younger countrymen and women, Evita's controversial reputation continues almost undiminished among them. For generations of Argentines, she remains the person who defines, "whose side are you on?"

years, Washington intervened at will in Latin and Caribbean affairs, ranging from Theodore Roosevelt's creation of Panama as a suitable place to build his canal to the sending of armed forces against Mexico and Haiti and the use of the Marines to squelch the rebels of General Sandino—the original Sandinistas—in Nicaragua.

After World War I, U.S. capital and finance took the vacated place of the Europeans with a rush. The dependence of the Central American **"banana republics"** on the plantations of the United Fruit Company was merely the most notorious example of the economic imperialism that was practiced throughout Latin America. Cuba's huge sugarcane farms and mills were 80 percent owned by U.S. investors; the big oil strikes in Venezuela were brought in by U.S. firms using U.S. engineers. Mexico's original petroleum fields were dependencies of U.S. firms until nationalization; 20 percent of the land surface of Mexico's border states was owned or leased by foreign investors in the 1920s, to name only a few examples.

But the story of Latin dependency on the United States has another side: had it not been for Yankee investment and commerce, the countries to the south would have

Pablo Neruda: "Cuba Appears" and "In Guatemala"

The Chilean poet Pablo Neruda (1904–1973), whose many books won him the Nobel Prize in 1971, both personified and articulated the sense of powerlessness, frustration, and resentment toward the United States shared by a large number of Latin American intellectuals in this century. For much of his life, Neruda was a spokesman for the Chilean Communist Party. He was outraged by the exploitation of the Indians and peons by the upper classes and used the communist ideology as a vehicle of protest. After 1959, these sentiments sometimes crystallized in poems glorifying the archnemesis of the United States, the Cuban Fidel Castro. The following excerpt from "Cuba Appears" is a typical example. The poem "In Guatemala"concerns the deposition of the elected president by a conspiracy organized by the U.S. Central Intelligence Agency in 1954.

Cuba Appears

But when tortures and darkness
seem to extinguish the free air
and it is not the spume of waves,
but blood among the reefs you see

Fidel's hand comes forth and in it
Cuba, the pure rose of the Caribbean.

And so history changes with her light
that man can change that which exists
and if he takes purity into battle
in his honor blooms a noble spring;
behind is left the tyrant's night,
his cruelty and his insensible eyes,
the gold snatched by his claws,
his mercenaries, his cannibal judges . . .

his high monuments sustained
by torment, disorder, and crime . . .
. . . And so Fidel came forth, cutting shadows
so that the jasmine tree could dawn.

In Guatemala

Just as in Sandino's time
I saw the rose bloom in Guatemala.

I saw the poor man's land defended,
and justice arrive in every mouth.
Arbenz* opened amidst his people
his delicate and powerful hand
    and schools were a granary
of triumphant possibilities
    till the Canal's long claws
severed the dawn's path
    the North American arsonists
dropped dollars and bombs;
death built its finery,
the United Fruit† uncoiled its rope.
And thus Guatemala was assassinated

    And thus Guatemala was assassinated
in full flight, like a dove.

---

*Jacobo Arbenz Guzmán, Guatemalan president and Leftist reformer (1950–1954).
†The United Fruit Company, an American concern, exerted great influence in Guatemala.

SOURCE: *Songs of Protest, Poems* by Pablo Neruda, trans. Miguel Algaris, pp. 43, 59. William Morrow, 1976.

---

been even less developed economically and would have sunk deeper into their grossly obsolete system of production and consumption. Until World War II, it's largely true that the Caribbean and northern Latin America (with the exception of Cárdenas's Mexico) were U.S. colonies in everything but name. The bigger question remains: What would have been the Latins' fate in this period in the absence of the United States? Through their own efforts and expertise, they would never have achieved reasonable living standards for even a small segment of their peoples during the first half of this century (and perhaps not in the second, either). If the U.S. capitalists had not been involved, would the Latin Americans have found more benevolent and selfless sources of help outside the Americas? It seems very doubtful.

In Franklin D. Roosevelt's presidency (1933–1945), the United States embarked upon a **"Good Neighbor" policy**, treating the Latins more as sovereign nations than as colonies. For thirty years, no troops were landed to assure a "stability" acceptable to the United States, but still no one had any doubt where true sovereignty lay in the western hemisphere. With World War II and the coming of the Cold War, Washington became more concerned about the political allegiance of the Latin states. To obtain rights to airfields in Brazil so that bombers could be flown across the Atlantic, the U.S. government provided considerable financial and diplomatic support to Vargas. In treaties signed immediately after the war, the United States pledged political and economic assistance to the other signatories. In 1948, the **Organization of American States (OAS)** was founded under American auspices and served several useful commercial, cultural, and legal purposes besides its primary one of assuring democratic and pro-Western governments in the hemisphere.

But the real catalyst for U.S. activity was the coming of *Fidel Castro* to power in Cuba. Originally the organizer of a hopelessly outnumbered band of idealists, Castro surprisingly overturned the corrupt and unpopular Batista government at the beginning of 1959. After a period of increasing tension, he declared himself a Marxist and began systematically persecuting those who disagreed with that philosophy, while denouncing the United States as the oppressor of freedom-loving Latin Americans. After he nationalized the very extensive U.S. businesses in Cuba, a state of near war existed between the two countries, culminating in the abortive Bay of Pigs invasion by U.S.-financed anti-Castroites in 1961. A year later, the placement of long-range missiles on the island by the Soviets brought the world to the brink of nuclear war (see Chapter 54).

Since then, relations between the Castro government and Washington have remained frigid, but tolerable. The Cuban revolution, despite some real achievements for the people of the island (literacy, public health, technical education, housing), has proved unable to guarantee a decent material life especially since Castro's Soviet and Chinese supporters have withdrawn their aid. The revolution has also proved unsuitable for export to the rest of the continent, as Castro had once intended. No other Latin state ever "went communist," although one or two Marxist-leaning governments have been elected (notably, that of Salvador Allende in Chile in 1971) and several

■ **Fidel Castro in Havana.** The Cuban revolutionary leader enjoys his triumph in making his first address to the Havana populace after chasing out the corrupt Batista regime in 1959. The display of guns was a frequent note in Castro appearances during his early years in power.

guerrilla rebellions have been dominated by Marxists. None has succeeded, in part because of the extensive aid given to anti-Castro and conservative forces by the U.S. Central Intelligence Agency. (See Map 58.1)

⚜ THE U.S. ROLE IN RECENT LATIN AFFAIRS

In the early days of the Kennedy administration (1961–1963), the U.S. entered into an **Alliance for Progress** with the Latin American states. More than $10 billion were set aside for economic development loans and credits, more than twice the money allocated to postwar Europe under the Marshal Plan. But as so often happens with government programs that are intended to make a quick impression on the electorate, much of the money went to make the rich richer or wound up in the wrong pockets. The single most effective, externally funded program for Latin American development was the mutually supervised, quiet work on improving crop yields, done mainly in Mexico during the 1950s and 1960s. This botanical laboratory project gave a tremendous boost to world food grain production, resulting in some places in the Green Revolution

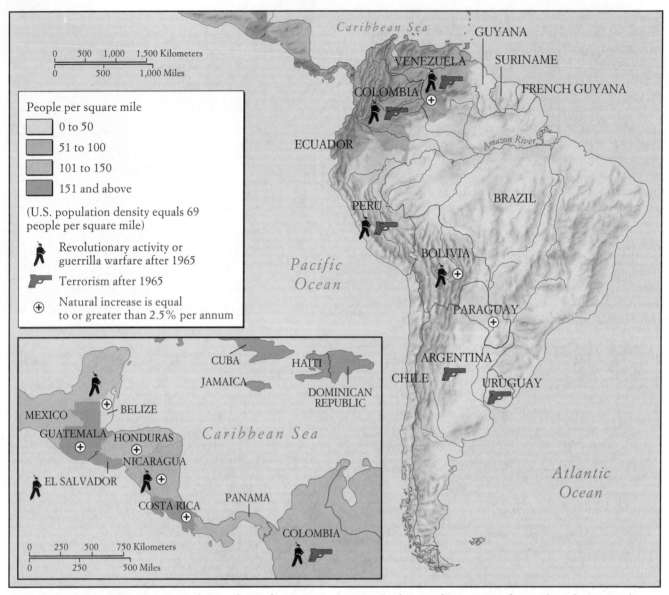

⦿ MAP 58.1   Population Density and Guerrila Warfare in Latin America. In the past thirty years, urban and rural terrorism has been a frequent occurrence, sometimes for political and more often for a mixture of political and monetary motives, such as the alliance between Colombian guerrillas and the narcotics lords. The rate of population increase is highest in Central America and the Andean countries where resources are fewest.

we have mentioned earlier. Its success is a main reason why the threatened world famine has thus far been confined to regions of Africa and has not menaced Latin America and the entire developing world.

In recent years, the U.S. involvement with the Caribbean nations has again become openly interventionary, but generally within dimensions that the OAS as a whole has been willing to approve. Presidents Ronald Reagan (Grenada,

Nicaragua), George Bush (Panama), and Bill Clinton (Haiti) have acted forcefully to protect what they conceived to be U.S. strategic, political, or economic interests in the area. But a return to the pre-1930 system of "gunboat diplomacy" by the United States is hardly possible, even if it were desirable. A major change will occur in the year 2000 when the Panama Canal is due to become part of the sovereign territory of Panama. Other pending questions include independence for Puerto Rico (a U.S. territory for the past century) and the possible surrender of the Guantánamo naval base in Cuba to a post-Castro government.

✤ CURRENT ISSUES AND PROBLEMS

In Latin America as elsewhere, economic and social issues are linked together. In Latin America as a whole, just as in Africa, probably the highest-priority social problem is controlling a rate (2.9 percent) of population growth that is too high. Also as in Africa, a number of governments would contest this assessment, saying that faulty or non-existent access to resources, both domestic and foreign, generates most social frictions in their countries. There is, in fact, something to be said for this argument. In the eyes of many Latin Americans, the developed world, and especially the United States, has taken unfair and short-sighted advantage of the underdeveloped world during the past century and continues to do so in the following ways:

1. The terms of trade, that is, the rate at which raw materials are exchanged for manufactures, consumer goods, and necessary services, are loaded in favor of the developed countries.
2. Financial credits have been extended to the underdeveloped American nations (in contrast to Africa) on an unrealistically "businesslike" basis (high interest and short terms), which guarantees that the loans cannot and will not be repaid on time, if at all.
3. Currently, the underdeveloped nations are being pressed to avoid using the main resources they possess—what Nature has given them—in order to assure a more secure future for the developed minority. Environmental concerns are being used to justify interference in internal affairs such as how many trees are cut down, or where beef cattle should graze, or how many fish should be caught.

What are we to make of these complaints? There can be little doubt that the Latin Americans, like the rest of the developing world, have been asked to accept consistently disadvantageous trade conditions, while getting only an occasional sop in the form of World Bank or bilateral loans and grants. Since World II, a ton of wheat, a bag of coffee, or a container of bananas purchases less and less of the electrical machinery, plate glass, or insurance policies that the developed countries sell to the underdeveloped.

Whether the second accusation is true is debatable. Much of the waste, corruption, or misuse of international

credits was indisputably the work of recipients in the developing countries, who had little fear of ever being held personally responsible. At the same time, the international lending community has rarely if ever "pulled" loans that were clearly being diverted to the illicit benefit of individuals. In any case, the terms of the international loans extended to the Latin countries in the past have been notably more severe than those granted to Africa. The efforts to repay have handicapped Latin America's domestic investment.

The third charge has a very complex background, but demands a decisive answer because it will affect us all in a powerful fashion. The Latin Americans (and others) are saying in essence: "You, the developed societies, are now waking up to the dangers of pollution and abuse of nature, but want us, the less developed, to pay the price of implementing rational policies while you have enjoyed the short-term benefits of irrationality." It was all right, in other words, for nineteenth-century American timber companies to cut down every tree over a foot thick in Michigan, but it is not all right for twentieth-century Brazilian timber companies to cut down mature mahogany in the Amazon basin. Multiply this example by hundreds, and you will have the position adopted by the Latin Americans and most other leaders of the developing countries in response to the environmental concerns of the developed world.

■ **Oil production in the Amazon.** The environmental devastation which often accompanies natural resource exploitation is dramatically apparent in this aerial photo over the Peruvian Amazon.

The developed world adds salt to the Latin Americans' wounds by paying too little for that mahogany tree compared to the cost of the chain saw that cut the tree or the insurance on the boat that transports the tree to a U.S. mill—both the saw and the insurance, of course, were supplied by the developed world. And further salting comes from the fact that the fine piece of furniture made from the tree will be too expensive to grace an ordinary Latin American home due to the high costs and profits of the U.S. manufacturer. What benefits, if any, the recent **North American Free Trade Agreement (NAFTA)** will bring to Mexico, and perhaps through Mexico to the rest of Latin America, is an interesting but unanswered question at this writing.

The *flight to the cities* we have already mentioned in connection with modern Africa is equally strong in Latin America. Towns such as Lima or Bogotá, which were still slumbering in the early twentieth century, have been overwhelmed with peasant migrants in the last thirty years. Mexico City, so far as anyone can tell, is now the largest metropolis in the world, with an estimated population of about 15 million. The majority live in shabby *barrios* or unfinished subdivisions that spring up like mushrooms in an ever-widening circle around the older town. Many of the inhabitants of these slums have established a settled, even secure life, but many others are living on a tightrope, balancing petty and sporadic income against constant demands for food and fuel. Much of the urban population seems to be "living on air," hustling up unskilled work on a day-to-day basis or depending on intricate networks of kin and friends to see them through until they can return the favor.

Rich and Poor

The *chasm between rich and poor* is deeper and more apparent in Latin American countries than anywhere else. Africa has relatively few very rich and not many people who are well-to-do. In most of Asia, wealth is fairly evenly distributed except in one or two cities in each country. But in South America, the extremes of very poor and very rich are growing, while the number of those in the middle is more or less stable. There are a great many very poor and a very small but growing number of rich—and the contrast between them is a powder keg in most Latin American countries.

So visible and disturbing is the polarization of Latin American society that the Catholic church, long the main bastion of conservatism and reaction, has taken the lead in country after country as a voice for the poor. A peculiar combination of Marxist social theory and Catholic humanitarianism has come to life in several countries, notably Brazil, to speak for the common people against a social and economic system that has exploited them for many generations. Hundreds of priests, nuns, and higher officials of the church have been imprisoned or even murdered by military and civilian reactionaries in the past fifteen years. Archbishop Oscar Romero of El Salvador was shot down while saying mass in his own cathedral for speaking out against the bloody excesses of the military in the civil war in El Salvador in the 1980s. The Romeros of a generation ago would have been blessing the army's guns.

Changing Styles in Government

In the 1960s, it appeared quite possible that Latin American Marxists, inspired by Castro's success, would attempt to seize power in several countries. Economic nationalism was faltering, and little social reform had been effected.

■ **Mexican Rebels Challenge Government.** In the extreme south of Mexico where small cliques have controlled the state government for many years, an armed rebellion broke out in 1995 under the leadership of a certain *Subcomandante* Marcos. After some hundreds of casualties, the federal government agreed to negotiations with Marcos which are still continuing.

Degree of Political Freedom

High

Moderate

Low

⊙ **MAP 58.2 Political Freedom in Latin American, 1995.** Categories are derived from data over the medium term (1990–1995). The low point of political democracy was reached in the 1970s when military men thrust aside elected governments throughout the continent because of fears of Leftist revolution. In the past decade, however, the democratic ideal has made a strong comeback.

Terrorist activity became a menace to the upper classes in Argentina and Brazil, where urban guerrillas operated. The military establishment in country after country pushed aside the ineffectual politicians and governed directly on a platform of law and order. The U.S.-sponsored Alliance for Progress was inaugurated in 1961 in the wake of the Cuban revolution. Encouraged by government policy makers, Western banks loaned huge sums to the Latin American nations; foreign debt in creased by more than twelve times in the 1970s, to a point where with the slightest reversal the Latin American nations could not pay even the interest on time.

The *1970s were the low point for constitutional government;* at one point in that decade, only three of the twenty Latin American nations were still ruled by elected governments. Everywhere else, the military attempted to meet the increasing demands for social and economic reform by going outside the political process. Almost always these attempts failed or were discarded before they had a chance to take hold.

A wild inflation was the main enemy of the reform plans; at one time, the value of the Argentine peso against the U.S. dollar was dropping at the rate of 10 percent per *day*. In Chile, the Marxist Salvador Allende was elected president in 1970, but was assassinated in a military *golpe* (coup) three years later. For the first time since the nineteenth century, Chile was then subjected to martial law and the brutal regime of General Augusto Pinochet, which lasted until he stepped down in 1989.

In the 1980s the pendulum swung back to civilian rule, and by the end of that decade, only a few countries were still ruled by men in uniform. Argentina and Brazil again led the way. The military in Buenos Aires stepped down in disgrace after foolishly provoking a war with Britain over the Falkland Islands in 1982, and a few years later, the Brazilian generals gave up power to the first duly elected government in a quarter century.

Latin America has thus tried several different forms of government, including socialism, corporatism, and populism in an effort to achieve greater social justice and economic prosperity. Most of these have quickly degenerated into dictatorship. All have proved either ineffective or corrupt or were unable to retain their momentum after a time. Castro's Cuba remains the one experiment with scientific socialism, and even its defenders acknowledge that it has failed its people economically in the last ten years.

Democratic, constitutional government is still a fragile flower most of the time in most of the continent. But it made some strong gains in the 1980s and 1990s. The replacement of a series of military *juntas* by elected civilians in all three ABC nations and several others as well is a hopeful sign. The ending of the Cold War has had a beneficial effect on U.S.-Latin American relations, as the United States no longer worries that some type of hostile, Marxist regime will be installed in these near neighbors. But the emergence from neocolonialism is a painfully slow process that will continue well into the twenty-first century even in the most hopeful scenarios. And the relative backwardness of Latin America, as part of the developing world, will cause it to continue to be a breeding ground for social discontent. The continent's future will depend largely on whether and how that discontent is resolved.

Summary

The twenty nations in Latin America in the twentieth century have many overriding similarities despite some differences. Everywhere, policy makers are concerned with the question of economic development—how to achieve it and how to manage it. Everywhere, the relationship between the United States and the Latin American nations is vital to the future stability and prosperity of the continent. Various types of economic nationalism, sometimes introduced by the military, have been the Latin American response to their status as poor relations of the more developed nations of the world. Cárdenas in Mexico, Perón in Argentina, and Vargas in Brazil were perhaps the most noted examples in the past sixty years, but many others have appeared and will continue to do so. Thirty-five years ago, Castro offered a Marxist response to neocolonial status in Cuba, but Marxism has had minimal appeal outside that country despite initial efforts to spread it. Its future is very dim.

Social problems, especially the maldistribution of wealth and the pressures generated by a high birthrate haunt the continent south of the Rio Grande. One of the most striking manifestations of these problems is the uncontrollable growth of the cities and their shantytown surroundings. Political solutions to Latin American problems have been at best sporadic and partial. But after the failure of the military regimes of the 1970s, there has been a vigorous recovery in parliamentary government. In the 1990s, there have been some hopeful signs that constitutional democracy will triumph permanently.

Test Your Knowledge

1. The most socially conscious Mexican president in this century was
   a. Lázaro Cárdenas.
   b. Porfirio Díaz.
   c. Benito Juárez.
   d. Pancho Villa.

2. In the 1970s, the government and politics of most Latin American countries experienced
   a. a swing toward the Marxist Left.
   b. intervention by military-based conservatives.
   c. a swing toward social welfare programs.
   d. a renewal of clerical influence.

3. The most widely recognized female in recent Latin American history was probably
   a. St. Theresa.
   b. Eva Perón.
   c. Carmen Miranda.
   d. Violeta Chamorro.

4. Which of the following countries did *not* experience U.S. military intervention in the twentieth century?
   a. Nicaragua
   b. Colombia
   c. Panama
   d. Haiti

5. After the Great Depression of the 1930s began, the larger Latin American states
   a. became totally dependent on imported goods.
   b. carried out long delayed agrarian reforms to favor the peons.
   c. started on a program of economic nationalism.
   d. suffered economic collapse.

6. Juan Perón was forced from power in 1955 by
   a. a mass uprising.
   b. a free election.
   c. U.S. intervention.
   d. a military plot.

7. In the later 1980s, Latin America has experienced a strong movement toward
   a. democratically elected governments.
   b. military coups d'état.
   c. Marxist dictatorships.
   d. Fascist governments.

Identification Terms

Alliance for Progress

banana republics

Cárdenas (Lázaro)

descamisados

Good Neighbor policy

North American Free Trade

Agreement (NAFTA)

Organization of American States (OAS)

Perón (Juan and Eva)

Vargas (Getúlio)

Bibliography

Several general histories of all of the American continent south of the Rio Grande are available; all contain good bibliographies for further research.

Fagg, J. E. *Latin America,* 1977. A standard history, though now somewhat out of date.

Graham, R. *Independence in Latin America,* 1994, and E. Williamson, *The Penguin History of Latin America,* 1992, are the most up-to-date.

Skidmore, T. E., and P. H. Smith. *Modern Latin America,* 1992. Focuses on recent times.

Tanenbaum, F. *Ten Keys to Latin America,* 1956. Is still relevant.

Individual Nations

Ferns, H. *Argentina,* 1969. A good survey to the date of publication. C. Scobie, *Argentina: A City and a Nation,* 1971, is worthwhile for its account of how the potentially richest country in the southern hemisphere failed its chances in the twentieth century. More current and less focused on Buenos Aires is D. Rock, *Argentina 1518–1987,* 1987. A good biography of Perón was written by J. A. Page in 1983.

Burns, E. B. *A History of Brazil,* 1980, is good, as is the more personalized and sensational R. DaMatta, *Carnivals, Rogues, and Heroes,* 1991.

Degler, C. N. *Neither Black nor White: Slavery and Race Relations in Brazil and the United States,* 1971. A classic comparison of the two biggest slaveholding societies in the New World.

Kinsbruner, J. *Chile: An Historical Interpretation,* 1973, and B. Loveman, *Chile,* 1988, are both good general histories, with the latter having an economic slant.

Mesa-Lago, C. *The Economy of Socialist Cuba,* 1981. An introduction to what Castro sought to do, and sometimes did. Another point of view is given in L. Perez, *Cuba: Between Reform and Revolution,* 1988.

Meyer, M. C., and W. L. Sherman, *The Course of Mexican History,* 1991. Very detailed for serious researchers. For material on L. Cárdenas, see J. Bazant, *A Concise History of Mexico,* 1978.

CHAPTER 59

THE REEMERGENCE OF THE MUSLIM WORLD

THE MUSLIM COUNTRIES UNTIL
WORLD WAR I

RESPONSES TO MUSLIM WEAKNESS

THE TURKISH REPUBLIC

PALESTINE

THE RETURN OF ISLAM

The Iranian Revolution

THE OIL WEAPON

The Gulf War

THE MUSLIM NATIONS TODAY

The Arabs

The Non-Arabic Nations

1917	Balfour Declaration on Palestine
1920s	Ataturk leads Turkey/Most of Middle East under British, French mandates/Saudi Arabia united by Ibn Saud
1946–1948	Mandate territories become independent states
1948	Israel founded and Israeli—Arab war begins
1956	Sury Canal nationalized by Egypt
1973	OPEC oil boycott
1979	Iranian Revolution
1991	Gulf War

For the first time in centuries, the Muslim peoples are at the center of world events and are playing major roles in international affairs. Muslims now number about one-fifth of humanity, and Islam is the dominant religion in thirty-eight countries reaching from Southeast Asia to the Atlantic coast of Africa. It is important to remember that the "Muslim world" includes far more than the Middle East or the Arab countries (see Map 59.1). The 148 million Arabs are mostly Muslims, but a great many of the nearly one billion Muslims are not Arabs.

This chapter, however, will focus on the Arab Middle East because that is where the major events defining the Muslim relationship with the world have taken place in this century. The single most important factor in Middle Eastern history over the last seventy years has been geology. By far the largest known oil fields in the world are located under Saudi Arabia and the other Persian Gulf countries, and their development has been the key to the massive change in Muslim–non-Muslim relations that the later twentieth century has witnessed.

✣ THE MUSLIM COUNTRIES UNTIL WORLD WAR I

We have seen in an earlier chapter (Chapter 42) that the three Muslim empires of earlier times in Asia were either overthrown or much weakened by the nineteenth century. The Mughals in India, the Safavid Persians, and the Ottoman Turks had been overwhelmed by Western military and financial powers where they came into conflict with them. By the mid-1800s the British had made India into an outright colony, and Persia was effectively divided between Russian and British spheres. The Ottomans had been repeatedly defeated by Russia in the Balkans and had been forced to watch as even the facade of their political overlordship in North Africa faded away; only in the Near East did some substance of Turkish control remain.

But these political and military weaknesses were not the only indicators of decline. The Islamic world would have to overcome a series of psychological and technical barriers if it were to reassert its equality with the West. The fundamental tradition of Islam, wherever it attained power, was to understand itself as a community of righteous believers who were actively spreading the word of God and establishing his rule on earth. For a thousand years, since the time of the Prophet, this viewpoint had

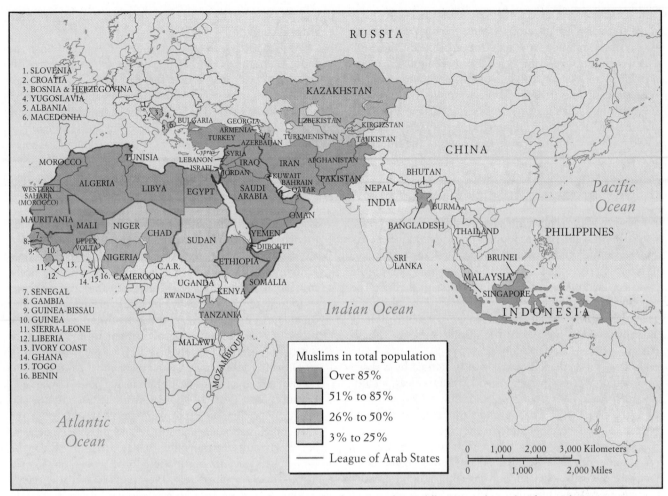

1. SLOVENIA
2. CROATIA
3. BOSNIA & HERZEGOVINA
4. YUGOSLAVIA
5. ALBANIA
6. MACEDONIA

7. SENEGAL
8. GAMBIA
9. GUINEA-BISSAU
10. GUINEA
11. SIERRA-LEONE
12. LIBERIA
13. IVORY COAST
14. GHANA
15. TOGO
16. BENIN

Muslims in total population

Over 85%

51% to 85%

26% to 50%

3% to 25%

—— League of Arab States

0   1,000   2,000   3,000 Kilometers

0   1,000   2,000 Miles

⊙ **MAP 59.1   Modern Islam, 1995.** Although the Islamic heartland remains the Middle East and North Africa, Islam is growing steadily in black Africa and is the faith of heavily populated Indonesia.

been the driving force behind the spread of the religion around the globe.

From about the middle of the eighteenth century, however, this view could no longer be sustained, as the Europeans took over former Muslim territories from the Balkans to the islands of Southeast Asia. The learned men of Islam reacted in two ways: some assumed that these reverses were temporary and would soon be made up, while others looked—for the first time—to the West for inspiration in technology and, above all, military science, to help them to counter and overcome Western superiority.

Unfortunately for Muslim ambitions, a mixture of these views resulted with the first trend prevailing over the second. The *ulema* and the *imams* of the Ottoman do-

mains could not accept the secularism of post–French Revolution Europe, but they recognized that Muslim practice would have to incorporate some Western elements if they were not to be overwhelmed by the Europeans. Yet they still believed in the inherent superiority of the community of God (the *Dar al-Islam*) over the unbelievers (*Dar al-Harb*). The result was a sporadic and inconsistent attempt to adopt some European science and technology without changing the very conservative cast of Islamic education and government, which frowned on innovation. Those few who attempted to bring Western ideas into Islam were opposed by a vast body of traditions and prejudices. Even some of the Ottoman sultans who recognized that resisting the West without Western science and education would be hopeless were unable to carry through their plans of reform against the twin obstacles of conservative opinion and fatalistic apathy. By the mid-nineteenth century, Islam, as a religious community and as a political association, was in a nearly moribund state and was quite unable to impede the triumphs of European imperialism. Unwilling to adapt beyond a few superficial phenomena, the Muslim nations were seemingly destined to a future in which they were the pawns of the European powers.

✤ RESPONSES TO MUSLIM WEAKNESS

By the end of the nineteenth century, this inability to resist external pressure had produced two quite different responses in the Muslim world. The first was the beginnings of what is now called *Islamic fundamentalism,* supported by armed action against internal or external enemies. The second was *pan-Arabism or Arab nationalism,* which are related but not identical attempts to create a sense of unity among the Arab peoples of the Middle East and North Africa.

Islamic fundamentalism was and is marked by a sharp rejection of Western influences and Western ideas, including such notions as political democracy, religious toleration, the equality of citizens, and various other offshoots of the Age of Enlightenment and the American and French Revolutions. To a fundamentalist (the word is a recent appellation), the task of civil government is to facilitate the reign of Allah and his faithful upon earth—nothing less and nothing more. Any obstacles that stand in the way of this process should be swept aside by persuasion if possible, but by force if necessary. There can be no compromise with the enemies of God, nor with their varied tools and facilitators such as secular schools, mixed-religion marriages, and nonconfessional parliaments. In the Mahdi's bitter resistance to the British in Sudan and Shamil's resistance to the Russians in central Asia, Islamic fundamentalism found its first heroes; it would find many others in the twentieth century (see the discussion of The Return of Islam later in the chapter).

Pan-Arabism is an outgrowth of Arab national feeling, which began to be articulated in the late nineteenth century especially among Egyptians and Syrians. The long delay in the rise of Arab nationalism can be attributed to the universal nature of Islam, which had no place for national divisions. (It is important to note that the word *Arab* or *Arabic* refers to an ethnic group, not a religious one. There are many Arab Christians in Egypt, Lebanon, and Syria, and they were among the leaders of Arab nationalism.)

Arab nationalism was originally directed against the Turkish overlords, and it had become so strong by the time of World War I that the British found the Arabs willing allies in the fight against the Ottomans. The Arabs' reward was supposed to be an independent state, reaching from Egypt to Iraq and headed by the Hussein family of *sheikhs* in Arabia, who had been among the most prominent of the British allies during the war.

The Arabs' dream of a large, independent state was ended, however, by the realities of the diplomatic deals made by the French, British, and Italians in 1916–1917. Intent on destroying their enemy the Ottoman state, the French had been promised much of the eastern Mediterranean coast while the British would take Palestine, Jordan, and Iraq. When it came time to write the peace treaties, Woodrow Wilson objected to these secret deals, so these intended Western colonies were converted into "**mandates**" in the care of the British and French until such time as the Arabs proved their ability to act as sovereign powers themselves.

The difference between a mandate and a colony proved exceedingly fine; for all practical purposes, Syria and Lebanon were French colonies from 1919 to 1946, and Jordan, Palestine, and Iraq were British ones. When the Hussein-led nationalists protested and rebelled, they were put down with decisive military action. Egypt, where the British had had an occupation force since 1882, got a slightly better arrangement; there nationalism was strong enough to induce the British colonial administration to grant the Egyptians technical independence in 1922. British troops remained, however, and real independence was withheld until the 1950s because of British concerns about the Suez Canal and their "lifeline to India." In sum, Turkish imperial rule had been replaced by European.

During the 1920s and 1930s, the small gains effected by individual Arab groups gave momentum to the Pan-Arab movement, which tried to get Arabs everywhere to submerge their differences and unite under one political center. The example of Saudi Arabia was held up as a possible model: under a fundamentalist sheikh Ibn Saud, most of the Arabian peninsula was unified in the 1920s by conquest and voluntary association and turned into a poverty-ridden and primitive, but sovereign state. But the Pan-Arabists could show few other gains by the time World War II broke out. The colonial grip was too strong, and the disunity and jealousies that had plagued Arab politics for a long time showed no sign of abating.

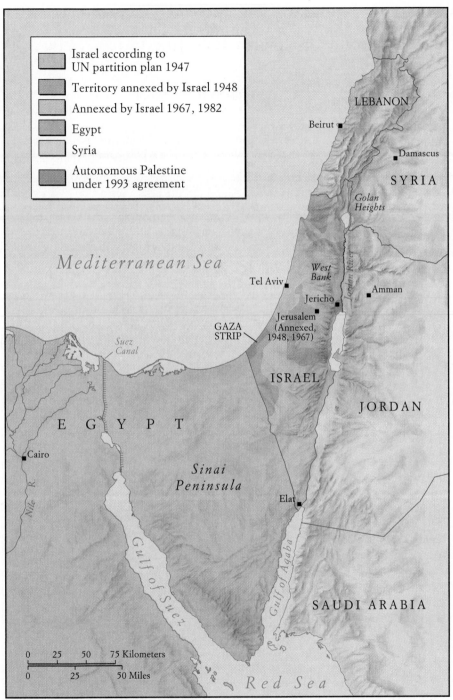

■ **Map 59.2 Israel and Its Arab Neighbors, 1947–1994.** The extraordinary complexity of the conflict between Jews and Arabs stems in large part from the many years of peaceable intermixing of populations, making it impossible to separate them and to place them under separate governments without coercion. As in the Balkan states, the very success of the past peace has made the current conflict more savage.

The Arab Viewpoint on Jewish Palestine

The most hotly disputed international question in the entire postwar era is probably not the fate of Berlin, or Korea, or Vietnam, but rather the question of Palestine. This former Ottoman province was ceded to British "mandate," that is, supervision, by the settlement of World War I. In the interwar era, the area had a solid majority of Arabs and a slowly increasing minority of Jews, many of whom were recent immigrants inspired by the vision of a Jewish state. The Arab leaders considered these Zionists intolerable intruders who were out to wrest political control of the territory from the Arabs while the British looked on complacently.

At the end of World War II, the United States and Britain created a commission to investigate the future of Palestine. The following excerpt from the Arab leaders' memorandum to the commission shows their fundamental opposition to the idea of a Jewish Palestine, or the state of Israel:

1. The whole Arab people is unalterably opposed to the attempt to impose Jewish immigration and settlement upon it, and ultimately to establish a Jewish State in Palestine. . . . They cannot agree that it is right to subject an indigenous population against its will to alien immigrants, whose claim is based upon an historical connection which ceased many centuries ago. . . .

2. Zionism is essentially a political movement, aiming at the creation of a state: immigration, land-purchase and economic expansion are only aspects of a general political strategy. If Zionism succeeds in its aim, the Arabs will become a minority in their own country; a minority which can hope for no more than a minor share in the government, for the state is to be a Jewish state, and which will find itself not only deprived of that international status which the other Arab countries possess but cut off from living contact with the Arab world of which it is an integral part. . . .

8. In the Arab view, any solution of the problem. . .
   i. must recognize the right of the indigenous inhabitants of Palestine to continue in occupation of the country and to preserve its traditional character.
   ii. must recognize that questions like immigration which affect the whole nature and destiny of the country should be decided in accordance with democratic principles by the will of the population.
   iii. must accept the principle that the only way by which the will of the population can be expressed is through the establishment of a responsible representative government.
   iv. This representative government should be based upon the principle of absolute equality of all citizens irrespective of race and religion. . . .
   vi. The settlement should recognize the fact that by geography and history Palestine is inescapably part of the Arab world; that the only alternative to its being part of the Arab world is accepting the implications of its position, that is, complete isolation, which would be disastrous from every point of view. . . .

The idea of partition and the establishment of a Jewish state in a part of Palestine is inadmissible for the same reasons of principle as the idea of establishing a Jewish state in the whole country. If it is unjust to the Arabs to impose a Jewish state on the whole of Palestine, it is equally unjust to impose it in any part of the country. . . . It would also be impossible to devise frontiers which did not leave a large Arab minority in the Jewish state. This minority would not willingly accept its subjection to the Zionists, and it would not allow itself to be transferred to the Arab state. . . . [A Zionist state] would inevitably be thrown into enmity with the surrounding Arab states and this enmity would disturb the stability of the whole Middle East.

SOURCE: Excerpted from *The Israel-Arab Reader,* 2d ed. edited by W. Laquer, Wildwood House, Ltd.

✤ THE TURKISH REPUBLIC

The great exception to the continued subordination of the Muslim states or societies was the new Republic of Turkey. In the aftermath of the defeat in World War I, the sultan's government had lost all credibility in Turkish eyes. Backed by Great Britain, the Greek government attempted in 1919 to realize the "Great Idea" of restoring the former Byzantine Empire and making the interior of Turkey (Anatolia) once more a Greek colony. A Greek army landed on the Turkish coast and began to move inland. At this critical point, a leader emerged who almost single-handedly brought his people back from the edge of legal annihilation. His name was **Mustafa Kemal,** but his people called him **Ataturk** (father of Turkey). Kemal had been a colonel in the Ottoman army and distinguished himself at the defense of Gallipoli in 1915. In 1919–1921, he organized the national resistance to the invaders and won a decisive victory against the poorly led Greeks. Alone among the defeated in World War I, Turkey was able to secure a drastic revision of the original peace treaty in the Treaty of Lausanne in 1923. The new treaty recognized the full sovereignty of the Turkish state within the borders it now has. The former Arab provinces were abandoned to the West.

But this was no longer Ottoman Turkey. Kemal induced the Turk leadership to abolish the 600-year-old sultanate and declare a parliamentary republic. Kemal himself was elected the first president (with near dictatorial powers). Until his death in 1938, Kemal retained the presidency and the support of most of his people as he drove Turkey and the Turks to a systematic break with the past. Modernization and Westernization were the twin pillars of Kemal's policies. Giving up any plans of reincorporating the former Ottoman provinces, he focused on separating Turkish civil society from Islamic culture, a massive task.

In every visible and invisible way Kemal could devise, the citizens of modern Turkey were distinguished from their Islamic ancestors. Western-style dress was introduced and even made mandatory for government workers; the veil was abolished; the revered Arabic script was replaced by the Latin alphabet; women were made legally equal and could divorce their husbands; polygamy was forbidden. Western schooling was introduced and made compulsory for both sexes. A new legal code was introduced, with no preference for Muslims. The capital was moved from half-Greek Istanbul to pure Turkish Ankara.

By the time of his death, Kemal had indeed kept his promise to do for the Turks what Peter the Great had attempted to do for the Russians: to thrust them forward several generations and bring them into Europe. Despite intense resistance from conservative Muslim circles, Kemal had managed to turn his people into a secular society in less than twenty years. He had also become a model emulated by reformers all over the non-Western world.

✤ PALESTINE

The thorniest of all problems in the Middle East after World War I was the fate of the British mandate of Palestine (Israel). During the war, the hard-pressed British had made promises to both the Ottoman-ruled Arabs and the **Zionists** who claimed to represent most European Jews. These promises conflicted with one another in the case of Palestine. In the **Balfour Declaration of 1917,** the British had agreed to support a "Jewish national homeland," but this could be achieved only at the expense of the Arab majority, who had shared Palestine with the Biblical Jews and had been the majority people there for many generations. To these Arabs, a "national homeland" sounded like a Jewish-controlled state in which they would be only a tolerated group, and they accordingly did not like the idea (see the Document in this chapter).

Jewish immigration to Palestine had begun in a minor way as early as the 1880s, but had only taken on potentially important dimensions after the founding of the Zionist movement by the journalist Theodor Herzl at the turn of the century. Under the well-meaning but muddled British colonial government, Arabs and Jews began to take up hostile positions in Palestinian politics during the 1920s. By the late 1930s, this hostility was taking the form of bloody riots, suppressed only with difficulty by the British police. Despite restrictions imposed from London, Jewish immigrants poured into Palestine from Hitler's Germany and eastern Europe where vicious anti-Semitism had become commonplace. At the outbreak of World War II, perhaps 30 percent of Palestine's inhabitants were Jews.

At the end of the war, the British in Palestine as elsewhere were at the end of their strength and wished to turn over their Middle East mandates as soon as possible to the United Nations. The pitiful remnants of the Jews of Nazi Europe now defied British attempts to keep them from settling illegally in Palestine. Attempts to get Arabs and Jews to sit down at the negotiating table failed, and the frustrated British announced that they would unilaterally abandon Palestine on May 14, 1948. Faced with this ultimatum, the United Nations eventually (November 1947) came out with a proposal for dividing the mandate into a Jewish state and an Arab state—a compromise that, needless to say, satisfied neither side. By the time the United Nations proposal was passed by the General Assembly fighting between Arab and Jewish militias was already under way. Full-scale war soon followed.

The results of the 1948 War—the first of six in the past half-century between Israel and its Arab neighbors—were strongly favorable to the new Jewish state. Unexpectedly, it had held its own and more against its several enemies. But the triumphant Israelis then expelled many hundreds of thousands of Palestinian Arabs from their ancestral lands, creating a reservoir of bitterness that guaranteed hostility for decades to come.

In 1964, after fifteen years of intermittent armed conflict and much intra-Arab dissension about how best to deal with the Israeli presence, the **Palestine Liberation Organization** (PLO) was formed by Arab extremists; its single goal was the destruction of the state of Israel, and it pursued that goal with terror and bloodshed for almost thirty years. In this effort the PLO was assisted by most of the Arab states, which saw Israel as both a religious and a secular enemy that could not be tolerated in their midst. This enmity, like all other conflicts during the Cold War era, became caught up in the general hostility between the United States and the Soviet Union, with the former siding strongly with the Israelis and the latter with the Arabs.

✦ THE RETURN OF ISLAM

Bernard Lewis, a leading expert on the Muslim world, recently wrote an essay entitled "The Return of Islam," which deals with the resurgence of Islamic devotion in the past few years. He emphasizes that the West has always misunderstood the nature of Islam and has tried to equate it with Christianity in Europe with unfortunate results. Islam is much more than a religion and is certainly not limited to the private sphere as Christianity has been since the French Revolution. Islam does not recognize the separation of church and state; rather, for the good Muslim the church and the state are one and always have been. They can no more be separated than can the human personality be parted from the body it inhabits.

Lewis goes on to say, "It was not nation or country that, as in the West, formed the historic basis of identity, but the religio-political community." For this reason, Arab nationalism has never been as successful as, say, French nationalism was; Muslim Arabs felt a higher identity embracing them than the mere fact of being Syrian or Egyptian. "The Fatherland of a Muslim is wherever the Holy Law of Islam prevails." This feeling is not new. Even at the high point of secular nationalism in the Middle East, during the interwar years when the Turkey of Kemal Ataturk was blazing the path, there was a strong under-current of religiously based patriotic feeling that rejected secularism as severely as it did Western imperialism. The original *Muslim Brotherhood* was founded in Egypt in 1928, and despite official repression, its numerous subdivisions have thrived there and in many other countries ever since, both legally and illegally.

But it is only in recent decades that Muslim fundamentalists have come into the spotlight in world affairs. In several countries—Algeria, Iran, Jordan, Libya, Sudan, and Yemen—they enjoy widespread and vociferous public support to the point of dominating public life and intimidating their civic rivals. In some others—Egypt, Saudi Arabia, Syria, and Turkey—they are a minority, but seem to be gaining ground against the secular moderates who still control the governments.

■ **The Palestinian Intifada.** Beginning in 1989 under PLO leadership, the Palestinian Arabs, in the Gaza Strip and the West Bank occupied territories, challenged Israeli claims to these areas. Rock-throwing youth rioted in the streets in a persistent "intifada," or uprising, which forced Israeli countermeasures and gave the Tel Aviv government a black eye in the world press. The intifada was the decisive element in bringing about the 1993 agreement.

The Iranian Revolution

Three outstanding events have taken place in the world of Islam in the twentieth century. Together, they have defined many of the spiritual and material bases of the Muslim universe. The first in time was the establishment of the secular Republic of Turkey by Mustafa Kemal Ataturk. The second was the oil boycott of 1973–1974 implemented by the Arab members of the **Organization of Petroleum Exporting Countries (OPEC).** The third was the Iranian Revolution of 1979, led by the Ayatollah Khomeini.

The modern state of Iran is the successor to the great Persian empires of ancient times. Its inhabitants, who are ethnically different from the Arabs, have been Muslims almost without exception since the Arab conquest in the 640s. In many epochs, the Iranians have been among Islamic civilization's most distinguished leaders. Nevertheless, they are separated from the majority of Muslims in one decisive way; they are Shi'ite Muslims and have been that sect's major stronghold for seven centuries.

Modern Iran came into being in the aftermath of World War I, when a military officer named Reza Shah Pahlavi (r. 1925–1941) seized power from a discredited traditional dynasty and established an authoritarian regime modeled on his Turkish neighbor. His son, **Shah Muhammed Pahlavi** (r. 1941–1979) followed him on the throne and continued his westernizing and secularizing efforts. By the 1970s, considerable progress had been made in the cities, at least. The country had a substantial middle class of professionals and businessmen, technically advanced industry (especially connected with petroleum engineering), an extensive school system, and mechanized agriculture. The immense oil deposits generated sufficient income to pay for large-scale government projects of every sort, and these proved very profitable for a select few contractors and their friends in the bureaucracy.

But the shah had neglected to see to the spiritual well-being of much of the urban and most of the rural population. Government corruption was universal, the army and police were all-powerful, and traditional religious values were held in more or less open contempt by the ruling clique. On top of that, the shah and his advisers were viewed by many as slavish puppets of the West, who had neither understanding nor respect for the greatness of Islamic Persia.

The upshot was a massive swell of protest, inspired and led by the exiled **Ayatollah** (theologian) **Ruhollah Khomeini** (see the Biography in this chapter). Under the banners of "Back to the Qur'an" and "Iran for the Iranians," Khomeini skillfully led his people into revolution and then returned in 1979 to take the helm of the government that succeeded the bewildered shah, who went into exile in his turn. For the next decade, the ayatollah implemented what he had promised Iran from afar: a thoroughly Islamic, uncompromisingly anti-Western, antisecular government. Resistance to this course was brushed aside by his authoritarian attitude that made no concessions. The atheistic Soviets were denounced almost as heartily as the Americans, whose long-standing support for the shah as a counter against the Soviets had earned Khomeini's especial hatred.

In the ayatollah's Iran, Muslim fundamentalism found its most dramatic and forceful exponent so far. But it was by no means a necessarily welcome or attractive scenario for other Muslim states, and within a year of the ayatollah's return, Iran was at war with a Muslim neighbor. In 1980, Iraq attempted to take advantage of the upheaval next door to seize some disputed oil-bearing territory from Iran. The eight-year conflict that followed was one of the bloodiest in recent history, claiming at least 1 million lives (mainly Iranian) and dealing both countries blows from which they have not yet recovered.

With its much smaller population, Iraq would have been defeated early in the war had it not been for the active financial support and armaments supplied by other states. Led by the Saudis, many Arab leaders thought that the ayatollah's brand of fundamentalism posed a serious threat to all of them and wished to see it contained or defeated. The rabid anti-Western positions embraced by Khomeini (notably, the taking of hostages at the U.S. embassy in 1979–1980) also induced the Western states to support Iraq in various covert ways, which they would soon regret.

✤ THE OIL WEAPON

In the 1970s, the biggest single story in international affairs was not the Cold War between the United States and the Soviet Union, or the American adventure in Vietnam, or even the rapid steps being taken toward European unity. It was the worldwide economic crisis started by the OPEC oil boycott.

In 1973, the consistent favoritism shown by the West and especially the United States toward Israel was answered during that year's brief Arab-Israeli conflict (sometimes known as the "**Yom Kippur War**" because it began on the Jewish holiday of Yom Kippur) by the Arabs' decision to withhold all oil shipments to the United States and its NATO allies. Since the Middle East had long been

Ayatollah Khomeini
1902–1989

Early in 1979 the massive street demonstrations that had become a daily occurrence in Tehran succeeded in persuading the shah of Iran to leave the country for exile. His place was quickly taken by an unlikely figure: the Ayatollah Ruhollah Khomeini, a blazing-eyed, ramrod erect man in his seventies, garbed in the long kaftan of a strict Muslim believer. Khomeini had been forced into exile by the shah's police fifteen years earlier. Now the tables had turned, and it would be Khomeini, not the once all-powerful shah, who ruled Iran's 40 million inhabitants until he died.

The ayatollah (the word means "theologian") was a member of Iran's leading sect: the Shi'ite Muslims, who make up only about 10 percent of the world's Muslim population, but have long been the dominant religious group in Iran. Since the 1960s, conservative Shia had opposed the secularizing policies of Shah Muhammed Reza Pahlavi. They believed in a rigid interpretation of the Qur'an whereby government should be the strong right arm of the religious establishment (the *ulema*). Not surprisingly, neither

the shah nor his close advisers shared this view. Using all the apparatus of the modern state, including a barbaric secret police, they made the lives of the ayatollah and his followers miserable and assassinated many. Among the dead was Khomeini's elder son, who was murdered in Iraq. At least one attempt was made on Khomeini's life while he was in exile. Later, he said that his preservation was a sign of Allah's benevolence toward his people.

With the resources of a modern army and police at his command, and with the full support of the U.S. government in his general policies, it seemed unthinkable that the shah's throne was in danger from a small group of unarmed religious fanatics. That was true until the mid-1970s when it became apparent that the government's initial social reforms—the White Revolution—were going into reverse gear, thanks in part to massive corruption. Always a country of economic extremes, Iran became the model of a society in which a tiny elite became fantastically wealthy while the ever more numerous poor got the merest crumbs from their table.

the dominant supplier of world petroleum markets, the impact was immediate and catastrophic. Prices of crude oil quadrupled within a few months. The economies of the Western nations and Japan were put under great strain; even the United States, which came closest to oil self-sufficiency of all the affected nations, faced shortages.

A major recession, the worst since the 1930s, with unemployment rates zooming to 13 percent in western Europe, was one of the results. Soaring energy costs caused consumer prices for practically every necessity of

life to spiral upward even as demand decreased. As mass unemployment was accompanied by double-digit inflation in the mid and late 1970s, a new word came into the vocabulary—*stagflation*. It referred to the worst of all economic worlds, the combination of stagnation and inflation. The postwar boom, which had lasted a quarter of a century, definitely ended, and most of the West remained in a painful business recession well into the 1980s. Some countries have never entirely recovered from the great oil shock; their labor markets have been perma-

Surrounded by his elite friends, the shah compounded the bad impression by spending huge sums on personal and familial luxuries.

Khomeini as a respected Shi'a clergyman had begun denouncing the shah's mistakes in the 1960s. When the shah addressed him condescendingly, Khomeini responded by calling him "Mr Shah," which earned the religious leader immediate imprisonment. A few months later Khomeini denounced the shah's dependency on U.S. aid and weapons and was forced into exile in Iraq. Even in exile he was regarded as the spirit of the opposition in Tehran. He was adept at linking the fanatical Shi'a in the villages with the urban middle classes and reform-minded intellectuals who were coming to hate the shah's misrule. The police attempt to beat the increasing numbers of street demonstrators into flight only created martyrs for the movement. Thousands were arrested weekly; their places were instantly filled by new recruits. The peasant soldiers watched their parents and relatives being beaten, and the army became too unreliable to be used against the demonstrators. From his waiting place, Khomeini's messengers flew back and forth carrying instructions to the faithful. They boiled down to one demand: the shah and all he stood for must go.

When Khomeini took over, the world knew nothing of him or what he desired. That changed very soon, as he imposed strict Qur'anic standards on every aspect of Iran's constitutional and social affairs. He generally opposed all non-Muslim views, but was especially contemptuous of the West and, above all, of the Americans. Regarding the U.S. government as the foreign power most responsible for Iran's corruption and distortion, he cut off all relations and began whipping up crowd hatred of the "Great Satan." In November 1979, the demonstrators broke into the U.S. embassy and took over fifty hostages in an attempt to force the Washington authorities to turn over the ailing shah to revolutionary justice in Tehran. The shah soon died of cancer, but the hostages were held for over a year until their release was negotiated.

By then, Khomeini (who never took an official post but directed all policy in Tehran) was looked upon in the West as a deranged tyrant. Iran's crusade against neighboring Iraq in a war that broke out in 1980 and lasted until 1988 was a relief to the Western countries, which supported the equally tyrannous but secular government of Iraq under Saddam Hussein.

Khomeini's rigid views and his conviction that he had supernatural approval made it next to impossible to approach him with realistic compromises. While the Cold War raged, the West was delighted to see him attack Iran's small Communist Party and to listen to his denunciation of "godless Marxism"; but he was equally adamant against the democracies and all they stood for. His own country seemed on the verge of civil war when he died, but the transition of power went smoothly, with clerics of the ayatollah's type giving way to more moderate but still anti-Western politicians.

Khomeini's legacies to his people will long be the subject of acrid dispute. While many conservatives regarded him as a saint, his ideas were always opposed by a hard core of resistance, which has grown since his death and the reinstitution of a parliamentary government.

nently altered by the disappearance of many blue-collar production jobs that depended on cheap energy. (The 1973 shock was later reinforced by events in Iran. In 1979–1980, international oil prices again quadrupled because of fears of a supply pinch following the Iranian Revolution and the Iran-Iraq War.)

Fears of a general collapse of the world economy proved to be unfounded; a combination of mandatory conservation efforts, non-OPEC oil, and divisions among the OPEC members defeated the attempt by the Arab members to coerce political realignments against Israel. The temporarily chaotic petroleum markets stabilized at the new higher price within a year or so. But the brief havoc in oil supplies—which the West had always thought were shielded from producer-country influence—established a *new respect for Arab political potency*. The surge in price made some of the major producers (notably, the largest of all, Saudi Arabia) immensely rich in dollars; and money here, as elsewhere, spelled both economic and political power.

This windfall in oil profits did not last more than a decade, and the OPEC nations were eventually forced to adjust their prices to a diminished world demand, but these facts were beside the point. What Western consumers knew after 1973 was that a handful of heretofore peripheral and insignificant Middle Eastern and North African kingdoms had risen on a tide of crude oil to become at least transitory major players in world politics. No longer could any industrial nation afford to ignore what OPEC was doing and planning, and very few could afford to flatly oppose the wishes of the Muslim majority of OPEC members. For the first time in at least two centuries, the Muslim East had attained importance through its own initiatives, rather than merely because of what one or another alien group was doing there.

The Gulf War

In 1990, the ambitious and bloodstained Iraqi dictator Saddam Hussein believed the time ripe for a settlement of accounts with his oil-rich neighbor at the head of the Persian Gulf, Kuwait. In an undisguised grab for additional oil revenues, Saddam invaded the tiny country and declared it annexed, thinking that he would present the world with *fait accompli* backed up by a large and well-armed army, veterans of the just-concluded struggle with Iran.

To his surprise, the West reacted violently and was very soon joined by a substantial majority of the non-Western world, including most Arabs. These latter feared the effects of opening up the question of the territorial borders derived from the colonial era, and they also rejected Saddam's transparent bid to become the pan-Arab arbiter of the Middle East. When even the Russians joined in the American-led pressure on Baghdad to vacate its conquest, almost all of the United Nations presented Saddam with the most unified front that organization had seen since its inception. The Iraqi dictator refused to back down, however, and it took a powerful air and ground attack upon his forces in 1991 to induce him to withdraw with heavy losses. As of 1995, multiple sanctions against Saddam's government imposed by the United Nations have as yet failed in their aim of toppling his brutal regime, however, and the clear-cut military victory has thus not been entirely successful in its further goals of restoring stability.

The Gulf War, as it was dubbed, was a high point in international collaboration against a disturber of the peace. The cooperation occurred largely because of the ending of the Cold War and the strong leadership exerted by President George Bush of the United States. Great hopes of continuing effective United Nations action against future aggressors and disturbers of domestic peace have not been fulfilled in Bosnia, Somalia, Rwanda, and other scenes of conflict, however, and the euphoria expressed in Bush's "new world order" quickly evaporated.

❧ The Muslim Nations Today

Muslim importance in the world has suffered since the end of the Cold War, for during its heyday both the United States and the Soviet Union attempted to influence and ally with many of the Muslim states. And in the mid-1990s, the energy crisis seems to have become ancient history. Crude oil prices are down to their 1960 levels in terms of real value, while OPEC has been signally unsuccessful in its attempts to impose marketing unity on its members. As a result, it has been tempting to some to dismiss the Muslim resurgence as a temporary "blip" that will have no lasting effects on the overall picture of Western domination.

The Arabs

For the first time in fifty years, the prospects of a lasting peace between Arabs and Israelis in the Middle East seem reasonably good. The peace treaty between Israel and Jordan as well as Israel and Egypt, the recognition of the Palestine Liberation Organization by Israel, and the creation of a quasi-autonomous Arab administration in the Gaza Strip have transferred the struggle for a mutually acceptable Jewish state from the battlefield to the negotiating table despite the desperate resistance of Arab and Israeli hard-liners.

If the Arab-Israeli conflict continues to be resolved peacefully, the Arab states will—for the first time since their creation—be able to focus their energies upon internal development and raising the living standards of their rapidly rising populations. In several countries, a high rate of population growth has checked or eliminated the benefits derived thus far from economic expansion and technological expertise. Egypt, with the largest population of the Arab world, is especially needful in this regard. With few resources beyond the fields of the Nile valley, it has become entirely dependent upon U.S. and World Bank assistance to maintain an even minimal living standard for its people. Economic desperation, especially in contrast to the oil wealth of the Saudis, Iraqis, and others, has added fuel to other resentments, which have given rise to a militant fundamentalism in Egypt and other nations.

But the potential resolution of the Arab-Israeli conflict also poses the danger that without the common enemy, the Arab nations will be forced to recognize what most leaders already tacitly acknowledge: they lack any mutual policies and goals except for adherence in one degree or another to Islam. And that fact will almost certainly fuel the rising antipathies between the fundamentalists and the current ruling group of secularist and nationalist politicians. The clash between these two focuses on the struggle for the allegiance of the rural majority: Will the villagers continue to support the urban politicians who have promised them a better life but have delivered on that promise only partially and sporadically since 1945? The secularists include such very different past and present personalities as **Gamal Abdel Nasser** and Anwar Sadat in Egypt, Saddam Hussein in Iraq, Ahmad Ben Bella in Algeria,

■ **An Historic Handshake.** Israeli foreign minister Rabin and Palestinian leader Arafat shake hands while their beaming host, President Clinton, congratulates them for finally agreeing on initial steps to restore peace to the Middle East. The 1993 Rabin-Arafat agreement on partial self-government for the Palestinians in Israel was a major breakthrough after decades of conflict. Unfortunately, Rabin was assasinated in 1995.

■ **Muslim Women: Street Scene in Tunisia.** Many Muslim women prefer to wear the traditional *chador*, or robe with head scarf, whenever they appear in public. In some of the strict Muslim countries such as Saudi Arabia, such dress is mandatory. Even in a relatively secular country such as Tunisia, women such as those shown here, often wear some adaptation of the chador.

King Hussein in Jordan, and Hafiz al-Assad in Syria. All of them wanted to lead their nations into a Westernized technology and economy, while giving lip service at least to Western-style political and civil rights.

On the other side of the equation are the Islamic fundamentalists, led by such men as the associates of Khomeini in Iran, Mu'ammar Qaddafi in Libya, the leaders of the Algerian and Egyptian Muslim Brotherhoods, and many others whose names are as yet unknown to the world. They are quite willing to accept most of the modern world's material and technical achievements, but only if the power of selection remains securely in their own hands, and if it is understood that the society utilizing these achievements must be fully in tune with the words of the Qur'an as interpreted by themselves. Between these two visions of proper government in the Arab world—and by extension, the Muslim world—there seems to be little common ground.

The Non-Arabic Nations

Outside the Arab nations, the Muslim countries of Africa and southern Asia have thus far shown little interest in coordinating their activity, foreign or domestic, with the Arabs. This is partly due to the circumstances in which Islam was introduced and grew in this part of the globe.

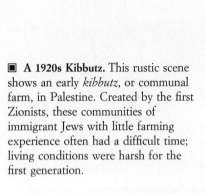

■ **A 1920s Kibbutz.** This rustic scene shows an early *kibbutz*, or communal farm, in Palestine. Created by the first Zionists, these communities of immigrant Jews with little farming experience often had a difficult time; living conditions were harsh for the first generation.

The product of converts with strong bonds to their previous culture, the African and Asian Muslims have never been as single-minded and exclusive as their Arab fellows in religious affairs.

Since attaining independence, *Indonesia,* the largest Muslim state and boasting the fourth largest population in the world, has felt its way forward by the well-known technique of "guided democracy," originally under the charismatic leader of the anticolonial struggle, Sukarno, and for the last twenty-five years under the secularist General Suharto. (Guided democracy claims to be more authentic in representing the popular will than the Western parliamentary governments. It purports to reconcile clashing points of view by the benign guidance of a single leader.) Preoccupied with the problems created by a burgeoning population with quite limited resources (rich oil deposits are by far the most important), the government has been wary of any international alliances, even with nearby Muslim states such as Malaysia. In this melting pot of religions, fundamentalism is almost nonexistent as a political force.

Pakistan and Bangladesh are the next largest Muslim states. Until recently, Pakistan has been entirely occupied with its generation-long quarrel with neighboring India over Kashmir, and Bangladesh has been struggling with abject poverty; its economy ranks as one of the world's poorest. Neither has shown any interest in making common policy with other Muslim countries (they could not get along even with one another in an earlier joint state). Both have been ruled by secularist generals or their civilian accomplices and puppets most of the time since

their creation (see the Biography in Chapter 61). Lacking any notable mineral or energy resources, both of these countries have remained on the periphery of both Muslim and world affairs and are heavily dependent on aid from foreign sources ranging from China (Pakistan) to the United States (both).

By the mid-1990s, the politics and governments of the Muslim states were still far from democratic in most instances. The monopolistic party with an authority figure at its head was the rule (Hosni Mubarak in Egypt, Saddam Hussein in Iraq, Hafiz al-Assad in Syria, Suharto in Indonesia). Ethnic minorities and/or religious "deviants" were treated roughly by the central authorities if they showed the slightest resistance. Civil wars, declared and undeclared, raged in several nations, both between competing sections of the Muslim populace and between Muslims and their religious and cultural rivals. Whole regions containing groups unfriendly to the regime were systematically punished, sometimes by armed force. The domestic economic condition varied from quite good (Malaysia, much of the Middle East,) to very shaky (most of North and West Africa). "Connections" with the bureaucracy were usually necessary for successful enterprise, corruption was rampant, and necessary investments in infrastructure (roads, airports, sewer lines, and the like) were still conspicuous by their absence. All in all, the reentry of Islam into a prominent place in the affairs of the modern world has not been easy, and the ride ahead promises to be perhaps even rougher, not only for the countries concerned but also for their non-Muslim neighbors.

Summary

The Muslim world has returned to an important role in world politics and economics during the twentieth century after two or three centuries of insignificance. Making up about one-fifth of the globe's population, Muslims from West Africa to Southeast Asia have been able to reassert themselves into Western consciousness, especially since the oil boycott of the 1970s. Although some observers think that this prominence will be transitory, most believe that the reviving religious vitality and the sheer numbers of Muslims will guarantee a continuing major role in a shrinking world.

The first real change in twentieth-century Muslim affairs was the creation of the secular Turkish republic after World War I. This state served as a model to many other Muslim thinkers and politicians and fostered the creation of nationalist associations throughout the Middle East and North Africa. The Arab-Israeli struggle over Palestine was a galvanizing force from the 1930s onward to the present. It was followed by the creation of the Arab-sponsored Organization of Petroleum Exporting Countries, the oil boycott, and the rise of an aggressive Islamic fundamentalism in the 1970s and 1980s. Some Muslim countries have experienced a tremendous burst of modernization, fueled by oil profits; others, lacking oil, have remained at or near the bottom of the world prosperity scale.

After a long oblivion, Islamic religious purists are staging a strong political comeback in several countries, notably since the revolution in Iran. Their uncompromising rejection of Western ideals such as religious toleration and political equality, combined with their appeal to an alienated underclass in poverty-stricken Muslim countries makes them a potentially dangerous force not only for their secular rivals at home, but also for international peace. Although all previous Pan-Arabic and Pan-Islamic appeals have foundered on personal and national rivalries, it is possible that such an alliance could be erected and maintained by the present surge of fundamentalism.

Test Your Knowledge

1. After World War I, the chief exception to continued colonial rule among Muslim countries was
   a. Egypt.
   b. Turkey.
   c. Iraq.
   d. Lebanon.
2. The historical movement to unite all Arabs under single political leadership is
   a. Arabs First!
   b. Pan-Arabism.
   c. the Arab Awakening.
   d. Arab Unity.
3. The state of Israel traces its creation to
   a. an Arab-Jewish understanding in World War II.
   b. a United Nations decision to create two states from British Palestine in 1947.
   c. U.S. military intervention after World War II.
   d. a war against Egypt and Syria in 1963.
4. The Iranian Revolution in 1979 was aimed against
   a. the shah of Iran and his Soviet backers.
   b. the shah and his U.S. backers.
   c. the communists who had seized power.
   d. the Sunni Muslims who had captured the shah.
5. The trigger for the Arab-sponsored oil boycott in 1973 was
   a. the U.S. air raid on Colonel Qaddafi in Libya.
   b. the Israeli raid on Yasir Arafat's headquarters in Tunisia.
   c. the support given by the West to Israel in the Yom Kippur War.
   d. the revenge of Saudi Arabia for the West's support of the shah in Iran.
6. The Muslim state with the largest population is
   a. Pakistan.
   b. Indonesia.
   c. Algeria.
   d. Saudi Arabia.
7. Kemal Ataturk believed that
   a. Turks must remain Muslim to retain a national identity.
   b. Turks must expand beyond their old borders to solve their national woes.

    c. Turks had an obligation to liberate their Muslim comrades in Europe.

    d. Turks must adopt a Western lifestyle.

8. At the time of the Balfour Declaration on Palestine, that country's population

    a. was almost in its majority Muslim Arabs.

    b. was about half Arab and half Jew.

    c. was almost zero.

    d. was polled on its preferences for the postwar era.

Identification Terms

Ataturk (Mustafa Kemal)

Balfour Declaration

Khomeini (Ayatollah Ruhollah)

mandates

Nasser (Colonel Gamal Abdel)

Organization of Petroleum

Exporting Countries (OPEC)

Palestine Liberation Organization

Shah Muhammed Pahlavi

Yom Kippur War

Zionists

Bibliography

Arab-Israeli Conflict

All of the following are generally fair-minded in their treatment of this extremely sensitive topic:

O'Brien, C. C. *Siege: The Saga of Israel and Zionism,* 1986.

Reich, B. *Israel: Land of Tradition and Conflict,* 1985.

Smith, C. *Palestine and the Arab-Israeli Conflict,* 1988.

Individual Countries

Goldschmidt, A., Jr. *Modern Egypt,* 1988. Treats the recent years better than any other source.

Keddie, N. *Roots of Revolution: An Interpretive History of Modern Iran,* 1981. Takes the story through Khomeini's coming.

Munson, H., Jr. *Islam and Revolution in the Middle East,* 1988. Looks at Iran and the Arab countries in the last three decades.

Pelletiere, S. C. *The Iran-Iraq War,* 1992.

International Affairs/Muslim Fundamentalism

Bill, J. A., and R. Springbork. *Politics in the Middle East,* 1990. A comprehensive study.

Donohue, J., and J. Esposito. *Islam in Transition,* 1982. An anthology of Muslim writers' views on social organization.

Gellner, E. *Muslim Society,* 1980. A sympathetic account of the rise and growth of Muslim fundamentalism. Another view is reflected in S. Sullivan and F. Milan, *Iranian Women since the Revolution,* 1991.

Odell, P. *Oil and World Power,* 1986.

Voll, J. O. *Islam: Continuity and Change in the Modern World,* 1982. The final chapters give a compact overview of recent Islamic history from Indonesia to North Africa.

THE MARXIST COLLAPSE

In 1989, an astounded world watched the spectacle of the impossible happening in eastern Europe: the collapse of the Marxist communist system. A year later, the doubly impossible happened in the Soviet Union: the peaceable abolition of the Communist Party's control of government. One year after that, the Soviet Union itself was abolished, and its component ethnic regions became independent states.

Rarely, if ever, has such a totally unexpected and complete reversal of the existing state of international political affairs occurred. The Cold War—which had defined all other international arrangements for a long generation—was abruptly terminated. And an integrated system of political and military controls, governing an economic apparatus that had ruled from fifty to seventy-five years over 300 million people, was simply thrown into the ashcan and the table swept clean.

✣ THE IMMEDIATE POSTWAR ERA

The Communization of East Europe

As we saw earlier, the Soviet government under Josef Stalin emerged from the "Great Patriotic War" triumphant. The Red Army stood in the center of Europe, hailed by some, at least, as the liberator of the East and Central Europeans from the Nazi yoke. While the exhausted British tried to get their breath, and the impatient Americans quickly demobilized their forces, Stalin proceeded to reap the fruits of his very costly victory over the Nazi enemy.

Under the Yalta Agreement of 1945, the Russians were to carry through free, democratic national elections in the East European countries as soon as conditions permitted. The divisions among the Big Three (Britain, the Soviet Union, and the United States), which became evident at the war's end, made it impossible to specify more exactly when and how the elections should be held. The Yalta Agreement, insofar as East Europe was concerned, was an unwilling acknowledgment by the West that Stalin and his Red Army would be in control east of the Elbe for at least the immediate postwar years. The best that Washington and London could hope for was the election of governments that would be Soviet-friendly without being outright puppets.

But Stalin, whose suspicion of the West was approaching paranoia, was not inclined to accommodate himself to any type of independent leadership among the East Europeans. The Balkan states were quickly brought into line. As early as 1944, in *Bulgaria, Yugoslavia, and Albania* communists had seized power through armed resistance movements that had fought the Nazi occupiers and their domestic collaborators. In the next year, the communists legitimatized their position by holding elections, which returned solid majorities to a coalition of parties led by the communists, although the governments were not yet clearly satellites of Moscow.

In *Romania and Hungary,* the Soviet-supervised intimidation of the numerous anticommunists took longer. Peasant anticommunist parties held on until 1947, when they were finally eliminated by arresting and executing their leaders. In *Greece,* however, a wartime agreement between Stalin and Winston Churchill resulted in Stalin's abandoning the Greek communists when they attempted to seize power through an uprising. Stalin's failure to support the communists in the civil war (1944–1948) that ensued assured the eventual victory of the royalist side supported by the West. In *Czechoslovakia,* a neutral government headed by respected prewar politicians attempted to walk the tightrope between West and East, but gradually was forced to make decisive concessions to the strong Communist Party. Alone among the East European states, the Czechs had never had unpleasant experiences with tsarist or Soviet Russia, and the Czechoslovak Communist Party had sizable popular support. Backed by Soviet power, which was too obvious to need mentioning in negotiations, the communist leaders pulled off a bloodless *coup d'état* in early 1948 and immediately installed a thoroughly Stalinist regime.

But the vital test case of whether the West would accept Stalin's plans for East Europe was *Poland.* The Polish wartime government-in-exile, like several others, had its headquarters in London and had been promised the firm support of the Allies in ousting the Nazis and recovering their country. Poles fought bravely in the British Royal Air Force (RAF) and other Allied armed forces during the war and distinguished themselves in the Italian and French campaigns. In 1944, Stalin broke with the Polish government in London over the massacre in the Katyn Forest (thousands of Polish army officers had been murdered in Soviet-occupied Poland in 1940) and put together a group of Polish communists to act as his cat's-paw in liberated Poland. He made sure that most of the anticommunist leaders of the Polish Resistance would be removed from the scene by refusing to send the nearby Red Army to aid the Poles in their Warsaw Uprising in late summer of 1944. Despite Western protests, the pro-Soviet group, backed by the Red Army, gradually made political life impossible for their opponents, and after a series of highly predictable elections under Soviet supervision, Poland's decidedly anticommunist and anti-Russian population was forced in 1947 to accept a Soviet satellite regime. The Baltic countries of Estonia, Latvia, and Lithuania received even less consideration; the advancing Red Army simply treated them as recovered provinces of Soviet Russia.

Thus, throughout eastern Europe, a total of about 110 million people from the Baltic to the Adriatic Sea had been forced under Stalinist rule by Soviet puppets. If truly free elections had been held in most of the area, the Communist Party would have received perhaps 10 to 20 percent of the vote, but that fact was irrelevant.

The Stalinist Economy

For the first several years, the postwar era was a continuation of already familiar Soviet goals and methods, both in the Soviet Union and in its new satellites. The lion's share of investment went into either new construction or reconstruction of war-ravaged heavy industry and transportation. Thanks partly to stripping the Soviet Zone of Germany of all industrial goods, and also to the forced "cooperation" of the satellites, *the Soviet Union recovered rapidly* from the horrendous damage caused by the Nazi invasion. The first postwar Five Year Plan reached its goals in considerably less time than planned. By 1950, the Soviet Union was an industrial superpower, as well as a military one; it surpassed faltering Britain and still overshadowed recovering Germany, France, and Italy. New Soviet oil fields in central Asia, new metallurgical combines in the Urals, and new Siberian gas and precious metal deposits were coming on stream constantly.

But in basic consumer goods, the postwar era was even worse than the deprived 1930s. The housing shortage reached crisis proportions in the cities; to have a private bath and kitchen, one had to be either a high Party official or an artistic/literary favorite of the day. Personal consumption was held down artificially by every means available to a totalitarian government: low wages, deliberate scarcity, diversion of investment to heavy industry, and constant propaganda criticizing the materialism of the hostile West and stressing the necessity of sacrificing to "build a socialist tomorrow."

⊙ **MAP 60.1   The New Eastern Europe and Former Soviet Union.** Although in East Europe only Yugoslavian borders were changed as a result of the dissolution of the communist regimes, the borders of the Soviet Union were radically rearranged into four independent states and eleven members of a Commonwealth of Independent States (CIS). The Russian Republic is by far the most important of these, followed by Ukraine and Kazahkstan.

East Europe under Stalin

The suffering of the Soviet population in Stalin's final years was replicated in the East European communist states. Their backward agrarian economies were changed by the same methods employed in the Soviet Union in the 1930s: coercion of the peasantry, forced (and wildly inefficient) industrialization, and the absolute control of the national budget and all public affairs by a small clique within the single party. The East European Communist Parties and their leaders were more or less exact replicas of the Soviet Communist Party and Stalin from the late 1940s until at least the late 1950s. The positive and negative results they obtained resembled those obtained in the Soviet Union fifteen to twenty years earlier, with the important exception that they were never able to inspire their populations by playing the nationalist card. Unlike Stalin, who became a Russian nationalist when it suited him, the Soviet puppets in East Europe were never able during his lifetime to appeal to the deep-seated nationalism of their own peoples. On the contrary, they bore the burden of being in the general public's eye what they were in fact: minions of Stalin and the Soviet Union.

In 1948, Stalin declared the Yugoslav leader Marshal *Tito* an enemy of communism and undertook a campaign against him that embraced everything but actual war. Tito's crime was that he had objected to the complete subordination of his party and his country to Soviet goals—a process that was well under way everywhere else in East Europe.

After a period of hesitation, the United States decided to assist Tito with economic aid. By so doing, Washington allowed the Yugoslav renegade to escape almost certain catastrophe for his country and himself. Tito, still a stalwart Marxist, responded by changing his foreign policies from unquestioning support of the Soviet Union to a prickly neutrality. By 1956, Yugoslavia was busily experimenting with its own brand of social engineering, a peculiar hybrid of capitalism and socialism that for a time seemed to work well enough to attract considerable interest among many African and Asian nations.

✣ FROM STALIN TO BREZHNEV

Tito's heresy was the beginning of the slow breakup of international Marxism into two competing and even hostile camps. The phases of the breakup can best be marked by looking at the Soviet leadership and its policies after the death of Stalin (by a stroke, supposedly) in 1953.

Goulash Communism

Nikita Khrushchev (1894–1974), a longtime member of the Politburo, succeeded to the leadership first of the Communist Party and then of the Soviet state by gradual steps between 1953 and 1955. A son of peasants, Khrushchev was a very different sort of individual than Stalin, and having suffered in fear through the Stalinist purges himself, he was determined that the Communist Party, and not the secret police, would be in the position of final power. By 1957, the dreaded KGB had been put back into its cage, and Khrushchev, after a couple of close calls, had succeeded in breaking the Stalinist wing of the party who considered him to be the ignorant underminer of the system they believed indefinately necessary.

Khrushchev's difficulties within the hierarchy of the CPSU largely revolved around his crude and volatile personality, but substantive frictions occurred over foreign and domestic policy as well. In foreign policy Khrushchev committed the Soviet Union to *peaceful coexistence* with the capitalist West, until such time as the alleged communist superiority at providing a better life for people would make itself overwhelmingly apparent. He allowed the tensions with the Maoist Chinese party to reach a complete break in 1959, splitting the vaunted unity of the world Marxist movement and introducing the unheard-of scandal of competing Marxist governments. In 1961, he challenged the West and particularly the new U.S. president John F. Kennedy by ordering the Soviets' East German satellite to build the *Berline Wall* in defiance of existing access agreements. Finally, Khrushchev took and lost the huge gamble of the *Cuban Missile Crisis of 1962*. To save Fidel Castro's vulnerable regime in Cuba, the Soviets tried to introduce atomic missiles within ninety miles of Florida (see Chapter 54) and were forced to give way by the United States.

But Khrushchev ultimately was brought down more by his domestic political innovations than by his foreign policy. Most important by far was his *attack on Stalin* at the Twentieth Congress of the CPSU in February 1956. At this highest party meeting, Khrushchev gave a long, supposedly **secret speech** in which he detailed some (though by no means all) of the sins of the dead idol, whom a generation of Russians had been trained to think of as a genius and incomparable savior. Khrushchev's denunciation, which immediately became known as well as inside Russia, marked a turning point in international Marxist affairs: never again would Stalin occupy the same position in the communist pantheon and never again would a European communist leader be looked upon as a demigod.

Foreign reactions soon appeared: in the autumn of 1956, first the Poles and then the Hungarians attempted to act on Khrushchev's revelations about Stalin by shaking off Soviet political controls. Both were unsuccessful, but the Soviet party would never again have the same iron control over its satellites. Grudgingly, the CPSU had to admit that there were "many roads to socialism" and that each party should be allowed to find its own way there.

Secondarily, Khrushchev's "harebrained" attempts to change the structure of the CPSU and to install a mistaken agrarian policy backfired badly. Party leaders came to see him more as a debit than an asset to Russian power and prestige, and in 1964 Khrushchev was unceremoniously ushered into premature retirement by his enemies within the Politburo. He lived out his final years in seclusion, but at least was not executed by the new authorities—a welcome departure from the Stalinist model.

Khrushchev confidently expected the Soviet system to outproduce the capitalists in the near future and devoted much effort to improving the lot of the Soviet and East European consumers during his ten years in office. He coined the telling phrase "goulash communism" to explain what he wanted: a system that put meat in the pot for every table. Some progress was indeed made in this respect in the 1950s and 1960s when consumption of goods and services rose substantially. The very tight censorship over the arts and literature imposed by Stalin was also loosened temporarily. But the Khrushchev era was by no means a breakthrough into democracy from political fear and repression; it was an advance only in comparison to what went before.

Stagnation

Khrushchev was replaced by **Leonid Brezhnev** (1906–1982), an *apparatchik* who had climbed the Party ladder by sailing close to the prevailing winds. Worried about the long-term effects of the denunciation of Stalin, Brezhnev and his associates allowed a degree of *re-Stalinization of Russian life.* He cracked down hard on writers who did not follow Party guidelines and on the small but important number of dissidents who attempted to evade censorship by *samizdat* (self-publishing). At the same time he endorsed Khrushchev's policy of increasing consumption. In the 1970s, the living standards of ordinary Russians finally reached levels that had been current in West Europe in the Great Depression of the 1930s.

The hallmark of Brezhnev's foreign policy was a determination to retain what had been gained for world communism without taking excessive or unnecessary risks. The best example of this attitude was the so-called Brezhnev Doctrine applied in Czechoslovakia in 1968. Several months earlier, Alexander Dubček, a reformer, had been voted into the leadership of the still-Stalinist Czech Communist Party and proceeded to attempt to give his country "socialism with a human face." The Soviet leadership watched this loosening of the reins with intense and increasing concern. The Soviet generals warned that if Czechoslovakia were allowed to escape its satellite status, even though it remained communist, it would soon become a partner of the West Germans and the NATO forces behind them.

In **August 1968** Brezhnev acted: Soviet and East European army units poured into Czechoslovakia in overwhelming numbers. The Czechs had no alternative but to surrender. Dubček was forced out, and a faithful puppet installed in his place. Despite verbal denunciations, the Western countries accepted this resolution of the issue without lifting a hand. As in Hungary twelve years earlier, it was clear that the NATO nations were not prepared to risk a world war on behalf of the freedom of East Europeans under Soviet rule. Anticommunists in the satellite nations realized that their freedom to act independently could only come about if (1) the Soviet Union gave them leave or (2) the Soviet Union itself changed radically its system of government. Neither prospect seemed likely within a lifetime in 1968.

Brezhnev remained in power (1964–1982) longer than any Soviet leader except Stalin, but his effect on the Soviet state was in no way comparable. Where Stalin had turned the Soviet Union on its head, Brezhnev was intensely conservative; he would move on an issue only when delay could no longer be tolerated—and sometimes not even then. (There is one glaring exception: his decision to invade Afghanistan in 1979 for reasons that were unclear then and are still obscure.) His eighteen years as chief of the state and Party were marked by a general *loss of momentum in every aspect of Soviet life* except the military. Opportunists and career seekers completely dominated the CPSU. Corruption in its top ranks (starting with Brezhnev's own son-in-law) was rampant and went unpunished. Using Party connections to obtain personal privileges, such as rights to buy in special stores and permission for foreign travel, was taken for granted. Intellectuals and artists had once considered it an honor to join the Party, but now its prestige had degenerated to the point that authentically creative people refused to join.

For a time, the increased emphasis on consumer goods in the 1970s masked what was happening to the **command economy**: the overall *productivity* of Soviet labor was *declining* while government investments were being misapplied. Pushed by his generals, Brezhnev went along with a huge increase in the military budget in order to match the U.S. atomic weaponry. Always given an abnormally large share since the early Stalin years, the military now received by NATO estimates about a third of Soviet total spending. These funds could only come out of the civilian investment budget. Two forces thus converged to squeeze Soviet consumers from about 1975 onward: increased unproductive investment in military hardware and personnel, and declining civilian gross national product.

The *era of stagnation,* as it was later dubbed, made itself apparent in daily life in different ways. For many people, the most depressing was that Soviet living standards continued to lag behind the West. Instead of catching up by 1980 as Khrushchev had once rashly predicted, the gap was increasing. After sixty-five years of communist promises, Soviet consumers still faced long lines outside shops selling inferior goods; unexplained shortages of meat, produce, and even bread in the cities; a housing shortage that never seemed to improve; and five-year waits to buy the cheapest and least desirable automobiles.

The Soviet Union was actually slipping backward, not just compared with the United States and West Europe, but also relative to Japan, South Korea, and Taiwan. In fact, the *Soviet Union was rapidly becoming a Third World country* in every way except military technology and power. The entire postwar communications revolution had bypassed East Europe; even a private telephone was a rarity for all but the higher Party ranks and a few favored urbanites. Computers and their electronic spin-offs were few in number and obsolete compared with those in the West. The efficiency and productivity of communist industry and agriculture in both the Soviet Union and the satellites were far below world standards. They showed no signs of improvement as the ailing Brezhnev wheezed on into the 1980s. Had it not been for recently opened Siberian gas and oil resources, the U.S. Central Intelligence Agency estimated that Soviet domestic product would have actually *diminished* in the last years of Brezhnev's era.

The problems were not limited to the Soviet Union. By the 1980s, the gerontocracies (rule of the aged) of East Europe were also beginning to show signs of doom.

✣ THE END OF COMMUNIST RULE

Poland, the largest of the Soviet satellites, was the catalyst. The Polish leaders had failed to provide sufficient consumer goods for years and were almost ousted by a workers' peaceable protest in 1980–1981. This **Solidarity** movement, which was led by a shipyard electrician **Lech Walesa,** was then repressed by a communist general, who tried to rule by martial law for the next several years against massive popular resistance. Although Poland was the most dramatic example, by the mid-1980s all of the East European states were experiencing a rising tide of popular rage at the inability of the Marxist leaders to provide a decent standard of living. Yet the leaders insisted on clinging to their obsolete and discredited ideology.

In 1985, **Mikhail Gorbachev** (b. 1931) rose to the leadership of the Soviet Union promising to reform both the sputtering economy and the CPSU itself. He pushed his program of **perestroika** and **glasnost** (restructuring and openness) slowly, however, as it became apparent that both the Party and much of the populace were fearful of a future in which the old rules might not hold anymore. Two full generations of Soviet citizens had accustomed themselves to "the system," and they had learned that reforms and reformers tended to disappear in disgrace, while the system went on.

Nevertheless, it became clear that economic restructuring and the regeneration of the tired party could not proceed without basic political reforms that allowed free criticism and initiative. In 1987–1988, Gorbachev took the plunge in this direction, spurred by heroic Soviet dissidents like the physicist Andrei Sakharov, by his own

■ **Gorbachev at the Soviet Parliament, 1990.** Having invited a much wider and more authentic electoral process to fill the seats in the new Parliament, party leader Gorbachev found himself in the unheard-of position of having to defend his policies before it. Resolute critics such as the great physicist Andrei Sakharov were not easily silenced or put off.

convictions, and by the necessity of reducing the tremendously costly arms race with the United States. As long as that race went on, the money necessary for productive economic investment would not be available, and the communist world would fall further behind the West.

Gorbachev therefore initiated a *rapid winding down of the Cold War,* meeting several times with his counterpart President Ronald Reagan of the United States to sign agreements on arms control and troop reductions in divided Europe. Gorbachev also made gestures of reconciliation to China, and in 1989, he withdrew Russian troops from Afghanistan. They had been engaged there in a highly unpopular war—the Soviet Vietnam—on behalf of native communist rulers since 1979, while the United States supported the opposing guerrilla forces. Afghanistan proved to be the last of the surrogate wars fought between the two rival systems all over the globe since 1946.

The most remarkable of Gorbachev's domestic initiatives was his drive to *separate the Communist Party from the government of the Soviet Union.* Between 1988 and 1991, the CPSU first secretary presided over a series of moves that transformed the Soviet state. He initiated a multiparty democracy with a parliament and a revised

Mikhail Gorbachev

b. 1931

No one realized it at the time, but the accession of Mikhail Gorbachev (b. 1931) to supreme power in the Communist Party of the Soviet Union was the beginning of the end of the reign of the communists and, eventually, of the Soviet Union itself. This was hardly the intent of the Party members who elected him in 1985 to the position of First Secretary of the CPSU; they expected him to grapple with the many serious problems that were afflicting the country after twenty years of weak leadership and to restore the communist state to a condition of parity with the United States. Above all, the Party members were hoping that Gorbachev could break up the logjam in the Soviet economy that had prevented them and their fellow citizens from obtaining the consumer goods that the capitalist West had enjoyed for a generation. They were very tired of the stagnation that had overtaken the Soviet Union since the 1970s in every area except military hardware.

Gorbachev seemed a proper choice for this difficult job. At fifty-four, he was the youngest leader the Party had seen in almost half a century. He was a well-educated lawyer with a reputation for practicality and great energy. His early speeches made it clear that he perceived the economy's failings and was determined to do something about them. Assisted by his charming wife, he was an instant hit ("Gorby! Gorby!") in his ventures abroad as spokesman for a "new USSR," a country that was quite ready to drop its previous threatening gestures and take its place in a rational and peaceable world. Within two years, he had collaborated with President Ronald Reagan to end the Cold War and begin real disarmament in Europe and around the world.

Gorbachev insisted that the communist government and especially its economic aspect needed *perestroika* (restructuring) to be competitive with the West and satisfy the needs of the citizenry. His attempts to begin this were fiercely opposed by many of the Party leaders, who were more concerned about retaining their privileges under the old system than improving the economy. And his measures never went far enough to satisfy the liberal elements. They saw that as long as the so-called command economy existed in Russia, the hoped-for loosening of political and social controls could not be attained. They therefore pushed Gorbachev to reform the government and the organs of censorship, in step with a reformed economy.

Gorbachev responded, but only grudgingly and partially. He truly believed in the Communist Party's mission to bring about a more just and more rational

constitution. The CPSU's seventy-year monopoly on political life was abolished. Any group claiming to represent a legitimate interest or a recognized ethnic, professional, or social group could now register as a political party and solicit votes. A Congress of People's Deputies and a Supreme Soviet (a standing parliament) were elected under these rules and took office in 1989. Immediately, bitter conflicts arose between the worried communist hard-liners in the parliament and its sizable noncommunist minority.

The conflicts were the result of Gorbachev's cautious moves toward democracy, which had greatly upset the old guard CPSU activists and bureaucrats, but had not gone nearly far or fast enough to satisfy the growing numbers of anticommunists and the supporters of thoroughgoing reform. A convinced believer in the possibilities of Marxism, the Soviet Union's last president also knew that radical reforms were necessary. Gorbachev was a classic case of the moderate who is criticized by both extremes and cannot bring himself to join either one for survival (see the Biography in this chapter). The result was his political death in the summer of 1991. An attempted coup by CPSU hard-liners was foiled by the reformers led by *Boris Yeltsin,* but simultaneously revealed how naive Gorbachev had been about his friends and his enemies. He was discredited and was soon pushed aside by Yeltsin.

The failed coup ended not only Gorbachev's prestige, but also the authority of the Communist Party. Yeltsin had already demonstratively resigned from the Party, and

society, not only in Russia but everywhere. He could not accept the view that communism's day had ended, and he therefore wished to keep the Party in control of the country's politics. He believed that if the CPSU were reformed along the lines he wished, it could legitimately claim that position.

The attempt to change the economy gradually through restructuring was a fiasco; it satisfied no one and had resulted in shortages of all sorts by 1988. At the same time, Gorbachev marched with the liberals toward a truly open and democratic political system. The Party's monopoly on electoral candidates and on the whole political system was dismantled by 1989; multiparty elections for a new Soviet parliament were held in that year. For the first time in two generations, Soviet citizens could express themselves without fear, travel abroad, and deal freely with foreign visitors. The political atmosphere and social conditions were literally transformed. Dissidents were released from the jails; the once dreaded KGB and other police forces were openly criticized and their powers abolished. Rock music could be freely played; Western books and newspapers were available to anyone who could afford them. Even the Soviet newspapers printed the news without censorship. All of this was collectively termed *glasnost,* or openness such as Soviets had never seen.

But Gorbachev's problems mounted faster than he could solve them. The non-Russian nationalities ev-erywhere used their new freedom to protest against Russian domination and their own lack of authority in the various Soviet republics. Soon, several of them declared themselves independent of Moscow and began fighting among themselves for supremacy in the regional scene. The stagnant economy did not respond as hoped to the partial free market introduced by Gorbachev's advisers; instead, the already shaky production and distribution system broke down even further. Russians blamed Gorbachev for their mounting troubles; non-Russians wanted "out" of a system that was abhorrent to them.

In late summer 1991, the final blows fell on *perestroika* and on Gorbachev himself. The hard-line element in the Communist Party attempted a poorly-organized *coup d'état* against the government. It failed miserably, not because of Gorbachev but because of the resistance mounted by his chief rival, the dema-gogic ex-communist Boris Yeltsin. In December the belatedly disillusioned Gorbachev resigned his party and presidential posts and turned over power to Yeltsin. Assured of a good pension but otherwise ignored by a public that had no use for him, he withdrew to become the director of a "think tank" in Moscow, surrounded by the ghosts of what might have been.

---

he was now joined by millions of others who recognized the CPSU as a law-breaking and corrupt organ. Within a few months, the Party was declared illegal in Russia (though this decree was later reversed by court action), and its ranks faded to a few hundreds of thousands of embittered and demoralized members. To use Leon Trotsky's cruel words to the anti-Bolsheviks in 1917, it had been "thrown on the ash-heap of history." Its enormous property and financial resources were declared forfeit and either taken over by the government of Yeltsin or offered to private hands, in line with a vast "privatization" campaign which was introduced slowly and with considerable difficulty into the economy as a whole. The dismantling of communism was going to prove as challenging as its introduction had been some three quarters of a century earlier.

✤ THE BREAKUP OF THE SOVIET UNION

Gorbachev had failed to recognize the depth of discontent in the Soviet Union. Above all, the fires of *nationalism* were finding steady fuel from the possibility—for the first time in a century of tsarist and communist rule—of expressing ethnic discontents openly. Indeed, *glasnost* proved to be a tremendous boost to the many peoples in this truly multiethnic union who wished to end their connection with Russia as well as with communism. Among them were Turkic and Mongol Asiatics who were second-class citizens in their own countries, Muslim fun-damentalists who rejected Russia and communism with equal passion, and Ukrainian and Baltic nationals who had never accepted their coerced incorporation into the

■ **Boris Yeltsin Defies the Attempted Coup.** In August 1991, Yeltsin, the president of the Russian Republic, mounted a tank drawn up before the Parliament Building to read out his refusal to surrender governmental powers. At this time, Soviet leader Gorbachev was being held under arrest by the hard-line coup participants.

Soviet Union. Once the reins were loosened, all of the western and southwestern borderlands of the Soviet Union were potential breakaways.

But the breakup turned out to have a grim as well as a hopeful side. Within two years of the initiation of *glasnost,* Armenians and Azeris were fighting one another over ancient disputes in the far Caucasus, Russian immigrants were being hunted down by wrathful Kazakhs in the new Kazakhstan, and the three Baltic republics of Latvia, Estonia, and Lithuania were demanding total independence. They were soon joined by Ukraine, Georgia, Moldova, and some of the Muslim provinces along the southern borders of Siberia. By mid-1991, the Soviet political structure of a federation dominated by the huge Russian Republic was in a state of collapse. The end came in August 1991 with the bungled coup, whose conspirators claimed their goal was to reestablish the union, though they actually aimed to restore the rule of the Communist Party.

What eventually emerged from the events of 1991 was the **Commonwealth of Independent States (CIS),** whose very name reflects the difficulty of finding some common ground among the various nationalities, once the lid of communist rule was blown off. Eleven of the fifteen Soviet republics opted to join the commonwealth, while four (the Baltic states and Georgia) refused. The CIS is a very weak confederation—the smaller members would not agree to anything else—and is politically, economically, and territorially dominated by the huge Russian Republic. If the 25 million Russians living in other CIS republics are counted,

Russian ethnic dominance becomes even more pronounced.

The CIS faces every conceivable type of problem, not the least of which are the mutual suspicions of its members. The non-Russian members suspect that Russia will try to reestablish the tight centralized controls over the minorities that marked the communist era and are determined to frustrate this. On their side, the Russians see a mass of irresponsibly nationalistic peoples, who need Russian expertise and culture to lead them from the wilderness of mutual antagonisms and general backwardness in which they wallow. What the confederation's future will be is very difficult to know, but most observers believe that *the CIS cannot endure in its present state.* It must either gravitate toward tighter bonds in all areas (which would give Russia still more weight) or become a kind of loose, merely economic arrangement.

President Yeltsin's role is crucial, and he has thus far walked an uncertain and unpredictable line between democratic reforming politician, arrogant party boss, and befuddled spectator. The bloody dispersal of his parliamentary opponents in 1993 and the mishandled repression of the Chechnya independence movement within the Russian state in 1995 gave much ammunition to those who see him in the second and third roles.

✤ East Europe's Revolution of 1989

The rejection of Marxist ideology was at least as thorough in the former satellite states of East Europe as in the

Soviet Union. In the fantastic Fall of 1989, the governments of Czechoslovakia, East Germany, Bulgaria, and Romania were thrown out by peaceful protests or more violent means. Earlier, the Hungarian communists had saved themselves temporarily by agreeing to radical changes, and the Polish Communist Party had in desperation agreed to share political power with Walesa's Solidarity. A bit later, in 1990, the Yugoslav and the Albanian Communist Parties were cast aside. What Zbigniew Brzezinski called "the Grand Failure" had finally been dispersed. Soviet-style communism was decisively rejected by almost all who had had the misfortune to live under it for a long generation in East Europe.

As in the Soviet Union, the *primary cause of the East European breakaway* was the failure of the system to deliver on its promises of economic advance (see Chapter 54). This failure reinforced the nationalist resistance to Russian dominion, which most East Europeans traditionally felt, but which had been temporarily silenced in the face of military might and communist indoctrination during the postwar years. When Gorbachev showed that he believed in democratic ideas and was not inclined to keep East Europe under communist control by force as his Soviet predecessors had, the cork came flying out of the bottle of discontent.

■ **Vaclav Havel.** After an irresistible wave of public protests brought down the former regime, the playwright and political dissident, Vaclav Havel was inaugurated as the first post-communist president of Czechoslovakia in 1990. Because no lives were lost during the uprising, the Czechoslovak revolt against the communist government is known at the "Velvet Revolution."

The means of ridding their nation from communism varied from the massive, peaceful protests mounted by the East Germans and Czechs (the "Velvet Revolution" in Prague), to the more gradual pressures brought by a wide spectrum of anti-Marxists in Bulgaria and Albania, to the lethal street fighting in Romania. In all countries, the Communist Party attempted to retain some validity by renaming itself and participating as a legal party in the free elections held throughout postcommunist Europe in 1990 and 1991. A number of "reform communists" were able to vindicate themselves in the eyes of their fellow citizens and retained important posts in the Baltics, Hungary, Romania, and other states.

Generally speaking, the discredited old leaders were allowed to retire without being subjected to witch-hunts and there was no attempt to bring any but the most hated to trial for injuries done to their fellow citizens during the postwar period. The most respected of the anticommunist leaders, like Walesa of Poland and **Václav Havel** of the Czech Republic, were inclined to put the past behind them as rapidly as possible and to forgive and forget those who had harassed and imprisoned them in the name of "the future."

⚜ PROBLEMS OF THE POSTCOMMUNIST ERA

The *economic and financial problems* of the new governments of East Europe and the former Soviet Union were immense. As in the former Soviet Union, they had to cope with a technologically backward, collectivized agricultural system that required far too much of their available labor and produced too little. Markedly inadequate consumer distribution networks and services had been the rule for forty years. The interest payments on the foreign debt accumulated by communist governments seeking popularity in the 1970s were eating up an intolerable percentage of the gross national product. Above all, the industrial sector, packed with superfluous workers by a policy of maintaining full employment through artificial means, was performing miserably. Most companies were actually bankrupt, but had been protected by government ownership and subsidies. The biggest plants were almost always the products of Stalinist design and were antiquated, polution-ridden, and inefficient. Their low-quality output could not be sold in hard currency markets and had to be forced upon the domestic market or other communist countries.

The postcommunist democratic governments had to make the difficult choice between adopting free market

The End of the Berlin Wall

The ultimate symbol of the Cold War between East and West came to be the ten-foot-high concrete line of the Berlin Wall. Erected by the East German government with Soviet approval and assistance in August 1961, it ran along the boundary between East and West Berlin in an attempt to stem the increasing numbers of East Germans who sought asylum in the free and economically prospering West Germany. The "death zones" on the eastern side of the wall were just that; hundreds of people lost their lives attempting to sneak or burst their way across the barrier in the 1960s and 1970s. President John F. Kennedy's "Ich bin ein Berliner" speech at the wall in 1963 committed the Western alliance to the defense of the West Berliners and the eventual removal of the hated barrier to German unity.

The abrupt decision of the tottering East German government in November 1989 to allow free passage across the Berlin boundary signaled the end of the wall and of the Cold War. It heralded the demise of communism in East Europe and, a little later, in the Soviet Union. On November 9, the demoralized East German border guards gave up their defense of a collapsing state. The American historian Robert Darnton gives his eyewitness account:

> The destruction of the Wall began in the early evening of Thursday, November 9th, soon after the first wave of East Berliners . . . burst upon the West. A young man with a knapsack on his back somehow hoisted himself upon the Wall . . . he sauntered along the top of it, swinging his arms casually at his sides, a perfect target for bullets that had felled many other Walljumpers . . . border guards took aim, and fired, but only with power waterhoses and without much conviction. The conqueror of the Wall continued his promenade, soaked to the skin, until at last the guards gave up. . . .
>
> A few minutes later hundreds of people . . . were on the Wall, embracing, dancing, exchanging flowers, drinking wine . . . and chipping away at the Wall itself.

Another view comes from an East Berlin woman:

> I was performing with my cabaret group in Cottbus, about three hours' drive away from Berlin, when someone said they'd heard on the radio that the Wall had been opened. We all dismissed that as rumor. But you didn't know what to believe, there were so many rumors going around. About an hour after the performance, we were driving back and heard it on the radio ourselves. When we arrived in Berlin, we immediately drove across into the West. . . . The city center, on Ku'damm, was one big party. After an hour we came back, and my friend dropped me off at my home.
>
> Bert, my husband, was away on a business trip and the kids were already asleep. Thirty minutes later, my friend called me back and said he couldn't sleep. I couldn't, either! so we decided to go back again. It was something like two or three in the morning . . . I didn't come back till it was time for my kids to get up.
>
> The next weekend Bert and I and the kids went off on a trip to West Germany. People were passing out drinks along the autobahn. There were huge lines. I took a glass of something and thought: what kind of funny lemonade is this? It was champagne!
>
> That first week people were marvelous. There was an openness, a new spirit.

SOURCE: Robert Darnton, *Berlin Journal, 1989–1990.* p. 75. W. W. Norton, 1991.

capitalism in one sudden sink-or-swim shift, or attempting to achieve a mixed economy less traumatically through a gradual transition from state to private ownership. With the exception of Poland, which introduced capitalism all at once, the governments opted for the gradual approach. At the time of this writing, the Poles appear to have been more successful, but regardless of the ultimate choice, all the countries were having severe difficulties. Rapid inflation, increasing unemployment at the former state-owned enterprises, and resentment at the increasing and highly visible division of society into haves and have-nots were the first fruits of the postcommunist economic order.

Summary

Stalin's last years, the Soviet Union experienced a uation of the fierce political and cultural repression ier decades, combined with a rapid climb in military onomic might before the dictator died in 1953. His sor Khrushchev relaxed the paranoid terror that had imposed upon his people and his satellites in urope and denounced Stalin's tyranny in a famous 1. But Khrushchev's crudeness and repeated mis- in foreign policy weakened his prestige at home; his efforts at reforming agriculture and the highly ucratized Communist Party failed, he was turned office by his associates in 1964.

ezhnev then became the frontman in a collective ship that lasted in spirit until 1985, though Brezh- imself died in 1982. While attempting to continue goulash communism" begun by Khrushchev, the and government showed declining ability to meet routine demands after about 1975. Economic prob- steadily became more severe and were exacerbated e unpopular adventure in Afghanistan. By the end of the gerontocratic Brezhnev era, the Soviet Union was entering an economic and political crisis that reverberated through all the East European communist states as well.

Gorbachev then took the reins with visions of an open, communist society emerging from the stagnation that gripped the Soviet Union. But Gorbachev's success in winding down international tensions was not matched by his overly cautious and wavering initiatives at home. An attempted communist *putsch* in 1991 pushed him out of office and led directly to the collapse of the Soviet Union and the discrediting of the CPSU. Even before this, East Europe had taken advantage of the new spirit to peace- ably free itself from the decrepit Marxist grip. For a brief year or two, the spirit of democratic freedom seemed to triumph, only to face massive challenges from rampant nationalism and economic discontent. Both the Common- wealth of Independent States (CIS), which succeeded the Soviet Union, and the ex-satellites in East Europe seem- ingly face a long and difficult struggle to find the way to a stable, just, and prosperous society.

Test Your Knowledge

he Western Allies considered the most vital country their foreign policy in postwar East Europe to be

Czechoslovakia.

Poland.

Hungary.

Yugoslavia.

alin's main objective in eastern Europe in the imme- ate postwar era was

to hunt down and punish Nazis and their sympa- thizers.

to secure military assistance against a possible West- ern attack.

to generate a better supply of consumer goods.

to repair war damage to the Soviet Union and assure communist control.

major reason for Khrushchev's sudden expulsion om leadership of the CPSU in 1964 was

his submission to the Maoists.

his embarrassment over the attempt to place mis- siles in Cuba.

c. his disregard of the building pressure for consumer goods.

d. his efforts to emulate Stalin too closely.

4. The creator of the term "goulash communism" was

a. Gorbachev.

b. Khrushchev.

c. Stalin.

d. Yeltsin.

5. The Brezhnev Doctrine

a. put the world on notice that the Soviet Union was preparing an invasion.

b. asserted that the Soviet Union would always be the leader in world Marxism.

c. said that East Europe must choose between com- munism and capitalism.

d. said that an existing socialist state cannot be al- lowed to become neutral or capitalist.

6. After being deposed in 1989, the leaders of the various East European Communist Parties generally were

■ **The Wall Comes Down.**
willing volunteers turned
November 9, 1989 and ev
succeeding day for a mont
smash down the hated Wa
divided Berlin and the Be
almost two decades.

The sour realities of the situation began to sink in as soon as the brief celebrations of restored freedom were over. Many citizens, especially the older generation, have been embittered at the surging crime rates, the appearance of a "mafia" of newly rich *biznezmeni,* and other unsavory phenomena of a wounded and dislocated society. At least a decade will be required to repair the civic damage of the previous forty years. Whether the East European peoples will wait that long before turning in desperation to adventurers and demogogues is a troubling question.

Most of the East European states (Romania has been an exception) quickly installed complete personal freedom, honest elections, a free press, and effective justice and security. But these political changes were not enough to ward off a certain disillusionment with the fruits of the 1989 revolutions. Already, the disappointment has been sufficient to allow the renamed communist parties to make a strong comeback in several countries, although with a different and more moderate set of socioeconomic goals.

As the 1990s went on, the democratic governments, like their Marxist predecessors, were discovering that political stability could only be purchased through sensitivity to nationalist desires and some "meat in the pot" for the common people. If economic conditions were too grim or if resentment of the illegal maneuvers of foreign and domestic capitalists or the unprecedented conse-

quences of an open immigration policy ran
stability that all the new governments h
would be permanently shattered.

The East Europeans are laboring un
handicap. They have never had a prolon
political freedom and constitutional goverr
of their countries, the years of parliament
could be measured on the fingers of bo
Chapter 48). The postwar Marxist rep
educated and the middle classes and its
posed "class solidarity" have made the ne
sus for parliamentary give-and-take even r
achieve. Worst of all, the violent, negative r
was the curse of the early twentieth centur
below the Marxist surface, as the spectac
disintegration of former Yugoslavia afte
strated. The civil war between Armenians
the repression of the Chechnya rebellion
other severe blows to hopes for an easy
communist coercion to democratic harmo

Clearly, the tasks of establishing effec
and just government in these countries ar
will not be solved until well into the twent
at all. Whether Marxist or free, East Euro
continuing challenge to a world that se
peaceable development.

a. hunted down and accused of crimes against their people.

b. imprisoned without trial or shot.

c. allowed to retain their posts if they changed their party affiliation.

d. sent into retirement without being accused of crime.

7. In economics, the postcommunist governments of East Europe generally

a. continued with the Marxist system without change.

b. introduced a completely free market in a short time.

c. sought to convert to a free market in gradual steps.

d. retained the basic idea of a "command economy."

8. As the head of the Communist Party in the late 1980s, Gorbachev's fundamental problem

a. was his inability to see the need for change.

b. came from foreign sources such as the Afghan war.

c. was his indecision about the extent of necessary reforms.

d. was his continuing belief in the probability of war against the United States.

Identification Terms

August 1968

Brezhnev (Leonid)

command economy

Commonwealth of Independent States (CIS)

Revolution of 1989

glasnost

Gorbachev (Mikhail)

Havel, Václav

Khrushchev's secret speech

perestroika

Solidarity

Walesa, Lech

Bibliography

East Europe

Ash, T. G. *The Magic Lantern: The Revolution of 1989 as Witnessed in Warsaw, Budapest, Berlin, and Prague,* 1990. See also the same author's *The Polish Revolution: Solidarity,* 1984. Both are written with flair and insight.

Banac, I., ed. *Eastern Europe in Revolution,* 1992. A collection of mainly good articles.

Brown, J. F. *Eastern Europe and Communist Rule,* 1988. A rich source of information on postwar affairs, unfortunately published just a year before everything changed.

Cohen, L. *Broken Bonds: The Disintegration of Yugoslavia,* 1993. A clear account of how and why that state fell apart after the communist lid was raised.

Glenny, M. *The Return of History,* 1991. A British journalist's account of why the East Europeans rebelled against communism. The same author's *The Fall of Yugoslavia,* 1992, gives the story of the civil war through late 1992.

Rothschild, J. *Return to Diversity: East Central Europe since 1989,* 1992. One of the best of the vast crop of political histories of eastern Europe under communism and after.

Valenta, J. *Intervention in Czechoslovakia, 1968,* 1979.

The Former Soviet Union

Brzezinski, Z. *The Grand Failure: The Birth and Death of Communism in the Twentieth Century,* 1988. An important explanation of why Gorbachev could not save the Soviet Union.

Gwertzman, B., and M. T. Kaufman, *The Decline and Fall of the Soviet Empire,* 1992. The same pair put together *The Collapse of Communism,* 1991, which is similarly composed of contemporary newspaper accounts from the *New York Times.*

Laqueur, W. *The Long Road to Freedom,* 1988. Why *glasnost* and *perestroika* came, and why they could not succeed as Gorbachev desired.

Shipler, D. K. *Broken Idols, Solemn Dreams,* 1983. A perceptive journalist's summary of life in the final years of the Marxist society; what was wrong and why it could not be fixed.

Smith, G. *The Nationalities Question in the Soviet Union,* 1990. A good review of more than twenty nations and how they reacted to Gorbachev's program in the late 1980s.

Smith, H. *The New Russians,* 1990. Written just prior to the collapse of the Communist Party and the Soviet government, this very readable analysis by a *New York Times* Moscow correspondent is an updating of an earlier book, also on Russian society.

White, S. *Gorbachev and After,* 1991. Also see R. G. Kaiser, *Why Gorbachev Happened,* 1992.

CONTEMPORARY WORLD SOCIETY: SELECTED ASPECTS

1948–1973	Economic boom in West
1960s–1970s	Shortened labor week/Increased labor mobility
1970s–1980s	Female economic equality drive
1960s–present	Sport and leisure-time activities multiply

One of the noteworthy contradictions of the contemporary world is the fact that as advances in electronics are making physical distance almost irrelevant to communication, economic and social factors are splitting the human community into pieces that seem to have little to communicate to one another. The northern hemisphere abounds in personal luxuries and social resources of every type; the southern hemisphere has few and is unable to generate them. Several countries have already experienced a Third Industrial (or Postindustrial) Revolution, but it has not begun in many others, some of which, indeed, have not yet undergone the first two Industrial Revolutions. Patriarchal structures have been abolished by statute or changed by custom in many countries, but women still face important handicaps.

Contemporary society is a kaleidoscope of significant differences, often concealed beneath a thin veneer of similarities that are generated in the West and then adopted worldwide. Women apply much the same cosmetics, for exactly the same reasons, throughout the modern world; from Kenyan villages to New York apartments, children play with plastic toys mass-produced in Taiwanese factories. But these superficial uniformities of cultural behavior are deceptive. A better acquaintance or the arrival of a crisis lays bare the lasting differences.

✤ THE ECONOMIC BASIS: CONTRASTS

Despite the best efforts of well-meaning individuals in the leadership of international organizations, the income gradient from the heights of developed countries to the lower slopes of the underdeveloped remains as steep as ever, perhaps steeper. According to the World Bank, in 1950 the average per capita income of the developed countries was ten times that of the underdeveloped. In 1995, it is almost twenty-five times! In 1994, cash income *per capita* in Malawi, the poorest nation in the world, was about *one–two-hundredth* of that in the United States.

Both the socialists and the supporters of the free market have advanced various schemes for improving living standards, but in general, these have failed. This is partly the result of the unforeseen consequences of the advances in public health that have kept more people alive for longer. An increase in population is, of course, not itself an economic depressant. But when it is not accompanied by a significant increase in employment or productive investments—as has been the case throughout the developing world—then it becomes one. More mouths and the same quantity of food available add up to less per person—a statement underlined again and again in sub-Saharan Africa, South Asia, and parts of Latin America in the past couple of decades.

But what about the touted Green Revolution in agriculture? Didn't the United Nations and Western banks make immense funds available to developing countries for industrial-technical development? Indeed, the world's food supply did increase significantly in the 1960s and 1970s, and a large number of industrial projects were financed by international agencies in the same years. But the benefits of the Green Revolution went disproportionately to large producers, not to the poor peasants. Sometimes the new seeds and fertilizers were aimed at industrial export crops, such as sunflower seeds, cotton, and peanuts, rather than food for local consumption. West Africa is a notable example of this unfortunate misallocation of scarce resources.

The attempts made by the postwar nationalist leaders to substitute locally produced items of general consumption for imported ones were only briefly successful. The idea was to give badly needed factory employment to their own people and to bolster national pride in home-produced consumer goods. But it was soon discovered that the peasant majority lacked the necessary disposable income to purchase the new products, just as earlier they had had insufficient money to buy the foreign goods. Impoverished Tanzanian villagers, for example, who were worried about their next meal, did not care where the handsome porcelain offered in local stores had been made. The villagers could not afford it in any case, and both the domestic workshop that made it and the shop that attempted to sell it soon had to close.

This dismal state of declining opportunities was the total opposite of what was happening in the developed world, especially during the quarter-century between 1948 and 1972. As we saw in Chapter 59, the Arab oil boycott marked the first serious reversal of a boom that had begun with the American decision to help the West Germans and other Europeans rather than risk a communist Europe. As the Korean War (1950–1953) increased the demand for raw materials, the Western world entered on a production-consumption cycle unprecedented in history. Even the countries of the communist bloc, at this juncture, were making considerable progress in industrializing their backward economies.

Looking back from the present vantage point, we can see that in the early postwar years the West was on the threshold of the *longest sustained economic advance in modern history,* which would result in important social, political, and cultural changes by the century's end. At the same time, the failure of most of the less-developed nations to provide anything like a comparable living for their citizens has created a *dangerous gap between the two worlds* of rich and poor. Here we will briefly compare three aspects of these worlds: occupations and the mobility between them; educational opportunity and who gets it; and efforts at redistribution of wealth by government.

Occupational Mobility

People in the poorer developing countries still hold almost the same occupations as their ancestors. For the big majority, taking a man's or woman's role in society means performing some task in almost the same way and for much the same rewards as in one's parents' time. The work may now be performed on a clock-driven basis rather than seasonally, and the worker may be paid in cash rather than produce. But the tending of animals, tilling of fields, and buying and selling of necessities are essentially unchanged in their demands and returns to the laborer. Mobility among these tradition-dictated jobs is minimal for reasons ranging from climate and terrain to ingrained customs. Only by leaving the village to try their luck in the city can these uneducated and unskilled people find any real mobility, but doing so is a risky gamble.

In the developed countries, on the other hand, **labor mobility** has expanded tremendously in terms of both the nature and prestige of jobs and geographically. It is now quite possible for a Belgian baker, for example, to take a bakery job in Italy without facing any more red tape or employer prejudice than an Italian would. But our baker might want to escape the physical labor and difficult hours of his job. So in Milan he decides to take some courses in his off time, and within a year or two, he is qualified to become an accountant. His next job is keeping the books for an elegant French hotel. Our baker has left the working class and become a *bourgeois.* Such mobility has become as commonplace within the European Community as it was a generation earlier in North America. It is one of the chief reasons why average incomes (measured in real buying power) are much higher now than thirty or forty years ago.

Educational Opportunity

The baker is able to change occupations because he had access to specialized education. This access is denied to most people in general in the developing world and to

■ **Economic Feminism, 1970s.** The battle for women's rights shifted during the 1960s and 1970s from a political to an economic and social focus as millions of single and married women entered the western workforce for the first time. Here, some United States women march in a street demonstration for equal pay and benefits.

almost all females in particular. Education in the most primitive terms—the mastering of some literacy in the national language—is still by no means assured to many rural dwellers from Morocco to Indonesia. The average length of schooling outside the West is only three years, partly because of tiny education budgets and partly because of the still-vigorous prejudices of some cultures against formal education, especially for females. Although the average is three years, a given individual's actual school experience may be only several months. After that, a majority of rural people in the developing countries never see a classroom of any type again. Only the urbanites who are either relatively well-to-do or very ambitious will go beyond elementary school and into some form of technical or professional training.

Redistribution of Wealth

The success or failure of government policies aimed at promoting the **redistribution of national wealth** is the controlling factor in any modern economy. Not only the failed communist regimes, but also democratic socialism and even free-market capitalism are committed verbally, at least, to improving the lot of the poor. To a degree, this means redistributing existing wealth. How loudly politicians proclaim this goal and how determined they may be to put it into action vary greatly. But to advocate any other policy in the age of mass democracy would be a political impossibility.

The prime means of redistribution is taxation, though there are several others. In the Western countries, progressive income taxes, that is, higher rates on those who have more, have been accepted as a fundamental principle for a

century. Corporate taxes on profits are also accepted as a legitimate exercise of governmental authority. The bulk of all central government revenues stem from those two sources in all modern economies.

In many developing countries, however, a different view prevails. They make no attempt to redistribute wealth; rather, governmental policy is normally aimed at protecting the well-to-do from the demands of the poor. The bulk of taxation falls on the consumers through indirect taxes that they pay daily in the form of higher prices for ordinary necessities. When governments have attempted to impose an effective income tax or a land tax on large landholders, they have faced either a conservative revolution or massive resistance and evasion until the traditional tax system is restored. Both patterns have occurred frequently since World War II in most of the underdeveloped world.

✤ SOCIAL REFORM—EAST AND WEST

The collapse of the Soviet communist bloc in 1989–1991 was the unforeseen end of a system of economics and politics that had haunted the Western democracies for seventy years. In the interwar years and immediately after World War II, communism seemed likely to spread throughout the world either by revolution or by parliamentary procedure. In the underdeveloped lands, many millions saw it as the best hope at a decent material life for them and their children. In some countries such as China and Cuba, it did bring an initial surge of social and economic justice to the masses and earned their strong support for a generation. They were willing to pay for their better economic prospects by giving up the political

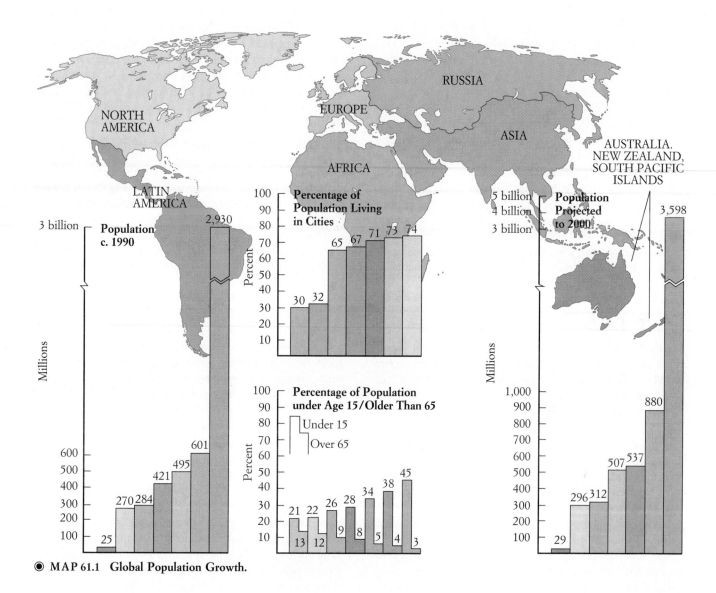

● **MAP 61.1 Global Population Growth.**

and social freedoms they had only minimally and imperfectly enjoyed under the previous, capitalist system.

But this was not true of the Western countries, including the East European countries, which fell under Soviet dominion at the end of World War II. Here, when the people had a choice, they firmly rejected the political, economic, and intellectual sacrifices demanded by communism. The socialist parties severed all connections with Soviet communism during the 1950s and even distanced themselves from many of the long-treasured ideas of Karl Marx. Reformism rather than revolution and gradualism

rather than radical change became the order of the day among the social democrats.

What had previously been considered a peculiarly American viewpoint, that the secret of social harmony was in making a bigger pie rather than rearranging the slices, came to prevail in all the Western nations. And, although never clearly admitted, this view came to be the new Soviet orthodoxy after Stalin's death. Revolution in the eyes of a Brezhnev or even Khrushchev was reserved for developing countries, where any other means of effecting change was out of the question. And such a revolution was only desirable where it served Soviet foreign policy; its efficacy as a catalyst of desirable social and economic reform was incidental. By the 1970s, it is fair to say that only Castro in Cuba and Mao in China gave more than lip service to Marx's original doctrines of social and economic egalitarianism.

Thus, if societal improvement was to be achieved, it would have to come from the new possibilities afforded by Western material and nonmaterial wealth since 1945. The Marxist dream of humans fulfilled in an earthly heaven was put on the shelf indefinitely. So long as the economic boom in the West lasted, social changes *did* come as both a reflection and a cause of vast improvement in the workers' living and working conditions. Indeed, these improvements were what nullified the appeal of communism in Europe, as the Soviet system proved unable to generate anything like them.

Prosperity in the Developed Societies

Western workers (extending "Western" to mean Japan since about 1980) work about one-fourth fewer hours weekly to earn wages that purchase about two and a half times as much in real terms as in 1950. They have guarantees of job security, wage or salary increases, vacation and sick time, insurance against accidents and ill health, unemployment pay, family leave, and other benefits that would astound workers of the 1940s. Material conditions have vastly improved also. In the United States, most salaried and about half of the wage-earning people own their homes. In Europe, where rentals are the standard, working-class families can afford more space, and automobiles are now commonplace. Upward mobility out of the working classes into the technical or professional groups has become commonplace. In this very real sense, social reform in the West has been extensive and effective since 1945, though it has not been carried out in the name of an ideology or even a set of principles.

Losing Ground in the Developing Countries

Again, the developing world shows a different pattern. Social mobility has increased, but only a small number of persons with access to education and "connections" have moved upward. *Downward mobility* has probably been more common in Africa and Latin America, where large groups of previously independent landowners or tribal community members have been forced out of their traditional niches by economic pressures. The near total absence of independent organizations such as trade unions or farmers' associations leaves these people vulnerable to changes imposed by modern urban life with no one to help defend their interests. The Latin American peon and African mineworker can rarely improve their economic or social prospects except by migration to the city with its attendant dangers.

⚜ LEISURE, PLEASURE, AND SPORT

Life is not made up solely of work and education. Certainly, that is not the case today; the amount of **leisure** enjoyed by both blue-collar and white-collar workers has doubled and tripled over the course of the twentieth century. But the uses people make of their nonwork time give rise to controversy and even dismay. The 38-hour workweek, which is now the norm among West European trades people and office workers, means that the job occupies less than a fourth of the week's time. Subtracting time for sleeping and eating, commuting, and other necessities still leaves about 40 hours per week with no specific activities—more time than is spent in working for pay. A good deal of this time is usually spent on tasks and engagements that are not wholly by choice (visiting relatives, education, seeking information, communication, cooking). But most people still have much free time, or leisure, in which they have no prescribed or imposed tasks. How do they spend it?

As physical labor has declined dramatically over the last generations, people have begun to substitute participation sport for it in the interests of promoting muscular and glandular well-being as well as entertainment. It is no coincidence that the rise of *mass participation sports* like soccer in Europe and baseball in the United States closely parallels the decline of the use of human muscle for routine tasks. Both these team sports became professionalized and organized into leagues of contestants in the last decades of the nineteenth century. At that time the Second Industrial Revolution was sharply reducing the need for heavy physical labor, and the cities, which supply the necessary concentration of paying spectators for professional sports' profitability reached great size.

Sports of both the participatory and the spectator types have steadily increased in importance in ordinary life from the middle years of the twentieth century. Television has been partially responsible, as it presents an ever greater variety of professional sporting events to appeal to mass audiences. The determination (first evident in the United States, but spreading throughout the Western world in the 1960s) to remain youthful looking and slender lifelong is another stimulus for participatory sport. In the 1990s, watching or engaging in some type of strenuous sporting exercise is a major consumer of leisure time.

The term *pleasure* defies precise definition, no matter what the contextual restrictions. Certainly, leisure can give rise to pleasure, but it does not necessarily do so. On the contrary, too much leisure can become exceedingly annoying to most persons. But most of us would also agree that leisure and pleasure are mutually reinforcing, and that pleasure often is contingent upon having leisure. Contemporary society has a great deal of leisure by the measures of older generations, but it is by no means clear that the ratio of pleasure has kept up. A basic axiom of twentieth-century sociology seems to be a slight variation on the law of diminishing returns: pleasure diminishes as leisure increases beyond a certain point. Where is that point? It is impossible to say with precision without dealing with individual tastes, but it also seems clear that the West as society has either already reached it or is fast approaching it.

As the *modalities and means* of attaining pleasure increase with every increase in leisure time, the *satisfaction and intensity* of pleasure become more evanescent. To some perceptive non-Western observers, though we may be armed with every electronic aid ever dreamed of, we are still chasing our tail.

✤ THE OTHER HALF OF HUMANITY

In the year 1964, a French wife and mother had to obtain the written permission of her husband to open a bank account in her own name. Ten years later, after a ferocious verbal battle, the French parliament legalized abortion. These two facts symbolize the changes in the status of women brought about by the struggle for **"women's liberation"** in the last several decades.

The *second sex,* as Simone de Beauvoir's influential book called women, has been steadily closing the vast gap that once stood between them and men in the social and economic arenas of the Western world. Most countries now have laws on the books (sometimes unenforced) that prohibit paying women less than men for the same work, discriminating on the basis of gender for promotions or entry into a profession, refusing credit to women, denying them contractual rights, denying women custody of minors, and so on. In the 1990s, women make up half of all university graduates, up from 20 percent in the 1950s. Almost a third of the students entering U.S. law schools are women; 14 percent were women in 1979 and only 4 percent in 1965.

These indications of rapid social change are by no means limited to the economic and labor sectors. About a quarter of American women between eighteen and forty-five were single in 1960; almost half were by 1990. More than half of all first marriages end in divorce. In the United States, one-fifth of firstborn babies are born to unmarried women, up from about 8 percent thirty years earlier. Unwed motherhood has become so common in some sectors of the population that it no longer requires explanation. Thirty years ago, it would have been grounds for social ostracism.

✤ FAMILY AND THE INDIVIDUAL

The dramatic changes in family life over the past generation are evident in more than the increased frequency of single motherhood. The entire family has come under

◾ The transfer of identities and loyalties from a neighborhood or a family to the far more impersonal professional athletic teams can perhaps best be witnessed during a baseball World Series.

Virginia Woolf, *A Room of One's Own*

In 1929, the novelist Virginia Woolf (1882–1941) published an essay that has become one of the landmarks of modern feminism. *A Room of One's Own* is an expanded version of a lecture delivered by Woolf to a women's college at Cambridge, where she was asked to speak on the topic "Women and Fiction." Instead, she seized the opportunity to point out the handicaps that have confronted women of talent and ambition for many centuries in Western culture. In the final paragraph, Woolf parodies the words of those who claimed that women and men were equal in status in England and that women's lack of accomplishment in the intellectual and artistic spheres was attributable to their natural inferiority to men.

> Let me imagine, since facts are so hard to come by, what would have happened if Shakespeare had a wonderfully gifted sister, called Judith, let us say. Shakespeare himself went, very probably, to the grammar school, where he may have learned Latin—Ovid, Horace, and Virgil—and the elements of grammar and logic. He was, as is well known, a wild boy who poached rabbits, perhaps shot a deer, and had, rather sooner than he should have done, to marry a woman in the neighborhood, who bore him a child rather quicker than was right. That escapade sent him to seek his fortune in London. He had, it seemed, a taste for the theatre, he began by holding horses at the stage door. Very soon he got work in the theatre, became a successful actor, and lived at the hub of the universe, meeting everybody, knowing everybody, practicing his art on the stage, exercising his wit in the streets, and even getting access to the palace.
>
> Meanwhile, his extraordinarily gifted sister, let us suppose, remained at home. She was as adventurous, as imaginative, as anxious to see the world as he was. But she was not sent to school. She had no chance of learning grammar and logic, let alone of reading Horace and Virgil. She picked up a book now and then . . . and read a few pages. But then her parents came in and told her to mend the stockings or mind the stew and not moon about with books and papers. . . .
>
> Soon, however, before she was out of her teens, she was to be betrothed to the son of a neighboring

great pressure to adapt or die out as the prevalent form of basic social relationship. This trend is far more apparent in the richer countries and among persons below age forty; among, say, rural Norwegians over forty the changes described here would be minimally apparent, if at all. But most people are not rural Norwegians, and we are concerned here with majority trends.

First, the two-parent, two-generation, male breadwinner and female housewife model, which has been the norm for Western urban families since the nineteenth century, has clearly become but one of several *alternative lifestyles.* With most mothers working outside the home, children under six are commonly cared for by paid employees. The removal of the biological mother from primary responsibility for the young child's welfare during the most impressionable years will presumably have wide-ranging but as yet unknowable effects upon the importance and permanence of the nuclear family relation.

Second, the increasing *numbers of female-headed households and unmarried females* in all Western and some non-Western countries are putting women into a position of potential political and social power quite unparalleled in recent history. But so far this potential power has not been realized. Women have shown themselves generally unmoved by appeals to feminism as a political, as contradistinct from a socioeconomic, force. As divorce and abandonment by the male grow more common, so does common-law marriage where enforcing legal responsibility for maintenance of spouse or children is difficult, if not impossible. Annually, many millions of women, from the villages of Africa to the ghettos of U.S. cities, find themselves thrown into permanent poverty by the breakup of their living arrangements with a man. Grappling with acute problems of survival, poor women have had little interest and/or energy to consider longer-term political goals.

The social and economic identification that individuals in the past received from their family has largely become superfluous. It is the individual, not the family or the clan, who exercises choice, creates opportunity, accepts respon-

wool-merchant. She cried out that marriage was hateful to her, and for that she was severely beaten by her father....

She made up a small parcel of her belongings, let herself down by rope one night, and took the road to London. She was not seventeen. The birds that sang in the hedge were not more musical than she was. She had the quickest fancy, a gift like her brother's, for the tune of words. Like him, she had a taste for theatre. She stood at the stage door; she wanted to act, she said. Men laughed in her face.... She could get no training in her craft. Could she even get her dinner in a tavern, or roam the streets at midnight? ... At last, Nick Greene the actor-manager took pity on her; she found herself with child by that gentleman, and so—who shall measure the heat and violence of the poet's heart when caught and tangled in a woman's body?—killed herself one winter's night and lies buried at some crossroads where the omnibuses now stop outside the Elephant and Castle.*

That, more or less, is how the story would run, I think, if a woman in Shakespeare's day had had Shakespeare's genius....

Young women ... you are, in my opinion disgracefully ignorant. You have never made a discovery of any sort of importance. You have never shaken an empire or led an army in battle. The plays of Shakespeare are not by you, and you have never introduced a barbarous race to the blessings of civilization. What is your excuse?

... May I remind you that there have been at least two colleges for women in existence in England since the year 1866; that after the year 1880 a married woman was allowed by law to possess her own property; and that in 1919—which is a whole nine years ago—she was given a vote? May I also remind you that the most of the professions have been open to you for close to ten years now.... When you reflect upon these immense privileges and the length of time during which they have been enjoyed, and the fact that at this moment there must be some two thousand women capable of earning over five hundred [pounds Sterling]† a year in one way or another, you will agree that the excuse of lack of opportunity, training, encouragement, leisure and money no longer holds true....

*A well-known tavern in south London.
†Woolf believed that a woman of talent needed "A Room of One's Own" and about 500 pounds per year to maintain her personal independence and thus allow her to pursue her gifts.

SOURCE: Excerpt from Virginia Woolf, *A Room of One's Own,* © Harcourt, Brace and Company.

sibility, earns renown, and generally makes his or her mark in the twentieth-century Western world (and increasingly, everywhere else). While this may be seen as a further large step toward democracy and fair play, it also has very definite negative aspects for both individual and society. The feeling of alienation from others that was mentioned in the chapter on modern high and low cultures is highly stressful. It has been most apparent in those locales where the traditional family has become weakest: the urban, mobile, wealthy West where the individual is an *atom among atoms* rather than a link in a chain. The degree to which this has become true can be easily demonstrated by a simple question to the reader of these lines: Do you

■ **Isolation in a Tokyo Apartment.** The extraordinary costs of housing in the Japanese capital are dramatized by this dormitory scene. The young woman will have to spend a large part of her leisure time in these surroundings; anything more spacious is beyond her means.

Benazir Bhutto

b. 1953

In November 1988, the first national election in many years allowed Pakistanis to select a new parliament and prime minister. The voters responded by selecting the first woman ever to head a Muslim country as their choice: Benazir Bhutto, head of the Pakistan People's Party.

Bhutto had been involved deeply in politics since her twenties, when she returned from American and English university life to her native land. Her father, Ali Bhutto, was then the prime minister; he had been the People's Party leader since several years earlier, when he had won a much disputed election against the candidate of the Pakistani army. Only a few months after his daughter's return, in September 1977, Ali Bhutto was removed from office and placed under army arrest. Eighteen months later, he was put on trial for murder, found guilty by a military court, and executed despite worldwide protests.

Meanwhile Benazir Bhutto was placed under

house arrest along with other members of the family; she remained there for the better part of the period between 1977 and 1984. The military clique that ruled Pakistan in that epoch was clearly apprehensive of the political appeal "this impetuous girl" exerted on her father's followers. Bhutto had gained some experience in politics during her undergraduate years at Radcliffe College (the female undergraduate school at Harvard) and more at Oxford, where she was the first foreign woman to be elected head of the debating club, the Oxford Union. Even while being held under arrest, she was able to take the reins of the People's Party and become its acknowledged leader. General Zia Khan, the president of the republic, repeatedly tried to persuade Bhutto to agree to be silent and take no part in public affairs in return for her freedom; but she was not so inclined despite occasional bouts of solitary confinement as punishment. In 1984, Zia forced her into exile.

---

know where you are going to be buried? Probably, you have no idea where this traditionally most sacred rite will be carried out or who will do it—an unthinkable thing to confess until very recently in human history.

✤ THE FINAL HEALTH PROBLEM: DEATH AND DYING

There is a fascinating diversity in the approaches to the "problem" of death in late twentieth-century society. On the one extreme is the attitude in the United States and some parts of Europe that death is an unfortunate and presumably temporary obstacle in the march of medical progress. In this view, an individual's passing from life to nonlife is rather like failing an important exam; unhappily, it is not yet possible to take the exam over.

Despite deep-rooted Christian beliefs in immortality, in the West the cessation of earthly life is a sad and rending experience to be delayed as long as possible through all the devices of the modern hospital and pharmacy. In the other camp are most Muslims, Asians, and the entirety of the nonindustrial societies. They believe, to speak very generally, that death is the natural culmination of life, inevitable and thus not to be feared. Some consider it a

In 1986, a discouraged military stepped down from day-to-day political leadership and revoked the martial law it had imposed nine years earlier. Bhutto came home at once and was greeted by the largest crowd ever seen at a political function since Pakistani independence forty years earlier. It took her caravan six hours to come into the center of Karachi from the airport, normally a ride of ten minutes.

Bhutto demanded that Zia permit immediate elections instead of waiting, as already announced, until 1990. But the general was able to stall for two more years, as opposition to the idea of a female leader jelled among tradition-minded voters. Finally, national elections were permitted in 1988. Bhutto displayed a flair for campaigning, riding to her rallies atop the cab of a truck with her trademark red-tinted glasses and clearly enjoying "pressing the flesh" of her constituents.

Her party won a solid plurality, which put her in the office of prime minister, a post she held for less than a year when she was forced out on trumped-up charges of corruption. The real issues were gender and the political hatreds generated by her father. Bhutto then overplayed her hand somewhat, and her party lost the 1990 election to a coalition of right-wing and traditionalist parties. In the chaos of Pakistani politics, however, nothing seems to be of long duration, and in the elections in 1993, the People's Party came back again, and Bhutto with it.

She has proven notably capable at riding the domestic tiger. Her foreign policy has continued in more or less conventional, neutralist lines except for her initiatives toward peace with India, which have been greeted in New Delhi and Western capitals as a distinct turn for the better.

Pakistan's support for the militant Muslim separatists in India's Kashmir province has been sharply reduced. The pressures created by the overcrowding of the million or more Afghani refugees within Pakistan has been gradually reduced through resettlement aid provided by the United States. However, urban violence by unknown groups of street thugs has been on the increase.

The prime minister married—by family arrangements—a wealthy Pakistani from her own socially prominent class in 1987 and has had three children by him. (Her husband has taken no overt political role despite rumors of behind-the-scenes influence.) Western reporters have repeatedly attempted to get Bhutto to comment on her private life, both before and after her marriage. She has defeated all these efforts by insisting that she is "a Muslim woman, in a Muslim country," and that she has no intention of saying or doing anything that would offend the moral principles of her devout and patriarchal fellow citizens. She knows too well that one of the potentially most effective weapons in the hands of her political enemies is the suspicion that this Western-educated, vivacious, and attractive woman must have at times deviated from the strict standards of feminine behavior imposed by fundamentalist Islam. Thus far, she has proven more than a match for them.

transition from one form and mode of life to another and understand that an indestructible spirit goes on after the body has returned to dust.

Much of the Western world has sunk enormous sums in one fashion or another into the pursuit of a longer life. It has been restrained from sinking still more only by the unavoidable other demands on the national budget. As unpleasant reminders that all these efforts have ultimately been defeated, death and dying have been ruled out of bounds in the good life, at least as far as is humanly possible. They are unfit topics for children to hear or see; for 80 percent of the American population, death comes in hospitals rather than at home. (Two generations ago, the reverse proportion ruled.) But in most of the remainder of the global village, almost everyone dies among their family or cohort of friends, avoiding to the end the indignities of the hospital ward and the indifferent strangers who pass through it. But they also die earlier, and perhaps more painfully, and from disease or accident that would be routinely overcome in a Western medical environment.

Which of the two approaches, the Western or the non-Western, is more constructive and more realistic is not yet clear (and perhaps never will be). But it seems apparent that some compromise must be struck in the

West between expenditures for physical health and long life, and those demanded by a lengthening list of other and equally urgent needs. To a rapidly increasing number of people, it makes little sense to prolong a life that has exhausted both its capacity and its desire to live, even though doing so is within the possibilities of modern medicine.

Summary

Contemporary society in what has truly become a closely linked global village offers a full palette of contrasts and variations. These are frequently obscured by the adoption of superficial Western habits and customs in the non-Western three-quarters of the world's population. In labor mobility, educational opportunity, and occupational variety, the industrialized and the preindustrial countries remain significantly different. The place of women is also quite distinct in the underdeveloped world, where the patriarchal habit of mind is sometimes anchored in statutes but always in more powerful unwritten custom. The second sex labors under many handicaps in its struggle for occupational and social equality, even where it has obtained legal and political equity.

The family has been placed under severe strain by changing socioeconomic conditions, and in the West, it seems to have disintegrated in several fashions shocking to traditionalists. Individual atoms are replacing the former aggregations of family and clan. Leisure has become superabundant by the measures of previous generations, and the task of filling it constructively sometimes becomes burdensome. Participatory and spectator sports have come to occupy a place unthought of in previous times.

Death in the West at the end of the twentieth century is considered an unfortunate and guilt-inducing disruption of the life course, though most of the world views it as the natural consequence of living. The necessity of allocating scarce funds in national budgets brings these opposing views into ever sharper focus and will presumably soon compel a choice.

Test Your Knowledge

1. In the last generation, the differential in per capita income between the developed and least-developed countries has
   a. diminished steadily.
   b. stayed about what it was.
   c. increased slightly.
   d. risen from about ten to twenty-five times.
2. In the Western world, the years between 1948 and 1973 were a period of
   a. slowly declining buying power for most people.
   b. unparalleled prosperity for the consumer.
   c. recurrent industrial shortages.
   d. declining income for the lower or working class.
3. In the developing world, government generally sees its domestic task as
   a. trying to make the nation fully independent in trade.
   b. protecting the masses from exploitation.
   c. encouraging investment and development through high tax rates on the wealthy.
   d. protecting the upper classes from new demands from the lower.
4. In European countries in recent times, labor mobility
   a. has been limited to a few jobs and a few situations.
   b. has increased markedly through international agreements.
   c. has been limited for women but increased markedly for men.
   d. has changed relatively little.
5. Female "liberation" has recently been
   a. successful in civil rights but not in obtaining economic equality.
   b. successful in economic affairs but not in political and social areas.
   c. much more successful in the developing countries than in the West.

d. unable to make any real headway against male opponents.

6. A striking change in the last several decades in the West is
   a. the rise in households headed by a single female.
   b. the decrease in babies born out of wedlock.
   c. the governments' readiness to abolish taxes on income.
   d. the resurgence of traditional patriarchal values.

7. Which of the following has *not* contributed to making sport more popular than ever in the West?
   a. The influence of Buddhism's insistence on bodily mastery

b. Television
c. Better diet for more muscular bodies.
d. The desire to remain slender and youthful

8. Benazir Bhutto
   a. was raised in a peasant home.
   b. was the first Muslim female to lead her country.
   c. was originally put into power by the Pakistani military.
   d. has upset her fellow citizens by remaining unmarried.

Identification Terms

labor mobility   leisure   redistribution of national wealth   women's liberation

Bibliography

Banks, O. *Faces of Feminism,* 1982. A comparison of British and American feminist movements.

Cherlin, A. *Marriage, Divorce, Remarriage,* 1981.

Critchfield, R. *The Golden Bowl Be Broken: Peasant Life in Four Cultures,* 1988. Very engagingly written account of ordinary life in the developing world.

Dudly, W. *Death and Dying,* 1992. One of the *Opposing Viewpoints* series published by Greenhaven Press particularly for students.

Guttmann, A. *From Ritual to Record: The Nature of Modern Sport,* 1978. An excellent analysis. See also S. Freeman and R. Boyes, *Sport behind the Iron Curtain,* 1980 for a view of how the communist lands employed sport as propaganda.

Iglitzin, L., and R. Ross, eds. *Women in the World: A Comparative Study,* 1976. An anthology concerning the freedoms or restrictions placed on women in the recent era.

Kubler-Ross, E. *On Death and Dying,* 1974. One of the best-known works on the "ultimate health problem" and how it can be faced.

O'Neill, W. *Coming Apart,* 1971. A highly readable account of the critical decade of the 1960s in the United States and in much of the Western world.

Smith, B. G. *Changing Lives: Women in European History since 1700,* 1989.

CHAPTER 62

AT THE END OF THE TWENTIETH CENTURY: THE ROAD AHEAD

A SHORT AND VIOLENT CENTURY

THE UNITED NATIONS AND NATIONAL SOVEREIGNTY

CONTROL OF NUCLEAR WEAPONS

ENVIRONMENTAL DETERIORATION

CHOICES

1945	United Nations founded in San Francisco
1945	First use of atomic energy
1963	Nuclear Atmospheric Test Ban, U.S.A. and U.S.S.R.
1970	Recognition of environmental crisis begins in West
1986	Chernobyl nuclear plant meltdown
1991	Atmospheric pollution documented over Antarctica
1990s	Global warming trends suspected

Our globe has shrunk incredibly since the opening of the twentieth century. Mass communications and instantaneous transfer of data and ideas from one corner of the earth to the others have worked a transformation that contemporary human beings have not yet fully grasped. We do not yet understand the dimensions of the problems that have arisen, let alone their solutions.

A chief difficulty is that our technology has far outrun our political culture. We can do things that have infinite power for good or evil in the lives of human beings—our own and those in the future—but we don't know how to determine "good" or "evil" in a consensual fashion. In a world that has become immensely more interdependent, the old chimera of "I win, you lose" is still being pursued by rivals of all types. This is as true in economic development and environmental protection as it is in international wars and ethnic conflicts. The results are often chaotic and sometimes fatal.

Will the East versus West struggle of the postwar era be replaced by the North versus South competition, as some fear? Have we put the Cold War behind us, only to be faced by beggar-thy-neighbor rivalries? Can we find a way to guarantee justified autonomies while avoiding the extremes of ethnic wars? The human species will have to learn to do much better—or we will assuredly do much worse.

❧ A SHORT AND VIOLENT CENTURY

A recent book by the well-known historian John Lukacs claims that the twentieth century really lasted only the seventy-five years between the outbreak of war in 1914 and the collapse of communism in 1989. But this short time (less than a modern Western lifetime) has seen more upheavals occur at a more rapid pace than any of the longer centuries before. According to Professor Lukacs, the two world wars towered like mighty mountains over the twentieth century, and when the Soviet system finally went down, the shadows thrown by those mountains lifted, and a new era began.

A good deal can be said for this interpretation. Leninist communism has come to be recognized as a passing infatuation, rather than a lasting marriage, between some humans' recurrent idealism and their lust for power. And Leninist communism was a child that was born of World War I, grew to adulthood in World War II, and died of senility in the 1980s. An out-of-control nationalism, not communism, was the true menace to world civilization in the twentieth century, Lukacs insists. Recent events seem to support his thesis.

❖ THE UNITED NATIONS AND NATIONAL SOVEREIGNTY

One of the touchiest of all political topics in the 1990s is the degree to which national sovereignty must be surrendered to a supranational organization in order to preserve peace. The *United Nations Organization (UN)* was founded in 1945 by the victorious Allies to do what its predecessor, the League of Nations, was unable to do: guarantee international peace.

Unlike the League, the UN has a potentially very powerful executive organ in the Security Council. Its permanent members are the Big Five powers of the post-World War II era: the United States, Russia, Britain, France, and China (after 1972, the People's Republic of China). The Security Council has wide authority, including the power to take air, sea, and land military action against aggression. But any of the permanent members can veto any such initiative.

The UN *General Assembly* has no such powers and can only debate and recommend to the Security Council. All states of the world have an equal vote in the Assembly, which in effect means that the developing countries have a very large voice in the UN's nonmilitary aspects, such as labor, cultural affairs, and public health through the International Labor Organization (ILO), the United Nations Educational, Scientific, and Cultural Organization (UNESCO), and the World Health Organization (WHO), respectively. These organs have played an important and positive role in world affairs for the last fifty years, even while the political and military performances of the UN were disappointing to many sympathetic observers.

The reason for their disappointment was that ultimate powers were retained by the sovereign states and not by the UN Secretariat (executive office). When a major state saw that its interests were being threatened by UN intervention of some type, it either exercised its veto in the Security Council or ensured by other means that there would be no effective interference. Throughout the Cold War era, the UN was able to intervene effectively only on the very few occasions when both blocs could agree that a given conflict was intolerably dangerous (namely, the Israeli-Arab contest) or when one side chose to boycott the proceedings (namely, the UN decision to defend South Korea in the 1950s). The smaller powers, on the other

■ **The United Nations in Plenary Session.** This photo shows a cross-section of the General Assembly as it met in 1995. The African, Asian, and Latin American representatives far outnumber the Western ones but are still not able to implement policy reforms when such reforms are opposed by the traditionally powerful nations.

hand, were frequently forced to conform to Security Council resolutions aimed at controlling their political and military inclinations and initiatives. Thus, the UN's *guardianship of the peace* was *applied on two levels,* one for the powerful, and another for the less so.

In the most recent times, the relative collaboration between the United States and Russia in international affairs has given the UN an unprecedented freedom of action in maintaining peace and redressing injustice that might lead to war. The successful coalition against Iraq in 1991 was an outstanding example of what can be done. Perhaps this type of vigorous action in the name of the UN will become more common now that there is truly only one superpower and Cold War maneuvering has ended. But it is equally possible that the anti-Iraq coalition was an exceptional response to a clear-cut case of regional aggression, which disturbed even nations that might otherwise have been inclined to support the acts of fellow Muslims. Instead, the frustrations and failure that have marked the attempted intervention in the Yugoslav civil wars may be the rule.

The entire question of political sovereignty promises to be extremely thorny for the coming generation. Most of the nation-states created from the old colonies since World War II are by no means inclined to give up their newly won sovereignty to a supranational organization. On the other side, none of the great powers, led by Russia and the United States, are willing to be "told what to do" by an organization whose decisions will be strongly influenced, if not controlled, by a pack of little nations, especially when most of those smaller nations are alien in race and culture and sometimes have a large list of complaints and animosities against the ex-colonial powers.

❧ CONTROL OF NUCLEAR WEAPONS

Another pressing problem awaiting solution is the proliferation of nuclear weaponry. So long as only the United States, the Soviet Union, Britain, and France had atomic weapons, the "deadly secret" of creating them could be contained. But in the late 1960s, the Chinese under Mao went ahead with their own research effort, and by the mid-1970s, they had cracked the atomic code. The Israelis and South Africans were next, followed closely by the Indians and Pakistanis. Currently, the U.S. Central Intelligence Agency estimates that at least twelve nations have sophisticated, lethal atomic weapons, and that another fifteen are nearing the end of their quest. The mushroom cloud is spreading over wider territories and can be set off by more and more hands. Many think that it is just a matter of time before some terrorist band or desperate government attempts atomic blackmail.

❧ ENVIRONMENTAL DETERIORATION

We have all heard so much about the threats to the continued survival of the human race that we may be tempted to throw up our hands and trust to good luck or hope that another habitable planet is found before this one becomes unlivable. Nevertheless, certain environmental dangers are both real and can be addressed effectively, if only we have the will to do so. The most urgent near-term problems facing us in the 1990s seem to be the following:

- *Excessive and unbalanced consumption of nonrenewable energy.* Each year the average U.S. citizen consumes roughly thirty-five times as much energy (fossil fuel, water, electric) as a person in India and about three times as much as an individual in Italy or France. The tremendous difference between the developed North and the underdeveloped South in global affairs is nowhere more apparent than in energy consumption. The less-developed countries consume only 12 percent of the energy produced in the world; the rest is consumed by the developed countries. And if per capita use remains the same in 2030 as it is today, the world will need to produce 50 percent more energy just to keep pace with population growth.

- *Food production in Africa.* Due to sharply rising populations and the systematic use of marginal land for agriculture, African food supplies have been actually declining in large areas of the continent. Several countries, including Somalia, Sudan, Chad, and Tanzania, are now permanently dependent on imported food and have become beggars in the world economy.

- *Reduction of the tropical forest belt.* Some of the rainforest countries around the equator (Malaysia, Brazil, Indonesia) are attempting to check the generation-long decimation of this vital resource, but their efforts are belated and are pushed only halfheartedly by governments that are often in league with the timber companies and need the foreign exchange timber brings. It has only recently been recognized that the tropical forests, as the purifiers of the polluted atmosphere and the stabilizers of world climate, are absolutely vital to the whole world.

- *Pollution and radioactive wastes.* Many developing countries are almost entirely ignorant of or disregard the most elementary pollution control measures. Their

■ **Industrial Pollution, Novokuznetsk, Russia.** The former communist states were among the worst offenders in creating intolerably bad pollution of the air and waters. It has been estimated that it will take thirty years of clean-up work to remedy the damage done in East Europe.

industries and mines—frequently controlled by owners in the developed countries—poison the earth, air, and water on a large scale. The meltdown at the Chernobyl nuclear plant in Ukraine a few years ago was the most spectacular example of the dangers posed by inadequate or nonexistent policing and protection. Many others might be cited. These potential catastrophes have no respect whatever for national borders, and the long-term, slow effects of pollution may be worse than the occasional explosive event like Chernobyl.

This list is by no means comprehensive and deals only with what the author of this book believes to be the problems with the most immediate international repercussions. Many other complications arise from the disturbance of nature by conscious human actions such as pollution of the sea by leaking tankers and dumping of garbage, overuse of underground water reserves for agricultural irrigation, and the extinction of thousands of plant and animal species. During the life spans of students reading these lines, the developed world (the United States foremost) will either master the most urgent of these problems or substantially change the hitherto known environment of human beings from a life with nature to a *life against or outside nature.* Whether this latter style of life is possible and at the same time "humane" is an open question.

✣ Choices

We earthlings live on a small planet, which is only a minor part of a nine-planet solar system, which is itself one of hundreds, perhaps, within a still expanding cosmos. We will soon either succeed (temporarily) or fail (perma-

nently) in our attempt to keep the earth livable for creatures like ourselves. It is now quite possible for humans to damage their habitat so drastically that it will no longer be a fit place for the species. What will be done in these regards in the next decades is largely up to people like yourselves, the educated men and women of a powerful country.

At bottom, there are only two rational approaches to the solution of basic environmental problems: *conservation, which is the attempt to retain (conserve) existing systems, and technology, which is the attempt to discover superior replacements.* The conservationists argue that the earth's natural systems are the results of eons of slow

■ **Atomic Rockets Being Dismantled in Russia.** One of the chief benefits of the ending of the Soviet-US Cold War was the beginning of meaningful disarmament in the two countries. Pictured here are medium-range Soviet missiles, capable of carrying nuclear warheads, being prepared for destruction in 1993.

evolution; that of all earthly beings, humans alone rebel against those systems rather than live with them; and that this rebellion, though it may be successful in the short run, spells ruin in the longer. The technicians argue that evolution is only one path to an acceptable, sustainable system and that humans can and must try to find other paths when the natural one proves inadequate or has been blocked. The choices that must be made between these differing approaches will largely determine the quality and character of your lives.

Indeed, choices of every kind lie before you, as they have before all of your predecessors. Like them, you will often not be sure of what must be or should be done. Like them, you will have to seek guidance from many sources: religion, science, parents, and the study of history. The answers from history especially will often be unclear or cryptic; they may have sections missing or lend themselves to more than one interpretation. But it is the historical answer that will usually be most applicable and most comprehensive: this is what humans, in all their variety, have done successfully to meet and overcome problems somewhat like those you currently encounter. And like all your predecessors on this earth, you will have to hope that you have understood correctly and have taken a constructive, viable path as you join the long parade of men and women, moving forward into the infinite future.

Bibliography

Brown, L., ed. *Reports by the Worldwatch Institute.* This publisher has issued an annual report on the state of the environment since the 1970s; they are accepted as the most reliable and insightful of their kind.

Clark, A. *Profiles of the Future: An Inquiry into the Limits of the Possible,* 1984. By the renowned sci-fi author.

Lorraine, J. *Global Signposts to the 21st Century,* 1979. A very interesting discussion of what one man sees as the coming age's characteristics.

Lukacs, J. *The End of the Twentieth Century and the End of the Modern Age,* 1993. A stimulating, opinionated, sometimes maddening discussion of the challenges facing the West after the demise of communism. A different focus rules in the various works of A. and H. Toffler, who have led in the creation of a new intellectual discipline—futurism. See, for example, their *Previews and Premises,* 1984.

Kennedy, P. *Preparing for the Twenty-first Century,* 1993. Focusses on economic challenges and the changing structure of American population.

Meadows, D. L., and D. H. Meadows. *The Limits of Growth,* 1974. Argues that the globe has become overburdened and that the supply of natural resources has become dangerously low.

Moorcroft, S., ed. *Visions for the Twenty First Century,* 1993. An anthology of short, very wideranging topical essays, written by experts or interested amateurs in their fields.

Schell, J. *The Fate of the Earth,* 1982, and P. Harrison, *Inside the Third World,* 1986, are very illuminating surveys that warn without sensationalizing the plight of the two-thirds of humanity who live in the underdeveloped countries. See also A. B. Mountjoy, ed., *Third World: Problems and Perspectives,* 1978. Particularly good for a statement of the non-Western viewpoint that time has validated is M. ul-Haq, *The Poverty Curtain: Choices for the Third World,* 1976.

Wager, W.W. *The Next Three Futures: Paradigms of Things to Come,* 1991. A wellknown academic futurist provides scenarios of what is successively awaiting us in the twenty-first century World Commission on Environment and Development. *Our Common Future.* 1987.

GLOSSARY

A

Abbasid dynasty The caliphs resident in Baghdad from the 700s until 1252 C.E.

Abbot/abbess The male/female head of a monastery/nunnery.

Abstractionism A twentieth-century school of painting that rejects traditional representation of external nature and objects.

Act of Supremacy of 1534 A law enacted by the English Parliament making the monarch the head of the Church of England.

Age of the Barracks Emperors The period of the Roman Empire in the third century C.E. when the throne was repeatedly usurped by military men.

Agricultural revolution The substitution of farming for hunting/gathering as the primary source of food by a given people.

Ain Jalut A decisive thirteenth century battle in which the Egyptians turned back the Mongols and prevented them from invading North Africa.

Ajanta Caves Caves in central India that are the site of marvelous early frescoes.

Alienation The quality of feeling oneself isolated or misunderstood.

Alliance for Progress The proposal by President John F. Kennedy in 1961 for large-scale economic assistance to Latin America.

Alliance of 1778 A diplomatic treaty under which France aided the American revolutionaries in their war against Britain.

Anabaptists Radical Protestant reformers who were condemned by both Lutherans and Catholics.

Anarchism A political theory that sees all large-scale government as inherently evil and embraces small self-governing communities.

Anghor Wat A great Buddhist temple in the jungle of Cambodia, dating to the twelfth century C.E. Khmer empire.

Angola-to-Brazil trade A major portion of the trans-Atlantic slave trade.

Animism A religious belief imputing spirits to natural forces and objects.

Anschluss The German term for the takeover of Austria by Nazi Germany.

Anthropology The study of humankind as a particular species.

Apartheid The Dutch term for segregation of the races in South Africa.

"Appeasement" The policy of trying to avoid war by giving Hitler what he demanded in the the 1930s; supported by many in France and Britain.

Archaeology The study of cultures through the examination of artifacts.

Ark of the Covenant The wooden container of the two tablets given to Moses by Yahweh on Mount Sinai (the Ten Commandments); the Jews' most sacred shrine, signifying the contract between God and the Chosen.

Aryans A nomadic pastoral people from central Asia who invaded the Indus valley in c. 1500 B.C.E.

Assurbanipal An Assyrian king of the seventh century B.C.E.

Audiencia The colonial council that supervised military and civil government in Latin America.

August 1991 coup The attempt by hard-line communists to oust Gorbachev and reinstate the Communist Party's monopoly on power in the Soviet Union.

Ausgleich of 1867 The compromise between the Austro-Germans and Magyars that created the "Dual Monarchy" of Austria-Hungary.

Avesta The holy book of the Zoroastrian religion.

Axis pact The treaty establishing a military alliance between the governments of Hitler and Mussolini; signed in 1936.

Axum The center of the ancient Ethiopian kingdom.

B

Babylonian Captivity The transportation of many Jews to exile in Babylon as hostages for the good behavior of the remainder; occurred in the sixth century B.C.E.

Babylonian Captivity of the papacy The period from 1305 to 1378 when the pope was located in the city of Avignon and was under French royal influence.

Bakufu The government of the Japanese shogun.

Banana Republics A dismissive term referring to small Latin American states.

Bantu A language spoken by many peoples of central and eastern Africa.

Barbarian Greek for "noncomprehensible speaker"; uncivilized.

Bedouin The original Arab converts to Islam.

Behaviorism A school of psychology that holds that observation of what humans do is the key to understanding them.

Berbers Pre-Arab settlers of northern Africa and the Sahara.

Bhagavad-gita The best-known part of the *Mahabharata*.

Bill of Rights of 1689 A law enacted by Parliament that established certain limits of royal powers and the specific rights of English citizens.

Black Death An epidemic of bubonic plague that ravaged most of Europe in the mid-fourteenth century.

Boer War/Boers The armed conflict 1899–1902 between the Boers (the Dutch colonists who had been the initial European settlers of South Africa) and their British overlords; won by the British after a hard fight.

Bolsheviks The minority of Russian Marxists led by Lenin who seized dictatorial power in the October revolution of 1917.

Boule The 500-member council that served as a legislature in ancient Athens.

Bourgeoisie The urban upper middle class; usually commercial or professional.

Boxer Rebellion A desperate revolt by superstitious peasants against the European "foreign devils" who were carving up China in the New Imperialism of the 1890s; quickly suppressed.

Bread and circuses The social policy initiated by Augustus Caesar aimed at gaining the support of the Roman proletariat.

Brest-Litovsk Treaty of 1918 The separate peace between the Central Powers and Lenin's government in Russia.

Brezhnev Doctrine The policy proclaimed by Soviet leader Brezhnev after the Czechoslovak effort to install a reform communist government in 1968; aimed at ensuring the retention of Soviet-friendly governments within the "socialist camp."

Bronze Age The period when bronze tools and weapons replaced stone among a given people; generally about 3000–1000 B.C.E.

Brumaire (November 1799) The coup d'état by which Napoleon took power in France.

Burning of the books China's first emperor attempted to eliminate Confucian ethic by destroying the Confucian writings and prohibiting its teaching.

Bushido The code of honor among the samurai.

C

Caliph Arabic for "successor" (to Muhammed); leader of Islam.

Cape-to-Cairo project Cecil Rhodes's plan to build a transcontinental African railway under British control.

Caste A socioeconomic group that is entered by birth.

Caudillo A chieftain, i.e., a local or regional strongman, in Latin America.

Censors Officials with great powers of surveillance during the Roman Republic.

Chaeronea The battle in 338 B.C.E. when Philip of Macedon decisively defeated the Greeks and brought them under Macedonian rule.

Chartists A British working class movement of the 1840s that attempted to obtain labor and political reform.

Cheka An abbreviation for the first Soviet secret police.

Civilization A complex, developed culture.

Cold War The ideological and diplomatic conflict between the United States and the Soviet Union that lasted from 1946 until 1991.

Collective Security The guiding policy of the democratic powers during the interwar years until its abandonment in 1936.

Columbian Exchange The interchange of techniques and goods between Europeans and non-Europeans following the sixteenth-century voyages of discovery.

Comintern Abbreviation for the international network of communist parties and agents under Soviet control from 1919 to 1943.

Committee of Public Safety The executive body during the Reign of Terror during the French Revolution.

Commonwealth of Independent States (CIS) The much looser confederation of eleven of the fifteen former Soviet republics that was formed after the breakup of the Soviet Union in 1991.

Conciliar movement The attempt to substitute councils of church leaders for papal authority in late medieval christianity.

Constitution of 1889 Japan's first modern constitution; written by politically conservative, economically progressive daimyo.

Consuls Chief executives of the Roman Republic; chosen annually.

Corpus Juris "Body of the law"; the final Roman law code, produced under the emperor Justinian in the mid-500s C.E.

Council of Nicaea A fourth-century conclave that defined essential doctrines of Christianity under the supervision of the emperor Constantine.

Council of Trent The council of Catholic clergy that directed the Counter-Reformation against Protestantism; met intermittently from 1545 until 1563.

Creationism A cosmology based on Christian tradition that holds that the universe was created by an intelligent Supreme Being.

Crimean War Conflict fought in the Crimea between Russia and Britain, France, and Turkey from 1853 to 1856; ended by the Peace of Paris with a severe loss in Russian prestige.

Criollo Creole; term used to refer to whites born in Latin America.

Cuban Revolution Led by Fidel Castro, guerrillas fought against the corrupt Havana government until they were victorious in 1959 and then proceeded to apply Marxist principles and methods for transforming their underdeveloped society.

Culture The human-created environment.

Cuneiform Mesopotamian wedge-shaped writing begun by the Sumerians.

Cynicism A Hellenistic philosophy stressing poverty and simplicity.

Cyrus the Great The founder of the Persian empire in the 500s B.C.E.

Czechoslovakian intervention Occurred in August 1968 when Soviet armed forces chased out a reform communist government in Czechoslovakia.

D

Dada A brief art movement in the early twentieth century that repudiated all obligations to communicate intelligibly to the public.

Daimyo Japanese nobles who controlled feudal domains under the shogun.

Dao de Jing (Book of Changes) Daoism's major scripture; attributed to Lao Zi.

Daoism (Taoism) A nature-oriented philosophy/religion.

Dawes Plan A plan for a dollar loan and refinancing of post World War I reparation payments which enabled recovery of the German economy.

Deductive reasoning Arriving at truth by applying a general law or proposition to a specific case.

Delian League An empire of satellite *polei* under Athens in the fifth century B.C.E.

Deme The basic political subdivision of the Athenian *polis*.

Demesne The arable land on a manor that belonged directly to the lord.

Dependency In the context of national development, the necessity to reckon with other states' powers and pressures in the domestic economy and foreign trade.

Descamisados "Shirtless ones"; the poor working classes in Argentina.

Detente Relaxation; the term used for the toning down of diplomatic tensions between nations, specifically, the Cold War between the United States and the Soviet Union.

Dharma A code of morals prescribed for one's caste in Hinduism.

Dhimmi "People of the Book": Christians, Jews, and Zoroastrians living under Muslim rule and receiving privileged treatment over other non-Muslims.

Diaspora The scattering of the Jews from ancient Palestine.

Diffusion theory The spread of technology through human contacts.

Directory The executive organ that governed France from 1795 to 1799 after the overthrow of the Jacobins.

Divine right theory The idea that the legitimate holder of the Crown was designated by divine will to govern; personified by King Louis XIV of France in the seventeenth century.

Diwan A council of Islamic government ministers in Istanbul during the Ottoman Empire.

Dorians Legendary barbaric invaders of Mycenaean Greece in c. 1200 B.C.E.

Dream of the Red Chamber The best known of the eighteenth-century Chinese novels.

E

East India Company A commercial company founded with government backing to trade with the East and Southeast Asians. The Dutch, English, and French governments sponsored such companies starting in the early seventeenth century.

Economic Nationalism A movement to assert national sovereignty in economic affairs, particularly by establishing freedom from the importation of foreign goods and technology on unfavorable terms.

Edict of Milan A decree issued by the emperor Constantine in 313 C.E. that legalized Christianity and made it the favored religion in the Roman Empire.

Edict of Nantes A law granting limited toleration to French Calvinists that was issued in 1598 by King Henry IV to end the religious civil war.

Eightfold Path The Buddha's teachings on attaining perfection.

Ekklesia The general assembly of citizens in ancient Athens.

Emir A provincial official with military duties in Muslim government.

Empirical data Facts derived from observation of the external world.

Enclosure movement An eighteenth-century innovation in British agriculture by which formerly communal lands were enclosed by private landlords.

Encomienda The right to organize unpaid native labor by the earliest Spanish colonists in Latin America; revoked in 1565.

Encyclopedie, The The first encyclopedia; produced in mid-eighteenth-century France by the philosophe Diderot.

Entente The understanding between Britain and France in 1904 that each would come to the other's aid if attacked; joined by Russia in 1907.

Epicureanism A Hellenistic philosophy advocating the pursuit of pleasure (mental) and avoidance of pain as the supreme good.

Equal field system Agricultural reform favoring the peasants under the Tang dynasty in China.

Equity Fairness to contending parties.

Era of Warring States The period of Chinese history between c. 500 and 220 B.C.E.; characterized by the breakdown of the central government and feudal war.

Era of Stagnation The era of Brezhnev's government in the Soviet Union (1964–1982), when the Soviet society and economy faced increasing troubles.

Essay concerning Human Understanding An important philosophical essay by John Locke that underpinned Enlightenment optimism.

Estates General The parliament of France; composed of delegates from three social orders: clergy, nobility, and commoners.

Ethnic, Ethnicity The racial or linguistic affiliation of an individual or group of human beings.

European Economic Community An association of West European nations founded in 1957; now called the European

Union, it embraces fifteen countries with several more in candidate status.

Excommunication The act of being barred from the Roman Catholic community by decree of a bishop or the pope.

Existentialism Twentieth-century philosophy that was popular after World War II in Europe; insists on the necessity to inject life with meaning.

Exodus The Hebrews' flight from the wrath of the Egyptian pharaoh in c. 1250 B.C.E.

Extended family Parents and children plus several other kin group members.

F

Factory Acts Laws passed by Parliament in 1819 and 1833 that regulated hours and working conditions in Britain.

Factory system Massing of labor and material under one roof with a single proprietorship and management of production.

Fallow Land left uncultivated for a period to recover fertility.

Fascism A political movement in the twentieth century that embraced totalitarian government to achieve a unity of people and leader; first experienced in Mussolini's Italy.

Fathers of the Church Leading theologians and explainers of Christian doctrine in the fourth and early fifth centuries.

Fertile Crescent A belt of civilized settlements reaching from lower Mesopotamia across Syria, Lebanon, and Israel and into Egypt.

Feudal system A mode of government based originally on mutual military obligations between lord and vassal; later often extended to civil affairs of all types; generally supported by landowning privileges.

First Emperor (Shi Huangdi) The founder of the short-lived Qin dynasty and creator of China as an imperial state.

Five Year Plan First introduced in 1929 at Stalin's command to collectivize agriculture and industrialize the economy.

Floating world A term for ordinary human affairs popularized by the novels and stories of eighteenth-century Japan.

Forbidden City The center of Ming and Qing government in Beijing; entry was forbidden to ordinary citizens.

Four Noble Truths The Buddha's doctrine on human fate.

Fourteen Points The outline for a just peace proposed by Woodrow Wilson in 1918.

Frankfurt Assembly A German parliament held in 1848 that was unsuccessful in working out a liberal constitution for a united German state.

G

General theory of relativity Einstein's theory that introduced the modern era of physics in 1916.

Gentiles All non-Jews.

Ghana The earliest of the extensive empires in the western Sudan.

Glasnost The Russian term for "openness"; along with *perestroika,* employed to describe the reforms instituted by Gorbachev in the late 1980s.

Golden Horde The Russia-based segment of the Mongol world empire.

Gothic style An artistic style, found mainly in architecture, that came into general European usage during the thirteenth century.

Great Elector Frederick William of Prussia (1640–1688); one of the princes who elected the Holy Roman Emperor.

Great Leap Forward Mao Zedong's misguided attempt in 1958–1960 to provide China with an instantaneous industrial base rivaling that of more advanced nations.

Great Proletarian Cultural Revolution The period from 1966 to 1976 when Mao inspired Chinese youth to rebel against all authority except his own; caused great damage to the Chinese economy and culture.

Great Purge The arrest and banishment of millions of Soviet Communist Party members and ordinary citizens at Stalin's orders in the mid-1930s for fictitious "crimes against the State and Party."

Great Reform Bill of 1832 Brought about a reform of British parliamentary voting and representation that strengthened the middle class and the urbanites.

Great Reforms (Russia) Decrees affecting several areas of life issued by Tsar Alexander II between 1859 and 1874.

Great Schism A division in the Roman Catholic church between 1378 and 1417 when two (and for a brief period, three) popes competed for the allegiance of European Christians; a consequence of the Babylonian Captivity of the papacy.

Great Trek The march of the Boers into the interior of South Africa where they founded the Orange Free State in 1836.

Great Zimbabwe The leading civilization of early southern Africa.

Grossdeutsch versus **Kleindeutsch** The controversy over the scope and type of the unified German state in the nineteenth century; *Kleindeutsch* would exclude multinational Austria, and *Grossdeutsch* would include it.

Guild A medieval urban organization that controlled the production and sale prices of many goods and services.

Gupta dynasty The rulers of most of India in the 300–400s C.E.; the last native dynasty to unify the country.

H

Habsburg dynasty The family that controlled the Holy Roman Empire after the thirteenth century; based in Vienna, they ruled Austria until 1918.

Hacienda A Spanish-owned plantation in Latin America that used native or slave labor to produce export crops.

Haiku A type of Japanese poetry always three lines in length.

Hajj The pilgrimage to the sacred places of Islam.

Han dynasty The dynasty that ruled China from c. 200 B.C.E. to 221 C.E.

Hanoverians The dynasty of British monarchs after 1714; from the German duchy of Hanover.

Hare Krishna A Hindu sect popularized in the eighteenth century.

Hegira "Flight"; Muhammed's forced flight from Mecca in 622 C.E.; marks the first year of the Muslim calendar.

Hellenistic A blend of Greek and Asiatic cultures; extant in the Mediterranean basin and Middle East between 300 B.C.E. and c. 200 C.E.

Helots Messenian semislaves of Spartan overlords.

Hetairai High-class female entertainer-prostitutes in ancient Greece.

Hinayana Buddhism A stricter monastic form of Buddhism.

Hohenzollerns The dynasty that ruled Prussia-Germany until 1918.

Hominid A humanlike creature.

Homo sapiens "Thinking man"; modern human beings.

Horus The falcon-headed god whose earthly, visible form was the reigning pharaoh in ancient Egypt.

Hubris An unjustified confidence in one's abilities or powers.

Huguenots A term for French speaking Calvinists.

Hungarian Revolution The Hungarians' attempt to free themselves from Soviet control in October 1956; crushed by the Soviets.

Hyksos A people who invaded the Nile delta in Egypt and ruled it during the Second Intermediate Period (c. 1650–1570 B.C.E.).

I

Ideographs Written signs conveying entire ideas and not related to the spoken language; used by the Chinese from earliest times.

Inductive reasoning Arriving at truth by reasoning from specific cases to a general law or proposition.

Infamia Roman term for immoral but not illegal acts.

Infanticide The killing of children soon after birth by their parents.

Institutes of the Christian Religion John Calvin's major work that established the theology and doctrine of the Calvinist churches; first published 1536.

Investiture Controversy A dispute between the Holy Roman Emperor and the pope in the eleventh and early twelfth centuries about which authority should appoint German bishops.

Iranian Revolution The fundamentalist and anti-Western movement led by the Ayatollah Khomeini that seized power from the shah of Iran through massive demonstrations in 1979.

J

Jacobins Radical revolutionaries during the French Revolution; organized in clubs headquartered in Paris.

Jacquerie A French peasant rebellion against noble landlords during the fourteenth century.

Janissaries From *yeni cheri* meaning "new troops"; an elite troop in the Ottoman army who gained much political power in the seventeenth and eighteenth centuries; created originally from Christian boys from the Balkans.

Jesuits Members of the Society of Jesus, a Catholic religious order founded in 1547 to combat Protestantism.

Jewish War A rebellion of Jewish Zealots against Rome in 66–70 C.E.

Jihad Holy war on behalf of the Muslim faith.

Joint-stock companies/corporations The dominant form of industrial and financial organization in the twentieth century.

Judea One of the two Jewish kingdoms emerging after the death of Solomon when his kingdom was split in two; the other kingdom was Samaria.

July Monarchy The reign of King Louis Philippe in France (1830–1848).

Junkers The landowning nobility of Prussia.

Jus gentium "Law of peoples"; Roman law governing relations between Romans and others.

K

Ka The immortal soul in the religion of ancient Egypt.

Kabuki A type of popular Japanese drama.

Kadi An Islamic judge.

Kami Shinto spirits in nature.

Karma The balance of good and evil done in a given incarnation in Hinduism.

Karnak The site of a great temple complex along the Nile River in Egypt.

Kashmir A province in northwestern India that Pakistan also claims.

Kellogg-Briand Pact A formal disavowal of war by sixty nations in 1928.

KGB An abbreviation for the Soviet secret police; used after Cheka and NKVD.

Khmers The inhabitants of Cambodia; founders of a large empire in Southeast Asia.

Kiev, Principality of The first Russian state; flourished from c. 800 to 1240 when it fell to Mongols.

King of Kings The title of the Persian emperor.

L

Latifundia Huge agrarian estates in the Roman Empire and later.

Late Manzhou Restoration An attempt by Chinese reformers in the 1870s to restore the power of the central government after the suppression of the Taiping rebellion.

League of Nations An international organization founded after World War I to maintain peace and promote amity among nations; the United States did not join.

Left The reforming or revolutionary wing of the political spectrum; associated originally with the ideals of the French Revolution.

Legalism A Chinese philosophy of government emphasizing strong authority.

Legislative Assembly The second law-making body created during the French Revolution; dominated by the Jacobins.

Legitimacy A term adopted by the victors at the Congress of Vienna in 1815 to explain the reimposition of former monarchs and regimes after the Napleonic wars.

Levee en masse General conscription for the army; first occurred during the French Revolution.

Leviathan A book by Thomas Hobbes that supported the necessity of the state and, by inference, royal absolutism.

Liberum veto Latin for "free veto"; used by Polish nobles to nullify majority will in the Polish parliament.

Little Red Book Contained the thoughts of Chairman Mao Zedong on various topics; used as a talisman during the Cultural Revolution by young Chinese.

Locarno Treaty An agreement between France and Germany in 1925.

Long March The 6,000-mile fighting retreat of the Chinese communists under Mao Zedong to Shensi province in 1934–1935.

Lyric poetry Poetry that celebrates the emotions of the poet.

M

Maastricht Treaty Signed in 1991 by members of the European Community; committed them to closer political-economic ties.

Maghrib or **Maghreb** Muslim northwest Africa.

Mahabharata A Hindu epic poem; a favorite in India.

Mahayana Buddhism A more liberal, looser form of Buddhism.

Mahdi A Muslim leader who organized a serious rebellion against European rule in the Sudan in the 1890s.

Mali The African empire that was the successor to Ghana in the 1300s and 1400s.

Manchester liberalism The economic practice of exploiting the laboring poor.

Mandarins Chinese scholar-officials who had been trained in Confucian principles and possessed great class solidarity.

Mandate Britain and France governed several Asian and African peoples after World War I, supposedly as agents of the League of Nations.

Mandate of heaven A theory of rule originated by the Zhou dynasty in China.

Manichaeism A Zoroastrian cult that emphasized the evil of all fleshly things; later became a major Christian heresy.

Manor An agricultural estate of varying size normally owned by a noble and worked by free and unfree peasants/serfs.

Manzhou Originally nomadic tribes living in Manchuria who eventually overcame Ming resistance and established the Qing dynasty in seventeenth century China.

Marathon The battle in 490 B.C.E. in which the Greeks defeated the Persians, ending the first Persian War.

March on Rome A Fascist demonstration in 1922 orchestrated by Mussolini as a preliminary step to dictatorship in Italy.

March revolution of 1917 The abdication of Tsar Nicholas II and the establishment of the Provisional Government in Russia.

Maritime Expeditions, (China's) Early fifteenth-century explorations of the Indian and South Pacific Oceans ordered by the Chinese emperor.

Marshall Plan A program proposed by the U.S. secretary of state George Marshall and implemented from 1947 to 1951 to aid western Europe's recovery from World War II.

Masscult The banal culture that some think replaced the elite culture in the twentieth century.

Matriarchy A society in which females are dominant socially and politically.

Maya The most advanced of the Amerindian peoples who lived in cities located in southern Mexico and Guatemala.

Medes An early Indo-European people who, with the Persians, settled in Iran.

Meiji Restoration The overthrow of the Tokugawa shogunate and restoration of the emperor to nominal power in Japan in 1867.

Mercantilism A theory of national economics popular in the seventeenth and eighteenth centuries. It aimed at establishing a favorable trade balance through government control of exports and imports as well as domestic industry.

Meritocracy The rule of the Meritorious (usually determined by examinations).

Messenian Wars Conflicts between the neighbors Sparta and Messenia that resulted in Messenia's conquest by Sparta in c. 600 B.C.E.

Messiah A savior-king who would someday lead the Jews to glory.

Mestizo A person of mixed Amerindian and European blood.

Mexican Revolution The armed struggle that occurred in Mexico between 1910 and 1920 to install a more socially progressive and populist government.

Middle Kingdom The period in Egyptian history from 2100 to 1600 B.C.E.; followed the First Intermediate Period.

Milan, Edict of A decree issued by the emperor Constantine in 313 C.E. that legalized Christianity and made it the favored religion in the Roman Empire.

Minoan An ancient civilization that was centered on Crete between c. 2000 and c. 1400 B.C.E.

Misogyny The fear and hatred of women by men.

Missi dominici Agents of Charlemagne in the provinces of his empire.

Modernism A philosophy of art of the late nineteenth and early twentieth centuries that rejected classical models and values and sought new expressions and aesthetics.

Moksha The final liberation from bodily existence and reincarnation in Hinduism.

Mongol yoke A Russian term for the Mongol occupation of Russia.

Monotheism A religion having only one god.

Mughal A corruption of "Mongol"; refers to the period of Muslim rule in India.

Mulatto A person of mixed African and European blood.

Municipia The basic unit of Roman local government; similar to a present municipality.

Muslim Brotherhoods Associations of Islamic groups that have strong fundamentalist leanings and practice mutual aid among members.

Mycenaea The most important town in the first Greek civilization; flourished c. 1500 B.C.E.

Mystery religion One of various eastern Hellenistic cults promising immortal salvation of the individual.

N

Nantes, Edict of A law granting toleration to French Calvinists that was issued in 1598 by King Henry IV to end the religious civil war.

Napoleonic settlement A collective name for the decrees and actions by Napoleon between 1800 and 1808 that legalized and systematized many elements of the French Revolution.

National Assembly The first law-making body during the French Revolution; created a moderate constitutional monarchy.

Navigation Acts Laws regulating commerce with the British colonies in North America in favor of Britain.

Nazism The German variant of Fascism created by Hitler.

Negritude A literary term referring to the self-conscious awareness of African cultural values; popular in areas of Africa formerly under French control.

Neo-Confucianism A revival of Confucian thought with special emphasis on love and responsibility toward others.

Neolithic Age The period from c. 7000 B.C.E. to the development of metals.

New China movement An intellectual reform movement in the 1890s that attempted to change and modernize China by modernizing the government.

New Economic Policy (NEP) A policy introduced at the conclusion of the civil war that allowed for partial capitalism and private enterprise in the Soviet Union.

New Imperialism The late nineteenth-century colonialism of European powers interested in strategic and economic advantage.

New Kingdom or **Empire** The period from c. 1550 to 700 B.C.E. in Egyptian history; followed the Second Intermediate Period. The period from 1550 to c. 1200 B.C.E. was the Empire.

Nicaea, Council of A fourth-century conclave that defined essential doctrines of Christianity under the supervision of the emperor Constantine.

Ninety-five Theses The challenge to church authority publicized by Martin Luther, October 31, 1517.

Nineveh The main city and capital of the Assyrian empire.

Nirvana The Buddhist equivalent of the Hindu *moksha*; the final liberation from suffering and reincarnation.

NKVD An abbreviation for the Soviet secret police; used after Cheka but before KGB.

Non-aggression Pact of 1939 The treaty between Hitler and Stalin in which each agreed to maintain neutrality in any forthcoming war involving the other party.

North American Free Trade Agreement (NAFTA) An agreement signed by the United States, Canada, and Mexico in 1993 that provides for much liberalized trade among these nations.

North Atlantic Treaty Organization (NATO) An organization founded in 1949 under U.S. aegis as a defense against threatened communist aggression in Europe; primarily a military association with some cultural affairs.

Nuclear family Composed of parents and children only.

Nuclear test ban The voluntary cessation of aboveground testing of nuclear weapons by the United States and the Soviet Union; in existence from 1963 to the present.

Nuremberg laws Laws defining racial identity that were aimed against Jews; adopted in 1935 by the German government.

O

Occupation of the Ruhr The 1923 attempt by the French government to pressure Germany to pay reparations on schedule; stimulated disastrous inflation.

October revolution of 1917 The Bolshevik coup d'état in St. Petersburg that ousted the Provisional Government and established a communist state in Russia.

Oil boycott of 1973 The temporary withholding of oil exports by OPEC members to Western governments friendly to Israel; led to a massive rise in the price of oil and economic dislocation in many countries.

Old Kingdom The period of Egyptian history from 3100 to 2200 B.C.E.

Old Testament The first portion of the Judeo-Christian Bible; the holy books of the Jews.

Olmec The earliest Amerindian civilization in Mexico.

Omdurman The battle in the Sudan where the Mahdists were defeated by Britain in 1898.

Opium Wars Conflicts that occurred in 1840–1842 on the Chinese coast between the British and the Chinese over the importation of opium into China. The Chinese defeat began eighty years of subordination to foreigners.

Organization for African Unity (OAU) The present name of the association of sub-Saharan African nations founded in 1963 for mutual aid.

Organization of American States (OAS) An organization founded in 1948 under U.S. auspices to provide mutual defense and aid; now embraces all countries on the American continents except Cuba.

Organization of Petroleum Exporting Countries (OPEC) An organization founded in the 1960s by Arab governments and later expanded to include several Latin American and African members.

Origin of Species, On the Charles Darwin's book that first enunciated the evolutionary theory in biology; published in 1859.

Ostpolitik German term for Chancellor Brandt's 1960s policy of pursuing normalized relations with West Germany's neighbors to the east.

Ostracism In ancient Greece, the expulsion of a citizen from a *polis* for a given period.

P

Paideia "Education and upbringing" in classical Greece.

Paleolithic Age The period from the earliest appearance of homo sapiens to c. 7000 B.C.E., though exact dates vary by area; the Old Stone Age.

Paleontology The study of prehistoric ancient things.

Palestine The traditional name for modern Israel.

Palestine Liberation Organization (PLO) An organization founded in the 1960s by Palestinian expellees from Israel; until 1994 aimed at destruction of the state of Israel by any means, but now is in uneasy partnership with the Israeli government to achieve a solution to Muslim-Jewish enmity.

Pan-Arabism A movement after World War I to assert supranational Arab unity, aimed eventually at securing a unified Arab state.

Pantheism A belief that God exists in all things, living and inanimate.

Pariah An outcaste; a person having no acknowledged status.

Paris Commune A leftist revolt against the national government after France was defeated by Prussia in 1871; crushed by the conservatives with much bloodshed.

Patents Royal documents conferring nobility.

Patria potestas The power of the father over his family in ancient Rome.

Patriarchy A society in which males have social and political dominance.

Patricians (*patres*) The upper class in ancient Rome.

Pax mongolica The Mongol peace; between c. 1250 and c. 1350.

Pax romana The Roman peace; the era of Roman control over the Mediterranean basin and much of Europe between c. 31 B.C.E. and 180 C.E. or later.

Peaceful Coexistence The declared policy of Soviet leader Khrushchev in dealing with the capitalist West after 1956.

Peloponnesian War The great civil war between Athens and Sparta and their respective allies in ancient Greece; fought between 429 and 404 B.C.E. and eventually won by Sparta.

Peon A peasant in semislave status on a *hacienda*.

Perestroika The Russian term for "restructuring," which, with *glasnost*, was used to describe the reforms instituted by Gorbachev in the late 1980s.

Persepolis With Ecbatana, one of the twin capitals of the Persian empire in the 500s B.C.E.

Persians An early Indo-European tribe that, along with the Medes, settled in Iran.

Petersburg Soviet The council of workers and soldiers under Bolshevik control that vied for power with the Russian Provisional Government in the summer and fall of 1917.

Petrine succession The doctrine of the Roman Catholic church by which the pope, the bishop of Rome, is the direct successor of St. Peter.

Philosophe A French term used to refer to the writers and activists during the Enlightenment.

Phonetic alphabet A system of writing that matches signs with the sounds of the oral language.

Plastic arts Those that have three dimensions.

Platea The land battle that, along with the naval battle of Salamis, ended the second Persian War with a Greek victory over the Persians.

Plebeians (*plebs*) The common people of ancient Rome.

Pogrom Mob violence against local Jews.

Polis The political and social community of ancient Greece.

Polytheism A religion having many gods.

Popular Front The coordinated policy of all anti-Fascist parties; inspired by the Soviets in the mid-1930s as a policy against Hitler.

Porte, The A name for the seat of Ottoman government in Istanbul.

Post-Impressionist A term for late nineteenth-century painting that emphasized color and line in revolutionary fashion.

Praetorian Guard The imperial bodyguard in the Roman Empire and the only armed force in Italy.

Precedent What has previously been accepted in law.

Pre-Socratics Greek philosophers prior to Socrates who focused on the nature of the material world.

Primogeniture A system of inheritance in which the estate passes to the eldest legitimate son.

Principate The reign of Augustus Caesar (the *princeps*) from 27 B.C.E. to 14 C.E.

Proconsuls Provincial governors and military commanders in ancient Rome.

Proletariat Poverty-stricken people without skills; also, a Marxist term for the propertyless working classes.

Provisional Government A self-appointed parliamentary group exercising power in republican Russia from March to October 1917.

Psychoanalysis A psychological technique that employs free associations in the attempt to determine the cause of mental illness.

Punic Wars The three conflicts between Rome and Carthage that ended with the complete destruction of the Carthaginian empire and the extension of Roman control throughout the western Mediterranean.

Purdah The segregation of females in Hindu society.

Purgatory In Catholic belief, the place where the soul is purged after death for past sins and thus becomes fit for Heaven.

Pyramid of Khufu (Cheops) The largest pyramid; stands outside Cairo.

Q

Qing dynasty The last Chinese dynasty, which ruled from 1644 until 1911; established by Manzhou invaders after they defeated the Ming rulers.

Quadruple Alliance The diplomatic pact to maintain the peace established by the Big Four victors of the Napoleonic wars (Austria, Britain, Prussia, and Russia); lasted for a decade.

Quanta A concept in physics indicating the expenditure of energy.

Quechua The spoken language of the Incas of Peru.

Qur'an The holy scripture of Islam.

R

Raison d'état The idea that the welfare of the state should be supreme in government policy.

Raja Turkish for "cattle"; used to refer to non-Muslims.

Red International See Third International.

Reign of Terror The period (1793–1794) of extreme Jacobin radicalism during the French Revolution.

Reparations Money and goods that Germany was to pay to the victorious Allies after World War I under the Versailles Treaty.

Rerum novarum An encyclical issued by Pope Leo XIII in 1890 that committed the Roman Catholic church to attempting to achieve social justice for the poor.

Revisionism The adaptation of Marxist socialism that aimed to introduce basic reform through parliamentary acts rather than through revolution.

Romanov dynasty Ruled Russia from 1613 until 1917.

S

Safavid The dynasty of Shi'ite Muslims that ruled Persia from the 1500s to the 1700s.

Sahel The arid belt extending across Africa south of the Sahara; also called the Sudan.

Sakoku Japan's self-imposed isolation from the outer world that lasted until 1854.

Salamis The naval battle that, with the battle of Platea, ended the second Persian War with a Greek victory.

Samaria One of the two kingdoms into which the Hebrew kingdom was split after Solomon's death; the other was Judea.

Samsara The reincarnation of the soul; a concept shared by Hinduism and Buddhism.

Samurai Japanese warrior-aristocrats of medieval and early modern times.

Sanhedrin The Jewish governing council under the overlordship of Rome.

Sanskrit The sacred language of India; came originally from the Aryans.

Sati The practice in which a widow committed suicide at the death of her husband in ancient India.

Satrapy A province under a governor or *satrap* in the ancient Persian empire.

Savanna The semiarid grasslands where most African civilizations developed.

Schutzstaffel (SS) Hitler's bodyguard; later enlarged to be a subsidiary army and to provide the concentration camp guards.

Second Front The reopening of a war front in the west against the Axis powers in World War II; eventually accomplished by the invasion of Normandy in June 1944.

Second Industrial Revolution The second phase of industrialization that occurred in the late 1800s after the introduction of electricity and the internal combustion engine.

Second International Association of socialist parties founded in 1889; after Russian Revolution 1917 the Second International split into democratic and communist segments.

Secularism The rejection of supernatural religion as the arbiter of earthly action; emphasis on worldly affairs.

Self-Strengthening The late nineteenth-century attempt by Chinese officials to bring China into the modern world by instituting reforms; failed to achieve its goal.

Seljuks Turkish converts to Islam who seized the Baghdad government from the Abbasids in the eleventh century.

Semitic languages A major family of Middle Eastern languages.

Serfdom Restriction of personal and economic freedoms associated with medieval European agricultural society.

Shang dynasty The first historical rulers of China; ruled from c. 1500 to c. 1100 B.C.E.

Sharija The sacred law of Islam; based on the Qur'an.

Shi'ite A minority sect of Islam; adherents believe that kinship with Muhammed is necessary to qualify for the caliphate.

Shiki Rights attached to parcels of land (*shoen*) in Japan.

Shinto Native Japanese animism.

Shoen Parcels of land in Japan with *shiki* (rights) attached to them; could take many forms and have various possessors.

Shogun The military and civil regent of Japan during the shogunate era.

Shogunate The government of medieval Japan in which the shogun served as the actual leader while the emperor was the symbolic head of the state.

Sino-Tibetan languages The family of languages spoken by the Chinese and Tibetan peoples.

Social Darwinism The adaptation of Darwinian biology to apply to human society in simplistic terms.

Social Democrats Noncommunist socialists who refused to join the Third International and founded independent parties.

Solidarity The umbrella organization founded by Lech Walesa and other anticommunist Poles in 1981 to recover Polish freedom; banned for eight years, but continued underground until it was acknowledged as the government in 1989.

Song dynasty The dynasty that ruled China from c. 1127 until 1279 when the last ruler was overthrown by the Mongol invaders.

Springtime of the Peoples The spring and summer of 1848 when popular revolutions in Europe seemed to succeed.

Stalingrad The battle in 1942 that marked the turning point of World War II in Europe.

Stalinist economy Involved the transformation of a retarded agrarian economy to an industrialized one through massive reallocation of human and material resources directed by a central plan; imposed on the Soviet Union and then, in the first years after World War II, on eastern Europe.

Stamp Act A law enacted by the British Parliament in 1765 that imposed a fee on legal documents of all types and on all books and newspapers sold in the American colonies.

Stoicism A Hellenistic philosophy that emphasized human brotherhood and natural law as guiding principles.

Structural Adjustment Programs (SAPs) Programs designed by the World Bank to achieve economic improvement on a national scale in developing countries.

Stuprum A Roman legal term denoting acts that were both immoral and illegal.

Sturmabteilung (SA) The street-fighting "bully boys" of the Nazi Party; suppressed after 1934 by Hitler's orders.

Sudan The arid belt extending across Africa south of the Sahara; also called the Sahel.

Sui dynasty Ruled China from c. 580 to c. 620 C.E.

Sumerians The creators of Mesopotamian urban civilization.

Sunni The majority group in Islam; adherents believe that the caliphate should go to the most qualified individual and should not necessarily pass to the kin of Muhammed.

Supremacy, Act of A law enacted in 1534 by the English Parliament that made the monarch the head of the Church of England.

Suzerain The superior of a vassal to whom the vassal owed feudal duties.

Swahili A hybrid language based on Bantu and Arabic; used extensively in East Africa.

Syndicalism A doctrine of government that advocates a society organized on the basis of syndicates or unions.

T

Taipings The followers of anti-Manzhou rebels in China in the 1860s.

Taj Mahal The beautiful tomb built by the seventeenth century Mughal emperor Jahan for his wife.

Tang dynasty Ruled China from c. 620 to c. 900 C.E.

Tel el Amarna The site of great temple complexes along the Nile River in Egypt.

Tenochtitlán The Aztec name of Mexico City.

Teotihuacan A large palace-city of Toltec origin in central Mexico.

Test Act Seventeenth century English law barring non-Anglican Church members from government and university positions.

Tetrarchy "Rule of four"; a system of government established by Diocletian at the end of the third century C.E. in an attempt to make the Roman Empire more governable; failed to achieve its goals and was not continued by Diocletian's successors.

Theocracy The rule of gods or their priests.

Theravada Buddhism A stricter, monastic form of Buddhism. Same as Hinayana Buddhism.

Thermidorean reaction The conservative reaction to the Reign of Terror during the French Revolution.

Third International An association of Marxist parties in many nations; inspired by Russian communists and headquartered in Moscow until its dissolution in 1943.

Third Republic of France The government of France after the exile of Emperor Napoleon III; lasted from 1871 until 1940.

Third Rome theory A Russian myth that Moscow was ordained to succeed Rome and Constantinople as the center of true Christianity.

Third World A term in use after World War II to denote countries and peoples in underdeveloped; formerly colonial areas of Asia, Africa, and Latin America; the First World was the West under U.S. leadership, and the Second World was the communist states under Soviet leadership.

Tianamen Square, massacre on The shooting down of thousands of Chinese who were peacefully demonstrating for relaxation of political censorship by the communist leaders; occurred in 1989 in Beijing.

Tilsit, Treaty of A treaty concluded in 1807 after the French had defeated the Russians; divided Europe/Asia into French and Russian spheres.

Time of Troubles A fifteen-year period at the beginning of the seventeenth century in Russia when the state was nearly destroyed by revolts and wars.

Titoism The policy of neutrality in foreign policy combined with continued dedication to socialism in domestic policy that was followed by the Yugoslav Marxist leader Tito after his expulsion from the Soviet camp in 1948.

Toltec An Amerindian civilization centered in the Valley of Mexico; succeeded by the Aztecs.

Torah The first five books of the Old Testament; the Jews' law code.

Tories A nickname for British nineteenth century conservatives.

Totalitarianism The attempt by a dictatorial government to achieve total control over a society's life and ideas.

Trent, Council of The council of Catholic clergy that directed the Counter-Reformation against Protestantism; met from 1545 until 1563.

Tribunes The chief officers and representatives of the plebeians during the Roman Republic.

Triple Alliance A pact concluded in 1882 that united Germany, Austria-Hungary, and Italy against possible attackers; the members were called the Central Powers.

Triumvirate "Three-man rule"; the First Triumvirate was during the 50s B.C.E. and the Second in the 30s B.C.E. during the last decades of the Roman Republic.

Twelve Tables The first written Roman law code; established c. 450 B.C.E.

U

Ulema A council of learned men who applied the *sharija* in Islam; also, a council of religious advisers to the caliph or sultan.

Ummayad dynasty The caliphs resident in Damascus from 661 to 750 C.E.

Uncertainty principle The theory in physics that denies absolute causal relationships of matter and, hence, predictability.

Upanishads The Hindu holy epics dealing with morals and philosophy.

Utopian socialism The label given by Marx to previous theories that aimed at establishing a more just and benevolent society.

V

Vakf An Islamic philanthropic foundation established by the devout.

Vassal In medieval Europe, a person, usually a noble, who owed feudal duties to a superior, called a suzerain.

Vedas The four oral epics of the Aryans.

Verdun, Treaty of A treaty concluded in 843 that divided Charlemagne's empire among his three grandsons; established what became the permanent dividing lines between the French and Germans.

Vernacular The native oral language of a given people.

Villa The country estate of a Roman patrician or other wealthy Roman.

Vizier An official of Muslim government, especially a high Turkish official equivalent to prime minister.

W

Wandering of Peoples A term referring to the migrations of various Germanic and Asiatic tribes in the third and fourth centuries C.E. that brought them into conflict with Rome.

Warsaw Pact An organization of the Soviet satellite states in Europe; founded under Russian aegis in 1954 to serve as a counterweight to NATO.

Wars of the Roses An English civil war between noble factions over the succession to the throne in the fifteenth century.

Wealth of Nations, The The short title of the pathbreaking work on national economy by Adam Smith; published in 1776.

Wehrgeld Under early Germanic law, a fine paid to an injured party or his or her family or lord that was equivalent to the value of the injured individual.

Weimar Republic The popular name for Germany's democratic government between 1919 and 1933.

Westphalia, Treaty of The treaty that ended the Thirty Years' War in 1648; the first modern peace treaty in that it established strategic and territorial gains as more important than religious or dynastic ones.

Whigs A nickname for British nineteenth century liberals.

"White man's burden" A phrase coined by Rudyard Kipling to refer to what he considered the necessity of bringing European civilization to non-Europeans.

World Bank A monetary institution founded after World War II by Western nations to assist in the recovery effort and to aid the Third World's economic development.

Y

Yalta The site of a conference in 1945 where Franklin D. Roosevelt, Josef Stalin, and Winston Churchill (the "Big Three") met to attempt to settle postwar questions, particularly those affecting the future of Europe.

Yamato state The earliest known government of Japan; divided into feudal subdivisions ruled by clans and headed by the Yamato family.

Yin/yang East Asian distinction between the male and female characters in terms of active versus passive, warm versus cold, and the like.

"Yom Kippur War" A name for the 1973 conflict between Israel and its Arab neighbors.

Young Plan A plan for refinancing Germany's reparations payments to the Allies in the 1920s.

Z

Zhou dynasty The second Chinese dynasty; ruled from c. 1100 to c. 400 B.C.E.

Zionism A movement founded by Theodor Herzl in 1896 to establish a Jewish national homeland in Palestine.

Zulu wars A series of conflicts between the British and the native Africans in South Africa in the late nineteenth century.

Answers to Test Your Knowledge

CHAPTER 1
1. d, 2. a, 3. c, 4. c, 5. b, 6. d

CHAPTER 2
1. a, 2. b, 3. b, 4. d, 5. b, 6. b, 7. d

CHAPTER 3
1. c, 2. c, 3. c, 4. c, 5. b, 6. a, 7. b

CHAPTER 4
1. b, 2. b, 3. d, 4. b, 5. b, 6. c, 7. c

CHAPTER 5
1. c, 2. a, 3. b, 4. b, 5. c, 6. a, 7. b

CHAPTER 6
1. c, 2. a, 3. b, 4. c, 5. c, 6. a, 7. d, 8. d

CHAPTER 7
1. a, 2. b, 3. c, 4. a, 5. b, 6. b, 7. d, 8. d

CHAPTER 8
1. b, 2. b, 3. b, 4. c, 5. a, 6. d, 7. b, 8. b

CHAPTER 9
1. b, 2. b, 3. c, 4. b, 5. a, 6. c, 7. c

CHAPTER 10
1. a, 2. c, 3. d, 4. d, 5. c, 6. c, 7. a

CHAPTER 11
1. a, 2. a, 3. a, 4. d, 5. d, 6. b, 7. b, 8. d

CHAPTER 12
1. c, 2. b, 3. d, 4. d, 5. d, 6. c, 7. a, 8. c

CHAPTER 13
1. d, 2. b, 3. d, 4. b, 5. b, 6. c, 7. c

CHAPTER 14
1. a, 2. b, 3. c, 4. d, 5. a, 6. b, 7. b, 8. b

CHAPTER 15
1. b, 2. b, 3. c, 4. d, 5. a, 6. d

CHAPTER 16
1. b, 2. d, 3. d, 4. b, 5. d, 6. a, 7. c, 8. c, 9. a

CHAPTER 17
1. b, 2. d, 3. b, 4. b, 5. b, 6. b, 7. b

CHAPTER 18
1. a, 2. a, 3. a, 4. c, 5. b, 6. d, 7. c, 8. d

CHAPTER 19
1. a, 2. a, 3. c, 4. b, 5. b, 6. a, 7. d, 8. b

CHAPTER 20
1. b, 2. b, 3. d, 4. c, 5. c, 6. d, 7. a, 8. d

CHAPTER 21
1. a, 2. c, 3. c, 4. d, 5. d, 6. c, 7. a

CHAPTER 22
1. c, 2. a, 3. a, 4. d, 5. c, 6. d, 7. a, 8. b

CHAPTER 23
1. b, 2. a, 3. c, 4. a, 5. d, 6. b, 7. b, 8. c

CHAPTER 24
1. d, 2. a, 3. a, 4. d, 5. b, 6. a, 7. d, 8. c

CHAPTER 25
1. b, 2. a, 3. d, 4. c, 5. a, 6. c, 7. c, 8. b

CHAPTER 26
1. b, 2. c, 3. a, 4. c, 5. a, 6. a, 7. d

CHAPTER 27
1. b, 2. a, 3. c, 4. d, 5. b, 6. c, 7. a, 8. a

CHAPTER 28
1. c, 2. a, 3. c, 4. d, 5. a, 6. c, 7. a, 8. d

CHAPTER 29
1. b, 2. c, 3. c, 4. c, 5. d, 6. b, 7. c, 8. a

CHAPTER 30
1. d, 2. d, 3. a, 4. a, 5. d, 6. a, 7. a

CHAPTER 31
1. b, 2. a, 3. b, 4. d, 5. d, 6. a, 7. a, 8. d

CHAPTER 32
1. b, 2. a, 3. b, 4. b, 5. d, 6. b, 7. a, 8. a

CHAPTER 33
1. c, 2. a, 3. b, 4. d, 5. d, 6. a, 7. c, 8. d

CHAPTER 34
1. a, 2. c, 3. d, 4. c, 5. c, 6. d, 7. a, 8. b

CHAPTER 35
1. d, 2. b, 3. b, 4. d, 5. a, 6. a, 7. b, 8. a

CHAPTER 36
1. d, 2. c, 3. a, 4. c, 5. b, 6. b, 7. c

CHAPTER 37
1. a, 2. d, 3. a, 4. a, 5. b, 6. b, 7. a, 8. b

CHAPTER 38
1. c, 2. b, 3. a, 4. d, 5. b, 6. b, 7. b, 8. b

CHAPTER 39
1. c, 2. c, 3. a, 4. c, 5. a, 6. b, 7. a

CHAPTER 40
1. d, 2. b, 3. b, 4. b, 5. c, 6. d, 7. c

CHAPTER 41
1. c, 2. d, 3. a, 4. c, 5. b, 6. c, 7. c, 8. b

CHAPTER 42
1. d, 2. c, 3. a, 4. b, 5. b, 6. b, 7. d, 8. a

CHAPTER 43
1. d, 2. b, 3. c, 4. b, 5. b, 6. c, 7. c

CHAPTER 44
1. b, 2. b, 3. b, 4. b, 5. a, 6. c, 7. d, 8. c

CHAPTER 45
1. c, 2. b, 3. d, 4. c, 5. c, 6. b, 7. d, 8. c

CHAPTER 46
1. b, 2. b, 3. d, 4. d, 5. c, 6. a, 7. c

CHAPTER 47
1. a, 2. c, 3. d, 4. d, 5. a, 6. c, 7. b, 8. d

CHAPTER 48
1. c, 2. a, 3. c, 4. a, 5. c, 6. b, 7. c

CHAPTER 49
1. b, 2. b, 3. c, 4. c, 5. d, 6. b, 7. c

CHAPTER 50
1. a, 2. b, 3. a, 4. a, 5. a, 6. c, 7. d

CHAPTER 51
1. c, 2. c, 3. a, 4. c, 5. d, 6. a, 7. b

CHAPTER 52
1. b, 2. b, 3. c, 4. b, 5. b, 6. b, 7. c

CHAPTER 53
1. c, 2. c, 3. c, 4. a, 5. c, 6. b, 7. b, 8. d

CHAPTER 54
1. d, 2. a, 3. a, 4. b, 5. b, 6. a, 7. c, 8. b

CHAPTER 55
1. c, 2. c, 3. d, 4. c, 5. d, 6. b, 7. b

CHAPTER 56
1. d, 2. d, 3. d, 4. c, 5. c, 6. b, 7. b, 8. c

CHAPTER 57
1. a, 2. c, 3. b, 4. d, 5. c, 6. b, 7. a, 8. c

CHAPTER 58
1. a, 2. b, 3. b, 4. b, 5. c, 6. d, 7. a

CHAPTER 59
1. b, 2. b, 3. b, 4. b, 5. c, 6. b, 7. d, 8. a

CHAPTER 60
1. b, 2. d, 3. b, 4. b, 5. d, 6. d, 7. c, 8. c

CHAPTER 61
1. d. 2. b, 3. d, 4. b, 5. a, 6. a, 7. a, 8. b

Photo Credits

INDEX